Social Psychology and Modern Life

CENTRAL CONNECTICUT STATE COLLEGE **Patricia Niles Middlebrook**

CONSULTING EDITOR: **Philip G. Zimbardo** STANFORD UNIVERSI

Social Psychology and Modern Life

ALFRED A. KNOPF · NEW YORK

Cartoons drawn specifically for this book by Al Jaffee appear on pages 3, 22, 34, 37, 66, 75, 81, 84, 86, 98, 131, 134, 148, 189, 201, 222, 247, 264, 275, 281, 284, 292, 301, 344, 388, 392, 403, 425, 428, 432, 436, 453, 458, 463, 466, 479, 530, 554.

Credits for chapter opening photos: (2) R. Lynn Goldberg and James M. Wall; (3) Joe Molnar; (4) Keystone Press Agency; (5) R. Lynn Goldberg; (6) Marine Corps; (7) The Bettman Archive; (8) a. Patricia Hollander Gross/Stock, Boston, b. Joe Molnar, c. George W. Gardner, d. Michael Philip Manheim, e. David Glaubinger/Jeroboam; (9) Thomas H. Brooks/Stock, Boston; (10) The New York Times; (11) Jean Raisler.

THIS IS A BORZOI BOOK PUBLISHED BY ALFRED A. KNOPF, INC.

First Edition
9 8 7 6 5 4

Library of Congress Cataloging in Publication Data

Middlebrook, Patricia Niles, 1936–
 Social psychology and modern life.

 Bibliography: p.
 1. Social psychology. I. Title.
[DNLM: 1. Psychology, Social. HM251 M627s 1973]
HM251.M4618 301.1 73-12802
ISBN 0-394-31726-2

Manufactured in the United States of America

To Solomon Asch, who introduced me to social
psychology and who made me want to write this text,
and to Steve Middlebrook, my husband, who
made it possible for me to do so.

INTRODUCTION

Since my father did not go beyond the third grade himself, it is no wonder that he was fond of telling me and my college-educated friends the story of how one little Italian shoemaker won a confrontation with a dozen tough, young thugs—and did so not with book learning but with street wisdom. I would like to retell it to you because there are other morals to be drawn from it, which I believe illustrate some of the virtues of this textbook as your introduction to the field of social psychology.

Nunzi, the shoemaker, was hard at work in his new store, singing along with the Saturday broadcast of the opera from the Met, when his voice was drowned out by shouts outside his door—"Dirty WOP!" "We don't want Guineas in our town!" "Greaseball, go back to Sicily!"—obscenities, and then garbage thrown against the door. Nunzi grabbed the handiest, biggest iron bar and ran out cursing (in Italian, of course) at this gang of young, American boys. They ran off but only to return the next day and resume their taunting. This time Nunzi tried to reason with them, to persuade them that it was not fair or decent for native-born Americans to do what they were doing to naturalized citizens in this beautiful land of the free. Did they know he paid his taxes, contributed to charities, did good shoe repairing? And . . . they laughed, shouted him down, and became so menacing he retreated in fear.

He rejected the counsel of various family members to go to the police, to report his tormentors to their parents, to sit tight and wait it out, or to put iron grates over his windows and doors. "There must be a way to get them to want to stop this foolishness themselves, so that they won't come back again," he thought aloud. He was so deep in thought for a solution to his problem that he did not even finish his Sunday pasta. Nunzi knew that the boys' "game" might erupt into violence soon, if he couldn't convince them of its folly.

Shortly after 3:00 P.M. the next day the gang approached, and Nunzi stood waiting for them in front of the store. Before they could begin their attack, he waved a fist full of dollar bills and summoned them to come closer. "Don't ask me why," he said, "but I will give each one of you a new dollar bill if you will shout at the top of your lungs ten times: 'Nunzi is a dirty Italian swine,' 'Guineas go home,' and 'No greaseballs in our neighborhood.'" Eagerly the boys took their crisp bills and gleefully screamed the chants in unison. "What a crazy old idiot," they thought as they left, a little bit hoarser for all their shouting.

After school on Tuesday, Nunzi again beckoned the gang to his door and said, "A shiny half dollar to every boy who will kick against my door here, scream the same shouts I told you yesterday, and make up at least one new one."

With obvious relish and a half dollar in hand, the boys went to it once more, shouting and stomping until weary.

The next day, in anticipation of dealing out more of their subsidized bigotry, the boys headed for the shoemaker's shop as soon as school was out.

Nunzi was there, but this time with a sad expression on his face as he said: "I'm very sorry but today I can only give each of you a shiny dime if you will repeat your marvelous performance of yesterday. Business has not been good and that is all I can afford for the favor."

"You really must be crazy," said the ringleader, "to think that we would knock ourselves out screaming and cursing and kicking for a lousy dime." "Yah, said another, "we got better things to do with our time than to do favors for dumb Guineas for only a dime." And away they went.

Never again did Nunzi miss singing along with his favorite tenors on Saturdays; nor did he ever leave his Sunday pasta unfinished.

What can we learn from this story in addition to "You don't have to go to college to have brains"? At the most obvious level, there is the proposition that people create problems for other people, or put differently, the existence of other people, although often comforting to you, can sometimes complicate your life. When people in certain situations are social problems (for example, drug pushers, protestors, parents who batter their children, vandals, racists, slum lords), the most typical solution is to try to change those people directly by means of a range of strategies for interpersonal control. These include education, persuasion, behavior modification (via selective reward and punishment), coercion, therapy, isolation, confinement, banishment, and ultimately execution. An alternative approach to the analysis of social problems seeks to understand those environmental-situational forces that were operating on the person(s) in question and most likely elicited the problem behavior. In this approach, then, those undesirable elements of the situation are changed with the expectation that the problem behavior will, in turn, be affected or changed indirectly.

However, social change is complex and costly, and time is often required before results are seen. In addition, such an analysis implicates society to some extent in the "evil deed" for having allowed the instigating conditions to prevail. The preference in our society among legislators, law-enforcement personnel, and authority figures in general is to attribute social problems not to defects or inequities in the social system (*their* social system) but rather to defects and inadequacies in particular people. Massive institutions, then, are erected everywhere to deal with these problem people—to make "them" clearly different from "us." This difference itself is considered sufficient basis to warrant whatever treatment or mistreatment they receive. "We" are comforted by the illusion that we could never have behaved as they did—robbed, cheated, raped, hurt, or killed—because they are not comparable to us.

Our little Italian shoemaker's final strategy was not to solve his social problem either by changing the people involved or by changing the situation! Instead, his effectiveness was achieved by changing the way people perceived the situation. What he did was to provide an extrinsic reward for a behavior that was originally intrinsically motivated by the boys' desire to have fun, to attack a scapegoat, to belittle an adult, to engage in mindless physical acts, to mimic adults, and who knows what else. Why do you solve puzzles or read books "you don't have to"? Because there is an inherent pleasure derived from the activity itself. When the activity becomes merely a means to another end, an instrumental response for obtaining a goal, then the activity will persist only as long as the reward is sufficient to justify the expenditure of effort. Many elementary teachers have used this principle effectively to get students to *not* read poetry or indeed anything for which there is no immediate, tangible, extrinsic reward. The boys in our story ceased what once had been an inherently satisfying activity after it was made contingent on a large reward and the large reward was no longer forthcoming.

The systematic analysis of the influence of extrinsic rewards on modifying intrinsic motivation is at this time just beginning in several social psychology laboratories. The initial findings from this research imply that the principle that Nunzi utilized does, in fact, generalize to other situations. Thus we discover that there is an important limitation to the laws of reinforcement that we learned about in general psychology: namely, even positive reinforcement might have a counter-productive effect on the emission of certain behaviors that would have been practiced for their own sake, but cease in the absence of the gold star, dollar bill, or pat on the back.

The recognition that people think, are influenced by their values, attitudes, beliefs, and perceptions, react in complex ways to an anticipated loss of freedom or to concern about how others will evaluate them has been part of the reason for a recent dramatic shift in the status of the field of social psychology. Until a few short years ago, social psychology was on the periphery of psychology, a distant cousin with too much sociological blood to suit many of the purists. Little serious attention was paid to social psychology as long as behaviorism ruled the psychological roost. General laws of behavior were to be discovered by studying the behavior of simple organisms (rats, pigeons, and even paramecium) in sterile, artificial environments. To apply these laws at the human level required only the changing of a constant or a parameter here or there in the grand equation. The methodology was one of precise experimentation, with a lot of "brass instruments" and numbers coming out of recorders, a molecular level of analysis of the individual *in vacuo*.

Many are the reasons for the decline in the political power of American behaviorism, among them, the failure to extrapolate from the results in these overly simplified situations to the complex reality of human behavior. The fact that humans use language and can manipulate abstract symbols introduces concepts of time, space, illusion, fantasy, self-awareness, knowledge of death, and a score of others that change the fundamental basis of many psychological laws. The research of Kurt

Lewin, the pioneering figure in modern social psychology, and his students demonstrated not only some of this complexity, but that it could, nevertheless, be analyzed theoretically and carefully studied empirically.

But perhaps the greatest impetus for moving social psychology to its present position close to the very center of psychological study is the demand from college students as well as the average citizen for solutions to our pressing and apparently escalating list of social problems. We cannot afford the luxury of armchair social sciences that are out of contact with the world in which we must survive. Although the term *relevance* has been much abused, it has served the corrective function of changing priorities so that the study of the social behavior of people has been elevated to a level where it is a more central concern in psychology departments, in research-funding agencies, and in the undergraduate curriculum.

This text, which Pat Middlebrook has written for you, has emerged as the finest account available of why social psychology has come of age now. She has the natural gift of being able to combine a thoroughly rigorous and systematic presentation of the state of knowledge in this field with an awareness of how to make it a lively, meaningful experience for you, the reader. Pertinent examples are in abundance throughout, not only to clarify concepts but to extend them and reveal the links between apparent abstractions and your own everyday experience. These links are further strengthened by the judicious use of contemporary illustrations, cartoons, photographs, and selections from our mass media. You will notice that a fine balance is sustained in every chapter between a thorough, systematic, up-to-date scientific social psychology and an imaginative, readable, provocative treatment of our social behavior. There is no shortage of authors who have written either sound hard-headed or interesting soft-headed social psychology texts. It has remained for Pat Middlebrook to show the way in which humanism, social relevance, and the research tradition can be effectively integrated in an introductory social psychology text. I'm only sorry that her text was not available to introduce me to this exciting field when I was a student. However, I can take joy in knowing that as a consulting editor I helped shape this book into one from which you will derive many hours of enjoyable, informative reading.

Philip G. Zimbardo
SAN FRANCISCO, CALIFORNIA

P.S. Rejoinder to Father:

Book learning may not be the whole answer, but without it I'd be working in Nunzi's shoe store instead of being a college professor with the freedom to do things I like for their intrinsic interest and not simply because I have to work to make a buck and survive.

PREFACE

Even before students begin a course in social psychology, they encounter many social phenomena in their daily lives. Social interactions take up a considerable portion of their time. Television commercials try to persuade them to buy an advertiser's product by pointing out the utility of that product to other people. As any observer on a campus in the spring has noticed, dating and romantic love are not rare phenomena. Conformity pressures on campus are strong, too. Students see many social problems around them and wonder what social psychology has to offer to solve these problems.

It is, therefore, very clear that social psychology can be one of the most exciting psychology courses taught today. Moreover, the discipline no longer has to excuse itself because it is a young science. It is young, but in its short history it has amassed a fascinating set of information. Student interest *is* there—if a text can capitalize on that interest and not kill it with jargon and endless repetition of studies irrelevant to the concerns of most students.

How, then, to present social psychology as the relevant and interesting discipline it is without getting bogged down in endless detail? My own answer has been to write a text that can provide the student with (1) a rigorous, research-oriented approach that, at the same time, is sufficiently concerned with contemporary, real-life problems, (2) a coverage of the field that is intermediate in scope and provides an in-depth treatment of the most important areas in social psychology in the 1970s, and (3) an effective learning device.

My principal goal has been to do justice both to the discipline and to the student's natural concern with real-life problems. Extensive research has gone into the preparation of the manuscript. Over 1,100 references are cited, many of which are 1972 or 1973 publications, studies that are in press, and unpublished works. To show my bias that a thorough grounding in research is basic to the student's comprehension of the field, I have opened the text with a chapter devoted exclusively to that subject. Basic concepts, terminology, and experimental artifacts are thoroughly discussed. Then, within the substantive chapters, key experiments are reviewed in detail so that the student can evaluate and understand the procedure used to arrive at the results. Thus the research results are not given as cut-and-dried, and as a result the student can become more actively involved in the research process as well as in understanding the meaning of research results.

Although the text is organized according to topics and not theories, theories are emphasized in all relevant chapters. For example, social comparison theory is discussed in Chapters 2, 5, 8, and 11; attribution theory is summarized in Chapter 8; and cognitive dissonance theory is covered in Chapter 1 as well as in several other chapters. The interrelationship between theory and research is emphasized throughout the book.

A scholarly, research-oriented approach does not dominate the book, however. When traditional topics of social psychology, such as attitude change, are discussed, students are invited to apply the findings to designing their own programs, for example, a program for changing attitudes about traffic safety. To interest the students in research, sometimes a difficult task, I have opened Chapter 1 by discussing the application of various research tactics to the question of whether or not job discrimination against women exists, and a controlled experiment on that topic is summarized.

In addition to the more traditional topics, subjects of high student interest are included. Although social psychologists have only recently begun to do research on romantic love, students discovered it long ago. Accordingly, I treat the topic at some length, as well as dating, courtship, and marriage, in Chapter 9. Chapter 2 deals with the problem of evolving an identity and arriving at self-understanding. To make the concept of the self a little less slippery, I have supplemented the discussion of the principal aspects of the self with the related autobiographical comments of one of my former students. Police interrogation techniques are detailed in Chapter 4. Chapter 5 discusses the incidence of loneliness, as well as some of the psychological and sociological causes. Conformity pressures, communes, and encounter groups are summarized in Chapter 11.

Students frequently ask what social psychology has to offer in solving social problems. Here again, I must betray a bias. I think that applying the results of social psychological research offers the best chance of solving many of the problems that exist in our society today. Admittedly, not all of the answers are in, and in some cases the questions have not yet begun to be asked. But through science we have the best chance of gaining insight into solutions. Thus I discuss the application of research results to social problems in Chapter 1, give speculations about how to control aggression and to increase the incidence of altruism in Chapters 6 and 7, and set out some ideas of how to meet the loneliness problem in Chapter 11.

Throughout the book, then, an attempt is made to balance the research-oriented approach with the real-life approach. It is my belief that focusing on both strengthens each. Without the scientific, rigorous approach, the student cannot have a good introduction to the research methods and results of the discipline. Without the real-life approach, the student may reject the entire discipline as a crashing, irrelevant bore. With both, he will, hopefully, learn what the discipline of social psychology has to say about human social phenomena and apply that learning to his own life.

My second objective was to write a book that was intermediate in scope—not a too-long and superficial summary of the entire field, but an in-depth treatment of the most important areas in the field in the 1970s. Accordingly, I chose to cover research; the self; attitudes and their formation; attitude change; affiliation; aggression; altruism; person perception; the dyad; group formation, structure, and leadership; and groups in action. Although this coverage may not include every social psychologist's favorite areas, it does cover most of the principal topics of interest.

My third objective was to create an effective learning device for students. Twelve years of teaching experience have given me a number of ideas as to how a text could be written to secure maximum student involvement and to explain complicated concepts in a comprehensible way. Many of the ideas in the text and the methods of presenting information evolved from students' reactions to my lectures and to earlier drafts of the text. All of the chapters have been critiqued by anonymous student reviewers, as the materials were used in my classes, and have been more thoroughly reviewed by selected students. Their reactions and criticisms were fully considered in preparing the final draft of the manuscript.

To make the book effective as a teaching device, I have tried to write in a highly readable style and to maximize student involvement. I have also included a number of student-learning aids and a full program of drawings, graphs, cartoons, and photographs.

The paragraphs and sentences in the text are unusually short. Words and phrases that are familiar to the average student were chosen. When technical terms are introduced, they are defined in the text. Numerous examples that are familiar to students are provided for complex concepts. Each chapter opens with a section designed to stimulate student interest in the particular topic. For example, Chapter 6 begins with a discussion of the massacre at Mylai as a means of illustrating how violent civilized men can become when certain conditions are present. Chapter 8 opens with a series of photographs of anonymous individuals as a device to show how people form their impressions of others from minimal information.

To maximize student involvement, I repeatedly ask readers how they would react in a hypothetical situation before giving the results of an experiment related to that situation. Occasionally, readers are also asked how they would criticize an experiment or derive a testable hypothesis from a particular theory. The discussion questions are designed to stimulate the application of important concepts, findings, and theories and to recall the concepts, results, and theories discussed.

Student-learning aids include outlines at the beginning of each chapter, summaries within each chapter of the major sections, and summaries of the chapters themselves. Terms are defined both in the text and in a glossary provided at the end of the text. Materials that are supplementary to the main points made in a chapter are provided in boxes. Discussion questions that emphasize the main points made in the chapter are included at the end of each chapter.

Students like illustrations in texts. In our magazine-reading, television-watching society, pages of straight type can be intimidating. Thus 184 photographs, graphs, drawings and cartoons—38 of which were prepared specifically for this text—are included. Moreover, the illustrations are closely coordinated with the written text. Each has been designed to emphasize an important concept, theory, or study. For example, in Chapter 2 the difficult distinction between the normative and comparative functions of a reference group is illustrated by two cartoons.

These are the most important comments about the text, but some other points should also be made. The organization of the text is topical—not theoretical. After the opening chapter on research, the text focuses on the influence of other people on the individual, in the forming of his self-concept, his attitudes, and his motives. Person perception is then discussed, and the text concludes by reviewing how people interact with one another. However, the instructor need not follow this organization. In none of the chapters is it assumed that the student has read any of the earlier chapters, except for Chapter 1. If a theory or finding that was discussed earlier is mentioned in a later chapter, it is briefly summarized. Thus the chapters are independent of one another, and the instructor can choose the number and sequence of topics to be covered.

Although I wrote the text and any errors in it are my responsibility, many people contributed to the project. The consulting editor, Philip G. Zimbardo, of Stanford University, has given the entire manuscript a line-by-line review and has provided many helpful criticisms. Professor Zimbardo is a gifted social psychologist whose work has made many outstanding contributions to the discipline. He is also an author who knows how to write clearly and to hold the fine balance between rigor and student interest in a text. His constant encouragement throughout the book's preparation has been of invaluable help to me.

Professor Ivan Steiner of the University of Massachusetts reviewed seven chapters of the manuscript and provided many valuable criticisms and comments. Professors Irving Janis of Yale University and David Kanouse of UCLA each read an outline of the entire manuscript and gave me some very sound advice about overall organization and scope. Additional helpful comments and criticisms were provided by those who reviewed portions of the manuscript: Kenneth Gergen, of Swarthmore College, who read Chapter 2; Harry Triandis, of the University of Illinois at Urbana-Champaign, who reviewed Chapters 3 and 4; Harry Kauffmann, of Hunter College, who reviewed Chapters 6 and 7; Robert Kleck, of Dartmouth College, who reviewed Chapter 8; Paul Swingle, of the University of Ottawa, who reviewed the bargaining section of Chapter 9; Ellen Berscheid, of the University of Minnesota, who reviewed all of Chapter 9; and Marvin Shaw, of the University of Florida at Gainesville, who reviewed Chapters 10 and 11. A debt of gratitude should also be extended to Vello Sermat, of York University, who not only graciously provided me with an extensive account of his fascinating, as yet unpublished work on loneliness, but also reviewed and critiqued my account of his work in Chapter 5. Thanks should also be given to Kenneth Eells who provided me with background information on his marijuana and LSD survey at California Institute of Technology and who reviewed my description of his study in Chapter 1.

Acknowledgment and thanks should also go to the 300 students who read my manuscript in various stages of polish over the past three years. The contributions of some of these students should be specially noted. Augustina Musumeci, Sebastian Pappalardo, and Carol Graboski spent many hours with the *Psychological Abstracts* and provided line-by-line reviews of several of the chapters. Kathy Elliott also contributed significantly to the library research. But above all, Renée Windmuller, who provided invaluable aid in the many tedious chores of research in the *Psychological Abstracts*, xeroxed hundreds of articles, and helped in compiling the references for the text, should be acknowledged and thanked. Shirley Harris accurately and patiently typed many drafts of the manuscript. Both she and Elizabeth Walden also helped with the final reference checks.

The delightful cartoons of Al Jaffee and the careful copy editing of Cynthia Harris should be acknowledged. Many of the members of the staff at Alfred A. Knopf contributed immeasurably to the project. Richard Kennedy provided initial encouragement and support for the concept of this book. Lynn Goldberg did the research on the picture program for the text and obtained permission to use the photographs and drawings selected. James Wall worked out the layout of the book, and Paul Shensa provided coordination as college editor. For her patience, good sense, humor, and fine editorial hand, special thanks are extended to Elaine Rosenberg, who, as project editor, led me through all phases of the book's preparation.

Patricia Niles Middlebrook

AVON, CONNECTICUT JULY 1973

CONTENTS

3
**Attitudes
and Their
Formation**

**6
Aggression**

**7
Altruism**

8
Person Perception

**9
The Dyad**

**10
Group Formation,
Structure, and
Leadership**

11
**Groups
in Action**

BOXES

BOXES

STUDENT REACTION BOXES

PSYCH QUIZZES

Social Psychology and Modern Life

Does job discrimination against women exist? To the 30,795,000 American women who work, this question is obviously one of great practical importance. Unfortunately, even statements made by women on this

issue are sometimes inconsistent—as the following two comments illustrate:

There's no discrimination against women like they say there is. Women themselves are just self-limiting. It's in their nature and they shouldn't blame it on society or men.

[Mrs. Saul Schary, executive secretary and forthcoming president of the 23-million member National Council of Women, quoted in *The New York Times*, August 26, 1970.]

Television, like most areas of big business, does not offer equal opportunities to women.

[Barbara Walters, of NBC's "Today Show," quoted in *The New York Times*, August 27, 1970.]

Which of these two statements is correct? Is there or is there not job discrimination against women? How would one go about proving whether or not there are equal job opportunities for women?

Before giving your reactions to these inconsistent statements, you could first examine various types of evidence. You could, for example, review your own personal experience. Have you ever seen any discrimination? Consider the experience reported by one female electrical engineer:

My undergraduate degree was in electrical engineering. When the companies came around to interview senior engineering students, interviewers looked at me as if I were some sort of a freak. One pair of men actually laughed in my face. I finally was hired in an office with 20 other electrical engineers but was called a computer aide so that my pay could be $100 less.

[Kresge, 1970, p. 7.]

Does this one experience from everyday life settle the issue of whether or not job discrimination exists? The woman felt that she was discriminated against, but does her experience prove the general existence of discrimination? Clearly not. She may have misinterpreted the situation. Rather than being discriminated against because she was a woman, she may have been discriminated against because she was not a good student. Or she may not really have been discriminated against at all. Finally, even if she actually was discriminated against, others may have very different experiences.

Another approach would be to read what a number of contemporary writers have to say about job discrimination against women. You might consult Kate Millett's book, *Sexual Politics* (1970), or you might read what Lawrenson (1971), another feminine "authority," has to say on the issue. Yet if you chose these particular references, they would provide little help, for these two authors stand directly opposite each other on the question. Referring to "authorities" to establish the truth is a risky business—especially when different authorities do not agree. And even if they do agree, how do they know? What is their evidence?

Still a third way to assess whether or not job discrimination exists is to resort to "common sense"—what everybody "knows" to be true. Without thinking about how you knew, you might have reacted to the question because you "just knew—it was so clear." But people may differ in their assessment of what "everybody knows is true." Further, even if everyone agrees, there are many documented cases in which what everybody knew was true turned out to be completely wrong. For a long time the conventional wisdom was that the earth was flat, but we believe otherwise today.

If neither personal experience nor authority nor common sense is adequate to "prove" a statement or to resolve a question, how can one establish the truth about the existence of job discrimination or, indeed, about any question concerning human behavior? The answer is to use the techniques of scientific research. Let us see what information scientific research has provided regarding the question of job dis-

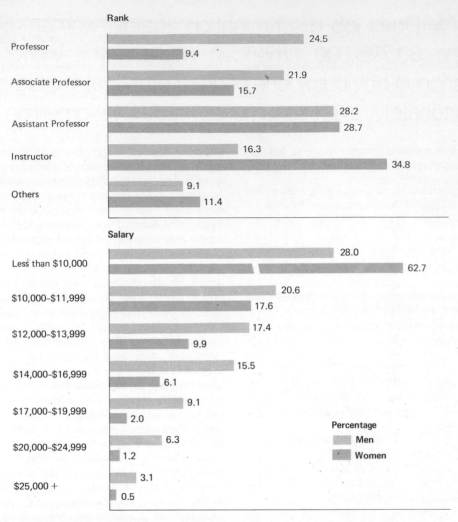

Rank

Professor	24.5 / 9.4

Salary

FIGURE 1-1 **1972 and faculty women are still not equal. To support charges of bias in higher education, one investigator found that 62.7 percent of female faculty members have jobs paying less than $10,000 a year compared to 28 percent of men.** (Analysis by Maeroff, 1972; adapted from The News of the Week in Review, *The New York Times,* October 8, 1972, p. 10. © 1972 by The New York Times Company. Reprinted by permission.)

crimination. Since the question of whether or not discrimination exists in all jobs would be a very large one to cover, let us limit the question to whether or not there is sex discrimination in hiring women to teach psychology and sociology at colleges and universities.

As many research processes do, our investigation of this question might begin by observation. At the 1969 Convention of the American Psychological Association, all of the women who participated in the Women's Caucus, a

group concerned with the role of women in psychology, reported personal observations of discrimination in hiring (Kaplan, 1970). Since these combined reports relate the experiences of a number of individuals, they are stronger evidence than the report of one individual case of discrimination would be. However, there are still problems in interpretation. Proving that discrimination exists is difficult, for events in everyday life are determined by many factors. You apply for a job and are turned down. How do you know *why* you were rejected? Is it possible that if you are concerned about discrimination, you may tend to interpret any job rejection as an indicator of discrimination when other factors, such as the presence of better qualified applicants, might really be responsible? Further, your thinking that you had encountered discrimination might be partially responsible for your attending a meeting concerned with the role of women in psychology, and it was at such a meeting that these personal observations were recorded.

To obtain a more representative sample of female respondents, you might interview or give a questionnaire to a sample—say all of the women who belong to the American Psychological Association—and ask them about their experiences in regard to job discrimination. Since the number of women involved in the survey would represent a larger group than the Women's Caucus, the results might produce stronger evidence for your hypothesis. Yet, here too, there are problems in interpretation. Even if many of the respondents reported what they thought was discrimination, we would still not know whether or not their sex was responsible.

A more direct approach would be to study the actual jobs women hold in colleges and universities. A 1970 study of positions held in sociology departments showed that women held lower level jobs and taught at less prestigious colleges than men (Rossi, 1970). A 1972 study of the status of faculty women in all disciplines showed that women still had not attained equal status. A male faculty member is two and a half times more likely to become a full professor and is almost twice as likely to earn $10,000 or more than a female faculty member (Maeroff, 1972). (See Figure 1-1.) Although these findings show a clear relationship, or "correlation," between sex and employment status, they do not explain *why* the facts were as they were. Perhaps women did not remain in college teaching as long as men, or perhaps they did not work as hard. Or perhaps they were discriminated against.

To test directly whether or not women are discriminated against, a controlled experiment would be necessary. By keeping all other variables in the situation the same, or controlled, the investigator can see the effects of the change he or she is making in one variable. For

instance, if hypothetical job applicants with identical qualifications, including PhDs—half of whom were described as men and half of whom were described as women—elicited different reactions from potential employers, one could infer that sex discrimination was the explanation. This result was obtained in just such a study. Men were offered higher level jobs than women: 46 percent of the men were offered a job at the associate professor level, and only 37 percent of the women were given a similar offer. Further, the potential employers tended to give more enthusiastic evaluations of the male applicants than they did of the female applicants. Since all of the applicants' qualifications were exactly the same except for sex, the different reactions could only be related to the sex of the applicant (Fidell, 1970).

This study illustrates the use of the "controlled experiment"—a research technique that enables the investigator to eliminate alternative explanations for a given situation by manipulating one variable in that situation. In this experiment the variable was the sex of the applicants, and we can conclude, therefore, that this factor alone caused the different reactions.

Scientific research procedures offer the best way to answer questions about human behavior and are basic to social psychology. This chapter will be devoted to the four major research techniques: (1) observation, (2) questionnaire-interview, (3) correlation, and (4) the controlled experiment. Since the controlled experiment is the best way to assess cause-and-effect relationships between variables, our discussion will focus primarily on this research method. We will examine the published report of a controlled experiment in order to enable you to see at first hand some of the practical problems involved in conducting and interpreting this type of research as well as some of the contemporary problems in research.

At this point you may be feeling distinctly uninterested. Students frequently feel that research is dull, routine, and uncreative. In high-school science courses, dull-sounding discussions of research as a routine following of certain basic and given steps may have perpetuated your stereotyped view. In fact, this stereotype of research as dull and uncreative includes many of the oversimplifications and errors typically found in stereotypes. As we shall see, doing research involves originality, creativity, and some trial and error. Further, obtaining an understanding of what research results mean involves considerable intellectual exercise. Although an investigator may have felt that all variables in the situation were controlled, there may have been other variables that could also have been responsible for the effect observed.

To sharpen your critical abilities, we will focus repeatedly on some of the contemporary problems in research. However, to note that there may be problems with a particular approach or study is not to say that the work is not any good. Designing and interpreting research is a complex procedure. Many decisions have to be made, and sometimes the requirements are inconsistent. For instance, an experimenter may not wish to deceive his subjects, but he may see no other way to test his hypothesis.

As you read about some of the problems, two things should be kept in mind. First, without scientific research procedures, we would still be answering questions by referring to our own experience, authorities, or common sense. Second, progress in any science involves constant attention to possible defects in the research methods and a continuing effort to eliminate these defects so that accuracy can be increased.

Observation

A basic technique of science is observation. Many hypotheses have been derived from what a scientist first noticed casually. For instance, a series of studies on the causes of senseless acts of destruction, termed "deindividuated" behavior, first began with one scientist's informal observation of the high frequency with which senseless acts of aggression occur in contemporary American life (Zimbardo, 1969). Murder, riots, mob violence, vandalism, and uncontrollable violence of many types are reported daily in newspapers and on television.

On the basis of these observations, the psychologist began to *theorize* about the causes of these acts, to ask why these events occur. One possible answer that occurred to him was that these events would be more likely to occur when the individual feels anonymous. If others cannot identify you, they cannot punish you, and you are free of responsibility for your actions. In observing the high frequency of violence and theorizing about its causes, this psychologist followed a process quite similar to what writers and philosophers have been doing since Plato. But his theorizing went beyond philosophical speculations because he *tested* his theory to see if it was correct. Obtaining evidence to prove or disprove a theory is the unique contribution of the scientist.

To test his theory, Zimbardo set up a laboratory experiment in which half of his subjects, college girls, were made to feel anonymous. (They wore a hood over their head while they were in the experiment, and the experimenter avoided any mention of their names.) The other half of the subjects were given large name tags to wear. Thus their individuality was emphasized. The task used to measure aggression was the number and intensity of electric shocks each subject would deliver to another girl. Making the subjects anonymous in this manner had a significant effect on their aggressive behavior: The total duration of shocks given was twice as high in the anonymous group.

Although these results clearly support the anonymity-aggression theory, the theorist wondered if an even stronger support for that theory could be obtained outside the laboratory, since the formal laboratory setting (including a responsible, observing adult) might have inhibited the subjects' expression of aggression. Anonymity might lead to more extreme forms of aggression outside the laboratory.

In the real world feelings of anonymity are very strong in large cities, like New York. On a busy street no one knows the names of those he passes by. In contrast, in a smaller town, like Palo Alto, California, people often know each other by name. To test the effects of anonymity on aggression, the investigator had a car left unattended on a street in New York City for sixty-four hours. At the same time a car was left unattended on a street in Palo Alto. The license plates of both cars were removed to make them look abandoned. Then, unseen observers kept around-the-clock watch from a nearby window to see what would happen.

What happened in New York City was incredible. At 3:25 on a Friday afternoon, ten minutes after the car was left, the first vandals appeared: a well-dressed family of three. The mother kept watch while the father and son searched the trunk, glove compartment, and motor, and then removed the battery and radio. As a result of twenty-three similar incidents, the car in New York was virtually demolished. In strong contrast, the Palo Alto car was not vandalized once during its sixty-four-hour abandonment. In fact, when it began to rain, one passer-by lowered the hood so that the engine would not get wet.

The behavior observed in these two real-life situations strongly supports the anonymity-aggression theory. Not many laboratory studies would yield information such as this. Vandalism is not socially acceptable, and subjects in a laboratory setting might be much more reluctant to engage in vandalism than were those persons observed in the New York City vigil. In the New York City setting the persons observed were in their own environment, and they were completely unaware of their being observed; thus they were completely "natural." If the vandals had known that their behavior was being observed, they might have acted quite differently.

Different terms have been used to refer to the distorting effect of observation when the subjects are aware that they are being observed, such as the "measurement effect," the "reactive effect of measurement," or the "guinea pig effect" (Campbell, 1957; Selltiz et al., 1959). Whatever term is used, minimizing the effect of the observer is one of the biggest problems in observational studies. A variety of techniques have been used. In some cases, as in the abandoned car study, the observers are concealed. In others the observers may become an accepted part of the group being measured.

Measures that can be obtained without the individual's awareness (so-called unobtrusive measures) may also be used to overcome the guinea pig effect. For instance, one investigator who wanted to learn how much whiskey was consumed in a town that was officially dry did so by counting the number of empty liquor bottles in trash cans. Another investigator, who wished to measure the effect of the introduction of television on the amount of reading people do, did so by comparing the number of books withdrawn from local libraries before and after the advent of television. The relative popularity of museum exhibits has been measured by comparing the relative wear on the flooring materials around the exhibits (Webb et al., 1966, p. 2). You may be able to think of other unobtrusive measures. For example, one possible way to determine how much time students spend reading their textbooks would be to measure the amount of "wear and tear" their books show.

All of these techniques—concealment, participant observation, and unobtrusive measures—may well decrease the measurement effect, but they also pose ethical problems. Is it ethical to invade an individual's privacy and observe his personal behavior? If someone checks out your trash, is he going too far? These ethical problems share some common characteristics with the ethical problems involved in other types of research. We will be examining these problems in more detail in connection with our in-depth analysis of one experiment.

The last step involved in observation is to record what was observed. This step also involves problems. Assume, for instance, that you are trying to take down everything two people say in a conversation that lasts for five minutes. If you have ever tried to do this, you know how difficult it is. A lot happens in five minutes—people talk, change facial expressions, move around, make gestures. In any event you would probably not be able to record everything that happened, so you would summarize—either by indicating on a form whether or not a given behavior occurred or by summarizing in narrative form.

Whichever form your summary takes, the observational report can involve a significant amount of subjective interpretation. In the process of interpretation, the observer's own feelings and biases may influence what he sees. For instance, when middle- and lower-class boys looked at exactly the same event, they were found to "see" different things. Behaviors that seemed to be aggressive to the middle-class boys were seen as being playful by the lower-class boys (Selltiz et al., 1959). Thus in observational studies it is important to check the *reliability* of the observation, by assessing whether or not different observers, looking at the same thing at the same time, agree in what they see. To the extent that different observers agree, confidence in the accuracy of the observation increases. However, even when there is observer agreement, there may be consistent errors. Two middle-class mothers watching their children playing with lower-class children would agree that the lower-class children were behaving aggressively, while lower-class mothers watching the same events would not "see" the aggression.

Although observation can suggest hypotheses and provide information about what people may do in their natural environment, it cannot provide cause-and-effect information. Too many aspects of the situation are varying. For instance, in the comparison of vandalism in New York and Palo Alto, other factors in addition to the size of the two cities differed. The typical resident of Palo Alto may be more affluent than the average resident in New York City and therefore less tempted to vandalize. In New York people may be more accustomed to seeing cars vandalized than in Palo Alto, so that they may be more likely to imitate what they have seen others do. Because of the extremely crowded parking conditions in New York City, cars may be seen as enemies and sources of frustration in New York, while they may be seen as necessities for transportation in California.

Likely or unlikely as any of these particular hypotheses seem, on the basis of observational evidence, we really don't know why the car in New York was vandalized. Although an anonymity-aggression explanation fits the findings, other explanations are also possible. Since no one observational study can settle the question, other methods of research are necessary.

Questionnaire-Interview Research

Suppose you wanted to know how many students at a particular college were using marijuana or LSD. You might use some of the observation techniques already discussed. However, since the use of these drugs is illegal, students would probably tend to conceal their practices, thus making direct observation very difficult or ineffective. Further, concealed observation techniques—such as disguising oneself as a fellow student or using hidden recording devices—would pose many ethical and practical problems.

A far better approach might be to ask the students, or to obtain a "self-report" measure. Asking the students would be less time-consuming, less expensive, more efficient, and would not invade their privacy to the same extent as a concealed observation.

The two self-report measures most frequently used to obtain information are the questionnaire and the interview (either in person or by telephone). Both methods involve presenting questions in order to obtain information. In the interview the questions are asked in a two-person conversation; on a questionnaire they are presented and answered in writing.

Self-report techniques are used in many ways. They may be used to obtain information from, or to "survey," everyone in the relevant group, or the "population." The population may range in size from a few persons to millions. One example of a survey that involves a very large population is the United States census, which is an attempt to obtain information concerning every resident of the United States.

Sampling

Surveying large groups of people is so very expensive and time-consuming that another procedure is used more frequently: the sample survey. The general idea of sample surveying, or "polling," is to interview a small group, or a "sample," selected so that it accurately represents the larger group from which it is drawn. If the sample is an accurate representation, the pollster can generalize from the responses of the sample to the population.

Suppose, for instance, that you wished to know the incidence of drug use among all American college students. If you had a lot of time and money, you could conceivably question all of the 6,048,496 full-time and part-time college students (Harth, 1972). Or you could select a group that represents the population, question the group members, and then generalize from their responses. However, if you wish to generalize from the responses of your sample, your basis for selection must give some reasonable assurance that all members of the population have an equal chance of being included. When this assurance is given, the sample is known as a "random sample."

If you wish to generalize from the sample to a population, you must identify the population to which the results are to be generalized and then devise a procedure that will enable you to sample randomly from that population. This is easier said than done. First, the investigator must obtain a list of all of the members of the population. For large populations such lists may not be readily available. (Imagine the problems involved in obtaining a list of the names of 6,048,496 American college students.) Next some procedure for selecting members of the sample must be devised so that all the members of the population have an equal chance of being selected. Although, as you may have learned in an elementary statistics course, there are more elegant ways to select the sample, you could place each of the names on a separate piece of paper, place the pieces of paper in a container, shuffle them thoroughly, and then draw out as many names as are to be included in your sample. All of the names selected must be included if the sample is to represent the population. Thus the investigator must locate all the people selected and convince them to participate in the study.

As you can see, it is difficult to obtain a random sample for very large populations. Thus other sampling methods, such as "area sampling" (which involves the random sampling of geographical areas rather than the random sampling of all the individuals in the population) and "quota sampling" (which involves the selecting of a sample that represents the basic attributes of the population) are frequently used. Although area and quota sampling are less precise than random sampling, they are less expensive and easier to use if large populations are involved. And when they are very well done, they can be exceedingly accurate.

For instance, the Gallup Poll, in which approximately 1,500 people selected to represent a true cross section of the American voting population are interviewed, has failed only once to pick the winner in the United States presidential elections since it began in 1936 (*U.S. News & World Report,* October 16, 1972, p. 26). In the 1972 presidential election, the polls were highly accurate. See Table 1. But to attain the accuracy of a Gallup Poll is no easy feat, as our discussion of the problems encountered in one survey study will show.

Table 1. How the Polls Made Out

The Final Polls	Nixon	McGovern	Others, Undecided
Gallup	62%	38%	
Harris	59%	35%	6%
Sindlinger	59.8%	35.6%	4.6%
The actual vote	61%	38%	1%

Source: U.S. News & World Report, November 20, 1972, p. 18.

To see how an actual survey is done, let us return to our initial problem—how to assess students' use of marijuana and LSD—and follow some of the steps used in one well-designed study of this topic. In 1967 a psychologist at Cal. Tech. conducted a survey to answer this question (Eells, 1968). As a counseling psychologist at the Cal. Tech. Health Center, the investigator became aware that the use of marijuana and LSD at Cal. Tech. was more extensive than most administrators or faculty members believed, and he decided to do a survey to find out just how extensive it was. He also noted that despite the social importance of the question, at that time relatively few studies had been done on the incidence of drug use among college students. The accumulation of new or additional information about a topic of interest or concern is a frequently cited reason for research. In such cases it is essential to determine what work has already been done on the topic. Box 1, page 12, discusses the most practical way for a psychologist to do this.

For the marijuana-LSD study the population the investigator was interested in consisted of all the students on the Cal. Tech. campus. To study this group, the investigator mailed a questionnaire to every student in the college. In this case, then, no sampling was involved: All of the population was surveyed.

Ninety percent of the students returned their questionnaires. Although this rate is unusually high for a mailed questionnaire dealing with a sensitive issue, there is still the question of what the 10 percent who did not return their questionnaire were like. Were they systematically different from the 90 percent who did? Perhaps they were drug users who did not want to report their usage. Or they may have been nonusers who were not sufficiently interested to complete the questionnaire. We have no way of knowing who they were.

BOX 1 THE PSYCHOLOGICAL ABSTRACTS

When you are attempting to locate previously published research, the most useful reference is the *Psychological Abstracts,* which contains brief summaries, or abstracts, of books and articles from journals that publish psychological research. Almost all of the American journals as well as many foreign journals are covered in the *Abstracts.*

To find research done on the topics of "drug incidence" and "drug attitude," you would look in the subject index of the abstracts, which contains a listing of the numbers of the abstracts done on these topics. (The abstracts are arranged in chronological order.) The portion of the index that includes Eells' study is shown below and the Eells citation is circled:

Drug Effects—Human
(see also specific drugs, Drug Therapy—Schizophrenia, Drug Addiction, Drugs)

18140, 18387, 18402, 18413, 18422, 18423, 18428, 18430, 18469, 18613

Drug Therapy

18019, 18374, 18387, 18430, 18880, 18950, 18951, 18955, 18957, 18959, 18961, 18962, 18963, 18964, 18965, 18966, 18967, 19078, 19100

Drug Therapy—Schizophrenia

18944, 18956, 18958, 18960

Drugs
(see also Amphetamine, Chlorpromazine, Lysergic Acid Diethylamide, Reserpine, Tranquilizer)

18031, 18430, 18512, 18887, 19022, 19023, 19102

[*Psychological Abstracts,* December, 1968, subject index, p. iv.]

Or if you know a particular investigator has published work in an area, you could look up the investigator's name in the author index and then find the abstract number. See below for the Eells citation:

Eells, K., 19022

[*Psychological Abstracts,* December, 1968, author index, p. xv.]

After you have located the abstract number, the next step is to locate the abstract, which is a brief summary of the article. The abstract of Eells' study follows:

"**19022.** Eells, Kenneth. (California Inst. of Technology) Marijuana and LSD: A survey of one college campus. *Journal of Counseling Psychology,* 1968, **15**(5, Pt. 1), 459–467.—Utilized special procedures to achieve a 90% return of an anonymous questionnaire dealing with the extent and use of marijuana and LSD by college students, and with attitudes of the Ss toward these drugs. Data are reported concerning (1) incidence, nature, and recency of usage of both marijuana and LSD, (2) plans for future use, (3) judgments as to beneficial-harmful nature of the drugs, (4) reasons for using or not using the drugs, and (5) attitudes toward legal controls. The value of a college wide survey in promoting communication between the generations regarding drug use questions is pointed out.—*Journal abstract.*"

[*Psychological Abstracts,* December, 1968, p. 1885.]

If the abstract indicates that the study is relevant to your research, the final step is to locate the journal article. The citation, or reference information, is given in the abstract immediately after the number. The name of the investigator is given first, then the title of the article, then the title of the journal, the year of publication, the volume, and finally, the page numbers.

If a representative sample is to be obtained, those selected must be persuaded to participate. No matter how carefully the sample is selected, it will not represent the population unless it is actually measured. Thus developing techniques to persuade selected respondents to participate is a very important part of questionnaire-interview research. So far the techniques used have been derived rather informally from what has been found to work. Potential respondents may be told that the work is important, that their responses will be confidential, and that the questionnaire will not take much time to complete. If the questionnaire concerns personal information, questionnaires may be returned anonymously.

Writing items

Once a sample or a population has been selected, the investigator must translate his rather generally defined interests into specific terms. For instance, in the marijuana-LSD study the investigator had to write items so that the respondents would be able and willing to give honest answers. Although there are no simple approaches to the drafting of questionnaire items, a few general principles are widely followed.

Asking Questions So That the Respondent Is Able to Answer There are a number of reasons for a respondent's not being able to answer a question. First, he may simply have *forgotten the information*. If an event occurred a long time ago or it seemed relatively unimportant to the respondent, he may not be able to remember it. Or *the respondent may never have had the information requested*. If someone who has never heard of the strategic arms limitations talks (SALT) is asked to indicate his opinion about them, he might become embarrassed and resentful at being asked a question that reveals his lack of information. In addition, if *the items do not communicate clearly and accurately*, the respondent will not be able to answer. This may seem so obvious that you think it hardly needs saying, but it is extremely difficult to write clear and accurate items. If you were interested in the amount of aspirin consumed by middle-aged housewives, asking

about the incidence of their drug intake might not produce valid information.

Asking Questions So That the Respondent Is Willing to Answer Honestly One of the important issues of questionnaire-interview research is the willingness of respondents to answer truthfully. There are many studies showing that respondents do falsify information and that, moreover, they do so in a manner that enhances their image. For instance, respondents have underreported the amount of liquor they drink (Lamale, 1959) and the amount of their automobile loans (Lansing and Blood, 1964). On the other hand, they have overreported their charitable contributions (Parry and Crossley, 1950).

What can be done to counter this tendency to falsify? The importance of the research and the utility of the findings to the respondent may be emphasized. Questionnaires can be completed anonymously, as they were in the marijuana study. Also, questions should be written so that respondents do not find it easier or more socially acceptable to answer in a particular way. See Psych Quiz 1, page 14.

However, no matter how carefully the questions have been written and the explanation, directions, and persuasive appeals prepared, it is essential to try them out, or to "pretest" them. As many an investigator has found, what seems completely clear to him can be highly ambiguous to his subjects.

Analysis of the questionnaire responses

When the previous steps are completed, the investigator will have obtained a specific body of information. The next step is to quantify these data in a meaningful way. One simple method is to report the relative frequency of responses in terms of percentages. This type of analysis was used in the Cal. Tech. study, and it was found that 19.8 percent of all undergraduate students who answered the questionnaire reported having used marijuana one or more times "at any time during his lifetime."

Since approximately 20 percent of those responding at Cal. Tech. had used marijuana at least once, could one generalize that probably about 20 percent of all American college stu-

PSYCH QUIZ 1

Writing items that meet the criteria discussed in the text sounds simple. But if you try your hand at writing some items of your own, you will soon find that writing items that people are able and willing to answer is difficult. You will be asked to find the flaws in some items illustrating common defects. First, however, it might be helpful to see some examples of good items: items that ask respondents about information they know and that communicate clearly. Below are three items from the marijuana study.

1. During my lifetime, I have used marijuana:
   _____ Never
   _____ Once or twice
   _____ Three to five times
   _____ Six to nine times
   _____ Ten or more times

2. My plans for the possible use of marijuana *in the next year* may be described as:
   _____ I definitely expect to use it more than once or twice
   _____ I definitely expect to use it once or twice, but probably will not continue using it beyond that
   _____ I might use it once or twice, but I'm not very sure
   _____ I have no present plans for using it, but I might easily change my mind
   _____ I am quite sure that I will not use it

3. Based either on my own personal experience or on what I have read or heard about marijuana, my present belief is best described as:
   _____ This is a beneficial drug, whose values outweigh any likely harmful effects
   _____ This is a fairly harmless drug, with no marked positive value, but with no very serious harmful effects either
   _____ This is a possibly harmful drug, whose dangers are important enough to outweigh possible beneficial effects
   _____ This is an extremely dangerous substance, with little or no beneficial effect
   _____ This may be an extremely dangerous substance, but the benefits more than offset the possible risks
   _____ I have no opinion as to possible benefits or dangers of this drug

If the items had not been as specific, if they had not included all of the possible alternatives, or if they had been worded in emotional terms, they would have been flawed. See if you can find the flaws in the following items; the flaws are given upside down at the end of the quiz.

1. How many times have you used marijuana during your life?
   _____ 1 or more times
   _____ 3 or more times
   _____ 6 or more times
   _____ 10 or more times

2. How many times have you used drugs during your life?
   _____ Never
   _____ 1 or more times
   _____ 3 or more times
   _____ 6 or more times
   _____ 10 or more times

3. How do you feel about heroin and marijuana?
   _____ Strongly approve
   _____ Approve
   _____ Neutral
   _____ Disapprove
   _____ Strongly disapprove

4. How many times have you damaged your body by taking LSD?
   _____ 1 or more times
   _____ 3 or more times
   _____ 6 or more times
   _____ 10 or more times

Flaws:

Item number 1 is based on the assumption that you have used marijuana at least once during your life and provides no alternative answer for a person who has never used the drug.

Item number 2 is too generally worded. "Drugs" may be interpreted as meaning different things by different people. Some might classify everything from aspirin to LSD as a drug, and others might think only of such items as marijuana and LSD.

Item number 3 refers to two different matters. In this "double-barreled" item, the respondent is unable to express his opinion about either issue. For instance, how would a student be able to indicate his disapproval of heroin and his approval of marijuana—if that is how he felt?

Item number 4 uses highly emotional language, is unclear, and does not provide all of the alternatives needed. How would a student reply who had never taken LSD? Or how would a student answer who took LSD frequently, but did not believe that it had damaged his body?

dents had also done so? The answer to this question is emphatically No. Only if the sample has been randomly selected from the entire population is there any justification for making inferences about that population from the sample. Thinking about the Cal. Tech. sample, we can see many ways in which these students might not represent all students. The standards for admission to Cal. Tech. are extremely high; the school is a private, all-male, science-engineering school. These students may be quite different from those at other schools in the United States.

An unexpected finding of the Cal. Tech. study was that the relative incidence of marijuana use varied according to campus residency. Although 15 percent of the undergraduate students living off campus had used marijuana ten or more times, only 4.7 percent of those living on campus reported a similar frequency of use. Why do you think off-campus students were more likely to "turn on"? This finding suggests that there may be some interesting psychological differences associated with on- and off-campus residency. Perhaps students living off campus feel freer from possible sanction from the university. Or students living off campus may be more curious and adventurous and thus more willing to try something new. Or they may be more subject to peer pressures to turn on. In this study, as in any other, unanticipated findings may suggest other research.

Assessing validity and reliability

Now that we have progressed through the various stages of this questionnaire study, two questions remain—its validity and its reliability.

Validity How do we know that the students were giving truthful answers about their reported marijuana and LSD use? This question of the "validity" of the questionnaire responses, or the extent to which the items accurately measured what they appeared to be measuring, is not unique to the Cal. Tech. study. In fact, establishing the validity of questionnaire-interview responses is one of the most difficult problems in this type of research. We have already noted the importance of designing questionnaire items that the respondent is able

and willing to answer. The whole point of all of the questionnaire procedures is to obtain an accurate assessment of some behavior or belief; if the measures are not valid, the entire process is pointless.

How do researchers establish validity? One approach is to *compare the questionnaire-interview responses with some other measure of the same thing.* For instance, if you were interested in assessing the validity of the students' responses on the Cal. Tech. questionnaire, you might obtain some independent measure of which students smoke marijuana and then compare what they did with what they said. But this is easier said than done. How in the world would you obtain an independent measure of the incidence of marijuana use? In surveying other topics, such as voter preference, however, it is relatively simple to compare the poll's predictions with actual voting returns. Obviously, the ease or difficulty of using some other measure to validate questionnaire results varies according to the topic being measured.

Another approach to establishing validity is to *see if there is any evidence that would indicate that the respondents were lying.* In discussing the possibility of different types of falsification, or invalidity, the Cal. Tech. investigator noted that two types of falsification were possible: overreporting and underreporting. Although there was no evidence to suggest overreporting, underreporting was a possible source of error. Student rumors about underreporting were widely circulated, but it was simply not possible to determine the extent to which this kind of bias distorted the data.

Reliability The "reliability," or consistency, of measures also has to be established. Reliability may be considered in two ways: (1) the consistency of answers given by an individual, or "intrapersonal reliability," and (2) the amount of agreement between two different people evaluating the same information, or "interpersonal agreement."

Intrapersonal reliability can be measured in two ways: (1) by comparing responses given to related questions in the same questionnaire or (2) by comparing answers given to the same question on successive occasions. When either method of establishing reliability is used, well-conducted questionnaire-interview studies have been found to have acceptably high levels of reliability (Campbell and Katona, 1953).

In addition to the problem of the consistency of each individual's responses, we need to determine whether or not the persons evaluating the questionnaire data will interpret the data reasonably consistently. If two social psychology instructors who are teaching the same course content to the same level of student read one student's essay exam, and one instructor gives it an "A" while the other gives it a failing grade, the objectivity of their ratings will be highly questionable. If interpersonal agreement between those scoring the same materials is high, confidence in the objectivity of their ratings is increased. Measuring the extent to which various judges agree is a basic problem in all of the social sciences and in all situations in which judgments are used—not just in the questionnaire-interview approach.

Summary

In this section we have seen some of the strengths and problems of the questionnaire-interview approach. To assure a valid study, three steps are essential. First, if you wish to generalize from the responses of a sample to a population, your basis for selecting the sample must provide some reasonable assurance that all members of the population have an equal chance of being included. Second, once the sample has been selected, those selected must be persuaded to participate. Third, questions must be devised so that the respondent is willing and able to answer them.

After all of the information has been collected and analyzed, there are two last extremely important considerations—establishing the validity and reliability of the responses. Although a number of studies have shown that the intrapersonal reliability of well-designed questionnaire-interview studies is very high, establishing the validity of the responses has proved to be a much more difficult matter. In cases such as the study of the incidence of student use of marijuana, independently establishing the validity of the questionnaire reports may be extremely difficult.

Since questionnaire-interview research is so basic to social psychological research, virtually every aspect—from interviewer bias to validity—has been researched. When research is done on research, the problems involved in the procedures emerge and, then known, may be controlled. However, to say that there are certain technical problems in polling is not to minimize the contribution of well-conducted surveys. Without scientific polling to determine voter preferences, political pulse taking would be reduced to "guesstimates" from various authorities about the voters' inclinations.

Correlation

A third, frequently used research approach is to obtain measures on two variables and then assess the extent to which they are related, or correlate. Perhaps two simple examples will indicate precisely what a correlation is.

That lovers tend to gaze more often into each other's eyes than other people is an assumption of psychological folklore that has received some empirical support (Rubin, 1970). To illustrate the use of a correlational approach, let's assume that we have first administered a "love scale" to ten couples. Scores could vary from 1, which would indicate indifference, to 10, which would indicate intense love and involvement

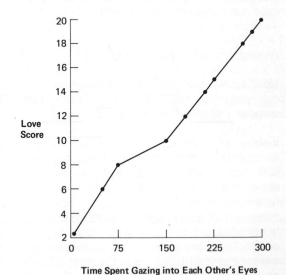

FIGURE 1-2 Positive correlation: Love and gazing.

Table 2

Couple's Love Score	Number of Seconds Spent Gazing into Each Other's Eyes
20	300
19	285
18	270
15	225
14	210
12	180
10	150
8	75
6	50
2	0

with the other person. To obtain a measure of the total attraction, the scores of both members of the couple would be added, so that the highest score possible for a couple would be 20; the lowest score 2. Then the amount of time each couple spent gazing into each other's eyes during a five-minute period would be measured. Let's assume that the scores are as shown in Table 2.

Clearly, in this hypothetical example there is a highly positive relationship between the two sets of scores. By just looking at either the love score or the gazing-time score, you can make a better than chance prediction about what the other score will be. Graphically, the relationship may be shown on a "scatter diagram," in which each point on the graph represents the two scores obtained by the couple. (See Figure 1-2.)

A correlation is a statistically based measure of the degree of the relationship between two sets of scores. The better one score predicts the other score, the higher the correlation is. For instance, if there were complete predictability from love scores to gazing time, the correlation would be +1.00. If there were no relationship at all, the correlation would be 0. For instance, there probably would not be any systematic relationship between the number of freckles students had and the excellence of their test scores in social psychology, and these two measures would probably generate a correlation of 0. There are statistical procedures available for calculating the magnitude of relationships in between correlations of 0 and 1.00. The larger the correlation is, the more predictable one score is from the other.

A correlation does not have to be positive to yield high predictability. A strong negative correlation also means that one score can be predicted very accurately from the other. To see how this works, let's again assume some hypothetical data. Both common sense and some empirical evidence suggest that the degree of one's satisfaction with the present social-economic system is negatively related to the level of his political activism (Gold, Friedman, and Christie, 1971). Assume that we have administered a test measuring "satisfaction with the system," in which scores could vary from 10, indicating extreme satisfaction, to 1, indicating extreme dissatisfaction. Also, assume that the amount of political involvement of each individual has been measured on the same numerical basis, with 10 representing extensive involvement and 1 representing very little or no involvement. From these measures the scores shown in Table 3 might have been obtained:

Table 3

Political Satisfaction	Political Involvement
10	1
5	5
1	10
7	3
9	2
3	8
2	9

There is clearly a highly negative relationship between the two sets of scores. The more satisfied the individual is, the less likely he is to be politically active. Graphically, the relationship is shown in Figure 1-3.

In real life an investigator rarely obtains correlations that yield complete predictability—either positive (+1.00) or negative (−1.00)—since so many other variables influence the variables being measured. Moreover, no matter how high a correlation may be, it does not allow one to infer cause-and-effect relationships. In our example of the negative correlation between satisfaction and involvement, there are many possible reasons for the relationship. For instance, personality factors may be responsible for both the level of satisfaction and the level of involvement. Social pressures not to

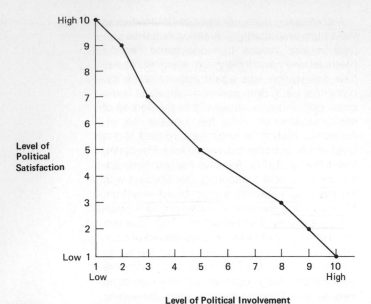

FIGURE 1-3 Negative correlation: Political satisfaction and political involvement.

Plot axes: Level of Political Satisfaction (Low 1 to High 10) on vertical axis; Level of Political Involvement (Low 1 to High 10) on horizontal axis.

become involved may be stronger among persons who are satisfied. Or some other variable—which we are not aware of—may be responsible for the relationship. To give a ludicrous example, people who are satisfied may tend to be less active physically. No matter how high the correlation is, it does not allow us to infer *why* the relationship exists. Unless everything in the situation except the one variable studied is controlled, so many things are varying that it is not possible to draw meaningful conclusions about how the relationship came about. To determine the "why" of any relationship, a controlled experiment is necessary.

Correlation is nevertheless a very useful technique for assessing the *extent* of relationships, and it has been used to study a variety of problems in social psychology. For instance, it has been found that intelligence and conformity are negatively related; persons who are more intelligent are less likely to conform (Nord, 1969). Anti-Semitism is positively correlated with other forms of prejudice; persons who are highly anti-Semitic also tend to dislike members of other minority groups (Adorno, Frenkel-Brunswik, Levinson, and Sanford, 1950). Cigarette smoking and emotionality are positively correlated; persons who smoke are rated as

more "emotional" by their friends than non-smokers are (Smith, 1967). The examples could continue indefinitely.

You may have noticed a feature that is common to correlational research. Variables that develop over a long period of time or are difficult if not impossible to create in a laboratory experimental setting are frequently studied by the correlational approach. These would include such variables as socioeconomic background, personality factors, personal experiences, and deeply experienced emotions. Correlations do not allow us to infer the direction of cause and effect, but they do provide information that allows prediction. In our first hypothetical example, for instance, we really don't know *why* gazing and love were related, but the correlation did tell us they were highly related.

The Controlled Experiment

Suppose you were interested in the question of whether or not an individual is more apt to like a group that he joins if he goes through some discomfort as a part of the initiation process. To investigate this question, you might consider using some of the techniques previously discussed. For instance, you might try observing the reactions of persons who have gone through initiations of varying levels of severity. Although you might note some interesting reactions, you would also encounter some problems. Finding people who have gone through initiations of differential severity might be difficult. Also, your subjects may have differed in their initial enthusiasm about joining the group, and their reactions to the group might therefore reflect not only the severity of their initiation but also the relative level of their initial enthusiasm.

You might use the questionnaire-interview technique and simply ask people if they liked groups more when they had to go through a severe initiation in order to become a member than when they did not. However, many respondents might not know themselves what effect the severe initiation had on their overall reaction. Determining the validity of their answers might be very difficult.

Still a third approach would be to calculate the correlation between the severity of initiation in a number of groups and the members' enthusiasm about those groups. Although this approach would measure the extent of the relationship between severity of initiation and liking, it would not allow you to isolate the effect of initiation from all of the other aspects of the situation. Some other variables, such as differences in the attractiveness of the groups, might be influencing the correlation.

Consequently, the original question remains. How could you test the effect of the severity of initiation on the individual's liking for the group in such a way as to eliminate alternative explanations? The best way would be to set up a controlled experiment. In a controlled experiment the experimenter manipulates one or more variables, called "independent variable(s)," in order to see the effect produced on one or more other variables, called "dependent variable(s)." By attempting to control all other, extraneous variables that might influence the relationship, the investigator seeks to assure that any effects observed are due only to variations in the independent variable.

If there are any systematic differences in the experimental sessions other than those in the independent variable, the study results will be ambiguous. In an initiation study, for instance, if one very attractive group is used in the severe initiation condition and an unattractive group is used in the moderate initiation condition, any variation in the extent to which individuals are attracted to their groups could be attributed to the differences in the attractiveness of the groups, to the differences in initiation, or to some combination of these two variables.

Results arising out of situations in which more than the independent variable is changing are referred to as being "confounded"—that is, the effects of other variables are varying along with the effects of the independent variable. For instance, if the attractiveness of the group varied as well as the severity of the initiation, you would say that attractiveness was confounded with severity of initiation. Other terms, such as "lack of control" or "lack of internal validity," are used to mean roughly the same thing as confounded (Campbell, 1957). No matter what term is used, making sure that nothing except the independent variable systematically varies so that all alternative explanations of the results can be eliminated is not easily done.

In observation, questionnaire-interview, and correlation research, alternative explanations of the results plague the investigator. The controlled experiment greatly reduces the number of possible alternative explanations, as we shall see, but no one experiment can eliminate all alternative explanations. For instance, if severity of initiation is manipulated through the level of humiliation inflicted on pledges, pledge resentment—rather than severity of initiation— may be responsible for the results obtained. Only through a series of successive experiments can alternative explanations of the effects of the independent variable be made less and less probable.

The best way to develop an understanding of the enormous complexity involved in maintaining control is to consider in detail all of the decisions and problems encountered in designing and conducting one experiment. Further, examining one study in detail may sharpen your critical skills in interpreting experimental results. As we shall see repeatedly in this text, results may not mean what they seem to on the surface. To understand experiments, you have to know some of the possible problems involved in maintaining control so that you will be alerted to confounding and alternative explanations. Of course, to point out possible confounding in a particular study is not to say that the experiment is "no good." If the experiment were not of value, it would not be discussed here. However, as you shall see, there are many different problems and possibilities for very subtle sources of confounding.

Our step-by-step analysis will be of a study in which the experimenters sought to investigate the relationship between severity of initiation and liking for a group (Aronson and Mills, 1959). (This experiment has also been analyzed intensively by Aronson and Carlsmith, 1968.) The topic is of practical interest, since so many groups seem to assume that a severe initiation binds the new member more closely to the group. Further, the issue of whether or not severity of initiation is related to the members' attraction to the group is relevant to two topics that will be discussed later in the text— affiliative behavior and groups in action. The experiment also relates to cognitive dissonance theory, which has had a major effect on the field of social psychology. Most important, however, the published report of this work furnishes us with an excellent example of how experiments are designed, conducted, and reported. Extensive excerpts from the published report will be quoted so that you can see what a published report of a well-run psychological experiment looks like.

As this experiment is being analyzed, you should remember that designing and conducting an experiment so that all extraneous variables are completely controlled is an ideal that is seldom—if ever—realized. In interpreting experimental results, the experimenter has to attempt to evaluate the degree to which possible confounding might have influenced the dependent variable. Some confounding is obviously much more serious than others.

Also, you are encouraged to design your own study as you read the analysis of this experiment. If you were interested in the general hypothesis, how would you have done the study? By taking the role of the experimenter, you will become more actively involved in the process of experimental design. The best way to learn about research is to become as actively involved in it as you can.

Before we begin the analysis, one more point should be made. The actual progression of research may or may not have followed the sequence given in the research report. There has been relatively little work on the way research is actually done. What little evidence there is indicates that the published report is much more formal than the actual process.

Getting the idea

The introduction to a report usually includes the experimenter's reasons for doing a study. Aronson and Mills' introduction is quoted in the shaded box.

It is a frequent observation that persons who go through a great deal of trouble or pain to attain something tend to value it more highly than persons who attain the same thing with a minimum of effort. For example, one would expect persons who travel a great distance to see a motion picture to be more impressed with it than those who see the same picture at a neighborhood theater. By the same token, individuals who go through a severe initiation to gain admission to a club or organization should tend to think more highly of that organization than those who do not go through the severe initiation to gain admission.

Two questions are relevant here: 1. Is this "common observation" valid, that is, does it hold true when tested under controlled conditions? 2. If the observation is valid, how can it be accounted for? The relationship might be simply a result of differences in initial motivation. To take the case of initiations, persons who initially have a strong desire to join a particular club should be more willing to undergo unpleasantness to gain admission to it than persons who are low in initial interest. Therefore, a club that requires a severe initiation for admission should be joined only by those people with a strong desire to become members. On the other hand, a club that does not require a severe initiation should be joined by some individuals who like it very much, and by others who are relatively uninterested. Because of this self-selection, one would expect persons who are members of clubs with severe initiations to think more highly of their club, on the average, than members of clubs without severe initiations.

But is there something in the initiation itself that might account for this relationship? Is severity of initiation positively related to group preference when motivation for admission is held constant? Such a relationship is strongly implied by Festinger's (1957) theory of cognitive dissonance. The theory of cognitive dissonance predicts this relationship in the following manner. No matter how attractive a group is to a person it is rarely completely positive, i.e., usually there are some aspects of the group that the individual does not like. If he has undergone an unpleasant initiation to gain admission to the group, his cognition that he has gone through an unpleasant experience for the sake of membership is dissonant with his cognition that there are things about the group that he does not like. He can reduce his dissonance in two ways. He can convince himself that the initiation was not very unpleasant, or he can exaggerate the positive characteristics of the group and minimize its negative aspects. With increasing severity of initiation it becomes more and more difficult to believe that the initiation was not very bad. Thus, a person who has gone through a painful initiation to become a member of a group should tend to reduce his dissonance by overestimating the attractiveness of the group. The specific hypothesis tested in the present study is that individuals who undergo an unpleasant initiation to become members of a group increase their liking for the group; that is, they find the group more attractive than do persons who become members without going through a severe initiation.

[Aronson and Mills, 1959, p. 177.]

How did the investigators arrive at their hypothesis that "individuals who undergo an unpleasant initiation to become members of a group increase their liking for the group"? Two answers are given in the introduction. First, this is a commonsense assumption that seems to be widely applied. You may have noticed that members of fraternities, who have undergone an initiation, seem more loyal to their group than do residents of a dorm, who have not had to suffer for their "membership." Without consciously realizing that they are doing so, many groups may set up a stressful initiation in order to increase the loyalty of their members. Certainly, some of the rigors of professional training—such as the long hours required of a medical intern—may be seen as a kind of hazing. As the experimenters note, however, the only sure way to test whether or not the presumed initiation-liking effect really exists is to demonstrate the relationship in a controlled experiment.

Second, the hypothesis follows from a particular psychological theory—the theory of cognitive dissonance. Before that theory is described, however, a word or two about the importance of theory in social psychology and the relation of theory to research is necessary.

Obviously, the goal of the science of social psychology is to derive an understanding of its subject matter: how people influence one another. But why are theories necessary to do this? Why not simply have a science in which investigators study questions that are of particular interest to them? For instance, those interested in the effects of the severity of initiation could pursue that area; those interested in consumer behavior could study that; and those interested in what leads people to change their attitudes could concern themselves mainly with that issue.

Studies have been done in each of these areas. In the study being discussed in this section, it was found that people are more attracted to groups when they have had to undergo a *severe* initiation. In another study it was found that the *higher* the price a consumer pays for a product, the more he will like it (Doob, Carlsmith, Freedman, Landauer, and Tom, 1969). And in a third experiment it was found that subjects were more willing to change their negative attitudes about fried grasshop-

pers when they ate them for a nasty experimenter than when they ate them for a nice experimenter (Zimbardo, Weisenberg, Firestone, and Levy, 1969).

And so it could go. A series of separate studies yielding highly specific findings about human behavior could be done. But what would the results of such a-theoretical studies tell us about human nature in general? Not much. In contrast, a theoretical approach would focus on an orderly, systematic understanding of how variables influence one another. For example, one theory—cognitive dissonance—is consistent with all three of the findings cited in the preceding paragraph.

The basic concept of dissonance theory is that simultaneously believing two ideas or opinions that are psychologically inconsistent arouses dissonance. Because dissonance is unpleasant, we try to reduce it by removing the inconsistency. To achieve consistency, or "consonance," we may change one of our beliefs to make it consistent, or we may add others (Festinger, 1957).

A number of ingenious experiments have shown that a wide variety of situations that arouse dissonance result in the predicted dissonance reduction. As we will see, in the initiation experiment people were made to like an objectively dull group by being made to go through some unpleasantness in order to join it. The dissonance explanation of this relationship is that the knowledge that you have suffered is inconsistent with the notion that the group for which you have suffered is dull, so you reduce your dissonance by changing your evaluation of the group. Dissonance theory also provides an explanation of the higher price–higher liking relationship. The more you pay for a product, the more dissonance is aroused by the realization that there are things about it that you don't like; so you emphasize the positive aspects of the product. Again, dissonance theory explains the greater persuasiveness of a disliked experimenter. Knowing that you are crunching away on something as repulsive as a fried grasshopper is dissonant with your believing that you are doing this for a nasty experimenter. One way to reduce your dissonance is to change your attitude about the grasshoppers. (For a dissonance explanation of reactions to dancing-partner choices, see Psych Quiz 2, page 22.)

PSYCH QUIZ 2 DISSONANCE AND DANCING

The man at right is making a choice between two equally attractive women. Try to provide a dissonance explanation for what is happening. One dissonance explanation is printed upside down at the bottom of this quiz.

[Festinger, 1962.]

The two girls are equally attractive, as shown in the first panel. However, as shown in the third panel, once a choice is made, all of the information about the positive features of the rejected girl is dissonant with the boy's knowledge that he is not choosing her. Also, any information about the negative aspects of the chosen girl is dissonant with the knowledge that he has chosen her. Both kinds of information—positive about the rejected girl and negative about the chosen girl—are inconsistent with the desire to have made the best decision; so the chooser tries to reduce the dissonance by emphasizing the positive aspects of the chosen girl and the negative aspects of the rejected girl, as shown in the third panel.

The predictions from dissonance theory, which generated more research in social psychology in the 1960s than any other theory, do not seem commonsensical or readily derivable from any other theory. The theory enables experimenters to make predictions about what will happen in a wide variety of situations, generates ideas for research, and provides an organizing principle for the findings of seemingly disparate studies, thus giving us a more coherent view of human nature.

However, if you consider the derivations from the theory, you may see some of the weaknesses of dissonance theory—weaknesses that it shares with other theories in social psychology. The specification of the central theoretical assumptions is somewhat ambiguous. What situations arouse dissonance? What makes beliefs inconsistent? Once dissonance is aroused, how can we predict which strategies will be used to reduce it?

Since social psychology is a relatively new science, much of its theorizing has not yet attained the mathematical elegance of theorizing in the physical sciences. But the usual criteria for evaluating theories in any discipline—simplicity, testability, generation of novel predictions, and internal consistency—can be applied, so that, through a process of testing and refinement, theory in social psychology may become more sophisticated. Thus theoretical research that tests the derivations of existing theories is highly important. Without theories a chaotic goulash of information would be all that would result from scientific research.

Translation of the general idea into experimental procedures

As in any experiment, a number of decisions are involved in going from, or "translating," the general hypothesis to experimental procedures, or in making the concepts "operational." The hypothesis tested in the initiation study concerned the effect of severe initiation on the members' liking of a group.

One of the first decisions the investigators had to make was whether to do the experiment in the laboratory with experimentally created groups or to do the study with existing groups in a "field experiment." If they had used a field approach, the investigators could have used fraternities that seemed equal in all other characteristics but that used differentially severe initiation procedures. Although a field experiment would have had the advantage of being more natural and eliminating the subjects' knowledge that they were in an experiment, control of all of the relevant variables would have been much more difficult. For instance, it would have been extremely difficult to assign all subjects randomly to the various experimental conditions—a very important consideration, since random assignment assures that the chance of there being any systematic differences initially between the subjects in the various experimental conditions is minimal.

Since these experimenters could think of a way to set up realistic conditions in a laboratory setting—as many other investigators have also been able to do—they decided to perform their study in the laboratory. However, we should note that whether a field or a laboratory study is the more appropriate depends on what is being studied. For example, if you wished to study the effect of crowd size on people's attraction to a group, it might be more natural to test that effect in a "live" setting than in the laboratory.

Further, the investigators had to decide whether to test for one independent variable or for several. For example, they could have manipulated two independent variables: (1) severity of initiation and (2) attractiveness of the group. To do so, however, would have required more subjects and a good operational definition for both group attractiveness and severity of initiation. Since the investigators were primarily interested in severity of initiation, they decided to focus all of their energies on testing for its effect. (See Box 2, page 25, for an example of an experiment involving more than one independent variable. Such a study is referred to as a "factorial design.")

Once the investigators decided to perform their experiment in the laboratory and to investigate only one independent variable, there were still many decisions remaining. What should be done to set up a "severe initiation"? Should people be shocked? made to perform difficult tasks? embarrassed? How should "liking" be measured? by watching how people acted? by administering questionnaires? What should be done to make the whole experimental procedure seem "sensible" to the subjects? Is it ethical to make people undergo a severe initiation in order to find out their reactions?

These are just a few of the many questions involved in designing and conducting an experiment. In designing any experiment, the investigator will think of many ways in which his hypothesis could possibly be tested. His problem is to select the way that is the best solution to the problems posed by that experiment. Although this may sound a little vague, a consideration of some of the concrete problems facing the investigators in the initiation experiment should make it clearer. Before discussing these problems, however, we will need to know what procedures were actually followed in this experiment. Accordingly, excerpts from the method section of the experiment are quoted in the shaded box.

In designing the experiment it was necessary to have people join groups that were similar in every respect except for the severity of the initiation required for admission—and then to measure each individual's evaluation of the group. It was also necessary to randomize the initial motivation of subjects (Ss) to gain admission to the various groups in order to eliminate systematic effects of differences in motivation. These requirements were met in the following manner: Volunteers were obtained to participate in group discussions. They were assigned randomly to one of three experimental conditions: A *Severe* initiation condition, a *Mild* initiation condition, and a *Control* condition. In the Severe condition, Ss were required to read some embarrassing material before joining the group; in the Mild condition, the material they read in order to join the group was not very embarrassing; in the Control condition, Ss were not required to read any material before becoming group members. Each S listened to the same tape recording which was ostensibly an ongoing discussion by the members of the group that he had just joined. Ss then evaluated the discussion.

The Ss were 63 college women. Thirty-three of them volunteered to participate in a series of group discussions on the psychology of sex. The remaining 30, tested at a somewhat later date, were "captive volunteers" from a psychology course who elected to participate in the group discussions on the psychology of sex in preference to several other experiments. Since the results obtained from these two samples were very similar, they were combined in the analysis presented here.

Each S was individually scheduled to "meet with a group." When she arrived at the experimental room,

she was told by the experimenter (E) that he was conducting several group discussions on the psychology of sex. E informed her that she was joining a group that had been meeting for several weeks and that she was taking the place of a girl who had to leave the group because of scheduling difficulties. E stated that the discussion had just begun and that she would join the other members of the group after he had explained the nature of the experiment to her. The purpose of the foregoing instructions was to confront S with an ongoing group and thus make plausible the recorded discussion to which she was to be exposed.

E then "explained" the purpose of the experiment. He said that he was interested in investigating the "dynamics of the group discussion process." Sex was chosen as the topic for the groups to discuss in order to provide interesting subject matter so that volunteers for the discussion groups could be obtained without much difficulty. E continued as follows:

"But the fact that the discussions are concerned with sex has one major drawback. Although most people are interested in sex, they tend to be a little shy when it comes to discussing it. This is very bad from the point of view of the experiment; if one or two people in a group do not participate as much as they usually do in group discussions because they are embarrassed about sex, the picture we get of the group discussion process is distorted. Therefore, it is extremely important to arrange things so that the members of the discussion group can talk as freely and frankly as possible. We found that the major inhibiting factor in the discussions was the presence of the other people in the room. Somehow, it's easier to talk about embarrassing things if other people aren't staring at you. To get around this, we hit upon an idea which has proved very successful. Each member of the group is placed in a separate room, and the participants communicate through an intercom system using headphones and a microphone. In this way, we've helped people relax, and have succeeded in bringing about an increase in individual participation."

The foregoing explanation set the stage for the tape recording, which could now be presented to the S as a live discussion conducted by three people in separate rooms.

E then mentioned that, in spite of this precaution, occasionally some persons were still too embarrassed to engage in the discussions and had to be asked to withdraw from the discussion group. S was asked if she thought she could discuss sex freely. She invariably answered affirmatively. In the Control condition S was told, at this point, that she would be a member of the group.

In the other two conditions, E went on to say that it was difficult for him to ask people to leave the group

BOX 2 — EXAMPLE OF A FACTORIAL DESIGN

Suppose an investigator is interested in two questions: (1) the relative drawing power of groups composed of attractive and unattractive females and (2) the relative drawing power of groups of one person and of fifteen people. To study these two independent variables, group size and group attractiveness, the experimenter might test each variable at two different levels. In total there might be four experimental conditions:

1. One person, attractive female
2. One person, unattractive female
3. Fifteen people, attractive females
4. Fifteen people, unattractive females

This design is shown below.

Diagram of a Fictitious Factorial Experiment: Percentage of Passers-by Stopping

		Group Size 1 Person	Group Size 15 People
Attractiveness	Low	20 percent	90 percent
	High	90 percent	20 percent

Note that the effect of one independent variable, group size, depends on the level of the other independent variable, group attractiveness. In this frivolous example, if the group is small, 90 percent of the passers-by stop if the girl is attractive; if the group is large, 90 percent of the passers-by stop if the girls are unattractive. The effect of one of the independent variables changes according to the level of the other. This kind of result is called an "interaction," and there are statistical procedures to test for its existence. Only when factorial designs are used can the presence of an interaction be determined. Thus if an investigator hypothesizes that the effect of one independent variable changes according to the level of another, the factorial design may be the best choice.

Obtaining an interaction does not preclude assessing the effects of each independent variable separately. This information can still be obtained by looking at the experimental results. Thus the effects of any one independent variable can be analyzed separately. In this sense, interaction is completely different from confounding. When confounding occurs, there are no ways to assess the relative contribution of the independent and the uncontrolled variable.

---

once they had become members. Therefore, he had recently decided to screen new people before admitting them to the discussion groups. The screening device was described as an "embarrassment test" which consists of reading aloud some sexually oriented material in the presence of E. S was told that E would make a clinical judgment of her degree of embarrassment, based upon hesitation, blushing, etc., and would determine whether or not she would be capable of participating in the discussion group. He stressed that she was not obligated to take this test, but that she could not become a member unless she did. Only one S declined to take the test. She was excluded from the experiment. . . .

In the Severe condition, the "embarrassment test" consisted of having Ss read aloud from 3 × 5 cards, 12 obscene words. . . . Ss also read aloud vivid descriptions of sexual activity from contemporary novels. In the Mild condition, Ss read aloud five words that were related to sex but not obscene, e.g., prostitute, virgin, and petting. In both the Severe and the Mild conditions, after each S finished reading the material, she was told that she had performed satisfactorily and was, therefore, a member of the group and could join the meeting that was now in progress.

It was of the utmost importance to prevent the S from attempting to participate in the discussion, for if she did, she would soon find that no one was responding to her statements and she would probably infer that the discussion was recorded. To insure their silence, all Ss were told that, in preparation for each meeting, the group reads an assignment which serves as the focal point of the discussion; for this meeting, the group read parts of the book, *Sexual Behavior in Animals*. After the S had indicated that she had never read this book, E told her that she would be at a disadvantage and would, consequently, not be able to participate as fully in this discussion as she would had she done the reading. He continued, "Because the presence of a participant who isn't contributing optimally would result in an inaccurate picture of the dynamics of the group discussion process, it would be best if you wouldn't participate at all today, so that we may get an undistorted picture of the dynamics of the other three members of this group. Meanwhile, you can simply listen to the discussion, and get an idea of how the group operates. For the next meeting, you can do the reading and join in the discussion." Ss were invariably more than willing to comply with this suggestion. The above instructions not only prevented S from attempting to participate in the discussion but also served to orient her toward the actual content of discussion.

Under the guise of connecting the S's headphones

and microphone, E went into the next room and turned on the tape recorder. He then returned to the experimental room, put on the headphones, picked up the microphone, and pretended to break into the discussion which supposedly was in progress. After holding a brief conversation with the "members of the group," he introduced the S to them. Then he handed the headphones to her. The tape was timed so that at the precise moment that S donned her headphones, the "group members" introduced themselves and then continued their discussion.

The use of a tape recording presented all Ss with an identical group experience. The recording was a discussion by three female undergraduates. It was deliberately designed to be as dull and banal as possible in order to maximize the dissonance of the Ss in the Severe condition. The participants spoke dryly and haltingly on secondary sex behavior in the lower animals, "inadvertently" contradicted themselves and one another, mumbled several *non sequiturs,* started sentences that they never finished, hemmed, hawed, and in general conducted one of the most worthless and uninteresting discussions imaginable.

At the conclusion of the recording, E returned and explained that after each meeting every member of the group fills out a questionnaire expressing her reactions to the discussion. The questionnaire asked the S to rate the discussion and the group members on 14 different evaluative scales, e.g., dull-interesting, intelligent-unintelligent, by circling a number from 0 to 15. After completing the questionnaire, S made three additional ratings, orally, in response to questions from E. Nine of the scales concerned the S's reactions to the discussion, while the other eight concerned her reactions to the participants.

At the close of the experiment, E engaged each S in conversation to determine whether or not she was suspicious of the procedure. Only one S entertained definite suspicions; her results were discarded.

Finally, the true nature of the experiment was explained in detail. None of the Ss expressed any resentment or annoyance at having been misled. In fact, the majority were intrigued by the experiment and several returned at the end of the academic quarter to ascertain the results.

[Aronson and Mills, 1959, pp. 177–179.]

Translating the Conceptual Independent Variable into Operations, or Providing an "Operational Definition" All controlled experiments involve a translation of a concept into a specific operation. In the initiation study the general concept of the independent variable was severity of initiation. But how could this general concept

be made operational in the laboratory in such a way that other variables would not be involved also? A number of operations, such as the subjects' receiving electric shocks, eating raw eggs, walking long distances, or being humiliated, could have been used as the operational definition of the concept of a severe initiation.

Why did these investigators decide to use the "embarrassment test," reading a list of dirty words and paragraphs, as the operational definition of the independent variable—severity of initiation? This is a difficult question. When an experimenter sets up an operational definition of an independent variable, a number of considerations are involved: control, impact, ethical problems, etc. Constructing the specific operations for an independent variable is a very complex process for which no easy formula can be given. The experimenter must use his experience and imagination and try to arrive at something that works (Aronson and Carlsmith, 1968).

The task of constructing an independent variable is further complicated by conflicting criteria for a good independent variable. For instance, an experimenter who wishes to maximize the *effectiveness of the independent variable* may nevertheless be concerned about the *welfare of subjects.* A more severe initiation would increase the effectiveness of the independent variable but would be more upsetting to the subjects. A weak initiation would decrease the effectiveness of the independent variable but would be less upsetting to the subjects. The solution is to select a procedure that is effective and yet is not harmful to the experimental subjects.

Another set of conflicting requirements is *control* versus *impact.* The great contribution of the experiment is that it controls for everything except the independent variable. If the independent variable is so weak that it has no impact, the most perfect controls will be completely useless. On the other hand, if, in the initiation study, a more severe initiation had been used—such as having subjects go through a real sorority pledge period—the impact would have been greater but control less. Thus the problem is to select a procedure that will have the desired impact but will still be controllable.

The embarrassment test was a compromise

manipulation, which met all of the necessary requirements for the independent variable. It did not severely injure the subjects and was therefore acceptable on ethical grounds. It did seem to be an effective way to manipulate the severity of initiation, but it was within the control of the experimenter.

Although the respective demands of control and impact must be balanced, one requirement of control cannot be compromised. All subjects must be randomly assigned to the various treatment conditions so that differences in subjects are not confounded with the independent variable. If, for instance, in the initiation experiment all of the subjects in the severe condition had been captive volunteers and all of the subjects in the mild condition had been true volunteers, we would not know whether any differences in ratings were caused by the different experimental conditions or by the initial differences. Unless subjects are randomly assigned, a study is not a controlled experiment (Aronson and Carlsmith, 1968). In the initiation experiment the subjects were randomly assigned to one of the three experimental conditions.

Once the experimenter has juggled all of the considerations of ethics, control, and impact plus other practical considerations in order to construct an independent variable, one question remains. How does he know the procedures will have the desired effect?

To be specific, how do we know that the subjects in the severe group, who read aloud "12 obscene words," plus "two vivid descriptions of sexual activity from contemporary novels," really suffered more than subjects in the mild condition, who "read aloud five words that were related to sex but not obscene, e.g., prostitute, virgin, and petting"?

One cannot assume that because the words look more embarrassing in the severe condition that subjects who read them were actually more embarrassed. Indeed, subjects may have developed other, quite different reactions to the whole procedures, as two psychologists noted in their analysis of the effects of the experimental procedures used in the Aronson-Mills experiment:

Was it to demonstrate the effect of feelings of relief when people discover that a task (the group discussion) is not as painfully embarrassing as the embar-

rassment test led them to believe? No. Was it to demonstrate the effect of success in a difficult task (passing the embarrassment test) on task evaluation? No. Was it to demonstrate the displacement of vicarious sexual pleasure from a discomfiting, but sexually arousing, situation to a more socially acceptable one? No.

[Chapanis and Chapanis, 1964, p. 4.]

As in any experiment, the problem is to ascertain that the specific operations used in the study had the desired effect on the subjects. If, to take one of the alternative interpretations suggested, the embarrassment test simply aroused the subjects, so that they began to think about sex and were doing this when they rated the discussion, the conceptual definition of the independent variable would not have been tested.

Thus finding out if the manipulation had the desired effect is a very important part of experimentation in social psychology. There are several ways to do this (Aronson and Carlsmith, 1968). The investigator can pretest all of his procedures. To do this, he may first begin with rather informal pretesting, in which he exposes a small number of subjects to the experimental procedures and then interviews them to see if there are any problems with the procedures. Then, he can conduct more formal pretesting, in which subjects who are very similar to those who will be used in the experiment are tested and all of the materials are tried out.

Another technique is to obtain some information from the experimental subjects on their reactions to the procedure—either by asking them or by observing them in the procedure. This technique is known as a "manipulation check" and provides information to support the contention that the manipulation of the independent variable really had the desired effect and no other.

How did Aronson and Mills validate their manipulations? The published report does not indicate that any pretesting was done, but three indirect measures of validity were provided. First, the procedures for the different levels of severity of initiation are described, and the reader can infer whether or not the levels of severity seem to be different (a "face validity" approach). Second, the agreement between the experimental results and the predicted effect of the manipulation, according to cognitive dissonance theory, is another indicator of validity. Third, in the interviews conducted at the end of the experiment, subjects were given an opportunity to indicate their feelings about the procedure.

All of these indicators are indirect, and a more direct proof of validity might strengthen our confidence that the manipulation had the desired effect and no other (that is, that it did result in discomfort rather than in sexual arousal). Why didn't the investigators include more direct verification? Both investigators are highly competent social psychologists, who have done a number of excellent experiments. Why the omission? Perhaps there were procedural reasons, which are not indicated in the report, or perhaps the need for a manipulation check was overlooked. In an area as complicated and demanding as designing and conducting experiments, it is very easy to overlook a possible control. Further, designing experiments is highly ego-involving, so that those who are most immediately involved may be less able to see possible flaws than others. The difficulty experimenters have in detecting flaws in their own procedures has been demonstrated in this author's classes. Repeatedly, students have presented what they thought was a perfect experimental design only to have other students detect numerous possible confoundings.

Providing a Rationale for the Procedures In order for the independent variable to influence the subjects, the experimental procedures must seem reasonable. Making procedures seem reasonable has been described as the "concoction of a context—a setting within which the basic manipulations and measurements make sense and have impact, and which integrates all the necessary aspects of the experiment" (Aronson and Carlsmith, 1968, p. 37).

But why must the subjects be deceived in a concocted setting? Why not simply tell them the truth? Consider what might have happened in the initiation experiment if an "honest explanation" of the experimental procedure had been given. The explanation might have gone something like this:

Tonight, we are trying to determine whether or not the severity of initiation into a group influences one's liking for that group. To simulate "initiation" we are going to make you read out loud some embarrassing, obscene words. After you do this, you will then listen, through intercom devices, to a group of persons having a discussion about sex. Direct interaction will be avoided, since we want to keep your reaction to the group as standardized as possible, and this will be easiest if we avoid all face-to-face contact. At the end of the discussion we will want you to evaluate the group and the discussion, and for this purpose you will be furnished a questionnaire.

How valid would any results obtained from this experiment be? To begin with, each of the subjects would be acutely aware of the artificiality of the simulated initiation and its lack of any meaningful connection with the discussion group. Moreover, some subjects might become bored or disinterested in the procedures because of their inability to associate them with a real-life experience. In short, the subjects' reactions would have been badly confounded with their knowledge of the true purpose of the procedures, and little about the effects of severity of initiation would have been learned from the study.

Clearly, a false rationale, or a "cover story," was necessary. In the initiation study the experimenters used the cover that they were interested in the "dynamics of the group discussion process." The investigator said that in order to study this he was conducting a series of group discussions on the psychology of sex, which was chosen as a topic because of its interest. From this cover a justification of all of the experimental procedures followed. The embarrassment test, the operational definition of the initiation to the group, was explained as necessary to assure that persons participating in the discussion on sex could discuss sexual matters freely within the group. Next, since the different subjects would have heard different discussions if they had interacted with a real group, a tape recording of a fictitious group discussion was presented by means of an intercom system. Thus all of the subjects heard an identical group discussion, and so the discussion was completely controlled. The rationale for this was that separation of group participants by means of an intercom device made it easier for them to discuss sex freely. Finally, the experimenter justified asking each subject to rate her feelings about the group—the dependent variable—by explaining his request as "customary procedure."

Clearly, in this case deception well served the experimenter's purpose. The cover story provided a reasonable explanation for all of the procedures, kept the subjects from becoming suspicious (thereby preventing them from providing their own rationales, which might have differed from subject to subject), and made the subjects take the procedures seriously. Nor is this study alone in its use of deception. Two recent studies of the frequency of deception in social psychological research have shown that it is very frequently used—around 40 percent of all research was found to involve some deception (Seeman, 1969).

Deceiving subjects may allow the experimenter to create a realistic experimental setting in which to test his hypothesis, but deception has its disadvantages, too (Kelman, 1967). First, of course, ethical problems are involved. In ordinary life it is generally considered unethical to lie to another person. It can be argued that deception in an experimental context is just as much of a violation of the basic dignity and respect with which others should be treated as it is in ordinary life. When the experimental deception involves imparting false information that may be potentially harmful to the subject, the ethical problems become even graver. In one study, for instance, male undergraduates were led to believe that they had been homosexually aroused by viewing photographs of men (Bramel, 1963). After the experiment was over, of course, the deception was elaborately explained to the subjects, but we can wonder, as we shall see later, whether or not the dehoaxing was entirely successful.

Second, the use of deception introduces a number of methodological problems. Some subjects may become suspicious, and this may influence their behavior (Stricker, 1967). Although not all of the evidence shows that suspicious subjects react differently from those who are not suspicious (e.g., McGuire, 1969b), enough evidence exists to indicate that in at least some cases suspicious subjects react differently from nonsuspicious subjects (e.g., Stricker, Messick, and Jackson, 1967), so that experimenters have to be concerned with controlling for subject suspicion.

How would you find out if the subjects were suspicious? So far, amazingly little research has been done on the problem of detecting suspicion (Rubin and Moore, 1971). The most

usual procedure is to assess subject suspicion by means of either a questionnaire or an interview at the end of the experiment, which is what was done in the initiation experiment. At the end of each experimental session, the experimenter talked with each subject to see "whether or not she was suspicious of the procedure." Only one subject "entertained definite suspicions; her results were discarded." However, detecting suspicion by interview poses some problems. How do we know the subjects were being honest when they said that they were not suspicious? Perhaps some of the captive volunteers, the students from a psychology course who were required to participate, were vaguely apprehensive about the possible effect of expressing such suspicions on their grades, or perhaps they were afraid their suspicion would require them to participate in another study.

If deception involves so many problems—both ethical and methodological—what can be done to minimize or eliminate these problems? A number of possibilities have been proposed (Kelman, 1967). First, investigators should become actively aware of the problems involved in deception. Although in many cases there may be no other alternative than to use deception, in each case the investigator should actively consider whether or not such deception is necessary or justified. Second, when subjects have been deceived, the investigator should make sure that all possible steps have been taken to minimize any possibly negative effects of deceptions. For instance, subjects should be selected in a way that will avoid anyone who might be especially vulnerable to the possibly harmful effects of the deception. In the debriefing interview the reasons for the deception should be explained fully, and the subject should be allowed to work through his feelings about having participated in the study.

Third, new experimental techniques could be developed to eliminate the need for deception. One such technique is role playing. Instead of manipulating variables, the experimenter describes a situation to a subject and asks him to react *as if* he were in that situation. For instance, in the initiation experiment the girls in the various experimental conditions would have been asked to react as if they were subjected to these conditions. With one or two exceptions (e.g., Horowitz and Rothschild, 1970), however, the results of studies using this technique cast serious doubt on its validity as an overall replacement for more traditional experimental procedures. (See Miller, 1972, for a review.) As you know, people are not always aware of how they would react in a novel situation. Moreover, even if they were, they might be reluctant to be honest and would respond in the way they think they *should* react. The information provided by role-playing studies really constitutes guesses from a group of subjects about their reactions—not controlled reactions (Freedman, 1969).

Thus there is no easy answer to the ethical and methodological problems of using deception as an experimental technique. Although the investigator should be aware of the problems of deception and attempt to minimize them if he uses the technique, in the last analysis he is the only one who can settle the ethical question of whether or not he is justified. See Box 3 for an analysis of the ethical problems in one well-known study.

Obtaining Subjects If you were going to replicate the initiation experiment, where would you get subjects? If you are like Aronson and Mills and most other investigators, you'd probably use college students. It has been estimated that about 80 percent of the published research is done on the 6.3 percent of the adult population that attends college (Smart, 1966). Since social psychologists are presumably interested in understanding the social behavior of all people— not just that of college sophomores who are taking a psychology course—this limitation on the population of subjects studied may be seriously limiting the extent to which experimental findings can be generalized to other populations.

College students differ from the general population in a number of ways that seem very relevant to their psychological reactions. College students obtain higher scores than others on standardized tests of verbal skills (Fleming, 1958). Students are a young group, mainly between the ages of eighteen and twenty-four. Also, the college student population includes more upper- and middle-class people than the general population (Fleming, 1958). With all these distinctions, we can readily wonder

whether, and to what extent, one can generalize from this group to the rest of the general population.

As if largely limiting the subject population used in social psychological research were not biasing enough, many research studies have used subjects taking an introductory course in social psychology. This reliance on introductory psychology students as subjects may influence research results in a number of ways. First, as part of the course requirements in many introductory psychology courses, students are required to participate in a certain number of psychological experiments. Understandably, students may be less than enthusiastic about their compulsory participation. In one study of the attitudes of 251 students at New York University toward this requirement, 40 percent of the students felt negatively about it—with feelings ranging from irritation to fear and apprehension (Gustav, 1962). Somewhat predictably, the negative attitudes of the captive volunteers could make them perform differently from subjects who enter the experiment through their own free choice. Such differences were found in one recent study (Cox and Sipprelle, 1971). In the initiation experiment, however, there were no significant differences between the reactions of captive volunteers and those of actual volunteers.

A second major disadvantage of using introductory college students as subjects is that many of them may have participated in previous studies that involved deception. Being deceived and then being made aware of the deception may influence the subjects' performance in later experiments. Studies comparing the performance of subjects who have been deceived in previous experiments with subjects who have not been deceived previously have yielded inconsistent results. Sometimes a history of being deceived has significantly influenced the subjects' behavior in later studies (e.g., Silverman, Shulman, and Wiesenthal, 1970), and sometimes it has not (Brock and Becker, 1966). Until more experimental evidence is accumulated, the safest policy may simply be not to use subjects who have been in other experiments that involved deception.

A third disadvantage of using psychology students as subjects is that their increasing knowledge of psychology will influence their

BOX 3
A CASE HISTORY IN ETHICS: THE OBEDIENCE EXPERIMENT

The American Psychological Association has set forth basic ethical principles for researchers who work with human subjects:

"a. Only when a problem is of scientific significance and it is not practicable to investigate it in any other way is the psychologist justified in exposing research subjects, whether children or adults, to physical or emotional stress as part of an investigation.

"b. When a reasonable possibility of injurious aftereffects exists, research is conducted only when the subjects or their responsible agents are fully informed of this possibility and agree to participate nevertheless.

"c. The psychologist seriously considers the possibility of harmful aftereffects and avoids them, or removes them as soon as permitted by the design of the experiment."

[*Casebook on Ethical Standards of Psychologists,* 1967, pp. 70–71.]

In order to see how difficult it is to apply these seemingly clear standards, let us consider one well-known study—that of Milgram's work on obedience. Under the guise of teaching the correct response in a learning study, the experimenter directed his subjects to administer increasingly severe levels of electric shocks to another person, who was supposedly participating in the learning study. The shocks were graded from "Slight Shock" to "Danger: Severe Shock." In fact, the "learners" were experimental confederates who actually received no electric shocks. The subjects were not aware of this fact, however, and the "measure of their obedience" could therefore be validly determined by the highest intensity of shock they would administer. Unexpectedly, of the forty subjects tested, twenty-six administered the highest level of shock possible, and many showed extremely high levels of tension (Milgram, 1963).

The question that has been extensively debated is whether or not Milgram's work violated the rights of the subjects who participated in his study. One prominent critic of Milgram's work has argued forcefully that he did violate their rights (Baumrind, 1964). According to her, the self-respect of those who complied and administered the maximal shocks may have been irreparably harmed, and the subjects may have lost a certain amount of their ability to trust authority figures. Only if the results of a potentially dangerous experiment were of immediate and clear benefit to humanity—like the polio vaccine—*or* if the subjects were warned of the potential damage would such studies as Milgram's be defensible according to this critic.

As you might imagine, Milgram has not remained silent while his work has been criticized. In rebuttal, he has advanced a number of arguments (1964). First, a careful postexperimental interview was conducted to dehoax the subjects and, at the same time, allow them to work out their feelings about the experiment. Subjects were told that many others had reacted as they had. Further, a questionnaire was sent to all of the subjects who had participated, and of the 92 percent who returned the questionnaire, 84 percent indicated that they were glad they had participated. For some subjects there was evidence that having gone through the trauma of the obedience experiment strengthened their belief in their own responsibility for their own actions. As a final precaution, a psychiatric interview was held with forty of the subjects, who were thought to be most likely to have been affected by the experiment, and none of them showed any signs of having been psychologically harmed.

Thus Milgram has gathered an impressive array of rebuttals to his critics. But, of course, whether or not he has met the three ethical guidelines set forth at the beginning of this box remains a question of personal values. How would you react if you heard that a well-trained psychologist were going to replicate the obedience test at a college that a very close friend of yours attends? If the test were done, what safeguards would you want to see implemented?

reactions to studies. Once you know about conformity and the standard experimental ways of testing it, you may be much less susceptible to group pressures. Experimental support for the biasing effect of the subject's increasing knowledge about psychology on his performance has been obtained (Page, 1968).

If the investigator expands his source of subjects and asks for volunteers in general, he may still fail to obtain a sample that represents the general college population. A person who volunteers may feel some commitment to the experiment, since he knows that he has freely offered his services and that no coercion is involved in his participation. The evidence is not completely consistent, but it seems that volunteers generally possess a superior intellectual ability, have greater self-confidence, and tend to be more sociable and more unconventional than nonvolunteering students (Rosenthal, 1965). These differences in personal characteristics between volunteers and nonvolunteers would suggest that the two types of subjects might react differently in some experimental situations. The results of a recent study show that this was the case in at least one situation. Subjects who volunteered disclosed a significantly greater amount of personal information than did nonvolunteers (Hood and Back, 1971).

These comments about the ways in which subjects' characteristics can influence their reactions in particular psychological experiments should not be interpreted as a condemnation of the evidence accumulated through experiments using the typical subject for social psychological experiments (Oakes, 1972). The phenomena revealed in working with these students are real in the population sampled. The problem is to establish whether or not these phenomena exist in other populations. Most of them undoubtedly do. No matter what group is studied, conformity pressures are probably very high. But the occurrence of some phenomena may be limited to the populations studied so far. For instance, social rewards have been found to have different effects on college students and "real people"—subjects recruited through advertisements in New York City newspapers (Oakes, 1972). Only more work with a number of different populations will enable us to understand how different subject populations react to various experimental conditions.

Avoiding Confounding Perhaps the most important requirement in setting up any controlled experiment is to develop the experimental conditions in such a way as to minimize the number of alternative explanations for the results obtained. For instance, we saw that the problem of translating "severity of initiation" into a laboratory procedure was to minimize the possibility of the results being caused by anything other than severity of initiation.

In addition to the many possible sources of confounding discussed so far, some other possible sources, called experimental "artifacts," have received widespread attention. Experimental artifacts are particular demands of the experimental situation that may have an effect on the behavior of the subject and the experimenter. The experiment is a social situation involving the interaction of the experimenter and the subject. Each has a clearly defined role to play. Usually, the experimenter is testing a hypothesis, and the subject knows his reactions to the experimental conditions will help determine the validity of that hypothesis (although he is rarely told what hypothesis is being tested). Further, the subject may be apprehensive about how the experimenter will evaluate his reactions. Both the experimenter's and subject's roles can influence the subject's behavior in the experiment.

A series of studies have shown that the *experimenter's expectations* can sometimes significantly influence the subject's behavior (Rosenthal, 1966). The experimenter's hypothesis about what he expects to happen in the various experimental conditions may lead him to behave differently toward the subjects, without his consciously realizing that he is doing so, so that his expectations become self-fulfilling prophecies. In some cases subjects may act as they do, not because of the independent variable, but because of the experimenter's differential treatment of them.

In an early study the significant effect of the experimenter's expectations, or the "Rosenthal effect," as it has come to be known, was dramatically shown. College undergraduates, enrolled in an experimental psychology course, were told that they were to do an experiment on rates of maze learning in rats of differing abilities. Half of the students were told that they were going to be working with "maze-bright" rats, which would learn well; the other half of the students were told that they had been assigned "maze-dull" rats, which would probably show very little evidence of learning. Actually, the rats had been randomly assigned to the students, so that there were no real differences in their abilities. The independent variable in this study was the student experimenters' expectations about their rats' performance.

Despite the fact that initially there had been no differences in the rats' abilities, rats that had been identified as being maze-bright showed significantly more learning than the rats labeled as maze-dull. The rats performed as the student experimenters expected them to perform. (See Figure 1-4, page 34.) Apparently, without knowing it, the different student experimenters had treated their rats differently, and their expectations produced the expected results (Rosenthal and Fode, 1963).

Teachers' expectations have also been shown to have a significant impact on student performance. In one study teachers were told that some children in their class were "intellectual bloomers who will show unusual intellectual gains during the academic year." Although these children had been randomly selected from the class, so that there was no objective reason to expect them to perform better than the other students, they did what was expected of them and did show more intellectual development than the other children (Rosenthal and Jacobson, 1968).

The power of expectations in shaping behavior is extremely interesting. The Rosenthal effect may be a potent determinant of behavior in many situations. For instance, some have argued that the poor academic performance of many ghetto schoolchildren may be due to their teachers' negative expectations about their levels of performance. Before the teachers actually have any contact with the children, they have a stereotype of ghetto children as slow learners. The covert communication of these expectations may result in the prophecies being fulfilled (Clark, 1965).

That the Rosenthal effect can occur in some situations is clear. The remaining and intriguing questions are when and how it occurs. Research to answer these questions is just beginning. However, the results of one study suggest that the Rosenthal effect is more likely to occur with human subjects who feel apprehensive about being evaluated (Minor, 1970). Perhaps the subject's apprehensiveness about being in the experiment makes him more sensitive to the subtle cues through which the experimenter conveys his expectations. Exactly how experimenters or teachers convey their expectations is not yet clear. The present evidence suggests that expectations are conveyed in the quality of the interpersonal interaction. For instance, when teachers were told that certain children were gifted (when actually the children in question had been randomly selected from the class), the teachers were observed to call upon and praise the "gifted children" more often than children they did not think were gifted (Rubovits and Maehr, 1971).

Interesting as the Rosenthal effect is as a social fact, however, it is obviously a very serious possible source of confounding if it is not controlled. Although not all studies have replicated the effect (e.g., Barber and Silver, 1968), there is enough evidence to show that sometimes it can occur.

A number of techniques for controlling the effect have been suggested. Since subjects may be most likely to fulfill the experimenter's hypothesis when they are apprehensive, any procedures that will reduce the level of their apprehensiveness might reduce the chance of the Rosenthal effect's occurring. Another strategy is to keep the experimenters who are testing the subjects as ignorant of the hypothesis as possible. If they are not told what to expect, they are much less likely to "shape" the behavior of their subjects to fit their expectations (Rosenthal, 1966).

As was said earlier, the subject also has a role to play, and his role may also influence his reactions in the experiment and become confounded with the independent variable. Four such subject roles have been described. One is that of the "good subject," the subject who tries to give responses that he thinks will validate the experimenter's hypothesis. To the extent that the experimental procedures make explicit what the experimenter is trying to prove—or, to use the technical term, to the extent that there are "demand characteristics" in the experiment

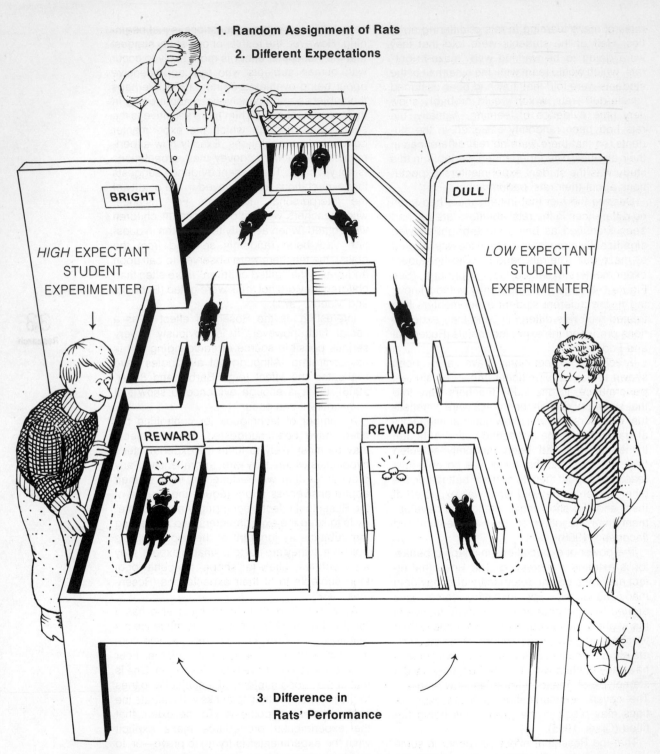

1. Random Assignment of Rats

2. Different Expectations

BRIGHT

DULL

HIGH EXPECTANT
STUDENT
EXPERIMENTER

LOW EXPECTANT
STUDENT
EXPERIMENTER

REWARD

REWARD

**3. Difference in
Rats' Performance**

FIGURE 1-4 Even rats do what is expected of them: A characterization of the Rosenthal-Fode experiment.

(Orne, 1962)—a subject's playing the good subject role may confound the experiment. In support of the confounding effect of this role, studies have shown that when the subjects have been explicitly told the experimental hypothesis, they have generally tended to substantiate the hypothesis more than subjects who were not informed (Weber and Cook, 1972).

As we have already seen, subjects can be very apprehensive about being evaluated, and this "evaluation apprehension" describes a second type of subject role. A series of studies have shown that subjects respond in terms of what they are told are norms of psychological health, maturity, and intelligence (Rosenberg, 1969). Indeed, evaluation apprehension is probably a stronger motive in many subjects than the desire to play the good subject role (Sigall, Aronson, and Van Hoose, 1970).

The other two subject roles have not been as thoroughly documented as the two just discussed. One is that of the "negativistic subject," a subject who does the opposite of what he thinks the experimenter wants him to do. The other is that of the "faithful subject":

someone who believes that a high degree of docility is required in research settings and who further believes that his major concern should be to scrupulously follow experimental instructions and to avoid acting on the basis of any suspicions he might have about the true purpose of the experiment.

[Weber and Cook, 1972, p. 275.]

Controlling for these subject roles is more difficult than controlling for the experimenter's expectations. At present there is no rigorous evidence suggesting when students will adopt a given role or precisely how their roles will influence their behavior. For instance, in an experiment on attitude change an apprehensive subject might change his attitude more easily if he thinks that makes him look good, or he might become more resistant if he thinks that being independent will win favor. In any event, the fact that a number of studies show that bias results from a subject's learning the hypothesis suggests that the less obvious the hypothesis is from the experimental procedures, the less likely subject roles are to influence and distort the subjects' reactions.

Further, the problem of subject roles may vary according to the experimental topic and setting. In areas in which there is a clear norm about good performance, evaluation apprehension may become very great. For instance, administering a test of prejudice in a college atmosphere in which prejudice is clearly unfashionable may result in the students' presenting themselves as being less prejudiced than they are in fact. In another situation, in which the experimenter exerts a great deal of pressure on the subject, a negative reaction might be more likely. And if the subject knows that confirmation of the hypothesis is very important to the experimenter, he may be more likely to play the role of the good subject. In situations that seem conducive to the appearance of one or more of these subject roles, the careful experimenter will attempt to minimize cues that could lead to these types of role behavior.

Were these various experimental artifacts operative in the initiation experiment? Clearly, the investigators had definite ideas of what they were looking for—a substantiation of their hypothesis that increasing the severity of initiation into a group tended to increase the members' liking for the group. Did this hypothesis affect their conducting of the experiment? We do not know for sure, since the investigators did not control for this artifact.

Why didn't they? One answer is that the study was done in 1958, five years before Rosenthal published the report of his first experiment on the effect of the experimenter's expectancy. Until an artifact is documented, experimenters can hardly be expected to control for it. As more information about research is accumulated, more potential artifacts are discovered and then controlled for. In order to control an experiment completely, the investigator would have to know all of the variables that could influence behavior—a complete psychology.

What about the problem of "subject roles"? Here it would appear that the possibility of an artifact is even less likely. Since the experimenters very cleverly disguised the true purpose of the experiment, it seems reasonable to assume that the severity-liking hypothesis was obscured sufficiently to eliminate any meaningful possibility of the subjects' consciously or unconsciously distorting their questionnaire responses by playing a role.

Translating the Dependent Variable into Experimental Procedure The problems in this translation are similar to those discussed in connection with manipulating the independent variable and eliminating confounding. You wish to select experimental procedures that will closely resemble the conceptual dependent variable. You also want your subjects to take the procedures seriously and to respond to them honestly—not in terms of demand characteristics. Also, practical concerns and concerns about the welfare of the experimental subjects are relevant. Constructing a measurement that meets all of these criteria is a difficult business.

In the initiation experiment the investigators wished to measure the members' liking for a group. How could they do this? One way would be to obtain a "behavioral measure," or let the subjects do something that seemed to express their liking for the group. In this experiment a variety of behavioral measures could have been used. For instance, a series of "discussion sessions" could have been scheduled, and the number of sessions that a subject actually attended could have been counted.

Another approach would be to measure the subject's intention to perform activities that seem indicative of his liking—a "behavioroid measure" (Aronson and Carlsmith, 1968). In one study, for instance, the subject's liking for an experimenter was assessed by counting the number of telephone calls a subject promised to make on behalf of the experimenter (Aronson and Cope, 1968).

Still another way to measure liking would be to use "self-report measures," either by interview or questionnaire. For instance, to find out whether or not subjects liked the fictitious groups, an experimenter could ask them to indicate their feelings about the group participants and the discussion. This is how Aronson and Mills obtained their measures of liking for the fictitious groups. Subjects were asked to rate the discussion and group members on seventeen scales (e.g., "dull-interesting, intelligent-unintelligent") by circling a number from 0 to 15.

Which of these three approaches is the best? Each has its advantages and its disadvantages. One advantage of a behavioral measure is that it requires more effort and commitment from the subjects than the self-report and the behavioroid measures do. Yet, behavioral measures have disadvantages, too. Behavior may reflect a variety of motives. For instance, a subject's attending a meeting might be an index of loneliness as well as an index of liking for the group. Also, obtaining behavioral measures may be more time-consuming and expensive than obtaining either of the other two forms of measure.

Self-report measures are easier to administer than behavioral measures and may seem more clearly related to the conceptual variable than a behavior does. If you are trying to find out whether or not a subject liked a group, what could be more direct than asking him?

The problem is that it may be too direct. In some studies, as we saw in the discussion of demand characteristics, the experimenter's intent is rather clear. Such knowledge of the experimenter's intent can create invalidity in a number of ways. For instance, if subjects go through the severe initiation procedure and then are asked to rate the group, they might have a desire to appear to be good sports and thus give the group a good rating.

Behavioroid measures are a compromise between self-report and behavioral measures, and as such, they possess some of the advantages and disadvantages of both techniques. A behavioroid measure is easier to obtain than a behavioral measure but is less committing. Saying you plan to attend a group meeting may be more committing than checking "very favorable" on a questionnaire, but it is less committing than actually attending a given number of times.

Although all of the measures have advantages and disadvantages, the most frequently used measure is the self-report—especially in attitude research. In fact, in experimental social psychology the use of either behavioral or behavioroid measures is unusual. Why is this the case? Two prominent social psychologists have suggested that

> . . . all too often it appears that the questionnaire is chosen because it is simpler to concoct and easier to administer. With more effort and ingenuity, many studies could be designed to include behavioral data.
>
> [Aronson and Carlsmith, 1968, p. 56.]

Conducting the Experiment, or "Running" the Subjects After an investigator has worked hard to develop all of the experimental procedures, the time finally comes to conduct the experiment. How should this be done? Most would agree that the experimenter should be a constant in all of the experimental conditions; his behavior should be standardized. To accomplish this standardization, experimenters are usually given the same set of experimental "directions," which are to be followed verbatim. Standardized instructions were used in the initiation experiment. Indeed, the exact comments made by the experimenter in introducing the embarrassment test were included in the research report. Providing directions for the experimenter is very typical; in fact, the usual research report indicates that all experimenters read identical directions to the experimental subjects.

But does providing standard instructions really result in "standardized," unchanging experimenters? Little research has yet been done directly on this question. What has been published seems to show that in spite of standard instructions, experimenters may vary considerably in some cases.

In order to see how experimenters actually behaved, one investigator photographed twenty-nine experimenters, who were male graduate students in educational psychology, while they tested female subjects, who were enrolled in lower division undergraduate courses at the University of North Dakota. Neither the experimenters nor the subjects were aware that they were being photographed. All experimenters were given the usual type of standard instructions to read from a mimeographed sheet (Friedman, 1967).

How standardized were the experimenters? Not very. The experimenters differed in a number of ways, such as in the greeting they gave when the subject entered the room, their interpersonal behavior (degree of smiling, eye contact, etc.), their tone and emphasis in reading the instructions, and the degree to which they modified the instructions. To illustrate this variability, two examples of the different greetings the experimenters gave are quoted below:

Experimenter #1
E (S walks in and sits down.): How are you this evening?
S: Fine. What's going on?
E (Laughs.): I can't tell you.

Experimenter #2
E (S walks in. E is busy putting away rating sheets from previous Ss. He has them spread over the table. Looking down and continuing his work.): Hi.
S: Excuse me.

[Friedman, 1967, p. 75.]

FIGURE 1-5 Subject reactions to variations in the experimenter's behavior.

The atmosphere of the first E-S exchange is clearly quite different from that of the second E-S exchange. In the first the situation is much more friendly and less formal; E and S are joking about the secrecy. Contrast this with the atmosphere in the second exchange. The situation is so chilly that the S reacts by being apologetic: "Excuse me." (See Figure 1-5.)

Variations among experimenters have even been noted in their reading of standardized instructions. Since providing written instructions has been assumed to produce uniformity, this variability is quite interesting. Experimenters changed the directions by omitting words and changing the order of the material that was supposed to be read. In addition, the tone of voice in which the experimenters read the standard directions varied. Summarizing his series of studies, the investigator concluded:

I have been concerned with a discrepancy between the ideal and the real. Psychological experiments are supposed to be standardized, controlled, replicable, objective. These experimental sessions were unstandardized, uncontrolled, different, heterogeneous. Psychological experimenters are supposed to be inflexible, mechanical, "programmed," standardized in their behavior. These experimenters improvised and ad-libbed and were nonconforming, different, variable in their behavior.

[Friedman, 1967, p. 106.]

What could be done to decrease experimenter variability? One obvious approach, which is frequently followed, is to use the same experimenter in all of the various experimental conditions. However, even if the same experimenter is used, his style of dealing with the subjects may influence the effects of the independent variable. A warm, friendly experimenter, for example, might have obtained results in the initiation experiment that were far different from those obtained by an aloof, cold experimenter.

Another suggestion, which is more difficult to implement, is that all of the social interactions that occur in an experimental session be standardized. More occurs in an experiment than just reading the experimental directions. The experimental session is also a social interaction, with all of the attendant social behaviors.

Whenever people interact, there will be a greeting of some sort. If there are no explicit rules to govern the behavior of the experimenter, each experimenter will greet subjects in his own manner. To be sure that all experimenters are responding in the same way, the investigator should give them recommended procedures for all of the behaviors that occur. However, even with such recommendations, one might doubt that all inter-experimenter differences would be eliminated.

Another possible approach to eliminating experimenter variability is to use some type of "canned" directions, such as tape-recorded or printed directions. These devices have the advantage of complete standardization, but a live experimenter can make the subjects take the experiment more seriously and can respond to unforeseen events, such as equipment breakdown. Thus the live experimenter is not just a potential source of experimental error; he can also be a source of experimental authenticity. Which he is depends largely on how standardized he can keep his behavior.

Conducting the Postexperimental Interview Whether or not any deception is used in an experiment, each subject should be interviewed at the end of the experiment in order to obtain his general reactions to the procedures and also to explain what was done and why. This interview also gives the experimenter an opportunity to thank his subject for his time and effort. When deception is involved in an experiment, the postexperimental interview assumes an even greater importance. It provides an opportunity for the experimenter to see if the deception worked and to remove the deception, or to "dehoax" or "debrief" the subjects. Such a dehoaxing interview was held at the conclusion of the initiation experiment.

If deception is involved and if more experimental sessions are scheduled, the subjects should be asked not to discuss the experiment with anyone. The subjects' maintaining secrecy is of utmost importance, since if even one subject discusses the experiment, subjects who participate later may be aware of all of the details of the procedure—including the false cover story. And screening these forewarned subjects from naïve subjects would be extremely difficult.

How well do these pleas for secrecy work? Do subjects who have been asked not to discuss an experiment in fact maintain secrecy? So far, the little empirical research that has been done on this question has yielded inconsistent results. In one study undergraduate experimental confederates said they were going to be participating in an experiment and tried to obtain information on the experiment from three friends who had recently participated; none of the subjects revealed what the true purpose of the experiment was to the confederate (Aronson, 1966a).

In contrast, other studies have shown that the secrecy pleas may not be effective. One investigator asked subjects who had previously been sworn to secrecy if they had "talked to people about this research," and 64 percent of the subjects said they had (Wuebben, 1967). Whether or not a subject reveals the experimental "secret" may depend on the effectiveness of the particular plea as well as on how he is asked and by whom. In the study in which none of the subjects revealed the secret, the confederate said that he was going to participate subsequently in the study. It may be that subjects may feel the prohibition against discussing the experiment applies only to persons whom they know will be actively involved.

If deception has been involved in the experiment, how effective are the dehoaxing procedures? Available research results indicate that dehoaxing may not be as effective as experimenters hope. Although comparatively little research has been done on the effectiveness of dehoaxing, two experiments have shown that even after a lengthy and thorough dehoaxing, subjects continued to act as though the dehoaxing had not occurred: The subjects' reactions continued to be influenced by the fictitious information even after they had been told that it was not true. For instance, in one study in which subjects were given fictitious "sociability scores," even after dehoaxing, subjects who had been given high fictitious sociability scores rated themselves higher on sociability than subjects who had received low fictitious sociability scores (Walster et al., 1967).

These residual effects after dehoaxing are particularly surprising in view of the fact that the subjects seemed to be thoroughly dehoaxed:

It is disturbing that in the present experiment . . . , even after a very lengthy and thorough debriefing (probably atypical in thoroughness), subjects still behaved to some extent as though the debriefing had not taken place. Subjects behaved in this manner even though they had voiced to the experimenter their understanding that the manipulation was false, their understanding of the true purpose of the experiment, and even though, by their manner and replies, the experimenter had been satisfied that they did indeed understand the nature of the deception.

[Walster et al., 1967, p. 380.]

Clearly, much more work is needed to determine the effectiveness of various debriefing procedures and the long-term effects of such procedures—especially in view of the high frequency of studies using deception. Subjects are told a wide variety of fictitious things, and if it is found that debriefing does not wipe out the effects of the deception, the ethical problem will be even more intense.

Analyzing the data

The goal of all of the procedures discussed so far has been to find out if there is a relationship between the independent and the dependent variable. The experimental procedures have been devised to eliminate confounding and error; subjects have been run, etc.; and now the effect of different severities of initiation on liking can be measured.

You will recall from our previous discussion that all of the subjects in the various experimental conditions answered seventeen questions rating the group discussion and the participants. Larger numbers meant more favorable evaluations: 0 was the worst rating a participant could give on a particular item; 15 was the most favorable. Thus the total score for each subject could vary between 0 and 255 (or 17×15).

To obtain the average rating given by the subjects in each of the conditions, all of their ratings would be added and then divided by the number of subjects in the condition. In the initiation experiment the average rating of the discussion group was 166.7 for subjects in the control condition, 171.1 for subjects in the mild condition, and 195.3 for subjects in the severe condition. That is, subjects in the severe condition gave more favorable ratings than did subjects in either the mild or the control condition. In fact, the average rating in the severe condition was 24.2 points higher than the average for the mild condition.

Do the differences in the ratings substantiate the hypothesis that more severe initiation leads to greater liking? Not yet; one more step is needed. A statistical test of "significance" must be done to assess the probability that the differences between the ratings could be due to chance factors, such as sampling variation. You will recall that since all of the subjects in the initiation experiment were randomly assigned to the various experimental conditions, it was assumed that there were no initial differences among the subjects in the various groups. However, what if, by chance, the girls assigned to the severe condition were more predisposed to like their group than the girls assigned to the other two conditions? Such an initial difference is not likely, but it is possible. A statistical test of significance assesses the chances that random assignment of the subjects could have resulted in the differences obtained.

To assess statistical significance, a number of tests are used. Although the procedures involved differ, all of these tests have the common purpose of deriving a probability that the findings could have occurred by chance.

The exact value of the probability that chance alone could have produced the results is reported in decimal form and is read accordingly. For instance, a probability of .01 indicates that there is less than one chance in a hundred that the obtained results were caused by chance factors, and a probability of .05 indicates that there are less than five chances in a hundred that the differences were caused by chance. Although conventions vary among investigators, the usual practice is to consider any results that meet a .05 level of probability or better as being "statistically significant." Thus if a result reaches the .05 level or the .01 level, it increases our confidence that the independent variable is responsible for the effect. Throughout the text, when differences between various experimental conditions are said to be "signifi-

cantly different," this is the sense in which the term will be used.

To return to the results of the initiation experiment, you will recall that the average rating was 171.1 for subjects in the mild condition and 195.3 for subjects in the severe condition. Thus the difference between the averages in the two conditions is 24.2 points. The investigators reported that a statistical test of significance showed that the probability was less than five chances in one hundred that the difference of 24.2 points could be obtained by chance alone. Or, in the terminology that will be employed throughout the text, the subjects in the severe condition were significantly more attracted to their group than were the subjects in the mild condition. There was no significant difference between subjects who had gone through a mild initiation and those who had had no initiation at all (the control condition).

One last point about the definition of the term "significance." In this section we have been talking about "statistical significance," a statistical assessment of the role of chance factors in creating a particular experimental result. Note, however, that "significance" may also be used in another sense—that of "psychological significance," the importance of a particular result. If we measured the height of 6 million Mainland Chinese and 6 million Americans, we would probably find that Americans on the average are taller and that the differences in height are statistically significant. But would the difference be psychologically significant? Does it make an important contribution to our understanding of behavior? Does it have immediate practical implications? The answer to these questions is a matter of judgment, and various psychologists might differ.

Summarizing and interpreting the data

In their summary and conclusions section, the investigators who conducted the initiation experiment make the statement which appears in the shaded box.

An experiment was conducted to test the hypothesis that persons who undergo an unpleasant initiation to become members of a group increase their liking for the group; that is, they find the group more attractive than do persons who become members without going through a severe initiation. . . .

. . . The results clearly verified the hypothesis. Subjects who underwent a severe initiation perceived the group as being significantly more attractive than did those who underwent a mild initiation or no initiation. There was no appreciable difference between ratings by subjects who underwent a mild initiation and those by subjects who underwent no initiation.

[Aronson and Mills, 1959, pp. 180–181.]

Clearly, subjects in the severe initiation condition were more attracted to the group. However, the question of *why* they were, or the interpretation of the results, remains. The explanation offered by the investigators is that the differences were caused by differences in the severity of initiation. Once a person has suffered to gain admission to a group, his thinking that the group is dull arouses dissonance. To reduce this dissonance, the individual persuades himself that the group is really attractive.

However, there are other interpretations that would fit the initiation study results as well as the cognitive dissonance explanation (Chapanis and Chapanis, 1964):

1. *The relief hypothesis.* After subjects in the severe condition had read the obscene words, they were so relieved to find that the group discussion was dull that they gave it a high rating.

2. *The pride hypothesis.* Subjects in the severe condition were so pleased with themselves after having successfully passed the embarrassment test that they gave the group discussion a good rating.

3. *The displaced sexual arousal hypothesis.* After subjects in the severe condition read the list of obscene words and descriptions of sexual activity, they were aroused and continued to think about sex. Thus they were reacting to their own thoughts when they rated the discussion.

So we see that various interpretations are possible for the Aronson-Mills experimental results. Why is this the case? Why can't the experimenter test for just the effects of severity of initiation?

The reason is that the general concept, sever-

ity, has to be tested by some laboratory procedures. Severity can never be tested directly; it must always be tested by means of some operations that are supposed to manipulate severity. Thus in the translation from the general concept, severity, to the specific operations, reading obscene words, some distortions may result. The laboratory procedures may either (1) not arouse severity or (2) arouse other reactions in place of or in addition to severity. Because general concepts can only be tested indirectly by means of operations, interpreting experimental results is always a problem.

Consequently, the process of interpretation involves first being aware that reactions other than those you hoped for might have occurred and then examining the results and procedures for indicators of these. Alternative interpretations may be tested in replications of the experiment.

Replication

One approach to assessing the extent to which the findings of a particular study can be generalized to other subject populations and to other manipulations of the independent variable is through "replication"—trying the procedures again. There are at least two different types of replication: (1) "exact replication," a repetition of a study in which research procedures either are as similar to the original as possible or vary in some specified, relatively minor way (such as using students at a different university as subjects), and (2) "conceptual replication," an attempt to test the conclusions of a previous study by using different procedures that overlap with the original procedures in a general way (Rose, 1953). The contributions and problems of both types of replication will be discussed below.

Exact Replication If an exact replication of the initiation experiment were done and the results obtained were similar to those of the original study, confidence in the reproducibility and generality of the findings would be increased. In fact, one such exact replication of the Aronson-Mills study has been done. Two of the conditions (the severe initiation condition and the control condition) were repeated, and similar results were obtained. Subjects in this study's severe condition also gave higher ratings to the fictitious group than did subjects who had not undergone an initiation (Schopler and Bateson, 1962).

A successful exact replication increases confidence in the generality of the original findings; unsuccessful replications are more difficult to interpret. First, even though the investigator thinks he is replicating a study exactly, he may not be doing so. Although someone who wanted to replicate the initiation study could learn about the materials used, the subjects, the cover story, etc., from the journal write-up, he might not learn about relevant contextual and interpersonal variables in the experiment (Friedman, 1967). Or different results could be due to chance factors.

Conceptual Replications You will recall from the discussion of the Aronson-Mills results that a variety of interpretations in addition to the investigators' could explain the data. For instance, the sexual-arousal interpretation fits the actual manipulations used by the investigators as well as the severity-liking interpretation. Consequently, there is still some doubt as to whether it was suffering or sex that caused the subjects in the severe condition to give the higher ratings.

One way to eliminate alternative explanations of the results is to design an experiment that tests the same conceptual variable, suffering, but in which the experimental procedures differ in as many ways as possible from the original. If widely differing operational definitions of suffering produce the same results, confidence in the conceptual variable, suffering, as the best explanation for the results is increased.

Such a conceptual replication of the Aronson-Mills study has been done (Gerard and Mathewson, 1966). To eliminate the sexual explanations of the original study, the investigators used severity of electric shock as the operational definition of suffering, and the tape-recorded group discussion was on cheating rather than sex. Even with a different operational definition of suffering, similar results were obtained. Subjects who had been given severe electric shocks gave a higher rating to the group discussion than did subjects who had received mild shocks. When similar results are obtained whether subjects are made to suffer

by reading a list of dirty words or by getting an intense shock, we become more confident that suffering—no matter how it is induced—increases liking. If another conceptual replication were done, in which still another operational definition of suffering were used and the original findings were again replicated, our confidence in the conceptual variable of suffering as indeed causing the results would be further increased.

Concluding comments

During our analysis of the Aronson-Mills experiment, a few themes have emerged. First, designing and conducting a good, well-controlled experiment is far from a simple process. Although it may sound easy to say that a controlled experiment simply involves manipulation of an independent variable(s), measurement of a dependent variable(s), and the elimination of confounding, it is not easy to perform these tasks. In the analysis of the initiation experiment, some of the investigators' decisions, problems, and solutions were discussed. Designing a well-controlled experiment is a highly creative act. Far from the stereotype of the mechanical researcher, researchers must, like architects, propose a solution that best meets all of the demands of their problem. And, like playing chess or painting a picture, this kind of creative activity can be highly exciting and rewarding.

Second, research on the problems of research is an important area of social psychology. When certain artifacts, such as the Rosenthal effect, are discovered, researchers can then control for these artifacts. Thus with the discovery of the Rosenthal effect, researchers could control for the effect of their own expectations. Further, the experimental situation is also a social situation, and what happens there may reveal what happens in other social interactions. Psychological folklore has long assumed that people do what others expect them to do ("Tell a boy he is a thief enough times, and eventually he will become one"), and the substantiation of the Rosenthal effect shows that interpersonal expectations can indeed be a potent determinant of behavior.

The orientation in this section has been a

critical one. The problems in research have been emphasized to give you a better understanding of the complexities involved and to sharpen your own critical skills. However, this criticism should not be interpreted as a minimization of the already tremendous contributions to knowledge made through the use of laboratory experiments in social psychology. The beginning of experimental social psychology can be dated to 1898, when the first laboratory experimental work was done on the differences in the way people perform tasks when they are alone and when they are with others (Triplett, 1898). In the seventy-six years that have followed, tremendous additions have been made to our knowledge of how people interact with one another and the effects of social influences on the individual.

For instance, literally hundreds of studies have yielded consistent findings on the prevalence of conformity and have documented the variables that influence its occurrence. Similarly, that stress increases people's desire to be with others has been shown repeatedly. The list of findings firmly established as "facts" in the discipline of social psychology could go on and on, and this is the knowledge that this text summarizes. After reading the text and completing your social psychology course, you may be surprised at how much more is known about social psychology than your informal observations and common sense would tell you. In the last analysis perhaps the best measure of the validity of an approach is the information it yields. And, as you shall see, empirical social psychology—social psychology based on the research methods outlined in this chapter—has already provided a great deal of information about social influences and processes.

Is the Controlled Experiment Always the Best Research Method?

The theme throughout this chapter has been that the controlled experiment is the best way to assess a causal relationship. This is true. Yet to say that does not mean that the controlled experiment is always the best research method. Which technique is best depends on what you want to do. There are times when observation, the questionnaire-interview technique, or a cor-

relational approach might better suit your research problem.

For instance, observation might open completely new areas of research. This was the basic technique Freud used when making many of his discoveries about psychological functioning that have subsequently been verified by other research methods. Observation may be the best research method when the problem is one that cannot be translated into experimental procedures. For instance, one psychologist observed that the age of a patient's children may influence his or her psychological health:

. . . in the study of several cases of rather sudden precipitation of psychoses, the ages of the children of the patients were not considered to be particularly relevant. Then it became apparent that these patients' children were at an age at which the patients themselves had had rather severe traumatic experiences.

This readily becomes: The probability of becoming psychotic increases as a result of beholding intimately my child who is now as old as I was when (say) my parents died.

[Hilgard, 1953, in Bakan, 1969, p. 92.]

Questionnaire-interview studies may yield information about what people think, feel, and say in a variety of circumstances. If you want to predict the outcome of a presidential election, this method may clearly be the most appropriate. Or if you want to find out how many students on your campus smoke marijuana, it would be the most appropriate method.

Correlational methods yield information about the extent to which two variables are related. If the variables are such that they cannot easily be translated into experimental procedures or created in a laboratory, then a correlational approach may be the best research method. If you want to find out if smokers are more emotional than nonsmokers, it would be very difficult, not to say unethical, to create habitual smokers in a laboratory setting.

Of course, the controlled experiment remains the best approach if you wish to assess cause-and-effect relationships. Indeed, most research in social psychology falls into this category. Some psychologists have argued, however, that an insistence that *all* research be experimental may have impeded the progress of psychology as a science. Forcing all research into the mold of the controlled experiment may interfere with the discovery and understanding of new phenomena. An insistence that experimental research is "best" may force an investigator to use this method when it is not appropriate for him to do so. Also, restricting the area of researchable questions to only those that fit the experimental method may eliminate whole areas of important behavior from study (Bakan, 1969).

The Relevance of Social Psychology to Solving Social Problems

It is hardly news to anyone that contemporary society is beset by a wide variety of social problems. Violence, racial confrontation, urban decay, feelings of loneliness and alienation—the list could go on and on.

What is social psychology doing to help solve these problems? How relevant are the findings of seventy-six years of research in this discipline? If the research isn't relevant to solving social problems, what good is it?

The issue of relevance has become a highly complicated and controversial topic among social psychologists. Some would argue that the criterion of relevance is irrelevant in the assessing of the worth of their research (McGuire, 1967). The most efficient procedure for understanding social influences and social interaction is the patient study of basic theory and phenomena—whether or not they have any immediate applicability. Furthermore, these psychologists would argue, the concept of what is most relevant changes from year to year. In the 1960s, when campus confrontations were rampant, research on the reasons for campus unrest was relevant. In the 1970s, when many people are concerned about controlling pollution, developing techniques to discourage polluters would be relevant. What was relevant yesterday may not be relevant tomorrow.

The proponents of basic research ask how a systematic and integrated understanding of social processes can ever emerge if the social scientist constantly shifts his focus to whatever the relevant issue of a given year may be. They urge an emphasis on understanding social processes through repeated studies on theoretically important issues.

In support of this approach, psychologists

can cite several cases where the ultimate result of basic research had enormous applicability. Perhaps the best-known example of the huge payoff of basic research is the widespread application of Skinnerian operant conditioning. As you may remember from your introductory psychology course, the basic principle of operant conditioning is that animals and people tend to repeat behavior that is rewarded. After years of theoretically oriented research with animals, the principles of operant conditioning have been firmly established. Today, these principles of learning are being applied to modify behavior in many, many settings, including classrooms, mental hospitals, prisons, outpatient therapy, and factories.

Other psychologists, however, would argue that social psychologists should focus actively on making their research relevant by studying those problems that have a strong and immediate human concern. In a time in which there are so many social problems, they argue, the most efficient way for social psychology to contribute to a better society is to study those issues that are of immediate concern.

The proponents of relevant research can also show how the knowledge obtained from their work is being applied to contemporary social problems. The examination of the topics to be covered in this text will demonstrate that much of the research concentrates on areas of great practical concern and that there are many practical applications of the findings from this research.

We can also cite several examples not otherwise covered in this text. In the famous 1954 Supreme Court decision barring racially segregated schools, research by social scientists on the harmful effects of segregation was used to support the Court's opinion (Clark, 1955). The principles of group interaction that emerged from the early work on group dynamics has led to the contemporary sensitivity groups, which are attended by many people. Management and administrative procedures in businesses and government have been modified on the basis of the results of research on group processes and management goals. Programs such as Head Start were stimulated by research on the negative effects of early environmental deprivation on learning. Numerous presidential commissions on such diverse social issues as the causes and prevention of violence, the impact of televised violence, and the use of marijuana have called on prominent social scientists to serve as consultants.

Even though the present knowledge in social psychology already includes a considerable body of knowledge with practical implications, some "activist" social psychologists argue that social psychologists should focus even more actively on making their research relevant to social problems and should apply that knowledge even more intensively. For instance, some have argued that *only* problems that have a strong and immediate concern should be studied (Sanford, 1965). Further, some feel that social psychologists should become more involved in "action" research by applying their laboratory-tested hypotheses to designing and evaluating real social programs. As the founder of the group dynamics movement, Kurt Lewin, has said, "no research without action, no action without research" and "nothing is so practical as a good theory" (Lewin, quoted in Ring, 1967).

In other words, develop a theory through laboratory research, but then test it outside the laboratory. The immediate application will result in information that can sharpen future laboratory work. Lewin argued that by fusing theoretical and practical approaches to research, social psychologists would most efficiently reach their two goals: (1) the scientific understanding of social man and (2) the application of that knowledge to improving human welfare.

Thus the activists argue that social psychologists should take a highly active role in social planning. Decisions about social programs that influence our society are made every day. Every time a decision is made about whether or not to change the present welfare system, the prison system, antidrug programs, someone has to decide what to do. If the decision is not based on the results of social research, it will be made on the basis of commonsense psychology, expediency, or political considerations.

Further, the activists believe that once a social program has been instituted, it is important to assess its effect. Any change in our current welfare system, for example, can be seen as a massive social experiment. Obviously, very valuable data will be lost if there is no attempt to measure the variables that make the

revision effective or ineffective. Thus there is need, the activists would argue, for social psychologists to be involved not only in the social planning process but also in the evaluation of plans already adopted.

We cannot resolve in this space which approach to research—basic, relevant, or activist—can make the greatest contribution to knowledge and to the successful application of that knowledge. All three approaches have undeniably contributed a significant body of knowledge that is applicable to social issues. Perhaps the more immediate question is: If the application of the results of social psychology can contribute so much to the resolution of social problems, why hasn't the discipline been more successful in this endeavor? First, at present, the discipline of social psychology has not yet accumulated enough knowledge about some of the enormously complex problems of our times. Although beginnings have been made in research on urban problems, much more precise knowledge is needed before social psychologists can offer a firm set of recommendations for solving those problems (Korten, Cook, and Lacey, 1970).

Second, even when research does result in knowledge that social psychologists feel is relevant to solving problems, they do not have the power to implement their policies. They can only recommend and provide information on which others take action. You may be able to think of many research findings and commission reports that have been largely ignored. Critics of integration ignore the controlled studies that demonstrate improved achievement for black children in genuinely integrated schools (Goodall, 1972). (See Figure 1-6.) The National Commission on Marihuana and Drug Abuse recommended that the possession of marijuana for personal use be legalized, but the recommendation has not resulted in any sweeping changes in legislation. In view of the number of people arrested by state and federal agencies on marijuana charges (estimated by the Commission to be over 190,000 in 1970), the question of marijuana laws is far from an academic one for many (see Figure 1-7).

Why aren't recommendations based on the results of scientific research implemented more often? Again, the answer is complex. First of all, change—any change—is strongly resisted. No

FIGURE 1-6 In this 1972 near-mob scene, white parents are protesting the enrollment of massive numbers of black children into their previously predominantly white school. The setting is Canarsie, a community located in Brooklyn, New York. *(New York Daily News)*

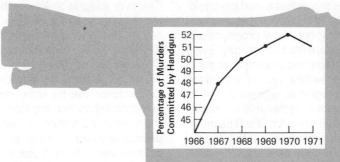

FIGURE 1-8 Percentage of murder by handgun. In 1971 over half of all homicides in the United States were committed with handguns. (Adapted from *F.B.I. Uniform Crime Reports*, 1972.)

FIGURE 1-7 This eight-cell jail is packed with attempted harvesters of a wild marijuana crop which was found growing in ditches and pastures in a small midwestern town. Twenty-four young men and women were arrested and placed in jail on charges of possessing marijuana leaves. (UPI)

DARING DRUG EXPOSE

SHAME HORROR DESPAIR

MARIHUANA
WEED WITH ROOTS IN HELL

MISERY

SMOKE THAT GETS IN YOUTH'S EYES

WHAT HAPPENS AT MARIHUANA PARTIES?

LUST
CRIME
SORROW
DESPAIR
HATE
SHAME

WEIRD ORGIES WILD PARTIES UNLEASHED PASSIONS

FIGURE 1-9 Views about the dangers and evil associations of marijuana are not unique to contemporary society. In this 1930s poster, the drug is connected with a potpourri of social ills. (Courtesy, Mel Romanoff)

matter how uncomfortable and miserable an individual is (within limits), he is more comfortable with the known than the unknown. People who have been following fixed procedures for a long time may feel threatened by any suggestion to modify what they are doing. Further, they may have an investment in the status quo. If the present system is working well for them and yielding good economic rewards, why should they want a change? Thus the findings of social psychologists studying aspects of courtroom procedure have met with hostile reactions from some lawyers. Many lawyers feel that precedent—rather than research evidence—is the most valid indicator of what should be done in the courtroom. Of course, not all lawyers or law schools feel that way. Indeed, some law schools, such as Yale, have specifically attempted to integrate law and psychology more closely. For the most part, however, psychology has had very little impact on legal procedures. Even though it has been shown repeatedly that a person's memory becomes inaccurate very rapidly, jury trials are sometimes held two or more years after an alleged crime.

Other, more specific, factors are also involved in the resistance to implementing social scientists' recommendations. Political considerations may influence policy makers more than scientific evidence. The fact that very strong and efficiently organized lobbying groups oppose gun control may be more important to a congressman seeking reelection than scientific evidence, recommendations, or all the documented evidence available (see Figure 1-8, page 46).

Popular misconceptions may be more influential than commission reports. For instance, the popular image of marijuana is that it is exceedingly harmful and that its use almost inevitably leads to the use of hard drugs. (See Figure 1-9, page 47.) Although the National Commission on Marihuana and Drug Abuse found little evidence to support these popular misconceptions, many people do believe them, and a majority opposes the use of marijuana. (In fact, 64 percent of the adult public surveyed in one study cited by the commission said that "using marijuana is morally offensive.")

Even if social scientists or others are successful in implementing a change, the program may be passively resisted and subverted by those involved. One classic example of this is provided by the failure of a program introduced at Yale to train secondary-school teachers. Shortly after the first Russian space missile had been launched, the president of the university decided to inaugurate a program for future teachers that would emphasize subject matter in the student's area and minimize methods courses. The object was to attract students from good liberal arts colleges, who might be turned off by the usual education program, to Yale's Master of Arts in Teaching program (MAT).

However, a vital fact overlooked by those initiating the new program was that the faculty was very hostile to the whole field of education. In fact, shortly before the program was begun, the faculty had approved a motion to eliminate the university's department of education on the grounds that the department was *"alien to the scholarly and research traditions of the university"* (Sarason, 1971, p. 51). Even in the face of this obvious hostility, the initiators of the new program took no steps to involve the faculty or persuade them of the program's merits. Rather, they simply assumed that enrolling the MAT students in the Yale graduate courses would have the desired effect: the production of gifted teachers who were well grounded in their disciplines and confident of their abilities.

As you might imagine, this was not the result that occurred. In a setting in which academic scholarship was and is highly valued, the students enrolled in the MAT program felt that the program was not a success. In fact, when twenty-two of the students were interviewed about their reactions to the program, fourteen indicated that they were bitterly discontented. They felt that their needs were being completely ignored in graduate courses that focused only on the interests of the doctoral students. Many sensed that other graduate students and professors condescended to them and assumed that they were less intelligent than the other students because they were enrolled in the MAT program (Levine, 1968).

The failure of the Yale MAT program shows the complexities involved in implementing social change. Social systems are complex; the individuals within them have vested "rights" and attitudes; and any change may be regarded with suspicion. If the change is one that conflicts with the values of the majority, they may subvert it through passive resistance.

There is one other source of resistance to the implementing of social scientists' recommendations concerning social problems. Social engineering may arouse mixed emotions in people and summon the specter of 1984. Among the community of psychologists, the issue of how much social engineering is enough is highly controversial. In one camp there are those who argue that in our time of tremendous social change and social problems, unplanned, piecemeal solutions to the problems of the future may lead to chaos and perhaps to the destruction of society as we know it. Perhaps the best-known advocate of this position is B. F. Skinner, who states in *Beyond Freedom and Dignity* that a technology of behavior—with planned control—is our only alternative to chaos.

As you know, not all agree with Skinner. His position has been attacked by politicians, journalists, theologians, and other psychologists. Many find the idea of a planned, controlled "technocracy" repellent and contrary to their ideas of individual freedom. They would argue that each person should have a choice about his own destiny—rather than being programmed into a particular pattern of behavior by operant conditioning. And, of course, there is the problem of the possible side effects of social engineering. As chemists found out when they developed DDT, sometimes the cure is worse than the problem. The same kinds of difficulties might be encountered with social engineering. The specter of an Establishment social science linked to the interests of an Establishment government raises the possibility of a combination that would be very difficult for the public to control.

At present, we know very little about the *process* of social change—planned or unplanned. One investigator, who has observed the reactions to a number of changes introduced in a large school system, has summarized the complexities involved as follows (Sarason, 1971). First, any theory of social change must consider the complexities of the social setting. For instance, people of different status in the group may respond differently to the change. Second, the opposition must be explicitly recognized, and ways to deal with it must be considered. The failure of the Yale MAT program is a classic example of what happens if opposition is ignored. However, there is not yet enough information to indicate precisely how complexity and opposition can best be dealt with. If social psychology is going to be able to solve pressing social problems, it must provide not only the correct solutions, but also a knowledge of how to get people to accept change.

It is not the purpose of this text to determine the most appropriate role of social psychological research in modern society. The important fact is that this type of research *has* a definite role. The real argument involves the more sophisticated question of how actively the role should be played. Between the two extreme positions of complete and minimal social engineering are a number of intermediate positions. Doubtlessly, the debate as to how the discipline can best aid the complicated process of social planning will continue well into the 1970s and beyond.

SUMMARY

Without scientific research, our knowledge of social behavior would be reduced to that obtained from authorities and commonsense psychology—both of which have frequently been found to be in error. Four major research techniques have been considered in this chapter: observation, questionnaire-interview, correlation, and the controlled experiment.

1. Observation A basic technique of science is observation. Many hypotheses have been derived from what a scientist has first casually noticed, and observation can provide information about what people do in their natural environment. However, there are some problems with the technique of observation. If subjects are aware that they are being observed, their behavior may change. To counter this reactive effect of measurement, many techniques have been used, including concealing the observer and using unobtrusive measures, or measures that can be obtained without the individual's awareness. Further, in observational studies the investigator is faced with the problem of recording what was observed and establishing the reliability, or interobserver agreement, of his observations.

2. Questionnaire-Interview Research The questionnaire and the interview are two of the most widely used research techniques for both applied and theoretical research. To assure a valid questionnaire-interview study, three steps are essential. First, if you wish to generalize from the responses of a sample to a population that the sample represents, your basis for selecting the sample must give some reasonable assurance that all members of the population have an equal chance of being included. Second, once the sample has been selected, those chosen must be persuaded to participate. Third, questions that the respondent is willing and able to answer must be devised.

After all of the information has been collected and analyzed, there are two extremely important considerations—establishing the validity and the reliability of the responses. Although a number of studies have shown that the reliability of well-designed questionnaire-interview studies is very high, establishing the validity of the responses has proved to be a much more difficult matter. In some cases, as in the political polls, it is relatively simple to establish validity by comparing election returns with the poll results. In other cases, however, such as a study of the incidence of student use of marijuana, independently establishing the validity of the questionnaire reports may be extremely difficult.

3. Correlation A third frequently used research approach is to obtain measures on two variables and then assess the extent to which they are related. The better one score predicts the others, the higher the correlation is. However, no matter how high a correlation may be—whether it is positive or negative—it does not allow one to infer cause-and-effect relationships. Too many alternative explanations of the

relationship are possible. To determine the "why" of a relationship, a controlled experiment is necessary.

4. The Controlled Experiment The research technique that best enables one to establish a cause-and-effect relationship is the controlled experiment—an experiment in which one or more variables, the independent variable(s), are manipulated in order to determine the effect produced on one or more other variable(s), the dependent variable(s). By attempting to control all other extraneous variables that might influence the relationship, the investigator seeks to eliminate alternative explanations for the observed results. If there are any systematic differences in the experimental sessions other than those in the independent variable, these variations will be confounded with the independent variable. Of course, although the controlled experiment greatly reduces the number of possible alternative explanations for the results, no one experiment can eliminate all of them.

To illustrate the enormous complexity involved in maintaining control, the various steps involved in one experiment—the initiation-liking study—were analyzed in detail.

What led the investigators to believe that severity of initiation might be related to the members' liking of a group? First, that severity of initiation is related to liking is an assumption of commonsense psychology that seems to be widely applied. Second, the hypothesis followed from cognitive dissonance theory, which is an important theory in social psychology. Knowing that you have suffered through an unpleasant initiation would be inconsistent with the knowledge that the group you have suffered for is dull. The dissonance prediction would be that to remove this inconsistency, you would tend to view the group favorably.

Theory-related research is basic to evolving an understanding of social interaction. Without it social psychology would be a hodgepodge of unrelated findings. Theories enable one to make predictions about what will occur in a wide variety of situations, generate research, and unify the findings of seemingly disparate studies. Thus theories yield a more coherent view of human nature.

Once an investigator has decided to test a

hypothesis, he has to make a number of decisions in going from, or translating, the general hypothesis to experimental procedures. The conceptual independent variable must be made operational in the study in such a way that other variables are not also involved. In doing this, the experimenter must consider many factors as, for instance, control versus impact. Of course, to see that the operations had the desired effect on the subjects, a manipulation check should be done after the experiment has been completed.

In order for the independent variable to influence the subjects, the other experimental procedures must seem reasonable. Most usually, the investigator makes them seem reasonable by concocting a cover story, so that the subjects will remain unaware of the true hypothesis being tested. Although a good cover story can provide a reasonable explanation for all of the procedures, deception has its disadvantages. Ethical problems are involved, and the subjects may become suspicious.

For most experiments the subjects are college students—typically sophomores taking a psychology course—and they may be captive volunteers. The use of such subjects poses several problems: (1) They differ from the general population in a number of ways; (2) they may resent being required to participate; and (3) they may have participated in previous studies involving deception, which may influence their behavior. It should be emphasized, however, that the phenomena revealed in working with the college student population are real in the group sampled. And probably most of these phenomena do exist to some degree in the general population.

The most important requirement with any controlled experiment is to minimize the number of alternative explanations for the results obtained. Although there are many possible sources of confounding, two in particular have received widespread attention: (1) the effect of the experimenter's expectations, or the Rosenthal effect, and (2) the effect of the role that the subject assumes. As has clearly been shown—both in and out of the lab—a person sometimes can make others act as he expects them to act. A number of techniques have been used successfully to control for the effect of the experimenter's expectations.

Another possible artifact in an experiment is the role the subject plays. Four such roles have been documented: (1) the good subject, who seeks to give responses that will validate the experimenter's hypothesis, (2) the apprehensive subject, who is concerned with making a good impression on the experimenter, (3) the negative subject, who wants to do the opposite of whatever the experimenter wants him to do, and (4) the faithful subject, who meekly follows directions without trying to "psych out" the experiment. Although controlling for the effect of subject roles is more difficult than controlling for the Rosenthal effect, generally, the more thoroughly the true purpose of the experiment is concealed from the subject, the less likely he is to distort his responses by playing one of the four roles.

The problems involved in translating the dependent variable into experimental procedures are very similar to those involved in manipulating the independent variable. One or more of the three forms of measures are generally used: behavioral, behavioroid, and self-report. Although each of these measures has advantages and disadvantages, the self-report measure is the most frequently used.

When "running the subjects," the experimenters' behavior should be standardized. To accomplish this, the investigator usually gives the experimenters a set of experimental directions that are to be read verbatim. However, studies of experimenters in action show that even when they are given standard instructions, their style of dealing with subjects may vary. If the same experimenter runs all of the experimental conditions, this source of confounding can be significantly reduced.

After the experiment is over, the experimenter typically interviews each subject in order to obtain his general reactions to the procedure and, if deception was involved, to explain the deception and to ask him not to disclose it to any other persons who might participate in the experiment. Whether or not the dehoaxing procedures are successful in motivating the subject not to reveal the deception or in removing the effects of false information given during the experiment is not yet clear.

The typical procedure in analyzing the data is first to measure the differences in scores on the dependent variables among the various groups, and then to assess whether or not the differences are statistically significant—that is, whether or not the findings could have occurred by chance alone. By convention, if there are less than five chances in one hundred that the differences could have occurred by chance alone, the results are deemed significant.

Once the data have been analyzed, the question of interpretation remains. Conceptual variables must be translated into operational definitions, and some distortions may occur in this process. Thus other explanations of the findings may also be possible. Of course, the question is: Which explanation fits the results best?

Through replication, the extent to which the findings of a particular study can be generalized to other subject populations and to other manipulations can be assessed. There are two different types of replication: exact and conceptual. When exact replications confirm the original findings, they support the generality of the phenomena; conceptual replications can eliminate alternative explanations of the original findings.

Our analysis of the initiation experiment has been a somewhat critical one. The problems in research have been emphasized to give you a better idea of the complexities involved and to sharpen your own critical skills. However, this critical analysis should not be interpreted as a minimization of the already tremendous contributions to knowledge made by the use of experimental social psychology.

5. Is the Controlled Experiment Always the Best Research Method? Which research technique is best depends on what you want to do. If you wish to assess a causal relationship, the controlled experiment is the best approach. However, there are times when observation, the questionnaire-interview technique, or a correlational approach might suit your research problem better than a controlled experiment.

6. The Relevance of Social Psychology to Solving Social Problems The proponents of both basic and relevant research can show how the knowledge obtained from their work has been and is being applied to contemporary social problems. Much of the research does concentrate on areas of great practical concern.

Yet if the findings of social psychology are so relevant, why hasn't the discipline been more successful in solving social problems? First, the discipline has not yet accumulated enough knowledge about some of the enormously complex problems of our times. Second, even when research does result in knowledge that social psychologists feel is relevant to solving problems, they do not have the power to implement their policies, and in many cases, the implementing of their policies is met with resistance. In general, change—any change—is strongly resisted. In addition, specific resistances may be encountered: Political considerations may influence policy makers more than scientific evidence, and popular misconceptions and passive resistance may hinder the implementation of change. Finally, the very idea of applying the results of psychological research—social engineering—may cause resistance.

At present, it is clear that research is relevant to creating an improved society. What is debatable is how actively social psychologists should become involved in social engineering.

DISCUSSION QUESTIONS

1. How would you test to see if job discrimination against women exists in the field of law?
2. List some unobtrusive ways of measuring the amount of time students spend working for a particular class.
3. Why is the controlled experiment the best way to detect a causal relationship between two variables?
4. Why do you think it is difficult for an experimenter to spot the confoundings in his own experiment?
5. Would randomly selecting names from the telephone directory of a community yield a random sample of all of the members of that community?
6. Assume that you had given out a questionnaire in which the respondents were asked to indicate the make and year of the car they owned. How could you assess the validity of their responses?
7. In your everyday experience, have you ever seen any evidence of the Rosenthal effect at work?
8. What criteria do you feel are important in assessing psychological significance?
9. Which approach to research—basic, relevant, or activist—do you think can make the greatest contribution to knowledge and to the successful application of that knowledge?
10. For what problems do you think the correlational technique would be a good approach?
11. Why are theories important in social psychology?
12. For what problems do you think a field approach would be preferable to a laboratory experiment?
13. Under what circumstances would a factorial design be preferable to a study in which only one independent variable was manipulated?
14. If you were on a committee to revise the American Psychological Association's ethical standards, what basic ethical principles would you formulate about the precautions researchers should take in their work with human subjects? How would you attempt to balance the rights of the individual subject with the researcher's need for freedom of inquiry?
15. We saw that the controlled experiment greatly reduces the number of possible alternative explanations. Why is it that no one experiment can eliminate *all* alternative explanations?
16. How could the behavior of experimenters be standardized within the experimental situation?
17. Do you think that extensive social engineering in the twenty-first century would improve or worsen the quality of life for the average American?
18. Design a conceptual replication of the initiation study. Indicate how you would do each of the following: (a) get the idea, (b) provide a rationale, (c) obtain subjects, (d) provide an operational definition of the independent variable, (e) avoid confounding, (f) translate the dependent variable into experimental procedures, (g) conduct the experiment, (h) conduct the postexperimental interview, and (i) analyze and interpret the data.

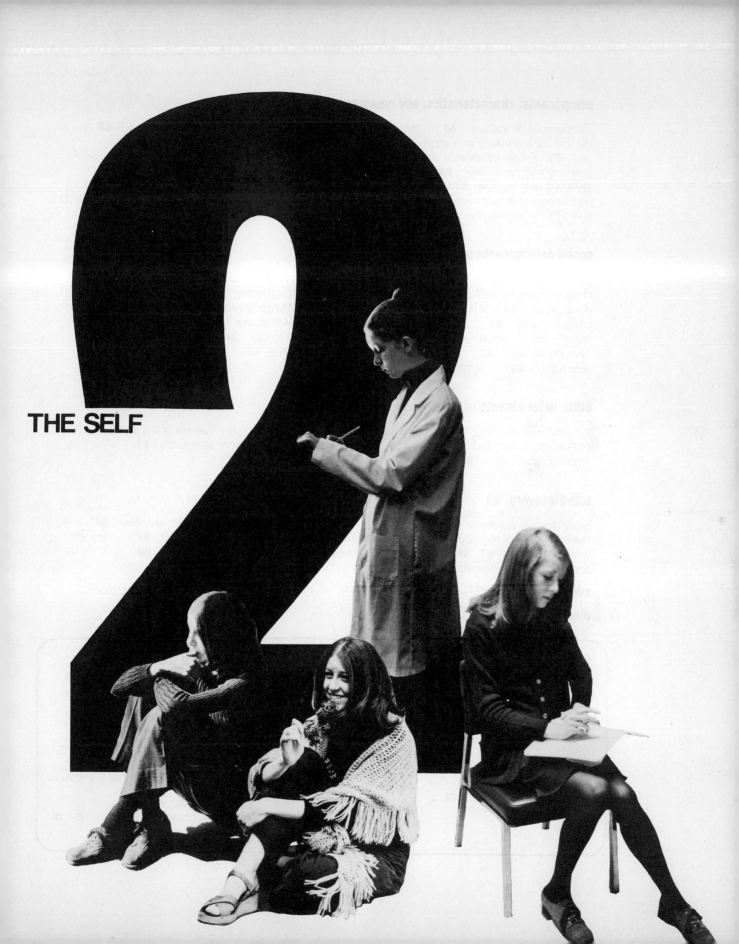

THE SELF

How do you see yourself? In terms of specific, tangible characteristics or in more philosophical ways? When asked the question, "Who are you?" four randomly selected students gave the following replies:

I don't know who I am—someone trying to take hold of some part of my life.

Someone trying to reach the goals I've set for myself.

John Z., a student majoring in business administration, engaged to Anne D., and worried about getting a job after graduation.

Someone located inside my body—just behind my eyes is the center of myself.

These answers reflect just a few of the many ways in which the term "self" has been defined. Self is not just a technical, psychological term. In and out of class students discuss themselves and their identity. "Knowing myself," "finding an identity," "discovering who I am" are familiar student topics. Your conception of yourself is at the center of your concern for what you are all about. Indeed, you may not be able to remember a time when you did not possess a feeling of self-awareness.

This all-absorbing involvement with our own self creates a paradox for many of us. On the one hand we strive for a sense of our own uniqueness, wanting to be singled out for recognition, status, and love. On the other hand, though, our feeling of separateness can sometimes give rise to isolation and loneliness. Thus our self-awareness has both positive and negative aspects, often placing us in conflict as to our social needs. We will see evidence of this conflict throughout this chapter and this text.

People of college age are particularly concerned with achieving a unified, coherent self, or an "identity." See Student Reaction Box 1. At the end of childhood the individual's earlier ways of defining himself and relating to the world are no longer adequate; he must evolve a new identity. This involves testing his new identity components, integrating aspects of the self, and attaining a sense of the reality of the new

self (E. E. Erikson, 1968). The process is not easy. Many people have great difficulty evolving a sense of who they are, and some never do. (See Figure 2-1.) As the thirty-four-year-old Biff said, in Arthur Miller's *Death of a Salesman,* "I just can't take hold, Mom, I can't take hold of some kind of a life."

As we shall see in this chapter, the process of identity formation is significantly determined by the social environment. (This is why the self is part of a social psychology text.) The important point here is that many students are concerned about evolving and knowing themselves, and they have their own ideas of what this process involves. The variety of definitions in ordinary usage makes the term "self-concept" ambiguous.

The technical literature has, if anything, added to this ambiguity. Since the beginning of their disciplines psychologists and sociologists have been concerned with the self. One work on this topic noted the existence of over 2,000 titles on the subject (Gordon and Gergen, 1968a). In addition to discussing the basic nature and characteristics of the self, the authors of these studies have attempted to measure the individual's self-concept scientifically and to relate that concept to everyday behavior. Yet in spite of the large number of studies, the understanding of the conscious self and its influence on behavior is far from complete. In fact, as Pepitone has said, "the analysis of the self and its functioning has been woefully simplistic" (1968, p. 347). With such confusion and lack of understanding has emerged a multiplicity of definitions of the term "self."

Perhaps a historical digression will explain this current state of affairs. In the early years of psychology, when it was breaking away from philosophy, the self was an important theoretical concept. William James (1910), the most influential American psychologist in the 1880s

STUDENT REACTION BOX 1

THE PROBLEM OF EVOLVING AN IDENTITY

Many of the concepts relating to the self are amorphous and somewhat difficult to understand. The reactions of one undergraduate, Anne G., will be quoted at length throughout this chapter in order to make these concepts more concrete. Her reactions are not intended to represent those of all college students or even of all female college students. Rather her comments are included only to illustrate one individual's reactions.

About evolving an identity, Anne wrote:

"I guess if you posed the question to me of "Who are you?" I would have to say I don't know. A new me has appeared in the last year, but the old me has existed for the past twenty years, and I'm trying to resolve the confusion that the new me has brought on. The new me evolved without my noticing it, but sure enough my family and old friends made me sit up and take note of it. At first I vehemently denied that there was a new Anne, yet I knew that I was behaving, dressing, and speaking differently. My ideas about all sorts of things changed and so did my reactions to people. The problem is that while all my family and friends have almost forgotten the old Anne, I haven't. Is the real me, the new Anne, the cool, hippie, freaky chick or is she the old straight Anne who is just playing the freaky role? Am I really still the straight, hard-working, family-pleasing Anne? I just don't know who I am.

"Now I feel I am a different person at different times. With my family and my professors, I am a sincere, hard-working, straight student. With my friends, I am a hippie, partying chick. But I really don't know who I am or even who I want to be. In the past year I've been so many different people, the freaky Anne, the straight Anne, Mommy and Daddy's Anne, the future graduate student or a just-getting-by student, or just me—whoever that is. Right now all I can say is that I am still confused about which one I really will become."

---

and 1890s, extensively and insightfully analyzed the properties of the self. Psychology's concern with the self was part of its broader concern with conscious experience in general. As psychology was then defined, the study of conscious experience was its basic goal, and in the early years many studies were based on conscious experience. Early psychologists, for example, were interested in such questions as whether "pure thought" could occur without any accompanying mental images. The psychological journals were filled with verbal descriptions of conscious experience and the inevitable disagreements.

Why disagreements? Assume that you and a friend of yours have gone through a pleasant, happy experience and that the two of you differ in your descriptions of the experience. How can you resolve the difference? Each of you, by definition, can only be aware of your own feelings of happiness.

Because conscious experience could not be verified, and because much of the early work was sterile, a group of American psychologists came to reject the study of inner, mental experience in favor of the study of behavior. Hence the term "behaviorists." In 1913 John Watson began to argue persuasively that psychology should study only objective events—events that are public. Behaviorism gradually won more and more converts, so that by 1930 it was clearly the dominant approach in American psychology. With the advent of behaviorism and its emphasis on public events, such as classical conditioning, the study of the self went into a decline. The behaviorists defined what was appropriate for psychological study, and private experience—even that as immediate as our sense of being—was off limits. A few psychoanalysts continued to be interested in the functioning of the self, which they called the ego, but in general the self was out of fashion until quite recently.

Within the past twenty years there has been a revival of interest in the self. The ignoring of a large part of human experience because it doesn't fit into preconceptions about "areas appropriate for psychological inquiry" has

FIGURE 2-1 **A diffusion of a sense of identity and a lack of unity are prime symptoms of the identity crisis experienced by many persons moving from childhood to adulthood.** (R. Lynn Goldberg)

seemed unnecessarily narrow to many. Accordingly, many contemporary psychologists have moved toward a more "humanistic" psychology, one that is self-oriented, uses human subjects, is interested in topics such as social dynamics and personality, and makes a certain amount of use of speculation and intuition.

The reawakening of interest in the self has been, in part, a reaction to the narrowness of behaviorist psychology, which focuses exclusively on stimuli and responses, uses animal subjects, and assumes an "empty organism." It has also been a result of existential philosophy. According to that philosophy (particularly as it is set forth by Kierkegaard, Husserl, and Sartre), the essential problem of modern man is to develop his own being in a meaningless and absurd world.

So the self is in again, and along with it, theories that emphasize its determinants and importance as well as the need to return to the study of conscious experience—or the "phenomenological method," as it is called. Maslow's theory of motivation, for example, emphasizes the importance of the optimal development, or "actualization," of the self. Carl Rogers stresses the importance of self-acceptance for healthy personality functioning. Binswanger, May, Allport—to name some others—all believe that the subjective experience of the individual as he strives to realize himself should be the prime focus of psychology. These theories each cover very different aspects of the self, and they differ from one another in critical ways; but they are grouped together here to point up the emphasis that is now being given to the study of the self in a social environment.

The increase of interest in the self, as well as the whole humanistic movement, is clearly an important development. Still the behaviorists' objections to the phenomenological method and its abuse remain valid. The self is a slippery concept. Much of our evidence concerning the self is derived from the insights of autobiographies and case histories, which may have attendant biases of small, unrepresentative samples and personal slant. Many of the terms concerning the self are vague: How would one define self-actualization? What is the difference between an actualized and a nonactualized person? Would people agree in their judgments

concerning who is actualized? The bulk of the research must depend on self-report measures, or people reporting how they feel, and with such measures there is the attendant problem of detecting when the respondents are being untruthful. In order to avoid the mistakes made in the early part of this century, it is imperative that the research questions concerning the self be formulated in terms that can be closely tied to objective research procedures. In this respect the behavioral approach may be quite helpful. The behaviorists have provided a workable methodology and a sense of rigor, which the self theorist can use to study ephemeral concepts, such as the self, more scientifically.

So we see in the self, perhaps more than in any other area of social psychology, the tension between the demands for rigor imposed by research and the demands for subtlety imposed by the phenomenon. What is needed in this area is a rigorous operational definition of the self—how it is determined, how it is known, and how it influences behavior—a definition that can be experimentally verified, but is not simplistic. A systematic, clear theory of the self is needed to generate hypotheses that will unite the scattered research findings.

In this chapter the focus will be on both the conceptual ideas of the self theorists and their translation—both actual and possible—into research procedures. In reviewing these concepts and procedures, you may be able to think of other ways in which the nature of the self could be tested. In studying the self, we all have one case history that we are most familiar with—our own selves. Each of us feels he has access to information about himself that no one else has.

Components, Characteristics, and Measurements of the Self

Components of the self

The self is that part of our experience that we regard as essentially us. When we participate in a competitive athletic event, such as a race, we join with others in the performance of complex acts—running, jumping, and so on—but the physical effects on our own bodies are individually felt. All thinking activity is dominated by the process of conceptualization—classifying and sorting experience into common categories. When a conceptualization of the self is developed, this process is used to label those components of experience that are most personal to the individual (Gergen, 1971).

Just what these "components of the self" are has been the subject of countless works in social psychology. Because the process of self-conceptualization is necessarily an internal one, no commonly agreed upon description has been found. In the following discussion, we will utilize an approach first developed many years ago (James, 1910). Like all other approaches, it has its flaws and its critics, but it describes aspects of the self experienced by many within Western culture. See Student Reaction Box 2.

The Material Self Perhaps the first aspect of "us" that comes to mind is the "material self." We are located inside a physical body, which is uniquely ours. We care when it hurts, and we try to make it attractive. For many the material self may include more than the body. Any material object that a person cares deeply about can arouse the same intensity of feeling as his physical body. Seeing one's new car smashed by another car may arouse as much concern as a physical injury to one's body.

Although we may be attached to material objects, however, the basic anchor of our sense of self is composed of the stream of sensations that relate to our bodies. We may be only vaguely aware of these sensations most of the time, but together they form a basic picture, or schema, of ourselves. When our picture of our own body corresponds to objective reality, we may hardly be aware of the complexities of the picture. But when the reality and the picture diverge, the fact that our experience of our bodies is a construct becomes very clear. The phenomenon of the "phantom limb" shows the importance of our body image. Persons who have had a limb amputated may continue to feel the limb in its usual position and to experience movement in the phantom limb, and this experience may continue for years (Simmel, 1966).

Further, the experience of the self is intimately related to a location in the body. A number of studies have been done on the part of the body most often associated with the self. Most persons designate an area midway between and

STUDENT REACTION BOX 2

COMPONENTS OF THE SELF

Below Anne has written about what she thinks of when she considers herself. Earlier, we saw that she is concerned about evolving her identity. The following comments show many of the components discussed in this section.

"I guess when I think about myself, I think I'm a different person in different situations. When I'm going out or meeting people for the first time, I usually am mainly concerned about my outward appearance. As a child, I always felt self-conscious about being tall and thin, I guess it was because I was teased a lot about being skinny and looking like a toothpick. But lately, I've become very proud of being tall and slim. I don't know how my feeling changed, but lately I've gained a lot of self-confidence and think of myself as being very good-looking and attractive. I've even seriously considered modeling.

"When I'm with my family or good friends, I'm much less concerned about my appearance. Then, I begin to think of myself as Anne, the future graduate student. 'Man, she's going to make it big someday. She's going to be the best.' But then I realize that I'm also going to have to work my ass off to get it. I know I wasn't given the greatest intelligence in the whole world, but I'm a worker, the 'old slugger' who really works for the grades.

"You see when I think of myself, I think of many Annes: Anne the student, Anne the freak, Anne the clotheshorse, Anne the future professional, and many others, such as Anne, the daughter of immigrant parents, the once Catholic, now atheist, etc. But of all the Annes, there is one part of myself that remains constant. It is the insecure part of me that rates itself in comparison with others. I never really feel confident of my own abilities. I need constant reassurance: that the guy I'm going out with really does love me; that my grades really do show I'm smart and can make it; that my friends really do like me."

slightly behind the eyes (Claparède, 1924). When an individual is not disturbed, he assumes that the self resides in his body.

Yet sometimes the self does become disassociated from the body. When you have been very tired or upset about something, you may have had the experience of watching your body talk and behave—sort of like your spaceless self watching your physical self go about its business. Temporary dissociation is a common, fleeting experience in normal people. Among many schizophrenics it is a chronic condition. The person consistently feels separated from his body. One psychotherapist wrote of a patient who complained that although his body would have sexual intercourse with his wife, his mental self could only look on as an observer (Laing, 1965, p. 86).

The Actual, Psychological Self A second aspect of the self is the actual, psychological self—what you think of when you think of "me." You may think of an interrelated set of attitudes, beliefs, judgments, and so forth. The actual self is your view of who you are at any particular time and provides a standard against which all other information is judged. Experiments in which subjects judge weights provide a clear and simple example of how this judgment process works. Assume that people are judging the same one-pound weight. Person A has been lifting weights of five pounds, ten pounds, and twenty pounds. When he lifts the one-pound weight, he thinks how light it is. Person B, however, has been lifting weights of one ounce, three ounces, and five ounces. When he lifts the one-pound weight, he thinks how heavy it is. Whether the weight is judged as light or heavy depends on the person's past experience or his "frame of reference."

All experience is interpreted against the standard provided by the self. Your evaluation of all aspects of yourself is determined by your own past experiences and your ideals as to what you ought to be. If you are the second best Ping-Pong player in the world and your ideal is to be the first, you may be disappointed and feel ashamed of yourself. As we shall see, how you define yourself is to a large extent determined by how others react to you and label you. Yet your reactions to the reactions of others is

filtered by your own evaluation of others and your own view of yourself. If you are praised for something but you do not think it merits praise or do not believe the person who is praising you, you may discount that praise.

The Self As a Thinking and Emotional Process A third element in the self consists of one's own experience of the process of experiencing. In contrast to the "actual, psychological self," which focuses on the end result of our thinking and emotional processes, here the emphasis is on the actual processes of our thinking, imagining, and sensing. This phenomenon has been described as the "stream of consciousness": "The very core and nucleus of our self, as we know it, the very sanctuary of our life, is the sense of activity which certain inner states possess" (James, 1910, in Gordon and Gergen [Eds.], 1968, p. 43).

Although these thinking and emotional processes are clearly part of the self, they have not been emphasized in contemporary work on the self (Wylie, 1961). However, the self as a thinking and emotional process and as a capacity for these processes is clearly important. The thinking process and the development and perfection of it may be highly important to a person who views himself primarily as an intelligent, problem-solving being.

The Social Self The material self, the actual, psychological self, the self as a thinking and emotional process—all of these are important aspects of our view of our self. But we all live in a world in which we interact with others, who also have a view of us. As we shall see, the reactions of other people are the most significant influence on the formation of the self. In part the social self is a consequence of the roles one plays. When he is in uniform, a physician's social self is in large part a consequence of the role he plays. The self is also constructed of labels—assigned by others and self-imposed. In fact, someone's identity can be modified if those in his social environment change the way they label and respond to him.

Our private and public selves influence each other, and usually the view others have of us corresponds somewhat to our view of ourselves. Usually, the two correspond to such an extent

FIGURE 2-2 In searching for the components of an ideal self, many persons tend to focus on characteristics they do not themselves possess. (Mark Haven)

that we are not aware of the interplay and interaction between them. When they do separate, the effect can be very unsettling—as when a person who thinks of himself as a "person who doesn't need anyone" learns that to others he seems very lonely.

The Ideal Self A fifth aspect of the self is your idealized self—what you would like to be. Irrespective of what you actually are, you have dreams about what you would like to be, as shown in Figure 2-2. Perhaps you wish you were fatter or thinner. Or perhaps you wish you were talented and could make a great artistic contribution or that you could be the best Ping-Pong player in the world. The ideal self need not be objectively worthy. It simply is what you would like to be.

Two questions arise in connection with the ideal self: (1) How are your goals, or "level of aspiration," formed? and (2) Once they are formed, how do these goals influence your reactions to your behavior? Our focus will be on the second of these two questions.

How pleased would you feel about making $83 per week? Clearly, your feelings would depend on your personal goals. If you felt—as many middle-class respondents in San Antonio, Texas, did—that you'd be "really well off" with $318, that you could "barely survive" on $60, and that your goal was $230, you'd be dissatisfied. In contrast, if you felt—as the lower-class, Spanish-speaking respondents did—that the lowest possible income for survival was $30 and that "plush living" began at $83, you'd be pleased (Sherif, 1967, p. 236). To know how a given, objective event will affect someone, one must know his goals and expectations.

Although this fact is extremely obvious, it can be too easily forgotten. For example, many people do not realize, in assessing the "progress" of black people, that black expectations and goals have been rising faster than objective gains. This imbalance may help explain the continuing level of black discontent in the face of objective improvements.

Characteristics of the self and their behavioral implications

Although it is helpful to examine the self in segments as we have just done, it is doubtful that anyone ever thinks of his self-experience in such anatomical fashion. The normal self, after all, is a cohesive whole functioning as a single unit and presenting a single image to those who view it at any given time. In this section, then, we will focus on this unitary concept of the self and identify some of its most predominant characteristics and their behavioral implications.

The Self Is Organized and Consistent Organization and consistency are characteristics emphasized by many writers on the self (e.g., Heider, 1958). The parts of the self are thought

STUDENT REACTION BOX 3

ONE OR MANY SELVES?

How consistent is the self? Is there one you or many yous? In answer to this question Anne wrote:

"There are many facets and sides of Anne. In fact, there are many Annes that different people interacting with her encounter. She is a hippie chick, a conscientious student, a snotty spoiled brat, an insecure little girl, and so on. There are so many different mes that I am confused about who I really am. It seems that I change according to who I'm with: My parents think I'm really hard-working and dedicated to getting good grades and doing well. My friends think I'm a real party girl. And I don't know who I think I am."

to interrelate, to form a unified, consistent entity. When the self isn't unified—as when the individual is going through an "identity crisis"—some have theorized that highly pathological symptoms may result. The individual may be unable to act or to relate to others (E. E. Erikson, 1968). In addition, many writers have emphasized the consistency of the self in many different settings. Although a person at a party may seem different from the way he acts in the office, the changes are only superficial. The real self basically stays the same.

These analyses, based for the most part on informal observational data, can be generally summarized as follows: (1) At a given moment in time the individual seeks consistency of the various parts of the self, and (2) in different situations the individual is consistent. These two statements may seem to be true when we think about ourselves, but some of the available evidence suggests that they may be open to challenge.

CONSISTENCY AT A GIVEN MOMENT Let's assume that at a given moment in time the self moves toward consistency and that a particular individual has a poor opinion of himself. He views himself as someone who cannot win. The consistency theory would predict that if this individual should be exposed to favorable information about himself, an inconsistency in the self would arise, causing him to refuse to believe the information. To maintain self-consistency, such an individual would seek substantiating, negative information about himself. In such a manner, an unbreakable cycle of self-depreciation would develop in which the individual would repeatedly seek derogatory evaluations.

But clearly this is not always the case. As we shall see, people have a strong need to think well of themselves, and they use a variety of techniques to seek out positive information—especially when they are feeling insecure. You may have noticed your friends' attempts to gain reassurances about their personal worth after some failure. Experimental results support both the consistency and the positive-information-seeking predictions. In one study subjects who were made to have a low opinion of themselves subsequently rejected success (Aronson and Carlsmith, 1962). In other studies, however, subjects with a negative opinion of themselves did not reject success (e.g., Cottrell, 1965).

As may be the case whenever inconsistent experimental results are obtained, other, crucial variables, which were not controlled by the experimenter, may have interacted with the main variables. Other aspects of the situation may have an influence on whether or not a discouraged individual seeks consistent or pleasant information. The *person's certainty* about his low self-appraisal has been found to influence his behavior: If subjects were certain about their negative self-evaluations, they were more likely to seek negative information (Jones and Schneider, 1968). Another investigator found that the *relevance of the issue* to the individual also influenced his reaction: Subjects were less likely to reject an unexpected success in an area that was irrelevant to their self (Mettee, 1971).

Further work is needed to identify other variables that influence whether an individual with a negative view of himself seeks consistent or positive information. Identifying these variables has more than academic value. Research has shown that some members of minority groups have accepted negative stereotypes concerning themselves and so feel that they are unworthy and incompetent. Feeling this way about themselves, they expect and may even invite failure. Developing ways for changing ingrained negative self-expectancies and self-images is clearly an important step in combating some of the most invidious effects of racial and ethnic prejudice.

CONSISTENCY IN DIFFERENT SITUATIONS A popular concept is that the self is stable and constant. When you meet a friend who is in a bad mood, you may say, "he was not himself today." Students wanting to "find themselves" imply that there is a stable unity to find. Many self theorists would agree with this concept of the self as an enduring object (Allport, 1955).

But not all theorists agree. Some have argued that an individual does not have one stable self, but rather is composed of a number of separate selves, each of which relates to a group in which he participates (Sorokin, 1947). The self may be thought of as an image that the individual presents in order to maximize the approval he receives from others. See Student Reaction Box 3.

A series of recent experiments support the notion of multiple selves rather than a single self (summarized in Gergen, 1972). It was found that the subject's self-image varied according to the other person in the situation, the demands of the situation, and the individual's motives. Typically, these experiments involved initially measuring the subject's level of self-esteem, exposing him to a situation predicted to change that level, and then measuring his self-esteem again. For example, in one study (Gergen and Wishnov, 1965) subjects rated themselves initially. Then a month later half of the subjects were asked to describe themselves to a partner who was made to seem very egotistical; the other half described themselves to a "humble" partner, one who confessed to many weaknesses. The characteristics of the partner influenced the subjects' self-ratings. Subjects working with the egotistical partner gave themselves more favorable ratings; those working with the humble partner gave themselves more

negative ratings. It was as if, when working with the braggart, the subjects made themselves look better to minimize the difference between themselves and their partner. When working with the humble partner, they felt free to admit shortcomings of their own.

To assess the authenticity of the change, the investigators asked the subjects how honest and open they felt they had been during the information exchange. Over two-thirds said either that they had been completely honest or that their second responses were not any different from those given earlier. On the basis of these subjects' reactions, the investigators hypothesized that the change in the level of self-esteem was not a conscious one, but rather reflected "habitual and unconscious modes of relation to others" (p. 304). Thus the individual is not a single self, but many selves, which change somewhat as the individual shifts from situation to situation and person to person. We are, in short, what the situation demands (Gergen and Wishnov, 1965).

Or are we? Is our sense of self really this chameleon-like? Several other interpretations of these self-presentation findings are possible. They may have been the result of artifacts in the experimental situation. The subjects may have felt that their self-esteem ratings were expected to change as a result of the experimental treatment and obliged. Later, when asked about their honesty, the subjects may have simply lied. After all, part of playing the role of "good subject" involves saying you are honest.

Although it is possible that the results of any one study may be due to artifacts in the situation, the large number of studies that have shown a shifting definition of the self in different social situations makes this interpretation improbable. In another study, for instance, a group of fifty naval-officer trainees wrote a description of themselves. A month later half of the subjects were assigned to two-man work teams, and the other half were assigned to two-man "leisure" teams and told that their focus should be on getting along well with each other. Then all of the subjects were asked to write descriptions of themselves. The subjects in the work groups described themselves as significantly more organized, logical, and efficient than they had earlier. The subjects in the leisure groups changed in the opposite way;

they said they were freer, more easygoing, and friendlier than they had earlier (Gergen and Taylor, 1969). In short, subjects in each group adopted the proper self for the social occasion.

You may feel that these studies show only the very transient effects of an experimental situation. The subject may have changed his level of self-esteem or his view of himself, but only temporarily. If something very pleasant happens to you, you may be temporarily elated, but as you return to the usual course of events, your view of yourself returns to its usual level. However, people continually operate in "temporary" settings, and these settings consistently bend people in one direction or another.

To determine the degree of consistency within the self, we must first determine what would constitute a "change." There are several possible approaches to this problem. One would be to measure the long-term effects of changing situations on the person's self-concept. Another would be to measure the relative importance to the individual of the various components of his self-image, and to see if the more basic elements of a self-image can be changed by varying the situation. If a basic part of your picture of yourself is that you do not conform, this aspect of your self may remain constant in many social situations, while some relatively unimportant parts of your self may change from situation to situation.

FIGURE 2-3 "It's your favorite dessert, I know. But I want you to eat it for Mommy, Aunt Bertha, and Grandma!"

The Self Is Seen As the Origin of Behavior   People feel that they cause their own behavior. In deciding whether to go to class or to sleep late, you feel that you are making your own decision. As has been emphasized in the theory of "psychological reactance," any lessening of the freedom to act is highly unpleasant. People do not like being compelled to do things, and they react by trying to reassert their freedom (Brehm, 1966). (See Figure 2-3.)

For example, assume that a student usually goes home for Thanksgiving dinner and looks forward to the welcome relief from college food and the opportunity to see old friends and relatives. On a particular Thanksgiving he has decided to go home, but when his mother tells him he must come home because she is having a group of relatives from a distant part of the country for the holiday dinner, his feeling of pleasure and anticipation turns to dissatisfaction and resentment. The more intensely she demands that he *must* come home for Thanksgiving, the more intensely he wants to stay away. His freedom of choice has been threatened. His psychological reactance has been aroused. From such reactance we can predict: (1) a decrease in the attractiveness of the "forced activity," (2) emotional dissatisfaction, and (3) less involvement and poorer performance at the forced task.

Experimental evidence supports these three predictions. When an experimental confederate demanded that subjects select a particular object out of two possible alternatives, the subjects tended to want the other alternative (Worchel and Brehm, 1971). Subjects who were given arbitrary, step-by-step directions for a task disliked the task more than subjects who were given a feeling of freedom and self-direction (Kuperman, 1967). Also, subjects who were required to perform were less motivated and performed more poorly than those who were not forced to perform (Kuperman, 1967).

Behavioral freedom, in addition to allowing the individual to choose his activities, makes the situation more predictable for the individual. When the college student made his decision freely, he could control what he did and could know what to expect. If control and predictability are important, their loss should have the same upsetting effects that a loss of freedom has. Experiments have shown that people prefer knowing what will happen—even if it is bad and they have no control over it—to not knowing (Lanzetta and Driscoll, 1966). In situations that are both predictable and controllable, the impact of electric shocks has been reduced. For example, when subjects believed that they could terminate electric shocks (but actually could not), the unpleasant effects were reduced (Glass, Singer, and Friedman, 1969).

Although most people feel that their self is the origin of their behavior, people differ in the extent to which they see themselves as determining their own acts. Do you feel that your behavior is largely determined by your own choosing? Or do you think that your acts are primarily determined by external forces, such as luck or chance? A test, termed the "Internal-External" test, has been devised to measure the generalized expectancies of people concerning the degree to which they control their behavior (Rotter, 1966). People who indicate that they themselves primarily determine their acts have been termed "internals." Those who feel that their actions are mainly determined by external forces are called "externals."

A number of studies have been done in which scores on the Internal-External test have been correlated with behaviors. In general, it has been found that people who see their behavior as being determined by internal forces are more effective in dealing with their environment (e.g., Phares, 1968). These findings are consistent with the basic assumption of many existentialist philosophers that the loss of freedom of choice is debilitating. Since man is basically free and responsible, any diminution of that condition threatens the core of his existence.

The Self Is Separate and Unique Imagine your walking into a room filled with exact replicas of yourself—people who looked just like you, talked just like you. How do you think you would feel? Many psychological writers would predict that you would feel very anxious and insecure. (See Figure 2-4.) Many agree that man has a need for a separate and unique identity (e.g., Maslow, 1962). Feelings of sameness, a loss of identity, or a feeling of not being differentiated from other people—all these would arouse similar kinds of negative feelings. See Student Reaction Box 4.

STUDENT REACTION BOX 4

AM I "TYPICAL"?

Below Anne has written of her desire to be unique.

"If someone really wants to bug me, all they have to do is to tell me that I'm a 'typical chick.' I can't stand that. I despise being called a typical chick and pride myself on being unique. I want to be Anne, period. I feel proud of what I am and who I am; and I don't want to be like everyone else."

FIGURE 2-4 Despite pressures toward conformity in today's society, seeing aspects of yourself exactly duplicated in another person can still be disconcerting. (James M. Wall)

That feelings of undistinctiveness do, in fact, have these unpleasant effects has been shown in a series of experiments. For example, when experimental subjects were provided with fictitious test results that showed they were very similar to their peers, the students felt upset and tried to assert their uniqueness by emphasizing their dissimilarity (Fromkin, 1968).

In another study it was found that students who had been made to feel undistinctive showed a marked preference for unique experiences. After receiving bogus test results, subjects were told that they could spend time in one of four "psychedelic chambers," which were either available or unavailable to other students. Students who had been told that they were very similar to others preferred the chamber that was not available to others, almost as if they felt that some unique, restricted-to-them-only experience was necessary to prove their identity. This reaction is similar to the clinically observed tendency of some extremely depressed persons to seek out thrills and sensations—again as if to prove to themselves that they do exist.

Yet, strong as the desire for uniqueness may be in some situations, in others people may not desire to be different. As we shall see in Chapter 11, there are also extremely strong pressures for people to be like others, to conform. Going to a party and seeing that you are dressed in a very different manner from all of the other guests would be upsetting.

In fact, there may be a sense of ecstatic joy in the loss of identity resulting from physical intimacy, psychedelic experiences, and crowds. These experiences may even be sought, in part, precisely because they do weaken the sense of self-identity. Having a sense of a separate and unique self has its negative aspects, too, for a sense of loneliness and alienation from others can accompany it. The philosopher Nietzsche wrote about the "glorious transport which arises in man, even from the very depths of his nature" (1956, p. 22) at the shattering of his sense of individuality.

The bursting of the bonds of self and separateness allows the "reduction of inner restraints" (Festinger, Pepitone, and Newcomb, 1952). Once the individual has been "submerged in a group," or "deindividuated," his restraints are lifted, and he is freer to do what he wants. According to this formulation, being an anonymous member of a crowd should lead to more antisocial behavior as well as to very pleasant feelings. As we saw in Chapter 1, more aggressive acts are performed by individuals who are made to feel anonymous (Zimbardo, 1969).

In one study another form of restraint decreased when college students were made to feel anonymous. Half of the subjects, groups of college males and females, spent an experimental session in a lighted room. The other half of the subjects interacted in a room in which there was no light. In the anonymity of darkness, subjects engaged frequently in purposeful touching. Almost 90 percent of the subjects in the dark room touched each other, but none of the subjects in the light did so. Half of the persons in the dark room hugged another person in contrast to none of those in the light. Sexual excitement was significantly higher in the dark room: 80 percent of those in the dark said that they felt excited, and only 30 percent of the subjects in the lighted room indicated feelings of excitement. Feelings of closeness in the dark room were not limited to sex. The students also felt a sense of close friendship with the other members of the group. As the investigators noted, "by simply subtracting light, a group of perfect strangers can be moved within approximately 30 minutes to a stage of intimacy not often attained in years of normal acquaintanceship" (Gergen and Gergen, 1971, p. 15). Interestingly, the subjects in the dark room indicated that they were not eager either to identify the others or to be identified. Thus clearly, they enjoyed their anonymity.

Thus we are faced with a paradox. Sometimes people want to be separate and unique, and sometimes they wish to blend into the crowd. What circumstances would influence whether an individual will seek to make himself more unique or choose to deindividuate himself? Both the aggression study and the dark-room experiment provide some leads. As long as the individual feels that he can reverse events and once more assume a separate identity, he may enjoy playing at a loss of identity. Or perhaps there is an optimal level of separateness, in which case departure in either direction would result in an attempt to move one's identity level back to its optimal level.

Or it may be that when the individual's gains from being anonymous outweigh his losses, he will seek anonymity. Walking up to and hugging a stranger in broad daylight would expose you to the possibility of rebuff and embarrassment, but doing the same thing in a dark room offers less of a possibility for negative consequences. When the environment offers the possibility for sanctions for your behavior, anonymity may be preferable. However, if there is a possibility of something pleasant happening, you may wish to make yourself as individual as possible. Experimental verification of these hypotheses has been provided. Subjects who anticipated a positive environment made a significantly greater effort to individuate themselves than did subjects who expected to be punished for making errors (Maslach, 1972).

The Self Evaluates Itself People have general feelings about their own adequacy and their relative competency. If a person feels that he is worthy, that he can control events, that his work is worthwhile, he is said to have a high level of self-esteem. In contrast, if a person feels that the work of others is better than his, that he doesn't count for much, and that his efforts usually produce poor results, his self-esteem is low. The actual self is constantly, and unthinkingly, being measured against the ideal self. To the extent that the two match, the person feels good about himself and his abilities.

Most people feel somewhat pleased with themselves. In one test of self-esteem, in which test scores could vary between 40 (extremely low self-esteem) and 100 (extremely high self-esteem), the average score was 82.3. If the scores were normally distributed, then 68 percent of the subjects who took this particular test scored between 70.7 and 93.9—relatively high levels of self-esteem (Coopersmith, 1967). This finding replicated the generally positive levels of self-esteem reported in a number of studies.

The individual's general level of self-esteem would be expected to have important effects on his general "style" of perceiving and interacting with his environment. Low self-esteem would have a pervasive and debilitating effect. People who feel themselves to be unworthy and incompetent would be expected to be unhappy and displeased with themselves. As predicted, persons with a low level of self-esteem report a higher level of anxiety and a lower level of happiness (Coopersmith, 1967). A number of studies have shown that the level of self-esteem is generally lower in neurotic than in more healthy subjects (Wylie, 1961).

These feelings of inadequacy and unworthiness among people with low self-esteem may also result in their seeking to minimize painful confrontations with their own perceived inadequacy. It has been found that college students who were dissatisfied with themselves were more inclined to use drugs of all types (Brehm and Back, 1968). Other data have suggested that low self-esteem is also correlated with the development of alcoholism (Wahl, 1956).

People with low self-esteem may avoid what they think would be negative information about themselves. For example, they have been found to use the defense mechanism of "projection" (attributing their own traits to others) more often than persons with high self-esteem, and they have been found to be less accurate in perceiving threatening stimuli (Wylie, 1965).

People who see themselves as incompetent also lack confidence in their ability to cope with the environment successfully. They set lower goals for themselves than those with high self-esteem and feel less able to meet even these lowered goals (Coopersmith, 1967). Even though actual popularity is not correlated with self-esteem, persons low in self-esteem feel less able to make friends and to interact successfully with other people (Coopersmith, 1967). Persons with a low level of self-esteem were found to cheat significantly more than those having a favorable view of themselves (Aronson and Mettee, 1968). Cheating may be easier for someone with a low level of self-esteem, since it is consistent with his view of himself as an inept person who does unworthy things.

Correlational studies have also shown that people who feel they are inept and incompetent rely more heavily on the opinions of others. Persons with low self-esteem are more easily persuaded (Janis, 1954), are influenced more by group criticism (Stotland et al., 1957), and

STUDENT REACTION BOX 5

TRYING FOR HER IDEAL

Anne feels a great deal of pressure to meet her personal goals. At times, as she notes below, the desire to actualize herself is her main motivation:

"At many times, there are pressures both outside of myself and within me to become the ideal self that I picture. At times, the need to actually become my ideal self is the main motivating force in my life. Sometimes I get so caught up in whatever I want at that time for myself that it is the only thing in my life. When I was a junior I decided that I wanted very much to go to graduate school, and since then getting into graduate school has been the only thing that mattered to me. I made the Dean's List every semester since then; I ate, slept, and drank grad school. Now I say I'm not so sure, but I continue working like hell. I'm not even sure that I'm not sure."

scanty. Second, even if the self-report measures are valid, one still cannot establish a causal relationship on the basis of a correlation. Still, the correlations have been obtained in a number of different areas, and the style of perception and behavior for the person with low or high self-esteem has generally been supported. The person with low self-esteem almost seems to give up before he starts.

The Self Seeks Actualization Many self theorists, including Maslow and Rogers, have assumed that self-realization, or "actualization," is an extremely important motive in human behavior. The process of actualization is frequently discussed in terms of the individual's urge to develop his actual self so that it will correspond more closely with his ideal self. (See Student Reaction Box 5.) One seeks to become what he wishes he were. In addition to referring to the individual's reaching to attain his ideal self, the term "actualization" is sometimes used to refer to a desire to obtain a healthy, optimal form of psychological functioning.

What would a fully actualized person be like? Maslow (1961) has theorized that such a person feels more unified and whole and, at the same time, more able to fuse with the world. The person's abilities and power seem fully realized. He can function effortlessly, ably, spontaneously, and creatively. He feels completely self-determined, and yet has lost all self-consciousness—a person such as Aldous Huxley, who:

. . . was able to accept his talents and use them to the full. He managed it by perpetually marveling at how interesting and fascinating everything was, by wondering like a youngster at how miraculous things are, by saying frequently, "Extraordinary! Extraordinary!" He could look out at the world with wide eyes, with unabashed innocence, awe and fascination, which is a kind of admission of smallness, a form of humility, and then proceed calmly and unafraid to the great tasks he had set for himself.

[Maslow, 1971, quoted in Bugental, 1972, p. 18.]

Although everyday observation would suggest that people seek actualization, both in the sense of moving toward their ideals and in the sense of attaining certain healthy modes of personality functioning, verifying this empiri-

conform more (Coopersmith, 1967) than those with high self-esteem. In addition, persons with low self-esteem do not have the independence necessary for creative work, which involves relative independence from the criticism of others (Coopersmith, 1967).

Thus self-esteem has been correlated with a large number of variables. Typically, an investigator obtains a self-report measure of an individual's level of self-esteem and then correlates that measure with some other variable. Such an approach, however, involves some difficult methodological problems. First, whenever self-report measures are used, there is the problem of assessing their validity. As we shall see later, evidence on the validity of the most commonly used measure of self-esteem is

cally poses enormous difficulties. If you wished to test this experimentally, what would you do? The concept of actualization is extremely difficult to define operationally. One approach might be to designate actualized persons and then study the characteristics that they possess in common to see what the empirical attributes of fully actualized persons are. But try to get a group of people to agree on who is a fully actualized person. See Psych Quiz 1.

Only when a clear, operational definition of actualization can be evolved will the general actualization hypotheses become more than interesting philosophical speculations. With such a definition, research could begin on what may be the most interesting hypothesis in the self literature. This research could first explore the characteristics of actualized persons and then the antecedents and consequences of actualization. If the existence of the phenomenon could be demonstrated, the question of what allows some people to become actualized would be a fascinating one to pursue. Of course, it may turn out that a person's situation plays a large part in determining the extent to which he can become actualized. A person who is actualized in one set of circumstances might not be in another. As we shall see in Chapter 10, someone who is a leader in one situation may not be in another.

Measurement of self-esteem and self-concepts

A concept is only as good as its measurements. No matter how subtle the phenomenon and how philosophically literate the discussion, what the concept can actually contribute to psychological research and theory is determined by the degree to which it can be translated into testable terms. An important vehicle for this translation is the development of standardized tests that validly and reliably measure the phenomenon. Unfortunately, the majority of the tests used most frequently to measure self-esteem and self-concepts have serious limitations (Wylie, 1961).

Measuring Self-Esteem by Means of the Q Sort
The most frequently used measurement of self-esteem is the Q sort (Stephenson, 1952), in

---

PSYCH QUIZ 1

WHO'S ACTUALIZED?

To see how difficult it is to reach agreement about who is a fully actualized person, first indicate whether or not you think the following people are actualized. Then list some characteristics they possess in common. Compare your reactions with those of the other students in the class. You may be surprised at the diversity of reaction.

	Actualized	Not Actualized
Ralph Nader		
Richard Nixon		
Pablo Picasso		
B. F. Skinner		
Gloria Steinem		
Eleanor Roosevelt		
Ethel Kennedy		
Joan Baez		

---

which subjects are first asked to sort characteristics along a continuum ranging from "like me" to "unlike me." For example, an individual may be asked to indicate the extent to which the following statement applies to himself: "I put on a false front." Then he is asked to rate the same characteristics in terms of whether or not he would like to possess them. The discrepancy between what the individual thinks he is and what he would like to be yields a measure of self-esteem.

Although this technique sounds like an interesting and objective way to measure self-esteem, in practice it has involved serious problems. The main difficulty is determining the extent to which the subject's answers are influenced by his desire not to say unpleasant things about himself. It doesn't take a very subtle mind to detect that "I doubt my sexual powers" or "I despise myself" are negative statements. People do not like to admit that such negative attributes characterize themselves, and they may simply check those characteristics that they think make them look good. The Q sort then, as its opponents argue, may simply measure the individual's ideas of what is socially acceptable. This criticism seems to have considerable validity. Several studies have shown that Q sort scores are highly influenced by the social desirability variable (Edwards, 1957).

In addition, the Q sort technique has other attendant difficulties. Frequently, the tests are administered in an impersonal group setting, so that the opportunity for the investigator to develop rapport (and so increase the extent to which the respondents take the test seriously) is limited. The technique has not been standardized. For instance, different investigators use different sets of statements.

In view of all of these shortcomings, it is not surprising that the results of studies on the reliability and validity of the Q sort technique have tended to be equivocal. At the present time the question of the Q sort's reliability and validity is still very open.

Measuring Self-Concepts Although the Q sort can also be used to measure the individual's self-concept, other, more indirect measures may also be used.

One such promising approach involves asking the subjects to write fifteen different answers to the question "Who am I?" in no more than six or seven minutes. Each person's spontaneous answers reveal how he views himself. An analysis of the different answers reveals the actual contents of the subject's self-representations.

In one study this self measure was administered to 156 high-school students. The answers were then classified according to the predominant themes, or kinds of answers given. The most frequent answer was an expression of age, student role, and sex. Eighty-two percent answered in terms of their age, and 80 percent answered in terms of their student role. Seventy-four percent answered in terms of their sex. See Table 1 for the themes of the other student

Table 1. How Students View Themselves (Examples of Answers in Each Category Are Shown in Parentheses)

Theme	Percentage of Students Replying
How they typically related with others ("fair")	59
Judgments, tastes, or activities ("a football player")	58
How they typically act and feel ("happy")	52
Physical appearance ("pretty")	36
Freedom to determine their own fate ("someone who decides things for himself")	23
Sense of moral worth ("self-respecting")	22
The reactions of others to them ("popular")	18
Their material possessions ("a car owner")	5
Their unity or lack of unity ("mixed-up")	5

answers, listed in order of their frequency (Gordon, 1968).

This technique of self measurement has a number of very interesting possible applications. In addition to identifying common referents of a person's self-concept, it could be used to study differences in self-concepts among members of various populations as well as changes in self-concepts during times when these might be expected—as during the college years. Further, the interrelationships between the various reported aspects of the self might yield the information necessary to build a theory of the development and structure of the self.

However, promising as the technique is, it also has attendant problems. The technique involves classifying the respondents' answers into one of thirty categories, which is obviously very time-consuming. Once the statements are classified, the investigator must be sure that his classifications are sufficiently objective, so that another rater would classify them in the same way (the reliability problem). And, as always in the case of self-report measures, there is the problem of validity: assessing whether or not the respondents are telling the truth about themselves. Still, this measurement approach offers real promise of adding to the empirical and theoretical knowledge of the self.

Summary

Components of the Self. Five components of the self were discussed: (1) the *material self,* our physical body and those possessions that are uniquely ours, (2) the *actual, psychological self,* what you think of when you analyze your thoughts and ideas, (3) the *self as a thinking and emotional process,* one's own experience of the process of experiencing, (4) the *social self,* the self as defined in one's own interactions with others, and (5) the *ideal self,* what you would like to be.

Characteristics of the Self. Five characteristics of the self were considered.

1. With regard to the *consistency of the self,* we saw that some of the available evidence casts doubt about the degree to which we are consistent, either at a given moment or in different groups. The individual may not be a single, unchanging self, but may be many selves, which change somewhat as the person shifts from situation to situation.

2. *People feel that they cause their own behavior,* and any lessening of their freedom to act is highly unpleasant—as has been emphasized in the theory of psychological reactance. Once reactance is aroused, the forced activity becomes less attractive; the individual is dissatisfied; and he performs poorly at the forced task.

3. *People sometimes feel a strong desire to be separate and unique.* In some cases the individual's being made to feel undistinctive has been shown to upset him. Yet, strong as the desire for uniqueness may be in some situations, in others people may not desire to be different. Once the individual has been submerged in the group, his restraints are lifted, and he is freer to do what he wants. Whether individuation or deindividuation is sought may depend on a number of variables, including the individual's feeling of control over his separateness, and whether or not the individual's gains from deindividuation outweigh his losses.

4. *The actual self is constantly being measured against the ideal self.* To the extent that the two match, the person has a high level of self-esteem, as most people do. Those with a low level of self-esteem are unhappy and see themselves as incompetent in a variety of situations.

5. *Self-actualization* is an important motive for many people. The individual may feel a strong desire to develop his actual self so that it will correspond more closely with his ideal self. In addition, some may feel a desire to attain a healthy, optimal form of psychological functioning. However, operationally defining the term "actualization" is extremely difficult.

Measurement of Self-Esteem and Self-Concepts. A concept is only as good as its measurements. Unfortunately, the tests used most frequently to measure self-esteem and a person's self-concept have serious limitations. In the Q sort test the extent of the discrepancy between what the individual thinks he is and what he would like to be gives a measure of self-esteem. In another type of measure subjects are asked to write different answers to the question: "Who am I?" The person's spontaneous answers reveal how he views himself. In both measures, however, it is very difficult to determine the extent to which the subject's answers are influenced by his desire not to say unpleasant things about himself.

Social Determinants of the Self

How have you developed your own self view? Unclear as it may be at times, we all have at least a vague sense of our own identities. How was this formed? Is our sense of self determined by the unwinding of an innately given genetic uniqueness? Or in response to objective appraisals of our own skills and abilities? Or by our own reactions to us? Or by our interactions with people?

The most frequently given answer to these questions is that our self-concept emerges as the result of a series of interactions with significant other people. This has been a persistent theme in a number of social psychology theories, as we shall see in this section. The earliest formulation of the theory was that the self reflects the imagined reactions and appraisals of others (Cooley, 1902), as is shown in Figure 2-5. This "looking-glass" concept was made more explicit in a later theory, which said that the child's self is determined by his imitation of the reactions of significant others and by their reactions to him (Mead, 1925).

The way in which other people influence the development of one's self-concept is more explicit in contemporary social determinant theories. All of the contemporary theories agree that our self-concept is to a great extent formed by our comparing ourselves to others who matter to us, by our absorbing their reactions to us, and by our seeing ourselves as we believe they see us. (See Student Reaction Box 6.) In fact, social feedback is an essential component of self-knowledge. As we shall see in Chapter 5, when people are isolated from others, their sense of identity may become confused. The social determinant theories may differ in their emphasis on *who* and *what* is crucial in this development, and give different emphasis to the *processes* by which the development occurs. Nevertheless, since all of the theories are variations on the basic theme that our self-concept is determined by others, there is a considerable amount of overlap among them.

Psychologically compelling situations and self-concepts

How do you think your self-concept would be modified if you were convicted of theft, imprisoned, and then treated as the prisoner quoted here wrote that he had been treated?

FIGURE 2-5 A characterization of the "looking-glass" concept of the self.

I was recently released from "solitary confinement" after being held therein for 37 months [months!]. A silent system was imposed upon me and to even "whisper" to the man in the next cell resulted in being beaten by guards, sprayed with chemical mace, blackjacked, stomped, and thrown into a "strip-cell" naked to sleep on a concrete floor without bedding, covering, wash basin, or even a toilet. The floor served as toilet and bed, and even there the "silent system" was enforced. To let a "moan" escape your lips because of the pain and discomfort . . . resulted in another beating. I spent not days, but months there during my 37 months in solitary. . . .

Maybe I am an incorrigible, but if true, it's because I would rather die than to accept being treated as less than a human being. . . . I know that thieves must be punished and I don't justify stealing, even though I am a thief myself. But now I don't think I will be a thief when I am released. No, I'm not rehabilitated. It's just that I no longer think of becoming wealthy by stealing. I now only think of "killing." Killing those who have beaten me and treated me as if I were a dog. I hope and pray for the sake of my own soul and future life of freedom, that I am able to overcome the bitterness and hatred which eats daily at my soul, but I know to overcome it will not be easy.

[Zimbardo, 1971b, p. 1.]

Although this is an extreme example, most observers agree that prison life demeans prisoners. In many ways the guards, the prison routine, and the prisoner role itself systematically convey a highly negative view of the inmate, which has a powerful, self-shattering effect on his view of himself (Goffman, 1968). Humiliation begins during the admission procedure. All personal possessions are signed away; the individual is bathed, searched (even to the extent of rectal examinations), and fingerprinted, and then issued institutional clothing and a number. The dehumanizing details of the admission procedures convey the prisoner's new, low status. Further, his sense of pride in his personal appearance is weakened by the removal of all of the props necessary for maintaining a socially presentable self. Murtagh and Harris (1958) have written of the despair of obese prisoners "confronted by the first sight of themselves in prison issue." Presenting a good appearance is an important part of maintaining a good self-image, and forcing the individual to face his physical defects is a basic assault on the self.

Degradation is continued and amplified in the day-to-day prison routine. (See Figure 2-6.) Humility is forced on the inmate by the physical surroundings and by the rituals in which he is constantly mortified. The total lack of privacy—toilets without doors or partitions—means that others can easily see the prisoner in humiliating circumstances. The prison rules, which usually include a provision for routine searches and many meaningless chores, emphasize his reduced status. The inmate may have to ask permission to mail a letter or to use the telephone. To all of these blows to his self-esteem are added the verbal and gestural obscenities from the guards and other inmates. For some prisoners the most degrading part of prison life is their being forced to participate in homosexual activities. Further, the institution conveys a total lack of self-determination for the inmate. He has no choice about any aspect of his life. He must wear what he is told to wear; he must do what he is told. His lack of self-determination may even include a loss of control over his own body. When the guards want him to move, they may simply push him where they want him to go.

All of these intentional and unintentional ways of humiliating the prisoners combine to make them feel worthless. This exposure to consistently degrading views of themselves, combined with the many other factors in the inmates' backgrounds and the prison culture, may contribute to the extremely high rate of released prisoners who return to crime.

You may feel that these negative effects of prison life could have a self-shattering impact only on people who initially had a poor view of themselves. After all, people in prison are there usually because they could not cope with life in the outside world. However, the results of a recent study show that in less than a week the prison situation can transform mature, emotionally stable, physically healthy, and law-abiding, middle-class college students into either the traditional prison guard or inmate role (Zimbardo, Haney, Banks, and Jaffee, 1972).

FIGURE 2-6 Prisoners filing into the dining room at Sing Sing prison for dinner. This woodcut was done in 1876. (The Bettman Archive)

To investigate the psychological consequences of being either a prison inmate or a guard, the investigators created a simulated prison. (See Figure 2-7.) Twenty-one volunteer students were involved in the experiment. To ensure that only emotionally stable students participated in the experiment, the investigators gave all of the subjects an intensive clinical interview and a personality test before the study began. Only those whose scores fell within the middle range of a "normal" comparison population were allowed to participate. Half of the subjects were randomly designated as "prisoners" and the other half were assigned to be "guards." All were paid fifteen dollars a day to participate in the study. Thus before the study began, there were no significant differences between the prisoners and guards; nor were there any differences between the subjects and a "normal" population (to which you probably belong).

Although the simulated prison was not a literal simulation of a prison (which might include sexual degradation for some of the prisoners), it did include many of the significant psychological features of imprisonment. The prisoners were unexpectedly picked up at their homes by a city policeman in a squad car, taken to the station house, where they were searched, handcuffed, fingerprinted, and booked, and then taken blindfolded to the simulated jail. There they were stripped, issued a uniform, given a number, and put into a six-by-nine-foot barred cell, which they were to share with two other convicts. There were no windows in the cells, and the prisoners could be continuously observed by the guards. Toilet facilities (without showers) were in a nearby corridor. After ten o'clock at night all toilet privileges were denied, so that the prisoners had to use buckets if they wished to relieve themselves. No clocks or any other personal effects were permitted. To perform routine activities—such as writing a letter or smoking a cigarette—the prisoners had to get permission from the guards.

Thus the "Stanford County Prison" reproduced many of the debilitating conditions found in other prisons. The prisoners were humiliated and made to feel anonymous. Since the guards had complete power, the prisoners were dependent on them for functions as basic as going

FIGURE 2-7 A prisoner being led to his cell at the "Stanford County Prison." (Philip G. Zimbardo)

to the toilet. With no windows, no clocks, and minimal external distractions, time passed very slowly. The unwashed bodies in the summer made the prison smell. Further, television and films had provided them with information about how prisoners are expected to behave.

The setting was highly realistic for the guards, too. They were given billy clubs, whistles, handcuffs, and the keys to the cells—all symbols of their power. They were told that they should maintain "law and order" and that they would be responsible for any difficulties that might develop. Sixteen prison rules, including one that "prisoners must address each other by their ID number only," were provided, and the guards were told to enforce these to the letter.

After six days in this environment, the majority of the subjects had thoroughly absorbed their role. Despite a lifetime of learning in which they had thoroughly established their self-concepts, within less than a week, their behavior, thinking, and emotional reactions were changed to fit their roles. Many of the "prisoners" became "servile, dehumanized robots who thought only of escape, of their individual survival, and of their mounting hatred of the guards" (Zimbardo, 1971b, p. 3). The extent to which they internalized their prisoner roles is shown by the following statement from one prisoner:

I began to feel that I was losing my identity, the person I call [subject's *name*], the person who put me into this place, the person who volunteered to go into this prison . . . was distant from me, was remote until finally, I wasn't that. I was #416—I was really my number.

[Zimbardo et al., 1972, p. 12.]

The impact of the prison on the guards was equally marked. Soon after the experiment began, the guards began to abuse their power:

They made the prisoners obey petty, meaningless and often inconsistent rules, forced them to engage in tedious, useless work such as moving cartons back and forth between closets and picking thorns out of their blankets for hours on end. Not only did the prisoners have to sing songs or laugh or refrain from smiling on command, but they were encouraged to curse and vilify each other publicly.

[Zimbardo et al., 1972, p. 10.]

Not all of the guards were equally tyrannical. About one-third arbitrarily used their power to demean the prisoners. Some of the guards played their role as "tough but fair" correctional officers, and a few of the guards were friendly with the prisoners and did small favors for them. However, none of the guards ever protested against the arbitrary orders given by the tyrannical guards, and none ever intervened on behalf of the prisoners.

The guards' and prisoners' acting out their respective roles intensified the differences in their behavior:

As the guards became more aggressive, prisoners became more passive; assertion by the guards led to dependency in the prisoners; self-aggrandizement was met with self-deprecation, authority with helplessness, and the counterpart of the guards' sense of mastery and control was the depression and hopelessness witnessed in the prisoners.

[Zimbardo et al., 1972, p. 9.]

This cyclic interaction—as well as the two different roles of guard and prisoner—led to significant differences in the frequencies of

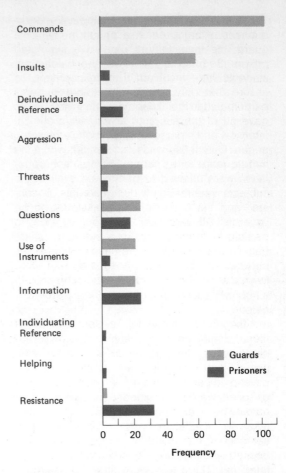

FIGURE 2-8 Interaction profile of guard and prisoner behavior on twenty-five occasions during the six days in the simulated prison environment. (Adapted from Zimbardo et al., 1972, Figure 1.)

guard and prisoner behavior. On twenty-five separate occasions the interactions between guards and prisoners were video recorded and subsequently analyzed. As can be seen in Figure 2-8, the guards' most typical response with prisoners was to give orders. Their control was abusive—as shown by the frequency of their insults, their threats, and their use of night sticks and other instruments to keep the prisoners in line. Further, the guards frequently referred to the prisoners in anonymous deprecating ways, such as, "You ass hole, 5401, come here."

Although initially many of the prisoners resisted the guards and asked questions, over time they stopped resisting and, indeed, almost ceased reacting altogether. As can be seen in Figure 2-8, there was a very low rate of response for prisoners in all of the categories analyzed. In the prison setting a prisoner's asking questions sometimes led to punishment, so that over time, the prisoners may have thought the safest way to behave was not to behave—a reaction noted by some ex-prisoners: "The only way to really make it with the bosses [in Texas prisons] is to withdraw into yourself, both mentally and physically—literally making yourself as small as possible" (Mike Middleton, Ex Con, *Christian Science Monitor Series* in Zimbardo et al, 1972, p. 18).

As the differences between the guards and prisoners became more apparent, the prisoners—smelly, passive, and demoralized—invited further degradations. Eighty-five percent of the comments the prisoners made about their fellow prisoners were deprecating. Ninety percent of the prisoners' conversations focused on plans for resistance or ways to ingratiate themselves with guards to obtain a small favor—such as permission to go to the toilet. Thus the prisoners mirrored the negative image of themselves indicated by the guards' actions. After awhile almost any indignity seemed "fair game" to some of the guards, one of whom wrote: "I was surprised at myself. . . . I made them call each other names and clean the toilets out with their bare hands. I practically considered the prisoners cattle, and I kept thinking I have to watch out for them in case they try something" (Zimbardo et al., 1972, p. 9).

After six days of what was originally intended to be a two-week experiment, the study had to be broken off. It had become too real. Five prisoners had had to be released, four because of either severe emotional depression or acute anxiety attacks, one because he developed a psychosomatic rash over his entire body. Some of the guards had become too brutal. And all of these effects occurred in a sample of "normal, average" college students representative of an educated, white, middle-class sample.

When men are in real prisons, subjected to the demands of prison life for extended periods of time, imagine how much more debilitating the prison experience is—for both prisoners and guards. In only six days the demands of the situation and the assumed roles made many normal students act either as sadistic brutes or as submissive passivists. (The investigators who conducted the prison study have attempted to maximize the social value of the implications of their work by presenting their findings to a Congressional Subcommittee on Prison and Prison Reform, to those in correctional facilities, to student groups, and to groups of taxpayers.)

From the study of these real and simulated prison experiences, we can hypothesize that an individual's self-concept and behavior can be changed extensively by the demands of any psychologically compelling situation. A similar plasticity has in fact been found in other situations in which the demands to enact a certain role are extremely strong and of long duration. In a classic study persons who had functioned as bureaucrats for extended periods of time, and thus had been exposed to strong demands to fit the bureaucrat's role, were found to fit the stereotypes of impersonality and compulsiveness (Merton, 1940). For other examples of the effect of a psychologically compelling environment on one's self-concept, see Box 1. As we saw in the discussion of whether people possess one or multiple selves, we may be what the situation demands us to be.

The influence of parents on the child's emerging self-concept

Almost all personality and self theorists agree that parent-child interaction plays a crucially important part in determining the child's self-concept. There are many ways in which learning could occur as a result of parent-child interaction. Early establishment of the attachment relationship, early sensory experience, classical conditioning, instrumental conditioning, and imitation—all of these processes combined provide a powerful determinant of the child's emerging distinction between himself and others and his subsequent definition and evaluation of himself. (See Figure 2-10.) Although they differ in the specification of precisely how this occurs, social evaluation theories all emphasize that the formation of the self-concept is a basic part of the socialization process. The child's view of himself is a reflection of how he thinks his parents view him. See Student Reaction Box 7.

BOX 1 LEARNING TO HATE YOURSELF

Prison is not the only place where you can learn to hate yourself. A number of studies have shown that the negative views held by a majority group toward a persecuted, minority group may be absorbed by members of the minority group. In recent years self-hatred has been shown among American Jews and blacks. Anti-Semitic attitudes have been demonstrated among Jews (Sarnoff, 1951). Instances of self-hatred among blacks have been shown in many studies. (See Figure 2-9.) Blacks have been found to have basically the same prejudices and stereotypes about many ethnic groups, including their own group, as do whites. In surveying 160 Negro college students from schools throughout the United States, one investigator found that approximately 19 percent had negative attitudes toward themselves (Maliver, 1965). What this can mean to an individual black person's sense of self-identity is perhaps shown most clearly in an individual quotation:

"I have many fantasies that I am not a Negro. I don't want to be a Negro woman. . . . My jealousy and need to be on top is from the effort to divorce myself from Negroes and prove I'm not inferior. To stop competing and fighting would mean I would have to go back to this feeling of inferiority."

[Kardiner and Ovesey, 1968 reprint of a 1951 book, p. 292.]

Self-contempt seems to begin early among black children. When shown dolls that were identical except for skin color and asked to "give me the doll you like best," the majority of the black children (from ages three to seven) indicated a preference for the white doll (Clark and Clark, 1947). Further, it has been shown that the black child's self-rejection is related to the degree of discrimination in the community. When shown pictures of black and white children and asked which child they would prefer as a playmate, the majority of the black children—both in the North and South—expressed a preference for the white child. However, the percentage of black children preferring the white playmate was higher in the South (78 percent) than in the North (53.7 percent) (Morland, 1970). Thus the black child absorbs the negative attitudes about himself held by those in his community.

This existence of a negative self-image concerning blackness is shown in yet another way. Until quite recently, with the advent of the "black is beautiful" movement, many American blacks spent a lot of money trying to make themselves look less black. In the 1930s and 1940s hair straightening and oiling to eliminate the kinkiness of black hair was a popular beauty treatment among both men and women.

You probably noticed that most of the citations for the self-contempt studies were from the 1950s and 1960s. With the emphasis given to black pride and racial awareness in the late 1960s and early 1970s, one can wonder if the results would be quite different if the studies were done in the 1970s. Some of the most recent studies have yielded inconsistent results. In one study, conducted in an interracial setting in Lincoln, Nebraska, it was found that when black children were given a choice between white and black dolls, they chose black dolls (Hraba and Grant, 1970), but another study, conducted in de facto segregated settings in Newark, New Jersey, replicated the earlier findings of a black preference for white dolls (Asher and Allen, 1969). Apparently black is not equally beautiful in all parts of the country and in all settings.

The continuing existence of self-contempt, the most crippling legacy of white racism, emphasizes the need for research on ways to increase black self-pride.

FIGURE 2-9 Impoverished ghetto surroundings can lead to self-hatred among an oppressed minority. (Joe Molnar)

STUDENT REACTION BOX 7

THE INFLUENCE OF ANNE'S PARENTS ON HER SELF-CONCEPT

"My parents first and above all have had an enormous influence on me. The spoiled little brat in me is probably due to my mother. She has always been the parent to go through to get what you want. If there was something I wanted, I always knew how to manipulate Mom into getting it for me. Until recently I didn't respect her because I thought of her as a pushover. But now I'm beginning to love my mother more and to respect her. I guess it is because she has realized that I'm not a baby anymore.

"My father is the original model for the authoritarian personality. If my mother is responsible for the spoiled brat in me, he is responsible for the insecure, submissive part of me. All my father thought he had to do was to open his mouth and everyone in the family should be ready for the command. You only asked my father once and he only answered once. He was not an affectionate man: I still can't recall his ever saying he loved me. At times, I resented him a good deal, while I loved and respected him. He, too, has changed recently. Since I've decided to go to graduate school he seems to have realized that I must have a head on my shoulders and has loosened the reins a little."

Since controlled experiments are impossible (for ethical reasons), the research on the effects of parent-child interaction on the child's self-concept has been correlational. In their attempts to relate certain critical aspects of the parents' behavior with their children's self-concept, researchers have had difficulty obtaining reliable and valid information about both the children's and their parents' behavior. Frequently, investigators have asked children to rate aspects of both their own behavior and their parents' behavior. The validity of the child's ratings is somewhat open to question. Further, much of the work on the antecedents of the self in the parent-child relationship has been largely a-theoretical in nature and has not focused on those aspects of the parent-child interaction emphasized by various self theorists. Thus the findings of many of the correlational studies have been somewhat difficult to conceptualize.

A recent study by Coopersmith (1967) has gone a long way in meeting both methodological and theoretical criticisms. The customary questionnaires that the children (ages ten to twelve) filled out, rating their own level of self-esteem and their interactions with their parents, were supplemented by four other kinds of evidence: (1) teachers' ratings of the children's self-esteem, (2) an intensive clinical evaluation of the children, (3) observation of the children in a series of situations "theoretically related to self-esteem," and (4) an intensive series of interviews conducted with the children's mothers.

To tie his research procedures as closely as possible to the various self theories, the investigator reviewed a number of those theories to find the factors that were most often related to high self-esteem. Two emerged: (1) a history of success and competency and (2) parental acceptance.

The research results provide an interesting

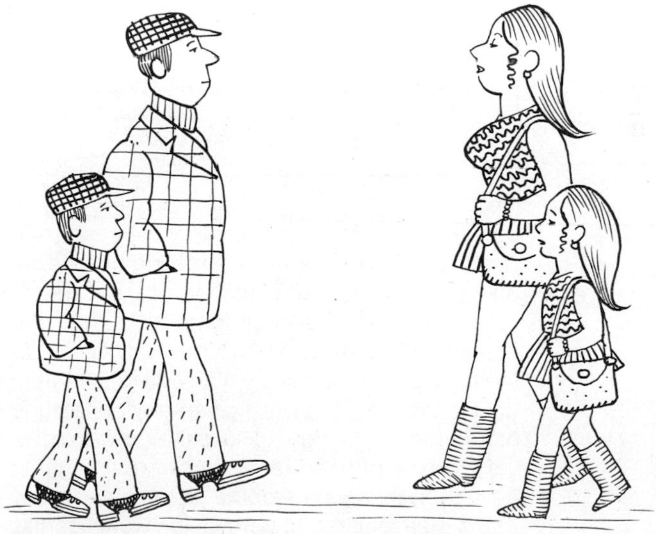

FIGURE 2-10 The strength of parental influence in determining the child's self-concept.

STUDENT REACTION BOX 8

ANNE'S REFERENCE GROUP

Obviously, Anne's friends influenced her view of herself. In this way, one of her reference groups—that is, her friends, including Lee and Marcia—influenced her ideas and values. Anne was also influenced by a group to which she did not belong yet: professional psychologists. As we see below, she also evaluated herself in terms of this group, which she aspired to:

"I guess my ideal self has changed many times, but it keeps returning to Anne being a professional psychologist. The faculty in the Psychology Department has had a lot to do with this. I've come to think of the Psychology Library as my second home. I admire the faculty very much, especially Dr. G. He always knows what he's talking about and he makes it all so interesting. He's cool! Liking and respecting so many of the profs has made me want grad school and academia for the rest of my life. That's why I've got to keep my grades up and work hard. Dr. G.'s counting on me. He doesn't say much, but I'd hate to tell him that I'd gotten a bad grade—especially in a psychology course."

children with high self-esteem emphasized the need for their children's independence. Children were encouraged to develop their own standards for evaluating their own behavior and to avoid relying on the judgments of others to evaluate their own worth.

The parents of children with a high level of self-esteem had a high level of self-esteem themselves and were very accepting of their children. Thus the parents of children with high self-esteem provided a model of competent, realistic persons, who conveyed their high regard for their children in a warm, close, and loving relationship with them.

Although it is clearly impossible to show the direction of causation in this correlational study, these findings may be interpreted as supporting the importance of both competency and loving acceptance in the development of self-esteem. By providing clear limits, the parents structure the world of their child, so that he can more accurately gauge his own successes and failures within those limits. By accepting the child, parents convey a warm, approving reflection of the child, which he then incorporates into his concept of himself.

The reference group theory

According to the reference group theory (as ably summarized by Pettigrew, 1967), the individual identifies with the standards and beliefs of certain groups—termed "reference groups" (Hyman, 1942)—and then uses these as a standard against which he defines and evaluates himself. For most people the groups to which they actually belong, or "membership groups," serve as the measuring standard, or reference group. For a student his friends may serve as his reference group.

Nevertheless, the membership group and the reference group do not always coincide. Occasionally, a group the individual does not actually belong to may fulfill this measuring function. Any group against which the individual evaluates himself, whether he actually belongs to it or not, is termed a reference group. An individual may have more than one reference group, and some of the groups may have conflicting standards. See Student Reaction Box 8.

confirmation of the two central elements emphasized by self theorists: a feeling of success and competency, and acceptance by critical others. The parents of children with high self-esteem had clearly set and enforced limits for their children's behavior. Within these "benign limits" the children were given a wide latitude of freedom. Their right to have their own point of view was supported, and they were thought to have a right to participate in making family plans. Reasoning and persuasion were used as discipline techniques. Further, the parents of

Functions of the Reference Group Once the individual has identified with a particular group, exactly how does that reference group influence his behavior? Say you associate with a group of freaks on your campus and that you view yourself as a freak. First, you may feel subtle and not-so-subtle pressures to conform to what others in your group do—the "normative" function of a reference group (Kelley, 1952). If all your friends wear bell-bottomed jeans and army jackets, you may feel pressure to dress similarly. If you don't, you will probably receive some negative reactions (as Anne noted in Student Reaction Box 6, page 74). Conformity pressures are extremely strong and pervasive in group processes.

A second function of the reference group is the "comparative" function. You use your group as a source to judge your beliefs about many aspects of reality—including yourself. Without the other members of your group making any overt attempts to influence you, you look to them to see what is correct. To decide, for example, what sorts of things you should be concerned about, you may look to your friends to see what concerns them and use this as a standard for your own beliefs. Or to make a judgment about your own level of physical attractiveness, you may compare your appearance with the models shown in magazines. Even when you have no desire to be liked or accepted by other people, you may use them as a source of information. See Figure 2-11 for an illustration of the comparative and normative functions of a reference group.

Although the normative and comparative functions of reference groups can be distinguished, in real life they are closely interrelated. The normative function may mediate what seems to be a comparative function: You may internalize the standards of your group to avoid being ridiculed for nonconformity. Or the comparative function may mediate the normative: You may conform because you have internalized the standards.

Both the normative and comparative functions of the reference group—especially when they are combined—make the reference group an important source for beliefs and values. You may define yourself as your group does. A number of studies have shown the power of the group in determining the self-concept of its members. For instance, it has been found that college undergraduates described themselves in the way that they thought others whom "they valued" saw them (Mannheim, 1966). Several studies have shown a positive correlation between the individual's view of himself and the group's view of him (e.g., Miyamoto and Dornbusch, 1956). In addition to the correlational evidence, several controlled experiments have shown that a person's view of himself can be influenced—at least momentarily—by how others in an experiment react to him. Persons who are given negative reports have been found to see themselves more negatively; those given positive information see themselves more positively (Gergen, 1965; Tippett and Silber, 1966).

However, as we shall see, the individual's view of himself is not completely determined by his group's evaluation of him. The individual "screens" the information in a number of ways. And there is a strong desire in each person to see himself in a favorable way. Thus a number of studies have shown that although the individual's rating of himself tends to reflect what others say, that rating is generally more favorable than those given to him by the other members of his group (e.g., Reeder et al., 1960).

Strengths and Weaknesses of the Reference Group Theory This relatively early social evaluation theory emphasized the importance of the group in defining and evaluating all aspects of the social situation, including the individual's self, and in policing adherence to the group's definitions and evaluations. Reference group theory has provided a fundamental insight into the way in which group membership influences the individual: The reference group not only actively coerces the individual to meet its standards, but also indirectly influences him by providing information about what is acceptable. Throughout this text, we will repeatedly see ways in which the normative and comparative functions of a group influence the behavior of its members.

However, a basic shortcoming of the theory is that it does not describe clearly how an individual comes to select a particular group as his reference group (Pettigrew, 1967). When the

FIGURE 2-11 (A) Comparative function of a reference group. (B) Normative function of a reference group.

reference group is one that the individual belongs to, the process of choice seems clear. College students compare themselves with other college students—not with peach pickers. There are, however, puzzling instances in which the person does not identify with his membership group, but rather evaluates himself against the standards of other groups or even against the standards of a fictitious group created by the individual. For example, a writer may compare his work with the ephemeral reference group "great writers of all time" rather than with his contemporaries.

Merton (1957) has suggested four variables that cause individuals to select reference groups they do not actually belong to: (1) The relative ability of the membership and nonmembership groups to *provide rewards.* When the actual membership group cannot provide as many potential rewards as another group, the individual is more likely to select a rewarding, nonmembership group. (2) The individual's *status* in his membership group. People who are marginally involved in their membership groups are more likely to choose nonmembership groups as reference groups. (3) The *rate of social mobility.* When people have rapid, upward patterns of social mobility, they are more likely to choose higher status groups as reference groups. (4) The *individual's own personality and view of himself.* People are likely to choose groups that seem similar to themselves in some way.

Although these suggestions provide some promising leads about the process of selecting a reference group, empirical evidence has not yet been accumulated. Since an empirically supported analysis of the central concept of reference group theory has never really been provided, the theory has remained somewhat vague and has frequently been used to "explain" findings after the fact.

Social comparison theory

Clearly, our views of ourselves do reflect the opinions of others. The question is why, when, and how this happens. Why do we compare ourselves with others? When are we most likely to compare ourselves? To whom do we compare ourselves? Once we have compared ourselves, what are our reactions? One highly systematic set of answers to these questions is provided by Festinger's social comparison theory, which applies to many areas of social psychology, as well as to the development of one's self-concept. Social comparison theory provides an analysis of the way in which the components of the self are evaluated. In his formulation of social comparison, Festinger considered the comparison of abilities and opinions. Others have extended the theory to include the comparison of emotions and personality traits. In the process of comparing aspects of yourself with others, your overall level of self-esteem is determined (Singer, 1966).

The effects of social comparison on the person's self-concept has been shown clearly in one study (Morse and Gergen, 1970). The student-subjects thought that they were being interviewed for a job. In the first part of the experiment, all of the students completed a measure of self-esteem. Then they saw "another job applicant." For half of the students, the competitor was very impressive-looking, and for the other half of the students, the competitor

was very messy-looking. Then all of the subjects completed a second measure of self-esteem. As predicted, the self-esteem of those who had met "super" candidate decreased significantly, and the self-esteem of those who had met the messy candidate increased.

In relatively few of the social comparison studies has the direct social comparison of the self as a whole been considered. As we review the literature comparing components of the self, we should keep in mind the question of whether or not the same processes function in the social comparison of the total self.

Why Do We Compare Ourselves with Others? For Accuracy or Aggrandizement? Festinger assumed that the main motive for social comparison was accuracy. People need to evaluate their opinions and abilities, and when no "objective" means is available, people do so by comparing their opinions and abilities with those of other people (Festinger, 1954, p. 118). Since objective means of evaluating abilities, opinions, and other aspects of the self are rarely available, it would follow from this theory that people would have an extremely strong drive to compare all of the components of the self as well as the total self. To get an accurate idea of how good a skier you are, you would compare your skiing ability with that of other, similar people.

A number of studies have shown that people do seem to want an accurate social comparison in evaluating their abilities, opinions, emotions, and personality traits. For example, the intensity and pervasiveness of the desire of persons attending human relations training sessions "to be told point blank how other people perceive them" has been noted (Bennis et al., 1968, p. 224). Management trainees have reported an urgent desire for "respected superiors to give them absolutely objective, point-blank feedback" on their potential as managers (Bennis et al., 1968, p. 225). Anne, the student whose comments have been quoted, remarked: "When I'm with people, I'm constantly wondering what they think of me."

But do people always want accuracy when that closest and dearest of all entities, their self, is being compared? If you are discussing some very important aspect of yourself with a friend, do you really want him to be honest? When our interactions with others relate to our definition and evaluation of our total self or aspects of the self that are very important to us, how often do we really want or allow honest appraisals and reactions?

A number of theorists would say "not very often." One psychologist feels that so very few social exchanges involve honest disclosures about the self that to give an honest disclosure requires real courage (Jourard, 1964). Usually, highly censored versions of ourselves are presented to others, who have, in turn, similarly laundered their own public selves. (See Figure 2-12.) Goffman has emphasized the ritualization of social interactions that allow for mutual enhancement of one's public image, or "face," and the avoidance of honest self-disclosure. Social interaction is governed by an elaborate set of rules, which allow everyone to keep face and preclude honest interactions:

> Whatever his position in society, the person insulates himself by blindness, half-truths, illusions, and rationalizations. He makes an "adjustment" by convincing himself, with the tactful support of his intimate circle, that he is what he wants to be and that he would not do to gain his ends what the others have done to gain theirs.

> [Goffman, 1955, p. 230.]

We can see many examples of attempts to maintain a favorable image of ourselves in everyday life. In fact, it was found that positive evaluations of people in a group circulated much more freely than negative ones (Blumberg, 1972). Still, at least occasionally, we do seem to want honest and accurate information about ourselves. Indeed, one theorist has emphasized that honest and realistic self-disclosure is essential for a healthy functioning of the self (Jourard, 1964). The puzzle is the relative strength of the accuracy and the aggrandizement motives in the social comparison of the self.

In your own interactions with other people, which motive, accuracy or aggrandizement, is stronger? When do you really want accurate information about the self? We could theorize that the relative strength of these two motives is determined by the conflict between factors impelling the person toward self-knowledge and those restraining him. If you are highly curious, feel a strong need for self-definition, or are very uncertain about a particular aspect of yourself, you may strive for accuracy. In contrast, if you are afraid of what you may discover and your overall level of self-esteem is so low that you cannot tolerate an unfavorable opinion, you may avoid an authentic exchange.

Although the empirical evidence on the relative strength of accuracy and aggrandizement is very sparse, what is available indirectly supports the hypothesis that the need for favorable information is a strong motive in interpersonal comparisons of the self. For instance, in one study it was found that subjects chose to make a social comparison that provided less ac-

FIGURE 2-12 Keeping face in social interaction.

curate information about themselves and avoided the possibility of obtaining negative information (Hakmiller, 1966). This finding raises an important issue. Often in order to obtain self-information, the person must expose himself to a group. But being with other people also allows them to see his weaknesses and may result in negative evaluations. In some cases people may avoid others because of this fear of negative evaluation—rather than because of a disdain of others.

At this point, it is not at all clear that accuracy is the main motive behind social comparisons concerning the self. The pervasiveness of the accuracy motive in much of the social comparison work may reflect the relatively uninvolving nature of the laboratory procedures. Perhaps subjects can only afford to be honest with themselves when they don't really care.

When Are We Most Likely to Compare Ourselves?
Festinger assumed the existence of an evaluative drive. Given this drive, the next question concerns the variables that influence its intensity (Latané, 1966). Depriving an animal of food increases his hunger drive; conversely, giving him food decreases it. One might expect the depriving and giving of information to have a similar effect on the individual's need to know. Increasing the individual's level of uncertainty would be expected to increase his desire for social comparison and decreasing his level of uncertainty, to decrease his need to know the reactions of others.

A number of experiments have provided supporting evidence for this hypothesis. One investigator found that the more uncertain an individual was about his own opinions, the greater was his desire to be with other people (Radloff, 1959). It has also been found that providing an individual with information that supported his point of view decreased his desire to compare his opinions with those of other people (Gordon, 1966). From these results we might conclude that the degree of someone's uncertainty about his opinions is directly related to the intensity of his desire for social comparison.

However, the results of a recent study complicate this simple hypothesis (Latané and Wheeler, 1966). After being exposed to the extreme emotional arousal and uncertainty involved in a body search at the site of a Boeing 707 airplane crash, men who were usually emotionally unresponsive reported that they had communicated more than usual, but men who were usually emotionally responsive communicated less. The uncertainty explanation of social comparison would predict that all of the men exposed to this highly unusual situation would have an increased tendency to communicate and compare. Why, then, didn't the highly emotional men share their experience? One possibility is that being involved in such a grisly chore may have raised the level of anxiety in the persons who are usually highly emotional to the point where they could no longer bear to talk or think about the experience. The intensity of emotional arousal may have overwhelmed the need for social comparison.

With Whom Do We Compare Ourselves?
Festinger (1954) theorized that when people wish to obtain accurate information about themselves, they compare themselves with someone who is *similar*. Let's assume that a psychology major wishes to get an idea of how he stands with respect to his ability in psychology. He might compare his grades with those of other psychology majors at his school. Information about the grades of physics majors might not be helpful, since the grading standards might differ in the various academic departments. And information about the grades made by psychology majors at different colleges might not tell him much either, since their grading standards might also differ. The grades made by persons who are most similar would provide the most information. See Student Reaction Box 9.

Of course, the real-life process of social comparison usually occurs in an automatic and unthinking way. We do not consciously deliberate about who would be the best person to compare ourselves with, and we are likely to make our comparisons with minimum effort. This, in turn, suggests that we look primarily to our friends, whom we generally consider to be similar to ourselves (Lundy, 1958). Thus the experimental evidence on the choice of a comparison person may be more applicable to situations in which the individual is allowed a wider variety of potential comparisons than

STUDENT REACTION BOX 9

ANNE'S CHOICE OF COMPARISON PERSONS

"I really have no idea when or why I choose certain people to compare myself with. Sometimes I compare myself with people who are very similar and, at other times, I seek out people who are as dissimilar as I can find. For instance, my best friend Marcia initially seemed very dissimilar: I thought she had everything I wanted. Gradually, as we grew closer, I found that she and I had many things in common. And nobody could have seemed more dissimilar than Lee when I first met him.

"Sometimes I seek out people I think will be good for me even though I don't think they are similar. Like George. He's hard-working, stable, and so intelligent. I think he is the brightest person on this campus. He isn't like any of my friends, he doesn't view life as I do, we disagree about everything, but I respect him a great deal and do compare myself with him."

depend on: (1) the motive behind the person's making the social comparison, (2) the information available to the subject, and (3) the definition of "similarity" in the particular experiment.

THE INFLUENCE OF MOTIVES ON COMPARISON CHOICE As we have seen, social comparisons are not always aimed at obtaining accurate information; sometimes people want pleasant, self-aggrandizing information. If you want reassurance about your own worth, you may seek out someone you think will provide that—similar or not—and if your main motive in interacting with others is to exercise your influence, you may choose someone who is dissimilar so that you can try to influence him. One study showed that when subjects who were very sure of themselves were given a choice of being with similar or dissimilar persons, they chose dissimilar persons (Gordon, 1966).

Still another reason for social comparison might be self-improvement. If you wish to improve yourself in an area that is important to you, you may select someone who provides a complete and positive example of that trait. Experimental evidence for this kind of "upward choice" was provided in a study showing that persons who were highly motivated to attain a certain characteristic chose comparison persons who were objectively better than themselves (Wheeler, 1966a). The choice of a comparison person clearly depends on the person's particular motive for social comparison.

usually obtain or to situations in which the individual is highly motivated.

Although a number of studies have confirmed Festinger's hypothesis concerning the importance of similarity in interpersonal comparisons (e.g., Darley and Aronson, 1966), some have not. As is usual with new, broad theories, the psychological processes mediating social comparison have been found to be more complicated than originally thought. By formulating a definite, testable prediction, Festinger has encouraged experimental work that can be incorporated into an elaborated version of the original theory.

The experimental results show that the selection of someone for social comparison seems to

THE INFLUENCE OF THE INFORMATION AVAILABLE ON THE COMPARISON CHOICE If you wished to obtain accurate information about yourself, whom would you choose for comparison? The answer seems to depend, at least in part, on the amount of information you already have. If, for example, you were beginning a new job and had no idea of the range of salaries, you might be interested in finding out the company president's salary. This would tell you what the upper limits would be. In contrast, if you wanted to answer the question of where you stood in relation to other people who had begun to work with you, you might want to know what your contemporaries were making. Whether you want similar or extreme scores may depend on whether you wish to make an absolute comparison, which involves knowing the whole distribution, or a relative comparison, which means learning about those most similar to you. This pattern of results has been obtained in two experiments: When subjects were told the range of scores possible on a test, they chose to see similar scores, but when subjects were not told the range of scores, they wished to see the extreme scores (Thornton and Arrowood, 1966; Arrowood, 1966).

OPERATIONAL DEFINITION OF SIMILARITY   If you were asked to compare your goals in life with someone who was similar, whom would you choose? Someone with a similar personality? Someone in the same situation? Someone with a similar background? Since similarity can be defined in so many ways, isolating the critical elements of similarity has been the concern of much of the social comparison literature.

Frequently, similarity has been defined in terms of the similarity of scores on a bogus test given during the experimental session. Whether people wish to see similar or dissimilar scores seems to depend on whether they feel that the test measures a positive or a negative aspect of themselves. For example, one investigator told subjects he was giving them a projective test of "hostility toward one's own parents." After the test he informed each subject of his "score" and then asked him whether he wanted to see a similar or a dissimilar score. In this situation, in which a negative trait was being rated, the subjects did not wish to see the scores of a similar subject. However, when the trait that was allegedly measured by the test was more positive, the subjects preferred to see similar scores (Wheeler, 1966a).

The desire to share the same immediate psychological situation has also been found to influence the selection of someone for social comparison. If you're going through an upsetting experience, you may want to share your reaction with someone who is in the same situation. For example, it was found that subjects who thought they would be going through a painful experimental procedure preferred being with others whom they thought were in a similar situation (Darley and Aronson, 1966).

Similarity in personality, however, may be an even stronger determinant in the choice of a person for social comparison than situational similarity. Subjects who thought they would be participating in a painful experiment preferred being with others who had similar personalities, even though they were not going to be in the painful experiment, to being with people who had dissimilar personalities but were going to be in the same experiment (Miller and Zimbardo, 1966).

Clearly, specifying the critical aspects of similarity is a difficult business. The choice of comparison persons will be discussed in more detail in Chapter 5.

Once We Have Compared Ourselves, What Are Our Reactions? Say that you have compared your values with your friends' values, and you find that they differ. What do you do? Festinger has hypothesized that three outcomes are likely: (1) You may change your own values; (2) you may try to change your friends' values; or (3) you may reject those people whose opinions remain divergent. In everyday life we see many examples of these three effects.

One of the most extensively documented findings of social psychology is that people do not like to be different from the other members of their group. We saw this in Anne's uncomfortable reaction when she was dressed differently from the other people in her group. A common reaction when one sees that he is different is to change, so that he becomes more similar to others.

If he does not change, members of the group will try to persuade him. As we have seen, one of the main functions of the reference group is to enforce conformity to the group values. Outside the laboratory you may see examples among your friends of attempts to persuade others. When one person differs, the others may subtly or not-so-subtly try to influence him, so that his behavior moves closer to what is acceptable.

Or if conversion fails, people may reject those whose opinions and behaviors deviate too much. After a number of unsuccessful attempts to persuade a friend to view a situation as you do, you may lose interest in that person. You associate with people who provide a reassuring amount of agreement.

Summary

Psychologically Compelling Situations and Self-Concepts. In situations in which the individual's former sense of self is systematically assaulted and the demands of the situation for him to play a certain role are clear and compelling, his self-concept can be molded to match what the situation demands. In prison the prisoner's identity becomes merged with the role of prisoner.

The Influence of Parents on the Child's Emerging Self-Concept. Almost all personality and self theorists agree that parent-child interaction plays a crucial part in determining the child's self-concept. In particular, a parent's providing his child with a history of success and competency and with loving acceptance have been found to be important. Parents who do this have been found to have children with high self-esteem.

The Reference Group Theory. The individual identifies with the standards and beliefs of certain groups—termed reference groups—and then uses them as a standard against which he defines and evaluates himself. Reference groups serve two functions for the individual: (1) the *normative function,* which pressures the person to conform to what others in the group do, and (2) the *comparative function,* which gives him information against which he can judge himself. When both the normative and comparative functions are combined, as they frequently are, the reference group is an important determinant of all of one's beliefs—including his definition of his self.

The Social Comparison Theory. This theory provides a highly systematic explanation of the way in which our views of ourselves are influenced by others. Although in many situations the person's main motive for social comparison is accuracy, people sometimes desire enhancement rather than honest feedback when comparing the self. Generally, people are most likely to engage in social comparison when they are uncertain about themselves. Usually, people compare themselves with others who are similar. However, the motive behind the individual's making the social comparison, the information available to the person, and the definition of similarity have all been found to influence the choice of a comparison person.

Once social comparison occurs, three outcomes are likely: (1) you may change your own values; (2) you may try to change your friends' beliefs when they differ from yours; or (3) you may reject those people whose opinions remain divergent.

Similarities and Differences Between the Four Theories. All four social evaluation theories agree on the importance of others in determining the individual's self-concept. However, they differ in their emphasis on who is crucial in this interaction and on the process by which it occurs. The "compelling situation" approach emphasizes the importance of the immediate situation. People in prison reflect their immediate environment and do what is expected of them. In contrast, the parent-child approach emphasizes the importance of early experience in forming a stable self-concept.

Reference group theory emphasizes the importance of the group and to some extent overlaps both the compelling situation theory and social comparison theory. In a prison setting the other inmates and guards may be viewed as the individual's reference group. Clearly, they serve both a powerful normative and comparative function. Outside prison an individual has a variety of reference groups, so that the power of any one group is not total, but in prison the individual is largely cut off from all groups except those in his immediate surroundings. Social comparison, too, can be seen as an extension of reference group theory, since it makes explicit how one function of the reference group, the comparative function, operates.

Other Determinants of the Self

To return to our original question, why do we think of ourselves as we do? In the preceding section we saw the important role our interactions with other people play in forming our self-concept. Parent-child interactions may be argued to form the core of the child's self-concept. Later, interactions with others—in psychologically compelling situations, with reference groups, or through social comparison—influence our self-concept. Clearly, the reactions of significant others are very important in forming one's self-concept. The question is whether or not the self is completely determined by social interactions.

Not all would agree that it is. Some theorists have argued that our perceptions of our actual abilities have a critical effect on the defining of our self and our self-esteem. Others have emphasized the active role of the self in determining the evolution of the self. Both of these explanations overlap the social evaluation approach. Frequently, abilities are evaluated by others. The grades you obtain in a particular area may indicate your ability in that area. Further, the original "core" component of the self, theorized to exert an active role on further development of the self, may have been completely determined by your parents' view of you. All three determinants of the self—the reactions of others, your perception of your own abilities, and your own self—overlap. A complete theory of the formation of the self would have to specify the relative contributions of each determinant.

The influence of perceived competency on self-esteem

Several theorists have emphasized the importance of perceived competency in defining self-esteem, although this determinant of self-esteem has not been as extensively researched as social determinants. For instance, it has been argued that a sense of competency is basic to the development of self-esteem (White, 1959). Your feelings about your ability to cope with the environment would determine how favorably you view yourself.

What research has been done supports the importance of perceived competency. The results of a number of "level of aspiration" studies (done in the 1940s and 1950s) suggest that perceived failure on relatively uninvolving experimental tasks influences an individual's goals. Consistently, when subjects were made to think that they had succeeded, their level of aspiration rose; when they thought they had failed, it fell (Pepitone, 1968).

Success or failure at a more involving task has been found to have an effect on the overall level of self-esteem (Koocher, 1971). In the YMCA summer camp where the study was done, the ability to swim was very important. Success in learning to swim was found to be related to a significant increase in the learner's level of self-esteem. However, the evidence on the self-esteem effects of success at basic and ego-involving tasks has been correlational, since success and failure at such tasks cannot be experimentally manipulated for ethical reasons.

There is one puzzle. Competency, as evaluated by others, does not always correspond to the individual's own view of his abilities. People whom others consider highly competent may view themselves as incompetent and thus have a low level of self-esteem. The reverse may also occur. In one study both types of discrepancy between the socially mediated and private standards were noted (Coopersmith, 1967). Not all individuals accept their socially rated self; some seem to reject the commonly accepted social criteria for success and judge themselves by their own internal standards, which are either more or less demanding.

The influence of the self on self-development and evaluation

Many examples of the independence of self-evaluations from the reactions of others are to be found in psychological research. According to one theory, the most advanced stage of moral development involves the individual's judging his actions by his own ethical principles rather than giving the judgments that will please his peers (Kohlberg, 1969). History provides other examples of independence. Freud did not give up his work when his contemporaries considered it obscene and unscientific. Many black Americans have not settled for a second-class citizenship despite the existence of negative stereotypes and discrimination. Jews did not accept the Nazi view of their "inherent inferiority" even after the devastating effects of Nazi genocide. (See Box 2.)

Yet, paradoxically, we have also seen the power of the group in influencing the individual's definition and evaluation of himself. People seem to differ in their relative reliance on personal and social evaluations of themselves. Marked individual variation has been shown, for example, in conformity behavior—an area conceptually close to social evaluation. Some individuals "go along with the group" much more

BOX **2** THE INDEPENDENCE OF GROUPS AND
INDIVIDUALS FROM THE MAJORITY

Individuals and groups do not always absorb the majority's opinions of them, of their beliefs, or of their work. As shown in two very different situations below, a variety of factors may account for the group's or the individual's being able to withstand the social pressures of the majority.

Christian Martyrdom

Despite over 250 years of persecution, the early Christian faith grew rapidly. Persecution began in the very early days of Christianity with the martyrdom of several disciples in Jerusalem. As Christian missionaries spread the faith through the Roman Empire, the pattern of persecution followed (Daniélou and Marrou, 1964).

Christians were persecuted for a variety of reasons—both political and social. Some of the Roman emperors who actively persecuted the Christians felt that Christianity had to be eradicated, since it subverted the religious traditions of ancient Rome and interfered with the emerging cult of emperor worship. Early Christians also did not follow many of the customs that other Romans did. By differing in all of these ways, the early Christians earned the wrath of the Roman rulers and people.

Although the persecutions made some Christians flee or conform to the required form of Roman worship, the overall effect of the persecution was to encourage the growth of the Church. Thousands—no one knows how many —suffered martyrdom during the various persecutions. Believing that being martyred absolved the individual of his sins and assured a place in heaven, many seemed almost to seek confrontation and persecution. Rather than making the early Christians conform to Roman dictates, persecution increased their sense of fellowship.

Walt Whitman

Another example of persistence in the face of public scorn and ridicule is that of Walt Whitman, who continued his work in the face of extremely negative critical reactions. In 1855, when the first edition of Whitman's now classic *Leaves of Grass* was published, the critical reaction was extremely negative. Whitman's work was dismissed as crude, vulgar, obscene, and brutish. Initial sales of the work were so poor that Whitman himself tried to sell it to booksellers, most of whom were decidedly unenthusiastic. Afraid that being the publisher of *Leaves of Grass* would hurt business and possibly result in legal prosecution for obscenity, Whitman's publisher dropped him (Winwar, 1941).

Whitman's reaction to this almost universally negative reaction passed through a number of stages. At first he defended his poems against the critics. Gradually, he became more and more self-praising in his articles, saying such things as "An American bard at last!" These laudatory self-reviews may be interpreted as either egotism or an attempt to deny the negative hurtful reactions of others.

Notwithstanding his bravado, Whitman's self-doubts began to grow, and he went off alone to wrestle with the problems of whether he or the critics were right. After several months of isolation, he returned to his writing, secure in his own knowledge that his work was good and time would bear this out. For the next four years, even while *Leaves of Grass* was without a publisher, he continued his work. In 1860, with the publication of another edition of his poems, the critical reaction began to soften, and Whitman's fortunes improved.

---

frequently than others. What contributes to this individual difference?

Two hypotheses have been advanced: (1) The higher the individual's level of self-esteem is and the more differentiated his standards are, the more likely he is to rely on his own evaluation of his abilities and himself, and (2) the more the individual filters out information that is inconsistent with his standards, the more likely he is to judge himself by his own standards. Indirect evidence supports both of these hypotheses.

Refusing to Accept Majority Standards Once an individual attains a clear sense of his own identity, he relies on internal standards in evaluating his own performance and defining his own sense of worth (E. E. Erikson, 1968). For example, a musician with a high level of self-esteem may have incorporated his standards for a good performance from his music instructors and from listening to great musicians. Having formed these standards, he may have become his own most critical audience. Even though he may be so competent a musician that no one else can detect a very slight flaw in his performance, his own knowledge of the flaw may upset him. Thus the critics' and the audience's favorable reaction to his performance may not prevent his own feeling of distress because of his inability to meet his own standards.

Research evidence indirectly supports the hypothesis that if the individual thinks well of himself and has clearly formulated internal standards, he may be likely to judge his performance according to his own standards. As we saw previously, high self-esteem is correlated with a relative freedom from group pressures; persons with high self-esteem conform less. Evidence from the area of attitude change indicates that the most clearly articulated attitudes are the most resistant to change.

Filtering Information A common theme in the many definitions of the self is a monitoring, filtering, active self. The self does not passively accept all information about itself from others. We may choose our own way of evaluating ourselves. Each person can protect his self-image by selecting as characteristics "that really count" the ones that he possesses and by setting goals that he thinks he can realistically achieve. Or we may project our unfavorable characteristics onto others.

The individual also protects his favorable view of himself by interpreting and selecting social feedback from other people. Since hard, objective social facts are a rarity, the individual is free to interpret the usually ambiguous information in a positive way. In addition to interpreting social reactions, the individual selects the reactions that he pays attention to. In large part, friends are selected because a person feels they like him. Thus people are exposed most frequently to people who overtly and covertly reflect largely positive information. As one writer noted, "Friendship is the purest illustration of picking one's propaganda" (Rosenberg, 1968, p. 343). Positive information may be sought in other ways. It was found in one study that all subjects—whether they believed that they had succeeded or that they had failed at an experimental task—preferred positive evaluations of their performance (Skolnick, 1971). People are kind to themselves.

As an illustration of how the distortion and filtering of information might diminish the effects of social evaluation, let us speculate about how a person who is being opposed by many of his peers could "close out" criticisms. Critics might be denied or denigrated. People

who do agree might be intensively sought out —as illustrated by Freud's close attachment to those who supported his work. Absolute and unequivocal support might be demanded from friends. Again, this is illustrated by Freud's impatience with any attempts to modify his theory. Any ambiguous information might be favorably interpreted. And finally, the individual might begin to reward himself with his own positive self-evaluation.

Self-Discovery

How do you come to know yourself? Existentialists and college students have long emphasized the tremendous difficulty in gaining self-knowledge. We think we know ourselves better than anyone else and that we have access to private thoughts that no one else has access to; yet at the same time we acknowledge our own tremendous capacity for duplicity. Self-deception is a predominant theme in much of contemporary literature. Earlier in this chapter we saw how the individual sometimes seeks out favorable, self-aggrandizing information. A basic tenet of psychoanalysis is that the individual refuses to acknowledge those aspects of himself that are too painful. The desire not to know those aspects of the self that are upsetting is so strong that only the intervention of a skilled psychotherapist can sometimes bring these to consciousness.

Even when neutral areas of the self are involved, self-knowledge is difficult. One can hardly imagine a less threatening aspect of self-perception than the individual's knowledge of his arm's length. If you were asked to estimate the length of your arm without looking at it, how accurate do you think you'd be? If you reacted like some subjects, you would not be very accurate. Indeed, they complained that they did not have a clear picture of what they looked like (Orbach et al., 1966). Try closing your eyes and forming an image of your physical body. How clear is it? Or how clear is your image of your own voice? Listening to a recording of your voice can be a disturbing experience. Even though your friends insist that the voice sounds "just like you," it may seem strange and foreign to you (Holzman, 1971).

Discovering other aspects of yourself—

including aspects as basic as emotions and motives—involves similar difficulties. Complicated interpretive processes are involved. As the self-aspects being judged become more involving, the forces that come into play in the self-knowledge process increase.

Experiencing emotions and motives

How do you know when you are afraid? How do you know when you are hungry? Our emotions and motives seem to be experienced so directly and related so clearly to what has happened to us that it is difficult to believe there is a problem in self-perception in this area. Someone says we are going to get an electric shock, and we feel afraid. A nurse gives an injection, and we feel pain. Six hours after our last meal our stomach rumbles, and we feel hungry. Our emotions and motives seem to be directly related to our physical environment and our physiological reactions. The more intense an electric shock is, the more it hurts. The longer we have gone without food, the hungrier we are.

Straightforward and appealing as this view is, it is not correct. Cognitive factors, our beliefs and interpretations of situations, play an enormously important role in our experiences. Even in an experience as basic as pain, expectations and interpretations influence the intensity of pain experienced. Perhaps you have had the experience of having a headache leave as you were in the process of swallowing an aspirin. Obviously, the medication has not had time to have a physical effect, yet you feel better. Expectations of relief have been shown repeatedly to produce relief.

The strongest evidence in support of our own self-curing powers is the documented effectiveness of the "placebo," a harmless, inactive substance that the patient thinks will reduce his pain. In a review of approximately one hundred studies on the effects of placebos on a wide variety of symptoms and illnesses (including cancer), an average of 27 percent of the patients reported that they were experiencing less pain after taking the medication (Haas, Fink, and Hartfelder, 1963).

The Cognitive Theory of Emotional Reaction
The plasticity of experience led Schachter and Singer (1962) to formulate a theory of emotional arousal that emphasizes the role of cognition. Their argument holds that no matter what emotion is aroused, the physiological reactions are very similar. Whether the emotion is anger or euphoria, one feels a kind of stirred-up set of internal reactions, including such things as a more rapid pulse rate. Since all of the physiological reactions are so similar, the only distinctive aspect of the emotion is the situation. If you feel all stirred up after someone has hit you, you label your feeling as anger and react appropriately. Conversely, if you feel all stirred up while watching a horror film, you call that fear. In short, Schachter and Singer analyze the emotional sequence as shown in the accompanying ruled diagram.

Something in the environment produces the physiological reaction.	$\longrightarrow$	You experience the general reaction and look at the situation to decide what is being experienced.	$\longrightarrow$	You attach a label to the reaction.

To make sense of your physiological arousal, you look to the situation for cues. However, to say that the individual uses situational cues to interpret his physiological arousal does not imply that this is a conscious process. In everyday life the physiological reaction and situations are so inextricably related that one is not aware of the interpretive process. Imagine that you are lying in bed at night, and you see a hand slowly raising your window. The situation, your pounding heart, and your feeling of fear will all seem to occur simultaneously.

How can the cognitive theory of emotions be tested? In effect, the theory says that the label given to a particular emotional-physiological arousal depends on the situation. Yet in real life these physiological reactions are inextricably related to the situation. But what if a general state of emotional-physiological reaction could be induced directly and the situations varied?

In an ingenious experiment, which has served as a model for a number of subsequent studies, two investigators directly induced a state of general emotional excitement by administering an injection of the stimulant adrenaline, which produces a general state of diffuse excitement very similar to (if not identical with) that produced by general emotional excitement. Of those given the drug, one-third were not told anything about the effects of the drug, one-third were misinformed about the drug's effects, and another third were given accurate information about the effects. Then these subjects were placed in situations designed either to make them angry or to make them happy and carefree.

The prediction was that those subjects who either had no explanation for their feelings or had been misinformed as to the drug's effects would experience the emotion dictated by the situation, whereas the subjects who had been accurately informed about the physiological reactions caused by the adrenaline would not be influenced by the situation.

The experimental results were as predicted. In the situation designed to produce euphoria, the subjects who had no explanation for their physiological state showed more euphoria. In the situation designed to elicit anger, subjects who had been aroused without a correct explanation of the drug's effects reacted with anger. Subjects who had been given a correct explanation of the drug's physiological effects experienced the physiological effects, but were significantly less affected by the situation. Those, for instance, in the situation designed to elicit euphoria reported a significantly lower level of euphoria than subjects who had not been informed of the drug's effects (Schachter and Singer, 1962). Subsequent studies have shown that subjects in a drug-induced state of general arousal can also be made to experience humor and anxiety (Schachter and Wheeler, 1962; Schachter and Latané, 1964).

Emotional experience seems very plastic. The emotion that is experienced is apparently the one that furnishes the most reasonable "explanation" for the arousal. But are naturally occurring states of emotional arousal this moldable? If someone were in a situation that really frightened him, could he be made to think he wasn't frightened? The results of several experiments seem to indicate that he could be "within the limits of plausibility." If he isn't highly fearful, his fear can be reduced by making him attribute it to other causes.

Half of the subjects were told that they would receive a mild electric shock; the other half were told to expect a severe shock. Then all of the subjects were injected with a placebo and told to expect a reaction. Half of the subjects in each group were told to expect a general level of physiological arousal, similar to what people experience when they are afraid, and the other half in each group were told to expect some highly specific reaction completely unrelated to the general physiological reactions that accompany fear. Thus there were four conditions: (1) subjects expecting a mild shock and a general level of physiological arousal common to emotions, (2) those expecting a mild shock and a reaction completely irrelevant to a general state of emotional arousal, (3) those expecting a severe shock and a general level of physiological arousal, and (4) those expecting a severe shock and an irrelevant reaction (Nisbett and Schachter, 1966).

The information about the placebo effect significantly influenced the reactions of those subjects expecting a mild shock. Those who were told that the placebo produced a general level of physiological arousal reported that they were less afraid, tolerated higher intensities of shock, and reported experiencing less pain than those anticipating an irrelevant physiological reaction. In contrast, among those expecting a painful shock, the "information" had no significant effect. Perhaps a situation that usually produces a mild level of emotion can be interpreted in a variety of ways. "I may be feeling excited because of the shock. But then it's not much of a shock, and I was told that my injection would make me feel this way. So I'm not really afraid." But when the situation clearly justifies the emotional reaction, that reaction is accepted as the explanation, and the emotion is very difficult to modify. Emotional reactions are not infinitely plastic.

Controlling fear is a pervasive problem in clinical practice, and any possible techniques deserve careful study. Even if not all emotional reactions can be modified by causing the individual to misattribute his feelings, some may be modified. If, for example, persons who are afraid of certain situations were given placebos to which they could attribute their fear, could they be made to think they were not afraid? Although the clinical effectiveness of such a technique can only be demonstrated through actual application, the results of several studies suggest that emotional misattribution may have clinical potential.

In one experiment purporting to investigate the effects of noise on performance, all of the subjects were made fearful by being told that they might receive an electric shock. However, half of the subjects were told that the noise would cause them to experience a set of physiological reactions—such as a general sensation of visceral upset—that corresponded with the usual physiological correlates of fear. The other half of the subjects were told that the noise would create symptoms unrelated to fear—such as ringing of the ears. Thus subjects in the noise-attribution condition could attribute their reactions to the noise bombardment; the other subjects were not provided with an alternative explanation of their reactions and so presumably attributed their physiological reactions to the potential shock. Then all of the subjects were given two puzzles to work on. Solution of one puzzle would allow the subjects to escape from the shock. Solution of the other puzzle would result in a monetary reward. As predicted, 60 percent of the subjects in the noise-attribution condition spent the majority of their time working on the money-reward puzzle, and 80 percent of the subjects in the shock-attribution condition spent their time working on the shock-avoidance puzzle. Even though all of the subjects were experiencing the same physiological reactions, those who had been given an alternative explanation for their reactions did not label their feelings as fear and turned their attention to seeking monetary reward (Ross, Rodin, and Zimbardo, 1969).

Further, if emotions can be controlled through misattribution, so can the behaviors mediated by these emotions. One reason people refrain from certain activities is that they are afraid of being punished. Just considering a particular act can cue off physiological reactions that are experienced as guilt or anxiety. To avoid further unpleasant emotional reactions, the individual refrains from the act. People may not commit crimes because they do not want to feel guilty. People may not cheat because they wish to avoid their negative feelings. There are individuals, however, who do not seem to experience the usual variety of emotions and who also frequently engage in antisocial activities. From this description you may have recognized one type of behavior disorder: the sociopath. Noting that sociopaths have more intense physiological reactions than others, two theorists have hypothesized that sociopaths have learned to disregard autonomic cues. Since they react strongly to all situations, there is nothing distinctive about the physiological experience, and they do not label or experience emotions (Schachter and Latané, 1964).

Direct evidence on the uninhibiting effects of misattribution has been obtained by two investigators, who found that subjects who were led to misattribute their emotional reactions to a placebo were more likely to cheat on a test. People who feel that their emotional reactions are being caused by medication are not motivated to assess the situation and to take action that would reduce their emotional reaction. If you are upset and think it is because you are considering cheating, you will be motivated to stop thinking about cheating and to resist the idea of actually doing it (Dienstbier and Munter, 1971).

So far the cognitive theory of emotional reaction has been confirmed. But you may be thinking that all of these situations are somewhat exotic. How often do people receive injections of various drugs? Since they are so unfamiliar with the reactions, they may simply reflect whatever the experimenter tells them. Do we have similarly plastic, moldable reactions for more familiar physiological reactions—like hunger? Don't we know when we're hungry simply by being aware of how many hours have elapsed since we ate last and by paying attention to the signs usually associated with hunger, like stomach "motility" (commonly heard as the rumblings in a twelve o'clock class)?

The Extension of the Cognitive Theory to Motives
A fascinating series of studies shows that even in knowing something as basic about ourselves as whether or not we are hungry, a process of interpretation is involved. Although some of us

eat because of our internal, physiological cues, these cues seem to make little difference to others.

Consider what governs your own eating. When are you likely to get hungry? After a set number of hours? When you walk by a pizza stand? When you see food commercials on television? When you watch other people eating? When you see an appetizing cake? When you feel empty? If physiological cues are the main determinant of eating behavior, we would expect people to stop eating when they are full.

This hypothesis has been tested. Normal and obese subjects (who were approximately 15 percent overweight) participated in the experiment. Half of the subjects were first given as many roast beef sandwiches as they wished to eat, and the other subjects were given no food. Then all the subjects were asked to sample crackers, and the number of crackers consumed by each subject was noted. Subjects of normal weight who had not eaten the roast beef sandwiches ate more than those who had just finished the sandwiches. To the fatties it made no difference whether they had eaten or not. After stuffing themselves on roast beef sandwiches, they moved on undauntedly to the crackers (Schachter, Goldman, and Gordon, 1968).

Apparently, the subjects differed in what motivated them to eat. For those of normal weight the internal, physiologically mediated cues set off eating behavior. But for the obese the internal cues made little difference. People differ in the cues that mediate hunger.

If internal cues do not control eating among the obese, what does? Obviously they eat, or they wouldn't be obese. One popular theory, which you are probably familiar with, is that the fat eat because they are anxious and unhappy, and food is a consolation. Yet there is little direct evidence in support of this theory (Schachter et al., 1968).

A consideration of the Schachter-Singer theory provides another possible explanation. If an individual knows he is "afraid" only because he is in a fear-arousing situation, the obese may eat only because the appropriate external cues are available. When enticing food is available, not eating is really difficult, as one former fatty indicates: "Tonight when I passed that pizza stand on Eighth Street that has that fresh frozen custard, it almost killed me" (Trillin, 1971, p. 62). (See Figure 2-13.) Any situation related to eating would set off eating behavior in the obese. For instance, it has been found that obese subjects ate more when they thought they were eating later than their usual dinner hour (Schachter and Gross, 1968).

If external cues mediate eating by the obese, the removal of these cues should cause them to eat less. This hypothesis has also been confirmed. When obese people who had previously eaten vast quantities of food were given only an unappetizing but nutritive formula, they curtailed their intake to about 400–500 calories. Persons of normal weight did not cut their calorie intake when they were on the same formula diet (Hashim and Van Itallie, 1965).

The work on hunger motivation shows that both the situation and the internal cues are important determinants of behavior. External cues govern eating for the obese, and internal cues control eating for those of normal weight. The demonstration of individual differences in how people perceive their own hunger opens a fascinating series of questions. What are the relative contributions of situational and internal cues in mediating the other physiological drives? For instance, to what extent is the sexual drive influenced by internal and situational cues?

Learning about the self

We have seen the complexity of the interpretive processes involved in understanding relatively simple and neutral aspects of the self. To know if we are angry or frightened, we look at least in part to the situation.

When we try to discover information about our general selves, the problems of knowledge multiply. (See Figure 2-14.) Knowing about that unique set of attitudes, motives, emotions, capabilities, and ideals involves learning about each of these as well as their interrelationships. Furthermore, knowing the self frequently is far from a neutral process. We may want to learn about ourselves, and at the same time we may be afraid to do so. We may be ashamed of ourselves. The disparity between what we are and what we want to be may be so painful that we cannot bear to contemplate our actuality. A

FIGURE 2-13 External versus internal cues in determining hunger.

dramatic illustration of this disparity is shown in Eugene O'Neill's *The Iceman Cometh* (1940). After years of an unhappy marriage in which Hickey made his wife miserable with his irresponsible drinking and gambling and unkept promises to change, he killed her. Hickey's account of the incident to his friends follows:

So I killed her. (There is a moment of dead silence.) And then I saw I'd always known that was the only possible way to give her peace and free her from the misery of loving me. I saw it meant peace for me, too, knowing she was at peace. I felt as though a ton of guilt was lifted off my mind. I remember I stood by the bed and suddenly I had to laugh. I couldn't help it, and I knew Evelyn would forgive me. I remember I heard myself speaking to her, as if it was something I'd always wanted to say: "Well, you know what you can do with your pipe dream now, you damned bitch." (He stops with a horrified start, as if shocked out of a nightmare, as if he couldn't believe he heard what he had just said. He stammers.) No! I never—!

[O'Neill, 1940, pp. 240–242, quoted in Fingarette, 1969, pp. 59–60.]

Obviously, Hickey has deceived himself. He has refused to acknowledge all of his feelings toward his wife and has distorted what he does acknowledge. From the situation and from his act of murdering his wife, he had initially inferred that his attitudes toward his wife were positive. From his physiological reactions and the situation, he inferred that his motives for the murder were almost altruistic—he had done it for her good. Although this seems a transparent deception to us, Hickey was so motivated to avoid recognizing his hatred and resentment that he distorted his interpretation. In real-life situations in which we do not wish to know certain things about ourselves, we may tell ourselves what we want to hear.

How Do We Lie to Ourselves? This question has puzzled psychotherapists for years. The classic answer provided by psychoanalytic theory is that when some aspect of our self or our experience is so painful that we cannot bear to consider it, we banish it from consciousness and no longer have the capacity to recognize it. Only under certain special, therapeutic circumstances can unconscious material be restored to consciousness.

The psychoanalytic approach to self-deception has traditionally emphasized the *motive* for lying: to avoid unbearable anxiety. But what is the actual process by which we deceive ourselves? Although several theories have been proposed, relatively little research has been done, so that our account is largely theoretical.

Most people are not particularly proud of some aspect of their self. Say a person feels that nobody really likes him. How would he go about deceiving himself about this feeling? He might simply avoid thinking about it. Whenever the thought occurred to him, he would try to shift away from it. He would not formulate his thoughts into words or focus on the problem, and he would avoid becoming explicitly aware of his avoidance.

Further, in addition to avoiding aspects of ourselves, we present a highly censored, socially acceptable image of ourselves to others. As children we may be taught not to reveal ourselves honestly to others. Honest self-revelation frequently is punished, so the child learns to censor what he says. He learns to act a part that he knows will meet with social approval. To return to our example, the individual who feels insecure about his relations with other people is not free to reveal this. Rather, he acts a part that masks his insecurity. Usually, social interaction is between a series of unrealistic, socially acceptable masks.

In deceiving others we also deceive ourselves. Paradoxically, although we know the public image is not really authentic, we begin to believe that it is really us. If this continues for a sufficient period, we may no longer be able to distinguish between our real selves and our various images; we may find it impossible to know ourselves. Many existentialist writers have discussed self-alienation—the separation of the person from himself.

Further, the public images interfere with close relationships with others. If each person is simply acting a part, both will sense that very little contact has been made, and they will still feel essentially lonely because no contact has

FIGURE 2-14 When it comes to gaining objective self-knowledge, we are all as blind as men without eyes. (Christopher S. Johnson)

been made with their real selves (Jourard, 1964).

Knowing Ourselves Through Honest Self-Disclosure The only way we can peel back the images and force ourselves to be honest in our self-knowledge is to disclose ourselves to others:

Through my self-disclosure, I let others know my soul. They can know it, really know it, only as I make it known. In fact, I am beginning to suspect that I can't

BOX 3

**SAMPLE ITEMS FROM JOURARD'S
SELF-DISCLOSURE QUESTIONNAIRE**

To illustrate the kinds of questions asked, two items from each area on the questionnaire are quoted.

Attitudes and Opinions

1. What I think and feel about religion; my personal religious views.
2. My personal views on sexual morality—how I feel that I and others ought to behave.

Tastes and Interests

1. My tastes in clothing.
2. My likes and dislikes in music.

Work (or Studies)

1. What I find to be the worst pressures and strains in my work.
2. What I feel are *my* shortcomings and handicaps that prevent me from working as I'd like to, or that prevent me from getting further ahead in my work.

Money

1. Whether or not I owe money; if so, *how much.*
2. Whether or not I have savings, and the amount.

Personality

1. The aspect of my personality that I dislike, worry about, that I regard as a handicap to me.
2. Things in the past or present that I feel ashamed and guilty about.

Body

1. My feelings about the appearance of my face—things I don't like, and things that I might like about my face and head: nose, eyes, hair, teeth, etc.
2. My feelings about my adequacy in sexual behavior—whether or not I feel able to perform adequately in sex relationships.

[Items selected from Jourard, 1964, pp. 161–163.]

even know *my own soul* except as I disclose it. I suspect that I will know myself "for real" at the exact moment that I have succeeded in making it known through my disclosure to another person.

[Jourard, 1964, p. 10.]

We saw that Hickey, the man who murdered his wife, came to realize his true motives as he recounted the situation to others. Discussing the events made him focus on his own feelings and made it impossible for him simply not to think about the whole event. As the words tumbled out, almost against his will, he realized his true feelings about his wife.

Whether or not he wished to be completely honest is not clear. Nor is it clear in many other situations in which people try to be honest about themselves. Although the person may want to be honest, he may be afraid at the same time about what he will find. Still, the increased imperative to be honest in an authentic self-disclosure situation makes the individual less comfortable with his familiar self-deceptions and avoidance tactics.

Finally, when a person honestly reveals aspects of the self, he provides a realistic picture of himself that can counter all of the false images, allowing him to relate more closely to another person. Hearing himself say certain things about himself could result in his internalization of what he hears. In the process of honest communication about the self, a closer, more intense relationship can develop with another person. Instead of the usual social exchange in which image relates to image, the person who engages in honest self-disclosure reveals himself. In turn, the other person may be more likely to reciprocate (Ehrlich and Graeven, 1971).

Research on Self-Disclosure In view of the importance of accurate self-disclosure in learning about ourselves, one might expect that such disclosures would be very prevalent. Such is not the case. Before beginning his research program on the determinants of self-disclosure, Jourard noted the relative rarity of authentic self-disclosures. Frequently, his patients would begin a confidence with "I've never told this to anyone before." To assess the frequency of self-disclosure in a nonpatient group, Jourard devised a questionnaire that listed sixty items concerning ten general areas of the self. (See Box 3.) In a series of studies subjects were asked to indicate whether or not they had discussed these aspects of themselves and with whom they had discussed them.

The results of Jourard's questionnaire indicated that the amount of self-disclosure varied according to the characteristics of the person, the aspect of the self being discussed, and the person in whom he was confiding (Jourard, 1971).

People varied widely in their willingness to disclose information about themselves. Female students disclosed more than males, and white students disclosed more than black students. Part of the male role in our society may involve not discussing the self, which, in turn, may add to the level of stress experienced by males and to their earlier death. The same kind of argument may apply to the racial differences. In not disclosing themselves, black students may add to their overall level of stress. National differences were also found. American college students disclose more than do "comparable students from Britain, the Middle East, Puerto Rico, and Germany" (Jourard, 1971, p. 102).

Not surprisingly, the subjects reported that they had disclosed more about some aspects of the self than about others. Less self-disclosure was reported in relation to money, personality, and body than in the other three areas: tastes and interests, attitudes and opinions, and work. On analysis, the items listed under the areas of lesser disclosure appear somewhat more threatening to the individual's self-image than those listed under areas in which great disclosure was found. The items on taste, for example, seem rather innocuous. In fact, discussing tastes in music and clothing could be used as a device to avoid more self-revealing, threatening discussions.

The college student folklore has it that the closest confidences pass between friends. The reactions of the college students surveyed did not support this (Jourard and Lasakow, 1958). On the contrary, unmarried students indicated that they had disclosed the most to their mothers, and less information to their father, male friends, and female friends. Since this study was reported in 1958, it would be interesting to see if these patterns of disclosure have persisted. (See Student Reaction Box 10.) Today

there may be more alienation between the generations, which would result in greater disclosure to peers than to a parent. Married students shared most of their confidences with their spouse and confided less with other people.

This work on self-disclosure is a first step. Jourard has shown that self-disclosure can be measured. The reliability of the measurement is high: The level of self-disclosure shown in answers to one-half of the test items correlated .94 with the level of self-disclosure shown in the answers to the other half of the items. The test's validity has also been shown. Scores on the test were compared to the amount of self-disclosure the subjects gave to an experimenter (Jourard, 1971).

However, Jourard's questionnaire approach does not tell us about the actual process of self-disclosure. How does it happen? Once it occurs, how does it influence a relationship? What is the effect of the passage of time on self-disclosure? What is the effect of the perceived similarity of the other person? Only by observing self-disclosing interactions in a controlled situation could we answer these questions. So far most of the research on self-disclosure has focused on reactions to questionnaire measures.

In a recent experiment the process of self-disclosure was studied under controlled laboratory conditions. The subjects were tested one at a time with an experimental confederate. The rationale of the experiment was that each subject was to discuss himself, so that the investigators could study the "sociology of conversation." The confederate spoke first and either gave personal, intimate information about himself (high-intimacy condition) or spoke in rather impersonal, conventional terms (low-intimacy condition). The hypothesis to be tested was that subjects in the high-intimacy condition would reveal more intimate information about themselves than those in the low-intimacy condition.

The experimental results supported the hypothesis. Subjects hearing a confederate reveal fairly personal, intimate material reciprocated by disclosing personal concerns of their own. There was not an exact reciprocity: If the confederate spoke intimately about his feelings on marriage, the subject might reply with intimate comments on his reactions to school and work. But the overall level of intimacy was reciprocated. To explain their findings, the investigators discussed a "norm of reciprocal self-disclosure." When someone tells you something personal, you are expected to reply with an equally personal revelation. Other explanations may be possible. Listening to someone else tell revealing things may remind you of your own concerns. Or it may make you feel safe. Once a person has opened up like this, he can be trusted. In any event, this experiment has shown

the powerful effect of reciprocity (Ehrlich and Graeven, 1971).

Asking the other person to disclose more about himself has also been found to influence significantly the amount the other person discloses. In a recent experiment both the intimacy of what the confederate disclosed about himself and the intimacy of the confederate's questions about the subject were varied (Sermat and Smyth, 1973). There were four experimental conditions. In group 1 the confederate matched in intimacy what the subject said about himself and kept his questions at the same level. In group 2 the confederate disclosed more intimate information about himself than did the subject, but did not ask intimate questions. In group 3 the confederate asked more intimate questions than the subject's current level of self-disclosure but did not exceed the subject's intimacy in his own self-revelations. In group 4 the confederate both disclosed more intimate information about himself than the subject did and asked for increasingly intimate self-disclosure from the subject.

As predicted, the highest level of subject self-disclosure was obtained in group 4, in which the confederate both asked for and gave intimate information. The lowest amount of self-disclosure occurred in group 1, in which the confederate neither asked for nor gave intimate information. Groups 2 and 3 produced an intermediate amount of self-disclosure and did not differ significantly from each other. To obtain maximal self-disclosure from another person, both increasing the intimacy of what you say yourself and asking increasingly intimate questions seems necessary.

SUMMARY

Many students are concerned about evolving their identity and knowing themselves, and they have their own ideas of what this process involves. The variety of definitions in ordinary usage makes the term "self-concept" ambiguous. The technical literature has, if anything, added to this ambiguity. Today the understanding of the conscious self, its determinants, and

its influence on behavior is far from complete. The current lack of knowledge may be largely due to the fact that the study of the self was out of fashion until quite recently.

1. Components, Characteristics, and Measurements of the Self When that portion of our experience that we regard as essentially us is analyzed, five components emerge: (1) the *material self,* our physical body and those possessions that are uniquely ours, (2) the *actual, psychological self,* what you think of when you analyze your thoughts and ideas, (3) the *self as a thinking and emotional process,* your own experience of the process of experiencing, (4) the *social self,* the self as defined in your interactions with others, and (5) the *ideal self,* what you would like to be.

Five characteristics of the self were considered.

a. With regard to the *consistency of the self,* some of the available evidence casts doubt about the degree to which we are consistent, either at a given moment or in different groups. The individual may not be a single, unchanging self, but may be many selves, which change somewhat as the person shifts from situation to situation.

b. People feel that they cause their own behavior, and any lessening of their freedom to act is highly unpleasant, as has been emphasized in the theory of psychological reactance. Once reactance is aroused, the forced activity becomes less attractive; the individual is dissatisfied; and he performs poorly at the forced task.

c. People sometimes feel a strong desire to be separate and unique. Being made to feel undistinctive has been shown to upset the individual in some cases. Yet, strong as the desire for uniqueness may be in some situations, in others people may not desire to be different. Whether individuation or deindividuation is sought may depend on a number of variables, including the individual's feeling of control over his separateness, and whether or not his gains from deindividuation outweigh his losses.

d. The actual self is constantly being measured against the ideal self. To the extent that the two match, the person has a high level of self-esteem, as most people do. Those with a low level of self-esteem are unhappy and see themselves as incompetent in a variety of situations.

e. Self-actualization is an extremely important motive for many people. The individual may feel a strong desire to develop his actual self so it will correspond more closely with his ideal self or attain a healthy, optimal form of psychological functioning. However, operationally defining the term "actualization" is extremely difficult.

Unfortunately, the tests used most frequently to measure self-esteem and self-concepts have serious limitations. In the Q sort test, the amount of the discrepancy between what the individual thinks he is and what he would like to be gives a measure of self-esteem. In another type of measure, subjects are asked to write different answers to the question: "Who am I?" The person's spontaneous answers reveal how he views himself. With both measures, however, it is difficult to determine the extent to which the subject's answers are influenced by his desire not to say unpleasant things about himself.

2. Social Determinants of the Self In *psychologically compelling situations,* in which the individual's former sense of self is systematically assaulted and the demands of the situation for him to play a certain role are clear and compelling, his self-concept can be molded to match what the situation demands. In prison the prisoner's identity becomes merged with the role of prisoner.

Parent-child interaction plays a crucial part in determining the child's self-concept. In particular, a parent's providing his child with a history of success and competency and with loving acceptance has been found to be important. Parents who do this have been found to have children with high self-esteem.

The individual identifies with the standards and beliefs of certain groups—termed *reference groups*—and then uses them as a standard against which he defines and evaluates himself. Reference groups serve two functions for the individual: (1) the *normative* function, which pressures him to conform to what others in the group do, and (2) the *comparative* function, which gives the individual information against which he judges himself. When both the normative and comparative functions are combined—as they frequently are—the reference group is an important determinant of all of your beliefs, including your definition of yourself.

Social comparison theory provides a highly systematic explanation of the way in which our views of ourselves are influenced by others.

Although in many situations the main motive for social comparison is accuracy, people sometimes seek enhancement rather than honest feedback when comparing the self. Generally, people are most likely to engage in social comparison when they are uncertain about themselves. Usually, people compare themselves with people who are similar. However, the motive behind the individual's making the social comparison, the information available to the person, and the definition of similarity have all been found to influence the choice of a comparison person. Once social comparison occurs, three outcomes are likely: (1) You may change your own values; (2) you may try to change your friends' beliefs when they differ from yours; or (3) you may reject those people whose opinions remain divergent.

All four social evaluation theories agree on the importance of others in determining the individual's self-concept. However, they differ in their emphasis on who is crucial in this interaction and on which process is used. For instance, the compelling situation approach emphasizes the importance of the immediate situation, whereas the parent-child approach emphasizes the importance of early experience in forming a stable self-concept.

3. Other Determinants of the Self Our perception of our own competency and our own self-concept also determine the evolution of the self. However, both of these explanations overlap with the social evaluation approach, since the original core component of the self may have been determined by the reactions of other people. Once a self-concept emerges, it too influences your self-definition and self-evaluation. Your own perception of your ability to cope with the environment determines how favorably you view yourself. People differ in their relative reliance on personal and social evaluations of themselves. It may be that the higher the individual's level of self-esteem is and the more differentiated his standards are, the more likely he is to rely on his own evaluation of his abilities and himself. Further, the more the individual filters out information that is inconsistent with his standards, the more likely he is to judge himself by his own standards.

4. Self-Discovery Paradoxically, even though we think we know ourselves better than anyone else, attaining self-knowledge is very difficult. Our emotions and motives seem to be experienced so directly that it is difficult to believe self-knowledge is a problem in this area. However, it has been shown that cognitive factors play an enormously important role in our interpreting of our emotions and motives.

No matter what emotion is aroused, the physiological reactions are very similar. To make sense of our physiological arousal, we look to the situation for cues as to what emotion is being aroused. The label given to a particular physiological arousal depends on the situation. Several studies have shown that the emotion that is experienced is apparently the one that furnishes the most reasonable explanation for the arousal.

Even knowing something as basic about ourselves as whether or not we are hungry involves a process of interpretation. Although some of us eat because of our internal physiological cues, these cues seem to make little difference to others, who eat because the appropriate external cues are available.

When we try to discover information about our general selves, the problems of knowledge multiply. The disparity between what we are and what we want to be may be so painful that we cannot bear to contemplate our actuality, and we may deceive ourselves. We may simply avoid thinking about unpleasant aspects of ourselves. Or in presenting a highly censored, socially acceptable image of ourselves to others, we may also deceive ourselves. Although we know that the public image is not really authentic, we may begin to believe that it is really us. If this continues for a sufficient period, we may no longer be able to distinguish between our real selves and various images.

The only way we can force ourselves to be honest is to disclose ourselves to others. When a person honestly reveals aspects of his self, he provides a realistic picture of himself that can counter all of the false images and allow him to relate more closely to another person.

Extensive questionnaire research on self-disclosure has shown that the amount of self-disclosure varies according to the characteristics of the person, the aspects of the self being discussed, and the person being confided in. For example, women tended to disclose more than men; less self-disclosure was reported in relation to money, personality, and body than in relation to other areas; and unmarried students indicated that they had disclosed the most to their mothers.

However, the questionnaire approach does not tell us about the actual process of self-disclosure. Recent experiments suggest that both reciprocity and questioning operate in the situation. Confederates who disclosed intimate information about themselves and asked increasingly personal questions about the other person obtained very high levels of self-disclosure from that person.

DISCUSSION QUESTIONS

1. Have you or any of your friends experienced any difficulty in achieving a unified, coherent self, or an "identity"? If so, in what form has the struggle manifested itself?

2. What arouses reactance in you? Once aroused, how does it influence your behavior?

3. Name the people—in order of importance—whom you feel *now* have the most significant influence on your view of yourself.

4. In the prison experiment we saw that in a psychologically compelling situation, the individual's self-concept and behavior can be molded to match what the situation demands. Can you think of any other highly compelling situations that might have the same effect?

5. Is your eating primarily determined by internal cues or by the situation?

6. Why are many people reluctant to be honest with themselves and with others?

7. Do you think humanistic psychology will ever become more dominant than behaviorism in American psychology?

8. Do you think you have one self—which stays basically the same—or do you think your self changes in different situations? Give evidence to support your answer.

9. In which circumstances do you think people prefer to be individuated? When do you think they wish to be deindividuated?

10. What determines your selection of a particular group as your reference group?

11. Which aspects of themselves do you think students on campuses today are least willing to disclose to others? Design a questionnaire study to test your hypotheses.

12. Do you agree with Jourard that the *only* way to attain valid self-knowledge is to disclose yourself to others?

13. When you think of your self, do any components not discussed in this chapter emerge? If so, what are they?

14. Design a study to test the effects of a situation that you hypothesize would produce a change in an individual's self-concept. Indicate your hypothesis, its supporting rationale, your independent variable, experimental procedures, and dependent variable.

15. In what ways does the individual's self influence his behavior?

16. People differ in their relative reliance on personal and social evaluations of themselves. Can you think of any variables, in addition to those discussed in this chapter, that influence the degree of the individual's independence from other people in defining and evaluating his self-concept?

17. Can you think of any ways in which the misattribution of emotions could be applied clinically to reduce anxieties and fears? Could misattribution be applied to modify other emotions in other situations?

18. What are the determinants and consequences of self-disclosure?

3

ATTITUDES AND THEIR FORMATION

Perhaps the best way to begin our discussion of attitudes is by providing some examples of one particular attitude—racial prejudice. In reading these examples, try to put yourself in the position of the person

exhibiting prejudice. What causes his reaction? Is it learned or instinctive? Is it based on his own experience, on what others have told him, or on emotional factors?

After a white soldier had been admitted to a hospital with an extremely severe sunburn, a black soldier began to stop in to straighten the room and to keep the white soldier company. Of this experience, the white soldier wrote:

Twice a day for about two weeks Private First Class Robinson called to sweep and mop my room, change the linens, carry out laundry; sometimes he brought snacks or magazines. We talked about sports, Robinson's foul luck in not having been selected for Officer Candidate School, and my own wish to quit the military. . . .

One night I stammered thanks. "Don't mention it," he said. "This is part of my life's work." I thought this over while Robinson expertly pushed the mop back and forth. "What were you in civilian life? A porter?" Robinson gave me a strange, unbelieving look. "No, Sergeant," he said. "I was a student in a seminary, studying to become a minister. I've had three years of college." He never came back.

[King, 1971, pp. 42–43.]

Of white people, James Baldwin's black fictional characters had this to say:

"Caleb," I asked, "are all white people the same?"
  "What do you mean, the same?"
  "I mean—you know—are they all the same?"
  And Caleb said, "I never met a good one."
  I asked, "Not even when you were little? In school?"
  Caleb said, "Maybe. I don't remember." He smiled at me. "I never met a good one, Leo. But that's not saying you won't. Don't look so frightened."

[Baldwin, 1969, p. 47.]

While being kept waiting by Dr. Ralph Abernathy, Martin Luther King's successor as leader of the Southern Christian Leadership Conference, Norman Mailer wrote:

He [Mailer] was getting tired of Negroes and their rights. It was a miserable recognition, and on many a count, for if he even felt a hint this way, then what immeasurable tides of rage must be loose in America itself? . . . He was weary to the bone of listening to Black cries of Black superiority in sex, Black superiority in beauty, Black superiority in war. . . . He was heartily sick of listening to the tyranny of soul music, so bored with Negroes triumphantly late for appointments, . . . so weary of being sounded in the subway by Black eyes, so despairing of the smell of booze and pot and used-up hope and blood-shot eyes of Negroes bombed at noon, so envious finally of the liberty to abdicate from the long-year-end decade-drowning yokes of work and responsibility that he must have become in some secret part of his flesh a closet Republican—how else account for his inner, "Yeah man, yeah, go!" when fat and flatulent old Republicans got up in Convention Hall [at Miami] to deliver platitudes on the need to return to individual human effort?

[Mailer, 1968, quoted in King, 1971, pp. 143–144.]

Of white guilt, a white city dweller wrote:

Out of old guilts, compassion, expediency—who knows?—I became so generous in small coins to bands of young black beggars that I became known to them as "The Money Man"; a mark, a John, Big Whitey, a target for increasing demands, hustles, put-ons, and condescending attitudes.

[King, 1971, p. 147.]

These quotations illustrate some of the complex and varied beliefs, emotions, and reactions of blacks and whites regarding each other. Perhaps without his being aware that he did so, the white soldier assumed that all blacks did menial work for a living. On the basis of his personal experience, one of James Baldwin's fictional characters made clear his assumption that all whites were bad. Norman Mailer was ashamed of his self-insight that he was tired of black demands. The white city

FIGURE 3-1 Black-white confrontations, often resulting in violence and bloodshed, are still very much a part of the American scene. A policeman in San Francisco, California, is shown restraining a participant in a riot. (Alan Copeland)

dweller was so torn by guilt and fears that he compensated by becoming an easy mark to bands of young black beggars.

In addition to attitudes about race, people have attitudes about many other things: marijuana, President Nixon, their social psychology classes, their cars, their mothers—the list could go on and on. For instance, to analyze one attitude, you may have certain *beliefs* about the effects of marijuana smoking. You may feel that it is relaxing and not harmful, or you may feel that it is injurious to your health. You may also have an *emotional reaction* to marijuana: either positive, neutral, or negative. And your beliefs

and emotions influence your *behavior.* If you believe that marijuana is not harmful and you have had pleasant associations with it, you may continue to smoke it.

In order to understand what an attitude is and what influences its formation, we will focus predominantly on a particular attitude—that of black-white racial prejudice—in this chapter, although many examples of other attitudes will also be given. The decision to emphasize this attitude was influenced by the enormously destructive impact that black-white prejudice has had in the United States and its duration over many years. (See Figure 3-1.) As with any attitude that creates unfavorable results, an understanding of how prejudice is formed may give useful insights into how it can be eliminated. Ways to change prejudice will be discussed at the end of this chapter, and specific techniques for changing attitudes will be the subject of the following chapter.

Components of Attitudes

What is an "attitude"? One way of understanding the concept is to think of it as an overall, learned, core disposition that guides a person's thoughts, feelings, and actions toward specific others and objects. For example, out of his beliefs that blacks had been wronged by whites and his feelings of guilt, the white city dweller attempted to compensate by becoming overly generous. Or you may think of an attitude as a general predisposition to respond to an object in either a favorable or an unfavorable way. Attitudes may also be regarded as internal biasing mechanisms. Because of his ingrained belief that all blacks did menial work, the white soldier simply could not conceive of his black friend as having had any other occupation.

Each of these definitions gives us some insight into what an attitude is, but it may be even more useful to think in terms of the three components that have generally been found to be common to all attitudes: (1) cognitive (or beliefs), (2) emotional (or feelings), and (3) behavioral (or action) (Kothandapanl, 1971).

In this chapter and the next we will consider a concept to be an attitude only if it possesses, to at least some degree, each of these three components. Thus our belief that man has been to the moon is simply a cognitive experience with no emotional or behavioral reaction and is thus not an attitude as we will be using the term. Similarly, our pained reaction to a bee sting and our moving our legs while walking are, respectively, purely emotional and behavioral; they are not attitudes either. Only when the three components are working together to some extent—as in our forming an opinion of the NASA program, spraying ourselves to prevent insect bites, or walking to get exercise—are we expressing an attitude.

Of course, attitudes differ in the extent to which they possess each of these components. In some attitudes the belief component may predominate—with little emotional or behavioral content. You may believe that Crest toothpaste is effective in reducing cavities, but not be thrown into a panic if the drugstore is out and you have to buy another brand. Or you may have an attitude with a very strong emotional component and minimal belief and action components. You may have had the experience of forming an immediately negative reaction to a stranger with little real understanding of why you felt that way and with no translation of your feelings into action. Or your behavior may be determined more by the situation than by your feelings and beliefs—as in the case of a white employer who believes that Negroes are lazy and dislikes them, but hires them to avoid being prosecuted for violation of federal fair employment practices legislation.

Before considering the specific components of an attitude, we need to identify the attitudes that constitute a "prejudice," since our main focus will be on this type of attitude. In general, we can say that an attitude has become a prejudice when a distinct combination of beliefs, emotions, and behaviors—usually negative—has led one to a fixed way of thinking about a person or an object (a bias) and that way of thinking does not readily change on the basis of newly acquired information or experiences. Thus black-white racial prejudice is a fixed set of negative and generally irrational beliefs, emotions, and behaviors that many blacks and whites have formed about each other. (See Figure 3-2.)

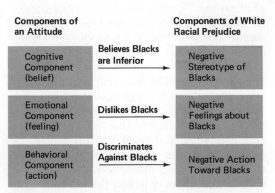

FIGURE 3-2 The components of an attitude and their relationship to one attitude—racial prejudice.

The cognitive component

The cognitive component of an attitude includes an individual's beliefs about the "attitudinal object." Frequently, the cognitive component of racial attitudes is termed a "stereotype" or a "picture in the head" regarding a social or racial group (Lippmann, 1922). The white soldier in our example clearly had beliefs about blacks including what the typical black person did for a living—menial work. When he saw a black man do menial work as well as a variety of other, nonmenial tasks, such as talking with him and bringing him magazines, he emphasized that which was consistent with his beliefs and made the mistaken inference that his friend had formerly been a porter. Irrespective of whether the beliefs are true or false, they summarize what the individual has learned in the past and influence his interpretation of subsequent events.

Why do people have beliefs? To take a less emotive topic, why do you believe that all oranges are round? On the basis of what you have seen and been told, you form ideas about the general properties of objects and groups of people. These beliefs perform a wide variety of functions (Katz, 1960). They summarize previous experiences and make future interactions with the world more predictable and meaningful. Once a belief is formed, the person thinks he knows what to expect from certain objects and groups and how to interpret and make sense of what he sees. Without beliefs we would be overwhelmed by the complexity of our environment. Beliefs simplify and organize what we see. Further, beliefs provide a context for experience and, to some extent, determine what information one will seek out (Freedman and Sears, 1965a).

Beliefs may also express the person's emotions and personality. Believing negative things about blacks may drain off hostility due to other things or preclude the recognition of negative traits in oneself. Beliefs also "justify" emotions and behaviors. Believing that all whites are destructive racists, the Black Panthers can justify their dislike and mistrust of whites as well as their own program of action. Beliefs are clearly an important component of many attitudes.

Frequently, investigators measure beliefs by presenting respondents with a question and several alternative answers—a "fixed-alternative" measure. People may be asked to indicate whether they agree or disagree with a statement, and the results may be reported in terms of the percentage of respondents expressing agreement. A 1971 Harris survey on black and white racial beliefs used fixed-alternative items of this agree-disagree type. The members of a national sample of 1,200 black households were asked to indicate whether they agreed or disagreed with a number of statements concerning whites. As the percentages in Table 1 show, the majority of the blacks polled had negative beliefs about whites and felt that whites had negative beliefs about blacks.

Table 1. Black Perception of Whites

	Percentage of Blacks Agreeing with Statement
Whites feel blacks are inferior.	81
Whites give blacks a break only when forced.	79
White men secretly want black women.	76
Whites are really sorry that slavery was abolished.	70
Whites have a mean and selfish streak.	68

Source: The Harris Survey, October 4, 1971.

The Harris organization has repeatedly measured white attitudes about blacks since 1963. Thus the responses given on a 1971 national survey of 1,445 white households not only indicate how whites feel about blacks now, but through a comparison with the 1963 responses, can also show whether or not white prejudices are changing. As the percentages in Table 2 indicate, although a sizable minority of whites still have negative beliefs, the number has declined since 1963. The survey also shows that the number of whites holding negative stereotypes about blacks is not as high as the blacks think. Although 81 percent of the blacks agreed that "most whites think that blacks are inferior," only 22 percent of the whites sampled admitted this belief.

How do beliefs develop? Why do you believe that oranges are round or that fried grasshop-

Table 2. White Perception of Blacks

| | Percentage of Whites Agreeing with Statement | |
	1971	1963
Blacks are inferior to white people.	22	31
Blacks have less ambition.	52	66
Blacks smell different.	48	60
Blacks have lower morals than whites.	40	55
Blacks breed crime.	27	35

Source: The Harris Survey, October 4, 1971.

pers taste bad or that Jews are "pushy"? Personal experience, what others tell you, and your own emotional needs—as we shall see later in this chapter—are the main determinants of your beliefs. The source of a belief may also influence its content. For instance, a person whose beliefs reflect his own personal experiences with a particular object in a wide variety of situations may have highly accurate and clearly articulated beliefs. In contrast, someone whose racial attitudes simply reflect the prevalent stereotype may have more simplified beliefs and may be prone to overgeneralization. Further, once an individual has assimilated racial stereotypes in childhood, he may respond to the label and not to a particular person. For this reason, racial prejudices acquired from other people become extremely resistant to change.

Beliefs vary in a number of ways. Some are much more basic than others. Our belief in the accuracy of our own senses and in the accuracy of what reliable people tell us may be two of our most basic beliefs. You don't doubt what you see, and probably, you don't doubt the validity of much of what your friends tell you. From these very basic beliefs, many others are derived. If you value your money and your friends tell you that a certain person is a spendthrift, you may conclude that he would be unlikely to repay debts and so not lend him any money.

Beliefs vary, too, in the *amount* and *type* of evidence on which they are based. Some of your beliefs, such as your belief that oranges are round, may reflect hundreds of experiences. The bigoted white soldier's belief that all Negroes did menial work may have been based in part on a few experiences with blacks, but primarily on what others had told him. Further, beliefs vary in their *openness to change*. Information inconsistent with the beliefs may change some beliefs. If you saw a series of oval oranges, you might begin to doubt your belief that all oranges are round. However, the bigoted white soldier's seeing a number of blacks holding professional jobs might not modify his beliefs. Indeed, this irrational refusal to consider the objective evidence has been suggested as a defining characteristic of prejudices and stereotypes.

Of course, beliefs vary in their *accuracy*. Never having tasted frogs' legs, you might assume that they taste very unpleasant, while your belief that oranges are round is based on many experiences and is more likely to be accurate. Many of the negative stereotypes whites have of blacks are based on what others have told them rather than on direct personal experience with blacks. Some beliefs are much more *important* to a person than others. Your belief in your own competency is clearly more important to you than your beliefs about the qualities of avocados.

Further, beliefs may vary in their *complexity*. Some may be composed of only one basic assumption, whereas others are composed of a number of beliefs. For example, Norman Mailer's belief about blacks comprised his beliefs that Negroes kept him waiting in order to demonstrate that they could; that they claimed to be better in music, war, and sex; and that they shunned responsibilities that Mailer met. All of these beliefs were unpleasant, and Mailer's overall belief was somewhat negative.

But what happens if some of the beliefs are *inconsistent* with each other? Prior to 1969, when a girl riding with Senator Ted Kennedy was killed because he drove his car off a bridge, you may have believed that Senator Kennedy was a very able and good man. How did the news of this event influence your beliefs? If you reacted as a number of important theories predict you should (consistency, congruity, dissonance reduction, balance, and so on), you sought to remove the apparent inconsistency between your beliefs concerning Kennedy and the incident. To obtain consistency, you could have used a number of strategies. You could have modified your favorable beliefs about Kennedy to make them consistent with your negative reactions to the accident. Or you could have reinterpreted or denied the negative aspects of the accident by thinking: "The incident only showed that the senator was understandably distraught."

An impressively large number of laboratory studies have shown that, as consistency theories predict, inconsistency among various beliefs does motivate individuals to move toward consistency in their beliefs. Consistency between beliefs may be one criterion people use to evaluate the validity of their assumptions. When experimental subjects are exposed to information that is inconsistent with their previously held attitudes, frequently these beliefs are modified.

But in real life are people always motivated to seek consistency among their beliefs? Are all of your beliefs consistent? Some psychologists do not believe that they are (e.g., Abelson, 1968). People are not always aware of the many inconsistencies in their beliefs, and even when they are, they are not always motivated to reduce them. The bigot who clings to his beliefs even in the face of strongly contradictory evidence illustrates the inconsistency of human thought.

The results of a recent field study on reactions to the Kennedy accident show a high tolerance for inconsistency. Subjects, who had initially had a favorable attitude toward Kennedy, were classified into those who had changed their mind about Kennedy and those who had not. A consistency theory would predict that those who had not changed their attitude were likely to hold generally positive beliefs about the incident, for example, that he was "definitely not aware that he might have been sacrificing the girl's life by his delay." However, a number of people did not change their favorable beliefs about Kennedy, but nevertheless agreed with negative assessments of the incident. Of those who did *not* change their beliefs, "65% admitted the possibility, if not the probability, that the girl's life could have been saved had he not delayed; 20% admitted the possibility that he was aware of this when he did delay; and 64% thought that his delay was probably or definitely based, at least in part, on his concern for his reputation" (Silverman, 1971, p. 176). Apparently people are not always motivated to remove inconsistencies.

The emotional component

To understand the second component of an attitude—the emotional reaction—listen to a group of people discussing the merits of busing their children to achieve racial balance. One important dimension of all attitudes is the emotional reaction to the attitudinal object. This component is usually measured on a continuum running from "extremely negative" through "neutral" to "extremely positive."

Emotional reactions may be far more complicated than a simple negative-to-positive scale would show (Ostrom, 1969). If Norman Mailer were asked to indicate how positively or negatively he felt about the black protest movement, he might be able to place a check mark along a continuum. But when he discussed his full range of feelings, a number of widely differing emotions were associated with his attitude—guilt, annoyance, shame, irritation. And if you have observed pro-Negro bigotry ("bring your token Negro along"), you may be aware of the mixture of emotions in the overly gracious, overly friendly whites: a combination of fear, condescension, and curiosity (Owens, 1971).

Not only does the emotion attached to the attitudinal object vary, but so does the degree of emotional involvement with a particular attitude. Not all attitudes are equally important. The person's involvement is influenced both by the way in which he perceives information related to the attitude and by the attitude's resistance to change (Sherif et al., 1965).

What determines how you feel about a particular object or group? In many cases beliefs may dictate the emotional reaction. If a white student believes that Negroes are lazy and he objects to laziness, he may have a negative emotional reaction to Negroes. Or emotional reactions may be determined by experience. As in the case of James Baldwin's character, direct, negative experiences may cause an individual to have a negative feeling. Or an emotional reaction to a particular object may be an expression of other emotions that the individual is not consciously aware of. In some cases negative feelings toward a particular social group may really be an overt expression of unconscious emotions or of frustrations which the individual does not knowingly relate to his attitude.

How can the emotional component of an attitude be measured? One way would be to ask the individual. Another is to measure the individual's physiological reactions. As you may recall from your introductory psychology course, intense levels of emotional arousal result in changes in bodily processes. For example, prejudice may cause fear or anger, and when you are afraid or angry, you perspire more profusely. Rather than ask a person about his attitudes, the researcher looks directly at the indicators of emotion—heart rate, galvanic skin response, and pupil dilation—to determine the level of emotion aroused. This technique of measuring physiological reactions is perhaps best known from the popular literature as the "lie-detector test," made famous in television crime drama.

Of all the physiological measures, the galvanic skin response (GSR), which is a measure of changes in the skin's electrical conductivity caused by changes in the degree of perspiration, has been used most frequently to assess levels of prejudice. In the GSR studies to date, highly prejudiced white subjects have been found to have more intense physiological reactions to black-related stimuli than subjects who are less prejudiced. For example, white subjects who were highly prejudiced (as measured by a self-report test) had significantly more intense GSRs when interacting with black experimenters than did subjects who were not as highly prejudiced (Porier and Lott, 1967).

The behavioral component

A third component of an attitude is behavior—how the person acts in relation to an object or a group. Beliefs and emotional reactions influence behavior. If a white student has a stereotype that most blacks are stupid or if he dislikes most blacks, then what would he be expected to do in a black-white setting? He might be expected to discriminate or refuse to treat a particular black person according to his merits.

Conversely, behavior can also influence the other two components of an attitude. One theory, called radical behaviorism, would say that we come to know our own attitudes in much the same way we come to know those of other people (Bem, 1967). If you want to know how your friend feels about woman's lib, you observe what he says and does, how consistent he is over a period of time, what he says when he is high or really gets into the topic, etc. To infer how he really feels, you take the whole situation into account to see what the various behaviors mean (Kelley, 1967). Some would contend that exactly the same processes operate in our learning about our own attitudes. Unless our thoughts are very clearly articulated, our observation of our own behavior is the most powerful determinant of our attitudes. As E. M. Forster said, "How can I tell what I think 'till I see what I say?"

If we do infer some of our attitudes from what we say and do, it should follow that these attitudes could be changed simply by our changing what we say and do. No matter how you felt about socialized medicine previously, simply listening to yourself defend socialized medicine would cause you to infer that you supported this position. As we shall see in the next chapter, a number of role-playing studies, in which subjects were asked to defend attitudes that they initially opposed, seem to show that this is what happens. However, although these findings may be interpreted to support the hypothesis that we directly infer our attitudes from what we say, another interpretation is possible. In the process of marshaling arguments to make a good defense, the individual is forced to become familiar with reasons that support his position, and so the merits of the argument may convince him. In reality, though, both the direct inference of our attitudes from our behavior and our behavior's forcing us to think of arguments to support our behavior may combine to make our behavior a powerful determinant of our beliefs and emotions.

It might seem that the behavioral component of an attitude would be the easiest of the three attitudinal components to measure, but this is not the case. If you wanted to set up situations that would measure prejudice, what would you do? One possible test might be to ask a person to agree to sign a release for increasingly wider distribution of a photograph showing him with a black student, as deFleur and Westie (1958) did. Or you might stage a situation in which a person had to agree or not agree to have a black roommate, to attend an NAACP meeting, to show black students around the campus, or to sign a petition urging more civil-rights legislation.

Even though behavioral measures are immediate, committing, and highly realistic, they are much more time-consuming and costly than self-report measures. Moreover, the relationship between beliefs, emotions, and behavior is not always clear. In situations where an individual is free to do as he pleases and is not afraid of sanctions, his behavior may be consistent with the other components of his attitudes. In many situations, however, behavior is dictated more by the demands of the situation than by the individual's beliefs and emotional reactions. A student's refusing to attend an NAACP meeting may mean either that he is prejudiced or that he has other commitments for the evening in question.

The relationship between beliefs, emotions, and behavior

How do the three components of an attitude relate to each other? A number of theorists have conceived of attitudes as a consistent system of beliefs, emotions, and behaviors organized around a single object (Rosenberg, 1960). According to this view, an individual who held largely negative beliefs about black Americans would be expected to have largely negative emotions about blacks and to act negatively toward them.

From this view it would follow that changing one of the three components would induce a tension toward change in the other two. For instance, if the emotional component were directly modified, the cognitive component would be expected to change so that it would become consistent with the changed emotions. In an ingenious test of this hypothesis, one investigator modified the affective component of attitudes by means of hypnotic suggestion (Rosenberg, 1960). The beliefs of subjects concerning a number of issues, including blacks moving into white neighborhoods, were measured before and after subjects were given hypnotic suggestions. Subjects who were given the suggestion to favor and feel happy about blacks moving into their neighborhoods changed their

beliefs so as to make those beliefs more consistent with their changed emotional reactions. These results clearly support the consistency model of the relationship between beliefs and emotions.

But the relationship between beliefs, emotions, and behavior is more complex. Are your emotions and behaviors consistent with your beliefs concerning racial issues? If you are like many of the subjects studied in this area, sometimes they are, and sometimes they are not. Research results have shown both consistency and inconsistency among the three attitudinal components (Wicker, 1969). The problem is to determine the circumstances under which the three components are consistent. The research results suggest that whether beliefs and emotions are translated into consistent behaviors depends on a number of variables, including the accuracy with which a person's beliefs are measured, his attitudes about other aspects of the situation, his fear of punishment, and the extent to which he feels he is able to act on his attitudes and is personally involved with the issue.

In the typical research procedure to test the consistency between beliefs, emotions, and behaviors, paper-and-pencil, self-report measures of attitudes are obtained and then related to emotions or behaviors. If the respondents are not truthful and simply say what they think the investigator wants to hear, their questionnaire answers may not relate to what they do. For instance, in a college setting in which a norm of racial tolerance prevails, students may not feel free to express bigoted opinions. Thus in one recent study in which the racial attitudes of white college students were measured by a questionnaire and then their behavior toward a black co-worker was unobtrusively measured, there was a negative relationship. The students who indicated that they were the least prejudiced engaged in the most covert rejection of their black partner (Weitz, 1972). However, under conditions in which there is no clearly socially acceptable response, attitudes may be highly predictive of behavior. The attitudes expressed by low-income, married, Negro women about the use of contraceptives correlated .81 with their intention to use these measures and with actual use (Kothandapani, 1971).

Behavior is determined by attitudes about

various aspects of the situation. Although you may have a negative attitude about cutting classes in general, your attitude about cutting the classes of a particular professor, whom you think is dull, may be different. To predict how frequently you would cut, one would need to know your attitude about cutting in general as well as your attitudes about the professor. When such "combinational" attitude approaches have been used, correlations as high as .78 have been obtained between attitudes and behavior (Rokeach and Kliejunas, 1972).

No matter how bigoted a white individual is, he probably would not express his feelings should he find himself in the midst of a Black Panther meeting. Potential punishment and norms clearly influence the expression of attitudes. Prejudiced Southern workers may not express their prejudices when interacting with blacks in integrated labor unions for fear of losing their jobs (Killian, 1952). Conversely, if punishment is not expected, behavior may express prejudices (deFleur and Westie, 1958). Also, your beliefs about what others expect you to do in a situation and your motivation to comply with these expectations will influence the extent to which you act in accordance with your attitudes (Ajzen and Fishbein, 1972). Acting the role of the gracious restaurant proprietor may dictate that a prejudiced restaurateur serve blacks even though he continues to dislike them privately.

If you see yourself as the kind of person "who takes actions on things he believes in," this feeling has an important effect on your acting according to your beliefs (Freedman and Fraser, 1966, p. 201). Evidence of the importance of a person's self-perception as a "doer" has been provided by a recent experiment (McArthur, Kiesler, and Cook, 1969). After subjects had been told that they had a "doer personality," they were much more likely to act in a manner consistent with their expressed attitudes.

Further, the personal importance of the issue may partly determine whether or not attitudes are translated into action. In areas in which racial integration has been very slow, such as housing, highly personal issues of great importance to the individual are often involved (Katz and Gurin, 1969).

Summary

One way of thinking about attitudes is to analyze them in terms of their three components: (1) cognitive, (2) emotional, and (3) behavioral. When these three components are negative and highly resistant to new information or experience, we think of the resulting attitude as a prejudice.

The cognitive component of an attitude includes an individual's beliefs about the attitudinal object—clearly an important component of many attitudes, as a number of self-report studies have shown. People have beliefs in order to (1) adapt to the world by summarizing previous experience and thus making future interactions with the world more meaningful and rewarding and (2) express their emotions and personality.

Beliefs vary in a number of ways—in the extent to which they are basic to other beliefs, in the amount and type of evidence on which they are based, in their openness to change when inconsistent information is presented, in their accuracy, in their complexity, and in their importance to the individual.

The degree to which people are motivated to maintain consistency between their various beliefs is not yet clear. Although a large number of studies have shown that inconsistency in beliefs can motivate individuals to move toward consistency, some studies have not. In real life people may not always be aware of the many inconsistencies in their beliefs, and even when they are, they may not always be motivated to remove them.

A second important dimension of all attitudes is the emotional reaction to the attitudinal objects. Emotional reactions may be influenced by beliefs, by experience, or by other emotions that the individual is not consciously aware of. The emotional component of an attitude may be measured by either self-report measures or the individual's physiological reactions.

A third component of an attitude is behavior—how a person acts in relation to a particular object or a group. In some cases beliefs and emotional reactions determine behavior, but in many other cases the demands of the situation may determine what the individual does to a far greater extent than the other components of his attitudes. Thus measures of the behavioral component are sometimes very difficult to interpret. Behavior can also influence beliefs and emotions. Unless our beliefs are very clearly articulated or our emotions intense, our observation of our own behavior will be a powerful determinant of our beliefs and emotions.

A number of theorists have conceived of attitudes as a consistent system of beliefs, emotions, and behavior organized around a single object. Although there may be a pressure toward a consistency between beliefs and emotions, the relationship between beliefs, emotions, and behavior is complex. The extent to which beliefs and emotions are translated into consistent behavior depends on a number of variables, including the accuracy with which a person's beliefs are measured, his attitudes about other aspects of the situation, his fear of punishment, the extent to which he feels he is able to act on his attitudes, and the extent to which he is personally involved with the issue.

Attitude Formation: An Overview

How did you acquire your attitude about the food served in your university's dining hall? You may have eaten there on several occasions, or you may have observed the reactions of other people who were eating there. In either event your feeling would be based primarily on your personal experience.

If I were to offer you a dinner of rattlesnake meat, chocolate-covered ants, and fried grasshoppers, you would probably be repelled. Why would you react this way? You probably have never tasted these foods. The answer would be that you have acquired this attitude from influences in your culture.

And if, after a particularly frustrating day in which nothing has gone right, you begin to feel hostile toward everyone, including minority groups, your negative attitude might be an escape valve for your own emotions.

Our own personal experiences, the influence of others, and our own emotional reactions are the three main determinants of our attitudes. Since many of these attitudes concern objects that are remote from our immediate personal experience—like the rattlesnake meat—and that do not seem to relieve emotional pressures, it is commonly assumed that social influences

are the single most important source of most attitudes.

For instance, in response to a questionnaire, many college students were able to describe people they had rarely met, such as the "typical Turk." Many Americans have never met a Turk and probably would not recognize one unless he were wearing a fez. Yet, despite the lack of personal contact, the Turk's image was not good: 9 percent of the college students surveyed saw Turks as cruel, 13 percent as treacherous, 14 percent as physically dirty, and so on (Karlins, Coffman, and Walters, 1969).

Further, a number of studies have shown the emergence of a form of embryonic bigotry in preschool white and black children who have had minimal opportunities, if any, to interact with members of other races. Both black and white preschoolers have been found to have racial preferences: White seems more beautiful to both. When preschool white and black children in segregated settings were asked to select a picture of either a white child or a black child as someone they would like for a playmate, 80.5 percent of the Southern whites selected the picture of a white child and so did 78 percent of the black children (Morland, 1970).

Because of findings such as these, a number of social psychologists have argued that most—if not all—attitudes are based primarily on the information provided by social sources: family, friends, the mass media, school courses, and so on. But there is little empirical evidence on what actually happens in the process of attitude acquisition, and this is an assumption rather than a proven fact (Brigham, 1971).

Personal Experience and Attitude Formation

If you consider the whole range of your attitudes, you may find that many of them are based on personal experience. Your attitude about going to the dentist may, for example, be based very directly on what has happened to you in the dentist's chair. See Box 1 to see how one person's personal experience influenced her racial attitudes.

BOX 1

TO KNOW WHAT IT'S LIKE, YOU'VE GOT TO EXPERIENCE IT YOURSELF

Can a white person ever really know about the prejudice and discrimination experienced by blacks? White people can read about bombings and racial epithets and all of the rest of the great American traditions, but to really understand how prejudice affects a black, one has to have a black skin. Two white people have tried to do just that. John Howard Griffin and Grace Halsell took medication that temporarily turned their skins black and then went to live as blacks in the black community. Since Halsell's experiences are more recent (1969), her reactions will be summarized here.

During her life as a black, Grace Halsell lived and worked in Harlem and Mississippi. She wrote of the prevalence in Harlem of a feeling of futility, entrapment, and pointlessness; of the difficulty of survival in the ghetto; and of escape through the use of drugs and alcohol. She also noted white prejudice and discrimination. When, for example, she went to Harlem Hospital with infected blisters so painful that she could barely hobble, a white physician conveyed his prejudice in a rather unsubtle way:

"'You people,' he lectures me, 'should bathe more often. Your feet are *dirty!*' He says there is nothing wrong with my feet. 'Just blisters.' Again he utters the stern injunction that I must bathe myself and my feet every day. He gives me no treatment or medication. I leave wondering if he talks to all 'colored people' as he has talked to me, indicating that we were all dirty, somehow less than human."

[Halsell, 1969, pp. 76–77.]

In Mississippi Miss Halsell found that although her life was very different, her blackness was just as difficult to bear. For example, despite the removal of "whites only" signs from Southern bus depots, waiting rooms were still segregated in 1968, and the "black facilities" were barely adequate. "Black jobs" consisted mainly of household work (five dollars for an eight-hour day). The Ku Klux Klan was still strong enough to be feared by many Negroes, which was

a realistic fear, as shown by the earlier murder of Medgar Evers and other civil-rights workers. Overall, there was the constant assumption by whites that blacks were somehow not quite human and should "know their place." Halsell wrote:

"A house has a sign out front: 'Room for Rent.' I muster my courage, rap on the door, and am greeted by a white woman who studies me like an apparition.

"'I'd like to see your room,' I say. And I couldn't have shocked her more if I'd slapped her.

"'I have no room!' She gazes at me incredulously.

"'But you put out a sign.'

"'Why, you *black bitch!*' she shouts, and furiously slams the door."

[Halsell, 1969, p. 145.]

Perhaps her most dramatic revelation of what it is like to be poor and black came when Miss Halsell was working as a domestic. The white man of the house arrived home early one day, while his wife was out, and immediately began making sexual advances to Miss Halsell. As a white woman who was only temporarily black, Miss Halsell fought off her attacker and fled, unpaid for her day's work. Afterward, she wondered whether or not she could have afforded this reaction if she had really been poor and black. If she had had children at home who needed her salary, could she have afforded to flee the white man's lust without being paid? Could she have afforded to jeopardize her job? Economic considerations might have forced her to submit to this added "duty" for her five-dollar, eight-hour workday.

(Courtesy, The Advertising Council)

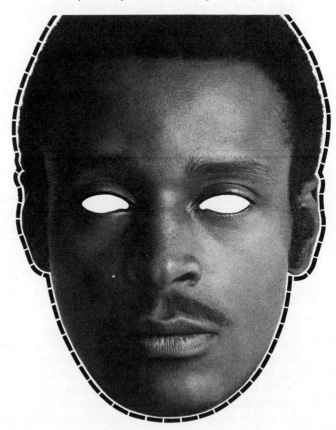

Unfamiliarity breeds contempt

Since most white people in the United States live in racially segregated residential areas, their opportunities for interracial contact are extremely limited. How does this lack of familiarity influence interracial attitudes?

The unfamiliar may be feared and disliked simply because it is strange. To get some idea of the intensity of the fear of the unknown, watch a young child in an unfamiliar situation. Or more immediately, you may recall your own lost, frightened feelings when you first arrived at college.

Mere familiarity may be an important determinant of emotional reactions. Repeated exposure to something may make it more attractive. For instance, frequently presented nonsense words have been found to elicit more positive emotional reactions than those that are presented only a few times (Zajonc, 1968). Although not all of the evidence has been consistent (Harrison and Crandall, 1972), a number of studies have shown that subjects have a preference for the reasonably familiar. (Obviously, this reaction has its limits. Seeing *Gone with the Wind* ten times consecutively might break the spirit of even the staunchest fan.)

The familiarity-liking relationship may account for the development of racial prejudices in white children. As we saw, racial preferences develop before children have any opportunities for interracial contact: Preschool white children in segregated areas preferred white dolls to black dolls. Since most white children have had very few opportunities to meet black children, it may be that they initially prefer white simply because it is more familiar. Thus the emotional reaction—the dislike of black—may first develop as a result of a complete lack of any experience with blacks rather than as the result of specific experiences.

If this hypothesis is correct, it would follow that the only way to prevent the emergence of a preference among whites for their own race would be to provide opportunities for whites to interact with blacks at a very early age. Either integrated preschools or residential areas would provide such opportunities.

The relative unfamiliarity of most whites with blacks may also contribute to racial prejudice in another way. In the absence of any contact, the only information available to whites about blacks is that contained in the culturally mediated stereotypes, which emphasize black-white differences. Further, without any contact, many whites may assume that members of other races are different simply because they are unknown. A number of studies have shown that the dissimilar is disliked. See Box 2.

Experience and impressions

How do your experiences with people and objects influence your beliefs about what they are "really like"? How have you evolved your impression of your social psychology course? Without any conscious intention of doing so, you have taken all of the varied experiences you have had with it and put together a cohesive, meaningful, and perhaps accurate impression of what it is like. No matter what you are forming an impression of, whether another person, an abstract entity, such as the social psychology course, or an extended group, such as a national group, your experiences influence your impressions.

The forming of an impression of something involves a complicated interaction between the person forming the impression, the situation in which it is formed, and the objective attributes of the person or thing being considered. In this process the person forming the impression is far from passive. When you form an impression of your social psychology course, your own motives, interests, and past experiences influence your evaluation. The situation in which the impression is formed also shapes your impression. Whether the class meets at eight o'clock in the morning or at a more civilized hour will influence your reactions. And, of course, the objective characteristics of the class influence your impression. If you are at all accurate, you are more likely to have a favorable impression of the course if it is objectively good.

The Influence of the Perceiver To cite a truism, two people looking at the same thing may see something quite different. A twenty-year-old college student in Stockholm, Sweden, will form a rather different impression of that city than his parents would. The impression derived reflects

BOX 2 DOES RACIAL PREJUDICE REALLY EXIST?

Assume that you have to choose one of two people to spend some time with. One is a person of a different race whose beliefs coincide exactly with your own; the other is someone of your own race whose attitudes are completely inconsistent with your own. Which would you choose? If you reacted as several other college students have when they were faced with this choice, you would probably select the person whose beliefs were the same as yours, whether he was black or white (e.g., Rokeach, 1960; Hendrick, Bixenstine, and Hawkins, 1971).

For example, in a recent experiment two white and two black confederates staged a conversation with a white subject. One of the white and one of the black confederates always agreed with the white subject—no matter what he said. The other two confederates always disagreed with him. After the staged discussion was over, the subject was asked which two of the four confederates he would prefer to have join him for coffee. Typically, the subject selected the confederates who had agreed with him. Similarity of beliefs was more important than race in determining preference in this situation (Rokeach and Mezei, 1966).

People like interacting with others who share their attitudes. There is noth-

ing so pleasant as finding out that others agree with the infinite wisdom of your own attitudes (Heider, 1958). Maximizing your pleasure in a particular social interaction would mean choosing someone who is similar. Thus what may seem to be preference based on racial grounds in everyday life may really be caused by a tendency to assume that people of different racial groups have different beliefs (Rokeach, 1960). But if you find out that a person is really similar to yourself, race becomes relatively unimportant in determining preference. So the answer to our question—does racial prejudice really exist?—would seem to be that preference based solely on race may not exist, but prejudices against people who are different influence social choices.

Case proven? Have the studies shown that similarity of beliefs is always a more important consideration than race? In your own social choices are there ever times when race seems more important than similarity? Many of the studies in which beliefs were found to be more important than race involved testing college students in situations that were clearly experimental. The demands of the experimental situation and the college environment in general may have combined to make the subjects avoid looking prejudiced.

Race may become important when people exercise social preferences that involve more intimate relationships. When people are deciding about dating, marriage, and family relationships, race may be a more important consideration than attitude similarity. And this is what a number of studies have shown (Triandis and Davis, 1965; Willis and Bulatao, 1967).

Why should race be a more important consideration in these more involving, intimate social interactions? Social pressures and sanctions against interracial interactions are strongest in the most intimate social interactions (Mezei, 1971). Although your family and friends might not care about interracial coffee drinking, marriage is quite another thing. To avoid social disapproval, people may be forced to choose their intimates on racial grounds.

The fact that intimate social interactions are still primarily determined by race should not obscure the importance of the findings that similarity of beliefs is the prime consideration for less involving interactions. Through the publicizing of white-black similarities and of the similarities of the problems and concerns of blacks and whites, the wall of assumed dissimilarity that motivates much interracial avoidance may be broken down.

---

the past history, culture, interests, motives, and beliefs of the person forming the impression as much as the actual characteristics of the person or situation being judged (Campbell, 1967).

For example, if you have talked with any foreigners, you may have noticed some of the ludicrous possibilities for cross-cultural misunderstandings. Say an American boy, traveling through Greece, meets a Greek girl and asks her out. In the United States a date is not a very involving commitment; the American therefore may be very surprised when the Greek girl believes his invitation involves a more intimate

relationship than he does (Triandis, Vassiliou, and Nassiakou, 1968).

The perceiver's own background will also influence what he tends to notice in different settings. That which is familiar to him will have less impact than that which is unfamiliar. Take, for example, an American college student visiting a country in which transportation is still provided by horses and mules. Since American transportation differs so dramatically, the means of transportation will very likely be included in the student's impression of the country (Campbell, 1967).

Further, the tourist may be more likely to notice behavior that his society disapproves of. If you have been taught that breast-feeding infants in public is wrong and you visit a country in which this is done, the women's breast-feeding will probably be a prominent part of your impression (Campbell, 1967).

Your own beliefs about what traits "go together" will also influence your impressions. If you believe that someone who earns his living by manual labor is probably strong and not too bright, you will, when observing a group of people involved in manual labor, undoubtedly conclude that these people are unintelligent.

All of these perceiver variables clearly influence the way in which whites form impressions of blacks. Cultural differences between the two groups may lead to misunderstandings. The perceiver's own background may influence what he notices. For instance, whites may interpret the fact that many blacks do physical labor as indicating that they are less intelligent.

The Influence of the Situation The conditions under which observations are made influence one's impression by setting limits as to what can be observed and by providing a context within which a particular event is judged. Thus in meeting the requirements of his role, the white policeman in a black ghetto must exert control and maintain order. In doing this, he inevitably concentrates on those ghetto residents who are breaking the law. His repeated involvement with the fights, drugs, and problems of the ghetto reinforces his negative stereotype of inhabitants of that ghetto.

The black ghetto dwellers' view of whites is in turn biased because they see mostly the white policeman who pushes their people around. Thus in meeting the requirements of his role, the white policeman reinforces the stereotypes of whites held by some blacks.

Further, events are interpreted in context. In the tense interactions between black ghetto residents and white police, the usually innocuous act of giving a motorist a traffic ticket may have a very different meaning. To the white policeman, it is yet another instance of black irresponsibility. To the black ghetto dweller, it is yet another instance of white racism.

The Influence of the Actual Characteristics of the Attitudinal Object In everyday life we assume that our impressions of people and objects have some validity. You may think that your impression of your social psychology course reflects in some measure what it is really like. And you may feel that your stereotypes of minority groups reflect what they are really like.

Believing that stereotypes are accurate is so unfashionable in today's college scene that this explanation is rarely mentioned. Students may think there may be some accuracy—some "kernel of truth"—in at least a few stereotypes and not say so. And, indeed, some contemporary evidence does suggest that there may be.

Until quite recently, the statement that all stereotypes are false and irrational has almost been a truism in social psychology. Some social psychologists have even defined the term "stereotype" as an inaccurate, irrational overgeneralization, which, once formed, persists even in the presence of contradictory evidence and is used to justify discriminatory behavior.

This definition does apply to some stereotypes. The irrational bases and harmful effects of many stereotypes are too obvious to require documenting. In part, then, the traditional emphasis in social psychology on the irrational inaccuracy of stereotypes may be seen as a healthy counterbalance to the everyday assumption of their accuracy.

The complexity of forming an impression of a large group may impel the individual to resort to stereotypes. If you should try to form an impression of "what Englishmen are really like" while you were in England, you would see that the task would be incredibly complicated. The people you met would vary in many, many ways. And how would you know whether or not those you met were typical Englishmen? If you did begin to form an impression, how would you know whether or not you were correct? (See Figure 3-3.)

When confronted with the hopelessly complex task of forming an impression of an extended group, the overloaded information processor may simply blow a cognitive fuse and resort to more irrational methods of information processing. In desperation the traveler may form a hypothesis based on a couple of instances and ignore inconsistent information. Or he may seize on some readily observable aspect of the situation—like the impression that all Englishmen wear bowler hats and carry umbrellas. Or he may simply accept the stereotyped view of the English.

Further, some stereotypes have been scientifically shown to be inaccurate. One classic study of Armenian laborers in southern California in the 1920s showed that the Armenians were stereotyped as being dishonest, deceitful, untruthful, and troublesome, but the objective facts were that they were arrested less often than other California residents, applied less often for charity, and had credit ratings as good as other Californians (LaPiere, 1936).

Although many stereotypes are inaccurate, not all are. For example, when the actual characteristics of people from different regions of Pakistan were compared with the stereotypes concerning them, some of the stereotypes corresponded with real differences in behavior. Specifically, people from the Noakhali region were stereotyped as pious by other Pakistanis, and the Noakhalis' reported frequency of prayer was found to be higher than that of people from other areas of Pakistan (Schuman, 1966).

If some stereotypes do have a kernel of truth, the next problem is to determine the conditions that influence their accuracy. In considering

your own impressions and stereotypes, do you think that some have more validity than others? Those that refer to groups with which you have had contact might be expected to be more valid. When people have an opportunity for contact with different groups, their impressions of group differences may reflect real differences.

Although the mutual dislike of the white policeman and the black ghetto resident suggests that there are limits to the familiarity-accuracy relationship, some support for the relationship has been obtained. In one study it was found that as the amount of contact Americans had with Greeks increased, the Americans' stereotypes of Greeks became more differentiated and reflected more accurately what the investigators took to be the "real" characteristics of Greeks (Triandis and Vassiliou, 1967). Although there is the awkward problem of independently defining the actual characteristics of a national group, these results lend support to what one might ordinarily expect—that increased familiarity leads to increased accuracy.

Further, the distribution of traits within a particular group might be expected to influence the accuracy of observers' impressions. If all of the members of a group possessed about the

FIGURE 3-3 The traveler's dilemma. All of the figures below represent "Englishmen." What is the characteristic common to all of them?

Solution: They are all smiling when they are wearing a hat or carrying an umbrella.

same degree of a particular trait, it might be easier for outsiders to form an accurate impression (Triandis, 1971). Further, the more complete and more representative the sample of behavior from the group is, the more accurate you might expect the impressions to be. If all of a white person's contacts with blacks are with blacks acting in a servant capacity, his impressions will reflect only the behaviors possible in that situation.

Experience and emotions

Consider the way in which your experience with your social psychology course has influenced your feelings and behavior toward it. Your experience determines your impression of the course, and consistent emotions and behavior follow from that. If your experience has been good, you may believe that social psychology is an interesting and relevant course, and so you may have positive feelings about it and may even be doing the work assigned.

Confirmation of this "cognitive-mediational" hypothesis has been obtained in a recent study. After some Americans living in Greece had gotten to know some native Greeks well, they began to think that Greeks were somewhat inefficient in their general approach to business. Since the Americans valued business efficiency, their overall emotional reaction toward Greeks became less favorable. The Americans' impression of inefficiency may also have influenced the way they behaved toward Greeks. For example, expecting deliveries to be late, the Americans would order before they really needed the merchandise (Triandis and Vassiliou, 1967).

Sometimes experience can influence emotions without necessarily being mediated by beliefs. Say that initially you are neutral about political candidate Bombast. But after attending a series of delicious political dinners at which candidate Bombast speaks (briefly), you begin to associate Bombast with the delicious foods and thus develop a positive reaction to him. Just like Pavlov's dog, you have been conditioned and so react positively whenever you see Bombast.

Impossible? Not really. In fact, subjects who were given a free lunch became more favorably

inclined toward political slogans that were presented while they were munching the free food (Razran, 1940). A number of other studies have also shown that attitudes can be established by means of classical conditioning. For example, presenting a neutral stimulus, such as the word "light," just before a person receives a painful electric shock results in his having a more negative evaluation of that word (Zanna, Kiesler, and Pilkonis, 1970).

It is agreed that emotional reactions can be classically conditioned. However, there is considerable controversy as to *why* the effect is obtained. Some contend that subjects are aware of the expected relationship between the stimulus and the electric shock and simply comply (Kiesler, Collins, and Miller, 1969). Others feel that the subjects' awareness has nothing to do with the conditioning, and the simple pairing of the word and the shock results in the conditioning (Staats, 1969). Several recent studies have demonstrated conditioning in situations in which it is highly unlikely that the subjects were aware of the relationship between the electric shock and the attitude assessment; these studies make the hypothesis that the subjects' awareness causes the conditioning less probable (e.g., Zanna, Kiesler, and Pilkonis, 1970).

Even though the explanation of the effect is not clear, that there is such an effect is clear. But before the political campaign managers begin hiring gourmet chefs to prepare "conditioning meals," some limitations of the conditioning of attitudes should be noted. The usual procedure involves the association of some neutral stimulus with either a positive or a negative stimulus and then an immediate assessment of the conditioning effects. Consequently, the question of the permanency and magnitude of the effect remains open. How long would such conditioning last? And would the same results be obtained if the stimulus were not quite so neutral? If Bombast said stupid things and fell down in a drunken stupor, would feeding his followers tenderloin steaks keep them faithful? And how would social interpretations of the situation influence the impact of the food? If the free food were seen as obligating the potential voter, might not reactance be aroused, so that Bombast's barbecue would boomerang?

Summary: what you've seen has some relation to what you think

In this section we have seen that what you yourself have experienced in relation to attitudinal objects does influence your attitudes. The unfamiliar may be feared and disliked simply because it is strange. Thus negative attitudes toward blacks may develop among many whites as a result of their complete lack of experience with blacks.

Specific experiences also influence impressions. An impression is the product of a complicated interaction between the person forming the impression, the situation in which the impression is formed, and the objective attributes of the person or thing being considered. Many aspects of the perceiver—his culture, interests, motives, and beliefs—will influence his interpretation of personal experience. The conditions under which he is making observations will also influence his impressions by setting limits as to what he can observe and by providing a context against which he can judge a particular event. Finally, the object or group being judged influences the impression. Although many stereotypes have been shown to be inaccurate and irrational, some contain a kernel of truth—especially those relating to groups the individual has had extensive contact with.

Experience also influences the emotional and behavioral components of an attitude. Either indirectly, by influencing your impressions of an object, or directly, by conditioning an emotional reaction to an object, experience influences emotional reactions.

Other People and Attitude Formation

Let us begin this section with a quiz.

	Yes	No
1. Do you have an attitude about heroin?		
2. Have you ever used heroin?		
3. Do you have an attitude about Senator Edward Kennedy?		
4. Have you ever met Senator Kennedy?		

The not-too-subtle point of this test is that many, if not most, social attitudes are not based on personal experience. Without having used heroin, you can still have an attitude about it. Your particular attitude—like the rest of your attitudes—is predictably determined by the particular social influences you have been exposed to. Given William F. Buckley's wealthy, conservative family background, including conservative schools and conservative friends, and his penchant for conservative literature, his conservative attitudes are almost inevitable. And just as predictably, Julian Bond's social history determines his nonconservative attitudes. So we are all very much the products of the people with whom we interact.

If you were to list the names of the people who have been most influential in the forming of your attitudes, you'd probably mention your parents and friends first and then the names of relatives, teachers, clergymen, and so forth. Although you'd also note that television and the other media have had a significant impact on your attitudes, you would probably emphasize the role of other people. Despite the gloomy forecasts about the ability of the mass media to exert a kind of thought control, "the major influence upon people is people" (Bem, 1970, p. 75). See Box 3.

That nothing is more effective than face-to-face contact has been known by fund raisers and election campaigners for a long time. Assume, for instance, that you are working in a political campaign to get a revision of your city charter passed and that you have a choice of three campaign methods: (1) personally contacting each voter and trying to persuade him to vote in favor of the charter, (2) sending repeated mass mailings in favor of the charter, or (3) placing a series of ads in the mass media. If the voters in your town are anything like those in Ann Arbor, Michigan, personal contact would be the most effective method: 75 percent of the voters who were personally contacted voted in favor of the revision, whereas only 45 percent of those who received the mailing and 19 percent of those who had been exposed to the ads did so (Eldersveld and Dodge, 1954).

Why is direct face-to-face contact more effective? If you have ever been coerced by a friend into making a donation to a charity about which you knew little and cared less, you know why

BOX 3 GETTING IT TOGETHER IN COLLEGE

What do students themselves say about the "forces that have influenced them"? Some of the autobiographical comments that students made in this connection are quoted below.

Students tend to rebel against their parents. Trixie said:

"Every time I went home and talked to my father he convinced me that religion was something real. But now I find that I just can't accept that at all. I don't even talk with my father anymore about it; he has sort of given up on me or something. This is partly the result of psychology, because I can see in my personality development what has turned me against religion; it is all part of this rebellion against my parents. My rebellion against God is almost exactly equal to my rebellion against my father."

[Madison, 1969, pp. 25–26.]

But not always. Bob said:

"I've at least fulfilled the major wish of my parents, that I get a degree in something before I start fooling around."

[Madison, 1969, p. 97.]

Friends influence attitudes, too. As Bob said when asked how he had come to develop his attitudes:

"I think it's mainly been through discussions with my fellow students. For instance, our House is about as diverse a group as you can find, and there are constantly arguments being waged about this and that and the other thing. It's difficult not to have a stand on something when you can hear the ideas of this person being presented and you know you don't agree with them. . . .

"Fred [another student] has been responsible for a good deal of my education. . . . He makes you think. He'll come out with some answer which is so cynical or so . . . well, if I come up with some statement, like 'I want to be a tutor in the educational program for deprived children,' Fred says 'What for?' Even though he is also a tutor there, he'll ask me exactly why; he'll give me a lot of reasons why I shouldn't be. He just makes you look at every side of every question and think about it."

[Madison, 1969, pp. 104–105.]

To some extent, so does the faculty, as Sidney noted:

"My philosophical interest was nurtured by a graduate instructor in an introductory philosophy course. He took a personal interest in me, and we are still friends. His example of rigor, combined with depth of thought, helped me to make a transition from the vagueness of literary interests to careful examination of basic philosophical problems like problems of God."

[Madison, 1969, p. 66.]

As do the courses and reading assignments, as Sidney noted:

"What are my moral values, how deep do they go? I have just finished reading Gide's *L'Immoraliste.* I don't think I live by the golden rule, but society smiles upon this. Is my desire for acceptance the reason for my surface moral values? I must probe deeply the question: What is right?"

[Madison, 1969, p. 75.]

this is so. When your roommate asks you to donate to the "needy Wombangu," you may make the donation, not because you care about the Wombangu but in order to avoid irritating your friend or looking cheap. Contrast your reaction to your friend's request with your reaction to a mailed circular on behalf of the Wombangu. To the delight of all, the wastepaper basket provides a potential final resting place for unwanted mail, which doesn't talk back, look at you reproachfully, or think "wait 'til you want a favor." In face-to-face interactions, even with a stranger, the social norms governing appropriate reactions and the fears about the effects of disagreeing are always present.

In this section we shall discuss each of the various social sources that determine one's attitudes—parents, friends, the mass media, and school and church. To the extent that these are consistent, the attitude may be so thoroughly internalized that the person is not even aware that he has an attitude—it is just his assumption about what the world is really like. But sometimes the information is not consistent. Your parents, for instance, may believe that marijuana is harmful and leads to heroin, and your friends say just the opposite. Many of you may be experiencing this kind of conflict just now. Traditionally, the four years of college have been the time when many people are first exposed to a wide variety of opinions.

The cultural context

All of the elements of culture—the shared beliefs, values, and expectations about the appropriate ways to behave in certain situations—influence our attitudes, including our racial prejudices. Without even knowing that we are doing so, we automatically accept the prejudices and stereotypes of our group. If the culture provides racist information as well as pressures to conform to these teachings, we will tend to accept prejudice simply as a means of functioning effectively in a racist society and with others who are racist (Pettigrew, 1971). In support of the acculturation theory of prejudice, Pettigrew (1971) estimates that roughly three out of every four white Americans who are prejudiced are simply reflecting their culture. See Box 4.

White Americans may not be aware of any specific "teachings" concerning blacks. But if you think about some of the elements of middle-class white culture, you can see that prejudice pervades many aspects. In addition to the obviously racist stereotypes and prejudices, racist assumptions are included more subtly in many other beliefs and values. "Nice neighborhoods" don't have black residents, unless the resident is a Bill Cosby or some other, equally acceptable, token black. Certain jobs, usually menial, may be thought of as "Negro jobs." The middle-class values, emphasizing money, status, and material things, also contribute to antiblack attitudes. Only those who have "made it" are worthy of respect; lower-class people are regarded with contempt. Since fewer blacks than whites are middle-class, this value also contributes to antiblack attitudes.

BOX 4 INSTITUTIONAL RACISM: IT DOESN'T HAVE TO BE PLANNED TO HURT

People and institutions can injure minority groups without any deliberate attempt to do so. Simply doing business as usual, eating in the same restaurants, buying at the same stores, attending the same church—all can result in injury to black Americans if these institutions discriminate.

For a number of years the American Psychological Association has been concerned about racial prejudice and has emphasized that it has neither condoned nor engaged in racial prejudice or discrimination. Yet while the APA was assuring itself that it was not discriminating, its printer was. The APA's largest expenditure of funds for conducting its business was to the Lancaster Press, which printed nine of the fourteen APA journals. Curiously, in 1969 the Lancaster Press reported that although Lancaster's population of 63,000 included approximately 10,000 blacks and Puerto Ricans (about 15 percent), only one of its 300 employees was black, and he worked as a "wash-up" man for $1.75 per hour. In justifying this state of affairs, the Lancaster Press

indicated that its hiring practices were not racially discriminatory, but that the "low educational level among black persons in Lancaster prevented their employment" (Senn and Sawyer, 1971). Hearing this, the Board of Directors of the APA considered its "resolution to promote equality in employment among all firms with which APA deals" and decided that its discussion with Lancaster Press had met the intent of this resolution.

At this point another organization of psychologists, called the Psychologists for Social Action (PSA), began independent action to persuade the Lancaster Press to employ more nonwhites. Two members of PSA and a highly placed member of the APA visited the Lancaster Press and made it clear that if the press did not end its discriminatory hiring practices, the PSA members would attempt to pressure APA to take away its substantial business (over $600,000 per year). A program outlining what they expected the press to do and a request for periodic progress reports were left with the management.

Since this forceful call for action the press has complied. Approximately 50 percent of the new employees hired between October 1969 and September 1970 were black. In fact, the minority hiring program of the press is currently being used as an example of what other Lancaster firms can do to decrease racial discrimination.

The interesting thing about this example is the apparent absence of any overt, negative intent. What the firm was doing was "explained" as an unfortunate consequence of differences in background and training. But when external incentives became sufficiently large, the firm could modify its hiring practices and did so successfully. Habit, comfort, "doing it the way we've always done it" may result in more injury to blacks than the rantings of the minority of frothing bigots.

You may want to consider whether or not you are involved in any "institutional racism." What are the social consequences of your actions?

A

FIGURE 3-4 The popular culture tends to perpetuate white stereotyping of blacks. (A) A scene from the Paramount Picture film "Among the Living" in which the only black actor in the scene is shown as a shoeshine boy. (B) In Alabama, a group of black children lounge near a pile of watermelons—a typical stereotype of black culture. (A—The Bettman Archive; B—Alan Mercer)

B

How are the racist elements of the white middle-class culture conveyed? In addition to the direct, obvious ways, they are taught through folklore, humor, and language. (See Figure 3-4.) Until recently the comically terrified Little Black Sambo was a staple of many white nurseries. Until the early 1960s the caricature Negroes of "Amos 'n' Andy" were staples of radio and later television. Everyone's stereotypes were supported in that show. Legal "opinions" in the mouth of the inevitably limited Lawyer Calhoun emerged as garbled nonsense. Andy was obsessed with chasing loose and high-living black ladies, and Lightnin, the office boy, was so lazy that breathing seemed an effort. And George ("Kingfish") Stevens was a sly, dishonest Negro who would try to steal or con others out of anything that wasn't nailed down. And as an example of what the others could have been if they hadn't been so foolish and immoral, Amos was portrayed as having the white man's virtues of thrift and hard work.

Although the television image of blacks may be better in the 1970s, we still see subtle forms of support for our stereotypes in contemporary programs. Archie, the "lovable bigot," may be a ridiculous figure, but he is still saying the old familiar racial epithets and mouthing the old familiar stereotypes. (See Figure 3-5.) And Flip Wilson's "Geraldine" shows the same familiar propensity for "loose living" as the characters did on the "Amos 'n' Andy" show.

Racism even pervades our language. Without necessarily having any racist intent, people

FIGURE 3-5 In the popular television show "All in the Family," Carroll O'Connor has achieved fame as "Archie Bunker," the American bigot incarnate. (Courtesy, CBS Television Network)

**FIGURE 3-6 Parental impact on child develop-
ment and, in particular, on attitude formation is
very strong. Here a child imitates her mother in an
everyday homemaking scene—probably without
conscious awareness by either that a behavior
pattern is being set.** (Donald Wright Patterson, Jr./
Stock, Boston)

may use figures of speech that are obviously
anti-Negro: Working hard may be expressed as
"working like a nigger." You may have heard
other crudely anti-Negro expressions. Somewhat more subtly, the very word "black" has
generally connoted negative, evil, sinful things,
and "white" has symbolized what is good and
pure (Williams, 1970).

Parents

That parent-child interactions have an enormous impact on a child's attitudes and values
as well as on his personality is a truism of
psychology. Many studies have shown that the
attitudes of children tend to resemble those of
their parents. (See Figure 3-6.) For example, 76
percent of a national sample of high-school
seniors favored the same political party favored
by both of their parents (Jennings and Niemi,
1968). Racial prejudice also follows this general pattern. The racial prejudices of white elementary school children tend to resemble those
of their parents, as do the racial prejudices of
black elementary school children (Horowitz and
Horowitz, 1938; Epstein and Komorita, 1966).

Such similarities are not surprising in view of
the total dependency of the child on his parents. Like a government-controlled communications network in a totalitarian country, the
parents have total control over what information
is given to the young child and thus can ensure,
quite without any conscious intent to do so, that
he hears only the "party line." Since the child
has no attitudes as an infant, he starts his life by
absorbing uncritically whatever his parents say.
Once these parental-based attitudes are acquired, they influence the way in which he
reacts to all subsequent information. Further,
the rewards and punishments received from the
parents are more powerful than any received in
most other social situations. The emotional relationship that develops between parent and
child intensifies the effect of the parents' rewards and punishments.

What is the end result of these powerful
forces? Usually, the parents are thought to pass
along their own attitudes, based on their culture, personal experience, and personality, and
thus to create attitudinal miniatures of themselves. But this is not the inevitable result of
attitudinal socialization. Sometimes, especially
in situations of rapid social change, parents
may adapt what they teach their children to fit
what they think their children will face as adults
(Hyman, 1969). For example, when schools are
being integrated, some prejudiced parents may
express their own opposition but tell their children that they "should make the best of it"
(Valien, 1956, quoted in Hyman, 1969). Assuming that integration is inevitable, the parents
may urge their children not to imitate their
views, but rather to do what will work.

Powerful as the parental impact is, it is clearly limited. As the child grows older, he interacts
with many more people, has a wider variety of
experiences on which to base his attitudes, and

is increasingly impressed by what he hears on television and by what he reads. Predictably, a number of studies have shown that the correspondence between the attitudes of parents and those of their children decreases with age. In terms of political preference, for instance, it has been found that the percentage of children who prefer the same political party as their father declines from 80 percent for elementary school children to 50–60 percent for college students (Hess and Torney, 1967; Goldsen et al., 1960).

The correlations between the attitudes of parents and their college-age children, however, though smaller than those between parents and younger children, are still significant. It is, for example, well documented that the attitudes and values of campus radicals and their parents are similar. Despite the different hair lengths and dress styles, both college activists and their parents have been found to be more liberal than their peers and they have been found to agree in their ethical and religious values. Both value "intellectual and esthetic activities, humanitarian concern, and self-expression" and devalue "personal achievement, conventional morality, and conventional religion" (Flacks, 1967, p. 68; description quoted from Bem, 1970, p. 86). Ironically, when the student activists do criticize their parents, their negative comments are directed at their parents' failure to live up to their own values rather than at the values themselves. In a sense, then, the activists think of themselves as providing purer examples of their parents' own attitudes. Thus apparent differences between parents and college-age children may mask basic similarities (Bem, 1970).

FIGURE 3-7 Peer power.

Peers

At the same time that your parents' influence on you is decreasing, your friends' influence is increasing. (See Figure 3-7.) How, for instance, did you make your decision about whom to vote for in the 1972 presidential election? By talking with your parents? By reading newspapers? By watching television? By talking with your friends? If you are like most college students, your friends' comments and actions provide the strongest single influence on your attitudes, even though the other sources are important.

Repeatedly, the peer group has been shown to be enormously influential in molding a wide variety of attitudes and behaviors among high-school and college students (Coleman, 1961). The way your friends vote influences the way you vote (Rose, 1957). Your friends' aspirations influence yours (Coleman, 1961). And your friends' prejudices also influence yours. Black students, for instance, have noted that the main factor affecting their dating white students or otherwise associating with them was how they thought their black friends would react (Margolis, 1971).

When we analyze the social situation of the college student, this peer dependence becomes very understandable. Facing the highly ego-involving dilemma of evolving an identity amid the complexity of college life, the student is highly motivated to talk with others who are facing similar problems and who therefore sympathize with him. The college situation provides a unique opportunity for this. Dormitory living arrangements and the general informality of the college situation make it easy to get to know other students. Further, the student has time. Before becoming totally absorbed in the demands of a profession or child rearing, he has

time to spend talking with others about his concerns. (See Figure 3-8.)

The process of discussion itself, which sometimes involves confiding highly personal thoughts and concerns, intensifies the student's involvement with his fellow students. As friendships evolve, in part because of the shared confidences, the students take more seriously what their friends say and care more deeply about their friends' approval.

Although this analysis clearly shows why friends would be so powerful in molding the attitudes of college students, it leaves a number of questions unanswered. What is the extent of the influence? Do students differ in their susceptibility to the influence of their peers? How permanent are the effects? After college does the student revert back to his precollege attitudes?

In a classic study Newcomb (1943) studied

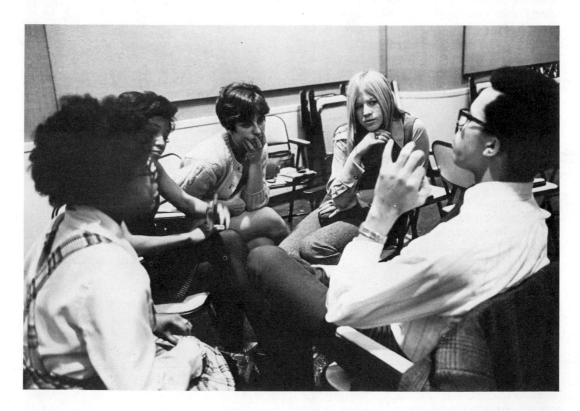

FIGURE 3-8 College rap sessions afford an opportunity for students to go beyond surface acquaintance-ship and communicate fully their day-to-day concerns. Through such meetings, the views of similar others in like surroundings can exert powerful pressures on attitude formation. (Sylvia Plachy)

the evolution of the political attitudes of students attending Bennington College between 1935 and 1939. These girls came from affluent and highly conservative political backgrounds in which praising Franklin Roosevelt would have been as acceptable as praising George Wallace to a group of Black Panthers today. The girls experienced a marked contrast when they arrived at highly liberal Bennington College. Although Bennington had not yet earned a reputation for being liberal, it had a highly liberal faculty, who had ample opportunity to disseminate liberal ideas and values. How the girls resolved this contrast between their conservative family background and the liberal college atmosphere was the subject of Newcomb's study.

The longer the girls were at Bennington, the more politically liberal most of them became. During the presidential election campaign of 1936, for example, over 60 percent of the students' parents favored the Republican candidate, Landon. The percentage of students endorsing Landon decreased steadily, however, from 62 percent among freshmen, to 43 percent among sophomores, to 15 percent among juniors and seniors. Conversely, the percentage of students endorsing more liberal candidates increased. Only 9 percent of the freshmen endorsed either the Socialist or Communist presidential candidates, whereas 30 percent of the juniors and seniors did so. Only 29 percent of the freshmen preferred Roosevelt as compared to 54 percent of the juniors and seniors.

Whether the students became more liberal or remained conservative seemed to depend on the relative strength of their parental and their college relationships. If the student continued to look primarily to her family for information and approval, even though she was physically separated from it, then she remained conservative. (Her family remained her reference group.)

Conservative students were less active in the college community, were less popular with the other students, and sometimes even deliberately insulated themselves from the other students. The following quotation illustrates one girl's strategies and reasons for resisting the liberal college atmosphere:

Family against faculty has been my struggle here. As soon as I felt really secure here I decided not to let the college atmosphere affect me too much. Every time I've tried to rebel against my family I've found how terribly wrong I am, and I've very naturally kept to my parents' attitudes.

[Newcomb, 1943, p. 124.]

In contrast, those students who became more liberal were highly involved in the college community, were highly popular, and were regarded by their peers as "most worthy to represent Bennington College in a national convention." Becoming involved with the members of the college community and looking to them for information and approval seems to have been crucial in the liberalizing of the students.

Not all of the students who became more liberal did so for the same reason. Some simply adopted what was socially acceptable in order to fit into the college group and to avoid criticism. Without any regard for the merits of the issue, they simply said what the group said:

It's very simple, I was so anxious to be accepted that I accepted the political complexion of the community here. I just couldn't stand out against the crowd unless I had made many friends and had strong support.

[Newcomb, 1943, p. 132.]

For others the desire for social acceptance was mixed with the acquisition of new information about the merits of the liberal point of view:

I became liberal at first because of its prestige value; I remain so because the problems around which my liberalism centers are important. What I want now is to be effective in solving the problems.

[Newcomb, 1943, p. 136.]

To see how permanent the liberalization was, Newcomb and his associates reinterviewed the Bennington students twenty-five years later and found that the college-induced liberalism had persisted (1967). In the 1960 presidential election, for example, 30 percent of a group of women who were comparable to the Bennington graduates in economic and social terms preferred Kennedy to Nixon, and 60 percent of the Bennington graduates did so. And the college conservatives hadn't changed much either. For example, 67 percent of the college conservatives were married to men who preferred Nixon to Kennedy.

How had the political attitudes remained so stable over the twenty-five-year period? Newcomb and his associates suggested that when the girls graduated from Bennington, they selected post-college social environments that supported their attitudes. Friends, jobs, husbands—all were chosen in part because they were consistent with the girls' attitudes. Thus the graduates' daily social interactions provided supporting, consistent information— conservative social pressure and information for the conservatives, liberal for the liberals. Many of the decisions concerning friends, jobs, and husbands were made soon after college and were committing once they were made, which may have intensified the continuing influence of Bennington.

Clearly, the original study and the twenty-five-year follow-up show the importance of the reference group in the forming and maintaining of a person's attitudes. One could say that what you believe depends to a large extent on what your reference group believes. Or one could say—on the basis of the same relationship between college involvement and attitudes— that what you believe determines how readily you are accepted by others. Newcomb's basic finding of the relationship between involvement in the college community and liberal political attitudes could, like any correlational finding, be interpreted to show either that being in-

volved created the attitudes or that having the attitudes contributed to a girl's involvement.

Today, prejudice is very unfashionable on American college campuses. The normative and informational pressures from students and faculty would therefore be expected to make college students less prejudiced and the results of several studies support this prediction. Even in the deep South college seniors have been found to be significantly less prejudiced than freshmen (Caffrey, Anderson, and Garrison, 1969).

The mass media

Try to imagine what your world would be like with no television, radio, newspapers, or magazines. After a week of this, you'd be so desperate for information that you'd be reading the print on the back of cereal boxes. The media provide much of our information about what is happening in the world. The evening news brought the Vietnam War into the American living room. Commercials teach us what to want—to smell good, for example, so that others will like us. And the media try, and often succeed, in making us do things. Although many unadvertised brands of aspirin are medically as effective as Bayer and the buffered types, the more expensive, highly advertised brands continue to sell well (Bem, 1970). Clearly, the mass media are a powerful influence on our attitudes. (See Figure 3-9.)

Just how powerful has been debated for some time. Citing the immediacy of the media and their capacity to reach and involve millions simultaneously, many have argued and sometimes shown that the media have almost limitless powers. Perhaps one of the most dramatic examples of the power of the media was the panic aroused in over a million Americans who heard Orson Welles' now famous 1938 science-fiction radio broadcast describing an invasion of the United States by Martians (Cantril, 1940). Further, as everyone knows, people spend a lot of time with the media. Children and adolescents have been found to spend between one-half and one-fourth of all of their waking time in front of a television set (*To Establish Justice*, 1970, p. 159).

Establishing the limits of media power has

FIGURE 3-9 "Look what my little girl learned from watching television."

enormous practical implications. If, for instance, the outcome of political campaigns is controlled by the media, then assuring equal coverage for all candidates becomes vitally important. And if the media can mold viewers, then the sex and violence that permeate the media may make the viewers more aggressive and arouse them sexually.

Although speculations are readily available, there is surprisingly little solid research on the effects of the media. Experimental studies are difficult to perform without destroying the relaxed atmosphere of most television viewing. How would you do an experiment on the effects of televised football on a typical Sunday-afternoon, football-game viewer, beer in hand, without completely altering his usual viewing conditions? Interviews and correlational studies, with their usual limitations, have been used most frequently to measure media effects.

Transmitting Information The media transmit much of our information. Children can learn the alphabet from "Sesame Street," and most people obtain the news from media sources. Approximately 50 percent of the American public first learned of President Kennedy's assassination through radio or television, and one-half hour after the media had announced the assassination, over two-thirds of the public was aware of the event (Hill and Bonjean, 1964; Sheatsley and Feldman, 1964). More complicated information is also effectively transmitted through television. Six months after viewing a CBS-TV program on United States' constitutional law, high-school students scored significantly higher on a test of constitutional law than did a comparable group of student nonviewers (Alper and Leidy, 1970).

The media also impart information more indirectly. First, people may pass information they obtain from the media on to other people. This effect has been termed the "two-step" flow of communication (Katz, 1957). For example, when you decide which car to buy, your decision may be influenced by the advice you receive from someone you respect—an "opinion leader." Your friend's advice may be based on what he has read in various magazines about the relative virtues of automobiles. Thus the media have influenced your decision indirectly by influencing your friend.

In addition to explicit verbal messages, the mass media convey images of people and events which may influence our beliefs. (See Figure 3-10.) For instance, does seeing blacks depicted as middle-class people in the media change the white's image of the typical black person? Clearly, the image of blacks in the media has changed. In 1950, 94 percent of the blacks shown in ads in nationally circulated magazines were laborers or servants; in 1968 only 3 percent of the blacks shown were depicted in this way (Cox, 1970). Whether or not the changed black image has affected basic white beliefs about the blacks is not yet clear, however.

Effective as the media are in transmitting information, there are limits. Attempts to teach complicated intellectual material like calculus through television have not been very successful (Wiebe, 1970). Sometimes, in fact, people even have trouble remembering what they hear on the evening news. When people were telephoned a few hours after the evening news, the average listener could recall only one item correctly out of the nineteen covered in the program (*Time,* October 18, 1971).

Further, since people choose what they want to see, a person can be influenced only to the extent that he opens himself to the media. In selecting television programs, you may choose what you think will be useful to you or what you're interested in. And you may deliberately watch programs that support your point of view and avoid those that don't ("selective exposure"). Republicans may listen only to Republican candidates and avoid Democrats.

Although utility and interest clearly govern one's choice of programs, there is considerable controversy as to whether or not people deliberately seek out information that supports their point of view. Laboratory experiments on selective exposure have had very mixed results. Sometimes people have sought out consistent information, and sometimes they haven't (Sears, 1968). Of course, one could argue that since the subjects are participating in an experiment, they may feel more pressure to be fair and to hear both sides of an argument than they do outside the laboratory, when they are not being observed. It is clear that in everyday life people are more frequently exposed to information that is consistent with their point of view. Whether

"All right," said Carol. "But we don't have a grandmother in our family."

"I don't think I want to play house," said Bobby. "Isn't that a girl's game?"

"I don't see why," said Carol. "After all, there has to be a father. A boy can be a father better than a girl can."

"After we play house for a while," said Bobby, "let's play something else."

"All right," said Nancy and Carol. "We'll play one of your games next."

What do you think the children did when they played house? Have you ever played house? What people do you have in your play family?

Is it sometimes hard to think of things to do? What do you like to play?

34

After a while, Bobby said, "I'm tired of playing house. Let's play office. I'll be the boss, like my Dad is. He goes to his office and gives his secretary letters to write."

"What is a secretary?" Nancy asked.

"I'll show you," said Bobby. "Here is a big box for my desk. I send letters to people and do other work. You are my secretary, Nancy. I tell you what to say in the letters, and you write it on your paper. Then you write the letters on a typewriter and mail them. That is what a secretary does."

"Oh, I see," said Nancy.

"All right," said Bobby. "Please take a letter. Dear Mr. Brown . . ." Bobby stopped. Then he said, "I don't know what to say in the letter."

35

FIGURE 3-10 Two pages from a children's reading book. By conveying traditional images of the sex roles assumed by adult men and women, the illustrations and the text influence the child's belief as to the appropriateness of these roles. (From C. W. Hunnicutt and Jean D. Grambs, *I Know People*, © 1957 by L. W. Singer Company, Inc.—illustrations by Guy Brown Wisen.)

the fact that there are proportionately more Democrats in an audience when a Democrat speaks reflects a deliberate attempt to avoid inconsistent information or other motives (such as commitment to a political party) is not clear.

Even though there are limits to the media's effectiveness in transmitting information, it is clear that they do transmit a great deal of information. What is not clear, however, is the effect of this informational input on attitudes. For instance, do the media actually form attitudes in some cases? Or do they only sustain prevailing ones? Unfortunately, there is very little evidence on these questions. One might speculate that only under certain situations can the media have a significant impact on creating attitudes: (1) when the individual initially has either no attitude at all or a very weakly articu-

lated attitude and (2) when the information builds on another attitude. People do not have deep emotional involvements with their brands of toothpaste; advertising may therefore be an effective device for forming a person's attitude toward a particular brand. The value of personal cleanliness is basic to many middle-class Americans, so advertisements that build on this value may be effective. One can doubt the immediate impact of the media on an attitude as deep-seated as racial prejudice. Even there, however, the media may have a cumulative effect and influence opinion leaders, who, in turn, influence others.

Arousing Emotions and Motives The tearful audience at a sentimental film like *Love Story* shows that the media can arouse emotions. But

136
Social
Psychology and
Modern Life

do they always? What determines whether or not they will? Does the cumulative exposure to certain kinds of materials have long-term emotional-motivational effects? Several well-controlled studies recently done in connection with *The Report of the Commission on Obscenity and Pornography* provide some information about the effects of viewing one kind of arousing material—erotica.

The proportion of people who can be aroused by viewing erotic materials was investigated. Subjects, typically college students, were shown films, and immediately after, their level of sexual arousal was measured by both self-report and physiological measures. Consistently, between 60 and 85 percent of both male and female subjects became sexually aroused when reading or viewing erotica (*The Report of the Commission on Obscenity and Pornography,* 1970).

Clearly, some materials are more arousing than others, and some people are more easily aroused. In general, erotic films have been found to be more arousing than still photographs or textual material. Scenes of usual sexual activity, such as heterosexual petting or intercourse, were more arousing than scenes of more unusual activity. The circumstances under which the material was viewed also influenced the level of arousal. Higher levels of arousal were reported by subjects tested alone and in an informal setting. Further, there were marked individual differences in the reactions to the pornography. Persons who were sexually experienced, young, educated, and religiously inactive reported the highest level of sexual arousal (*The Report of the Commission on Obscenity and Pornography,* 1970). From each of these findings and others made by the commission, there is little doubt that exposure to erotica can arouse emotions, although the cumulative effect of this exposure is not yet clear.

Impelling Us to Action How effective are the media in controlling our actions? Their effectiveness varies from action to action. If an action is relatively uninvolving (like purchasing mouthwash) or something that we already want to do (like engaging in sexual activity), then the media may influence behavior. But if the action is highly involving, if other interpersonal influences counter the media's message, and if

the action is difficult, then the media's impact may be rather limited.

Advertising does seem to influence what we buy. The usual way in which the effectiveness of an advertising campaign is determined is to: (1) measure sales before the campaign, (2) introduce the campaign, and then (3) remeasure sales. Many studies have shown that increased sales do follow advertising campaigns. These increased sales strongly suggest that the campaigns were effective, but do they prove the case? Maybe the competitors raised their prices during the campaign. Until all of the variables that could influence sales are controlled, inferences from sales figures are not conclusive proof of the effectiveness of advertising campaigns. But even though advertisers may not know the precise effects of their advertising, they may feel that they have to advertise to retain their section of the market. And even if a particular campaign can generate only one or two additional percentages of sales, these increments may mean substantial increases in profits.

Exposure to sexually arousing materials does affect the frequency of usual sexual behavior among some persons. Although the majority of persons reported no change at all in the frequency of their sexual activity after viewing erotic materials, some did report a temporary increase. For example, between 14 and 30 percent of the unmarried and sexually experienced males reported increased frequencies of masturbation during the twenty-four-hour period following their viewing pornography. However, none of the subjects reported engaging in sexual behaviors that they had not already engaged in. Exposure to erotica can motivate the individual to do what he usually does more often, but it cannot drive him out, lust-ridden, to ravage the first person he meets (*The Report of the Commission on Obscenity and Pornography,* 1970).

The effect of the media on more complexly determined behaviors, such as voting, is even weaker. If you consider why you voted as you did in the 1972 presidential election, you will see that a wide variety of forces influenced you: your party affiliation; your demographic characteristics, such as age, sex, social class, and religious affiliation; your past history of voting; your perception of the issues; and mainly, what your family and friends were saying and doing—as has been shown in a series of studies (e.g., Berelson, Lazarsfeld, and McPhee, 1954).

Although the results of these studies suggest that the media's role in elections is limited, the media do have several effects. First, as we noted earlier, they are an important source of information and images. What is shown about the issues and candidates may influence voting. After the first Nixon-Kennedy debate in 1960, Kennedy's image improved markedly, and Nixon's did not change (Carter, 1962). Even if Kennedy's improved image only resulted in one or two additional percentage points of votes, the televised debate could have been a highly significant event in an election as close as the 1960 one. Further, since opinion leaders are likely to be exposed to the media in their area of expertise, people who rely on such leaders when forming their voting preferences may be indirectly molded by the media.

Still another possible way in which the media could influence voting is through the nationally televised and broadcast announcements of early election returns. When computer-based "predictions" are broadcast while people are still voting in a presidential election, there is no significant influence on voter turnout or switching (Fuchs, 1966). However, in the more changeable, less emotionally involving situation of a nonpartisan referendum on one issue, early election returns have been found to influence voting patterns (Mann, Rosenthal, and Abeles, 1971).

Thus the media do influence voting. The extent of their contribution is not really known, but in events as chancey as national elections, every percentage point is valuable. The faith of the professional politicians in the power of the media is testified to by the expenditures of time, effort, and money in marketing candidates and by the debates over the need for equal television exposure for all candidates.

School and church

School   A number of studies have shown that the more education one has, the less prejudiced he is. For example, in a study assessing the existence of anti-Semitism, 16 percent of those with a college education were anti-Semitic, as compared to 66 percent of those with only a grade-school education (Selznick and Steinberg, 1969). Of course, people who have attended college differ from those who have not in a number of other ways besides the extent of their formal education. Even when these other variables are controlled, however, the correlation between educational attainment and lack of prejudice still obtains. In one study comparing the prejudice levels of college freshmen and seniors, where social class and intellectual level could be expected to be similar, significantly less prejudice was found among the seniors (Caffrey, Anderson, and Garrison, 1969).

These studies suggest that something in the educational process itself reduces prejudice. There is relatively little solid research on how this phenomenon works, but thinking about how college has influenced your own racial attitudes may provide some leads. Clearly, education involves the acquisition of specific information. Also, you are exposed to a variety of ways to analyze and solve problems, and these alternative approaches teach you about the danger of overgeneralizing and oversimplification. Further, you are exposed to faculty members and other students who also have attitudes and set the tone of what is socially acceptable, as we saw in the case of the faculty and students at Bennington College. Since we have already discussed the enormous influence of the college reference group in modifying attitudes, we shall focus here on the intellectual effects of information provided in the formal education setting.

One possible way in which attending school could influence your racial attitudes would be by providing specific information. Unfortunately, few schools teach much about the contributions of minority groups. What did you learn in high school about the contribution of blacks and other minorities to American history? Did you know that a black man founded the city of Chicago? That many black soldiers fought in the Revolutionary War? That black men played a very active part in settling the American West? (Katz, 1971). If you are like most white and black students, you were taught a white-only version of American history, which overlooked the many contributions made by minority groups.

Although the coverage given to minority groups in social studies courses has improved in recent years, a complete picture is still not given in many schools (*Negro History Bulletin*, 1970).

Since little is taught about minority groups, the decline in prejudice associated with increasing educational attainment cannot be attributed simply to the amassing of specific information combating prejudice. The more likely explanation is that attending college exposes one to a way of thinking that combats the oversimplifications of prejudice, and places one in a social environment that resoundingly rejects the existence of prejudice. The available evidence does not yet allow us to separate the relative contributions made by these two aspects of the college situation.

There is evidence to support the hypothesis that attending college reduces simplistic and overgeneralized thinking. If the process of higher education increases the individual's ability to think constructively, it should make him more critical, more likely to reject oversimplifications, and more likely to make subtle distinctions than someone who is not exposed to college training. As the student's intellectual sophistication increases because of his academic work, he may develop a more complex thinking process and reject all oversimplifications—including those of racial stereotypes (Selznick and Steinberg, 1969).

Some preliminary evidence is consistent with the hypothesis that attending college increases the complexity of one's cognitive style. In one study it was found that 26 percent of the elementary-school graduates believed in astrology compared to 5 percent of the college graduates. Differences in the complexity of the beliefs of grade-school graduates and college graduates were also obtained on other items (Selznick and Steinberg, 1969).

Church　A number of studies have shown that involvement with the church is also related to prejudice. What form do you think the relationship would take? Would you expect that persons who attend church would be more or less prejudiced than those who do not? Since all of the major religions emphasize the brotherhood of man and the importance of love, one might expect that those who attend church would be

less prejudiced than those who do not. Not so. Many studies have shown that those who attend church are more prejudiced than those who do not (as summarized in Allport and Ross, 1967).

In view of the commonly emphasized religious values, this finding seems paradoxical. Why do you think that churchgoers are more prejudiced? From your observations of people who attend church, do you think that all churchgoers act on the same motives? Some may use religion to meet their need for social acceptance, security, and status. For others, who are truly involved with religion, their faith and its practice are the most important things in their lives. These two types of churchgoers might be expected to act very differently in a number of areas, including racial prejudice (Allport and Ross, 1967).

There is some evidence to show that the degree of personal religious commitment is related to prejudice. A person who is completely involved with his religion would probably attend his church or synagogue very frequently—more often than the conventional one day per week. A number of studies have shown that those who attend their church or synagogue once or twice a month are more prejudiced than those who do not attend at all, and those who attend very frequently (eleven or more times per month) are the least prejudiced (Struening, 1963). Further, persons who said that religion was something basic and important in their lives were less apt to be prejudiced than those who answered that they saw religion in terms of what it could do for them (Allport and Ross, 1967).

Summary: what you've been told has some relation to what you think

Many, if not most, social attitudes are determined by the particular social influences the individual has been exposed to. Although the media may influence attitudes to some extent, nothing is more effective than face-to-face contact.

All of the elements of culture—the shared beliefs, values, and expectations about the appropriate ways to behave in certain situations—influence our attitudes, including our racial prejudices. If the culture provides racist information as well as pressures to conform to these teachings, the individual will tend to accept prejudice simply as a means of functioning effectively in a racist society.

That parent-child interactions have an enormous impact on a child's attitudes and values is a truism of psychology. Many studies have shown that the attitudes of children tend to resemble those of their parents. As the child grows older, however, the correspondence between the attitudes of parents and those of their children decreases.

Among high-school and college students, the peer group has been shown repeatedly to be enormously influential in molding a wide variety of attitudes. In the Bennington study we saw one classic demonstration of the power of peers. Students who were highly involved in a liberal college community assimilated the college's liberal norms and retained them over a twenty-five-year period.

The mass media influence attitudes, too—primarily by transmitting information. Effective as the media are in this function, however, there are limits. It is clear that in everyday life people are more frequently exposed to information that is consistent with their point of view. Thus it is not clear whether the media actually form attitudes or merely sustain existing ones. Further, it has been shown that exposure to the media—at least to erotica—can temporarily arouse emotions. The effectiveness of the media in controlling actions varies from action to action. If the action is relatively uninvolving or something that the individual already wants to do, the media may influence behavior. But if the action is highly involving or if other interpersonal influences counter the media's message, the media's impact may be rather limited.

Both school and church influence attitudes. The more educated one is, the less likely he is to be prejudiced. Since few schools teach much about the contributions of minority groups, the liberalizing effects of education are probably explained by the exposure in college to a more complex way of thinking and to a social environment that resoundingly rejects prejudice. Involvement with the church is also related to prejudice. Although persons who attend their church or synagogue once or twice a month are more likely to be prejudiced than those who do not attend at all, those who attend

very frequently are the least likely to be prejudiced.

Emotions and Attitude Formation

We have emphasized the rational, problem-solving function of attitudes—how attitudes meet the individual's need to know what exists, to cope effectively with the environment, and to get along with other people. But not all attitudes are focused on a realistic adjustment to the environment. Some seem self-destructive. For instance, had Hitler been able to control his anti-Semitism during the closing days of World War II and not persisted in using badly needed German soldiers and war matériel to continue exterminating the Jews, he might have been able to delay the Allied victory. The extreme prejudice shown by Southern lynch mobs, which mutilated the corpses of their black victims, was also aimed at goals other than a realistic adjustment to the environment. The main function of these attitudes seems to be the expression of the individual's emotional reactions—either those aroused momentarily by some frustration or those related permanently to the individual's personality. (See Figure 3-11.)

Of course, the dichotomy between emotionally and rationally based attitudes is an oversimplification. It might be more accurate to think of the relationship as a continuum with these two alternatives, emotional and rational, as the extremes. Thus many, if not most, attitudes would serve varying proportions of both functions. Consider, for instance, the workingman's generally negative attitude toward people on welfare. Is this attitude founded on his own, personal experience with welfare recipients and what his enlightened friends and the media have told him? Or is it based on frustration and anger because others seem to collect nearly as much as he does without having to work for it?

Distinguishing between attitudes that are rationally based and those that are more emotional in origin does permit us to understand the essential differences between the ways in which the two types are acquired. And since not all attitudes serve the same functions, the procedures most effective in changing one type might not be as effective with the other type.

Frustration-aggression

Picture a day in which just everything goes wrong. Your car won't start; a friend forgets an appointment and leaves you waiting for an hour; you lose the heel off your shoe; and you find out that you are flunking a course required in your major. To say the least, you'll be feeling frustrated, angry, and probably aggressive (Dollard et al., 1939). Ghetto frustrations clearly contributed to the inner city riots of the 60s and 70s. As we will discuss further in Chapter 6, how you express your anger and to whom you express it depends on your assessment of what is safe. Sometimes frustrations are difficult to blame on anyone in particular. At other times you may be afraid to express any hostility to the person responsible. In those situations you are likely to displace your anger to other people or things—people who are vulnerable, who won't fight back, who are available, and toward whom you may feel "justified" in acting aggressively (Harding, Proshansky, Kutner, and Chein, 1969).

Minority group members have the dubious distinction of meeting many of these criteria. A number of correlational studies have shown that people who are frustrated are more prejudiced. For example, people who are dissatisfied with their own economic status were found to be more prejudiced than people who are contented (Campbell, 1947). A frustration-

FIGURE 3-11 A lynching in the South: An extreme example of racial prejudice. (Danny Lyon/Magnum)

displacement analysis of this finding would be that people who are economically dissatisfied are frustrated and cannot express it directly to the vague power structure responsible for their plight. Therefore, they displace it onto a safe, vulnerable, socially acceptable source—a member of a minority group.

Direct experimental evidence in support of the frustration-displaced hostility hypothesis has been obtained. The prejudice shown by a group of eighteen- to twenty-year-old camp counselors toward Mexicans and Japanese increased significantly after the counselors had been frustrated (Miller and Bugelski, 1948). Other experiments showed that highly anti-Semitic college students were more likely to act aggressively with either a neutral bystander or an obviously Jewish person after they had been frustrated (Berkowitz, 1959; Weatherley, 1961).

One generalization from these studies might be that people do indeed react more aggressively toward minority group members after frustration. But is this always the case? If you are white and you have been frustrated, have you displaced your aggression to minority group members? Say you were working on a project with a black partner, who was trying to be helpful. Despite his and your best efforts, though, the project didn't turn out well. Do you think you would take your frustrations out on your black partner? Whether you would or not would depend on the extent of your frustration, your own prejudices, your guilts about your prejudices, your assessment of the social acceptability of your expressing your prejudices, and your interpretation of whether your black partner had worked effectively and had really tried. In face-to-face social interactions a minority member is more than a one-dimensional figure to be rated on a scale.

In just such a situation white college students did not displace their aggression to a black student. In fact, white students working with a black partner reacted more favorably toward their black partner when they were told that they had failed than when they were told that they had succeeded (Burnstein and McRae, 1962). Thus the frustration did not result in displaced hostility. On the contrary, failure made the whites' hearts grow fonder.

So far we have been talking about prejudice as a "safe" aggressive reaction to frustration in general. However, frustration may also be caused by competition with members of the minority group. Competition for economic security, status, and sexual advantages has been thought to play a major role in prejudice (Dollard, 1938). In a person's attempt to obtain status or a good job, he may conveniently accept highly negative attitudes toward the members of minority groups that are competing with him. His negative stereotypes then justify his ruthless exploitation, and he can pursue his own goals without feeling guilty.

A number of correlational studies are consistent with this hypothesis. For instance, it has been found repeatedly that antiblack prejudice is much more prevalent among lower-class whites, who feel that they may have to compete with blacks for available jobs, than among middle-class whites (Selznick and Steinberg, 1969).

Direct experimental confirmation of the relationship between competition and prejudice has been provided by a recent study in which one white and one black subject worked together as a team to solve a series of problems. In one condition the white subjects were made to think that they and their black partners each gave the same number of correct answers and so contributed equally to the success of the team. In another condition the white subjects were made to believe that they had given the majority of the correct answers. Then the white subjects in both conditions were asked to indicate whether or not they would like to continue working with the black subject and to rate his problem-solving ability. You may guess what happened. Even though the objective performance of the black partner had been better in the equal contribution condition than in the unequal contribution condition, the white subjects in the equal condition rated their black partners more negatively than did the white subjects in the unequal contribution condition (Katz and Cohen, 1962).

Competition does not seem to make the heart grow fonder—especially if it is with a member of a minority group and he seems to be doing as well as you. Further, highly prejudiced subjects may have found the black's success particularly difficult to bear, since they may have viewed it as showing a weakness in their own skills. Nobody loves a successful competitor, but to have someone you think is inferior do as well as you may be particularly galling.

Unconscious emotions and attitudes

Freud was the first to advance the theory that attitudes can be an expression of an individual's own unconscious desires. Thus a negative attitude about homosexuality may express the individual's repressed conflict about homosexuality. Or a negative attitude toward authority in general might be an expression of unconscious resentment of one's parents. The bigot obsessed with black sexuality may be viewed as someone who is unable to admit his own sexual impulses and therefore projects them onto a minority group.

The Freudian approach to prejudice is best illustrated by a classic study on the anti-Semitic personality (Adorno, Frenkel-Brunswik, Levinson, and Sanford, 1950). Performed at the University of California at Berkeley (and hence generally referred to as the "Berkeley study"), this research has been the model for countless studies to determine the make-up of the authoritarian personality.

The first part of the Berkeley study involved a survey of over 2,000 white, non-Jewish Californians who belonged to organizations. Three multiple-choice questionnaires were distributed. The first questionnaire was designed to measure anti-Semitism (and came to be known as the "A-S" scale). Assuming that anti-Semitism consisted of hostile, stereotyped notions of Jews, the investigators devised fifty-two items, each characterizing Jews as offensive, threatening, deserving of discrimination, seclusive, or intrusive. Agreement with any item gave the subject a high A-S score for that item. One sample item: "One trouble with Jewish businessmen is that they stick together and connive, so that a Gentile doesn't have a fair chance in competition."

The second questionnaire measured a general dislike of all people who were different from the white middle-class norm (and was called the "ethnocentrism" or "E" scale). One sample item gives an idea of what was being measured: "Certain religious sects who refuse to salute the flag should be forced to such a patriotic action or else be abolished." As the investigators predicted, scores on the A-S scale were highly correlated (.80) with those on the E scale. People who didn't like Jews didn't discriminate; they didn't like anybody or anything that was different from themselves.

Having established these correlations, the researchers next sought to determine how the personalities of prejudiced people differed from those of people who were not prejudiced. Because anti-Semitism had been so strongly related to fascism in Hitler's Germany, they hypothesized that people who were anti-Semitic would be high in their potentiality for fascism. Accordingly, they devised what they called the "implicit antidemocratic trends or potentiality for fascism (F) scale."

But, specifically, what would a potential fascist be like? On the basis of Freudian theory and their previous survey and clinical work, the investigators hypothesized that the potential fascist would have the following personality pattern. First, he would adhere rigidly to all conventional values—especially those involving authority and traditional morality. Thus he would be expected to agree with the statement: "Obedience and respect for authority are the most important virtues children should learn." Second, he would believe that any deviation from the conventional way should be strongly punished. He would agree that "homosexuals are nothing but degenerates and ought to be severely punished."

Third, he would be preoccupied with power and toughness in human relations. For instance, he would agree that "no weakness or difficulty can hold us back if we have enough will power." Coupled with this preoccupation with power would be a destructive, cynical attitude about human beings: "Human nature being what it is, there will always be war and conflict."

Fourth, he would project his unconscious, emotional impulses outward into the world and resist serious introspection. He would agree that "when a person has a problem or worry, it is best for him not to think about it, but to keep busy with more cheerful things" (Adorno et al., 1950, pp. 255–257).

Highly conventional, obsessed with power, subservient to authority, and unanalytical. Do you know of any people who fit that description besides Archie of "All in the Family"? It seems that the characteristics do fit together. And a subsequent analysis of the internal consistency of the F test confirmed the researchers' hypothesis. The items are highly interrelated (Eysenck, 1954). Further, the F test scores were highly related with the E and A-S scales (.75). Thus people who were anti-Semitic were also ethnocentric and possessed a number of personality characteristics generally associated with the authoritarian personality.

In the second, clinical part of the Berkeley study, eighty subjects, half of whom had obtained very high scores on the E scale and half of whom had obtained very low E scores, were given projective tests and an intensive, open-ended, nonstructured interview. There were no set questions. Interviewers were given a set of suggested probes, which they could use or not as they found appropriate. All interviewers knew what the questionnaire scores were for the people they were interviewing.

From these interviews and the other clinical data, the researchers concluded that the prejudiced person differed significantly in personality, cognitive style, and early family history from the nonprejudiced person. The picture of the authoritarian personality was consistent with that presented by the F test. The subjects with authoritarian personalities rejected any possible negative comments about themselves or their parents and engaged in what the investigators termed "self-glorification." Neither they nor their parents ever experienced the all-too-human vices of fear, aggression, or laziness. They were, in short, too good to be true. When they did have self-critical thoughts, they did not recognize the element of criticism, preferring to treat such thoughts as "ego-alien."

What about the early childhood of the authoritarians? A psychotherapeutic nightmare. Their parents were concerned about status, were cold and unloving, severely punished deviations from what they considered acceptable behaviors, and were not reluctant to use physical punishment to enforce their particular point of view. Thus the sick authoritarian has so many painful, unresolved fears about his own adequacy, is so frustrated by the severe discipline, and at the same time has so many conflicts over expressing his own anger directly toward his parents that he projects his own feared inadequacies onto minority groups and consciously accepts what his parents tell him is right.

He pays a psychological price for this projection. As is the case with any neurotic symptom, his prejudiced thinking becomes very rigid and closed off from experience. Because his prejudices allow him to exist psychologically, he cannot confront the possibility that they might not be true, and so his thinking processes become very rigid and closed to evidence. He sees things in absolute terms and cannot tolerate ambiguity. Good people are all good; bad people are all bad. His ideas are not consistent, but he is not aware of it. Thus, for instance, an anti-Semitic individual believes that Jews are, at the same time, clannish and intrusive.

Thus the Berkeley findings may be divided into two major parts: the objective aspects of a prejudiced personality and the interpretation of why these patterns obtain. The interview and questionnaire data showed that persons who were highly anti-Semitic were also generally prejudiced toward other "non-American" groups, possessed highly distinctive personality traits, came from harshly disciplined home environments, and had a rigid cognitive style.

What conditions fostered the formation of certain psychological and social attitudes that contributed to prejudice? To the Berkeley investigators the answer was the pathological home environment, which produced high levels of repressed hostility and in turn led to the other parts of the authoritarian syndrome—the prejudice, the personality, and the cognitive style. As we shall see, critics of the Berkeley study have suggested other interpretations of the interrelationships found by the Berkeley investigators.

Everything about the Berkeley study was massive. It was one of the most ambitious studies ever attempted in social psychology. Literally hundreds of studies have been done using the F test, which is now a classic in social psychology. And although the rate of publication in this area has slowed down somewhat, work with the F test continues.

In the original Berkeley study, the unconscious conflicts derived mainly from the individual's unpleasant early childhood experiences. But other conditions might also be expected to elicit unconscious conflicts. During a period of great unemployment and economic uncertainty, such as the Depression of the 1930s, people might also be expected to feel highly threatened and to express their unconscious emotions in the same patterns of authoritarian behavior found in the Berkeley study. Confirmation for this hypothesis was obtained in a recent study in which it was found that the frequency of a number of authoritarian behaviors was higher in the 1930s than in the 1920s, a period of economic prosperity. For instance, magazines were rated for the degree to which they emphasized power and toughness, and it was found that magazines emphasizing these characteristics sold more widely during the Depression than they did in the 1920s—even though people had less money in the 1930s. And when figures for the 1930s and 1920s were compared, it was found that there were significantly higher levels of financial support for police forces, and prison sentences for sexual crimes were longer during the Depression (Sales, 1972).

The volume of criticism of the Berkeley study has also been massive. Four years after *The Authoritarian Personality* was published, an entire book devoted to its criticism was published (Christie and Jahoda, 1954). Before we summarize some of the criticisms of the questionnaire portion of the study, you might try to do your own critical evaluation of the method followed. Do you see any flaws in the Berkeley investigators' procedures? Were their sampling procedures unbiased? Can the wording of the questionnaire items be criticized?

As you will recall, the subjects included in the Berkeley survey sample all belonged to organizations and were white, non-Jewish, California residents. Since this sample clearly is not a random sample of the general population of the United States, one can question whether the findings would generalize to other portions of the American population. Several other studies, which have used different samples, have shown similar correlations between prejudice and the other attitudes and personality variables found in the original Berkeley study. For instance, Jews who obtained high scores on the F scale were also highly anti-Semitic and ethnocentric, and showed some of the same rigidities of thought (Radke-Yarrow and Lande, 1953).

The questionnaire items in the Berkeley study were worded so that agreement with an item always gave the individual a high F score on that item. Thus a high score on the F scale could mean either that the subject really had a high tendency toward fascism *or* that he had a strong tendency to agree with questionnaire items. To separate the effects of the wording of the questionnaire items from what was being measured, several researchers have set up studies in which the consistent relationship between agreement and high scores was removed (e.g., Couch and Keniston, 1960). The general finding of these studies is that although a tendency to agree with the items did contribute somewhat to the original F scale scores, it was not a major factor (Brown, 1965). Thus subsequent work has indicated that the major criticisms of the questionnaire portion of the Berkeley study were not serious enough to cause us to question the basic validity of the survey results.

The criticisms of the interview portion of the Berkeley study are more serious. You will recall that the interviewers knew each individual's questionnaire scores *before* interviewing him. In an interview that is flexible and involves interpretation, such preknowledge creates extremely serious problems in potential bias. Further, the people who coded the interviews were well acquainted with the expected interrelationships between personality, cognitive style, and childhood experiences, so that their coding decisions may have been influenced by the overall content of the interview. In addition to these two serious sources of bias, the clinical portion of the study omitted all subjects who scored in the mid ranges. Thus the clinical portion of the study does not seem quite as solid as the survey portion.

However, although not all of the interview findings have been supported by subsequent work, many have been. For instance, similar relationships between a high F rating and support for the attitudes of those in power have been reported (Izzett, 1971), as well as similar relationships between high F scores and the personality traits reported by the Berkeley group (e.g., Smith and Rosen, 1958). Harsh and discipline-oriented early childhood backgrounds have been found to be related to high F scores (e.g., Martin and Westie, 1959), and so have cognitive rigidity and intolerance for ambiguity (Steiner and Johnson, 1963).

Another serious criticism is of the interpretation of the Berkeley findings. This interpretation holds that the authoritarian syndrome is caused by repressed hostility, created by overdemanding and unloving parents, which expresses itself in prejudiced attitudes, a particular personality, and a rigid cognitive style. Other interpretations of the same pattern of relationships are possible. Considering all of the findings discussed so far, how would you account for the interrelationships?

One possible interpretation is that the authoritarians came from authoritarian homes, and as children they simply imitated their authoritarian parents. Repressed hostility and projection would not be necessary to explain the fact that a child reared by parents who seemed power-oriented in their interpersonal relationships would also be power-oriented in his interpersonal relationships.

Another possible interpretation is that low education and low socioeconomic status (SES) were responsible for the pattern of relationships obtained in the original study. Persons who have high F scores have also been found to have less education and to be of a lower SES than persons who obtain low F scores (e.g., Hyman and Sheatsley, 1954). Not having been exposed to the abstractions of higher education and having accepted the norms of their class, uneducated persons may simply be reflecting their class characteristics rather than a personality dimension when they answer the F scale questionnaire.

But finding that there is a higher proportion of authoritarians among those with little education and those who are in the lower socioeconomic class does not eliminate the Freudian interpretation. Perhaps there is simply a higher percentage of disturbed persons among these people. Because of the difficulties of their existence, the authoritarian syndrome may occur more frequently in these groups. Moreover, subsequent work has shown that even when education is controlled, many of the correlations between F scores and other attitudes and personality attributes remain high (Roberts and Rokeach, 1956). Thus although the original empirical findings of the Berkeley study remain, the question of accounting for these interrelationships is still very much an open one.

The Berkeley group saw prejudiced people as emotionally disturbed; "you're not prejudiced, you're sick" would be their approach to understanding prejudice. In contrast, a number of others see prejudice as primarily reflecting conformity to social norms. "The members of your reference group are prejudiced, and you have absorbed their attitude." Which explanation do you think accounts for most prejudices? How would you go about testing whether pathology or conformity accounts for most prejudices? One way might be to select people from two areas where the amount of prejudice differs, such as the North and the South in terms of antiblack prejudice, and then compare their scores on the F scale. If authoritarian personality trends account for prejudice, one would expect stronger indications of authoritarianism in an area in which prejudice is stronger.

Several such comparisons of the F scores of Southerners and Northerners have been done. Unfortunately, the results have not been consistent. In one classic study Southerners scored no higher on the F scale than did Northerners. Further, as the conformity hypothesis would predict, in the South, where prejudice is the accepted norm, people who were found to be more conforming were more prejudiced (Pettigrew, 1959). These findings have been widely interpreted as suggesting that social conformity may be responsible for the bulk of typical racial prejudices.

In contrast, other studies have shown that the F scores are higher in the South than in the North. For example, 52 percent of a Southern college sample indicated that the most important thing to teach children was obedience to their parents, but only 31 percent of a Northeastern sample of college students agreed (Williams, 1966). Further work, involving more representative and larger samples, is required to settle the issue of whether or not there are regional differences in F scores. Further, even when higher F scores are found in the South, they may be interpreted as reflecting different cultural patterns, in much the same way that many have interpreted the relationship between F scores and SES status.

Summary

The main function of some attitudes seems to be an expression of the individual's emotional reactions—either those aroused momentarily by some frustration or those related permanently to the individual's personality. Frustration—caused either directly by competition with minority group members or indirectly by other sources—can lead to aggression. Whether or not aggression is expressed depends on the individual's attitudes and his perception of the situation.

Another explanation of prejudice is that it expresses a disturbed personality and protects the individual against his own unconscious desires. The results of a classic study are consistent with this Freudian explanation. It was found that people who were anti-Semitic were also ethnocentric and possessed several common personality traits—they were highly conventional, obsessed with power, subservient to power, and unanalytical.

Although the original study had some methodological flaws, the original pattern of relationships has been obtained in a number of replications. However, the question of accounting for the pattern of relationships is still very much an open one. The Berkeley interpretation was that the authoritarian syndrome is caused by repressed hostility, created by overdemanding and unloving parents, which expresses itself in prejudice, a particular personality, and a rigid cognitive style. However, other interpretations of the same pattern of relationships are possible. Since the authoritarians come from homes described as authoritarian, they may have simply imitated their parents. Low education and low socioeconomic status may also be responsible for the pattern of relationships.

Changing Racial Prejudice

Changing racial prejudice is easier said than done. Many people learn and relearn prejudices from all of their important sources of information. Opportunities for direct experience with blacks is limited for many white Americans because of segregated housing and schools. Consequently, the social sources of information become particularly effective in transmitting prejudices. The white child of prejudiced parents is exposed to their prejudices first; his own embryonic prejudices are formed before he is

out of the nursery. His friends, largely children from other white middle-class, prejudiced homes, do not contradict the lessons of prejudice taught by his parents. Until quite recently, the media have contributed to the problem either by completely omitting all mention of blacks or by depicting them in an unflattering, demeaning way. And education in the public schools hasn't been much better. Usually, the black man has not been mentioned at all or mentioned only in connection with the Civil War.

Once absorbed, racial prejudices become self-perpetuating. Whites gain because of prejudice. What they initially believed simply because it was taught to them becomes something they have a personal stake in. Believing that blacks are inferior is a nice justification for having informal racial quotas in one's union or keeping one's neighborhood all white. Prejudices also provide escape valves for temporarily frustrated or emotionally disturbed people.

Because of the intensity, consistency, and pervasiveness of racial attitudes and the economic and political costs of changing them, it may be premature to suggest immediate applications of social psychology to this problem. Clearly, if the answers were simple, the problem would have been solved a long time ago. However, even though some of the following suggestions may be speculative, scientific speculation seems preferable to the alternative of haphazard, commonsense solutions or no solutions at all. Time is short. The American racial truce is an uneasy one. Although the race riots of the early 1970s have not been as extensive or as widely publicized as those of the 1960s, a slight shift of events could bring the United States into open racial conflict once again. (See Box 5, page 148.)

There are two main problems for black Americans: white racial prejudice and the deficit in their social and economic attainments resulting from over 300 years of unequal treatment. Even if all white prejudice disappeared tomorrow, blacks and whites would not have an equal share in American prosperity. (See Tables 3 and 4, page 149.) The legacy of inequality in employment, education, housing, income, and health would remain. (See Box 6, page 150.) But since our focus in this chapter has been on the acquisition of attitudes, our focus here must

BOX 5

In the 1960s, with the ghettos in many American cities in flames, documenting the existence of racial tension and violence in the United States was about as necessary as proving the human need for oxygen. But in the mid-1970s white Americans may be feeling that American racial tension has decreased.

You may be surprised to learn that during the first eight months of 1971, 176 major and minor civil disorders occurred in the United States. Unless one of them occurred in a community in which you lived, you may not have read about them. With the exception of major upheavals, such as that which occurred in Albuquerque, New Mexico, in June 1971, civil disorders are not given extensive coverage outside the communities in which they occur, because they have become so commonplace. Thus it could be argued that what has decreased since the 1960s is the coverage the mass media are giving to civil disorders rather than the disorders themselves.

Other signs of racial tension persist into the 1970s. In the United States Navy racial rioting and disorders have occurred so frequently on board ships that a congressional investigation of the matter has resulted (Holles, 1972). Furthermore, a New York City Commission on Human Rights has warned about an ominous trend toward the violent resistance of integration in some all-white neighborhoods. In some communities in which there is blockbusting, several cases of violence have occurred. During an eighteen-month period in 1972 and 1971, there were eleven cases reported in which minority-owned homes had been set afire or vandalized (Shipler, 1972).

Some have suggested that the major arena for racial clashes in the 1970s may be prison uprisings rather than massive civil disorders. As John Naisbett, president of the Urban Research Corporation, noted: "Look at the list of demands made by the prisoners at Attica. Better education, narcotics treatment, legal assistance, better recreation, more black workers, the search for dignity. These are the demands of the ghetto" (quoted in Herbers, 1971, p. 34).

There is continuing tension between police and blacks, and there is some evidence that the number of police being killed or wounded by ambush is actually increasing. Between June 1970 and July 1971, 1,081 policemen were killed or wounded in violent clashes; unprovoked ambush attacks are now the leading cause of police deaths. The extent to which these acts of terrorism reflect racial tension as opposed to other causes is not yet clear. It is obvious, however, that racial tension is, at the very least, a contributing factor.

Further, although the 1970s have seen a cooling of tension on American college campuses, the incidence of racial clashes in high schools has been increasing. Many of these have involved violence. The list of incidents or examples of racial tension could go on and on. The headlines in the evening news show that racial tension, many times violent, continues in many aspects of American society: in the cities, in the school, in the armed forces, in prisons. Try carefully reading a newspaper for a week and checking for stories of racial tension. You may be surprised at the number of incidents you find.

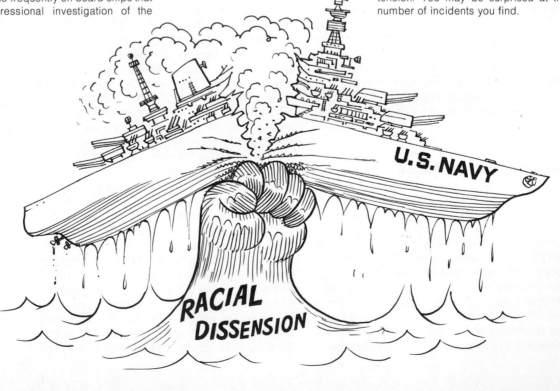

Table 3. Blacks Have Scored Striking Advances in Education But Still Have Not Attained Equality

Median Years of Schooling Among Adults, Age 25–29	1960	1970	Percent Who Are College Graduates Among Adults, Age 25–34	1960	1970
Blacks	10.8	12.2		4.3%	6.1%
Whites	12.3	12.6		11.7%	16.6%

Percent with 4 Years of High School or More Among Adult Males, Age 25–29	1960	1970	Percent Who Are Illiterate Among People Age 14 and Older	1959	1969
Blacks	36%	54%		7.5%	3.6%
Whites	63%	79%		1.6%	0.7%

Source: U.S. News & World Report, August 23, 1971, p. 31.

Table 4. In Terms of Dollars, the Gap Between Nonwhite and White Incomes Widened from 1960 to 1970. The Difference Grew from $2,602 in 1960 to $3,720 in 1970.

	Median Family Income		
	Nonwhite	White	Nonwhite Income as a Percentage of White Income
1960	$3,233	$5,835	55%
1970	$6,516	$10,236	64%

Source: U.S. News & World Report, August 23, 1971, p. 30.

be on changing white racial prejudice and not on the removal of these underlying deficits.

How can racial prejudice be reduced? There are a number of approaches, many of them just beginning to be used effectively—such as introducing black studies into elementary-school curricula, improving the black image in the mass media, legislating against prejudiced behavior, and treating black-white confrontation through psychotherapy. Space limitations prohibit a thorough discussion of all of these techniques, however, and we will concentrate on one of the most effective and widely recognized methods—interracial contact. In the following chapter, we will be discussing general techniques for changing any attitude, and some of these techniques could also be applied to changing racial prejudice.

Most black-white prejudices result from a lack of contact, thereby suggesting that if an opportunity can be provided for blacks and whites to get to know one another, these prejudices will disappear. Integrate the schools, build interracial housing projects, have blacks and whites work together, and prejudice will go away.

But will it? Does interracial contact always lead to liking? Clearly not. The extensive contact between the black ghetto resident and the white policeman has hardly led to mutual affection. Whether or not contact results in decreased prejudice depends on what happens in the particular contact, the racial attitudes held by the significant people in the person's life, and the individual's own racial attitudes and personality. For example, if a white student were in an integrated high school in which there were a number of racial disturbances, his parents and friends were highly prejudiced, and he himself disliked Negroes violently before he ever met any personally, he probably would not become less prejudiced because of interracial contact.

What aspects of an integrated setting are most crucially related to decreasing white prejudice? To get some leads about this question, we can contrast some studies in which interracial contact decreased prejudice with those in which it did not.

One of the most dramatic reductions in racial prejudice took place in the United States Army in 1945 when black platoons were assigned to

What is it like to be a black American? One way to answer this question would be to cite the familiar litany of statistics that document the catastrophic problems of black Americans. But general statistics refer to discrimination that is so vast the human mind may not be able to comprehend the magnitude of the problem.

To make the problem more concrete, we could consider one important aspect of contemporary black life in some detail—the question of whether or not job discrimination exists. Fantasize for a moment that there are two people who are identical except that one is black and one is white. In the 1970s would the white person have employment advantages over the black person?

How could we go about answering this question? Read newspaper accounts? Ask black people whether or not they have experienced discrimination? Look at the 1970 United States Census figures to see how black employment figures compare to white? Whatever the source, the consistent picture that emerges is that having a black skin is still a handicap: Jobs aren't as available; when blacks do find work, they are relegated to the less prestigious and lower-paying jobs; even when they do obtain more skilled jobs, they

are frequently paid less *(The Social and Economic Status of Negroes in the United States, 1970)*.

But do the census figures prove discrimination? Are people of different races with equal backgrounds and qualifications being treated differently? The comparative figures from the United States Census do not answer this question. All they reflect is the difference in the economic indicators for the typical white and black at a given point in time. But, as is common knowledge, blacks have suffered 300 years of oppression and systematic discrimination, and have not had equal opportunity and training. The employment rates and incomes do not separate the differences resulting from differences in preparation from those resulting from racial discrimination.

To show discrimination today, we would have to establish a different reaction to two people who are identical in everything but skin color. A comparison of the incomes of black and white persons in equivalent jobs or with equivalent academic training might give us a clearer picture. Several such comparisons have been done, and most tend to confirm that even when all other variables are equal, the average black receives less pay than his white coun-

terpart for equal work. Black college graduates earn $3,000 less than white college graduates *(Newsweek,* November 20, 1967). Black skilled workers earn less than white skilled workers. Black plumbers earn 60 percent of the wages paid to white plumbers (Ashenfelter, 1970).

Even when the average salary of blacks and whites is comparable, discrimination against blacks can take other forms. Equal salaries have been found to exist among black and white psychologists. The black psychologists surveyed, however, reported more intangible forms of discrimination, such as a feeling of isolation from the mainstream of American psychology, a feeling of having to guard against rejection by limiting job choices to the predominantly black colleges in the South (which have traditionally been limited in terms of facilities and research funds), and the personal cost of being apprehensive about the possibility of racial slight. All of these limit the opportunities for professional development (Wispé, Awkward, Hoffman, Ash, Hicks, and Porter, 1969).

Look around. What is the price of simply having a black skin in your community?

previously all-white combat infantry companies. After the white soldiers had an opportunity to fight side by side with black soldiers, their racial prejudices decreased significantly. For example, 64 percent of the men in the integrated companies thought that it was a good policy to assign blacks to combat roles, as compared to only 18 percent of those enlisted in all-white divisions (Star, Williams, and Stouffer, 1965).

Another example in which interracial contact decreased prejudice is provided by a study in which a white community voluntarily desegregated its schools before the Supreme Court's

1954 ruling. In this situation emphasis was placed on interracial cooperation. The children began the first grade in an interracial setting. When the racial attitudes of a group of fifth graders in this school setting were compared with those of children attending all-white schools in a comparable community, the children in the voluntarily integrated schools were much less prejudiced (Singer, 1964).

In contrast, in some other integrated situations, prejudice has not been reduced. For example, one study showed that after six months of attending an integrated high school, some white students had become more prejudiced, and others had become less. Whether or not the students' prejudices were reduced was closely correlated with how prejudiced their parents and friends were (Campbell, 1958). In another study the racial attitudes of eighth, tenth, and twelfth graders were measured before and after five months of integration. Although the younger children became less prejudiced, the attitudes of the twelfth graders remained unchanged (Whitmore, 1957).

After considering these situations, do you have any ideas about what aspects of the integration experience are crucial in reducing prejudice?

Why was the army integration effective? In that situation the men were relying on each other, and they had to cooperate closely in order to survive. Once the men began to act cooperatively, they may have begun to feel cooperative. As we saw earlier in this chapter, we may infer our own attitudes from what we see ourselves doing. Further, the front-line combat conditions involved a close, intimate association in which everyone was in the same miserable situation. Everyone had the same status. The army had equalized pay, privileges, and other working conditions. Neither black nor white could avoid intensive interaction. Finally, the black volunteers in the combat unit were excellent soldiers, which helped to contradict their racial stereotype. The army study may be interpreted as showing the importance of four variables in the interracial contact situation: degree of cooperation, relative status of the participants, intimacy and intensiveness of the interactions, and the character of the minority group members.

Several of the other examples suggest the importance of another variable—social norms. For instance, the reduced prejudice found among fifth graders in the voluntarily desegregated schools could have been a reflection of the community norm. Since the town residents had decided voluntarily to desegregate their schools, we might assume that the majority of residents were opposed to prejudice. By emphasizing interracial cooperation, the schools reflected the prevailing town sentiment. Further, since most of the parents and teachers were pro-integration, it would seem reasonable for most of the children to be also.

The characteristics of the people involved in interracial contact may also make a difference. The more highly prejudiced the individual is, the less effect interracial contact may have on modifying his prejudices—no matter how objectively pleasant the contact is. Age has been found to be related to the development of prejudice. Although children as young as five have racial preferences, they are not as articulated and intense as those held by older children and adults. That the prejudices of younger children are decreased more by interracial contact than are those of older children has been shown in several studies (e.g., Whitmore, 1957).

To move beyond these relatively untested hypotheses about the prejudice-reducing aspects of interracial contact, we need both a theory of the processes involved and some controlled experiments to test scientifically which variables are most significant. Cook (1969) has made a major contribution in this area. He believes that the effectiveness of integration can be directly related to specific variables in the situation, the type of person involved, and the things that that person does.

In one highly realistic laboratory study, the subjects, female college students from the border South, never knew they were in an experiment; they all thought they were working in a series of part-time jobs (Cook, 1969). Initially, all of the subjects were recruited by a fictitious organization called the Educational Testing Institute to take a number of tests on abilities and attitudes, including some items on racial prejudice. Forty-six of the girls who scored as highly antiblack on the initial test were used in the actual experiment. Half of these girls were telephoned by a faculty member at St. George College and asked if they would play a management game, which involved their operating an imaginary railroad system. In reality, this was the experimental manipulation of interracial contact. For twenty days the girls in the experimental group spent two hours a day with two experimental confederates, one white, the other black.

Five variables from Cook's interracial contact theory were simultaneously manipulated during the interracial sessions: equality of status, need for cooperation, dissimilarity of the black confederate from the social stereotype, intimacy of interaction, and antiprejudice social norms.

Since both the experimental confederate and the experimental subject were working as equals in the same job, they had equal status. If the group was to succeed at the management game, a high level of cooperation was needed. The black experimental confederate was extremely personable, ambitious, and able. An intimate, close association was provided in the face-to-face contacts and coffee-break conversation. Antiprejudice social norms were manipulated by having the white experimental confederate express, in the black's absence, strong opposition to segregation and prejudice.

Several months after the twenty-three experimental subjects completed the game, they and their twenty-three control counterparts were again contacted by the Educational Testing Institute and asked to take more tests. In this way, the racial attitudes of the experimental subjects after they had experienced interracial contact were compared with the attitudes of girls whose initial tests showed they were equally antiblack and who had not been in a program of interracial contact.

How many of the experimental subjects do you think changed their attitudes? All? Most? Half? After forty hours of intensive contact under theoretically ideal conditions, 35 percent of the subjects in the experimental condition showed a lower level of prejudice, and 9 percent of the subjects in the untreated control group showed a similar decrease. Thus the net prejudice-reduction rate was 26 percent (35 percent less the 9 percent reduction, which apparently would have occurred anyway).

Some leads as to the personality differences between the changers and the nonchangers were also found. Most of the girls who became less prejudiced also had a more positive attitude toward people in general, were more responsive to social influence, and acknowl-edged a discrepancy between what they were and what they wished to be.

Whether you are impressed or discouraged by these findings may depend on what you expected. All that effort and such a small percentage of change is one reaction. Or, conversely, you may be impressed at the strength of the manipulation. If we consider the thousands of hours of "prejudice lessons" that each of these girls had lived through, a net prejudice-reduction rate of 26 percent after forty hours of interracial contact may be a hopeful finding.

Cook's experimental procedures provide a convincing demonstration that aspects of the interracial contact situation can be manipulated. In this preliminary study five aspects were varied simultaneously, but in further work these and other variables could be manipulated separately. For example, the amount of suffering an individual must go through in order to stay in a group may influence his attraction to the members of that group, black and white, and thus suffering could be an important variable.

Once a tested model for prejudice reduction through racial interaction has been developed, its social contribution could be enormous. Southern schools are desegregating, and there are signs that the Northern suburban communities may be required to integrate their schools with those of the central cities. If social psychology provides a model of effective conditions for integration, integration conducted along the lines of this model might radically decrease prejudice. Although local political considerations might prevent people from following a model if it were available, they surely can't follow what isn't available. Developing and testing a model of interracial contact could be social psychology's greatest contribution so far to social progress.

SUMMARY

Since no other attitude has had the long-lasting, nationally destructive impact of black-white racial prejudice, this chapter has focused primarily on the acquisition of racial attitudes. However, the comments made about racial attitudes apply to other attitudes as well.

1. Components of Attitudes One way of thinking about attitudes is to conceive of them as an overall, internalized, core disposition that guides thoughts, feelings, and actions toward specific others and objects. However, attitudes may be more usefully analyzed in terms of their three components: (1) cognitive, (2) emotional, and (3) behavioral. An attitude becomes a prejudice when these components become fixed and highly immune to new information and experiences.

The cognitive component of an attitude includes an individual's beliefs about the attitudinal object. People have beliefs for two reasons: Beliefs summarize previous experiences, and they express the individual's emotions and personality. Beliefs vary in a number of ways—in the extent to which they are basic to other beliefs, in the amount and type of evidence on which they are based, and in their openness to change when inconsistent information is presented. A prime characteristic of one type of belief—sometimes called a stereotype—is its resistance to change when inconsistent information is presented. The degree to which people are motivated to maintain consistency between their various beliefs is not yet clear.

A second important component of all attitudes is the emotional reaction to the attitudinal object. Emotional reactions may be influenced by beliefs, by experience, or by other emotions that the individual is not consciously aware of. A third component of an attitude is behavior— how the person acts in relation to a particular object or group. In some cases beliefs and emotional reactions determine behavior, but in many other cases the demands of the situation may determine what the individual does to a far greater extent than the other components of his attitudes. Conversely, behavior can also influence beliefs and emotions. Unless our beliefs are very clearly articulated or our emotions intense, our observation of our own behavior is a powerful determinant of beliefs and emotions.

2. Attitude Formation: An Overview Attitudes are based on our own personal experience, the influence of other people, and our emotional reactions. Of these three sources, other people seem to be the most important for most of our attitudes.

3. Personal Experience and Attitude Formation A complete absence of any experience with a particular object tends to lead to negative reactions. What we have experienced with a particular object influences our attitude. The forming of an impression is a complicated process involving an interaction between the person forming the impression, the situation in which the impression is formed, and the objective attributes of the person or thing being judged. Experience also influences the emotional and behavioral components of attitudes.

4. Other People and Attitude Formation A wide variety of social sources influences our attitudes: culture, parents, peers, mass media, and the school and church. To a great extent, we are the products of the social sources we interact with, the most effective source being face-to-face contact.

Culture is an important determinant of attitudes. Without our even being aware that we are doing so, we automatically accept many of the beliefs of our culture. If these are racist, we are unknowingly brainwashed into racism.

Of all the social interactions, the parent-child interaction is the strongest single influence. The attitudes of parents and children tend to resemble one another all through life, even though the correspondence decreases with age.

The influence of peers is especially strong among high-school and college students. As Newcomb's classic Bennington study showed, when parents and peers clash, peers generally win.

Although the mass media are not as powerful as face-to-face interactions, they sometimes influence beliefs and behavior, as the people who listened to Orson Welles' 1938 radio broadcast could testify. A number of studies have shown that the media can transmit information, arouse emotions and motives, and sometimes make people do things that are rather uninvolving or that they already wanted to do. However, the media's impact on more important and complexly determined behavior—like voting—is limited.

School and church also influence attitudes. Those who have received a higher education are less prejudiced than those who have not—probably because of the combination of antiprejudice peer pressures and the increased intellectual sophistication resulting from academic work. Church membership is also related to prejudice. Those who attend church conventionally are more prejudiced than those who are not involved with the church, but those who are truly committed to their religious values are the least prejudiced.

5. Emotions and Attitude Formation Not all attitudes serve the primary function of organizing the environment and allowing the individual to adapt to what exists. Some have as their main function the expression of the individual's emotional reactions—either those momentarily aroused by some frustration or those more permanently related to the individual's personality.

Prejudices may sometimes be an outlet for frustration. A number of studies have shown that persons who are frustrated in general are more prejudiced than those who are not and that intergroup competition may lead to hostility. However, there are limits to these relationships: Anticipated punishment, the intensity of the frustration, and the demands of the situation, may determine whether or not frustration leads to aggression.

In some highly prejudiced persons antiblack attitudes may be an expression of their disturbed personality and a protection against their own unconscious motives. The classic Berkeley study showed that persons who were highly anti-Semitic were generally prejudiced toward "non-American" groups, possessed highly distinctive personality traits, came from harshly disciplined home environments, and had a rigid cognitive style. Although the study has been criticized, most of the basic findings have been replicated. What is not yet clear is *why* the syndrome exists.

6. Changing Racial Prejudice Since the lessons of prejudice are so thoroughly taught, prejudice is extremely difficult to modify. Of the different approaches, one seems to offer the best chance for reducing prejudice: interracial contact. Interracial contact does not always lead to a reduction in prejudice, however. Prejudice can be reduced in an interracial situation when there is equality of black-white status, a need for cooperation, a dissimilarity between the black members of the group and their negative social stereotype, intimacy of interaction, and antiprejudice social norms.

DISCUSSION QUESTIONS

1. How would you measure the behavioral component of prejudice?

2. Have you ever had the experience of not knowing what you think until you have heard what you've said? How would you explain this phenomenon in terms of attitude formation theory?

3. Which of the three determinants of attitudes—personal experience, social sources, and emotions—do you think is the most powerful determinant of most attitudes?

4. Why do you think the educational process reduces prejudice?

5. Have there been any incidents of racial tension in your community within the last year? If so, describe them.

6. Research has shown that inconsistency between beliefs does not always motivate the individual to move toward consistency. Under what conditions do you think people would not be motivated toward consistency?

7. When do you think behavior is likely to be consistent with beliefs and emotions?

8. Why is face-to-face contact generally more effective than the mass media in forming a person's attitude? Can you think of any situations in which the media might be more powerful?

9. Have you observed or been directly involved in any institutional racism? If you have, give an example.

10. Do you think the college history texts you have read give an accurate description of the black's role in American history?

11. The Bennington study showed the impact of the college reference group on the students' forming of attitudes. In what other settings do you think the reference group has an equally decisive role?

12. We saw some evidence that competition between whites and blacks increases the white's racial prejudice. Yet we also saw that the expression of aggression depends on the sanctions for overt aggression. Some people have suggested black capitalism—infusing large sums of money into the black community so blacks can become more involved in business—as a solution to racial prejudice. What effects would you expect a highly successful program of black capitalism to have on white prejudices?

13. Under what circumstances do you feel stereotypes may contain a kernel of truth?

14. On reflection, can you detect any racist elements in your culture?

15. Five aspects of interracial contact have been shown to be significant in reducing white racial prejudice: equality of black-white status, need for cooperation between the blacks and whites, dissimilarity of the black confederate from the social stereotypes, intimacy of interaction, and antiprejudice social norms. Can you think of any other aspects of interracial contact that would be related to the prejudice-reducing aspects of that contact for whites? For blacks?

ATTITUDE CHANGE

BOXES

Every year thousands of Americans die in automobile accidents. More people were killed on the highway in 1968 (54,862) than during the entire United States' involvement in Vietnam from 1961 to

1971 (44,475) (*The New York Times Encyclopedic Almanac, 1972*, pp. 305, 637). Although faulty highway design and poor safety design in automobiles contribute to the high rate of traffic fatalities, so do certain attitudes about driving, such as the belief that drinking "makes you a sharper driver" or that good driving is fast driving and you should never be passed.

Suppose you had the job of persuading all of the freshmen at your college to change their attitudes about fast driving. How would you proceed? If they enjoy driving fast and have done so safely on many occasions, if their friends also drive fast and have related the pleasure in controlling a fast-moving machine, and if driving fast relaxes them when they are tense, why should they change their attitude? It is supported by their personal experience and by what others have told them and may also serve as an emotional outlet.

If you had total power over them, it would be easy to change their behavior. If you rode in the back seat of a student's car and told him that he'd be shot if he drove over sixty miles per hour, he would probably comply with your demand. But his compliance wouldn't necessarily mean that his attitudes about driving had changed.

When you do not have complete power over another person, the problem of persuasion is much more difficult. Which techniques work depends on what functions the particular attitude serves. If driving fast and recklessly is an outlet for aggressive urges, then reducing the individual's level of aggression—perhaps through psychotherapy—might be the most effective way to modify his attitudes. As we shall see, psychotherapy is one approach to modifying emotionally based attitudes.

If the attitude's primary function is to provide a way for the person to interact realistically with

his world and it is based on his own experience or what others have told him, the only way to get him to change his attitude is to introduce some inconsistency in his present attitudes and values. If a student had a "close call" while he was speeding, he might change his beliefs about the safety of speeding and thereafter drive more slowly. Or if students were shown statistics documenting the relationship between speeding and accidents, they might be persuaded. To change attitudes based on personal experience and social sources, the basic tactic is to introduce information that is inconsistent with the individual's present attitudes and then make it difficult for the individual to dismiss the material. A classic use of this tactic is wartime propaganda. (See Figure 4-1.)

It is very difficult, however, to make a person accept inconsistent information. For instance, if you tell cigarette smokers about the dangers of smoking, they may dismiss your information by rationalizing that driving a car is more dangerous than smoking or that smokers who become ill would have become so anyway—even if they hadn't smoked (Canon and Mathews, 1972). Someone who enjoys driving fast might rationalize his behavior by thinking that he is such a good driver the statistics do not apply to him. People resist persuasion. In order to change someone's attitudes, you have to introduce the inconsistency in a forceful way so that he cannot dismiss it easily.

How do you do that? To get some leads, you might consider how people try to persuade others in everyday life. Advertisers, for example, may try to get you to buy their products by having celebrities give testimonials—Brand X cosmetics are just great according to Zsa Zsa. They may try to frighten you into buying. If you don't gargle twice a day with Listerine, you'll offend everyone, and no one will go out with you. Or they may try to lower your resistance to

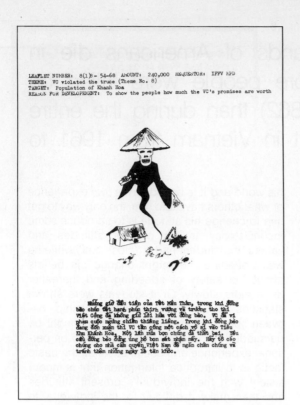

LEAFLET NUMBER: 8(1)B - 54-68   AMOUNT: 240,000   REQUESTOR: IFFV RPD
THEME: VC violated the truce (Theme No. 8)
TARGET: Population of Khanh Hoa
REASON FOR DEVELOPEMENT: To show the people how much the VC's promises are worth

FIGURE 4-1 A sample of the propaganda used by U.S. Intelligence in the Vietnamese war. The message, addressed to South Vietnamese villagers who were suspected of sympathizing with the Viet Cong, tells how the Viet Cong have violated a truce agreement and destroyed villages. (U.S. Army Photograph)

their persuasive messages through humor. (For a sample of advertising appeals directed to safe driving practices, see Figure 4-2.)

You might also get some ideas from history, literature, religion, law, and current events. Hitler (1933), for example, felt that simple, emotional appeals were much more effective than complicated, rational arguments. Machiavelli (1532, translated 1906) urged that persuasion be disguised. Guilt-arousing and fear-arousing appeals have long been used by religious evangelists, who first frighten people with the specter of the fires of hell and then tell them they can be saved by committing themselves to Christ. The lawyer Louis Nizer (1961) has noted the importance of looking each juror in the eye. And Charles Manson, convicted in 1971 for masterminding a mass murder, was reported to have "hypnotic eyes."

Or perhaps you can get some ideas from the material on attitude formation covered in the previous chapter. There we saw that most attitudes are based on social information. If most are formed on the basis of what others tell us, then it would seem that the most effective way to change attitudes would be to have other people provide information inconsistent with the attitude in question. Perhaps the best way to make your subjects drive more carefully is to have other people provide information inconsistent with the attitudes you are trying to change.

If, however, you decide to use information from other people as the basis for your safety program, you still have a number of questions facing you. Which source would introduce the most conflict with the attitudes you are trying to change? A highly respected and expert governmental agency, such as the National Safety Council? Ralph Nader? The president of General Motors? Clearly, the person who provides the information makes a difference.

If you presented the information yourself, what would you say and how would you go about saying it? Would more conflict be induced if you talked to the students individually than if you showed them all a film? Would you use a picture showing the bloody details of some accidents or use a more low-keyed approach? Would you try to refute arguments that defective highway design and faulty cars are more responsible for accidents than poor driving or would you just concentrate on your recommendations?

And what about the audience? How actively would you try to involve it? If the members of the audience played the role of someone who has just been involved in an accident, would this introduce more conflict than having them watch a film? Would you try to get the people in the audience to commit themselves to driving more safely immediately after your program?

Finally, how would you measure the influence of your program after you had presented it? By questionnaire? By interview? By observing the way your subjects drove? How would you determine how permanent the effects were?

Your decisions involve four areas: (1) the *source* of your communication ("*who* says it"), (2) the *message* and *how* it is delivered ("*what* is said"), (3) the audience ("to *whom* it is said"),

The drunk driver.
He helps to eliminate the overcrowding in our classrooms.

Drunk drivers kill and injure our children.

Last year, almost 6,000 children under 15 years old were killed in traffic accidents. Countless thousands were seriously injured.

No one can be sure how many drunken drivers were responsible. But even one death or one injury is one too many.

What can you do?

Remember, it's not the drink that kills. It's the drunk, the problem drinker, the abusive drinker, the drunk driver.

Remember, drunk drivers may be sick, and we've got to give them help.

But first we've got to get them off the road. For their sake and yours.

To find out what you can do, write the National Safety Council, Dept. A, 425 North Michigan Avenue, Chicago, Illinois, 60611.

Scream Bloody Murder.

Advertising contributed for the public good.

A. _____

FIGURE 4-2 Try to determine the type of appeal that is being used in each of these advertisements. Compare your answers with those of other students. How effective do you think each ad is in stimulating attitude change? (Courtesy, The Advertising Council)

and (4) the *effects* of the communication (Lasswell, 1948).

The Source of the Communication

If the president of General Motors contends that failures in automotive safety have little to do with traffic fatalities, is this as persuasive as Ralph Nader's saying the same thing? Social psychologists have found repeatedly that the source of a communication influences its acceptance. (See Figure 4-3.) But which aspects of the source determine its effectiveness? According to one psychologist, the source's credibility, attractiveness, and power are the crucial determinants, and each of these determinants leads to attitude change through different psychological processes. When you are trying to

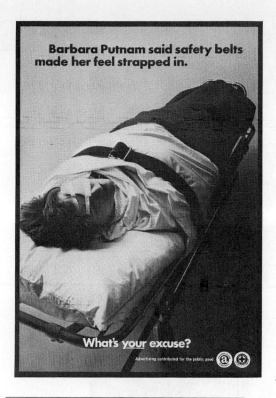

B. _____

C. _____

Here's Johnny...
plaid and fancy in
an out-going
Spring suit.

All the right colors have
banded together to make this
the all-right suit of the
season.

It's a 100% texturized woven
polyester that looks just like
seersucker. It's got all the
right detailing, all the right
coloring. And the two-way
stretch that's built into the
fabric makes it very, very
comfortable.

As always, there's a shirt and
tie especially created to
complement this suit.

See the Johnny Carson
Wardrobe at fine stores
throughout the United
States and Canada.

JOHNNY CARSON
APPAREL, INC.
77 GOODELL STREET
BUFFALO, NEW YORK 14240

FIGURE 4-3 Advertisers believe that testimonials from celebrities are effective in selling products. (Courtesy, Hart, Schaffner & Marx)

find the truth, you are persuaded by people who know what they are talking about and whom you believe are not lying (*high-credibility* sources), and you *internalize* their messages—you privately accept what they say, since you think their information is correct. However, if your prime motivation is to establish a personal relationship with the communicator, the most influential characteristic may be his *attractiveness.* You adopt his position to *identify* with him—to be like him—and you accept his position only as long as he advocates it or you wish to maintain the relationship. And if someone has *power* over you, you may comply publicly with his persuasion to avoid punishment with no private attitude change (Kelman, 1961).

Credibility *In general, high-credibility sources are more effective in changing attitudes than low-credibility sources.*

"Prestige," "image," "charisma"—what is termed "credibility" in social psychology goes by a number of different terms outside the laboratory. Credibility is generally thought to consist of two main components: expertness (how much the source knows) and trustworthiness (how honest he is about it).

Expertness Experiments have shown repeatedly that expert sources are more persuasive than nonexperts. In one study students who had evaluated nine stanzas of poetry negatively were given communications from someone who had praised the poetry. These communications were from either T. S. Eliot or Agnes Stearns, "a student at Mississippi State Teachers College." The students' attitudes were then measured again, and not too surprisingly, their reactions to the poetry were influenced more by the expert, T. S. Eliot, than by the nonexpert, Agnes Stearns (Aronson, Turner, and Carlsmith, 1963). If a message is attributed to an expert, people tend to believe it.

But is this true of any message? If T. S. Eliot makes a pronouncement about chicken feed, will his influence still be greater than that of a less well known person? Advertisers clearly think so when they have experts in one area give testimonials about areas in which they have no expertise—as when beauty expert Zsa Zsa gives testimonials about car transmission repair shops. And there are some limited research results that indirectly support their belief. Whether, in these situations, the expertise of the expert is generalized to other areas in which he is not an expert, or whether the persuasiveness of his message is due to other characteristics, such as personal attractiveness or power, is not yet clear.

Who is considered an expert depends on the topic and the audience. Whom would you consider experts on rock music or the future of professional football? You may have ideas about who is expert in these areas, but you may be surprised to learn that not everyone shares your opinions. Whenever one manipulates source credibility, he should check the reactions of those in the audience to make sure they share his opinion about a source's credibility level.

In laboratory experiments source credibility is usually manipulated directly by giving the subjects an introduction to the "communicator." But in real life credibility is conveyed much more subtly. When you talk with someone, how do you judge his expertness? By what he says? By the way he is dressed? By his age? By the way others react to him? By his gestures? Laboratory work on the cues that communicate credibility is just beginning (e.g., Sharp and McClung, 1966; Mehrabian and Williams, 1969).

However expertness is communicated, studies have shown repeatedly that expert sources increase attitude change. Why should the expert's arguments be more effective? Perhaps people pay closer attention to what an expert says and so learn his arguments better (Hovland, Janis, and Kelley, 1953). Although this seems like a reasonable hypothesis, research results have not supported it. Repeatedly, laboratory studies have shown that the members of an audience retain the arguments made by low-credibility sources just as well as those presented by high-credibility sources (e.g., Hovland and Weiss, 1951). Whether or not audiences outside the laboratory pay as close attention to low-credibility sources is an open question.

Credibility seems to act directly on the individual's acceptance of the message. If, for instance, you are not paying much attention, the easiest way to arrive at your attitude may be to use the credibility of the source. Rather than work through all of the arguments, you may simply react to the communicator. If he is an expert, you accept what he says as true. Or the communicator's credibility may influence the way you interpret his message. The arguments may seem more reasoned and more objective when they come from T. S. Eliot (Asch, 1952).

However, the effect of the communicator's credibility is limited. When highly involved students read communications from high- and low-credibility sources, the source did not influence their judgments; yet when students were not involved, it did (Johnson and Scileppi, 1969). Further, if the material to be judged is highly personal—such as the subjects' own personality traits—communicator credibility does not influence the subjects' attitudes (Johnson and Steiner, 1968). Or if the communication is completely implausible, communicator effects may disappear. Still, in most situations

communicator expertness has been found to be a highly significant variable in attitude change.

Trustworthiness What characteristics do you associate with trustworthiness in friends? In teachers? In political figures? As certain politicians have discovered to their dismay, when they make statements that are later contradicted by objective evidence or when they change their views to coincide with what is popular, a "credibility gap" may develop, and people may cease to pay attention to what they say. If you think someone has something to gain, you may disregard everything he says. Although common sense and the bulk of the experimental results support the hypothesis that untrustworthy communicators are not as effective as trustworthy ones, the results have not been completely consistent.

In a study by Hovland and Mandell (1952), trustworthiness was manipulated by presenting an attitude-changing communication from two equally expert communicators, one of whom appeared to have something to gain from the change. In the low-trustworthiness condition, a speech advocating the devaluation of American currency was attributed to the head of a large importing firm, which had a lot to gain from devaluation. In the high-trustworthiness condition, the same speech was attributed to a professor of economics, who had nothing to gain or lose from devaluation. The commonsense prediction would be that the communication from the disinterested, neutral professor would cause more attitude change. But this did not happen. Although the students rated the professor's speech as more fair and honest than the importer's speech, the degree of attitude change did not differ significantly. In this experiment the topic was highly complex, and the students may have felt that the professor's knowledge was somewhat academic, and that the importer, even though he did have an ax to grind, knew more about the practicalities of the issue.

It is very difficult to manipulate trustworthiness in an experimental situation in which all communicators are clearly trying to persuade. Rather than indicate the communicators' trustworthiness by stating their backgrounds, some experimenters have tried more indirect approaches. Suppose, for instance, that someone argues against his own best interests. If a convicted criminal argued in favor of a stronger police force, you would have difficulty seeing what he had to gain, so you might be persuaded by his arguments. This predicted reaction was obtained (Walster, Aronson, and Abrahams, 1966).

Or if a communicator did not know his comments were being overheard, he would have little reason to lie. A number of studies have shown that when subjects are led to believe they are overhearing a conversation, they show more attitude change (e.g., Walster and Festinger, 1962).

> **Attraction** *In general, liked sources are more persuasive.*

A nasty salesman isn't going to sell much; the more likable he is, the more persuasive he'll be. This seems almost too obvious to be stated. As a lot of research has shown, people like those who are similar to themselves or whom they think are similar to themselves, so that whenever communicators appear to be similar to the audience, or seem to be likable in some other way, they should be more persuasive.

Why should someone who is likable be more persuasive? One answer is that when you like someone, you wish to make yourself more like him by adopting his attitudes (Kelman, 1961). Another answer would be that people who are likable are persuasive because they convey more information. For instance, you might be more persuaded if a friend of yours told you about the dangers of LSD and used his personal experiences as the basis for his argument than if an expert delivered exactly the same message. You might feel that your friend knows what he is talking about, since he has experienced LSD himself, is using values similar to yours in making his judgments, and is giving you the straight information with no ax to grind. Similarity and likableness, then, may be seen as having indirect effects on the communicator's credibility (Hovland, Janis, and Kelley, 1953).

Similarity Advertisers frequently assume that similarity gives someone magically persuasive

powers. The sweaty guy in his undershirt with the Imperial margarine crown on his head is a testimony to the advertiser's faith in the appeal of someone with whom the audience can identify. The results of a number of experiments support this faith. For example, in one field study a paint salesman who established his similarity to the customer by claiming to have just bought the same amount of paint that the customer was going to buy was much more persuasive than an "expert salesman" who had recently purchased twenty times as much paint (Brock, 1965).

Communicators who are dissimilar from their audience may even create a negative persuasion effect. Indirect support of this hypothesis was obtained in a recent field experiment in which students opposed to the United States' involvement in Southeast Asia delivered persuasive talks in the homes of a number of residents in their college town. Instead of persuading the residents, however, the talks had the opposite effect—they boomeranged. After the talks, the citizens were less convinced that the United States should reduce its involvement. Apparently, by appearing to the residents as radicals and by invading the privacy of their homes, the students created a negative persuasion effect (Nesbitt, 1972).

Clearly similarity sells, but what aspects of similarity are important? Consider your interactions with others. What kinds of similarity in others makes them influential? Similarity of beliefs? Similar background? Racial similarity? Similarity of their situation? Similar personality? Not all kinds of similarity are equally important in making someone influential. When the similarities in the communicator are relevant to the issue at hand, they make the communicator more effective, but irrelevant similarities have no influence (Berscheid, 1966). In considering the attributes of a maximally effective similar other, you might find some of the work from social-comparison theory on the determinants of similarity helpful.

Are there any limits to the effects of similarity? Would increasing similarity between the communicator and his audience inevitably increase his effectiveness? Clearly not. In the previous section we saw that T. S. Eliot, a dissimilar and expert source, was more effective than Agnes Stearns, a similar but inexpert source. A number of laboratory studies have shown that experts are more persuasive than similar communicators.

Why was the expert, T. S. Eliot, more persuasive when the topic was poetry, and the inexpert but similar paint salesman more persuasive in pushing paint? Perhaps both T. S. Eliot and the inexpert salesman were seen as the best source of information. "T. S. Eliot knows about poetry and is not tempted to lie; the man who has purchased the same amount of paint also knows about his subject and appears to have no reason to lie."

Further, if the communicator has an attribute that is similar to the target person but is undesirable, the similarity would not be expected to make him more persuasive. For instance, if the communicator has a personality similar to the target person's and both are former residents of a mental hospital, this similarity would not make the communicator more effective (Novack and Lerner, 1968).

Likableness It seems clear that a communicator who is liked would be more effective than one the audience is hostile to or feels neutral about and that a neutral communicator would fare better than one who is disliked. Although the results are not completely consistent, this relationship has generally been obtained in laboratory experiments. In one field experiment the relative effectiveness of an insulting and a neutral communicator was determined. Not only was the insulting communicator significantly less effective than the neutral one in persuading the audience to his point of view, but after the members of the audience heard the insulting communicator, they moved in the opposite direction from what he was advocating (Abelson and Miller, 1967).

Why would the nasty communicator be less effective? The unpleasant dimension of his character may convey information. "If this stupid, nasty boob supports this position, there must be something wrong with it." Conversely, when the communicator is likable, a member of the audience might think, "If this highly pleasant person—who is clearly similar to me—thinks this, his reasons must be good and his conclusions sound."

Although most studies have supported the commonsense prediction that communicators who are liked are more effective, not all have. When could someone who is nasty, snobbish, demanding, and tactless be more effective than someone who is nice? Suppose you're doing something you consider unpleasant—like eating fried grasshoppers. You might have difficulty justifying your agreement to do this for someone who is nasty, so the only way you can make any sense out of your action (or reduce your dissonance) is to convince yourself that you really don't mind doing it, or to increase your liking for the grasshoppers. And this is what happened in a recent experiment. Army reservists who complied with a nasty experimenter's request to eat fried grasshoppers ended up liking the grasshoppers more than subjects who ate the grasshoppers for the nice communicator (Zimbardo, Weisenberg, Firestone, and Levy, 1965). Perhaps a negative communicator is only more persuasive than a positive one when you are doing something unpleasant.

> **Power** *In general, powerful sources are more persuasive than sources without power.*

A man who doesn't "agree" when a gun is pointed at his head would be rare indeed. Usually, increasing the power of a communicator increases the incidence of the target person's compliance. In real life power buys media exposure, legitimacy, the capability to reward, police support, and so on. In face-to-face interactions a communicator who cares whether or not you agree, who can see what you are doing, and who can punish you if you do not agree would probably be most persuasive (McGuire, 1969a). If the communicator does not care whether or not you agree, he will not punish you if you disagree. Nor can he punish you if he is unable to see your actions.

The communicator's increased ability to elicit compliance when he can reward you for agreeing with him or punish you for disagreeing with him has received experimental support (e.g., Raven and French, 1958). In Chapter 2 we saw how the power of a prison setting could mold the individuals' behaviors and beliefs to fit what was expected of them. When power is total, the individual is likely to comply. Sometimes when the individual complies, he internalizes the attitude the communicator is trying to change. Thus in the prison study we saw that some "prisoners" not only acted the role of prisoners but also seemed to feel and believe the way prisoners would.

But there are limits to power. Even when power is total, the individual may comply publicly but not change his beliefs and emotions. If the communicator's power is unlimited and obvious, the subject can use it to explain his compliance while his private attitude remains unchanged. This hypothesis has been supported. Under some conditions mild threats have been found to be more effective than severe ones in changing the person's attitudes (Aronson, 1966b). The dissonance created by a person's complying with a communicator for a minimal reward can best be reduced by his changing an attitude. Further, the threat of power may increase the individual's reactance and make him more resistant. Something you have looked forward to doing may become unattractive if you feel you are being made to do it (Brehm and Wicklund, 1970). Thus the relationship between power and attitude change is not a simple one.

Summary

If you had to select either a credible, a liked, or a powerful communicator to present your traffic safety program, which would you choose? A highly credible source, such as a highway safety expert? Your audience would probably think he knew his facts and was honest. Or would you select someone who was similar to and liked by your audience, such as a highly popular student? He would be similar, would share the audience's values, and might be seen as less preachy. Or would you pick someone with considerable power, such as the chief of the local police, who might say that he makes a lot of arrests for unsafe driving? He would certainly have the ability to enforce his own attitudes, but would students simply be irritated by the implied threats and drive even more recklessly? The relative strength of each of these communicator variables is still uncertain; but it is reasonably clear that, within the limits

discussed in this section, all have a positive effect on inducing attitude change.

The Communication

Is a lecture on safe-driving techniques as effective as a technicolor film? Is a film that is meant to scare the audience as effective as a more reasoned appeal? Both *what* you say (the message) and *how* you say it (the channel of communication) influence acceptance. In this section we will examine a number of communication techniques that have been used to change attitudes. Of necessity, we will analyze these techniques separately, but in real life many are often used in one communication. Remember also that variations in the source of the communication, which we have just discussed, and the audience itself, which will be analyzed in the next section, influence the amount of acceptance of the message.

> **Channel of communication** *In general, face-to-face communication is the most persuasive.*

If you had a budget of $500 to persuade the freshmen at your college to drive more safely, what medium would you use? According to Marshall McLuhan, the way in which you present your information may be more important than what you say (McLuhan and Fiore, 1967). In your safe-driving program, would you present your information to each student on a one-to-one basis? Present it personally to groups of students? Show films? Show slides? Distribute printed materials? In deciding which medium to use, you would have to consider the practical aspects, the particular materials available, and the audience. Since comparatively little research has been done on the effects of various media, many of your decisions would have to be made on a commonsense basis.

You might try face-to-face persuasion, which, as you recall from Chapter 3, is generally assumed to be the most persuasive. This would enable you to modify your arguments to fit the motives and characteristics of the person you are persuading, counter his objections, and answer his questions. The social relationship established during the interaction might motivate him to accept what you are urging.

If you should decide to use this method, how could you make yourself most effective? Since communicator credibility, attractiveness, and power generally make communicators more persuasive, anything you do to give yourself these characteristics should increase your effectiveness. In everyday life this seems to work. Doctors may be more effective persuaders in their starched white laboratory coats than they would be in a sports shirt. Communicators can make themselves more attractive and likable by meeting the eyes of the person they are talking with, by nodding their heads attentively and "un-huhing," and by looking pleasant (Mehrabian and Williams, 1969).

Even the distance between the communicator and the target person can influence the communicator's persuasiveness. How far away should you stand? One or two feet? Four or five feet? Fourteen or fifteen feet? One recent study indicated that communicators who stood fourteen to fifteen feet away from the person were more effective than those who stood at either the medium or the close distance (Albert and Dabbs, 1970). Why should this be? Maybe the novelty of the longer distance made the communicator's arguments seem more impressive. Or the subjects may have had to pay closer attention to hear. Or maybe they felt less pressured to change at the longer distances.

Effective as the individual approach is, it might not be practical for persuading an entire freshman class. If you can't meet each freshman individually, you might meet a few influential students individually and assume that they will persuade the others (Rosnow and Robinson, 1967). This technique is used frequently in public relations work, but there is very little research on its effectiveness. Also there is the problem of finding out who the influential freshmen are.

In order to save time you might use a group method. You could either lecture small groups of students or conduct group discussions on traffic safety. Which would be more effective? A number of early studies showed that group discussions are more persuasive than lectures, but more recent work has not duplicated these results (Lewin, 1947; Bennett, 1955). The later research showed that persuasion was highly effective—regardless of whether it was done in a lecture or a discussion setting—when the members of the group were made to commit themselves (Bennett, 1955). The effectiveness of group discussion also depends on the attitudes of the people in the group. With a topic like traffic safety you might assume that everyone would agree with your position. But when the topic is more controversial, some group members might argue against your position.

You could also show a motion picture—an approach that is popularly thought to be more persuasive than using printed material. When something is shown on film, it may seem more real and compelling. The enjoyment people generally experience in viewing films may make them pay close attention to the film. The visual material may reinforce the points made in the sound track. And since verbal material has been found to be more persuasive than printed material, the sound tracks may add to the overall level of effectiveness (Cantril and Allport, 1935).

In a classic study it was found that when subjects saw a film, their knowledge of the factual material contained in the film increased significantly. When tests on the information presented in the film were administered after the film, 51 percent of those who had viewed the film could answer the items correctly, whereas only 29 percent of those who had not viewed the film knew the material. Further, the film significantly influenced attitudes specifically related to the film (Hovland, Lumsdaine, and Sheffield, 1949).

Using printed material, however, may be the easiest and fastest approach, and when access to your audience is difficult, it may be the only way to distribute information. Further, some audiences may find printed media more believable than filmed material. One psychologist, for example, has noted that people of higher socioeconomic status tend to give greater credibility to newspapers than to television (McGuire, 1969a, p. 231).

After deciding what medium to use, you would still have to make a number of decisions about what you would say. Should you use scare appeals? Should you present your pitch directly or in a more disguised way? How often should you repeat your message? The research

When you're
16 years old, you're
never going to die.

That's something
to think about,
puff after puff
after puff.

AMERICAN CANCER SOCIETY
THIS SPACE CONTRIBUTED BY THE PUBLISHER

evidence concerning these questions and other "message" variables will be considered below.

> **Fear-arousing appeals** *Whether strong or mild fear appeals are more effective depends on other variables.*

Scare appeals are widely used. (See Figure 4-4.) To persuade teen-age drivers to be more careful, the Connecticut state police show films of gory traffic fatalities to high-school audiences. In antismoking campaigns some groups have shown a technicolor film purporting to be a case study of a young man whose cigarette smoking leads to the removal of his cancerous left lung. Included in the film is an actual surgical procedure during which the camera is focused throughout at the site of the incision in the patient's chest. All of the procedures, from the initial incision to the suturing of the opening, are shown in close-up.

Yet despite wide use of scare appeals and almost twenty years of research effort, the question of whether or not scare appeals are more effective than less emotive appeals has not yet been answered. Although most studies have shown that highly fear-arousing communications are more effective, not all have. The effectiveness of scare appeals seems to depend on a number of other variables in the situation (Janis, 1967).

In a now classic study the effects of fear-arousing appeals at three different intensities were measured (Janis and Feshbach, 1953). All of the communications contained the same recommendations about dental hygiene, but the amount of fear-arousing material included in them differed. The high-fear lecture emphasized the painful consequences of tooth decay and included colored slides of examples of severe tooth decay and mouth infections. The moderate-fear communication described the consequences in less personal terms and used photographs of less severe cases of oral pathol-

FIGURE 4-4 An example of a scare technique in advertising. Do you think a less emotive, more reasoned argument against smoking would be more effective than this one in stimulating smokers to give up cigarettes? (Courtesy, The American Cancer Society)

ogy. The minimal-fear communication used diagrams and photographs of completely healthy teeth. Somewhat surprisingly, the minimal-fear communication was the most persuasive: 36 percent of the subjects in the low-fear condition reported favorable changes in their dental hygiene practices, as compared to 22 percent in the moderate- and 8 percent in the high-fear condition.

In another study, however, increasing the intensity of fear arousal resulted in more persuasion. Fear arousal was manipulated by showing gory technicolor sound films for four different durations (eight, sixteen, twenty-four, and thirty-two minutes). These films showed the victims of serious accidents at the scene of the crash. In this study the subjects exposed to the greatest amount of scare material showed the greatest adherence to the safe-driving recommendations that were made in all four conditions (Leventhal and Niles, 1965). Increased intensities of fear arousal have also been found to increase persuasion levels for a number of other topics, including dental hygiene (Leventhal and Singer, 1966).

How does one account for these strikingly different effects? Since the level of fear itself does not have a consistent effect, we need to look for other variables in the situation that may also influence persuasiveness. Consider what it would take to make you change your own attitudes about an issue such as your driving habits. If you are to be persuaded, you must want to change your attitudes, and you must know how to take the recommended action. Ordinarily, you may not think much about traffic safety or feel any desire to modify your driving patterns. Before you will change, your desire to change has to be stimulated. Arousing your fears about automobile accidents might have that effect. But what if your fears became too intense? Seeing corpses of accident victims might frighten you so much that you would no longer be able to bear the fear; instead you might begin to defend against it. Past a certain intensity, then, fear arousal may become less persuasive. Both very low and very high degrees of fear arousal would probably have negligible persuasive effects, and a moderate level would be most persuasive (Janis, 1967).

How would you test this curvilinear theory? You might measure the intensities of fear re-

ported by the subjects in the high-fear conditions in the dental-hygiene and auto-safety experiments to see if they differed. Unfortunately, the absolute levels of fear experienced by the subjects in different experiments cannot be measured directly; instead, the curvilinear theory has to be tested indirectly.

People who are always fearful, or neurotically anxious, would have more fear initially, and increasing their level of fear would push them past the "drop-off" point on the fear continuum, so that they would be less affected by fear-arousing appeals that are effective for nonanxious people, as has been shown by Janis and Feshbach (1954). Further, people who feel vulnerable to a threat, who feel that something like the threat depicted could really happen to them, would be more easily moved past the drop-off point and so would be persuaded less by highly fear-arousing communications (Niles, 1964).

Anything that counters an individual's tendency to rationalize and defend against high levels of fear can be expected to make fear-arousing techniques more effective. In an experiment in which the subjects played the extremely frightening role of a smoker who was being hospitalized with lung cancer, the subjects in this condition were persuaded much more than those who listened to a tape recording of one of the role-playing sessions. The girls who actually played the part of the cancer victims showed a significantly greater decrease in the number of cigarettes they smoked over an eighteen-month period than did their more passive counterparts (Mann and Janis, 1968). Thus the emotional involvement in role playing may act as an effective counter to the usual tendency to defend against extremely high levels of fear arousal.

Whether or not a person knows what to do, feels he can do it, and feels it would be effective also determines the extent to which he accepts a recommendation (Leventhal, 1970). A number of studies support the importance of this "coping" variable. For example, in one study students who had been given specific directions about where to obtain a tetanus shot were much more likely to obtain an injection than those who were not given specific directions (Leventhal, Singer, and Jones, 1965). The level of fear aroused did not significantly influence the subject's shot-getting behavior; 29 percent of the subjects in both the high- and the low-fear conditions followed the recommendation to get a tetanus shot once they knew where to go. Their knowing how to act and that some action was expected of them appeared to be more persuasive than the level of fear aroused.

The emotional and the coping variables in fear-arousal studies are not mutually exclusive. People who can cope may be able to take higher levels of fear arousal and thus may be persuaded by a higher level than others.

To return to our example of presenting safe-driving recommendations, you might conclude that the effectiveness of fear-arousing materials would be enhanced both by arousing moderate levels of fear and by giving specific directions for following your recommendations.

> **Style** *Whether or not variations in style influence communication persuasiveness is not yet clear.*

You might expect material that is presented in a competent, dynamic, and humorous way to be more effective than bumbled, dull, unfunny communications. Certainly, in everyday life speakers attempt to be competent, dynamic, and humorous. However, not all of the studies on the effect of communication style have supported these everyday assumptions (McGuire, 1969a).

Speeches that included a large number of deliberate mispronunciations were as persuasive as those with very few mispronunciations (Addington, 1965). Poorly organized messages were as effective as well-organized ones (Thistlethwaite, de Haan, and Kamenetsky, 1955). A few studies, however, have shown that the effectiveness of the speaker's delivery did correlate significantly with his rated persuasiveness (Bettinghaus, 1961). Of course, rated persuasiveness is not the same thing as a measure of actual persuasiveness.

Whether or not the speaker's skill is related to his persuasiveness may depend on the absolute level of competency. Perhaps the studies in which the speaker's delivery did not relate to his persuasiveness did not tap the depths we know possible in speaker incompetence and disorganization.

Nor have the research results concerning the question of a dynamic versus a subdued delivery been consistent. Although a dynamic delivery may hold the audience's attention, it may also seem more propagandist. In some situations a dynamic style has been less effective than a subdued one (Dietrich, 1946); in others there have been no differences (Hovland, Lumsdaine, and Sheffield, 1949); and in still others the dynamic approach has been more effective than the subdued one (Bowers and Osborn, 1966). Differences in topics, audiences, and the operational definitions of dynamic and subdued speeches may have contributed to these inconsistent results.

The businessman practicing his opening jokes is part of executive folklore. Once again, however, the research on humor has not supported the assumption that humor makes speeches more interesting and persuasive. Adding humor to speeches did not increase either their judged interest level or their persuasiveness (Lull, 1940). But from this limited evidence we cannot conclude that humor is never effective. The humor used in the research may not have been very funny. The message may have been so subtle that the audience missed the point. Humor may be effective only in gaining an audience's attention. Or the persuasiveness of humor may vary with topics and audiences. It is unlikely that your telling a few sick jokes as you showed a gory film of an automobile accident would endear you to your audience.

One variation in style that has been found to be related to persuasiveness is the use of rhetorical questions—creating a dramatic effect with no expectation of an answer—rather than making the same point in a statement. Asking the question, "Wasn't Frank Myers a threat to his own daughter?" would be more effective than saying, "On this night and in this condition, Frank Myers was a threat to his own daughter." Support for this hypothesis has been obtained in a recent study (Zillmann, 1972). Why are rhetorical questions effective? Two possibilities have been suggested. First, putting the information in a question form may emphasize it. Or it may be that the use of rhetorical questions makes the communicator seem less intent on persuading the audience.

> **Conclusion drawing** *In general, explicitly drawing the communication's conclusion is more persuasive.*

When you present your traffic-safety program, should you use an implicit form of communication, that is, present the evidence about the need for safe driving and then stop, hoping that the audience will draw the conclusion you want it to? Or should you use an explicit form, that is, present the evidence and then draw your conclusions about the need for safer driving practices? If you let the audience draw its own conclusions, the members may feel that they have made up their own minds, but the danger of letting the audience draw its own conclusions is that some members may not see the implications of the facts you present. (See Figure 4-5.)

The more complicated the issue is, the greater is the advantage of explicitly stating your conclusions. In one study involving the merits of United States' currency devaluation, a highly complicated topic, half the subjects were given only the arguments favoring devaluation (current economic issues and the United States' poor financial status). The implication of these arguments—that United States' currency should be devalued—was not explicitly stated. The other half of the subjects were given both the arguments and the explicit recommendation that United States' currency be devalued. When the conclusions were explicitly stated, more than twice as many subjects changed their attitude in the direction advocated (Hovland and Mandell, 1952). Since the devaluation issue was so complicated, the students who did not hear the speaker's conclusion may not have understood the implications of the arguments.

But an explicitly stated conclusion may not always be more persuasive. If the members of the audience are highly intelligent or the issue is a very simple one, they would be more likely to draw the appropriate conclusion (Thistlethwaite, de Haan, and Kamenetsky, 1955). Indeed, stating it for them under these circumstances could be insulting. Further, if the audience is hostile, the members might label the communicator's explicitly stated recommendations as propaganda, in which case letting the

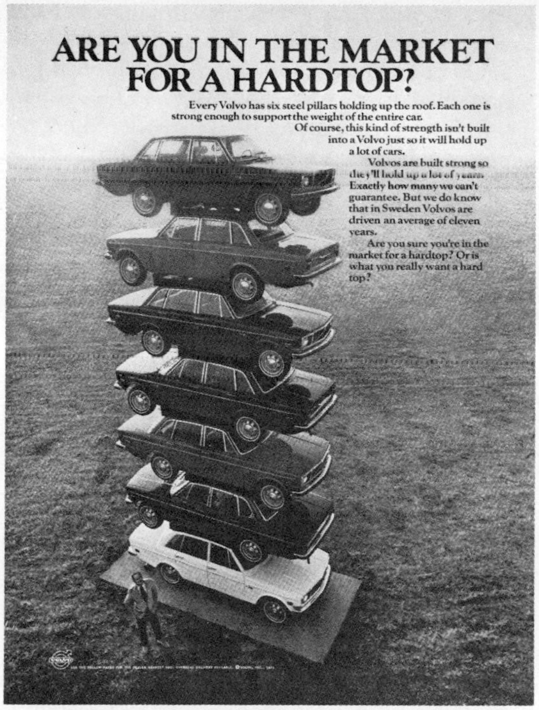

FIGURE 4-5 Volvo apparently believes that explicit ads are highly persuasive. (Courtesy, Volvo of America Corporation)

audience draw its own conclusions might be more effective. In deciding whether or not to explicitly draw the conclusions, you must decide whether you gain more by providing information or lose more by irritating the audience and appearing as though you were trying to persuade them.

> **One-sided versus two-sided communications** *When an intelligent audience initially disagrees with you, knows that there are two sides, or will soon hear the other side of the issue from someone else, present both sides.*

In your safety program should you simply present the recommendations to drive safely or should you include and refute the arguments that faulty highway and car design are more responsible for the high accident rate than unsafe driving? If you present arguments in favor of your recommendation along with some arguments in support of the opposing view (the two-sided communication), you appear more objective, more knowledgeable, and less intent on trying to persuade. If you present only the arguments supporting your position (a one-sided communication), you don't provide your audience with arguments for the opposition, and your communication is less complicated.

Whether a one-sided or a two-sided communication is more persuasive depends on the audience's initial attitudes, its level of education, and whether or not it knows that there are two sides to the issue. If the audience is initially opposed to your recommendation, a two-sided communication is more effective (McGinnies, 1966). For educated persons a two-sided communication is also more effective (Hovland, Lumsdaine, and Sheffield, 1949). Simply telling your audience that there are two sides to an issue, without telling it any of the counterarguments, also makes communications more effective (Jones and Brehm, 1970). Further, two-sided communications are more effective in producing resistance to counterpropaganda (Lumsdaine and Janis, 1953).

Under some circumstances, however, a one-sided communication can be more effective. If the audience initially supports your position, is relatively uneducated, doesn't know that there are two sides, and isn't likely to find out, then a one-sided communication would be more effective. If the audience has no familiarity with arguments supporting the opposition, you may just confuse and weaken your own case by presenting both sides of the issue. If you can't effectively refute the opposition's arguments, presenting them may also weaken your own position.

Repetition *Within limits, repeated arguments are more persuasive.*

How often should you tell your freshmen to drive more slowly? Once? Twice? Ten times? Fifty times? The well-known indoctrinator Adolf Hitler felt that repetition was very important in persuasion:

The receptivity of the great masses is very limited, their intelligence is small, but their power of forgetting is enormous. In consequence of these facts, all effective propaganda must be limited to a very few points and must harp on these in slogans until the last member of the public understands what you want him to understand by your slogan.

[Hitler, 1933, quoted in Downs, 1956, p. 125.]

Some repetition might help your audience remember your arguments, but beyond a certain point boredom and reactance would set in. How many times do you have to see a commercial before you begin to hate it? The point at which repetition of a message decreases its persuasiveness is an important practical question for advertisers, some of which seem to believe that there is no such thing as satiation.

Presenting a message several times has been found to be more persuasive than presenting it only once. In one study, for instance, a tape of a "court suit for damages caused by an allegedly defective vaporizer" was played three times for one group and once for another. Not only did the subjects remember the repeated arguments better, but the repeated arguments were also more persuasive. One week after the subjects had listened to the tapes, their acceptance of the arguments was measured and the repeated arguments were accepted more (Wilson and Miller, 1968).

Primacy–recency *Whether presenting your arguments first or last is more effective depends on the time elapsed between the arguments and the attitude assessment.*

If you were debating another student who contended that faulty automotive design is the primary cause of accidents, would you prefer to present your side first or last? If you presented your arguments first, they might be learned better and thus have a greater influence—a primacy effect. On the other hand, the audience might be more apt to remember what was presented last—a recency effect. Whether primacy or recency effects are obtained depends on both the length of time between the first and second communication and the time between the second communication and the assessment of the attitude. Acceptance is related to how well the individual has learned the message of the two communications. On the basis of the usual effects of time on forgetting, one would predict the following primacy–recency effects:

1. If the second communication is presented right after the first, and attitudes are tested immediately after that, the retention of the two should be equal, and neither primacy nor recency should occur.

2. If there is a long delay between the first and second communication, and another equally long delay between the second communication and testing, neither primacy nor recency would occur, since both communications would be forgotten.

3. If, however, there is a long delay between the first communication and the second, and the individual's attitudes are assessed immediately after the second communication, the most recent message should be the most influential, since he would remember it better.

4. If the two communications are given one right after the other, and then there is a slight pause before attitudes are measured, the first argument should be slightly more influential, since the message of the first communication is usually learned better.

Confirmation for these four hypotheses has been obtained (Miller and Campbell, 1959).

Although the lapsing of time does offer one approach to understanding primacy–recency, other approaches are possible. For instance, when would members of the audience begin to combine the arguments from both positions and construct compromise positions? How would hearing the first information influence the person's interpretation of the second argument? How would hearing two inconsistent arguments influence the perceived expertness of both communicators or the perceived truth of both positions? No single approach to primacy–recency is sufficient to explain all of the find-

ings in this area (McGuire, 1969a; Luchins and Luchins, 1970).

> **Discrepancy** *Communications that are moderately discrepant from the audience's views are more persuasive than either extremely or minimally discrepant communications.*

How discrepant should your communication be from the audience's initial attitudes? If you are trying to persuade an audience of people who are opposed to the legalization of abortion, what should you say? Should you argue a position that is mildly discrepant from their view—such as that abortion should be legal only in limited cases, as, for example, when the pregnancy results from rape or when continuation of the pregnancy would endanger the life of the mother? Or would it be best to present an extremely discrepant communication urging the legalization of abortion for all women who want an abortion?

Most of the studies have shown a curvilinear relationship between discrepancy and persuasiveness. Both too much and too little discrepancy are ineffective; maximum persuasiveness comes when communications are moderately discrepant from the audience's view (e.g., Peterson and Koulack, 1969).

Why should moderately discrepant communications be the most persuasive? There are two theoretical answers. One approach is dissonance theory. When the members of the audience find that someone disagrees with them, dissonance may be aroused, which in turn motivates a number of resolutions. On hearing moderately pro-abortion statements, a person opposed to abortion could change his attitudes. But if the arguments are too discrepant, he may be more likely to reduce his dissonance by denigrating the communicator (Aronson, Turner, and Carlsmith, 1963).

The second theoretical approach focuses on the way people judge attitudes. Our own attitudes provide a standard against which all attitudes are judged. When attitudes coincide exactly with our own or differ moderately from them, we are likely to listen, and we may be persuaded. If an attitude is too discrepant, however, it falls within our "latitude of rejection," which means that we automatically reject it (Hovland, Harvey, and Sherif, 1957). To obtain the optimal level of discrepancy, one would have to know an individual's "latitude of acceptance" and present a communication maximally discrepant within that range.

Any variable that influences the width of the latitude of acceptance would, then, influence the optimal level of discrepancy. One such variable might be ego involvement. Frequently, people who are involved with an issue are less tolerant of opinions differing from their own, and so their optimal level of discrepancy is low. A number of studies support this hypothesis. For instance, when the issue was an increase in their school's tuition, students were influenced much less by communications urging very large increases than by communications urging smaller increases (Rhine and Severance, 1970).

These two approaches to understanding discrepancy are not necessarily mutually exclusive. Whether a statement is in the latitude of acceptance or rejection may influence the way in which a person reduces dissonance. When statements differ too much from his own views, he may simply laugh at the communication, denigrate the communicator, or leave, if he can. When statements are within his latitude of acceptance, he may reduce dissonance by changing his attitudes.

You may be somewhat surprised by the generalization that novel arguments are more persuasive. Since we saw in Chapter 3 that familiarity leads to liking, you might expect familiar arguments to be liked more and so to be more persuasive.

But think about your reactions when someone begins to repeat arguments you have heard before. You may not pay close attention, since you were aware of these arguments when you formed your attitude. You may not think about changing your attitudes until you hear something new. And you may believe that the novel information is more current and, therefore, more apt to be correct. In our culture novelty may be associated with being "one up," and it is the in thing to follow new trends. (See Figure 4-6.)

The hypothesis that novel arguments are more persuasive was indirectly supported in a recent experiment. Although all of the subjects were exposed to identical communications, half were told that their communications contained novel arguments and information, and the other half were told that their communications contained familiar information. The subjects who thought they were reading novel information were significantly more influenced. This study appears to demonstrate, therefore, that even without variation in actual novelty, a communication can achieve greater effectiveness simply by seeming to be novel (Sears and Freedman, 1965).

Reinforcement *Primary and secondary reinforcement of attitudes is persuasive.*

As you present your safe-driving recommendations, should you provide the members of your audience with soda and peanuts? Should you nod and smile every time a member of the audience indicates that he wishes to drive more slowly? As we saw in Chapter 3, both primary and social reinforcers can influence attitude acquisition. They can also modify attitudes.

Presenting primary reinforcements, like food, while you present your persuasive materials can be an effective technique. Subjects who read persuasive communications in a room well stocked with soft drinks and peanuts changed attitudes more than subjects who read the same communications in a room where no food was available (Janis, Kaye, and Kirschner, 1965).

It has been found repeatedly that if an experimenter reinforces a particular attitude by smiling, nodding, and saying such things as "good," the subject will agree with the experimenter's attitude. For instance, after a series of interchanges in which the experimenter said "good" whenever the subject said something positive about pay television, the subject began

Social
Psychology and
Modern Life

to move in the rewarded direction and to say more positive things about pay television (Insko and Cialdini, 1969).

This is hardly news. People have been doing this at parties for years. Unless something is very important to an individual (and sometimes not even then), he doesn't usually offend others by disagreeing with them. The more he likes another person, the more likely he is to agree with that person. In the food experiment the subjects may have liked the experimenter more because he provided soda and peanuts, and so they may have been more likely to agree with him. In the social reinforcement study the experimenter's smiles and nods conveyed his attitude and may have made subjects like him, thereby producing a high rate of agreement.

Dissonance *Arousing dissonance can change attitudes.*

At the beginning of this chapter, we saw that the only way an attitude can be changed is by introducing inconsistent material that is difficult for the target person to dismiss. All of the variables that have been found to influence attitude change can be interpreted in terms of this inconsistency model. For instance, since subjects believe that what a high-credibility communicator says is true, someone who likes to drive fast experiences more inconsistency when a high-credibility communicator says that fast driving is dangerous than when a low-credibility communicator says the same thing. Or, to take another example, novel arguments may introduce a greater inconsistency because the subject values novelty and is more likely to pay attention to new information. Introducing dissonance is yet another way to introduce inconsistencies.

A number of experiments with widely different techniques have shown that dissonance arousal is a very effective tactic in changing attitudes. Although dissonance has been mentioned several times, we will consider it in more detail here, since the largest body of dissonance research has been in connection with attitude change.

As we saw in Chapter 1, the basic concept of

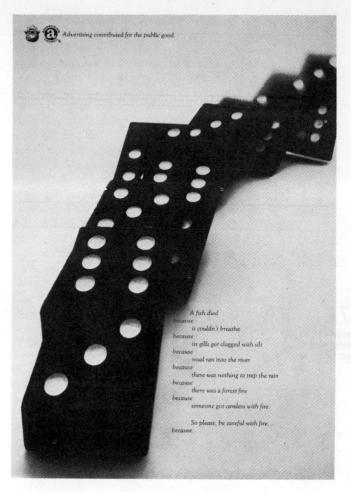

FIGURE 4-6 For many years, forest fire prevention ads have featured Smokey the Bear urging forest users to be careful. This ad takes a quite different approach to the problem. Do you think its novelty makes it more effective than a Smokey ad? (Courtesy, The Advertising Council)

dissonance theory is that when someone simultaneously has two ideas or opinions that are psychologically inconsistent, dissonance is aroused. Because dissonance is unpleasant, he tries to reduce it by removing the inconsistency. To achieve consistency, or "consonance," he may change one of his beliefs, or he may add other beliefs (Festinger, 1957). Let us use one of Festinger's examples. For a cigarette smoker, the belief that smoking leads to lung cancer is dissonance-arousing, since people do not ordinarily want to believe they are injuring themselves. To reduce the dissonance, the smoker could criticize the evidence linking cigarette smoking with lung cancer. He could rationalize that smoking adds so much pleasure to his life that a shorter, cigarette-filled life is preferable to a longer, cigarette-less one. Or he could stop smoking.

A number of ingenious experiments have shown the wide variety of situations that arouse dissonance and cause people to change their attitudes in order to reduce dissonance. In the analysis of the initiation experiment in Chapter 1, we saw that people come to like a group if they have to suffer in order to belong. The idea that you have suffered to join a group is inconsistent with the notion that the group is dull, and so you reduce your dissonance by changing your evaluation of the group (Aronson and Mills, 1959).

Earlier in this chapter, we saw that when people agree to do something unpleasant such as eat fried grasshoppers, they are more apt to change their attitudes when they dislike the communicator than when the communicator is pleasant. Why? Again dissonance provides an answer. Knowing that you are crunching away on something as repulsive as a fried grasshopper is dissonant with your belief that you are doing this for a nasty experimenter. One way to reduce your dissonance is to change your attitude about the grasshoppers (Zimbardo, Weisenberg, Firestone, and Levy, 1965).

A mild threat to keep you from doing something you'd like to do can make you derogate what you originally wanted to do. Sound strange? Dissonance provides the explanation. Whenever you don't do something you want to do, you experience dissonance. Knowing that you want to do something is inconsistent with the fact that you're not doing it. If you are refraining from a pleasant activity because of a severe threat, your dissonance is reduced. But when the threat is mild, you have to add other justifications, such as denying that you really wanted to do what you're prevented from doing (Aronson and Carlsmith, 1963).

Simply making a decision can make you have more favorable feelings about what you have chosen and more negative feelings about what you have rejected. Why? The belief that there is something negative about what you have chosen is dissonant with your having chosen it. And the belief that there are pleasant aspects to

something you have rejected also arouses dissonance. To reduce this dissonance, you emphasize the positive aspects of what you have chosen and see only negative things in what you have rejected (Brehm, 1956).

After seeing a number of dissonance derivations, you may want to try one yourself. Suppose all subjects are told that they are going to perform a dull task. Then half the subjects are told that what they are doing is of no value, since all the necessary experimental data has already been collected. The other half is told that their participation is of great value. Which group would experience more dissonance?

The subjects who were told that their data had no value would be expected to experience dissonance, since doing something dull is dissonant with the idea that the activity has no value. One way for them to reduce their dissonance would be to convince themselves that the task was not really dull, which is what the subjects did in an experiment testing this hypothesis. Students who were told their work had no value said they enjoyed the task (Freedman, 1963).

This small sample from the vast dissonance literature may give you an idea of some of the strengths and weaknesses of the theory. The predictions from dissonance theory, which generated more research in social psychology in the 1960s than any other theory, do not seem to be commonsensical or readily derivable from any other single theory. Today, the validity of these predictions and the strength of the theory are hotly debated. See Box 1, page 180.

Summary and concluding comments

Some of the more important variables that influence a communication's persuasiveness have been discussed in this section. (For other types of appeals, see Figure 4-7.) We saw that, in general, face-to-face communication is the most persuasive. Whether strong or mild fear appeals are more effective depends on other variables. Past a certain intensity, fear arousal may become less persuasive. The individual's ability to cope may also determine the effect of fear arousal. People who can cope may be able to take higher levels of fear arousal. With the exception of the technique of asking rhetorical

FIGURE 4-7 In addition to the message variables on which research evidence is available, advertisers use many other appeals. Analyze each of the following ads to see what appeal you think is being used. One analysis of the appeals used in these ads follows upside down. (A—Courtesy, Virginia Slims; B—Courtesy, Bulova Watch Company, Inc.; C—Courtesy, Steuben Glass; D—Courtesy, R. J. Reynolds Tobacco Company; E—Courtesy, Mercedes-Benz of North America, Inc.; F—Courtesy, Parfums Carven; G—Courtesy, The Fresh Air Fund; H—Courtesy, Sony Corporation)

If you've got the guts, we've got the watch.

This Bulova Oceanographer was designed for the man who is very brave. Or slightly crazy. Or terribly accident-prone. It was *also* designed for the man who absentmindedly dunks his watch in his soup.

If you *really* find yourself in the soup (like our friend in the photograph), you may decide you're in over your depth. But, as long as the depth is less than 666 feet, you can depend on your automatic Oceanographer, with its elapsed time indicator, to tell you when it's time to get yourself out of there.

BULOVA OCEANOGRAPHER

A

You've come
a long way, baby.

VIRGINIA SLIMS.

Slimmer than the fat cigarettes men smoke.

VIRGINIA SLIMS
FILTER

VIRGINIA
SLIMS
MENTHOL · FILTER

Regular: 18 mg. "tar," 1.2 mg. nicotine—Menthol: 18 mg. "tar," 1.3 mg. nicotine av. per cigarette, FTC Report Apr. '72

Fashions by Willi Smith for Digits

C

LUDWIG VAN BEETHOVEN: Glass design by Donald Pollard · Portrait by Robert Ziering · Height, with marble base, 11¾" Limited edition · $7,600.00 · For 80-page Christmas catalogue in full color, send $1.00

STEUBEN GLASS

FIFTH AVENUE AT 56th STREET · NEW YORK · N.Y. 10022 · (212) PL 2-1441

(continued on page 178)

questions, whether or not variations in style influence a communication's persuasiveness is not yet clear.

In general, explicitly drawing the communication's conclusion is more persuasive. Within limits, repeated arguments are more persuasive. When two arguments are presented in sequence the relative persuasibility of each will depend on (a) the time elapsed between the two presentations and (b) the time elapsed between the last presentation and the attitude assessment. If, for instance, the two communications are given one right after the other, and then there is a slight pause before attitudes are measured, the first argument should be slightly more influential, since the message of the first communication is usually learned better.

Communications that are moderately discrepant from the target person's initial attitudes are more persuasive than either extremely or minimally discrepant communications. Novel arguments tend to be more persuasive. Primary and secondary reinforcement of an attitude is persuasive, and so is arousing dissonance.

Most of the studies in this section focused on "main effects"—are humorous appeals more effective? Are one-sided communications more effective than two-sided ones? Although this approach yields information about the particular variable studied, it does not tell us how these variables interact with others.

Some of the inconsistencies in the experimental results may be due to this main-effect conceptualization. Just as the effective level of fear arousal seems to depend on other variables, so may the effective level of any given communication variable depend on other variables. For instance, whether a humorous or straight approach is more effective may depend on the topic. Whether a one-sided or a two-sided communication is more effective may depend on the audience's level of intelligence. Focusing on interactions rather than main effects might be a better way to approach research on attitude change now that the main-effect approach has established a number of basic findings. Suggesting an interactional approach in no way discredits the work already done, however. The general findings that came out of this work provide a foundation to build the interactional approach on so that even more precise predictions are possible.

BOX 1   A CRITIQUE OF DISSONANCE THEORY

The criticisms of dissonance theory relate to four major areas: specification of dissonance-arousing situations, predictions concerning which strategies will be used to reduce dissonance, methodological problems in the dissonance research, and the relation of dissonance to other social-psychological theories (Aronson, 1969b).

As you read about the dissonance experiments, was it always clear to you whether or not a given situation would arouse dissonance? The general definition of "psychological inconsistency" doesn't seem to help too much. Why is it inconsistent to think that dull work has no value? Defining dissonance-arousing situations has been a constant problem, which has not yet been resolved. Festinger listed four types of inconsistency that produce dissonance: (1) logical inconsistency, (2) inconsistency with the cultural mores, (3) inconsistency between a particular belief and a more general belief, and (4) inconsistency with past experience. All of these may be subsumed under the general rubric "violation of an expectancy." But does this list clarify what will be dissonance-arousing? Perhaps not. Determining when an expectancy is violated may be as difficult as determining psychological inconsistency.

Since there are many ways of reducing dissonance, the theory must make clearer when a person is most likely to change his attitude to reduce dissonance. Although dissonance theory does not yet have any clear statements about the circumstances that dictate the choosing of one strategy over another, some studies are beginning to focus on the influence of the situation on the choice of ways to reduce dissonance (Walster et al., 1967).

Dissonance theory has also been criticized because of the methodological problems in some of the dissonance experiments. However, replications of many of the earlier studies with methodological improvements have supported the findings of the original, somewhat flawed studies. In the Aronson-Mills experiment, for instance, you will recall that some psychologists criticized the dissonance explanation of the girls' favorable reactions to the unpleasant initiation. But you will also recall that in replications using other operational definitions of suffering, the suffering-liking relationship continued to obtain.

Finally, dissonance theory has been criticized on the grounds that it overlooks the contributions of other theories. Clearly, people are not always motivated primarily by their desire for consonance; they frequently do things to seek rewards and avoid punishments. To use Aronson's example, a man who has just spent an enormous amount of money on a new house will see water in his basement even though it arouses dissonance. The price for consonance in this case is too high.

Perhaps the best approach to understanding the overlap between dissonance and other theories is to study the situations that determine which theory is applicable. For example, a dissonance approach to the water in the basement would predict that the man wouldn't see it because it would mean that he had made a mistake. A reward-incentive theory would predict that he would be sensitive to the problem now so that he could avoid bigger problems in the future. The water level in the basement might determine which prediction would be correct. If there is just "a little dampness" in the basement and the contract is signed, dissonance reduction might be his main motive. But as the water rises, the importance of dissonance reduction may decrease. Some recent work has begun to isolate the variables relevant to the strength of the two motives (Aronson and Ross, 1964).

The Audience

People resist pressure and persuasion. Going to a party because you want to go may be very pleasant, but if you were required to attend the same party, you might really hate it. The strength of people's desire to resist inroads on their freedom is emphasized in reactance theory. Whenever a person feels that his freedom to choose an activity or attitude is threatened, psychological reactance is aroused, as noted in Chapter 2. Whether or not an attempt to persuade will be successful, then, is determined by the relative strength of the compliance motives set up by the communicator and his message and the individual's desire to resist persuasion, that is, his reactance motivation. When the communicator is highly credible, the message is persuasive, and the individual feels little threat to his freedom, he may change his attitude. But if the communicator is inept, the message is weak, and the individual feels pressured, he is likely to reject the persuasive message. If reactance is sufficiently strong, he may even change his attitude in the opposite direction of that advocated.

The importance of reactance has been shown in an ingenious experiment (Sensenig and Brehm, 1968). The attitudes of the subjects were first measured on a variety of issues. Each subject was then told that he would be working with one other subject to prepare separate essays on five of the attitudes previously measured. In all of the experimental conditions, it was arranged that each subject always wrote an essay supporting his original position.

In the control condition, each subject was told that both he and his partner would have to support the same point of view on five issues, and he was made to believe that he had participated with his partner in deciding which point of view was to be endorsed. In the high-reactance condition, the subject was also told that he and his partner had to support a common position on the five issues, but he was made to believe that his partner had unilaterally decided what the common position on the five essays would be. The need for unanimity and the dictatorial approach was also used in the low-reactance condition, but for only one of the five essays. For the other four topics, the subjects were told they could choose to write what they wished.

As hypothesized, reactance did significantly influence the amount of attitude change. Post-experimental measures showed that control subjects tended to endorse more strongly the positions they had originally taken and that subjects in the reactance conditions tended to move away from their originally preferred positions. Among the reactance subjects, those who thought that their partners were dictating the position to be taken on all five issues showed significantly more change away from their original views—which the subjects were required to defend during the experiment—than did subjects who were being dictated to for only one such issue.

Exactly what does one have to do or say to arouse reactance? The subtlety of reactance arousal in this experiment is interesting. In the control condition the subject was told that his partner preferred to take a given position "if it's all right with you." In the reactance conditions the subject was simply told that his partner had "decided we both will agree" on this position. These slight changes in wording resulted in significantly different amounts of attitude change. As the diplomats know, niceties of language can make an enormous difference in human interactions.

Other aspects of the situation may also influence reactance reduction. For instance, if you thought that you would have to continue interacting with someone who was pressuring you, you might express your reactance differently than if you thought it was a one-shot encounter. If you expected to continue interacting with the person, you might express your reactance by feeling hostility toward him, instead of feeling more negative about an attitude. This hypothesis has been confirmed (Pallak and Heller, 1971). Really intense levels of reactance may lead to interpersonal hostility. Or we might speculate that the importance of the issue would influence the amount of reactance aroused. You might not care if you were pressured about something small, but if your choices on something important, like choosing a career, were being limited, you might feel a lot of reactance.

Reactance includes all of the audience's strategies to resist persuasion. When someone tries to persuade you, how do you resist? Perhaps you do not really pay attention. Or if you do listen, you may criticize the arguments, reject them, argue with the source, make fun of him, or misinterpret the communication. Or you may leave the situation.

In this section we shall discuss a number of tactics to overcome audience defenses (role playing, distraction, inoculation, commitment, forewarning, and dimensions of the attitude). We shall also consider how systematic differences in both attitudes and people can affect susceptibility to persuasion. Although one might argue that some of these tactics could be classified under the "how" and "what" of the attitude change procedure, they are treated here because each provides a way of overcoming some of the audience's methods of resisting persuasion. As we consider each of these, ask yourself: Which aspect of audience resistance is the persuasion tactic directed against? Could the particular tactic be fitted into reactance theory?

Role playing can be very persuasive.

Instead of having the members of your audience see a film on safe-driving practices, you might have them play the role of someone who has been hospitalized because of an automobile accident. They could be asked to act out a number of scenes: being visited in the hospital by family members, having their driver's license suspended, being told that their insurance has been canceled. If your audience reacts anything like the subjects who have been involved in a number of role-playing studies, this would be a highly effective way to get them to drive more carefully. Although role playing is not always more persuasive than the more passive techniques, a number of studies have shown that it can be a very powerful technique.

As we have seen, role playing has even been found to be effective in convincing cigarette smokers they should smoke less. Those who played the part of a cancer victim showed a significant decrease in the number of cigarettes they smoked even after an eighteen-month period (Mann and Janis, 1968). And role playing has been effective in reducing racial prejudice, a highly resistant attitude. Prejudiced whites who role played the part of a black showed much more favorable attitudes toward blacks after their role playing (Culbertson, 1957).

In fact, one could argue that one of the basic means of socializing human beings involves their playing their various occupational and sexual roles. After a person plays a role for a while, he may internalize it.

As psychotherapists and novelists have long known, there is something particularly compelling about acting the part of another person or putting yourself in another situation. Why is this such an effective technique? Psychologists are divided on this question. Some attribute the phenomenon to an "incentive theory" (Janis and Gilmore, 1965); others believe it is best explained by dissonance theory (Festinger, 1957).

According to the incentive theory, when a person agrees to play a role, he tries to think of all the good supporting arguments he can for his assumed position. He considers all of the facts he knows, concentrates on those that support his role, and ignores the others—an effect that is termed "biased scanning." In the process of improvising his own arguments, he persuades himself. The stronger the reward is

for his role playing, the better job he does, the harder he works, and the more persuasive are the arguments he amasses. Thus increasing the reward for role playing should increase the amount of attitude change (a "maximum-reward" effect).

As you may have foreseen, dissonance theory makes exactly the opposite prediction about the effects of reward on the persuasiveness of role playing. The knowledge that what you are saying is inconsistent with your beliefs arouses dissonance and thus a tendency to remove that dissonance (possibly by changing your beliefs). If, however, there is some justification for this discrepancy, such as a powerful reward for lying or a powerful punishment for telling the truth, the discrepancy will not arouse dissonance, and as a result, you will not change your attitudes. Thus according to dissonance theory, increasing the reward for role playing will only decrease the predicted attitude change (a "minimal-reward" effect).

Since incentive and dissonance theory differ so clearly, the effects of reward on role playing have been investigated extensively. In the study that began the whole controversy, all of the subjects worked on a very dull task for a considerable length of time. Then subjects were asked, but not required, to tell "another student waiting to start the experiment" that the tasks were interesting. Some subjects were offered one dollar to lie; others were offered twenty dollars. After each subject played his role and told the "waiting subject" that the study was interesting, his own attitudes about the experiment were measured by a "departmental investigator." And as dissonance theory would predict, the subjects given one dollar were more positive about the dull experimental task than the subjects given twenty dollars (Festinger and Carlsmith, 1959).

Contrast the procedures in this experiment with those followed in a study designed by an advocate of the maximum-reward effect. While waiting to "participate in an experiment run by a psychology professor," the subjects, students at Ohio State University, were told to report to an "education graduate student," who was running another study. This study involved their writing an essay arguing that the Ohio State football team should not be allowed to play in the Rose Bowl, a position at variance with what most of them believed. To write their essay, they were paid either fifty cents, one dollar, or five dollars. After they had written their essays and handed them in to the "graduate student," they reported back to the "psychology professor," and their attitudes about the team's trip to the Rose Bowl were then measured. As the incentive theory would predict, subjects who had been given the five-dollar reward more strongly supported the position that their football team should not be allowed to play in the Rose Bowl than the subjects given lesser amounts of money (Rosenberg, 1965).

The results of the two experiments appear to be completely inconsistent. Could the differences in the procedures used account for the different results? In the first experiment the subjects were asked to lie to a fellow student. In this context the twenty dollars may have been seen as a bribe, especially since it was offered while the subject was making up his mind. In the second experiment there was no moral problem. The student could easily rationalize his writing the essay as an example of a classic debating technique. The reward could not have been seen as a bribe; it may have been viewed as a "gold star" for good performance (Steiner, 1970). The essay writing was anonymous, whereas in the first experiment the subjects had to endure embarrassing eye-to-eye contact with their fellow students. The topic in the second experiment was more complex, so that there may have been more opportunity for the students to evolve rational arguments in support of the position they were asked to take.

Clearly, the circumstances do influence the effects of reward. These inconsistent results led the dissonance theorists to conceptualize more clearly just what inconsistencies would create dissonance. According to the most current conceptualizations, the minimal-reward effect occurs when one or more of the following variables are present: (1) the person feels that what he is doing is nasty, (2) he has a choice, (3) the experimental reward is seen as a bribe, (4) the role-playing procedure publicly commits him to what he is advocating, (5) the role playing does not give him an opportunity to evolve arguments or the issue is too simple for many arguments to be evolved, and (6) the person feels personally responsible for the aversive consequences of his role playing. Either direct or indirect support

for the influence of each of these variables has been obtained (Cooper and Worchel, 1970; Steiner, 1970; Sherman, 1970; Carlsmith, Collins, and Helmreich, 1966; Hoyt, Henley, and Collins, 1972).

The controversy about the effects of reward on role playing has preoccupied social psychologists almost to the exclusion of other variables. Yet if you were going to have the members of your audience play the role of an accident victim, you would have to make many decisions in addition to how much you were going to pay them. For instance, would it be enough merely to have the members of the audience think they were going to role play, so that they would begin marshaling their arguments, or would they actually have to play the role? The results of a recent study suggest that people are more likely to change their attitudes if they actually play the role (Cialdini, 1971).

Would you give your subjects a prepared script or would you let them improvise? Experimental results are not completely consistent, but the available research suggests that if subjects are interested and can think of good arguments, improvisation produces more attitude change (King and Janis, 1956). Would the amount of effort they expended in their role playing influence its persuasiveness? If they had to deliver persuasive speeches under the effortful conditions demanded by delayed auditory feedback (a quarter second delay between speaking and hearing what one has just said), they would show more attitude change (Zimbardo, 1965).

Would the reaction of the audience listening to the role player's presentation influence his attitudes? Under some circumstances audience approval will result in more attitude change, since the role player is rewarded for his performance (Wallace, 1966). If, however, the role player takes the audience's disapproval as a challenge to devise more persuasive arguments, disapproval might result in more attitude change in the role player than approval.

Role playing is a highly complicated psychological process. Although the incentive theory provides an intriguing explanation of how role playing could influence attitude change, it has not been investigated extensively, and what evidence there is on the marshaling of arguments is not completely consistent (Sherman, 1970). Further research in this area is necessary, not only to perfect our understanding of when rewards should be used in role playing or of how arguments can best be assembled, but also to develop a clearer notion of how the whole process of role playing functions.

> *Generally, distracting the audience increases attitude change.*

Would persuasive messages concerning safe-driving techniques be more effective if you presented an irrelevant film while you gave the driving recommendations? Consider your own reactions when someone says something you disagree with. You may covertly think up counterarguments or you may ridicule the communicator's arguments and presentation. Your own critical resistance decreases the impact of what the communicator says. But if you are distracted while listening to his communication, these counterarguing processes may be slowed, and you may be persuaded more by what he says. According to this hypothesis, distracting an audience should be a way of overcoming its resistance to persuasive communications (Festinger and Maccoby, 1964).

Another view, however, is that distraction would decrease attitude change. According to this view, attitudes change because the audience learns the content of a communication, and anything that interferes with learning would decrease a communication's persuasiveness (McGuire, 1969a).

Early studies on the effects of distraction yielded inconsistent results. Sometimes it increased the persuasiveness of a communication (Festinger and Maccoby, 1964), and sometimes it decreased persuasiveness (e.g., Haaland and Venkatesen, 1968). Typically in these studies a communication was presented along with some distracting stimulus, such as an irrelevant film, and then attitudes relevant to the communication were measured. If you were listening to a persuasive communication while watching a film, which would you focus on? There was no control over what the subjects were "set" to pay attention to in many of these

studies. Thus the results may have been inconsistent because sometimes the subjects paid more attention to the distraction and sometimes they paid more attention to the persuasive message.

Support for this explanation was obtained in a recent study (Zimbardo et al., 1970). Some subjects were exposed only to a message advocating that the college's summer vacation be shortened to one month (message-only condition). The other subjects were asked to add numbers while listening to the same message. Half of these subjects were told to concentrate on the numbers (number-set condition), and the other half were told to concentrate on the message (message-set condition). Then attitude changes were measured. The subjects' focus, or set, was found to have a significant effect: The acceptance rate of the persuasive message was 90 percent in the message-set distraction condition, 15 percent in the number-set distraction condition, and 45 percent in the message-only condition. These results strongly confirm the experimental hypothesis that the inconsistent results of the previous experiments were the result of uncontrolled variations in what the subjects were paying attention to. When the subjects are set to attend to the message, the presence of other distracting stimuli increases attitude change. But when they are set to attend to the distraction, its presence decreases attitude change. Whether or not hiring hecklers and providing distractions increases a communicator's persuasiveness, then, depends on what the audience listens to.

When the audience is set to attend to the communication, why should distraction increase a message's persuasiveness? The original hypothesis was that distraction interferes with the production of counterarguments. The evidence on this, however, is far from consistent. After the subjects had heard the persuasive communication in the set experiments, they were asked to recall how much time they had spent "thinking about arguments against the position taken by the speaker." Surprisingly, the message-only and message-set distraction groups did not differ significantly (Zimbardo et al., 1970). In other studies, however, less counterarguing has been found in distraction conditions. For instance, when subjects were asked to write down counterarguments in a three-minute time period after they had heard the persuasive message, subjects who had been distracted wrote significantly fewer counter-arguments than those who had not been distracted (Osterhouse and Brock, 1970).

A better measure of counterarguing *while* the audience is listening to the persuasive communications is needed. How do we know that asking people to *recall* either how much time they spent counterarguing or their specific counterarguments is a valid measure of their counterarguing?

Even though we do not know *why* distraction works or the limits of the effect, it is clear that as long as it does not markedly impair the audience's learning of the persuasive communication, distraction is an effective persuasive technique.

In recent work investigators have begun to focus on which situations are distracting. If, for example, you were viewing a television program in which the video portion was distorted, would intermittent distortion or continuous distortion be more distracting? You might be able to adjust to continuous distortion; thus intermittent distortion would be more distracting and would be expected to lead to more attitude change.

Confirmation of this hypothesis was obtained in a recent study in which the amount of video distortion of a television program was manipulated. In all three experimental conditions the audio portion of the program was clear. In one experimental condition the video portion was clear also; in another condition the video portion was continuously distorted; and in a third condition the video portion was intermittently distorted. As predicted, the subjects in the intermittent condition showed the most attitude change: 59 percent. Forty-four percent of the subjects in the no-distortion condition changed their attitudes, as compared to only 30 percent of the subjects in the continuous-distortion condition. Continuous distortion may be a source of annoyance and so lead to less attitude change (Keating and Latané, 1972).

The members of an audience can be inoculated against persuasion.

Assume that you knew the subjects involved in your safe-driving program were going to hear a talk the following week that would link defective auto design, rather than poor driving habits, with accidents. What could you do to make the audience more resistant to this counterpropaganda?

The individual's defenses against persuasion can be strengthened in several ways. One method would be to increase his general ability to evaluate persuasive messages critically. If people are aware of certain persuasive techniques and of how arguments are structured, they might be expected to be more resistant to persuasion. Logical as this sounds, real-life training programs to give people this awareness have been "only marginally successful" (McGuire, 1969a, p. 260).

Or the individual might be provided with additional supporting arguments for your position. You might strengthen your audience's ability to withstand the "faulty safety devices" counterpropaganda by providing additional arguments supporting the idea that careless driving is the primary cause of automobile accidents. You might cite statistics showing the number of accident victims who had been drinking. Since the individual would then have more arguments with which to refute the counterarguments, he would be less persuaded by those counterarguments.

Or you might provide weakened forms of the counterargument along with refutations of that counterargument—that is, you would "inoculate" the audience against the counterpropaganda. If one views the persuasion situation as being similar to a situation in which a person is being attacked by a disease, whether or not the person will be persuaded (become ill) depends on the relative strengths of the persuasive message (virus) and the individual's defense, either his general ability to resist persuasion (health) or his ability to refute the specific message (antibodies). Inoculating the individual with a weakened counterargument that allows him to build up effective refutations may be the most effective way of making him more resistant.

Again, to take our safe-driving example, you might acknowledge that there is an argument holding engineering design flaws as being primarily responsible for automobile accidents, but you would then point out weaknesses in that argument, and say that it is not a very good one. Then, when your audience is exposed to the faulty design argument, it will presumably be more resistant to this argument because of your attitudinal inoculation.

In a study confirming this hypothesis, the subjects were divided into three groups. One group was given additional supporting arguments (support condition); another group was given weakened forms of the counterargument along with refutations (inoculation condition); and a third group was given neither additional supporting arguments nor inoculation (control condition). Then all subjects were submitted to very strong counterpropaganda. As predicted, subjects who had received no information were the most persuaded by the counterpropaganda; those who had received additional supporting arguments were persuaded less than those in the control group; and those who had been inoculated were found to be the most resistant to counterpropaganda (McGuire and Papageorgis, 1961).

Clearly, inoculation works, but how it does so is not clear. One might theorize that when people are exposed to the weakened counterargument, they are motivated to accumulate more arguments supporting their beliefs. Experimental results do not confirm this (Rogers and Thistlethwaite, 1969), possibly because the measures used to assess the presence of counterarguments were inadequate.

Or one might theorize that when people are exposed to weakened forms of counterarguments along with attacks on those counterarguments, the credibility of persons subsequently asserting those arguments is weakened. Suppose you have been told that "some foolish people misguidedly blame traffic accidents on poor automotive design." When you then encounter the faulty-design communicators, you may conclude automatically that they are uninformed and biased. Several studies have confirmed this hypothesis (e.g., Papageorgis and McGuire, 1961).

Commitment can persuade and also make the audience more resistant to counterpropaganda.

If the members of your audience could be made to take some action consistent with their attitudes, would that influence their attitudes? If they had to make their attitudes about safe driving public, would that influence their attitudes and their resistance to counterpropaganda? If they felt that these attitudes were irrevocable, what influence would that feeling have on their attitude-making process? All of these questions concern different operational definitions of "commitment." They are included in the general question of whether or not a person's taking some binding action influences his attitudes and provides him with effective resistance to counterpropaganda.

We have already seen the crucial role of various kinds of commitment in dissonance theory, where the individual's commitment to some action is seen as an important component of dissonance arousal (Brehm and Cohen, 1962). There can be no postdecisional dissonance unless there has been a commitment of some sort. However, as we shall see, taking some binding action has effects independent of dissonance.

Acting on an Attitude: The "Foot-in-the-door" Technique If you want someone to do something big for you, get him to do something small but committing first. This is the lesson of one study (Freedman and Fraser, 1966). The investigators, presenting themselves as members of a nonprofit service organization, asked two sets of people to post a large, unattractive sign, which read "Drive Carefully," in their front yards. One set of people had been approached previously by another group of investigators, who asked them to perform one of a number of lesser tasks, such as sign a petition urging their senators to work for safe-driving legislation. The other group was being approached for the first time.

As you might expect, the people who had already expressed a willingness to perform a lesser task responded far more favorably than the previously unapproached group. Over 55 percent of those who had complied with the initial small request agreed to post the ugly sign, and only 17 percent of those who were being approached for the first time agreed to do so.

If this technique works in other situations, it

could have enormous practical implications. How could you use it in your safe-driving campaign? By getting people to sign a petition urging stricter drunk-driving legislation, you might gradually involve them in more effortful safe-driving behaviors.

As the investigators pointed out, it is not entirely clear why the foot-in-the-door technique works. Do you think it would be dissonance-arousing to refuse to post a sign after you have signed a petition? Would your signing the petition change your attitude? Or would signing the petition make you pay more attention to safe driving and talk about it with your friends?

Making Your Attitude Public If you agreed to make a tape recording of your views, would that modify your attitudes and make them more resistant to counterpropaganda? The results of several studies suggest that it might. Students who initially believed that scholarships should be awarded on the basis of need came to support their position even more strongly after indicating a willingness to state their position on tape (Jellison and Mills, 1969). In studies in which subjects actually made a tape recording, however, commitment did not have any effect on their views (Kiesler and Sakumura, 1966). The discrepancy between these two studies opens the fascinating possibility that the process of recording may somehow undo the effects of the initial commitment (Jellison and Mills, 1969).

Making your decision public also increases your resistance to counterpropaganda. If you commit yourself publicly, say by signing a petition in favor of an issue, you become more resistant to attack and may even become more extreme in your attitudes if you are attacked. This was shown in a recent field study (Kiesler, Mathog, Pool, and Howenstine, 1971). Half the women in a group that favored disseminating birth-control information in the local high school were asked to sign a petition urging that this be done. On the following day half of those who had signed the petition received a leaflet attacking this stand. Then on the following day the women's attitudes about birth control and their willingness to do volunteer work for a group distributing birth-control information were measured. As in earlier work, signing the petition increased the intensity of the women's

attitudes. Women who had initially felt favorably about the issue felt even more so after they had signed the petition. Commitment also influenced their reaction to attack. After they had committed themselves, reading contradictory information increased their willingness to act on behalf of their attitude. Over 40 percent of those who had signed the petition and had had their position attacked agreed to do volunteer work, as compared to only 10.5 percent of those who had signed but had not been attacked.

Getting someone to commit himself and then attacking his position may be an excellent way of intensifying his attitudes. Additional confirmation of the power of this technique has been obtained in another recent study (Pallak, Mueller, Dollar, and Pallak, 1972). In fact, the process related to commitment may furnish one explanation of the polarization of attitudes among persons who have publicly committed themselves. After a student radical has publicly advocated a given position, his own attitudes may become even stronger and more resistant to any evidence that is inconsistent with his publicly stated position.

Why does making a decision public intensify it and make it more resistant to counterpropaganda? Is this because you know that other people expect you to be consistent? Or does commitment provide information with which you judge, and thus formulate more clearly, your own attitudes? Or in the process of justifying your attitudes, do you become more sensitive to supporting arguments? In an experiment supporting this last hypothesis, people who had committed themselves learned more information that was consistent with their position than people who had not committed themselves (Salancik and Kiesler, 1971).

Making Your Decision Irrevocable In many dissonance studies commitment has been important in arousing dissonance. But does the act of making an irrevocable decision have any other psychological effects? A number of studies suggest that if you know a decision will be committing, you may try to be unbiased and as objective and accurate as possible before you make the decision (Janis and Mann, 1968). Evidence in support of this hypothesis has been obtained in several studies. If, for instance, an adult is warned that his decision will be binding, his decision making is more cautious, and he is less confident about the correctness of his decision (Mann and Taylor, 1970). Children as young as four or five years old have also been found to approach a decision more carefully if they are warned that it will be committing (Mann, 1971).

Commitment—no matter what form it takes—has been shown to have a powerful effect. However, different forms of commitment may produce different psychological effects. Although it has been assumed in the research that all kinds of commitment are interchangeable, this may not be the case. For instance, in publicly stating your attitude you may be more concerned about the impression this makes on others, whereas in making irrevocable decisions you may be more concerned about being correct.

> *The effects of forewarning may depend on the audience's level of commitment to the issue.*

Should you forewarn the members of your audience that you are going to try to persuade them to drive more carefully? The experimental evidence on the effects of forewarning has not been consistent. Sometimes forewarning the members of an audience has resulted in their being less influenced by a communication. For example, teen-agers who were told ten minutes ahead of time that they were going to hear a talk entitled "Why Teen-agers Should Not Be Allowed to Drive" showed significantly less attitude change than teen-agers who were not warned in advance (Freedman and Sears, 1965b). That a warned audience would be less persuasible seems predictable. If you knew that in ten minutes you'd be hearing a talk on why you should not be allowed to drive, you would probably start thinking of reasons why you should be able to drive, and you might become a little hostile toward anyone presumptuous enough to try to deny you that right.

Yet forewarning has also resulted in an audience's showing more attitude change. Telling subjects in advance that their attitudes about the high probability of a Communist takeover in Latin America would be attacked resulted in more attitude change (McGuire and Millman, 1965). Why should forewarning increase persuasion? Perhaps when the issue is complex, people are afraid they will not be able to resist persuasion. Thus when they know they will be exposed to a communication that opposes their views, they misinterpret their own initial position and persuade themselves that they really adhered to the attacker's position all along. Obviously, there are limits to this phenomenon. Only when a person's initial beliefs are ambiguous and he views change as a threat to his self-esteem does forewarning motivate him to make a protective change (McGuire and Millman, 1965).

Why should forewarning teen-agers that they are going to be persuaded they shouldn't drive have a different effect than forewarning people that they are going to be persuaded to change their beliefs about Communist takeovers? One clear difference between the two situations is the degree to which the subjects are committed to their beliefs. For teen-agers, prohibiting their driving is equivalent to prohibiting their breathing, whereas the students may have cared little about Communist takeovers in distant lands.

As we have seen, when people who are committed are attacked, they become more intense about their attitudes. If we assume (as Kiesler, 1971, has) that forewarning is like an attack, it may follow that the effects of forewarning depend on the level of the person's commitment along with the strength of the attack. If the attack is very strong or the person's commitment very weak, the forewarned person may accept the attacker's position. But if his commitment is strong or the attack weak, the forewarned person may be more resistant and may even become more intensely committed to his own position. Support for this hypothesis has been obtained (Kiesler and Jones, 1971).

> *Dimensions of the attitude and its associated cognitive structure influence its resistance to persuasion.*

Are all of your attitudes equally open to change? Obviously not. Persuading you that your mother is a fink might take a lot more effort than convincing you that a particular mouthwash is ineffective. If your reactions resemble those of college students tested in a recent experiment, it would be more difficult to persuade you that the tuition at your university should be increased by $600 than to persuade you that Allentown, Pennsylvania, should add 240 acres to its parks (Rhine and Severance, 1970). An increase in the tuition at your university is a highly ego-involving issue, whereas the acreage of the parks in a town that may be thousands of miles away is relatively unimportant to you.

That highly *ego-involving attitudes* are much more resistant to change has been shown in a number of studies. Imagine your reactions and those of your friends if a speaker from the state legislative body should speak about the merits of increasing the tuition at your university. (See Figure 4-8.) Your own opposition might make you distort what he says, stop listening, start thinking up your own counterarguments, and denigrate the speaker. If the situation permitted, your friends might start to heckle the speaker. As we have already noted, your involvement in the issue could also narrow the range of positions that you would consider as possible compromises. You might feel that anything over $50 would be completely unacceptable for tuition expenses, although you would consider a much wider range of possibilities for the park acreage in Allentown. As you become more ego-involved, the range of what you consider acceptable narrows (Sherif, Sherif, and Nebergall, 1965; Rhine and Severance, 1970).

Moreover, many of your most ego-involved attitudes may be so linked with each other that they produce an *"anchoring"* effect. An attack on any one attitude in this interrelated structure would threaten the whole structure and thus produce an especially high level of resistance. As a number of experiments have shown, the more integrated the person's belief system is and the more salient the internal logical relationships among the beliefs is, the more resistant the person is to persuasion directed at any one specific belief in the system (e.g., Holt, 1970). In the tuition issue, for instance, your attitude about increased tuition may be closely related to your attitudes about the Establishment, student protest, and so forth. And it may also be related to other goals and values: If the tuition were increased, you might have to work

FIGURE 4-8 Trying to change attitudes that are important to the audience is risky business.

BOX 2 — ARE SOME PEOPLE MORE PERSUASIBLE THAN OTHERS?

A vast amount of research has been done to isolate individual differences that relate to persuasibility. Before we discuss some of these results, take the following quiz to test the accuracy of your impressions. As you answer the questions, keep in mind that "being persuaded" involves two processes: comprehending the message and yielding to it (McGuire, 1969a).

	Yes	No	Depends on Other Variables in the Situation
1. In general, are women more persuasible than men?			
2. Is age related to persuasibility?			
3. Are some people more susceptible to persuasion than others?			
4. Are intelligent people more persuasible?			
5. Are people with low self-esteem more persuasible?			

The correct answer is Yes to the first three questions and "it depends" to the last two questions. That females are more persuasible than males is one of the most consistent findings in laboratory studies (e.g., Rosenthal et al., 1964). The feminine role in our society has traditionally emphasized passivity and yielding, so that when little girls are socialized into their roles, they may be trained to yield. Further, since females tend to be more verbal than males, they may understand complicated messages better.

Age is also related to persuasibility. Consistently, eight and nine year olds have been found to be maximally persuasible. Suggestibility seems to increase up to that age and then to decline steadily until the child reaches adolescence, after which it levels off (Barber and Calverley, 1964; Stukát, 1958). Up to the age of nine the child's ability to comprehend the message may increase rapidly. After nine comprehen-sion may still be increasing slowly, but the resistance to yielding may be increasing more rapidly (McGuire, 1969a).

There seems to be a trait of "general persuasibility"—some people are more likely to yield to persuasive messages regardless of the issue. In one study high-school students were exposed to messages that were contrary to their attitudes on a wide variety of subjects, and their attitude change scores on all of the issues were measured. As predicted, there were consistent individual differences. If the students changed on one issue, they were more likely to change on the others. The correlations were, however, relatively low (Janis and Field, 1959).

No clear relationship between intelligence and persuasibility has been found. Although people who are intelligent may be more likely to understand a message, they may be less likely to yield to it. Thus when the persuasive message is simple, intelligent people should be influenced less than others, but when it is complicated, they should be influenced more, since they would understand the message better (Hovland, Lumsdaine, and Sheffield, 1949).

The relationship between self-esteem and persuasibility is also complicated. In some studies people with low self-esteem have been found to be more persuasible; in others people with high self-esteem have been found to be more persuasible. The relationship between self-esteem and persuasibility may also depend on the complexity of the situation (McGuire, 1969a). This hypothesis has been confirmed. In a complicated persuasion situation people with high self-esteem were influenced more, but in a simple persuasive situation those with low self-esteem were persuaded more (Gollob and Dittes, 1965). Those with high self-esteem may comprehend better but yield less.

more hours at your spare-time job, or your summer job earnings might have to go for tuition rather than for the sports car you were planning to buy. And your attitude about tuition may be closely linked to what your friends think. Imagine your friends' reaction if you said that you thought a $600 tuition increase per semester would be a good idea.

The *perceived origin* of an attitude may also influence its resistance to change. If a person believes that a particular attitude is the product of learning rather than the result of "intrinsic characteristics of the object," it may be easier for him to change the attitude. For example, if someone feels that his attitude about abortion has been acquired solely through the teachings of others, it may be easier for him to modify that attitude than it would be for someone who believes that abortion is intrinsically wrong.

There is some correlational evidence confirming the predicted relationship between the perceived origin of an attitude and an individual's expectancy that it might change. Students were asked to indicate the origin of their attitudes and their expectancy that these attitudes could be modified. Those attitudes that were rated as being based on learning were seen as being significantly more open to change than those based on intrinsic characteristics of the situation (Levy and House, 1970).

Whether or not you think your attitudes are liable to change may be an important determinant in your reactions to persuasive communications. If you expect to change, you may open yourself to information, but if you feel that an attitude is immutable, you may cut off the information before it penetrates. If this analysis is correct, it follows that attitude change must involve not only an effective process of communicating persuasive material—the subject of our last three sections—but also an initial attempt to persuade the individual that his attitude can be changed (Levy and House, 1970).

Unfortunately, only a few theorists (Rokeach, 1960; McGuire, 1968) have given any attention to the attributes of attitudes that influence their openness to change. The majority of the research on attitude change has been devoted to techniques to induce change, such as the effect of fear appeals; some research has been devoted to the characteristics of an audience that relate to its acceptance of persuasive communications (see Box 2); but little attention has been given to the target of persuasion—the characteristics of the attitude itself.

Summary

All of the variables discussed in this section influence an individual's power to resist persuasion by affecting his ability to counterargue. Role playing focuses the role player's attention on his behavior and tends to divert his normal tendency to rebut the message of that role. Distraction may interfere directly with the counterarguing process. Inoculation may increase the audience's resistance to later counterpropaganda by bolstering its ability to counterargue. Commitment may inhibit counterarguing: Once you take action, you may no longer criticize or question the evidence. Forewarning of persuasive intent may decrease the effectiveness of a communication by giving the audience time to criticize the communicator and his message. People may resist persuasion most when they are highly involved with and committed to the attitude as well as when they feel that the attitude is the result of the intrinsic characteristics of the object.

The Long-term Effects of Persuasion

If you presented a film showing gory traffic accidents, how long would its influence on the attitudes and driving practices of those who viewed it last? When would the film's impact be the greatest? What could be done to increase the permanency of its effects? The answers to these questions are important because unless a persuasive message has lasting impact, it doesn't make much practical difference what one does.

Surprisingly little research has been done on the permanency of attitude change. This neglect becomes more understandable when you consider some of the research problems. If you wished to measure the long-term effect of your safe-driving films, what problems would you encounter? Contacting the subjects might be difficult. Once they left your experiment, you would have no control over them. Subjects who were in different conditions could contact one another and so confound the experimental treatments. Further, the experimental demand of repeatedly having their attitudes measured might influence the subjects' reactions. Finally, doing this research would be very time-consuming, since you would have to wait for a considerable period of time to elapse before the permanency of the effects could be validly tested.

> *Most, but not all, persuasive communications have short-lived effects.*

Although there is a great deal of variability in the duration of attitude change, it is often relatively temporary. In some studies there were no residual effects at all six months after the audience had been exposed to a communication. For example, immediately after a group of foremen had taken a two-week leadership-training course in which the importance of consideration for others was emphasized, the men indicated that they thought consideration for others was more important than they had previously. But when the on-the-job behavior of those who had completed the course was compared with a comparable group who had never taken the course, there were no consistent differences (Fleishmann, Harris, and Burtt, 1955).

More typically, persuasive communications continue to have an effect—about half the size of the immediate effect—for up to six months. For example, in one study mothers in an experimental group read a pamphlet urging them to begin toilet training their infants later than usual; mothers in a control condition were not given any information concerning toilet training. Immediately after the mothers read the communication, they indicated that they felt toilet training should be started later than they had previously thought. Six months later the pamphlet still had a significant effect on these mothers, although the effect was not as large as the immediate one. But one year later there was no significant difference between the control and experimental groups (Maccoby, Romney, Adams, and Maccoby, 1962).

In some cases, however, the effects of persuasive communications have continued on, undiminished, for very long periods of time. For example, eighteen months after cigarette smokers had played the role of lung-cancer victims, their smoking was still significantly less than that of subjects in a control group (Mann and Janis, 1968). This long-term effect is interesting in that the eighteen-month follow-up was conducted by someone that the subjects did not know was connected with the experiment. Although the results of this study suggest that role playing had extremely long-lasting effects, the investigators noted that during the eighteen-month interval, the surgeon general's report linking cigarette smoking and lung cancer had been released. This event may have reinforced the effect of the role playing, and thus necessitates some caution in interpreting the experimental results. Further, the investigators had to rely on the self-report measures of the smokers.

> *In some cases persuasive communications have a delayed-action, or "sleeper," effect.*

Although usually the effect of a persuasive communication is maximal immediately after exposure and then declines gradually until it is no longer significant, sometimes the effect is greater after a time delay. Such an effect was first noted in the 1940s, when several investigators found that the effect of a persuasive film was greater eleven weeks after the film had been shown than it was immediately after it had been shown (Hovland, Lumsdaine, and Sheffield, 1949). Since that time a number of other investigators have also reported delayed-action, or "sleeper," effects (e.g., Rokeach, 1971).

Why should the impact of a persuasive communication be greater after a period of time has elapsed? There are several possible answers. A persuasive communication may modify the way a person reacts to subsequent events. A cigarette smoker who role plays the part of a lung-cancer victim might become sensitized to information linking cigarette smoking to lung cancer and might become more emotionally aroused when reading such information. When questioned about their emotional reaction to the surgeon general's report, the role players said they had been more worried about lung cancer than did the students in the control group (Mann and Janis, 1968).

Further, if something in the persuasive situation interferes with immediate acceptance, the audience may tend to forget this interference over time while retaining the communication. If an incompetent communicator presented a persuasive communication, you might not accept what he said because you did not trust him. But over time you might tend to forget the source of the communication while retaining what was said. (How many times have you remembered something, but not been able to recall where you read it?) Thus subjects exposed to a negative communicator would show more attitude change over time than they would immediately after they had heard the communication. And those exposed to a positive communicator would show less attitude change over time. Their initial acceptance would be high because of their favorable reaction to the communicator, but over time they might forget the communicator and react to the message, which was contrary to their initial beliefs. This effect has been obtained (Hovland and Weiss, 1951). In the latter case, however, if the audience is reminded of the source of the message, the sleeper effect disappears, and the positive communicator once again has impact (Kelman and Hovland, 1953).

But some caution should be exercised in making this interpretation of the sleeper effect. In the time between the immediate and the delayed testing, the students in the various experimental conditions could have talked with one another. Those that received the communication from the low-credibility communicator could have found out that others had received similar messages from highly credible sources and so been more persuaded. One could argue that a sleeper effect may simply be due to the social interactions between the subjects (Festinger, 1955). Only when the subjects in the various experimental conditions have no opportunity to interact can this methodological problem be eliminated.

Another possible explanation of the sleeper effect is that when the communication is complicated, the person needs time for it to "sink in"

and to work out all of its logical implications. Several studies provide support for this hypothesis. For example, when students were made aware of inconsistencies between their values and their attitudes about civil rights, their attitudes had changed more three to five months later than they had three weeks later (Rokeach, 1971).

The audience's retention of the message's content, environmental support for the changed attitude, and the audience's being actively involved in the communication all affect the duration of persuasion.

Retention of the Message's Content   One might assume that the more a person retains of the persuasive arguments, the longer his attitudes will be changed. Thus any variable that increases the audience's retention of the message would increase the length of time attitude change persisted.

Unfortunately, the relationship between attitude change and the person's memory of a persuasive communication is not that simple. Correlations between the amount of material retained and the amount of attitude change have not been large, ranging from .21 to .53 (Janis and Rife, 1959; McGuire, 1957).

Environmental Support for the Changed Attitude
Your attitudes result from your own experiences with objects, what others say and do, and your own emotions. If someone showed you a film of automobile accidents, you might indicate immediately after the film that you intended to drive more safely. But once you got back to your usual social interactions, the forces that determined your original attitude would act to recreate that attitude. Thus on leaving the auditorium, you might speed again and enjoy it; you might see others driving recklessly and hear them bragging about their bravado; or you might really get angry and vent your emotions in your driving. Any attitude change caused by the momentary effect of a persuasive communication is inherently unstable, and the attitude will revert to its former state unless the individual's

social environment can be made to support it (Festinger, 1964).

When the individual's environment does support the changed attitude, it may persist for very long periods of time. Thus, as we saw earlier, girls at Bennington who became more liberal stayed that way over a twenty-five-year period, and their husbands tended to be more liberal than the average, thereby providing them with a supporting environment (Newcomb, Koenig, Flacks, and Warwick, 1967).

The Audience's Being Actively and Intensely Involved in the Communication As we have seen, several studies have shown that role playing exerts a longer lasting influence than passively reading the same information. While role playing the individual may become more involved, may have a more intense emotional reaction, and may look for information to support his role. Spontaneous comments made by the lung-cancer role players indicated that the experience was still extraordinarily vivid and effective in breaking down their feelings of personal invulnerability eighteen months later.

In another experiment in which the effects were remarkably durable, the participants were also actively involved in a highly emotional way (Rokeach, 1971). Students were made aware of inconsistencies and hypocrisies in their values and attitudes concerning civil rights—a peculiarly painful kind of dissonance. Students in the experimental group were asked to rank their values (including freedom and equality) and to indicate their attitude about civil rights. Then value rankings that were said to have been obtained previously from 298 college students were shown to the subjects, and the experimenter stated that most students ranked freedom as the most important value and equality as the eleventh most important value, a reaction showing that "students are, in general, much more interested in their own freedom than in other people's." To expose the students' inconsistencies even more pointedly, the experimenter told them that previous students who were unsympathetic with civil rights also ranked freedom high and equality low, whereas those students who were pro-civil rights ranked freedom and equality equally high. Students in the control group simply ranked their values

and indicated their attitude toward civil rights. No interpretations were given.

When the subjects were tested fifteen to seventeen months later, the students in the experimental group showed a significant increase in their ranking of equality, and they were much more pro-civil rights. Even more impressive than these paper-and-pencil changes is the fact that significantly more subjects in the experimental group responded favorably to an invitation to join the NAACP, which was sent out on NAACP stationery more than one year after the experiment. As the result of one forty-minute session, the students' values and attitudes were still changed more than a year later.

Again we have the question of why the experimental effect was so durable? Was the self-dissatisfaction aroused by exposing the inconsistencies within the self so painful that it continued to motivate the student to change? Was the experience so vivid that it continued to be remembered? Or did the subjects seek out social support for their changed values?

Irrespective of why such long-lasting effects occur, that they do is clear. This finding may make you feel somewhat ambivalent. It is encouraging to find that present-day techniques can produce such powerful and lasting attitude changes. But possessing the power to mold attitudes and values opens the ethical questions of who should make decisions about which values and attitudes to shape and in what direction to mold them (Rokeach, 1971).

Conclusion

The laboratory work on attitude change has yielded an impressive body of knowledge as to how varying aspects of the source, message, and audience contribute to a message's persuasiveness. At this point we have the beginnings of a technology of attitude change—techniques that can be and are being applied with impressive results. See Box 3.

We are beginning to know *what* works, but do we know *why* it works? Although the general theories of attitude change (learning theory, dissonance theory, and social judgment theory) have given rise to a lot of research, none of the

BOX 3 THE SELLING OF THE PRESIDENT IN 1968

In the 1968 presidential campaign, Richard Nixon's image and his solutions to the country's problems were marketed in just the same way any other product is sold. Sound impossible? If it does, you haven't read Joe McGinniss' account of the persuasive techniques used in that campaign (1970).

One of the main goals of the campaign was to alter Nixon's image—to make him seem less cold, aloof, and impersonal and more likable and more similar to his audience. Nixon was coached to smile more frequently and to include more humor, and he was always shown in an "unstaged setting"—leaning on a desk, informally interacting with people. In his live television shows an audience of loyal Republicans was primed to clap enthusiastically and to crowd around him when the show ended.

Nixon was also made to appear trustworthy and expert. None of the sweating and shifty eyes of the 1960 television debates were observable in 1968. Great precautions were taken to make sure that the television studios were cool, that he was provided with a handkerchief and off-camera opportunities to use it. Attention was given to using the proper make-up for his eyes ("slightly whiter make-up on upper eyelids") and to having him maintain eye contact with those he was addressing. A series of television shows in which Nixon was shown answering unrehearsed questions from a panel of six or seven voters made him seem more spontaneous and truthful. He was presented as a calmer, more thoughtful "new Nixon" and introduced in an appropriately presidential, dignified style, which emphasized his expertness. In the 1972 campaign the dignity of the presidential office was emphasized.

Efforts were also made to make him appear strong, masculine, dynamic, and youthful. In spot commercials he was shown in a wood-paneled set with an impressively large wooden desk.

When he answered questions, he was shown standing alone—ringed with people—which made him look "gutsy" as well as candid. He was encouraged to keep a good tan so that he would appear healthy, and campaign photographs were selected that made him look young and vital.

As many politician's speeches do, Nixon's speeches contained a number of platitudes and clichés. For example, the following sentence appeared in one ad: "We must stop talking to Americans as special interest groups and start talking to special interest groups as Americans" (McGinniss, p. 147). Who can argue against considering all Americans as Americans? Since you can't argue against them, platitudes and clichés may be particularly effective—as inoculation theory would predict.

In Nixon's spot commercials his words were accompanied by a series of photographs to illustrate the speech.

While Nixon repeated the same pat speech about law and order, the photographs of crime that flashed across the screen gave the speech an exciting, dynamic quality. The artful use of photographs distracted the audience from Nixon's words and made the words seem new.

One of Nixon's main campaign themes was the rising crime rate in the United States and the need for law and order. In one spot commercial a woman was shown walking down a lonely city street at night, while the announcer said that a violent crime was committed in the United States every sixty seconds. Seeing someone in such a threatening setting was an involving reminder to the audience that crime could happen to them too—if they didn't vote for the law-and-order candidate. This scare tactic may sound familiar.

Do you still think a president can't be sold?

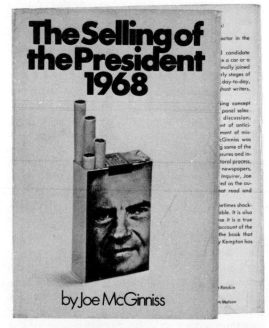

(Carl Fischer)

theories has been consistently confirmed. Thus after thirty years of focusing primarily on the question "What aspects of the source, message, and audience influence persuasion?" we still don't understand the processes involved in attitude change.

Perhaps the time has come to change the question being asked to "What are the processes involved in attitude change?" Intensively interviewing people about the way they change their attitudes might yield some testable hypotheses. For example, if counterarguing turned out to be an important theme, investigators could focus more directly on what facilitates or inhibits this process. Or researchers could investigate how the role player's production of supporting arguments influences his reaction to his role playing.

An Emotional Approach to Changing Attitudes

Imagine the reactions from an authoritarian type of person like Archie Bunker if you tried to modify his racial prejudices by telling him about the contributions of the blacks to American history. After a few moments of this, Archie would probably get angry, start yelling, defend his position with his own "arguments," and end up believing more firmly in his own prejudices. This reaction emphasizes the fact that not all attitudes are based on the individual's need to know and to relate realistically to the environment. As we have seen, some attitudes are primarily expressions of an individual's personality. Giving the person some insight into his personality and enabling him to accept his own impulses would be the best way to change these attitudes.

To find the most effective way to change an attitude, then, one must first know its motivational basis. For example, a housewife's negative attitude about frozen TV dinners might be based on her own personal experience, on information furnished by others, or on her own, perhaps unconscious, motives and emotions. She may not like frozen TV dinners because she has tried them and found them tasteless, or she may not like them because she feels guilty about not cooking dinner for her family. To

present advertising appeals that would be the most effective in getting her to purchase TV dinners, one would have to know not only her attitude, but also why she feels that way (Katz, 1960).

The need to first establish the basis for an attitude before one advertises has been emphasized by those who do motivational research. Their basic assumption is that people sometimes buy things for unconscious, irrational reasons (Dichter, 1964). Usually, advertisers ascertain the public's attitudes and the reasons behind these attitudes through the intensive study of small groups of consumers. These studies include projective tests, clinical interviews, and free associations. When they know the public's attitudes and motives, those who construct the advertising campaigns can attempt to counter the potential customers' resistances. If housewives feel guilty because convenience foods reduce what they do for their families, advertising campaigns can emphasize that convenience foods allow them to do other things for their families—time out of the kitchen can be spent playing with the children (Dichter, 1964).

Motivational research has resulted in some very successful advertising campaigns. After an advertising campaign that stressed how quickly a particular airline could get a businessman to his destination had failed, the motivational research people were called in to answer the puzzling question of why emphasizing speed hadn't worked. Through in-depth interviewing, the researchers found that the emphasis on the quickness with which businessmen could get away from their families made some men feel guilty. When the advertising format was changed to "In only _____ hours you can *return* from your business trip to your family," sales rose sharply. (For further examples of motivational research, see Vance Packard's *Hidden Persuaders*.)

Although motivational research provides an interesting approach to advertising, it does pose some problems. How, for instance, did the motivational researchers for the airline company establish that the men felt guilty about speedily getting away from their families? Interpreting projective tests and interviews for unconscious material is a tricky business. Does the success of the second campaign suggest that the guilt hypothesis was correct? As we saw in Chapter 3, sales figures cannot be used as a final measure of the effectiveness of an advertising campaign. Maybe the other airlines ran particularly obnoxious ads, which drove the passengers back to the speedy airline. Even if one really does know what the consumers' unconscious attitudes are, designing ad campaigns that overcome these attitudes is difficult. If the housewife is sufficiently guilty, she may continue resisting frozen TV dinners no matter what you say.

As we have seen, racial prejudices can also fill a variety of functions within the individual. If a person's prejudices primarily serve an ego-defensive function, helping him to develop insight into his own personality disturbances might be the most effective way to reduce those prejudices. Again, you would have to assess the basis of the prejudice before using the functional approach. Prejudice does not serve an ego-defensive function for all persons. People can be prejudiced because of their own personal experiences and their social influences as well as because of their own personal problems. Once you have determined the function an attitude serves, you are in a position to design communications that are directed at that particular function.

If you were interested in assessing the motivational basis of prejudice, how would you separate the people for whom the attitude serves primarily an ego-defensive function from those for whom it is the result of social or personal information? This problem has plagued many of the researchers in this area. And what kinds of communications would counter the ego-defensive attitude? Changing an individual's unconscious motives and defenses is not easy.

One classic study tested the hypothesis that those whose prejudices are based on ego defenses are influenced most by communications that provide some insight into the dynamics of prejudice. The relative impact of two sets of materials was tested: (1) ego-defensive material, which first explained the psychological processes involved in scapegoating and then gave a case history of a college girl, which clearly showed the relationship between her own personality problems and her prejudices, and (2) informational material, which stressed the achievements of black Americans and their contributions to American society.

All of the subjects (college students) indicated their attitudes about blacks and then took some tests designed to measure their ego defensiveness, including parts of the F test. On the basis of their scores on these tests, the students' attitudes were categorized as either ego-defensive or factual and were subcategorized as high, medium, or low. One week later the subjects were randomly divided into three groups. One group read the ego-defensive materials; another read the informational material; and a third group did not read anything. All of the subjects indicated their attitudes toward blacks immediately after the experiment and again five weeks later.

As predicted, the students whose attitudes were labeled low ego-defensive or moderate ego-defensive were persuaded more by materials designed to show them the dynamics of prejudice than by the factual materials. But for those whose attitudes were high ego-defensive, neither type of material was very effective. For these strongly defensive people, the persuasive communications may not have been sufficiently strong to counter the entrenched defenses involved in their prejudices (Katz, Sarnoff, and McClintock, 1956).

This study and subsequent ones (e.g., McClintock, 1958) provide support for the hypothesis that appeals based on ego-defensive material can be an effective means of persuasion for some people who hold their beliefs for emotional reasons. However, the procedures used involve a number of problems. First, how did the investigators know that the prejudices of the ego-defensive personalities really served a defensive function? Does the fact that a person is generally defensive mean that this is the prime motive for his prejudice? Defensiveness can be expressed in a variety of ways. Moreover, the measurement of the overall level of defensiveness involved serious problems (Sarnoff, 1965). You will recall that the F test, which was found to correlate with the prejudice scale developed by the Berkeley group, was used to measure the level of ego defensiveness. Thus the subjects who were classified as ego-defensive may have also been more prejudiced, and after hearing that prejudiced people are sick, these highly prejudiced subjects may have changed what they said so they wouldn't look bad in front of the experimenter.

In a more recent study participation in a sensitivity group was used to manipulate the subjects' self-insight and self-acceptance. If a person knows himself, he should have less of a need to take out his hostile impulses on minority groups. This prediction was confirmed. Subjects who participated in a two-week sensitivity-training session showed significantly lower levels of prejudice after the two-week session than did a control group, which did not participate in the sensitivity training (Rubin, 1967).

Although this study provides an interesting confirmation of the effectiveness of a motivational approach, it too has some limitations. Again, no attempt was made to assess the function that prejudice played in each of the participants. It was assumed that an increase in self-insight and self-acceptance would automatically result in a decrease in prejudice, as though prejudice served an ego-defensive function for everyone. The intensive social interactions during the two-week, residential training sessions may have been as responsible for the decrease in prejudice as was the increased self-acceptance. The participants may have been sensitized to the issue by the initial measuring of prejudice, so that antiprejudice group pressure may have been responsible for the change. Despite the various criticisms, however, the general hypothesis that increasing self-insight may decrease prejudice in certain types of people seems to have received some confirmation.

The hypothesis that the most effective appeal depends on the function of the particular attitude is not as well supported, however, because of the absence of a good way of assessing what function is being served by a particular attitude. A reliable technology for assessing the function of attitudes is badly needed (Kiesler, Collins, and Miller, 1969).

Intensive Indoctrination

A few years ago in New York City, after almost twenty-four hours of police interrogation, a young man confessed to having raped one woman and to having murdered three others. Subsequent evidence proved him innocent of all four crimes (Zimbardo, 1970). After three years of Chinese brainwashing, a well-known Shanghai physician confessed to having been involved with French and American espionage as well as to having inflicted "slanderous insults on the Chinese people." On his release he denied that his confessions had any validity (Lifton, 1963).

What kinds of powerful persuasive techniques can make men confess to crimes they are not guilty of when their confession may lead to lengthy imprisonment or even death? If certain techniques can persuade people to make false confessions, they may also serve as very powerful techniques for changing people's professed attitudes about other things.

Police interrogations and brainwashing are not the only intensive indoctrination situations in which old attitudes are weakened and new ones implanted. We have seen the power of parents to mold their young children's attitudes. Prolonged periods of intensive indoctrination also occur in adulthood. Education may be viewed as an intensive indoctrination. When you attend college, for instance, you not only learn facts but attitudes as well, as we saw in the Bennington study. Profound attitude changes may also occur during psychotherapy.

Intensive indoctrination may be necessary to secure really large and lasting attitude changes, and even with intensive indoctrination, an individual who yields during the indoctrination process may still revert to his former attitudes once he is released. For example, in 1965 more than 500 appeals were made by prisoners in New York State, who wished to have their cases, which were based on confessions, reopened (Zimbardo, 1970).

Police confessions

Over 80 percent of all criminal cases are solved by the suspect's confessing his crime during police interrogation. (See Figure 4-9.) Once the confession is admitted as evidence, the trial by judge and jury is largely a formality. How the suspect is "tried" by the police, then, becomes a matter of utmost importance. Although progress has been made in protecting the rights of suspects during interrogations, through the Supreme Court rulings providing that all suspects have the right to counsel during interrogation and requiring that they be told of their rights to remain silent, the question is whether or not these rulings have gone far enough in protecting suspects from undue psychological coercion. Clearly, in some cases they have not, since people have confessed to crimes and then been found to be innocent. As you read about some of the police interrogation tactics, you might consider whether or not you would confess to just about anything if you were subjected to some of these procedures.

There is very little direct evidence about what happens during police interrogations. More psychological analyses have been written about the experiences of men brainwashed by the Chinese Communists than about the strategies used to extract confessions in the local police station. To get the best evidence of how police interrogation works, one must consult procedure manuals developed by the police themselves. Since interrogation techniques are emphasized in police training, they have been treated at length in a number of police manuals (e.g., Inbau and Reid, 1962). The most extensive study to date of police interrogation procedures relies heavily on these manuals (Zimbardo, 1970). Much of the summary set forth here is taken from that study.

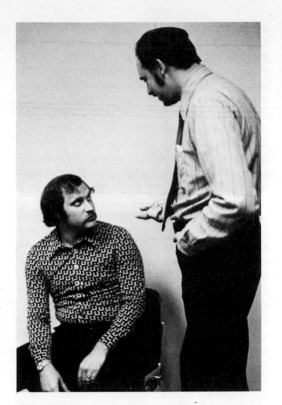

FIGURE 4-9 A simulated police interrogation. (R. Lynn Goldberg)

Demand Characteristics of the Interrogation
Suspects are questioned in an environment that "minimizes sensory stimulation, maximally exposes the subject's vulnerability, and provides for complete control and domination by the interrogator" (Zimbardo, 1970, p. 103). The interrogation takes place in a plain room that is free of all distractions, and all signs of a "policelike atmosphere" (such as bars) have been removed. In this quiet setting the monotony of the environment, with its reduced sensory input, may increase the suspect's suggestibility, as sensory deprivation has been found to do in other situations (Suedfeld, 1964).

As the police interrogator demonstrates his mastery during the interrogation, all social support is removed from the suspect. No one whom the suspect knows is present. No tension-relieving activities, such as smoking, are

permitted, and the suspect is usually seated in an armless, straight-back chair. To avoid distracting the suspect from the interrogation, the police officer is dressed in a conservative manner with no signs of police paraphernalia visible. To bring maximum pressure on the suspect, the interrogator stands or sits as close to the suspect as he can. The interrogator's complete power in the situation is even demonstrated in such small but effective ways as his telling the suspect when he can or cannot sit.

Perceptual and Judgmental Distortion The police use a variety of tactics during interrogation to misrepresent and confuse the situation. To get the suspect to confess, the interrogator may minimize the seriousness of the offense, or he may blame others, including the victim. For example, one manual suggests that in forcible rape cases "where circumstances permit, the suggestion might be offered that the rape victim acted like she might be a prostitute" (Zimbardo, 1970, p. 104). The police manuals even suggest ways for the interrogators to fabricate evidence. The interrogator may lead the suspect to believe that his fingerprints were found at the scene of the crime when they were not. Or in a fixed line-up the suspect may be falsely accused by police accomplices pretending to be honest witnesses. Or the suspect may be accused of a crime far more serious than the one he is being held for. Someone being questioned about a burglary might be glad to confess to that crime after being accused of murder.

After being questioned for several consecutive hours, the suspect may begin to be confused about what is true and what is not. When made to play the role of a guilty party with the details of his crime repeatedly suggested to him, the suspect may begin to believe what is said about him and what he may falsely say about himself. As one suspect who was convicted of first-degree murder on the basis of an alleged confession said: "They were asking so many questions, I don't know when they started or when they stopped or anything. Everything is so mixed up, I don't know what I told them" (*Asbury Park Evening Press,* November 12, 1966, quoted in Maslach, 1971, pp. 145–146).

Social-Psychological Distortion During the interrogation the police officer attempts to develop a warm social relationship with the suspect, thereby seeking to make the suspect want to earn his approval. A variety of tactics are used to create rapport—including flattering the suspect, patting him on the shoulder, or offering to do him a small favor, such as getting him a glass of water. Sometimes an interrogator who seems pleasant alternates with a cruel, relentless interrogator to increase the suspect's belief in the friendly interrogator's sincerity. (This is known as the "Mutt-and-Jeff approach.")

If there are two or more suspects, they may be played off against each other. One may be detained in a waiting room and told that his accomplice, who is detained separately in an interrogation room, has just confessed to the crime. A secretary is then brought from the interrogation room to the waiting room to "type up the confession" allegedly made by the prisoner's accomplice. As she does so, she asks the waiting suspect questions that make him

believe his accomplice has not only confessed to the crime but has implicated him thoroughly. Then when the waiting suspect is questioned, he confesses from spite.

Clinical Approach The interrogator also plays upon the suspect's guilts and fears. Many people have deep-seated guilts about real or imagined crimes committed during their childhood, and these can only be relieved by confession. Some theorists hold that all of us have some need to confess, to be punished, and to receive absolution (Reik, 1941). The interrogator sizes up each suspect to determine his weaknesses. If he seems nervous and guilty, he may be left alone to sweat it out. If he doesn't seem to feel guilty, the interrogator tries to instill guilt by repeatedly accusing the suspect and by calling attention to the physiological symptoms of guilt. One manual suggests that the interrogator should focus on the dryness of the suspect's mouth, his shaking hands, and the "peculiar feeling inside" caused by his guilty conscience in order to suggest the suspect's guilt to him (Inbau and Reid, 1962). Guilt may be stimulated in young men by asking them how often they masturbate. After the suspect has been fully upset by unrelated guilts, he may be relieved to change the topic to his alleged crime.

Semantic and Verbal Distortion The phrasing and asking of questions has been polished to a fine art by police interrogators. For young people, emphasizing the effects of the crime on the suspect's mother is a highly effective tactic. Anger-arousing terms are avoided. Homosexuals are never called perverts, since that would only arouse unproductive antagonism. The way in which questions are phrased is closely tailored to fit the suspect's educational level. Even the interrogator's tone of voice is controlled. As one manual says, "Care must be exercised as to tone of voice, because a very soft voice seems to lull the subject into a state of tranquility" (Inbau and Reid, 1962, in Zimbardo, 1970, p. 106).

Ethics of Police Interrogation Since police interrogation procedures have been known to make innocent people confess, they are clearly highly persuasive. Are such tactics necessary to maintain law and order? The available evidence suggests that unhampered interrogation tactics may not be necessary for effective law enforcement. In areas where the suspects' rights have been defended and interrogation procedures have been controlled, the rate of the increase in crime has been lower than in comparable areas where police have been free to interrogate in any way they wished (Zimbardo, 1970). Relying on excessively harsh interrogation techniques may be easier than amassing other kinds of evidence.

How can the use of such interrogation tactics be controlled? Interrogation takes place in the heavily guarded privacy of the police station. Procedures to make interrogations more public might protect the suspects' rights. Video tapes of interrogations might be made so that courts could decide if a particular confession had been illegally coerced. Further, both experimental evidence concerning the effects of various interrogation tactics and case histories of personal reactions to these tactics are badly needed. This is an enormously immediate question. If you were to be arrested tomorrow, these tactics might be used on you. The best way to resist being persuaded is to be aware of the techniques that might be used against you.

Chinese thought reform (brainwashing)

Usually police interrogations take place over a limited period of time—perhaps a day or two at the most. But the intensive indoctrination practices used by the Chinese Communists in the thought reform of some European civilians went on for a period of two to four years in an atmosphere even more totally controlled than that in the police interrogation.

There is nothing new in their tactics, however. Brainwashing is not the result of some mysterious new mind-controlling chemical or psychiatric insight. All of the specific tactics—such as the use of group pressures—have been used by the Chinese police for a long time. The physical hardships experienced by those being brainwashed in Chinese prisons are typical of life in a Chinese prison. What was new in the Chinese brainwashing was the systematic application of a wide variety of persuasive techniques, along with a great emphasis on the use of fellow prisoners as indoctrinators. The Chinese found

that under this concerted and powerful persuasive attempt the great majority of prisoners would confess without being physically tortured. It had been known for a long time that when maximal physical torture is used (as in the Spanish Inquisition), just about anyone can be made to say anything. The Chinese experience showed that concerted psychological pressures are at least as effective as old-fashioned torture—and perhaps more so. (See Figure 4-10.)

Our discussion of brainwashing procedures is based on Lifton's intensive interviews (which typically lasted fifteen to twenty hours) with Westerners who had been through the brainwashing procedure (1956, 1963) and, in particular, on one interview with Dr. Vincent, whose experiences were fairly typical. To minimize the distorting effects of time on memory, Lifton interviewed these brainwashing veterans immediately after their release from China. Of course, as with any interview, one can question whether or not the accounts were accurate. After having cooperated with the Chinese and having given highly anti-Western public confessions, the interviewees may have exaggerat-

FIGURE 4-10 Characterization of Chinese brainwashing techniques.

ed the rigors of their treatment in order to justify their compliance. However, in cross-checking the stories of twenty-five people, Lifton found that the versions of Chinese thought reform varied little from account to account.

Assaulting the Self The initial step is to weaken the individual's sense of identity along with all of his attitudes. The "reactionary" who enters the prison must die, and in his place a new man, cast in the communist image, must emerge. The prisoner's identity is annihilated by the removal of all feelings of social support, the demands of lengthy interrogations, and the physical and emotional stress induced by the prison situation.

Immediately after his arrest, all signs of physical identity were stripped from Dr. Vincent. He was addressed only by his prison number, not his name, and he was issued a drab prison uniform. Strong social pressure to confess was then brought to bear on him by his fellow prisoners. He was placed in an eight-by-twelve-foot cell with eight other prisoners, all Chinese who were advanced in their own personal reform and eager to reform Dr. Vincent. Dr. Vincent was ordered to sit in the center of the cell while the others stood in a circle around him, denouncing him as a spy and demanding that he confess everything to the government.

After several hours of this intensive group pressure, Dr. Vincent was subjected to his first interrogation. There a vague sense of guilt was implanted in him as he was accused for ten hours of "having committed crimes against the people." During the course of the interrogation, the interrogator obtained numerous personal details from Dr. Vincent, which later formed the nucleus of his "confession." When Vincent did not immediately yield and confess, the interrogator ordered that his hands be fixed behind his back with handcuffs and that chains be placed around his ankles.

Once he was back in his cell, his Chinese cell mates continued attacking him, both psychologically and physically. The unrelenting pressure to confess continued whenever he was not being interrogated, so that he could not sleep. One European businessman remembered:

they would put me in the middle of a cell and walk around me. Each one as he passed would spit in my face and hit me in the stomach.

[Lifton, 1956, p. 178.]

Combined with the psychological and social pressures, the handcuffs and chains were almost unbearable. Standing all day with his hands behind his back, the prisoner was reduced to the most basic biological level. As Dr. Vincent observed:

You are obliged to stand with chains on your ankles and holding your hands behind your back. They don't assist you because you are too reactionary. You eat as a dog does with your mouth and teeth. You arrange the cup and bowl with your nose to try and absorb broth twice a day. If you have to make water they open your trousers and you make water in a little tin in the corner. . . . In the w.c. someone opens your trousers and after you are finished they clean you. You are never out of the chains. Nobody pays any attention to your hygiene. Nobody washes you. In the room they say you are in chains only because you are a reactionary. They continue to tell you that if you confess all, you will be treated better.

[Lifton, 1963, p. 22.]

The Breaking Point Ill, tired, demoralized, vaguely guilty, depressed, and hopeless after eight days of constant pressure, Dr. Vincent became confused and began to lose his own sense of identity. He had confessed a great deal of personal information, which his cell mates and interrogators used in their pressures. At this point Dr. Vincent—like most of the prisoners—gave up and became "psychological Jello." Some prisoners became suicidal or psychotic, but most—like Vincent—gave in. Of the moment when he saw that his only hope of psychological survival was to yield to the environment, to cease resisting, and to start doing what the interrogators wanted, Dr. Vincent said:

From that moment, the judge is the real master of you. When he asks how many "intelligences" you gave to that person, you just put out a number in order to satisfy him. If he says, "Only those?" you say, "No, there are more." If he says, "One hundred," you say, "One hundred." . . . You do whatever they want.

[Lifton, 1963, p. 23.]

Leniency and the Gradual Emergence of a Confession Once the prisoner yields, his situation improves noticeably. In Dr. Vincent's case his chains were removed; he was allowed to sit while being interrogated; and his interrogators became warm and friendly. Rather than being attackers, his cell mates became more friendly, "fellow students." Further improvements in his condition were promised if he cooperated. He was told that if he confessed to his crimes, the government would be lenient with him and release him. His continued well-being as well as his hopes for the future were contingent on his continued compliance.

The Cell Study Group Once the person has yielded and given a rudimentary confession, the cell mates continue the pressure to yield further. The group imparts feelings of guilt, inundates the individual with information on communism, and requires him to adopt actively the communist point of view. For ten to sixteen hours per day the prisoners in the cell discuss and criticize the views of everyone in the cell. The individual is constantly made to criticize others and to accept criticism, so that guilt becomes a way of life. Somewhat like group psychotherapy, there is a massive concerted pressure to express "bad" thoughts—only in this situation they are phrased in Marxian terminology rather than psychotherapeutic terminology. Day-to-day interactions with others are analyzed in Marxian terms. If Dr. Vincent drank too much water, he was "draining the blood of the people." If he took up too much space while he slept, his action was "imperialist expansion."

The prisoner is taught to think in communist terms, and thus his guilt is channeled into his confession. Through hours of discussing communist material and definitions of crime with his interrogators and cell mates, the prisoner learns to verbalize material from the "people's standpoint." For example, according to the official communist point of view, there is no distinction between news, information, and intelligence. Thus any passing of news could be classified as espionage. The prisoners are made to verbalize this and show why it is a crime. After this endless role playing, the prisoner begins to internalize what he says and to use his new perspective to organize his confession into a more logical system, with his guilts artfully attached to fancied wrongs and real events in his life. As Dr. Vincent wrote:

In the cell, twelve hours a day you talk and talk—you have to take part—you must discuss yourself, criticize, inspect yourself, denounce your thought. Little by little you start to admit something, and look to yourself, only using the "people's judgment."

[Lifton, 1963, p. 27.]

For his successful role playing, the prisoner is given both social and material rewards. As he continues to become more "progressive," his lot improves. His food becomes better, and he is treated still more kindly by his interrogators. For his conformity to the group, he receives the satisfaction of being included in a group after months of ostracism. Always, there is the threat that unless he continues to improve, he will be returned to the miserable conditions of the beginning of his imprisonment.

The Clinical Approach In addition to capitalizing on the prisoner's guilts, the interrogators use the considerable amount of personal information the prisoner provides about his life and personality to attack other areas of weakness and so discredit the prisoner's life patterns. For example, the hypocrisy of one priest's saying that he was a servant of the Lord while he was served by others was pointed out in an exchange between an interrogator and the priest:

Are you familiar with the Biblical saying, "I came on earth to serve, not to be served?"
   "Yes, as a priest it is my creed."
   "Did you have a servant in your mission?"
   "Yes, I did."
   "Who made your bed in the morning and swept out the floor?"
   "My servant did this."
   "You did not live up to your doctrine very well, did you father?"

[Lifton, 1956, p. 187.]

The Final Elaboration After one year of this reeducation, Dr. Vincent was once again subjected to intensive indoctrination, and the details of his confession were expanded. Gradually, his confession was elaborated to include a more organized and coherent account of his "crimes." In final form Dr. Vincent's confession comprised eight crimes, including slanderous insults to the Chinese people.

After the prisoner has ceaselessly repeated the confession, reality begins to be blurred with the confessions. Most prisoners are aware of the distortions, but some come to believe at least some details of the confession. Rare is the prisoner who doesn't at least feel hazy at times about the line between fact and fiction after thousands of hours of learning the Chinese point of view and verbalizing his guilt. For example, after a third year of working through his confession with his cell mates and interrogators, Dr. Vincent came increasingly to believe in his own confession.

You begin to believe all this, *but it is a special kind of belief.* You are not absolutely convinced, but you accept it—in order to avoid trouble—because every time you don't agree, trouble starts again.

[Lifton, 1963, p. 31.]

The more he complied with what his captors wanted, the better he was treated. As his confession moved toward its final state, he was transferred to a more pleasant part of the prison and was given an hour of outdoor recreation per day. Finally, he was summoned for the formal signing of his confession in front of representatives from the Western press. Then he was sentenced to three years of imprisonment (which the Chinese considered he had already served) and released.

The Effects of Brainwashing These brainwashing procedures were effective in eliciting false confessions from most of the prisoners. But what of the other goal—converting the prisoners to Chinese communism? Powerful as the techniques were, they were not too successful in meeting this goal. Dr. Vincent's reactions were fairly typical. Immediately after his release he was very confused, frightened, and felt that he was being manipulated: "I have a certain idea that someone is spying on me because I came from the Communist world." On leaving China, he felt that he was venturing into alien territory:

When I left China I had this strange feeling: Now I am going to the imperialist world. No one will take care of me. I'll be unemployed and lost—everyone will look on me as a criminal. Still, I thought, there is a Communist Party in my country. I am coming out of a Communist world; they must know I have had reform training. Perhaps they will be interested in keeping me.

[Lifton, 1963, p. 33.]

But once the prisoner returns to his former environment, the influence of the brainwashing greatly diminishes. After a few weeks in English-held Hong Kong, Dr. Vincent was more "himself" again, saying, "I have the feeling that if I meet a Communist in my country, my first reaction toward him will be violent."

Intensive indoctrination shows, curiously, both the power of persuasion and the power of people to resist that persuasion. Police confessions and brainwashing show that "just psychological" approaches can create enormous changes in attitude. Had Dr. Vincent continued in an environment supportive of communism, one can wonder if the effects would have lasted and if he would have internalized his conversion to communism. But once the person returns to his usual environment, even indoctrination as intensive as brainwashing has limited effects.

SUMMARY

The most effective technique for changing a particular attitude depends on the function that attitude serves. If an attitude primarily serves an emotional function, modifying the underlying emotion is the most effective way to change someone's attitude. However, if the attitude primarily provides a way for the individual to interact realistically with his environment, the only way to get him to change his attitude is to introduce some inconsistency in his present attitudes and values. Since most attitudes are based on social information, the most effective way to change attitudes is to have other people provide the inconsistent information.

Research in attitude change has focused on four areas: (1) the source of the communication (who says it), (2) the message and how it is delivered (what is said), (3) the audience (to whom it is said), and (4) the effects of the communication.

1. The Source of the Communication Three aspects of the source determine its effectiveness: credibility, attractiveness, and power. Each leads to attitude change through different psychological processes. When the individual is motivated to find the truth, he is persuaded by people who know what they are talking about and whom he believes are not lying. However, if the individual's prime motive is to establish a personal relationship with the communicator, the most influential characteristic may be the communicator's attractiveness—usually determined by his similarity and likability. In this situation the individual will adopt the position of the communicator to be like him. If someone has power over the individual, he may publicly comply with that person's persuasive message to avoid punishment, but there may be little change in his beliefs and emotional reactions.

2. The Communication In general, the most persuasive communication is a face-to-face communication. With the exception of the technique of asking rhetorical questions, whether or not variations in style influence a communication's persuasiveness is not yet clear. Whether strong or mild fear appeals are more effective depends on their absolute intensity and the individual's ability to cope. In general, explicitly drawing the communication's conclusion and repeating the arguments are persuasive communication techniques. When two arguments are presented in sequence the relative persuasibility of each will depend on (a) the time elapsed between the two presentations and (b) the time elapsed between the last presentation and the attitude assessment. Communications that are moderately discrepant from the target person's initial attitudes are more persuasive than either extremely or minimally discrepant communications. Novel arguments tend to be persuasive. Primary and secondary reinforcement of an attitude is persuasive, and so is arousing dissonance. However, the most effective type of communication in any given situation may depend on other variables. For instance, whether a humorous or a straight approach is more effective may depend on the topic.

3. The Audience A number of variables seem to influence an individual's power to resist persuasion by affecting his ability to counterargue. Role playing focuses the role player's attention on acting his role and tends to divert his normal tendency to rebut the message of that role. Distraction may interfere directly with the counterarguing process. Inoculation may increase one's resistance to later counterpropaganda by bolstering his ability to counterargue. Commitment may inhibit counterarguing. Forewarning of persuasive intent may decrease the effectiveness of a communication by giving the audience time to criticize the communicator and his message. People may resist persuasion most when they are highly involved with and committed to the attitude and when they feel that the attitude is the result of the intrinsic characteristics of the object.

4. The Long-term Effects of Persuasion Although there is a great deal of variability in the duration of attitude change, it is often relatively temporary. Usually the effect of a persuasive communication is maximal immediately after exposure and then declines gradually until it is no longer significant. However, sometimes the effect is greater after a time delay—an effect known as the delayed-action, or sleeper, effect. The audience's retention of the message's content, environmental support for the changed attitude, and the audience's active involvement in the communication tend to increase the duration of persuasion.

Today, there is an impressive body of knowledge on which aspects of the source, message, and audience contribute to a communication's persuasiveness. The underlying processes of attitude change are less clearly understood.

5. An Emotional Approach to Changing Attitudes Some attitudes are primarily expressions of the individual's personality. For these emotionally based attitudes, giving the individual some insight into his personality and enabling him to accept his own impulses are the best way to change his attitudes. As we saw in Chapter 3, some individuals' prejudices are based on ego defense. Despite the various criticisms of studies on the emotional approach to changing attitudes, the hypothesis that increasing self-insight may decrease prejudice in certain people seems to have been confirmed.

6. Intensive Indoctrination In both police interrogations and brainwashing, a variety of powerful forces are brought to bear on the individual to make him change his attitude. Since over 80 percent of all criminal cases are solved by the suspect's confessing his crime during police interrogation, the techniques used in police interrogation are obviously very powerful. During interrogation suspects are questioned in an environment that minimizes sensory stimulation, maximally exposes the subject's vulnerability, and provides for complete control and domination by the interrogator. The police use a variety of tactics to misrepresent and confuse the situation. During the interrogation the police officer attempts to develop a warm social relationship with the suspect, thereby seeking to make the suspect want to earn his approval. The interrogator may also play on the suspect's guilts and fears.

In brainwashing a wide variety of persuasive techniques are applied along with an emphasis on the use of fellow prisoners as indoctrinators. Initially, the person's sense of identity is assaulted through the removal of all signs of personal identity and physical and psychological attacks on him. After days of constant pressure the individual may become confused and see that the only hope of psychological survival in the environment is to yield and confess. Once a rudimentary confession is given, social and physical pressures continue so that the individual yields further, until the final confession is elaborated. However, powerful as the pressures are that are exerted both in police interrogation and brainwashing, once the individual escapes from the pressure situation, the influence of both tactics greatly diminishes.

DISCUSSION QUESTIONS

1. What advice could you give to a politician who wished to avoid a credibility gap?
2. Why is face-to-face persuasion more effective than more impersonal appeals?
3. Under what conditions would you expect adding humor to make a communication more persuasive?
4. Why do you think role playing is such an effective persuasive technique?
5. What principle of persuasion would predict that intermittently blurring the video portion of televised political broadcasts would increase the effectiveness of the broadcasts?
6. Even if police interrogation tactics are powerful, why would anyone who is innocent confess to a crime he did not commit?
7. Why do you think the effects of persuasion are often short-lived?
8. Whom do you think would be the most effective source for a communication to college students on the need to drive safely?
9. Although increasing the power of a communicator has generally been found to increase the incidence of compliance, sometimes it has not had that effect. Under what circumstances would you predict that increasing power would *decrease* a communicator's effectiveness?
10. How could you use the technique of commitment to modify a friend's attitude on some topic? Which of the various forms of commitment—getting him to do something small but committing, making his attitude public, or making him feel his decision is irrevocable—do you think would be the most effective? Why?
11. Why is it so difficult to change a person's attitude?
12. Laboratory studies of attitude change have shown a much higher percentage of attitude change than studies conducted in the field—say in assessing the impact of the media on voting. Why do you think a higher percentage of change is typically found in laboratory studies?
13. It has been proposed that a moderate level of fear arousal is more persuasive than either a minimal or a maximal level. How could you test this hypothesis?
14. What do you think are the basic *processes* that mediate attitude change?
15. If you wanted to ensure that the effect of a persuasive communication would endure in undiminished form for at least a year, what persuasive tactics would you use?
16. Assume that you wished to convert conservative William Buckley to a liberal point of view. Outline the details of a persuasion campaign based on the techniques discussed in this chapter and any others that you think would be effective.
17. The attitudes of Americans toward the United States' involvement in Vietnam changed from general support in the early 1960s to opposition by most people in the 1970s. What factors do you think led to this change?
18. Design a study to test the effect of some source, communication, or audience variable not mentioned in this chapter. (Hint: Think about some of the tactics used by advertisers and historical figures who have been effective persuaders.)

AFFILIATION

5

How much time do you spend with other people? Probably you eat with others regularly and seek the company of others in recreation—even in such passive things as watching television and going

to the movies. When you are concerned about a personal problem, you may share your feelings with another person. In short, you probably spend a considerable amount of your time with other people. When 120 of the author's students at Central Connecticut State College were asked how much time during their sixteen waking hours was spent with or in the presence of others, the average answer was about fourteen hours.

Why do people need contact with others? If all of your biological needs were satisfied in a perfectly programmed physical environment in which you were continuously alone, what would you miss? (Before reading any further, see Psych Quiz 1.)

There is no single answer to this question. Different people have different reasons for needing others. From the considerable literature on the subject, however, we can suggest

PSYCH QUIZ 1 LIFE ALONE

What do you think you would miss if all of your physical needs were met and you were continuously alone? Below are some of the reasons that people need contact with others. Please indicate the extent to which you feel each of these applies to you. When you finish, you might find it interesting to compare your answers with those given by some of the other students in the class and with the subsequent material in this chapter.

Reasons for Social Contact	Applies to Me	Not Sure	Does Not Apply to Me
1. So that I may be loved by another person			
2. So that I may love another person			
3. So that I can share experiences			
4. So that my life can be ordered and structured			
5. To provide diversion and avoid boredom			
6. For the joy of finding that another person is pleased or impressed with me			
7. To provide information about myself and events			
8. To make me less upset when I'm worried about something			
9. To share work with me			

Of all of the reasons for being with others which do you think is the most important to you? _____

some of the more common needs that affiliation fulfills. Without other people many persons miss the feeling that they are loved. As Freud and many others have noted, the feeling that you matter to someone else and are worth loving is very important. When others are absent, there is no one else to care for you or to receive your love. Some people need to bestow love on others as much as they need to be loved themselves.

Without others you are unable to share your experiences. If something particularly pleasant or upsetting occurs, you have no one to discuss it with. All alone, you have complete responsibility for your daily routine. There is no one else to give any structure to your life. You have to do everything yourself, whether or not you want to and whether or not you are good at it.

Life alone can also get pretty boring. If you have ever spent a weekend in an empty house, you know that life alone can be very quiet. With no one to talk to, you will eventually find yourself longing for someone you can interact with. No matter how interesting a book or a television show is, it can never completely replace the stimulation of social interaction.

When you are all alone, the stimulation of the social "games" people play is missing. What fun is there in putting on a particularly attractive outfit if there is no one to admire you? Mastering a particularly difficult intellectual task will not be as much fun either. The joy you feel when you find that another person is pleased with your appearance or performance is real and rewarding.

Alone, you are also cut off from an important source of information when making judgments about complicated events. Much of the information people are exposed to in the mass media is highly complicated and inconsistent. Depending on which commentators you read in the 1972 presidential election, Richard Nixon's image was comparable either to Adolf Hitler's or to that of a statesman engaged in creating a lasting world peace. Faced with such inconsistent information, how did you make your own decision about Nixon's character? As we saw in Chapter 3, what other people say is an important determinant of our attitudes.

If something happens that upsets you and you are alone, how are you to be comforted? Many times when people have personal prob-

lems or are upset about some event, they turn to others for help. You may have done this yourself. If you were very involved with another person and the relationship soured, you may have poured out your feelings to a close friend. Alone, of course, you would have no one with whom to share your grief, no one to reassure you and to comfort you.

The needs that are fulfilled when we interact with other people are so basic and being with other people is such a pervasive part of our existence, that usually we are not very conscious of our need for others. But, just as the lack of oxygen can very quickly cause us to focus on its importance, so can we gain insight into the extent of our need for people by going through a period of social isolation. To begin our discussion of the affiliation motive, then, we will examine the experiences of some people who have been totally deprived of the company of others.

Social Isolation

Men have been isolated in a number of situations. Examples include, to name a few, prisoners in solitary confinement, explorers, survivors of shipwrecks, high-altitude flyers, hermits, men in religious orders, and men in space capsules. The sensations and behavior of one man, Richard Byrd, illustrate some of the reactions to this kind of experience.

Byrd, who was in command of an exploratory expedition to the South Pole in 1933, volunteered to spend six months completely alone in a weather station that was inaccessible to the main base of the expedition. Byrd's reactions to the experience of physical isolation are valuable for two reasons. First, they provide a relatively pure case of the reactions to isolation. Unlike many prisoners in solitary confinement, Byrd had an adequate food supply, was well stocked with reading material, was in continual radio contact with persons he knew, and had a demanding schedule of daily activities in order to maintain the weather station. His reactions, therefore, may be ascribed primarily to the absence of the physical presence of people rather than to other factors such as monotony, punishment, torture, or hunger. Second, since Byrd volunteered for his isolation, we might assume that he was not unduly sensitive to being alone. Indeed, he wrote that he was looking forward to the experience so that he might rest and "take inventory":

Aside from the metereological and auroral work, I had no important purposes. There was nothing of that sort. Nothing whatever, except one man's desire to know that kind of experience to the full, to be by himself for a while and to taste peace and quiet and solitude long enough to find out how good they really are.

[Byrd, 1938, p. 4 (1958 edition).]

How did Byrd respond? His initial reaction was one of exhilaration. On the evening of the first full day he had spent alone, Byrd wrote:

About one o'clock in the morning, just before turning in, I went topside for a look around. The night was spacious and fine. Numberless stars crowded the sky. I had never seen so many. You had only to reach up and fill your hands with the bright pebbles. Earlier, a monstrous red moon had climbed into the northern quadrant, but it was gone by then. The stars were everywhere. . . . If great inward peace and exhilaration can exist together, then this, I decided my first night alone, was what should possess the senses.

[Byrd, 1938, p. 57 (1958 edition).]

The following days were very busy ones for Byrd. Many things had to be done to prepare his weather station for the impending Arctic night, to maintain the instruments at the weather station, and to observe and record weather conditions. But after twenty-four days of solitude, Byrd wrote of his "brain-cracking loneliness":

This morning I had to admit to myself that I was lonely. Try as I may, I find I can't take my loneliness casually, it is too big. But I must not dwell on it. Otherwise I am undone.

At home I usually awaken instantly, in full possession of my faculties. But that's not the case here. It takes me some minutes to collect my wits; I seem to be groping in cold reaches of interstellar space, lost and bewildered. The room is a non-dimensional darkness, without shadow or substance; even after all these days I sometimes ask myself: Where am I? What am I doing here? I discover myself straining, as if trying to hear something in a place where no sound could possibly exist.

[Byrd, 1938, pp. 95–96 (1958 edition).]

The extent of Byrd's loneliness and resulting boredom can be further gauged by his reactions to an ice quake. Even though the sound was a signal of possible danger, he wrote that he welcomed it, since it broke the silence of his world:

A moment later there came a tremendous boom as if tons of dynamite had exploded in the Barrier. The sound was muffled by distance; yet it was inherently ominous breaking through the silence. But I confess that any sound which interrupts the evenness of this place is welcome.

[Byrd, 1938, p. 103 (1958 edition).]

As have many others who have been isolated, Byrd tried to dispel his loneliness by imagining familiar scenes and people:

Yet, I could, with a little imagination, make every walk *seem* different. One day I would imagine that my path was the Esplanade, on the water side of Beacon Hill in Boston, where, in my mind's eye, I often walked with my wife. I would meet people I knew along the bank, and drink in the perfection of a Boston spring.

[Byrd, 1938, p. 116 (1958 edition).]

After sixty-three days of being alone, Byrd's concern with religious questions and the meaning of life greatly increased:

The universe is not dead. Therefore, there is an Intelligence there, and it is all pervading. At least one purpose, possibly the major purpose, of that Intelligence is the achievement of universal harmony.

Striving in the right direction for Peace (Harmony), therefore, as well as the achievement of it, is the result of accord with that Intelligence.

It is desirable to effect that accord.

The human race, then, is not alone in the universe. Though I am cut off from human beings, I am not alone.

[Byrd, 1938, p. 185 (1958 edition).]

From these reactions we can see that isolation, even under what might be called optimal circumstances, is a stressful experience. Although Byrd's initial reaction was one of exhilaration, after a time he became lonely and began to feel depressed and bored. To fill his world, he sought escape in fantasy and became preoccupied with thoughts concerning religion and the general meaning of life. These reactions occurred even though Byrd was in continual radio contact with others and was well supplied with food and reading material. (See

BOX 1   SOLITARY CONFINEMENT

During World War II Christopher Burney, an English spy, was arrested by the Germans and placed in solitary confinement for eighteen months. During much of that time he had nothing to read, no work, nor any other diversions. Added to the rigors of this situation were hunger, threats of torture, and on one occasion, actual torture. Since his situation included these deprivations in addition to social isolation, it is difficult to determine the relative contribution of social isolation and of these other deprivations in eliciting his reactions. Nevertheless, in reading some of these reactions, as recorded in his book *Solitary Confinement,* we can see patterns of behavior similar to those noted by Admiral Byrd.

Fantasy

"But at this point I abandoned calculation and sailed gaily off to a dreamland of camps of prisoners-of-war, where only English was spoken, where no one worked, and where daily arrived thousands of enormous parcels of food. Into the parcels I delved and romped in a heap of hams and plum puddings and bathed in condensed milk."

[p. 65.]

In fact, Burney became so involved in his fantasies that after awhile he rejected any opportunities for social contact:

"I did not like to admit that the real reason was that I was so used to silence and so privately engaged in my own thoughts that I found conversation an embarrassment."

[p. 152.]

Rituals to Fill the Time

"To shorten the morning lap of this daily marathon, after I had washed, I used a series of pastimes which I regarded as ridiculous but useful. I started by manicuring myself with a sliver of wood. . . .

"When the manicure was finished, I sat on my stool and, with what even then appeared ridiculous solemnity, forbade myself to rise again before I had catalogued the counties of England, Scotland, Wales and Ireland and after them the states of America and their capitals."

[p. 19.]

Another ritual that Burney described was husking the oats in his straw mattress:

"On the other hand, I found a new activity, which was more enervating but seemed more useful than promenading. My straw mattress was filled with oat-straw, and I found that many of the oats had been left over from the threshing. I decided to eat them and spent many hours collecting, husking, and amassing them in a little pile. When this seemed to be a small mouthful (perhaps twice a day if I worked hard), I ate it with due ceremony, thinking a little smugly that God helped those who helped themselves."

[p. 111.]

Concern with Religious Questions and the Meaning of Life

Burney wrote that the second Sunday of his imprisonment he considered the Christian parable of the Prodigal Son, and felt that he himself resembled the Prodigal Son. Consequently,

"knowledge and reason had failed to serve me, saying only of my problem that they could find no answer to it. But I wanted an answer, as everyone must, and the old and often despised parable had given out: that I could hope. . . . Here were rest and fullness, and if my stomach were still empty, there was a calf to come. It was assured, and who was I to doubt?

"So I slept that night, dreaming of banquets and homecomings."

[pp. 42–43.]

Box 1 for the reactions of a man who was locked up alone for eighteen months with nothing to read, little to do, and very limited food.)

Although Byrd's reactions are those of only one individual, other biographical accounts of men who have lived isolated from their fellow-men reflect many of the same reactions. All of these accounts, however, suffer from some common problems. First, they are frequently written long after the isolation period is over, so that the distorting effects of time on memory may be present. Second, the accounts relate to very personal reactions, and consequently the writer may censor some of his feelings. Moreover, the people who write accounts of their isolation may not be typical of all people or even of isolates. People who are willing to undergo prolonged isolation may not be comparable to the general populace. Of those who do go through an isolation experience, maybe only those with dramatic reactions or those who are highly verbal write accounts of their experiences.

Still, even with the problems inherent in such autobiographical accounts, such accounts do provide some information about man's reaction to isolation. The picture that emerges is one of a difficult experience that frequently produces fantasy and anxiety-like symptoms. There may be indications of nervousness, of depression, of a general going-to-pieces. In summarizing the reactions of many persons who have been socially isolated, Schachter (1959) has noted that "anxiety, in some degree, is a common concomitant of isolation" (p. 12). People seem to need contact with others to continue functioning in a healthy manner.

Acquisition of the Need for Social Contact

How do people acquire their need for social contact? Does it come from mother-child contact? Most writers in this area would agree that human infants form strong and persistent ties to their mother or to some other person who cares for them. From this intimate relationship the child's love for his mother and for other people is formed.

But how does the relationship develop? And how does it come to generalize beyond the original person involved? Clearly, people need more than their mothers if their needs for social contact are to be met. Undeniable as the close mother-child relationship is, there is considerable disagreement as to how it comes about and how it develops into a "social response" of wanting to associate with other people. Three very different theories have been given.

Imprinting

If you were to see a group of goslings following their mother, you would be less surprised than if you were to see the same group following a distinguished-looking man. Just such a change in the natural order of events was demonstrated in a classic experiment (Lorenz, 1935). A set of eggs laid by a goose was divided into two groups. One-half of the eggs were hatched by the mother goose, who thus became the first living thing the goose-hatched goslings saw. Predictably, they followed her around and kept close to her. But the other half of the eggs were hatched in an incubator, and a scientist was the first living thing they saw. The goslings reacted to the scientist in the same way the other

goslings had reacted to their mother. They followed the scientist and kept close to him.

Thus the early exposure to a moving stimulus during a "critical" period of the bird's life—even without any tangible rewards such as warmth or nourishment—produced the attachment. After being "imprinted" on a particular stimulus, the goslings made their "social" responses to that object—no matter what it was. Since the original work with imprinting it has been found that imprinting can occur only during a limited period of life (Hess, 1959), and that it occurs in a wide variety of birds and in some mammals, including the guinea pig (Shipley, 1963).

It has been suggested that human infants may form their social attachment by an imprinting-like process, in which the basic social responses of the infant (sucking, clinging, and smiling) are elicited by a "releaser stimulus," usually the mother (Bowlby, 1958). Like the mother goose with the goslings, the mere presence of the human mother at a critical time in the infant's life may result in the formation of an attachment between the infant and his mother. After the social responses to a particular social stimulus have been acquired during the critical period, they later generalize to other, similar social objects. Humans imprinted on humans would respond to other humans, and humans imprinted on ducks would respond to ducks.

Interesting as this imprinting theory is, experimental verification with humans is obviously unattainable for ethical reasons. To demonstrate that the social response is determined by exposure to a stimulus at a critical point, human infants would have to be exposed to nonhuman stimuli—just as the goslings were exposed to a member of another species. What mother would volunteer her baby for this kind of experimental work at such a critical stage in his life? Nevertheless, further testing of the imprinting theory with higher animals, such as chimpanzees, is possible, and could provide further indirect evidence for the possible existence of this phenomenon in human beings.

Conditioning love

The learning theory holds that the infant becomes attached to the mother because her face and form have been associated with the alleviation of certain primary drive states, primarily hunger and thirst. Every time a baby is fed by his mother, he learns to associate her with the warm, comfortable feelings that come from the relief of his hunger. In short, the literally millions of times a baby is cared for by his mother or others could be thought of as times (or trials) when human beings are associated with pleasant situations. Gradually, through this process of conditioning, the child learns to "love" mother, and this love generalizes to other people. Affection, or the need for others, becomes—as the behaviorists would describe it—a "learned drive" (Dollard and Miller, 1950). Just as a pet kitten learns to "love" its human mother because she feeds him, so does the human infant learn to love his mother because she is constantly associated with pleasant experiences.

If you have had a course in introductory psychology, you do not need to be reminded of the power of classical conditioning in learning. Pavlov's famous dog, which salivated when a bell that had been associated with food was rung, has made this process famous. And, of course, you have seen that classical conditioning is a pervasive learning process at the human level. Further, conditioning may be remarkably resistant to extinction, or forgetting. One woman, for instance, was reported to have developed an unreasoning fear, or phobia, of public places, which lasted months after she had narrowly escaped death in a disastrous night club fire in which hundreds of people were burned to death (Cobb and Lindemann, 1943, in Janis et al., 1969).

As clearly shown by the reaction of one three-month-old baby, very young children can become classically conditioned after just one association. When the baby was approximately three months old, she had a series of painful inoculations at her pediatrician's office. The injection, of course, hurt, and she screamed loudly. One month later, when the baby was taken to the same doctor's office for her second polio shot, her mother recorded the following reactions: "began to scream and shake with racking cries and sobs as soon as she approached the doctor's examining room. Increased volume of sound when he appeared . . ." (Church, 1968, p. 13).

The instinctive-component theory

Conditioning is a pervasive and important learning process and offers a sound explanation of the development of the attachment between mother and child. Another equally plausible theory is that certain aspects of the mother, such as her warmth and softness, might instinctively set off certain social responses in the human infant, such as smiling, clinging, and sucking. The mother's softness or warmth—not the frequency of her association with any pleasant stimulus—would be responsible for the development of the infant's attachment to her.

These two theories are clearly inconsistent. Whereas the learning theory holds that the development of affection is completely determined by the frequency of pairing primary reinforcements such as food with mother, the instinctive-component theory holds that the development of attachment is determined by the pairing of certain aspects of the mother—some of which are not yet known—with the infant's social responses. Certain aspects of the mother, such as intimate physical contact, may instinctively arouse affection responses in the infant.

Which of these two theories offers the better explanation? What is most important in the development of the mother-child attachment: the association of primary drive reduction with the mother or cues, such as physical contact, that instinctively set off an attachment response? These theories have not been tested directly at the human level. Although designing such a study might be simple enough, there are obviously ethical problems involved in conducting such research with human beings.

To test whether food or contact comfort is more important in the development of affection, one investigator has run a series of experiments using infant macaque monkeys as subjects (Harlow, 1958; 1959; Harlow and Harlow, 1962). These animals are believed to exhibit strong similarities to humans in their basic responses, such as nursing, clinging, and visual and auditory exploration.

In an early study two artificial, surrogate "mothers" were constructed. One mother was built of wire mesh. A second mother, designed to resemble the first in size and shape, was made of terry cloth so that she could provide contact comfort.

In one subexperiment a cloth mother that did not dispense milk and a wire mother that did were placed in cubicles attached to the individual cages of newborn monkeys. (See Figure 5–1.) By observing which of the two mothers the infant monkeys spent the most time with, that is, preferred, Harlow felt that he could gain some insight into the relative validity of the learning and instinctive-component theories. The learning theory would predict that the monkeys would respond more to the wire mesh mother, since she would become associated with hunger reduction. The instinctive-component theory, in contrast, would suggest greater affiliation with the soft, terry cloth mother, since she would provide contact warmth.

During the 165-day period that the infant monkeys spent with both mothers, a distinct preference was shown for the cloth mother. By the end of the time period, the baby monkeys were spending an average of sixteen hours per day on the cloth mother as compared to an average of only one and a half hours on the wire mother. Clearly, the need for contact comfort produced more of an affiliation response than the need for hunger reduction.

The Harlow experiments, of course, do not settle the issue of how social attachment is learned in human beings. Whether these results show the workings of an imprinting-like process in the forming of attachments in monkeys or a drive for contact comfort that is stronger than the drive for food is, of course, debatable. Nevertheless, the results do emphasize the importance of aspects of the mother, other than her association with food, in eliciting an attachment relationship.

Further work on the characteristics of a "super mother" has indicated that "mothers" that are soft and mobile are more attractive than soft, stationary mothers (Harlow and Suomi, 1970). More experimental work is required to establish the maternal attributes that can influence the attachment relationship, but these findings could have dramatic implications for understanding the formation of attachment at the human level. For example, the folklore has long held that rocking soothes a crying baby.

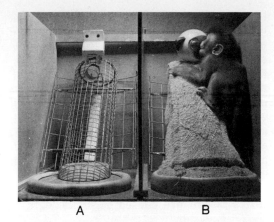

A   B

FIGURE 5-1 Two examples of Harlow's surrogate mothers. (A) A wire mesh mother with a provision for a milk-dispensing device. (B) A cloth-covered mother. (Wisconsin Primate Laboratory)

Perhaps this rocking movement also influences the formation of an attachment relationship.

The importance of the attachment relationship

Although these three explanations emphasize different aspects of the learning process, it is possible that in real life all three aspects combine to produce the very strong attachment that usually exists between infants and those who care for them. Imprinting on the mother, the thousands of pleasant associations with the mother, and her warmth and softness may all combine to produce the extremely strong affiliation motive present in most people.

Regardless of *how* the attachment relationship between an infant and the person or persons who care for him is formed, its formation is crucial to normal social development. For obvious reasons isolation experiments are never done on children. There are situations, however, in which the closeness of attachment is minimal. Infants raised in orphanages, for instance, may receive relatively little personal care and stimulation.

In one situation seventy-five babies were observed in an institution in which each infant was kept enclosed in a glass-partitioned cubicle and was fed with his bottle propped up in his crib. After four months in this environment, the babies began to show a number of differences from babies reared in the usual home setting. They showed very little vocalization; they did not coo or babble. By eight months of age they had begun to lose interest in the external environment. Body rocking became very common, and they seemed to lose interest in their toys (Provence and Lipton, 1962). A number of other "maternal deprivation" studies have shown similar results. Although many of the studies may be criticized for methodological flaws, the evidence consistently shows the severe disturbance caused by social deprivation (Yarrow, 1961).

Evidently, social interaction is necessary for normal development—even in areas that do not seem to be socially determined, such as paying attention to the environment. Further, in the formation of the infant's attachment to the person who takes care of him, we see the core relationship from which all other social relationships and social learning derives. For instance, the pattern established in the child's relationship with his mother will determine his view of other people. It has been theorized that the child's trust of his mother determines the extent to which he can trust other people in other relationships (E. H. Erikson, 1950).

Further, once the child has become attached to his mother, the way is open for social influences, such as her approval or disapproval, to play a part in what he does. As we will see in Chapter 6, social rewards are a powerful factor in the modification of an individual's behavior. Once the attachment relationship between mother and child is formed, the child has gone a long way toward becoming a social being.

FIGURE 5-2 Striving to attain a goal is obviously not limited to the classroom. Here we see the power of the achievement motive in sports. (David Tenenbaum/Editorial Photocolor Archives, Inc.)

BOX 2 WHAT MAKES PEOPLE RUN?

One answer to the above question is motivation. People react selectively to their environment. You don't eat every time you see food, but if you have been without food for eight hours, you are probably hungry and will eat. If you're feeling a little lonely, you may pass up eating immediately and wait to join some friends for dinner. The common core of a motivational approach to understanding human behavior is that there are inner directing forces that guide behavior. To predict what a person will do, one has to know what that person wants.

Even though we think and act in motivational terms in everyday life, not all psychologists agree that motivation is an important determinant of behavior. Some object to the concept of motivation on the grounds that it is frequently used in unclear and fuzzy ways. Teachers may explain the behavior of poor performers by saying that they are not motivated, when in truth they may be motivated in ways that the teachers don't recognize or acknowledge. More important, some radical behaviorists claim that motivation is not necessary to explain behavior. Reinforcers, they argue, are the important factor. Motiva-

tion simply refers to conditions that make reinforcers effective, and the real progress in psychology is to be gained by focusing on the effects of reinforcers (Reynolds, 1968).

These critics have pointed out some legitimate problems in motivational research, but it seems premature to banish the concept. Although radical behaviorists may emphasize that the study of behavior is best advanced by studying the effectiveness of reinforcers, it is still important to know *what* reinforces and *why*.

What are the motives of man? As you may recall from a previous psychology course, motives are usually divided into the basic, biological needs, which are necessary for survival, and the social motives. Hunger, thirst, the need for oxygen, sex, and so forth, are usually included among the biological motives.

However, an examination of what impels much of your own daily behavior will show you that the biological motives are not sufficient to explain most human behavior. In our affluent society these biological needs are normally met quite easily, thus leaving us free to focus on the "higher" social motives (Maslow, 1954). Your reading of this text, for in-

stance, is hardly related to your fulfilling of hunger or thirst motives. Much of human behavior is determined by the so-called social motives.

The three social motives to be discussed in this text are the affiliation motive, the aggression motive, and the altruism motive. The selection of these three motives is based on their pervasiveness in American society and the resulting importance that seems to be attached to them. In addition, there are a number of other motives. If you examine your own behavior, you may realize what some of these are. You may go without sleep to *achieve* on an examination. (See Figure 5-2.) You may work hard in a club to achieve a position of *dominance.* You may puzzle through a problem, even though it is inconvenient, because your *curiosity* has been aroused. You may rebel against doing something even though you really want to do it, to show your *independence.* And as we saw in Chapter 2, you may go through considerable discomfort to reach *self-actualization.* (For a further listing of social motives, see Cofer and Appley, 1964.)

Affiliation Motivation: An Overview

Whether the need to be with other people is learned or innately released through certain critical cues, it is clear that affiliation is a very strong social motive among many people. (For a discussion of social motives, see Box 2.) Accordingly, a number of studies have been done on people's desire to be with others, or as it has been called in the literature, the affiliation motive. Since 1959, when the pioneering work in affiliation was first published, nearly one hundred studies have appeared in psychological journals.

In this chapter we will explore the way in

which the affiliation motive works from three different vantage points: (1) *When* do people affiliate? What situations increase an individual's desire to be with others? (2) *Why* do people affiliate? What purposes are served by being with others? and (3) *What kind of people* affiliate? Is the desire for affiliation a persistent personality trait? What kinds of activities or personality traits are associated with persons high in the need to affiliate? In addition, since being with others serves a variety of badly needed functions for the human being, we will consider how well the need for human contact is being met in our contemporary society.

FIGURE 5-3 Mourners at the John F. Kennedy funeral. At times of great national tragedy, people have been shown to exhibit a high degree of affiliative behavior. (UPI)

When Do People Affiliate?

Under what circumstances do people want to be with others? One possible answer is that they want to be with others when they are in a stressful situation. In reviewing the effects of social isolation, Schachter (1959) has noted that distress, or anxiety, is a fairly common reaction to isolation. If this hypothesis is correct, *increasing the level of stress (or distress) that is experienced might result in an increase in the desire to affiliate.*

Many events in everyday life support this hypothesis. Misery does seem to love company. If, for instance, you were having problems with someone you loved, you might seek out someone you could discuss your problems with. You might want to get someone else's reaction to your problem. Just talking might reduce your worrying. You might want someone to sympathize with you.

News of some tragic situation on a national level can also stimulate an affiliation need. President Kennedy's assassination provided an opportunity to test the effect of a highly stressful situation on affiliation behavior (Cole, 1965). (See Figure 5-3.) A few weeks after the assassination, college students were asked to indicate whether or not they had sought to affiliate during the critical three-day period following the assassination. The majority of the students (64 percent of the men and 57 percent of the women) reported that they had wanted to be with others during that period. The majority of the students in the author's social psychology classes showed a similar preference for affiliation in another stressful situation. Of the one hundred students polled, 60 percent indicated that they had wished to be with others during the East Coast blackout of 1965 (an electric power failure that affected large portions of the entire eastern area of the United States).

These studies provide useful information on reactions to stressful situations. They do not, however, indicate the true effects of stress on affiliative behavior, since the other aspects of the situation are not controlled. Further, when people are surveyed, they may not remember accurately or, if they do remember, they may not report accurately what they did. Also, since the percentage of people reporting a desire to affiliate is not measured against the usual percentage of people who would like to be with others under nonstressful conditions, the reports of affiliation preference may tell us comparatively little about the effects of stress on affiliation.

To assess accurately the pure effects of stress on affiliation, controlled experiments would be necessary. In a controlled experiment everything but stress would be held constant and the subjects' reactions measured. Fortunately, one psychologist has designed a series of experiments testing the effects of increasing the level of stress on the frequency of affiliation (Schachter, 1959). Since Schachter's procedures were the original ones used in this area and a number of subsequent studies have been based on his paradigm, his study will be discussed in some detail.

Schachter's experiment on stress and affiliation

The object of Schachter's experiment was to compare the amount of affiliation behavior that would occur under stress conditions with the amount that would take place in the absence of stress. The subjects were female students in introductory psychology courses at the University of Minnesota, who had signed up to participate in the experiments in order to obtain extra credit on their final exam.

The experimental sessions were conducted with groups of five to eight girls at one time. Since friendship between the subjects could influence their wanting to be together or alone, an attempt was made to use subjects who did not know one another before coming to the experiment. Also, an attempt was made to prevent the subjects from talking with one another while waiting for the experiment, since conversation with a particularly pleasant girl might also influence a subject's reaction. To minimize the opportunity for conversation, the experimenter asked each subject to fill out a long questionnaire on biographical information.

There were two experimental conditions. In one subjects were led to believe that they would be given a series of painful electric shocks (painful-shock condition). In the other they were told that they would receive a series of very mild electric shocks that would not be painful at all (nonpainful-shock condition). Actually, neither group received any shocks. The deception was used to arouse different intensities of stress.

In the painful-shock condition both the appearance of the experimenter and the experimental setting were designed to frighten the subjects. As the girls arrived at the laboratory, they were greeted by a man wearing a white laboratory coat with a stethoscope hanging out of his pocket. Behind him was a formidable array of electrical equipment. After a few initial comments, the experimenter began the session by saying:

Allow me to introduce myself, I am Dr. Gregor Zilstein of the Medical School's Department of Neurology and Psychiatry. I have asked you all to come today in order to serve as subjects in an experiment concerned with the effects of electric shock.

[Schachter, 1959, p. 13.]

After an ominous pause Zilstein continued with a seven- or eight-minute lecture on the importance of research in this area, citing electroshock therapy and so forth. He concluded by saying:

What we will ask each of you to do is very simple. We would like to give each of you a series of electric shocks. Now, I feel I must be completely honest with you and tell you exactly what you are in for. These shocks will hurt, they will be painful. As you can guess, if, in research of this sort, we're to learn anything at all that will really help humanity, it is necessary that our shocks be intense. What we will do is put an electrode on your hand, hook you into apparatus such as this [Zilstein points to the electrical-looking gadgetry behind him], give you a series of electric shocks, and take various measures such as your pulse rate, blood pressure, and so on. Again, I do want to be honest with you and tell you that these shocks will be quite painful but, of course, they will do no permanent damage.

[Schachter, 1959, p. 13.]

Obviously, some of the procedures in this condition were far from reassuring. (See Figure 5-4.) Being subjects under the ominous Dr. Zilstein's power, looking at the equipment, and being told that they were going to receive painful electric shocks that would not do permanent damage to them must have left the girls feeling upset.

In the nonpainful-shock condition the experimenter was the same; but there was no electrical apparatus in the room, and the subjects were told that the electric shocks would be quite mild and not painful. After introducing himself, Zilstein stated:

I have asked you all to come today in order to serve as subjects in an experiment concerned with the effects of electric shock. I hasten to add, do not let the word "shock" trouble you; I am sure that you will enjoy the experiment.

[Schachter, 1959, p. 13.]

FIGURE 5-4 Characterization of the Schachter experiment: Painful-shock condition.

Then, after an identical lecture on the importance of the research, Zilstein concluded by saying:

What we will ask each one of you to do is very simple. We would like to give each of you a series of very mild electric shocks. I assure you that what you will feel will not in any way be painful. It will resemble more a tickle or a tingle than anything unpleasant. We will put an electrode on your hand, give you a series of very mild shocks, and measure such things as your pulse rate and blood pressure, measures with which I'm sure you are all familiar from visits to your family doctor.

[Schachter, 1959, p. 14.]

The remaining experimental procedures were identical for the two conditions. First, in order to find out whether or not the stress manipulations had worked, the experimenter measured the amount of fear the subjects in the two conditions experienced. The subjects were asked, "How do you feel about being shocked?" and answers were checked off on a five-point scale, which ranged from "I dislike the idea very much" to "I enjoy the idea very much."

The experimenter then continued with the next part of the experiment, which was designed to determine whether the subjects wished to affiliate or to be alone. Subjects were told that there would be a ten-minute delay while the room was prepared for the shocking procedure and were asked whether they wished to wait alone or with others. The experimenter's actual dialogue follows:

Before we begin with the shocking proper there will be about a ten-minute delay while we get this room in order. We have several pieces of equipment to bring in and get set up. With this many people in the room, this would be very difficult to do, so we will have to ask you to be kind enough to leave the room.

Here is what we will ask you to do for this ten-minute period of waiting. We have on this floor a number of additional rooms, so that each of you, if you would like, can wait alone in your own room. These rooms are comfortable and spacious; they all have armchairs, and there are books and magazines in each room. It did occur to us, however, that some of you might want to wait for these ten minutes together with some of the other girls here. If you would prefer this, of course, just let us know. We'll take one of the empty classrooms on this floor and you can wait together with some of the other girls there.

[Schachter, 1959, pp. 14–15.]

The experimenter then passed out a sheet on which the subjects indicated whether they preferred to wait alone or with others and the extent of their preference. A sample of the items on the questionnaire is given below:

Please indicate below whether you prefer waiting your turn to be shocked alone or in the company of others.
_____ I prefer being alone.
_____ I prefer being with others.
_____ I really don't care.

Finally, to obtain another measure of the effectiveness of the stress manipulation, the experimenter passed out another sheet of paper on which each subject indicated whether or not she wished to continue with the experiment. The experiment was then over. None of the subjects actually received shocks, and the experimenter explained in detail the purpose of the experiment and the need for the various deceptions involved.

Thus the independent variable, stress, was manipulated by telling the subjects either that they would receive a series of painful electric shocks or that they would be given very mild shocks. The dependent variable, affiliative tendency, was measured by the subjects' questionnaire responses, which indicated whether they wished to wait alone or with others before receiving the electric shocks.

In examining the results of the experiment, we need to determine first whether or not the stress manipulation worked. Were the subjects in the painful-shock condition really under more stress than the subjects in the nonpainful-shock condition? On both indicators of stress (the rating of fear about being shocked and the indication of a desire to drop out of the experiment), subjects in the painful-shock condition reported more fear about being shocked than did the subjects in the other condition; and approximately 19 percent of the subjects in the painful-shock condition refused to continue in the experiment, whereas none of the subjects in the other condition refused to continue.

Once it was established that the electric shock manipulations worked, the next question was whether or not the level of stress influenced the subjects' desire to be with others. As shown in Figure 5-5, subjects in the painful-shock condition showed a significantly greater desire

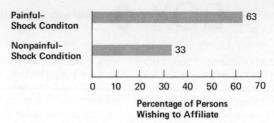

FIGURE 5-5 Stress and the affiliative tendency.

to be with others. Sixty-three percent of the subjects in the painful-shock condition wanted to wait with other subjects, as compared to only 33 percent of the subjects in the nonpainful-shock condition.

Thus in this study *the arousing of stress increased the tendency to affiliate.* As in any study, however, there are some limitations, which should be noted. (See Box 3.) First, the reader must be careful not to generalize beyond the actual subjects tested and the procedures used. A technically correct summary of Schachter's results would be that groups of girls who were students in introductory psychology courses at the University of Minnesota, who had signed up to participate in psychological experiments in order to get extra credit on their final exams, and who did not know each other and had not talked to each other were more likely to indicate on a questionnaire that they wished to wait together when they were told by a particular experimenter that they would get a painful electric shock than when they were told that they would get a mild electric shock.

This summary is technically correct, although it is a writer's nightmare and almost incomprehensible. The simpler generalization "the arousing of stress increases the tendency to affiliate" is much easier to remember, but is not an accurate summary of the Schachter results. As Schachter has noted, we can wonder whether or not people in other anxiety-arousing situations will tend to affiliate more. After Schachter published his original findings, a number of replications were done in an attempt to demonstrate the generality of the stress-affiliation relationship. Of the six replications done, all but one have duplicated the original finding that the increasing of stress increases the desire to affiliate (e.g., Kissel, 1967). The consistency of

BOX 3 HOW WOULD YOU EVALUATE THE SCHACHTER EXPERIMENT?

The basic areas involved in conducting an experiment and some questions relevant to these areas are listed below in the order in which these areas were discussed in the analysis of the Aronson-Mills initiation experiment. Consider the implications that these areas and the accompanying questions have for the Schachter procedure. As you consider these, you may think of additional problems.

1. *Translating the Independent Variable into Experimental Procedures.* Although we have been treating the conceptual variable as "stress," Schachter thought he was manipulating a particular type of stress, namely, anxiety. Do you think that telling subjects they are going to receive a severe electric shock would be more likely to make them anxious or fearful? Can you differentiate between feeling anxious and feeling fearful? Would you expect the reactions that follow fear to be different from those that follow anxiety?

2. *Providing a Rationale for the Procedure.* To obtain a measure of the dependent variable, the wish to be with others or alone, the experimenter said there would be a delay while the equipment was being set up and then passed out a questionnaire on which the subjects indicated their preference. Do you think the subjects could have been suspicious about the delay, since the experiment had been scheduled in advance? Do you think the readily available mimeographed forms might have aroused their suspicions about the spontaneity of the procedure?

3. *Obtaining Subjects.* The subjects were girls at the University of Minnesota who were taking an introductory psychology course. They had volunteered to participate in the experiment in order to receive extra credit on their final exam. Do you see any ways in which their being psychology students or their volunteering might have influenced their reactions to the experimental procedures?

4. *Avoiding Confounding.* Schachter's experiment was published in 1959, several years before attention was called to the possible biasing effects of the experimenter's own expectations and the demand characteristics of the situation. Do you see any ways in which these two artifacts might have confounded the experimental variable? Also, do you think that testing the girls in groups might have influenced their reactions? Might they have looked to see how others were reacting both before the experiment began and during the experimental session?

5. *Translating the Dependent Variable into Experimental Procedures.* Schachter measured whether or not the subjects would like to be with others by asking them to complete two questionnaire items, on which they indicated whether or not they would like to be with others and how strongly they felt about their inclination. Can you think of a behavioral measure that could have been used? Do you think similar results would have been obtained?

6. *Conducting the Experiment.* Although Schachter states what the experimenter said, he does not discuss *how* the experimenter said it. Was the experimenter cold and impersonal? Or informal? Would the experimenter's manner influence the subject's reactions?

7. *Conducting the Postexperimental Interview.* During the postexperimental interview, the subjects were asked not to discuss the experiment with others. Is there any chance they may not have kept the secret? If they didn't, could that have influenced the results of later experiments?

---

the subjects' reactions to the anticipated painful electric shock, across a variety of populations and in a variety of experimental settings, increases confidence in the generality of the relationship. All of the replications, however, have used in whole or in part the same manipulation of stress that Schachter used—the threat of an electric shock.

Moreover, the results of a field study have also confirmed the findings of the numerous laboratory studies on the relationship between stress and affiliation. Subjects who had been involved in a severe rainstorm in which twenty-two inches of rain fell within a twenty-four-hour period were given a questionnaire designed to measure their affiliative tendencies during this period. Those who had found themselves in extremely serious situations (such as in buildings that were flooded with three or more feet of water) reported a significantly higher affiliative tendency—saying that they had "tried to remain in the company of others constantly"—than did those who had been subjected to only a slight danger or inconvenience (Strümpfer, 1970).

Assuming that there is a relationship between stress and affiliation raises a whole series of questions about *why* it exists. Why did the subjects want to be with others when they were under stress? Was it to console each other? To distract each other? To compare the way they were feeling and thinking with the way others in the situation were reacting? As we shall see in the next section, many experiments have been done to answer this question of why.

Further, Schachter's results showed wide individual differences in the reactions to the stress manipulation. Not all of the subjects in the painful-shock condition wished to be with others. Out of thirty-two subjects nine indicated that they did not care, and three said that they wished to be alone. These findings raise questions about the extent to which subjects differ in their desire to affiliate or be alone. As we shall see, there are permanent consistent differences between people in the extent to which they wish to affiliate. Although affiliation may be more likely to occur in some situations than in others, some people may be more or less likely to affiliate in a wide variety of situations.

A further question arising out of the Schachter experimental procedure is: What emotion was aroused by the anticipated painful shock? We have been referring to stress arousal, but Schachter assumed that the particular kind of stress he was creating was anxiety. He began with the concept of anxiety and then evolved experimental procedures that seemed to be related to that emotion. His procedures were the operational definition of his conceptual variable.

As with any operational definition of a concept, the question remains as to whether Schachter manipulated what he was interested in or something else. For instance, you will recall that some commentators contended that the Aronson-Mills initiation experiment may have manipulated sexual arousal rather than the level of suffering, as the experimenters claimed. Two investigators have contended that in threatening the subjects with a painful electric shock, Schachter induced a state of fear, not one of anxiety (Sarnoff and Zimbardo, 1961). If so, so what? Does it make any difference what the emotional state the subjects experienced is called?

What is anxiety?

Two investigators have contended that whether fear or anxiety was aroused would make an enormous difference in affiliative behavior (Sarnoff and Zimbardo, 1961). Their reasoning was based on Freud's (1933) distinction between the two concepts: (1) *Fear* is aroused when a person is confronted with something that is objectively dangerous and likely to produce pain; (2) *anxiety* is typically aroused by innocuous stimuli that are subjectively upsetting but not related to objectively dangerous stimuli in the environment. If, for instance, you saw a poisonous snake while walking, you would feel fear, not anxiety, according to Freud's definition of these terms. If, however, for no explicable reason, you suddenly began to feel very upset, you would be feeling anxiety. Receiving a severe electric shock is clearly a painful, objectively unpleasant event, and thus being concerned about it would seem closer to the concept of fear than to that of anxiety.

Further, fear and anxiety have very different effects on behavior. When anxieties are aroused, people become concerned with the restoration of their inner self-control. Also, since the anxious person may be concerned about the inappropriateness of his feelings, he is reluctant to communicate his feelings to others who, he thinks, do not have similar reactions and, as a result, might ridicule his feelings. In contrast, in a fearful situation the individual realizes that most people share his feelings and thus feels that he can communicate with others. Therefore, when anxiety is aroused, people would be expected to seek solitude, but when fear is aroused, they should seek affiliation.

To test whether or not anxiety and fear do have different effects on affiliation, these investigators designed a factorial experiment in which two levels of fear and two levels of anxiety were manipulated. Fear was manipulated by using a slight modification of Schachter's procedure of having subjects anticipate either painful or innocuous electric shocks. Anxiety was manipulated by arousing a motive assumed to be anxiety-arousing in some subjects—what in Freudian terminology would be called oral libido, which is a repressed desire to obtain pleasure by sucking objects clearly related to infantile nursing experiences. To arouse the oral motive, and thus the anxiety that should follow its arousal, the investigators told the subjects, who were male Yale undergraduates, that they would have to suck a number of objects that are related to the oral period, including large nipples and pacifiers, for two minutes apiece. Subjects in the low-anxiety condition were told that they would have to put some objects that are less directly related to sucking pleasures, such as whistles and balloons, in their mouth. The desire to be alone or with others was then measured by the standard Schachter procedure.

The results were consistent with the experimental hypothesis. Although there were no significant differences in the affiliation tendency in the two low-arousal conditions, increasing the intensity of fear increased the subjects' desire to be with others, and increasing the intensity of anxiety decreased the subjects' desire to be with others. Ninety-five percent of the subjects who thought they were waiting for an intense electric shock wished to wait with others, and only 46 percent of those who thought they were waiting to suck nipples expressed such a preference.

These experimental results show why one has to distinguish between emotions in order to predict the effect of their arousal on affiliation. Thus to predict accurately the effects of arousing an emotion on affiliation, one must know which emotion is aroused and how strongly it is experienced.

This last comment is consistent with another interpretation of the nipple-sucking experiment: an embarrassment interpretation. Suppose that for some subjects in the high-anxiety condition, anticipating that they would have to suck nipples aroused embarrassment—not anxiety. Sucking nipples is hardly consistent with the Yale student's image of himself. Knowing that they would have to act in such an undignified and childish way may have made some subjects embarrassed and thus stimulated a desire for isolation because of embarrassment, not because of anxiety. Confirming evidence for the embarrassment hypothesis was obtained in some survey data collected by the author. When one hundred CCSC students were asked whether they wished to be alone or with others when

they were embarrassed, 76 percent indicated that they wished to be alone.

Whichever explanation is correct, the findings of the nipple-sucking experiment clearly indicate that in some situations increasing the intensity of the emotion may decrease the desire to affiliate. The tendency to affiliate may be increased only when emotions are stimulated in a manner that permits the subjects to assume that their reaction is appropriate and shared by others in a similar situation.

Practical implications and speculations

One form of stress—fear arousal caused by the expectancy of electric shock—has been found to increase the affiliation motive. Stress in another form—anxiety or embarrassment caused by the subject's expecting to suck on a nipple—decreased the affiliation motive. These findings have some interesting practical implications. As we shall see in Chapter 10, groups are often brought together when people are faced with an external threat. When people experience a stressful situation together, whether a common enemy, a drastic economic setback, or a natural disaster, they often work together and cooperate more closely than they did before they faced a common problem. As Homans has noted, joint and successful operation in a dangerous environment may vastly increase the feelings of friendship between the various members of a group, which tends to make their "interaction especially frequent and sentiment especially intense" (Homans, 1950, p. 117).

In the army, for instance, the primary group (the men who are buddies and interact frequently) is of great importance to the individual soldier. As we saw in Chapter 4, one of the techniques used in the Chinese Communist brainwashing procedures was to separate the man from his primary group. Without others to share his experiences with or to support him, the individual was thought to be much more susceptible to brainwashing procedures. And there is some indirect evidence to show that the Chinese were correct in their assumption (Lifton, 1963).

Before going on to the next question of why

people wish to affiliate, we might speculate about the effects of some other situations on the desire to affiliate. Although there are many possible situations that could be studied, two in particular interest this writer.

One area, suggested by Schachter, is the effect of joy. If the desire to affiliate is produced by the desire to communicate feelings that the individual assumes are acceptable and shared by others, one might predict that increasing joy would increase the desire to affiliate. Clearly this prediction is supported by commonsense observations. The idea of wanting to share good news with a friend is almost a cliché.

Another possibility for further research is the relationship between fatigue and the subject's desire for affiliation. Social interaction takes effort, and one might speculate that an increase in the level of fatigue might decrease the desire to be with others. After working hard for several days, a subject might be far less likely to want to be with others.

These are only speculations concerning two situations that interest this writer. Probably you can think of many other situations that would seem intuitively to increase or decrease your desire to be with others. (See Box 4 for some students' affiliation reactions to thirteen situations.)

Why Do People Affiliate?

Most of the research on the reasons for affiliation has focused on reactions in stressful situations. Several investigators have conducted experiments to determine why people wish to be with others when they are anticipating a painful shock. You may wonder why experiments were necessary to answer this question. Why not simply ask people why they wish to affiliate?

Several investigators have done precisely that by including in their experimental procedures questionnaire items on the reasons subjects chose either to be alone or to be with others. In one such experiment the reason cited most frequently by subjects anticipating a mild electric shock was social curiosity. ("I want to see who the others are.") Subjects who were anticipating painful electric shocks cited three basic reasons for their desire to affiliate: for comfort, for emotional comparison ("I'll know my own reaction better if I compare myself to others"), and for catharsis ("Just talking helps to reduce worry") (Zimbardo and Formica, 1963).

Since these reasons are so clearly indicated by the questionnaire responses, why is further work on the motives for affiliation necessary? As in any self-report study there is the question of the validity, or accuracy, of the responses. In an area such as this, in which the subject may not be completely aware of all his motives, the question of validity is even more critical than in some simpler, less complicated areas.

Consequently, some of the hypotheses as to why people tend to affiliate when they are afraid have been tested by means of controlled experiments. Although a number of possible reasons for the relationship between affiliation and fear exist, two explanations in particular have received major emphasis.

The first explanation states that a fearful person's desire to be with others is determined by his need to evaluate his own emotional state. The presence of other people gives an individual an opportunity to evaluate his own level of emotion by comparing it with others. If a situation is ambiguous and thus an individual is unclear about how he should feel, the responses of others may indicate the proper level of emotion. This explanation is referred to as the "social comparison" explanation of affiliation.

A second, frequently advanced, explanation is that a person's desire to be with others is determined by his need for a direct reduction of fear. People expect that through affiliation their fear will subside. They may find sympathy or reassurances from others, or they may simply feel that being in the physical presence of others will somehow minimize the fear-producing stimulus. This explanation is referred to as the "direct fear-reducing" explanation of affiliation.

Social comparison and fear reduction have emerged as major reasons for affiliation when subjects are under stress. But in everyday life people frequently wish to be with others when things are going well for them. As we saw at the beginning of the chapter, people need contact with others for a number of reasons: to love and to be loved, to provide diversion, to share work,

BOX 4 STUDENT AFFILIATION PREFERENCES IN THIRTEEN SITUATIONS

The author asked one hundred of her students (at CCSC) to indicate whether they wished to be with others, alone, or had no preference when they were in thirteen different situations. The questionnaires were handed in anonymously.

Situation	Percentage of Students Who:		
	Wished to Be with Others	Wished to Be Alone	Had No Preference
When depressed	42	48	10
When worried about a serious personal problem	52	44	4
When physically tired	6	85	9
When mildly ill (e.g., with a cold)	32	49	19
When very happy	88	2	10
When feeling very guilty about something you have done	45	43	12
When embarrassed	16	76	8
When you want to cry	8	88	4
When in a good mood	89	0	11
When busy	12	70	18
After an extensive period of social contact—after being with others for a long time	12	75	13
On Saturday night	85	1	14
When you are in a strange situation or doing something you've never done before	77	13	10

and so on. In nonstressful conditions some of these reasons may be major ones for affiliation behavior. As we shall see later, preliminary evidence on some of these other reasons is beginning to develop.

Social comparison

Social Comparison Theory As we saw in Chapter 2, people need to evaluate their opinions and abilities, and when no objective means are available, they do so by comparing their reactions with those of other people. *The more uncertain people are, the stronger is their need for social comparison.*

In many situations the validity of one's opinions or emotional reactions cannot be readily ascertained. Objective reality may be either very complicated, inaccessible, or irrelevant. For instance, in a situation in which students are boycotting classes because of an administrative decision to fire a popular faculty member, what would be the relevant, objective physical evidence on which to base an opinion? Had the professor adequately met the requirements of his job? Had his hearing been fair? Answers to these and to many other questions would be very difficult, if not impossible, to establish. In such ambiguous situations individuals will turn to the opinions of others to evaluate what is the "correct" opinion. And the more ambiguous the situation is, the more likely such a social comparison process is.

With whom do we compare ourselves? As you will recall from Chapter 2, Festinger theorized that people seek out *others who are similar* to themselves in order to evaluate their reactions. If another person is similar to you, his reactions will provide an accurate baseline for your own judgments. The opinion of other college students about marijuana may be more informative to you than your grandfather's opinion on the subject.

What happens once the individual begins comparing his reactions with those of similar people? According to Festinger, he attempts to reduce any discrepancies that exist between himself and the others. *Once individuals in a group begin comparing themselves with others, there are strong pressures toward uniformity.* Since each person is looking to the reactions of others as his source of knowledge about what is correct, inconsistency is upsetting. If one member of a group feels that marijuana is harmless and another feels that it is not, the discrepancy between their opinions may be unsettling to both. Consequently, there are strong pressures for the group to arrive at a uniform reaction (Festinger, 1954).

Social comparison theory clearly provides one explanation of why subjects who are expecting painful electric shocks would wish to affiliate. Most students are not used to receiving electric shocks, so they would be unclear about how they should feel and react. Since there is no physical reality they can use to test the appropriateness of their reactions, the subjects will tend to refer to the experience of the others. Given a choice, students would prefer to compare their experiences with others who are similar. And once the social comparison process begins to operate, there is a tendency

toward persuasion and resultant uniformity of reaction (Schachter, 1959).

We now turn to an examination of each component of social comparison theory and its relationship to affiliation motivation.

Increasing Uncertainty Concerning an Emotional Reaction Will Increase the Desire to Affiliate
A basic hypothesis of social comparison theory is that the more uncertain one is concerning a reaction, the more he will wish to compare his reaction with others. Support for this hypothesis has been provided by several studies. For instance, in one study, in which a slightly modified version of Schachter's procedure was used, subjects were first told that they would be receiving electric shocks and were then given one of three types of information: (1) fictitious information about how other subjects in the experiment were reacting, (2) fictitious information about how they themselves were reacting, and (3) no information. The subjects then chose whether they wished to wait alone or with others before receiving the shocks.

By providing or not providing this fictitious information, the investigators manipulated the degree of uncertainty the subjects felt about their reactions. If the subject's motive for affiliating was to compare his reactions with those of others, why would he seek affiliation if he already knew how they reacted? On the other hand, if he had not been given any information or had only been given fictitious information about his own reactions, he would be curious about how others were reacting and would want to be with others. As predicted, there was a significantly lower desire to affiliate when the subjects thought they knew the reactions of others than when they had been given either no information or fictitious information about their own reactions (Gerard and Rabbie, 1961).

The clearly documented relationship between uncertainty, affiliation, and social comparison explains a number of social phenomena. For instance, you will recall from Chapter 2 that no matter what emotion is aroused, the physiological reactions tend to be very similar. Whether the emotion is anger or euphoria, one feels a kind of stirred-up set of internal reactions. Since all of the physiological reactions are so similar, the only distinctive aspect of the emotion is the situation and how others are reacting. If you feel stirred up after an emotionally arousing experience, but are unclear as to how to label your emotions, and someone else in the same situation is acting angry, you label your feelings as anger (Schachter and Singer, 1962). Thus whenever you're not clear as to how to interpret your emotional arousal, an increase in the level of your arousal should increase your desire to compare your reactions with others.

Confirmation of this hypothesis has been obtained in a recent study. Subjects given a drug and not told that it had a stimulating effect showed a significantly higher desire to affiliate than subjects who were given the same drug and told that it was a stimulant (Mills and Mintz, 1972).

Another practical implication of the relationship between uncertainty and affiliation is the role that uncertainty plays in rumor. It has long been observed that uncertainty is one of the conditions that encourages rumor. Rumors are born, circulate, and flourish when an event is important and the actual facts are ambiguous or difficult to obtain (Allport and Postman, 1947). Thus, for example, in riot situations, where the normal sources of reliable information have been disrupted, rumor plays a significant role. Affiliation under conditions of uncertainty, the labeling of emotions, and the rumor process can all be viewed as manifestations of the same basic social process: When reality is unclear, people seek information from others and, in so doing, may begin to evolve their own interpretations of that reality—which may or may not be accurate. When clear and objective information is not provided, people may fabricate their own.

Increasing the Similarity of Persons with Whom One Expects to Affiliate Will Increase Affiliation
Confirmation of this hypothesis was obtained in a second experiment by Schachter (1959). Following the same procedure he used in his earlier experiment, he set up two conditions for subjects who expected to be given a painful shock. Half of the subjects were given the choice of waiting alone or with others "who will be taking part in the same experiment"— people who were similar, since they were going through the same experience of waiting for the painful experiment. The other half of the subjects were given the choice of waiting alone or with others who were "waiting to talk to their professors and advisers"—girls who were not sharing the unpleasant experimental procedure. If the desire to affiliate were a general desire simply to be with others, no matter whom, there should have been no difference in the percentage of girls choosing to affiliate in the two experimental conditions.

However, there was a difference. Subjects much preferred being with others who were in a similar situation. Sixty percent of the subjects in the similar-waiting condition chose to affiliate with the other girls, but none of the subjects in the dissimilar-waiting condition preferred to affiliate with the girls who were not participating in the experiment. As Schachter pointed out, this finding would mean that the old saying "misery loves company" should be modified to "misery loves miserable company."

These results clearly show that increasing the similarity of persons with whom one expects to affiliate will increase affiliation. However, since similarity can be defined in so many ways, isolating the critical aspects of similarity has been the concern of much of the work in this area.

If you were given a choice of waiting with someone who was similar while you were preparing to receive a painful electric shock, whom would you choose? Someone in the same situation? Someone with a similar personality? Someone with a similar socioeconomic background? Someone of similar intelligence and ability? Someone of the same race? Someone with similar physical dimensions? Someone with similar attitudes? Frivolous as some of these variables may sound, all have been found to be important in predicting interpersonal attraction. (We will explore these findings further in Chapter 9.) In relation to affiliation preference, two aspects have been studied in detail: (1) situational similarity and (2) personality similarity.

As we saw, *situational similarity* is a powerful determinant of affiliation. Subsequent investigators in this area have tried to isolate the crucial aspects of situational similarity that lead to affiliation. Why should people want to affiliate with someone in a similar situation? Is it to compare their *emotional reactions?* To see how others are taking the whole procedure? Or is it for *intellectual reasons*—to see if the other person has any additional information about the experimental procedure?

Both emotional and intellectual reasons have been found to be important. In one study subjects who were going to participate in a fictitious pain-tolerance experiment were given the choice of either having no one with them during the experiment or having one of four fictitious others with them: (1) a student who was participating in the same experiment, (2) a student who had just completed the experiment and was waiting for his test results, (3) a student who was not going to be involved in the pain-tolerance experiment, or (4) a physiologist, who could give the subject physiological information on his reactions. If a subject chose to participate in the experiment with a physiologist, the strength of the intellectual comparison motive would be shown; if he chose to wait with another subject who was participating in the same experiment, the strength of the emotional comparison motive would be illustrated.

The results obtained supported the strength of both the emotional and the cognitive comparison motives. Sixty-eight percent of the subjects wished to be with the other person when he was described as a physiologist, 62 percent when he was described as someone participating in the experiment, 52 percent when he was someone who had just completed the experiment, and 51 percent when he knew nothing at all about it. In summary, there was a significantly higher desire to affiliate either when the other person was participating in the same experiment, and thus was emotionally similar, or when the other person was a physiologist who could provide information about the subject's reactions (Becker, 1967).

Another type of similarity, *similarity in personality,* may have an even stronger influence on affiliation behavior. In real life affiliation may not be directed toward strangers—even those who are sharing an unpleasant situation with us. All of the patients waiting to see a dentist are situationally similar; yet the incidence of affiliative behavior may be rather negligible. When faced with a personal problem, we may be more likely to share our feelings with a friend than with a stranger who is having the same personal problem.

To test the relative strength of situational similarity versus similarity of personality traits and interests, investigators gave subjects in one experiment a choice between three alternatives: (1) waiting alone, (2) waiting with someone who was in the same experiment but had a different personality, and (3) waiting with someone who was in a different experiment but had a similar personality. Which aspect of similarity was more powerful? Among those who chose to wait with others, 59 percent chose to wait with persons of similar interests and personality, and only 41 percent chose to wait with others who had dissimilar personalities but were in the same experiment (Miller and Zimbardo, 1966).

Before one uses this result to generalize that similarity in personality is always a more powerful determinant than situational similarity, a word of caution is necessary. In this study the description of the persons with a dissimilar personality may have caused a negative reaction. If someone says, as the experimenter did in this study, that a person is "just not like you," you might interpret this to mean that he is somewhat unpleasant. Certainly, if these words were used to describe a potential blind date, they might sound ominous.

The crucial aspects of similarity have just begun to be explored. Most of the work has focused on two aspects of similarity in a stressful situation. The aspects of similarity that are most important in determining affiliation may vary from situation to situation. If you're feeling very happy, you may prefer someone in a similar mood. Nothing can bring you down faster than a dour companion. If you are discussing a political issue that is important to you, you may prefer someone with similar attitudes. The results of a recent study showed that people preferred working with others who had highly similar attitudes to working with persons with different attitudes (Castore and DeNinno, 1972). On a Saturday night you may want someone who is physically attractive, irrespective of whether he is similar or not. As we shall see in Chapter 9, there are many dimensions of similarity that can influence interpersonal attraction. In fact, under some circumstances you may prefer someone who is dissimilar. Two equally dominant people may have trouble settling "who's in charge" in a relationship, as many dating and married couples have found out.

Once Affiliation Occurs, There Is a Tendency Toward a Uniformity of Reaction When people are in a situation in which emotional reactions are discrepant, there will be pressures toward uniformity. Since each person is looking to the reactions of others for his knowledge of what is correct, discrepant reactions are upsetting. When discrepancies exist, people may modify their own reaction in order to come closer to the reactions of the other group members. At the same time they may also try to modify the opinions of others in the group to make those opinions resemble their own more closely. If neither of these tactics works, they may simply cease comparing themselves with those in the group who are very different.

This tendency toward a uniformity of emotional reaction has been clearly shown in the typical stress-affiliation experiment (Wrightsman, 1960). Subjects were first told that they would be receiving a series of painful injections; then they were asked to indicate how uneasy they felt about this procedure on a scale from zero to one hundred, with one hundred indicating that they felt very uneasy. After this question was answered, subjects were assigned to one of three experimental conditions: alone, together-talk, or together-no-talk.

In the alone condition subjects were left completely alone for five minutes and were told that they could read or smoke if they liked. In the together-talk condition four subjects were brought together and told that they could talk about the experiment or anything else. In the together-no-talk condition four subjects were brought together and were asked to remain silent.

After a five-minute wait in one of these experimental conditions, each subject was again asked to rate the intensity of his uneasiness on the same uneasiness scale that was used previously. Changes in the subjects' responses on this scale were the measure of changes in emotions.

In both of the together conditions there was a significantly greater decrease in variability of emotions than in the alone condition. For instance, subjects who initially were very uneasy became less uneasy when confronted with others who were less uneasy than they were, and subjects who had been relatively calm became more uneasy when confronted with persons who were more upset than they were.

In this situation, interestingly, the tendency toward uniformity of reaction occurred whether or not the subjects were allowed to talk with one another. There was as much uniformity in the together-no-talk condition as there was in the together-talk condition. As we shall see in Chapter 8, much human communication takes place on a nonverbal level. By noting the facial expressions and gestures of others and many other subtle cues, people can tell how others are feeling and react accordingly.

Also, it should be noted that the uniformity effects observed in the injection study occurred after only a five-minute period of social interaction. In longer time periods the pressures toward uniformity may be much greater. As we shall see in Chapter 11, pressures toward uniformity of opinion and behavior are pervasive in everyday situations. If you have any doubts about the prevalence of uniformity, take a look at the similarities of dress patterns on a college campus. Whether the students in a particular group wear short or long hair, sweaters or fringes and beads, the similarities within a group are striking.

Fear reduction

People exposed to the threat of an electric shock may also want to affiliate in order to reduce their fears (Schachter, 1959). Being with others may provide reassurance. By discussing one's feelings with others, one may reduce his overall stress level. When asked why they wished to be with others, subjects in the standard Schachter procedure have frequently mentioned the desire for comfort: "Just talking with others reduces worry" (Zimbardo and Formica, 1963, p. 152).

Observational Evidence A number of observations are consistent with the fear-reducing explanation of affiliation under stress. Under combat conditions, for instance, the soldier knows that if he gets into difficulty, he can count on his buddies to help him. If he is wounded, he can depend on both his buddies and the medics to take care of him. Further, maintaining his responsibilities to his buddies is a matter of loyalty and pride. When fighting with the men in his unit, the soldier learns to trust and depend on them and therefore feels safer with them (Mandelbaum, 1952). (See Figure 5-6.)

In fact, the fear-reducing effect of affiliation has sometimes been so pronounced that it has impelled men to expose themselves to further dangers. Many combat crew members in the United States Air Force during World War II reported that they suffered more when they were safely on the ground and their crew was flying without them than when they were on a combat mission (Grinker and Spiegel, 1945). A medical officer in the Royal Air Force wrote of a similar group loyalty that was stronger than the desire for physical safety:

Everyone looked forward to the completion of his tour, but so strong was the crew spirit in bomber command that it was not an uncommon occurrence for a man to volunteer to do as many as ten extra trips so that he and his crew could finish together, if for any reason he had joined them with more to his credit than they had done.

[Stafford-Clark, 1949, p. 15.]

Affiliation has also been reported to reduce the level of fear in other stressful situations. For example, being with others has been observed to produce reassuring effects under conditions of natural disaster (Marshall, 1951) and to make children less fearful when exposed to stressful conditions (Burlingham and Freud, 1943). In riot conditions being with other policemen may make an individual policeman feel less fearful, as described in Box 5. In fact, one might speculate that the reassuring effect of being with others accounts for the observed strength of groups that are under stress—such as in an army setting.

Fear-Reducing Effects of Being with Strangers

If you were waiting to get an electric shock, would you be less afraid if you waited with other people—even if you didn't know them? A number of studies in this area show that being with others does reduce the level of stress—but only for some people.

The injection study summarized in the preceding section was an early study on the fear-

FIGURE 5-6 Under the highly stressful conditions of combat, a fellow soldier may provide sorely needed comfort, an effective means of fear-reduction. (U.S. Army Photograph)

reducing effects of being with others. As you will recall, subjects in this study were first frightened, then assigned to one of three waiting conditions: alone, together-talk, or together-no-talk. The amount of fear expressed by the subjects in the three conditions was compared.

If simply being with others reduces fear, subjects who were in either the together-talk condition or the together-no-talk condition would be less afraid than subjects who were alone. However, this did not occur. Although, as we noted, the *variability* in levels of fear stabilized in the together conditions, there were no statistically significant differences in the *amount* of fear expressed by the subjects in the different conditions. Among one subgroup of subjects, however, subjects who were first-born or only children, there was significantly less fear when they were with other people than when they were alone. As we shall see later, there is a substantial amount of evidence indicating that first-born and only children tend to be higher than others in affiliation motivation (Wrightsman, 1960).

In interpreting the results of this experiment, we should note two limitations. First, those participating in the experimental together conditions did not know each other prior to the experiment. Strangers may not feel free to discuss their fears, and if a free discussion does not develop, opportunities for catharsis and comfort may be severely limited. Moreover, the together conditions were limited to five-minute periods, so that the opportunity for relationships to develop was somewhat restricted.

Fear-Reducing Effects of Being with Friends
The effectiveness of other people in giving comfort may depend on their familiarity. To test this hypothesis, one experimenter exposed subjects to a stressful condition (induced failure on a task) under three social conditions: (1) alone, (2) with a stranger, or (3) with a friend. The amount of stress experienced by each subject under these conditions was measured.

If stress reduction is greater with friends, one would expect a lower stress level among those subjects tested with a friend than among those subjects tested with a stranger. This hypothesis was confirmed. In fact, there was no significant difference between the amount of stress experienced by those tested alone and those tested with a stranger (Kissel, 1965).

Why should being with a friend make you less afraid in a stressful situation? You may feel a kind of strength in numbers. You may joke about your feelings. Your friend may reassure you. You may frankly discuss your fears and in so doing reduce them. Or the physical presence of a friend may remind you of many pleasant things that distract you from the immediate unpleasantness. The exploration of the processes underlying the reduction of stress when one is with friends remains an intriguing research problem and one that has enormous practical implications. Stress situations are so pervasive in contemporary society that the exploration and use of fear-reducing strategies would constitute a helpful, preventive approach to the problems caused by excessive stress—such as the reactions of some students to the strains of college life.

On some occasions, however, being with a stranger can be more reassuring than being with a friend. The cliché about the instant intimacy of anonymous passengers on planes and trains would point up one advantage of strangers. Since more than likely the passengers will never see each other again, maintaining self-images becomes less important. Consequently, they can express feelings without concern about what others will think of them or to whom their confidences will be revealed.

The superiority of strangers to friends in reducing stress in some situations was shown by the results of one study. While viewing a technicolor film of a primitive culture, male college students saw graphic illustrations of puberty rites in which deep incisions were made into the genitals of young men. Half of the students watched the film with a stranger; the other half with a friend. More tension was shown when the subjects viewed the film with a friend than when they viewed it with a stranger (Gordon, 1971).

Why should the students viewing the film with a friend have been more upset than those viewing it with a stranger? There are at least two possible answers. First, those viewing it with a friend may have been more embarrassed about their own reactions. The film was powerfully arousing, and many subjects may have been concerned that their friends would think they were overreacting. They may have worried about whether or not they were betraying the intensity of their reaction in front of a friend whom they would continue seeing.

Or the friends may have scared each other. Friends may be more responsive to each other's reactions than strangers. If one person becomes scared, it is easy for the emotion to spread. Some of you may have been in a situation in which you were initially calm but became upset because of what your friends said. For instance, when preparing for an examination, one of the author's students wrote:

Everyone's saying that the instructor is *real* difficult. Flunks many students. Respecting the opinions of others, I feared that their arguments were correct, and my ideas of the instructor being human and fair were defeated. Then, too, I think I'm prepared until I hear others studying things I just passed over.

The "contagion" of other's fears has been noted by a number of observers of disaster situations. One clear example is furnished by a series of interviews with people who listened to Orson Welles' 1939 broadcast, *The War of the Worlds,* in which a fictitious invasion from Mars was described in a highly believable fashion. (See Figure 5-7.) The program is estimated to have frightened at least a million Americans. Thousands were panic-stricken (Cantril, 1940, 1966 reprint).

One of the recurrent themes found to account for the panic reaction of those interviewed was the reactions of other people. This contagion effect seemed to increase fear in a number of ways. Initially, other people's behavior corroborated the broadcast:

I was *resting when an excited person phoned* and told me to listen to the radio, that a big meteor had fallen. I was really worried.

[Cantril, 1940, 1966 reprint, p. 140.]

I had just gone to the store to get some last-minute things for my daughter's party. When I came in my son said, "Mother, something has come down from Mars and the world is coming to an end." I said, "Don't be silly." *Then my husband said, "It is true." So I started to listen.* And really, I heard 40 people were killed and there was gas and everybody was choking.

[Cantril, 1940, 1966 reprint, p. 141.]

FIGURE 5-7 A Martian war machine creates panic among a terrified citizenry. Illustration to H. G. Wells, *The War Between the Worlds* **(1898).** (The Bettman Archive)

Sometimes the sight of others who were frightened *increased the emotional tension* of the initially calm individual:

I was getting worried when my friend came in and *his face was ghastly white*. He said, "We're being invaded," and *his conviction impressed me.*

[Cantril, 1940, 1966 reprint, p. 142.]

The presence of other people also acted as a *disturbing influence,* interfering with the individual's intellectual ability to evaluate critically the information. In the tumult of a group the individual was not able to concentrate on and assess the situation:

My wife kept outwardly calm too. But *there were so many people around that neither of us had a chance to collect our wits* and see what was really the matter.

[Cantril, 1940, 1966 reprint, p. 142.]

From the "Martian invasion" and from the puberty rite film, we can see that friendly others do not always serve to reduce fear. Although friends are sometimes more reassuring than strangers, under some circumstances they can add to the level of stress aroused.

Friends versus Strangers   Just as in any area in which contradictory effects are found, a number of variables may influence the relative comfort value of friends and strangers. One may be the *social acceptability* of the emotion aroused in the situation. You will recall that in the study in which friends were found to be more comforting, the stress manipulation was an induced failure on an experimental task. Once the subjects found that their friends shared their reaction to failure, they may have overcome their embarrassment about their own reactions. In such a situation they may have been free to share their feelings with their friends and may have found support in the comfort of a known face. In contrast, in the puberty rite film study, which showed that the presence of strangers was less upsetting than the presence of friends, the students may have been concerned about their friends' reactions—both to the film and to themselves.

The *physical demands* of the situation may also influence your reactions to friends and to strangers. If you are in a situation in which there is physical danger and the others you are with

are dependable people whom you know will not desert you, their presence may be reassuring. Strangers are unknown entities. On the other hand, if your friends react emotionally and irrationally, their presence may increase your own level of fear.

Fear reduction versus social comparison

Sometimes people may want to affiliate in order to compare their reactions with those of others; sometimes they may want to be with others in order to reduce their level of fear. We've seen evidence showing the power of both motives.

Which of the two motives is more powerful? Evidence on this point is somewhat inconclusive. In one study social comparison was shown to be a stronger motive for affiliation than stress reduction (Darley and Aronson, 1966). In a typical Schachter shock procedure, subjects were given information about the fear reaction of two people—one of whom was said to be slightly more afraid than the subject and one of whom was said to be considerably calmer. If fear reduction were the individual's main reason for affiliation, one would predict that the subjects would have chosen the considerably calmer subject. However, the subjects chose to wait with the person who was more similar to them—the person whose fear level deviated only "slightly" rather than "considerably" from their own.

In another study, however, fear reduction seemed to be the stronger motive. Subjects, again in a Schachter electric shock procedure, were asked to indicate the strength of their desire to affiliate with persons who were highly fearful, moderately fearful, and calm. If one assumes that being with a frightened person would increase the intensity of the fear experienced, a fear-reduction explanation of affiliation would predict that individuals would avoid the highly fearful person.

This hypothesis was confirmed. All of the subjects showed the least preference for a highly fearful person—even those subjects who were highly fearful themselves (Rabbie, 1963). Apparently misery may not love miserable company if it gets too miserable.

Whether social comparison or fear reduction

is the stronger motive for affiliation may depend on the intensity of the fear that the other person is experiencing. Social comparison may be the stronger motive at moderate levels of fear, but when the other gets too upset—whether he's comparable to ourselves or not—our main desire may be to avoid him and seek a calmer person. You may have seen this in yourself around the time of finals. Even if you're really concerned, you may avoid others whom you know are concerned, because talking with them will just upset you.

Other reasons for affiliation

We have focused primarily on why people wish to be with others when they think they're going to receive a painful electric shock. In other situations, however, the reasons for affiliation may differ. Although very little experimental work has been done on the reasons for affiliation in nonstressful situations, we may speculate that any of the reasons mentioned at the beginning of this chapter may motivate affiliation. For instance, if you're feeling uncertain about whether or not you're loved, the desire to reassure yourself that someone does care for you may be a powerful force behind your affiliation behavior. Or if you need to care for another and your opportunities to do so have been limited, you may want to affiliate with someone on whom you can bestow love.

If you have been deprived of an opportunity to play "social status games," you may choose to affiliate with someone whom you think will fulfill this need. For instance, if you've just mastered a difficult intellectual task, you may prefer to affiliate with someone whose opinion you value or whose acceptance you wish to earn.

Speculation aside, there is some evidence suggesting that people affiliate for at least two other reasons: (1) to receive protection and comfort and (2) to relieve boredom.

Protection and Comfort If something occurs to make you feel very threatened, you may wish to be with someone who is powerful and can protect you. As we shall see in Chapter 10, people may cling to leaders whom they feel can take care of them. For instance, one of the appeals of Hitler to the German people in the late 1920s and 1930s was their belief that he could extricate them from the severe social and economic problems they faced during that period.

A recent study provides experimental evidence supporting the importance of seeking protection and comfort as a reason for affiliation. First a high level of stress was induced in second- and third-grade children by warning them that they were about to have an important test. Then they were allowed to choose between waiting for the test with another classmate, with whom they could compare their reactions, or waiting with an adult, who would comfort them. As would be predicted by a protection-nurturance approach, the children preferred affiliation with the adult (McIntyre, 1971). When there are no strong normative pressures against affiliating with a powerful person, troubled people may prefer someone whom they think can protect them from harm.

As you may have noticed, there is some overlap between a fear-reduction and a protection-comfort explanation of affiliation. Both point to the importance of the subject's desire to reduce his concerns about expected events. However, a protection-comfort explanation would predict that the frightened individual would choose someone who is powerful and can protect him from the threat, whereas a fear-reduction hypothesis would predict that the frightened person would choose whoever can reduce the fear the most. Of course, in some situations both hypotheses might predict the same source for affiliation. However, it may be that protection becomes a particularly important reason for affiliation when people are feeling very helpless or when they see an opportunity to affiliate with someone they think can solve their problems.

Boredom Relief At times being alone with your own thoughts can be pretty boring. All alone at breakfast—without television, a newspaper, or anyone to talk to—you may feel restless, uncomfortable, and vaguely anxious.

People need stimulation. As you may recall from your introductory psychology course, a number of studies have shown that when people are deprived of outside stimulation, they experience a variety of negative reactions. For instance, if you were lying on a bed in a small soundproof cubicle, twenty-four hours a day, sitting up only to eat meals and being released only to go to the toilet, wearing plastic goggles that prevented clear vision, wearing cotton gloves to restrict touch stimulation, and having your ears covered with a foam-rubber pillow to reduce auditory stimulation—with all variations in sensory stimulation minimized—you'd probably experience a variety of negative psychological reactions. (See Figure 5-8.) You might think that such an experience would be pleasant, but literally hundreds of studies have shown that most subjects are very disturbed by sensory deprivation. You'd probably become restless and bored. Your thought processes would be disturbed, and you'd have difficulty concentrating. Your performance on standardized intelligence tests would decrease. You'd probably daydream, and in some rare cases you might hallucinate. Thus for most people to continue normal psychological functioning, a certain amount of outside stimulation appears to be necessary (Zubek, 1969).

Other people are an important source of outside stimulation, and when we are deprived of their presence, we may become less efficient and more preoccupied with our own inner thoughts. Unfortunately, most of the experiments in this area have involved depriving the individual of opportunities for both sensory stimulation and social interaction. There is not much evidence on the effects of social isolation alone. However, in the few experiments in which the effects of social isolation and sensory deprivation were manipulated separately, it has been found that social isolation alone does produce impairments in psychological functioning. In one study, for instance, subjects who were kept alone but were provided with outside stimulation were found to become less efficient in their thought processes and to become more involved with their own thoughts, dreams, and memories (Zuckerman, Persky, Link, and Basu, 1968). The anecdotal reports provided by Admiral Byrd and others also suggest that social contact may be important in keeping us firmly fastened to outside reality.

A desire for social stimulation may motivate much of social interaction. If you should ever be home alone with a highly contagious illness for several weeks without seeing or talking with anyone, even people you usually consider bor-

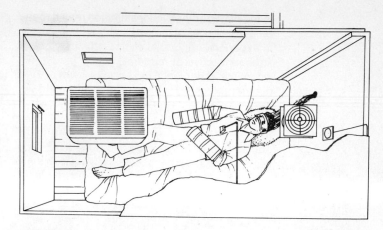

FIGURE 5-8 In a series of experiments at McGill University, each subject remained in a small soundproof cubicle, as shown above, and for several days severely deprived himself of sensory stimulation. An air conditioner (left) and a fan (right) masked outside noise. The wires attached at the top of the subject's head enabled the experimenters to study brain waves. (From "The Pathology of Boredom," Woodburn Heron, *Scientific American,* January 1957. Copyright © 1957 by Scientific American, Inc. All rights reserved.)

ing might begin to look good. The longer you are isolated, the more pressing the need for social stimulation may become. The importance of the need for stimulation as a reason for social behavior was shown in a recent study (Sales, 1971). People who had been classified as needing a greater variety of outside stimulation than others were found to participate more frequently in group discussions.

Excessive affiliation

Although being with others may frequently be motivated by a desire to escape boredom, there is such a thing as too much social contact. If you've ever spent an entire day with someone who talked all of the time, your main reactions may have been irritation and a profound desire to escape to peaceful solitude. (See Figure 5-9.) Just as some investigators (e.g., Berlyne, 1960) have theorized that people try to maintain an optimum level of overall stimulation—not too much and not too little—so, too, may people try to maintain an optimum level of social stimuli. You don't want to be alone all of the time, but you may not want people around constantly either.

FIGURE 5-9 The solace of solitude. (Thomas H. Brooks/Stock, Boston)

Both anecdotal and experimental evidence show that there are negative reactions when people are in constant contact with others. People seem to need time alone too. Laboratory studies of men confined together over a period of days have repeatedly shown that the subjects tend to withdraw into themselves more and more over the period of confinement. For instance, in one study of pairs of men confined together for eight days, the men spent about 50 percent of their waking time together during the first four days, but during the last four days the time the men spent interacting declined to about 25 percent of the day (Altman, Taylor, and Wheeler, 1971). Over a longer period of intensive interaction, the tendency toward mutual withdrawal might have increased even more. Witness the reaction of one subject who had been confined for a twelve-week period with five other men:

> We all felt the need not to express ourselves completely. It is close in here at times. I don't want to get involved. Have to be here for two more months. You learn to ignore people more.
>
> [Cowan and Strickland, 1965, pp. 37–38.]

Interpersonal frictions are commonly found in isolated groups. In laboratory experiments, over time, the subjects frequently become hostile, rude, and uncooperative with one another (Haythorn and Altman, 1967). Anecdotal reports of working groups in real life also indicate the presence of hostile impulses. When the members of the group know that they must depend on one another to accomplish their mission and perhaps to survive, they may engage in elaborate rituals to avoid confrontations. For instance, in one study of two men who spent thirty days in a simulated space flight, the men were found to avoid emotionally involving topics and to keep the conversational material neutral (Hagen, 1961).

Of course, variations in the situation influence the incidence of irritation. As you might expect, people who are compatible with one another are less likely to become irritated. When confinement is lengthy and under crowded conditions, interpersonal stress has been found to be higher. Further, when two men are confined together, stress is higher than when three men are kept together (Smith and Haythorn, 1972).

Another reaction commonly found in groups of people confined together is boredom. In most studies of long-term confinement of a small number of people, subjects have mentioned boredom and monotony as major problems (Smith, 1966). For instance, despite the fact that magazines and recreational facilities were available to the members of a submarine crew, many complained of their intense boredom (Levine, 1965). When recreational facilities are more limited, boredom may become an even more intense problem.

Why do people react with withdrawal, irritation, and boredom when confined with other people? There are a number of possible answers. Since their contact with the outside world is limited, they may retreat into their own thoughts. In the closeness of a contained group, events that ordinarily would not be noticed may become highly irritating and cause the members to withdraw mutually from contact and thus become bored. (Imagine how you would react to someone who constantly cracked his knuckles if you knew you were going to have to listen to that for thirty days.) Or an extremely strong need for privacy may be involved. Or all three factors may combine to make confinement the stressful experience that so many people have found it to be.

Summary

People affiliate for a variety of reasons. In the stressful situation of anticipating a painful electric shock, people may affiliate for social comparison. As social comparison theory would predict, (1) increasing uncertainty concerning an emotional reaction increases the desire to affiliate; (2) increasing the similarity of the persons with whom one expects to affiliate increases affiliation; and (3) once affiliation occurs, there is a tendency toward a uniformity of reaction.

People also affiliate in a stressful situation to reduce fear. Sometimes people are less afraid when they can face a stressful situation with another person. At other times, however, being with others can increase the level of stress. The conditions under which friends or strangers are more reassuring are not yet clear.

Which is a stronger motive for affiliation under stress—social comparison or fear reduction? The evidence here is not yet clear either. In some studies social comparison has been shown to be the stronger motive; in others, fear reduction. Whether social comparison or fear reduction is the stronger motive for affiliation may depend on the intensity of the fear experienced by the person one is affiliating with.

In situations that are not fear-arousing there may be other reasons for affiliation. Although very little experimental work has been done in nonstressful situations, we may speculate that any of the reasons mentioned at the beginning of the chapter may motivate affiliation. We saw specific evidence that in some situations people may affiliate for protection and comfort or to relieve boredom.

We have been trying to isolate the various reasons for affiliation. In real life, however, the various causes for affiliation may be cumulative. A person may affiliate with a particular person for a variety of reasons, some of which may overlap greatly. You may wish to be with a particular person because you want to compare yourself with him, because he makes you feel calmer, and because he is amusing.

People may differ in their reasons for affiliating. We have been focusing on controlled experiments showing how the situation can arouse affiliation behavior. But, as the results of the original Schachter study showed and as you have probably observed among your friends, people differ in the intensity of their desire to affiliate. Consistently, in many different situations, some people have a much stronger motive to be with others than do other people. It is to this question of consistent, individual differences in the strength of the affiliation motive that we now turn.

FIGURE 5-10 (James M. Wall)

Loners versus Joiners

Let's begin this section by taking a test. Look at Figure 5-10, and spend about five minutes making up any kind of story you like about it. Since this is a test of creative imagination, be sure to make the story vivid and dramatic. Please include answers to the following questions in your story.

1. What is happening? Who are the people?
2. What has led up to this situation? What has happened to precipitate it?
3. What are the people in the picture thinking? What do they want? Why do they want it?
4. What will happen?

The test you have just taken is a variation of a well-known correlational procedure (McClelland et al., 1953). In the real test you would be shown four or five pictures and then asked to write a story for each. As you may have gath-

ered, this test is not really concerned with creative imagination; rather it is an attempt to measure the intensity of a variety of social motives—including the desire for achievement, power, and sex, and the motive we are primarily concerned with here, affiliation. All stories are scored for the presence of certain content. To see roughly how this is done, let us look at the contents of two stories, one high in affiliation motive, the other low:

Story A

Two college women, roommates I think, are studying together. While one of them is trying to work, she is really wondering whether the other one likes her or not. They have been rooming together for several weeks now and she just can't figure out where she stands. Sometimes, the other girl is very friendly and then she thinks they are good friends. And then something happens when she finds out that her roommate has made plans and not included her at all. Since she is a transfer student and lonely, this relationship is important to her. And she knows that she can't be pushy—she just has to sit back and see what happens. But this uncertainty makes her lonely; in some ways she wishes she were by herself completely so she could stop worrying.

Story B

A college student is studying hard for a test in her dormitory room. Since the test is in organic chemistry, which is a required course for pre-med students, she is really working. Her last test scores have been low and she's afraid she might flunk the course if she doesn't pull her grades up. And she is really worried since she wants to go to med school more than anything else in the world. She's been working so hard that she had a sandwich and a soft drink in her room to save the time involved in going out to eat. She's really sweating it—hunched over her notes and notebook.

As you no doubt have guessed, story A is high in affiliation imagery. It centers on the theme of "establishing, maintaining, or restoring a positive effective relationship with another person" (Atkinson, Heyns, and Veroff, 1954). Moreover, there is concern over the possible loss of the friendship and an emphasis on the importance of the relationship. In contrast, story B contains almost no mention of friendship or interpersonal relationships. There is no reference to the other person in the picture. All of the emphasis is on achieving a goal—passing the test. The student is seen as trying to achieve, to do better. Story B would indicate a high score in the achievement motive, which has also been frequently measured by this procedure.

Measuring motives

Since people vary in the motives that "make them run," a measure of the relative intensities of motives within people would be very useful. However, as you might expect, accurately measuring human motivation is extremely difficult. A variety of techniques have been used, each of which has some inherent problems.

Self-Report Measures One technique would be to use a self-report measure, or to ask the individual to indicate his desire to be alone or with others. A good example of this kind of approach is furnished by Schachter's affiliation scale. In his study girls were asked to "be perfectly honest and let us know how much you'd like to be alone or together with other girls" on the following scale:

_____ I very much prefer being alone.
_____ I prefer being alone.
_____ I don't care very much.
_____ I prefer being together with others.
_____ I very much prefer being together with others.

But would the response given to this question accurately reflect the person's real motives? Individuals may be dishonest and rate themselves according to the way they would like to appear to others. Or if they rate themselves accurately according to how they see themselves, their self-perception may be inaccurate. How many of us can be completely objective in our self-appraisals? Even when the rater is being as honest as he can, all he can reflect is what he himself knows about himself. To the extent that his self-perception is inaccurate, the self-rating must necessarily be inaccurate.

Behavioral Measures If self-ratings can be distorted, either because of conscious deception or because of inaccuracies in self-perception, one might be able to obtain better information by observing an individual's affiliation behavior. For example, one could observe the amount of time an individual spends with other people, the number of clubs he belongs to, and so on, in order to infer the strength of his affiliation motive. But the problem with this method is that there may be a variety of possible motives underlying one particular behavior. For instance, two individuals might belong to a very large number of organizations—one because he has a strong desire to be with other people, another because of social pressure from his parents, who consider extensive social activity a sign of social success. Thus there are also problems with the behavioral approach to measuring motivational strength.

A Projective Measure: The Thematic Apperception Test A third approach to measuring human motivation is through a variation of the "projective technique," which is based on the assumption that what a person sees in an ambiguous situation reveals his own personality. In the thematic apperception test (TAT) the subject is required to make up imaginative stories in response to a series of pictures that can be interpreted in a variety of ways. The stories are then analyzed for the subject's motives. In our fictitious TAT example respondent A saw concern over friendship and social acceptance, and B saw concern over a failure to achieve, although the picture that the two respondents saw was exactly the same. These differences in their reaction to the same picture presumably reflect differences in their motives. Respondent A would be considered higher in the need to affiliate than B.

However, like the other measures of the affiliation motive, the projective approach also has problems. Scores on self-report measures of affiliation have sometimes yielded low or insignificant correlations with those obtained by the TAT (McClelland, 1958). There has also been some disagreement about the appropriate way to score the TAT stories. Some psychologists have defined the need for affiliation as primarily a positive motive—people seek out others because they have learned that others are a dependable source of pleasure. Others using the TAT, however, have focused on affiliative behaviors as reflecting the need to avoid being rejected or left out—a negative approach to affiliation motivation. Still a third approach—the one most commonly used—is to score both positive and negative examples of affiliation and cumulate them for a total affiliation motivation score. Thus a person could earn a high affiliation score either by telling stories filled with loneliness and feared rejections or by telling stories filled with happy people lovingly interacting (Atkinson, Heyns, and Veroff, 1954). When this scoring method is used, many persons who differ psychologically may be classified as high in affiliation.

Even with these problems, however, the TAT measure of affiliation has been shown to have a number of strengths. The reliability, or consistency, of the test scores has been found to be high. When the TAT stories have been scored independently by a variety of experienced scorers, the correlations in affiliation scores have been impressively high (Atkinson, Heyns, and Veroff, 1954). A number of other studies have also shown the validity, or accuracy, of the TAT. It seems to measure accurately the kinds of affiliative behavior one would generally expect from people high in affiliation motivation. For instance, people obtaining high affiliation

scores have been found to engage in more friendly behavior in a small group setting than those with low affiliation scores (Fishman, 1966).

Characteristics of those obtaining high need-for-affiliation scores

If the TAT is a valid way to measure the need for affiliation, or "n-affiliation," in a person, it can also be used as a starting point for identifying those behaviors and characteristics that are most common in persons who are high or low in n-affiliation. Following this thought, researchers have, in a number of studies, administered the TAT to their subjects in order to measure the intensity of n-affiliation and then correlated the resulting scores with specific personality traits and behavior patterns.

Before we summarize the results of this considerable literature, you might try to envision what someone would be like who is very concerned with establishing, maintaining, or restoring good relations with others. Perhaps you see a person whose childhood taught him to seek out others. Or you may see someone who is very sensitive to social cues. Or perhaps you see someone who spends a lot of time with others, tries to get along with others, and is concerned about being accepted in a group situation. Although the results have not been completely consistent, in general this is the picture of a person high in n-affiliation that emerges from the correlational literature.

Background Factors One aspect of personal background that has been extensively investigated is *birth order*. The question of whether or not children who are first-born or only children differ from others in the intensity of their desire to affiliate was first studied by Schachter (1959). Using his standard threat-of-electric-shock procedure and female subjects, he found that birth order was related to n-affiliation. First- and only-born females showed a significantly greater preference for waiting with others than females who were later-born. This finding has been replicated in in a number of studies. (See Warren, 1966, for a review.) Several other studies have also confirmed that first- and only-born children generally rank higher than later-borns in n-affiliation scores (e.g., Dember, 1964).

What is there about being a first-born or an only child that would make him more affiliative? One answer is that the psychological climate surrounding a first birth may differ from that present at later births. The first birth may be more important to the parents. The experience is new to them; family pressures to produce an heir may be great; and the birth signifies the full sexual capacity of both husband and wife. Further, many parents are relatively inexperienced when their first child is born. The combination of the child's importance and the mother's inexperience may make the inexperienced, insecure, and concerned mother more responsive to the first-born. She may respond to more signals from the baby, respond more quickly, spend more time with the baby, and in general, be more effective in meeting all of the child's needs. This overprotectiveness may result in the child's becoming dependent. Since the first-born finds that his mother takes excellent care of him, he learns to rely heavily on her and, through a process of generalization, to rely on and need other people (Schachter, 1959).

This theory seems reasonable. Nevertheless, although a number of studies have shown that first-borns—especially first-born women—desire the company of others more than later-borns, not all of the evidence is consistent. A number of studies have shown no significant relationship between birth order and affiliative behavior (Schooler, 1972). For instance, in one study, involving over 400 subjects, no significant differences in n-affiliation scores were found on the TAT (Rosenfeld, 1966). In another study of over 200 male and female college freshmen, no differences in affiliative behavior (as reflected in their requests for roommates or single rooms) were found (Masling, 1965).

As in any area in which inconsistent results are obtained, it may be that other, uncontrolled variables influence the way birth order affects affiliation. You may be able to think of some possible explanations. For example, the atmosphere surrounding the first birth may differ from one family to another. Some may consider it an extremely important event, and others may take it in a more matter-of-fact way. Mothers who came from large families may have had so much child-care experience that they are as well prepared to attend to the needs of their first-born as they are to care for their later children.

Other aspects of the family structure may also be important, and these may interact with the birth order affiliation effect. The number and sex of children in the family and the age span between them may influence the relationship. The psychological climate for the oldest girl in a family of four girls may be quite different from that of a first-born girl with three younger brothers. If the births of the first and second child are separated by a very long period of time—say ten or more years—both may be treated like first-borns. When all of the possible family combinations are taken into account, birth order can become an immensely complex variable. Consistent findings about birth order and affiliation may not emerge until some of these variations are taken into account (Schooler, 1972).

Birth order, of course, is not the only background factor that relates to n-affiliation. The effect of sex and cultural differences are discussed in Box 6, and you may be personally aware of several other factors.

Sensitivity to Social Cues People high in n-affiliation might be expected to react to social cues differently from people who are less concerned about contact with others. By definition, persons with a high level of affiliation motivation are concerned about social matters. They may therefore be more sensitive to social cues in general and pay more attention to social than to nonsocial cues. However, since social contacts are so important to the person high in n-affiliation, he may, because of his overinvolvement, be less accurate in making fine discriminations in judging others than someone more neutral about social matters. He may care too much to be objective.

In general, these hypotheses have all been supported by the correlational findings. For instance, people high in n-affiliation have been found to watch their partners more carefully for signs of reactions than have persons low in n-affiliation (Davage, 1958). Yet persons high in n-affiliation have been found to be less accurate than others when perception of other people involves fine discriminations. If you are highly motivated toward something, you may see it when only minimal cues are presented. Thus when subjects high and low in n-affiliation were asked to distinguish between films showing "intense" levels of love and "medium" levels of love, subjects high in affiliation were unable to distinguish accurately, and subjects scoring low on affiliation were able to do so (Dayton, 1967).

Behavioral Differences As you might expect, persons who are high in n-affiliation are more likely to act "affiliatively." They spend more time in contact with others. It has been found, for instance, that such people belong to more social clubs (Smart, 1965), react more affiliatively when they are in groups, communicate more (Exline, 1962b), and act in a friendlier manner (Fishman, 1966).

Further, since persons high in n-affiliation seek to maintain the approval of others, you might predict that they would avoid mentioning potentially irritating subjects and would conform more to what the others in the group are doing and saying. Although the results have not been completely consistent, generally these expected relationships have been found (Exline, 1962a; McGhee and Teevan, 1967).

In general, persons high in n-affiliation are more concerned about maintaining good relationships with other people. They are more anxious about their group standing and are seen by their friends as actively seeking social approval (Byrne, 1961). They like other people more and see themselves as being popular (Mills and Abeles, 1965; French and Chadwick, 1956). Some persons high in n-affiliation may, however, be objectively less popular than persons not so high in this need (Groesbeck, 1958). People who want to be liked may try too hard. Also, since TAT scoring can classify persons with negative affiliation feelings as being high in n-affiliation, it is possible that these persons may have, in fact, been rejected by others.

Summary

People differ in the intensity of their desire to be with other people. In this section three basic measures of affiliation motivation were discussed: self-report measures, behavioral measures, and a widely used projective measure—the TAT. Although all of the motivation measures have inherent problems, the projective approach has proved to be the most reliable and valid, and has been used in many studies investigating the ways in which persons high in affiliation motivation differ from those lower in affiliation motivation. In general, although the evidence is not completely consistent, persons scoring high in the need to affiliate are first- or only-born children, are sensitive to social cues, and show a variety of affiliative behaviors—including spending more time in contact with others, being more friendly in groups, avoiding alienating others, being more anxious about their group standing, and liking other people more than persons low in affiliation motivation.

Affiliation Needs in Contemporary Society

Throughout this chapter we have seen the extent to which people need other people. (See Figure 5-11.) Being with others serves a variety of badly needed functions for the human being. But how well is this need for human contact being met in our contemporary society? If the writings of some poets, novelists, philosophers, and psychological theorists are to be believed, the answer is not too well.

Several notable psychological theorists have emphasized the prevalence of social isolation in contemporary society. According to Erich Fromm, for instance, most people have experienced loneliness at one time or another, and some people suffer much more from it than others. In his analysis of the conditions producing widespread loneliness in contemporary society, Fromm emphasizes a long-range historical emancipation of the individual from the power of traditional social groups. No longer must the individual remain in the town of his birth, pursuing the trade of his family. For the freedom of individuality, however, contemporary man has paid a large psychological price. A pervasive sense of loneliness has resulted from his lack of primary ties with other people (Fromm, 1941).

Although presenting a different explanation for the prevalence of loneliness, another classic social psychological theory also emphasizes the prevalence of the feeling of social isolation (Riesman, 1950). Even though the middle-class contemporary American is very sensitive to the actions and wishes of his peer group, and is

FIGURE 5-11 People need reassurance and acceptance from other people. If they can't get it live, they may someday be forced to resort to "canned" affection.

ready to conform to gain the approval of others, each person is separated from the others by the fear that he doesn't measure up.

Persuasive as literature and theorizing are about the prevalence of loneliness, there is also more solid evidence. Perhaps in talking with your fellow college students in their more candid moments, you may have heard them admit to experiencing profound feelings of loneliness. As one student said: *"I feel so lonely, excluded. I'd like to call some friends but I'm not sure I have any. I don't really feel accepted as a person"* (Seeman, 1971a, p. 84).

The popularity of telephone services for troubled people and the content of the calls made to them also show the frequency of loneliness in contemporary society. For instance, out of the 16,000 calls received in 1970 by the Toronto Distress Center, a telephone service for Toronto residents with problems, approximately 80 percent of the callers complained about their extreme loneliness in addition to their other problems (Sermat, 1972). In the New York City Help Line Telephone Center, over 7,800 callers specifically mentioned loneliness as their major problem (Help Line Telephone Center Release, 1970). Typifying the comments made by these lonely people are those made by a widow in a Davenport, Iowa, help-line setting: "I'm a widow living in this house alone. I was so lonesome tonight I had to talk to someone. What bothers me is the loneliness, not talking to anyone" (*Time,* August 1, 1969, p. 56).

In fact, the popularity of general radio talk shows in which the listeners call in their questions and comments may be viewed as an indirect indicator of the pervasiveness of loneliness. People like to hear themselves talk and to feel that someone is responding. To the sad and the lonely, calling in provides one way to maintain contact with others. For people with no friends, the radio personality may act as a substitute friend (*Time,* May 22, 1972, p. 79).

Of course, a more direct way to find out about the incidence of loneliness would be to ask people. Despite the widespread speculations and the importance of the issue, there is relatively little direct self-report evidence on the pervasiveness of loneliness. This may be, in part, because of the feeling that the incidence of contemporary loneliness is so self-evident it doesn't have to be documented. As the existen-

tialist philosophers have reminded us, each person is born alone, must lead his own life, and dies alone. However, self-evident as man's essential separateness may be, we've seen other self-evident truisms that did not turn out to be so true when subjected to empirical test.

The assumption that many people are lonely may turn out to fall into this category. Surveys on the incidence of loneliness have shown percentages of persons reporting feeling lonely ranging from 10 percent to 80 percent. In a survey of 400 Los Angeles workers only 10 percent of those questioned agreed with the statement "I often feel lonely" (Seeman, 1971b). Other surveys, however, have yielded much higher figures. In a poll of psychiatric patients more than 80 percent of those interviewed stated that their loneliness was the main reason for their seeking psychiatric help (Graham, 1969). This high percentage is consistent with that reported by one college counselor who notes that most of the students seeking counseling do so, not because they are mentally ill or seriously disturbed, but because they feel isolated—they have "trouble breaking down the barriers that separate them from other people" (Sermat, 1972).

These wide discrepancies may be more understandable if we consider the possibility that the frequency of loneliness may vary widely among persons with different personalities, among persons in different periods of their lifetime, and among persons in different situations. On some occasions you may have felt very isolated, and on other occasions you may have felt immersed with other people.

The low percentage of loneliness reported among the Los Angeles workers may be related to the fact that in our society work provides many people with needed social contact. In fact, in another survey 50 percent of the workers questioned said that they had close friends in the same line of work (Seeman, 1971b). Subtract the friendly job contacts or add other psychological pressures, and the incidence of loneliness may rise dramatically.

For instance, among freshmen college students—separated from home and old friends, placed in an unfamiliar university setting, and preoccupied with the problem of finding their own identity—the percentage of those experiencing loneliness may be much higher. (See

BOX 7 — THE PERVASIVENESS OF LONELINESS AMONG COLLEGE STUDENTS

One investigator obtained biographical essays (half of which were autobiographical and the other half of which were written about someone known well by the student) on loneliness from 401 students at four universities—the University of Oregon, San Francisco State, the University of Toronto, and York University in Canada (Sermat, 1972). These essays were scored to provide information about the overall extent of feelings of loneliness, and the following results were obtained.

Degree of Severity of the Loneliness Experience Described in the Essay	Frequency Among Male College Students	Frequency Among Female College Students	Total Frequency
Trivial	0	0	0
Relatively mild	7	16	23
Moderate	24	35	59
Quite upsetting, but not really severe	66	69	135
Very upsetting, but without psychiatric signs of emotional disturbance	63	66	129
Highly upsetting, with apparent psychiatric disturbances	13	23	36
The most severe emotional trauma that an individual is ever likely to experience	4	3	7
The individual made an actual suicide attempt	5	6	11
Not sufficient evidence to judge	0	1	1
Total	182	219	401

Box 7.) For suburban housewives—with their husbands and children gone for much of the day—the frequency of social isolation may be relatively high. And for retired people—severed from the social life provided by their jobs, faced with the loss of many of their friends, and sometimes further isolated by the death of their husband or wife—the feelings of separation and loneliness may be still higher.

If we acknowledge the affiliation motive as a basic social need, then loneliness, which represents the deprivation of this need, is a social problem. (See Figure 5-12.) In its worst form, loneliness can lead to destructive acts designed to attain recognition, including acts of self-destruction. Even in its passive form loneliness stifles good communication and hence thwarts full understanding among people—and perhaps a person's understanding of himself, as we saw in Chapter 2. It is therefore useful to examine the phenomenon and its causes in some detail so that we may become better able to understand it and to evolve ways of dealing with it.

FIGURE 5-12 Loneliness—a social problem in American society. (Sculpture by Michael Lawrence; photo by Dagmar)

Psychological causes of loneliness

To discover some of the correlates of loneliness, one researcher and his associates have done a series of studies. Lengthy questionnaires, including many items on background and personality, have been administered to several samples of subjects, mostly of college age or people in their mid-twenties. In addition, biographical and autobiographical essays of over 400 college students have been analyzed. From the analysis of all of these data, it has been hypothesized that there are at least six different psychological causes of loneliness (Sermat, 1972).

Existential Loneliness One type of loneliness seems to be caused by the realization of the limitations of human existence—the anxiety about death and the meaninglessness of life emphasized in some philosophical writings. Although it is not generally related to severe loneliness experiences, the feeling pervades the lives of many people in a mild form. Occasionally, it can become very intense—as shown by the contents of some suicide notes.

Loneliness Caused by Traumas Related to Largely Unavoidable Losses and Disasters Losing someone close to the individual was found to be a frequent cause of severe loneliness. The essays referred to in Box 7 showed that the severity of the loneliness experienced was greatest when its cause was beyond the control of any of the people involved. The severity of loneliness when the separation was initiated by some other person was intermediate, and self-initiated social isolation resulted in the smallest percentage of severe loneliness. Obviously, loneliness resulting from uncontrolled events would be expected to occur even more frequently among older people as an increasing number of their friends and relatives die.

Loneliness Caused by Lack of Support from One's Environment, Due to "Mismatching" of Assets and Skills and Needs, or to Discrimination or Persecution Loneliness is experienced by people who are misplaced "and suffer from the mismatching of what they have and want, and what the surrounding community has, approves of, or is interested in offering them or taking from them" (Sermat, 1972, p. 2). For instance, a young divorcee with children may be rejected in a family-centered community that sees her as a threat. Or recent immigrants may suffer because their values are mismatched with the community in which they currently reside.

An important case of mismatching occurs when a child's parents are cold and distant with him. As might be expected, the early childhood home environment has also been found to correlate significantly with loneliness. From the materials discussed in Box 7, it was found that many of those students who felt chronically lonely without any precipitating crisis came from homes that were "unhappy, lacking in emotional demonstrativeness, with lack of communication and emotional distance between the child and one or both of his/her parents" (Sermat, 1972, p. 7). Correlational studies of a number of college students and of a sample of the general population also support this hypothesis: "The more lonely the person feels to be, the more negative are his feelings toward his parents, and his perception of his parents' feelings toward him" (p. 8).

Loneliness Due to Internal Crises and a Sense of Failure People who have had blows to their self-esteem that have demoralized them and made them feel "empty" may withdraw from contact with others. For example, after she was punished—along with the other members of her class—for a conflict between students and teachers, one sixth-grade girl withdrew from social interaction and later wrote:

It didn't seem to bother the other kids that much, but with me it cut my self-esteem to just about nothing. I was exceptionally ashamed of myself, and even though my two older brothers knew about it, I couldn't bring myself to tell my parents. . . . The result: I withdrew from everyone. I wouldn't do a lot of things now, for fear that somehow they would end up with me getting in trouble again. After that, I never got back with my friends.

[Sermat, 1972, p. 3.]

Thus one would expect that people who feel lonely might feel that they have failed in something or that they have not lived up to their own expectations. As predicted, the correlation between perceived failure and loneliness was very high among men (.49). The correlations were not as high for female college students. Again, the culture may dictate that achievement is more important for men than for women, so that failing to live up to internal standards for achievement may be more destructive to the self-esteem of men than women.

Loneliness Due to Overreliance on Roles—Prescribed, Safe, but Relatively Impersonal, "Socially Pleasant" Relationships People who are very socially adept on the surface but who feel that they lack deeper levels of involvement may suffer from this type of loneliness. Although they may have superficial relationships with other people, they may feel that no one knows them as they feel they really are. When female college students were asked to rate how they saw themselves and how others saw them, those with high loneliness scores showed a significantly greater discrepancy between their self-perception and their ratings of how they thought others saw them (Moore, 1972). Feeling that you have authentic relationships with others who know you as you are may be very important in avoiding loneliness.

Additionally, people who are lonely frequently report that they have nobody with whom they can communicate about personally important matters. Several studies have shown the importance of "sharing one's innermost thoughts and concerns" with some understanding and close person. This was a factor mentioned, for instance, in 75 percent of 401 biographical and autobiographical essays written by college students (Sermat, 1972). Most of the students reported feeling lonely because they could not communicate about personally important matters—either because they felt that others would either not understand or dismiss their problems, or because they were afraid of the negative reactions they would receive from others if they revealed their true concerns.

Loneliness Due to Lack of Social Skills or Maladaptive, Offensive, or Unrewarding Behavior Toward Others Many chronically lonely people engage in maladaptive social behaviors or lack interpersonal skills. People who are overtly hostile would not be expected to be popular, nor would people who are excessively submissive. In a recent study it was found that female college students who reported feeling very lonely also obtained significantly higher scores on a measure of hostility and submissiveness (Moore, 1972).

In order to have satisfying interpersonal relationships, sometimes certain risks have to be taken—such as asking a favor, approaching someone you do not know well, or moving a conversation from a superficial to a more intimate level. People who see themselves as lonely, therefore, might be expected to see these actions as more risky, and to have greater reservations about undertaking such risks. A questionnaire was developed that measured the amount of perceived risk in various social overtures and the willingness to take the actions in spite of the risk. Scores on the risk-taking questionnaire were then correlated with the intensity of self-reported loneliness among approximately 150 Canadians from various geographical locations and occupations. For males, the judged level of risk and the reported readiness to take action were both highly and significantly correlated with loneliness. However, for women, these correlations were low and nonsignificant (Sermat, 1972).

The risk-taking questionnaire findings also suggested that different aspects of social risk-taking may be related to loneliness in men and women. Although the overall scores on risk-taking did not correlate significantly with loneliness for women, the individual items measuring difficulties with the expression of intimate feelings and dependency needs did correlate highly with self-reported loneliness among women. For men, the key items dealt with risk-taking in task-oriented and relatively impersonal situations. In our society, men and women may depend on different role-prescribed behaviors in satisfying their interpersonal needs. For a woman, expressing intimate feelings and dependency needs may be crucial if she is not to feel lonely, while for a man, being able to function socially in task-oriented and impersonal stiuations may be crucial in fending off loneliness.

For both men and women, one would further expect that persons lacking in social skills would not be popular with other people they interact with. This prediction has been confirmed. In a series of sensitivity groups, the members were rated on their social skills, and these scores were correlated with the friendship choices the participants made at the end of the session. Those who, for instance, were dogmatic, withdrawn, manipulative or judgmental toward others, and attributed responsibility for their problems to others, were not liked as well as participants who scored higher on social skills (Sermat, Cohen, and Pollack, 1970).

Sociological causes of loneliness

To isolate causes of loneliness, one may look at specific factors within the individual—as we did in the preceding section. However, another way to approach the understanding of causes of loneliness is to look at factors that operate for all people in our society—to approach the question from a sociological viewpoint. In a society in which many people are surrounded by other people, why are feelings of isolation so pervasive? Although no one knows for sure, there are a number of possible factors, which may be acting cumulatively.

Changes in family patterns are frequently cited as a cause for the prevalence of feelings of isolation. The immediate family is smaller in the 1970s than it was in the 1920s, so that both adults and children have fewer contacts within their immediate family (Bowman, 1955). Intensive family attachments are gradually becoming restricted to the nuclear family of husband, wife, and children; contact with grandparents and cousins is less frequent than it was formerly. Even within the nuclear family there is less stability. As we shall see in Chapter 9, approximately one out of every three American marriages now ends in divorce proceedings. Close ties between the immediate family members are therefore not exempt from disruption. The children of such marriages, as well as the marriage partners themselves, may be upset by divorce procedures, with the forced choice between mother and father and the artificiality of visitation rights.

The *increasing size of the organizations people must cope with and the dwelling units they live in* may also add to the individual's sense of isolation. Working for a large company or attending a university with an enrollment in the thousands may make the individual feel isolated. Increasingly, Americans are becoming an urban-dwelling people. The United States Census Bureau estimates that by 1975, 65 percent of all Americans will live in urban areas (Packard, 1972). Compressed tightly together in anonymous, high-rise, urban apartments or cramped together in suburban areas, people may keep more social distance between themselves as a way of maintaining a modicum of privacy. Also, with the increasing incidence of crime, strangers are understandably wary of each other.

Another factor contributing to the feeling of social isolation for some may be the *frequency with which Americans move.* One popular theorist has concluded that the American people have become isolated, indifferent to their communities, and shallow in their interpersonal relationships because they move so frequently. To support these conclusions, he cites some impressive statistics: 40 million Americans (or 20 percent of the population) move at least once a year; the average American moves fourteen times during his lifetime; people between the ages of eighteen and twenty-five constitute one-fourth of all the movers, and the incidence of their mobility has been rising sharply in recent years. Over time the percentage of mobility may increase, so that by, say, the year 2000 our society will be considerably more mobile (Packard, 1972).

Whether or not moving has all of the pathological effects Packard claims it does is not yet clear. Some people may adapt easily or may even benefit from moving. For others, however, it may contribute to their feelings of isolation. After all, if you know that you are working for a company that has a policy of transferring its personnel every two or three years, establishing deep roots and close friendships in a community may seem rather futile.

Other theorists have cited the *pervasiveness of the spirit of individualism and competition* as a cause for growing loneliness. Since everyone is out for himself and competition is the norm, people may be reluctant to form close personal relationships, or they may lack the time and energy to do so. Especially in job settings, where people are competing against one another for advancement, people may consciously keep personal relationships at superficial levels to avoid being hurt or disappointed.

What is the result of feelings of isolation? During the 1960s a number of speculations emerged stating that alienation—including feelings of powerlessness, social isolation, and self- and cultural-estrangement—was responsible for many of the ills of a mass society. Everything from political apathy to drug addiction was traced back to urban alienation. Despite the prevalence of speculation, there is very little rigorous evidence relating alienation in general or its specific aspects, such as social isolation, to behavioral problems. What little there is casts some doubt on the conventional wisdom concerning the effects of alienation (Seeman, 1971b). However, since we don't yet know precisely how widespread feelings of social isolation are, "explaining" society's ills in terms of this as-yet-unmeasured variable is a bit premature.

Still, even if we can't prove that social isolation is responsible for everything from drug addiction to race riots, loneliness isn't a pleasant feeling. What could be done to reduce the incidence of social isolation? Since the causes of contemporary loneliness seem inextricably related to the general patterns of contemporary urban living, obviously there is no easy or immediate answer to this problem. Encounter groups and communes have both been offered as solutions. How well these alternatives work and some of their problems will be discussed in Chapter 11.

SUMMARY

1. Social Isolation People need others for many reasons. They seek to love and to be loved, to share experiences, to give and receive information, to reduce fear, and to relieve boredom. A solitary existence, even for a strong man like Admiral Byrd, who volunteered for isolation, can be harrowing.

2. Acquisition of the Need for Social Contact Although most theorists would agree that the need for social contact among adults is derived from the infant's intimate relationship with the person who cares for him, exactly how the mother-child relationship develops is not yet clear. Three different theories have been given. According to an imprinting explanation, the infant's exposure to a moving social stimulus during a critical period produces the attachment. The learning theory explanation is that the infant's association of the mother with rewards is all-important in the forming of the attachment relationship. The instinctive-component theory is that certain aspects of the mother, such as her warmth and softness, instinctively set off social responses in the human infant. Irrespective of exactly how it is formed, a strong mother-child relationship is crucial in determining the child's subsequent relationship with people.

3. Affiliation Motivation: An Overview The way in which affiliation motivation works may be considered from three different vantage points: (1) When do people affiliate? What situations increase an individual's desire to be with others? (2) Why do people affiliate? What purposes are served by being with others? and (3)

What kinds of people affiliate? What kinds of activities or personality traits are associated with persons high in the need to affiliate? In addition, since being with others serves a variety of badly needed functions for the human being, it is necessary to consider how well the need for human contact is being met in our contemporary society.

4. When Do People Affiliate?

Varying a situation can significantly influence the incidence of affiliation. Placing subjects in a stressful situation in which they expect to receive an electric shock has been shown repeatedly to increase affiliation, as Schachter's classic experiment first showed. However, an anxiety-arousing situation, such as one arousing the subject's repressed oral desires, has been found to decrease affiliation.

5. Why Do People Affiliate?

People have been found to affiliate for a variety of reasons. In the stressful situation of anticipating a painful electric shock, they may affiliate primarily for social comparison or for fear reduction. As social comparison theory would predict, (1) increasing uncertainty concerning an emotional reaction increases the desire to affiliate; (2) increasing the similarity of the person with whom one expects to affiliate increases affiliation; and (3) once affiliation occurs, there is a tendency toward a uniformity of reaction.

As would be predicted from a fear-reduction explanation of affiliation, people are sometimes less afraid when facing a stressful situation with another person than when facing the same situation alone. At other times, however, being with others can increase one's level of stress. Whether social comparison or fear reduction is the stronger motive for affiliation may depend on the intensity of the fear experienced by the other person.

In situations not involving electric shocks or similar fear-arousing procedures, there may be other reasons for affiliation. Although very little work has been done in these nonstressful situations, any of the reasons for a person's needing contact with others may motivate affiliation. We saw evidence that in some situations people may affiliate for protection and comfort or to relieve boredom.

6. Loners versus Joiners

People differ in the intensity of their desire to be with other people. In general, people scoring high in the need to affiliate were found to be first- or only-born children, to be sensitive to social cues, and to show a variety of affiliative behaviors—including spending more time in contact with others, being more friendly in groups, being more anxious about their group standing, and liking other people more than persons low in affiliation motivation.

7. Affiliation Needs in Contemporary Society

Throughout this chapter we have seen the extent to which people need other people. Although the precise proportion of people in various situations who feel lonely is not yet clear, it has been shown that feelings of loneliness are widespread—at least among some segments of the population. Six different causes of loneliness have been discussed: (1) existential conflict, (2) traumas related to largely unavoidable losses and disasters, (3) lack of support from one's environment, (4) internal crises and a sense of failure, (5) relatively impersonal social relationships, and (6) a lack of social skills.

Different psychological factors would be expected to be related to these different types of loneliness. This hypothesis has been supported by several studies. People who are hostile, overly submissive, afraid to take social risks, and lacking in social skills have been found to be lonely. Failure has also been correlated with loneliness, as has superficiality of interpersonal relationships. Relationships with parents are also correlated with loneliness. The more lonely the person feels, the more negative are his feelings toward his parents.

In addition to psychological causes of loneliness, one can also look at factors that operate to cause loneliness for all of the people in our society. No one is really sure why these feelings are so pervasive, but four variables are generally cited as significant: (1) changes in family patterns, (2) the increasing size of working and living units, (3) the frequency with which Americans move, and (4) the American emphasis on individualism and competition.

DISCUSSION QUESTIONS

1. In the text a number of reasons why people need contact with others were mentioned. Can you think of any additional reasons?
2. Do you think the three assumptions of social comparison theory accurately reflect your own social behavior?
3. Why do you think being with others in a frightening situation is reassuring?
4. If you had your choice, how much time per day would you spend interacting with friends? How much alone? Do you think people differ in what they consider an "optimum amount" of social contact?
5. The frequency of loneliness reported in surveys has varied from 10 to 80 percent. In what situations do you think you would find a high incidence of loneliness?
6. Why do you think first-born and only children are generally higher in affiliation motivation?
7. Harlow's work showed that softness and mobility are important characteristics in surrogate mothers. Can you think of any other characteristics that might make a mother more attractive to an infant monkey?
8. In what situations have you noticed a high incidence of affiliation?
9. Can you think of any situations in which increasing the level of uncertainty would not increase the intensity of the individual's desire to affiliate?
10. Why do you think there are negative reactions when people are in constant contact with others?
11. Can you think of any reasons, other than those given in the text, as to *why* people wish to affiliate?
12. Six types of loneliness were discussed. Which type do you think occurs most frequently among college students? How could you verify your hypothesis?
13. Which variables do you think influence the relative strength of the social comparison and the fear-reduction motives for affiliation?
14. The TAT is a frequently used test to measure the intensity of an individual's affiliation motivation. Can you think of a behavioral measure of affiliation that is not open to a variety of alternative explanations—one that would measure affiliation motivation "purely"?
15. Psychological and sociological reasons for loneliness were discussed. In your opinion, are psychological or sociological factors more responsible for the loneliness experienced by college students? Defend your answer.
16. In some studies friends have been found to be more reassuring than strangers, and in other studies strangers have been found to be more reassuring than friends. What variables do you think influence the relative comfort value of friends and strangers?
17. Similarity of situation and of personality have both been shown to be important in determining affiliation behavior. In what situations do you think situational similarity would be more important than similarity in personality? And when would similarity in personality be more important?
18. Design a study to show the effects of varying a situation that you hypothesize would influence the incidence of affiliation. State the reason for your hypothesis, the procedures you would use to manipulate the independent variable, and the procedures you would use to measure the incidence of affiliation.

6

AGGRESSION

On March 16, 1968, three platoons of American troops, one of them led by Lt. William Calley, Jr., entered Mylai 4, a small village in South Vietnam, and systematically massacred between 450 and 500

people—most of them women, children, and old men. Those killed were not resisting the American troops. Quite the contrary, many of the shootings were of groups of villagers that had been rounded up and were being guarded:

Calley then turned his attention back to the crowd of Vietnamese and issued an order: "Push all those people in the ditch." Three or four GIs complied. Calley struck a woman with a rifle as he pushed her down. Stanley remembered that some of the civilians "kept trying to get out. Some made it to the top. . . ." Calley began the shooting and ordered Meadlo to join in. Meadlo told about it later: "So we pushed our seven to eight people in with the big bunch of them. And so I began shooting them all. So did Mitchell, Calley . . . I guess I shot maybe twenty-five or twenty people in the ditch . . . men, women, and children. And babies." . . . He remembered that "the people firing into the ditch kept reloading magazines into their rifles and kept firing into the ditch and then killed or at least shot everyone in the ditch."

[Hersh, 1970, p. 63.]

These soldiers were not the only ones in the platoon who participated in the killing. Although the accounts of which men were involved differ, one observer estimated that he saw at least thirty GIs killing Vietnamese civilians. So many civilians were killed that observers have difficulty recalling exactly how many were killed. (See Figure 6-1.)

These details of the Mylai 4 massacre are no doubt familiar to you. They were widely publicized during the trials of personnel allegedly connected with the massacre. Who was involved? How many were killed? Who was to "blame"? These questions were widely discussed. Yet there is another question: How does such an atrocity come to happen? Why did armed and presumably decent Americans shoot hundreds of unresisting Vietnamese civilians?

Nor, as we all know, is this one violent

incident unique in contemporary American life. Violence permeates our society. (See Figure 6-2.) In the 1960s a number of prominent political figures, including John F. Kennedy, Robert Kennedy, Martin Luther King, Jr., Malcolm X, Medgar Evers, and George Rockwell were assassinated. Assassinations continue into the 1970s—as the 1972 attempt on George Wallace's life shows. The crime rate has been rising continuously; according to the Federal Bureau of Investigation, over 5.5 million serious crimes were recorded during 1970—an 11 percent increase over 1969. In 1970 firearms were used in 10,340 murders, 80,000 assaults, and 138,900 robberies. Between 1963 and 1968 civil disorders resulted in more than 9,000 casualties, including approximately 200 deaths (The New York Times Encyclopedic Almanac, 1971, 1972).

Violence surrounds us—not only in real life but in our entertainment. Films emphasize it. John Wayne has attained almost legendary status for his countless screen battles, and the violence of the Western film is as American as cherry pie. Indeed, the realism with which film violence is staged is ever increasing. Improved techniques allow close-ups of realistically bruised and mutilated bodies. Television, both in its news reports and in its entertainment, provides a steady diet of violence. Riots, uprisings, wars, terrorists' raids as in the 1972 Olympics—all are a part of our daily lives in the evening news. Even children's toys can encourage aggression. (See Figure 6-3.)

Violence permeates sports too. In broadcasts of football games microphones are placed so that the thuds of body contact can be heard better. Roller Derbys—with their violence—are popular. Boxing continues as a major sport. (See Figure 6-4.) There have been several soccer game riots in which hundreds of fans were injured or killed. And the fighting involved in hockey reaches such heights that it is a ques-

FIGURE 6-1 The Mylai massacre, March 16, 1968. (Ronald Haeberle)

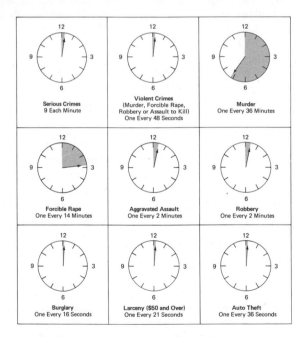

FIGURE 6-2 "Crime clocks" showing the frequency of crime in the United States. (Adapted from *The New York Times Encyclopedic Almanac*, 1971, p. 275. © 1970 by The New York Times Company. Reprinted by permission.)

tion of whether fans go to hockey matches to see the game or to watch the teams battle.

Nor is violence new to the American scene. Bloody riots over the draft occurred in New York City in the 1860s. Seventy years ago, when the United States was involved in a lengthy guerrilla war in the Philippines, American correspondents uncovered evidence of American atrocities. Civilians were being killed, tortured to extract information, shot as hostages, or herded into concentration camps (*The New York Times*, March 20, 1971, p. 29). (See Figure 6-5.) During a sensational atrocity trial of a marine major, the defense contended that the major was simply following his commanding general's orders to take no prisoners, to shoot all males over the age of ten, and to desolate the countryside in retaliation for the ambush of an American company.

The pervasiveness of violence and aggression in our society impels us to study these phenomena. Why are people aggressive? What can be done to control aggression? If our society is not to become even more aggression-centered, it is imperative for us to answer these questions. The world depicted in the film

FIGURE 6-3 (At left) Two examples of children's toys which can both teach and serve as an outlet for aggressive behavior—a model guillotine complete with head-chopping block and a kit for building monsters. (*The New York Times*)

FIGURE 6-4 (Above) Boxing is perhaps the purest form of aggressive behavior in sports. In this photograph, taken at an amateur bout in Milwaukee, the camera has captured the full impact of the victor's fist as it hits the loser's face. (UPI)

FIGURE 6-5 (Below) American War in the Philippines in 1900. The order attributed to General Jacob Smith, the commanding general, was to "kill everyone over ten." (*The New York Times*)

Little Murders, in which urban residents amuse themselves by shooting each other with rifles, is a foreboding picture of what the future may hold if aggression continues to increase.

Definition of "Aggression"

So far we have assumed a rough, everyday definition of the term "aggression." People do have a general idea of what the term means: Killing civilians at Mylai would be an example of aggression; kissing a baby would not be. Yet as we review the literature on aggression, it will readily be seen that the term is alternatively used in an emotional, motivational, or behavioral sense. If the difference between these three approaches is not understood, the meaning of aggression will be a constant source of confusion. Accordingly, before discussing the literature, we need to examine each of these approaches in some detail.

Emotional definition

Aggression is popularly thought to be an outgrowth of the emotion of anger. Something happens to make you angry; you become increasingly angrier; and finally you act aggressively. A series of insulting remarks is made by another person; you feel rage boiling up in you; and finally, if you can, you do something to injure the person who has made you angry.

You probably have been angry yourself. After someone has insulted you or hurt you deeply in some way, you may have had the experience of your cheeks flushing and your hands clenching. You may have felt a white-hot anger. A very young child who has been frustrated provides a clear example of the emotion of anger and the resulting aggression. Crimes of passion also demonstrate this emotional definition of aggression. For instance, imagine the intensity of emotion the murderer must have felt in the following case:

A resident surgeon who had an argument with his girl friend, a woman physician working with him at Methodist Hospital in Brooklyn, stabbed her 25 to 30 times.

[Zimbardo, 1969, p. 247.]

Motivational definition

Another way to define aggression is to focus on the motives behind the act: An act is aggressive when it is *intended* to hurt another. Of course, this definition overlaps the emotional definition to some extent. The surgeon who killed his girl friend in a crime of passion intended to hurt her. However, as the law recognizes, one can make distinctions in the amount of reasoning behind an aggressive act. By definition, first-degree murder involves premeditation, and second-degree murder does not. For example, the Palestinian terrorists' raid on the Israeli Olympic team in 1972 clearly involved extensive planning and was not the release of a sudden surge of rage.

According to a motivational definition of aggression, whether or not the act hurts another is less important than the reason behind it. If an angry boy's punch misses its target, the act is just as aggressive as his successful attempts, since the intent is the same.

The punch that missed is clearly aggressive; few other motives could lie behind someone's taking a swing at another person. But what of other, more ambiguous behaviors? What of the helpful friend who conveys a malicious remark that someone else made about you? "I thought you'd want to know that George said you really looked fat the last time he saw you." Is that aggressive? Is your friend conveying the message in order to hurt you? Or is his telling you an indication of his friendship? "Discussing the comment is unpleasant, but I'm willing to put up with the discomfort so that you may be informed and protect yourself." Assessing *why* someone is doing something—the intent of the act—is sometimes very difficult. Because of these ambiguities and the difficulty of determining people's thoughts and feelings, many psychologists have tended to dismiss the motivational and emotional approaches and to focus more on observable behavior.

Behavioral definition

According to a behavioral definition, aggression is simply "a response that delivers noxious stimuli to another organism" (Buss, 1961, p. 3). To classify a behavior as aggressive, all one

BOX 1 WHAT BEHAVIORS ARE VIOLENT?

The results of a national sample of 1,400 white and black American men showed that they differ in their classification of acts as violent (Kahn, 1972). Blacks are more likely to think of the polices' use of force as violent, and whites are more likely to see protest as a form of violence. The percentage of whites and blacks classifying nine different situations as violent are reported below:

Situation	Percentage of Whites Classifying the Situation as Violent	Percentage of Blacks Classifying the Situation as Violent
Police beating students	52	82
Police shooting looters	32	59
Police stopping people to frisk them	13	34
Denying people's civil rights	46	70
Looting	87	74
Burglary	64	70
Student protest	39	23
Sit-ins	23	15
Draft-card burnings	59	51

has to know is that it is hurtful. This definition may appear more objective and easier to implement than the motivational approach, but it too has limitations. How is "hurtful" defined? According to whether or not a particular recipient is injured? How is injury to be defined? See Box 1.

Classifying all hurtful acts together may obscure important differences in their motivational antecedents. For instance, what of unpleasant, painful behavior done for the recipient's benefit? The dentist's drilling, the surgeon's operating—are these done for the same sort of reasons as the giving of an angry punch? Further, accidental aggression may have very different antecedents than planned aggression, although a Freudian view would be that some events, which are apparently accidental, are, in fact, motivated by repressed emotions, which

the person himself is not aware of. What about self-inflicted hurt? Suicide, the fifth leading cause of death among fifteen to nineteen year olds (Jacobs, 1971), may be caused by different motives than other forms of hurtful behavior. To atone for their "sins," martyrs and flagellants may seek self-destruction or mutilate themselves, whereas a far different set of considerations may motivate the participants in a riot.

Further, the individual's assessment of *why* another person is hurting him influences his reaction to the injury. For instance, if a friend were pouring you a cup of coffee and the top of the pot fell off causing you to be burned, your reaction to the accident would differ markedly depending on whether you thought the act was accidental or had been premeditated.

Even though the behavioral definition does involve some problems, it is the one most commonly used, since it has the advantage of being easier to measure objectively than the other definitions. Counting the number of electric shocks one subject will administer to another or measuring the intensity of those shocks is far easier than attempting to measure the subject's emotional reactions and motives.

Overlap between the definitions

In real life the three aspects of aggression frequently operate together. The events at Mylai 4 can be considered as examples of aggression whether the emotional, motivational, or behavioral definition is used. The men were angry; they planned the execution of the civilians, as the methodical herding of the villagers to the ditch showed; and injury was inflicted on the villagers. Since the incident was so undeniably aggressive and has received extensive publicity and analysis, it will be referred to several times to illustrate the concepts being discussed in this chapter.

Causes of Aggressive Impulses: An Overview

What causes aggressive impulses in people? Six different answers have been given: (1) People are naturally aggressive; (2) they are aggressive because of crowding; (3) they learn to

FIGURE 6-6 Aggression as an inherent part of human nature.

be aggressive; (4) they are aggressive because of frustration; (5) they are aggressive because of group pressures; and (6) they are aggressive when the negative consequences of aggression, or the "restraining forces," are reduced.

Each of these factors will be analyzed separately. However, it should be noted that in real life the factors can cumulate. Even if one assumes that aggression comes naturally to the human animal, his level of aggression can still be meaningfully affected by the relative density of his living conditions, by learning, by the relative level of frustration in his daily life, and by the pressures toward or against aggression exerted in the various group settings he participates in.

Aggression as an Inherent Part of Human Nature

Many people feel that violence is basic to human nature (Wheeler, 1968). (See Figure 6-6.) Such a belief springs from many sources and is stated in a variety of ways. Christian theology has long assumed that man is both innately good and innately evil. Thomas Hobbes, a political philosopher, coined the saying "Man is [like] a wolf to [his fellow] man," indicating that man is possessed by an overriding cruelty toward his fellow-man.

Two major schools of contemporary psychological thought—the psychoanalytic theorists and the ethologists (scientists studying life in its natural habitat)—have supported the instinct concept of violence.

Freud's theory of the aggressive instinct

In his theoretical writings in the 1920s, Freud saw aggression as an innate primary drive representative of the death instinct. Life consists of an eternal conflict between two innate drives: a creative, or growth, force and a destructive force. From the moment of conception each man carries the urge to destroy as well as an urge to live and create.

Although Freud hoped that human reason could eventually control the most destructive and pointless expressions of this deadly force, he assumed that the drive to kill and destroy could never be abolished—that it was as basic as the need to breathe. Individuals involved in social situations would inevitably experience constraints and frustrations, which would perpetually activate the innate destructive force. Wars, violence against others, and violence against the self (such as suicide) would then follow. Freud felt that, given these realities, our efforts could best be directed toward lessening aggression by redirecting it toward less objectionable targets.

It should be noted that Freud's assumption of a death instinct is a highly controversial part of his theory. Freud himself never developed the concept of the death instinct as completely as he did his concept of the life instinct. Today, many psychologists feel that all of the phenomena Freud explained in terms of the death instinct can be explained by other factors that elicit aggression—particularly frustration (Maddi, 1968).

Lorenz's theory of the aggressive instinct

Freud stressed the negative aspects of the destructive drive. Lorenz (1966), on the other hand, has argued that the aggressive instinct has made a major contribution to the evolution and survival of animals—including man. The aggressive instinct underlies the vital functions of protecting one's territory against invasion, of defending the young, and of engaging in contests to select the strongest specimens for reproduction. The urge to defeat others, he believes, is basic to the survival of an animal species.

The problem is not with the urge itself, but with the way it is expressed in man. Man, Lorenz argues, suffers from an insufficient discharge of a high aggressive drive. The norms of most cultures—especially middle-class Western societies—inhibit the expression of even mild forms of aggression. Consequently, the drive mounts up until it may be strongly and viciously expressed.

In most animal species aggression is apparently counteracted by inhibitions that stop a victor from killing after he has defeated his opponent. As an example, Lorenz gives the following outcome of a fight between two dogs:

When the loser of a fight suddenly adopted the submissive attitude, and presented his unprotected neck, the winner performed the movement of shaking to death, in the air, close to the neck of the morally vanquished dog, but with closed mouth, that is, without biting.

[Lorenz, 1966, p. 133.]

Man, however, has lost this inhibition. Obviously, men can and do fight to the death. Lorenz theorizes that man has lost his inhibitions because most human slaughter occurs at such a distance that the victims' "postures of submission," which should elicit mercy, are not seen. People might be much more reluctant to kill other people if they had to murder with their bare hands (or their teeth) rather than use long-range weapons—such as guns and bombs.

Some objections to instinct theories

A general objection to instinct theories is that they are of limited explanatory value. To say that all aggression is instinctive does not explain the observed variation in aggressive behavior. Some anthropologists argue that there are cultural differences in the amount and style of aggression (e.g., Mead, 1935). Within a given society, some people are more aggressive than others; aggression is more likely to occur in some situations than in others.

You could argue that all people have aggressive instincts and that any differences in degree are attributable to learning. Such a response, however, only emphasizes the limited understanding of aggression that the instinct explanation offers. Human aggressive behaviors—whatever their basic origins—have been so modified by learning that it may not be helpful to spend much time on the extent to which their origins are instinctive in nature.

In addition to these general difficulties with the instinctive approach, there are specific problems with the individual theories. Thus, for example, Lorenz's inferences about human behavior are drawn mainly from his ethological studies of animals, with some anecdotal support from informal observations of people. Although these observations are interesting and thought-provoking, they clearly do not prove the case; generalizing from animals to people is dangerous business. And Freud's inferences were not based on a representative set of typical human behaviors either. Rather, they were based on his observations of destructive behavior during war and in his clinical practice. Today, there is little evidence supporting this portion of his theory.

A physiological approach to aggression

Another approach to explaining aggression as an inherent part of human nature is to search for physiological antecedents. Over the past few decades some very interesting relationships have been found. The fighting behavior in mice, for example, has been shown to depend on the concentration of the male sex hormone (Scott and Fredericson, 1951).

Brady (1960) has shown that different parts of the brain generate and inhibit aggression. Electric stimulation of certain portions of a cat's hypothalamus will produce attack behavior (Wasman and Flynn, 1962), although the probability of attack varies with the environment. If no suitable object of attack is visible, the animal is much less likely to attack even when stimulated (Levison and Flynn, 1965). Box 2 illustrates some recent findings on the relationship between brain damage and human violence.

Further, sociopaths—persons who engage in antisocial behaviors and do not seem to experience the intensity of emotional experience that normal people do—have been found to be more responsive physiologically to virtually every exciting event than normal persons. The sociopath reacts sympathetically to events that frighten others, but he also reacts to events that are neutral to others. Constantly experiencing the physiological reactions that accompany emotional arousal, sociopaths may have learned not to apply emotional labels to their physiological states. This would account both for their antisocial behavior and their "emotional flatness." Experiencing little or no guilt or fear, they are not motivated to avoid events that frighten others or make them feel guilty (Schachter and Latané, 1964).

Clearly, however, these findings indicate that the roots of violence are multiple and complex. Physiological factors may contribute to some of the enormous individual differences in temperament, the ability to be aroused, and self-control. Although more research on the physiological correlates of aggression is needed, this approach, like the instinct approach, must be supplemented with an understanding of how the environmental setting contributes to aggression.

Crowding and Aggression

It is popularly assumed that crowding has highly negative effects on human social behavior. (See Figure 6-7.) Newspaper accounts have related crowding to effects as diverse as physical disease, crime, riots, psychological withdrawal, and aggression (Zlutnick and Altman, Unpublished paper). The Massachusetts Mental Health Commissioner has been quoted as saying that "there is a toxic reaction caused in an individual when overcrowded by others" (in Freedman, Levy, Buchanan, and Price, 1972).

A number of studies on animals have demonstrated the detrimental effects of crowding. Under conditions of very high population density, normal social behavior has been observed to break down, and the number of the population decreases sharply (e.g., Calhoun, 1962). However, it is always dangerous to generalize from the results of animal studies to human reactions. Man has a remarkable ability to adapt to his environment.

The very few studies that have been done on the effects of crowding on human social behavior have yielded inconsistent results. One study of children showed that they were more aggressive when less space was available (McGrew, Unpublished paper). However, in another study, in which twenty different groups were observed, density had no effect on aggressiveness (Price, 1971). In some conditions high density has been found to result in a lower incidence of aggression. When the incidence of aggression among two- and three-man groups that spent twenty-one days in either a small (70-cubic-foot) or a large (200-cubic-foot) room was compared, it was found that less hostility was expressed by the men in the small rooms (Smith and Haythorn, 1972).

These inconsistent results suggest that fac-

FIGURE 6-7 How do you think the crowded conditions of this bus influence the passengers' reactions? (George W. Gardner)

tors in the situation may influence the human reaction to density. Two recent experiments were done to investigate the overall effects of density on aggression and to explore dimensions of the situation that might influence the reaction to crowding (Freedman et al., 1972). In one study 136 high-school students were assigned—four at a time—to work either in a small room (five feet square) or in a larger room (eight and a half feet square). Each room contained four comfortable chairs. In the smaller room the knees of one subject "didn't quite touch" the knees of the person sitting opposite him. In the larger room the chairs were placed so that the distance between them "seemed comfortable." All of the subjects spent four hours in either the large or the small room and participated in a variety of activities. The major measure of aggression was the amount of competition the subjects displayed in a game in which they could act either competitively or cooperatively.

Crowding had no overall significant effect on competition. However, there was a significant difference in the reactions of the male and the female subjects to the crowding. The high-school boys were significantly more competitive in the small room than in the large room, and the high-school girls were somewhat less competitive in the small room than they were in the large room.

Intrigued by these results, the investigators decided to do a second study in a different setting and with a different population of subjects. For the first study temporary rooms had been built of unpainted plywood. In their second study the investigators used existing rooms. To obtain subjects, the investigators ran a classified ad in *The New York Times,* and anyone over eighteen was eligible. The people who answered the ad were a very heterogeneous group, ranging in age from eighteen to eighty and representing a wide variation in socioeconomic status. The experiment was represented as a mock jury situation, and five taped courtroom trials were presented to the subjects during the three hours of the experiment. The measure of aggression was the severity of sentence the subjects indicated.

Again, the subjects were divided into groups (this time consisting of ten members per group), and each group was assigned either to a small room or to a large room. In the small room

(approximately 100 feet square), the chairs "touched those on either side and there was just about enough space in the middle of the room for the subjects to stretch their legs without touching those of the person opposite" (Freedman et al., p. 536).

As in the earlier study, density had different effects on the men and the women. Although density had no overall effect, all female groups were more lenient in the crowded room than in the uncrowded room, and all male groups were more lenient in the uncrowded room. Further, when the subjects were asked to indicate how pleasant and interesting the sessions had been, women who had been in the small room responded more positively than those who had been in the large room. The size of the room had the opposite effect on the reactions of men: Those who had been in the large room reacted more positively than those who had been in the small room.

So far, all of the groups had been tested in single-sex groups—either all-men or all-women. To test the effect of density in groups containing both sexes, the investigators tested mixed-sex groups in the jury-simulation procedure and asked them to make judgments about the severity of sentence. Surprisingly, density had no overall effect, and there was no significant difference between the reactions of males and females in the large and small rooms. Thus the interaction between density and sex seems to be limited to groups consisting of either all males or all females.

Why should women react positively to crowding and men react negatively when they are in single-sex groups? One possible explanation is that close physical contact is more acceptable between women than it is between men. Being close to each other may mean friendship and warmth to women, whereas it may have homosexual overtones for men, make them uncomfortable, and so make them react aggressively. In a mixed-sex group physical contact may have the same meaning to both men and women.

The effect of crowding may therefore depend to a large degree on the specific circumstances in which it occurs. The results of these studies show that men and women react differently to crowding in single-sex groups—perhaps because it has different meanings for them. A number of other variables may influence the reaction to crowding. The length of time the person is crowded may influence his reaction. In these studies the maximum length of time the subjects spent in a small room was four hours. With longer confinement in close quarters, different reactions might develop. Further, all of the subjects were volunteers who knew they were participating in an experimental study in which they were given directions as to what to do. Little physical activity was involved. Modifying any of these variables might influence the reactions. Four people trying to cook in a crowded kitchen may respond differently to the density than four people sitting in chairs.

Further, whether or not the person feels crowded may be a more important determinant of his behavior than the actual amount of space he has available. A high density of people in a subway car may make the riders feel crowded, but the same density might not irritate people at a cocktail party.

Many of the popular assumptions about the negative effects of crowding seem to refer to the *feeling* of being crowded rather than to actual physical density. The research so far shows that high density alone does not necessarily lead to a feeling of being crowded nor to overall negative results. Further research may show that people do indeed react aggressively when they feel crowded.

Social Learning

Another major theory is that aggression is learned in the same way other behaviors are learned. (See Figure 6-8.) Since learning has been shown to be such an important determinant of a great number of behaviors, we will explore this determinant of aggression in some detail.

Most social psychologists agree that learning is a major determinant of aggression. They differ, however, on the question of whether or not *all* aggressive behaviors are learned. Some argue that a few rudimentary aggressive behaviors (such as crying at certain forms of discomfort) may be instinctive, but argue that even these are transformed and elaborated through learning into the complex, selective behaviors of the aggressive-acting adult. Other theorists deny that there are *any* innately determined aggressive behaviors and hold to the

FIGURE 6-8 Bayonet practice in the United States Marine Corps. Every recruit is required to spend several hours of his basic training learning how to kill with a knife strapped to his rifle. In this typical scene, the marine is required to run at full speed, yelling "kill, kill, kill" as he goes, and then to thrust the bayonet into the body of his mock enemy. (Richard Lawrence Stack/Black Star)

belief that all aggressive behaviors are learned.

Consider the way in which an eighteen-month-old child reacts to frustration. Mommy takes away a toy, and the baby cries, rolls on the floor, bites or hits Mommy. Mommy, who does not like this, tries to teach the baby that certain aggressive responses are taboo. Biting is out, kicking is bad, and so on. This same baby, however, after being punished for hitting Mommy, may later be rewarded by her for fighting with his friends to stick up for his rights (Bandura and Walters, 1959). The child thus learns through a series of experiences when it is appropriate to act aggressively, what forms of aggression are permissible, and to whom he can express aggression without disapproval or punishment.

The acquisition of this complicated set of behaviors is effected through a variety of learning processes. Without intending to do so, parents administer a series of rewards and punishments for aggressive behavior. Norms showing the child how he should react in different situations are transmitted through this process. Social motives are acquired: The male child may learn that to be a "real boy" he has to defend his honor in certain situations. ("Only sissies don't defend themselves.") The parents also influence the child indirectly by serving as models that the child imitates and identifies with. Day in and day out through innumerable instances children are influenced by their parents.

Although the parents are the most important influence, there are many other sources from which the child learns and obtains reinforcements. If, for example, he accidentally hits another child and as a result the other child relinquishes a toy, then his hitting is reinforced. He may learn from a variety of other models: other members of the family, family friends, other children, the mass media.

Since the child learns from both parents and other persons, the relationship between parental discipline patterns and the behavior of children is a complicated one. We might expect that physically aggressive, punitive parents would tend to have physically aggressive children. Aggressive parents set an aggressive example for their children (see how Daddy yells at things that upset him) and may also reward their children when they engage in aggressive acts. Research results confirm this expectation: There is considerable evidence indicating that such parents are apt to have physically aggressive children (e.g., Sears, Maccoby, and Levin, 1957).

But what of the permissive parent? He does not engage in or reward aggressive behaviors. Are his children therefore less aggressive? Not necessarily. Even though the permissive parent neither rewards aggressive behaviors nor acts as an aggressive model, his children may be allowed to get away with aggressive behavior and may interpret their parents' seeing and not punishing their aggressive play as a sign that aggressiveness is appropriate. The results of several studies support this hypothesis. For instance, two investigators found that preschoolers played more aggressively when they were watched by a permissive adult than when no adult was present (Siegel and Kohn, 1959). Correlational studies have shown that either a mother's aggressiveness or her permissiveness is related to aggressiveness in her child (Sears, Maccoby, and Levin, 1957).

To date, however, studies assessing parental influences on aggression have entailed a problem generally found in studies of child-rearing practices: the enormous difficulty of obtaining a valid measure of actual parental behavior. If you wanted to assess how mothers treated their children, what would you do? You might try observation, but if mothers knew they were being observed, their behavior would change; concealed observation presents practical and ethical problems. In the Sears et al. study (1957) the mothers were asked to rate their own behavior. Unfortunately, as we saw in the earlier discussion of questionnaire validity, respondents are not always truthful. They may want to convey an impression of what they wish they were doing rather than what they actually do.

Correlational studies on the relationship between parental discipline and children's behavior provide one approach to studying the effects of social learning on aggression. Another approach is to study experimentally the effects of specific learning processes, such as reinforcement, punishment, and modeling.

Reinforcement

As you may remember from your introductory psychology course, a basic principle of learning is that responses that are rewarded tend to occur more frequently. This principle applies to aggressive responses as well as others. Numerous studies have shown the importance of reinforcement: When aggressive responses are rewarded, they tend to occur more frequently (Buss, 1966; Geen, 1968).

Many, if not most, reinforcements at the human level involve the approval or affection of others. Such rewards are termed "social reinforcers." Just as food pellets influenced Skinner's pigeons, many studies have shown that children will learn a particular response when they are praised for making it (Stevenson and Hill, 1966). Another person's praising you for doing something demonstrates his approval of what you are doing and conveys information. How do you know whether or not what you are doing is right? One way is to see how others react. Thus someone's smiling or saying "good" can convey information about what is correct as well as social approval and affection.

The importance of social reinforcement in modifying the frequency of aggressive behavior has been shown in several studies. In one study, for instance, nursery school teachers were instructed to ignore aggressive behavior and to reward cooperative behavior with attention and praise. After two weeks there was a significant decrease in physical and verbal aggression (Brown and Elliot, 1965). Conversely, providing social reinforcements for aggressive responses can result in an increased incidence of aggression. In a recent study male college students were given social reinforcements for saying either aggressive, neutral, or helpful words, and then subsequently all of the subjects had an opportunity to give an electric shock to another individual. Those reinforced for aggressive verbalizations delivered the strongest shocks; those who had said neutral words delivered an intermediate level of shock; and those reinforced for helpful words delivered the lowest intensity of shock (Parke, Ewall, and Slaby, 1972).

The effects of different patterns of reinforcement have also been studied. In one study children were rewarded with marbles for hitting a toy (Cowan and Walters, 1963). Some children were rewarded each time they hit the toy; others were rewarded intermittently. As in many other learning situations, when the reinforcement was partial and intermittent the learning was more resistant to extinction than when reinforcement was constant. Since many rewards in real life are given intermittently, this finding emphasizes that aggressive habits may be highly resistant to extinction.

Punishment

Physical punishment is a less efficient means of shaping behavior than reinforcement. Spanking a child for hitting may not produce the effect the parents desire. First, the child's main response to the spanking may be one of anger and frustration—reactions that are incompatible with his learning other, more socially acceptable responses. Second, the feelings aroused by the spanking may lead to aggressive acts against "safe," nonpunishing objects in the environment. Third, the punishment effects may extend only to behavior in the presence of the parents: The child may refrain from hitting while he is with them, but as soon as he is out of their

sight, he will do what he wants. The parents, by punishing aggression with aggression, have also provided an aggressive model for the child to imitate, and as we shall see in the next section, imitation is one of the most powerful processes of learning. The parent who spanks the child is in effect saying, "I obviously approve of aggression in some circumstances because that's what I'm doing to you now."

In some limited circumstances vicarious punishments may be effective (Walters, 1966). If a child observes others being punished for a given act, the chances of his imitating that act may be decreased (Lefcourt et al., 1966). People may not do things because they fear the expected punishment: You may refrain from smoking marijuana because you fear arrest, just as a middle-aged taxpayer may refrain from cheating the Internal Revenue Service for the same reason. Vicarious fear does not involve many of the detrimental components accompanying physical punishment. The threat of punishment does not, for example, usually arouse aggression; nor is there an aggressive model to imitate, such as the spanking parent.

Modeling

Imitation is another important learning process. All people, but particularly children, imitate others. (See Figure 6-9.) A young girl watches her mother baking cookies, and then pretends she is doing the same thing. Parents may encourage this imitative tendency by providing toy replicas of everyday objects. Imitation extends to all behaviors, including aggression. A child observes his parents being aggressive and copies them. He sees his father shout when he becomes angry, so the child shouts when he becomes angry.

Experimental Evidence That Aggression Is Imitated A series of experiments by Bandura and Walters and their associates have demonstrated the effect of the child's watching an adult—a "model"—act aggressively. In one study (Bandura et al., 1961) nursery school children watched a woman play with a set of tinker toys and a BoBo doll (a five-foot, inflated plastic toy). In the aggressive condition the adult began by playing quietly with the tinker

FIGURE 6-9 Imitation is a powerful learning process—especially in children. A child watches the behavior of others ("models") and sometimes follows the models' behavior. Here the child-observer has become a part of a parade of arms-carrying sailors. (Henri Cartier-Bresson/Magnum)

toys. After a minute she stopped playing with the tinker toys, approached the doll, and began to play aggressively with it. She hit it, sat on it, and tossed it into the air. While she was playing aggressively, she shouted such things as "sock him in the nose" and "pow." This aggressive play continued for nine minutes. In the control condition the model played quietly with the tinker toys for the entire ten-minute period.

To assess the effects of observing an adult act aggressively, the experimenter left each child alone with a number of toys, including the BoBo doll. The children who had observed the aggressive model behaved much more aggressively than those who had not. They punched, kicked, and hammered the doll and made the same aggressive comments the adult had. After observing the adult's aggression, they had, through the process of imitation, become more aggressive *in the laboratory situation.*

Aggressive models (both live and filmed) have been repeatedly imitated immediately

after they were seen by subjects in the same setting in which the violence was observed. It would be premature, however, to conclude that increased aggression could be generalized from the laboratory situation to other situations, to longer periods of time, and to all forms of aggressive models. As with any discovery of a very significant phenomenon, further evidence is needed to understand when and why it occurs.

A crucial question is whether or not children who behave aggressively in the experimental situation would be more likely to behave aggressively in *other situations*—with playmates or parents. Evidence is not conclusive on this point.

Another question is the permanency of the effect: How long after the child has seen an aggressive model does his tendency toward increased aggressiveness persist? Most studies test for an effect immediately after the aggressive model is seen. In real life one is rarely provided with an opportunity or an instigation to express aggression immediately after exposure to a film or television sequence showing aggression.

Variables That Influence the Amount of Imitation

There are enormous variations in the ways in which aggression may be displayed and in the conditions surrounding the viewing. Aggression may be seen as being rewarded or punished, justified or unjustified, real or fictional. It may be displayed by a live person or in films or on television. Several studies have shown that the behavioral effect caused by seeing an aggressive model is influenced by a number of variables.

Whether the aggressive model is rewarded or punished has been found to influence the extent to which aggression is imitated. In one experiment children were exposed to one of three conditions: (1) They viewed on film a successful aggressive model who was enjoying the fruits of his victory; (2) they viewed, also on film, an aggressive model who was severely punished by the intended victim; or (3) they did not see any film (control condition). In a subsequent testing situation the children who saw the aggressive model rewarded showed more aggression than the children who either saw the model punished or saw no model. Thus the tradition in the Western of always punishing the villain may have a deterrent effect on the viewer's imitating aggressive behaviors.

The consequences of a model's behavior may serve as a cue to the kind of behavior that is permissible in a given social context. If an aggressive model is punished, the individual may expect to be punished, too, if he acts similarly. Seeing an aggressive model rewarded may lead him to believe he will be rewarded if he acts similarly.

In real life, also, whether or not an aggressor is rewarded may be a crucial determinant of imitation. For instance, after Lieutenant Calley's court-martial and conviction, American soldiers may have been more reluctant to kill Vietnamese civilians than before the court-martial took place. Conversely, if an aggressor is not punished, one might expect his actions to be imitated much more readily. Thus the reaction to the experience of Captain Marasco, a Green Beret officer whom the U.S. Army charged with murdering a Vietnamese man and subsequently released, might have been quite the opposite from the reaction to the Calley proceedings. (See Box 3).

Other variables have also been found to influence the amount of imitation. Consistently, children have been found to imitate powerful, *high-status dominant models* (Hetherington, 1965). This finding is hardly surprising; in real life adults also imitate those who are successful and powerful. The relative effectiveness of *live and filmed models* has also been tested (Bandura and Mischel, 1965). Surprisingly, the filmed model elicited just as much imitation as a live model. What is seen on television may, in some circumstances, be a powerful molder of behavior—as we shall see in the next section. Characteristics of the observer can also influence the incidence of imitation. *Angry observers* have been found to imitate more readily than calm observers (Hartmann, 1969).

Violence that is seen by the viewer as being *ethically justified* is imitated more frequently than unjustified violence. In one study subjects viewed a two-and-one-half-minute film clip from the "CBS Evening News with Walter Cronkite" (November 3, 1969) in which a group of South Vietnamese soldiers had a brief encounter with the enemy and captured a prisoner. Subsequently, the prisoner was executed by being knifed in the chest. Some of the subjects were told that the prisoner had been an enemy assassin; the explanation given to others was that the South Vietnamese simply did not wish to be bothered with any prisoners. When the subjects were later given an opportunity to act aggressively, the enemy-assassin explanation—obviously a more justifiable cause for killing the prisoner—was found to produce a higher level of aggression than the annoyance explanation (Meyer, 1972).

Further, *the presence of stimuli usually associated with violence*—such as a gun—increases the incidence of imitation (Berkowitz and LePage, 1967). *If the viewer identifies with the person who is acting violently,* as in the case of a movie viewer who imagines that he is the winner in a fight film, he is more likely to imitate the aggression shown (Turner and Berkowitz, 1972).

Overt action on the part of the model is not necessary for imitation of aggressive responses

Russell Baker, a columnist for *The New York Times,* described an appearance of Captain Marasco on the "Dick Cavett Show":

"About midnight several days ago, a man appeared on the television screen in the cellar of our house to tell about a killing he had committed. . . .

"It was the 'Dick Cavett Show' and it had begun, as usual, with Dick's monologue, and a promise of pleasant anesthesia as Dick read off the cast of show biz people on hand to plug their various enterprises.

· · ·

"Then Dick was back with his next guest. He introduced Capt. Bob Marasco. The audience applauded. Down in our cellar, the pleased smile may have shown a trace of frown. Captain Marasco? The name was vaguely familiar. Was it somebody who had just made a new Andy Warhol movie?

"It was not. Dick said that Captain Marasco, who lived in Bloomfield, N.J.,

was a former Green Beret officer who had been charged by the Army some time ago with murdering a Vietnamese man and then discharged from the service after the murder charge had been dropped. . . . Bob appeared to be a tall, broad-shouldered, athletic young man. His clothing style was mod without being odd. 'Carefully groomed' would be the cliché. A careful man, a methodical man. Perhaps even a finicky, fastidious man when it came to details. Very neat in his habits one would guess. A good worker.

"Bob's account of the killing seemed to bear this out. He answered Dick's questions with details which a less fastidious man might have glossed over in his recitation. Yes, Bob said, Dick was right: two shots in the fellow's head. Of course, he had been pumped full of morphine before the shooting, which made it as humanitarian as you could possibly make something as awkward as killing a man, Bob volunteered.

· · ·

"What do you do now for a living? he

[Dick] asked Bob. Bob smiled slightly, knowing he was going to get a laugh, already indicating he would rather not. He said he sold life insurance. The audience laughed. . . . Dick asked about putting the body in a mail sack and weighting it with tire irons and dumping it from a rowboat into several hundred feet of water in the China Sea, and he asked why Bob thought the body had not been found. Bob smiled the smile of a man who knew something unpleasant and said the waters were 'shark-infested.'

". . . Bob said he had what amounted to an official execution order from the C.I.A. An order to 'eliminate with extreme prejudice.' Everybody who worked with the C.I.A. knew what that meant, Bob said. He had done it to serve his country, to serve us in the audience, to serve me down there in my cellar. He was not telling it now for profit, was not making any money, in fact, from his story. He just wanted us to know what duty we were all exacting from our army."

[Baker, 1971, p. 13.]

to occur. An adult's saying that aggressive behavior would be appropriate has been found to increase significantly the amount of aggression displayed by children. In a recent study children were assigned to one of three conditions: (1) one in which an adult acted very aggressively with some toys, (2) one in which an adult said that games played with the toys should be violent and gave specific suggestions about what he would do, and (3) a control condition in which no model was present. Although children who heard the aggressive behavior described acted significantly less aggressively than did those who saw the behavior, they nevertheless showed significantly more aggression than did those in the control condition (Grusec, 1972).

The fact that violence can be learned through the observation of an aggressive model has

many implications. Certainly, the findings emphasize the importance of parental action and words as a determinant of a child's behavior. The parent is the adult most frequently observed by the child. Setting a good example may be an extremely important aspect of the child-rearing situation. What parents say is important, and what they do is even more influential.

Television and aggression

Turn on your television set and what do you see? Dramas in which people are stabbed, shot, beaten, or poisoned; cartoons in which animals inflict injuries on one another in an amazing number of ways; the evening news with its daily recital of violence and death;

specials showing close-ups of baby seals being clubbed to death and skinned. Along with scattered situation comedies and quiz programs, the daily TV fare shows us innumerable ways in which one person can injure others.

A number of studies of the content of television programming confirms the accuracy of the popular impression that violence is pervasive on television. For instance, in one study of over fifty hours of prime time and Saturday morning programming on the three major network programs shown in Philadelphia between 1967 and 1969, it was found that the rate of violent episodes remained constant—at a rate of about eight per hour—over the three-year period. In this study violence was defined as "the overt expression of physical force against others or self, or the compelling of action against one's will on pain of being hurt or killed" (Gerbner, 1971). Despite network protestations that they are controlling violence, the amount of violence shown in cartoons, programs popular with children on Saturday morning, increased from 1967 to 1969.

Conflicting Theories on the Effects of Televised Violence Many feel that the steady diet of televised violence *increases the tendency of the viewers—especially children—to behave aggressively.* (See Figure 6-10.) Since young children spend so much time watching television and since we saw in the previous section

FIGURE 6-10 Aggression as learned from watching televised violence.

that viewing an aggressive model can influence aggression, it might follow that watching aggression on television can foster aggressive impulses among children. Through watching televised aggression, the child may learn techniques of aggression, become emotionally aroused, learn that aggression is acceptable, become accustomed to viewing violence, and so on. The National Commission on the Causes and Prevention of Violence concludes:

Each year advertisers spend $2 1/2 billion in the belief that television can influence human behavior. The television industry enthusiastically agrees with them, but nonetheless contends that its programs of violence do not have any such influence.

The preponderance of the available evidence strongly suggests, however, that violence in television programs can and does have adverse effects upon audiences—particularly child audiences.

[Eisenhower et al., 1969, p. 5.]

Not all agree with this view, however. There are two other positions. One, the "catharsis view," holds that watching violent television programs may *reduce* the incidence of aggression among viewers. In the course of daily life things happen that make people feel aggressive. They may be disappointed; someone may insult them; or they may feel ill. Usually, however, the individual who feels aggressive does not act aggressively, since there are constraints against his doing so: He may be punished. When the individual feels aggressive but cannot act out his feelings, aggression in his own fantasy, or in the fantasy of television programs, decreases his aggressive impulse. If he can't hit someone, seeing someone else do so may make him feel less aggressive.

A third view is that exposure to the various sorts of violence in the mass media has *no significant effect.* The main causes of aggression are situations that personally influence the individual (such as his own level of frustration) and the past history of rewards and models for aggression provided by his parents and friends. Although television may have some effect, it is a trivial cause of aggression.

Research Results: An Overview Unfortunately, as the recently published surgeon general's report, *Television and Growing Up: The Impact* of *Televised Violence* (1972) noted, the results of numerous studies in this area are not "wholly consistent or conclusive." However, after reviewing the many existing studies on television and aggression and commissioning a number of new studies on this question, the members of the Surgeon General's Advisory Committee concluded that a "modest relationship exists between the viewing of violence and aggressive behavior" (p. 9).

As we review the three sources of evidence considered by the Surgeon General's Advisory Committee, you will see the enormous research problems in this area and the consequent difficulty in obtaining conclusive answers.

Correlational Studies A number of surveys have correlated the number of violent television programs watched by children with the children's level of aggressive tendencies. Different measures of aggression have been employed in these studies, including the ratings given by the child of his own level of aggressive behaviors, ratings of his behavior by others, projective measures, and so on. Most of the correlations obtained were positive, but small—from 0 to .20, although some were as high as .30 or slightly above.

What do the results of these correlational studies show? First, the relationship between the two measured variables is not a very strong one. The highest correlations obtained, those of .30 and slightly above, do not indicate a great amount of predictability from one variable to another. Further, as you will recall from Chapter 1, the existence of a correlation between two variables does not indicate a causal relationship. Three different interpretations are possible: (1) The viewing of violence leads to aggression; (2) a tendency toward aggression leads to the viewing of violence; and (3) both aggression and a preference for violence on television are the result of other factors.

One variable that might possibly influence the observed relationship was suggested by the committee: parental emphasis on nonaggression. In families in which the parents discouraged their children from being "mean to other kids," doing "the bad things people do on television," and "fighting back" when another child is aggressive to them, the correlation

between viewing violence and the children's aggressive behavior was only .07—a very small correlation. In contrast, in families in which little stress was placed on the importance of nonaggression, the correlation between viewing violence and aggressive behavior was .26 (Chaffee and McLeod, 1971). The impact of televised violence may vary greatly according to parental attitudes about violence.

The correlational results do not allow a cause-effect interpretation, but they do show a small relationship between the amount of violence viewed and aggression among a number of children. Since there are difficulties in interpreting correlational data taken from real life, a controlled experiment may be needed.

Laboratory Experimental Studies As we saw in the discussion of modeling, a number of laboratory studies have demonstrated that viewing aggressive material increases the amount of aggression expressed by the subjects. This effect was shown repeatedly in a classic series of experiments conducted by Berkowitz and his associates (e.g., Berkowitz and Geen, 1966). Experimental subjects were exposed to an aggressive stimulus (frequently a seven-minute segment of the prize-fighting film *Champion*); control subjects viewed a nonaggressive stimulus (frequently a seven-minute film of a track race between the first two men to run the mile in less than four minutes). To assess aggressive behavior, the experimenter placed the subjects in a fictitious learning experiment in which they administered electric shocks to a confederate of the experimenter.

A number of experiments showed that the subjects exposed to aggressive stimuli delivered more intense electric shocks to their "learning partners." After seeing a boxing film, for example, subjects inflicted more intense shocks to their learning partners than subjects who had not seen the film.

It should again be noted, however, that these results occurred in a laboratory situation. The question remains as to how this finding and the theory relate to the more usual situation of watching violence on television.

Clearly, there are a number of differences. Giving an electric shock in an experimental setting may be quite different from acting aggressively in real life. Administering an electric shock is a relatively impersonal form of aggression; the subject pushes a button and is not physically involved in the aggression. The fact that the experimenter requires a subject to administer the shock sets up a very permissive atmosphere; clearly, the subject will not be punished for his aggression. In fact, it is clear that he is expected to administer shocks. If he doesn't, he'll spoil the experiment. Further, the experimenter at least implicitly assumes responsibility for the aggression and its consequences. Because the subject has been told to administer shocks to correct the confederate's "errors," the subject may not label his behavior as aggressive, but, instead, may think of himself as teaching.

Furthermore, the experimenter cannot tell what the subject guesses about the aggressive stimulus and its relationship to the administering of electric shocks. The rationale given for showing the aggressive film is that the film contains elements involved in the learning part of the experiment. However, when the experimental task, learning pairs of letters, is presented, this rationale may not sufficiently explain the showing of the film. The subjects may begin to suspect the true connection between the film and the so-called learning procedure. Briefly, the demand characteristics of the experimental situation might possibly influence the aggressive response.

Field Experimental Studies To obtain the advantage of being able to infer cause-effect relationships and to eliminate some of the artificialities of the laboratory work on modeling, an obvious solution would be to assess the effects of viewing aggressive television programs in a natural setting. This has been done in several studies, and the results have been inconsistent. In some, viewing aggressive programs increased the amount of violence in children who were initially highly aggressive; in others, viewing violent television had no measurable effect; and in still other experiments, viewing aggressive television reduced the level of aggressive behavior. See Box 4.

In one study, conducted in a nursery school setting, the investigators first observed the behavior of ninety-seven boys and girls for a period of three weeks to obtain a measure of the initial level of their aggressive behavior. Each child's level of aggressiveness during that period was rated. Then the children were assigned to one of three diets of television programming, which lasted for a four-week period. The aggressive-programming condition consisted of twelve twenty-minute episodes of "Batman" or "Superman" cartoons. The neutral programming consisted of programs on nature or travelogues. The "prosocial" programming consisted of a program that emphasized sharing and cooperative behavior, "Misterogers Neighborhood." The amount of aggressive behavior shown by all of the children during the four-week period of the study and during a two-week follow-up period was measured.

No overall effects were found in the three different conditions. However, among the children who were initially classified as highly aggressive, those who viewed the aggressive films increased their level of aggressive behavior, and those exposed to the neutral programming did not. Moreover, there was an interaction between the child's socioeconomic status and his reaction to the programming. Among children of low socioeconomic status, viewing the prosocial program produced a significant increase in helpful and cooperative behavior. The prosocial programming did not significantly increase this type of behavior among children of higher socioeconomic status, but viewing the aggressive programming significantly increased the incidence of helpful behavior among children of high socioeconomic status. Why viewing aggressive programming should have this effect on children of high socioeconomic status is not clear. Perhaps these children felt guilty after seeing the aggression, and atoned for their feelings by being more helpful. Whatever the reason, it is clear that the effect of the program content varied for different types of children (Stein and Friedrich, 1971).

In another study the investigators ingeniously arranged to have three different versions of a popular prime time television program broadcast in three different cities. In one of the versions (antisocial with negative consequences), a young man violently robs and destroys a series of charity collection banks and is

A consideration of some of the problems involved in field experiments on the effects of viewing aggressive television programs may also help explain the inconsistent results obtained in such studies. First, the investigators must classify the programs as aggressive or nonaggressive. Was the slapstick in "Laugh-In" aggressive? What about the intent of violence? Although very little injury occurred in "Lost in Space," one of the major characters was constantly attempting to injure the others. In one study in which watching violent programming was associated with a decrease in the level of aggression, the following classification of programs was made (Feshbach and Singer, 1971). If you remember these programs (see box below), would you agree with the investigators' classification?

Further, keeping control is difficult in field studies. The environment may be more natural, but this is acquired at a price. For instance, at the time one of the studies was done, "Batman" was an extremely popular program. Originally, it was not included in the television programs for the nonaggressive-programming condition, but the boys in this group demanded to see "Batman," so all of the subjects viewed this program. Since considerable violence was shown on this program, the fact that all of the boys saw it may have contributed to the results.

Still another problem involves the measurement of aggression. The measure most frequently used is a rating of the amount of aggression the subject shows. However, the effects of televised aggression may occur at a deeper level. Viewing aggressive television may not make a child behave more aggressively; but it might make him more tolerant of others' behaving aggressively, cause him to be more "turned on" by violence, or make him more callous to aggression in general and to the victims of aggression in particular.

Most of the field studies have involved relatively short periods of exposure to media violence. The longest duration of time studied in the research reported here was six weeks. However, the effects of televised violence may cumulate slowly over a long period of time. Watching televised violence for years may have quite different effects than watching it for weeks.

Aggressive Programs	Nonaggressive Programs
"Combat"	"NBC Sports in Action"
"FBI"	
"Get Smart"	"Gilligan's Island"
"I Spy"	
"Perry Mason"	"Lost in Space"
"Virginian"	
Wrestling	"Lucy Show"
	"Yogi Bear"

ultimately arrested. In a second version (antisocial without negative consequences), the same man is shown destroying the charity banks but escapes to Mexico to enjoy his money. In a third version (prosocial), the man contemplates breaking the banks, but changes his mind at the last moment. Then samples of viewers of each version of the program were invited to receive a free gift. However, when they arrived at the distribution center, they were met with a sign saying that free gifts were no longer available and a charity bank resembling the one shown in the television programs. A screwdriver and a hammer were conveniently at hand.

There was no significant difference in the incidence of breaking the bank among the subjects in the three conditions (Milgram and Shotland, 1973). However, as the committee noted, one cannot conclude from this study that television content has no significant effect. The act measured was one that was very directly related to the content of the program. The study involved adults, not children. And, as with most studies in this area, the cumulative, long-term effects of the content of television programming were not measured.

In a third study support for the catharsis theory of viewing aggression was obtained. Six hundred twenty-five boys were randomly assigned to watch six weeks of aggressive or nonaggressive television programs. The boys involved in the experiment were at boarding schools—either privately owned college-preparatory schools or publicly owned institutions for homeless boys. During the six-week period of the experiment, ratings were made of the level of aggressive behavior shown by each boy (Feshbach and Singer, 1971).

The main effect of viewing aggressive television in this experiment was to *reduce* the amount of aggression. Boys who saw the aggressive television programs showed less aggression than did boys who viewed the nonaggressive programming. Further, the effects of viewing aggressive television varied according to the populations of boys studied. In the private schools exposure to aggressive or nonaggressive television had little effect, whereas in the publicly owned institutions the viewing of aggressive television programs significantly *reduced* the level of aggression.

One possible explanation relates to the consequences of aggression shown in the violent programs. The investigators used real television programs in order to make the situation as natural as possible, and punishment was a common theme in these programs. The villain was always punished for his aggression; good always triumphed. Thus the pervasiveness of punishment for aggression may have inhibited the expression of aggressive impulses.

The reality of the violence may determine whether catharsis or increased aggression results from viewing violent television programming. Forty children, between nine and eleven years old, saw a six-minute film clip of a campus riot. Half of the children were told that it was a report of an actual event; the other half were told that it was a Hollywood film. Then the level of the children's aggressive behavior was measured. Those who had been told that the violence was real subsequently acted more aggressively than those who had been told that the film was fiction (Feshbach, 1971).

The number and complexity of variables that influence the individual's reaction to televised violence help explain the inconsistent results. The initial level of the individual's aggressiveness, his socioeconomic status, the presence of punishment for aggression, and the reality of the violence in the programming—all of these and many other factors may influence the individual's reactions. Of course, many other incidents in the person's life—in addition to what he watches on television—are influencing his level of aggressiveness.

So many variables are involved that trying to find a simple answer to the question "What is the effect of televised violence?" may be unrealistic.

And If It Sells? Even if it were conclusively established that televised violence significantly contributes to the incidence of aggressive behavior, what then? Violence is big at the box office—as has been shown repeatedly by the enormous popularity of such films as *The Godfather* and *The French Connection*. Television network officials seem to think that "action"—which to them usually means violence—is the best way to attract an audience. And as long as the networks must compete against each other for sponsors, they will continue to offer what the public wants and seems to like.

Further, the prevalence of violence in other aspects of society may increase the public taste for blood. Surrounded by violence and crime, the public may really want its media to be violent. If you think that there is a possibility of your experiencing real violence, you may want fantasy that is related to what you fear. Exposing yourself to a weakened version of violence may allow you to master your fear of experiencing real violence (Fenichel, 1939).

A tragic event at the University of Wisconsin provided an opportunity to test this hypothesis. A coed at the university was stabbed to death early on a Sunday morning in May, 1968, while she was walking alone on the campus. The week before the murder two films had begun playing at theaters near the university. One film was *In Cold Blood*, a violent account of the psychopathic murder of a family. The other was *The Fox*—an account of a lesbian relationship. When attendance figures for the two films were compared for the period before and after the murder, it was found that attendance at the violent film showed a significant increase over the attendance before the murder. Attendance at the other film decreased significantly (Boyansky, Newtson, and Walster, 1972).

If violence sells and the public wants it, who will stop it? Even if the networks and the public could be convinced that violence in the media should be regulated, how would the censorship be carried out? Would only children's programs be regulated? Children watch adult programs. Or would the violence in adult programming be curtailed also?

Summary

Most theorists agree that learning is a major determinant of aggression. The acquisition of aggressive behaviors is effected through a variety of learning processes. Without always intending to do so, parents administer a series of rewards and punishments for aggressive behavior, and also influence the child indirectly by serving as models that the child imitates and identifies with. Peers, other adults, and the mass media may also serve as models.

Since the child learns from both his parents and other sources, the relationship between parental discipline patterns and the children's behavior is a complicated one. However, correlational studies have shown that either parental aggressiveness or parental permissiveness is related to aggressiveness in a child.

A basic principle of learning is that *responses that are rewarded* tend to occur more frequently. This principle applies to aggressive responses as well as others. At the human level many, if not most, reinforcements involve the approval or affection of others. Such rewards are termed social reinforcers. The importance of social reinforcement in modifying the frequency of aggressive behavior has been shown in several studies.

Physical punishment is a less efficient means of shaping behavior than reinforcement. However, in some limited circumstances vicarious punishments may be effective. If a child observes others being punished for a given act, the chances of his imitating that act may be decreased.

Aggression may also be learned through *imitation*—another important learning process. A number of laboratory experiments have shown that children who observe aggressive models subsequently behave much more aggressively than children who do not observe such models. However, the evidence is not conclusive on the crucial question of whether or not children who behave aggressively in the experimental setting would also be more likely to act aggressively in other situations.

The behavioral effect of seeing an aggressive model is influenced by a number of variables. The tendency to imitate an aggressive model is increased when the model is rewarded for his aggression or is powerful and dominant. Further, if the violence is seen as ethically justified, it is imitated more frequently, and if the observer is initially angry or can identify with the person who is acting violently, he will also be more likely to imitate the violence. The presence of stimuli usually associated with violence, such as a gun, increases the incidence of violence. Overt action on the part of the model is not necessary for imitation of aggressive responses to occur. An adult's saying that aggressive behavior is appropriate can increase a child's level of aggression.

Televised violence may also provide a model for aggression. A number of social psychologists feel that children's viewing televised violence *increases* their tendency to act aggressively. Not all agree with this view, however. There are two other positions. One, the catharsis view, holds that watching violent television programs may *reduce* the incidence of aggression among viewers by providing an outlet for aggressive impulses. A third view is that exposure to the various sorts of violence in the mass media has *no significant effect*.

The recent report of the Surgeon General's Advisory Committee concluded that a "modest relationship exists between the viewing of violence and aggressive behavior." Correlations between the number of violent television programs watched by children and their aggressive tendencies have been positive, but small. Of course, one cannot infer causation from correlational studies.

As we saw in the discussion of modeling, a number of laboratory studies have demonstrated that viewing aggressive material increases the amount of aggression expressed by the subjects. Of course, since there are a number of differences between the experimental setting and the usual situation when one watches violence on television, there is a question of whether or not these findings generalize to real life.

To obtain the advantage of being able to infer

cause-effect relationships and to eliminate some of the artificialities of the laboratory work on modeling, several investigators have done studies to assess the effects of viewing aggressive television programs in a natural setting. The results of these studies have been inconsistent. In some, viewing aggressive programs increased the amount of violence in children who were initially highly aggressive; in others, viewing violent television had no measurable effect; and in still others, viewing aggressive television reduced the level of aggressive behavior.

The number and complexity of variables that influence the individual's reaction to televised violence—including his socioeconomic status, the presence of punishment for aggression, and the reality of the violence in the programming—may help explain the inconsistent results.

Even if it were conclusively established that televised violence significantly contributes to the incidence of aggression, what then? Violence is big at the box office. Further, the prevalence of violence in other aspects of society may increase the public taste for blood. Even if the networks and the public could be convinced that violence in the media should be regulated, how would violence be censored?

Frustration and Aggression

Another major theory is that aggression is the outgrowth of frustrating experiences. (See Figure 6-11.) As the theory was initially proposed by a group from Yale (Dollard and others, 1939), the only cause of aggression is frustration: Frustration inevitably leads to some form of aggression, and whenever aggression occurs, some form of frustration is responsible. The strength of the aggressive impulse is proportional to the intensity of frustration. The strength of the frustrated motive, the degree of interference, and the number of motives blocked determine the intensity of the aggression.

Expression of the aggressive impulse is determined by the expected rewards and punishments. No matter how frustrated a prisoner-of-war is in a prison camp, he isn't likely to act aggressively toward his guards because he

would probably be severely punished. If an individual expects an act of aggression aimed directly at that which is frustrating him to result in punishment, he will express his aggression in a modified way—either indirectly (by mimicking his guards behind their backs) or by displacing it to other, "safe," nonpunishing objects.

Once the aggressive impulses have been aroused by frustration, only acting aggressively or fantasizing about aggression—for instance, by viewing a violent film such as *The Godfather*—can release the tension. This release is termed catharsis. After a series of frustrating events, blowing off steam makes the individual feel better.

Frustration-aggression was one of the factors contributing to the events at Mylai. By all three indicators of the strength of frustration (strength of the frustrated motive, degree of interference, and number of motives blocked), the men involved in the Mylai massacre were intensely frustrated. Frustration was involved in most aspects of their daily routine: frustration at being in Vietnam, separated from family and friends; frustration at the dirt and grime of living in the field; frustration at not being able to catch and actively engage the elusive enemy. These general frustrations were heightened by an incident that had occurred just two days before the men entered Mylai: Two men from the unit were wounded and one was killed in a booby trap. As one man recalled: "It was a kind of gruesome

FIGURE 6-11 Aggression as a reaction to frustration.

thing. We were good and mad" (Hersh, 1970, p. 35). The threat to survival from an uncatchable enemy brought the frustrations to a peak.

Since aggressing against those directly responsible for the frustrations was not possible, it could be argued that the men displaced their aggression onto the Vietnamese civilians whom they encountered. The real object of their frustration was either intangible (the Establishment responsible for their being in Vietnam) or unavailable (those who set the booby trap). Aggressive impulses were therefore channeled to others who were seen as accessible, safe, and appropriate. Killing women and children was seen as justified, since most Americans in Vietnam had heard stories of women and children injuring American soldiers. Further, the Americans did not really consider the Vietnamese human. The Americans referred to them as "gooks" and believed them to be a very inferior people.

Also, the civilians themselves were a direct cause of frustration, for their duplicity and unpredictability had frustrated the troops on more than one occasion. Thus two sources of aggression—one caused by displacement and one caused by direct frustration—combined, and after about two months in Vietnam the atrocities began in the company: "As they filed through a hamlet, Carter offered a 'papa-san' a cigarette. As the man took it, Carter suddenly began to club him with his rifle butt. He broke his jaw and ribs. Most of the company watched" (Hersh, 1970, p. 31).

The day of the massacre at Mylai was a particularly frustrating one for the men. They had entered the village with the expectation of finding the enemy, who, as usual, had escaped. This frustration on top of all of the previous frustrations could be argued to have resulted in the killing of several hundred defenseless civilians.

According to the frustration-aggression hypothesis, the overt expression of aggression should have brought great release. And during the massacre the GIs seemed to be enjoying themselves: "The boys enjoyed it. When someone laughs and jokes about what they're doing, they have to be enjoying it." A GI said, "Hey, I got me another one." Another said, "Chalk up one for me" (Hersh, 1970, p. 56).

Nevertheless, the killings stimulated other killings. They did not stop after one or two killings, but went on for several hours. And afterward some of the men felt more tense, not less. The commander of the whole company, Captain Medina, seemed worried about the details of the massacre "leaking out"; some of the other men felt guilty. The men's reaction to the massacre was not completely consistent with the catharsis aspect of the original frustration-aggression hypothesis, which would have predicted a lessening of tension.

The incident at Mylai generally fits the frustration-aggression hypothesis. Aggression followed frustration; when the aggression could not be aimed directly at those responsible for the frustration, it was displaced. The evidence for catharsis is not completely consistent: For some of the men, expressing aggression reduced tension levels, but for others, it increased their tension levels.

Reactions to frustration

The relationship between frustration and aggression in the Mylai massacre is not unique. As we saw in Chapter 3, evidence that frustration tends to arouse aggressive impulses comes from a wide variety of sources. However, research has shown that, in addition to aggression, frustration can produce a variety of other behaviors, including a general increase in the amount of ongoing activity; an impairment in attention, thinking, planning, and other mental processes; and fantasy and withdrawal (Barker, Dembo, and Lewin, 1941). Also, as we saw in Chapter 3, frustration can sometimes result in no overt aggression at all. The contemporary approach to the frustration-aggression hypothesis has been to isolate those aspects of a frustration situation that lead to aggression, after considering all of the variables in the total situation.

Determinants of the strength of aggression

Five variables have been found to influence the amount of aggression elicited by frustration and the form which that aggression will take: (1) environmental blocking versus attack, (2) arbitrariness of the frustration, (3) expectations, (4) cues from the situation, and (5) anticipated results of aggression.

Environmental Blocking versus Attack So far in our discussion a general definition of frustration has been assumed: Frustration is any interference with, or blocking of, a goal-directed behavior. Placing a barrier between children and toys they want to play with is an example of blocking. According to this definition, frustration may occur because of a physical object that blocks what you want: You can't enter a theater because a door is locked. Or it may stem from someone's blocking you from what you want: You and a friend are competing for the same prize, and his winning means that you have to lose. Or frustration may result when two, competing, inconsistent motives operate within you to prevent you from attaining mutually exclusive goals: You want to help someone who is in trouble, but, at the same time, you don't want to get involved. All of these forms of interference are generally referred to as "environmental blocking."

A quite different source of frustration is physical or verbal "attack." Suppose, for example, someone insults you, thereby interfering with your goal of pleasant self-contemplation. Just as you are thinking how clever you are, someone rudely intimates the contrary by saying that you are stupid. Or suppose that you are involved in an automobile accident in which you believe you are without fault, but the other driver strikes you "for being reckless." In both of these cases you would undoubtedly experience a high degree of frustration.

Are your reactions to environmental blocking and attack equally aggressive? One theorist has argued that they are not; he contends that aggression is much more likely to occur as a result of attack, or insult, than as a result of environmental blocking (Buss, 1966). Reacting aggressively to an insult may be much more vital to one's successful functioning, for others may take advantage of an individual who never retaliates.

Several studies have compared the relative amount of aggression elicited by attack, environmental blocking, and no frustration (e.g., Berkowitz and Geen, 1966). Consistently, attack—usually in the form of a confederate's insulting the subject—has elicited stronger aggression than environmental blocking. However, the aggressive response to verbal insult is not viewed by all as being consistent with the frustration-aggression hypothesis. Some have theorized that an aggressive reaction to attack is simply a realistic, adaptive response. Reciprocating when attacked physically may be basic to survival; returning an injury for an insult is a strong desire in civilized man. The norm of reciprocity—"I do to you what you do to me"—governs much social behavior.

Arbitrariness of the Frustration A number of studies have shown that the relationship between frustration and aggression is markedly influenced by the person's perception of the reason for the frustration (Buss, 1961; Fishman, 1965; Epstein and Taylor, 1967). When the frustration can be attributed to a reasonable or otherwise acceptable cause, it is apt to elicit far less aggression than when it is given arbitrarily. For example, compare the effect of a week's solitary confinement in a narrow cell on someone who views this as an unearned punishment with its effect on someone who is voluntarily participating in a research project on the effect of confinement. The prisoner may see this as a very harsh punishment and react with aggression, whereas the volunteer feels that since he has volunteered, his being in the situation is his own responsibility (Feshbach, 1964).

Expectations A person's expectations are a powerful determinant of frustration. Expected unpleasant situations are much less frustrating than unexpected ones. Evidence of the importance of expectancies comes from a variety of sources.

When expectations rise faster than fulfillment, the thwarting of hopes breeds frustrations, as in ghetto riots. Once poverty-stricken groups have begun to hope for equal opportunity and material possessions, the inability to fulfill their expectations is frustrating. In a series of experiments by Berkowitz (1962) on the importance of expectations, subjects were exposed to negative judgments about themselves. Half of the subjects had expected the negative reactions; to the other half they were a surprise. Predictably, the unexpected negative comments were much more upsetting than the expected ones.

This outcome adds further support to the hypothesis that frustration is largely determined by expectations.

Cues from the Situation In a contemporary reformulation of the frustration-aggression hypothesis, Berkowitz has theorized that frustration produces a general arousal which then activates whatever response tendencies are elicited in the situation. Aspects of the situation, the individual's past history, any specific response cued off by the arousal—all of these determine whether or not, aggression follows frustration. That is, frustration creates an undifferentiated arousal, which is channeled into expression by all aspects of the situation.

Once frustration increases the level of activity, the situation determines which responses emerge. For example, one aspect of the situation that may affect the nature of the response is the presence or lack of "aggressive stimuli," such as guns or films of violence. It has been found that if, after an individual is frustrated, he sees a film of two prize fighters battling in the ring, he will be more likely to respond aggressively than if he had not observed any violence (Berkowitz and Geen, 1966). Further the presence of a gun increases the level of aggressive-

ness displayed by frustrated subjects (Berkowitz and LePage, 1967).

Anticipated Results of the Aggression Earlier, we saw how expected rewards and punishments affect the likelihood of an aggressive response. (See Figure 6-12.) In some cases it is not possible to aggress directly against the assumed cause. In these situations the individual can express his aggression in other ways. He may engage in *indirect acts of aggression* against the real object of his frustration: He may have dreams in which unpleasant things happen to the tormentor or ridicule the tormentor behind his back. Observations of American soldiers during World War II showed some of the ways in which aggression was indirectly displayed when a direct expression was severely punished. Four main patterns were seen: (1) griping about the alleged stupidity and cruelty of the officer, (2) gossiping about the officer's weaknesses, (3) mimicking the mannerisms and speech of the officer, and (4) "goldbricking," or avoiding work (Janis, 1945).

Or the individual may *displace his aggression to others.* Earlier, we saw the way in which the American troops involved in Mylai may have displaced their aggression to Vietnamese civil-

FIGURE 6-12 Anticipated results are a powerful determinant of whether frustration will result in aggressive behavior.

ians. What determines how aggression is displaced? This is a complicated question to which the present experimental results have provided only a partial answer.

One observation is that aggression is sometimes displaced to minority groups. As we saw in Chapter 3, when individuals are frustrated, their aggression is released on socially sanctioned targets of aggression: persons about whom very unfavorable stereotypes persist, persons who are not able to retaliate, persons toward whom aggression is sanctioned by the individual's friends, persons who are believed to be partially responsible for a particular frustration, or persons who seem similar to the source of frustration.

As shown in Chapter 3, experimental support for the effect of frustration in increasing hostility toward minority groups has been obtained (Miller and Bugelski, 1948). In a real-life setting frustration was imposed on the subjects by confining them to camp and giving them a series of dull, boring tasks on the night they usually had off. The subjects were given tests that included items on attitudes about various minority groups, and considerably more negative prejudices were expressed toward these minority groups after the frustration than before.

The social implications of this and other similar findings are clear. In a society that maintains negative attitudes toward various minority groups, the potential for scapegoating is high. If aggression against these groups is not precluded by possible punishment, then when frustration reaches a certain level, scapegoating will very likely occur. The extreme to which this can lead is shown by the Nazi destruction of over 6 million Jews.

Could a similar phenomenon happen in the United States? If frustration became intense enough, could a similar fate befall this country's black population? Some black writers have expressed concern over this possibility. In fact, they feel that the history of white persecution of blacks by such organizations as the Ku Klux Klan has laid the foundation for further actions. In opposition, many contend that the civil-rights laws passed in the 1960s have increased the punishments for such scapegoating and that these laws may, over time, be internalized and so lead to a change in attitudes.

Not all displaced aggression is directed toward minority groups. In your own experience when you have felt aggression, whom have you taken it out on? Perhaps people you see and feel comfortable with, such as family and friends. They are available, and you think they will forgive your "irritability." Availability may be a prime determinant of the expression of aggression.

Experiments have shown that similarity among individuals may constitute an important aspect of displacement. A frustrated individual may attack someone who physically resembles the source of his frustration. Or similarity of name may influence displacement. You may have had the experience of being introduced to someone whom you didn't like only to realize later that the person had the same name as, or resembled in some other way, someone you knew and disliked. Experimental evidence for this kind of displacement has been obtained (Berkowitz and Knurek, 1969).

Catharsis

So far in this section the relationship between various aspects of frustration and aggression has been discussed. But what happens after the aggressive impulses have been expressed? According to the original frustration-aggression hypothesis, once aggressive impulses are aroused, only aggressing will produce a decrease in tension. After acting aggressively, the individual will feel relieved and less tense because energy has been consumed through catharsis. (See Figure 6-13.)

This idea seems plausible: After you encounter a series of frustrations, letting off steam may feel good and may reduce your level of aggressive impulses, so that you are less likely to behave aggressively after the release. This all follows clearly from the theory.

However, experimental studies in this area have shown an inconsistent relationship between expressing aggression and catharsis. In some studies (Feshbach, 1955; Thibaut and Coules, 1952) aggressive behavior has lowered subsequent aggression; in others it has produced an increase in aggression (Kenny, 1953; deCharms and Wilkins, 1963).

Clearly, the effect of acting aggressively depends on other variables. What might some of

FIGURE 6-13 "Bashing the boss." In Japan, several companies provide a special room where workers can take out their aggressions on a toy replica of their "boss" to relieve their tensions. (Michio Chiboshi)

these be? Let's return to the example of how you feel after letting off steam. You may feel guilty about your actions; you may feel foolish if you think your behavior was somehow inappropriate to the particular situation; you may feel tired; or you may become worried because your aggression angered someone with power over you.

The consequences of the aggression determine whether or not it is a satisfactory release. This is clearly demonstrated in many everyday situations. Imagine that you really blew up at a professor you thought had been grading your tests unfairly. Would you feel cleansed? You might temporarily, but then you might begin to worry about the results of your losing control. Would your final grade be affected? How would you be treated in class? After the outburst you might be more tense. In contrast, yelling at someone who has been giving you a hard time and who has no power over you might make you feel good. Evidence for the differential effect of aggressing against high- and low-status aggressors was obtained in a number of studies (Hokanson and Shetler, 1961; Hokanson and Burgess, 1962a, 1962b). The existence of ten-

sion as well as release following the Mylai incident was already noted.

Summary

As we saw in Chapter 3, evidence that frustration tends to arouse aggression comes from a wide variety of sources. However, since research has shown that frustration can produce a variety of behaviors in addition to aggression, the contemporary approach to the frustration-aggression hypothesis has been to isolate those aspects of a frustration situation that can lead to aggression. From this research, the following conclusions have been drawn: (1) *Personal attack* results in more aggression than environmental blocking; (2) *arbitrary frustrations* are more likely to result in aggression than reasonable frustration; (3) *expected* unpleasant situations are much less frustrating than unexpected ones; (4) *certain cues from the situation*—such as the presence of guns or films of violence—can significantly increase the level of aggression; and (5) the *anticipated results* of the aggression determine whether it is expressed directly, indirectly, or displaced toward others.

According to the original frustration-aggression hypothesis, once aggressive impulses are aroused, only aggressing will produce a decrease in tension, or catharsis. However, experimental studies in this area have shown an inconsistent relationship between expressing aggression and catharsis. Whether expressing aggression results in an increase or a decrease in tension depends on a number of other variables—including the individual's guilt about his actions, his fear of punishment, and the possibility of embarrassment.

Aggression in an Interpersonal Context

So far in this chapter we have considered variables that increase the tendency toward aggressive impulses within an individual. The translation of those impulses into acts of aggression, however, usually requires interaction with other people. For instance, although you may feel aggressive because you've been frustrated, you may not act out your aggression unless you think that someone else has wronged you. In this section we will consider two approaches to how the social context and patterns of social interactions influence the intensity of the aggressive impulse and its expression.

Transactional aggression

As George and Martha amply demonstrate in Edward Albee's *Who's Afraid of Virginia Woolf?*, it takes two to fight. (See Figure 6-14.) Interpersonal aggression grows out of a sequence of escalating violence in which both parties contribute to at least some extent. If neither one breaks the chain of escalation, acts of extreme violence can occur. For instance, in their on-

stage fights George and Martha each keep reciprocating the attacks of the other by intensifying the level of attack until, in their final confrontation, they each seek to inflict maximum injury on the other.

To discover common themes in the sequence of behaviors leading to violence, one investigator has analyzed 444 assaults on policemen, as described by the policemen themselves, and has interviewed 77 inmates and parolees, each of whom has a record of several violent encounters (Toch, 1969). His conclusion from these studies is that violence tends to follow a fairly standard pattern: (1) *provocation* by one or the other of the individuals—for instance, a man announces to a woman he has been living with that he intends to leave her—and (2) *escalation* and *confrontation*—the woman reacts by nagging and cursing the man; he retaliates with

FIGURE 6-14 Richard Burton as "George" and Elizabeth Taylor as "Martha" go at each other in a scene from the Warner Brothers film, *Who's Afraid of Virginia Woolf?* by Edward Albee. In the background, at the left, George Segal as "Nick" joins in the fray. (The Bettman Archive)

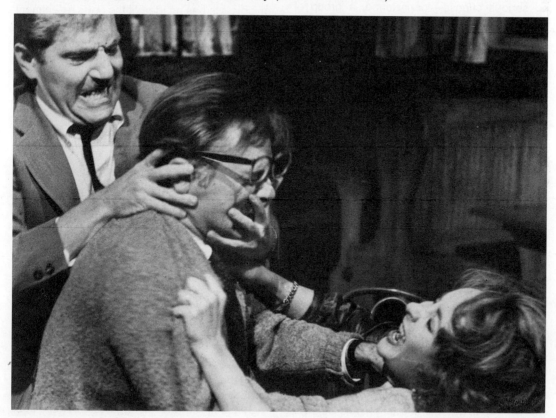

obscenities; and they ultimately engage in physical battle.

Provocation A variety of situations can provoke a violent reaction in another person. One violent incident, which ended with a man's killing his girl friend, began by his girl friend's refusing to turn over any of her paycheck to him. He reciprocated by announcing that he was leaving her and went out to get a couple of cans of beer. When he returned, his girl friend became angry and started to nag him. Amazingly, the man didn't understand how his announcement of departure could make her react as she did, and he interpreted her anger as an attack out of the blue. He therefore rationalized his brutal act as one of self-defense.

In police assaults, the main focus of Toch's study, over half of the assaults were caused by the suspect's reaction to a verbal approach by an officer—such as a simple request for identification or other routine questioning. Typically, in these incidents the assailant has committed no serious offense—for instance, a group of boys may be told to move, or a suspect may be questioned as to what he is doing. These individuals apparently regard the policeman's approach as a threat to their personal autonomy and therefore the approach causes deep resentment. To the policeman, it is simply part of his job.

One case cited in the study clearly illustrates the mutual misunderstanding and the provocative effect that the officer's approach and questioning can have. One officer, ordered to investigate reports of firecrackers being exploded, saw an adolescent Negro boy sitting on a bench in the school playground. Deciding to investigate, the officer stopped his car and approached the boy. The boy, a member of a solid middle-class family, reports what happened then:

So he said, "What are you doing here?" I said, "I was just sitting here." So he says, "Come around here." So the set-up was that there was a long fence, and I was sitting right in the middle of it. . . . So he said, "Come all the way around," and I said, "I was on my way toward home."

So he said he wanted to talk to me. So I said, "Well, I haven't done anything wrong. I'll tell you my name if you tell me what I did wrong." . . . And he says,

"Look, I don't want any trouble from you." And I said, "Look, I don't want any trouble either."

So he walked to one end, to the opposite side of the fence; so I started walking in the other direction, up to the end of the bench about ten or fifteen feet. So, he walks up that way and I walk back the other way. So he says, "Listen here, I don't want any trouble from you." I said, "I don't want any trouble either. Just tell me what I did wrong and we can talk. I haven't done anything wrong."

So he gets into his car and he drives up to one end of the fence. And all of a sudden, I'm thinking to myself, you know, "this is a dumb cop." . . . So I started running to the other end of the playground and I yelled to him, "You'll never catch me this way."

[Toch, 1969, pp. 104–105.]

This incident illustrates a number of common themes of provocative incidents. As in a marital quarrel, neither participant seems to take the other's point of view into account. The boy sees the policeman's demands as arbitrary and unreasonable, reacts in a stubborn and resentful way—with no attempt to see the policeman's side of the issue. The policeman is equally myopic. He has no idea of the boy's resentment of his approach, does not attempt to deal with the boy's view of the situation, focuses exclusively on his own concept of the situation, and reacts by feeling hampered and frustrated by someone whom he convinces himself is deranged and dangerous. If either had made a conciliatory gesture—if the policeman had explained why he wanted to talk with the boy or the boy had identified himself—the level of violence might not have escalated.

Assaults on policemen were also found to arise frequently out of police intervention in conflicts between two civilians. When a police officer intervenes in a domestic argument, for instance, he may be seen as illegitimately interfering in the couple's private business, as taking sides with one of the parties, or as posing a threat of arrest. Further, when violence already exists and the combatants are highly aggressive, it is easy to transfer this violence to a policeman—especially if the individuals initially have negative attitudes toward the police generally.

Escalation and Confrontation Each person reacts to what the other does, with a gradual increase in the level of aggression, until either one of the participants breaks off the sequence or a final confrontation occurs, in which the maximal injury possible—consistent with the situation and the participants' personalities—is given. In interactions between police officers and resisting civilians, the officer will frequently escalate his requests to orders, and then to threats or arrests. In turn, the civilian's resistance will grow increasingly intense and will include verbal abuse, attempts to flee, and sometimes assault on the officer.

To see how escalation can occur in a specific interaction between a policeman and a civilian, let us return to our example of the adolescent boy—this time as described by the officer, who tells of the events that surrounded and followed the boy's running away:

He [the boy] ran out east, through the gate, and slammed it as he was running down the road, and he was laughing like crazy, you know. And I hear him yell something about, "You're going to die," or some stupid thing. . . . He's gone, you know, it's very obvious to me that I'm never going to apprehend him, he was running like a deer. . . . So I run back to my vehicle, get on the radio and I told them that there was a possible 50–50 loose, which is from the Welfare and Institute's code, referring to a person that is mentally unbalanced. He had yelled something that in my opinion was a possible threat to my life, and I think that we should get somebody up there and flush him out before he hurts somebody.

[Toch, 1969, p. 106.]

Thus in round one of their interaction, both the boy's resistance and the officer's perseverance have escalated. The boy's defiance of authority has now escalated from his initial running back and forth along the fence to running away from the scene. The officer, after having made his opening moves, is convinced that he is dealing with a dangerous lunatic and has called for help. Since the boy's account and the officer's description of what the boy said differ, we cannot know what the boy really said. However, if the boy's account is true, the officer has seriously misinterpreted the boy's playful remark, "You'll never catch me this way," by thinking he said, "You're going to die." The situation might have ended there had the boy not decided to renew his interaction with the officer and returned to the scene. What happened then is described by the officer:

I'm walking at him like this, you know, talking to him because I honestly believe at this point that the guy is a nut. . . . Well, I says, "Look, if I have to chase you, there's going to be a real problem. . . ." And he's still backing away, only now he's taking bigger steps. . . . So, then I come out with, "Now look, I don't want to shoot you." Which was the classic statement. I didn't have my revolver out, and I would never have taken it out 'cause naturally a misdemeanor . . . is certainly no grounds. But it did shock him enough, so that he stopped and said, "What do you mean, shoot me?" And when he stopped I grabbed him by the right arm. I got sort of a half-nelson on him, and I'm walking him back to the car, and I says, "Look, you get in the car." And then the beef starts. He comes out with, "Get your hands off me, you [obscenity], I'm not getting in no police car." And the beef's on. The kid was big, and I don't mind telling you, he gave me one hell of a hassle, we were all over the street.

[Toch, 1969, p. 107.]

By the boy's returning to what he thought was an entertaining game, the policeman is made even angrier. His belief that the boy is a lunatic and his anger at being defied again result in his threat to use his weapon—at which point the boy stops and the policeman grabs him. Reacting to being grabbed, the boy swears at the policeman, and the fight is on.

Once the fight begins, both participants are filled with panic, and neither can communicate at all with the other. According to the boy's account, he was willing to talk once the officer grabbed him, but the officer saw the confrontation as a desperate fight to the death—as he recounts below:

So, then I really start putting the heat on him. And he starts bucking a little bit. All you can hear out of him, "You're choking me." See, but he's starting to slow down a little bit. So I figure, well, this is it. Boy, I'm getting tired, I'm either going to have to do him in now, or forget about it. So, I gave it all I had and finally put the kid on the ground. . . . As I recall, I had exerted so much strength that my left arm, I couldn't even unfold my hand the muscles were so cramped up. . . . And this is what it took to get the kid down. And he's put into the car.

[Toch, 1969, p. 109.]

Escalation and confrontation in aggressive encounters isn't limited to police-civilian interactions. See Figure 6-15 for an illustration of escalation in a domestic quarrel.

BOX 5 VIOLENT MEN

It has been hypothesized that an individual's propensity toward violence can be predicted from his overall personality—from the way he views himself and others and from his characteristic reactions and needs. To test this hypothesis, one investigator interviewed sixty-nine men with a history of violence and evolved a rough classificatory scheme of their underlying motives (Toch, 1969).

Two different motives emerged: (1) Approximately 76 percent of the men used violence to bolster their ego—to enhance both their self-image and their reputation with other people—and (2) roughly 24 percent of the men saw themselves (and their needs) as the only social fact of relevance and therefore used violence to gain their own ends. Within these two major groups, the investigator found several subcategories.

Over half of the men in the first group felt that being formidable and fearless was an important part of their self-image. Their fights were designed to impress their victims or their audience with their own strength so that they would not be regarded as weaklings or cowards. "Being tough" was extremely important to them, and they were very sensitive to any slight on their masculinity or to any hint that another person did not accept them as being tough.

The next largest subcategory in this group included those who used violence to meet the demands of a role. For instance, the leader of a juvenile gang would act violently because he knew it was expected of him, rather than because violence was important to his self-concept. Another subgroup engaged in violence for "norm-enforcing" reasons. These individuals acted violently because they thought it was the only appropriate response in a particular situation. Members of still another subgroup used violence because they perceived other people as dangerous or because they could not cope with a situation in any other way.

The second major group includes people who are extremely self-centered and use violence when it serves their purpose. Some may enjoy bullying others whom they think are unable to fight back. Or people who exploit others may use violence as a last resort when others will not cooperate. Some people may assume that others exist only to satisfy their needs, and when the other person does not comply, they apply violence. They feel that they should be able to do whatever they like, whenever they like, and they become very upset and violent when things don't work out as they would like them to. A last, and relatively rare, motive for violence among those in

the second major group was cathartic—the use of violence to discharge accumulated internal pressures.

Of course, this classification is only a beginning in the understanding of individual differences and motives for violence. Reliability among different judges in classifying the cases has been shown to be acceptable (seven errors out of thirty-five classifications in one reliability test). However, the classification system is limited to a small sample of prison inmates and parolees. In a larger sample the relative frequencies of the reasons for violence might be different, and there might be additional reasons for violence.

This beginning does point to the importance of violence, to some people, as a part of their self-image. In the case of the policeman interacting with the boy, for instance, we can wonder to what extent the violence was a product of the policeman's need to prove himself rather than a result of the objective requirements of the situation. Understanding that being tough may play an important part in the self-image of both many police and many civilians, for instance, might have implications for police-training procedures and for modification of police practices in approaching suspects.

In addition to the escalation involved in these reaction-counterreaction patterns, it is clear that the participants' previous interactions, their expectations about each other, and their personalities contribute to the intensity of violence in their ultimate confrontation. After a husband and wife have had a series of violent quarrels, each may be more likely to interpret an innocuous remark as provocative. After years of squabbling over a mother-in-law problem, mere mention of the mother-in-law might be sufficient to set off a new transaction in violence. After a civilian experiences a series of incidents that he regards as police harassment, he may be

likely to regard all policemen in a negative manner. And the level of physical aggressiveness people engage in varies from person to person. Hurtful verbal aggression is the most intense level of aggression that some people use; others may be more prone to engage in physical violence. See Box 5.

The subculture of violence

People generally accept the attitudes, values, and patterns of behavior of those around them. For instance, in Chapter 3 we saw that many

1. Man comes home and can't get into house because it is locked.

2. Woman has company—another boyfriend. Landlady lets the other boyfriend out the back door and lets regular boyfriend in the front door.

3. Man comes in, sees house in mess, also no food, says he is leaving tomorrow. Goes out and buys a pint of whiskey, drinks, and goes to bed.

4. Woman walks back and forth, swearing at the man.

5. Man tells woman to shut up.

6. Woman continues to swear at man.

7. Man decides to get even, gets up and grabs mirror; the mirror flashes on the ceiling.

8. Woman sees light against the ceiling and jumps out the window, thinking the mirror is a knife or something. Woman then calls the police. The police arrive, and the woman tells them that the man is reaching for a gun. Police grab man, and they wrestle.

9. Man wrestles and knocks policeman on bed.

FIGURE 6-15 Escalation on the home front. (Adapted from Toch, 1969, p. 31.)

girls from relatively conservative backgrounds became more liberal when exposed to the liberal intellectual community of Bennington College. There are segments of our society in which violence is widely accepted and highly valued, and many individuals living in that type of subculture will inevitably come to accept its values. (See Figure 6-16.)

Two investigators have conducted a series of studies that tend to show that the incidence of violence is much higher in some groups than in others (Wolfgang and Ferracuti, 1967). For instance, there are several parts of Italy in which violence is the acceptable reaction to personal affronts. In such subcultures of violence, all of the factors of usual social interaction press the individual toward acceptance of the cultural norms. Many—if not most—of the people surrounding him accept the norm that violence is appropriate in a large number of situations; to maintain successful relationships with others who accept the premise of the subculture, he must, therefore, act as expected. Sometimes a formal initiation into the group makes these group values explicit and forces him to accept violence publicly. The life-style and activities of the group are predicated on its beliefs and values, and he may internalize the group norms, so that they become part of his own private beliefs, if they accord with other aspects of his personality and he does not have other reference groups with conflicting norms.

Initiation and Socialization If an individual wishes to belong to a group, he must conform to the norms important to the other group members. The communication of what is acceptable and what is believed is usually done informally. By observing what others say and do, the individual learns about reality as his group sees it. But sometimes a formal initiation makes the group's values explicit and forces the individual to accept violence publicly—as shown by the initiation ceremony of the Mafia:

Such groups evolve elaborate and often secret rituals to dramatize the severity of their codes and to bring mutual reinforcement of unifying values to bear. From time immemorial the initiation rites of secret societies have served such functions, taking on a decidedly religious tinge. Such a rite is reported of the Mafia in Sicily. When a new recruit, after a long period of trial and observation, is admitted to membership, he is led solemnly through a candle-lit assembly of the members to a table displaying the image of a saint. He offers his right hand, and blood is drawn and sprinkled on the effigy. Before the saintly figure covered with blood, he takes an oath which binds him indissolubly to the association. Soon thereafter he is called upon to carry out an execution ordained by the association [Reid, 1952, p. 33]. In the new world [the

United States], according to Joe Valachi, the Cosa Nostra maintains a similar rite.

[Nieburg, 1969, p. 109.]

Beliefs, Values, and Norms In a subculture of violence, violence is valued; many situations are interpreted as menacing and requiring an aggressive response; and people are expected to follow the socially accepted ways of believing and reacting—the norms. If they do not, they are ostracized, or they may become the victims of those who do accept the norms.

For instance, in a Philadelphia study of 588 criminal homicides, it was found that young black males had the highest crime rate: Black men between twenty and twenty-four years of age had a rate of 92 crimes per 100,000 population as compared to a rate of 3.4 crimes per 100,000 persons in a population of white males of the same age (Wolfgang, 1958). In summarizing his impressions of this black subculture of violence, the investigator wrote:

The significance of a jostle, a slightly derogatory remark, or the appearance of a weapon in the hands of an adversary are stimuli differentially perceived and interpreted by Negroes and whites. . . . Social expectations of response in particular types of social interaction result in differential "definitions of the situation." A male is usually expected to defend the name and honor of his mother, the virtue of womanhood . . . and to accept no derogation about his race (even from a member of his own race), his age, or his masculinity. Quick resort to physical combat as a measure of daring, courage, or defense of status appears to be a cultural expression, especially for lower socio-economic class males of both races. When such a cultural norm response is elicited

FIGURE 6-16 Aggression as a result of belonging to a subculture of violence.

from an individual engaged in social interplay with others who harbor the same response mechanism, physical assaults, altercations, and violent domestic quarrels that result in homicide are likely to be common.

[Wolfgang, 1958, pp. 188–189.]

Sanctions for Deviation from the Norm of Violence Persons who deviate from the norm are not accepted by the group. In a group that values violence, the comparatively nonviolent individual may be ostracized. If he lives in an area in which violence is accepted, those who have accepted the norm may be indifferent toward him, treat him with disdain, or actively avoid him. Although he may not generally be prey for violent assaults and homicides—which usually occur between friends and relatives—if he should be forced into a situation in which he must interact with others who accept the values of violence, he may find himself a potential victim (Wolfgang and Ferracuti, 1967).

Prestige in the Group and Readiness for Violence If violence is valued, being violent is one way to attain status in the group. For instance, in prison one way to attain status is to gain a reputation as a tough guy (Toch, 1969). Violence may also be necessary in such a setting to save face. The desire to save face, combined with the social support of a friend encouraging you to prove yourself, may erupt into violence—as the following incident shows (S is the subject; I is the interviewer):

S: . . . We were watching these cats play cards, and we were standing behind this colored dude. He was one of these big iron lifters, you know. About ninety feet wide, you know, he was one of those. And he turned around and told us, "Whitey, man, don't stand behind me, punk, when I'm playing," you know. And I just looked at my partner and he looked at me, you know, and didn't say nothing, just stood there. 'Cause we were running the barracks anyway. We felt we did.
I: Who was Whitey?
S: He was my partner. I just looked at him for his reaction, and he looked at me for mine. I just smiled and he smiled and we stood there. We felt like, you know, more or less, what I said was, "Do what you want, I'm with you." And he looked at me like, you know, "You there?" You know, because he wasn't about to whip that big sucker. And he turned around again and he said, you know, "I told you not to stand

behind me." And he said, you know, "Bless you, man." And the dude got up man, so I hit him on one side and the other dude hit him, and we were both on him, man. And we beat him to a pulp. Fixed him up bad, man. And nobody jumped in, you know. Course we had about six or seven partners in the barracks and at the time there was only about four colored dudes in there. . . . And after that I felt like a king, man. I felt like, you know, "I'm the man." You're not going to mess with me.

[Toch, 1966, pp. 164–165, in Megargee and Hokanson, 1970.]

Fun and Games The beliefs, values, and usual patterns of behavior may be clearly reflected in the games of a group. People who value intellectual attainment may play chess. People who value violence may play games that are highly conducive to violence. One such game is "playing the dozens," which involves systematically insulting your opponent and trying to build up a reason for violence. This game is popular in slums and in prisons. One session of this game is described as follows:

One of the tormentors will make a mildly insulting statement, perhaps about the mother of the subject, "I saw your mother out with a man last night." Then he may follow this up with "She was as drunk as a bat." The subject, in turn, will then make an insulting statement about the tormentor or some member of the tormentor's family. This exchange of insults continues, encouraged by the approval and shouts of the observers, and the insults become progressively nastier and more pornographic, until they eventually include every member of the participants' families and every act of animal and man. . . . Finally, one of the participants, usually the subject, who has actually been combating the group pressure of the observers, reaches his threshold and takes a swing at the tormentor, pulls out a knife or picks up an object to use as a club. This is the sign for the tormentor, and sometimes some of the observers, to go into action, and usually the subject ends up with the most physical injuries.

[Berdie, 1947, p. 120.]

Internalization of the Norm Many but not all of those who are exposed to the subculture internalize its values and norms. For instance, it has been found that most lower-class boys see themselves as tough, powerful, and aggressive. Further, they would like to be even tougher than they feel they are, and they feel that their prestige in their group is directly dependent on their toughness (Fannin and Clinard, 1965).

However, not everyone exposed to a subculture of violence absorbs it equally. Differences in personality make some more predisposed to internalize the culture than others. It may be that persons with a weak sense of their own identity are more likely to absorb completely the norms of violence (Toch, 1969). Further, the individual may belong to more than one reference group. He may play on a basketball team at a local YMCA, which exposes him to a different set of values. The subculture will also usually allow for individual variation in the expression of violence. Some may seek out violence, and others may simply react to it. If, for personal reasons, a person internalizes the violence norm completely and becomes highly aggressive, he may become too aggressive even for the subculture of violence and be ostracized. Still others, who may have acquired special skills highly valued by the subculture of violence, may be exempted from the usual norm. Earl Monroe, a professional basketball player, has recalled how he was allowed to pursue his athletic ability while growing up in a tough Philadelphia neighborhood:

"Even today, Philadelphia is a gang town," he says. "Not just problems with black gangs and white gangs, but with the Mafia, race riots, everything. Most of the guys I grew up with were involved with the gangs. They tried to get me into it, but my cousins were in it, and they kept me out of it. They just say, 'He's a basketball player, leave him alone'; and everybody did."

[Anderson, 1973, p. 35.]

Summary

The translation of aggressive impulses into acts of aggression usually requires interaction with other people. In this section we considered two approaches to how the patterns of social interaction and the social context influence the intensity of the aggressive impulse and its expression: (1) *transactional aggression,* and (2) *the subculture of violence.*
Interpersonal aggression frequently grows

out of a sequence of escalating violence in which both parties contribute to at least some extent. If neither one breaks the chain of escalation, acts of extreme violence can occur. An analysis of a number of incidents of violence has led one investigator to conclude that violence tends to follow a fairly standard pattern: (1) *Provocation* by one or the other of the individuals. In the case of police assaults, for instance, many of the subjects have been found to interpret the officer's initial verbal approach as an infringement on their freedom. (2) *Escalation* and *confrontation*. In the case of police assaults the officer may escalate his initial requests to orders and then to threats or arrests. In turn, the civilian's resistance increases, moving from verbal resistance to abuse and then to attempts to flee or sometimes to an assault on the police officer. The participants' previous interactions, their expectations about each other, and their personalities can also contribute to the level of violence that will be reached in their ultimate confrontation. Persons who feel that being formidable and fearless is an important part of their self-image may be especially likely to resort to physical violence in the final confrontation.

In some segments of our society, violence is widely accepted and highly valued. Some individuals living in that type of subculture will inevitably come to accept its values and engage in a higher proportion of violent acts than people not living in such a subculture. In these subcultures all of the factors of usual social interaction press the individual toward acceptance of the cultural norms. Many—if not most—of the people surrounding him accept the norm that violence is appropriate in a large number of situations; to maintain successful relationships with others who accept the premise of the subculture, he must, therefore, act as expected. Sometimes a formal initiation into the group makes these group values explicit and forces him to accept violence publicly. The group's life-style and activities are predicated on its beliefs and values, and he may internalize the group's norms, so that they become part of his own private beliefs, if they accord with other aspects of his personality and he does not belong to other reference groups with conflicting norms.

Aggression Caused by the Reduction of Restraining Forces

In the preceding section we noted that for aggressive impulses to erupt into aggressive action, the presence of other people is usually needed. But even when other people are present, we do not act aggressively every time we feel aggressive; sometimes we do and sometimes we don't. If someone cut you off while you were driving, you would probably express your anger. You might mutter colorful things about the other driver, blow your horn, or glare at him. In contrast, if a professor is very late for an appointment, you might feel very angry but not express it. What determines when aggressive impulses result in aggressive acts?

In general, the expression of aggressive feelings depends on the relative strengths of the aggressive impulse and the negative consequences of the aggression, or the "restraining forces." In addition to variables that increase aggressive impulses, there are many negative forces that tend to restrain aggressive behavior: fear of the consequences or guilt feelings about those consequences, social pressures, and so forth. Conversely, any circumstances that weaken the strength of these restraining forces will increase the chance that aggressive impulses will lead to aggressive behavior.

The distinction between strengthening the aggressive impulse and weakening restraining forces, however, is not an absolute one. Group membership for the men involved in the Mylai 4 massacre could be viewed as both increasing the intensity of aggressive urges and decreasing constraining forces. The fact that the various rifle companies staged competitions for the highest score in rifle kills may have strengthened the aggressive urge. At the same time, being a member of a group may have made the men feel less vulnerable to punishment and so weakened the restraining forces.

The quality of aggressive behavior may be related to the relative strengths of the impulse and the restraining forces. Aggression that occurs because the impulse has reached an enormous intensity may be different from aggression that occurs because restraining forces are weakened. As we saw in Chapter 1, one investigator has noted the presence of what he terms deindividuated aggression, or mindless, impulsive, irrational, and regressive behavior. Once this behavior begins, the individual loses all awareness of anything except his act; he becomes completely immersed in it—like the bloody self-intoxication shown by sharks, which sometimes become so incensed while feeding that they begin biting each other. At the human level, too, crimes of passion can show this same kind of immersion and irrationality.

In contrast to this kind of mindless aggression, sometimes aggression is very carefully premeditated—as in the case of a murderer who carefully plots his crime over an extended period of time. One could speculate that the deindividuated crime of passion results from aggressive urges that are so intense they burst through the individual's constraints. The more thoughtful, calmer crime, on the other hand, may evolve from a weakening of restraints. To date this hypothesis has not been tested, but the analysis of phenomenological differences between passion-based and premeditated aggression would be a fruitful source for future research.

Two main variables appear to affect the strength of restraining forces: (1) fear of punishment and (2) moral considerations.

Reducing the fear of punishment

In the discussion of displacement we saw the effect of anticipated punishment. In general, any variables that decrease the fear of punishment increase the chances of aggressive impulses resulting in direct aggressive action.

Reducing the Chances of Being Punished Any variable that reduces the *chances* of a person's being punished should similarly reduce his *fear* of being punished. Again, the Mylai incident illustrates this general rule. The area in which Mylai was located had been designated a free-fire zone, which meant that it was legitimate to fire upon anything that moved. On a number of previous occasions, men in the unit had killed or tortured Vietnamese civilians, and no disciplinary actions had resulted. The whole climate of Vietnam glorified violence, as the following quotation shows:

Among the highly touted colonels in Vietnam in 1967–1968 was P_____ . . . who was commandant of the 11th Armored Cavalry Regiment just south of Quang Ngai. His unit had the motto: "Find the bastards and pile on." He would exhort his men before combat by telling them, "I like to see the arms and legs fly." He once told his staff, "The present ratio of 90 percent killing to 10 percent pacification is just about right." P_____ celebrated Christmas in 1968 by sending cards reading: "From Colonel and Mrs. P_____ Peace on Earth." Attached to the cards were color photographs of dismembered Viet Cong soldiers stacked in a neat pile.

[Hersh, 1970, p. 9.]

Being a member of a group also creates a kind of *anonymity,* which reduces the chances of any one individual being punished for his aggressive acts. Increasing anonymity has been shown to increase the amount of aggression. (See Figure 6-17.) As we saw in Chapter 1, several different sources of evidence support the anonymity-aggression hypothesis. A controlled experiment has shown that making students feel anonymous significantly increased their aggressiveness: The total duration of electric shocks delivered by girls made to feel anonymous was twice as high as the duration of shocks delivered by girls whose individuality was emphasized (Zimbardo, 1969). This finding has been replicated (Baron, 1970). Further, a car made to appear abandoned in the anonymity of New York City was virtually demolished by vandals, whereas a car left in a smaller community for the same period of time was not vandalized (Zimbardo, 1969).

Additional support for the anonymity-aggression hypothesis has been provided by a three-year study of the crime rate in public housing in New York City—primarily moderate-income housing occupied by families with children. The conclusion of the study was that high rise equals high crime. Sixty-eight felonies per 1,000 families were reported in the high-rise buildings (thirteen to thirty floors), in which the residents were anonymous. In mid-rise buildings (six to seven floors), the rate dropped to 41 per 1,000, and in walk-ups (three floors), the rate was 30 felonies per 1,000 families. (See

FIGURE 6-17 Anonymity has been found to increase the degree to which aggressive impulses are translated into aggressive behavior. Hoods, eye-masks, and an elaborate ritual allow the members of the Ku Klux Klan to downplay their individuality. (George W. Gardner)

Figure 6-18.) The most hazardous living quarters were high-rise buildings with apartments on both sides of the hall. In these buildings the corridors are "a nether world of crime and fear" in which it is difficult to distinguish residents from strangers.

A relationship was also found between building height and the areas in which crimes were committed. Although the rate of crimes committed inside apartments and on the outside grounds did not differ significantly according to height, there was a striking difference in the incidence of crime committed in interior public space—elevators, lobbies, and corridors. The overall crime rate was approximately twice as high in high-rise buildings as in walk-ups, but the rate of crime in the public spaces inside these high-rise buildings was seven times higher than in comparable spaces of other buildings. Interior spaces in high-rise buildings are extremely anonymous. No one feels that they

have a proprietary interest in them; residents cannot distinguish strangers from other residents; and it is difficult for the residents to observe what is occurring in these spaces. In contrast, in a walk-up the hall becomes an extension of the individual's home. He knows his neighbors. Further, in walk-ups parents can supervise their children at play outside—thus extending what the investigators term "defensible space" to the street as well as to the interior public spaces (Newman, 1972).

Reducing the Saliency of Punishment Even if the objective possibilities of being punished remain constant, any variables that decrease the prominence of the consideration of a possible punishment will increase the incidence of aggression. The effect of alcohol in reducing inhibitions has long been noted. For instance, in one study of homicides in Philadelphia, it was found that in 64 percent of the cases either one or both of the people involved had been drinking—usually excessively and over a long period of time (Wolfgang, 1958). The stereotype of the pugnacious drunk is part of our folklore.

There is also some evidence suggesting that methamphetamines ("speed") may lead to a change in the state of consciousness and a lessened awareness of the saliency of punishment. After the initial exhilaration caused by the drug comes an anxious, depressed down trip. To avoid this, some speed users take repeated injections—up to ten a day for several days. The result of the repetitive shooting up is that the speed freak develops a variety of symptoms, including agitation, anxiety, irritability, and paranoia, which make him very susceptible to becoming violent—as one observer of the Haight-Ashbury drug scene has noted (Smith, 1969).

Involvement in the physical act of aggression may also obscure any thoughts of possible punishment. Once a person begins hitting, he may not be able to think of anything but the hitting. Zimbardo's observations of some students destroying a car with a sledge hammer are relevant here:

There [was] considerable reluctance to take that first blow, to smash through the windshields and initiate the destruction of a form. But it [felt] so good after the first smack that the next one [came] more easily with more force, and [felt] even better. Although everyone knew the sequence was being filmed, the students got carried away temporarily. Once one person had begun to wield the sledge hammer, it was difficult to get him to stop and pass it to the next pair of eager hands. Finally they all attacked simultaneously. One student jumped on the roof and began stomping it in, two were pulling the door from its hinges, another hammered away at the hood and motor, while the last broke all the glass he could find. . . . They later reported that feeling the metal or glass give way under the force of their blows was stimulating and pleasurable.

[Zimbardo, 1969, p. 290.]

FIGURE 6-18 **High rise equals high crime—public housing crime in relation to building height. Felonies per thousand families, based on the number of crimes reported in 1969 to the New York City Housing Authority.** (Analysis by Professor Oscar Newman, New York University; adapted from *The New York Times,* October 26, 1972, p. 41. © 1972 by The New York Times Company. Reprinted by permission. Photo by UPI.)

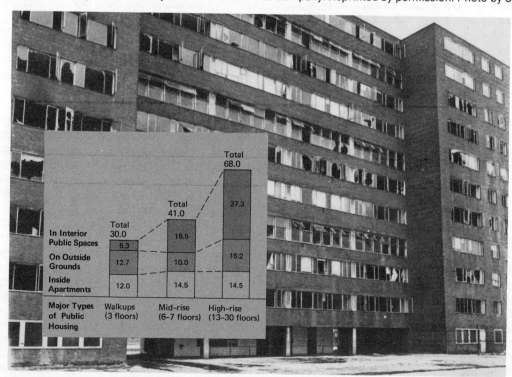

Major Types of Public Housing	Walkups (3 floors)	Mid-rise (6-7 floors)	High-rise (13-30 floors)
	Total 30.0	Total 41.0	Total 68.0
In Interior Public Spaces	5.3	16.5	37.3
On Outside Grounds	12.7	10.0	16.2
Inside Apartments	12.0	14.5	14.5

Involvement in aggressive situations may also result in a state of dissociation, or detachment, in which one views his own actions or those of others with little emotional involvement. Bernhardt, one of the men who refused to take part in the Mylai massacre, is reported to have had such an experience:

He was not moved by compassion as he watched the slaughter but by a sense of how ridiculous and illogical it all seemed. "I wasn't really violently emotionally affected. I just looked around and said, 'This is all screwed up.'" . . . What he does remember best are a few gruesome vignettes—one soldier, in particular, who laughed every time he pressed the trigger. ("He just couldn't stop. He thought it was funny, funny, funny.")

[Lelyveld, 1969, pp. 1, 26, quoted in Opton, 1971, p. 67.]

Reducing guilt

During the socialization process most individuals learn to feel guilty about certain forms of aggressive behavior. The idea of murdering another human being is repugnant to most people. In order for an incident such as Mylai to occur, these moral constraints must be removed.

The group may provide "sanctions for evil" (Sanford and Comstock's term, 1971) in a variety of ways (Duster, 1971). Members of a group might feel, for example, that what they are doing is morally required. In fact, many of history's most bloody, aggressive acts have been characterized by a feeling of righteousness. Nazis were saving their country from the greedy exploitation of the Jews when they exterminated over 6 million people. During the Inquisition heretics were tortured and executed so they would be saved from the tortures of hell.

In order to defend the United States against communism, the enemy in Vietnam had to be defeated, and only the army could do that. Each soldier owed his complete loyalty to the army. Loyalty to the group is more important than any other consideration and, indeed, obliterates the individuality of the individual. Soldiers' uniforms constantly reinforce the lesson that they are part of the army and not individually responsible. These beliefs combine to produce an ideology for massacre.

If an individual feels that he is not personally responsible for his actions and is simply carrying out orders—a line made famous by Adolf Eichmann—he may feel little guilt and engage in extremely aggressive acts. In Chapter 1 we saw the intense levels of aggression manifested by subjects "under orders" to inflict electric shocks (Milgram, 1963). When told to do so, 65 percent of the subjects inflicted the maximum level of shock possible, a level several steps higher than that at which the person being shocked pounded on the wall for mercy. Replications of the obedience experiment have yielded rates of subjects' inflicting the maximum level of shock as high as 85 percent (Rosenhan, 1969).

This same kind of blind obedience to authority may have contributed to the Mylai massacre. A survey of a national sample of 989 persons, representative of the American population over eighteen, was conducted two months after the Calley trial. At the beginning of the interview, before the Calley trial was mentioned, the respondents were given a hypothetical situation: "Soldiers in Vietnam are ordered to shoot all inhabitants of a village suspected of aiding the enemy—including old men, women, and children" (Kelman and Lawrence, 1972, p. 45). Then the respondents were asked what they thought most people would do in this situation. Sixty-seven percent of the respondents replied that they thought most people would follow orders and shoot. Fifty-one percent said that they themselves would shoot if placed in this situation; they seemed to consider following orders a moral obligation that outweighed any other consideration. As one respondent said: "I'm a great disciplinarian. In this type of situation, if I had been told to do it and trained to do it, I would follow orders" (Kelman and Lawrence, 1972, p. 45).

Further, when the members of the sample were questioned about their attitude toward the Calley trial, 58 percent disapproved of the trial against Calley; 34 percent approved; and 8 percent had no opinion. Interestingly, the reason given most frequently by those disapproving of the Calley trial was that "it is unfair to send a man to fight in Vietnam and then put him on trial for doing his duty." As one respondent who disapproved of the trial said: "They should not draft a man, then send him to prison for doing what he is sent out to do" (Kelman and Lawrence, 1972, p. 45). Those who approved of Calley's being tried most frequently supported their position by saying that "even a soldier in a combat situation has no right to kill defenseless civilians and anyone who violates this rule must be brought to trial" (Kelman and Lawrence, 1972, p. 44).

Studies such as Milgram's work on obedience and the Calley survey raise the question of the potential of Americans to follow orders, even when the orders contradict their own moral standards. Clearly, not everyone obeys orders no matter what they are. Not all of the subjects in the electric-shock experiments inflicted the maximum shock, nor did all of the soldiers under Calley's command follow his orders to kill unarmed civilians. Yet both the results of the electric-shock experiments and the answers to the hypothetical questions about following orders and killing unarmed civilians suggest that a majority of Americans feel they must follow orders—no matter how aggressive these orders are. Of course, making inferences from their answers to questions about a hypothetical situation as to what people would do in the actual situation is a risky business. However, the results "suggest quite strongly . . . that there is a *readiness* for violent actions of the type committed by Calley and his men in large segments of the American population" (Kelman and Lawrence, 1972, p. 81).

Conversation among group members may also be an effective technique for developing rationalizations and social support for violent activities. Schell has described such a search for justification:

At dinner . . . the pilots began to make jokes in which they ridiculed the idea that the bombings they guided were unnecessarily brutal by inventing remarks that might be made by men so blood thirsty that they took delight in intentionally killing innocents. The joke tellers appeared to bring out their remarks with considerable uneasiness and embarrassment, and some of the pilots appeared to laugh unduly long in response, as though to reassure the tellers. . . . "Bruce got a bunch of kids playing marbles," said Major Nugent. The group laughed again. "I got an old lady in a wheelchair," Lieutenant Moore said, and there was more laughter. . . . Lieutenant Moore was so severely racked with laughter that he could not swallow a mouthful of food, and for several seconds he was convulsed silently and had to bend his head low with his hands over his mouth. Tears came to his eyes and to Major Nugent's. "Oh, my!" Lieutenant Moore sighed, exhausted by all the laughing. Then he said, "I didn't kill that woman in the wheelchair, but she sure bled good!" Nobody laughed at this joke. A silence ensued. Finally, Captain Reese suggested that they might find out what movies were playing on the base that night.

[Schell, 1968, pp. 139, 142, quoted in Opton, 1971, pp. 55–56.]

Guilt is also reduced when the target of aggression is *dehumanized.* We feel empathy with other human beings, and so, in a sense, we also hurt ourselves when we injure others (Feshbach, 1964). But if we conceive of another as not being human, the inhibitions against acting aggressively toward him are reduced.

There is ample evidence that at least some American soldiers began to think of the Vietnamese as nonhuman. The army names for the Vietnamese—"gook," "dink," and "slope"— suggest the feelings the Americans had for the people. As one private from Texas said: "No one has any feelings for the Vietnamese. . . . They're lost. The trouble is, no one sees the Vietnamese as people. They're not people. Therefore, it doesn't matter what you do to them" (Schell, 1968, pp. 43–44, quoted in Opton, 1971, p. 55).

Inhibitions against injuring another are also reduced when feedback from the victim is reduced. The inhibiting effect of feedback has been shown experimentally. For instance, in an experiment in which subjects had been made to feel aggressive and were then allowed to administer electric shocks to a confederate, victims who consistently maintained eye contact with the subjects received significantly fewer shocks than victims who consistently averted their gaze (Diebold, 1971). In an electric-shock obedience experiment, it was also found that when subjects had an opportunity to observe the suffering of their victim, they were less likely to administer severe shocks (Milgram, 1965b).

Modern technology has created destructive weapons that afford very little—if any—feedback. Pilots who bombed villages in Vietnam were not immediately aware of the damage done. In this connection, it is interesting to recall Lorenz's thesis that signs of surrender in the victim inhibit the aggressor. Long-range, sophisticated weaponry has eliminated many of these cues.

Summary

In general, the expression of aggressive feelings depends on the relative strengths of the aggressive impulse and the negative consequences of the aggression, or the restraining forces. Two main variables appear to affect the strength of restraining forces: (1) fear of punishment and (2) feelings of guilt.

Any variable that reduces the chances of the person's being punished should similarly reduce his fear of being punished. In the anonymity of a group, the chances of any one individual's being punished are reduced. A number of studies have shown that increasing anonymity increases the amount of aggressive behavior. Further, even if the objective possibilities of being punished remain constant, any variable that decreases the prominence of the consideration of a possible punishment will increase the incidence of aggression.

The idea of murdering another human being is repugnant to most people. In order for an incident such as Mylai to occur, the guilt that most people would feel about murdering has to be reduced. This can be done in a number of ways. The group may sanction the act by emphasizing that what is being done is morally

required. If an individual feels that he is not personally responsible for his actions and is simply carrying out orders, he may feel little guilt about engaging in extremely aggressive acts.

Conversation among group members may also reduce guilt by providing social support and rationalization for violent activities. If people dehumanize the enemy, their guilt over murdering him is reduced. And inhibitions against injuring another are reduced when feedback from the victim is reduced, as it is by our modern technology of destructive weapons that afford very little—if any—feedback.

Controlling Aggression

By discussing many of the variables that lead to, or are otherwise related to, aggressive behavior, we have implicitly recognized methods that could be used to control that type of behavior. However, since controlling violence is such an important contemporary problem, these implications should be made explicit.

First, however, one might ask *why* aggression should be controlled, since violence has been part of human history for thousands of years. Admittedly, deciding that violence should be controlled involves a value judgment—that there are more constructive ways to deal with human problems. With the ever increasing efficiency of destructive weapons, man's failure to control aggression may mean his destruction. The potential of nuclear war has been present for so long that people may have become accustomed to it. Still the threats of possible destruction are real.

The beginning of this chapter reviewed statistics showing that violence within our society is increasing rapidly. We saw, for instance, that personal crime is increasing faster than the population. Factors that seem to contribute to violence are themselves on the increase: The frustrations and stresses involved in contemporary urban life are increasing. Visualize some of the stresses on someone who lives in a large city, such as New York: Every day the individual contends with frustration, feelings of anonymity, helplessness, and alienation. Without some effort to control aggressive behavior, our society

FIGURE 6-19 Man of the future.

may move to a level of aggression that will make the 1970s seem like a tranquil era. (See Figure 6-19.)

Before we consider ways of controlling aggression, it should be emphasized that the suggestions are speculative and only loosely based on research findings. In contemporary American society a number of factors contribute to violence—including unemployment and drug use. Once a violence-inducing situation is entrenched, it is difficult to distinguish determinants of violence from its consequences. For instance, do feelings of helplessness lead to aggression, or does aggression lead to feelings of helplessness? Further, it is not clear whether or not overt aggression occurs only when several variables are working simultaneously. If this is true, several factors might also have to be functioning simultaneously in order for violence to be controlled. Evidence from controlled, rigorous experiments is simply not available in many of these areas.

One might contend that social psychologists should refrain from making applications until they have firm evidence that they can apply. Perhaps this position has merit, but unfortunately the only alternatives to acting on the limited information we now have are either to do nothing or to act on the basis of common sense. Further, each decision, whether it is to do something or not to do something, influences the expression of violence. A mother's praising her child after his first fist fight increases his potential for violence, and a city council's not acting to correct some of the grievances of ghetto residents also increases the potential for violence. Since, obviously, not all action will be suspended until all the evidence is in, acting on the best evidence available seems the most sensible approach.

Controlling violence is a two-step problem: First a decision has to be made as to what will decrease violence, and second, that decision has to be implemented. Implementing some of the following suggestions would be difficult because it would involve social change, which—as we saw in Chapter 1—is usually resisted. For instance, giving urban dwellers more responsibility over their living conditions would involve changes in local government, and persons and institutions presently holding power are not going to welcome relinquishing it.

A research program on the effects of brain damage

At present relatively little research is being done on the relationship between brain damage and violence. Assessing the extent and generality of the relationship would be a basic step toward understanding the psychology of violence. For example, how many violent criminals are suffering from a form of brain damage that causes them to be violent? Traditional methods of rehabilitation with such men may be futile until their medical problems can be controlled.

Modification of child-rearing practices

Two generalizations emerged from the discussion of child-rearing practices: (1) Rewarded behavior tends to reoccur, and (2) children learn by imitating what their parents do. These two findings suggest that parents should not reward aggressive behavior and, more importantly, should not act aggressively themselves. Assuming that most of you will be or already are parents, these generalizations are of obvious personal relevance to you. How might you personally apply reinforcement and modeling techniques? To teach your child nonviolence, you would praise him when he demonstrates control of an aggressive impulse. You would also, to the extent that you reasonably could, refrain from aggressive behavior yourself in situations where such behavior might be expected. For example, you would substitute logic and reason for spankings and harsh words when the child misbehaved.

A crash program on the effects of television on aggression

Although the Surgeon General's Advisory Committee concluded that a modest relationship exists between the viewing of violence and aggressive behavior, the research on the effects of television has not yet provided conclusive or completely consistent evidence. What is urgently needed is a series of long-term field studies to determine the variables that influence the effects of televised violence. Since children spend so much time viewing television, isolating these variables should be a top priority research project.

Guns and aggression

Two experts on criminal homicide have estimated that "probably less than 5 percent of all known killings are premeditated, planned, or intentional" (Wolfgang and Ferracuti, 1967, p. 189). The other 95 percent occur in the heat of passion or as the result of one person's intention to harm, but not to kill, another. The availability of a gun makes it easier for an individual to use the weapon impulsively. (See Figure 6-20.) Earlier in the chapter we saw that the presence of a gun can increase the intensity

of electric shock subjects are willing to inflict.

These findings suggest the need for stricter gun legislation—especially the regulation of handguns. In further support of this proposal, it has been found that some countries with very strict gun control laws have much lower homicide rates than the United States. In Japan, for instance, it is illegal for any resident—except members of the armed forces, the police, ballistics researchers, and sporting marksmen—to own a handgun. The use by those permitted to have handguns is very carefully regulated. In 1970 the total number of murders in Tokyo, with a population of 11,398,801 people, was 213. During the same period 1,117 murders were committed in New York City—which has a population of 7,895,563 (Halloran, 1971). Although there are many differences between Japanese and American society, which might account for the different homicide rates, police officials in Japan feel that their gun laws—coupled with their very strict drug laws—have significantly reduced the incidence of homicide.

FIGURE 6-20 The explosive impact of a pistol is captured in this high-speed photograph. Guns are readily available and offer an easy, immediate, and dramatic outlet for aggressive impulses. (Leonard Kamsler)

Decreasing the level of frustration

Since frustration often results in aggression, one obvious way to reduce the incidence of aggression is to reduce the incidence of frustration. This is easier said than done. There was some progress in civil rights during the 1960s and early 1970s, for instance, but the progress has not kept pace with the rising level of black expectations. Even after the upheaval of the civil disorders of the 1960s and early 1970s, community action has sometimes been slow. Attempts to relieve frustration will only be successful if (1) the persons affected are not given unrealistic expectations of what is possible, and (2) the persons implementing change progress at a rate that is consistent with realistic expectations.

Decreasing anonymity

Urban living arrangements foster anonymity. City residents who live in a high-rise apartment house may neither know nor want to know their neighbors. Although the values and traditions of the group foster this kind of impersonal anonymity, so do the physical arrangements of the apartments. In the usual high-rise apartment house, there are no provisions or incentives for groups of tenants to meet, and therefore occupants are discouraged from spending time outside their own apartments. Earlier in this chapter we saw that the crime rate was significantly higher in high-rise buildings. One obvious implication of this finding is that families should not be placed in high-rise buildings in large public housing projects. Of course, walk-up buildings would mean a lower density of people—about fifty units to an acre. In most parts of the country, however, this lowered density would not be a problem. Where high-rise housing is the only housing solution possible, the tenants should be encouraged to have a stronger proprietary interest in the interior spaces, or provision should be made to make those spaces safer through good lighting, television monitoring, or the frequent presence of security personnel. Attention should also be devoted to designing buildings and communities in a manner that curtails crime. See Box 6.

BOX 6

DESIGNING A CITY TO BRING PEOPLE TOGETHER

All too often cities separate people. Sometimes in the largest, most populated cities, people feel the most lonely and alienated. In some of the new cities being built today, however, the human dimension has been taken into account. These cities are being developed to provide for people's needs: recreational facilities, good housing, and, perhaps above all, interaction with other people.

Fostering a sense of neighborliness was one of the central goals in planning Columbia, Maryland. From the major plan down to small details, encouraging people to meet and interact was a principal concern. Rather than housing all 110,000 residents in one core city with sprawling suburbs, the designers of Columbia deliberately set up thirteen areas: twelve residential "village" groups around a "core city." Further, each of the villages consisted of a neighborhood of not more than 1,000 families grouped around shops and schools. Even mailboxes were placed to encourage interaction. They were clustered outside houses so people would meet there.

Increasing a sense of personal responsibility

Feelings of helplessness and irresponsibility may foster aggression in two ways. First, a feeling of powerlessness is, in itself, frustrating and upsetting. Second, the lack of a feeling of personal responsibility makes it easier to be violent. If you smash a window in a city-owned housing project, you are smashing the government's window, not your neighbor's.

When members of the community are given more responsibility for their own area, the results can be encouraging. In Hartford, Connecticut, for example, the author observed that the incidence of vandalism decreased considerably when the residents of a city-owned housing project were given more responsibility. Tenant committees were formed and given broad powers to regulate such matters as parking and waste disposal. The operation of a community center was turned over to the adults and children who used it; they had authority to regulate the use of the building and to prescribe dress requirements and codes of appropriate conduct for such functions as group meetings and dances. Following these developments, residents who continued to commit acts of vandalism found that they were now subject not to the impersonal threats and punishments of an absentee landlord but rather to the specific sanctions of their own peer group.

This constructive result is consistent with the increased productivity and improved morale observed in industrial settings when the members of a group participate more fully (Coch and French, 1948). However, increasing the level of community involvement may be difficult. The residents may be so alienated that they may resist becoming involved, or authorities with vested power may not wish to see more community participation. These and other problems can make increasing the level of participation difficult.

Investigation of the effect of speed on aggression

As noted earlier, there is some evidence suggesting that the use of speed leads to aggressive behaviors. For instance, the director of a free medical clinic in San Francisco's Haight-Ashbury section is convinced that the enormous increase in violent crimes in the district is related to the increased use of speed (Smith, 1969). Since speed is widely used in some groups, ascertaining its effects on aggression is of great importance.

Countering the sanctions for evil

As we saw previously, the inhibitions against acting aggressively are reduced if the group justifies the aggression as moral or if the enemy is dehumanized. If one feels that a certain aggressive act is critical to the obtaining of something that is right, then the aggression can

be justified. Similarly, if an enemy is seen as not being human, the inhibitions against acting aggressively are reduced.

Countering the sanctions for evil may be extremely difficult, since they are part of our moral code. These sanctions involve our assumptions of basic values—assumptions of what is important and how we should act. Perhaps we should reassess our basic values, including our assumptions of what is important and how it should be attained. For instance, the most basic defense against dehumanizing the enemy might well be to change our basic assumption about the meaning of "being a human" from "people who are like us" to "all men" so that there is a greater emphasis on all human worth (Sanford, Comstock et al., 1971).

Prison reform

Seventy percent of prison inmates released return to patterns of crime, and their crimes are more violent after imprisonment than they were before (Zimbardo, 1971b). These facts make it very clear that the present prison system is failing to rehabilitate prisoners. Instead, the prisons are training grounds for aggression.

How could prisons be improved? The social psychologist who performed the prison experiment discussed in Chapter 2 and who has had extensive contact with several ex-convicts has made a number of suggestions—some of which follow (Zimbardo, 1971b).

The cloak of secrecy must be removed from prisons so that the taxpayers, the people who pay to maintain the system, can see what is going on. At present, "neither lawyers, judges, the legislature, nor the public are allowed into prisons to ascertain the truth unless the visit is sanctioned by 'authorities' and until all is prepared for their visit" (Zimbardo, 1971b, p. 9).

There should be an ombudsman in each prison—someone responsible only to the courts, state legislature and the public—who could report on violations of human rights within the prison. The presence of such an ombudsman would act as a check against dictatorial guards and violent inmates, and would eliminate the prisoners' sense of being totally powerless under the system.

The training given the guards should be

improved. At present, most guards receive minimal training—similar to that given to the guards in the prison experiment—for their demanding work. Social scientists and business-training personnel could help design a training program to prepare the guards more adequately for their work. As part of that training, the guard's role would be changed from that of "someone who keeps order" to that of a "teacher" or "counselor" and the prisoners would be "trainees." Bonuses and advancement for each guard would be contingent on the trainees learning "new social and technical skills which will enable them to leave the 'training-rehabilitation' center as early as possible, and not come back" (Zimbardo, 1971b, p. 10). Since the guard's own advancement would depend on the prisoners' learning, the guards would be highly motivated to teach the prisoners, and the training program would emphasize that rewards are a much more effective means of teaching than threats and isolation.

Many people are in jail because they are deficient in the social skills needed to interact successfully with other people. As we saw earlier in this chapter, one man who killed his girl friend didn't understand why his saying that he was leaving her would make her angry. Professional social scientists could train prison inmates who are deficient in social skills by providing them with an opportunity to be responsive to others and to be responsible for themselves. After an initial training period, some of the more responsive prisoners could act as psychiatric aides and social workers and care for the more disturbed prisoners. Working with others and contributing to their rehabilitation would seem to be an excellent way for these people to improve their sense of self-worth and community—as well as a good way for them to learn how to interact with others.

Further, the relationship between the prisoner and his community must be maintained. So that the prisoner can cope with the rapidly changing society to which he will eventually return, his continued relationships with his friends and family should be encouraged. More educational opportunities should be offered so that the prisoner can be a self-supporting member of his community when he is released. Once a prisoner has finished his rehabilitation and is judged ready to return to society, "there should be no stigma attached to his training, no need to report to prospective employers that he/she was a 'prisoner'" (Zimbardo, 1971b, p. 11). At the present time employers are extremely reluctant to hire ex-cons, so it may be very difficult for an ex-prisoner to support himself honestly.

Although there is no guarantee that implementing these suggestions will drastically reduce the incidence of violence on the contemporary American scene, there is some evidence to indicate that their implementation would probably have some positive effect. And if we continue without changing some of the conditions that produce violence, there is every reason to believe that the incidence of violence will continue to rise—as it has in the past decade.

SUMMARY

The pervasiveness of violence and aggression in our society impels us to study these phenomena. Why are people aggressive? What can be done to control aggression? If our society is not to become even more aggression-centered, it is imperative for us to answer these questions.

1. Definition of "Aggression" Aggression is alternatively used in an *emotional, motivational,* or *behavioral sense.* Aggression is popularly thought to be an outgrowth of the emotion of anger. It is also common to focus on the motives behind an act of violence: An act is aggressive when it is intended to hurt another. However, because of the difficulty of determining people's emotions and motives, many psychologists have tended to dismiss the motivational and emotional approaches and to focus more on observable behavior. According to a behavioral view, aggression is simply a response that injures another. In real life, however, the three aspects of aggression frequently operate together.

2. Causes of Aggressive Impulses: An Overview What causes aggressive impulses in people?

Six different answers have been given: (1) People are naturally aggressive; (2) they are aggressive because of crowding; (3) they learn to be aggressive; (4) they are aggressive because of frustration; (5) they are aggressive because of group pressures; and (6) they are aggressive when the negative consequences of aggression, or the restraining forces, are reduced.

3. Aggression as an Inherent Part of Human Nature Two major schools of contemporary psychological thought—the psychoanalytic theorists and the ethologists—have supported the instinct concept of violence. *Freud* saw aggression as an innate primary drive representative of the death instinct. *Lorenz* has argued that the aggressive instinct has made a major contribution to the evolution and survival of animals. However, the problem with an instinctive explanation of aggression is that it does not explain the observed variations in aggressive behavior.

Another approach to explaining aggression as an inherent part of human nature is to search for *physiological antecedents.* Electric stimulation of different parts of the brain has been shown to generate and inhibit aggression. Further, sociopaths—persons who engage in antisocial behaviors and do not experience the intensity of emotional experience that normal people do—have been found to be more responsive physiologically to virtually every event than normal persons and so may have learned not to apply emotional labels to their physiological states. Experiencing little or no guilt, they may not be motivated to avoid events that make others feel guilty. Clearly, these findings indicate that the roots of violence are multiple and complex. Although more research on the physiological correlates of aggression is needed, this approach, like the instinct approach, must be supplemented with an understanding of how the environmental setting contributes to aggression.

4. Crowding and Aggression Although it is popularly assumed that crowding has highly negative effects on human social behavior—including increasing the tendency to act aggressively—the very few studies done on the effects of crowding on human social behavior have yielded inconsistent results. *Sometimes crowding has been found to increase the incidence of aggression, sometimes to decrease aggression, and sometimes to have no significant effect.* These inconsistent results suggest that a number of variables may influence the human reaction to density. One variable found to be related to people's reactions to crowding is sex. All female groups were less aggressive in a crowded room than in an uncrowded room, and all male groups were more aggressive in a crowded room. A number of other variables— including the length of time the person is crowded, the amount of physical activity required, and whether or not the person feels crowded—may also influence the individual's reaction to crowding.

5. Social Learning Most theorists agree that learning is a major determinant of aggression. Without always intending to do so, parents administer a series of rewards and punishments for aggressive behavior, and also influence the child indirectly by serving as models that the child imitates. Correlational studies have shown that *either parental aggressiveness or parental permissiveness is related to aggressiveness in a child.*

A basic principle of learning is that *responses that are rewarded* tend to occur more frequently. This principle applies to aggressive responses as well as others. *Physical punishment* is a less efficient means of shaping behavior than reinforcement. However, if a child observes others being punished for a given act, the chances of his imitating that act may be decreased.

Imitation is another important learning process through which the child can learn aggression. Children who observe aggressive models subsequently behave much more aggressively than children who do not observe such models. The behavioral effect caused by seeing an aggressive model is influenced by a number of variables. The tendency to imitate an aggressive model is increased when the model is rewarded for his aggression or when he is powerful and dominant. Further, if the violence is seen as ethically justified, it is imitated more frequently; and if the observer is initially angry or can identify with the person who is acting violently, he will be more likely to imitate. The presence of stimuli usually associated with violence, such as a gun, increases the incidence of violence. Overt action on the part of the model is not necessary for imitation of aggressive responses to occur. An adult's saying that aggressive behavior is appropriate can increase the level of aggression.

Televised violence may also provide a model for aggression. A number of social psychologists feel that viewing televised violence *increases* a child's tendency to act aggressively. Not all agree with this view, however. There are two other positions. One, the *catharsis view*, holds that watching violent television programs may *reduce* the incidence of aggression among viewers by providing an outlet for aggressive impulses. A third view is that exposure to the various sorts of violence in the mass media has *no significant effect.*

The recent report of the Surgeon General's Advisory Committee concluded that a *"modest relationship exists between the viewing of violence and aggressive behavior."* Correlations between the number of violent television programs watched by children and their aggressive tendencies have been positive, but small. As we saw in the discussion of modeling, a number of laboratory studies have shown that viewing aggressive material increases the amount of aggression expressed by the subjects. Of course, since there are a number of differences between the experimental setting and the usual setting when one is watching violence on television, there is a question of whether or not these findings generalize to real life.

In order to be able to infer cause-effect relationships and to eliminate some of the artificialities of the laboratory work on modeling, several investigators have conducted studies to assess the effects of viewing aggressive television programs in a natural setting. The results of these studies have been inconsistent. In some, viewing aggressive programs increased the amount of violence in children who were initially highly aggressive; in others, viewing violence on television had no measurable effect; and in still others, viewing aggressive programs reduced the level of aggressive behavior.

The number and complexity of variables that influence the individual's reaction to televised violence—including the reality of the violence in the programming—may help explain the inconsistent results. Further, even if it were conclusively established that televised violence significantly contributes to the incidence of violence, the networks and the public might not be willing to renounce it.

6. Frustration and Aggression Evidence that frustration tends to arouse aggression comes from many sources. However, since frustration can produce a variety of behaviors in addition to aggression, the contemporary approach to the frustration-aggression hypothesis has been to isolate those aspects of a frustration situation that can lead to aggression. From this research, the following conclusions have been drawn: (1) *Personal attack* results in more aggression than environmental blocking; (2) *arbitrary frustrations* are more likely to result in aggression than frustration imposed for a good reason; (3) *expected* unpleasant situations are much less frustrating than unexpected ones; (4) *certain cues from the situation*—such as the presence of guns—can significantly increase the level of aggression; and (5) the *anticipated results* of the aggression determine whether it is expressed directly, indirectly, or displaced to others.

Experimental studies have shown an inconsistent relationship between expressing aggression and catharsis. Whether expressing aggression results in an increase or a decrease in tension depends on a number of other variables—including the individual's guilt about his action, his fear of punishment, and the possibility of embarrassment.

7. Aggression in an Interpersonal Context Interpersonal aggression frequently grows out of a *transaction* between two people in which a sequence of escalating violence, to which both parties contribute to at least some extent, occurs. If neither one breaks the chain of escalation, acts of extreme violence can occur. Violence tends to follow a fairly standard pattern: (1) *provocation* by one or the other of the individuals and (2) *escalation and confrontation.* In the case of police assaults, the civilian may interpret the officer's initial verbal approach as provocative. The officer may escalate his initial requests to orders and then to threats or arrests. In turn, the civilian's resistance increases. The participants' previous interactions, their expectations about each other, and their personalities contribute to the level of violence that will be reached in their ultimate confrontation.

In some segments of our society, violence is widely accepted and highly valued. Some individuals living in that type of subculture will inevitably come to accept its values and engage in a higher proportion of violent acts than people not living in such a subculture. In these *subcultures of violence,* all of the factors of usual social interaction press the individual toward acceptance of the norms. To maintain successful relationships with others who accept the premise of the subculture, he must act as expected. Sometimes a formal initiation into the group makes explicit these group values and forces him to accept violence publicly. The group's life-style and activities are predicated on its beliefs and values, and he may internalize the group norms, so that they become part of his own private beliefs, if they accord with other aspects of his personality.

8. Aggression Caused by the Reduction of Restraining Forces   The expression of aggressive feelings depends on the relative strengths of the aggressive impulse and the restraining forces. Two main variables affect the strength of restraining forces: (1) *fear of punishment* and (2) *feelings of guilt.*

Any variable that reduces the chances of a person's being punished should similarly reduce his fear of being punished. In the anonymity of a group, the chances of any one individual's being punished are reduced. A number of studies have shown that increasing anonymity increases the amount of aggressive behavior. Further, even if the objective possibilities of being punished remain constant, any variable that decreases the prominence of the consideration of a possible punishment will increase the incidence of aggression.

The idea of murdering another human being is repugnant to most people. In order for an incident such as Mylai to occur, the guilt most people would feel about murdering has to be reduced. This can be done in a number of ways. The group may sanction the act by emphasizing that it is morally required. If an individual feels that he is not personally responsible for his actions and is simply carrying out orders, he may feel little guilt about engaging in extremely aggressive acts. Conversation among group members may also reduce guilt by providing social support for violent activities. If people dehumanize the enemy, their guilt over murdering him is reduced. And inhibitions against injuring another are reduced when feedback from the victim is reduced—as it is in our modern technology of long-range weapons.

9. Controlling Aggression   The incidence of violence within our society is rising rapidly. Although evidence from controlled rigorous experiments is not available on many of the causes of violence, the only alternatives to acting on the limited information we now have are either to do nothing or to act on the basis of common sense. Acting on the best evidence now available seems the most sensible approach.

Ten ways to control violence were discussed. Intensifying the research on the relationship between brain damage and violence would be a basic step toward understanding the psychology of violence. Parents' applying reinforcement and modeling techniques to teach their children nonviolence would reduce the incidence of violence. A crash research program on the effects of television on aggression would isolate the variables that influence the effects of televised violence. Stricter gun legislation would make it more difficult for people to shoot others impulsively. Since frustration often results in aggression, one obvious way to reduce the incidence of aggression is to reduce the incidence of frustration.

Decreasing urban anonymity—through designing buildings and communities in a manner that would bring people together and increase their defensible space—would reduce crime. Giving the members of a community more responsibility in making decisions about their own area might also decrease the incidence of violence. Speed is widely used in some groups, and ascertaining its effects on aggression is important. Since inhibitions against acting aggressively are reduced if the group justifies the aggression as being moral or if the enemy is dehumanized, a greater emphasis on human worth would tend to undermine these aggressive incentives. Because the prisons, as they are presently run, are training grounds for aggression, prison reform is urgently needed.

DISCUSSION QUESTIONS

1. How do you think most people define "aggression"?
2. How does being crowded influence your emotional reactions and behavior?
3. Have you ever observed any instances of a child's acting aggressively as a result of imitating an adult or something he has seen on television?
4. How does viewing aggression on television or in a film make you feel?
5. Have you yourself ever experienced a sequence of escalating violence—either verbal or physical—in an argument?
6. Why do you think many people feel that they are not responsible for their actions if they are carrying out orders?
7. Do you feel that violence is basic to human nature? Give evidence to support your answer.
8. Why do you think parental permissiveness is related to aggressiveness in children?
9. A number of variables that increase a child's tendency to imitate an aggressive model were discussed in the text. Can you think of any other variables that might increase the tendency toward imitation? Any that would *decrease* the tendency?
10. Why do you think aggressive entertainment is so popular?
11. Can you think of any situations in which increasing anonymity would *not* lead to an increase in aggression?
12. Do you think the behavior of guards and wardens would be modified if they were required—as part of their job training—to spend two months incognito as a prisoner?
13. Under what conditions do you think crowding would make people more aggressive? Design a study to test your hypothesis. State the evidence supporting your hypothesis, your manipulation of the independent variable, your procedure, your dependent variable, and your expected results.
14. Design a field experiment to test the effect of real, as opposed to fictional, violence on children's reactions to televised violence.
15. Can you think of any aspects of a frustration situation—not mentioned in the text—that would increase the frustrated individual's tendency toward aggression?
16. How could police procedures in approaching suspects be modified so as to make the approaches less provocative?
17. Design a three-story apartment house to minimize tenant anonymity. In your plans focus on mailbox placement, entrances and exits, stairwell placement, and other interior spaces that may have common use.
18. In this chapter some suggestions for prison reform were discussed. Do you have any additional suggestions?
19. Assume that it could be proven that viewing televised violence did not stimulate you to commit violent acts but did lower your emotional reaction to violence committed by others. Would this be beneficial or detrimental to you? To society? Why?

ALTRUISM

7

BOXES

Acts of altruism abound in our society, even though they rarely command the front-page space more commonly reserved for sensational forms of aggressive behavior. (See Figure 7-1.) In a Philadelphia

suburb, for example, Joe Muldoon, a volunteer fireman, gropes his way through a blanket of smoke in a flame-filled house to rescue an infant. He feels for and finds the baby and then staggers to an open window. There another volunteer takes the baby, and Muldoon, overcome by smoke, falls to the floor (Winchester, 1969).

On a Los Angeles freeway George Valdez, forty-nine, rescues two girls involved in a serious car accident. At considerable risk to his own life, he runs across four lanes of fast-moving freeway traffic to give first aid to one of the victims as she lies inert in the fast lane of the southbound traffic. After applying a tourniquet to the girl's leg, he moves her to the shoulder of the road and then goes back to retrieve her severed leg, which has been cut off in the accident (Blank, 1970).

In San Francisco Bay two tankers collide, spreading a foul oil slick. Hundreds of birds are rescued and cleaned by swarms of volunteers working throughout the night in bird-receiving stations (White, 1971).

For six years Barkley Moore worked eighteen to twenty hours a day for seven days a week as a Peace Corps volunteer in Iran. In addition to his other Peace Corps duties, he rented a house for himself and fourteen boys, who were too poor to consider school, and became their foster father. He spent all of his $150 monthly Peace Corps salary to support "his boys," and now, out of the Peace Corps, he is still supporting these boys so that they may finish their schooling. In addition, he is paying the tuition so that eight other boys can have the same opportunity (Hampton, 1971).

After a newspaper publishes the story of George Brost, a thirty-nine-year-old salesman who is dying from an incurable kidney disease, some sixty-five persons volunteer to give a kidney. One of the volunteers, Mrs. Luedicke, who has never met George Brost, explains why she wants to give up a kidney for a total stranger: "I'm single, and he's got nine kids to live for. That's the best excuse in the world. I just need one kidney, so what's the difference" (*Newsweek,* March 4, 1963, p. 76).

The three nuns at St. Michael–St. Edward's Church in the Fort Green section of Brooklyn spend their days distributing communion, visiting the sick, helping the elderly, and walking around the neighborhood, being available to respond to the needs of the residents (Blau, 1973).

FIGURE 7-1 How likely is it that you would see this photograph of a donor giving blood carried on the front page of your newspaper? If a man were instead being apprehended for the commission of a crime, would his picture be more likely to appear on page one? (Irene Stein)

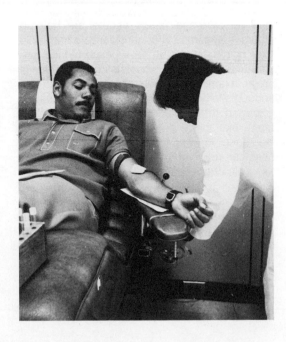

BOX 1 PROGRAMS IN ACTION

Since July 1, 1971, seven volunteer programs have come under the direction of one United States agency called ACTION. Each program is briefly described below.

Peace Corps

Organized in 1961, the Peace Corps reached a high point of 12,313 volunteers working in fifty-two countries in 1966. In 1972 there were 7,500 people working in sixty countries. Since its inception a total of 50,000 people have served in the Peace Corps.

VISTA—Volunteers in Service to America

This program is the domestic counterpart of the Peace Corps. In 1972 there were approximately 4,000 volunteers.

University Year for ACTION (UYA)

UYA is a new program organized in 1971. In 1972 it involved about 1,000 American college students, and the number participating is expected to grow. In this program a college student spends a year performing services in health, education, and housing. The student pays the usual college tuition, receives $200 per month from the federal government for his services, works under academic supervision, and receives full credit for his year's work toward his degree.

Foster Grandparent Program

This program began in 1965, and 6,000 people were enrolled in it by 1972. Each foster grandparent spends two hours daily with each of the two children assigned to him. The volunteers work twenty hours per week and are paid the minimum wage.

Retired Senior Volunteer Program (RSVP)

RSVP is a part-time program for people who want to help in their community but who do not need extra income. The projects in this program include tutoring and helping at hospitals and libraries in the volunteer's community. The 1972 enrollment was about 2,000, but ACTION hopes to increase the number to 40,000 eventually.

Service Corps of Retired Executives (SCORE) and Active Corps of Executives (ACE)

In both SCORE and ACE business executives offer professional advice to small businessmen. The only difference between the two programs is that SCORE involves retired executives, and ACE involves executives who are still working. In 1972 SCORE had 4,200 part-time volunteers, and ACE had 2,500 (*U.S. News & World Report*, November 27, 1972, pp. 86–87).

In all of these cases people are helping others, sometimes with considerable danger to their own safety or at the expense of their free time and frequently without being paid. Each of these examples is selected from day-to-day accounts in newspapers and magazines, usually buried in the back pages. These acts, and many like them, give strong evidence of the existence in many people of an apparently unselfish motivation to help others. (For an example of governmentally sponsored altruism, see Box 1.)

What makes people help others? What leads people to recognize the need for help? Which variables in a situation elicit helping? These questions will be explored in this chapter as well as the question of what contributes to nonhelping, or apathetic, behavior. We would not even recognize altruism as a phenomenon were it not for the fact that it stands in sharp contrast to the indifference, apathy, and reluctance of many people to intervene in someone else's behalf. If the "Good Samaritan" effect is to be noticed, there must be others who are not Good Samaritans.

A clear example of apathy is provided by the reactions of thirty-eight people who witnessed the murder of Miss Catherine Genovese without even calling the police (Rosenthal, 1964). After working late as a manager of a local bar, Miss Genovese returned to her home in a middle-class area of Queens at about 3:20 A.M. The murderer was lurking in a lot where Miss Genovese parked her car. As she left her car, he followed her and then attacked her with a knife. She screamed, "Oh my God, he stabbed me! Please help me! Please help me!"

Some lights went on, and windows were raised. A man called out, "Let that girl alone!" The murderer was frightened off and got into a car and drove away. Yet none of the thirty-eight people watching called the police.

The lights in the apartment building went out, and the killer returned to again attack Miss Genovese, who was now trying to get to her apartment building. When the attacker stabbed her a second time, she screamed, "I'm dying! I'm dying!"

Windows were opened; lights went on; and once again the assailant got into his car and drove away. But still no one called the police.

The assailant returned once more. By this time Miss Genovese had crawled to the entrance of her apartment house. Here the killer found her and made his third and fatal attack. (See Figure 7-2.)

The murder took thirty-five minutes. When the police were finally called, at 3:50, they were at the scene in two minutes. Had they been called earlier, Miss Genovese would have lived.

Why didn't any of these people call the police? All of them found this question difficult to answer. Police investigating the case reported that most of them said they were afraid but could not explain what they feared. One couple, who had put out their bedroom lights so they could see the action more clearly, shrugged and said they didn't know why they had not called. One man said he went back to bed because he was tired. A housewife said she thought it was a lover's quarrel.

The extent of the apathy shown by the Genovese case increased interest in altruism among social psychologists. Psychologists in general have long studied man's defects and problems—such as prejudice, anxiety, aggression, conflict—rather than his virtues. In a sense, social scientists have been problem-oriented, perhaps in an effort to learn how to cope with these problems. But with the publicity given the Genovese case, apathy and its opposite, altruism, have emerged as central areas in social psychology research.

Many published studies of altruism refer to the Genovese case as showing a peak of human indifference. If people would not, when they were safely in their homes, telephone the police to stop a murder in progress, how apathetic had contemporary urban life become? Further, this one incident is not an isolated one. Other crimes have been reported in which passers-by did not call the police and simply ignored the incident. For instance, shortly after the Genovese case a secretary was raped in an office building in the Bronx and escaped naked down the stairs, pursued by her attacker. She shouted for help to a crowd of nearly forty people who had gathered near the entrance. No one helped, and the assailant

FIGURE 7-2 At 3:20 A.M., March 13, 1964, Miss Catherine Genovese drove into the parking lot at Kew Gardens railroad station and parked (1). Noticing a man in the lot, she became nervous and headed along Austin Street toward a police telephone box. The man caught and attacked her (2) with a knife. She got away, but he attacked her again (3) and again (4). (From A. M. Rosenthal, 1964.) (*The New York Times*)

began dragging her back up the stairs. Fortunately, police who were coincidentally passing by rescued her (*The New York Times,* May 6, 1964, p. 38).

Definition of "Altruism"

The term "altruism" is one of the most difficult to define in all of social psychology. The examples of helping behavior given in Box 2 provide some idea of how elusive the concept is. In this section we will focus on both the motivational and the behavioral approaches to the term "altruism"—the same approach that was used when we considered the definition of "aggression."

Motivational definition

One definition of altruism emphasizes the motives, or reasons, for performing a helping act. According to this definition, a helping act is altruistic when it is motivated primarily by an anticipation of its positive consequences for another individual. The altruistic individual acts more out of concern for another than for "what he's getting out of it." This motivational definition seems to accord closely with popular usage, at least as the author's students have defined the term.

However, when discussing the motivational definition of altruism in class, students have expressed doubts that *any* behavior is motivated primarily by a concern for others rather than the self. Support for this student skepticism may be obtained from prominent psychological theories; both reinforcement theories and psychoanalytic theories hold that all behavior is basically motivated by self-concern. This line of reasoning argues, for instance, that if a soldier throws himself on a grenade, he does so to maintain consistency with his ideal self, to win the admiration of others, or for other self-advancing reasons that he may not be conscious of.

As we saw when aggression was being defined, assessing the reasons for any action is extremely difficult. As we shall see when we

---

BOX 2 WHAT IS ALTRUISM?

Is this altruistic?
(Circle your choice)

	yes	no
1. J makes a twenty-five-dollar contribution to charity and gets a chance to play tennis with a celebrity.	yes	no ✓
2. C, a white college student, spends eight hours per week tutoring a black child from a city ghetto.	yes ✓	no
3. S, a white college graduate, joins VISTA.	yes ✓	no
4. N, an army chaplain, rescues ten wounded men while under heavy enemy fire.	yes ✓	no
5. Following President Eisenhower's 1968 heart attack, Y volunteered to donate his heart to save Eisenhower.	yes	no
6. T, a fireman, rescues an elderly woman trapped in a fire and is injured.	yes	no
7. N, a high-school student, spends ten hours each week cleaning trash from a local river.	yes	no
8. J, a heart surgeon, saves a patient's life with a skillful operation.	yes	no

Compare your reactions to these situations with those given by another student. You may be surprised to see the extent of your disagreement. There are no right or wrong answers. What you classify as altruism depends, of course, on how you define the term.

consider some examples of altruism in real life, persons may not be completely aware of their motives. A decision to help someone may be made very quickly without any conscious thought. Or persons may distort their motives to make them conform to what they know is socially acceptable. Because of the difficulty of determining people's thoughts and feelings, many psychologists have tended to dismiss the motivational approach and to focus more on observable behavior.

Behavioral definition

According to a behavioral view, altruism is any conduct that helps another, regardless of the helper's motives. Research based on this definition focuses on behavior that is clearly beneficial: helping someone who has fallen down, giving directions to a stranger, reporting a lost wallet, giving up a few hours or minutes to participate in experiments, and so forth. All of these acts would qualify as altruistic, since they help another, even though they could be motivated by selfish reasons or could be accidental.

Although this approach avoids some of the assessment problems posed by a motivational approach, it too poses problems. Classifying all helpful acts together may obscure important differences in their motivational antecedents. Altruism that is motivated by a belief that it will be rewarded—sending flowers to your employer's sick wife—may be determined very differently from altruism that is motivated solely by your concern for someone who needs help. Helpful acts done by people in occupations that require them to act helpfully—the "institutionalized altruism" of priests, social workers, surgeons, and teachers—may have still different determinants. See Box 3.

Further, the individual's assessment of *why* the other person is helping him influences his reaction to the aid. For instance, if you thought someone was being kind to "win points" with you, your reaction would be quite different than if you thought there was no ulterior motive behind the kindness.

Even though the behavioral definition does involve some problems, it is the one most commonly used in the scientific literature, since it is easier to measure behavior objectively.

Recording whether or not people help someone who has fallen down is far easier than attempting to measure the subject's motives. Further, there are many situations in which helpful results are crucial regardless of the motives. Had any of the spectators at the Genovese murder called the police, for whatever reason, Catherine Genovese might have lived. She would not have cared about their underlying motives.

Is Altruism Learned or Instinctive?

Complicating the definition problem further is the debate over whether altruism is learned or instinctive.

Helping as an instinct

Campbell (1965) has argued that altruistic behavior may be in part instinctive. Since any particular individual, animal or human, is more likely to survive when living with others than when living alone, the more cooperative, social beings would be more likely to survive and reproduce, so that gradually—over thousands of years—evolutionary processes would favor the development of innate social, helping motives.

To emphasize the adaptive value of social life, consider how well you would survive if you lived a completely solitary life. You would have no one with whom to share ideas; you yourself would have to obtain everything you needed; if you were attacked, no one would be available to help you; and you could not reproduce yourself.

Experimental evidence concerning the adaptive value of social behavior comes from studies of aggregations of animals. Allee has suggested that the tendency of animals to cluster together is a basic biological principle, since the survival rate of groups is higher than that of individuals. In testing his hypothesis, Allee found that animals in groups survived longer in an experimentally created hostile environment than individuals did:

In one simple but dramatic demonstration, goldfish were placed either singly or in groups of ten into bowls of poisoned water (containing colloidal silver).

BOX 3 PUBLIC ATTITUDES ABOUT THE ALTRUISM OF TWENTY OCCUPATIONS

Four samples of subjects, including 296 college students, 50 secretaries from a small town in Connecticut, and 50 teachers from the public schools of the same small town, were asked to rate the relative altruism of twenty different occupations. The subjects were asked to rate an occupation as "1" if they felt that "this group is concerned mainly with the good of others and . . . will sacrifice a great deal for others." An occupation was to be rated as "2" if the subjects felt that those in the group "are out to help others but when actions involve important interests of their own, they will protect their own interests." And if the subjects felt that the members of a group are "usually out for themselves but they will make some effort to help others if they have nothing to lose by doing so," the occupation was to be rated as "3." In spite of differences in educational level and geographical location, the subjects gave remarkably similar ratings. These ratings, arranged from most to least altruistic, are shown below.

Occupation	Average Altruism Rating
Clergymen	1.29
Physicians	1.46
Psychologists	1.65
Psychiatrists	1.67
Dentists	1.71
Judges	1.71
High-school teachers	1.84
College professors	1.87
Lawyers	1.97
Law enforcement officials	2.06
TV news reporters	2.27
U.S. Army generals	2.42
Newspaper columnists	2.45
Plumbers	2.54
TV repairmen	2.64
Auto repairmen	2.72
Labor union officials	2.72
Executives of large companies	2.81
Politicians	2.86
Used-car salesmen	3.37

[From Rotter and Stein, 1971, Table 3.]

Repairmen, labor union officials, executives of large companies, politicians, and used-car salesmen did not get high altruism ratings. Do you agree with the ratings given here?

The seventy goldfish placed individually in the bowls lived an average of only three hours, whereas the seventy fish exposed to the same poisonous conditions in groups of ten lived an average of almost eight and one half hours.

Subsequent chemical analysis showed that the goldfish secreted a slime which changed much of the silver into a less toxic chemical. In nature, such a "sharing" of the potentially fatal dose of poison might allow some animals to escape death if the dose were moderate, or at least to gain time for wind, rain, or some other intervention to rescue some members.

[Allee, 1931, cited in Ruch and Zimbardo, 1971, p. 463.]

The view that man may be instinctively altruistic provides an interesting alternative to the traditional view in psychology that man is naturally self-centered. Both reinforcement theory and psychoanalytic theory agree in assuming that people are basically motivated by hedonistic concerns. According to reinforcement theory, people tend to learn best that behavior which produces pleasurable effects. According to psychoanalytic theory, people are basically selfish, id-driven creatures.

However, as we saw in the discussion of whether or not man is instinctively aggressive, proving the existence of an instinct in man is extremely difficult. The question has been approached by analyzing the existence of altruism in infrahuman animals, but the evidence about animal altruism has so far proved very difficult to interpret.

For a while it looked as though altruism existed in as unexpected a place as the albino rat. Two investigators found that albino rats were more likely to press a bar when it lowered a struggling rat than when it lowered a block of plastic (Rice and Gainer, 1962). One interpretation of this finding is that the rats were responding to the distress of another rat. However, before we conclude prematurely that altruism is at work, we must eliminate alternative explanations. The distressed rat is not as quiet as a plastic block, and the "altruistic" rat might have been seeking as much to reduce an unpleasant sound as to lend help to his fellow rat. Further work supports the hypothesis that the reactions in the distressed-rat experiment were simply a reaction to the unpleasant sounds (Lavery and Foley, 1963).

Helping behavior has also been observed in higher forms of animals. Hebb and Thompson (1968) noted that "there is definite evidence in other animals of . . . something we call altruism, defined as intrinsically motivated concern for others" (p. 744). For instance, chimpanzees have been observed to give food to chimps in adjoining cages. The food given, however, was their least preferred, and it was usually given only when it was solicited (Nissen and Crawford, 1936).

As is the case with human helping behavior, it is difficult to determine the reasons behind the helping acts. Were the chimps giving food in order to gain more food from another? Or to help another? It is very difficult to draw any conclusions concerning motives from comparative research.

Even if altruism were basic to human nature, an instinctive explanation would not explain the variations in helping behavior. Some people are much more helpful than others. Those who are more concerned with themselves are less likely to be altruistic (Berkowitz, 1970). Self-centered persons are less likely to realize how their behavior will affect others or to empathize with others. By contrast, those who feel that the welfare of others depends on their own actions and who assume a personal responsibility for others are more likely to act altruistically (Schwartz, 1970). Human altruistic behaviors, whether partly instinctive in nature or not, have been so influenced by learning that studying the instinctive component may not be very helpful.

Learning to be altruistic

How children learn to be altruistic is not yet completely understood. However, it seems obvious from everything discussed in Chapters 2, 3, and 6 that two primary conditions facilitate the learning of any behavior: being rewarded for performing the act and observing someone else engaging in the act (and getting reinforced or at least not punished for it). Altruism is no exception. A number of studies have shown the influence of reinforcement and imitation on the incidence of altruism.

The Role of Reinforcement As we have seen repeatedly, behavior that is rewarded tends to reoccur more frequently than unrewarded behavior. A number of studies have shown that when altruism is rewarded—either materially or with social reinforcers—the tendency of subjects to be altruistic in that particular situation increases. For example, one investigator found that four-year-old children were more likely to share marbles with another child if, after sharing, they were rewarded with bubble gum (Fischer, 1963).

A number of studies have shown that reinforcement has immediate effects, but the existing experimental studies do not allow us to assess the long-term effects of reinforcement or the extent to which the altruism reinforced in one situation generalizes to other situations. Evidence on these questions might come from naturalistic studies of the effects of reinforcing altruism.

Another consideration is the question of what reinforces. Clearly, material rewards do: Children will learn to behave in a certain way if they are given candy. And social reinforcers also produce learning: If a parent shows approval when a child helps, the helping behavior will be reinforced.

Empathy may also reinforce altruism (Aronfreed, 1970). Once a child learns to empathize with others—that is, to experience their thoughts, feelings, and motives vicariously—his empathy may provide another source of reward and punishment. If you can feel pain when you see another's pain, you may attempt to reduce his pain and so reduce your own. If you feel joy when another person is happy, you may wish to make him happy and so increase your own happiness.

For those believing in a self-centered psychology the concept of empathy may be a difficult one to accept. Yet there is evidence that empathy does occur. In several studies the physiological reactions of observers exposed to another person's suffering have been measured. For instance, two investigators found that observers exposed to someone who was in pain showed peripheral autonomic indices of pain themselves (Bandura and Rosenthal, 1966).

Further, it has been shown that empathy can result in altruism. In one study the physiological reactions of subjects who observed an experimental confederate receive rewards and punishments were measured. Since previous work has shown that a person's believing that he is similar to another person increases his tendency to empathize, some of the subjects were told that they were similar to the confederate, and others were not told that they were similar. The "similar" subjects showed greater physiological reactions to the confederate's plight, reported more feelings of empathy, and behaved more altruistically (Krebs, 1970).

The extent to which empathy results in altruism depends on a number of situational and personality variables. Two of these, acquaintance with the victim and the individual's tendency to take action to relieve his own feelings of discomfort, have been shown to increase the amount of altruism (Liebhart, 1972). If you know a person who is in trouble,

you would be expected to have greater empathy for him than for a stranger. Empathizing with the problems of a friend is much easier than imagining the suffering of a stranger. Further, the more likely one is to take action to relieve his own discomfort, the more likely he is to act altruistically to relieve the distress of another.

The Role of Models It has been shown repeatedly that observing a helpful model encourages the observer to be helpful himself in that particular situation. By analogy it might be argued that long-term personality differences in helping behavior are similarly learned: If a child has a parent who is helpful and who tells him about helping, he will grow up to be a helpful person. He will have observed and identified with his helpful parent and will thus become a helpful adult. Helpful parents would be expected to have helpful children—according to the identification hypothesis.

Although there have been relatively few studies on the relationship between the altruism of parents and that of their child, and in those studies that have been done the results have not always been consistent (as noted in Kohlberg, in press), several studies have offered support for the identification hypothesis. The idea for one very interesting study originated during the Eichmann trial, in which, amid the horrors revealed about the treatment of Jews in concentration camps, testimony was given about a Christian who rescued Jews from those camps. A California rabbi saw this rescue attempt as a "glimmer of redemption" from the "horrendous image of man" revealed in the Eichmann trial and wrote a magazine article urging that Christian rescuers be identified and honored. This idea was picked up by NBC, and on Christmas Day, 1962, NBC presented a network documentary in which some of the rescuers were interviewed.

As a result of all of this publicity, several social psychologists sought to interview some of those who had risked their lives to save Jews in order to see if there were any personality traits common to all of the rescuers (London, 1970). Finally, after a great deal of searching, twenty-seven rescuers were located in the United States and in Israel. All of these people were asked to describe their rescue activities, the events that led up to their becoming involved in rescue work, and personal details about themselves, which revealed their personality characteristics.

During the course of the interviews the investigators found a wide variety both of altruistic acts and of motives underlying the rescue attempts. The amount of risk the rescuers assumed varied widely. For some it was a life-and-death matter; for others it involved minimal personal risk. And in still other cases minimal risks were involved when the rescue attempts began, but these became much greater as circumstances changed. The rescuers' motives varied greatly, too. Some began the rescue attempts deliberately out of a sense of benevolence. Others became involved because of social pressures from others to help.

Still others, some of whom may have misunderstood the risks involved or how long they would have to continue taking them, "fell into" the rescue business through almost chance events. For instance, one famous German rescuer, who spent four years doing rescue work at tremendous personal cost and who saved about 200 people, reported that he initially became involved in rescuing Jews when his secretary came to him, said that the Germans were going to kill her Jewish husband, and begged him to hide her husband in his office over the weekend. Although the German rescuer initially did not believe his secretary's fears were realistic, he did allow her husband to hide. When the German found that the fears of the Jews were justified, he became increasingly involved in the rescue operation.

Although situational variables or miscalculations may explain the rescuer's initial helping efforts, they do not account for the help performed over a long period of time. The single factor that emerged most frequently during the interviews was the important effect of a strong identification with a parent who had very firm opinions on moral issues and who served as a model of moral conduct. The importance of this factor is shown in the comments made by the German rescuer:

My mother said to me when we were small, and even when we were bigger, she said to me . . . "Regardless of what you do with your life, be honest. When it comes the day you have to make a decision, make the right one. It could be a hard one. But even the hard ones should be the right ones."

[London, 1970, p. 247.]

Other studies have also shown the important influence of identification with a moral parent on altruistic behavior. For instance, two investigators found that boys who were themselves rated as generous also saw their fathers as warm and nurturing (Rutherford and Mussen, 1968). And a group of active civil-rights workers were found to have a close relationship with at least one altruistic parent (Rosenhan, 1970).

In the face of the general apathy of most Germans and the residents of German-occupied countries who refused to take any action to interfere with the massacre of some 6 million Jews, the fact that a small minority of Christians did help rescue some Jews stands as a testimony to the personal strength of the rescuers. Generalizing from such a small sample is hazardous, but the importance of parental identification in motivating these courageous people, who helped under highly hazardous conditions, suggests the extreme importance of identification as an influence on altruism.

Summary

Some have argued that altruistic behavior may be in part *instinctive*. Since any particular individual is more likely to survive when living with others than when living alone, the more cooperative, social beings would be the more likely ones to survive and reproduce, so that gradually—over thousands of years—evolutionary processes would favor the development of innate social, helping motives. This view provides an interesting alternative to the traditional view in psychology that man is naturally self-centered, but proving the existence of an instinct in man is extremely difficult. The evidence about animal altruism has so far proved very difficult to interpret. Further, even if altruism were basic to human nature, an instinctive explanation would not explain the variations in helping behavior. Some people are much more helpful than others.

Two primary conditions facilitate the *learning* of any behavior, including altruism: *reinforce-*

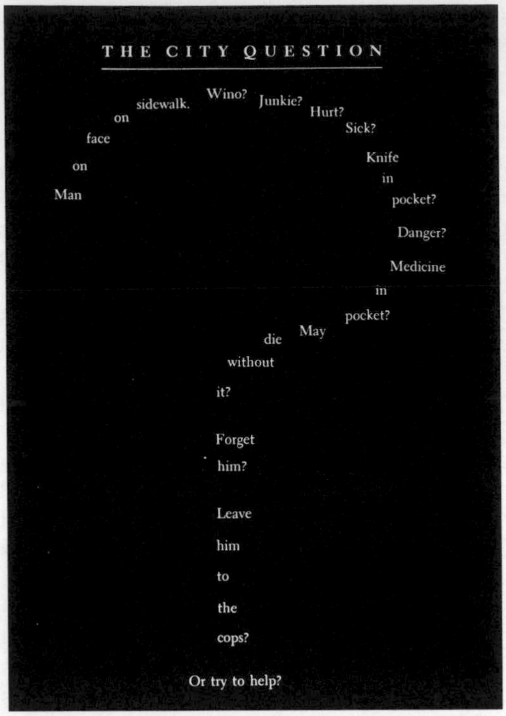

THE CITY QUESTION

Man
face
on
sidewalk.
Wino? Junkie?
on
Hurt?
Sick?
Knife
in
pocket?
Danger?
Medicine
in
pocket?
May
die
without
it?
Forget
him?
Leave
him
to
the
cops?
Or try to help?

FIGURE 7-3 (From *Street Poems* by Robert Fro-
man © 1971, Saturday Review Press.)

ment and *imitation*. A number of studies have shown that when altruism is rewarded the tendency of subjects to be altruistic in that particular situation increases. Another consideration is the question of what reinforces. Clearly, material rewards do and so do social reinforcers. Empathy may also reinforce altruism. If you can feel pain when you see another's pain, you may attempt to reduce his pain and so reduce your own. There is evidence that empathy does occur and that it can result in altruism. Acquaintance with the victim and the individual's inclination to take action to relieve his own feelings of discomfort have been shown to increase the amount of altruism motivated by empathy.

It has been shown repeatedly that *observing a helpful model* encourages the observer to be helpful himself in that particular situation. If a child has a parent who is helpful and who tells him about helping, he will grow up to be a helpful person. Although the relatively few studies on the relationship between the altruism

of parents and that of their children have not yielded consistent results, they have offered some support for the identification hypothesis. For instance, when Christians who helped rescue Jews in Germany and German-occupied territory were interviewed, an intense identification with a parent who had very firm opinions on moral issues was found in all of the rescuers.

Awareness of a Need to Help and the Acceptance of Personal Responsibility

Despite differences as to the definition of altruism and whether altruism is learned or instinctive, most social psychologists agree that people will engage in helpful acts to the extent that they are (1) *aware* of the need for help, (2) predisposed to *accept personal responsibility* for helping, and (3) *motivated* to help. Variables relating to the awareness of the need for help and to the acceptance of personal responsibility are discussed here. (See Figure 7-3.) Motivation will be covered in later sections.

The bystander effect

When you interpret events, the reactions of other people are a very important source of information, particularly when an event is ambiguous, as we saw in the discussion of social comparison theory. Suppose you were participating in an experiment in which you and another subject were filling out market research questionnaires. During the course of the experiment an accident occurs in an adjoining room. A loud crash is followed by a woman's screaming, "Oh, my God, my foot . . . I . . . I . . . can't move it. Oh . . . my ankle. I . . . can't get this . . . thing . . . off me." The cries continue for about a minute before becoming gradually more subdued. Finally, the woman gasps that she is going outside and thumps to the door, knocking over a chair as she pulls herself to her feet. The entire incident takes about two minutes.

If you are like the many subjects who have participated in such staged-distress studies, you would be much less likely to help the victim when you were with another person than when you were alone. In this particular experiment, for instance, 70 percent of the subjects who were alone when they heard the staged accident tried to help, whereas only 40 percent of those who were with another person whom they did not know did so (Latané and Rodin, 1969). Repeatedly, it has been shown that people are much less likely to help in an emergency when they are with others than when they are alone—the so-called bystander effect. The bystander effect is not limited to emergencies. It has been shown that groups of people are less likely to take action than individuals when an experimental confederate demands to be admitted to a room in which either the single subject or the group is working (Levy, Lundgren, Ansel, Fell, Fink, and McGrath, 1972).

What is it about being with other people that inhibits the individual's taking action? One theory is that in order for an individual to take action, he must first notice that something is happening, decide whether it really is an emergency, and then decide if he will take personal responsibility for action (Latané and Darley, 1969). (See Figure 7-4.) At each point in the individual's decision-making process, the presence of other people can influence the way he reacts.

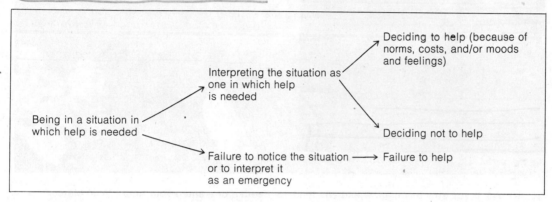

FIGURE 7-4 Steps involved in helping.

Many emergencies begin as ambiguous events. A man staggering may be suffering from a coronary, or he may be drunk. A person who has fallen may be seriously injured, or he may only be embarrassed at his own clumsiness. Before a bystander can decide what to do, he must first decide what is going on. (See Figure 7-5.) This is not to say that the decision process is a highly conscious, clearly thought out one. Quite the contrary. The individual may not be fully aware of all the factors influencing his interpretation or even of the fact that he is making an interpretation. When one interprets events, he looks to the reactions of other people for information, particularly when an event is highly ambiguous. If you were in a situation in which someone fell in an adjacent room, you might not be sure what had happened. To find out what others thought, you might discuss the situation with them, or you might infer their reactions from their actions. If they ignored the incident and continued with their work, you might infer that they did not think anything serious had happened. And other persons in the room might be watching you to see your reaction.

In the process of each person's covertly watching the other to see how he is reacting lies a common source of error. Each person may be attempting to hide his feelings, to appear "cool." No one wants to be the first to appear upset and to act in a foolishly inappropriate manner. It may be safer not to act than to act and risk embarrassment. Being with others, then, may distort the expression of feelings, as each person tries to avoid overreacting. As a result, the *group members may define the situation as less critical than they would if they were alone* and so be much less likely to take action. Until someone positively indicates that he feels the situation is a serious one, each member may conceal his belief that the situation may be

FIGURE 7-5 If you saw this man, would you think he needed or wanted your help? (Alan Mercer)

serious. Each individual is supported in his cool interpretation by the cool interpretation of the others, and so the distortion grows.

Once exposed to a general situation, the members of a group may be predisposed to avoid interpreting a given event as an emergency, for the knowledge that someone needs help may be upsetting. They may not know what to do or may not want to take the time and effort to help. (See Box 4.) Thus both by defining the significance of the situation and by providing social support for avoidance, the reactions of others are crucial in determining one's *awareness* of the need to help.

Further, the presence of other people influences the individual's decision about whether he will take personal responsibility for action. If you are faced with an emergency when you are alone, you know that if you do not help, no one else will. When others are present, however, each person in the group may think that someone else will help. Further, since all of the

people present are equal in status in their role as experimental subjects, it is not clear which one should help. Thus being with others *diffuses the responsibility* for helping.

The importance of both of the group-induced variables, *minimization of the situation* and *diffusion of responsibility,* were shown by the subjects' reactions in the lady-in-distress experiment. After the experiment the investigators interviewed the subjects to determine why they had reacted as they had. Those who had helped usually said they did so either because the fall sounded serious or because they were unsure about what had happened and felt they should investigate. Many of those who had not helped also claimed they were unsure about what had happened (59 percent). Some were unsure but decided that it was not too serious (46 percent). However, the noninterveners claimed that in a "real emergency," a situation that was serious and in which they alone were responsible, they would be among the first to help the victim.

BOX 4 AN EXTREME CASE OF THE BYSTANDER EFFECT

It is estimated that over a million people know of children who are physically abused by their parents but have not reported the case to the authorities (Gil, 1968). The following case, in which a mother had abused her child over a period of years, illustrates the extreme to which a conspiracy of silence and of inactivity may be carried:

"Jody was four years old when her parents brought her to Colorado General Hospital. She had suffered from severe child abuse all her life and demonstrated one of the most severe cases of malnutrition that we have seen. She weighed only seventeen pounds and was covered with bruises and abrasions. . . .

"For years Jody's mother had expressed to her husband and other members of the family and community her concern about this child and the manner in which she was able to care for her. No one had been willing to accept his responsibility, and no help was offered the mother [until she arrived at the Child Abuse Center in Denver]."

[Helfer and Kempe, 1968, pp. ix, x.]

How clear does the need for help have to be? Below is Jody upon admission to the University of Colorado Medical Center. (Courtesy, Drs. Ray E. Helfer and C. Henry Kempe, from their book, *The Battered Child*, 1968, p.x.)

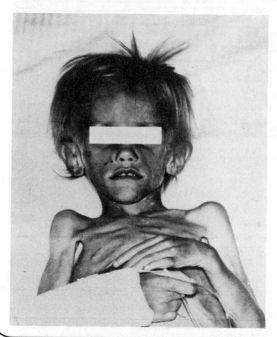 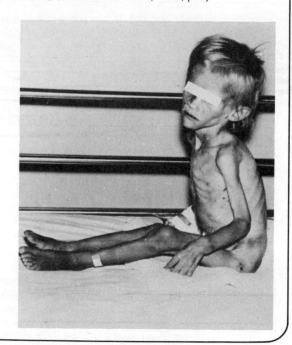

Diffusion of responsibility was also clearly shown by the subjects' reactions. Twenty-five percent of the subjects reported that they thought other people would or could help, so that they alone were not responsible. Regardless of whether these were truthful accounts of the subjects' reactions or mere rationalizations for their failure to help, these results do emphasize that the nonintervener's behavior was consistent with his interpretation of the event and influenced by diffusion of responsibility.

From this analysis of the decision-making process involved when one decides to take action in an emergency—or indeed in any situation—it follows that any variation in the situation that makes the individual less likely to interpret the event as one demanding action or that diffuses the responsibility for taking action among the individuals present will influence the incidence of helping.

Variables that influence the subject's interpretation of the situation

Suppose you were working with an experimental confederate who remained very calm during the lady-in-distress experiment. During the accident the other person looked up, shrugged his shoulders, and continued working on his questionnaire. Seeing his cool reaction would make you more likely to interpret the accident as one that did not require action. Just these results were obtained in a variation of the original lady-in-distress experiment. The presence of a nonresponsive confederate significantly influenced the incidence of subjects' helping. You will recall that 40 percent of the subjects helped when they were with another naïve subject. In the presence of a nonresponsive confederate, however, only 7 percent of the subjects helped. This finding replicates an earlier finding that subjects in a room that is filling up with smoke are less likely to take action if a calm, passive confederate is present (Latané and Darley, 1968). In both of these experiments the subjects may have looked at the calm, cool confederate and decided that nothing was wrong: "The other person is just continuing the experiment, and I'll look stupid if I make a fuss." Further confirmation of the importance of the reactions of others in defining a situation has been obtained in a more recent study (Bickman, 1972).

The bystander effect is thought to be caused by the ambiguity of the situation and the lack of response by others present in the situation. If the emergency is very clear, however, one would predict that the presence of others would have less of an inhibiting effect on the individual's helping.

Confirmation for this hypothesis was obtained in an experiment (Clark and Word, 1972). Accidents of varying ambiguity were staged. In one condition the subjects heard a staged accident in which a maintenance man fell over and cried out in agony—an incident that was clearly an emergency. The other subjects heard a more ambiguous incident—the same fall but without any verbal signs of injury. As predicted, when subjects were with others and heard the ambiguous accident, the incidence of helping was significantly lower than when they were alone. In the presence of others who remained calm, the subjects interpreted the event as one that did not require any action on their part. In fact, most of those who did not help reported that they thought the maintenance man had just dropped something. When the staged event was one that was very clearly an emergency, people alone still responded faster than those in groups, but the differences in frequency of helping were much smaller than when the accident was ambiguous.

Variables that influence the decision to accept responsibility

Taking action in an emergency is an emotionally arousing experience, which people may try to avoid. If you were a subject in the lady-in-distress experiment and heard the fall, you might wonder what you should do; you might feel capable or incapable of acting; you might wonder what others were going to do; and you might consider your own obligation to help. In a group setting all of your negative feelings about getting involved may be rationalized if you think someone else will take action. However, if aspects of the situation make it difficult for you to believe that others will help, you may be more likely to feel responsible and to take action. Research has demonstrated that several variables in the situation can counter the bystander effect.

If a person is forced to get involved or to feel responsible for the well-being of another, he is more likely to help the other person. This hypothesis was clearly supported in an experiment (Tilker, 1970). Using the basic Milgram electric-shock procedure (in which a "teacher" administers increasingly severe electric shocks to a "learner"), the investigator had naïve subjects observe the experimental procedure. Those given total responsibility for the other person's well-being and maximum feedback from that person regarding his need for help stopped the experimental procedure significantly earlier than the subjects given less responsibility and less feedback.

Diffusion of responsibility does not occur if the other bystanders are seen as being unable to help. In one experiment subjects were tested either alone, with another subject who was in an adjoining cubicle, or with another subject who was in another building (Bickman, 1971). An emergency was staged and the incidence of helping recorded. The incidence of helping did not differ significantly between subjects tested alone and those tested with another person thought to be unable to help. As was found in earlier studies, subjects who thought that another person was in a position to help helped significantly less frequently than subjects who were alone. To produce the bystander effect, the others must be seen as being able and likely to take action.

When another bystander does seem clearly competent to handle an emergency, an individual may feel much less responsible. In the lady-in-distress experiment, for instance, if you had been told that one of the other subjects "was a premedical student who worked three nights a week in the emergency room of a local hospital as part of a training program," you would probably feel that he was the obvious person to render help and so feel that you were off the hook. Just this result has been obtained in an experiment (Schwartz and Clausen, 1970). As predicted, the subjects responded less quickly when they thought that one of the other subjects was medically competent.

People may not help because they don't know what to do. Their concern about exposing their own inadequacies may make them likely to rationalize that others will help. However, if people are given precise instructions about how they can help, they are more likely to take action. In one study a seizure was staged. Half of the subjects had been told by the "victim" that he was subject to seizures, and if one occurred, he should be given the medication in his coat pocket. Other subjects were given no information about what to do in the event of a seizure. Eighty-two percent of the subjects who knew what to do tried to help, and only 61 percent of those who had no information tried to aid the victim (Schwartz and Clausen, 1970).

Countering the bystander effect

If group pressures to play down an emergency, diffuse responsibility, and avoid embarrassment make people in groups less likely to help

others than people who are alone, then what can be done to counter these group pressures? Sometimes a person who is in a group helps others in emergencies. Have you ever done so or at least witnessed such altruism? A recent study showed that under some conditions even supposedly blasé New York City subway riders in groups could be aroused to come to the aid of someone in trouble (Piliavin, Rodin, and Piliavin, 1969).

Three investigators staged collapses on a subway in New York City and measured the frequency with which bystanders helped. The collapses were staged in a very dramatic manner. On each trial the victim, a man between twenty-five and thirty-five, stood next to a pole in the center of the "critical area" of a subway car. (See Figure 7-6.) About a minute after the train began to move, he staggered forward and collapsed. He remained stretched out on the floor, looking at the ceiling, until he received help. All of the collapses followed the same basic pattern, but the type of victim (drunk or ill) was varied. For the drunk trials the victim "smelled of liquor and carried a bottle wrapped tightly in a brown bag"; for the ill trials the victim carried a cane.

A tabulation was made of the time it took men to respond when there were from one to three men, four to six men, and seven or more men in the immediate area of the collapse. (Since the incidence of helping has generally been found to be much higher among males than females, the investigators assumed that the number of males in the immediate area would be the best indicator of the number of potential helpers.) As shown in Table 1, the average speed of response was consistently faster for groups of seven or more. These results clearly do not show the bystander effect—the inhibiting effect of the presence of a number of people on helping.

In the subway-collapse experiment the bystanders could see the victim collapsed on the floor of the subway, so that the need for help was clearer than in the lady-in-distress experiments, in which the victim was in another room. Also, in the subway experiments the subjects could see what others in the situation were doing (or not doing), so that it was much more difficult for subjects to rationalize their not helping by thinking that someone else had.

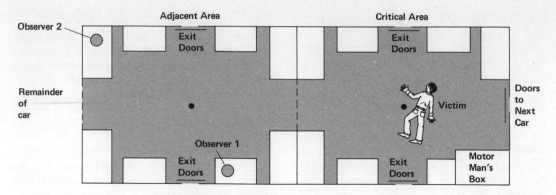

FIGURE 7-6 Layout of adjacent and critical areas of the subway car. (Adapted from Piliavin, Rodin, and Piliavin, 1969, Figure 1, p. 291.)

Table 1. The Effects of Group Size on the Average Speed of Helping

Number of Males in Immediate Area	Average Time Taken to Help Ill Victim (in Seconds)	Average Time Taken to Help Drunk Victim (in Seconds)
1–3	15	309
4–6	18	149
7 or more	9	97

Source: Adapted from Piliavin, Rodin, and Piliavin, 1969, Table 5.

Further, the apparent cause of the emergency had a highly significant effect on the speed of helping. For instance, when one to three men were in the immediate area of the collapse, the average time that elapsed before they helped the ill victim was 15 seconds; the average time taken to help the drunk victim was 309 seconds. The bystanders may have feared that helping the drunk would expose them to violence or foul odors, whereas helping the invalid may have seemed easier, and the invalid may have been seen as being in greater need of help.

But what would happen if the victim were very ill? One might expect more help when the need is greater. Yet, paradoxically, the more the victim needs help, the less capable the bystanders may feel, thereby making them less likely to help. Support for this hypothesis has been obtained in a more recent subway experiment. As in the earlier study, collapses were staged. In this study, however, the victim with a cane either "bled from the mouth" following his collapse or did not. As predicted, the bystanders were slower to help the bloody victim

than the victim who was not bleeding. The fear and revulsion that many people feel at the sight of blood—coupled with a lack of knowledge about how to help—may have increased the costs of helping (Piliavin and Piliavin, 1972).

Summary

It has been shown repeatedly that people are much less likely to help in an emergency when they are with others than when they are alone—the so-called *bystander effect.* What is it about being with other people that inhibits the individual's taking action? In order for a person to take action, he must first notice that something is happening, decide whether it is really an emergency, and then decide if he will take personal responsibility for action. At each point in the individual's decision-making process, the presence of other people can influence the way he reacts. When people are with others, they are likely to *minimize the seriousness of the incident.* Further, the presence of other people *diffuses responsibility* for taking action. The importance of both these group-induced variables has been shown by the lady-in-distress experiments.

Any variation in the situation that makes the individual less likely to interpret an event as one demanding action or that diffuses the responsibility for taking action among the individuals present will decrease the incidence of helping. When experimental confederates who remain very calm during the emergency are present, the incidence of helping decreases significantly. If the emergency becomes very clear, however, the presence of others has less of an inhibiting effect on the individual's helping.

If aspects of the situation make it difficult for the individual to believe that others will help, he may be more likely to feel responsible and to take action. If a person is forced to accept responsibility for the well-being of a person in distress, he is more likely to help the other person. Diffusion of responsibility does not occur if the other bystanders are seen as unable to help. However, if another bystander clearly seems competent to handle the emergency, the individual is less likely to help. Conversely, increasing the individual's own feelings of competency makes him more likely to help—as does giving people precise instructions about exactly how they can help.

If conditions in the situation counter the group pressures to play down the emergency, to diffuse responsibility, and to avoid embarrassment, people who are in a group will help others in emergencies. Groups of supposedly blasé New York City subway riders could be aroused to come to the aid of someone in trouble—although they were much quicker to aid someone who was ill than someone who was drunk. In the subway experiment the bystanders could see the victim collapsed on the floor, so that the need for help was clearer than in the lady-in-distress experiments, in which the victim was in another room. Further, in the subway experiment the subjects could see what others in the situation were doing, so that it was much more difficult for them to rationalize their not helping by thinking that someone else had helped.

An Overview: Why Do People Help?

In reply to the question of why people help, three main answers, each of which overlaps the others, have been given. Before they are discussed in detail, an overview of the three may be helpful.

Norms

During socialization children are taught rules of appropriate conduct. "Be nice to others"; "help those who have helped you"—these and many other rules, including rules about when one should help others, have been learned by most members of our society. If a properly socializated human being departs from these norms, he subjects himself to negative consequences, which may include disapproval by others and feelings of guilt. To avoid these feelings, the individual adheres to the various norms. Two helping norms have been explored extensively: (1) the norm of "social responsibility," that a person should help others who are dependent on him, and (2) the norm of "reciprocity," that a person should treat others as they have treated him.

A cost analysis

In contrast, a cost analysis is that the incidence of helping behavior in a particular situation depends completely on the relationship between the costs of and the rewards for helping. Costs would be the negative consequences to the individual; rewards, the positive consequences (Darley and Latané, 1970).

Moods and feelings

Still a third analysis of helping is that moods and feelings influence the incidence of helping. If someone is in a good mood, his "warm glow" leads to a greater incidence of helping. When an individual is happy, he may be less self-preoccupied and so be more open to the needs of others (Berkowitz, 1972). People may also help others in order to minimize their own feelings of guilt. If you wrong another person, say deliver an electric shock to him, you may feel guilty. One way to relieve your guilt is to do something nice—either for the person you originally wronged or for someone else. Recent experiments have identified two other feelings that may stimulate altruism when someone is injured, even if the helping person has not caused the injury. One of these feelings is based on the human desire to believe that the world is a fair place. Seeing someone unjustly injured disturbs this belief. The second feeling is one of sympathy—a feeling of compassion toward people who have been harmed by another.

BOX 5 REASONS FOR JOINING THE PEACE CORPS

One of the most frequently asked questions of a Peace Corps volunteer is "Why did you join?" Two investigators analyzed the replies 2,612 applicants gave to the question "What do you hope to accomplish by joining the Peace Corps?" (Gordon and Sizer, 1963).

Many of the volunteers indicated that they were interested in helping people. Some expressed a belief in the Peace Corps itself and said they wished to further its goals: working for peace, helping to improve international relations, and participating in the progress of developing nations. Further, the Peace Corps was said to offer people a chance to do something to help others attain a better life.

More than half of the applicants mentioned potential personal gains: experience, knowledge, and a chance to develop as individuals. Many described the personal satisfaction that would result from helping others or from feeling that they were involved with a worthwhile cause. The advantage mentioned most frequently was the opportunity the Peace Corps provides for gaining intercultural experience: learning about other cultures, knowing and working with people of other nations, and becoming familiar with other customs and ways of life.

General moral and ethical beliefs provided the rationale for many applicants: One should join because this is the right thing to do. A duty to one's country or to one's fellow-man motivated others.

In addition to summarizing the general themes, the two authors did a content analysis of the narrative statements. The answers given most frequently are reported in the table below.

Why Volunteers Say They Wish to Join the Peace Corps

Answer	Percentage of Volunteers Who Gave This Answer
1. To help people, humanity	35
2. To improve international relations, represent the United States, promote international understanding	31
3. To gain intercultural experience	27
4. Belief in the Peace Corps as an organization or an instrument of social change	24
5. To serve or strengthen the United States, become a better United States or world citizen	24
6. To work for peace or against war	23
7. To give of oneself, serve, work hard	19
8. To learn or gain general or specific experience	19

Source: Adapted from Colmen, 1966, Table 7.

These answers illustrate the overlapping of the three approaches to altruism. Although more than half of the applicants mentioned potential personal gains, many also cited moral and ethical beliefs. Although none of the volunteers mentioned moods or feelings, these may have played a role—perhaps without the volunteers being fully aware of them. For instance, some may have joined to expiate guilt about living in an affluent country while much of the rest of the world is starving.

Overlapping of the three approaches

Aspects of the situation will determine which of the three approaches is the "best" explanation of altruism. In some situations the social responsibility norm may be so thoroughly learned that it completely explains altruism. Imagine, for example, the tension that would be aroused by not helping an aged parent who is in real need. In other situations to which the social norm responsibilities do not apply as clearly, the occurrence of altruism may depend on the relative effort required. The cost analysis may be a valuable supplement to a normative analysis in situations calling for a considerable amount of effort (Berkowitz and Daniels, 1964).

In some situations moods and emotions may also overlap norms. If you are feeling particularly happy, you may be more responsive to social norms. Also, a situation that makes the individual feel guilty may make the social norm salient: If you feel guilty about neglecting your parents, you may be more likely to help someone else. Further, people who are performing the same helping acts may be doing so for different reasons. See Box 5 and Figure 7-7.

The Normative Explanation of Helping Behavior

The "social responsibility norm," which requires that a dependent individual be helped, and the "reciprocity norm," which calls for the repayment of benefits received from others, have been theorized to account for a number of helping behaviors (Goranson and Berkowitz, 1966).

The social responsibility norm

The moral norm that an individual should help those who are dependent on him and need his assistance is widely accepted in our society. When an individual who has adopted this norm learns that a dependent person needs his help, he feels obligated to aid that person, even when no direct return benefits are anticipated. At times people act to help others, not for material gain or social approval, but simply to do what is right (Berkowitz, 1972).

Public appeals to contribute to a charity frequently focus on the fact that a given group needs help and it is up to you, the public, to provide it. No promise is made that a contribution will directly benefit the donor; pointing up the existence of the need and the personal responsibility are thought to be sufficient to elicit help. (See Figure 7-8.)

FIGURE 7-7 Why do you think this Peace Corps volunteer is helping? Because of norms? The relative costs and rewards? Guilt feelings? (ACTION/Peace Corps)

We will make it...

With some help from our friends.

UNITED FUND OF GREATER NEW YORK
It's a lot of New Yorkers helping each other.

FIGURE 7-8 This advertisement illustrates the common assumption that there is a norm of social responsibility that motivates people to help others who are in need. (Courtesy, United Fund of Greater New York)

Normatively Motivated Helping Will people help when there is little in it for them? According to a social responsibility explanation, they will. This theory contrasts with another view of human social interaction—the social exchange theory—which holds that all of an individual's actions are determined by the rewards he thinks they will bring. Although a few people, who are "virtually saints," may work "without thought of reward and even without expecting gratitude," most people require an incentive, such as the expectation of reciprocal or anticipated benefits or the social approval of others, if they are to help others (Blau, 1968, p. 453).

External incentives are obviously important in determining whether or not a person will help, but a normative approach to altruism holds that many people will help even when they do not expect reciprocal or future benefits. In support of this approach, a series of studies has shown repeatedly that American college students will work hard to help someone who needs help even when there is little in it for themselves, the recipient does not know who has helped him, and the experimenter is not aware of their helping.

If someone else knows that you are helping him, your helping could be argued to be motivated by your desire to win the social approval of the person you are helping. But what if the opportunity for the recipient to thank his benefactor were eliminated? Would subjects still help even if they thought that their partner would not learn of their help for several weeks, if not months? To find out, two investigators led their subjects to believe that they were taking part in a test of supervisory ability in which the subjects ("workers") would be supervised by a peer (the "supervisor"). Half of the subject-workers were told that if they performed well, their supervisor would win a prize; the other half were told that their performance had nothing to do with the supervisor's chances to win a prize. Even though the subjects thought that their supervisor-partner would not learn of their help for several weeks, the subjects worked harder when they thought their performance influenced their partner's chances (Berkowitz and Daniels, 1963).

Again, however, it is possible to interpret these altruistic acts as reflecting a selfish motivation. Even if the partner did not know that the subjects had helped him, the experimenter knew what had happened; and this could have motivated the subjects to work hard in order to win the experimenter's approval. However, the results of a subsequent worker-supervisor study cast doubt on this explanation. Experimenter awareness of helping was manipulated by telling half of the subjects that the experimenter would keep close watch on their productivity throughout the session. The other half of the subjects were told to put their work in a closed carton that would not be opened for more than a month. Whether or not the experimenter was aware of the subjects' helping had no significant effect on the amount of help the subjects gave their partners. Again, subjects who believed that their partner was dependent on them worked harder than those who thought that their partner was not dependent (Berkowitz, Klanderman, and Harris, 1964).

Thus people have been shown to help others

332
Social Psychology and Modern Life

who are dependent on them when there is no possibility of social approval from either the recipient or the experimenter. If one wants to play the game of "find the reward," he might argue that the subjects' reward for helping was their own knowledge that they had done the right thing. However, to argue self-reward may be equivalent to saying that people are motivated to adhere to social norms of helping.

Limits to Dependency in Eliciting Altruism   We have seen that the presence of need or dependency elicits help even when the helper has nothing to gain and, moreover, may even have to suffer a little to give the help. But there are limits to the effectiveness of dependency. People do not automatically help everyone who needs help or contribute to every charity appeal they see. Some types of dependency are much more apt to elicit help than others. (See Figure 7-9.)

The importance of the cause of dependency has been shown in several studies. For instance, two investigators analyzed the contributions made to *The New York Times' 100 Neediest Cases* (Bryan and Davenport, 1968). The greatest number of contributions were made to cases in which the victims were in need because of circumstances beyond their control, such as children who had been abused and persons suffering from physical illnesses. Cases involving psychological illness and moral transgressions drew comparatively few contributions, perhaps because these persons' troubles were seen as "their own fault."

Experimental support for the importance of the cause of dependency has been obtained (Berkowitz, 1968). Dependency that was thought to have been caused by forces beyond the individual's control elicited much more altruism than dependency for which the individual was believed to be personally responsible. If the recipient's need is his own fault, dismissing him may be easy: "It's all his own fault, so why should I be put out?"

Another influence on the incidence of helping behavior is the degree to which the dependency of another interferes with one's perceived freedom. Sometimes people react with resentment when they feel they are being pressured to help another. A charity appeal that overdramatically emphasizes the extent of need may create resentment in its audience rather than sympathy.

One analysis of this dependency boomerang is provided by Brehm's reactance theory (1966). As we saw in Chapter 2, a central postulate of this theory is that people wish to feel free to choose their own behaviors. Any attempt to restrict an individual's perceived freedom of behavior results in psychological reactance, and the individual then attempts to reassert his freedom. If you feel pressured to go to a party, you may refuse to go. Similarly, any appeal that curtails the prospective helper's freedom will decrease his inclination to help.

Reactance may be aroused in a number of ways. If a person is ordered to help, he obviously does not feel that he has made a free choice.

FIGURE 7-9 How likely do you think you would be to give money to this minstrel beggar? What considerations might influence your decision? (Charles Gatewood)

In one experiment it was found that college students were more willing to help someone requiring assistance when they had a choice about helping than when they were required to help (Horowitz, 1968). Further, the circumstances surrounding the appeal may influence whether or not reactance is aroused. On Halloween you expect to see children out collecting goodies and sometimes soliciting for UNICEF But how would you feel if you opened your door and saw an adult in Halloween costume taking up a collection for UNICEF? You might feel that pressure was being put on you to donate; you might feel resentful and give less than you would to a child or not give at all. Just this result was obtained in one experiment (Fraser and Fujitomi, 1972).

Adhering to the social responsibility norm

To say that most persons in our society have learned a social responsibility norm does not explain the great variations observed in helping behavior. People may act very generously in some situations and be completely unresponsive in others. In this section variables that increase adherence to the social responsibility norm will be explored.

Observing a Helping Model Observing another person who is helping may make the norm salient and increase motives to help. In Chapter 6 and earlier in this chapter, we noted that people are likely to imitate what they see others do—and this applies to altruism too. In a number of studies it has been found that both adults and children are more likely to be helpful after observing a model helping. Two investigators, for example, found that motorists were more likely to stop and help a woman fix a flat tire if they had previously driven past a model helping a confederate fix a flat tire (Bryan and Test, 1967). Passers-by have been found to be more likely to donate money to a Christmas Santa Claus if they have observed a model making a donation (Macaulay, 1970).

What exactly does the model have to do in order to elicit imitative helping? In Chapter 6 we saw that a model who merely indicated that aggressive behavior was appropriate could

elicit imitation. However, children may be more predisposed to act aggressively than to help. Aggression involves no self-denial, and for some, acting aggressively may be pleasant. Thus to elicit the imitation of helping, the model may have to do more than merely say that helping is appropriate; he may himself have to engage in helping behavior.

Confirmation of the hypothesis that moral exhortations alone are ineffective has been obtained in several studies. In one such study in which eight to ten year olds participated, moral exhortations about the desirability of sharing did not increase the incidence of helping (Bryan, 1970). This finding has been replicated in a recent study (Grusec, 1972). Subjects were in one of three experimental conditions: (1) They were exposed to a model who shared; (2) they were exposed to a model who himself did not share but who indicated that sharing was appropriate; and (3) they were not exposed to any model—the control condition. In this study the boys exposed to the model who shared showed significantly more sharing than those exposed to the model who talked but did not himself share. In fact, the subjects in the "exhortation" condition did not differ significantly from those in the control condition. Apparently, deeds count more than words in eliciting altruism.

In general, why does observing a helping model facilitate help giving? Four answers have been given. Seeing someone else helping: (1) makes the social responsibility norm salient, (2) provides information about what is allowable or appropriate in the situation, (3) supplies information about the consequences of various courses of action, and (4) reduces constraints against helping.

First, seeing someone else helping makes the social responsibility norm salient. In the flat-tire experiment, for example, motorists driving down the freeway may have been thinking about many things: personal concerns, business problems, planning, and so forth. When they saw a man helping a woman fix a flat tire, they were reminded of their duty to help others in distress.

Second, seeing someone else helping provides information about what is allowable or appropriate in the situation. As discussed previously, other people play a crucial role in defining the situation and in defining appropriate behavior for the situation. On entering a new situation, a person may not have a clear idea of how he should act. By observing what another is doing, he gains information about what is appropriate. A precedent is established. If he is not sure how he should act, he may simply conform to what others are doing in the same situation.

But the observer is not automatically influenced by what a model does. Rather, the observer views the whole situation, considering characteristics of the model that are relevant to his own helping and other information about the model's motives. In the flat-tire experiment, for example, the viewing of a male model helping would not be expected to have much effect on a woman's helping in a similar situation. Tire changing is not thought of as a woman's function in our society. In one experiment helping behavior occurred more often when a model was similar to the potential helper (Hornstein, Fisch, and Holmes, 1968). Furthermore, if a model is seen as helping because he is forced to, the model's influence declines if the subject does not feel he is subjected to the same pressures (Hornstein, 1970). If the model is to be effective, the observer must feel that the model's behavior is relevant to his own behavior.

Third, observing a helping model may supply information about the consequences of various courses of action. If a helping model shows that he has enjoyed his helping, the observer might expect similar favorable consequences should he help. "If someone else enjoys working for that charity so much, so will I." This hypothesis has been supported by several studies. In one experiment subjects were exposed to a model who helped another person by returning his lost wallet. Half of the models indicated that they were pleased to help, and the other half said that they were annoyed at the inconvenience of returning the wallet but were doing so anyhow (Hornstein, 1970). As predicted, 70 percent of the subjects exposed to the model who was pleased about helping returned a wallet, whereas only 10 percent of the subjects exposed to the irritated model did so.

Finally, observing that someone else has helped may reduce constraints against helping. People may be concerned that they will look foolish if they help when no one else is helping,

so seeing someone else helping is reassuring. One investigator has quoted the reactions of one woman, which support this interpretation:

I've passed them (the boxes) a couple of times shopping. Giving to children is a good thing. Santa makes a difference. I (didn't) give to the box that didn't have a Santa because no one else was. Perhaps I was embarrassed.

[Macaulay, 1970, p. 53.]

In any particular situation one or a combination of these processes may facilitate helping. For example, in the flat-tire experiment the helping model may have made the norm of social responsibility salient and defined appropriate behavior for the situation. In the lost-wallet experiment all four processes may have been involved: The positive reaction of the person who was planning to return the wallet made the norm salient, defined the situation, provided information about the consequences of helping, and reduced constraints against helping.

Being Reminded About Social Responsibility In addition to being reminded by models, individuals are reminded about their social responsibilities in other ways. They may, for example, be asked directly to be charitable. In real life verbal appeals are frequently made for charities. If you want someone to do something, you may remind him of his duty to do that particular thing.

A person may also be reminded of his responsibility to help others by reading religious writings. As the following quotations show, the Bible and the Talmud make clear one's social responsibility to help others:

Thou shalt love thy neighbor as thyself.

[Matt. 19:19.]

He who saves a single life, it is as though he has saved the entire world.

[Talmud.]

Let your light so shine before men, that they may see your good works.

[Matt. 5:16.]

Inasmuch as ye have done it unto one of the least of these my brethren, ye have done it unto me.

[Matt. 25:40.]

FIGURE 7-10 The many charitable activities of the Salvation Army provide a clear example of the institutionalized altruism of a religious organization. Here, at a Salvation Army summer camp, nurses are on duty at the camp hospital for routine care or for emergency help. (Courtesy, The Salvation Army)

The Biblical commitment to helping others, combined with the image of Jesus as the ultimate model of an altruistic man can be argued to contribute significantly to the benevolence of many individual Christians as well as the institutional altruism of organized churches and other Christian organizations. (See Figure 7-10.) Many, if not most, churches devote a considerable amount of money to helping others. For instance, in 1969 the Episcopal Church in the United States spent $31,608,034 on benevolences, 15.91 percent of their total income; the Seventh Day Adventists spent $102,730,594, 71.78 percent of their total income; and the Lutheran Church, Missouri Synod, spent $49,402,590, 21 percent of their total income

(Jacquet, 1971). Of course, other religious faiths also direct considerable money and effort to charities. In 1970 Jewish Federations spent over $56,200,000 on such activities as youth services, family and child care, hospitals and health, and care of the aged (Fine, Himmelfarb, and Jelenko, 1972).

The reciprocity norm

Another norm that governs much of social behavior is the reciprocity norm, which states that people should help those who have helped them (Gouldner, 1960). If a friend has done you a favor, you return the favor when he needs a favor. And if a friend has denied you help when you needed it, you deny it to him when he is in need.

The Power of Reciprocity In a number of laboratory experiments subjects have been found to be much more likely to help another person when that person had previously helped them. Two investigators, for example, found that undergraduate females did more work for "supervisors" after the supervisors had helped them voluntarily, even though the girls did not expect to see the supervisors again (Goranson and Berkowitz, 1966). The reciprocity effect has been replicated in many studies. For instance, in a recent study it was again found that subjects reciprocated and gave help to another person solely on the basis of the amount of help that person had given to them (Kahn and Tice, 1973).

If the person who helped originally is not available, the recipient is likely to generalize his debt to others. He will be more likely to help a third person. In one study, for instance, it was found that workers who had received help from a confederate were much more likely to help another person than were persons who had not received help (Berkowitz and Daniels, 1964).

The reciprocity norm has important practical implications in a number of areas. For instance, the United States has given large sums of foreign aid to many countries on the assumption that the aid would build good will toward the United States. However, if people seek reciprocal relationships, their receiving gifts with no strings may create hostility and resentment—a reaction that has occurred in many countries that we give aid to. People may not want to be considered "charity cases." Instead of building strong ties of friendship with the United States, our foreign aid program seems to have had the opposite effect in many countries. People may prefer those with whom they have a reciprocal relationship.

A cross-cultural study provides support for this hypothesis (Gergen, Maslach, Ellsworth, and Seipel, in press). In Japan, Sweden, and the United States, each subject was first required to gamble with the other five subjects in the experiment. The betting was rigged, so that all of the subjects lost a lot of their chips. Each impoverished bettor received a gift of ten chips

just as he was about to run out of chips, supposedly from one of the other players. Three different conditions surrounded the gift. In one, the low-obligation condition, the gift was given with no strings—the note accompanying the chips said that the recipient need not bother to return the chips. In another condition, the reciprocal condition, the note asked the recipient to return the ten chips at the end of the game. And in the third condition, the high-obligation condition, the note requested the recipient to return more than the ten chips he had been given.

After the game was over, the subjects in all three conditions were asked to rate how much they liked the person who had given the chips. There was a significant preference for the person who provided help through a reciprocal exchange agreement. In no country was the charitable giver, who did not ask for a return, liked as much as the one who wanted a straight reciprocal arrangement.

In both the United States and Japan the giver who wanted to capitalize on his gift wasn't liked as much as the one who simply wanted back what he had given. In Sweden, however, the subjects had a tendency to like the person who wanted back more than he had given better than any of the other givers. This finding suggests the possibility that charging interest may have different connotations in Sweden than it does in the United States and Japan. In Sweden someone who charges interest may be regarded as very clever, and this feeling may result in the higher ratings that the Swedes gave to the "interest chargers." In contrast, in the United States and Japan someone who charges interest may be seen as greedy. The main point, however, is that in none of the three countries was the charitable giver liked as well as the one who wanted his gift reciprocated chip-for-chip.

This finding has very interesting implications for the United States' foreign aid policies. If people resent charity, perhaps a more reciprocal form of help—such as interest-free loans that would be repaid by the recipient country—would be more effective in improving our relationships with other countries.

Reciprocity holds in the business world, too. If a person feels that his employer is not paying him enough to compensate him fairly for the effort he is expending, he may curtail his work, so that its quantity and quality matches his compensation. Confirmation for this hypothesis was obtained in a study of the job output of cashiers and package handlers in a number of supermarkets (Clark, 1958). One of the ways in which an employee can assess whether or not he is being compensated fairly is to compare his salary to that of others who are doing comparable jobs. For instance, if a package handler found that he was not being paid the same as the cashier, he might feel that he was being treated unfairly and slow down on the job. Just this result was found when the efficiency of package handlers (measured in the number of man-hours required per $100 worth of sales) was correlated with the amount of inequity existing between the salaries of cashiers and those of package handlers. When the cashiers and package handlers' salaries were equivalent, the package handlers' efficiency was much higher than when the salaries were not equivalent.

Conversely, if people feel that they are being overpaid, they should increase the quality of their work in order to reciprocate. Confirmation for this hypothesis was obtained in one study (Adams and Jacobson, 1964). As predicted, the subjects who thought they were being overpaid did a better job than those who felt they were receiving an appropriate amount of money for the job required. This finding has very interesting implications for the way in which businesses pay their employees. If the employees think they are being overpaid, they will work harder in order to reciprocate the pay. Note that it is not the amount of money involved that increases performance. It is whether the person thinks he deserves it.

Variables That Influence Reciprocity Although reciprocity has been demonstrated in a number of instances, it doesn't always occur. Lending money to a close friend may be a quick way to lose the friend, since he may feel overly obligated by the loan. Predicting when reciprocity will occur is a very complex matter. So far research has been done on five variables: (1) the apparent reasons for the favor, (2) the degree to which the favor obligates the recipient, (3) the recipient's assessment of the resources of the person who has given the favor, (4) the recipient's expectations about receiving the favor,

and (5) social-class differences in reactions to favors.

THE REASONS FOR THE FAVOR When someone else does a favor, you attempt to understand *why* he is doing it. You consider what you know of the other person and the situation in order to understand his behavior. If someone who has a history of acting very competitively suddenly becomes cooperative and helpful, his behavior may be suspect. "Something must be going on for him to have changed so dramatically."

Moreover, the reactions to a favor have been found to depend on its appropriateness to the situation. If a person does an excessively generous favor, you may suspect his motives (Schopler, 1970). For instance, if someone you barely know volunteers to do something that would be extremely time-consuming, you might begin to suspect his motives. "He wouldn't be doing it if he weren't getting something out of it." Studies on inappropriate favors show that reciprocity is decreased when the motives of the benefactor are questioned (Schopler and Thompson, 1968).

If you think that the other person has voluntarily done you a favor, you are much more likely to reciprocate than if you think he was compelled to help. This hypothesis was supported in one study in which an experimental confederate helped a subject (Goranson and Berkowitz, 1966). The subjects who thought that the confederate had voluntarily helped them helped the confederate significantly more than did the subjects who thought the confederate had been required to help them.

THE DEGREE TO WHICH THE FAVOR OBLIGATES THE RECIPIENT If the recipient sees a favor as being obligating, he may not reciprocate. Someone's announcing that he is doing you a favor may turn you off, since you may feel that you are obligated to return the favor. Limitations on a person's freedom, even if they are caused by a favor, are unpleasant. "Binding" favors may result in irritation not gratitude (Brehm and Cole, 1966).

YOUR ASSESSMENT OF THE RESOURCES OF THE PERSON WHO HAS HELPED YOU If you think that the person who has helped you has limited resources, you are more likely to reciprocate than if you think the other has access to large resources. Confirmation of this hypothesis was obtained in one experiment (Pruitt, 1968). The subjects reciprocated more when they thought that the other person had given them a large proportion of their total holdings than when they thought he had given them a small proportion.

YOUR EXPECTATIONS ABOUT RECEIVING HELP What you expect from another person has a marked impact on how you react to what he actually does. For instance, suppose a friend who was getting very high grades in a course in which you were having problems promised that he would tutor you for the next examination in the course, and, at the last minute, refused to do so. If you are like the subjects tested in one experiment, you would tend to react much more negatively and be much less likely to help your friend than if he had neither promised to help nor helped (Morse, 1972). Conversely, an unexpected favor creates a more positive reaction and a greater desire to reciprocate than does the same favor when it is expected. Once you expect that someone will help you, his doing so doesn't win many points.

SOCIAL-CLASS DIFFERENCES IN REACTIONS TO FAVORS Not everyone responds the same way to favors. The reciprocity norm is much stronger in some individuals and groups than in others. One study showed that there are social-class differences in reciprocity tendencies (Berkowitz and Friedman, 1967). When adolescent boys were given an opportunity to help others, it was found that boys from entrepreneurial middle-class families (that is, boys whose parents were independent business owners) helped to the extent that they had been helped—regardless of whether they were working with the person who had originally helped them or someone else. In contrast, the help given by boys from a bureaucratic middle-class background (that is, boys whose parents worked for someone else) was relatively uninfluenced by a reciprocity factor.

Explanations of the Power of Reciprocity Why is the tendency toward reciprocity such a powerful force in social interactions? More than one

explanation of the effect of receiving prior help is possible. As we saw in the cross-cultural study measuring the attractiveness of reciprocal and nonreciprocal givers, reciprocity may increase liking for the person. Thus people may reciprocate because they like the person who has given them help on a reciprocal basis. Or the person may reciprocate because he feels that he may need help from the other person in the future and knows that if he does not reciprocate, the chances of his getting future help are very minimal. Finally, receiving help may remind the individual of his social responsibility. Reciprocity is a basic norm, which is thoroughly taught to us all. All of these interpretations are consistent with the experimental results. A clear separation of the motives for reciprocity requires further research.

The problem with a normative explanation of helping behavior

Although a normative explanation of helping behavior has generated a number of testable ideas, it does have one limitation (Darley and Latané, 1970). Suppose you saw someone slip and fall resoundingly on his backside. Would you feel that he wanted help? If he was hurt, clearly he would appreciate someone's helping. But if he was not, he might be embarrassed by someone's helping, which would just emphasize the incident. When something sufficiently embarrassing happens, a person may simply wish he could become invisible. In a particular situation contradictory norms may exist, and a normative explanation does not predict which norms—in this case helping or respecting another's privacy—will be applied. Without a careful specification of when the norms would be expected to apply, a normative theorist is in danger of using norms to explain *any* set of results. Giving an after-the-fact, or ad hoc, explanation for results may not add to an understanding of altruism.

Summary

The social responsibility norm, which requires that a dependent individual be helped, and the reciprocity norm, which calls for the repayment of benefits received from others, have been theorized to account for a number of helping behaviors.

At times people act to help others, not for material gain or social approval, but simply to do what is right—the *social responsibility norm*. This explanation of helping is in direct conflict with another view of human social interaction—the social exchange theory—which holds that all of an individual's actions are determined by the rewards he thinks his actions will bring. Although it may always be possible to argue that a helping person receives some reward for helping, several studies have repeatedly shown that American college students will work hard to help someone who needs help even when there is little in it for themselves, the recipient does not know who has helped him, and the experimenter is not aware of their helping.

Some types of dependency are much more apt to elicit help than others. If you feel that another individual is personally responsible for his plight, you may be less likely to help him. Your incidence of helping behavior may also be influenced by the reactance factor. Any appeal that limits the prospective helper's freedom decreases his inclination to help.

Repeatedly, it has been shown that people are more likely to be helpful after observing a model helping. What exactly does the model have to do in order to elicit imitative helping? Unlike aggression, where verbal exhortation to aggress may be enough to induce aggressive behavior, a model must actually engage in helping behavior to induce altruism in others.

Why does observing a helping model facilitate help giving? Four answers have been given. Seeing someone else helping: (1) makes the social responsibility norm salient, (2) provides information about what is allowable or appropriate in the situation, (3) supplies information about the consequences of various courses of action, and (4) reduces constraints against helping. In any particular situation one or a combination of these processes may facilitate helping.

In addition to being reminded by models, individuals are reminded about their social responsibilities in other ways. They may, for example, be asked directly to be charitable. A person may also be reminded of his responsibility to help others by reading religious writings.

The power of the *reciprocity norm,* which states that people help those who have helped them, has been shown in a number of laboratory experiments. Subjects have been found to be much more likely to help another person when that person had previously helped them. If the person who helped originally is not available, the recipient is likely to help a third person.

The reciprocity norm has important practical implications for international relations and business. For instance, if people prefer reciprocal relationships, foreign aid given on a "no strings" basis may only create hostility and resentment—a reaction that has occurred in many countries that we give foreign aid to. Cross-cultural work supports this hypothesis. In the business world, if a person feels that his employer is not paying him enough to compensate him fairly for the effort he is expending, he may curtail his work, so that its quantity and quality matches his compensation. Conversely, if employees feel that they are being overpaid, they may increase the quality of their work in order to reciprocate.

The occurrence of reciprocity is determined by: (1) the reasons for the favor, (2) the degree to which the favor obligates the recipient, (3) the recipient's assessment of the resources of the person who has helped, (4) the recipient's expectations about receiving help, and (5) social-class differences in reactions to favors. Reciprocity is decreased when the motives of the benefactor are questioned, when the other person has been compelled to help, and when the recipient sees the favor as being obligating. It is increased when the helping person is believed to have limited resources and when the helping acts are unexpected. The reciprocity norm is much stronger in some individuals and groups than in others. For instance, boys from entrepreneurial middle-class families were much more likely to reciprocate than boys from a bureaucratic middle-class background.

Why is the tendency toward reciprocity such a powerful force in social interactions? People may reciprocate because they like the person who has given them help on a reciprocal basis. Or the person may reciprocate because he feels that he may need help from the other person in the future and wishes to build up his "psychological capital." Finally, receiving help may remind the individual of his social responsibility.

Although a normative explanation of helping has generated a number of testable ideas, it does have one limitation. Social norms sometimes conflict with each other. Without a careful specification of which norms would be expected to apply in a given situation, a normative theorist is in danger of using norms to explain *any* set of results.

A Cost Analysis of Helping

Helping behavior is most likely to occur when the rewards for helping outweigh the costs. (See Figure 7-11.) Although norms may provide a general predisposition to help, the relationship between the various costs and rewards furnishes a more reliable predictor of whether helping will occur in a particular situation. Note that costs involve more than financial costs; they include all of the negative aspects that would be involved in helping. As we saw earlier in this chapter, for instance, the incidence of helping a drunk was less than that of helping someone who was ill—presumably because the subjects may have thought that greater risks were involved in helping the drunk.

To illustrate some of the components of costs, let us consider two requests for help: (a) A good friend asks for directions to a museum that is two blocks away, and (b) a stranger asks to be taken to the same museum. The second request clearly involves greater costs than the first. Walking two blocks takes more effort, may expose the benefactor to possible danger (since the person making the request may have more in mind than going to a museum), and may cause the benefactor embarrassment (since he may feel uncomfortable about relating to a stranger in this situation). Also, the rewards involved in the second request are less. The gratitude of a stranger probably is not as important as that of a friend. A cost analysis of these two requests would indicate that the incidence of helping would be much higher for the first request than for the second, since the second costs more. (See Box 6.)

Any variations in requests that increase the rewards of helping—that is, increase the chance that the altruism will "pay off" for the benefactor—would be expected to elicit more altruism. If the benefactor expects to be rewarded for his helpful act, he is more likely to help. Offering a reward for the return of a lost wallet would probably increase the chances of its being returned.

Other, less obvious, rewards may also increase the incidence of helping. The amount and kind of social approval gained as a result of an altruistic act would influence the incidence of helping. For example, helping when your good deeds will be widely publicized and so enhance your image would be more rewarding than if no one else knew of your altruism. Also, a benefactor might be rewarded by anticipating the joy of a potential recipient: Thinking how

FIGURE 7-11 The assumption that rewarding altruism increases the incidence of helping is clear in this advertisement. (Courtesy, United Fund of Greater New York)

BOX 6 A HYPOTHETICAL COST ANALYSIS

Rewards		Costs	
1. Material rewards	+3	1. Effort	−1
2. Social reinforcement	+4	2. Danger	0
3. Empathy with those who need help	+1	3. Possible embarrassment because of unfamiliar environment	0
4. Meaningfulness of the contribution	+2	4. Financial costs	−5
5. Maximizing one's sense of self-worth	+2		
	+12		−6

Assume a person—the potential help-er—has been asked to lend a friend fifty dollars, and assume that: (1) The friend has promised to repay the debt with 5 percent interest; (2) others know of the request and will admire the helper for making the loan; (3) the helper empathizes with his friend; (4) the helper feels that his loan will go to something worthwhile; and (5) the helper will increase his self-image if he makes the loan. In the list above values have been arbitrarily assigned to each of these rewards, and they add up to +12.

Hypothetical values have also been given to the various costs. A small amount of effort will be required, and there is some financial risk. There is no physical danger, however, and the environment does not pose a threat. Added together, the negative values equal −6.

Since the positive values are higher than the negative ones, the individual would be expected to help. This analysis is provided to give a general illustration of the cost-analysis approach, not to indicate that any theorist claims this is the way people actually decide whether or not to help. In real life the individual may not be aware of all of the rewards and costs; indeed, he may make his decision impulsively without any attempt to consider the various rewards and costs.

---

pleased someone will be may be a source of pleasure for the benefactor. The belief that one is making a meaningful contribution may also be a source of satisfaction, and the self-respect gained from helping may be gratifying.

Rewards and costs then refer to a variety of phenomena, ranging from the very obvious to the not so obvious. Rather than specifying an exact set of variables that are classified as rewards or costs, the cost-analysis interpretation of helping provides a general approach to analyzing helping behavior. Some of the studies that have explored the effects of various costs and rewards are reviewed below.

Increasing costs

Five aspects of cost have been investigated.

Type of Request In a series of interesting field studies, two investigators had ninety-three of their students in introductory social psychology courses at Columbia University go out on the streets of New York and make a variety of requests of passers-by (Darley and Latané, 1970).

Not too surprisingly, what was asked made a significant difference in the incidence of compliance. People were much more likely to give the correct time, give directions, or change a quarter than they were to give a dime or tell their name. (See Table 2.) Giving the correct time, giving directions, and making change for a quarter all involve relatively low costs to the benefactor. In contrast, telling one's name to a stranger involves a certain risk: Why does the person want to know? And giving a dime, though it is a minimal amount of money, does involve a financial cost.

Other studies have also shown that the relative cost of the help requested influences the incidence of helping. During the April 1971 peace demonstration, a young woman experimenter approached eighty randomly selected male participants and asked them to "help her friend who was feeling ill." She then began a series of requests for help that involved increasingly larger costs to the potential benefactor. As shown in Table 3, the percentage of subjects complying decreased as the costs of helping increased. Although 100 percent of those requested agreed to help her ill companion, only 11 percent agreed to provide bus fare for him (Suedfeld, Bochner, and Wnek, 1972).

Threat of Danger If you were riding in a subway in New York City and you overheard someone giving another person incorrect information about where the subway was going, how do you think you would react? Your reaction might depend on your assessment of the possible dangers involved in your providing the correct answer. How likely do you think you would be to correct someone who a few minutes before had shouted threats of physical abuse at another passenger who had inadvertently stumbled against the misinformer's feet? Or how likely would you be to correct someone who earlier had insulted another person on the subway? How likely would you be to correct someone who had not done anything when someone stumbled over his feet?

If you are like the subjects who participated in a realistic field study, the variations in the misinformer's potential nastiness would influence the likelihood of your correcting him (Allen, 1970). The study was conducted in a subway in New York City. A confederate approached a subject and asked whether the subway was going uptown or downtown. A second confederate who was standing next to the subject gave the wrong answer. The measure of helping was whether or not the subject corrected the incorrect answer.

Three different "characters" were established for the misinformer. Before the wrong-directions incident was staged, he sat with his feet stretched out, so that yet another confederate fell over them. His character was established by the way he reacted to this incident. In one condition he looked up from a magazine on muscle building and shouted threats of physical injury at the hapless stumbler (physical-threat condition). In another condition he looked up from his magazine on muscle building and made insulting

Table 2. Frequency of Response to Different Requests

Request	Number of People Asked	Percentage That Helped
"Excuse me, I wonder if you could		
a. tell me what time it is?"	92	85
b. tell me how to get to Times Square?"	90	84
c. give me change of a quarter?"	90	73
d. tell me what your name is?"	277	39
e. give me a dime?"	284	34

Source: From Darley and Latané, 1970, Table 1.

Table 3. Frequency of Response to Requests for Help

Request	Percentage of Subjects Complying
"Help me with him."	100
"Move [him] out of the way."	99
"Take [him] to first aid station."	66
"Take [him] home to Georgetown."	19
"Provide bus fare."	11

Source: Adapted from Suedfeld, Bochner, and Wnek, 1972, Table 1.

comments about the stumbler (embarrassment condition). In the control condition he did nothing.

Only 16 percent of the subjects corrected the physically threatening confederate; 28 percent corrected the insulting confederate; and 52 percent corrected the control confederate. Correcting someone whom you have seen either insult or physically threaten another person clearly involves your risking the same fate, and this risk makes you less likely to help. The incidence of helping in the insulting condition was only 12 percent more than in the physically threatening condition. The possibility of insult and embarrassment was almost as inhibiting as the threat of physical harm. Further, when the confederate had not done anything, approximately half of the subjects did not correct the false information. Intervening when two people are interacting may be qualitatively different from helping one person in a physically dangerous situation. If you saw a mother slapping her child, would you intervene? Or if a husband and wife were fighting, would you try to break it up? The norms about intervention are not clear, and so any intervention between two people may have relatively high costs—which would explain the low incidence of helping in this situation.

Further, in a large city, such as New York, people may generally be inhibited from helping because of their fear of physical vulnerability—a concern supported by urban crime statistics. Support for this hypothesis is provided by a study that compared the incidence of a helping act that required some trust of a stranger—allowing a stranger to enter one's home to use a telephone—in New York City with the data for several small towns in New York State (Altman, Levine, Nadien, and Villena, unpublished, in Milgram, 1970). As is shown in Table 4, strangers asking to use a telephone gained entrance much more frequently in small towns than in New York City. In fact, they did twice as well in the small towns. Fear of danger clearly seems to have played a part in the different reactions. Seventy-five percent of all the city respondents did not open their doors and responded by either shouting through closed doors or peering out of peepholes whereas about 75 percent of

the small town subjects opened their doors. (See Figure 7-12.)

Table 4. Percentage of Entries to City and Town Dwellings Achieved by Investigators

| Experimenter | Percentage of Entries Achieved | |
	City*	Small Town**
Male		
No. 1	16	40
No. 2	12	60
Female		
No. 3	40	87
No. 4	40	100

*Number of requests for entry, 100.
**Number of requests for entry, 60.

Source: From Milgram, 1970, Table 1.

Variables other than physical danger or embarrassment may be involved in threat of danger. A person may be less likely to help if helping involves a threat to his social status. In one study it was found that male undergraduates failed to help a highly dependent other when he was threatening their status (Schopler, 1967). Even though the cause was good, helping decreased when a threat to the potential benefactor's own status emerged. Perhaps it is not too far-fetched to analogize from this to the reactions of liberal, middle-class college alumni to their college's encouraging black enrollment. As long as the "liberalized" enrollment policy doesn't threaten them personally, they may encourage it. But if the revised policy impinges on their son's chances of being admitted, reactions may change quickly.

Familiarity with the Environment Suppose that as you were walking through an airport, you saw someone on crutches, with a bandage on his left leg, fall to the ground—clutching his knee and apparently in great pain. If it was your first trip to the airport, you might not know what to do, even if you wanted to help. You wouldn't know if there was an infirmary in the airport, where the closest taxi stand was, or how to locate a doctor. Because of your unfamiliarity with the physical environment, you might be afraid of looking silly and inept if you tried to help. The increased cost of potential embar-

FIGURE 7-12 The dangerous beggar. Fear of danger doesn't inevitably decrease the incidence of helping. Sometimes it may be more costly not to perform a "helping" act.

rassment would deter your helping. Preliminary correlational evidence has been obtained in support of this interpretation (Granet, unpublished, cited in Darley and Latané, 1970). A significant correlation was found between familiarity with the environment and responding to an emergency.

Financial Cost The amount of money involved is clearly another cost. Folk wisdom and the results of many fund-raising drives indicate that it is easier to obtain small donations than large ones. Persuading an impoverished college student to donate twenty-five cents to a charity is a lot easier than obtaining twenty-five dollars from him. Any variation that decreases the immediate financial cost can be expected to increase the amount of helping. Two investigators found that men made a larger charitable contribution when it was given in time-payment form than when it was deducted as a lump sum (Wagner and Wheeler, 1969). The fact that deferred giving increases the total amount donated has been used by many charities. For example, Community Chest fund drives routinely suggest that donations be made through payroll deductions rather than in one lump sum.

However, reducing the financial costs for helping may only increase the amount of helping when some cue—such as dependency—is present. Support for this hypothesis is provided by a recent field study (Schaps, 1972). The subjects were sixty-four shoe salesmen who worked on commission. When there were a number of customers, spending a lot of time with one customer meant that the salesmen would lose potential commissions from unattended customers. However, when there was one customer per salesman or fewer customers, the costs of helping were low. The customer's needs were manipulated, so that there were two levels of need. In the high-dependency condition a confederate limped into the store with the heel of her shoe broken and declared that she could walk no farther until she purchased a pair of shoes. In the low-dependency condition the confederate's shoes were intact. The amount of help provided by each salesman was measured by the amount of time he spent with the customer. When costs for helping were low, the salesman spent significantly more time with the customer with the broken heel than with the one whose heel was not broken. However, when the costs for helping were high, the amount of help given to the customer with the broken heel decreased significantly. In fact, under high-cost conditions there was no significant difference between the time spent with the woman with the broken heel and that spent with the other customer.

Time Pressures If people are busy, they are less likely to spend time helping another person. Dramatic support for this hypothesis is provided by the results of a field study conducted at Princeton Theological Seminary (Darley and Batson, 1973). All of the subjects reported to one building for the first part of the study and then were asked to report to another building for the second part of the experiment. While in transit, all of the subjects passed a "victim" who was sitting slumped in a doorway, coughing and groaning. Half of the seminary students were on their way to record a talk on "the Good Samaritan" parable; the other half were scheduled to talk on the vocational roles of ministers. Time pressures were manipulated so as to make the seminarians think they were either early, on time, or late for their scheduled talks.

The subject of the student's planned talk had no significant influence on the incidence of helping. The only variable which significantly predicted the incidence of helping was time pressure. Sixty-three percent of the early students helped. Among the on-time students, the incidence of helping was 45 percent, and only 10 percent of the late students helped. Ironically, even if the late person was hurrying to give a talk on the Good Samaritan, he was likely to hurry past someone who appeared to need help! Indeed, several of the seminarians rushing to talk on the Good Samaritan literally stepped over the victim as they rushed to their destination.

Increasing rewards

Any aspect of a situation that increases the rewards of helping will increase the frequency of helping. Rewards vary from material rewards to more intangible benefits.

Material Rewards   As we saw earlier, a number of studies have shown that giving material rewards increases the tendency of subjects to be altruistic in a particular situation. (See Box 7.)

Social Reinforcement   The admiration and approval of others is a powerful incentive for all behavior—including altruism. As you contemplate volunteering for a student-tutor program, you may imagine the complimentary things your friends will say. Many persons involved in helping activities have noted the importance of appreciative, positive reactions from others. An army chaplain, decorated for bravery in Vietnam, explained his feelings: "I feel it's a comfort to the men for us to be along. . . . When one of them comes up and says 'I'm glad you're here,' it makes it worthwhile" (Traester, 1968, p. 4).

Pride in being a member of a group organized to help others, such as a volunteer fire company, can also serve as an important source of social rewards:

[Volunteer firemen] love to parade. Prizes for the fanciest equipment are highly sought. It's not unusual for a volunteer company to buy a basic pumper for $16,750 and then spend another $20,000 for optional extras. . . . But the extras do serve a purpose. "If a company can win prizes in parades, it's great for the volunteers," said one official. "After all, they regularly risk their lives. A sense of pride welds them into a cohesive unit."

[Winchester, 1969, p. 99.]

Since the general effect of social reinforcement has been so thoroughly established, we will focus our attention on characteristics of the recipient that influence his effectiveness as a social reinforcer. Praise usually means more from someone you admire, think is an attractive person, like, or who is similar to yourself. It would therefore seem to follow that the incidence of helping would be higher for liked, attractive people and people who are similar to the benefactor.

HELPING FRIENDS Intuitively, we expect people to be more willing to help friends than strangers. You can probably think of a number of instances when you helped a friend in a way that you would not be likely to help a stranger. Empirical support for the relationship between friendship and helping has been obtained in several studies. The results of one study, for instance, showed that 40 percent of the experimental subjects agreed to help a confederate whom they liked, and only 10 percent agreed to help a confederate they disliked (Goodstadt, 1971).

However, the relationship between helping and friendship may not obtain in all situations. If you met someone you wished to gain as a friend, you might be more helpful to him than to someone you knew so well that you were confident of the relationship. One investigator found that third graders were more likely to give the more desirable of two toys to a stranger than to a friend (Wright, 1942). When the children explained their behavior, they said they wanted to gain a friend. One particular incident of giving or not giving a toy might not influence an existing friendship much, but it would have a marked effect on a new relationship.

HELPING PERSONS WHO ARE SIMILAR TO ONESELF   Although the evidence is not completely consistent, several studies suggest that people are more likely to help persons who are from the same group and country. In the face of the dangers of war, members of a combat unit may help the other members of their group—even when it involves a considerable amount of personal sacrifice.

Several studies have shown that people are more willing to help compatriots than foreigners. For example, one investigator found that Parisians and Athenians were more willing to give directions to their compatriots than to foreigners. Although the same study showed that Bostonians acted the same toward foreigners and compatriots when giving directions, it also showed that Bostonians were more likely to mail an unstamped letter for a compatriot than for a foreigner (Feldman, 1968).

Similarity in political attitudes has also been found to increase the incidence of helping. At the 1971 peace demonstration in Washington, when most of the demonstrators were opposed to President Nixon's Vietnam policy, demonstrators were more likely to help someone who displayed a "Dump Nixon" sign than someone who displayed a "Support Nixon" sign (Suedfeld, Bochner, and Wnek, 1972).

Similarity in dress style also increases the incidence of helping. When confederates, dressed either in hippie or straight clothing style, approached subjects who wore either hippie or straight clothing, hippies were more willing to lend money to a confederate dressed in similar hippie fashion than to someone wearing straight clothing. And those dressed in straight clothing were more willing to lend money to confederates wearing similar clothing than to those in hippie garb (Emswiller, Deaux, and Willits, 1971).

Why should people be more likely to help those who are similar to themselves? There are several possible explanations. When people share membership in a face-to-face group or in a nation, the implication is that they are similar, and a benefactor may find it easier to understand and therefore take seriously the problems of someone who is similar. A person is most sympathetic with his own problems, and this sympathy may be extended to others if they resemble him sufficiently. Another possible explanation is that persons like others who are similar to themselves. Further, the process may be cyclical. Increasing similarity may cause an increase in friendship, which will, in turn, result in more helping.

Empathy As a Source of Reward   Looking at someone who is upset can be upsetting. Thinking about the pleasure that someone else will be experiencing can be a source of pleasure. As we saw earlier in this chapter, empathy is a basis of altruism. You do helpful things to produce joy in others so that you can experience it vicariously, and you do things to reduce the unhappy feelings of those in distress because seeing their distress makes you unhappy.

The Meaningfulness of the Contribution   The need for human acts of altruism in our present society is so vast that the individual is often deterred from doing anything because he feels that nothing he could do would really make a difference. In order for people to help, they must feel that they are making a meaningful, powerful contribution. Appeals for VISTA, the Peace Corps, and other volunteer groups frequently emphasize the constructive, meaningful aspect of the work. Support for the role of this variable has been obtained in one study (Gore and Rotter, 1963). The investigators found that students from a southern college were more willing to help in a civil-rights project if they thought they could influence the course of events by so doing. One could hypothesize that any variables that increase the individual's sense of personal effectiveness will increase the chances of his helping. One task of agencies recruiting volunteers is to demonstrate the effectiveness of the work they would be doing.

Further, a dissonance analysis would predict that if a person can be persuaded to help in a situation in which there are some costs, he may eventually come to believe more in the value of his helping than he would if it involved relatively little effort. The belief that his helping had been valueless would be dissonant with the knowledge of the costs of helping. Dissonance would be reduced by the individual's believing in the effectiveness of his helping. Some evidence from persons who have donated a kidney is consistent with this interpretation (Fellner and Marshall, 1970).

Maximizing One's Sense of Self-Worth Occasionally, an individual may help someone when no one else—not even the person helped—knows about it. For example, a person may make an anonymous donation to a charity. In such cases, when there is no possibility of social recognition, what could motivate the individual? Perhaps his helping enhances his feelings of self-worth or self-esteem.

Although many religious writers have noted the joys of being involved with someone other than the self, and many works of fiction reflect this theme, comparatively little scientific work has been done on the effect that engaging in altruistic acts has on one's self-esteem. The limited evidence available does suggest, however, that after performing an altruistic act, the benefactor's self-esteem and his view of himself are enhanced. Two investigators, for instance, reported that after having donated a kidney, the donors said the experience had made them feel good:

(A forty-year-old, male donor, four weeks postoperatively.) I feel better, kind of noble. I am changed. I have passed a milestone in my life. I have more confidence, self-esteem . . . in every way, I am better. For realizing how far I could go for others, I am up a notch in life. . . . I value things more, big and small things. . . . I come in contact with others a bit more. My pleasures are bigger and have more meaning.

[Fellner and Marshall, 1970, p. 277.]

Studies of the personality changes that occur in college students working in mental health facilities also show that altruism results in positive personality changes. For instance, when the changes in self-acceptance and self-understanding in a group of volunteers were compared with the changes in a control group, the volunteers working with emotionally disturbed people showed significantly more positive changes (Holzberg, Gewirtz, and Ebner, 1964; Gruver, 1971). Further, the students who worked in a mental health installation seemed to have increased self-confidence and an enhanced sense of their identity (Scheibe, 1965).

The self can also enter into altruism in another way. Although most of the people in our society have accepted the general ideal that people should help others, few practice this ideal most of the time. Frequently, selfish concerns monopolize our interest. As a result, we may become upset because we are not as unselfish as we think we should be. Suddenly realizing the gap between what we are and what we wish to be can be a painful experience, as discussed in Chapter 2.

One way the person can reduce the inconsistency is to become more altruistic. In an imaginative experiment subjects were asked to complete two rating scales: a rating of their own selves and their ideal selves. Most students believed that the ideal self should be unselfish and altruistic and tended to classify their own selves as being somewhat selfish (V. Smith, 1969).

Half the subjects were asked to do something altruistic before they compared their actual self with their ideal self. The other half were asked to do something altruistic after comparing their actual self with their ideal self. The person's going through the act of comparing his two selves had a significant effect: Only 14 percent of those who were asked to take action before they were forced to note the discrepancy between reality and the ideal acted altruistically, whereas 54 percent of those who completed the two ratings first and thus were conscious of the discrepancy acted altruistically.

Difficulty with a cost analysis

Cost analysis provides an interesting and research-stimulating way of thinking about altruistic behavior. Like the norm explanation, however, it does not provide a clear definition of its two key terms, reward and cost. How do we know which variables will influence costs? If these terms are not defined independently of experimental results, the cost analysis can become an exercise in circular reasoning: (1) Increasing rewards increases altruism, and (2) since this manipulation increases altruism, (3) it increases rewards.

Summary

Helping behavior is most likely to occur when the rewards for helping outweigh the costs. Note that costs involve more than financial costs: They include all of the negative factors that would be involved in helping. Rewards include all of the benefits of helping.

Any variation that increases the costs of helping would be expected to elicit less altruism. Five aspects of cost have been investigated. The relative costs of the *help requested* influence the incidence of helping. The number of people complying decreases as the costs of helping increase. Helping is much less likely to occur if it involves the *threat of danger*—either physical threat, the potential for embarrassment, or a threat to social status. People are more likely to help if they are *familiar with the environment.* The increased cost of potential embarrassment if one tries to help in an unfamiliar situation deters helping. Generally, any variation that decreases the immediate *financial cost* can be expected to increase the amount of helping. However, reducing the financial costs for helping may only increase the amount of helping when some cue—such as dependency—is present. *Time pressures* decrease the incidence of helping. If people are busy and interested in what they are doing, they are less likely to spend time helping others.

Any aspect of a situation that increases the rewards of helping will increase the frequency of helping. Rewards vary from material rewards to more intangible benefits. Giving *material rewards* increases the tendency of subjects to be altruistic in a particular situation. *Social reinforcement* for helping also increases the incidence of helping.

Praise usually means more from someone you admire, think is an attractive person, like, or who is similar to yourself. The incidence of helping is higher for liked, attractive people and people who are similar to the benefactor. Although people are generally more apt to help friends than strangers, they may be more apt to help someone they wish to gain as a friend than someone they know so well that they are confident of the relationship. People are more willing to help compatriots than foreigners. Similarity in political attitudes and clothing style also increases the incidence of helping.

Empathy can also be a source of reward for helping. As we saw earlier in this chapter, empathy may motivate altruism. People do helpful things to produce joy in others so that they can experience it vicariously.

In order for people to help, they must feel that they are making a *meaningful, powerful contribution.* Any variables that increase the individual's sense of personal effectiveness will increase the chances of his helping. Further, a dissonance analysis would predict that if a person can be persuaded to help in a situation in which there are some costs, he may eventually come to believe more in the value of his helping than he would if it involved relatively little effort.

After performing an altruistic act, the *benefactor's self-esteem* and his view of himself are enhanced. For instance, college students working in mental health facilities have been found to show significantly more positive changes in self-acceptance, self-understanding, self-esteem, and clear identity formation than groups of students not engaged in this type of helping. The self can also enter into altruism in another way. Although most of the people in our society have accepted the general ideal that people should help others, frequently selfish concerns monopolize our interest. Suddenly realizing the gap between what you are and what you want to be can motivate altruism.

Cost analysis provides an interesting and research-stimulating way of thinking about altruistic behavior. Like the norm explanation, however, it does not provide a clear definition of its two key terms, reward and cost. If these terms are not defined independently of experimental results, the cost analysis can become an exercise in circular reasoning.

Moods and Feelings

Both moods and feelings influence the extent to which people are willing to help others. If someone is in a good mood, he is more likely to help than if he is in a bad mood. Or if someone feels that either he or someone else has injured another person, he may be more likely to help that person—out of sympathy, guilt, or a desire to maintain his view that the world is a fair place.

Moods

Imagine a day in which everything goes right for you. You find out that you got a very high test score on an important examination; you receive a large, unexpected check from home, which will finance a summer vacation in Europe; you finally succeed in making a date with someone you've wanted to go out with for a long time; and you spend a really pleasant afternoon with a good friend. You feel like you're on top of the world. The results of many experiments predict that if you are now given an opportunity to help another person, you will be much more likely to help that person than you would if you were feeling depressed.

In several experimental settings moods have been influenced by manipulating the subjects' success and failure at experimental tasks. Repeatedly, it has been found that subjects who experience success are more likely to help than those who experience failure. In one study, for instance, college students who had just succeeded on an assigned task were much more likely to help in a variety of ways, including donating money to a school fund and helping a young woman with an armload of books and cartons, than were persons who had not done well (Isen, 1970). The warm glow of success made them more helpful.

However, one can wonder whether the "successful" subjects were more helpful because they were in a good mood or because they felt competent. Feeling successful can put you in a good mood, but it can also make you feel more competent. Earlier in this chapter we saw that people who feel competent are more likely to help. Therefore, one could argue that the success experience increased helping because it increased the subjects' confidence in their own competency rather than because it put them in a good mood.

To eliminate the competency explanation of the success experiments, some recent investigators have manipulated the moods of the subjects in a more direct way. In one recent study the investigator manipulated mood by asking the subjects to read a series of fifty statements, which were designed to induce either elation or depression, and to try to "respond to the *feeling* suggested by each statement." The elation statements included such comments as "God, I feel great!" and the depression statements included such sentences as "I want to go to sleep and never wake up." Then, after some other manipulations which need not concern us here, two measures of the extent to which the subjects were willing to help the experimenter were obtained. First the experimenter asked the subjects to help him with a simple clerical task—numbering some forms he was planning to use in another experiment. Second, he asked the subjects if they would be willing to participate in an experiment that involved sitting in a very hot room for two hours. As predicted, on both measures the subjects who were in a good mood were significantly more willing to be helpful than those in a bad mood (Aderman, 1972).

Why are people in a good mood more willing to help? Although the answer to this question is not clear at the present time, there are several possible explanations. One is that being in a good mood frees you from self-preoccupation and allows you to empathize more with the needs and problems of others. When you are in a bad mood, your thoughts and feelings may focus exclusively on yourself and your problems. Another possible explanation is that people who are depressed are more likely to interpret another person's request for help as an infringement on their freedom, thus arousing reactance. When you are feeling low, you may think to yourself, "I've got troubles enough without someone bugging me about participating in some stupid experiment!"

Feelings

For most people, regardless of their mood, certain feelings are aroused when injury is inflicted on another person. Often these feelings lead to acts of altruism, directed at either the injured person or another person. In recent years a considerable amount of experimental work has been done to determine more specifically what feelings are aroused and which types of feeling are more likely to lead to helping behavior. The results of these experiments have shown that there are at least three separate reactions that can cause the helping effect. When the subject is responsible (or made to feel responsible) for the act, he will experience *guilt*. Regardless of his responsibility, he may experience a desire to correct the wrong so as to maintain his view that the world is a fair place. And he may experience *sympathy*—a compassion directed toward the injured person.

It is not always clear which of these three feelings is the most powerful in stimulating altruistic behavior. In part, the answer may depend on how the injury is caused—whether the individual is made to feel responsible or whether he is only a witness. In part, the answer may also depend on who is being helped—the injured person or another person.

Seeing another person injured does not inevitably result in helping. Under certain conditions the witness may justify the injury by derogating the victim or denying responsibility. For example, many Germans reacted to the persecutions of the Jews during World War II by thinking that the Jews were evil people who deserved their fate and by denying any personal responsibility. Whether helping or justification occurs when others are injured depends on a number of variables in the situation.

Injury-Helping Effect A number of studies have shown that people do, in fact, help those they have injured. In one experiment subjects administered either electric shocks or loud buzzes to an experimental confederate (Carlsmith and Gross, 1969). In the standard Milgram teacher-learner setup, an experimental subject was required to punish another subject (actually a confederate) whenever he made an error in a learning task. Half of the subjects administered electric shocks as punishment; the other half administered innocuous buzzes.

After the "learning" part of the experiment was over, each subject was asked to fill out a questionnaire. While this was taking place, the confederate asked the subject to telephone a number of people, as a favor, and try to enlist their support for a charity that was attempting to save the redwoods in California. The subject's willingness to help the confederate was the measure of altruism.

Whether the subjects had administered electric shocks or buzzes had a very significant effect on their willingness to help. Only 25 percent of those who had buzzed showed a willingness to help, but 75 percent of those who had administered the supposedly painful shocks agreed to assist the confederate. Three times as many subjects who had delivered shocks volunteered to help the individual they thought they had injured. Having been injured gave the victim real power over the harm-doer.

Similar results have been obtained with studies using other "harmful" acts and other measures of a willingness to help. When subjects are made to believe that they have ruined an experiment, broken someone's camera, deprived a partner of a desirable prize, or inflicted electric shocks, they are more likely to agree to help the person they have injured than when these guilt feelings have not been aroused. Novelists have long noted the power of guilt; the desire to make amends can be far more powerful than other, more obvious forces.

Further, reparation has been found to generalize to persons other than the victim. Another phase of the electric-shock experiment showed that the harm-doer would be more helpful even when he was not helping his victim. When a second confederate—posing as a subject who was observing the administration of the electric shocks—made a request of the subject, there was even more compliance than when the actual recipient made a request. On the average subjects agreed to make about twenty-four telephone calls for their victim and thirty-nine for the witness.

However, a higher incidence of helping someone else than of helping the actual victim may be limited to situations in which the victim can identify the person who has injured him. In the electric-shock experiment the subjects may have thought the victim could easily learn who had injured him and may have helped the victim less in order to avoid an unpleasant scene in which the victim might retaliate. In situations in which the victim does not know who has injured him, the wrongdoers might be expected to help the victim more than someone else.

Support for this hypothesis was obtained in an experiment in which subjects thought they were participating in a memory study. Guilt was aroused in half of the subjects by having them "overhear" the experimenter explain how to get a good score on the test. At the conclusion of the experiment, the subjects were given an opportunity to help either the experimenter or someone else. In this situation, in which the subjects thought that they had spoiled the study but that the experimenter did not know who had done it, the incidence of helping the victim was significantly higher (57.5 percent) than the incidence of helping someone else (40 percent) (Neumann, unpublished, in Berkowitz, 1972).

Even if a person is not personally responsible for someone else's being injured, seeing someone hurt sometimes increases the incidence of helping. Support for this hypothesis was obtained in one study in which there were three experimental conditions (Rawlings, 1970). In one condition subjects were led to believe that errors on their part were responsible for their partner's receiving ten electric shocks. Girls in another condition were told that their partner received ten electric shocks, but that there was no relationship between their own performance and their partner's fate. Subjects in the third condition were told that their partner had received no electric shocks. Then all of the subjects were given an opportunity to help a third person. Both the subjects who thought that they were responsible for their partner's being shocked and those who simply knew that their partner had been shocked helped significantly more than did the girls in the third condition (Rawlings, 1970).

Although witnessing misfortune may increase the incidence of helping, those misfortunes that a person feels personally responsible for may generally lead to a higher incidence of helping than those that he simply witnesses. Support for this hypothesis was obtained in one study (Regan, Williams, and Sparling, 1972). In a field experiment a male experimenter asked women in a shopping center to take his picture "for a project." It was arranged so that the camera would not work for all of the subjects. For half of the subjects the experimenter implied that they had broken the camera (guilt condition); the other half were told that the malfunctioning was not their fault (control condition). Soon after that an incident was staged in the shopping center so that a measure of helping could be obtained. A female experimenter carrying a broken grocery bag with items falling from it walked in front of the subject. Fifty-five percent of the subjects in the guilt condition informed the experimenter that she was losing some of her

groceries, and only 15 percent of the subjects in the control condition did so.

Explanations of the Injury-Helping Effect If an increased incidence of helping were limited only to situations in which the person himself was personally responsible for the injury, the explanation of the injury-helping effect would seem very clear. People feel guilty about hurting others. As children we are taught that harming others is bad, and therefore when we harm others or think we have harmed others, we feel disturbed, troubled, and guilty. Although these feelings are not subject to precise definition, it is commonly agreed that an individual is compelled to try to get rid of them—whatever they may be called. He does something to stop feeling like "a rat," to make restitution, to compensate somehow for his wrongdoing. If an individual thinks he has inflicted serious injury, guilt can rise to excruciatingly intense levels, which can only be reduced through confession and penance. Confession and penance lead to absolution, which then redresses the person's transgressions against God or society or whomever he has injured and "cleans the slate," allowing the individual to be reinstated within the body of accepted individuals.

This pattern can be seen very clearly when one person thinks that he has done something very wrong. The penance of one soldier who felt very guilty when his buddy was shot took the form of self-punishment. Thinking that "the bullet should have got me, not him," the soldier deliberately set out to destroy all that he valued about himself (Jackson, 1957). If the guilt becomes terribly intense, the person may no longer be able to handle it consciously, and irrational views of penance may evolve. For instance, in one case a young Jewish man from an orthodox family rejected the Jewish faith and married a Protestant girl. The father did not disown the son, but he made it very clear how deeply his son's actions had hurt him. Relations between father and son were strained while the father was alive, and the death of the father precipitated intense guilt feelings in the son— guilt that was almost unbearable. He sought help from a psychotherapist, but that did not help. Shortly after, when he became ill with infectious hepatitis and was hospitalized, he asked the hospital chaplain, "Is this also a punishment for my sins?" (Jackson, 1957, p. 100).

Penance can also take the form of helping another person. This is clearly shown in the case of an army captain whose mother died unexpectedly. Since the captain had never been able to get along with his mother, he had avoided visiting her. At the time of her death he had not seen her for ten years; so her death made him feel extremely guilty. Several weeks later he decided to adopt a war orphan. Although the captain may not have been aware of it, his decision was probably in large part related to a desire to do penance to relieve his guilt about the way he had treated his mother (Jackson, 1957). The relationship between guilt and altruism is also clearly illustrated by several instances in which the black sheep of a family has offered to donate a kidney in order to make up for past events and to be reinstated in the family group (Kemph et al., 1969).

The guilt explanation neatly fits the findings in the experiments in which one person thinks he has harmed another. You think that you have administered electric shocks to someone, and you do penance by helping him, so that your guilt will be reduced and you will obtain absolution. Guilt can also explain the act of helping a person other than the victim when circumstances prevent the giving of aid directly to the victim or the subject is unwilling to face the person he has injured. Penance can still be done by helping another.

But how does one explain the fact that people will help others more after seeing an injury that they did not inflict? One possible answer is that seeing someone injured arouses—either consciously or unconsciously—one's own feelings of guilt about his other transgressions. Seeing someone shocked, for instance, might remind a college student who has been neglecting his parents of his own wrongdoings and arouse guilt.

However, a vicarious-guilt explanation assumes that everyone has guilt feelings that can be easily aroused. This may be true of some people, but not all. For some people, seeing others injured may be upsetting because it disturbs their belief in a just world. These people, it has been theorized, wish to believe that everyone gets what he deserves. Seeing someone suffer when he has done nothing to deserve punishment threatens this belief and may motivate people to try to eliminate the unjust suffering or to help the victim. In addition, seeing unjust suffering may make people more sensitive to the suffering of others and motivate them to perform altruistic acts (Simmons and Lerner, 1968).

The just-world explanation, then, would hold that different factors are at work when one is personally responsible for injury than when one witnesses injury. If this hypothesis is correct, would you predict that mere witnesses to injury would react differently from those made to feel responsible for that injury? Say an experimenter contrived to make some of his subjects believe that the experiment they were participating in had been ruined and then told half of those subjects that this misfortune was their fault and the other half that it was not their fault. Would the subjects who believed the experiment was a failure be more likely to engage in subsequent helping behavior than those in a control group who thought that nothing had gone wrong? And if guilt feelings could be exorcised in some way other than helping, would the "guilty" subjects be less likely to help than the "witnesses"?

In an experiment designed to explore these questions (Regan, 1971), it was found that subjects who felt the experiment was ruined were more likely to help when an opportunity was provided immediately after the experiment than those subjects who believed that nothing had gone wrong. Then, to distinguish between guilt-motivated altruism and that motivated by a belief in a just world, the experimenter encouraged half of the subjects in the responsible condition and half of those in the nonresponsible condition to express and rationalize their guilt. Another measure of the incidence of helping among these subjects was then obtained. As you might have expected, expressing their feelings of guilt decreased the incidence of helping among subjects who felt responsible, but did not decrease the incidence of helping among those who were only witnesses to the misfortune. Thus guilt may be the source of altruistic acts when people see themselves as responsible for the injuring of another, but perceived injustice may be the prime motivating

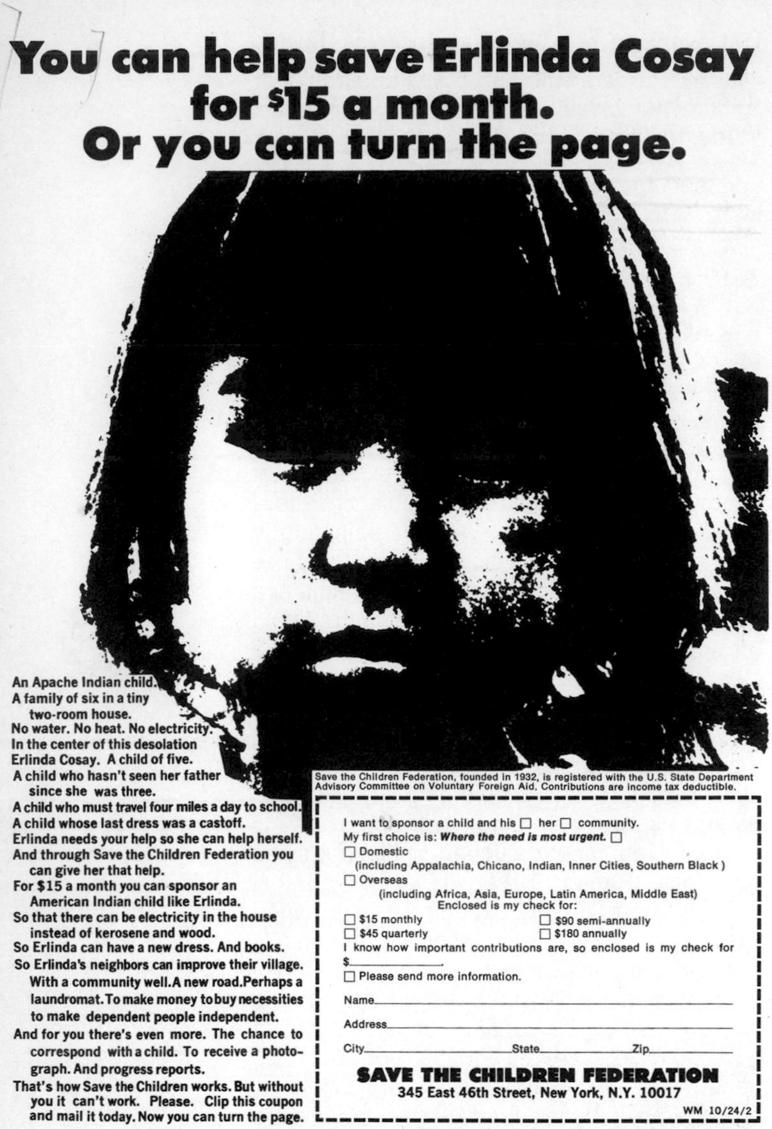

FIGURE 7-13 Clearly you are not personally responsible for Erlinda Cosay's problems. Yet many advertisements use the appeal of showing someone in need. What emotional reactions does this advertisement arouse in you? Vague guilt at your own affluence? Sympathy for her plight? Or a desire to make the world a fairer place in which needy children have a chance? (Courtesy, Save The Children Federation and Water-man, Getz, Miedelman Agency)

factor when they are only witnesses to misfortune.

Another explanation for the injury-helping effect is that the harm-doer or witness to the harm feels sympathy for the victim and wishes to do something that will make the victim feel better.

Although the sympathy theory seems plausible, the experimental data on it are inconsistent. In still another phase of the electric-shock experiment, the investigators had a subject watch a confederate who was ostensibly receiving painful shocks. The subject had nothing to do with the administration of the shocks; he was simply observing. In this condition the average number of telephone calls the subject agreed to make for the victim was significantly lower than the number the subjects who thought they were responsible for the shocking agreed to make (Carlsmith and Gross, 1969). Sympathy alone elicited surprisingly little helping in this situation.

However, a field study showed that sympathy was a very powerful motivator of helping—more so even than guilt (Konečni, 1972). The study was done on five rainy days on the streets of Toronto. In all conditions the experimenter dropped forty punched computer cards. The measure of helping was the number of subjects stopping to help the experimenter pick up the cards. There were four experimental conditions. In the control condition the experimenter let the cards slip out of a folder about four yards from the subject and said to the subject, "Please don't step on them." In the "restitution" condition the subject was made to think that it was his fault that the cards were dropped. The experimenter brushed his folder against the subject's arm so that the cards fell on the sidewalk in front of both the subject and himself. In the "sympathy" condition a confederate bumped into the experimenter and so appeared to cause the accident, and then—without any apology—simply walked away. In the "generalized-guilt" condition the subject was first made to think that he had caused a confederate to drop some expensive books. Then, after the subject had walked down the block, the experimenter let his cards slip out when the subject was four yards away.

In this experiment the highest percentage of subjects who helped pick up the cards was in the sympathy condition (64 percent). Forty-two percent of those in the generalized-guilt condition helped, as did 39 percent of those in the restitution condition. Only 16 percent of those in the control condition tried to help. It should be noted, however, that there was a possible confounding here. The experimenter's comment in the control condition, "Don't step on them," may have inhibited the subject's inclination to help and so have contributed to the low helping rate in that condition.

This experiment differed from the electric-shock experiment in several ways. First, the helping act was related directly to the injury that had been done, whereas in the electric-shock experiment there was no such relationship. Thus sympathy may explain helping only when it is possible for the person to undo some of the damage that has been done. Further, the sympathy manipulation in the computer-card study was very emotionally involving for the subjects. Many subjects in this condition made remarks about the confederate's lack of consideration. For sympathy to elicit helping, therefore, it may also be necessary for it to be strongly aroused.

Thus guilt, a desire to believe in a fair world, and sympathy can all contribute to the injury-helping effect. (See Figure 7-13.) In some situations all three may be involved. If you were to see a mugger attacking a woman who was the same age as your mother, you might feel guilty because you had not telephoned recently, you might resent the injustice of the situation, and you might feel sympathetic toward the woman. Or, as we shall see in the next section, you might feel that she deserved her fate.

Injury-Justification Effect As we saw earlier, people have a need to believe they live in a just world in which deserving people are rewarded and the undeserving are appropriately deprived or punished. (Imagine the threat of believing that the world is unjust or unfair. If you believed this, then everyone and everything would be a potential threat. Nothing would be predictable or under the control of the individual.) Given this need, when people are exposed to those who are suffering through no fault of their own, they experience a conflict. They can either decide that the world is not such a fair place after all—which disturbs their basic assumption and makes them uncomfortable. Or they can justify the victim's suffering through a variety of rationalizations (Lerner, 1970).

One way they can do this is to believe that the victim deserved his fate because he was basically bad. This effect was apparent to ancient philosophers. Tacitus, for example, noted: "It is a principle of human nature to hate those you

have injured." A number of studies have shown that harm-doers who feel guilty about injuring another person will derogate their victim. In one study, for instance, students who were hired to humiliate other students as part "of a research project" tended to convince themselves that those they were ridiculing were inferior and deserving of ridicule (Davis and Jones, 1960). One study of juvenile delinquents showed that the delinquents often defend their crimes toward others on the grounds that the victims are really homosexuals, bums, or possess other undesirable traits that make them deserving of punishment (Sykes and Matza, 1957).

Interestingly, several studies have shown that even if you do not inflict the injury yourself, there is a tendency to derogate the victim. In one study, for instance, half of the subjects saw a slide portraying scenes in which a white policeman was attacking a black civilian; the other half saw only that portion of the slide showing the heads of the black man and the white policeman. All subjects were asked to rate the attacker and the victim. As predicted, when the subjects thought the victim would not be allowed to see their ratings, they rated him more negatively when he was shown being attacked than when just his head was shown (Lincoln and Levinger, 1972). The desire to maintain their belief that the world is a fair place in which policemen do not attack people indiscriminately apparently motivated the subjects to believe the victim deserved his fate.

This finding obviously has widespread social implications. People may rationalize the injustices and cruelty of the present prison system on the grounds that the inmates are evil and deserve to be treated as they are. Or the same phenomenon may be at work to ease the conscience of affluent Americans who justify the financial hardships of those on welfare by thinking that the recipients are "lazy bums" who will not work. Or the discriminations against blacks may be justified by thinking that blacks are lazy and inferior and deserve their fate, since, "after all, my ancestors made it on their own" in this country.

Other ways may also be used to justify the victim's suffering. One may *deny responsibility* for the suffering. For example, in the electric-shock experiment a subject who thought he had shocked another person could have explained his behavior by convincing himself that he was not really responsible for the number of shocks administered: "The other person only got shocked when he was stupid enough to make an incorrect response." That harm-doers will often deny personal responsibility for their actions has been shown in several studies (e.g., Brock and Buss, 1962).

Another way to rationalize one's guilt is to *minimize the suffering* that has been caused. In the electric-shock experiment one might argue that the shocks were not really so painful. Several studies have shown that subjects administering shocks do not regard them as causing any significant suffering (e.g., Brock and Buss, 1962).

Determinants of the Reaction to Suffering
Whether seeing others being injured leads to helping or to justification of their suffering is determined by three variables: (1) the observer's power to take action, (2) the adequacy of the means available to him to make appropriate restitution, and (3) the believability of the justification attempt.

Seeing someone suffer when there is nothing you can do to aid him generally leads to justification of his suffering. In contrast, if an easy means of helping the victim is available, witnessing the suffering of another leads to an increase in helping. Support for this hypothesis was obtained in the study in which half of the subjects saw a black civilian being attacked by a white policeman and the other half saw only the heads of the two figures with all of the aggressive content masked out (Lincoln and Levinger, 1972). The subjects' ratings of the black victim were made under two different conditions. Half of the subjects thought that their ratings would be used only by the experimenter, and the other half thought that their ratings would be forwarded to a commission investigating the black man's case. When the subjects thought that their ratings would be seen only by the experimenter, they felt that there was nothing they could do to help, whereas when they thought that their ratings would be examined by a group investigating the case, there was clearly something they could do to help. As predicted, when the subjects felt powerless to aid the victim, they gave him a negative rating. When they felt that they could help

him, their ratings were significantly more positive.

The powerless-negative reaction findings have obvious practical implications. As society becomes more complex and as the individual feels a growing sense of powerlessness, witnessing the needs of another may lead to derogation rather than compassion. The less able we feel to give aid, the more likely we may be to derogate, which, in turn, helps spread a general sense of a lack of concern, indifference, or hostility. Thus, ironically, at a political level, those most in need of help, the powerless poor, may come to derogate others like themselves since they can't do anything to help them.

The more accurately the available means of restitution reflect the original injury, the more likely it is that the harm-doer will make restitution. If you injured another by administering electric shocks, you would probably help him out by making some telephone calls, but if your restitution were limited to a choice between giving him no money or giving him $100, you would probably do nothing to make amends.

According to equity theory, people attempt to maintain "equitable relationships" in which the proportion of each member's contributions and benefits is equal to that of the others (Adams, 1965). Consequently, when you injure another person, you wish to restore balance to the relationship by increasing what the other person is getting out of it. To make up for the injury, you do something nice for him, which is roughly equivalent to the injury done.

In other words, if you were to do something that on an imaginary scale of harmfulness was −3 units, you would wish to make restitution with a pleasant act that was +3 units. Two investigators have obtained experimental verification for this equity interpretation of restitution (Berscheid and Walster, 1967). In an experiment with women's church groups, these researchers led women to cheat others out of trading stamps in order to win additional stamps for themselves. Subsequently, when the women were given an opportunity to make restitution to the victim, the possible techniques of restitution influenced whether or not the victims were compensated. Women who could make restitution exactly by giving their partners the same number of books they had taken were much more likely to do so than women limited either to insufficient restitution (just a few stamps) or to excessive restitution (many more stamp books than they had taken).

This finding has implications for real-life restitutions. Frequently, when an individual has been hurt, he exaggerates the extent of his injury in an attempt to force another to make amends voluntarily. A person has an argument with a friend who hurts his feelings; to make it up, the friend should do something that is very important and meaningful. An equity analysis tells us that when the demanded reparation is much larger than the original injury, restitution is much less likely to be made.

A further complicating factor in real-life restitutions is that the two individuals involved may differ in their notion of what equity is. Very likely, the injured party always will experience more hurt than the injuring party imagines he has inflicted. Nothing hurts as much as our own pain. Thus, what is equity for the injured party may seem to be overcompensation for the injuror. Resolving this source of conflict in everyday restitutions is very difficult.

The believability of the justification for the victim's suffering also influences whether viewing or inflicting suffering will result in helping or justification (Scott and Lyman, 1968). If a wrongdoer can explain and justify his misdeed well enough to really believe his explanation, he will use this technique. Several factors are involved in whether a justification is believable.

The less distortion involved in a justification, the more believable the justification will be. If a person can rationalize his administering electric shocks by distorting only his view of the recipient, this rationalization will be more believable than if he has to distort many aspects of the situation. People like to feel that their views of a situation are correct.

The more public a justification must be, the less likely it is that a harm-doer will use rationalizations to restore equity. What one can accept in his own mind may not hold up under the close scrutiny of others.

The less contact the harm-doer has had with the victim, the more readily he will rationalize his acts. The more he knows about his victim, the more difficult it is for him to explain away his acts. If he has to watch the reactions of his victim, for example, it will be more difficult for

him to minimize the painfulness of the electric shocks.

Summary

Both moods and feelings influence the extent to which people are willing to help others. If someone is in a *good mood,* he is more likely to help than if he is in a bad mood. Although the answer to the question of why mood influences the incidence of helping is not clear at the present time, there are several possible explanations. One is that being in a good mood frees people from self-preoccupation and allows them to empathize more with the needs and problems of others. Another possible explanation is that people who are depressed are more likely to interpret another person's request for help as an infringement on their freedom.

For most people, regardless of their mood, certain feelings are aroused when injury is inflicted on another person. When the subject feels responsible for the act, he will experience *guilt.* Regardless of his responsibility, he may also experience a desire to correct the wrong so as to maintain his view that the world is a fair place, or maintain his feeling of *equity.* And he may experience *sympathy*—a compassion toward the injured person. Any one of these feelings can cause altruistic behavior.

When subjects are made to believe they have injured another, they are more likely to help the person they have injured than when these guilt feelings have not been aroused. Further, reparation has been found to generalize to persons other than the victim. The incidence of helping may be higher for the victim than for another person in situations in which the victim cannot identify the person who has injured him.

Even if you are not personally responsible for someone else's being injured, seeing someone hurt can sometimes increase the incidence of your helping. One explanation for this phenomenon is that for some people, seeing others injured may be upsetting because it *disturbs their belief in a just world.* Seeing someone suffer when he has not done anything to deserve punishment threatens this belief and sometimes motivates people to try to eliminate the unjust suffering or to help the victim.

Sympathy for the victim may also stimulate

altruistic behavior. Although the sympathy theory seems plausible, the experimental data on it are inconsistent. Sympathy may elicit helping only when the helping act is directly related to the injury that has been done or when the sympathy is strongly aroused.

Seeing another injured does not inevitably result in helping. Under certain conditions the witness may derogate the victim or deny responsibility—a *justification reaction*. When an individual is exposed to people who are suffering through no fault of their own, he may experience a conflict. He can either decide that the world is not such a fair place after all—which is disturbing—or he can justify the victim's suffering through a variety of rationalizations. He can convince himself that the victim deserved his fate because he was basically bad or that he is not really suffering much. If one is responsible for the victim's suffering, he can deny responsibility for the suffering.

Whether seeing others being injured leads to helping or justification of their suffering is determined by variables in the situation. Seeing someone suffer when there is nothing you can do to aid the person generally leads to justification of his suffering, whereas if an easy means of helping the victim is available, witnessing the suffering of another leads to an increase in helping. The more adequately the available means of restitution reflect the original injury, the more likely it is that the harm-doer will make restitution. And the easier it is to believe in the justification for the victim's suffering, the more likely it is that the justification will be used to support nonhelping behavior. Factors influencing the ease of justification are the extent of distortion involved, the publicity given to the justification, and the amount of contact between the harm-doer or witness and the victim.

Increasing Altruism

We have just spent a full chapter discussing variables that influence the incidence of altruism. After all the research is in and the theories are laid out, what does social psychology have to offer a world where there is all too much violence and all too little altruism? As we pointed out in Chapter 6, before we consider ways of increasing the incidence of altruism it should be emphasized that the suggestions are speculative and only loosely based on research findings. As in any other social behavior, a number of factors determine whether or not a person will act altruistically. Perhaps altruistic behavior can only occur when several variables are working simultaneously. For instance, it is possible that a person may help another only if he has absorbed the social responsibility norm and if the rewards for helping outweigh the costs. Further, once a situation is established which discourages altruism, how can determinants be distinguished from consequences? Are American cities so dangerous and crime ridden because people fail to assume responsibility for one another or do people fail to help others because they are fearful of being harmed in the process? Evidence from controlled, rigorous experiments is simply not available on many of these questions.

At present, there is too little helping in our society. At the beginning of the chapter, we saw that thirty-eight people, who were safely in their homes with telephones readily accessible, silently witnessed the murder of Catherine Genovese. In another incident, forty people witnessed a rape in progress and none of them intervened or attempted to get help. The author has seen a passenger injured and thrown out of a taxi cab in New York City only to have a number of passersby step over the wounded person and pass on with no attempt to help. Some American Indians go hungry on government reservations and many Americans ignore their plight. The list of apathy and neglect could go on and on. (See Figure 7-14.) If our society is not to become totally impassive, some action must obviously be taken now.

Implementing some of the following suggestions would be difficult because it would involve social change which—as we saw earlier—is usually resisted. Further, the competitive, every-man-for-himself philosophy is very much with us, and many people may not care whether or not altruism is increased. The need to decrease aggression may be an issue on which the members of our society are more unanimous. Very few are in favor of mugging. But how many people care whether our society is one in which people are kind to those who need help? The pressures of a society in which many are forced to compete, to rush around, and to be exposed daily to examples of hypocrisy and greed rather than truth and charity may make increasing the incidence of altruism even more difficult than controlling aggression.

Teaching altruism

Throughout the text we have seen two generalizations emerge from the discussion of child-rearing practices: (1) rewarded behavior tends to reoccur and (2) children learn by imitating what the adults around them do. These two findings suggest that adults interacting with children should reward altruistic behavior and—more importantly—should act altruistically themselves. Assuming that most of you will be or already are parents, these generalizations are of obvious personal relevance to you. How might you personally apply reinforcement and modeling techniques? To teach your child al-truism, you would praise your child when he voiced concern over the plight of others or when he helped another. You might devise games in which the child was provided an opportunity to act altruistically and reward him when he did so. Instead of buying dolls that are designed to look like soldiers—as the highly popular set of GI Joe dolls are—you might concentrate more on toy replicas of those who make a profession of helping others. Being kind to those who need help is the best way for an adult to teach a child to be altruistic. Donating blood, giving money to or working for local charities, expressing concern over the plight of those who need help, and emphasizing the importance of helping others will have a lasting impact.

Further, teaching altruism need not be limited to small children. Students of college age have been shown to undergo a number of changes in attitudes and behaviors during the four-year college period, as we saw in the Bennington study. Thus, you may encourage altruism in your peers by rewarding it when it occurs and by serving as an altruistic model to others.

FIGURE 7-14 An example of contemporary apathy to the needs of others. (Shelly Rusten)

Countering the bystander effect

Many people do not help when they are with others because social pressure may make them less likely to interpret an event as one demanding action and less likely to accept personal responsibility. Just knowing about the existence of this effect may make it less likely to apply to you. Knowing that others in a situation that may require action are as unsure as you and as likely to assume that someone else will take the necessary action may counter your own tendency not to act. Against the modest risk of embarrassment at offering help when it is not needed, you, by initiating helping behavior in an ambiguous situation, may lead others to perform in a similar way.

Further, the group-induced tendency to downplay the seriousness of a situation may be countered by the extent of the need being made clearer. At home, in school, and in churches and synagogues, children might be encouraged to role play the part of persons in various situations of need. Taking the role of a person who is ill in a public place might make children more sensitive to the needs of persons in such a situation. Taking children to visit those in need—say in convalescent hospitals—would counter their tendency to ignore the plight of these individuals. Greater media coverage given to those who need help—such as some of the very poor—also would make it more difficult for many middle-class Americans to ignore the needs of others.

Fostering a sense of personal responsibility for victims might make people more likely to assume responsibility for action. Programs that provide for helping on a person-to-person basis rather than an impersonal donation to a general cause may be more likely to lead to a continued involvement. In this respect, the program of the Save the Children Federation, for instance, which provides people with a chance to correspond with the child and to get his photograph and his progress reports, may result in more helping than one-shot charitable efforts from which the person can easily disengage.

Further, increasing the individual's feeling that he knows how to help may increase his tendency to assume responsibility and to take action. Circulating information about specific steps that can be taken to help in a variety of situations would be expected to increase the incidence of altruism. For instance, knowing the steps involved in calling for aid in the event of a car accident might make people more likely to take helpful action. Feeling powerless to do anything may be one of the biggest deterrents to taking action.

Increasing adherence to the social responsibility and reciprocity norms

Parents and teachers are in an excellent position to emphasize and reinforce the social responsibility and reciprocity norms. As we saw in the case of teaching altruism in general, actions may count for more than words in teaching children to adhere to these norms. Acting in a socially responsible way and providing live examples of helping may be much more effective in teaching the norms than an adult's verbally espousing them.

Giving greater publicity to acts of altruism would also be expected to make people more likely to adhere to the social responsibility norm. For example, increased distribution of the free magazine *Synergist* published by the National Student Volunteer Program in ACTION (806 Connecticut Avenue, N.W., Washington, D.C. 20525)—which describes a wide variety of student volunteer programs, resources for volunteers, and ways to make student volunteer programs more effective—might encourage students to become involved in volunteer programs. Instead of burying accounts of helping acts in the back pages of newspapers, they should be featured. Television interviews with some of the many people who have helped others, such as those involved in the many ACTION programs, would provide a model for helping. Further, the models should be encouraged to describe the joys of helping. For instance, students involved in working at a community mental health facility might be encouraged to speak in a psychology class or a meeting of a psychology club to describe the rewards their work has brought them.

Parents, in dealing with their children, and people of all ages, in dealing with others, could reward reciprocity and demonstrate reciprocity in their dealings with others so as to serve as models. Further, giving the recipient a chance to reciprocate may be more rewarding to both donor and recipient. Instead of sending a check to a nameless "they," aid might be given in a manner that enables the recipient to repay the donor. Middle-class Americans might feel much more positive about lending money to an impoverished student who wished to complete his education if they thought that it would be repaid, and the recipient might feel more comfortable about receiving a loan than a gift.

Reducing the costs of helping

People may not help because they are afraid they will be hurt if they do so. Even when a child has been thoroughly taught that he should behave responsibly toward others, if he walks down a street on which muggings occur frequently, his thoughts will probably not be on helping others but rather on his own safety. The high crime rate in many areas testifies to the fact that a concern for the urban dweller's own safety is a realistic one.

Consequently, if people are to help others, their own fears of physical danger must be reduced. One way to do this is to provide opportunities for people to report incidents and to retain their anonymity. A recent program in Hartford, Connecticut, provides an interesting example of how providing for anonymity increases the incidence of helping. To combat a high rate of heroin sales in the city, the police department instituted a "bust the pusher" program which was given extensive coverage in local newspapers and television programs. A telephone number which could be called at any time, day or night, was released, and it was emphasized that callers could report pushers without giving their names. All the callers had to do was to give the name of the alleged pusher and the area in which he peddled heroin. Thus the realistic fear of reprisals for reporting a suspected drug pusher were minimized, and hundreds of telephone calls were received.

People sometimes may not help because they are afraid they may be sued if they do or that their helping will involve them in time-consuming court cases. At the present time, in some states, a physician may be sued for malpractice by an accident victim who thinks the doctor did not act competently. Fear of malpractice suits may discourage a physician from coming to the aid of an accident victim. "Good Samaritan" laws to protect doctors who help accident victims under very adverse circumstances might make doctors more willing to give aid. Setting firm times at which a witness would give testimony would decrease the costs of acknowledging witnessing an accident. Under the present court procedures, a witness can sit in court for days waiting his turn to testify and have no idea when he will be called.

Making it easier and more convenient to help would also reduce the costs of helping. The Hartford "bust the pusher" program is a good case in point. To help, the Good Samaritan did not have to write a lengthy letter or go downtown to see an official. All that was required was a simple telephone call which could be made at any time. Providing free telephone "hot lines" to the police might make people more likely to report crimes. If charities, such as the Salvation Army, increased the number of bins and so made them more accessible to a greater number of people, more people would probably donate.

Increasing the rewards for helping

Providing material rewards for altruism would probably increase the incidence of helping. If the New York City police department had had a policy of rewarding reports on attempted crimes with $50, do you think one of the thirty-eight witnesses of the Genovese murder might have telephoned? The chances are that someone might have. To paraphrase the water pollution bounty hunters quoted earlier in this chapter, being socially responsible is good, but so is money.

Increasing the social rewards for altruism might also increase the incidence of altruism. Those who have helped others might be given medals and extensive publicity. Cities and towns sponsoring a "Good Samaritan of the Month" contest might stimulate some to help others whom they might otherwise ignore. Social support for helping might be increased by those in existing charitable groups emphasizing the helping function of their groups. Additional groups that are dedicated to helping, such as Nader's Raiders, could be created, and the social support and conformity pressures in these groups would probably result in increased dedication.

Countering the tendency to denigrate the victim

Whether seeing others being injured leads to helping or to justification of their suffering is in part determined by the observer's power to take action. Earlier in this section, we emphasized the need to make people feel competent to take action. For events which can be handled by one person, specific training may increase the feeling of competency. For larger problems which cannot be solved by action of any one person, the individual can be shown how his work has contributed to the group's progress toward its goal. Providing training which shows the potential helper a wide variety of possible ways to help others may make the means available to make appropriate restitution.

Countering the tendency to justify the victim's plight might also be accomplished by having potential helpers take the role of the victim. After reading about prison conditions, you may not get too involved with the idea that prison reform is necessary. But if you were to play the role of a prisoner in the Stanford County Jail and have another student, acting the part of a guard, yell obscenities at you and harrass you, you might find your interest in reform growing.

There is, of course, no guarantee that implementing the suggestions made in this section will drastically increase the incidence of altruism on the contemporary American scene. However, there is some evidence to indicate that their implementation would probably have a positive effect. And if we continue without changing some of the conditions that produce apathy, there is no reason to believe that its incidence will decrease. In fact, the unchecked pressures of competition and fear may make altruism a rarer phenomenon in the future than it is today.

SUMMARY

Acts of altruism abound in our society, even though they rarely command the front-page space more commonly reserved for sensational forms of aggressive behavior. These helping acts stand in sharp contrast to the indifference, apathy, and reluctance of many people to intervene in someone else's behalf—as was shown by the Genovese case.

1. Definition of "Altruism" Altruism may be defined in either motivational or behavioral terms. According to a motivational definition, a helping act is altruistic when it is motivated primarily by an anticipation of its positive consequences for another individual. According to a behavioral view, altruism encompasses any conduct that helps another, regardless of the helper's motives. Neither of these approaches are perfect, but the behavioral definition is the one most commonly used in the scientific literature, since behavior is easier to measure objectively.

2. Is Altruism Learned or Instinctive? Some have argued that altruistic behavior may be in part instinctive. Since any particular individual is more likely to survive when living with others than when living alone, the more cooperative, social beings would be the more likely ones to survive and reproduce, so that gradually—over thousands of years—evolutionary processes would favor the development of innate helping motives. This view provides an interesting alternative to the traditional view in psychology that man is naturally self-centered, but proving the existence of an instinct in man is extremely difficult. Further, even if altruism were basic to human nature, an instinctive explanation would not explain the variations in helping behavior.

Two primary conditions facilitate the learning of any behavior, including altruism: reinforcement and imitation. A number of studies show that when altruism is rewarded—with either material or social rewards—the tendency of subjects to be altruistic in that particular situation increases. Empathy may also be a source of rewards for altruism. If you can feel pain when you see another's pain, you may attempt to reduce his pain and so reduce your own. Acquaintance with the victim and the individual's inclination to take action to relieve his own feelings of discomfort have been shown to increase the amount of altruism motivated by empathy.

Observing a helpful model encourages the observer to be helpful. Parents who are helpful and who tell their children about helping can be expected to have helpful children—according to the identification hypothesis. Relatively few studies on the relationship between the altruism of parents and that of their child have been done, and the results have not always been consistent; but in general these studies do support the identification hypothesis.

3. Awareness of a Need to Help and the Acceptance of Personal Responsibility It has been shown repeatedly that when people are with others, they are much less likely to help in an emergency than when they are alone—the so-called *bystander effect*. When people are with others, they are likely to *minimize the seriousness of the incident*. Further, the presence of other people *diffuses responsibility* for taking action. Any variation in the situation that makes the individual less likely to interpret an event as one demanding action or that diffuses the responsibility for taking action will decrease the incidence of helping. However, if the situation is clearly an emergency or if aspects of the situation make it difficult for the individual to believe that others will help, he may be more likely to feel responsible and to take action. If a person is forced to accept responsibility for the well-being of a person in distress or if the other bystanders are seen as unable to help, then the individual is more apt to help.

4. An Overview: Why Do People Help? Three main answers, each of which overlaps the others, have been given to this question. One is the *normative* approach. Two helping norms have been explored extensively: (1) the norm of *social responsibility,* that a person should help others who are dependent on him, and (2) the

norm of *reciprocity,* that a person should treat others as they have treated him. According to a normative analysis, helping will occur when the helping norms become salient. In contrast, the *cost-analysis* approach holds that the incidence of helping behavior in a particular situation depends completely on the relationship between the costs of and the rewards for helping. Costs would be the negative consequences to the individual; rewards, the positive consequences. Still a third analysis of helping is that *moods* and *feelings* influence the incidence of helping. If someone is in a good mood, he will be much more likely to help than if he is in a bad mood. Feelings of guilt and sympathy and a belief in a just world may all induce helping behavior after a person has witnessed harm being done to another. Under certain circumstances, however, witnessing harm being done to another may lead to a justification of the injury rather than helping.

5. The Normative Explanation of Helping Behavior Two norms have been theorized to account for much of helping behavior.

The *social responsibility norm* is widely accepted in our society. At times people act to help others, not for material gain or social approval, but simply to do what is right. This explanation of helping is in direct conflict with another view of human social interaction—the social exchange theory—which holds that all of an individual's actions are determined by the rewards he thinks his actions will bring. Although it is always possible to argue that a helping person receives some reward for helping, a number of studies have shown that American college students will work hard to help someone who needs help even when there is little in it for themselves, the recipient does not know who has helped him, and the experimenter is not aware of their helping.

Some types of dependency are much more apt to elicit help than others. If you feel that another individual is personally responsible for his plight, you may be less likely to help him. The incidence of helping may also be influenced by reactance: Any appeal that limits the prospective helper's freedom decreases his inclination to help.

There are great variations in helping behavior. Repeatedly, it has been shown that people are more likely to be helpful after observing another person (a model) helping. What exactly does the model have to do in order to elicit imitative helping? Unlike aggression, where verbal exhortation to aggress may be enough to induce aggressive behavior, a model must actually engage in helping behavior to induce altruism in others.

In addition to being reminded by models, individuals are reminded about their social responsibilities in other ways. They may, for example, be asked directly to be charitable. A person may also be reminded of his responsibility to help others by reading religious writings.

The *reciprocity norm* has been demonstrated in a number of laboratory experiments. Subjects have been found to be much more likely to help another person when that person had previously helped them. If the person who helped originally is not available, the recipient is likely to help a third person.

The reciprocity norm has important practical implications for international relations and business. For instance, if people prefer reciprocal relationships, foreign aid given on a no strings basis may only create hostility and resentment—a common reaction to our foreign aid program. In the business world, if a person feels that his employer is not paying him enough to compensate him fairly for the effort he is expending, he may curtail his work, so that its quantity and quality match his compensation. Conversely, if employees feel that they are being overpaid, they may increase the quality of their work in order to reciprocate.

Reciprocity tends to decrease when the benefactor's motives are questioned, when the other person has been compelled to help, and when the recipient sees the favor as being obligating. Reciprocity tends to increase when the helping person is believed to have limited resources and when the helping acts are unexpected. The reciprocity norm is much stronger in some individuals and groups than in others.

Although a normative explanation of helping has generated a number of testable ideas, it does have one limitation. Social norms sometimes conflict with each other. Without a very careful specification of which norms would be expected to apply in a given situation, a normative theorist is in danger of using norms to explain any set of results.

6. A Cost Analysis of Helping Helping behavior is most likely to occur when the rewards for helping outweigh the costs. Note that costs involve more than financial costs: They include all of the negative aspects that would be involved in helping.

Any variation that increases the costs of helping would be expected to elicit less altruism. Five aspects of cost have been investigated. The relative cost of the *help requested* influences the incidence of helping. Helping is much less likely to occur if it involves the *threat of danger*—either physical threat, the potential for embarrassment, or a threat to social status. People are more likely to help if they are *familiar with the environment.* The increased cost of potential embarrassment if one tries to help in an unfamiliar situation deters helping. Generally, any variation that decreases the immediate *financial cost* can be expected to increase the amount of helping, particularly when some cue, such as dependency, is present. *Time pressures* decrease the incidence of helping. If people are busy and interested in what they are doing, they are less likely to spend time helping another person.

Any aspect of a situation that increases the rewards of helping will increase the frequency of helping. Giving *material rewards* increases the tendency of subjects to be altruistic in a particular situation. *Social reinforcement* for helping also increases that tendency, particularly reinforcement from someone you admire, think is an attractive person, like, or who is similar to yourself. Although people are generally more apt to help friends than strangers, they may be more apt to help someone they wish to gain as a friend than someone they know so well that they are confident of the relationship. People are more willing to help compatriots than foreigners. Similarity in political attitudes and clothing style also increases the incidence of helping. *Empathy* can also be a source of reward for helping. In order for people to help, they must feel that they are making a *meaningful, powerful contribution.*

Any variables that increase the individual's sense of personal effectiveness will increase the chances of his helping. When a person performs an altruistic act, *his self-esteem and his view of himself are enhanced.* The self can also enter into altruism in another way. Although most of the people in our society have accepted the general ideal that people should help others, frequently self-concerns monopolize our interest. Suddenly being made to realize the gap between what you are and what you want to be can motivate altruism.

Cost analysis provides an interesting and research-stimulating way of thinking about altruistic behavior. Like the norm explanation, however, it does not provide a definition of the two key terms, reward and cost. If these terms are not defined independently of experimental results, the cost analysis can become an exercise in circular reasoning.

7. Moods and Feelings Both moods and feelings influence the extent to which people are willing to help others. Someone in a *good mood* is more likely to help than someone in a bad mood, perhaps because he is relatively free from self-preoccupation and more able to empathize with the needs and problems of others. People who are depressed may be more likely to interpret another person's request for help as an infringement on their freedom.

When subjects are made to believe that they have injured another, they are more likely to help the person they have injured than when these *guilt feelings* have not been aroused. Further, reparation has been found to generalize to persons other than the victim. The incidence of helping may be higher for the victim than for another person in situations in which the victim cannot identify the person who has injured him.

Even if you are not personally responsible for someone else's being injured, seeing someone hurt can sometimes increase your incidence of helping. Seeing others injured may *disturb one's belief in a just world.* When the victim has not done anything to deserve punishment, his fate threatens this belief and may motivate people to try to eliminate the unjust suffering he is enduring.

Sympathy for the victim may also stimulate altruistic behavior. Although this hypothesis seems plausible, the experimental data are inconsistent. Sympathy may elicit helping only when the helping act is directly related to the injury that has been done or when the sympathy is strongly aroused.

Seeing another injured does not inevitably result in helping. Under certain conditions the witness may derogate the victim or deny responsibility—the *justification reaction.* When an individual is exposed to people who are suffering through no fault of their own, he may experience a conflict. He can either decide that the world is not such a fair place after all—which is disturbing—or he can justify the victim's suffering through a variety of rationalizations. He can convince himself that the victim deserved his fate because he was basically bad or that he is not really suffering much. If one is responsible for the victim's suffering, he can deny responsibility for the suffering.

Whether seeing others being injured leads to helping or to justification of their suffering is determined by variables in the situation. Seeing someone suffer when there is nothing that you can do to aid the person generally leads to justification of his suffering, whereas if an easy means of helping the victim is available, witnessing the suffering of another leads to an increase in helping. The more adequately the available means of restitution reflect the original injury, the more likely it is that the harm-doer will make restitution. And the easier it is to believe in the justification for the victim's suffering, the more likely it is that the justification will be used to support nonhelping behavior. Factors influencing the ease of justification are the extent of distortion involved, the publicity given to the justification, and the contact between the harm-doer and his victim.

8. Increasing Altruism Six ways to increase the incidence of altruism were discussed. Parents and teachers applying reinforcement and modeling techniques to teach children to help would increase the incidence of altruism. The bystander effect might be countered by teaching about the inhibiting effects of groups on helping, by making clearer the extent of the need, by fostering a sense of personal responsibility, and by increasing the individual's feeling that he is competent to help. Adults' adhering to the social responsibility and reciprocity norms—as well as giving greater publicity to helping acts—would probably increase adherence to these norms.

Reducing the costs of helping—by reducing the fear of physical danger, law suits, and time-consuming litigation—would increase the incidence of helping. Making it easier and more convenient to help would also reduce the costs. Increasing the material and social rewards for altruism would probably increase the incidence of helping.

Whether seeing others being injured leads to helping them or simply justifying their suffering is in part determined by the observer's power to take action. Making people feel competent to help would decrease the justification reaction to suffering. Also, having potential helpers take the role of victims in various situations would make justification of the victim's suffering more difficult.

DISCUSSION QUESTIONS

1. Do you think a motivational or a behavioral definition of "altruism" accords more closely with the way most people use the term?

2. Have you ever seen any evidence of the bystander effect at work?

3. Examine the motives involved in your own helping behavior. Which of the three explanations given in the text—norms, costs, moods and feelings—do you think explains most of your helping?

4. Do you think people help when there is little in it for themselves?

5. On reflection about your own interactions with others, do you see any evidence of your behavior being governed by the reciprocity norm?

6. Of all the costs and rewards listed in the text, which one (or ones) do you think contributes most significantly to your own helping behavior?

7. How do you think children learn to be altruistic?

8. Several variables that influence an individual's decision to accept responsibility to help were discussed in the text. Can you think of any additional variables that would influence this process? Give evidence to support your answer.

9. Which types of dependency do you think are most apt to elicit help? Which types are least likely?

10. Why do you think people prefer reciprocal relationships to ones in which they receive gifts with no strings attached?

11. Under which circumstances do you think a person would be more likely to help a friend than a stranger? When might he be more likely to help a stranger than a friend?

12. Three variables were listed in the text that determine whether seeing others being injured leads to helping or to justification of their suffering. After considering historical and contemporary examples of the justification of injury, see if you can derive additional variables that increase the chances of justification.

13. Under what circumstances do you think the members of a group might be more likely to help than single individuals? Design an experiment to test your hypothesis.

14. If you could magically rearrange the circumstances of Miss Genovese's murder, how would you maximize the chances of a bystander helping her? Use all of the findings discussed on pages 322–329, as well as the insights offered by the three approaches to helping—normative, costs, and moods and feelings—in planning your setting.

15. Design an experiment to test the effects of arousing reactance on the incidence of helping. In addition to stating your proposed procedure, state how you would manipulate reactance, how

you would verify the effectiveness of your manipulation, and how you would measure the incidence of helping.

16. People who think they are being overpaid will work harder in order to reciprocate the payment. How could one apply this finding to increase the amount of work students do in a social psychology course?

17. A number of different aspects of costs and rewards for helping were discussed in the text. Can you think of any additional ones?

18. Three feelings—guilt, a disturbed belief that the world is just, and sympathy—can be aroused when a person sees someone else being injured. In which circumstances do you think each of these is the most powerful in stimulating altruistic behavior? Design an experiment to test one of your hypotheses.

19. In field studies which are staged under conditions that minimize helping, real people see others not helping. As a result, this may lower the probability that they will help subsequently in actual danger situations. Do you think this poses an ethical problem?

8

PERSON PERCEPTION

How do you form an impression of other people? Look back at the five photographs on page 369 and then answer the following questions about the characteristics, interests, and attitudes of the people shown.

Person *a* probably
_____ likes rock music.
_____ does not like rock music.

Person *b* probably
_____ supported Wallace for the Democratic nomination in 1972.
_____ opposed Wallace for the Democratic nomination in 1972.

Person *c* is probably
_____ a college student.
_____ not a college student.

Person *d* is probably
_____ materialistic.
_____ not materialistic.

Person *e* is probably
_____ pleasant.
_____ not pleasant.

On the basis of only the physical appearance and facial expressions of these people, you probably formed a fairly clear idea of how to answer these completion questions. Smiling people are pleasant and all police support Wallace. In fact, you probably went beyond the simple completion questions offered in the quiz and formed impressions of their motives, emotions, and interests. In "person perception" we are not content with simply seeing and noting the physical characteristics of others. We do not just say we see a man wearing a business suit and glasses in picture *d*. We go beyond these obvious features and infer, or "attribute," his underlying motives, interests, abilities, and thoughts. For example, we may form an overall impression of this man as dedicated, hard-driving, and conscientious—probably a busi-

ness executive or a lawyer. From the information provided by the picture alone, we try to organize a meaningful impression of the overall man.

As a more concrete illustration of how this works, let us consider the impression that John, a college senior, formed of Jean, a girl who recently stopped by his apartment with another girl that he knew:

Jean has a pretty face and is really built. No bra and she was great up top and just a little heavy below the hips. Her dress was casual—flared jeans, a blouse, very little makeup, and long and straight hair. She seemed a very natural girl—not materialistic like a heavily made-up airline stewardess type. She was very clean and very nice—probably contemplative and into existential philosophy a little. And she was liberated—not a prude.

As we talked, she sometimes averted her eyes and looked at her girl friend more often than she did at me. She seemed shy. As I talked, she nodded her head to show that she was agreeing with what I was saying and occasionally she smiled at me. She seemed to like me and to be interested in what I was saying— she seemed to be a warm and friendly person.

After a while, I started to play some music—one of my favorite groups, the Grateful Dead. She didn't respond at all. When I started talking about other well-known rock groups, she didn't seem to know what we were talking about. She didn't even react to the Rolling Stones. My initial feeling that she was a hip chick began to blur. To me, people who are into rock music are into their heads more—more contemplative. If they don't know anything about music, you begin to wonder about them. But maybe she's more the gentle Mozart type.

After the music was over, we all started talking about what we wanted to do after graduation. Jean said that she wanted to do social work. I wondered if she were just saying that to create a favorable impression. But when she talked about looking for a job and asked me if I knew of any employment possibilities, I began to be more convinced. And when she said that she planned to stay home this summer so she could intern in a social work program rather than party it up on Cape Cod, I was more convinced about her genuine interest and sincerity.

All and all, Jean is a very attractive and well-built chick who seems warm, friendly, concerned with helping others, and intelligent. I hope to see her again.

This example shows some of the main characteristics of impression formation. On the basis of Jean's appearance, her reactions to him, her behavior, and other social cues, John formed a first impression of Jean as a gentle, nice, clean contemplative girl. As they talked, he tried to determine whether this impression was accurate. For example, when Jean initially indicated an interest in social work, John was not sure whether this demonstrated a real interest on her part or an attempt to impress other people with her "nobility." But when she indicated that she planned to give up a summer of fun to work in an intern program in the hot city, he became more convinced of her sincerity.

Once the available cues provide some specific information about another person, the perceiver tries to organize this information into a meaningful, consistent picture. For example, John felt—on the basis of Jean's appearance and actions—that she was with it. But in John's opinion all people who are with it are into rock music, so he was puzzled by Jean's unfamiliarity with rock music. It didn't seem to fit with the other things he had observed about her. To "explain" the inconsistency, he invented an explanation—maybe she liked classical music. Mozart might be more appropriate for a gentle, shy girl than acid rock.

Note also that in the process of forming his impression, John himself played a significant role. His initial interest in Jean's figure reflected his normal interests as a man. His interpretation of other cues to tell him "what she was like" reflected his own experiences and preconceptions. His assumption, for example, that girls who wear little make-up are less materialistic than those who are heavily made up is a product of his own experience and may or may not be accurate.

Because our impressions of others vary so from person to person and involve so many

inferences, there are many possibilities for error. In reality Jean may be far from gentle, shy, and contemplative. She may simply know what kind of façade to present to create the image she wants.

We might ask why people have to make so many inferences as they form their impressions of others. Why didn't Jean simply tell John what she was really interested in? Why the inference game? As we saw in Chapter 2, people frequently present a false, socially acceptable front in society. "Never give a base motive when a noble one will do" is a lesson learned early in our society. Thus we must try to separate contrived behavior, which is designed to impress others, from real behavior, which more genuinely reflects the person. This is a complex process, which is highly susceptible to error.

Once impressions of another person are formed, these impressions determine how we act toward that person and, in turn, how he reacts to us. As John talked with Jean, his own pleasant feelings toward her were undoubtedly communicated in various subtle ways, which he may not even have been aware of. In Chapter 1 we saw that experimenters can communicate their hypotheses to their subjects even though neither they nor their subjects realize that communication is taking place (Rosenthal, 1966).

Person perception is a complex process. Generally, people are not aware of the cues that dictate their impressions or of the way in which they combine information. (Try writing a description of what made you feel the way you do about a particular person. You may find this surprisingly difficult.) Overall impressions are formed quickly—frequently without our being aware of the reasons for them. Thus John's analytical discussion of how he formed an impression of Jean is a deliberate slow-motion assessment of what happened—certainly not a reconstruction of the way people typically operate.

Our main focus in this chapter will be on the manner in which people form their impressions of others. As illustrated by our brief example, first impressions are largely based on the physical appearance of the person being observed. Then, as interaction develops, we use a variety of other cues, such as facial expressions, gestures, words, and deeds, to develop the impres-

FIGURE 8-1 Preoccupation with physical appearance is evident in the enormous amounts of time and money spent beautifying the human face and figure. Above, Revlon Plaza in a New York department store. (Shelly Rusten)

sion in greater detail. Throughout this process various abilities, attitudes, and motivations are being attributed to the other person, and an attempt is being made to bring all of these impressions into a cohesive whole. The close of the chapter will include a description of how the perceptual process works interactively—in real-life situations where each person is perceiving others and being perceived by them.

Our review will be a piece-by-piece analysis of the elements of interpersonal perception. Admittedly, the approach is an artificial one, but it reflects the approach taken to date in the literature and is probably a necessary beginning to understanding the complexity of the process. However, the eventual research goal is to be able to say how the separate elements do in fact interact in combination.

Appearance and Impressions

As most people know, physical appearance is an important cue in person perception. In everyday life people act as though their appearance is an important determinant of the view others have of them. A billion-dollar cosmetics industry testifies to the number of people who believe that appearance is important. (See Figure 8-1.) How-to-do-it manuals for college grads give advice about how to dress for job interviews. When getting together with people you want to impress, you may take care to wear clothes you think they approve of.

A number of studies support this common-sense assumption that physical appearance is important. The typical procedure used in these studies is to present photographs of people whose physical appearance varies in some way and then have the viewers rate the people on a number of traits.

Many physical aspects have been found consistently to influence impressions. Persons wearing glasses, for example, have been judged to be more intelligent, reliable, and industrious than those without glasses (Manz and Lueck, 1968). Irrespective of whether or not people who wear glasses really are more likely to possess these character traits, people viewing them think they do. Thus the widely held stereotypes about certain aspects of physical appearance do contribute to the impressions people form of others.

Consider the way you form your impressions of people. You may have accepted the popular adage that blondes have more fun and are more attractive. Like John, you may think that girls who do not wear bras are liberated and that girls who do not appear heavily made up are more contemplative and less materialistic. And you may think that people whose style of dress is similar to yours are more likely to have attitudes and interests that are similar to yours.

As we review the evidence about some variations in appearance that have been found to influence impressions, keep in mind that this list is not exhaustive.

Clothing

The effect of clothing styles on people's impressions has been heavily emphasized in commonsense psychology. The need to dress conservatively for a job interview is almost a college student's truism. Imagine the reaction if a college student should go to a job interview wearing torn jeans and a dirty sweater. No matter what social setting you are in, the clothing you wear is an important determinant of how others view you. In relatively homogeneous groups there is considerable agreement about the impression created by a particular costume.

Subjects in one experiment felt themselves qualified to judge such diverse characteristics as personality, occupation, morality, educational level, and hobbies on the basis of clothing alone. When shown photographs of outfits from current fashion magazines, girls thought they could describe what kind of woman would wear

each costume. For example, one dress was seen as likely to be worn by a "21-year-old model who is snobbish, fun-loving, anything but shy, rebellious and gay, with easy-going morals. She smokes and drinks, has lots of boyfriends and is on the way to a nightclub" (Gibbins, 1969, p. 306). These descriptions and judgments were, of course, simply impressions that the subjects formed; there was no test of how accurate the impressions were.

Clothing style also influences the way others react to you. If you wanted to get credit or a loan, how would you dress? One experimenting student found that he had better luck getting credit when he dressed like a clean-cut student than he did in hippie garb (*The Hartford Courant,* January 19, 1971, p. 7).

If you were trying to get signatures on a political petition, would you do better if you were dressed conventionally or unconventionally? If the people you were trying to persuade were similar to those studied in several recent studies, you would be more effective if you were dressed conventionally. In one such study conventionally dressed and hippie experimenters solicited signatures on an antiwar petition from adult passers-by in two large suburban shopping centers. As might be predicted, the percentage of signatures obtained by the conventionally dressed students was significantly greater than that obtained by the hippie students (Keasey and Tomlinson-Keasey, 1973).

This and similar findings have been widely interpreted as demonstrating the prejudice of conventional, mainstream Americans against those who differ (Zimbardo, 1971a). But one might ask whether such a reliance on dress and rejection of what is different is the exclusive property of middle America. The reactions given by Anne's friends (which we reviewed in Chapter 2) would suggest that a dislike of what is different is common to many cultures. The results of a recent study also support this hypothesis. During the Peace March on Washington in April 1971—when most people were unconventionally dressed—two experimenters, one conventionally dressed, the other in hippie garb, tried to obtain signatures on an antiwar petition. Although everyone in the audience was ostensibly opposed to the war, since everyone was participating in an antiwar rally, the hippie experimenter had significantly more success than the straight experimenter: 80 percent of those approached by the hippie experimenter agreed to sign, and only 65 percent of those approached by the straight experimenter agreed.

Admittedly, this study is confounded. Since only a single hippie and single straight experimenter were used, differences in audience reaction might be attributed to differences in individual characteristics of the experimenters as well as to differences in their dress. Nevertheless, the subject of the petition was obviously a popular one to the audience and would probably have outweighed individual differences in the experimenters, since the petitioner's contact with each member of the audience was extremely brief. It is plausible, therefore, that the 15 percent difference is at least primarily related to the two clothing styles—one of which matched that of the audience generally, and the other of which did not (Suedfeld, Bochner, and Matas, 1971).

Why does dress influence impressions in such a consistent way? To what extent does your choice of dress represent a conscious statement about the kind of person you feel you are? In Chapter 2 we saw that Anne's vacillation between being straight and hippie was clearly reflected in her dress. On hippie days she wore flared jeans and the rest of the hippie uniform; on straight days she wore a dress and ribbons in her hair. It is obviously too simple, however, to say that all those wearing hippie garb do so because they have consciously espoused hippie values. People do things for a variety of reasons. If hippie garb is in at your school, you may wear it without much thought about the values it represents—just as every executive who wears a dark, pin-stripe suit may not do so simply because he is convinced of the value of capitalism. Still, it is clear that clothing offers an easy and quick way to sort people.

Physical attractiveness

To what extent does physical attractiveness contribute to the impressions people form of others? One of the main assumptions of everyday psychology is that attractiveness is a very important determinant of impressions, and the research findings support this assumption.

From nursery school on the best is assumed about beautiful people—male and female—and agreement about who is beautiful is surprisingly high (Dion and Berscheid, 1972). Nursery school children whom adults have judged as being physically unattractive are not as well liked by their classmates as are other children, and their classmates assume that they misbehave more. Thus the child's physical appearance begins to influence the way other children see him even at this early stage.

Further, the child's attractiveness determines the way adults view him (Dion, 1972). An act is seen as less naughty when it is committed by an attractive child than when it is committed by an unattractive child. For example, when an attractive girl threw rocks at a sleeping dog, one adult subject concluded: "She appears to be a perfectly charming little girl, well-mannered, basically unselfish. . . . She plays well with everyone, but like anyone else, a bad day can occur. Her cruelty . . . need not be taken too seriously." When the same act was said to have been committed by an unattractive child, however, another adult concluded: "I think the child would be quite bratty and would be a problem to teachers. . . . She would be a brat at home. . . . All in all, she would be a real problem" (Dion, 1972, in Berscheid and Walster, 1972, p. 45).

Physical attractiveness may also influence the way adults judge a child's intelligence. Even when children have identical report cards, teachers have been found to assume that the attractive children were more intelligent, more popular, and more likely to go to college (Clifford and Walster, 1973).

Thus all of the social sources—peers, teachers, and adults in general—share a common, positive attitude toward the attractive child. Such expectations may have a self-fulfilling effect. As we saw in Chapter 1, children have been found to behave the way their teachers expect them to behave (Rosenthal and Jacobson, 1968). The same factors causing self-fulfilling prophecies may work for physical attractiveness. Always being expected to be bright, pleasant, and well-liked, the attractive children might begin to think of themselves in this way and to meet the expectations.

Somewhat more predictably, attractiveness has been found to be of overwhelming importance in the impressions adults form of other adults in a number of situations. Physical attractiveness was the single most important determinant of how much college students liked their dates at a computer dance—at which they assumed a computer had matched them on the basis of similar interests (Walster, Aronson, Abrahams, and Rottmann, 1966).

One might argue that because of the relatively short time the students had to form impressions, they may have relied more heavily on physical attractiveness than they would have in situations where they had a chance to know the other person better. However, the results of a correlational study suggest that in real life, physical attractiveness may be an extremely important determinant of favorable impressions—at least as men appraise women. In that study the correlation between physical attractiveness and frequency of dating for college women was .61 (Berscheid, Dion, Walster, and Walster, 1971).

This high correlation is especially interesting in view of its contrast to what college students say they are looking for in a date (Vreeland, 1972). Both men and women say that such traits as intelligence, friendliness, and sincerity are more important than physical attractiveness. Yet when confronted with real-life situations, they are not really looking for these traits. It may be that students think that judging others by their attractiveness is somewhat superficial, thereby making them reluctant to report honestly what they really are looking for. Or perhaps they are not aware of the key role of physical attractiveness.

In fact, students have been found to rate attractive people as more sensitive, kind, interesting, strong, poised, modest, sociable, outgoing, and exciting than less attractive people. Further, students think that attractive people are more likely to find good jobs, to marry well, and to lead happy and fulfilling lives (Dion, Berscheid, and Walster, 1972). Thus the positive traits that college students think they are reacting to as they favorably evaluate a particular person may be no more than a mirage caused by that person's physical attractiveness.

Since the favorable stereotype about attractive people is so widespread, one might wonder whether or not it is valid. Are attractive people as "golden" as others think they are? On the basis of the self-fulfilling prophecy phenome-

non, one would expect that the physically attractive person would, indeed, be better adjusted to society and more capable of fulfilling his own objectives. However, in one study in which student attractiveness was related to happiness and adjustment twenty-five years after college, the attractive coeds seemed to fare less well. Women who had been very attractive during their college years were less satisfied, less happy, and less adjusted in their late forties and early fifties than their less attractive contemporaries (Berscheid, Walster, and Campbell, 1972).

The negative relationship found in this study, however, may be limited to its special circumstances. As the looks of a once-attractive woman began to fade, she may have become resentful and unhappy. Or being attractive when she was young, she may have failed to develop other positive traits—feeling that she could win points on her looks alone. Thus it is possible that in other situations, attractiveness may be related to the positive traits normally associated with it.

Other aspects of appearance

Many other aspects of physical appearance have been found to influence the impressions formed of other people. (See Box 1.) In a study done during the early 1950s, women who wore lipstick were seen as more frivolous and interested in sex than a group of comparable girls who wore no lipstick (McKeachie, 1952). Since fashions in make-up have changed radically since that time, the contemporary reactions to different styles of make-up are somewhat different—but just as stereotyped.

Names are another aspect of appearance that may influence impressions. Try imagining the success of a movie star named Melvin Schmaltz. Or conjure up the image of a blind date named Grizelda. Smell may also determine impressions. Fortunes have been made because of the total acceptance by Americans that smelling good helps win social success. Perfume manufacturers have made much of the fact that different perfumes create different images. It would be interesting to see if variations in scent do, in fact, influence impressions. Manicured fingernails, height, age, teeth, the style of walk, the car a person drives—all these

BOX 1 SOME ASPECTS OF APPEARANCE THAT DETERMINE IMPRESSIONS

Such varied aspects of appearance as physique, amount of hair and hair color, facial features, and physical handicaps have been found to influence the impressions of other people.

How would you expect the impression of a well-built, muscular man to differ from that of a very thin or a very fat man? A number of studies have shown that muscular physiques are seen as belonging to men who are active, energetic, and dominant. Both excessively thin and excessively fat men are seen as withdrawn, shy, and dependent (Dibiase and Hjelle, 1968). Although the evidence is not as clear, the results of a recent study suggest that there are stereotypes about female physiques too. As Raquel Welch could have told us, large-breasted women are preferred to small-breasted women (Wiggins, Wiggins, and Conger, 1968). A next step would be to determine whether large-breasted women are thought to possess different personality characteristics than their less well endowed sisters.

Both the amount of hair and its color have been found to influence impressions. Among some American college students, men with a lot of body hair were seen as more virile, potent, and active (Verinis and Roll, 1970). A bearded, masculine face was seen as more potent than a clean-shaven male face (Roll and Verinis, 1971). And as a number of popular images in our society about blond females and dark men would suggest, hair color was a highly significant cue in impression formation. Blond women were seen as beautiful, entertaining, warm, relaxed, and feminine, whereas brunettes were seen as more intelligent, sincere, strong, and dependable. The stereotyped image of the dark man was also confirmed: Dark men were seen as more intelligent, ambitious, rugged, and masculine than blond or red-headed men (Lawson, 1971).

(George Malave)

Facial features also influence impressions. You may have heard the common stereotypes about the intelligence of those with high foreheads, the weakness of those with receding chins, and the sensuousness of those with thick lips. In one study people with low foreheads and short noses were seen as happy, generous, and youthful. Those with a narrow mouth were judged as more intelligent than those with a wide mouth (Bradshaw, 1969). (Interestingly, those with high foreheads were not seen as more intelligent than those with low foreheads.)

Physical handicaps influence impressions too. (See accompanying figure.) In your own reactions to handicapped persons, you may have noticed two con-flicting feelings. You may feel sorry for the handicapped person and want to help him and yet, at the same time, feel embarrassed and try to avoid contact with him. Research results have confirmed both of these conflicting tendencies. When you have to interact on a face-to-face basis, your desire to avoid contact may make you terminate your relationship with a handicapped person sooner than you would with a nonhandicapped person (Kleck, Ono, and Hastorf, 1966). However, when there is an opportunity to help the handicapped and you do not have to interact on a face-to-face basis, your pity motive may be the strongest determinant of your impressions and interactions (Doob and Ecker, 1970).

and many other aspects of appearance can influence impressions. As you meet people, try observing which aspects of their appearance you notice.

Is it all skin deep?

Although physical appearance is an important determinant of the impression people create, it is clear that other variables also influence our impressions of others. What people say and do has a marked influence.

The more information you have about a person, the less important appearance may be. John Lindsay, the most beautiful of the Democratic presidential candidates, was beaten in the 1972 Florida primary by an unglamorous Wallace. Once the voters heard what both candidates had to say, Lindsay's attractive appearance may have become less important. This hypothesis was confirmed in a recent study. When video tapes of people wearing glasses and sitting still were shown for very brief periods of time (fifteen seconds), they were judged to be more intelligent than when a video tape was shown of a person in the same situation who was not wearing glasses. However, when a longer time period was used (five minutes) and the subjects were shown being interviewed about their holidays abroad, the presence or absence of spectacles did not influence the impression they created (Argyle and McHenry, 1971).

Yet we do know of at least some situations in which physical appearance is likely to remain a potent determinant of impressions. When the impression is based on very limited information, or when the initial impression shapes the direction of future interactions, physical appearance may well be the single most important determinant of impressions. Unless an elegantly barbered and dressed man says something obviously stupid, it may be difficult for those seeing him to overcome their feeling that he must be sophisticated and intelligent.

Summary

Many physical aspects of a person have been found to influence impressions. Persons wearing glasses, for example, have been judged to be more intelligent and reliable than those without glasses. People have judged such diverse characteristics as personality, occupation, morality, educational level, and hobbies on the basis of clothing alone. Further, clothing style influences the way others react to you. The type of clothing that creates the most favorable impression and cooperation depends on the preference of the particular group.

Physical attractiveness is a very important determinant of impressions—both for children and adults. Attractive people have been rated more positively on a number of traits—including intelligence, modesty, and sensitivity —than less attractive people.

Many other aspects of physical appearance influence the impressions formed of other people, such as make-up, physique, amount of hair and hair color, facial features, and physical handicaps. However, there are limits to the effects of physical features on impressions. The more information you have about a person, the less important appearance may be.

Other Influences on Impressions

As you interact with someone in a face-to-face situation, you get a lot of additional information about the kind of person he is. You see whether he looks you in the eye, how close he stands, his gestures, and his facial expressions. You may see how others react to him and discover something about his usual role. And you hear his tone of voice. All of these nonverbal cues yield information about others. A person's words and actions may be subject to conscious control and thus to distortion, but his gestures and mannerisms may be much more difficult to control and thus may be more valid indicators of personality than his words in some situations.

Eye contact

Look at the Figure 8-2A and B. Assume that this girl is being interviewed for a job with your company. In each case the photograph represents the interviewer's first impression. Assume that you are the interviewer and then answer the following questions:

A   B

FIGURE 8-2 (Photos by Betsy Blackmer)

In which photo does the girl seem more alert?

_____A

_____B

In which photo does the girl seem more attentive?

_____A

_____B

If your reactions were similar to those of college students who rated these photos in a recent study, you found the girl more alert and more attentive in Photograph A than in Photograph B. Why? The photographs are identical in every dimension except one: the direction of the girl's glance. Photograph A shows the girl looking straight ahead; Photograph B shows her looking downward. On the basis of the direction of her glance alone, the girl was seen as more alert, receptive, secure, and active when she was looking straight ahead (Tankard, 1970).

This finding is consistent with the assumptions of novelists and with common truisms about the importance of the eyes in conveying emotions and in creating impressions. *Direction of glance* is supposed to reveal a lot about a person's character. Someone who won't meet your eyes when being questioned about a misdeed may be assumed to be guilty. The *type of look* conveys information too. The sexy, half-sleepy look of a female screen star is a standard gimmick to let the audience know she is more than casually interested in the hero. The *frequency of eye contact* is also important in the conveying of information. Lovers who keep psychological contact by gazing deeply into each other's eyes (see Figure 8-3) are as common a part of the folklore as the bad man in Western films who stares down all competitors and, if they don't back down, settles the issue by shooting them. Apparently, eyes can convey many meanings, and social psychologists are just beginning to investigate the information conveyed by variations in eye contact.

Direction and Type of Glance As we saw, the direction of a person's gaze is a powerful cue in person perception. When evaluating girls as job applicants, subjects saw the individual with the downward gaze more negatively. This impression, however, occurred in a job-interview context. In another situation, say one in which men were evaluating photos of girls as possible dates, the reactions to the direction of gaze might be very different. Instead of negative traits, downcast eyes might mean demure shyness—as Jean's downcast eyes did to John.

Length and Frequency of Glances If you talked with someone for five or ten minutes and he never once looked you in the eye, what would your impression of him be? Probably it would be somewhat negative. In one experiment, for example, two people were presented reading the directions for the experiment: One did not look up once as he read the directions, and the other glanced up twice. The person who glanced up was rated as less nervous and less formal (LeCompte and Rosenfeld, 1971). Generally, persons who have more eye contact are rated more favorably.

There are limits to this phenomenon, however. If the situation is one in which negative or embarrassing information is being discussed, the individual may respond more favorably to a person who deliberately avoids eye contact. In both psychiatric sessions and religious confessions, eye contact is avoided. Thus whether increased eye contact results in a more positive or a more negative impression of another person may depend on the situation. In one recent experiment, when the content of the interview was favorable, an interviewer who looked the subject directly in the eye was rated more positively. However, when the content of the interview was negative, the interviewer who

FIGURE 8-3 For two people in love, eye contact is as important a means of conveying emotion as words or embraces. (Irene Stein)

avoided eye contact was rated more positively (Ellsworth and Carlsmith, 1968).

Further, staring may have different consequences from looking. If you notice the patterns you follow in looking at other people, you will see that once someone notices you are looking at him, you will either look away, smile, or say something. This pattern of "appropriate looking" can be clearly seen in an elevator filled with strangers. No one quite knows where to look. All avoid staring and so look down at the floor or up at the ceiling. Seeing someone look at you without looking away or responding to you in any manner would probably make you very uncomfortable.

In a series of recent experiments just this situation was set up (Ellsworth, Carlsmith, and Henson, 1972). When motorists or pedestrians stopped at an intersection for a red light, they were stared at by experimenters. Compared to a control group of subjects who were not stared at, those who were stared at moved significantly faster through the intersection as soon as the light changed. This finding was replicated in a number of different situations with a number of different experimenters. In all of the experiments the reaction to staring was the same: avoidance. Once people realized that they were being stared at, "within a second or two, they would avert their own gaze and begin to indulge in a variety of apparently nervous behaviors, such as fumbling with their clothing or radio, revving up the engines of their cars, glancing frequently at the traffic light, or initiating animated conversation with their passengers" (p. 310). As soon as the light changed, they raced off.

Why did the stares have these effects? The subjects may have seen the stares as indicators of hostile intent—as a number of lower animals seem to see stares. Thus the stare may be an unlearned cue for aggressive intent. Or it may be that staring makes humans uncomfortable because it violates the general norms for looking. People are taught not to stare, and so they may be uncomfortable when someone else stares.

It may also be that the amount of eye contact directly mediates the amount of psychological contact between people. There may be an optimal level of such contact. People may want to feel that they are in contact with others, but still wish to retain some feeling of privacy and separateness. Thus either too much eye contact (staring) or too little (avoiding all contact) may be aversive and create a negative impression. Under this hypothesis, staring may be seen as an invasion of one's privacy.

Interpersonal distance and location

There are other ways to invade another's privacy in addition to staring—just try standing six inches away from a casual acquaintance as you talk with him. If you should do this, you might find the other person bewildered and embarrassed; probably, he would back away and try to reassert the "proper" distance between you and him. In any culture there are norms concerning the permissible range of distance between two speakers in a variety of situations (Hall, 1963). In the United States, for example, one investigator—on the basis of his observations—has theorized that distances of six to eighteen inches are typical for intimate personal interaction, and of thirty to forty-eight inches for casual personal interactions (Hall, 1964). Although the exact normative distances for a number of relationships remain to be established, the important point is there are norms about physical distances in social interaction. If you violate these norms by standing either too close or too far away, people become upset. It is as if there were assumptions about the appropriate amount of "personal space" (Sommer, 1969) the individual is entitled to in each situation.

The results of several studies make it clear that interpersonal spacing is a highly significant cue in interpersonal perception. Standing within the acceptable range of distance from another person may communicate liking for that person. In one study subjects were asked to report the degree to which another person liked or disliked them. When the communicator stood within the acceptable range, three feet, he was thought to like those he was talking with more than when he stood farther away than the usual norm, seven feet (Mehrabian, 1968).

Violating the norm by standing too close has also been found to have negative effects—perhaps even greater than those caused by standing too far away. In one study when the experimenter sat down about six inches from someone he did not know, most people looked uncomfortable and tried to leave the situation (Felipe and Sommer, 1966).

In addition to the absolute amount of space between people, the location of people within that space has been found to provide social information. If you were to join a committee meeting where people were seated at a rectangular table, where would you expect the chairman to be sitting? In American society the "head of the table" is usually reserved for the leader of the group or the most prestigious person in the group, so you might expect the chairman to be occupying that position. In several studies the person occupying this position has been judged more positively than those seated in other positions. For example, subjects in one study were shown photographs of girls seated around a rectangular table and asked to judge them on a number of characteristics. The girl seated at the head of the table was rated as significantly more talkative, persuasive, leaderlike, self-confident, friendly, and intelligent. She was also seen as contributing most to the group's performance (Davenport, Brooker, and Munro, 1971).

Body language and impressions

Do body gestures influence impressions of other people? Judge for yourself. Look at the two gestures in Figure 8-4A and B (page 382) and then report your impressions.

Does person A seem open to an opposing point of view?
_____Yes
_____No

Does person B seem thoughtful?
_____Yes
_____No

If you are like the majority of the students in the author's classes who have seen these pictures, you will have formed an impression of these people just on the basis of their gestures. Person A is generally seen as being closed to opposing arguments; person B is seen as thoughtful. In everyday life gestures are an

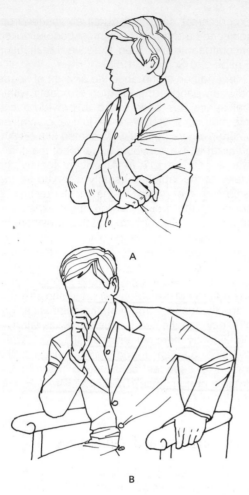

A

B

FIGURE 8-4

important part of interpersonal communication. Without our conscious awareness, we frequently use and interpret gestures. If you focus on what people do with their arms, legs, feet, and hands as they interact with others, you will see that many body gestures and movements accompany verbal and facial expressions.

What do these gestures communicate? Common observation suggests that they convey a number of messages—depending on the situation and the cultural context. At a middle-class party the way a person sits and uses his body may convey sexual receptiveness. A girl who sits or stands very stiffly, with her arms crossed against her chest, may be seen as being cold and unreceptive. Or a man who moves with the

grace of a Paul Newman may be seen as very sexy and masculine. (See Figure 8-5.)

Interpreting body language has been an important part of psychotherapy for a long time, and there are many anecdotal observations about body language and its meanings. Since words or facial expressions may not fully express what a patient feels, therapists have focused on the supplementary messages conveyed by body language. A suicidal patient, for example, may convey his depression not only by his words but also by his listless, drooping posture, flat voice, and limply crossed hands. More recently, in encounter group therapy the accurate use and interpretation of body language has been emphasized even more. It is hoped that if distortions in verbal communication are broken down and patients are made aware of the extent to which body language is used to communicate authentically, they will arrive at a greater measure of self-understanding. To do this, encounter groups may begin with "games" that make people more aware of body language and its messages. In one game, for example, the members of a group may move about a room with their eyes closed and touch the other members of the group with their hands. It is hoped that in so doing, each person will become more aware of his own gestures and of his reactions to the gestures of others. At the present, it should be noted that these encounter group procedures are based largely on hypotheses; they have not yet been tested thoroughly by experimental studies.

From an extensive clinical and applied literature, a number of speculations have been derived about the role of body language and what it communicates. In one recent popular book on body language, the "correct" interpretations for a wide variety of gestures are given in a kind of dictionary approach to understanding body language (Nierenberg and Calero, 1971). Clenched hands and crossed legs are seen as gestures of suspicion (p. 81); hands on the hips indicate readiness to do a particular task (p. 70); and so on.

Although these gestures may indicate what the authors claim they do, the kind of clinical-anecdotal evidence presented is clearly not enough to prove that they do. Unfortunately,

FIGURE 8-5 Body position and gestures can often suggest a person's mood even if his facial expression is not visible. (Charles Gatewood)

experimental interest in the area of body language did not begin in any significant way until the 1950s. However, since that time a considerable literature has accumulated.

To study body gestures experimentally, what would you do? Logically, the first step might be to see if body gestures convey any information when all other cues, such as facial expression or words, are eliminated. If people in a stressful or a pleasant situation are photographed with their heads covered, so that their facial expressions are eliminated, can subjects match the photograph of the body with the correct situation? In one experiment it was shown that they can (Ekman, 1964).

If body language does convey information, the next question is how this information differs from that conveyed by facial expressions or words. One of the popular assumptions of encounter groups is that language and facial expression may obscure and distort what the person is really feeling. As we saw in Chapter 2, we are all socialized to present socially acceptable pictures of ourselves to others; we are thus trained to make our faces and words polished deceivers. But we have not been as thoroughly schooled in using body gestures in deceit. People may not be aware that their gestures communicate, may not receive much feedback from their gestures, and thus may more realistically convey what they feel by those gestures.

To test the hypothesis that body gestures convey more accurate information than facial expressions, experimenters showed silent films of a psychiatric interview to subjects. Half of the subjects saw only the face and head; the other half saw only the body from the neck down. In one case a patient verbally denied the extent of her anxiety and tension—which she later admitted having felt. As predicted, observers who viewed only the patient's face and head were significantly less accurate than those who saw only the body. Most of the face viewers (70 percent) reported the apparent cheerfulness of the patient, and comparatively few sensed her underlying nervousness (18 percent). On the other hand, only 11 percent of the body viewers saw cheerfulness, and 68 percent of these viewers detected the nervousness that was actually there (Ekman and Friesen, 1969). Thus as the encounter theorists have long assumed, body gestures may provide more valid information about the person than his facial expressions and words in some situations.

Of course, the psychiatric interview is a special case of interpersonal interaction. A tense psychiatric patient may try to cover up his feelings, and so movements of his body—which may not be as subject to conscious control—may convey more information than his consciously controlled facial expressions. The expressions of a more normal person experiencing socially acceptable emotions, such as happiness or joy, may be more communicative than body movements. We must also remember that in this experiment words could not be heard. In many situations, what is said may be more communicative than either facial expressions or body movements.

Nevertheless, it is clear that body gestures do impart information and may be more valid in some situations than other means of communication. The next step is to focus precisely on what aspects of body gestures convey exactly what meanings. But here the research problems become formidable. Considering that body gestures and movements occur rapidly, how would you present a gesture in a controlled and realistic way? How would you select a particular gesture? How would you control the effect of context on the interpretation of gestures? Most who have written in this field agree that the context of the gesture—what has gone before—greatly influences the meaning of a particular gesture.

Because of the many technical problems, some of the experimental techniques discussed below may seem stiff and artificial to you. However, these procedures constitute an interesting beginning to an understanding of the role of body language.

The Pattern of Motion   Everyday psychology is full of observations about the effects created by certain patterns of movement. A woman who "glides" as she walks is seen as graceful. A man who moves with controlled power may be seen as menacing. Several studies support the belief that motion alone can convey impressions of character.

In one pioneering study a film was used in which three geometrical figures—a large triangle, a smaller triangle, and a circle—were shown moving in various directions and at various speeds in a field. When subjects were asked to report what they saw, the geometric figures were described as personalities with a definite character. Most of the subjects saw the large triangle as aggressive, mean, and bullying, and the small triangle was seen as a heroic figure, resisting the power of the big bully. The circle was seen as female and timid. The movements of the geometric figures were seen as a series of meaningful events, and the patterns of these movements were sufficient to make the subjects see the "characters" as fighting, bullying, hiding, chasing, and so on (Heider and Simmel, 1944).

More recent work has confirmed the hypothesis that patterns of motion alone are a significant factor in judgments of the "character" of geometrical forms (e.g., Thayer and Schiff, 1969). Whether or not motion patterns similarly affect impressions of real people interacting can only be determined by more research. Perhaps Marlon Brando's controlled movements were a major determinant in his sinister image in *The Godfather*.

Body Orientation   (the degree to which a person's shoulders and legs are turned toward another person). Here the evidence is not completely consistent. In one study it was found that the effect of body orientation on perception varied with the amount of eye contact. When the experimenter looked the subjects in the eye, the subjects interpreted lower frequencies of direct body orientation as meaning that the experimenter liked them less. However, when he did not look them in the eye, body orientation had no significant effect (Mehrabian, 1967). In situations other than an experiment, body orientation may have other meanings—with or without eye contact. On a date body orientation may be a highly significant cue.

Accessibility of Body (the openness of arms and legs). When subjects in one experiment were asked to infer the attitude of a seated communicator, body accessibility influenced the impression they formed of female communicators but not of male communicators. Females sitting in an "open" position, with their arms resting on their laps and their feet on the floor uncrossed, were seen as significantly more pleasant than females who were seated in a "closed" position, with their arms folded and their legs crossed (Mehrabian, 1968).

Body Relaxation Body angle is one indicator of relaxation. Both male and female subjects have been found to infer that a communicator had a more positive attitude toward them when he leaned slightly forward toward them than when he leaned backward away from them (Mehrabian, 1968). However, increasing relaxation is not an inevitable expression of increased liking. Relaxation is either very high or very low for a disliked person and is moderate for someone liked (Mehrabian and Friar, 1969). A person's relative status may also be inferred from his degree of body relaxation. It has been observed at psychiatric staff meetings that those of lower status (interns) are more tense than those of higher status (psychiatrists) (Goffman, 1961).

Some evidence is beginning to emerge that suggests that accuracy in interpreting the meaning of body gestures is an important component of successful interactions with others. In one study the comparative accuracy of happily and unhappily married couples in interpreting body gestures was compared. As a marriage counselor, who knows the importance of accurate communication in marriage, might predict, the happily married couples were significantly more accurate in interpreting body language than the unhappily married (Kahn, 1970).

Since body language has been found to be a significant determinant of interpersonal impressions, future work in this area might explore the "messages" conveyed by particular body gestures. In addition, consideration might be given to investigating factors related to different levels of accuracy in "reading" body language as well as to techniques to improve the accuracy of perception in this area.

Facial expressions and impressions

Can people tell whether you are happy, angry, or sad by looking at your facial expression? Of course, they can, you might answer. When the film director wants us to know what Richard Burton is feeling, the camera zooms in for a close-up of his face—not his feet. And when we look at Burton's face, we think that we can tell something of what he is feeling. If, on some occasions, he wants to keep a poker face and not betray his emotions, maybe he can hide his feelings. But if he allows himself to express what he feels, others can tell something of his emotions simply by looking at him. (See Figure 8-6.)

FIGURE 8-6 Marcel Marceau is probably the world's leading pantomimist. From his facial expression and gestures, can you determine what feeling he is trying to communicate here? (Courtesy, Ronald A. Wilford Associates, Inc.)

Whether in fact people are as accurate as they think they are in attributing specific emotions to specific facial expressions has been highly debated in social psychology for some time. Research in this area, dating back to Darwin's original work in 1872, has yielded inconsistent results. The typical procedure has been to present facial expressions (either drawn, photographed, or "live") to a group of subjects. These subjects are then asked to judge what emotion is being experienced. In some studies the subjects were not able to judge people's emotions with any accuracy from their facial expressions; in other studies the judges were highly accurate.

What could have interfered with the ability of some judges to "read" the facial expressions? In many of the studies with negative results, artist's drawings—which may or may not have accurately depicted emotional reactions—were used as the stimuli. Photographing people who are in situations designed to arouse particular emotions might be a more realistic way of depicting facial expressions. In one widely cited experiment just this procedure was used. Twenty-five persons, mostly psychologists who knew that the experiment concerned facial behavior and that photographs of their faces were being taken, were subjected in quick succession to seventeen different situations—as diverse as listening to music, looking at pornographic pictures, being shocked, and decapitating a live rat. When their photographed facial expressions were shown to a group of subjects, the subjects were not able to match the expressions with the emotions supposedly aroused in the situations. From these negative results the investigator and many others concluded that people are not able to judge emotions accurately from facial expressions alone (Landis, 1929).

Thinking about what your reactions would be if you were one of the persons photographed in this experiment may provide some clues about possible reasons for the subjects' lack of accuracy. Your reactions might be affected significantly by your knowledge of what the experiment was about. Further, you might try to mask your feelings. Rather than show your anger at being subjected to an electric shock, you might try to be a good sport. You might try to show no

emotion, or you might smile in a somewhat forced way. In support of this hypothesis, it was reported in the study that smiles were frequent in all of the situations—from the pornography to the rat decapitation.

Moreover, how did the investigator know what emotions the photographed persons were experiencing? Exposing people to the same stimuli does not ensure a uniform emotional reaction. The rapid fire of diverse emotional experiences may have also numbed the persons photographed. And still photographs of emotional reactions may not convey as much information as motion pictures; several studies have shown that subjects are more accurate in judging filmed emotional sequences than in judging still photographs (e.g., Kozel, 1969).

In a large number of more recent studies in which many of these errors have been corrected, people have been found to be able to detect emotions accurately from facial expression. For example, in one recent study an interview was staged in two parts: a stressful part and a reassuring part. During the beginning, stressful part the interviewer acted very unfriendly and challenging; in the second, reassuring part he acted very friendly and calming. Sixty-second film clips were made of subjects in the stress and nonstress conditions, and these were shown to subjects who were asked to judge whether the person felt pleasant or unpleasant (Howell and Jorgenson, 1970). In contrast to the earlier study, subjects could make this judgment accurately. In other studies, when actors have been asked to portray certain emotions by means of facial expressions, subjects have been able to read their emotions with even greater accuracy (e.g., Kozel and Gitter, 1968).

Although it now seems clear that people can accurately interpret at least some facial expressions, a host of other questions remain. Are there constants across cultures in the facial expression of emotion? Would a resident of a remote area in New Guinea interpret a sad face in the same way that a Westerner would? Recent evidence suggests that he would (Ekman and Friesen, 1971).

What is the relative contribution of facial expressions and other cues in determining judgments of others? In the previous section we saw that gestures are sometimes a more accurate indicator than facial expressions. Under what circumstances are facial expressions masked? If facial expressions conflict with other cues, such as the context, which prevails? In some studies in which the information provided by facial expressions and the context were inconsistent, the context was found to determine impressions (Munn, 1940). In other studies, however, just the reverse has occurred (e.g., Frijda, 1969). Whether facial expression or context prevails may depend on the relative strength and clarity of the two sources (Ekman et al., 1972). If the context is one that would clearly be expected to produce a particular emotion—such as a funeral—then the context may determine the interpretation of ambiguous facial expressions. However, if the expression is very clear—if someone is laughing at the funeral—the facial expression will determine how the emotion is judged.

Research in the area of facial expression has been in limbo for a long time because of the apparent inconsistencies and contradictions. However, it is now clear that at least under some circumstances facial expressions can be a valid and effective means of communicating information about a person. The next step in the experimental process will be to explore more specifically how and when this information is conveyed. Recently, a system has been evolved to measure the components of facial movements involved in facial expression (Ekman, Friesen, and Tomkins, 1971). Now that the components can be measured, it will be possible to vary parts of total expressions to find out exactly which aspect of the expression conveys information.

The voice and impressions

If you heard the rich, breathy voice of a woman you had never met, over the telephone, what kind of a person would you visualize? Then if you met her and she turned out to be a 250-pound woman with a faint but noticeable moustache, would you be surprised? You probably would be, since you would have visualized a sexy woman to match the sexy voice. And if you heard a high, squeaky man's voice, you might

be similarly surprised to find that he was a 250-pound football player. In everyday life we form impressions of other people partly on the basis of their voice. In situations where we cannot see the other person, as when we talk over the telephone, the voice may be a major determinant of our impressions of others.

What people say obviously influences our impression of them. But, in addition, how they say it—their pitch, rhythm, loudness, and accent—will have an effect. If we are to know how voice alone influences impressions, the content of the speech must be held constant. One way to do this is to have people with different voices read exactly the same material to a group of subjects, who then give their impressions on the basis of voice alone.

Repeatedly, it has been shown that people do form such impressions and that, moreover, they agree on the characterizatons of particular voices. For example, in one classic study 60 percent of the listeners who heard a voice characterized as "thick, mellow, and chuckling" thought it belonged to a short man (Allport and Cantril, 1934). In another study the majority of the subjects, who were gentile, reacted less favorably to a speaker with the accent of a Jewish immigrant than to one who spoke with a standard English accent (Anisfeld, Bogo, and Lambert, 1962). In other studies voice has been found to influence the impressions of such diverse characteristics as age, aptitudes and interests, intelligence, personality traits, and temporary emotional states (as summarized in Kramer, 1963). Thus irrespective of whether the judgments based on voice are valid—and there is real controversy in the literature as to whether or not they are—people do appear to accept vocal stereotypes.

Which aspects of the voice can create different impressions? Several aspects of speech have been found to be related to impressions. In one study pitch, loudness, and tempo were found to be influential: Persons with a high-pitched voice were judged as good and small-framed; persons with a loud voice were seen as bad and large; persons with a quick tempo of speech were rated as good and large (Phillis, 1970). In another study persons with a loud voice were rated as "extroverted and assertive" (Scherer, 1971).

The social context and impressions

So far our emphasis has been on those aspects of another person that have been found to influence impressions. We have seen, for example, that clothing, physical attractiveness, gestures, facial expressions, and many other cues can all have such an effect.

In real life, however, impressions are formed in a social context, not simply as a reaction to a series of cues. As John formed his impression of Jean, his main focus was on whether she would be a good date. What you focus on when meeting another person is largely determined by your interests—and the social situation determines these to a large extent.

Further, people's social roles influence your expectations and your evaluations of those people. John's expectations about what women are like may have influenced his perception of Jean to a significant extent. And the other people in a situation also contribute to the impressions formed. The reactions of others to the person you are evaluating may be a powerful determinant of your reactions. If everyone at a party acts as though they like your date, you yourself may be more favorably impressed.

Perceiver's Motives Motives can play a very important role in perception—especially when reality is ambiguous. (See Figure 8-7.) And in person perception reality is usually highly ambiguous. We are constantly trying to puzzle out what others are like on the basis of a few scanty cues.

Although there are persistent individual differences in the perception of others, the situational requirements can contribute significantly to the perceiver's motives. Even if a juror and a casual observer in a courtroom have overall similarities in their general motives and personalities, they will pay attention to very different things when they look at the defendant. The task for the juror will be to determine the defendant's guilt or innocence, whereas the casual observer may look instead at other aspects of the proceedings. Thus the requirements of the situation may determine what you pay attention to and how you interpret what you see.

In one study a tape-recorded "interview" between a psychologist and an ex-prisoner of war (who was alleged to have signed several Communist propaganda statements) was played before a group of Naval Air Cadets. Before they

FIGURE 8-7 Sometimes our own motives are so powerful that we are unable or unwilling to perceive the clearly expressed reactions of others.

Now that you've graduated from college, I think you should live here at home.

How can I tell what you think if you just sit there?

listened to the interview, each cadet was given one of two different "sets." Some were asked to imagine that they were a member of a judicial board of inquiry that was trying to decide whether formal charges should be preferred; others were told that they were members of a medical-psychological board that was trying to determine *why* the man had confessed. After hearing the interview, the subjects were given a number of different questions from which they chould choose the ones they wished to ask. As might be predicted, those given the judicial-legal set chose questions on the legal precedents involved, and those given the medical set chose medically related questions (Jones and deCharms, 1957). The different sets influenced what the subjects wished to get out of the situation and therefore influenced their focus in listening to the interview.

Further, your focus may be influenced by how closely your behavior is related to that of another person in a specific situation. For example, your focus on the aspects of the situation and your interpretation of the information available may differ according to whether the other person has power over you or not. The situations in which you pay the closest attention to another person and try to understand him best may be those in which the other person has a significant amount of power over you—perhaps a professor who is to give you an important grade or a friend whose continued affection is very important to you. And the harder you work in trying to form an accurate impression, the more confident you may be that you are accurate.

Support for this hypothesis has been obtained in one recent experiment. Subjects who played in a game in which another person had complete control over them were more confident of the accuracy of their impressions than were subjects who were not subordinate to another (Johnson and Ewens, 1971). Exactly how power influences the processes of interpersonal perception is not yet clear. The person in an unequal power situation may work harder to understand the other person, or since accuracy is so important, he may convince himself that his perception is accurate because the thought that he does not understand the person who has power over him may be too dissonance-arousing. No matter what the process is, however, it is clear that motives can influence interpersonal perception.

Social Roles and Impressions Most interactions take place in situations in which the participants' roles limit what they do themselves and what they expect others to do. The interaction between John and Jean was as carefully choreographed by their social and sexual roles as a Broadway musical. Common expectations about behaviors appropriate for men and women are widely shared by many members of our society. Women are expected to be romantic, passive; men are expected to be concerned about sports, their jobs, and power. Men ask women out; women, if they wish, accept. Although the exact content of the role may differ among various groups in our society, there are general concepts of what is appropriate masculine and femine behavior. If as Jean was leaving, she had asked John to go out with her, he would probably have been surprised and irritated. Pushy girl.

A role creates expectations about what others are likely to do, and these expectations determine how you perceive others. (See Psych Quiz 1.) If you expect women to be frivolous and passive, you will interpret any ambiguous act on their part as indicating frivolity and passivity. And if you, as a business manager, expect members of a union to be aggressive, argumentative, opinionated, and outspoken, you will see them in this manner if reality is at all ambiguous.

This last effect was shown in a study in which businessmen and members of a labor union were asked to describe the people in two photographs—one person was said to be a businessman, the other a union member. As you might expect, the descriptions given differed markedly depending on whether the businessmen and union members thought they were evaluating "their own kind" or "the enemy." For example, when the same picture was shown, 74 percent of the managerial subjects saw the person as honest when he was described as a businessman, and only 50 percent did so when he was described as a member of the union. In general, businessmen tended to see other businessmen as honest, mature, practical, and dependable and to see union men as aggressive, argumentative, opinionated, and outspoken. Labels had a similarly distorting effect for the union men; the photos looked better if the person was described as a union member rather than as a manager (Haire, 1955).

PSYCH QUIZ 1 EXPECTATIONS AND PERCEPTION

Take a quick look at the following photo, intended to show a male suspect hiding behind a car, and then cover the photo.

Now try to recall what kind of shoes the "suspect" was wearing: sneakers? boots? wingtips? high-heels? Check

your answer with the photograph. How much did the assumed role of male suspect influence your recollection?

(R. Lynn Goldberg)

Even when people actually interact with each other, their expectations concerning how the other will act may distort what they see. In one experiment several different managers were objectively rated in terms of the amount of criticism, correction, and supportive discussion they directed at their subordinates. When those subordinates were asked to make the same ratings, however, they failed to see any difference between managers (Webber, 1970). Even if a manager tries to fit the supportive, democratic, and participative image that is so highly regarded by management experts today, his

subordinates may still see his actions as fitting their own expectations of what an old-time, authoritarian boss does.

Other People The way other people in a situation react to a particular person is a powerful determinant of impressions. If you meet someone at a party and everyone seems to be very favorably impressed with him, you will probably be more apt to like him. As we have seen repeatedly, what others think is a powerful molder of opinions. Person perception is no exception. If others like a person, their actions provide information—"She can't be bad if everyone here likes her"—and also provide a certain amount of pressure, "If everyone likes her and I don't, will they continue to like me?"

In one study in which other people's evaluations were manipulated, the reaction of others was found to be a powerful influence. Girls who were provided with a fictitious "favorable reputation" were much better liked than a girl about whom "others had said highly negative things" (Jones and Shrauger, 1970).

In addition to providing information about whether or not they like a particular person, the reactions of other people in a situation provide a context against which the reactions of a particular person can be judged. If everyone at a party is looking cheerful, one person's gloomy expression may seem much more gloomy than it would if everyone looked slightly grim. Thus the reactions to a particular situation or facial expression would vary according to the context in which it appeared (Cline, 1956).

Summary

As you interact with others, you learn more about them. Eye contact, physical distance, gestures, facial expressions, and voice are all important sources of interpersonal information. For example, either too much *eye contact* (staring) or too little (avoiding all contact) has been found to create a negative impression.

Although the exact normative distances remain to be established, there are norms about appropriate physical distances in social interaction. If you violate these norms by standing either too close or too faraway, people become upset and react to you negatively. In addition to the absolute amount of space between people affecting impressions, the location of people within space provides social information.

Body language also conveys information. When other indicators of emotion, such as facial expressions and voice, have been eliminated, experimental subjects are still able to determine the relative degree of stress being experienced by another person from photographs of body gestures alone. Further, in some situations—as in a psychiatric interview in which a patient may be trying to conceal his feelings—gestures have been found to be even more accurate indicators of feelings than facial expressions.

Recent work on body language has isolated aspects of body gestures that convey meaning. Patterns of motion affect the judgments of the "character" of geometrical forms. Body orientation—the degree to which a person's shoulders and legs are turned toward another person—has also been shown to influence impressions, although the evidence on the effect of this variable is not completely consistent. And body angle, one indicator of body relaxation, has been found to influence impressions.

Whether people are as accurate as they think they are in "reading" emotions from facial expressions has been hotly debated in social psychology for some time. Although research in this area has yielded inconsistent results, in a large number of recent studies in which many of the errors of earlier work have been corrected, people have been found to be able to detect emotions accurately from facial expressions.

Aspects of the voice—pitch, rhythm, loudness, and accent—have an effect on interpersonal impressions. Persons with a high-pitched voice were judged as good and small-framed; persons with a loud voice were seen as bad and large; persons with a quick tempo of speech were rated as good and large. Persons with a loud voice were rated as extroverted and assertive. Gentile subjects reacted less favorably to a speaker with the accent of a Jewish immigrant.

Further, the social context determines what you focus on and how you interpret what you see. As in any perceptual situation, the perceiver does not simply passively record "what is there." The perceiver's motives can play a very important part in perception—especially when reality is ambiguous as it frequently is in person perception. Social roles create expectations about what others are likely to do, and these expectations determine how you perceive others. The way other people in a situation react to a particular person is a powerful determinant of impressions. In addition to providing information about whether or not they like a particular person, the reactions of others provide a context against which the reactions of a particular person can be judged.

But, of course, important as these cues are, what the other person says and does is the main determinant of your impression of him. How we try to puzzle out the meaning of the words and actions of others and fit them into a coherent view is the subject of the next section.

Interpreting Words and Deeds

When we interact with other people, we want to know what they are "really like." We are not satisfied to list what they do; we want to know *why* they do it. If someone does you a favor, you may wonder whether he has done it to help you or for some other reason. How you react to a given incident depends on how you interpret the event. If you attribute someone's doing you a favor to his generosity and genuine concern for you, then you may like the person and feel as though you would like to return the favor. But if you think that a favor was done for manipulative reasons, you may feel repelled—as has been shown in one experiment (Tesser, Gatewood, and Driver, 1968).

In our constant effort to puzzle out what others are really like, we look mainly to what they say

FIGURE 8-8 "You're always so good-natured. What's your angle?"

and do. Yet, as we all know from our dealings with people in real life, words and actions are not always an accurate reflection of another person's characteristics. Someone may compliment you because he genuinely likes what you are doing or because he wants to "butter you up." Consequently, without our necessarily being aware that we are doing so, we use a series of "tests" to determine whether another person's words and deeds reflect his underlying characteristics or are forced responses to the given situation. (See Figure 8-8.) Several theories about how this is done have been evolved (Heider, 1958; Jones and Davis, 1965; Kelley, 1967). Perhaps some examples will make clearer how we test our attributions in everyday life.

Suppose you are trying to decide how bright a particular person is. If he makes a clever pun at a party, you may feel that he is bright. But you may also think that you were having a good time and were ready to laugh. If, however, the person in question says bright things on a variety of other occasions, your confidence in the accuracy of your assessment (or attribution) that he is bright will be increased. Thus the *consistency* of the actions of another person influences your confidence in your attribution.

If some people that you know and respect confirm your impression, your confidence in the accuracy of your attribution will be increased even more. In the above example you might have originally wondered whether your favorable assessment of the punner reflected your penchant for punning. But if a good friend who doesn't like puns agrees that the other person is bright, you will be more certain about the accuracy of your original impression. The *consensus* of judgments influences the confidence with which you attribute characteristics.

As another example, say you were wondering what another student thought about George Wallace's candidacy. If a group of avidly anti-Wallace students were talking and the person in question made vaguely anti-Wallace statements, you might not be able to tell much about his true feelings. When the situation creates a social pressure not to praise Wallace, a pro-Wallace student might keep quiet in order to avoid the ridicule of others. A closet conservative might not voice his opinions in this situation because of *external pressures*.

Your own expectations about what a particular person is like would provide another guide in your attribution process. Without getting to know a fellow college student well, you might consider it safe to assume that he opposed the war in Vietnam. Many students did. In the absence of any inconsistent information, assuming that a particular student shares this *expected characteristic* might be the most accurate way of predicting what he really thinks.

The foregoing examples illustrate the four major criteria that attribution theorists hypothesize are used to verify impressions of others: (1) consistency, (2) consensus, (3) freedom from external pressures, and (4) prior expectancy of a behavior's occurring.

Consistency

If you have a dinner date with someone you have not dated before and he is late, you may believe his excuse about heavy traffic and car problems. But if he is late on another occasion, you may begin to wonder whether he is habitually late. And if he continues to be late for a number of different events, you will come to believe that being late is a part of his character.

From such real-life experiences one can hypothesize that the more consistent information about a particular behavior is, the more confidently people will attribute that behavior to the characteristics of the other person. Confirmation for this hypothesis has been obtained in a recent study (Kelley and Stahelski, 1970). The subjects watched two persons pretending to play the "prisoner's dilemma" game in which each player must decide whether he can win more points by playing competitively or cooperatively with his opponent. The sequence of competitive and cooperative moves of each player was manipulated. Not too surprisingly, when a player's moves were made to appear consistently competitive or consistently cooperative, the subjects more confidently attributed either a cooperative or a competitive motive to that player than when the player made inconsistent (some cooperative, some competitive) moves.

So far, so obvious. Even though you may not have been aware that you were looking for consistency as you tried to understand others,

you may recognize, now that the process is made explicit, that this is something you have been doing all your life. It is not so obvious, however, that the way you interpret consistency may depend on what you have done while interacting with another person, what others in the situation have done, and the characteristic you are trying to infer.

If, in the process of interacting with another person, you do something that you think will make a particular pattern of behavior likely to occur, then the consistency in the other person's behavior may tell you little about him. If, for example, you are having a discussion with another person and you act hostile and aggressive, his reciprocating the hostility and aggression will not tell you much about him. He may be acting this way because you have made him angry, or he may be acting this way because he is habitually aggressive. Only when you believe your own behavior was not a likely cause of the other person's behavior is his behavior informative. Confirmation for this hypothesis has been obtained in a recent experiment (Epstein and Taylor, 1967).

The reactions of others in the situation also influence your interpretation of another's consistency. If the other members of a committee are acting cooperatively and helpfully, the cooperative behavior of a particular member may not tell you much about his general level of cooperativeness. Is he being helpful because others in the situation are or because he generally is? If, however, he acts competitively even though others are being friendly and helpful, this may tell you more about his nature. If an individual's behavior differs from that of the other members of a group, the consistency of his behavior is more informative than if he is conforming to the expected norm. Again, this hypothesis has been confirmed (Kelley and Stahelski, 1970).

The characteristic you are trying to understand may also influence the way you interpret another person's consistent behavior patterns. Inconsistencies may provide more information about motivation than consistencies. Suppose you knew that one college student had achieved very high scores on the aptitude section of his college entrance exam and yet had earned just average grades in college, and that another student had received mediocre test scores and grades. How informative would each set of facts be if you were assessing each student's level of academic motivation? The discrepancy between grades and test scores would provide more information about the student's academic motivation than consistency of performance would (Kepka and Brickman, 1971). In general, an inconsistency between the various indicators of performance may be a prime cue when you are inferring motives. We may tend to think of people's abilities as being stable and thus attribute any day-to-day variations in performance to moods or motives.

Other variables may also influence the way you interpret consistency. The more disparate the situations in which you observe consistent behavior, the more informative the behavior may be (Kelley, 1967). If a person is pleasant when he is tired or frustrated as well as when things are going well for him, you may believe with more confidence that he really is pleasant. Or if time elapses between your observations, consistency may convey more information. Consistency between behaviors observed only minutes apart may not be as informative as consistencies observed over a period of months or years.

Informative as consistency is in the laboratory, interpreting consistency in real-life situations may be far more complicated. When subjects are given information that is obviously consistent or inconsistent, they may find it simple to detect and react to consistency. But in real life it is often much more difficult to determine what is consistent. For example, is someone's talking about ecology while tossing a paper cup out of a car window an inconsistency? Is the cup throwing a manifestation of a habit acquired over a number of years and the comments an indication of a genuine concern about the environment? Or is the apparent inconsistency a cue that the person is a talking, not a doing, ecologist?

Consensus

Assume you were trying to assess another student's intelligence. Even if all of the indicators were consistent, you might wonder whether your personal assessment was accurate or influenced by your own biases. If, however, some of your friends agreed that the person in question was bright, you would be more confident that your own initial judgment was accurate. As we have seen repeatedly, people look to others for information, especially when reality is not clear (Festinger, 1954). In person perception, when you rarely know whether your assessments of others are accurate, the influence of other people's reactions and evaluations is particularly important (Kelley, 1967).

Thus if others share your opinion about a particular person, your confidence in the accuracy of your judgment should increase, and if others disagree, your confidence should decrease. Support for this hypothesis was obtained in a recent study. College students were shown an "excerpt from a college admissions interview" of two students, one of whom was made to seem more able than the other. Then the subjects were asked to indicate which of the two students was more able. Later in the experiment the subjects were told how another student had rated the two interviewees. As might be predicted, subjects who received agreeing evaluations became more confident about the accuracy of their own initial ratings, and those receiving disagreeing evaluations became less confident (Goethals, 1972).

From this study it is clear that agreement can strengthen the confidence with which people judge others. However, the reaction to agreement might be expected to depend on why the other person is agreeing and who he is. If you think someone is agreeing with you simply to please you, his agreement may not increase your confidence in the accuracy of your judgments. For example, if someone who was working for you agreed with you, you might wonder whether he was doing so because of his genuine beliefs or because of his desire to win your favor. People may discount agreement that could be extraneously motivated. Confirmation for this hypothesis has been obtained (Ring, 1964).

Your reaction to agreement is also influenced by the person who is agreeing. People who can provide the most valid information can be expected to have the greatest impact (Kelley, 1967). Who would these people be? As we saw in Chapters 2 and 5, people who are similar to oneself—either in terms of situation or in terms of personality—are generally the preferred sources of information. If you are wondering how cool a friend is, your mother's reactions may not be very helpful. She may evaluate people by completely different criteria from what you use.

However, under certain circumstances a person who is dissimilar might be the best source of valid information. If you were trying to assess the brightness of a fellow student, a professor's comments might be more informative than those of another student. Because he is exposed to information about the student that is different from what is available to you, his agreeing with your assessment may be more informative than the agreement of another student, who has been exposed to the same information you have. According to attribution theory, whether a similar or a dissimilar other is preferred depends simply on the comparative amount of information each can provide.

And according to attribution theory, whether a similar or a dissimilar other can provide more information depends on other aspects of the situation. A beginning attempt to specify just what these aspects are was made in the admissions-interview experiment discussed earlier. In addition to the manipulation of the agreement-disagreement of the other judge's evaluation of the student being interviewed, two other variables were manipulated: (1) the similarity-dissimilarity of the other judge's *method of evaluation* (the subjects were told either that the other judge scored the same as they did on a test of how to judge people or that they scored differently); and (2) the similarity-dissimilarity of the *information* that the other judge was exposed to (the subjects were told either that the other judge had seen exactly the same section of the "interview" as they had or that he had seen another section).

In all of the conditions the judges were, in general, influenced more by other judges whom they thought used a similar method of evaluation. However, some of the interactions between similarity of method and similarity of information provide interesting leads about when dissimilar others might provide more information. When subjects were told that the other judge had been exposed to different segments of the interview from the segment they had seen, judges who were believed to have used a similar method of evaluation were more influen-

tial. But when subjects were told that the judges had been exposed to the same portion of the interview as they had, judges who were thought to have used a dissimilar method of evaluation tended to be more influential (Goethals, 1972).

What would account for these results? Think about which judge would provide more information. If the information that a given judge had been exposed to was different from what you had seen, a judge who used a similar method of evaluation would tell you more. His evaluation would tell you how you might react if you were to see the additional information. However, if the information the judge has been exposed to is the same that you have seen, you may learn more from the report of a person who uses a different method of evaluation. The different perspective may provide more information. Thus it may be that an intermediate amount of dissimilarity may be the most informative—just enough dissimilarity to show you that your evaluation is not unique to your own point of view, but not enough to challenge your whole perspective.

Freedom from external pressures

How much can you tell about a debater's true attitude on a topic that he has been assigned to defend? And how much can an employer tell about the enthusiasm of a potential employee during a job interview? To the extent that external pressures are clearly operating to force another person to act in a particular way, his behavior does not tell you much about his underlying characteristics. You cannot be sure whether to attribute his behavior to the situational pressures or to his own character. You may have noticed this kind of "discounting" in your own assessments of others. If a hostess at a party is friendly, you may wonder whether she is being friendly to play her role or because she genuinely likes you. That people discount pressured behavior has been shown in a number of studies. No matter what form the pressure takes, it has been found that acts committed under pressure are not very informative.

External pressures can be brought to bear in a number of ways. The most obvious is by direct assignment: An experimenter tells the subject that the person to be judged was either assigned a particular point of view or chose it freely. For example, in one recent experiment the subjects were told either that the person to be judged had chosen his position on the legalization of marijuana or that he had been assigned a particular position. Not too surprisingly, the subjects saw the freely chosen positions as being more informative (Jones, Worchel, Goethals, and Grumet, 1971).

Even if social pressures are not stated as explicitly as in the direct-assignment experiments, they can still exert a significant influence on how people interpret the behavior of others. For example, one of the "unwritten rules of the game" is that during job interviews, applicants are supposed to be enthusiastic and say what they think their potential employer wants to hear. Behavior that meets the demands of the job interview may be difficult to interpret, since the person could simply be playing along or his behavior could reflect his true characteristics.

Confirmation for this hypothesis was obtained in a well-known study. The subjects listened to a tape-recorded "job interview" in which an applicant was said to be trying to make a good impression. In half of the job interviews the job in question was that of a member of a submarine crew. The "ideal candidate" was described by the interviewer as being obedient, cooperative, and friendly. In the other half of the cases the job in question was that of an astronaut, and the interviewer described the ideal candidate as someone who was independent and had little need for social contact.

Half of the "job interview candidates" acted obedient, cooperative, and friendly, and the other half acted independent and showed little need for social contact. After hearing the job interview, the subjects were asked to state what they thought the candidate was really like as a person. When the candidate's behavior coincided with what was demanded by the job interview, the subjects could not make very positive attributions—their ratings were made with low confidence and were rather neutral. But when the applicant's behavior deviated from what was expected, the subjects attributed underlying characteristics consistent with the way the candidate acted. If it was expedient to be quiet and the candidate acted friendly, the subjects thought he really was friendly. Con-

versely, if it was expedient to be friendly and outgoing and the candidate acted quiet and withdrawn, the subjects thought he really was quiet and withdrawn (Jones, Davis, and Gergen, 1961). Thus in-role behavior didn't convey much information, whereas out-of-role behavior was very informative.

The hypothesis that in-role behavior is generally uninformative presents two problems, however. First, in real life it may be difficult to assess the expectations about "appropriate behaviors" for a particular role. Once it is announced what the "ideal job candidate" for a particular job is supposed to be like, there is little question about what is expected. But in the course of usual interactions as people play out a variety of roles, the expectations are not as clear. How much concern about injustices done to blacks is required among nominal campus liberals? How much humor is consistent with the professorial role? How much "social consciousness" is normative for today's enlightened executive? Thus when the attribution process involves less explicitly defined roles, we must first ascertain what the in-role behavior is.

Second, under some circumstances a person may be telling you something about himself even when he is knowingly playing a role. If you were interviewing a job applicant, would his acting out his role tell you anything about him? It might not tell you how he felt about you or the job, but it would tell you that he was sufficiently socially aware to know what his role was, that he had mastered it, and that he was sufficiently motivated to play his part.

The reason in-role behavior has been theorized to be relatively uninformative is that it is mediated by the many rewards for playing the part and by the punishments meted out for deviation. The direct effects of reward and punishment on attribution have been tested, and it has been found that, as predicted, behaviors that are rewarded are not very informative in the attribution process. Thus a person who is seen as doing a favor to gain something for his own advantage is seen as less sincere than someone who does a favor for no overt reward (Schopler and Thompson, 1968). Workers who are closely supervised by their superiors are seen as less motivated and less competent than workers who are supervised occasionally and produce the same level and quality of work (Strickland, 1958). People who defend a position for a large monetary reward may view themselves as less convinced than do those who defend the same view for small monetary rewards, as we saw in Chapter 4. Wherever the environment rewards a behavior, either directly by experimental fiat or indirectly through the working of roles, the behavior is generally seen as less informative about the person's true nature than unrewarded behavior.

It can be hypothesized that if rewarded, in-role behavior is relatively uninformative under most circumstances, then punished, out-of-role behavior is particularly informative. We saw this in the job-interview study. When, in another study, a communicator urging higher truck-licensing fees was represented as speaking to a hostile audience, the local union of truck drivers, he was seen as more sincere than when he was represented as speaking to a friendly group, the local union of railway men (Mills and Jellison, 1967). The judges may see the communicator who is willing to undergo highly negative reactions as feeling strongly about his views.

The espousing of unpopular causes may generally be a cue for attributing the unpopular behavior to a strongly held attitude, but could it mean anything else? Does someone's espousing unpopular beliefs always mean to you that he sincerely holds these beliefs? If someone were to champion a variety of unpopular beliefs, always changing to the opposite view from what most people were saying, you might begin to suspect that something other than the person's commitment to what he was saying was being revealed.

We have seen that external pressure, no matter what form it takes, tends to make behavior uninformative. But which form of pressure—hope of reward or threat of punishment—is seen as exerting more pressure? If someone took a bribe so he could buy a sports car, would he be seen as more greedy than if he took a bribe to pay off some badly overdue bills? Although the evidence is far from conclusive, it seems that avoiding punishment is seen as more pressing than seeking reward. In one experiment an athlete who was described as taking a bribe to improve his economic circumstances was seen as worse than one described as taking a bribe

to prevent a deterioration in his personal finances (Kruglanski and Yinon, unpublished paper).

Prior expectancy

Unless you have strong evidence to the contrary, you generally tend to think that people possess the characteristics you expect them to have. Since you know that most liberal college students have not been ardent supporters of Vice-President Agnew, you might assume that a particular liberal college student was anti-Agnew unless you had strong evidence to the contrary. And if you saw him making mildly pro-Agnew comments when he was compelled to do so (say in the interest of preserving family harmony at a Thanksgiving dinner), you might still think that he was anti-Agnew, since he was making the pro-Agnew comments under duress. However, if you saw this same college liberal vehemently supporting Agnew when there was no pressure for him to do so, you might believe that he really was a supporter of Agnew—perhaps even a stronger supporter than a conservative student who made exactly the same comments.

The importance of expectancy and its interaction with freedom of choice has been supported by several studies. In one recent experiment, partially reviewed in the previous section, subjects were asked to estimate the "true attitude" of a person after he read an essay in which he had either opposed or favored the legalization of marijuana. Four independent variables were manipulated: (1) the position taken in the essay (either pro- or anti-legalization of marijuana), (2) the intensity of support (either strong or weak support for the position taken), (3) the person's freedom to choose the position (either free choice or a mandatory assignment), and (4) prior expectancy of the person's position on the legalization of marijuana (Jones, Worchel, Goethals, and Grumet, 1972).

Prior expectations about the target person's attitude were manipulated by providing the subjects with the results of a questionnaire allegedly completed by the target person. All of the questionnaire items related to the general issue of whether people should be allowed to

Table 1. Experimental Conditions Listed in the Order in Which the Subjects Saw the Target Person As Being Opposed to Marijuana Legalization (the Larger the Mean, the More He Was Thought to Oppose the Legalization of Marijuana)

Position in Essay (Pro or Anti-legalization of Marijuana)	Target Person's Freedom to Choose Which Position to Support	Strength of the Essay	Expectancy About the Target Person's Attitude on Legalization	Degree of Opposition to the Legalization of Marijuana	
Anti	Free	Strong	Pro	5.79	
Anti	Assigned	Strong	Anti	5.57	Most opposed to legalization
Anti	Free	Strong	Anti	5.43	
Anti	Free	Weak	Pro	5.00	
Pro	Assigned	Weak	Anti	4.93	
Anti	Free	Weak	Anti	4.36	
Anti	Assigned	Strong	Pro	4.29	
Pro	Assigned	Weak	Pro	3.93	
Pro	Assigned	Strong	Anti	3.57	
Anti	Assigned	Weak	Anti	3.00	
Pro	Free	Weak	Pro	2.50	
Anti	Assigned	Weak	Pro	2.21	
Pro	Free	Weak	Anti	2.14	
Pro	Free	Strong	Pro	1.57	
Pro	Free	Strong	Anti	1.21	Least opposed to legalization
Pro	Assigned	Strong	Pro	1.21	

live their own lives with minimal governmental interference. Half of the subjects were given a set of answers that showed the target person was someone who systematically favored individual autonomy (thus creating the expectancy that he would favor the legalization of marijuana). The other half of the subjects were provided with a set of answers that showed the target person was someone who favored socially imposed restraints in a number of areas (thereby creating the expectancy that he would be opposed to marijuana legalization).

Next the subjects read the essays on the legalization of marijuana allegedly written by the target person. Half of the essays opposed marijuana legalization; the other half supported it. Half of the subjects were told that the target person had been free to either favor or oppose marijuana legalization in the essay. The other half were told that he had been assigned a given position on the subject. Half of the essays were strong, containing four arguments in support of their position; half of the essays were weak, containing two arguments in support of the writer's position and two in opposition.

In total, there were sixteen different experimental conditions, which are shown in Table 1 together with the degree to which the subjects saw the target person in that condition as being opposed to the legalization of marijuana. As predicted, the target person was seen as opposing legalization when the subjects expected him to have that attitude and their expectancy was supported by an essay in which he had freely chosen an anti-legalization position and had presented a strong argument. Similarly, when the target person had freely chosen to write a pro-legalization essay and was expected to believe in that position, subjects saw him as among the least likely to oppose legalization.

Subjects were also willing to give considerable weight to a person's position, either pro or anti, when he bore out their expectancies by writing a strong essay when the expected position was assigned to him. When a person is forced to take a position that people expect him to believe in and he supports it well, his behavior will strongly reinforce that expectancy; and he will be seen as believing what he writes.

In addition to these predictable results, however, there were some interesting interactions. The students seemed to be the most impressed when a person who was expected to favor legalization freely chose to write a strong anti-legalization essay. These persons were seen as even more anti-legalization than those who were expected to be opposed. Similarly, persons who were expected to take an anti-legalization position but freely chose to write a strong pro essay were seen as very unlikely to oppose legalization. Subjects were thus willing to discard their prior expectancies when confronted with evidence that the target person had chosen to take a strong position inconsistent with what was expected.

Why does expectancy interact with the person's choice in this manner? The effect of expectancy when the person is thought to have had no choice of position is fairly understandable. When someone has to defend a particular position, the best approach to assessing his real feeling is to base your estimate on what you think he probably feels. When he has a choice and says what you expect him to say, you attribute to him the attitude that matches both your expectancy and his behavior.

However, the contrast effect is a little more difficult to explain. Why should someone whom you expect to oppose legalization but who freely takes a pro position seem more pro than someone you expected to be pro all along? Do you pay more attention to unexpected comments and react more to them? Does the contrast between what you expected and what the other person says make his comments seem more extreme?

Biases in attribution

All of the attributional processes discussed so far seem very rational. Looking to the consistency of your own impressions over time and in a variety of situations, referring to the reactions of others, considering the pressure a person feels to act in a certain way, and thinking about your own expectations about what people are usually like—all of these are highly reasonable ways to approach the problem of understanding other people. However, we know from our own experience in forming impressions of other people that not all person perception is reasonable and unbiased. As we saw in Chapter 2, for instance, our perceptions of ourselves are particularly kind.

Do you interpret your own behavior differently from that of other people? If you do, this would suggest that either your perceptions of yourself are in error or that your perceptions of others are biased.

Comparing the way you view yourself and the way you view others may show some interesting contrasts. When the behavior in question is not particularly commendable or when you know little about the other person, you may be more likely to interpret his behavior as reflecting underlying motives, whereas you see your own acts as more a product of circumstances. For example, if you learned that a friend hadn't prepared for an important test, you might think he wasn't very interested in the course or didn't care much about grades. But if you yourself didn't prepare for a test, you might think that your personal problems or some other commitments had precluded your studying. Thus in such situations you may have a general bias toward interpreting the behavior of others as reflecting underlying characteristics and yet tend to see your own behavior as determined by many aspects of the situation.

Thus the same behavior would be interpreted differently—depending on whether you or someone else did it. In a recent experiment half of the female subjects were asked to observe another subject who was making a decision about whether or not to volunteer for a given task, and the other half were asked to decide themselves whether or not to volunteer. Then the actors and the observers were asked questions about why the actor had taken the action she had. In this case, where they had just met the other person and so had very limited information about her, the observers thought that the actor's volunteering reflected a general tendency, whereas the actors themselves did not interpret their own actions in this way (Nisbett, Legant, and Marecek, 1971).

Another way in which perceptions of the self and of others have been found to differ is in the kindness with which most people view themselves. In general, people want to see good things about themselves and avoid unpleasant information, as we saw in Chapter 2.

Thus it is not surprising that a number of studies have shown a systematic distortion in the way people interpret events that apply to themselves. In one study, for example, pairs of subjects thought that they were competing against other, similar pairs. Some of the subjects were made to think that they were losing. When the subjects were asked what had determined the outcome, the winning subjects attributed their success to their own sterling efforts, and the losing subjects blamed their fate on the other team (Streufert and Streufert, 1969). This sounds all too familiar. You don't have to look too far in everyday life to see similar patterns. People who are known to everyone but themselves—the Willy Lomans of the world—are common characters in literature.

You may be able to think of yet other ways in which your perception of yourself and others differs. Are you more attentive to what you do? Do you pay more attention to different aspects when considering your own behavior than you do when looking at another person? Are you less analytic when you look at yourself than when you look at others? Since your assessment of your own reactions forms the basic comparison for your perceptions of others, understanding the ways in which you come to know yourself provides a basic part of your understanding of how you see others.

The disparity between interpretations of self-behavior and of the behavior of others, as evidenced in the experiments we have just described, has interesting theoretical and practical implications. You will recall that earlier we discussed Bem's argument that people use exactly the same processes to infer their own characteristics as they do to infer the characteristics of others. Although people may sometimes do this, the results of the foregoing experiments make it clear that they do not always do so. And when people do not know each other well, they may tend to overinterpret the behavior of others. A chance nasty comment from a stranger may be seen as indicating underlying hostile feelings when in fact it may only be a reflection of a bad day on the job.

One might ask why people differ in their interpretation of their own behavior and that of others. There are several possible answers. First, the actor knows more about what he has done in the past. He knows whether or not he has volunteered in other situations, whereas an observer has a much more limited sample of behavior. And, above all, the individual may be motivated to avoid recognizing unpleasant information about himself.

Summary

In this section we have seen the complexity of the processes we use to interpret the words and deeds of other people. Since a person's behavior can be explained by attributing it either to some underlying characteristic or to other variables in the environment, we are constantly using a variety of tactics to sift out the meaning of what we see. Without being consciously aware that we are doing so, we use four highly rational techniques. In interpreting the behavior of others, people have been shown to consider (1) the consistency of the other person's behavior, (2) the reactions of others, (3) the degree of freedom from external pressures, and (4) their own expectations.

The more *consistent* information about a particular behavior is, the more confidently people will attribute that behavior to the characteristics of the other person. However, the way you interpret consistency may depend on what you have done while interacting with the other person, what others in the situation have done, and the characteristic that you are trying to infer. If in the process of interacting with another person, you do something that you think will make a particular pattern of behavior likely to occur, then the consistency of the other person's behavior may tell you little about him. If the individual's behavior differs from that of the other members of a group, the consistency of his behavior is more informative than if he is conforming to the expected norm. Inconsistencies may provide more information about motivation than consistencies.

In person perception, when you rarely know whether your assessments of others are accurate, the *influence of other people's reactions and evaluations* is particularly important. Thus if others share your opinions about a particular person, your confidence in the accuracy of your judgment is increased. However, the reaction to agreement depends on why the other person agrees and who he is. People may discount agreement that could be extraneously motivated. People who can provide the most valid information have the greatest impact.

To the extent that *external pressures* are clearly operating to force another person to act in a particular way, his behavior does not tell you much about his underlying characteristics. But when that behavior deviates from what the situation would normally require, you may regard the deviation as a particularly good indicator of underlying characteristics.

Unless you have strong evidence to the contrary, you generally tend to think that people possess the characteristics you *expect* them to have. However, if another person makes statements freely that are inconsistent with what you expected him to say, you would attribute underlying characteristics consistent with what the person said. In fact, you would see him as holding a belief more extreme than that of someone you expected to hear the statements from.

As we know from our own experience in forming impressions, there are *systematic biases in person perception*. When you know comparatively little about someone else, you may *overemphasize his behavior*. Further, there are *differences in the way we interpret our own behavior and that of others*. When the behavior is not particularly commendable or when you know little about the other person, you may be more likely to interpret his behavior as reflecting underlying motives, whereas you see your own acts as more a product of circumstances. Another way in which perceptions of the self and those of others have been found to differ is in the kindness with which most people view themselves. In general, people want to see good things about themselves and avoid unpleasant information.

Getting It Together

Once you have formed the impression that another person has a number of characteristics, how do you put the information together? On the basis of some of the cues discussed earlier, how would you see a person you thought had the following character traits?

> **intelligent skillful industrious warm determined practical cautious**

Asch's work

Some clues about the processes involved in putting information together are provided by a series of classic experiments done by Asch (1946). Since the procedure he used has been emulated in much of the subsequent work, his procedures and results will be outlined in some detail. In his experiments lists of character traits were read to subjects, who were then asked to write a sketch of the person described and to answer questions about him. When the above list was given, the subjects could form a unified and consistent impression of the person described. Just as people attribute certain character traits from situations, these subjects attributed an overall personality structure from the traits given. They had no trouble going from the list of traits to a complicated picture of what the individual was like. For instance, one subject saw the person as "a scientist performing experiments and persevering after many setbacks. He is driven by the desire to accomplish something that would be of benefit" (Asch, 1946, p. 263).

When the subjects were asked to select traits that would best fit the impression they had formed, their reactions were fairly uniform. For example, even though the list of traits did not contain any direct information about these characteristics, 100 percent of the subjects saw the person as serious; 98 percent saw him as strong; 88 percent as honest; etc.

Central Traits   Why did this list of traits call up such a uniform reaction from the subjects? When you think of someone as a warm person, you may see him as possessing other characteristics. Warm people may also be thought of as happy, sociable people. Further, in your informal theorizing of what traits go with what, some traits may be more important (or, to use Asch's term, more "central") than others. Asch theorized that warm and cold were two such central traits. To test this, he read two lists of character traits that were identical except for the words "warm" and "cold." To half of the subjects he read the list shown at the beginning of this section.

The other half of the subjects heard the same list except that the word "cold" was substituted for "warm." This substitution made a dramatic difference in the impressions formed. The warm person was described in positive terms (as in the description of the scientist given earlier). The cold person was seen in very negative terms, as shown by the following description: "A rather snobbish person who feels that his success and intelligence set him apart from the run-of-the-mill individual. Calculating and unsympathetic" (Asch, 1946, p. 263).

The dramatic difference in the impressions created is shown very clearly by the different traits checked off. Ninety-one percent of the subjects who heard "warm" thought the person was generous, and only 8 percent of those who heard "cold" thought so; 94 percent of the subjects who heard "warm" thought that the person was good-natured, and only 17 percent of those who heard "cold" thought so; 91 percent of the subjects who heard "warm" thought he was sociable, and only 38 percent hearing "cold" thought so.

There were also a number of characteristics that were not affected by the warm-cold variation. Both the warm and the cold persons were seen as reliable, strong, honest, serious, and persistent. Thus although the change of a central trait had a significant impact on the overall impression and on many components, it did not have a blanket effect on all aspects of the impression. Only those characteristics related to the central trait were changed.

If central traits can exert such a significant impact on impressions, their identification becomes important. What traits would you select as being central? Perhaps polite and blunt? These would seem to influence the way one would interpret a number of other traits. However, when Asch replicated his study, substituting "polite" and "blunt" for "warm" and "cold," the impressions created by the two traits were not substantially different.

Meaning Within Context   The meaning of a term depends on its context. The warmth of a shallow person may seem quite different from the warmth of a strong, self-sufficient person. When subjects were read the following list, the meaning of the term "warm" changed completely:

obedient	**weak**	**shallow**
warm	**unambitious**	**vain**

In this context "warm" became a "dog-like affection rather than a bright friendliness. It is passive and without strength." The quality of "cold" was also reinterpreted in the above context. Thus the meaning of the trait was transformed in a different context.

First Impressions   What happens if your first impressions of another person are unpleasant? Say you meet someone who freely picks his teeth and generally acts in a boorish way in initial encounters, but subsequently begins to show positive traits. Will your impression be influenced more by the early information than by the later information? A host of everyday observations attest to the common belief that first impressions are important.

To test the effect of the order in which information is given, Asch presented two lists of traits to different groups:

A.	**intelligent**	**industrious**	**impulsive**
	critical	**stubborn**	**envious**

B.	**envious**	**stubborn**	**critical**
	impulsive	**industrious**	**intelligent**

Note that the two lists contain the same traits with the order reversed. List A opens with positive traits (intelligent, industrious), proceeds to more ambiguous traits, which may be interpreted in a variety of ways (impulsive, critical), and then moves to the negative traits. List B opens with negative traits, moves to ambiguous traits, and then proceeds to positive traits.

As predicted, the impressions derived from the two lists differed significantly, and the information presented first exerted more influence (a primacy effect). (See Figure 8-9.) Generally, the impression derived from list A was that "of an able person who possesses certain shortcomings, which are not serious enough to overshadow his merits" (Asch, 1952, p. 212). In contrast, the person described by list B was seen as a "problem"—a person "whose abilities are hampered by serious difficulties" (Asch, 1952, p. 212). In many instances the ambiguous qualities (impulsive, critical) took on a positive content for those who heard list A and a negative content for those who heard list B.

Why did the order influence the impressions formed? Asch theorized that the beginning information influenced the way the later information was interpreted. If you begin with positive information, you interpret the subsequent information in a positive manner. If you think someone is intelligent and industrious, his critical ability can be viewed as a good-natured, creative kind of critical ability. But if you begin with a negative impression, his critical quality is seen as a small, petty, niggling criticism—criticism just for the sake of criticism.

FIGURE 8-9 Although the information given to the observer is exactly the same in the top and bottom sequences, the observer in the top sequence forms a more favorable impression of the other person—a primacy effect.

From the results and interpretations of Asch's studies, you may be able to see how Asch would answer the question of how we put our impressions together. As we use the separate pieces of information to form an overall, consistent picture of another person, each trait influences the way we interpret the others, and the total impression is not one that could be predicted from the individual traits alone. Some traits exert more of an influence than others, since they influence the way a number of other traits are interpreted. However, the whole context determines the meaning of any particular trait. The weak man's warmth is different from a strong man's warmth. And the order in which information is presented influences the meaning we attribute to the particular pieces of information. After one or two negative experiences, other traits, which might ordinarily be neutral, begin to take on a negative tinge.

Testing the Asch findings

Testing the generality of Asch's findings and his interpretation has preoccupied the majority of the researchers in this area since the publication of his studies. In general, the emphasis has been on three areas: (1) What determines the centrality of a trait? (2) What determines the relative importance of a first impression? and (3) How do we process the information about other people?

What Determines the Centrality of a Trait? Since several studies now show the centrality of the warm-cold trait, the bulk of the subsequent work in this area has tended to focus on the question of what makes a trait central. Asch's answer to this is that all of the traits present in a description interact, but that some traits have more of an impact in this process than others. Thus if a person is described as intelligent and warm or as intelligent and cold, the change in the central trait drastically changes the meaning of intelligent. "Warm and intelligent" summons up images of the friendly competency of a shaggy professor, whereas "cold and intelligent" brings up images of the ruthless capability of a hard-driving executive who would stop at nothing to attain success.

However, there is another approach to under-

standing how certain traits acquire their central characteristic. Rather than thinking of central traits as those that exert more influence than most traits on the interpretation of other traits, one can think of central traits as those that correlate with many other traits. People have ideas of what traits "go together" (or have an "implicit theory of personality"—Cronbach, 1955). We may tend to think that people who are warm will also tend to be sociable, generous, and popular, and that people who are cold will tend to be unsociable, ungenerous, and unpopular. Thus it is when the check list of adjectives describing a person includes many words that naturally correlate with "warm" and "cold" that the use of "warm" or "cold" significantly influences the overall description of that person.

To test this hypothesis, one investigator first asked 214 students to rate their college instructors on a number of traits. He then computed the correlations of each trait with each of the other traits. By looking at this pattern of intercorrelations, he could see that certain traits correlated with a number of other traits. He then picked out a set of new central traits—the terms "humane" and "ruthless"—and developed an adjective check list that included many of the terms that had been found to correlate with the humane-ruthless set. As predicted, there were significant differences in the responses to the adjective check list when the word "humane" was substituted for the word "ruthless" (Wishner, 1960).

Thus Wishner could argue that central traits don't have to be explained in terms of Asch's "change-in-meaning" hypothesis. He argued that if you know the intercorrelations between various traits and include a number of these intercorrelating traits on the check list used to test the effect of the central trait, you can predict that some traits will have a greater impact than others.

But, of course, the question is whether the correlational approach can account for all of Asch's findings. Clearly, it cannot. Although the correlational approach provides an interesting operational definition of a central trait—one that correlates with a number of other traits—it does not explain how context influences the meaning of terms. The fact that shallow-warm is interpreted differently from intelligent-warm seems to be explained best by Asch's approach. Indeed, the intercorrelations between traits depend on how a person is defining a particular term. A weak and expedient warmth might or might not be highly intercorrelated with sociable.

What Determines the Relative Importance of a First Impression? The importance of first impressions is commonly assumed. You may see this in your own behavior, both in the care you take to create favorable first impressions and in the impact your own first impressions have on the way you interpret the subsequent behavior of other people. You may have noticed your trying to create a favorable first impression when a potential relationship is important to you. A new employee may be on especially good behavior on the first day of the job. And you may have noticed that once you have formed an impression of someone else—either negative or positive—that impression influences the way you interpret and react to subsequent events. If you think a person is cold, his businesslike manner may be seen as cold, but if you think he is warm, the same businesslike manner may be seen as friendly competency.

The way we interpret ambiguous behavior depends to a large extent on what we expect to see. For example, if you were told that a guest lecturer, who was going to lead a discussion in your social psychology class, was a very cold person, you would be more likely to see him as a cold person. Just such a situation was arranged in an experiment. Half of the students were told that the guest lecturer was a very warm person; the other half were told that the lecturer was very cold. The lecturer came into the class, led a discussion for about twenty minutes, and then the students were asked to give their impressions of him. Even though all of the students had observed the same person, their descriptions of him varied according to what they had expected. Those who had been told he was warm saw him as warm, and those who had been told that he was cold saw him as cold. Further, those who had been told that he was warm participated more frequently in the discussion than those who expected him to be cold (Kelley, 1950).

Of course, a twenty-minute period isn't very

long, and what the instructor did in his class might have been interpreted in a variety of ways. Perhaps, then, this demonstration of the power of expectations may not impress you very much. But these results are not an isolated finding. Out of the many studies on the power of first impressions, most have shown that information presented first is disproportionately important in the determining of impressions (a primacy effect).

Even when the subsequent information completely contradicts the first impression, what is seen first may still determine the final impression. For example, in one study subjects were presented with two inconsistent paragraphs describing a boy named Jim. In one paragraph, referred to as the E paragraph, Jim was described as friendly, outgoing, and extroverted:

Jim left the house to get some stationery. He walked out into the sun-filled street with two of his friends, basking in the sun as he walked. Jim entered the stationery store which was full of people. Jim talked with an acquaintance while he waited for the clerk to catch his eye. On his way out, he stopped to chat with a school friend who was just coming into the store. Leaving the store, he walked toward school. On his way out he met the girl to whom he had been introduced the night before. They talked for a short while, and then Jim left for school.

[Luchins, 1957a, p. 34.]

In another paragraph, the so-called I paragraph, Jim was depicted as shy and introverted:

After school, Jim left the classroom alone. Leaving the school, he started on his long walk home. The street was brilliantly filled with sunshine. Jim walked down the street on the shady side. Coming down the street toward him, he saw the pretty girl whom he had met on the previous evening. Jim crossed the street and entered a candy store. The store was crowded with students, and he noticed a few familiar faces. Jim waited quietly until the counterman caught his eye and then gave his order. Taking his drink, he sat down at a side table. When he had finished his drink he went home.

[Luchins, 1957a, p. 35.]

As you might expect, subjects who read only the E paragraph saw Jim as a friendly person, and subjects who read only the I paragraph saw Jim as a quiet person. The interesting question is how subjects who read both paragraphs saw Jim. Although not all of our impressions of other people are completely consistent, we generally feel a desire to organize what we know of others into a consistent impression of them (Gollin, 1954). How would the order in which the information about Jim was presented influence the subjects' impression of him? Specifically, would subjects who first read the E paragraph and then the I paragraph see Jim differently from subjects who first read the I paragraph and then the E paragraph? As expected, the order in which the inconsistent information was presented did influence the impression. Subjects who read the E paragraph first saw Jim as more friendly than those who read the I paragraph first (Luchins, 1957a). Even when the information is inconsistent, that which is presented first has the greater impact. Thus the commonsense assumption about the importance of first impressions may have some validity.

Why do first impressions have this power? If you were a subject in the above experiment how would you react to the information in the I paragraph after reading the E paragraph? Would you think that maybe Jim had had a bad day in school, which accounted for his quiet after-school behavior? Or that he didn't like the girl he avoided? Or that some problem was bothering him? Your reading of the E paragraph might influence the way you would interpret the material in the I paragraph (Asch, 1946). Once you have read the E paragraph, you expect to see extroversion in Jim. As long as events can possibly be interpreted in this manner, you will reinterpret them to make them consistent with your initial impression of Jim (Luchins, 1957a). Thus first impressions may exert their influence by determining how you interpret subsequent information.

Support for this hypothesis has been obtained in several studies. The evaluation of individual traits has been shown to vary according to the context. In an interesting study which shows how this happens, students who believed that factory workers are generally unintelligent were given a list of traits describing a factory worker, and the list included the term "intelligent." The variety of ways in which the worker's intelligence was interpreted illustrates how the context can influence meaning. Some subjects simply ignored the presence of "intel-

ligent" on the list; some tried to resolve the inconsistency by promoting the worker to a higher position (He was a foreman); others tried to resolve the inconsistency by showing how other circumstances compelled the man to do factory work (He was lazy, or he hated office work) (Haire and Grunes, 1950).

Although a change-of-meaning hypothesis may partially account for the power of first impressions, it doesn't completely explain their importance. In fact, the results of some experiments have not supported the change-of-meaning interpretation (e.g., Tesser, 1968).

After you have formed a firm impression of someone, do you pay careful attention to what he does in subsequent interactions? If you think he is very pleasant and nice, do you carefully evaluate whether or not his response to you is nice on subsequent occasions? First impressions may be important simply because people pay less attention to later information.

To test this hypothesis, two investigators manipulated the attention subjects paid to a list of traits. Half of the subjects were told they would be tested for their memory of the traits, and the other half were not told they would be tested. As predicted, when the subjects thought they would be tested, the primacy effect disappeared. In fact, in one condition the traits presented later exerted a greater effect on the overall impression formed—a so-called recency effect (Anderson and Hubert, 1963). A number of other experiments have also shown that when the subject's tendency to ignore later information is countered, the primacy effect is weakened, or in some cases, a recency effect occurs (e.g., Stewart, 1965).

Still other variables may influence the occurrence of primacy or recency effects. If the information is presented over a long period of time, the information that came last may be remembered better and so have a greater impact on impressions (Luchins, 1957b). If people are warned about the dangers of forming first impressions, the primacy effect can be weakened (Luchins, 1957b). The use that a person plans to make of the information influences the occurrence of primacy or recency effects; if he has to make a prediction about what will happen next, that which occurred most recently will influence his reactions more than earlier events (Jones and Welsh, 1971).

Further the effect of the order of presentation is determined by the complexity of the materials. Several studies have shown that when more complicated materials are used, order may not have a significant effect. For example, when tape-recorded anecdotes about a person were presented to a group of subjects, the order in which they were presented had no significant effect (Rosenkrantz and Crockett, 1965).

Whether the information about the other person is conveyed by a sequence of trait descriptions or by a sequence of overt behaviors may influence the relative effectiveness of first impressions. For instance, Aronson and Linder (1965) have argued that increases in positive, rewarding behavior from another person have more impact on liking—and presumably on the impression of the other person—than constant pleasant rewarding behavior. If another person initially is very unfriendly to you and then gradually begins to be nicer to you, you may like him more than someone who was nice to you from the beginning of your relationship. As we shall see in Chapter 9, experimental support for this "gain-loss" theory has been obtained.

How Do We Process the Information About Other People? Underlying the various controversies about the importance of central traits and of first impressions are two very different theories about how we process information about other people. Asch's change-of-meaning hypothesis typifies one approach. As we have noted, he claimed that the whole context determines the meaning of any particular trait. For example, the term "irresponsible" alone will be viewed negatively, and "father" will be viewed positively. However, when the two traits are combined ("irresponsible father"), "father" will be rated negatively, and the combination will be rated more negatively than either of the two rated alone (Rokeach and Rothman, 1965).

The second theory dismisses the importance of context and instead concentrates on the independent value of a particular trait. According to this theory, impressions are derived from the separate ratings given to each trait—as shown in the following experimental approach. For example, if a person is described as "sincere, intelligent, and cautious," we would first seek to establish the values that a group of subjects would assign to each of these adjec-

tives. Let's assume that they think sincerity is an extremely positive quality and give it the highest rating possible, +3, that they also rate intelligent as +3, and that they rate cautious as +1. Then when subjects in a second group rate their overall liking for a person described as "sincere, intelligent, and cautious," their overall evaluation can be predicted on the basis of the combined ratings given previously to the single traits.

Among adherents of this "statistical" approach, controversy has centered on the best way of combining the ratings given to the traits. Is adding or averaging these values a better way to combine the information? According to the averaging approach, the overall impression is determined best by summing the values of all the component traits and dividing by the total number of traits. Thus you would have a more favorable opinion of a person who possesses two highly favorable traits (or is sincere and intelligent) than you would of one who possesses two highly favorable and one moderately favorable trait (or is sincere, intelligent, and cautious).

According to an additive approach, however, your impression is determined by the total number of positive points in a particular description, so that you would have a more favorable impression of someone who is sincere, intelligent, and cautious than you would of someone who is sincere and intelligent. Thus with the additive approach, the addition of any positive traits would increase the overall favorableness of the evaluation, whereas with the averaging theory, only the addition of traits that are not lower than the average so far could increase the favorableness of the evaluation.

Although a considerable amount of research has been done to test the relative validity of the two models, conclusive evidence is not yet available. Support has been obtained for both. In some cases the addition of only moderately favorable traits to a list of highly positive traits did not increase the subjects' overall evaluation (Anderson, 1965). In other studies the total amount of positive information was found to influence the evaluation: Five strongly positive adjectives were found to result in a more positive evaluation than two did (Fishbein and Hunter, 1964).

Many of the inconsistent findings can best be

explained by an averaging model in which some traits are counted more heavily than others—a so-called weighted-average model (Anderson, 1965). Just as a final examination score probably counts more heavily than a minor quiz score when a professor determines your final grade, some traits are weighted more heavily than others. In your reactions to other people, you may have noticed that you pay more attention to some kinds of traits, or "weight" them more heavily, than others. As we saw in the previous section, you may pay more attention to first impressions. You may discount inconsistent information, as the subjects in one experiment did (Bugental, Kaswan, and Love, 1970). Redundant traits may be discounted (Wyer, 1968). Highly positive or highly negative traits may be weighted more heavily (Anderson, 1968b). Trait descriptions given by highly credible people may be weighted more heavily (Rosenbaum and Levin, 1968). The list could go on and on. Obviously, the empirical problem in the weighted-average model is to determine the way in which weights are assigned.

Since experimental support has been obtained for all of these methods of processing information—from the change-in-meaning to the weighted-average approach—it may be that an attempt to specify one way in which all people process all interpersonal information is doomed to failure. Different models may be used by different people in different situations. The processes used to combine information may vary from person to person (Kennedy et al., 1966). People under stress may use simpler methods of combining information (Schroder, Driver, and Streufert, 1967). The situation may influence the way in which information is processed. And when a person wants to be very sure his judgment is correct, he may use more than one processing method.

Forever Asch?

In most of the studies reviewed in this section, Asch's procedure of presenting lists of adjectives to subjects and asking them to react to the person described has been used. The preoccupation of researchers with the Asch paradigm illustrates a general problem in social psychological research. Once a given approach is proven to be effective, it may be used exclusively in a given area. However, since the paradigm may be limited in scope or irrelevant to illuminating certain aspects of the phenomena being studied, its exclusive use may limit a full understanding of what is being studied.

The real question is whether we do in fact process information about other people through a trait list method. Does it seem that as you form impressions of other people, you think in terms of traits? Or do you proceed in a more global, nonanalytical way? Do you form an overall reaction—either positive, neutral, or negative—without first noticing a person's specific traits? Of course, you may think in terms of traits without realizing it. However, before the results of the trait-list research can be generalized to the way people actually process information about others, the relationship between the trait-processing approach and what really happens must first be established.

Although some of the few studies in person perception that have used more complicated, realistic materials have replicated the findings of the trait-list approach (e.g., Warr and Knapper, 1968), not all have. As we saw in the section on first impressions, the complexity of the material can influence whether or not primacy occurs.

An approach that more closely resembles real-life interpersonal perception was used in a recent experiment and provides some ideas about ways in which controlled and yet realistic materials may be used. Acted, video-taped scenes of an adult evaluating a child's performance were shown to adults, who were asked to describe the adult in the scene. The verbal content, vocal tone, and facial expressions were varied in the different scenes. In some cases the information conveyed by verbal content, vocal tone, and facial expression was consistent. In others it was inconsistent; one adult, for instance, was criticizing the child's performance and yet was smiling at him. Those who judged scenes in which the facial expressions were not consistent with the tone and content of what was being said relied heavily on the facial expressions to interpret the meaning (Bugental, Kaswan, and Love, 1970).

Summary

How do we make sense out of the information acquired about other people? One answer—given by Asch—would be that we go from separate pieces of information to form an overall, consistent picture of another person. When we do this, some traits—such as warmth and coldness—exert more of an influence than others on the impressions formed, and usually what is seen first is more influential than what is seen later. PRIMACY EFFECT

Testing the generality of Asch's findings and his interpretation has preoccupied the majority of the researchers in this area since the publication of his studies. In general, the emphasis has been on three areas: (1) What determines the centrality of a trait? (2) What determines the relative importance of a first impression? and (3) How do we process the information about other people?

Since several studies have shown the centrality of the warm-cold trait, the bulk of the subsequent work has tended to focus on the question of *what makes a trait central*. Asch's answer is that central traits are those that exert more influence than most traits on the interpretation of other traits. Another approach is to think of central traits as those that correlate with many other traits. Although the correlational approach provides an interesting operational definition of a central trait, it does not explain how context influences the meaning of terms—as context has been shown to do.

A number of studies have shown that *first impressions* are important. One possible reason is that first impressions determine the interpretation of subsequent information. Another explanation is that people pay less attention to later information. Support for both of these explanations has been obtained. Although in many cases first impressions are important (a so-called primacy effect), in some cases traits presented later have been found to exert a greater effect on the overall impression (a so-called recency effect). If the information is presented over a long period of time, if people are warned about the dangers of forming first impressions, if the person has to make a prediction, about what the other person will do next, or if the information is conveyed by a sequence of overt behaviors—rather than by trait descriptions—then a recency effect may occur.

There are two very different theories about *how we process information about other people*. Asch claimed that the whole context determines the meaning of any particular trait. A second, statistical approach dismisses the importance of context and instead concentrates on the independent value of a particular trait: Overall reactions are determined by the combined ratings given to each of the single traits. Among adherents of this statistical approach, controversy has centered on the best way of combining the ratings given to the traits. Should the values of the traits be added or averaged to predict the overall impression? Although a considerable amount of research has been done to test the relative validity of the two models, conclusive evidence is not yet available. However, many of the inconsistent findings can best be explained by an averaging model in which some traits are counted more heavily than others—a so-called weighted average model.

In most of the studies reviewed in this section, Asch's procedure of presenting lists of adjectives to subjects and then asking them to react to the person described has been used. To the extent that we do assign traits to others, the results of this trait-list research procedure has very useful things to say. However, the question is whether we do in fact proceed in this manner. Using video-taped scenes that show such characteristics as verbal content, vocal tone, and facial expressions may be a more realistic and yet controlled method of studying how impressions are really formed.

Interactive Perception

We have been viewing interpersonal perception as being essentially static—a perceiver forming an impression of another person. Most of the research on person perception has followed this paradigm. However, in real life we are being perceived—and we know it—at the same time that we are perceiving others. Further, as we saw in Chapter 3, we act on the basis of our perceptions of others and our perception of their views of us. Our reactions to others can modify the way they, in turn, react to us. All of these "interactive" aspects of real-life person perception greatly complicate the process.

Image seeking

Since people know that they are being perceived, they try to present a good image of themselves. As we saw in Chapter 2, much of social interaction can be viewed as a kind of "face work," in which people deliberately "sweeten" their own image and, at the same time, try to maintain the other person's "face" (Goffman, 1967). To present their own best image, people use a variety of tactics, such as avoiding potentially uncomfortable social interactions and disguising their own feelings to show feelings that are socially acceptable. To protect another person, they may avoid putting that person in a position potentially embarrassing to him.

Thus when interpreting the meaning of the cues discussed in this chapter, people must engage in a discounting process. Whenever we interact with another person, we must ask to what extent his actions and words are determined by what he really feels and to what extent they are determined by his image seeking. To what extent does President Nixon's presidential style of speech and dress reflect his true self and to what extent do they reflect his attempts to present a good image? To what extent does your friend's interest in existential philosophy represent a genuine interest as opposed to face work?

The emphasis in attribution theory on the interpretive element in person perception has made some of the discounting tactics people use explicit. But it should be noted that all of the cues in person perception—including appearance, gestures, facial expressions, and so on—must be filtered by the perceiver. And people, knowing that they are being observed, may use countertactics to make their behavior more difficult to interpret. If you don't want others to know how you feel, you may take deliberate steps to camouflage your feelings. And some people get pretty good at this. Someone who is feeling depressed may present a façade that convinces everyone he is really happy. Indeed, as we saw in Chapter 5, some

people who feel very lonely are seen by others as "lots of fun to be with."

Perception and reaction

The person perception process is also complicated by the influence of your perception on your reaction to the person perceived. As playwrights and novelists have known for a long time, our reactions to other people are not determined so much by the way they really are as by the way we think they are. Thus if you think another person is behaving aggressively toward you, you will behave aggressively toward him. And he, seeing your aggression, will be more likely to reciprocate and behave aggressively. Even if initially the other person had acted in what, objectively viewed, was a very neutral manner, you would be able to create just the behavior you first "saw" by acting as though it had been there all along. Thus your perceptions of others can act as self-fulfilling prophecies (Merton, 1957).

You may have observed the self-fulfilling nature of many of your own interpersonal perceptions. You may be nicer to people whom you think are friendly. Or if you are convinced that another person doesn't like you, you may avoid any contact with him and so eliminate any possibility of getting information that could change your opinion. And if you think another person is bright, you may—without being aware of it—act in such a way that the other person does indeed act brighter than he ordinarily would.

Confirmation for this hypothesis was obtained in one study. As we saw in Chapter 1, when teachers had been led to believe that some children were going to show improved scores on intelligence tests, the children did just what was expected of them and did show significant improvement—even though originally there was no real reason to believe they would obtain higher scores, since the "high-potential" students had been randomly selected from the members of the class (Rosenthal and Jacobson, 1968).

Thus both everyday observation and a number of experiments have shown the importance of the self-fulfilling prophecy in social interactions. What is not yet clear is exactly how this happens. What did the teachers do, for example, to make the children get higher test scores? Were they more friendly to the children they expected to do well, thereby motivating these children to try harder to succeed and so win their teacher's approval? Or did the teachers watch the "high-potential" children more closely and so reward their correct responses more quickly? Although research does not yet provide an answer as to what combinations of words, gestures, facial expressions, and other cues conveyed the information, that it was conveyed is clear. The fact that people can modify the behavior of others without even being aware that they are doing so shows the subtlety of the interactive process.

Your images of how others see you

Still another complicating factor in interactive person perception is the fact that your perception of how another person perceives you will influence your reactions to him and to others. If you think someone likes you, you will be impressed by his good taste and be inclined to like him. And if you think someone expects you to behave in a certain way and you wish to win his liking and approval, you may act the way you believe he wants you to act. Irrespective of what the other person really thinks of you, it is what you think he thinks that determines your behavior.

For example, if many women are convinced that men are threatened by intelligent females —irrespective of whether men actually are or not—they may try to hide their intelligence. Thus among a sample of high-school girls, those who thought that men disapproved of intelligent females were less likely to be committed to careers than those who did not feel this way (Matthews and Tiedeman, 1964). The same attempt to act the way they thought men expected them to was found among adult females. Those in the traditionally feminine occupations (such as homemaker and secretary) thought that men held the traditional stereotypes about appropriate masculine and feminine roles, but women who were in occupations that are not traditionally considered feminine

(such as medical doctor) did not think that men had stereotyped visions of masculinity and femininity (Hawley, 1971). Of course, since both of these studies are correlational, it is not clear whether the career choice caused or resulted from the different views of what men expected.

Reciprocal perspectives

Finally, to make interactive person perception still more complicated, in addition to perceiving another person and forming an impression of how he sees you, you tend to form an impression of what he thinks you think of him. (See Figure 8-10.) And others have the same spiral of "reciprocal perspectives" as they interact with you (Laing, Phillipson, and Lee, 1966). Playing a simple game in which another person has to decide whether to hide a coin in his right hand or his left hand illustrates how complex all of this can get. If he hides the coin in his right hand the first time, you will have to guess whether he will alternate and hide it in his left hand the next time. But you know that he knows you know this is the usual way to play the game. So you think he may try to fool you and hide it in his right hand the second time. But he also knows you know the usual rules, guesses that you might think he will hide it twice in his right hand, and so hides it in his left. Each of you forms guesses about what the other is thinking and about what the other thinks you are thinking. What you do is determined by these reciprocal views.

In close relationships—say in a husband-wife relationship—if these reciprocal views differ, the relationship is in trouble. If a husband thinks that he is considerate and his wife thinks he is selfish, complications can easily develop. If the two do not realize that their perceptions differ, serious communication problems can emerge.

For example, suppose a wife views her careful and close supervision of her children as a way of showing her love for her husband; he views her behavior as indicating a basic lack of love for him; and neither knows that the other sees the situation differently. The outcome of mutual feelings of hostility is not too difficult to imagine—as we shall see in Chapter 9. Although this is all obvious when it is spelled out

FIGURE 8-10 Reciprocal perspectives. (Feature Syndicate Inc. © 1962)

here, detecting such destructive patterns in real-life interactions may take a lot of skill. A recently developed test of the mutual perceptions of husband and wife may make these patterns easier to detect. In this test both husbands and wives separately indicate (1) how they view themselves, (2) how they think their spouses view them, (3) how they view their spouses, and (4) how they think their spouses view their view of the spouse. As might be predicted, couples who are happily married were found to agree more in their mutual perceptions of each other (Laing, Phillipson, and Lee, 1966).

The interesting question is, of course, what makes some couples agree so much more in their mutual perceptions? It is not so important for their views of each other to be accurate, but their sharing of a common, consensual view of themselves and of each other allows them to function successfully as a group. How and why some couples have more mutual perceptions than others is not yet clear. Is it because they try harder? Because they knew and understood their partner very well before marriage? Because they are more sensitive and perceptive than most in all interpersonal perception? Or for some other reason?

SUMMARY

First impressions are based largely on the physical appearance of the person being observed. Then, as interaction develops, we use a variety of other cues, such as facial expressions, gestures, words, and deeds to develop the impression in greater detail. Throughout this process various abilities, attitudes, and motivations are being attributed to the other person, and an attempt is being made to bring all of these impressions into a cohesive whole. This whole process is complicated in real life by the fact that at the same time that we are forming impressions of others, we know that they are forming impressions of us.

1. Appearance and Impressions Physical appearance is a potent determinant of impressions. People have judged such diverse characteristics as personality, occupation, morality, educational level, and hobbies on the basis of clothing alone. Further, your clothing style influences the way others react to you. Physical attractiveness is a very important determinant of impressions—both for children and for adults. Attractive people have been rated more positively on a number of traits—including intelligence, modesty, and sensitivity—than less attractive people. Make-up, physique, amount of hair and hair color, facial features, and physical handicaps have also been found to influence the impressions formed of other people. However, the more information you have about a person, the less important appearance may be in determining impressions.

2. Other Influences on Impressions As you interact with someone in a face-to-face situation, you get additional information, which determines your impression of him. *Eye contact, physical distance, gestures, facial expressions,* and *voice* are all important sources of interpersonal information. For example, either too much *eye contact* (staring) or too little (avoiding all contact) may create a negative impression. Although the exact normative distances remain to be established, there are *norms about appropriate physical distances* in social interaction. If you violate these norms by standing either too close or too far away, people become upset and react negatively. In addition, the *location of people within space* provides social

information. People sitting at the head of a rectangular table, for instance, were judged more positively than those seated at other positions at the table.

Body language also conveys information. In some situations—as in a psychiatric interview in which a patient may be trying to conceal his feelings—body language may more accurately convey what the patient is experiencing than his facial expressions. Recent work on body language has isolated aspects of body gestures that convey meaning. Patterns of motion, body orientation, and body relaxation have all been shown to influence impressions.

Whether people are as accurate as they think they are in reading emotions from *facial expressions* has been hotly debated in social psychology for some time. Although research in this area has yielded inconsistent results, in a large number of recent studies in which many of the errors of earlier work have been corrected, people have been found to be able to detect emotions accurately from facial expressions. Also, aspects of the *voice—pitch, rhythm, loudness,* and *accent*—have an effect on interpersonal impressions.

Further, the *social context* determines what you focus on and how you interpret what you see. As in any perceptual situation the perceiver does not simply passively record "what is there." The *perceiver's motives* can play an important part in his perception of others—especially when reality is ambiguous, as it frequently is in person perception. *Social roles* create expectations about what others are likely to do, and these expectations determine how you perceive the behavior of others. Also, the *way other people in a situation react* is a powerful determinant of impressions. In addition to providing information about whether or not they like a particular person, the reactions of other people in a situation provide a context against which the reactions of a particular person can be judged.

3. Interpreting Words and Deeds Of course, important as all of the nonverbal cues are, what the other person says and does is the main determinant of your impression of him. The way in which we try to puzzle out the meaning of the words and actions of others and fit them into a coherent view is the concern of attribution theory. The words and actions of other people are not always an accurate reflection of their characteristics, and so, without necessarily being aware that we are doing so, we use a series of tests to determine whether their words and deeds reflect their underlying characteristics or are the result of other forces in the situation. People have been shown to consider: (1) *consistency of behavior,* (2) the *reactions of others,* (3) the *degree of freedom from external pressures,* and (4) *expectations about what the other will do.*

The more *consistent information* about a particular behavior is, the more confidently people will attribute that behavior to the characteristics of the other person. However, the way you interpret consistency may depend on what you have done while interacting with the other person, what others in the situation have done, and the characteristics that you are trying to infer. If in the process of interacting with another person, you do something that you think will make a particular pattern of behavior likely to occur, then the consistency of the other person's behavior may tell you little about him. If the individual's behavior differs from that of the other members of a group, the consistency of his behavior is more informative than if he is conforming to the expected norm. Inconsistencies may provide more information about motivation than consistencies.

In person perception, when you rarely know whether your assessments of a person are accurate, the *influence of other people's reactions and evaluations* is particularly important. Thus if others share your opinions about a particular person, your confidence in the accuracy of your judgment is increased. However, the reaction to agreement depends on who the agreeing person is and why he is agreeing. For instance, people may discount agreement that could be extraneously motivated.

To the extent that *external pressures* are clearly operating to force another person to act in a particular way, his behavior does not tell you much about his underlying characteristics. But when the person's behavior deviates from what is expected, people attribute underlying characteristics that are consistent with the way the other person acts.

Unless you have strong evidence to the contrary, you generally tend to think that people possess the characteristics you *expect* them to have. However, when another person engages freely in behavior that is inconsistent with your expectations, you attribute underlying characteristics consistent with what the person does. In fact, you would see him as possessing the underlying characteristics to a more extreme extent than someone who acted as you expected him to.

There are *systematic biases* in person perception. When you know comparatively little about someone else, you may *overemphasize his behavior.* Further, there are *differences in the way we interpret our own behavior and that of others.* When the behavior is not particularly commendable or you know little about the other person, you may be more likely to interpret his behavior as reflecting underlying motives, whereas you see your own acts more as a product of circumstances. Also, people in general are more motivated to see good things about themselves and to avoid unpleasant information than they are when viewing others.

4. Getting It Together Once you have formed the impression that another person has a number of specific traits, you try to put the information together—to form a picture of the other person. How do we do this? One answer—given by Asch—would be that we go from the separate pieces of information to form an overall, consistent view of the other person. When we do this, some traits—such as warmth and coldness—exert more of an influence than others on the impressions formed, and usually what is seen first is more influential than what is seen later.

Testing the generality of Asch's findings and his interpretation has preoccupied the majority of researchers in this area. In general, the emphasis has been on three areas: (1) What determines the centrality of a trait? (2) What determines the relative importance of a first impression? and (3) How do we process the information about other people?

What makes a trait central? Asch's answer is that central traits are those that exert more influence than most traits on the way other traits are interpreted. Another approach is that central traits correlate with many other traits. Although the correlational approach provides an interesting operational definition of a central trait, it does not explain how context influences the meaning of traits—as context has been shown to do.

A number of studies have shown the importance of *first impressions.* Two possible reasons for the importance of first impressions have been advanced: First impressions may determine the interpretation of subsequent information, or people may pay less attention to later information. Support for both of these explanations has been obtained. Although in many cases first impressions are important (a so-called primacy effect), in some cases traits presented later have been found to exert a greater effect on the overall impression—a recency effect. If the information is presented over a long period of time, if people are warned about the dangers of forming first impressions, if the person has to make a prediction about what the other person will do next, or if the information is conveyed by a sequence of overt behaviors, then a recency effect may occur.

There are two very different theories about *how we process information about other people.* Asch claimed that the whole context determines the meaning of any particular trait. A second, statistical approach concentrates on the independent value of a particular trait: Overall reactions are determined by the combined ratings given to each of the single traits. Among adherents of this statistical approach, controversy has centered on whether the values of the traits should be added or averaged to predict the overall impression. Many of the inconsistent findings can best be explained by the weighted average model, in which some traits are counted more heavily than others.

In most of the studies in this area, Asch's procedure of presenting lists of adjectives to subjects and then asking them to react to the person described has been used. To the extent that we do assign traits to others, the results of this trait-list approach has very useful things to say. However, the question is whether we do in fact proceed in this manner. Using video tape scenes that show such characteristics as verbal content, vocal tone, and facial expressions may be a more realistic and yet controlled method of studying how impressions are really formed.

5. Interactive Perception Most of the research on interpersonal perception is essentially static—a perceiver forming an impression of another person. However, in real life we are being perceived—and we know it—at the same time that we are perceiving others. Our reactions to others can modify the way they, in turn, react to us. All of these interactive aspects of real-life person perception greatly complicate the process.

Since people know that they are being perceived, they *try to present a good image of themselves.* The emphasis in attribution theory on the interpretive element in person perception has made some of the discounting tactics people use explicit. However, people, knowing that they are being observed, may use counter-tactics to make their behavior more difficult to interpret.

Person perception is also complicated by the *influence that one's perception has on his reaction* to the person perceived. Our reactions to other people are not determined so much by the way they really are as by the way we think they are. If you think that another person is behaving aggressively toward you, you will behave aggressively toward him. And he, seeing your aggression, will be more likely to reciprocate and behave aggressively. Your perceptions of others can act as self-fulfilling prophecies.

Still another complicating factor in interactive person perception is the fact that *your perception of how another person perceives you will influence your reactions to him and others.* Irrespective of what the other person really thinks of you, it is what you think he thinks that determines your behavior. Finally, to make interactive person perception still more complicated, you also form an impression of what he thinks you think of him. And others have the same spiral of reciprocal perspectives as they interact with you. In any relationship each person forms guesses about what the other is thinking and about what the other thinks you are thinking. What you do is determined by these reciprocal views. In close relationships—say in a husband and wife relationship—if these reciprocal views differ, the relationship is in trouble.

DISCUSSION QUESTIONS

1. Why do you think physical appearance is such an important determinant of first impressions?
2. What are some of the contemporary stereotypes about characteristics associated with different styles of make-up?
3. Why does someone's looking at you without looking away or responding to you in any manner make you feel uncomfortable?
4. Have you ever noticed your evaluation of another person being influenced by the reactions of others?
5. Apply the four criteria of attribution theory to the way you have formed an impression of one person. To what extent did you use all four? Were any of the criteria more important than the others in determining your impression?
6. In your own interactions with other people, are first impressions or later impressions generally more important? Or does it vary according to circumstances?
7. Why do you think adults assume that attractive children are more intelligent?
8. Under what circumstances do you feel people seek eye contact? When do they avoid it? Give observational evidence to support your hypotheses.
9. In what ways—if any—do you think the information conveyed by body language differs from that conveyed by facial expressions or words?
10. According to attribution theory, four criteria are used to verify impressions of others. Can you think of any additional criteria not mentioned in the text?
11. When you know little about the other person, you may interpret his behavior—even when you know he was told to do what he is doing—as reflecting his underlying characteristics. In what circumstances do you think behavior would not be overemphasized?
12. What are some of the tactics people use to camouflage their feelings?
13. Under what conditions do you think physical attractiveness would be positively related to happiness and adjustment? When would you expect it to be negatively related? Give evidence to support your hypotheses.
14. Can you think of any aspect of physical appearance, in addition to those discussed in the text, that you think would influence impressions? Support your suggestions with observational evidence.
15. Observe the distance your friends maintain between themselves as they talk. Then design a study to test your observational evidence about conversational distance norms. Include (1) a definition of the type of interaction to be measured, (2) your procedures, and (3) your proposals to measure distances.
16. Does it seem to you that when you form impressions of other people, you think in terms of traits? Or do you proceed in a more global, nonanalytical way? For instance, do you form an overall reaction—either positive, neutral, or negative—without noticing and evaluating specific traits? Can you think of any way to test whether people do think in terms of traits when they form impressions of others?
17. In what ways do you think interactive person perception differs from the situation in which a perceiver is forming an impression of another person without interacting with him? If all of the static person-perception research were done in an interactive setting, which findings do you think would replicate? Which do you think might not?
18. To what extent do you think that environment (e.g., school, church, home, prison, or a foreign country) influences your impressions of others and their impression of you?
19. Often, when people meet each other for the first time, and each individual is free to create the impression he wishes, the conversation will move to a discussion of each person's past rather than the present. Why do you think this is so?

20. Do you think clinical psychologists are more accurate at person perception than other people? Design a study to test your hypothesis. Indicate (1) your hypothesis and (2) your procedures, including your techniques for assessing the true nature of the person being perceived.

21. Do you think that people could be trained so that they would be more accurate in person perception? Indicate your proposals for such a training program, giving specific details.

22. Which factors in the social context do you think increase the accuracy of person perception? Which factors decrease its accuracy? Support your hypotheses.

THE DYAD

With this chapter we begin a shift in emphasis from the orientation followed so far in this text. Heretofore we have been focusing on the individual in a social context, discussing the way in which others

contribute to the evolution of a sense of the self, the role played by significant others in molding an individual's basic attitudes, the impact of others in generating motives and reactions to those motives, and the way in which an individual's ideas and beliefs, as shaped by others, can affect his processing of information and his understanding of other people. We now turn from this emphasis on the social molding of individual behavior to an emphasis on the interaction of individuals in group settings. This chapter will explore the properties of the two-person group, or the "dyad."

We begin with a consideration of dyadic interaction for a number of reasons. First, a great deal of social interaction takes place on a one-to-one basis. Think of your own interacting experiences each day, and note how many occur with just one other person rather than in larger groups. Indeed, when one investigator and his students observed 7,405 informal interactions of pedestrians, playground users, swimmers, and shoppers, and 1,458 people in a variety of work situations, they found that 71 percent of both the informal and work interactions consisted of two people; 21 percent involved three people; 6 percent included four people; and only 2 percent of all the observed interactions involved five or more people. These findings suggest that the majority of social interactions may be dyadic (James, 1951).

Second, many of the most intensive, most influential relationships take place on a one-to-one basis. The power of dyadic interactions is shown by the impact a child's contact with his mother has on his personality. Another obvious example is the marriage relationship.

Third, dyadic interactions have important differences from interactions in larger groups—though the two are similar in many respects. In a two-person group emotions and feelings tend to be emphasized more than in larger groups (Hare, 1962), and, contrary to what you might expect, dyadic interaction has been found to be more emotionally strained and less overtly aggressive (Bales and Borgatta, 1955; O'Dell, 1968). Also, dyads are less stable than larger groups. If one of the two people involved in a dyad becomes disinterested, the relationship will collapse.

Fourth, dyads provide the simplest case of social interaction. Since only two people are involved, the sequence of action-reaction is easier to study than in larger groups. Examining the functioning of dyads can thus provide some general principles, which can later be applied to our study of larger groups.

In this chapter we shall discuss the formation, patterns of interaction, functioning, development, and dissolution of the dyad. Although there is an infinite number of dyads—from a shoe clerk and his customer to a mother and her child—for thematic consistency we will concentrate on the marriage relationship, a form of dyadic interaction that is common to virtually all of us whether through personal experience or the firsthand observation of our parents. Initially, however, we will be focusing on the factors that are influential in forming friendships generally, since those factors will be basic to our understanding of the formation of the more intense dyadic relationships.

Attraction

When people are free either to interact or not to interact, what draws them together? Of all the people you know, why do you like and spend time with some more than others? Why do you date the people you do? The answers provided by a considerable body of literature are, in general, that we tend to like others who:

1. Most would agree are objectively likable—who are physically attractive, have pleasant personalities, and are competent
2. Live close to us and are available
3. Like us, do favors for us, and praise us
4. Are similar in attitudes, interests, and personality
5. In some instances, are "complementary," or who possess characteristics that go nicely with our own.

All of these characteristics have been interpreted as being consistent with the generalization that we like people whose behavior is rewarding to us (Aronson, 1969a). Interactions with people who are intelligent, competent, and attractive will obviously be more pleasant than interactions with people who are dull, incompetent, and ugly. Since people who live close to us are more available than others, we can interact with them more easily. People who like us, praise us, and do favors for us are obviously more rewarding than those who don't like us, criticize us, and refrain from doing favors. Interacting with people with similar attitudes reassures us that our own beliefs are correct. And in some cases interacting with people with complementary personalities may be rewarding—as when a dominant man seeks out a submissive woman.

Neat as this reward-cost formulation sounds, it does not really allow us to predict in advance what draws two people together, since in real life it is very difficult to know what will be rewarding for different people in different circumstances: ". . . while a reward formulation may 'explain' attraction *after* the fact (if one is willing to play the game of 'finding the reinforcer'), it does very poorly at predicting, in advance, who will like whom" (Berscheid, 1972). For instance, being told that you have done a good job may be rewarding if you think you have and you respect the person who is praising you. However, the same words may have a negative effect if you don't believe you have done a good job or you don't respect the person who is praising you.

Further, determinants of attraction may vary in different kinds of relationships. One obvious distinction has been made between relationships in which sexual interests play a minimal role (friendships) and those in which they play a more significant role (dating, love, marriage). We shall first discuss the extensive literature on friendship and then talk about the little that is known about the determinants of dating, romantic love, and marriage.

Possession of valued traits

The most straightforward explanation of attraction is that people like those who are objectively likable. It is no great mystery that people tend to like individuals who are physically attractive, have a pleasant personality, and are competent. However, commonsensical and obvious as this cause-and-effect relationship may seem, it has definite limits and exceptions.

Physical Attractiveness In Chapter 8 we saw that beautiful people are generally liked more than homely people. Further, there is a stereotype that what is beautiful is good (Dion, Berscheid, and Walster, 1972). Physically attractive people, both men and women, are generally seen as possessing more socially desirable personality traits and are expected to lead happier and more successful lives than unattractive people. Further, the expectations of male and female subjects about the characteristics of attractive people did not differ. No matter whether a man was judging an attractive man or an attractive woman, he saw the attractive person as possessing socially desirable personality traits. Women reacted the same way to attractiveness—irrespective of whether they were rating other women or men. Thus even in same-sex friendships people may tend to prefer attractive people because they believe attractive people are pleasant and intelligent people who will be rewarding to know.

All of the research on the relationship between physical attractiveness and other variables has been in situations in which either the subjects were reacting to photographs of attractive and unattractive people or the amount of personal contact was limited. It may be that physical attractiveness is an important determinant of liking only in the initial stages of interaction and that as additional information is learned about the other person, the influence of physical attractiveness "decreases rapidly" (Berscheid and Walster, a, in press).

Pleasant Personality Characteristics   In one study college students were presented with a list of 555 adjectives and then asked to indicate how much they would like a person who possessed each one of these characteristics. Students generally agreed on what characteristics were likable (sincerity, honesty, loyalty, and so on); presumably, therefore, their reactions to people would be determined by whether or not the person in question was seen to have either the positive or the negative traits (Anderson, 1968a).

So far, so obvious. But explaining all attraction as a function of what others are "really like" is a little too easy. Although there may be a high degree of agreement about the rating of some traits, the rating of others may vary from person to person. A student who seeks intellectually and politically aware friends may value others who are interested in talking about art, philosophy, and world affairs, whereas another student with different interests may value someone who dates a lot, is extroverted, and has a high social standing. The findings of a recent study support this hypothesis. The traits that were valued varied according to the interests of the student who was doing the evaluating (Posavac, 1971).

Competency   Disliking competent people would be like being opposed to motherhood—who could possibly disapprove? If you want to have an effective friend whom you can respect, it would seem that the more competent the person is, the more you would like him.

Or would you? When you are in class, how do you feel about the student who always answers the professor's questions and who always gets the best scores on tests and term papers? Although you may admire his competency, you may also resent him just a little. His perfection may show you up and may make you feel uncomfortable or just plain stupid on occasion.

Thus if this superperfect student were to do something that showed he was human after all—such as trip over his chair when he stood up to answer a question—you might begin to like him more. In one study supporting this hypothesis, a highly competent person—one

who was shown answering 92 percent of some very difficult questions correctly—was liked more when he was shown clumsily spilling a cup of coffee all over himself than when he didn't commit the embarrassing blunder (Aronson, Willerman, and Floyd, 1966). From this you might be tempted to generalize that engagingly making blunders is a good way to endear yourself to others.

However, this isn't quite true. The effect of the blunder on attraction may depend on the difference between the person's level of competence and that of the beholder. In the same experiment a student of average competence (who answered 30 percent of the questions correctly) was also shown either spilling coffee on himself or not spilling it. The person of average competence who did not commit a blunder was rated as more likable than the person of average competence who drenched himself in his own coffee. Indeed, the blundering person of average competence received an extremely negative rating.

Why should the blunder of the average person have resulted in such a sharp drop in his judged attractiveness? One possibility is that the students in the experiment felt very similar to him and were perhaps concerned that they wouldn't be able to answer even as many questions as he did. The superior student was so far above their level of performance that they didn't feel competitive with him. The average student was too close, and when he made his blunder, the students used this as an excuse to denigrate him. Thus blunders may make people more likable only when the people being judged are comfortably superior to you. If they are comparable, the blunders may make them less attractive. Further support for this hypothesis has been obtained in a recent experiment (Mettee and Wilkins, 1972).

Proximity

Other things being equal, people tend to like those who are geographically close to them. That proximity influences attraction is one of the most frequently advanced generalizations derived from the research on interpersonal attraction. To verify this for yourself, visualize a map of where you live and then think of where your friends live. Chances are that your friends are among those who live closest to you.

The enormous impact of proximity has been graphically demonstrated in a classic study on the evolution of friendships in a housing project for married graduate students (Festinger, Schachter, and Back, 1950). All of the housing units in the project, except the end houses, faced onto a grassy court. Few systematic differences were found among the residents of the units, because the students could not choose their unit. They were simply assigned to a given unit when it became vacant. Accordingly, the setting provided an excellent opportunity to measure the effects of spatial arrangements alone on the evolution of friendships.

Two factors in the spatial arrangements emerged as crucial determinants of the friendships in the project: the sheer distance between the units and the direction in which each unit faced. As might be predicted, the residents were the most friendly with those who lived closest to them. In fact, friendships among students separated by more than four or five units were rare. And the direction in which the house faced also had a crucial impact on the social life of the project's residents. Those who lived in houses that faced the street rather than the court had less than half as many friends as those who lived in the houses facing the central court area. In fact, any architectural feature of the project that brought a resident into contact with other students in the project tended to increase his popularity. Students who lived near the entrances and exits of stairwells and those living near the mailboxes were more popular than those living farther away from the traffic area.

Although proximity in everyday life is usually thought of in terms of physical distance, the results of the student project study make it clear that the crucial variable is the *opportunity* to interact with others in a situation in which such interactions are socially acceptable. In an age in which feelings of loneliness and alienation trouble so many people, this finding raises fascinating possibilities. For instance, if spaces were arranged so that the probability of contact between the residents was maximized, would a higher frequency of friendships emerge? As we saw in Chapter 5, the designers of some experi-

mental cities—like Columbia, Maryland—have thought so and have grouped mailboxes to increase the possibilities for social interaction in the community.

Different theories have been advanced to explain the proximity-friendship phenomenon. Some have focused on the greater potential for rewarding interpersonal contacts with people who are close. The closer people live, the easier it is for them to interact with each other. Getting together with someone who lives next door is demonstrably easier than seeing someone who lives several houses away. Further, since one interacts more frequently with people who are close, he is more likely to have pleasant experiences with them and may actually try harder to be pleasant. Getting along badly with someone you see regularly is unpleasant, so you may try harder with those whom you think you will be seeing often. In general, the better you know someone, the more predictable and understandable his behaviors become, and the more likely it is that you will have pleasant relationships with him. Of course, there are limits to a predictability-liking explanation. (See Figure 9-1.) If someone becomes too predictable, you may become bored by him. Or if he predictably does unpleasant things, your knowledge of his predictable nastiness will not increase your fondness.

Other explanations of the proximity-attraction finding have focused on the cognitive factors in the relationship. The closer people live, the more opportunities each person has to acquire information about the others. This information has a number of effects. When you get to know someone, he becomes differentiated from the mass of people and can, therefore, be seen as a unique person. As we saw in Chapter 3, sheer familiarity can engender positive feelings. The more often you see a person, the more you may like him, simply because he is familiar.

You may also be motivated to emphasize the pleasant traits and to play down the negative traits of those who live close to you. Thinking that you have an unpleasant neighbor may arouse dissonance, since you know that you will be stuck with this person. You may, therefore, try to reduce your dissonance by playing down his negative traits. In one study subjects were given descriptions of two people and told that they would be interacting with one of them. The

FIGURE 9-1 Total predictability can be boring.

evaluation of the person they expected to interact with was more positive than that of the person they did not expect to see (Darley and Berscheid, 1967).

Finally, the norms of social interaction favor pleasant interactions among people who live close to each other. Contrast, for example, your reaction to a conversation started by someone who lives next to you in your dorm and a similar conversation initiated by a stranger in a shopping center. In the dorm you are expected to be friendly, and you expect others to be friendly. In the less involving context of a shopping center, however, you may be suspicious about the other person's motives.

Powerful as the proximity-attraction relationship is, there are limits to it. The effect of proximity is greatest when a number of people are first brought together. In the beginning days of college, before the freshmen have had a chance to get to know anyone, proximity may be

very important as a determinant of friendship. But once they have had a chance to get to know one another better and deeper levels of friendship have developed, proximity may decrease in importance, and compatibility of interests may become more important as a determinant of friendship. Just this result was shown in a study of the formation of friendships in a new farming community (Loomis and Beegle, 1950).

Further, in some situations familiarity does breed contempt—as the popular saying would have it. Think of all the people with whom you have interacted frequently. Are there any that you have ended up disliking thoroughly? Police records show that most violent assaults occur within the family or between neighbors and friends. When people interact intensively, the same forces that usually make proximity conducive to attraction can produce the opposite effect, if the interactions are negative. If the other person is thoroughly unpleasant, the desire to ignore his negative traits, discussed earlier, may not be enough to remove your feelings of hostility. The more you see this person, the more opportunities he has to be hostile, and the more you will come to dislike him. If he is nasty, the more often you see him, the more you will learn about the depths of his nastiness.

If a person is smotheringly close, you may dislike him because he has invaded your privacy and become predictably uninteresting. Imagine your reactions to a person who is always around you. Whenever you leave the dorm, there he is. No matter where you eat or try to study, there he is. After a short period of such total proximity, you might begin to dislike this "superavailable" person. As we saw in Chapter 5, people have a need for privacy, and someone who is too available may be unpleasant. Support for this curvilinear relationship between familiarity and liking has been obtained in a recent experiment. Stimuli that were shown to subjects very infrequently were rated negatively, as were stimuli that were shown a very high number of times. Those stimuli that were shown an intermediate number of times were the most preferred (Zajonc, Shaver, Tavris, and van Kreveld, 1972).

Reward-attraction effect

How attractive do you find people when it is ninety degrees in the shade and you are feeling surly? If you are like the subjects who participated in a recent experiment, your answer would be "not very" (Griffitt, 1970). How attractive are people who do favors for you? If you are like those tested, they probably look better than people who don't do favors (Jennings, 1959). And how attractive are people with the innate good taste to make flattering comments about you and like you? Again, if you are like the subjects in one experiment, you will probably like the person who praises you and indicates that he likes you (Jones, 1964).

A considerable number of experiments have shown that in general people tend to like others who are associated with pleasant events or "rewards." Anyone associated with a reward, whether it is material, as an attractive food snack, or psychological, as praise, will be more attractive than others. Furthermore, the more rewards associated with a person, the more you like that person (Lott, Aponte, Lott, and McGinley, 1969).

However, powerful as the reward-attraction effect is, it does not always hold. There are several exceptions to the general relationship between maximal reward and maximal attraction.

Ingratiation How would you feel about someone who praised you lavishly when she stood to gain something by ingratiating herself with you? If you were in a psychological experiment with a graduate student who wanted you to volunteer for another experiment, you might suspect that her praise for your performance was only intended to get you to participate in her experiment. This might make you suspicious of her. An experiment has shown that although praise under these manipulative circumstances would make you like the graduate student better than if she were criticizing you, it would not be nearly as effective as the same praise would be from someone who did not seem to have ulterior motives (Dickoff, 1961).

We all know that sometimes people try to manipulate us by ingratiatory tactics. When a person shows that he likes us, praises us, or does favors for us, his behavior may reflect genuinely positive feelings about us, but it may also reflect a manipulative intent. To know whether to attribute the rewards to ingratiation or to other motives, we all use—without being aware that we are doing so—a variety of informal "tests." One of these involves considering what the other person stands to gain by making us like him. If the other person obviously has something to gain—as the flattering experimenter did—then we tend to be suspicious of his motives and to disregard what he says.

Another test involves our comparing the praise with our own estimate of the situation. If a friend were to tell a beginning golfer who knew that his game was mediocre that he was as good as Jack Nicklaus, the person being praised would begin to doubt either the thinking power or the motives of the person passing out such a lavish compliment. We all have our own evaluations of ourselves and of what we do, and when compliments deviate too far from that evaluation, they become much less effective in making us like those who are doing the complimenting (Berscheid and Walster, 1969).

Thus to be effective, compliments must have a certain degree of realism. Telling the ugliest girl at a party how beautiful she is won't necessarily make her like you. But does that mean that compliments should always be totally accurate? Not necessarily. People may generally have a more positive view of themselves than total accuracy would suggest (Jones, Gergen, and Davis, 1962). Further, people may be tired of hearing compliments about their most obvious strengths. A very pretty girl may have heard that she is pretty innumerable times, so that telling her this again will not impress her much. In contrast, complimenting her on something about which she is uncertain may be much more effective (Jones, 1964).

Reward Imbalance A simple reward formulation of attraction would hold that the more rewards one person gives another, the more he will be liked. Yet your thinking about a situation in which another person has liked you more than you liked him will show that more is not always better. Such a situation can be awkward. Being polite and yet trying to discourage the other person is difficult. You may feel guilty because you are not returning, or reciprocating, the affection you are receiving. As we saw in Chapter 7, one of the strongest impulses in person-to-person interaction is reciprocity. People feel a strong urge to reciprocate in kind as they interact with others. If someone has done a favor for you, you feel a strong obligation to do a favor for him. If someone else likes you, you feel a certain amount of pressure to like him in return (Gouldner, 1960). If you don't, you feel uncomfortable.

Gains and Losses A general reinforcement approach to attraction would hold that the total amount of reinforcement is crucial in determining interpersonal attraction. Attraction of one person for another is simply a function of the number of times a person is associated with pleasant events. In contrast, the gain-loss theory of reward holds that "increases in rewarding behavior from another person (P) have more impact on an individual than constant, invariant reward from P" (Aronson, 1969a, p. 150).

To illustrate the difference between the total-reinforcement and the gain-loss approaches, let us imagine that we hear compliments either from a friend who usually says pleasant things to us or from a stranger. The total-reinforcement approach would predict that a compliment is a compliment and the pleasant remarks would have the same effect on our attraction regardless of the source. In contrast, the gain-loss prediction would be that the friend's comments would have far less of an impact. Since we are used to hearing compliments from our kind friend, hearing yet another compliment will not result in much of a gain in reinforcement; hearing the same compliment from the stranger will result in an appreciable gain.

In an experiment confirming the gain-loss hypothesis, subjects reacted more positively when a stranger was given as the source of a positive communication than when a friend was given. When the communication was negative, however, the subjects were much more upset and reacted more negatively when a friend, rather than a stranger, was given as the source (Harvey, 1962).

In addition to emphasizing the importance of the source of a compliment, the gain-loss formulation focuses on the importance of the sequence of remarks. A total-reinforcement position would be that the sequence of compliments has no effect; the sum is what matters. In contrast, the gain-loss approach holds that the sequence does matter. And common observations would seem to show that sequence does affect your reactions. You may have had the experience of winning someone over who initially did not like you. Converting someone is much more pleasant than the reverse—having someone start out by liking you and then gradually becoming more negative.

The importance of sequence was supported in an experiment in which the subjects were led to think that they had overheard a series of personal evaluations from an experimental confederate. Then they rated their liking for the confederate. In one condition the confederate's overheard evaluations changed gradually from positive to negative; in a second condition the evaluations changed from negative to positive; in a third condition the evaluations were all positive; and in a fourth condition they were all negative. Subjects were most attracted to the

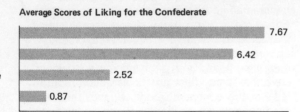

Average Scores of Liking for the Confederate

Sequence of Evaluations From the Confederate	Average Scores of Liking for the Confederate
Negative–Positive	7.67
Positive–Positive	6.42
Negative–Negative	2.52
Positive–Negative	0.87

FIGURE 9-2 Results of the gain-loss experiment.

confederate whose evaluations had gradually changed from negative to positive and least attracted to the confederate whose evaluations had changed from positive to negative (Aronson and Linder, 1965). (See Figure 9-2.)

Although the results of this study clearly support the gain-loss model, some other studies do not. For example, in one recent experiment in which the experimental confederate expressed his personal evaluation of the subject directly to the subject, the subjects liked those confederates whose evaluations were consistently positive the best (Hewitt, 1972). Thus whether the subject "overhears" the evaluation—as he did in the earlier study—or it is communicated directly to him may influence the subject's reactions. Since making negative remarks directly to someone is usually considered very rude and tactless, the subjects may have judged the confederate accordingly.

Similarity

One of the most consistent findings in the area of interpersonal attraction is that people tend to like others who are similar to themselves; the greater the similarity, the greater the attraction (Byrne, 1971). (See Figure 9-3.) The attracting power of similarity has been shown to apply to such diverse aspects of similarity as economic condition (Byrne, Clore, and Worchel, 1966), physical dimensions (Pearson and Lee, 1903), intelligence (Richardson, 1939), ability (Senn, 1971), race (Triandis and Davis, 1965), and less

FIGURE 9-3 "Notice how those squares always seek out their own kind."

consistently, personality (Byrne, Griffitt, and Stefaniak, 1967). But above all, it has been shown to apply to similarity of attitude, the variable that has been studied the most extensively in this area.

Repeatedly, with subjects as diverse as college students and female clerical workers and with experimental procedures as varied as reading a stranger's attitudes to judging a confederate, people have been shown to prefer others with similar attitudes (Byrne, 1971). Since the so-called imaginary stranger technique has been used in a number of experiments, it will be described in some detail. Typically, the subjects, college undergraduates, are given a questionnaire measuring their attitudes about such topics as belief in God and political party preference. Later in the semester, when the actual attraction experiment takes place, the subjects are told that they will be taking part in a study of interpersonal judgments. They are first given some information about another person—the "stranger"—who is described either as holding exactly the same attitudes as the subject or as holding opposing views. If, for example, the subject is strongly opposed to the legalization of marijuana, he is told, in the similar condition, that the stranger is strongly opposed to marijuana legalization, and, in the dissimilar condition, that the stranger is strongly in favor of marijuana legalization. After the attitude information is presented, the subject is then asked to indicate whether he would like or dislike the person and whether he would enjoy or dislike working with this person.

In these studies the subject never meets or even sees the stranger—all he has to go on in forming his impressions is what he is told about the stranger's attitudes. And in this experimental situation the usual result is that the more similar the stranger is said to be, the more the subjects like him.

The results of a recent field study suggest that the relationship found in the laboratory between similarity and attraction may generalize to real-life situations. The study also tells us something about how more realistic and yet controlled approaches to interpersonal attraction can be arranged.

In this experiment students at the University of Texas completed a fifty-item questionnaire. Later in the semester forty-four student couples

(one male, one female) participated in the experiment. Half were matched on the basis of maximum similarity; the other half on the basis of maximum dissimilarity. Each couple was introduced, told about the basis for their matching, and then asked to spend thirty minutes together on a "Coke date" at the Student Union. Afterward, their attraction to each other was measured by means of the standard rating scale as well as by how close they stood to each other after the date.

Both similarity and the subjects' physical attractiveness were found to be related to attraction immediately after the date as well as in a follow-up investigation at the end of the semester. Dates who were highly similar and were judged as physically attractive talked to one another more often in the time period after the date and indicated a higher desire to date each other than the other couples did (Byrne, Ervin, and Lamberth, 1970).

Explanations of the Similarity-Liking Effect

What is there about someone's agreeing with your attitudes that makes him attractive to you? A number of answers have been given by theorists in this field.

First, one might say that this is a specific instance of our general *desire for balanced relationships*. People try to make their relationships with others and the world harmonious. One way to do this is to strive for consistency in our relationships. If we are opposed to a political candidate, we want our friends to feel the same way that we do. Thus we avoid those who differ and prefer those with similar views (Heider, 1958).

It would also follow from this formulation that we may see more consistency than actually exists. Once we like a person, we may tend to see his attitudes as resembling our own more than they actually do. And there is evidence to show that this, in fact, happens. Several studies have shown that people see their friends' attitudes as resembling their own to a greater extent than they actually do (e.g., Levinger and Breedlove, 1966).

Another approach to the similarity-liking relationship is that *agreement is reinforcing*, because we assume that we will have more pleasant interactions with others who agree with us. Fighting over differences in political or re-

BOX 1 SOCIAL COMPARISON THEORY AND THE SIMILARITY-ATTRACTION RELATIONSHIP

Because of space limitations, we shall consider only how some of the social comparison findings might provide leads about the shape of the similarity-attraction relationship. First, social comparison theory holds that only when objective reality does not provide a basis for comparison do we use other people. From this it would follow that if attitudes are about events that can readily be verified (the president will go to China again in 1976), the need for, and hence the attraction of, someone holding similar beliefs will be less than if the attitudes concern events that cannot be verified. Support for this hypothesis has been obtained (Byrne, Nelson, and Reeves, 1966).

A number of social comparison studies have shown that the more uncertain the individual is, the stronger is his desire to be with others (e.g., Radloff, 1959). If the attraction of similar others is their potential for social comparison, it would follow that the more uncertain the individual is about the correctness of his attitudes, the greater the similarity-attraction relationship will be.

We have seen a number of social comparison studies in which the type of emotion aroused influenced whether people wished to be alone or with others. When subjects were frightened, they wished to be with others (Schachter, 1959). However, when they were made anxious (or perhaps embarrassed), they did not wish to affiliate (Sarnoff and Zimbardo, 1961). From these findings we might hypothesize that people wish to compare themselves with similar others only when they are not ashamed of, or preoccupied with, their own internal thoughts. Similarity of unsanctioned attitudes (about masturbation and homosexuality, for instance) might not result in attraction.

One of the most controversial issues in social comparison theory, as we have seen, is the specification of the crucial aspects of similarity. Which dimensions of similarity are preferred in what situations? This question applies to the similarity-attraction relationship too. What dimensions of similarity contribute most to liking? If you knew that one person had attitudes similar to yours and another had a similar personality, which would you prefer? And under what circumstances might you prefer someone who is dissimilar? If a friendship is based more on respect than on mutual attraction, might not your friend be someone who is dissimilar?

ligious opinion can be harrying. Similarity can also reinforce our confidence in the correctness of our attitudes. If the other person is reasonably competent and pleasant, and if we are not completely sure that our attitudes are correct (which we seldom are), then hearing someone agree with us will increase our belief that we are right, which is pleasant.

If, however, anything in the situation makes agreement unpleasant, then agreement will not result in liking. For instance, if someone with similar attitudes acted very obnoxiously during an experiment, we would not like him. Indeed, we might dislike him more than someone who had dissimilar attitudes and was obnoxious. Experimental support for this hypothesis has been obtained (Taylor and Mettee, 1971).

A third approach to the similarity-attraction finding is that we tend to like others who are similar because we assume that *they will like us.* From this formulation it would follow that if you are secure about others liking you, the preference for others who are similar would tend to disappear. Such a result occurred when college students were given a choice of joining a discussion group (talking about why people dream) comprising either persons who were similar (other college students) or persons who were dissimilar (psychologists, factory workers, etc.). When the students were told that the members of both groups would like them, they chose the dissimilar group. In contrast, when the students were told that the members of the groups probably would not like them, they chose to join the similar group (Walster and Walster, 1963).

A last explanation is that the similarity-attraction relationship is simply another manifestation of the *social comparison process* (Festinger, 1954). Repeatedly, we have seen that when objective reality offers no way for people to evaluate the accuracy of their beliefs, they look to other, similar people. Since attitudes usually refer to rather amorphous events, comparing our attitudes with those of others is an important way of our validating them. Since we gain the most information by comparing ourselves with others who are similar, it would follow that we would be attracted to similar others. See Box 1 for a discussion of some of the implications of social comparison theory for the similarity-attraction relationship.

Limitations to the Similarity-Attraction Effect
Are persons who are similar always preferred? The logical extension of the relationship would be that the more similar another person is, the more you will like him. Each person's ideal friend would be a carbon copy of himself.

Or would he? In Chapter 2 we saw that people have a strong desire to be unique, so that people who are too similar may become unattractive, since they threaten our individuality. Also, people who are too similar might prove to be dull. You know what you know, and a similar person may provide only a rehash of very familiar ideas and facts, whereas someone who is dissimilar could relieve your boredom.

And if someone already believes as you do, you have no opportunities to convert him. Persuading someone who always disliked Bill Buckley that Buckley isn't all bad may be a lot more fun than having someone simply agree with you. You may prefer someone you have converted to your opinions more than someone who has always agreed, as the results of one study showed (Lombardo, Weiss, and Buchanan, 1972).

Finally, whether you prefer similar or dissimilar others may depend on your own personality. If, for instance, disagreement is threatening to you, you might prefer similar others. Although the experimental findings about personality differences in the similarity-attraction relationship have not yielded consistent results, such personality differences have been obtained in some studies. (See Byrne, 1971.)

Complementarity

People have been shown to prefer others because of similarities in attitude, economic status, intelligence, ability, emotional state, and so forth. But do people tend to prefer persons who are similar in personality traits or do they prefer persons who are the opposite, or complementary? For example, do people who are dominant prefer others who are also dominant or do they prefer persons who are submissive?

Everyday psychology—with its two tired and

conflicting bromides, "Birds of a feather flock together" and "Opposites attract"—does not provide an answer. Nor do the results of a number of research studies. In some cases persons have been found to prefer others with similar personalities (e.g., Banta and Hetherington, 1963), and other studies have shown that people prefer opposites (e.g., Rychlak, 1965).

As in any area in which conflicting results have been obtained, a number of possible explanations present themselves. First, whether people prefer the personality of those who are similar or of those who are complementary may depend on exactly which personality trait is being measured. People may prefer others who are similar in terms of self-esteem, but may prefer those who differ in the level of dominance. Interacting with someone who has the same degree of pride and satisfaction with himself that you do may be rewarding, whereas interacting with someone who is as dominant as you are may lead to the two of you fighting for relative dominance and control of the relationship.

Second, whether people prefer people who are similar or different may vary according to the way in which preference is being measured. What people say they like may not reflect the way they would feel and react if they actually had to interact with another person. For example, in one study when student nurses were asked whether they would prefer a roommate who was similar or different in terms of dominance, they indicated that they would prefer someone who was similar. However, when the stability of the roommate pairs was measured, the most stable relationships were those between roommates who were complementary on dominance (Bermann and Miller, 1967).

Third, whether similarity or complementarity determines attraction may depend on the roles and demands of a particular relationship. Since it is generally assumed, for example, that in marriage the male is dominant and the female submissive, men and women who are complementary on dominance may be attracted to each other. If they both share a common view of what is appropriate "husbandly" and "wifely" behavior, potential conflicts about dominance may be minimized.

Determinants of attraction in the dating, love, and courtship and marriage relationships

It is safe to assume, as a general proposition, that factors that are influential in the forming of friendships generally will also be influential in the forming of the most intensive of human relationships—those involving dating, love, and courtship and marriage. Nevertheless, since the roles and motives of people involved in these sexual relationships differ from those of people involved in friendships, what draws people together in friendship may be somewhat different from what makes them fall in love and decide to marry. In this section we will discuss to what extent the various factors relating to friendship apply to these other relationships and whether there are other factors that uniquely contribute to dating, love, and courtship-marriage.

Dating What makes people attractive to members of the opposite sex? If you asked male and female college students to rank the relative importance of personality, looks, intelligence, and character as attributes of a date, they would probably indicate—as students did who were asked to rate these characteristics—that the most important characteristic of a potential date is personality. Students rated character second, looks third, and intelligence as the least important characteristic of a potential date (Tesser and Brodie, 1971).

How well do the students' answers reflect what really attracts them to a potential date? Assume that you are a freshman about to go to your first dance at college. You may be anxious about your own popularity with the members of the opposite sex, and you may be concerned about how others at the dance will react to your choice of partners. Once you arrive at the dance, you talk and dance with a number of other students of the opposite sex. You meet

FIGURE 9-4 "What drew me to you was your obvious intelligence."

one person who is bright, poised, interesting but not too attractive physically. And you meet another person who is not as bright, but is moderately good-looking. Which will you choose? The looker.

Physical attractiveness is of overwhelming importance in determining attraction in the dating setting. (See Figure 9-4.) In one study in which students assumed that a computer had selected their dates on the basis of similar interests, dates were actually assigned on a random basis. Each student's social skills, intelligence, and personality were measured as well as his or her physical appearance. At intermission time at the dance, the students were asked to rate how much they liked their date and how much they wanted to see that date again. The only variable found to be related to attraction was the date's appearance. Intelligence, personality, and social skills had no significant correlation with attraction. In this setting looks were everything (Walster, Aronson, Abrahams, and Rottmann, 1966). Other investigators, using the same computer-dance procedure, have similarly noted the importance of physical attractiveness. For instance, in one study the perceived physical attractiveness of a computer-dance date correlated .89 with the student's desire to date that partner again (Brislin and Lewis, 1968).

In analyzing these studies, one could argue that the limited amount of time available might have prevented the couples from getting to know each other, thereby giving an undue prominence to physical appearance. However, correlational evidence indicates that in everyday life a girl's physical attractiveness is correlated positively (.61) with the number of dates she has in a year—which suggests that physical appearance is an important determinant of dating choice. (Another possible explanation of the correlation is that unattractive girls make themselves less available.) The correlation between a male's physical attractiveness and his dating frequency was only .25 (Berscheid, Dion, Walster, and Walster, 1971). Physical attractiveness may be a more important criterion for men than for women in choosing dates. If women are more likely to view dates as potential mates, they may be looking for other attributes.

Why is physical attractiveness so important in dating? There are several possible answers (Berscheid and Walster, a, in press). One may be that we have internalized our culture's norm that we are only supposed to be sexually attracted to physically attractive people. Or it may be that people prefer attractive dates because of the prestige gained by associating with them.

The results of a recent study suggest that there is some basis in fact for the prestige explanation. Subjects were asked to give an overall impression of a man with a woman who was made to appear either extremely attractive or extremely unattractive. Half of the subjects were told that the woman was the man's girl friend; the other half were told that the woman had no connection with the man. The subjects' ratings of the man were most favorable when he was shown with a good-looking girl friend and least favorable when he was shown with an ugly girl friend. When the subjects thought there was no relationship between the man and the woman, the woman's attractiveness did not influence the ratings given to the man (Sigall and Landy, in press). Further, as we noted earlier in this chapter, there is a stereotype that "what is beautiful is good." People may prefer attractive dates because they assume that those dates will also be intelligent and pleasant.

Although everyone may want to date people who are physically attractive, many people may be concerned about the possibility of being rejected by someone who is much more attractive than they are. In a computer-dance setting in which you are matched for the evening and you do not have to be concerned about the possibility of rejection, physical attractiveness may completely determine the extent to which you like your date. However, in actual dating—when the possibility of rejection is present—the level of physical attractiveness of the dating couple would be expected to match. Confirmation for this matching hypothesis has been obtained in several studies. In one study the physical attractiveness of the photographs of ninety-nine couples who were engaged or going steady was rated, and the correspondence in physical attractiveness of the couples was compared with that of a control group of couples formed by randomly matching ninety-nine men and women. The correspondence in physical attractiveness of the engaged or steadily dating couples was signifi-

BOX 2 COMPUTER DATING—DOES SIMILARITY MAKE THE HEART GROW FONDER?

Computer dating is based almost entirely on the idea that people with similar interests and attitudes are compatible. In applying for a date, the person completes a questionnaire, such as the one below, and is then matched with a person of the opposite sex who has similar interests and attitudes.

KEY: A—Yes definitely!   B—Yes   C—Maybe   D—No   E—No definitely!

1.	Do you sometimes look down at others?	A	B	C	D	E
2.	Do you enjoy being the center of attention in group activities?	A	B	C	D	E
3.	Do you think it proper for unmarried couples to go on a trip by themselves?	A	B	C	D	E
4.	Do you think you would be content married to an unaffectionate mate?	A	B	C	D	E
5.	Do you believe that our schools should teach evolution?	A	B	C	D	E
6.	Do you find yourself getting angry easily or often?	A	B	C	D	E
7.	Do you usually prefer being with groups of people to being alone?	A	B	C	D	E
8.	Do you think that a theft is ever justifiable?	A	B	C	D	E
9.	Do you think that sex is over-exploited in advertising?	A	B	C	D	E
10.	Do you believe some religious instruction is necessary for all children?	A	B	C	D	E
11.	Do you feel that your life as a child was enjoyable?	A	B	C	D	E
12.	Do you ever go out of your way to avoid someone?	A	B	C	D	E
13.	Do you think it proper for a schoolteacher to smoke or drink in public?	A	B	C	D	E
14.	Do you think college campuses are too sexually liberated?	A	B	C	D	E
15.	Do you believe you could permit your child to choose a different religion?	A	B	C	D	E
16.	Do you find yourself happy more often than not?	A	B	C	D	E
17.	Do you feel there are many subjects you'd prefer not to discuss socially?	A	B	C	D	E
18.	Do you usually repeat good jokes or stories to other people?	A	B	C	D	E
19.	Do you think some lawyers are favored by certain judges?	A	B	C	D	E
20.	Do you become more aware of the opposite sex in groups?	A	B	C	D	E
21.	Do you believe we will be held responsible in the next world for our behavior now?	A	B	C	D	E
22.	Do you feel it is important to attend religious services regularly?	A	B	C	D	E
23.	Do you think that the "first" romance should continue throughout a marriage?	A	B	C	D	E
24.	Do you often feel that life is not worthwhile?	A	B	C	D	E
25.	Do you prefer a quiet mate to an extroverted one?	A	B	C	D	E
26.	Do you believe that women should run for public office?	A	B	C	D	E
27.	Do you dislike hearing so called "dirty" stories and jokes?	A	B	C	D	E
28.	Do you think religous people tend to be better people and better friends?	A	B	C	D	E
29.	Do you find your mood changes drastically without any apparent cause?	A	B	C	D	E
30.	Do you believe social clubs are a waste of time?	A	B	C	D	E
31.	Do you enjoy asking friends into your home?	A	B	C	D	E
32.	Do you believe an unsatisfactory marriage should be continued?	A	B	C	D	E
33.	Do you feel your marriage could exist without good sexual relationship?	A	B	C	D	E
34.	Do you believe God can control our lives?	A	B	C	D	E
35.	Do you find you can go to sleep easily and sleep soundly?	A	B	C	D	E
36.	Do you prefer to go out socially rather than stay at home?	A	B	C	D	E
37.	Do you approve of married women having lunch with other men?	A	B	C	D	E
38.	Do you feel that sexually suggestive entertainment is bad for the viewer?	A	B	C	D	E
39.	Do you give or receive affection easily?	A	B	C	D	E
40.	Do you believe churches are a strong force in improving moral standards?	A	B	C	D	E
41.	Do you at times experience vague aches and pains after a trying day?	A	B	C	D	E
42.	Do you find it difficult to accept criticism?	A	B	C	D	E
43.	Do you enjoy being active in social clubs?	A	B	C	D	E
44.	Do you believe women should initiate dates with men?	A	B	C	D	E
45.	Do you prefer someone you are fond of to openly display affection?	A	B	C	D	E
46.	Do you believe in life after death?	A	B	C	D	E
47.	Do you become uncomfortable with strangers?	A	B	C	D	E
48.	Do you think sex should be taught in public schools?	A	B	C	D	E
49.	Do you prefer being in the company of the opposite sex?	A	B	C	D	E
50.	Do you believe in the power of prayer?	A	B	C	D	E

This test will depict interest and values in areas of compatibility between persons and should not be construed as being able to afford psychological diagnosis.

Name_____   Age_____ Sex_____ Home Phone_____

Address_____   Business Phone_____Occupation_____

City_____State _____Zip_____   Single ☐   Widowed ☐   Divorced ☐

Mail this sheet only, in the enclosed postage paid, self addressed envelope to:

Operation Match Inc.
17 Barstow Rd., Great Neck, N. Y. 11021 Tel: (212) 969-1000 or (516) 482-2525

cantly higher than the correspondence of attractiveness in the control group (Murstein, 1972).

Earlier in this chapter we saw that similarity was also strongly associated with attraction in a dating situation. In another study physical attractiveness correlated .89 with the subject's desire to date a particular person, and perceived similarity of interests correlated .64 (Brislin and Lewis, 1968). Further, evidence suggests that physical attractiveness and similarity may interact. Someone who is similar may be thought to be more physically attractive than someone who is dissimilar. Support for this hypothesis was obtained in a study in which subjects discussed a variety of political issues with other students who either agreed or disagreed with their views. Then the subjects were asked to rate the physical attractiveness of the students with whom they had talked. Students who had agreed with their views were seen as more attractive physically than those who had disagreed (Walster, 1971a).

Physically attractive people may be seen as more similar than they really are. Since people want to associate with physically attractive people, they may try to steer their conversation toward areas of mutual agreement (Berscheid and Walster, a, in press). Thus the two very powerful determinants of attraction—physical attractiveness and similarity—may combine to reinforce the effects of each other.

Although research has emphasized the importance of physical attractiveness and similarity (see Box 2), you may be able to think of other variables that might influence attraction in the dating setting. For example, since each time a man asks a woman for a date he risks being rejected, we might expect that when a girl indicates her liking for a man, he may reciprocally view her as more attractive than another girl. In a setting in which students do not have ready access to transportation, proximity may also be an important factor.

Further, what is attractive in a potential date may depend on one's objectives in dating. As one survey of Harvard seniors taken in 1970 shows, students date for a variety of reasons. When the Harvard men were asked to indicate their most important or second most important motive for dating, sexual intimacy and a desire for friendship were the most frequently men-

tioned motives (52 percent each). Recreation was also frequently listed (49 percent). Another motive was a desire to enhance their reputation by dating attractive and popular girls (3 percent) (Vreeland, 1972). Clearly, what is attractive in a potential date depends on one's objectives.

Romantic Love What makes one person fall and stay in love with another? Although most theorists would agree that the need to give and receive love is basic to most human beings, very little work has been done on the determinants of male-female love—or, indeed, on the other kinds of love. Obviously, not all love occurs between adults of the opposite sex. Mothers may love their children; one man may love another; man may love God; a theorist may love his ideas. However, love as it affects the typical college student usually is in the form of romantic love with a person of the opposite sex. (See Figure 9-5.)

Before discussing why it happens, perhaps we ought to say what love is. What do you mean when you use the term? Although each of us may have a vague notion of what another means by "love," supplying a precise definition for the term could fill a season of TV talk shows. Popular culture, novelists, poets, and psychological theorists have defined the term in many ways—ranging from the Hollywood concept of love at first sight with internal bells ringing to the more responsible notions of care, responsibility, respect, and knowledge (Fromm, 1956). Generally, love is regarded as having two components: an intense, affectionate concern and an intense sexual desire. For some of the different definitions of love and a test of romantic love, see Box 3, page 438.

Although a precise definition of romantic love may not be available at the present time, it is clear that romantic love differs from friendship in a number of ways (Berscheid and Walster, b, in press). First, fantasy plays a much greater role in romantic love than in friendship. When in love, you may fantasize about the object of your love and visualize that person as a perfect creature who can meet all of your needs. Moreover, the initial intensity of passionate love seems to diminish over time, whereas liking does not. To the extent that passionate love is aroused more by the fantasies about the other

FIGURE 9-5 Love on campus.

person than by a realistic assessment, the information conveyed by the other as you interact may tarnish the perfection of the original fantasies. Further, liking generally is experienced as a pleasant emotion. However, passionate love is associated with a variety of conflicting emotions. When college students were given a chance to ask psychologists just one question about the nature of love, among the most frequently asked questions was: "Can you love and hate someone at the same time?" (Berscheid and Walster, b, in press).

Why do people fall in love? As we have noted, determinants of friendship are consistent with the general proposition that we tend to like people whose behavior is rewarding to us. Sometimes romantic love seems to follow this pattern too. We love those who are loving and kind to us. On some occasions, however, people love those who have rejected them. For instance, a woman may discover that her husband is deceiving her with another woman. The pain and suffering experienced by the wife at this discovery may cause her to realize how passionately she loves her husband (Walster, 1971b).

Why should suffering increase the woman's love? Schachter's two-component theory of emotion provides an answer. From the discussion of that theory in Chapter 2 you will recall that when a person experiences an emotion, two factors determine his reaction: (1) his physiological arousal and (2) the situation, which provides labels for the physiological reaction. If you are physiologically aroused by an injection but are in a situation designed to make you angry, you may interpret your physiological reaction as anger. In just the same way, any stimulus that increases your level of physiological arousal (such as jealousy) can make you experience the arousal as passionate love as long as the situation is such that the indicators are consistent with your notions of what love is (Walster, 1971b).

Thus any variable that increases your level of physiological arousal or increases your tendency to label your physiological arousal as love would be expected to intensify the amount of passion you experience. Berscheid and Walster (b, in press) have summarized the existing literature and have theorized what some of these variables are.

The first step in generating love is to generate *physiological arousal*. Such an arousal can be caused by either unpleasant or pleasant emotional experiences. One unpleasant emotion is fear. To test the hypothesis that fear aroused by an event unrelated to a woman can intensify a man's attraction to that woman, experimenters told half of the male subjects that they would receive painful electric shocks. The other half were assigned to a control group in which there was no mention of their receiving electric shocks. All of the men were then introduced to an attractive girl and asked to rate how much they liked her. As predicted, the men who had been aroused by the threat of electric shock were more attracted to the girl than the men in the control condition (Brehm et al., 1970).

Frustration can also be physiologically arousing. Sexual deprivation may lead to arousal that is labeled as romantic love. As in the case of Romeo and Juliet, parental interference can intensify the lovers' feelings for one another. To test this hypothesis, one investigator had dating couples complete questionnaires that measured the amount of parental interference they had experienced and the intensity of their love for each other. Parental interference was correlated .50 with the intensity of love reported by the dating couples (Driscoll et al., 1972). Of course, since these data are correlational, other explanations for the relationship are possible. Yet the relationship does suggest the possibility that parental attempts to break up a couple may boomerang.

Pleasant emotional experiences can also be arousing. One experiment has shown that even the mere belief that a woman has sexually aroused him increases a man's attraction toward that particular woman. College students were shown *Playboy* photographs of seminude women and told that their heart rate would be amplified and played back to them as they saw the slides. The feedback was manipulated so that the subjects thought their heart rate was altered when they viewed some of the slides and remained unaffected when they saw others. Then the subjects were asked to rate their preferences for the pinups. The men preferred the pictures they thought had aroused them (Valins, 1966).

Once an individual is physiologically aroused, he must label his arousal as love if he

BOX 3   WHAT IS THIS THING CALLED LOVE?

(Shelly Rusten)

Few people agree on what love really is. Perhaps no other single term has been defined in so many different ways. To give an idea of the range of definitions, some more or less randomly selected concepts of love are quoted below and then a recently evolved test of romantic love is discussed.

LITERARY DEFINITIONS OF LOVE

Love As Sex

"Love in young men, for the most part, is not love but simply sexual desire and its accomplishment is its end."
[M. Cervantes, *Don Quixote*, I, xxiv, c. 1605.]

Love As Bewilderment

"Love is the strange bewilderment which overtakes one person on account of another person."
[E. B. White and J. Thurber, *Is Sex Necessary?* 1929.]

Love As Illusion

"Love is merely the exchange of two fantasies and the contact of two skins."
[N. Chamfort, *Maximes et Pensées*, c. 1780.]

Love As Union

"Mature *love is union under the condition of preserving one's integrity,* one's individuality. *Love is an active power in man;* a power which breaks through the walls which separate man from his fellow men, which unites him with others; love makes him overcome the sense of isolation and separateness, yet it permits him to be himself, to retain his integrity. In love the paradox occurs that two beings become one and yet remain two."
[E. Fromm, *The Art of Loving*, 1956, pp. 20–21.]

Love As Unfailing Kindness

"Love suffereth long, *and* is kind; love envieth not; love vaunteth not itself, is not puffed up,

"Does not behave itself unseemly, seeketh not her own, is not easily provoked, thinketh no evil;

"Rejoiceth not in iniquity, but rejoiceth in the truth;

"Beareth all things, believeth all things, hopeth all things, endureth all things.

"Love never faileth."
[St. Paul, First Corinthians 13:4–8.]

(Stephen Shames)

(Sylvia Plachy)

THE MEASUREMENT OF ROMANTIC LOVE

One investigator has found that there are several internally consistent themes (or components) in the general expression of feelings by persons about their boyfriends or girlfriends (Rubin, 1973). From a seventy-item questionnaire given to University of Michigan students, three components emerged:

BOX 4

1. attachment (e.g., "If I were lonely, my first thought would be to seek _____ out.")

2. caring (e.g., "I would do almost anything for _____.")

3. intimacy (e.g., "I feel that I can confide in _____ about virtually everything.")

In a subsequent testing, thirteen items that clearly tapped these three components were administered to a second group of college students—typically those who had been dating a particular person for about a year. As might be expected, the scale had high internal consistency. If the subjects indicated "I would do almost anything for _____," they were likely to agree with the statement "One of my primary concerns is _____'s welfare." Further, the scores on the "Love Scale" were highly correlated with the subjects' own reports of whether or not they were in love. Even love may be measurable after all.

(Casta Manos/Magnum)

is to experience that emotion. In our society people are not clear about what the experience of passionate love is supposed to feel like—as shown by the frequency with which "Dear Abby" receives letters from teen-agers asking how they can tell if they are really in love. However, a common representation in our culture and the mass media is that people who are in love are physiologically aroused. "When your heart goes bumpety, bump . . . that's love, love, love" is the popular message (Berscheid and Walster, b, in press).

Thus when a person is physiologically aroused, he may have difficulty labeling his emotion because a number of different labels might be appropriate. When the individual is faced with this ambiguity, social influences provide cues as to how he should label his feelings. Our culture encourages people to interpret a wide variety of feelings as love. If a person becomes sexually excited and the situation has the "moonlight and roses" cues for romantic love, he may be more likely to label his feelings as love than as lust—since love may be a more socially acceptable feeling for him to have. An individual's own expectations about his susceptibility to "falling in love" may also influence the way he labels his feelings. If he thinks of himself as a romantic person, he may be more likely to label a wide range of physiological reactions as love.

The two-component theory of emotion provides an interesting approach to the question of why people fall in love and provides a framework within which the diverse findings in this area can be fitted. However, it should be emphasized that this account is still theoretical. As you might expect, there are no controlled experiments on the determinants of intense and passionate love. Think about how you would design such an experiment. Trying to achieve an adequate degree of realism without violating ethical precepts poses an enormously difficult dilemma. Correlational studies of persons who are in love might provide a better approach. (For poets', writers', and philosophers' views on the causes of love, see Box 4.)

Courtship and Marriage Why do people court the people they do? How do the deep personal relationships which often lead to marriage come about? Although you may have doubts about whether or not Americans will continue to marry in the future, at the present time more than 90 percent of Americans marry at least once during their life (Murstein, 1971). Given this high percentage, you might think that there would be a lot of information on the process of marital choice. Unfortunately, this is not the case.

A popular concept is that romantic love serves as the basis for most marriages. In one survey of male and female college students, approximately 67 percent of the males felt that they would not marry unless they loved their prospective wife, but less than 25 percent of the women indicated that love was the prime determinant of marital selection (Kephart, 1967). Apparently, the girls are less obsessed with champagne and roses than the men—popular stereotypes of the romantic female aside. Moreover, since the causes of love are not yet clearly understood, saying that people marry for love does not help us much in our understanding of the courtship-marriage relationship.

What we do know about the basis for courtship and marital choice has largely been provided by correlational studies of engaged and married couples. Repeatedly, it has been found that proximity, similarity, and complementarity all have an effect. Several studies have shown that the more physical distance there is separating potential marriage partners, the less likely they are to marry (e.g., Bossard, 1932). As we have noted, some studies have shown that people prefer persons with personality traits opposite to their own (e.g., Rychlak, 1965), although the evidence is not completely consistent. By far the most important variable in mate selection revealed by the correlational studies is similarity. When both partners are measured on such variables as age, religion, values, attitudes, education, race, height, and socioeconomic standing, they have been found repeatedly to resemble each other much more closely than chance would predict (Byrne, 1971).

Although the correlational approach yields interesting information about the sociology of courtship and marital choice, it is essentially a static view. As a relationship develops, the determinants of attraction may differ. Initially, appearance may be all-important, but after a dozen dates even the most beautiful girl may

BOX **4**

Love is probably the most thoroughly treated of all subjects in prose and poetry. The following excerpts from this vast literature point up the various determinants of the love relationship.

Possession of Valued Traits

"If you would be loved, love and be lovable."
[Benjamin Franklin, *Poor Richard's Almanac*, 1755.]

get boring if she is essentially dull and slow-witted. A recent theory of marital choice holds that a couple progresses through three stages before deciding to marry: (1) a so-called stimulus stage in which people are attracted on the basis of what can be seen, (2) a value stage in which the couple is concerned with evolving compatible values, and (3) a role stage in which

SOME LITERARY THOUGHTS ON THE CAUSES OF LOVE

Physical Attractiveness

". . . but women know perfectly well that the loftiest, and as we call it, the most poetic love depends, not on moral qualities, but . . . on the way of doing up the hair, the complexion, the cut of the gown."
[L. Tolstoy, *The Kreutzer Sonata*, Ch. 6, 1888.]

Proximity

"When I'm not near the one I love, I love the one I'm near."
[E. Y. Harburg, *Finian's Rainbow*, 1947.]

Reciprocity

"Love, and you shall be loved."
[R. W. Emerson, *Essays*, 1841.]

Rewardfulness

"I should have told you
that love is more
        than being warm in bed.
                More
than individuals seeking an accomplice.
Even more than wanting to share.

I could have said
that love at best is giving what you need to get.
But it was raining
and we had no place to go
and riding through the streets in a cab
        I remembered
that words are only necessary after love has gone."
[R. McKuen, *Stanyan Street and Other Sorrows*, 1970, p. 33.]

Complementarity

"I wanted you
that day at the beach
because you were different
and because you smiled
and because I knew your world
was different. "
[R. McKuen, *Stanyan Street and Other Sorrows*, 1970, p. 30.]

Frustration–Adversity

"The less my hope the hotter my love."
[Terence, *Eunuchus*, l. 1053, Act V, sc. 4, c. 160 B.C.]

"Some obstacle is necessary to swell the tide of libido to its height; and at all periods of history whenever natural barriers in the way of satisfaction have not sufficed, mankind has erected conventional ones in order to enjoy love."
[S. Freud, "The most prevalent form of degradation in erotic life," 1912.]

Idealization–Fantasy

"If thou must love me, let it be for naught
Except for love's sake only."
[E. B. Browning, *Sonnets from the Portuguese* XIV, 1850.]

Suggestion

"There are many people who would never have been in love if they had never heard love spoken of."
[La Rochefoucauld, *Maximes*, No. 136, 1665.]

Habit

"Habit causes love."
[Lucretius, *De Rerum Natura*, Bk. IV, l. 1283, c. 45 B.C.]

Glancing

"The power of a glance has been so much abused in love stories that it has come to be disbelieved in. Few people dare now to say the two beings have fallen in love because they have looked at each other. Yet it is in this way that love begins, and in this way only. The rest is only the rest, and comes afterwards. Nothing is more real than these great shocks which two souls give each other in exchanging this spark."
[V. Hugo, *Les Misérables*, III, vi, 1862.]

By Acting As If You Love

"Often the pretender begins to love truly and ends by becoming what he feigned to be."
[Ovid, *Ars Amatoria*, Bk I, 1, c. 3 B.C.]

For Human Contact

"There seems to be a cult of love in America. Perhaps this is so because today there are so few human contacts left except that one. Actually, only one person in a thousand ever really falls in love."
[Mary McCarthy, "Lady with a Switchblade," *Life*, September 20, 1963, p. 64.]

---

the partners are concerned about the adequacy of the "fit" between themselves. What draws the couple together, obviously, varies from stage to stage (Murstein, 1971).

In the initial, or stimulus, stage, when all each person knows about the other is what he can gain with minimal interaction, interpersonal attraction is a function of the person's perception of the other's physical, social, mental, or reputational attributes. During the initial contact each may try to find out more about those attributes that are particularly important. For a girl interested in making a financially advantageous marriage, for instance, the career aspirations of her date may be particularly important.

Not only does each person size up the other person and arrive at an overall evaluation, but both also have a concept of their own overall attractiveness. Through this process of other- and self-evaluation, people generally attempt to interact with those whose total level of attractiveness is roughly equal to their own. Even though there may be disparities on a given trait, the total attractiveness of one person should be roughly equal to the other's if they are to continue interacting. Indirect confirmation of this hypothesis has been obtained (Murstein, 1972).

In the second, or value, stage the main determinant of attraction is the couple's value and attitude compatibility. When a man and woman begin to date, they may talk about their attitudes and beliefs in a number of areas, and if they discover that their attitudes are similar, their attraction will be strengthened. Again, indirect evidence in support of this hypothesis has been obtained (Murstein, 1971).

In the third, or role, stage of the relationship, both members of the couple become more concerned about their ability to function as a unit. Successful interaction at this stage involves a working out of the way in which each person is expected to act in certain situations, or roles. When one person has some personal problem, how much comfort does the other give? As each sees how the other acts, each can compare what the other does with what he or she expects a future spouse to do. If the roles fit, the relationship is highly satisfying. At this stage of the relationship complementary needs and roles may become an important determinant of attraction. If the woman indicates that she feels a woman's prime interest should be in her home and her children and this is what her date wants his wife to feel, the fit is obvious.

Thus the stages theory of attraction makes clear that at different stages, different factors may be the main determinant of attraction. Physical attractiveness may be highly important in the initial stage, similarity in the second, and complementarity—for some—in the third. By the time the individuals have decided to marry, all of these factors may blend to produce a highly complex mixture of marital motives, as shown by the reasons one college girl gave for marriage:

Laurence gives me what I want—he remembers birthdays. We have a lot in common, we like to do things together. . . . It will be a sort of give-and-take relationship. Laurence doesn't need to dominate me and tell me what to do and that satisfies me, I need that. And I can ask for advice and get it, but he doesn't insist on his way being the only way. We like to do pretty much the same things. We like sports that we can do together, and we like to dance. And I just like being together with him, which was something I could never do with any other boys. . . . There's a physical satisfaction too—we're compatible. He isn't too pressing that way—neither am I—so there is a nice balance. I like someone I can talk over things with, and sort of come back to, like discussing the day's work. I like someone I feel loves me too; I feel that very strongly. I don't want criticism but someone who understands my moods.

[Burgess and Wallin, 1953, p. 200.]

What attracted this girl was determined by what she wanted. She didn't want to be dominated, and she wanted someone who could care about her and give her advice. Laurence met these qualifications, and she was attracted to him. Since people vary widely in what they consciously and unconsciously want, one would expect wide variations in what they seek in a potential mate. The intensive interviews that marriage counselors have with persons who are unhappily married provide some ideas of the diversity of marriage motives. People may marry, for instance, to escape from an unhappy home, to be like their friends, or to gain material wealth. In the intense emotional involvement of the courtship and marriage situation, people may not be consciously aware of what they really want to find in a marriage partner.

Summary

In general, we tend to like others who: (1) are objectively likable—who are physically attractive, have pleasant personalities, and are competent, (2) live close to us and are available, (3) like us, do favors for us, and praise us, (4) are similar in attitudes, interests, and personality, and (5) in some instances, are complementary—who possess characteristics that go nicely with our own.

All of these characteristics have been interpreted as being consistent with the generalization that we *like people whose behavior is rewarding to us.* Neat as this reward-cost formulation sounds, it does not really allow us to predict in advance what draws two people together, since in real life it is very difficult to know what will be rewarding for different people.

People tend to like people who *possess valued traits*—who are *physically attractive*, have a *pleasant personality,* and are *competent.* Even in same-sex friendships people may tend to prefer attractive people because they believe them to be pleasant and intelligent. However, as additional information is gained about the other person, the influence of physical attractiveness on liking may diminish. Although people generally agree on what personality characteristics are likable, and although their reactions to other persons are generally determined by whether or not those persons have either positive or negative traits, the traits that are valued may vary somewhat from person to person. Competency influences interpersonal attraction too. Blunders may make people more likable only when they are comfortably superior to you. If they are comparable, their blunders may make them less attractive.

Proximity generally increases attraction. The closer people live, the easier it is for them to interact, and they are more likely to have pleasant experiences with each other. Knowing that a person lives close may make you and the other person try harder to be pleasant. Powerful as the proximity-attraction relationship is, there are limits to it. In some cases familiarity breeds contempt. When people interact intensively, the same forces that usually make proximity conducive to attraction can produce the opposite effect if the interactions are negative. Further, if a person is smotheringly close, you may dislike him because he has invaded your privacy and become predictably uninteresting.

People tend to like others who are associated with pleasant events or rewards. Although in general maximal rewards result in maximal attraction, there are several exceptions to this generalization. If, for example, you think that someone is praising you in order to ingratiate himself with you, you will disregard what he says. If someone likes you more than you like him, you may be uncomfortable. Further, the gain-loss model of attraction has shown that the sequence of praise is important. People were most attracted to others whose evaluations of them gradually changed from negative to positive and least attracted to persons whose evaluations had changed from positive to negative.

One of the most consistent findings in the area of interpersonal attraction is that people tend to like others who are *similar* to themselves; the greater the similarity, the greater the attraction. Both in judging strangers and in a dating situation, similarity has been found to be related to attraction. What is there about someone's agreeing with your attitudes that makes him attractive to you? People may strive for consistency in their relationships. Agreement may be reinforcing because we assume that we will have more pleasant interactions with others who agree with us. We may tend to like others who are similar because we assume that they will like us. Or the similarity-attraction relationship may be simply another manifestation of the social comparison process. However, there are limits to the similarity-attraction relationship. People who are too similar may become unattractive because they threaten our individuality or because they become dull.

Research results on whether people prefer others who are similar or *complementary* in personality are inconsistent. Whether people prefer the personality of those who are similar or of those who are complementary may depend on exactly which personality trait is being measured, how preference is measured, and on the roles and demands of a particular relationship.

Many of the determinants that are influential in the forming of friendship relationships are also influential in the forming of dating, love, and courtship and marriage relationships. However, we also saw that the relative impact of these variables differs in such intense relationships and that there are some different causal factors.

In the *dating* relationship *physical attractiveness* plays a much more crucial role than it does in determining friendship. There are several possible reasons for the importance of physical attractiveness in the dating relationship. People may have internalized the cultural norm that they are only supposed to be sexually attracted to physically attractive people. Or it may be that people prefer attractive dates because of the prestige gained by associating with them. Although everyone may want to date people who are physically attractive, in actual practice they may be concerned about the possibility of being rejected by someone who is much more attractive than they are. Thus in actual dating situations the level of physical attractiveness of the dating couple matches.

Similarity is also strongly associated with attraction in a dating situation—although less so than physical attractiveness. Further, physical attractiveness and similarity may interact. You may think that those who agree with you are more attractive physically and may see physically attractive people as more similar to yourself than they actually are. Other factors may contribute to your attraction to a potential date, such as *assurance* that you will not be rejected by the other, *physical proximity,* and *your objectives in dating.*

What makes one person fall and stay in love with another? Very little work has been done on the determinants of love. Indeed, people differ in their concept of what constitutes love—although generally love is regarded as having two components: an intense, affectionate concern and an intense sexual desire. Why do people fall in love? As we have noted, determinants of friendship are consistent with the general proposition that we tend to like people whose behavior is rewarding to us. Sometimes romantic love seems to follow this pattern too. On some occasions, however, people love those who have rejected them.

A *two-component theory of emotions provides an explanation of the determinants of love: Any variable that increases your level of physiological arousal or increases your tendency to label your arousal as love would intensify the amount of passion you experience.* Thus the first step in generating love is to generate physiological arousal. This arousal can be caused by a variety of unpleasant or pleasant emotional experiences, including fear, frustration, and sexual arousal. Once a person is physiologically aroused, social factors will influence how he labels his reactions. Our culture encourages people to interpret a wide variety of physiological reactions as love. Although the two-component theory of emotion provides an interesting approach to the question of why people fall in love, it should be emphasized that this account is still theoretical.

Why do people court and sometimes marry the people they do? The popular concept that *romantic love* serves as the basis for most marriages—at least for men—was supported in one survey in which the majority of the men reported that they would not marry unless they loved their prospective wife. Correlational studies of engaged and married couples have shown the importance of proximity, similarity, and complementarity. However, as a relationship develops, the determinants of attraction may differ. One theory of marital choice holds that *a couple progresses through three stages before deciding to marry:* (1) a so-called *stimulus* stage in which people are attracted on the basis of what can be seen, (2) a *value* stage in which the couple is concerned with evolving compatible values, and (3) a *role* stage in which the partners are concerned about the adequacy of the fit between themselves.

Patterns of Interaction

We have seen some of the forces that can attract a man and woman to one another and in some cases cause them to marry. If they do decide to marry, they may be filled with affection for one another at the time of their wedding and have high hopes for their marriage. A few years later, however, hostility, resentment, and confusion may mark what was once a loving, friendly relationship. What happens to destroy so many relationships? Conversely, why do many marriages work out as well as they do?

In order for a relationship to survive, the participants must evolve a functional, customary way of doing things, or a "structure"; they must function; and probably their relationship must go through certain basic changes. If the relationship ceases to meet the participants' needs, it may be terminated by divorce or separation. Since divorce exerts extreme psychological and physical costs, causing suffering in the participants and their children, an examination in detail of what is known about the dyadic structure and functioning of marriage has obvious practical importance.

Evolution of the dyadic structure

That dyadic relationships have a "structure" may surprise you. It is much easier to see structure in larger groups. The beginning employee who wants to last on the job knows the status hierarchy in his company and doesn't demand to see the company president. Employees know their roles. Secretaries, for example, don't ask their bosses to get them coffee. And the norms are clear. You know that, unless you know someone very well, you are not supposed to inquire into how much money he is making.

Even though we are far less aware of it, dyadic relationships have a structure too. If you think about your relationship with a good friend or someone you date regularly, you will see that regular patterns of behavior have emerged. For example, the pattern of telephoning to suggest getting together may have evolved into one in which one person usually suggests activities and the other agrees. Unfortunately, at the present time there is relatively little experimental research on the determinants of dyadic structure. Therefore our discussion of the factors that determine the particular form a dyadic structure takes will be based on theory and the informal observations of marriage counselors.

One of the main determinants of the structure evolved in a marriage is the general cultural context. What husbands and wives expect of one another and indeed of the relationship itself does not emerge randomly as they interact. From birth on we have all been inculcated with certain expectations about the nature of the marriage relationship itself as well as with expectations concerning the marital status, roles, and norms of husbands and wives.

The assumption that a sexual relationship between an adult man and woman must be on a one-to-one basis that lasts for the participants' life is a good example of a culturally derived expectation about marriage. (See Box 5 for a discussion of the future of marriage in its present form.) There are other implicit assumptions, which may or may not correspond with the reality of contemporary marriage. That marriage means you and your spouse become one, that jealousy means you are in love, that marriage means you and your spouse will be together constantly and share as many activities as you can—these and many other assumptions make up a popular folklore about marriage. Think about your own assumptions about what marriage is like. You may be surprised to find the number of assumptions you have about the nature of the relationship. Irrespective of what your particular beliefs and expectations are,

they influence the way you act toward your partner and the way you interpret his or her actions. If both partners do not share a common definition of the relationship, it is easy for misunderstandings to develop.

The extent to which cultural context can influence the structure of a relationship has been clearly shown. Medical doctors are culturally defined as possessing more status than nurses and can elicit obedience from them. Without a particular nurse or doctor having any personal knowledge about each other, each reacts to the other in terms of the expectations given in the cultural context. The individual who is culturally defined as possessing more status is able to elicit obedience from those of lesser power. Thus twenty-one out of twenty-two nurses complied with an order from an unknown doctor to administer an excessive dosage of an "unauthorized" medication to a patient. Of course, once the nurse's obedience was measured, the order was rescinded (Hofling, Brotzman, Dalrymple, Graves, and Pierce, 1966).

Powerful as the effect of the cultural context is, however, other factors also influence the dyad's structure. One such factor is the personality or combination of personalities of the dyad members. One might expect, for instance, that persons with dominant personalities would be more influential in the relationship. However, one study showed that the relationship between personality and behavior depended on the sex of the individual. Men who were found to have dominant personalities were more influential than less dominant men in their interactions with their wives, but women who had high dominance scores were found to be less influential than less dominant women (Kenkel, 1961). It may be that because of the cultural taboo against dominant and pushy women, women who obtain dominant scores on personality tests and would presumably like to be dominant push too hard and arouse their husband's reactance.

The emergent structure is also influenced by the rewards and punishments attached to the behaviors that emerge. Each of the marital partners brings to the marriage his own personality, his own way of behaving, his cultural expectations, and his or her history of behavior with the other. As the marital relationship begins, each partner tries to probe the other;

BOX 5 IS MARRIAGE DYING?

Criticisms of legalized, traditional marriage abound today (Hall and Poteete, 1972). Some critics talk of the irrelevance of marriage to meaningful man-woman relationships. Advocates of the Woman's Liberation movement speak scathingly of marriage as a master-slave relationship and urge single girls not to marry into such a subordinate relationship. Increasingly larger numbers of American men and women under thirty-five are remaining single. In 1971, 56 percent of the men and 45 percent of the women under thirty-five were single in contrast to only 51 percent of the men and 37 percent of the women in 1960 (U. S. Bureau of the Census, 1971).

Although we won't know the fate of marriage in the 1970s until the decade is over, it can be argued that what we are seeing is a modification, not the death, of marriage. Instead of a legalized contract between one man and one woman that is expected to last a lifetime, new definitions of the monogamous relationship may be emerging. In fact, many of the forms of the future are already with us.

One case in point is divorce. Divorce statistics are usually cited to show the deterioration of the marriage institution. An examination of these statistics, however, shows that the vast majority of those who divorce remarry. Divorce allows people to dissolve unsatisfactory relationships and to replace them with others that suit their current needs better.

Another modification of the traditional marriage is a couple's living together without having been legally married. Although statistics on the incidence of this arrangement are difficult to obtain, it has been estimated that more than 5 percent of the young live together without a formal marriage ceremony (Thomas, 1971). But is this a departure from marriage? Hardly. Many of the conventions that apply to traditional marriages apply to the couple living together. Although customs vary from relationship to relationship, generally those living together are expected to be faithful to one another, to be concerned with one another, and so forth. In fact, they may be expected to show the tradi-

(Mark Haven)

tional values of marriage to an even greater extent than those who are legally married. As one coed argued, if you don't have to stay with someone, your staying voluntarily shows a much greater commitment. In addition, many unmarried couples may marry when they wish to have children.

Still another variation on traditional monogamy, involving an estimated 1 million Americans, is "swinging"—a couple's having sexual relations with at least one other person (Bartell, 1971). As a study of one sample of swinging couples showed, those who swing make all of the usual assumptions about marriage except that of sexual exclusivity. In fact, the swinger's assumption is that there should be no emotional involvement with the third person so that the emotional attachment to the spouse is not weakened. Amazing as it may sound, many swingers feel that swinging strengthens their relationship. It provides a common interest and relieves the monotony of suburban life. Whether or not this is true is not clear, since, at

present, there is very little systematic evidence on the effect of swinging on the marriages.

In recent years we have also witnessed a modification of the expectations of those in a legalized relationship. Rather than being trapped into carrying out sexual roles, each partner may define his role in the way that best suits the development of the couple involved (O'Neill and O'Neill, 1972).

The most dramatic change from traditional marriage is the group marriage in which men and women living together in a group consider themselves married to all of the members of the group. In these relationships, it is argued, individuals are free to love and be loved by many others. In practice, however, it rarely works out that way. Jealousy and conflict may emerge, and coordinating the group's activities may become cumbersome. Perhaps it is for these reasons that most group marriages are relatively unstable (Otto, 1971).

Marriage is changing, but it is not dying.

behaviors change; and reactions are noted. In the process some patterns—even unpleasant, punishing ones—become fixed (Homans, 1961). How this evolution occurs is shown in the following example:

Assume that through their interactions up to this time, a newly married man and woman, on their honeymoon, have established an unspoken "rule" that each is to fill the other's needs without being asked. Mary prepares John's favorite meals, compliments him, straightens his clothes; and John buys small gifts for Mary, compliments her cooking, makes all travel arrangements, and so forth. In this interaction, neither has to ask the other to fulfill his role according to their mutual expectations.

Now suppose that on the fifth day of the honeymoon, Mary . . . sees a ring which she would like to own and asks John if he will buy it for her. At this point, one unspoken rule of their relationship has been broken. Mary has asked for a gift.

[Lederer and Jackson, 1968, pp. 92–93.]

How this incident influences the emergent structure of John and Mary's relationship depends on how each reacts and how each, in turn, reacts to the other's reaction. If John complies cheerfully, a new rule that Mary has the right to make requests of John has been established, and Mary's requesting has been reinforced. If John complies grudgingly, the rule has been established that Mary may ask for things, but the price for doing so is listening to a surly husband. She may, therefore, become less likely to make requests in the future, or she may retaliate by being unpleasant to John. Or John may refuse to make the purchase. Mary's reaction to his refusal will, in turn, influence John's future refusing. If she cheerfully accedes to his refusal, his refusing will be rewarded. If she just accepts his refusal to avoid a scene, she may be resentful and give vent to her feelings later—perhaps by being unpleasant about something else or by refusing John something that he wants or by making him ask for what he had been given freely before.

From this simplified example we can see the enormous complexity of an emergent dyadic structure. And this is just one interaction on one issue. In a real marriage there are thousands of such incidents, and the structure of that marriage will be affected by the common patterns

of interaction that arise out of all of them. In some cases the structure is one that allows the two to interact in a mutually satisfactory way. In other cases the structure is destructive to the individuals and to their relationship.

Although a dyadic structure tends to be somewhat static once it emerges, it is not completely so. If either the participants or the situation changes, so does the structure. If, for example, John was an assistant plant manager at the time of his marriage and was later promoted to the presidency of his company, the structure of his relationship with Mary might change. His increased status in the job world might mean an increase in his status with his wife. Increased corporate responsibilities might mean that he has less time to spend with his wife and two sons, so that his wife may have to assume more family responsibilities. In this manner the roles of John and Mary may change. And if the requirements of his new job involve his traveling extensively, the norm of "togetherness," which he and Mary shared, may also be changed.

We shall focus on three aspects of structure: status (relative power), roles (expected behaviors), and norms (accepted and expected ways of believing and behaving). Although the three aspects of structure refer to different phenomena, there is some overlap between them. To some extent status overlaps with roles: Persons with higher status also have a general set of expected behaviors. Roles also overlap with norms. The expectation that a wife will be primarily responsible for cleaning the house may be seen either as an aspect of her role or as a marital norm.

There are other aspects of dyadic structure in addition to these three. Regular patterns of communication—how and when people communicate—may emerge. Regularities in "ecology"—the use of space and time—may also appear. For instance, who sits in what chair may become regularized.

Status, status, who's got the status?

What is the following argument between John and his wife, Mary, really about? Steak or status?

John: Darling, you're so fond of good meat, you really should try the rib-eye steak.

Mary: Thank you, darling, but I'd much prefer the filet mignon. It's a little more expensive than rib-eye, but I do think it has a better taste.

John (sensing that Mary has not accepted his superior knowledge of meat): But people order filet mignon because of snob appeal; only connoisseurs really know about the rib-eye cut. You'll be missing an opportunity if you don't order it. Many restaurants don't even carry it.

Mary: I really appreciate your advice, John, but I do feel like having a filet mignon tonight.

John: I'm not giving you advice. I'm just telling you facts.

Mary: You are giving me advice, and I don't need it. If it's all right with you, I'd like filet mignon—or do I have to order fish?

John: Order what you damn-well please!

[Lederer and Jackson, 1968, p. 165.]

Reviewing this scene, we can readily see that what John and Mary are arguing about is not the relative merits of filet mignon and rib eye, but rather who has more knowledge about meat, who has the right to decide about the steak, and who can influence whom. What is really at stake is the relative power of John and Mary.

In a situation in which two people are competing for relative power, someone has to lose. Obviously, if one gives in to the other, there is no conflict. But if both persist—as John and Mary did—then they are locked in a status struggle that may permeate all aspects of their marriage.

How is status usually allocated in marital couples? One way to study this question is to determine how decisions are made when the husband and wife disagree about areas that involve the family. For example, if a husband and wife differ in their choice of a new family car, who usually wins? In one recent study, when a representative sample of 776 husbands and wives in the Los Angeles area were asked who made the decisions in a number of areas, it was found that the relative number of decisions made by husbands and wives varied according to the issue being decided, the racial group, age, whether the marriage was a first or second one, and socioeconomic status. As might be expected, both husbands and wives reported that husbands were more influential than wives in making decisions about the husband's job,

the family car, and insurance. Both husbands and wives reported that wives were more influential in making decisions about house decoration, the dinner menu, and the wives' clothing. Husband power was greatest in Oriental couples and weakest among black couples; it was less in older couples and second marriages than in younger couples and first marriages. And husband power was greater among men of higher socioeconomic status and educational level than among those of lower socioeconomic status (Centers, Raven, and Rodrigues, 1971).

Although the results of this study give us an idea of the structure of conjugal power, it has some serious limitations. To obtain an overall measure of conjugal power, one would have to know the relative importance of each of the areas to the family's functioning. Deciding what is to be eaten at dinner may not be as important as deciding about a car. Further, some of the decision areas may reflect adherence to the traditional sex roles rather than actual power. The most sensitive indicator of conjugal power may be decision-making authority when both parties want to control the issue.

Also sociological studies of the shape of power and status tell us little about how status emerges. How pervasive are marital status struggles? Once they begin, what can the couple do to contain them? What are the foundations of power in the marital relationship? Evidence on the dynamics of status in married couples is exceedingly sparse. Case material from marriage counselors provides some evidence about the pervasiveness and destructiveness of the struggle and some suggestions for containing it once it begins. One suggestion is to devise workable and mutually agreeable rules about who is to take charge in which areas and under which circumstances (Lederer and Jackson, 1968). But since the counselors' suggestions for containing the status struggle are simply untested hypotheses, whether or not they will work is not certain. Getting couples to acknowledge that they are battling for status may in itself be a difficult problem; John and Mary may have thought that they really were disagreeing about the relative merits of steak.

Evidence about the basis of conjugal power is equally sparse. Some theorists have speculated that there are three main bases for conjugal power: (1) acceptance of cultural roles and norms about conjugal power, (2) relative ability to provide rewards and punishments, and (3) relative expertise (French and Raven, 1959).

In the survey studies of conjugal power, we saw the power of roles and norms: Husband and wife power was greatest in the "appropriate" man-woman areas. Support for the reward-punishment hypothesis comes largely from informal observations. If one spouse has a much greater ability to reward desired behavior and to punish undesired behavior, then he or she seems to have an edge in the status race. The third hypothesis—that expertise generates status—is derived from the common observation that greater knowledge and competence in a given area generally enables a person to exert more power in that area.

Of course, there may be differences in the tactics used by men and women, as well as by persons with different personalities, in order to gain power. Observing status struggles among your married and unmarried friends may provide you with some more leads about possible bases for status in dyads.

Roles

One unhappy ex-husband who felt that his long-term relationship with his girl friend had been ruined by a formal wedding ceremony made the following comment:

Before we married, everything was free and easy and really great. So, okay, we marry, and right away she begins to take me for granted. Now I'm a husband and should be emptying the garbage. Instead of working it out, like we did before, suddenly I'm *supposed* to do this, *supposed* to do that. You'd think she'd know me better, wouldn't you, after all we've been through together?

[O'Neill and O'Neill, 1972, p. 140.]

To paraphrase this unhappy husband, roles are what people are "supposed to do." A person taking the role of a mother of a small child is supposed to have warm, affectionate feelings toward the child and also to be able to control the child. Similarly, there are a number of expectations about husband and wife roles. In our society there is an extensive mythology about what men and women are "really like."

FIGURE 9-6 Role Playing. (Drawing by Lorenz © 1970, *The New Yorker Magazine*, Inc.)

Men are supposed to be tough, competitive, brave, strong, competent, and dominant, and women are passive, emotional, loving, and pliant. Along with the temperamental characteristics, the husband and wife roles also include a wide variety of expected behaviors.

All social interaction involves people acting out their assigned roles. (See Figure 9-6.) Take, for example, your everyday role as a shopper buying merchandise. When you have picked out your items, you will look for the person whose role prescribes that he accept your money and sell you the product—perhaps a check-out clerk. If, however, you tried to buy an item from another customer, as one investigator did, you would see how upset people can become when someone does not act appropriately for his role (Garfinkel, 1963). When the investigator approached other customers and tried to buy merchandise from them, they became embarrassed, angry, and upset. Some tried to escape from the situation entirely.

If all social interaction involves acting according to our various roles, then how do expectations about the roles of husband and wife create problems in the marriage relationship? First, people may differ widely in their concept of the husband and wife roles. If a man who assumes that the wifely role involves caring for him, his house, and his children marries a woman who wishes to have a career and feels that house chores should be equally divided between man and wife, there is obviously going to be trouble. Studies have shown that divorced couples are less likely to agree in their definitions of the husband and wife roles in marriage than are married couples (Jacobsen, 1952).

Second, the roles may not account for individual differences in people. Some women may enjoy house and child care; others may not enjoy it or may not be very good at it. Further, rigid adherence to what one is supposed to do may interfere with his or her doing what he wants to do. A woman who is highly competent in a given profession may not work because this would upset her husband. Her "sacrifice" may make her resentful, thus damaging their relationship. Or a man might wish to engage in some of the activities usually thought to be part of the wifely role and may be inhibited in his growth.

Third, the roles may not correspond to reality. Some have theorized that the husband role includes mainly those tasks involved in functioning realistically, paying bills, and solving job problems, and the wife role focuses mainly on meeting the emotional needs of the relationship (Parsons and Bales, 1955). This treatment of husband and wife roles is roughly parallel to the popular concept of women as being concerned with personal and emotional matters and men as being involved with achieving and coping.

Neat and expected as the division seems, however, observations of interactions between husbands and wives seem to indicate that reality is more complicated than the theory. In one study husbands and wives were observed in the process of decision making, and the relative influence of each was then measured in terms of whether the husband's or the wife's idea was finally accepted. True to prediction, husbands did have a higher number of com-

ments related to the issue being discussed and wives had a higher number of comments related to feelings and their relationship with their husband. However, the wives who were the most socially and emotionally expressive were also the ones who were the most influential (Kenkel, 1957). When the goal of marital power is at issue, women may simply be using different means than men to gain control.

Norms

John and Mary have been married for ten years, and they agree on virtually everything. They are both Republicans, both opposed to the legalization of abortion, and both feel strongly that the woman should stay at home raising the children—as Mary has done. Both are very pleased that John has risen to the level of assistant plant manager at the firm where he works. They agree that their two children, both boys, should attend college and try to earn good grades in high school. Further, both John and Mary believe that each is and should be faithful to the other. Thus they agree on what behaviors are expected and appropriate in their family, or the so-called norms. If either John or Mary should deviate from these accepted patterns of thinking and acting, the other would probably be somewhat upset. If the deviancy threatened either the goals of the marriage or the self-esteem of either John or Mary, very strenuous attempts to "bring the other back to the proper course" would probably be made.

Most of the experimental work on the formation and functioning of group norms has been conducted in groups larger than two people. In one pioneer study, however, the emergence of norms in groups comprising either two or three people was studied. In this experiment each subject was shown a stationary point of light in a completely dark room. Because of an optical illusion, light shown in this manner appears to move, although it is very difficult for the person watching the light to estimate exactly how far it seems to move. (This phenomenon is referred to as the autokinetic phenomenon.) When two or three subjects were brought into this highly ambiguous situation and asked to give aloud their estimates of the distance the light moved, their judgments tended to fall toward a common norm. One subject might first estimate aloud that the light moved five inches, while another subject would estimate only two inches. On the next estimate, however, the first subject might decrease his estimate to a little less than four inches, and the second subject might increase his estimate to a little less than four inches. Thereafter, with very slight fluctuations, both subjects would agree that the light moved a little less than four inches (Sherif, 1935, 1936).

It is very difficult for an individual to remain independent and ignore what another person says. Even if a subject had first seen the light alone and formed his own independent judgment about the distance it seemed to move, his later judgment would tend to converge with those given by others when he was with another person. The power of the group endures too. A year after subjects had first made their judgments with another person, they gave the normative judgments when they saw the light alone (Rohrer, Baron, Hoffman, and Swander, 1954). Further, the majority claimed that their judgments were not influenced by those that the other subject or subjects gave. Thus even what strangers say elicits pervasive, long-lasting, and unthinking compliance.

If strangers have this effect, how much more powerful must be the forces toward consensus in a relationship as intensive as marriage? Studies with larger groups have shown that the tendency toward convergence is greatest in groups in which the members like one another, think that the other is similar to them, and think that the issues under discussion are basic to the group's functioning (Jones and Gerard, 1967). For many issues in many marriages, these criteria are clearly met. Thus it is not surprising that the correlational studies of husbands' and wives' attitudes have so repeatedly shown a tendency toward similarity. Although people who are similar in attitudes may be initially attracted to one another because of their similarities, a continued interaction may enhance their initial similarities.

Why should other people's comments have such an impact on the individual's judgment? Repeatedly, we have seen that people use the information provided by other people when reality is not clear. Subjects in a novel or upsetting situation may want to be with other subjects to see how they are reacting. As we saw in Chapter 2, this informational pressure toward agreement has been termed the comparative function of groups.

In addition, we all know that sometimes other people do not take kindly to our disagreeing. Disagreement may mean arguments and hard feelings. If another person finds out that we disagree, he may use a variety of tactics to persuade us. He may try to reason with us or he may yell and use threats. If we persist in our difference, he may refuse to associate with us. These potential unpleasant events, which also tend to make us agree with others, are termed the normative effects of a group (Kelley, 1952). Because we are concerned both with being right and with avoiding the pressures exerted against deviancy, other people's statements frequently have a powerful effect.

Thus one might logically expect agreeing spouses to be happy spouses. The results of correlational studies have tended to support this hypothesis. Couples who were similar and thought that they were similar tended to be more satisfied with their marriages (Levinger and Breedlove, 1966). It is easy to see why agreement might facilitate marital satisfaction. By supporting the opinions of each other, both can avoid raising unpleasant doubts in each other's minds about the correctness of their views. Similarity would make a life more predictable and less filled with discussions of differences, which could easily turn into ugly quarrels. And it is easier to coordinate activities if couples agree on basic issues.

But is there a limit to the agreeable effects of agreement? If John always nods and says, "uh-huh" when Mary brings up an issue—no matter what she says—how will Mary react? Will she begin to wonder if the agreement is genuine or whether it is motivated by other reasons? She might attribute John's agreement to a desire to placate her or to avoid listening to what she is saying. And she may begin to be bored by his total agreement. If he always agrees, what does he contribute to her knowledge? Talking to him is like talking to herself. Thus for some people at least some disagreement might have the paradoxical effect of increasing the informational power of the other person.

Summary

Even though we are far less aware of a structure in a dyad than in larger groups, *regular patterns of behavior emerge in dyads*. In a marital relationship one of the main determinants of the structure is the general cultural context. From birth on we have all been inculcated with certain expectations about the nature of the marriage relationship itself as well as with expectations concerning the status, roles, and norms of husbands and wives. The personality or combination of personalities of the dyad members and the rewards and punishments attached to their behavior will also influence the regular patterns of action that emerge.

In a situation in which two people are competing for relative power, someone has to lose. If both persist, they are locked in a *status* struggle. How is status usually allocated in marital couples? Although the evidence is sparse, some theorists have speculated that there are three main bases for conjugal power: (1) the degree of acceptance of cultural roles and norms about conjugal power, (2) the relative ability to provide rewards and punishments, and (3) relative expertise.

All social interaction involves people acting out their assigned *roles*—doing what people in their position are "supposed to do." However, roles may create problems in the marital relationship because people differ widely in their definitions of the husband and wife roles. Moreover, the roles may not account for individual differences in people and may not correspond to reality.

In a marriage the partners agree on what behaviors are expected or appropriate in their family, or the so-called *norms*. If either deviates from these accepted patterns of acting and thinking, the other may become somewhat upset. If the deviancy threatens either the goals of the marriage or the self-esteem of the partners, very strenuous attempts to "bring the other back to the proper course" will probably be made. Norms emerge because it is very difficult for an individual to remain independent and ignore what another person says. And, of course, the expected negative reactions to disagreement will act as a deterrent to deviation.

Although status, roles, and norms refer to different phenomena, there is *some overlap* between them. For instance, to some extent status overlaps with roles: Persons with higher status also have a general set of expected behaviors. Further, although a dyadic structure tends to be somewhat static once it emerges, it is not completely so. If either of the participants or the situation changes, so does the structure.

Functioning

We have seen what attracts one person to another and the aspects of structure that emerge as two people interact. We will now focus on the dynamics of this structure—the functioning of a dyadic relationship in day-to-day activity.

All of the aspects of social functioning that we have discussed previously—imitation, reward and punishment, and the use of others to obtain information—apply to dyadic interactions as well as to other group interactions. Because of their extensive treatment elsewhere, they need not be discussed here. Instead, we shall focus on three aspects of social functioning that have been dealt with extensively in connection with the two-person relationship. First is the ability (or lack of ability) of each participant to see the interaction from the *other person's point of view*. Second is the *reciprocity* between the members of the dyad. Over time each person develops the part moral–part practical approach of doing unto the other what he has done unto him. Finally, because some conflict is inevitable in any prolonged dyadic interaction, there is the practice of *bargaining*, which, if successful, leads to the resolution of the conflict through cooperation or, if unsuccessful, leads to competition and strife.

Taking the other person's role

How many disagreements between people are caused by the inability of the participants to see the world from the other person's point of view? If a husband and wife are quarreling about his lack of attention and time spent at home, the wife may only be able to see all of the hard work she does around the house and the boredom and monotony of her life. Her husband may only be able to see his own difficulties on his job and his need for outside activities to progress on that job. Both may become so completely focused on their own view that they are unable to see the matter from the other's point of view. As one theorist emphasized, each person assumes that the other has the same view of the situation as he does (Mead, 1934).

Frequently, in our interactions with others, we may try to maximize our own rewards irrespective of what happens to the other person. We may neither know nor care what the other person wants or thinks; all we are concerned about is getting "ours." Such self-oriented social interactions do occur. People sometimes use others for what they can get out of them. One person may date another simply because of the sexual gains incurred without any genuine concern for, or acknowledgment of, the other person.

But people are not always so myopic (Argyle, 1969). Sometimes they try to disentangle themselves from their self-centered world perspective and see the world from another person's point of view. This "taking the role of the other" can occur in a variety of ways and for a number of different reasons. At the most self-centered level, one may take the other person's point of view into account in order to deal more effectively with him. In other cases, though, one may begin to identify with the other person after seeing the world from his view (Turner, 1956). The irritation of a hungry restaurant patron who has been kept waiting for his dinner may turn to sympathy when he notices that his waitress is perspiring as she hurries by and suddenly realizes the hectic pace that she is working. The patron may feel the same fatigue and weariness, in an attenuated form, that the waitress feels.

Irrespective of whether taking the role of the other is motivated by self-centered concerns or empathy with another, one might think that people would be able to interact more effectively if they could take the role of the other. Support for this hypothesis has been obtained in a study in which the people who did well in taking the role of another also did well in a test of social interaction (Feffer and Suchotliff, 1966).

However, seeing the other person's point of view may not always increase the effectiveness with which a person interacts with the other. If the other person's interests conflict with your own, empathizing with him may make you less effective. If a soldier really understood the perspective of his enemy in face-to-face combat, he might be unable to defend himself (Sarbin and Allen, 1969).

Reciprocity

If someone invites you to dinner, you will probably return the invitation. If someone is friendly and concerned about your problems, you will probably be receptive to his problems. If someone does you a favor, you will probably return it—just as the husband does in the following example:

A husband insists that the spare bedroom be converted into a study for his use even though the renovation is expensive. Several days later, his wife engages a cleaning woman. Previously both had considered a maid too expensive. When the husband gets the bill for the maid at the end of the month, he goes into his now-comfortable study, writes a check for the maid . . . lights a good cigar, and congratulates his wife on how clean the house is.

[Lederer and Jackson, 1968, p. 168.]

Without necessarily being aware that we are doing so, we tend to treat others as they have treated us. (See Figure 9-7.) As we saw in Chapter 7, if others have been pleasant to us, we reciprocate their pleasantness. Thus in the above example the husband reciprocated his wife's agreeing to have his study renovated by agreeably allowing his wife to hire a cleaning woman. And if people have been thoughtless to us, we also reciprocate that:

FIGURE 9-7 Reciprocity.

For example, if a husband comes home from a business trip and finds that his wife, without consulting him, has invited her mother to live with them for two months, and that the mother is now occupying his new study, he feels betrayed. . . . The way the husband responds here will depend on the nature of their relationship. He may react by insisting that the newly hired maid be fired. He may be surly and rude to his wife's mother. . . . He may start complaining about how bad business is and insist on unreasonable cuts in the household budget. He may start nagging his wife, saying that his boss is angry because he hasn't properly completed some work which he brought home. Thus he implies that he is failing at his job because his mother-in-law is in his study, and that his wife is to blame.

[Lederer and Jackson, 1968, pp. 181–182.]

That reciprocity is a pervasive force in social interactions has been shown in a number of experiments. For instance, people have been found to reciprocate favors. Someone who received help from another was found to be more likely to provide help for that person than someone who had been refused prior help (Goranson and Berkowitz, 1966). People have also been found to reciprocate self-disclosure. Subjects in one study disclosed more intimate information about themselves to other people from whom they had received intimate self-disclosures (Worthy, Gary, and Kahn, 1969). People will also reciprocate the injuries inflicted on them by others. In one study it was found that the more frequently a subject was shocked by another, the more frequently he would reciprocate with an electric shock (Helm, Bonoma, and Tedeschi, 1971).

Why do people reciprocate? There are several possible answers. Some theorists have argued that there is a social norm prescribing that people act toward others as the others have acted toward them (Gouldner, 1960). According to a normative explanation, people reciprocate irrespective of whether or not they have anything to gain by doing so. Thus if someone reciprocates a favor in a situation in which no future interaction is expected and no future gain can be anticipated, the normative explanation is supported. In one recent experiment subjects reciprocated in just this situation (Tognoli, 1968).

Another explanation is that reciprocity maximizes the amount of reward that each participant gets out of the social exchange. Acting nicely to people who have been nice to you may make them more likely to continue being nice in the future. Punishing those who have punished you may make them hesitate to injure you in the future. Indirect evidence in support of this explanation has also been obtained. In one study subjects were more likely to return favors to others when the others were expected to have large resources in the future (Pruitt, 1968).

Pervasive as reciprocity is, however, people don't always reciprocate. In fact, you may have been hurt by a friend who did not give you help when you needed it, even though you had helped him on many occasions in the past. There are a number of reasons why people don't reciprocate. If the person's main motive is to maximize his own immediate gain, he may not reciprocate favors because reciprocity does not serve his immediate ends.

Whether or not you reciprocate may also depend on your assessment of the motives behind the other's acts. If you think someone is being kind in order to manipulate you, you will be much less likely to return the favor (Schopler and Thompson, 1968). If you feel that the other person is so stupid he doesn't know what he is doing or that he is trying to fool you with some sort of tactic, you may not reciprocate his cooperativeness—as one theorist has recently hypothesized (Dorris, 1972).

Still other factors may determine the likelihood of reciprocity. You may be more likely to reciprocate in intimate relationships, when you know you will continue interacting, than in more casual encounters (Sahlins, 1965). You may also be more likely to reciprocate with persons of similar status. If a professor is very kind to a student and spends a lot of time listening to his troubles, how can the student reciprocate the professor's kindness? Would the student feel that under these conditions reciprocity was necessary?

Conflict and bargaining

Conflict between people, between groups, and between nations is a frequent occurrence. Many of these conflicts are settled in hostile and destructive ways: wars and armaments races between countries, strikes by labor against management, and bitter and destructive quarrels between husbands and wives. Sometimes more constructive and cooperative forms of negotiation are used: treaties between countries, collective bargaining agreements between union and management, and reasonable discussions between husbands and wives.

Since conflict and differences are not inevitably settled by hostile means, the important question is: Under what conditions are cooperative means used to settle a dispute?

To get some hints about the determinants of conflict resolution, let us look at one example of a marital quarrel. After a long series of quarrels this couple sought the help of a marriage counselor:

Therapist: Uh-huh. Well, let's start where you guys left off. What were you arguing about?

Mary: Money, as usual. . . . My husband gets extremely angry with me sometimes because I spend money to call my parents long distance.

Therapist: Um-hum.

Bill (bursting out): Sixty dollars in the last month!

Mary: This is a perfect example. He never lets me finish. First of all—

Therapist: Did you know the bill was sixty dollars?

Mary: Yes, I know. But my husband earns thirty-five thousand a year.

Bill: Well, I don't spend that calling my family.

Mary: All right. I call long distance. And if he'll be quiet, I'll tell you what he does that makes me feel that this is all right. First of all, he makes about thirty-five thousand a year, and my husband is an avid golfer and a sports fan and he spends about a good—a *good*—two hundred a month at the country club, golfing and buying the fellows drinks and whatnot. That's his form of recreation. I don't have anything like that. I'm not a big spender.

Bill: Goddamn it, recreation my eye. I hate to play golf, but my biggest client is a golfer. . . . I'm working as a CPA and my office looks crummy. I want to fix it up and my wife spends all my money, so I can't. In order to make money, you've got to spend some—on business, I mean. . . . Sixty bucks comes to a lot of money, and I'll be honest with you, it's the Goddamn principle of it, spending sixty bucks every time she's lonely—she just picks up the phone and calls her Goddamn mother in Los Angeles. And it has nothing to do with whether you've got the money or not; it isn't necessary to call one's family that much.

Mary: . . . And about the only time I call my mother is when he's out playing golf. But he takes *all* the money, the extra money, and wants to invest it and

then he criticizes me for taking money because he says he wants to invest it. To him, business is everything.

Therapist: What else does he do?

Mary: First, he's never at home. He doesn't ever have anything to do with the kids because he's too busy making money. They need a father a lot more than they need a new bicycle. And he doesn't like my family. He's rude to them under all circumstances.

[Lederer and Jackson, 1968, pp. 351–354.]

This conflict illustrates a number of variables that are generally involved in a conflict situation and that can influence the mode of resolution: (1) the motives of those in conflict, (2) the dimensions of the conflict, (3) communication between the participants and their perception of each other, (4) the negotiation tactics used, (5) the behavior of the other person in the bargaining situation, (6) individual differences between the participants in their approach to the issues, and (7) mediation by a third party. Because of space limitations we shall discuss only the first four of these variables, but it should be realized that each variable is an important determinant of whether competition or cooperation will occur.

The evidence on conflict resolution is somewhat limited. Obtaining information about real-life quarrels—either by asking married couples to describe what happens in their conflicts or by asking marriage counselors to describe what they see—would provide clinical insights into conflict, but would not allow one to disentangle cause and effect. For example, were Bill and Mary angry because the other was using poor negotiation tactics or because of some other aspect of the situation?

To obtain control, researchers have brought conflict into the laboratory setting. The bulk of the evidence about conflict resolution is based on experiments using various bargaining games. The most widely used game, the so-called prisoner's dilemma, is based on an old detective-movie clichéd situation in which two suspects have been apprehended by the police, are being questioned separately, and have the option of either confessing or not confessing to the crime that they are accused of. What happens thus depends entirely on whether each prisoner chooses to cooperate or compete with his fellow prisoner. There are three possibilities:

1. If neither prisoner confesses, neither can be convicted of the crime that he is accused of, but both could be convicted of other minor crimes (mutual cooperation result).

2. If one prisoner confesses and the other remains silent, the one who has confessed will be released for turning state's evidence, and the other prisoner will receive the maximum penalty (competition/cooperation result).

3. If both prisoners confess, both will be convicted, but they will be given some leniency (mutual competition result).

Typically, the game is played over several trials, and points are either awarded to or taken away from each player after each trial depending on the result. A player who confesses can gain the maximum number of points in a competition/cooperation result on one trial, but over several trials both players would make more points from mutual cooperation results than from mutual competition results. The dilemma for each player, then, is whether to remain silent (thus creating the best condition for maximizing the points over several trials for both players) or to confess repeatedly (thus focusing on the greater immediate gain of the competition/cooperation result).

This situation is similar to many encountered in everyday interactions. Say that a husband and wife have a certain amount of money in a joint savings account. If both trust that the other will not secretly withdraw the money, the most adaptive course of action may be to leave the money in the bank so that it will accumulate interest. However, if either party thinks the other might withdraw it, his best course of action is to take the money out first.

By varying conditions in the prisoner's dilemma game, investigators have been able to study bargaining behavior in a highly controlled setting. Typically, the subjects are college students who do not know one another and are not allowed to communicate with one another during the experiment. The usual result—when subjects are told to play to maximize their own advantage *and* when they are not given any explicit instructions about how to play—is that the majority of the subjects do not cooperate. Usually, between 60 and 70 percent of those

playing take the competitive strategy (Oskamp and Kleinke, 1970). Subjects have even been found to compete when a cooperative strategy would always result in a higher score (Minas et al., 1960). Systematically varying aspects of the prisoner's dilemma game provides information about variables that influence the incidence of cooperation and competition.

Thus these experiments have provided a first step toward understanding interpersonal bargaining and have made the isolation of crucial variables possible. Critics of the experimental game approach argue that what happens in the games may have limited application to real-life conflict resolution. The games take place in a highly artificial experimental setting with norms and requirements that may differ markedly from ordinary bargaining. In experimental bargaining little is at stake for the bargainers, since tokens are customarily used. The goals of laboratory bargaining may also differ from those in everyday negotiation. Since the subjects involved in the laboratory experiments typically do not know one another or expect to interact in the future, they may be free to focus on maximizing their individual returns, whereas in real-life bargaining situations, where the participants know one another, they may focus on both maximizing their return and maintaining the relationship. Real-life bargaining—as our quarreling couple illustrates—may take place over a period of weeks or years, whereas the laboratory bargaining is a one-shot affair.

Since at the present time there is very little evidence about the extent to which game behavior does or does not generalize to other bargaining situations (Sermat, 1970), our discussion of interpersonal bargaining will draw on anecdotal accounts as well as on the experimental game literature. By combining the information from the rich but uncontrolled anecdotal observations with the rigorous but artificial experiments on gaming, we may obtain a better understanding of the complexities of human bargaining as well as some ideas for more realistic experiments.

Motives of Those in Conflict What does the subject want to obtain when he plays the prisoner's dilemma game? Presumably, he wants to maximize the utility of his choice, which he can do by cooperating with the other player over the long run or by competing in a single game. The issue of whether to compete or to cooperate is exceedingly clear-cut, and it may not be very involving, since the student's main reason for playing may be that the experimenter asked him to.

In real-life conflict the motives are more complex, and it may be difficult to tell what the negotiators want. Were Bill and Mary fighting over money or something else? One could argue that their disagreements over money were symptomatic of other, more basic differences. In highly emotional disagreements those arguing may not be completely aware of what the issues are.

Further, in real-life arguments what the couple is negotiating about may change over time. The initial disagreement may be about some specific topic, but if the argument escalates, the initial cause of disagreement may be obscured by both parties' desire not to yield. As labor negotiators have known for a long time, keeping face is a pervasive motive in bargaining.

A series of fascinating studies have shown the power of the face-saving motive in bargaining. Subjects victimized and made to look foolish in front of others were much more likely to retaliate against their opponents than were other subjects who were victimized but not made to look foolish. Those who had been made to lose face retaliated even when they had to lose money to do so. But if the opponents knew how much the retaliation cost, the victimized subjects were less likely to retaliate than if the costs of revenge were private (Brown, 1971). Although generalizing from experiments to real-life bargaining would be premature, it is interesting to note the pervasiveness of face-saving devices in international diplomacy. For example, the need to give the Soviet Union a face-saving way out of the American-Russian showdown on the Cuban missile crisis was emphasized by several of President Kennedy's advisers (Hilsman, 1967).

In real-life bargaining the participants are sometimes concerned with maintaining the relationship as well as with gaining their particular objective. This concern can sometimes impose limits on the amount of force and power each person brings to the bargaining situation. Husbands and wives who wish to continue their relationship do not go into mortal combat over every issue. The "gentling" effects of the desire to continue a relationship have been shown indirectly. When subjects playing the prisoner's dilemma game thought they would be seeing their opponents in the future, they were more cooperative than when they did not think so (Marlowe, Gergen, and Doob, 1966). When students playing the prisoner's dilemma game were married to each other, they were more cooperative than when they were strangers (Schoeninger and Wood, 1969). From both of these findings one might hypothesize that any variable that enhances the chances that a relationship will continue would increase the incidence of cooperative behavior. And the more concerned the opponents are about maintaining a pleasant relationship, the more cooperative they will be.

Dimensions of Conflict Several experimental game studies have identified the structural aspects of conflict that most influence the incidence of competition and cooperation. As you might predict, the instructions given to subjects about how to play the game influence their choice to cooperate or not. If each player is told that he and the other player are partners and they can both win, they are both much more likely to cooperate than if they are told to win as much as possible for themselves or to try to defeat the other player (Deutsch, 1960).

If either the cooperative or competitive reaction has a larger payoff than the other reaction, the more rewarded approach will generally be selected (Rapoport and Chammah, 1965)—unless, of course, the subject is either retaliating or is primarily concerned with besting his opponent. The incidence of cooperation is also influenced by the length of time bargaining continues. Typically cooperation increases as the number of bargaining trials increases (Morehous, 1966). And the number of options for settlement may influence the nature of the resolution: Too many alternatives may confuse the bargainers, and too few may freeze them into a competitive position because they are afraid of losing face (Gallo, Funk, and Levine, 1969). The greater the conflict, the more difficulty the negotiators have in reaching a mutually beneficial solution (Deutsch, Canavan, and Rubin, 1971).

Each of these structural variables has obvious implications for the determining of patterns of cooperation or conflict in marital disagreements. Predispositions to compete or cooperate may influence what the partners do. Trust and communication may develop over the life of a relationship, so that the incidence of cooperation may be greater among persons who have been happily married for long periods of time. And the number of options may influence the resolution of marital quarrels. If either Bill or Mary can choose only between Mary's continuing to telephone her parents often or making no telephone calls at all, the conflict may reach a deadlock. Small conflicts over relatively unimportant issues are obviously easier to settle than disputes of major importance.

All of these findings can prove helpful in structuring optimal conditions for a cooperative bargaining process. At least some of the findings, however, do not always hold. Perpetuating the bargaining process, for example, will not always lead to a pressure to reach a cooperative result. In one recent experiment there was no tendency over time for the subjects to modify their goals according to what the other person wanted. Rather, the subjects repeatedly ignored what the other person wanted and stuck rigidly to their own initial goals (Pruitt and Drews, 1969). How extensively a similar myopia generally pervades negotiations is still an open question.

Similarly, the general finding that coopera-

tion increases as the possible payoff for cooperation increases has not always been borne out. In some cases subjects have been more cooperative when they were playing for imaginary dollars than when they were playing for real money (Gumpert, Deutsch, and Epstein, 1969). When observing the patterns of conflict resolution among married couples, we see a similar, paradoxical effect. Sometimes couples who seem to have a lot to gain by cooperating do so, but in other cases those who seem to have the most to gain persist in a highly destructive competitive pattern.

The dilemma of the prisoners may show how increasing the stakes can either increase or decrease the incidence of cooperation. If instead of a maximum of ten years in jail the penalty is either a life sentence or a twenty-year sentence, the motives both to defect and to cooperate are intensified. Only when both prisoners feel they can trust the other is the incentive to cooperate increased. If either thinks that the other may betray him, the incentive to compete will be higher. Thus mutual trust is a crucial determinant in the effects of reward on cooperation and competition.

Communication Although prisoner's dilemma experiments showing the effects of increased communication have not been completely consistent, it has generally been found that when the opportunities for the players to communicate are increased, the incidence of cooperation increases (e.g., Wichman, 1970). When the players are able to communicate, they can try to influence one another, so that the competitive choice may become less attractive. Also, with communication may come trust as the players get to know one another.

This general finding is consistent with what marriage counselors have long believed: Effective communication is basic to solving marital conflicts and to evolving a satisfactory marriage relationship. (See Figure 9-8.) Watching married couples quarreling certainly makes the assumption that communication is important seem reasonable. If neither Bill nor Mary understood what the other wanted, then negotiating their differences would be difficult if not impossible.

A number of correlational studies have shown

FIGURE 9-8 Communication is vital in resolving interpersonal conflict.

that happily married couples have more effective communication patterns than unhappily married couples do. In one study in which the communication patterns of twenty-four couples who had sought marriage counseling were compared with those of twenty-four couples who were presumably happily married, a number of differences were found. Those who were happily married talked more to each other, conveyed the feeling that they understood what was being said, had a wider range of topics open to them, kept the communication channels open, were more sensitive to each other's feelings, and paid attention to nonverbal as well as to verbal communication (Navran, 1967).

If communication is so basic to evolving adaptive solutions to joint problems and if most married people do not enjoy marital conflict, why can't they learn to communicate effectively with one another?

There is very little evidence on the determinants of effective communication in married couples, but some ideas about the crucial variables may be obtained from a study of what is lacking in the following example of poor communication:

A husband and wife, driven to the point of spontaneous combustion by their three small children and a few dozen other eroding pressures, escape for the evening to a party in their neighborhood. They have been looking forward to this evening for a week. The party is great. In about an hour, however, the wife develops a headache. After waiting a short while to make sure that the headache is not going to leave her, she dismays her husband with her entreaty, "You'd better take me home." He resists momentarily. "Every time we start having fun, you seem to get a headache." She doesn't feel like arguing. "You take me home and then you come back to the party." He pauses, rehearses in his mind all the reasons why he should return to the party and says, "Okay, let's go." They are both quiet during the drive home. Arriving home, he escorts her into the living room, asks if there is anything to do to help her get comfortable, and announces his departure. "Where are you going?" she asks. "I'm going back to the party." He notices the pained expression and a small tear welling up in the corner of her eye. "What's the matter now?" "You're leaving me alone." "But you told me I should go back to the party." "I know, but if you really loved me, you wouldn't want to."

[McCroskey, Larson, and Knapp, 1971, pp. 169–170.]

Why is this an example of poor communication? First, the emotional context of missing the party has tended to diminish the sensitivity of each partner to the other. Second, the interpretation of what is said has been distorted by unstated assumptions. The wife, assuming that it would be unthinkable for her husband to attend a party without her, may not really believe her husband will take seriously her suggestion for him to return to the party.

Third, both parties in their quiet drive home seem to be avoiding the real issue—her care versus his fun. Nor is there any apparent recognition of the nonverbal signs of what the other person is feeling, which, as we saw in Chapter 8, convey at least as much information about others as does the spoken word. Also, the wife, by nagging that her husband doesn't love her anymore, may make him even less likely to listen carefully to her in the future.

Commentators have noted several other factors that tend to produce poor communication among married couples. One is a tendency to overestimate the extent of mutual understanding and a consequent lack of any attempt to increase accuracy in expressing thoughts and ideas (Shapiro and Swensen, 1969). Another is the common habit of not listening closely to what the other person is actually saying. The cartoon image of a husband uncomprehendingly nodding as his wife drones on may sometimes have validity.

Poor communication can also result from saying destructive and hurtful things when one is angry, showing irritation and hostile feelings in one's voice, or being unable to say what one really feels (Bienvenu, 1970). As several other studies suggest, communications may also be misinterpreted because of inconsistencies, complexities, disorganization, and lack of objectivity (Mehrabian, 1972).

We have been tacitly assuming that there is no such thing as too much communication. The results of the prisoner's dilemma research, the insights of marriage counselors, and correlational studies of communication and marital satisfaction have all agreed that increasing communication will generally induce increased cooperation and reduce interpersonal conflict. Sometimes, however, clear communication can intensify conflict.

The effect of communication depends on the nature of the conflict and what is being communicated. If a conflict between a husband and wife is a very severe one that cannot be resolved, the more articulately the husband and wife communicate, the clearer the magnitude of their differences may become. To return to the quarrel between Bill and Mary, if Bill is happy only when he is working and he communicates this clearly to Mary, she may become more upset.

What is said also influences the effect of communication. If one is very clear in communicating hurtful information, the relationship may be weakened by effective communication. The one item on a questionnaire that most sharply separated couples with good communication patterns from those with poor communication was: "Does your spouse have a tendency to say things which would be better left unsaid?" Couples with good communication patterns answered No on this item (Beinvenu, 1970). This is not to suggest that nothing upsetting to the other should be communicated. Indeed, another item that distinguished those with good communication from those with poor communication measured a willingness to express disagreement with the spouse—those with good communication showing more willingness to express disagreement.

Tactics Close observations of numerous bargaining sessions have enabled commentators to identify a dazzling array of negotiating tactics. We will identify only some of these tactics and illustrate how markedly they can lead to a competitive or cooperative result. In addition, because of the enormous complexity of the negotiating process, our discussion of these few tactics must be somewhat simplified.

One of the oldest and most familiar negotiating strategies is to *inflate one's demands* over what one will ultimately accept. Mary, for example, might tell Bill that she will not consider cutting her phone bill to less than forty dollars per month when she really would be willing to settle for twenty dollars. Puffing demands is an old labor-management negotiation technique. If the other person does not know what you are really willing to accept, your statement about your maximal concession may dictate the point at which the bargaining begins. By conceding what you intended to concede all along, you make the other person feel pleased with the bargaining process (Chertkoff and Baird, 1971). On the other hand, if the other person interprets your inflated demands as indicating a negative attitude toward him or the negotiation process, the tactic might backfire. When the demands become exorbitant, the other may feel that he is being mocked and may break off negotiations.

Another negotiating tactic is to *make a series of small, unilateral and conciliatory gestures* (Osgood, 1962). Bill might show his good faith by voluntarily suggesting that Mary telephone her mother on a particular day or that Mary buy herself a new dress. Since Mary then knows that Bill is attempting to be nice to her and cooperative, she may be tempted to reciprocate and be nice to him. This is just what was found in a recent study. Subjects who were of equal power reacted favorably to the conciliatory overtures of their partners (Tedeschi, Lindskold, Horai, and Gahagan, 1969).

But again, there are limits to the effectiveness of making conciliations. What happens if the other person interprets the initial concession as a sign that the other has changed his position or is weakening? If Mary interprets Bill's conciliatory gestures as meaning that she can now call her mother as frequently as she likes or that Bill is about to give up the struggle, her resolve to defend her position may strengthen.

Still another tactic which Bill and Mary might use would be to *threaten one another*. If Bill tells Mary he will leave her if she doesn't reduce her telephone bill, will she be more likely to capitulate? Or if Mary threatens to divorce Bill if he doesn't spend more time with her and the children, will he be more likely to do so? That making and executing threats is an effective bargaining tactic has been a central assumption of American foreign policy for many years. For example, President Nixon's justification when he resumed the bombing of North Vietnam in 1972 was that this would pressure North Vietnam to negotiate for peace.

Obviously, it is difficult to generalize from the results of laboratory studies on bargaining to international diplomacy, and the experimental results on the effects of possessing and using threats are not completely consistent. However, it is clear that in some circumstances the existence of threats in a laboratory setting makes a cooperative solution less likely.

The unconstructive effects of threat have been shown in a classic game study in which two players were asked to assume that each of them owned a trucking firm (Acme or Bolt) and that each would be paid for transporting a load of merchandise from each firm's starting point to the firm's destination. The pay each was to receive was determined by the length of time the trip took. And that led to the conflict. Although longer, alternative routes were available, the shortest, most direct route for each player included a common section of road that could be used by only one player at a time. Since the only way in which either of the players could win points was to use this common section of the road, its use had to be divided between them. (See Figure 9-9.)

Threat was introduced into the experiment by giving some of the players "gates," which they could use to block the other player from the stretch of road in contention. In one experimental condition both players had gates; in a second condition only one player had a gate; and in the third condition neither player had a gate. As predicted, the incidence of cooperative use of the common route was greatest in the condition in which neither had a gate. There was the least cooperation in the two-gate condition. In the one-gate condition the player with the weapon initially did better than the player without, but during the experiment he gradually began to share the road more equally with his opponent (Deutsch and Krauss, 1962).

Why should the existence of threat decrease the incidence of cooperation? From the fact that the other has a threat, each bargainer may infer that the other has hostile intentions and plans to use his weapons. Assuming that, the parties involved are less likely to try to communicate about their differences. As predicted, the subjects communicated the least in the two-gate condition and the most in the no-gate condition (Deutsch and Krauss, 1962). Further, each player may be afraid that the other will think him chicken if he does not use the threat he has available. Once either person uses his threat potential, the other feels he must reciprocate, thus setting off the spiral of competition.

Moreover, as the threats become more powerful, each combatant is faced with the

problem that his threats may become less believable. Since it is such an extreme act, Bill may not believe that Mary will divorce him, so Mary is faced with the problem of maintaining her threat credibility. To do this, she may engage in tactics to show that she means what she says. She may commit herself irrevocably to her action—perhaps by telling her friends of her plans. Or she may display a recklessness to show that she doesn't care. As one writer remarked about the tactics of teen-agers playing chicken, the more irrational the better:

The "skillful" player may get into the car quite drunk, throwing whiskey bottles out the window to make it clear to everybody just how drunk he is. He wears very dark glasses so that it is obvious that he cannot see much, if anything. As soon as the car reaches high speed, he takes the steering wheel and throws it out the window. If his opponent is not watching, he has a problem; likewise if both players try this strategy.

[Kahn, 1965, p. 11, in Swingle, 1970, pp. 256–257.]

But the existence of mutual, powerful threats may also in some circumstances make the emergence of cooperative reactions more likely. If both players know that they can destroy one another, the need to limit their threats is

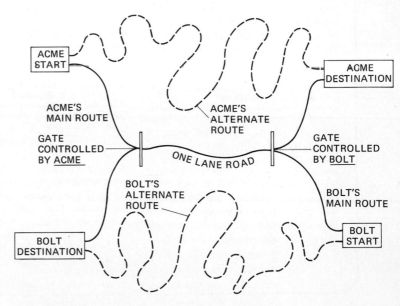

FIGURE 9-9 Map of the "Trucking Game." (Adapted from Deutsch, 1969, Figure 1, p. 1082.)

BOX 6 SOME TACTICS IN THE ART OF NEGOTIATING

Below are some classic negotiating tactics used by political figures and labor negotiators. See if any of these ploys have ever been used on you. (All of the examples are from Nierenberg, 1968.)

Surprise

Suddenly shifting your method. As Winston Churchill said,

"Surprise is a very effective bargaining strategy—as shown in the anecdote of the man who tried to give powder to a bear. . . . He mixed the powder with the greatest care, making sure that not only the ingredients but the proportions were absolutely correct. He rolled it up in a large paper spill, and was about to blow it down the bear's throat but the bear blew first."

[Pp. 112–113.]

Apparent Withdrawal

Seeming to withdraw while you really continue to be involved. In one situation in which a lawyer felt that the timing of a hearing was detrimental to his client, he pretended to withdraw from the hearing, but in reality, an associate of his was in the next room prepared to appear at the hearing if it was held.

Feinting

Using diversionary tactics to conceal your real goal or object. Even though a district attorney is theoretically obligated to disclose all of the information about a case, he may withhold information that is helpful to the defense. If the defense can convince the prosecution that it is in complete possession of the facts, the prosecution may not continue to withhold information.

Reversal

Turning the opponent's tactics back on him. In one case:

"In the days following World War II, the left-wing American Labor Party was prominent in New York politics. The ALP had formed an extreme aversion to a certain Brooklyn state senator, and had decided to 'go after' him. They entered a candidate in the Democratic primary in his district, and there was a possibility that they might not only beat him, but gain control of the Democratic party in that district.

"The senator refused to knuckle under and accept the endorsement of the American Labor Party. His problem was to prevent the ALP from 'making an example' of him.

"The senator and his staff decided on a strategy of reversal. They would make a bid to take over the American Labor Party in that district by entering a candidate in *their* primary. Squads of workers went out, and in two days enough signatures were accumulated to make an ALP primary fight feasible. Then the truce flag went up. The American Labor Party agreed not to fight the state senator if he would withdraw from their primary."

[P. 115.]

Blanket

Covering as many demands as possible. This tactic is illustrated by the following apocryphal incident:

"[A] young man . . . , whenever he went to the movies, picked out a seat next to a young lady. He would then suggest that she kiss him. His friend, on hearing this, said to him, 'I imagine that you get your face slapped quite a few times.' The young man replied, 'Yes, I do, but I also get an awful lot of good kissing.'"

[P. 118.]

Crossroads

Introducing several issues into the bargaining so that you can make concessions on some in order to gain on the others.

Participation

Using your friends to help you. International treaties are good examples of this form of negotiation.

Salami

Taking something bit by bit. The General Secretary of the Hungarian Communist party, Mátyás Rákosi, is credited with explaining this tactic:

"When you want to get hold of a salami which your opponents are strenuously defending, you must not grab at it. You must start carving for yourself a very thin slice. The owner of the salami will hardly notice it, or at least, he will not mind very much. The next day you will carve another slice, then still another. And so, little by little, the whole salami will pass into your possession."

[Pp. 120–121.]

Forbearance

Waiting out the opposition. This is used when members of a Quaker meeting disagree:

"When members of a Quaker meeting find themselves divided on a question, it is customary to declare a period of silence. If the division still persists, the clerk postpones the question for another time or a later meeting. This can go on indefinitely until the question is resolved."

[P. 112.]

FIGURE 9-10 In real-life situations, people resort to a wide variety of tactics to resolve their conflicts.

very obvious; they cannot afford to be irresponsible. Just as the United States and the Soviet Union began to evolve agreements about their use of power in 1972, players who are very powerful may act less competitively and more responsibly than players who are less powerful.

Confirmation for this hypothesis was obtained in an experiment in which the level of power was manipulated. When both players had the ability to damage the other substantially, the players were more likely to enact a number of "treaties" concerning the limitations on, and the penalties for, the use of power than when only one or neither of the players has such power capabilities (Thibaut and Faucheux, 1965). Thus it may be that only when both parties have powerful and approximately equal threat capabilities is either party motivated to develop norms about the limitations of power, as President Nixon has argued.

As we have indicated, people use a lot more bargaining tactics than just puffing, making concessions, and threatening. (See Figure 9-10.) Bill and Mary, for example, may use some of the tactics marriage counselors have seen

other couples use. Every time Bill criticizes Mary, she may begin to cry. When a difference emerges, one of them may take to his or her bed with a convenient ailment. One or the other may verbally capitulate but continue to do exactly as he or she pleases. One of them may nag or ridicule the other. One may try to enlist the support of allies—people who agree with his or her side of the issue. (For some tactics observed by one labor negotiator, see Box 6.)

Summary

We have discussed three aspects of dyadic functioning. First, we saw that *sometimes people see their interaction from the other person's point of view.* This can range from merely recognizing his view to empathizing with him and can take place because of a number of motives, ranging from a manipulative expediency to a less self-centered empathy.

Second, we saw that without our necessarily being aware that we are doing so, we tend to treat others as they have treated us. Although *reciprocity* is a general theme in dyadic functioning, there are limits to it. Whether or not we reciprocate depends in part on our own motives and on our assessment of the motives behind the other's actions.

Third, we discussed four of the variables that determine whether a competitive or a cooperative solution occurs when two people *bargain*. The *motives* of those in conflict determine their mode of resolution. In an experimental game the players presumably wish to maximize the joint gain of themselves and their partner or to maximize their gain relative to that of the other. However, in real-life conflicts the motives may be more complex. In fact, the bargainers may not be fully aware of what they want; their goals may change over time; and they may be more concerned with maintaining their relationship than with obtaining their stated objectives.

The *dimensions of the conflict* also influence the incidence of competition and cooperation. In the experimental situation instructions that emphasize the desirability of cooperative modes of playing, higher payoffs for cooperative than for competitive solutions, and longer periods of bargaining all tend to increase the incidence of cooperation. However, increases in the pressure to reach agreement and increases in the total payoffs for cooperation have not had completely consistent effects on the incidence of cooperation.

Communication between negotiators generally increases cooperation, as shown by both the experimental game studies and the anecdotal observations of marriage counselors. Although the importance of communication is generally acknowledged, improving communication in day-to-day interactions is extremely difficult.

Tactics also influence the outcome of bargaining. Within reason the puffing of demands can be an effective bargaining technique. Graduated conciliations may also be effective—if the other person doesn't interpret them as a sign of weakness. Although the assumption that making and executing threats is a highly effective bargaining technique has been an accepted part of American foreign policy for years, the experimental evidence suggests that at least in some circumstances the existence of threats makes a cooperative solution less likely.

Development

As we have seen, people tend to develop, from their thousands of interactions with other people, a limited number of relationships with certain people, and these relationships evolve a structure with certain patterns of functioning. In this section we will discuss how such relationships can change over time from an initial superficiality to a far more intensive and intimate interinvolvement.

Some of the changes that occur as a relationship becomes more intense may be shown by comparing Jane's reactions to John and their relationship after their first few dates with her feelings about him and their relationship ten years later. Just after their initial dates, Jane described her relationship with John as follows:

Whenever we go out, I'm always sure that I look my best—freshly shampooed hair and all that. I'm an independent woman but that might disturb John, so I'd never admit it to him. So far we've dated every couple of weeks—parties at friends' houses. I think I'm attracted to John because of his inner qualities, but I can't be sure. He is a sexy looking guy!

[Middlebrook, 1972, p. 3.]

Ten years later, after nine years of marriage, Jane gave quite a different description of her relationship with John:

How do I feel about John now? Well, I guess the simplest way to describe my feelings is to say that he is part of me. The initial fuss of always trying to look good and say the "right things" disappeared years ago. I just act like myself with him now. No put-ons. I say what I think and I hate to admit it, but if I'm in a bad mood, I sometimes let myself go. We have our differences, but I'm really involved with him. We don't do everything together—he hates shopping for women's clothes so I go alone—and I hate baseball so he goes to the games with a man friend. But we share most things. And I tell him everything—even some of the things about myself of which I'm not particularly proud.

[Middlebrook, 1972, p. 6.]

By comparing these two quotes, we can see that a number of changes have occurred in Jane and John's relationship as the years have passed. Why did these changes occur? How did they happen? And just what are some of the critical differences between an intense relationship and a more superficial one?

Time alone does not make a relationship become more intense. You may be able to think of people whom you've known superficially for years. According to one theoretical account, the growth of a relationship is a function of the relative rewards and costs incurred in the relationship, the personality characteristics of the participants, and the requirements of the situation (Taylor, 1968). If a relationship provides rewards for both parties, it is likely to develop (Taylor, Altman, and Sorrentino, 1969). If both people desire a close relationship, it may be more likely to evolve toward a more intimate relationship. And if the situation permits the relationship to develop, it will probably do so. Further, if a person feels that he is committed to a particular relationship, he may be less likely to try to exploit the other person (Marlowe, Gergen, and Doob, 1966).

How does a relationship develop from the acquaintance stage to a closer relationship? Does it move gradually, step by step from a less intimate to a more intimate relationship? Or does it go through a series of phases, as some have theorized (Argyle, 1969)? As has been observed repeatedly, people tend to disclose more intimate information about themselves when they are closely involved with someone. Do the disclosures gradually become more intimate? Or are there periods when there is little change followed by periods when the level of intimacy increases greatly? As yet there are no commonly accepted theories as to how the process works.

Irrespective of why or how close relationships emerge, it is clear that they differ dramatically from more superficial ones. Thinking about the way you feel about and act toward some of your own very close friends will give you some indications of what these differences are. When you are with people you do not know well, you may be concerned about the impression you are creating. You may try to look as attractive as you can, and your conversation may be deliberately unrevealing. But once you get to know someone well, you feel much freer to be yourself with him. If a good friend is coming over to see you, you may not bother to dress up or clean your apartment. If you feel surly, you may not be as concerned about letting yourself go.

That people who know each other well feel less constrained to be polite to one another was shown in a study that compared the behavior of married couples and strangers in a problem-solving situation. In general, the subjects were found to treat "strangers more gently, and generally more nicely than they did their spouses" (Ryder, 1968, p. 237).

As a relationship becomes more intimate, the two people are more likely to do things together—to function as a team. A study of the friendship patterns of male college students confirms this hypothesis. As the level of intimacy of a friendship increased, so did the number of activities shared. Moreover, the activities shared in close friendships were more intimate. Close friends were more likely to borrow money and exchange home visits with their close friends than with acquaintances (Peters, 1969). In very intense relationships a person may become almost as involved with the other as he is with himself. The extent to which identities can be merged is illustrated by the extreme grief reactions some spouses go through on the death of their mate. Unable to perform in their familiar "team" environment, they find even the activities they used to perform alone or with others no longer satisfying or meaningful. The void created by the death of their spouse has expanded to swallow the rest of their life.

As noted earlier, customary patterns of doing things emerge as a close relationship develops. Although the structure may be changed by changing circumstances, it tends to remain stable. Once an equilibrium is reached, both partners try to keep the relationship functioning in the usual patterns. Further, "rituals of solidarity" may be added to the other regular patterns of behavior—a couple may celebrate their relationship through anniversary celebrations. This serves both to reinforce the couple's feelings of solidarity and to make clear to others that the relationship is an exclusive and legitimate one (McCall et al., 1970).

Finally, more information is exchanged in intimate relationships than in superficial ones. We have seen that the attitudes of married couples tend to resemble one another. Although this is partly because persons who are similar are initially attracted to one another, the process may be heightened by repeated exchanges of information. It is not surprising that

FIGURE 9-11 Dissolution.

after a number of years of listening to the same information and conversing with one another, husbands and wives tend to have attitudes that resemble one another.

Moreover, the longer people interact, the more likely it is that the information they exchange will become more and more intimate, thus increasing the sense of closeness in the relationship. In a study of college friendships it was found that students tended to disclose more intimate information to close friends (Peters, 1969). A study of college roommates showed that they tended to reveal increasingly intimate information about themselves as the semester passed: More intimate information was shared during the ninth week of the semester than during the first week (Taylor, 1965). As a relationship develops, people may begin to trust one another and so feel free to risk revealing themselves. Once they do this, their feelings for the other person become even more positive (Gergen and Gergen, 1971). (For some thoughts on how a good marriage can be initiated and developed over time, see Box 7.)

Dissolution

Not all relationships survive. Many couples separate or divorce. (See Figure 9-11.) Current estimates of the incidence of divorce vary, but some estimate that roughly one in three American marriages will end in divorce (Lederer and Jackson, 1968). (See Figure 9-12.) High as this figure is, it is an underestimate of the number of marital relationships that cease to function. Two people may be very unhappy with one another and with their marriage and yet remain married.

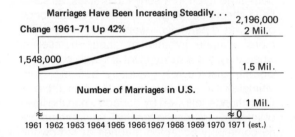

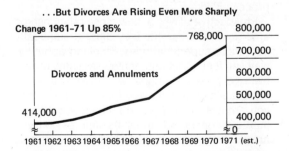

FIGURE 9-12 *Result:* For every three new marriages today, one old marriage ends in divorce or annulment. A decade earlier, there was one divorce or annulment for every four marriages. (Reprinted from *U.S. News & World Report*, Copyright 1972, U.S. News & World Report, Inc., August 14, 1972, p. 30.)

BOX 7 — GUIDELINES FOR BUILDING A HAPPY MARRIAGE

Every couple and every relationship is different, so there are no infallible rules for selecting a mate with whom you can maintain a happy and satisfying relationship. However, on the basis of problems encountered by marriage counselors and the research discussed in this chapter, some general guidelines can be suggested.

Before Marriage

1. Try to *distinguish sexual attraction from love.* Obviously, sexual attraction is an important component of love, but it is not enough to base an enduring relationship on.

2. *Examine your reasons for wanting to marry* this particular person. If you are marrying to escape from an unhappy homelife, to "reform" the other, to solve your own personal problems, or because all of your friends are marrying, don't. Analyze what you would gain and what you would lose should you marry.

3. *Keep the lines of communication open.* Discuss areas that will be important after marriage, such as the relationship between the two of you and your in-laws, money, religion, children, and the role of husband and wife. There should be no surprises in basic areas after the wedding ceremony. *Really get to know the other person.*

4. *Be analytical about the relationship you now have* with the other person. Patterns of interaction before marriage are your best clue as to what life with the other person will be like after marriage. Don't delude yourself that the other person will "change" after marriage. *What you see is what you're going to get.*

5. *Think about the characteristics of the other person.* Are you compatible in areas that are important to you? Complete similarity could lead to a boring relationship, but dissimilarity in important areas—such as attitudes about sex, religion, children, the husband and wife roles, and so forth—can be irritants after marriage.

After Marriage

1. *Be as concerned about the happiness, growth, and well-being of the other as you are about your own.*

2. *Keep the lines of communication open.* Don't store up grievances. Air important differences openly, but in a way that will not wound the self-esteem of your partner.

3. *Be tolerant.* Nobody is perfect. Accept the imperfections of the other that you can tolerate. Before criticizing the other, think about some of your own imperfections, and decide whether the issue is important enough to discuss.

4. *Don't try to make your partner into a carbon copy of yourself.* You married your partner because you liked and loved what was there; give the other person some breathing room. You'll both be more interesting to the other if you don't have total togetherness.

5. *Be aware of the other person's moods* and guide your reactions accordingly. Don't bring up an irritating subject when the other person is feeling tired or irritable.

6. *If you do get into an argument, keep the discussion limited to the issue at hand.* Hurtful remarks about areas irrelevant to the issue at hand will only interfere with the discussion. If you sense that the argument is escalating, break off the discussion. When tempers have cooled, resume the discussion.

7. *Be your partner's best friend.* Act in such a manner that the other person knows he or she is deeply loved. Be receptive to discussions of the other person's problems, but don't dwell exclusively on them. A marriage is not psychotherapy. Be sure you share pleasant events as well as problems.

8. *Be analytical about the meaning of your patterns of interaction.* Say what you mean and not what you think you should say. Be honest with one another.

9. *Make "marital rules" explicit.* Bargain openly and negotiate contracts about duties, obligations, and privileges. There are some unpleasant duties that must be performed, and how the chores are to be allocated should be made explicit.

You may know cases of embittered and frustrated spouses who have wearily stayed together "for the sake of the children."

Why do so many marital relationships fail to survive? In general, it has been found that whether or not a person continues in a relationship is largely determined by: (1) the relative number of pleasant and unpleasant aspects of the relationship, and (2) the strength of the constraints against terminating the relationship.

Unpleasant aspects of marriage

As long as the pleasant aspects of marriage—sexual gains, companionship, and so on—predominate, there will be little or no cause for the couple to move toward the dissolution of the relationship. When more unpleasant aspects emerge, however, dissolution becomes a realistic alternative.

What are the sources of difficulty in marriage? Obviously, if one of the partners has a *disturbed personality* before marriage, he will continue to have it after marriage. Thus some marital problems may be related to problems faced by one or both of the partners as separate individuals. However, the problems reported more frequently seem to relate to difficulties that arise when the two interact.

False expectations about the mate and marriage may contribute to marital breakups. A number of studies have shown that brevity of courtship is correlated with marital unhappiness (Dominian, 1968). During a brief courtship the couple may not have time to come to know one another. Unrealistic expectations about marriage may also lead to diminished satisfactions. If a person expects that once he is married he will never be lonely again, he may be sadly disappointed.

Problems in the external environment may also be a source of difficulty. If a couple doesn't earn enough money to meet its expenses, the tension from financial problems may make both partners irritable. If in-laws are overly involved, their interference may pose problems. If one or both of the partners is overworked, fatigue may enlarge what would otherwise be seen as small problems. People who marry at a very young age may be likely to face financial problems or difficulties with interfering in-laws, which may explain, to some degree, the very high incidence of divorce among those who marry young.

People frequently marry for companionship, love, and someone to care about them. If these *psychological needs* are not met, the marriage is in trouble. In one survey that compared the reactions of couples who were happily married with those who were unhappily married, the major difference that emerged was related to the warmth, love, and affection that the marriage provided. Those who were unhappily married complained significantly more often than those who were happily married about neglect, lack of affection, lack of understanding and appreciation, and loneliness. Further, those who were unhappily married complained that their spouse attacked their self-esteem by magnifying their faults, belittling their efforts, and making false accusations (Mathews and Mihanovich, 1963).

The *structure and patterns of interaction* can also contribute to marital breakdown. As we noted earlier, an unresolved status struggle may cause problems. The absence of structure can cause trouble too. If a working couple never evolves a standard procedure for both husband and wife to get out in the morning, daily chaos may be the result. Certain patterns of reconciling differences—such as fights in the style of *Who's Afraid of Virginia Woolf?*—can also be very destructive. If, whenever a couple argues over one issue, both try to hurt the other as much as they can, the very process of fighting will rip the relationship apart (Bach and Wyden, 1969).

Not all divorces occur because the couple has violent quarrels or the spouses feel unloved. Sometimes one or both of the individuals may wish to dissolve the relationship because it does not allow the *freedom to develop* a potential that could otherwise be developed individually. If two students marry in their early twenties, ten years later one or both of them may be quite a different person. Interests and values may change. One may mature while the other does not. Or the requirements of the particular marriage may make one of the partners feel stifled.

Constraints against terminating marriage

The power of the constraints against dissolving the relationship also determine whether or not the couple stays together. Unhappy as a particular marriage may be, the partners must also consider the rewards and costs of alternative courses of action (Thibaut and Kelley, 1959). Obtaining a divorce is expensive, painful psychologically, and still may be seen as socially unacceptable in some communities. Looking beyond the divorce, the individual also considers how pleasant his life as a single person would be. If he is afraid of the loneliness of a single existence, he may stay with a very unpleasant marriage just to avoid being alone. If someone feels very unattractive and completely unable to attract another person, he may stay with an unpleasant situation.

Painful as the dissolution of a marriage is, the legal and social problems of divorce provide additional indignity and difficulty for the suffering couple. It is a well-known fact that the legal grounds for divorce in many states bear little resemblance to the reasons people really wish to divorce. Although the most usual reason for divorce today is a mutually acknowledged incompatibility, the legal grounds frequently do not recognize this and, instead, include such items as desertion, adultery, bigamy, and cruelty. To provide the legally required grounds, one or both parties may have to perjure themselves. The present divorce proceedings in many states are based on an "adversary" system in which the business of the court is to have the contestants battle for allocation of the relative blame for the failure of the marriage. This, obviously, places the husband and wife in a very unpleasant situation. Laws generally favor providing alimony for the wife and not the husband, so that the divisive effects of relative greed may ruin what little was left of the relationship.

Further, divorce creates an awkward social situation. It is the only major change in status for which there are no "rites of passage." When a couple marries, there are elaborate rituals to signify the change in status, and everyone knows what the appropriate rules of conduct are. In contrast, there are no rituals surrounding divorce. The couple's friends may feel awkward in dealing with the couple. "Do we invite them both to the party or should we just ask him?" is a common concern of those who know the divorced couple. Even as simple a matter as circulating the information that the couple has divorced is awkward. Divorce causes a dramatic change in a person's life and is a commonly experienced event. Perhaps evolving some rituals and etiquette to surround the event might minimize its painfulness and awkwardness.

SUMMARY

This chapter explored the properties of the two-person group, or the dyad. A great deal of social interaction takes place on a one-to-one basis; many of the most intensive, most influential relationships are dyadic; and there are several differences between dyadic interaction and interactions in larger groups, although the two are similar in many respects.

1. Attraction In general, we tend to like and to be attracted to others who (1) are *objectively likable*, (2) are *proximate*, (3) *like us, do favors for us*, and *praise us*, (4) are *similar* in interests, attitudes, and personality, and (5) in some instances, are *complementary* in certain characteristics that go nicely with our own.

All of these characteristics have been interpreted as being consistent with the generalization that we *like people whose behavior is rewarding to us*. Neat as this reward-cost formulation sounds, it does not allow us to predict attraction in advance, since it is difficult to know what will be rewarding for different people.

People tend to like people who *possess valued traits*—who are *physically attractive*, have a *pleasant personality*, and are *competent*. Even in same-sex friendships people may tend to prefer attractive people because

they believe them to be pleasant and intelligent. Although people generally agree on what personality characteristics are likable and react positively to people who possess these pleasant traits, the traits that are valued may vary somewhat from person to person. Competency also influences attraction. Blunders may make people more likable only when they are comfortably superior to you. If they are comparable, their blunders may make them less attractive.

Proximity generally increases attraction. The closer people live, the easier it is for them to interact; and since people interact more frequently with people who are close, they are more likely to have pleasant experiences with them. Knowing that a person lives close may make you and the other person try harder to be pleasant. Powerful as the proximity-attraction relationship is, there are limits to it. When people interact intensively, the same forces that usually make proximity conducive to attraction can produce the opposite effect if the interactions are negative. If the person is smotheringly close, you may dislike him because he has invaded your privacy or because he is so predictable he has become uninteresting.

People tend to like others who are associated

with *pleasant events or rewards.* However, if the praise is thought to be made for ingratiating reasons, it may be disregarded. If someone likes you more than you like him, you may be uncomfortable. Further, the gain-loss model of attraction has shown that the sequence of praise is important. People were most attracted to others whose evaluations of them gradually changed from negative to positive.

People tend to like others who are *similar* to themselves, and the greater the similarity, the greater the attraction. People may strive for consistency in their relationships. Agreement may be reinforcing because we assume that we will have more pleasant interactions with others who agree with us, or we may assume that others who are similar will tend to like us. However, there are limits to the similarity-attraction relationship. People who are too similar may become unattractive because they threaten our individuality or become dull.

Research results on whether people prefer others who are similar or *complementary* in personality are inconsistent. Whether people prefer the personality of those who are similar or of those who are complementary may depend on which personality trait is being measured, how preference is measured, and on the roles and demands of a particular relationship.

Many of the determinants influential in forming friendship relationships are also influential in determining attraction in dating, love, and courtship and marriage relationships. However, the relative impact of these variables differs in heterosexual attraction, and there are some other causal factors.

In the *dating relationship, physical attractiveness* plays a much more crucial role in attraction than it does in determining friendship. People may have internalized the cultural norm that they are only supposed to be sexually attracted to physically attractive people, or they may assume that physically attractive people are intelligent and pleasant. Or it may be that people prefer attractive dates because of the prestige gained by associating with them. Although everyone may want to date people who are physically attractive, in actual dating, the level of physical attractiveness of the dating couple matches. *Similarity* is also strongly associated with attraction in a dating situation—

although less so than physical attractiveness. Physical attractiveness and similarity may interact. You may think that those who agree with you are physically attractive and may see physically attractive people as more similar to you than they actually are. Other factors may contribute to your potential date's attractiveness—such as assurance that you will not be rejected by the other, physical proximity, and your objectives in dating.

What makes one person fall and stay in love with another? Very little work has been done on the determinants of love. People differ in their definition of love, although it is generally regarded as having two components: an intense, affectionate concern, and an intense sexual desire. The general proposition that we tend to like people whose behavior is rewarding to us may sometimes apply to romantic love and sometimes may not.

A two-component theory of emotions provides one theoretical explanation of the determinants of love: Any variable that increases your level of physiological arousal or increases your tendency to label your arousal as love would intensify the amount of passion you would experience. Thus the first step in generating passionate love is to generate physiological arousal. This arousal can be caused by a variety of unpleasant or pleasant emotional experiences, including fear, frustration, and sexual arousal. Once a person is physiologically aroused, our culture encourages people to interpret that arousal as love whenever circumstances permit.

Why do people court and sometimes marry the people they do? The popular concept that romantic love serves as the basis for most marriages—at least for men—has been supported. Correlational studies of engaged and married couples have also shown the importance of proximity, similarity, and complementarity. However, as a relationship develops, the determinants of attraction may differ. One theory of marital choice holds that a couple progresses through three stages before deciding to marry: (1) a so-called *stimulus stage* in which people are attracted on the basis of what can be seen, (2) a *value stage* in which the couple is concerned with evolving compatible values, and (3) a *role stage* in which the partners are concerned about the adequacy of the fit between themselves.

2. Patterns of Interaction Regular patterns of behavior emerge in dyads. In a marital relationship the general cultural context and expectations concerning the marital status, roles, and norms of husbands and wives are both important determinants of the ultimate marital structure. The personalities of the dyad members and the rewards and punishments attached to behavior also influence the patterns of action that will emerge.

Although the evidence is sparse, some theorists have speculated that there are three main bases for conjugal power or *status* in a dyad: (1) degree of acceptance of cultural roles and norms about conjugal power, (2) the relative ability to provide rewards and punishments, and (3) relative expertise. All social interaction involves people acting out their assigned *roles*—doing what people in their position are "supposed to do." However, defining roles in the marital relationship may create problems, since (1) people differ widely in their definitions of the husband and wife roles, (2) assignment of the roles may not account for individual differences in people, and (3) in some cases the roles may not accurately reflect the behaviors of husband or wife.

In a marriage the partners agree on what behaviors are expected or appropriate in their family—the so-called *norms*. If either deviates from these norms, the other may become somewhat upset. If the deviancy threatens either the goals of the marriage or the self-esteem of the partners, very strenuous attempts will be made to make the other conform to the norms. Norms emerge because it is very difficult for an individual to ignore what another says. And the expected sanctions for deviation from the norms act as a deterrent to deviation.

Although status, roles, and norms refer to different phenomena, there is *some overlap* between them. For instance, persons with higher status also have a general set of expected behaviors, which accompanies their higher status. Further, although a dyadic structure tends to be somewhat static once it emerges, if either the participants or the situation changes, so does the structure.

3. Functioning Three aspects of dyadic functioning were discussed. First, we saw that *sometimes people see their interaction from the other person's point of view*. This can range from merely recognizing his view to empathizing with him and can take place because of a number of motives, ranging from a manipulative expediency to a less self-centered empathy.

Second, without our necessarily being aware that we are doing so, we tend to treat others as they have treated us. Although *reciprocity* is a general theme in dyadic functioning, there are limits to it. Whether or not we reciprocate depends in part on our own motives and on our assessment of the motives behind the other's actions.

Third, we discussed four of the variables that determine whether a competitive or a cooperative solution occurs when two people *bargain*. The *motives* of those in conflict determine their mode of resolution. In an experimental game the players presumably wish to maximize the joint gain of themselves and their partners or to maximize their gain relative to that of the other. In real-life conflicts the motives may be more complex. In fact, the bargainers may not be fully aware of what they want; their goals may change over time; and they may be more concerned with maintaining their relationship than with obtaining their stated objective.

The *dimensions of the conflict* also influence the incidence of competition and cooperation. In the experimental situation instructions that emphasize the desirability of cooperative modes of playing, higher payoffs for cooperative than for competitive solutions, and longer periods of bargaining all tend to increase the incidence of cooperation. However, increases in the pressure to reach agreement and increases in the total payoffs for cooperation have not had completely consistent effects on the incidence of cooperation.

Communication between negotiators generally increases cooperation. Although the importance of communication is generally acknowledged, improving communication in day-to-day interactions can be extremely difficult.

Tactics also influence the outcome of bargaining. Within reason the *puffing of demands* can be an effective bargaining technique.

Graduated conciliation may also be effective—if the other person doesn't interpret this technique as a sign of weakness. Although the assumption that making and executing threats is a highly effective bargaining technique has been an accepted part of American foreign policy for years, the experimental evidence suggests that at least in some circumstances the existence of threats makes a cooperative solution less likely.

4. Development Over time some relationships change from an initial superficiality to a far more intensive and intimate interinvolvement. If a relationship provides rewards for both parties, if both desire a close relationship, and if the situation permits the relationship to develop, it will probably do so. As a relationship becomes closer, people become less concerned about superficialities and are more likely to do things together, to become emotionally involved, and to exchange intimate information.

5. Dissolution Many couples separate or divorce. Whether or not two people will continue their marriage relationship is largely determined by (1) the relative number of pleasant and unpleasant aspects of the relationship and (2) the strength of the constraints against terminating the relationship. If the pleasant aspects of a relationship (e.g., sexual gains, companionship) outweigh the unpleasant aspects (e.g., disappointed expectations, problems with in-laws), the relationship is more likely to last. If the constraints against termination (such as the fear of loneliness and the pain of divorce) are greater than the unhappiness of those in the relationship, the relationship is also likely to continue.

DISCUSSION QUESTIONS

1. Do you think the majority of your own social interactions are dyadic?
2. Why do you think people who are attractive are seen as being good?
3. Do you have any friends who have attitudes dissimilar to your own on issues that are important to you? If so, what attracts you to these people?
4. In your own dating, which factor do you think is more significant in determining your attraction to a potential date—physical attractiveness or similarity of attitudes?
5. Think about your relationship with a good friend or someone you date regularly to see if regular patterns of behavior, or a structure, have emerged. If they have, describe some of them.
6. In your own relationships and those of others, what changes have you observed as the relationships developed from an initial superficiality to a more intensive interinvolvement?
7. Which of the five explanations of attraction do you think played the most significant part in determining your closest relationships with friends of the same sex?
8. Why do you think people generally prefer people who are similar to them?
9. Think about some of the dating couples you know and observe some that you don't know. To what extent do these couples match in their level of physical attractiveness?
10. Have you ever been in love? If so, what do you think made you fall in love with the person you did?
11. In your interactions with others, have you seen any evidence of reciprocity in interpersonal relationships? Since exact matching is sometimes impossible, how do people go about evaluating the actions of others in order to reciprocate?
12. As we saw, effective communication is very important in maintaining a successful dyadic relationship. There is no recipe for teaching people how to communicate effectively. However, on the basis of what you have read in this chapter and from your own observations, present a set of recommended ways for dating and married couples to increase the level of effectiveness of their communications. In your proposals, you might include ideas for verbal exercises the two

people could use, a plan for analysis of present communication difficulties, and any other proposals that you think could increase the effectiveness of interpersonal communication.

13. Five explanations of attraction were discussed in the text. Can you think of any additional determinants of interpersonal attraction?

14. What do you think most people mean when they use the term "love"?

15. Derive a hypothesis from the two-component theory of passionate love and design a study to test your hypothesis. Include (1) support for your hypothesis, (2) the independent and dependent variables, (3) proposed procedure, and (4) predicted results.

16. Under what conditions do you think mediation by an impartial third party would be helpful in a bargaining situation? When might mediation be detrimental?

17. No one can yet provide a sure-fire set of criteria to predict the chances of marital happiness for a given couple. However, on the basis of what you have read in this chapter and your own observations, try your hand at compiling a list of variables that you think are related to marital success. Indicate your assessment of the relative importance of the variables you list.

18. Write some additional items for the test of romantic love discussed in the text. How would you validate your test?

GROUP FORMATION, STRUCTURE, AND LEADERSHIP

How much of your time each day is spent in class with other students, playing on athletic teams, working on committees, talking with groups of friends, or interacting with your family or other people? If you

are like most people, a very large proportion of your time is spent with others. As writers since Aristotle have observed, man is basically a social animal.

Given the importance of your interactions with others, you may wonder how they come about. How do collections of people become a group? Once they do, how do they evolve roles, status, and norms? Why are some groups so much more tightly knit than others? How does the physical environment influence group formation and function? When and why do leaders emerge? In this chapter we will discuss how social psychologists have dealt with these questions.

Group Formation

Definition of a "group"

Before discussing why people form groups or join an existing group, we should first determine what a "group" is. Physical proximity alone does not make a collection of people a group. Six individuals walking down the same street, for example, do not make up a group, even though they may be close to each other in space. In fact, groups can exist without physical proximity. The moon-bound astronauts and their earth-based associates at Mission Control in Texas functioned as a group even though separated by many thousands of miles. For a group to exist, people must interact with a common goal in mind.

Suppose, for example, a number of people are lying on a beach. Suddenly a man in the water cries for help, and five of the people rush to help him. One runs for a lifeguard; three start out into the water; and the fifth person looks on. Eventually, the man is rescued, and the other five people resume their previous, separate activities.

The aggregate of people lying on the beach is not a functioning group, even though they are physically close to one another. They become a group only when, in concert, they try to help the swimmer in distress. When that goal is achieved, the group dissolves. In order for a collection of individuals to become a group, they must coordinate their activities toward a common goal.

In more permanent groups other characteristics, in addition to goal orientation, may emerge: (1) identification of the members with the group, (2) a structure, including leadership, (3) strong conformity pressures, and (4) changes in the behavior of the individual members as a result of their membership in the group. These are the characteristics of a highly organized group, and they can be seen clearly in one example of a group marriage commune—the Manson "family" (Smith and Rose, 1970). See Box 1.

The simple example of the five men reacting to a swimmer in distress and the more complex example of the Manson family represent the two ends of a continuum of characteristics of "groupness." In between these extremes there is, of course, considerable variation in the extent to which collections of individuals possess the various attributes commonly associated with groupness.

The unifying effects of common goals

What transforms a collection of separate individuals into a group or makes them join existing groups? In general, groups originate or are joined when the members think their best chance of obtaining a particular goal requires their interacting with other people. If a person thinks that he cannot handle a task alone or that it will be accomplished more easily through the combined efforts of several people, he may

BOX 1

THE MANSON FAMILY

In 1967 Charles Manson first began collecting girls for his harem. By 1969 the "family" consisted of approximately twenty people, including fourteen women and six men. To enter into the group, the members had to give up their social hang-ups—especially any sexual inhibitions. All activities and responsibilities were shared, including ideology and bedmates. The members eked out a meager living by renting out horses at a ranch and stealing food. The women of the commune shared the household chores and the raising of the group's children.

The undisputed leader of the group, whose orders were followed without question, was Charles Manson. Belief in Manson's sexual prowess and his philosophical abilities, in the supremacy of nature, and in the decadence of the Establishment united the group. If any member of the group did not subscribe completely enough to the group norms, pressure would be applied. Other members might refuse to have sexual intercourse with him or her, or they might talk at length to the individual. Strong social support was provided by the group members for the family's way of life.

combine with others to form a group. (See Figure 10-1.)

The strong influence of common goals on group formation has been shown in a classic series of studies performed in a boys' summer camp setting (e.g., Sherif, Harvey, White, Hood, and Sherif, 1961). Eleven- and twelve-year-old boys were chosen from different schools and neighborhoods so that there would be no preexisting friendships, which might influence group development. In addition, the boys were all selected from stable, white, Protestant, middle-class families so that prejudices would not affect group formation.

In what the boys thought was simply a summer camp, a number of investigators observed closely the process of group development. In one study, known as the Robbers' Cave experiment because of the name of the location where it was conducted, two separate busloads of boys arrived at the camp and settled into two separate cabins at a considerable distance from each other. During the first week of camp the boys in both cabins were given a number of activities that were very attractive but required cooperative activity in order to be performed effectively. For instance, canoes were placed near the cabins, which were a considerable distance from the water. One boy alone could not transport the bulky canoe to the water, so that if the boys wished to use the canoes, they had to work together.

With no directions or suggestions from the staff as to how they should proceed, the boys cooperated with each other and organized their activities. Elements of group structure, as we shall see later, emerged, as did a group feeling and a feeling of pride in the accomplishments of the group. Each boy's friendship choices were restricted exclusively to the members of his own group.

If common goals can unite a number of individuals into a group, it should follow that conflicting goals will make group formation less likely. This effect was also shown in the summer camp setting. You will recall that two busloads of boys came to the camp. Once two groups had evolved, a tournament of games was arranged between the two groups. It was predicted that since only one group could win the tournament, hostility would develop between the two competing groups, which is what happened. Although the tournament started amid spirits of good sportsmanship, intergroup hostility soon erupted. The boys in each group began to dislike the boys in the other and engaged in name-calling, scuffles, and raids on the other's campsite. Subsequent work has shown that the divisive effects of competition

FIGURE 10-1 The unifying effects of common goals.

are not limited to children. Similar effects have been observed in adolescents (Rabbie and Horwitz, 1969) and adults (Blake and Mouton, 1961).

Once competition between the two groups resulted in intergroup hostility, how could the two groups be reconciled? One possible answer was to provide opportunities for pleasant contacts. For instance, having the members of the conflicting groups eat together in the same dining room or go to movies together would give them opportunities for pleasant interactions, which might, in turn, tend to reduce intergroup hostility. Neat as this prediction seems, however, the tactic didn't work. When the members of the two groups were brought together, they called each other names and threw paper plates at each other.

To unite the two warring groups, the investigators eventually found it necessary to provide common goals for all of the boys at the camp. A series of urgent situations requiring all the boys to cooperate was created. For instance, the water supply to the camp was interrupted, and the boys from both groups had to work together in order to solve the problem. Although working together did not immediately dispel the preexisting hostilities, they were gradually replaced by positive feelings.

Groups may be formed to attain a variety of goals. One may think, for instance, of a group organized to obtain a work goal. If a task is too big for one individual or if it is more easily accomplished by a group of people, people may pool their skills and abilities. For instance, if a professor gives students the option of working together to prepare for a take-home examination, some students might divide the assignment, thereby reducing the work load for each individual, and assign to each student the subject area that he knows best.

Other groups may serve more emotional needs. As we saw in Chapter 5, people frequently want to be with others simply to avoid being alone. It could be argued that the pervasiveness of memberships in clubs shows the

BOX **2**

REASONS FOR JOINING A SENSITIVITY GROUP

Recently, the author surveyed fifty of her students (most of whom were either freshmen or sophomores) in her class in introductory psychology to assess their interest in attending a sensitivity group and their reasons for wanting to participate.

Fifty-two percent of the students indicated that they would be interested in attending a sensitivity group if one were available; 27 percent indicated they were undecided; and 21 percent said they would not be interested. When those who were either interested in attending or undecided were asked why they were interested, they gave the following reasons—listed from the most frequently stated reason to the least frequently given reason.

Reason	Percentage of Students Indicating That This Factor Was Relevant to Their Interest
Curiosity—to find out what happens in a sensitivity group	89
For personal development	84
To be able to relate more deeply to others	84
To gain insight into myself	82
To see how others view me	78
Because of interest in the field of psychology	54
To resolve personal problems	38
To make friends	36
Because friends or acquaintances have participated	18

intensity of this desire. Groups may serve other emotional needs too. To obtain a feeling of status, college girls may join a sorority (Willerman and Swanson, 1953). To be able to let themselves go without fear of punishment, a group of middle-aged men may attend an American Legion convention together. To obtain excitement, adolescent boys may join gangs.

In real life most groups serve a variety of goals. For instance, a girl might have joined Charles Manson's family for one or more of the following reasons: (a) to find sanctuary from the outside world, (b) to be with others who are similar, (c) to arrive at a greater understanding of herself, (d) to try to build a new and revolutionary way of life, or (e) to gain easy access to drugs and sex.

People, of course, may not always be aware of their reasons for joining a group. For instance, women who claim they are joining volunteer organizations because of the charity's goals may really be joining because they are lonely or desire status. Men in a business setting may think their meetings are primarily work-oriented while other motives are also being served. People at business meetings may hold back criticisms for fear of alienating the other members of the group, or they may compete with one another, to the detriment of the effectiveness of the group, in order to gain status. Thus the single-minded work group, objectively and rationally pursuing its goals, may be an abstraction seldom seen in real life (Bion, 1959).

The reasons for belonging to a particular group may also vary from member to member. One woman working for a charity may be involved because of genuine concern; another may be there simply because her neighbor belongs and it is therefore easy to attend meetings. For an analysis of the various reasons why students might wish to attend a sensitivity group, see Box 2.

Other variables in group formation

Given that specific individuals have some motivation to obtain a common goal, their evolution into a group may also be influenced by other variables. The *physical proximity* of individuals makes their formation into a group more likely. As we saw in Chapter 9, proximity is a powerful determinant of attraction. In the study of friendships in a housing project for married graduate students, the residents were most friendly with those who lived closest to them (Festinger, Schachter, and Back, 1950). The closer people live, the easier it is for them to interact with each other. Since one interacts more frequently with people who are close, he is more likely to have pleasant experiences with them. Knowing that a person lives close may make you and the other person try harder to be pleasant. If people who are geographically close to one another share a common goal, they are highly likely to become a group. Further, if a common goal did not exist before interaction, one may emerge in the process of interacting, as the people come to know one another and are attracted to one another. The power of proximity in group formation has been shown repeatedly. In one study of juvenile gangs, for instance, it was found that the members of each gang tended to consist mainly of boys living in the same neighborhood (Ahlstrom and Havighurst, 1971).

Similarity of members has also been found to influence group formation. Again, as we saw in Chapter 9, similarity is an important determinant of interpersonal attraction. A study of the patterns of gangs in one city showed that gangs usually had an ethnic basis—blacks in one, Puerto Ricans in another, and so on (Ahlstrom and Havighurst, 1971). In the dangerous but dull world of the inner city, boys are very likely to see that their best chance for protection and relief from monotony lies in their associating with others. And the others they are most likely to see are either those who are of a similar background or those who live in the neighborhood.

Individuals are also more likely to form groups in *highly stressful situations.* This phenomenon has been observed repeatedly. Disaster victims, for instance, are likely to work together with neighbors and friends to find shelter and rescue victims (Quarantelli and Dynes, 1972). During the student strikes and riots of 1969–1970 over the United States' invasion of Cambodia, at the University of California at Berkeley and at Stanford University, students who rarely, if ever, spoke with one another, organized themselves into work groups—putting out leaflets, setting up rumor-control centers, and so on (Zimbardo, 1972, personal communication). When people are under stress, it may become very clear that the best way to survive is to work with others, who can provide physical and emotional support. In a disaster situation one person may be unable to perform the demanding work of rescue; in a military setting the risks of combat may make group formation very adaptive.

There are limits to the group-inducing effects of stress, however. If the level of stress is too high or if the individual feels that he can better fend for himself alone, he may be more likely to remain independent of others. The incidence of group formation appears to have been relatively low among individuals exposed to the terrible deprivation of a concentration camp (Bettelheim, 1943). At the edge of survival and in the depersonalized setting of the concentration camp, individuals may have been unable to focus on more than their own immediate concerns.

Combat units in the Vietnam War have been observed to be less unified than those in World War II or the Korean War (Bourne, 1970). Two possible explanations have been offered for this reduction in group spirit. One is that the rotation system used in the Vietnam War, which guaranteed each soldier that he would be returned to the United States at the end of twelve months (or thirteen months if he was a Marine), tended to make the war a more individualized event for each man. The other explanation is that communications with the United States were much better in Vietnam than they were in previous wars. The mail service was more efficient, and it was possible to telephone the United States. Thus preexisting emotional ties could be used to meet some of the soldier's emotional needs (Bourne, 1970).

Subgroup formation

We have seen evidence consistent with the general hypothesis that people form groups or join existing groups when doing so serves their goals better than independent activity. Once a group is formed, the same processes that resulted initially in the formation of the group may result in the formation of subgroups. People form subgroups within larger groups if doing so serves their goals better than alternative courses of action. In a group of eighteen to twenty members, subgroups may be formed to allow the warm and intimate human contact that is possible in groups of five or less (Theodorson, 1953). (See Figure 10-2.) In a classroom setting small committees of students may be formed because communication is more efficient than in the overall class setting. In work settings subgroups may form because the workers are doing different tasks or because of physical proximity (Roethlisberger and Dickson, 1939). Subgroups may also be formed in voluntary organizations, such as the staff of a college newspaper, on the basis of relative compatibility and similarity of interests.

In certain situations some members of a group may form a *coalition*—a subgroup of people acting jointly to improve the outcome of their activities at the expense of others in the group (Thibaut and Kelley, 1959). Thus in a group of five card players, two may unite to gain mutual advantage over the other, uncoordinated players. Research has shown that a number of conditions make the emergence of coalitions more likely. The probability of the coalition's success will determine whether or not members will coalesce (Chertkoff, 1966). Further, the success or failure of the overall group in attaining its goals will influence the incidence of coalitions within the group. If the group has failed to attain its purpose, coalitions are more likely to evolve (Michener and Lawler, 1971).

Summary and conclusion

Physical proximity alone does not make a collection of people a group. In order for a group to

FIGURE 10-2 In the large setting of a clubroom, club members and their guests are likely to divide into subgroups. (George W. Gardner)

exist, its members must interact with a common goal in mind. In general, both groups and subgroups will tend to be formed when doing so serves the purposes of the members. When some motivation toward a common goal exists among a given number of individuals, their evolution into a group is made more likely by three other variables: their physical proximity, their similarity, and their being in a highly stressful situation.

Although we understand the general principles underlying the formation of both groups and subgroups, the evolution of groups cannot be predicted without an understanding of precisely those situations and conditions that make people feel group membership best fits their needs. Analyzing a group after it is formed and showing how group membership fits the goals of the individuals does not enable us to predict when a group will be formed. How, for instance, could one have predicted that the members of the Manson family would choose one another rather than other people?

With the exception of a few experimental studies, most of the evidence on variables that influence group formation is observational. Experimental evidence on the effects of the variables discussed in this section might enable us to understand better the exact processes involved. Under what circumstances, for instance, would increasing an individual's level of stress influence his desire to join a group? And what would be the effect of other variables—such as the structure of the group—on its attraction for the individual?

Group Structure

The elements of structure discussed in connection with the dyad also emerge in larger groups. With increasing size, however, comes increasing complexity and variability. As we shall see, the *roles, norms,* and *status* relationships become more organized, and the tasks of the various group members become more specialized. Other elements of structure may also vary as group size increases. *Group cohesiveness,* or the attraction of each member to the group, may be of more concern in groups than in dyads, since there are some indications that attraction to the group tends to decrease as

groups increase in size (Thomas and Fink, 1963). Further, *physical space* also plays an important part in determining the regular patterns of behavior that emerge in groups.

The development of roles, norms, and status

The Determinants of Overall Structure In any group the structure that is likely to emerge is determined chiefly by: (1) the requirements for efficient group performance, (2) the abilities and motives of the group members, and (3) the group's physical and social environment (Cartwright and Zander, 1968). For example, in the summer camp study the group's goal was to cope with the tasks required in the camp setting, and the structure pertained primarily to the division of work tasks. Roles emerged according to individual skills and personal characteristics as the boys divided their work. Boys who excelled in cooking took responsibility for meal preparation, and others who excelled in athletics led athletic activities. Some seemed to take a disruptive part, goofing off or teasing at inopportune times, and others consistently had good suggestions and contributed the skills that the group needed.

Gradually, in the give-and-take of social exchanges over a period of several days, the roles ascribed to the various group members began to stabilize, and a status hierarchy emerged. One boy in each group began to emerge as a leader, exercising control in a number of different situations; other boys assumed their ranks throughout the middle levels of the status hierarchy; and still others drifted toward the bottom of the hierarchy. One event that occurred during this formative period illustrates concretely the forms that the various roles and statuses assumed:

During a hike in the woods, the boys started to get hungry. They had been supplied with unprepared food. One boy started to build a fire, asking help in getting wood. Another attacked the raw hamburger to make patties. Others prepared a place to put buns, relishes, and utensils. Two mixed soft drinks from flavoring and sugar. One boy stood around without helping and was told by several others to "get to it." Shortly the fire was blazing and the cook had hamburgers sizzling. As soon as they became browned,

BOX **3** ROLES IN A SENSITIVITY-TRAINING GROUP

In one study of four sensitivity-training groups (sometimes referred to as T groups), seven roles, or styles of behavior, emerged. These groups focused on the need of each individual to learn about himself and his relationships with other people in a setting in which the leader, or "trainer," refused to give the group a precise structure (Mann, Gibbard, and Hartman, 1967). The different roles reflect different individual reactions to this approach and reveal some of the processes at work in sensitivity groups. They are reported in detail below:

"(1) *Hero*. One male member of the group takes over the effective leadership of the group, from which the trainer has abdicated, in the early stages. While accepting the trainer's suggestion that the group should study itself, he rebels against the trainer's authority and resists a dependent role. The rest of the group is hostile to the hero and asks the trainer to suppress him, which is refused. Even-

tually he is integrated into a cooperative and working group.

"(2) *Moralistic resister*. Another male member rejects the task of seeking personal change through analysis of the group. He is anxious and rebellious, and acts as spokesman for the group in favor of "balanced, sane discussion," and seeks a type of group interaction which is characterised by more nurturance and control.

"(3) *Paranoid resister*. A similar pattern to the last was found in all groups, in a more rebellious and paranoid reaction to the unexpected and incomprehensible behavior of the trainer. The paranoid resister is not popular, becomes hostile to the group, but is the main spokesman against T-group procedures in the group.

"(4) *Distressed females*. Most females in these groups are less active than the males; they are passive and dependent on the leader, and do not accept responsibility to get on with the defined

task. Toward the trainer they tend to be loyal and flirtatious.

"(5) *Sexual scapegoat*. An inconspicuous male member becomes the centre of attention at one point in the group's development. He is uncertain of his masculinity and asks the group to study him. He is loyal and dependent towards the trainer, while finding the latter rather frightening. He seeks the company of the distressed females and may become their spokesman.

"(6) *Male enactors*. Some of the male members accept the T-group task, and work together with the trainer, treating him as a colleague. Their initial rebellion gives way to loyalty.

"(7) *Female enactors*. Some female members similarly accept the group task, but with a more dependent attitude to the trainer and show greater anxiety and depression than the males. They are more sensitive and help to prevent members of the group from being hurt."

[Argyle, 1969, pp. 264–265.]

---

two boys distributed them to others. Several took turns pouring the drink. Soon the cook had eaten and it was time for the watermelon. A boy already ranked low in status took a knife and started toward the melon. Several boys protested. The most highly regarded boy took the knife and started to cut the melon, saying: "You guys who yell the loudest get yours last."

[Sherif and Sherif, 1969, p. 233.]

Group norms also emerged. In one of the two groups in the Robbers' Cave study, a norm of toughness evolved. It became the in behavior to swear, to act roughly, and to ignore minor injuries. In the other group a norm of conventional good behavior—being polite, praying, acting considerate—emerged. Further, as a more clearly differentiated structure evolved in the groups, each group developed its own nicknames, special jokes, special places, and so forth. For instance, in one group the tough and good-looking leader was named Baby

Face in honor of the gangster Baby Face Nelson (Sherif, Harvey, White, Hood, and Sherif, 1961).

In other types of groups with different members, different group goals, and a different environmental setting, very different group structures emerge from those arising out of a boys' camp. In committees, for example, roles may relate to the division of work; status may be determined by a member's relative effectiveness or by his initial status; and norms may relate to matters directly relevant to the task.

In a sensitivity group setting, the goal of self-discovery and increasing sensitivity in interpersonal relationships determines the existence of a very different structure. Roles may emerge according to the differences in the reactions of the group members to the sensitivity setting. See Box 3. Norms may pertain to the need for honest and authentic expression, and status relationships may not emerge in as clear a form as they do in other groups.

The characteristics of the members and the environment of the group can also determine group structure. If, for instance, some of the members of the group have a high need for structuring a situation, a more elaborate structure may emerge. Similarly, expectations about behaviors appropriate to the group setting may make certain norms and roles more likely to emerge.

Processes in the Emergence of Overall Structure

Exactly how does group structure emerge? Does the structure of all human groups go through predictable stages in its development? There are conflicting theories and evidence on this point.

One theorist has contended that *any* group, irrespective of its setting, will go through the following four phases: (1) initial orientation to interpersonal and task behaviors, (2) intragroup conflict, (3) the development of group cohesiveness, roles, and norms, and (4) use of group structure to perform the tasks required of the group. In the initial "forming" stage the members of the group try to discover, define, evaluate, and test their behaviors with respect to one another and to the group's goal in order to see what is appropriate. In the second, or "storming," stage the group members express their hostility to one another and polarize with respect to interpersonal issues. Harmony reasserts itself in the third, or "norming," stage, in which the group members accept one another, become highly cohesive, and develop norms and roles. Finally, in the fourth, or "performing," stage the group uses the interpersonal structure that evolved in the third stage to accomplish its work goals (Tuckman, 1965).

In contrast, "recurrent cycle" theories of group development hold that groups do not progress through a series of clearly demarcated stages and that groups are concerned with basic issues that may never become fully resolved. For instance, in addition to attempting to complete a task, the group members may be concerned about the distribution of power in the group and the appropriate amount of intimacy between the group members. These concerns will permeate the group and influence the formation of structure, both at the beginning and recurrently throughout the life of the group (Bennis and Shepard, 1956).

A number of studies have been done to test the accuracy of the various theories of group development. In these studies the interactions of a group, usually a therapy or a sensitivity group, are measured over a period of time. The originator of the "forming, storming, norming, and performing" theory reviewed the existing literature on group development and found that the majority of the studies were consistent with his model. However, as he noted, not all types of groups have been investigated. Many of the observations of the different types of groups are impressionistic and based on only one group. Further, the terms used to classify the groups vary from investigation to investigation (Tuckman, 1965).

Although the evidence is not completely consistent, the preponderance of it does indicate that groups develop through a number of stages. Whether all groups in all situations evolve through exactly the same stages is another question.

Permanency of Structure

Once a group structure emerges, it is somewhat independent of the group members. Although the personal characteristics of the individual occupying a particular role influence the way in which he will perform that role, the requirements of the role itself may be stable with respect to a number of different people. No matter who is taking the role of a T-group trainer, for example, he may be expected to do roughly the same sorts of things.

Further, even when the membership of a group changes, the structure tends to remain the same once it has emerged. Even if the structural element is highly arbitrary and extreme, it may persist for a long time. Thus in one study a cultural norm for the description of a visual illusion was developed. Then the original members of the group were removed, one at a time, and replaced by new members. The norm persisted for five generations of subjects, after which it disappeared (Jacobs and Campbell, 1961).

If the tradition is not arbitrary or extreme, it may persist for even greater lengths of time. In one study subjects could play an experimental game in a variety of ways. Two tactics for game play were introduced at the initial session, and then the original members of the group were removed, one at a time. One tactic was easy,

FIGURE 10-3 A graphic example of a highly cohesive group. Physical closeness is an obvious indication of cohesiveness, but there are many other, less tangible ways in which group members may express their commitment to a group. (Eleanor Pred/Editorial Photocolor Archives, Inc.)

reasonable, and functional; the other was functional but more difficult. As you might predict, the difficult tradition disappeared after three generations. However, the easy and functional tradition lasted for eleven generations—the entire number of experimental sessions (Weick and Gilfillan, 1971). If a greater number of sessions had been run, the tradition might have continued unchanged.

If you have doubts about the longevity of traditions, consider the many requirements of academic life. Courses may be required long after their original purpose has disappeared. Class meeting hours may be set because "that's the way it has always been done." The seating arrangement in classes may also be determined more by tradition than by practical considerations.

Cohesiveness

One group on your campus may be highly active and effective. Its members may be deeply involved with the group and its goals, very close to one another, and fiercely loyal to their group. (See Figure 10-3.) In contrast, a second group may be dying on its feet. Few of the members appear for meetings, and there is no enthusiasm for planning any group activities. Its members are not at all involved with one another, do not care about their group, and are not close to one another. The first group would be high in cohesiveness—the overall level of attraction of the members to a group—and the second group would be very low on this dimension. Groups vary widely in their level of cohesiveness. In this section we shall review how cohesiveness is measured and some of the antecedents and consequences of cohesiveness.

The Measurement of Cohesiveness The concept of cohesiveness seems simple enough to understand. In thinking about the groups to which you belong, you may be able to order them roughly along a continuum of cohesiveness. In some the members seem very loyal and dedicated to the group; in others the majority of the members may be indifferent. But if you wanted to measure cohesiveness scientifically, you might have difficulty thinking of a measure that captures this elusive quality.

The technique used most frequently is to measure the attraction of the group members toward each other, and is known as "sociometry" (Moreno, 1953). Each person is asked to indicate the other person he would most prefer as an associate for various activities. Then the proportion of people chosen from among the group members is compared to the proportion of persons chosen from outside the group. (See Figure 10-4 for an example of a sociogram showing how these preferences are portrayed.) This measure provides only an idea of the amount of attraction between the group members; it does not distinguish the individual's attraction to the whole group from his attraction to a smaller set of members within the group. As we saw, groups may break into subgroups in some circumstances.

Other measures have been evolved in an attempt to focus on the individual's attraction to the whole group rather than to the members within the group. For instance, members of a group may be asked to evaluate their group as a whole. In one study the members of a public utility crew were asked to indicate whether or not they agreed with the statement "Our crew is better than others at sticking together" (Mann and Baumgartel, 1952). Or people may be asked to indicate how closely they identify with a particular group. In another study the members of a work group were asked, "How strong a 'sense of belonging' do you feel you have to the people you work with?" (Indik, 1965).

Both the sociometric cohesion measures and the overall rating approaches to measuring cohesion seem to be measuring a part of cohesiveness. However, the studies in this area have not always shown that the two types of indicators are positively correlated—perhaps because of the existence of subgroups within the larger groups (Eisman, 1959).

Antecedents of Cohesiveness Why do some groups give off "good vibes" to their members? If you have ever had the misfortune to be president of a group low in cohesion, you may have wondered what you could do to bring the group back to life. The results of some laboratory and field studies indicate that a number of variables are related to cohesiveness.

The *initiation* into the group may influence the level of cohesiveness. As we saw in Chapter 1, persons who have endured a painful initiation may be more likely to be attracted to a group. The results of several subsequent laboratory studies have confirmed the initiation severity-liking effect. This effect was also confirmed in a study in which the severity of the hell week conducted in twenty-nine fraternities was correlated with the level of cohesiveness in the various fraternities. As might be predicted, the amount of stress in the initiation was highly correlated with the level of organizational solidarity (Walker, 1968). If you want members to stay and be loyal, there's something to be said for making them suffer to get into the group.

Once members have been admitted to an organization, their level of attraction to the group is determined by two general variables: (1) the extent to which the group meets the interpersonal needs of those who belong and (2) the extent to which the group accomplishes the goals for which it was formed.

Several variables influence the extent to which a group meets the interpersonal, affiliative needs of its members. In general, as you might expect, organizations in which the members are considered to be *pleasant* by the other

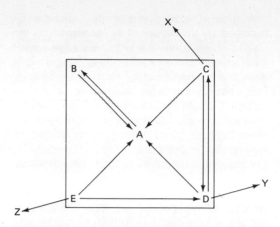

FIGURE 10-4 Sociogram of a cohesive group. Each member of a group is asked to name the individual or individuals he would choose to join him for some specific activity—such as work or leisure activities. The total pattern of choices can be plotted by using letters to represent people and arrows to represent choices in a "sociogram." In the sociogram shown here, the group consists of persons A through E. Persons X through Z are outsiders. (Some or all of these persons, of course, may be involved in the sociometric patterns of others not shown in this particular sociogram.)

Note that Person A is popular, or a so-called star; E is not chosen by anyone (an isolate); and there is mutual choice between A and B, and between C and D. Note also that eight of the choices are from among the group members, and only three outsiders have been designated. Since the number of people chosen from among the group members is significantly higher than the number of persons chosen from outside the group, this sociogram shows a highly cohesive group. (The direction in which the arrow points indicates the person chosen.)

members have been found to be highly cohesive (Lott and Lott, 1965). Also, as you might predict from social comparison theory, groups in which there is *similarity* in values, interests, and beliefs that are important to the group members have been found to be highly cohesive (e.g., Zander and Havelin, 1960). However, when an issue is irrelevant to the group's functioning, similarity may not be related to cohesiveness. In one study of industrial work groups, for instance, similarity of age and the educational level of the group's members was not related to the group's cohesiveness (Seashore, 1954).

A group's attractiveness may also be influenced by the nature of its *leadership*. In the United States a number of studies have shown that persons are more attracted to groups with a democratic, participatory form of leadership. For instance, college students in a group-centered classroom rated their class more favorably than did students in a leader-centered class (Bovard, 1951). Although most Americans may prefer a democratic form of leadership, people with different cultural backgrounds, values, and attitudes may prefer other forms of leadership. The situation may also determine whether or not people are more attracted to groups with a democratic form of leadership. Getting a job done in an emergency may require a dictatorial leader who has the brains or brawn to get the job done.

Other properties of a group may also influence its level of cohesiveness. Groups with a pleasant, warm, accepting feeling, or *atmosphere,* may be more likely to be cohesive (Dittes, 1959). As the *size* of a group increases, its cohesiveness decreases (Porter and Lawler, 1965). Since larger groups are more likely to have difficulties in achieving adequate communication and coordination between the members, the use of inflexible, bureaucratic rules will probably increase as the size of the group increases.

The extent to which a group accomplishes the goals for which it was formed also influences the level of its cohesiveness. If a number of the members have joined a group to attain a particular goal, then the attainment of that objective would be expected to increase the group's cohesiveness, unless, of course, the achieving of the goal ended the reason for the group's existence. Nothing may be quite so attractive to its members as a winning team. In general, this is what has been found (Lott and Lott, 1965). However, as those of you who follow sports may have noticed, under some circumstances the members of a losing team may be highly attracted to their group. The results of some experiments have also shown this paradoxical failure-cohesion effect (e.g., Wilson and Miller, 1961). This effect may be the result of the time and effort the members of the group spent as they jointly worked on the project. Or it may be a question of misery loving company. Or it may be that the failure-cohesion effect occurs when the members of the group feel that the group is not responsible for its failure.

Threats, irrespective of whether they arise from natural disasters, war, or competition with another group, also increase the level of group cohesiveness in much the same manner as they make group formation likely to occur. The level of group cohesiveness has been observed to be higher in communities affected by natural disasters than it had been before the disaster (Quarantelli and Dynes, 1972). Contrary to what military strategists thought would happen, light bombing of civilian populations in World War II sometimes increased the cohesiveness and morale of the populations (Janis, 1951). And as we saw in the boys' summer camp study, the threat of losing a prize in competition with the other group increased cohesiveness within each group (Sherif, Harvey, White, Hood, and Sherif, 1961).

Why should threat increase cohesiveness? There are several possible explanations. The common threat to all of the members may make them realize that the group represents their best chance for survival. Or threat may increase cohesiveness by making the members more aware of their "ingroup identity" (Coser, 1956). When the groups were competing in the boys' summer camp study, the boys in each group tended to exaggerate the virtues of their own group and to magnify the vices of the other group. Or the threat may distract the members from minor dissatisfactions with one another and with the group as a whole.

We have seen some of the antecedents of cohesiveness. You may have noticed the effect of these and perhaps other variables in your own observations of why some groups seem to be so cohesive. What is not yet clear is exactly how these sources combine to determine the overall level of group cohesiveness and whether the various antecedents of cohesiveness have different effects on the various aspects of group functioning (Cartwright, 1968).

Consequences of Cohesiveness How does the level of a group's cohesiveness influence the way its members feel about the group and act toward one another? As you might expect, it has generally been found that the members of highly cohesive groups are more pleased with their membership, communicate more often and in a more cooperative manner with one another, and have much more social influence on each other than the members of groups low in cohesiveness. As we shall see in Chapter 11, however, the relationship between cohesiveness and productivity is far from clear.

Almost by definition of the term "cohesiveness," it would seem to follow that the members of highly cohesive groups would be *more satisfied with their groups,* which is what has been found (e.g., Marquis, Guetzkow, and Heyns, 1951). Further, one would expect a *lower rate of absence* and a *greater amount of participation* in group activities in highly cohesive groups. Although the findings have not been completely consistent, this is the general pattern that has emerged (Cartwright, 1968). Further, those who are highly attracted to a group are more likely to assume responsibility in the group, participate more fully in meetings, and remain members longer (Cartwright, 1968).

Less predictably, it seems that there may also be a number of *personal consequences* for the group members arising from the level of cohesion in the group. There is some evidence that the level of cohesiveness is correlated with fulfilling the members' need for security, increasing the members' sense of personal worth, and decreasing the members' level of anxiety. For instance, workers in highly cohesive groups have been found to report less of a tendency to feel nervous or jumpy on their jobs (Seashore, 1954). Other studies have shown that the members of groups high in cohesiveness tend to have a higher level of self-esteem and to feel freer to report embarrassing events to their fellow members (Julian, Bishop, and Fiedler, 1966; Pepitone and Reichling, 1955). Thus groups high in cohesiveness clearly seem to meet the social-affiliative needs of their members better than those low in cohesiveness.

As you might expect, both the *quantity and quality of communications* are related to the level of group cohesiveness. Even when the opportunity for interaction between all group members is the same, there is a higher frequency of communication in highly cohesive groups than in low-cohesive groups (Lott and Lott, 1961). Further, the quality of the communications in groups that are highly cohesive is different from that in low-cohesive groups. In general, the communications in highly cohesive groups tend to be cooperative, friendly, and generally oriented toward coordinating the activities of the various members of the group (Shaw, 1971). On some occasions high cohesiveness creates a freedom to be more natural and less concerned with superficial politeness. In one study the members of an organized athletic team showed significantly more aggression toward the other members of their team than did a group of strangers who did not know each other (French, 1941). As we saw in Chapter 9, with familiarity and liking may come the freedom not to present one's best image. In the setting of a college athletic team, a rough, aggressive teasing may be the socially acceptable way of conveying liking to the other members of the group.

Cohesive groups exert *strong influences on their members,* as a number of studies in this area have shown. For instance, a study of a highly cohesive student housing project showed that the members of the project held uniform opinions and usually acted in accordance with their group's standards (Festinger, Schachter, and Back, 1950).

The observed correlation between high group cohesion and uniformity of opinion has led one psychologist to theorize that all social groups create a pressure toward uniformity and that the extent to which the members of a group attempt to reach consensus is determined by: (1) the extent of the differences in initial opinions, (2) the cohesiveness of the group, and (3) the relevance of the issue to the group (Festinger, 1950).

Before we describe an experiment that tested the effects of these three variables, try to predict the effect of manipulating each of these variables on the group members' attraction toward, and communication with, a group member who agrees with or differs from the attitudes held by the majority.

1. Would the group reject someone whose opinion differed from the majority?
   _____ yes
   _____ no

2. Would a cohesive group be more likely to reject a deviant than a noncohesive group?
   _____ yes
   _____ no

3. Would the relevance of the topic to the group's goal influence the subjects' reaction to deviance?

   _____ yes

   _____ no

4. If a member of a highly cohesive group deviated on a topic relevant to the group, how would his deviation influence the amount of communication the other members directed toward him?

   _____ increase communication

   _____ have no effect

   _____ decrease the amount of communication

In an experiment that was designed to test these variables (Schachter, 1951), students who had previously expressed an interest in joining some clubs that were to be formed were brought into the experimental setting, and each was arbitrarily assigned to one of the clubs. Each of the clubs was oriented toward one of the following topics: psychological case studies, movies, journalism, or radio.

Cohesiveness was manipulated through the assigning of the students to the different clubs. Since all of the students had expressed considerable interest in the case-study and the movie clubs, these were the high-cohesive clubs. Students assigned to the journalism and radio clubs, in which little or no interest had been shown, were in the low-cohesive groups.

Relevance was manipulated by making the task assigned to the members appropriate or inappropriate for the purpose of the club. No matter what the ostensible purpose of the club was, all of the subjects ended up doing the same thing: discussing a fictitious case history of a juvenile delinquent. For half of the clubs—the case-study club and the journalism club—the discussion was made to seem relevant. In the case-study group the relevance was self-evident; in the journalism club the subjects were told that this case was to be used as a basis for a feature story. In the two low-relevance conditions a short time was spent initially doing activities related to the ostensible purpose of the club, and then the case was introduced as a diversion.

The *extent of differences in opinion* expressed by the members of the group was manipulated during the group discussion. In each group (consisting of eight to ten members), there were three confederates who had been instructed previously to play various roles. At the beginning of the discussion, all of the naïve subjects indicated how they felt the delinquent should be treated. Since the case was written to produce a sympathetic reaction, most of the subjects recommended lenient treatment. By prearrangement, one of the confederates, the "agreer," supported what the majority of the naïve subjects said. Another confederate, the "slider," initially disagreed with whatever the majority of the group said and then gradually came to agree with the majority position. The third confederate, the "deviant," started out disagreeing with the majority opinion and continued to express his deviant opinions until the end of the discussion. In total, then, there were twelve experimental conditions. See Table 1.

During the discussion an observer kept a record of who spoke to whom and whether the comment was supporting or attacking. Then, to measure the group members' rejection of the three confederates, the discussion leader indicated that it might be necessary to reduce the size of the club and that each person should therefore list the names of the others he would like to have remain in his club. For an additional measure of the subjects' reactions to the three confederates, the members of the club were asked to nominate club members for one of three committees, which were described as differing greatly in importance.

As you might expect, all three variables significantly influenced the subjects' reactions. The deviant confederate was rejected from future club membership significantly more often than either the agreer or the slider. The level of club cohesiveness and the topic's relevance influenced the subjects' reaction to deviance. Rejection of the deviant was greater in the highly cohesive groups, and when the topic was relevant to the club's purpose, the deviant confederate was assigned to the unimportant committee significantly more often. Further, in the high-cohesive, high-relevance condition (case-study club), there was a tendency for the number of communications between the subjects and the deviant to decrease toward the end of the experimental session.

These findings go a long way toward providing an understanding of why cohesive groups exert so much influence over their members. In everyday life we have all seen what happens to the person who disagrees. Although disagreement may be tolerated or, more rarely, encouraged in some situations, the usual reaction to deviance is rejection. People do not like people who disagree with them. Since we all know this, the more a person cares about others liking him, the more motivated he may be to agree with them. The more relevant the topic is to the issue at hand, the more grating disagreement will be to the group, and the more likely the others will be to try to elicit the individual's agreement, causing him to fear the consequences of disagreement more.

The physical environment

We have seen how several psychological variables, such as roles, norms, and cohesiveness, influence group structure. To this list of determinants of group interaction, we must now add the physical environment.

Territoriality Suppose that midway through your social psychology course, you sit in the chair another student has been occupying all semester. You may have violated the territoriality of the other student. People frequently tend to assume possessive rights about objects in the environment, even when they have no legal right to feel that they own them. Even when students are not assigned seats and when they obviously have no legal claim to them, many college students tend to sit in the same seat class after class. If another student sits in "their" chair, they may be upset, and if they feel strongly enough, they may ask the other person to move.

That people establish territories has been shown in several studies. In one study of nine pairs of sailors, who initially did not know one another and who lived in a small room for ten days, the men showed strong evidence of territorial behavior. At the beginning of the study, their territoriality was limited to fixed geographical areas, such as a part of a room, and to highly personal objects, such as a bed. Later, as they spent more time in the environment, their territory began to expand to include more

Table 1. Conditions in the Club Experiment

Club	Cohesiveness	Relevance	Magnitude of the Difference in Opinion
Case study	high	high	agreer slider deviant
Movie	high	low	agreer slider deviant
Journalism	low	high	agreer slider deviant
Radio	low	low	agreer slider deviant

mobile and less personal objects, such as chairs (Altman and Haythorn, 1967).

Why do people seek a territory? The answer to this question is not clear. Some psychologists have speculated that people seek a territory in order to maintain their own identity. Thus the sailors may have claimed particular items in their environment to maintain a sense of their own separateness (Proshansky, Ittelson, and Rivlin, 1970). Or they may have done so to make their lives more predictable or to seek more privacy. Another explanation is that the allocation of space may be a necessary prerequisite for viable group functioning, as the results of one recent study suggest (Altman, Taylor, and Wheeler, 1971).

Groups of people also establish territories, perhaps for different reasons. Groups of students may establish "their" tables in the student coffee houses or libraries. For instance, one investigator studied the seating preferences of black and white students at two integrated colleges in New York City in 1953, 1963, and again in 1967. Consistently, territoriality was found. For instance, certain tables were consistently occupied by blacks, and some, but not all of these, were consistently avoided by whites (Zimbardo, 1966).

More dramatically, gangs may establish their "turfs," which are open only to them and which they may defend to the death against rival gangs (Whyte, 1943). In New York City the black territory in the 1960s began at Ninety-Sixth Street, which one writer has called New York's Berlin Wall (Pritchett, 1964). The exact boundary may shift slightly, but with few exceptions white gangs tend to stay on their side of the line, and black and Puerto Rican gangs on theirs, thus reducing the risk of overt racial conflict. Although segregation clearly does not have a long-term effect in reducing prejudice, it could be argued that the presence of a territory reduces the probability of immediate racial confrontations (Sommer, 1969).

Territories have important effects on group functioning. Once a group has established a territory, it will go to considerable lengths to defend that territory. Students may make others who sit at "their" table feel very unwelcome. A gang may openly attack a member of a rival gang who wanders into its territory. Individuals also defend their territory, as the results of a number of studies on the tactics of territorial defense have shown (Sommer, 1969). Territorial "markers," for instance, may be used to "reserve" territories. A sandwich wrapped in cellophane may be left on a college library table, or a sweater may be draped over the back of a chair, to ensure that no one else will sit in the space so marked (Sommer and Becker, 1969).

When one is in competition with others, being in one's own territory also seems to provide an advantage. It has long been observed that animals behave in a dominant manner on their home ground and usually win a conflict with an intruder. The same effect seems to obtain with people. The first principle given in police interrogation manuals is *never* to interrogate a suspect on his home ground. Always get him to the station, which is unfamiliar to the suspect but familiar to the detective (Inbau and Reid, 1962). Baseball coaches have long been aware of the advantage of playing in the hometown. Not only do the members of the team have loyal hometown fans, they also know the area better (Sommer, 1969). And they may simply feel more confident when on their home ground, as the results of one study suggest. When two male college students negotiated in one of the two men's dormitory rooms, the subject whose room was being used was more likely to win the negotiation (Martindale, 1971). As lawyers have suspected for a long time, whose office is used for negotiations may have a powerful effect on the outcome.

Physical Distance As we saw in Chapter 8, when people interact with one another, they are very careful to maintain an appropriate distance between themselves. If you come too close to another person, say an inch away from the face of a stranger, or stand too far away, say twenty feet, you will become aware of the disruptive effects of inappropriate spacing. The amount of physical space between people influences their interaction to a surprisingly large extent.

If you sit too far away from another, you have trouble interacting. Suppose, for example, that you belong to a four-man committee, which typically sits around a twenty-foot table, with two members sitting on either side and one on each end. The excessive distance between the committee members may interfere with the group's effective functioning, so that the group never really "gets it together."

If you sit too close, you will also have difficulty. Invading another person's personal space—that area around him that he feels belongs uniquely to him—produces a variety of negative reactions, ranging from simple avoidance to strong retaliatory actions, depending on the situation and the people involved.

To see some of the reactions to the invasion of personal space, some investigators have staged spatial invasions. In one study, done in a university library, subjects were approached by an experimenter who sat down a foot or less away from them. Over two-thirds of the experimental subjects left during a thirty-minute period, whereas only 13 percent of a comparable, control group of students, who were not crowded, left during the same time period. Flight was the most direct response to excessively close proximity. However, other reactions were also observed. Some subjects turned away from the experimenter or pulled in their elbows (Felipe and Sommer, 1966). In a less restraining environment than a college library, with its norms of silence and impersonality, the defense could well become more colorful. If you were in an uncrowded college dining room and someone sat down, uninvited, less than a foot away from you, how would you react? At the least, you might ask him to move. At the most, you might get rather unpleasant about it.

How much space do people try to keep between themselves and others when they interact? As you may know from your own observations, the amount of appropriate distance varies widely from situation to situation. Studies of how people arrange themselves in physical space (small-group ecology) have shown that the intimacy of the interpersonal relationship is a major determinant of what is appropriate distance. As your dating experience may show and as the results of several studies suggest, people tend to sit closer and stand closer to people they know well. In one study, for instance, when subjects were asked to play the part of a theater director and to place live actresses an appropriate distance apart from one another, the distance the subjects selected varied with what they were told about the closeness of the relationship: Friends were placed 15.5 inches apart; acquaintances were set 27.2 inches apart; and strangers were separated by 34.3 inches (Little, 1965).

This spacing study illustrates that the distance the subjects considered appropriate increased as the relationship became more formal. We should note, however, that this study did not deal with the distances people assumed as they actually interacted with one another. There is some evidence to suggest that in live person-to-person interactions, the appropriate distances may be larger. In one study when college students who did not know each other well were sent into a large lounge to discuss assigned topics, they sat approximately 5.5 feet apart (Sommer, 1969). In another study subjects sat 4.75 feet away from another person when they were instructed to be friendly, and 8 feet away when they were told to be unfriendly (Rosenfeld, 1965).

A number of other variables also influence interpersonal spacing. The necessity for cooperative action reduces interpersonal spacing. The members of groups making cooperative decisions have been found to sit closer to one another and to maintain more eye contact with one another than subjects who are not working together (Batchelor and Goethals, 1972). Cultural differences also influence interpersonal spacing. In one study first- and second-grade white children stood farther apart from each other on school playgrounds than did first- and second-grade black and Puerto Rican children (Aiello and Jones, 1971). The amount of stress that individuals are under may influence interpersonal spacing. Subjects under stress conditions were observed in one experiment to maintain significantly greater interpersonal distances (Dosey and Meisels, 1969). You may be able to think of still other variables that in-

fluence interpersonal distance. Under threat conditions or when the environment is noisy, people may tend to stand closer together. In informal situations, such as in conversations at home, people may tend to sit farther apart from one another. As all of the commercials would remind us, unpleasant breath or body odor would be expected to drive people apart.

Avoiding embarrassment can also motivate people to keep space between themselves and others. A student who has not written a required term paper may avoid his professor. Similarly, you may avoid being confined in close quarters—such as an elevator—with someone you know only slightly. In the enforced closeness of an elevator, you may feel you cannot ignore the other person and must talk with him; yet you may not know what to say (Goffman, 1967).

Why does space have such an impact on human interaction? Clearly, certain practical requirements limit the maximum distance possible. People cannot stand so far apart that they cannot hear one another. But within the limits imposed by the senses, what determines precisely how far people will separate themselves from one another? At present there is no precise answer to that question. Most of the studies have been concerned with establishing the normative interpersonal distances. Why these distances are chosen has yet to be studied. It may be that the critical dimension underlying the physical distance selected is the degree to which the other person is seen as related to or as alien from the self. Thus any condition that makes the other seem more a part of oneself may reduce interpersonal distance.

Furniture Arrangement Suppose you are having a party, and you line up all the chairs next to each other, so that the people sitting in them will be seated shoulder-to-shoulder. Will the furniture arrangement influence social interaction? As hostesses have suspected for a long time and as research is gradually showing, furniture arrangement has a surprisingly marked impact on social interaction. (See Psych Quiz 1.) It has been found that people have preferences for certain types of seating arrangements and that, moreover, these seating arrangements really do influence how much people interact.

Seating preference depends on: (1) the social background of those involved, (2) the en-

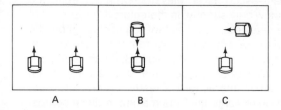
percent preferred this arrangement at a rectangular table (Sommer, 1969).

What the group plans to do also has a major impact on seating preferences. In one study each subject was asked to choose the seating arrangement he preferred for himself and another person from diagrams of a number of different possible arrangements at a rectangular table. For casual conversation the subjects chose either a corner-to-corner or face-to-face arrangement. For cooperative activity with another person, they preferred side-by-side seating, and a face-to-face position was preferred for competition with another person. For separate activity that involved no interaction with the other person (co-acting), diagonal seating across the table was preferred (Sommer, 1969). (See Figure 10-5.)

When larger numbers of people are involved, the function of the group also influences the preferred seating arrangements. In one recent study the subjects were given a task to perform and were instructed either to make individual decisions or to work together and come to a collective decision. They were then free to arrange their chairs anywhere they wished in a large room. As might be predicted, the shape of the seating formations in the two conditions differed. Those given the directions to work individually arranged their chairs along one wall, following a roughly j-shaped line, and did not arrange themselves so that eye contact could be maintained. Those given the directions to work together typically arranged their chairs in a rough semicircle, which allowed the maintenance of eye contact (Batchelor and Goethals, 1972). (See Figure 10-6.)

Why do people prefer certain seating arrangements? The answers given by some of the subjects indicated that their preferences were based on considerations of efficiency. For instance, tasks that require conversation are expedited by seating arrangements that allow the members of the group to remain close to one another and to maintain eye contact (Sommer, 1969). If the comments made by these subjects are accurate, it would seem to follow that manipulating seating arrangements so that they accord with personal preferences would influence social interaction. This is what has been observed in several studies. Thus if people prefer either a face-to-face or a corner arrange-

vironmental setting, and (3) the activity that the group is performing. When people are free to select their own seating location, their choice may reflect their perception of the meaning of different locations as well as their estimate of their own status. For instance, as we saw in Chapter 8, the seat at the head of a table is usually seen as a leadership position. In an experimental study of jury deliberations, it was observed that jurors from professional and managerial backgrounds were more likely to assume this position than were jurors from other backgrounds (Strodtbeck and Hook, 1961).

The environmental setting also determines preferences. Seating arrangements preferred at a round table may not be those that are preferred at a rectangular table. For instance, in one study 63 percent of the subjects polled preferred a side-by-side seating arrangement for conversing at a round table, and only 11

Seating Arrangement	Percentage of Subjects Choosing This Arrangement for:			
	Conversing	Cooperating	Coacting	Competing*
(corner seating)	42	19	3	7
(opposite ends, short sides)	46	26	32	41
(diagonal)	1	5	43	20
(far corners)	0	0	3	5
(side by side)	11	51	7	8
(opposite ends, long sides)	0	0	13	18

*This column does not total to 100 percent because of the rounding off of percentages.

FIGURE 10-5 Seating preferences for different activities at a rectangular table. (Adapted from Robert Sommer, *Personal Space: The Behavioral Basis of Design*, © 1969, Figure 3, p. 62. By permission of Prentice-Hall, Inc., Englewood Cliffs, N.J.)

ment for conversation, it might follow that if they were placed in either of these arrangements, conversation would be more likely to occur than if they were placed side-by-side. This hypothesis has been confirmed. When two chairs were arranged so that they were either side-by-side, at an angle to one another, or face-to-face, the least amount of conversation occurred in the side-by-side condition (Mehrabian and Diamond, 1971). The more direct the orientation is, the more likely eye contact is, and eye contact may be likely to stimulate conversation, since

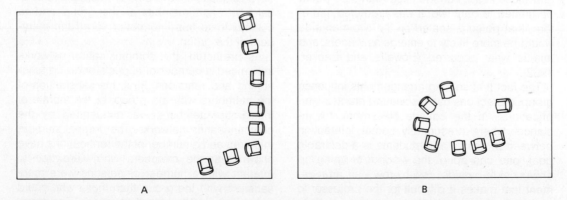

FIGURE 10-6 Arrangement of chairs in groups with different functions. (A) Placement of chairs in the group given directions to reach individual decisions. (B) Placement of chairs in the group given directions to reach a collective decision. (Adapted from Batchelor and Goethals, 1972, Figures 1 and 2.)

495

Group Formation, Structure, and Leadership

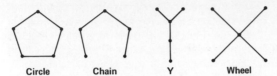

Circle   Chain   Y   Wheel

FIGURE 10-7 Communication networks. Each network represents a separate communication pattern for five subjects, each of whom is represented by a black dot. In the circle each subject has access to the two persons on either side of him and no access to the remaining two members of the group. In the chain three subjects have access to two persons in the group; the other two have access to only one person. In the Y three persons have only one-person access; the subject at the center of the Y has access to three persons; and one subject has access to two persons. The wheel illustrates one-person contact only for four of the subjects and full access to all members of the group for the subject in the center. (Adapted from Leavitt, 1951.)

looking away is awkward and looking at someone without talking is boorish.

Seating arrangements have also been found to influence the emergence of leadership in a group. As we have seen, people are more likely to interact with those they can see directly. If three people were seated on one side of a rectangular table and two were seated on the other, those seated on the two-man side of the table would have a potential audience of three, and those seated on the three-man side would be limited to only two. It was predicted, therefore, that persons seated on the two-man side would be more likely to emerge as leaders, and this is what occurred (Howells and Becker, 1962).

The fact that seating arrangements influence group interactions has fascinating practical implications. In the college classroom, for instance, where presumably social interaction between professor and students is a desirable goal, one can doubt the wisdom of lining up chairs, side-by-side, row-by-row—an arrangement that makes it difficult for the professor to maintain eye contact with many of the students and minimizes the opportunities for interaction among the students.

Communication Patterns Imagine a club in which only the president is aware of all of the activities of the members. How effective do you expect communication would be in such an environment? Just as furniture arrangement influences the frequency of social interaction, so does the level of opportunity for communication among the members of a group. In some groups all of the members feel free to communicate with all of the other members. In many groups, however, this is not the case. It has been found that when opportunities for communication are restricted, the pattern of communication opportunities, or the "communication network," has an important impact on member satisfaction with the group, the way the group processes information, the emergence of leadership, and as we shall see in Chapter 11, work efficiency.

Let us consider in detail the procedures of one classic experiment on communication networks since its procedures have been followed in much of the subsequent research in this area. Five subjects, separated from one another by vertical partitions, were seated around a table. The person with whom a subject could communicate was controlled by slots in the partitions, which could be opened and closed by the experimenter. Four networks of communication were used: the circle, the Y, the chain, and the wheel (Leavitt, 1951). (See Figure 10-7 for a diagram of these networks.)

At the beginning of the experiment each subject was given five symbols from a list of six (circle, triangle, diamond, square, plus sign, and asterisk). Each group had to discover which of these six symbols appeared on the list held by each member of the group and to communicate this information to all the members of the group.

As predicted, the communication networks influenced a number of aspects of group functioning and reactions. First, the satisfaction of the members with the group, or the morale of the group members, was influenced by the communication networks. The original study in this area and a number of the replications have shown that the members who were free to interact with a number of persons were more satisfied with the group than those who could only interact with one other person. The members of decentralized networks (the circle and the chain), in which most subjects could talk with the person on either his right or his left, were more satisfied than those in the centralized networks (the Y and the wheel), in which most of the subjects could interact with only one person. Moreover, in the centralized networks those in the center positions were happier than those in isolated positions (Leavitt, 1951). Apparently, being in the know is pleasant.

Second, the communication network also influenced the way the group processed information. In the centralized networks information was funneled from all of the members to the central person, who then distributed the answer to all of the members of the group. The persons who occupied the central positions and thus received all of the information were frequently named by their groups as the leader. In decentralized networks all available information was transmitted evenly to all of the group members (Shaw, 1954).

Summary

In this section we have discussed various elements of group structure. *Roles, norms,* and *status* emerge in groups, just as they do in dyads. Whether the process of structural development is invariant across all groups or variable is still not clear, but we do know that the form that the group structure assumes is likely to be determined by: (1) the requirements for efficient group performance, (2) the abilities and motives of the members of the group, and (3) the physical and social environment of the group. Moreover, once a group structure emerges, it is independent of the particular group members and may survive unchanged for a considerable period of time even when group membership changes.

Groups vary widely in *cohesiveness,* or the overall level of attraction of the members to the group. Although cohesiveness may be measured in a number of ways, the most frequently used procedure is to assess the attraction of the group members toward each other, a technique known as *sociometry.* The cohesiveness of a group is determined primarily by: (1) the extent to which the group meets the interpersonal needs of those who belong and (2) the extent to which the group accomplishes the goals for which it was formed.

A number of variables influence the extent to which a group meets the *interpersonal, affiliative needs* of its members. Organizations in which the members are considered by the other members to be pleasant and similar are highly cohesive. People are generally more attracted to groups with a democratic, participatory form of leadership. Groups with a pleasant, warm, accepting feeling, or atmosphere, may be more likely to be cohesive. Further, as the size of a group increases, its cohesiveness decreases.

The extent to which a group accomplishes the *goals* for which it was formed also influences the level of its cohesiveness. Nothing may be quite so attractive to its members as a winning team. However, under some circumstances the members of a losing team may be highly attracted to their group—perhaps because of the time and effort the members of the group spent as they jointly worked on the project or because the members of the group feel that the group is not responsible for its failure.

Threats also increase the level of group cohesiveness. A common threat to all of the members may make them realize that the group represents their best chance for survival. Or threat may increase cohesiveness by making the members more aware of their ingroup identity.

Members of highly cohesive groups are more pleased about their membership, communicate more often and in a more cooperative manner with one another, and have much more social influence on each other than the members of groups low in cohesiveness. Members of highly cohesive groups participate more frequently in group activities. Also, being a member of a highly cohesive group has personal consequences for the members. Members of highly cohesive work groups may feel less nervous or jumpy on their jobs than members of groups low in cohesiveness.

Both the quantity and quality of communications are related to the level of group cohesiveness. There is a higher frequency of communication between the members of highly cohesive groups than between members of low-cohesive groups. Further, the communications in highly cohesive groups tend to be cooperative, friendly, and generally oriented toward coordinating the activities of the various members of the group. High cohesiveness may also create a freedom to be more natural and less concerned with superficial politeness.

Cohesive groups exert strong influences on their members. All social groups may create a pressure toward uniformity, but the extent to which the members of a group attempt to reach consensus is determined by: (1) the extent of the differences in initial opinions, (2) the cohesiveness of the group, and (3) the relevance of the issue to the group. All three of these variables have been found to influence the pressures toward uniformity. In everyday life we have seen what happens to the person who disagrees. The usual reaction to deviance is rejection. Since we all know this, the more a person cares about others liking him, the more motivated he may be to agree with them. The more relevant the topic is to the issue at hand, the more grating disagreement will be to the group, and the more likely the others will be to try to elicit his agreement, causing him to fear the consequences of disagreement more.

Another major influence on social interaction is the *physical environment*. People tend to assume possessive rights about objects in the environment, or to establish a given area as their *territory*, in order to maintain their own identity, to make their lives more predictable, or to seek privacy. Groups of people also establish territories, perhaps for different reasons. Once established, territories have important effects on social functioning. An individual or a group will go to considerable lengths to defend a territory. When the person is competing with others in his territory, he seems to have the advantage.

When people interact with one another, they are very careful to maintain *appropriate distance* between themselves. If you sit too far from another, you have trouble interacting. Invading another person's personal space—that area around him that he feels belongs uniquely to him—can also produce negative reactions, ranging from simple avoidance to strong retaliatory actions. Studies of how people arrange themselves in physical space (small-group ecology) show that the intimacy of the interpersonal relationship is a major determinant of what is an appropriate distance. Also, the need for cooperative action, cultural differences, and stress may influence interpersonal spacing.

Furniture arrangement has a surprisingly marked impact on social interaction. People have preferences for certain types of seating arrangements, and these seating arrangements really do influence how much people interact. Seating preference depends on: (1) the social background of those involved, (2) the environmental setting, and (3) the activity that the group is performing. Why do people prefer certain seating arrangements? Tasks that require conversation may be expedited by seating arrangements that allow the members of the group to remain close to one another and to maintain eye contact.

When opportunities for communication are restricted, the pattern of communication opportunities, or the *communication network,* has an important impact on member satisfaction with the group, the way the group processes information, and the emergence of leadership. Members of a group who are free to interact with a number of persons have been found to be more satisfied with the group than those who could only interact with one other person. In centralized networks information is funneled from all of the members to the central person, who then distributes the information to the other members of the group. The person who occupies this central position is frequently named by the group as the leader. In decentralized networks all available information is transmitted evenly to all group members.

Leadership

Imagine a lecture class of one hundred students with no professor or a large corporation with no executives. Or think of a group of rescuers trying to save flood victims with no one person directing and coordinating their activities. Or consider a football team, where the quarterback is the leader. If the quarterback is hurt, even a backup quarterback with equal skills may not be able to move the team. What is lost to a group when its leader is lost? With no overall direction it may have a very difficult time coordinating its activities. Loss of the leader may also have a demoralizing effect. Leadership is vital to the effective functioning of a group. (See Figure 10-8.)

Definition of "leadership"

Although most people have a general notion of what is meant by the term "leadership," a number of different definitions have appeared in the psychological literature. Consider the various ways you use the term, say in thinking of a friend who seems to be a leader, and you may become aware of the many different ways the term can be defined. You may think of leadership in terms of *an individual's characteristics.* The aggressive, dominant, take-charge type of person is a leader in any situation. Or you may think of the *individual's relationship with a group.* A leader may be someone who holds a leadership office, such as the presidency of a group. Or a leader may be the group member who *possesses the highest level of skill for the task at hand.* In a newspaper setting the leader might be the person most knowledgeable about newspaper matters; in a sports setting he might be the most powerful person on the team. Or you may think of a leader as *someone who performs the leadership functions,* someone who can plan the group's activities, act as an example, and so forth.

Although each of these definitions emphasizes a different aspect of leadership, it can be argued that all of them include the common element of *someone who exerts more influence than the other members of the group.* Indeed, this is the definition that has been used most frequently in the literature. However, as you read the results of the various studies in this area, keep in mind the possibility that if leadership had been defined in another way, the results might have been different. For example, the results of one study suggest that members may expect more from elected leaders than from appointed leaders. Elected leaders had to perform better to maintain the members' support than did appointed leaders (Hollander and Julian, 1970).

Emergence of leadership

Clear leadership structures are much more likely to emerge in some groups than in others. If you and three friends are having a pizza, there may be no clear leader. No one has to coordinate the pepperoni and beer. If you are in a large group, with a short time in which to accomplish a complex and urgently desired goal, leadership is much more likely to emerge (Argyle, 1969).

Group size is an important determinant of the emergence of leadership. In small, leaderless groups the members may be able to coordinate their activities without a leader. In larger groups, however, a lack of leadership may result in chaos. This hypothesis is consistent with the findings of one study, in which the members of groups with over thirty members placed more demands on the leader for coordination and tolerated more directive leadership than did the members of smaller groups (Hemphill, 1950).

Decision time and task complexity may also determine whether or not a leadership structure will emerge. If the group members must reach decisions quickly, there may be a greater need for a leader to coordinate the group's activities. Similarly, if the task is complex, there may be a greater need for a leader. Imagine one hundred people at General Motors trying to design an

FIGURE 10-8 How effective do you think this karate class would be if its leader were to absent himself? Each member might continue to practice, but the class would probably lose its identity as a group functioning together. (Charles Gatewood)

FIGURE 10-9 John F. Kennedy and Richard M. Nixon in one of their television debates during the 1960 presidential campaign. Do you think that these men would have risen to a position of leadership in *any* situation? (UPI)

effective antipollutant emission system with no one in charge of the overall task.

The *importance of the activity* may also influence the emergence of leadership. If an activity is either trivial or urgent, the powers of the leader may be increased (Jones and Gerard, 1967). If the members of a group, say a group of teachers, are faced with a series of completely trivial tasks, such as deciding what brand of paper clips to order, they may delegate the authority to make decisions so as not to be bothered with such mundane things. Paradoxically, if the stakes are high, the members of a group may also be more likely to follow a leader. In times of war, for instance, a leader may assume more power than he would exercise in peacetime. And in one experiment subjects who were tested under stressful conditions were influenced more by the leader of their group than were subjects tested under nonstressful conditions (Hamblin, 1958). It may be that only when decisions are of an intermediate level of importance—not too trivial and not too important—that the members of a group are unwilling to concede their decision-making power to the most influential member of the group.

This analysis summarizes only some of the variables that influence the probability of leadership emerging in a group setting. You may be able to think of several other variables, such as the personalities of the members or the general cultural expectations of those involved. If conditions are such that a leader does emerge, and they usually are, who among the members of the group will assume that role? What will he do? What *should* he do to function effectively? The remainder of this section will be devoted to a discussion of these three questions.

Determinants of leadership

Are you a leader? Do you possess certain unique traits, a charisma, which means that your rise to leadership in any group situation is almost inevitable? How do you know whether or not you possess these unique traits? Or do you think that whether or not you become a leader in a given group setting is determined by a peculiar combination of circumstances that arise in that setting and make one member the most appropriate of those involved to assume the leadership functions? In J. M. Barrie's play *The Admirable Crichton,* for example, the lowly butler becomes a leader when he and his employer's family are shipwrecked and forced to eke out survival under novel conditions. Once the group is saved and returned to "normal" society, however, he resumes his position as the lowly butler. Perhaps there are many of us who possess the necessary skills for leadership in certain situations, but only perform them if and when the situation arises.

General Characteristics of Leaders If the main determinant of leadership is the possession of unique leadership traits, it would seem to follow that leaders would differ systematically from followers, regardless of the setting. (See Figure 10-9.)

To find out whether or not this is the case, you might first ask each member of a specific group to rate the other members in terms of their influence as leaders. Next you would test each of the members to determine the extent to which they possess traits that you hypothesize are related to leadership. Finally, you would assess the extent to which the traits measured correlate with the leadership ratings. This approach is known as the *trait approach* to the study of leadership. Between World War I and World War II literally hundreds of trait-approach studies were done in the United States. Almost every conceivable trait, from height and weight to more "psychological" characteristics such as self-confidence and dominance, was correlated with leadership in settings as disparate as nursery schools and prisons.

What was the result of this enormous amount of research? Some characteristics were found to correlate to a slight extent with leadership in the majority of the studies. Leaders tended to be taller, bigger, and heavier, to possess better physiques and health, to have higher energy levels, to be more attractive, and to be slightly more intelligent than followers. Further, they were found to be more self-confident, better adjusted, more dominant, and more extroverted, and to have greater interpersonal sensitivity (Gibb, 1969; Mann, 1959).

Many of the results, however, were inconsistent. There were no traits that correlated with leadership in all of the studies. Further, when correlations were found, they were generally quite low. Since the demands of leadership vary widely in different situations and with different people, the failure to find traits that correlated universally with leadership may not be too surprising.

In contrast to the trait approach, the contemporary *interaction approach* to leadership determinants holds that to predict who will assume leadership in a particular group, one must take into account the characteristics of the group members, the structure of the group, the situation, and the nature of the task facing the group, as well as the personal characteristics that may make one person more likely to emerge as a leader. Leadership is determined by the interaction of all of the members of the group. The person or persons who are most visible and who are seen by themselves and by the other members of the group as most apt to move the group toward its goals will assume leadership (Gibb, 1969).

From this interaction approach it follows that if the situation changes, the person who is acknowledged as the leader of the group may change, and many studies have shown that this occurs. Among naval personnel, for instance, the persons designated as leaders changed according to which officer was involved in

activities most central to the group at a particular time (Stogdill and Koehler, 1952).

Leadership Traits for Specific Situations From the interaction approach it also follows that if the situation remains basically the same, the group leaders will tend to possess common traits (Carter, 1953). In situations in which group membership, structure, goals, and setting are highly similar, the same kinds of people may be likely to emerge as leaders. The results of contemporary research suggest that there may be at least three kinds of situations in which leaders are likely to possess common traits: business, politics, and situations in which manipulative interpersonal bargaining pays off.

Is there such a characteristic as executive potential? Assume that you are in the position of choosing an executive for your corporation— say a senior vice-president for corporate planning. How would you go about doing it? If you followed the procedure that twenty large American corporations, including AT & T, IBM, General Electric, and Sears, Roebuck, have used in assessing more than 70,000 candidates during the past ten years, you would test prospective job candidates for their executive potential. Basically, the procedure is to give persons who are being considered for promotion to executive positions an elaborate series of tests, which simulate the basic situation they would face if they were promoted. Although each program differs slightly, since the exact demands of the different jobs may vary, all the programs contain tests designed to measure what is thought to be a set of characteristics necessary for all executive positions: leadership, ability to delegate authority, control, motivation, ability to sell ideas, originality, and ability to operate under time pressures (Byham, 1970).

A discussion of two exercises included in most of the assessment programs will give you a more precise idea of the tests involved. In the first, the so-called in-basket exercise, the candidate is asked to process an in basket filled with unfamiliar materials typical of the type he would have to handle if he were promoted. How well he does this provides some measure of his insight into unfamiliar problems. In a second test, the so-called leaderless group discussion test, the individual is put into an unstructured situation with a group of other candidates to discuss a topic, and at the conclusion of the meeting all of the members of the group rate the leadership shown by the other members of the group (Bass, 1949).

What are the characteristics of the candidates rated as possessing a high potential for management? Typically, they are highly motivated to advance in their company, show good interpersonal skills, are good in group relations, can withstand stress, have good insight and financial comprehension, and have good intellectual ability (Byham, 1970). (See Figure 10-10.)

The real question is whether men rated as having a high management potential actually perform better than men with a lower rating. Although the validity of the testing varies according to the particular set of tests used, in one study—in which the company was *not* informed of the assessment findings—it was found that 64 percent of the candidates rated as having high potential were promoted to middle management positions during the eight years after the testing, and only 32 percent of the candidates given marginal ratings were promoted during that same time period (Bray and Grant, 1966). Of course, whether or not these tests could predict promotion in other companies is not clear. If they could, it would seem that there might be some validity to the corporate assumption that there is such a characteristic as management potential.

FIGURE 10-10 Samuel J. Lefrak, President of the Lefrak Organization, the largest individual builder-landlord in the country. (Cyril Morris)

If successful executives possess characteristics that are different from others, it may also be possible that powerful *political figures*—men whose whole adult lives have centered on the pursuit of power—may also differ systematically from those who are not involved in politics. Presidents and scientists may differ, but strange as it may seem, Eisenhower, Kennedy, Johnson, and Nixon may all share common characteristics that differentiate them from others. As one writer has suggested, a characteristic that all politicians may have in common is an unusually high opinion of themselves (Mazlish, 1972).

Although there is very little evidence in this area, the results of at least one study suggest that some political men may differ from nonpolitical men. The reactions of twenty-three men who were active in politics in an eastern city were compared with the reactions of a comparable group of men (matched on religion, nationality, background, and business occupation) who were not engaged in politics. Interestingly, the characteristics of the politicians themselves differed according to how they had entered into their political careers. Men who had become involved in politics through the recruitment attempts of party leaders obtained higher than average scores on a test of the need to affiliate with others but otherwise resembled the nonpolitical men. In contrast, men who had initiated their own political activity scored significantly higher than average in their desire for success and power, expressed explicitly their desire for power and achievement through politics, aspired to higher office, and had lower than average scores on a test of the need to affiliate (Rufus, 1968). Although one cannot generalize about all politicians on the basis of this limited sample, it may be that the stereotype of power-hungry politicians has some validity—at least for those who initiate their own involvement.

To the list of specific situations in which those exerting greater influence may have common characteristics, we may add one final possibility—*situations in which coldly manipulative interpersonal bargaining pays off.* In certain situations people who are willing to use any tactics that work—however unprincipled—may gain influence over those who are not so willing.

Since 1532, when Machiavelli's account of

how to control people was first published, his name has been synonymous with an endorsement of the use of impersonally opportunistic tactics in controlling others, a belief in the baseness of most people, and a feeling that there are no absolute moral standards. (See Figure 10-11.) Recently, a test has been devised to measure the extent to which people endorse Machiavellian views—a so-called Mach scale (Christie, 1970). Some of the items from that scale are:

Tactics

High Mach: The best way to handle people is to tell them what they want to hear.

Low Mach: Honesty is the best policy in all cases.

Views about the nature of man

High Mach: It is safest to assume that all people have a vicious streak and it will come out when they are given a chance.

Low Mach: Barnum was very wrong when he said, "There's a sucker born every minute."

Morality

High Mach: The most important thing in life is winning.

Low Mach: All in all, it is better to be humble and honest than important and dishonest.

Presumably, those who endorse high-Mach statements more frequently than low-Mach statements are more likely to use exploitative and manipulative tactics when dealing with others. A series of studies has shown that this is the case (Christie and Geis, 1970).

In one study, for instance, three subjects (one of whom had a high Mach score, one of whom had a medium score, and one of whom had a low score) were told to bargain about the division of $10. The subjects were free to use any bargaining tactics they wished, and they could keep the money after the experiment was over. The only restriction was that the money had to be divided between two of the three subjects; one man had to be left out. Seven groups of three players each were tested.

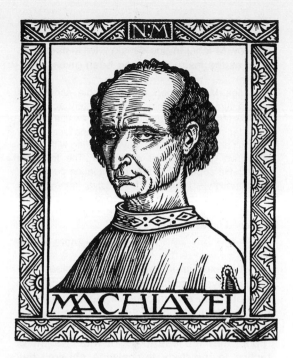

FIGURE 10-11 Niccolò Machiavelli, born in 1469, died in 1527. As you might gather from his facial expression, Machiavelli was a leading proponent of the tactic "whatever works" in manipulating others. (New York Public Library Picture Collection)

If there were no relationship between the players' Mach level and their performance in dividing the $10, you would expect the average winnings for the players at each of the three Mach levels to be one-third of the $10, or $3.33. This was not the case. The average winning for the high-Mach players was $5.57, for the middle Machs, $3.14, and for the low Machs, $1.29 (Christie and Geis, 1970).

How did the high Machs win? Although all of the subjects knew the $10 had to be divided between two of the three players, the low Machs seemed less willing to try to manipulate the other players, and their concern for the ethical problems of the situation may have interfered with their bargaining effectiveness. Since the morality of the situation was of little concern to the high Machs, they opportunistically bargained to form a coalition with one other player and pushed the limits to arrive at an agreement maximally advantageous to themselves. And the middle Machs, as you might expect, fell somewhere between the patterns of the high and low Machs. In one session, for instance, as soon as the instructions had been given:

The high Mach turned to the middle scorer and offered him $4. The middle immediately accepted. The low Mach then suggested that they wait a minute, consider the situation, talk it over, and see if they couldn't arrive at some fair way of dealing with it. The other two gave minimal responses. The low kept talking. He appeared to take the situation personally and seriously—"I don't like to fight over money." Over and over, he emphasized the need to find a fair way to handle the money situation. The high and middle remained unresponsive.

[Christie and Geis, 1970, p. 169.]

In this experiment the stakes were clear to all of the players, so the high Machs couldn't use deception as a manipulative technique. However, when the high Machs have more information than the other members of a bargaining group, they are free to use a wider variety of tactics. In one study, for instance, children, half of whom were high Machs and half of whom were low Machs, were told by an experimenter that they would be paid five cents for each unpleasant and bitter-tasting cracker they could persuade another child to eat. As you might predict, high-Mach subjects were more successful than low Machs.

In this relatively unstructured situation, high Machs used a variety of bargaining tactics. Deception was the most frequently used tactic. The high-Mach subjects were much more likely than low Machs to either distort or withhold information about the cracker. They also used bribery, offering to split the five cents with the other child if he agreed to eat the cracker. Moreover, the high-Mach children were more likely to attribute responsibility for their request to the experimenter: "She wants you to eat the crackers" (Braginsky, 1970).

High Machs do not always gain influence and win. In summarizing a considerable number of studies contrasting the behavior of high and low Machs, two investigators, who have done numerous studies in this area, have noted that only in ambiguous, emotionally arousing, and face-to-face situations do high Machs exert more influence (Geis and Christie, 1970). When no clear-cut procedures have been enunciated,

high-Mach subjects move in and take over. In one study, for instance, involving a leaderless group discussion in which the subjects were given just a very few directions, high-Mach subjects were rated higher in leadership (Geis, Krupat, and Berger, 1965).

In emotionally arousing situations the high Machs keep their cool. For instance, in one study high and low Machs had to bargain about issues that were either very emotionally involving (such as raising the minimum age for drinking to twenty-five) or relatively neutral (such as issuing a new postage stamp). As predicted, there was no difference in the incidence of winning between high and low Machs when the issues were neutral, but the high Machs won significantly more often in the game involving emotional issues (Geis, Weinheimer, and Berger, 1970).

The results of a number of studies also suggest that interaction has to be face-to-face in order for high Machs to do better than low Machs. High Machs seem to be less susceptible to the influence of others and more accurate in sizing up other people and situations. Whereas the low Mach is oriented toward trying to please other people, the high Mach intellectually appraises the situation in order to gain control and structure the situation to his own liking.

Situational Determinants If the emergence of leadership is not completely determined by the inevitable rise to power of "born leaders," what other factors determine it? Your thinking about the leaders in the many groups to which you belong may show you that a number of variables are at work: chance, the cultural and organizational context of the group, the characteristics of the members of the group, group structure, and group goals—all determine which member or members emerge as leaders. (See Figure 10-12.)

Not all leaders are chosen initially by the members of the groups they lead. Some are appointed. Although an appointed leader may eventually be replaced if he is sufficiently incompetent, the appointed individual is likely to be accepted as the group leader. The *power of appointment* was shown in one study. In a group of newly arrived naval recruits, one man was chosen at random to be acting petty officer—a position that involved various minor jobs, such as lining the men up for roll call. Subsequently, when these recruits were asked which man in their unit they would like to have lead them during combat, they chose the sailor who had been designated initially as their leader (Bell and French, 1950).

The *cultural context* can also influence who assumes leadership. Some group members may possess characteristics that are valued by the group in question, making them more likely to emerge as leaders. In one study of the selection of leaders among subjects in a mock jury, persons of high status, such as professionals, managers, and officials, were chosen significantly more often than were persons of low status, such as semiskilled workers and servants (Strodtbeck, James, and Hawkins, 1958). In another study white subjects gave a light-skinned Negro girl significantly higher leadership ratings than a dark-skinned Negro girl (Burroughs, 1970).

The *organizational context* of the group is also an important determinant of leadership. In large organizations the members of a group may prefer as a "formal" leader a person designated as a leader because of the office he holds—someone who has influence with the upper levels of the organization (Pelz, 1951). When selecting their "informal" leaders—men who have no official status but who wield power within the group—the members of the group may be more concerned about the individual's ideas and his liking for the other members of the group (Gibb, 1969). Thus satisfaction with formal leaders seems to be determined by different criteria than satisfaction with the leaders chosen by the group members.

The *pattern of personalities present in the group* influences both the group's preference for particular individuals as leaders and its preference for the kind of leadership exerted. In a classic study it was found that groups of authoritarian subjects preferred leaders who could help them attain their group goals and who did so by exercising their leadership in a strongly directive manner. In contrast, groups of equalitarian subjects preferred a leader who was warm and concerned about the quality of interaction in their group and who did not exercise a strong leadership unless the situation demanded it (Sanford, 1952).

Potential leaders *cannot be too different from the other members of the group*. They may differ slightly—they may be slightly more intelligent or higher in social status—but they cannot be too different. As we saw earlier, someone who persistently disagrees with the majority opinion may be excluded from the group, and certainly he will not be given a leadership position (Schachter, 1951). However, if a person's agreeing is to earn him points toward leadership, the others in the group must perceive his agreement as authentic. If they believe it is opportunistically motivated, his agreement may result in a lowered rating (Rosen and Einhorn, 1972).

The relative *competency* and *success* of the various group members in attaining the group's goals might be expected to influence the emergence of leaders and their retention of power. If attaining the group's goals is important to the members of the group, it would seem to follow that the person or persons seen as most competent and successful would also emerge and remain as leaders. Although the results have not been completely consistent (Jaffee and Lucas, 1969), at least one study has shown the importance of competency (Julian, Hollander, and Regula, 1969).

As we saw earlier, the subject who occupies a central position in the communication network often emerges as a leader simply because he has access to more information and communi-

FIGURE 10-12 "Yes, he's definitely assuming leadership. A case of the right ant in the right place at the right time, evidently." (Drawing by Richter © 1971, *The New Yorker Magazine*, Inc.)

cates more frequently with the other members of the group. This suggests that one important determinant of leadership is the *frequency of communication*. In many group situations, especially classroom discussions and other types of rap sessions, you may have noticed that group leadership often goes to those who talk the most. Since a primary function of these groups is to talk, it may not appear surprising that the most active talkers—those who contribute the most to this type of setting—will lead.

Several experimental studies have tested this common observation. In one study 108 three-man groups met to discuss a variety of problems (Morris and Hackman, 1969). Transcripts were made of the discussion, and a record of the participation of each group member was obtained. After the meetings all of the groups were asked to rate their members on leadership. As predicted, there was a significant correlation between the amount of participation and rated leadership. Of the 154 subjects who talked more than average, 66 percent were rated as above average by the other members of their group. Since the person who talks a lot is highly visible and may be helping his group reach their goals, it seems reasonable to believe that he would tend to emerge as a leader.

But what happens if the talkative person's comments aren't helpful? Doesn't *what* is said influence the emergence of leadership as much as simple quantity? Have you ever been in a class in which a not-too-bright bore monopolized the discussion? Respect is not usually the feeling he inspires. In this study 33 percent of those who participated more than average were rated as below average in leadership. These garrulous subjects who were not seen as leaders were distinguished from those who were by *what* they said. They tended to focus on negative comments about the group's effectiveness and emphasized activities inconsistent with a good group performance. In general, they seemed to reject the group, and the group seemed to dislike them. Of course, since the study is correlational, it is not clear which rejection came first. Did the members of the group move from liking to dislike because of the argumentative and critical nature of the talkative person's participation? Or did the group's initial rejection cause the high participators to become negative? Or did each of these two

factors reinforce the other in cyclical fashion?

Of course, someone's negative reactions to the group may not be the only reason he does not emerge as a leader. Someone who talks a lot and is ineffective—however pleasant he may be about it—may bore the other members of a group and so not be chosen. Or someone who seems to talk just to hear himself talk may irritate others.

As further evidence that a high participation rate alone does not guarantee a position of leadership, it was found that some subjects in these three-man groups were rated as above average in leadership even though they had participated with less than average frequency. Some 31 percent of the leaders were in this low-participation category. The emergence of these persons as leaders is puzzling. As the investigators suggest, it may be that they were seen as leaders because of their physical appearance (they may have "looked like leaders") or because they communicated forcefully at a nonverbal level. Or they could have been chosen simply because they lacked the negative aspects of others in the group. Further, whether or not low participators would emerge as leaders in larger groups is not clear. In a three-man group all of the members have a chance to become familiar with one another, but in a larger group someone who is relatively quiet may not be very visible.

Maintaining Leadership   We have been discussing the determinants of who will *attain* power. But once a leader gets his power, whether by election or by appointment, he must *maintain* it. Observations of informal groups suggest that once leadership emerges, a lot of energy goes into maintaining the status quo (Whyte, 1941).

How do leaders do this? Although there is relatively little experimental evidence on this question, your own observations of tactics leaders use to maintain their power may suggest that a number of strategies—somewhat different from those used in attaining power—are used. Leaders may buy loyalty from certain members of their group through favoritism. Or if the members are dependent on the group and cannot leave, the leader may use intimidation tactics. Or leaders may try to make themselves appear very competent in attaining the group's goals, by publicizing and perhaps exaggerating their own successes. Or if they are high Machs, they may use any number of effective and amoral tactics. For instance, they might create disharmony between members of the group who might possibly rival them for leadership. When reading the next section on how leaders function, keep in mind that behind much of leadership behavior lurks a survival motive.

Summary One early theory was that the main determinant of leadership was the individual's possession of unique leadership traits. Between World War I and World War II literally hundreds of *trait-approach* studies were done. Some characteristics were found to correlate to a slight extent with leadership in the majority of these studies. For instance, leaders tended to have high energy levels, to be more attractive, and to be slightly more intelligent than followers. Many of the results, however, were inconsistent. There were no traits that correlated with leadership in all of the studies. Further, when correlations were found, they were generally quite low.

A more contemporary approach to leadership determinants is an *interaction approach,* which holds that to predict who will assume leadership in a particular group, one must take into account the characteristics of the group members, the structure of the group, the situation, and the nature of the task facing the group, as well as the personal characteristics that may make one person more likely to emerge as a leader. Leadership is determined by the interaction of all of the members of the group. The person or persons who are most visible and who are seen by themselves and by the other members of the group as most apt to move the group toward its goals will assume leadership. Thus if the situation changes, the person who is acknowledged as the leader of the group will change.

However, *if the situation remains basically the same, the group leaders will tend to possess common traits.* The results of contemporary research suggest that there may be at least three kinds of situations in which leaders are likely to possess common traits: business, politics, and situations in which manipulative interpersonal bargaining pays off. People rated high in *executive potential* have been found to be promoted more frequently than men not possessing these traits. Although there is very little evidence on whether powerful *political figures* differ systematically from those who are not involved in politics, one study showed that men who had initiated their own political activity scored significantly higher than average in their desire for power and achievement, and aspired to higher office.

In certain situations people who are willing to use any tactics that work—however unprincipled—may gain influence over those who are not so willing. A test has been devised to measure the extent to which people endorse *Machiavellian* views—a so-called Mach scale. People who obtain high Mach scores have been found to be more likely to use exploitative and manipulative tactics when dealing with others. They may deceive the other person, distort or withhold information about the situation, use bribery, and attribute responsibility for the situation to others. However, high Machs do not always win. Only in ambiguous, emotionally arousing, and face-to-face situations do high Machs exert more influence.

A number of variables in the situation influence the *emergence of leadership.* When people outside the group *appoint* one person as a leader, the appointed individual's chances of being accepted by the group as a leader are increased. The *cultural context* also influences who assumes leadership. Some group members may possess characteristics that are valued by the group members in question. The *organizational context* of the group is also an important determinant of leadership. Informal leaders may be selected primarily because they are seen as liking the other members of a group, while a formal leader's power may be based on his influence with those in the upper levels of the organization. The *pattern of personalities present in the group* influences both the group's preference for particular individuals as leaders and its preference for the kind of leadership exerted. Potential leaders *cannot be too different* from the other members of the group. The *relative competency and success* of the group members in attaining the group's goals also influences the emergence of leaders.

One very important determinant of leadership

is the *frequency of communication.* There is a significant positive correlation between the amount of participation in group discussions and rated leadership. Since the person who talks a lot is highly visible and may be seen as helping his group reach its goals, it seems reasonable to believe that he would tend to emerge as a leader. But frequency of participation is no guarantee of leadership. People who participate frequently but make negative comments about the group's effectiveness do not emerge as leaders.

Once leadership emerges, a lot of energy goes into maintaining the status quo. How do leaders do this? Although there is relatively little experimental evidence on this question, observation suggests that leaders use a number of strategies to maintain power. For instance, they may buy loyalty through the promise of favors, or they may use intimidation tactics.

Leadership behavior

Once a person emerges as the leader of his group, how does he lead? The answer to this question is not as obvious as it might seem. Stereotypes aside, the research results in this area show that: (1) leadership includes a variety of behaviors, and (2) there are a number of different styles of leadership, the relative effectiveness of which depends largely on the situation.

Varieties of Leadership Behavior If you wanted to find out what leaders actually do, how would you proceed? A fairly straightforward approach, followed in a number of studies, is to ask group members to describe the behavior of their leaders. In one such study, involving the members of Air Force crews, the two predominant themes of leadership behavior that emerged were: (1) *consideration,* the extent to which the leader was characterized by warmth and trust in his personal relationships, and was willing to explain his actions to his subordinates and allow them to participate in decision making, and (2) *initiating structure,* the extent to which the leader organized the work done by the group, set standards of performance, followed routines, and made sure that the relationship between

BOX 4

Analyzing social interactions is a very complex task. Robert Bales (1970) has conducted a series of observational studies of the patterns of social interactions in conferences. In these studies he has classified the types of remarks and responses people made as they interacted to solve a problem. Typically, the subjects were told at the beginning that they were participating in a study of the processes of group discussion and that their behavior would be observed by people behind one-way mirrors. Then the groups, ranging in size from two to seven, were given a five-page report containing facts relevant to the case to be discussed—usually a complex human relations type of problem. The subjects were not told whether or not they had all been given the same information. They were given forty minutes in which to reach a consensus judgment.

All aspects of the group interaction, including words, gestures, and facial expressions, were recorded and analyzed. (Generally, fifteen to twenty acts occurred each minute.) After conducting a number of studies, Bales evolved four main categories into which all of the group members' behaviors could be classified: positive reactions, problem-solving attempts, questions, and negative reactions. These four main categories were divided further into three subcategories, so that there was a total of twelve categories. As shown in Figure A, 56 percent of the responses fell into the problem-solving category; the other 44 percent were distributed throughout the remaining three major categories. Thus the discussion process seemed to consist of two major components: problem-solving suggestions and reactions to the suggestions.

The relative frequency of behaviors falling in the twelve categories varied as the session progressed. During the first third of the meeting, information giving occurred most frequently—probably because each member of the group was uncertain as to whether or not his information on the case was the same as

INTERACTION IN CONFERENCES

			Percent
Positive Reactions	Shows Solidarity		3.4
	Shows Tension Release		6.0
	Shows Agreement		16.5
Problem-Solving Attempts	Gives Suggestion		8.0
	Gives Opinion		30.1
	Gives Information		17.9
Questions	Asks for Information		3.5
	Asks for Opinion		2.4
	Asks for Suggestion		1.1
Negative Reactions	Shows Disagreement		7.8
	Shows Tension		2.7
	Shows Antagonism		.7

0 10 20 30

A

FIGURE A. Types of acts in social interaction may be classed in four main categories: positive reactions, problem-solving attempts, questions, and negative reactions. The averages for 96 group sessions show that 56 percent of the acts fall into the problem-solving category. (Adapted from Robert F. Bales, "How People Interact in Conferences," *Scientific American*, March 1955, p. 33. Copyright © 1955 by Scientific American, Inc. All rights reserved.)

that given to the others. During the middle portion of the meeting, opinions were usually given most frequently. The frequency of suggestions was generally low in the first third of the meeting and highest during the last part of the meeting. Interestingly, the rate of both positive and negative reactions increased as the meeting progressed. The increase in negative reactions may be due to difficulties within the group in reaching a consensus. Once the decision point was reached, the incidence of positive reactions, including joking and laughing, which indicated solidarity and tension release, increased sharply. (See Figure B.)

After the group meeting was over, the members of the group were interviewed and asked to indicate who had the best ideas. Usually, this person had talked more than the other members of the group and provided more than the average number of suggestions and opinions. Subjects were also asked whom they liked best. Typically, the person who was liked had a higher than average rate of showing tension release (by laughing and smiling) and showing agreement.

FIGURE B. Group progress toward a decision is characterized by a change in the frequency of different types of social acts as the meeting wears on. Information giving decreases while suggestions and positive and negative reactions increase. (Adapted from Robert F. Bales, "How People Interact in Conferences," *Scientific American*, March 1955, p. 35. Copyright © 1955 by Scientific American, Inc. All rights reserved.)

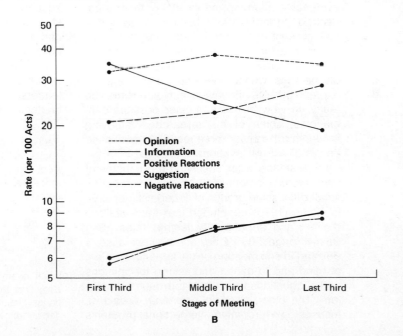

B

himself and his subordinates was clearly understood (Halpin and Winer, 1952). A number of other studies have confirmed the importance of these two factors in leadership behavior and have established that the two can act independently. A supervisor can be high in one and low in the other (Fleishman and Harris, 1962).

The results of these questionnaire studies depend entirely on what the group members see as leadership behavior in their own situation. Thus it is not surprising that in settings substantially different from the military setting of an Air Force crew, other leadership behaviors have been noted. For instance, when employees in an industrial setting were asked to describe their supervisor's behavior, five leadership patterns were noted: (1) his planning, organizing, and controlling of the group's work, (2) his use of control and authority, (3) his concern with maintaining good interpersonal relationships with his followers, (4) his concern with his own feelings of insecurity, and (5) his motivation toward self-achievement (Wofford, 1970).

The findings about the varieties of leadership behavior yielded by such questionnaire studies constitute useful information for group and leadership planning, and they are relatively easy to obtain. There is also some preliminary evidence confirming the validity of these studies (e.g., Stogdill, 1969), but they do nevertheless present the general difficulties of a questionnaire approach. One principal problem is that the accuracy of the results depends entirely on persons whose memories and ability to express complex behaviors may sometimes be faulty. In view of this and other possible deficiencies, some of the researchers studying leadership behavior more recently have relied on the direct observational technique.

For instance, after observing the patterns of interpersonal communication in a number of small discussion groups of college students, R. F. Bales (1970) concluded that there are two distinct and separate leadership roles. (See Box 4, page 508.) One, a *task specialist,* is devoted to commenting on the specific problem at hand and to giving and asking for opinions and suggestions for ways to approach the problem. The other, a *social-emotional specialist,* focuses on overcoming interpersonal problems

in the group, showing the solidarity of the group, and releasing tension through humor. If a group is to be effective, both of these roles must be filled. Whether or not one person usually fills both roles is not yet clear. In Bales' observations (1955) the roles were occupied by two different students. In other situations, however, in which the members of the group were highly committed to the task, one person has been observed to fill both roles (Turk, 1961).

In situations other than college discussion groups, additional leadership behaviors have been noted. What a leader must do is largely determined by the requirements of the situation. For instance, a successful T-group trainer has to become involved in the group, help the group members work through their encounters, make sure that none of them are psychologically damaged, and lend support to the group members (Aronson, 1972). In contrast, to be the successful mayor of a large American city, a person may have to become adept at the art of using political patronage, making deals with dissidents, and using the large city bureaucracies (Royko, 1971). See Box 5 for one psychologist's concept of what an effective committee chairman should do.

That leadership behaviors do vary from situation to situation has been shown in a number of studies (e.g., Carter et al., 1950). In combat rifle squads, for instance, three aspects of leadership behavior were observed: (1) a command and modeling function, (2) a therapeutic function, and (3) a housekeeping function (Clark, 1955). (See Figure 10-13.) In a street gang known as the Pirates an even wider variety of leadership behaviors—spread among four leaders—was observed:

Paulie was the man with "the final say in all important decisions." He was older than the others, held himself aloof, but masterminded the gang's burglaries and robberies. He established contact with older neighborhood gangs and with fences to sell the stolen goods. Like generals in battle, he directed but never jeopardized himself by taking part physically in the "hits." *Lulu* was second in command, and was the tactician and burglary expert. He would plan the details of the burglaries, and "had a tremendous talent for anything connected with tools or electricity." *Solly* was the diplomat who dealt with the frequent police "interference." "Solly played the part of the decent fellow commiserating with the police over the

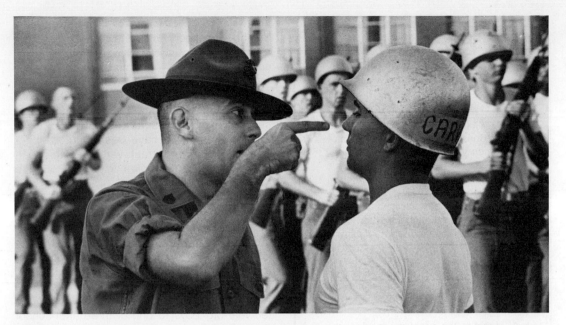

FIGURE 10-13 Leadership in the Marine Corps. The drill sergeant is exhibiting one of the key functions of leadership—command. (Richard Lawrence Stack/Black Star)

bad habits of the other Pirates." He had a talent for listening quietly to a long harangue from a cop and then pacifying him with an earnest but noncommital answer. *Blacky* occupied a very unusual position: "most of the time he played the clown, the butt of all the gang's earthy humor, which often took a brutal turn." But Blacky was supreme in the domain of sex, the field where the others were sadly lacking, and they looked to Blacky for leadership in matters relating to the opposite sex. He made available his personal "stable" of three or four girls to special friends in the gang.

In this way "the division of power allowed completely different personality types to function efficiently."

[Block and Niederhoffer, 1958, quoted in Ruch and Zimbardo, 1971, p. 485.]

In situations where the members of the group feel emotionally dependent on the leader, his main function may be to meet these emotional needs (Bion, 1959). For instance, a group of psychiatric patients who feel inadequate and immature may look mainly to their therapist-leader for his strength—his supposed omnipotence and omniscience. Nor is emotional dependency on the group leader limited only to therapy sessions. Citizens may feel this kind of emotional dependence on elected leaders, as the intense emotional reactions to President Kennedy's murder showed (Cole, 1965). And as seen in Chapter 11, sometimes the group's emotional dependence on a leader can cripple the members' ability to analyze his proposals.

In still other situations the leaders' behavior may differ very little from the behavior of other group members. For instance, in one study in which the behavior of four-man groups was observed, leaders did not differ significantly from followers in the frequency of comments indicating confusion, aggressiveness, and friendliness or in the amount of their support for the proposals made by others (Carter et al., 1950). In fact, sometimes in groups with well-established traditions the only way a leader can assume dominance is to accept the group's traditions and tell the members to do what they usually do (Merei, 1949).

Since leadership varies from situation to situation, it may be that what works well in one situation may not work well in another. Thus much of the contemporary work on leadership behavior has focused on the question of the relative effectiveness of various styles of leadership in different situations.

BOX 5

THE EFFECTIVE COMMITTEE CHAIRMAN

What makes a good committee chairman? Consider effective and ineffective chairmen you have known to see what the differences are. From the discussion in this chapter, we have seen that organization and coordination are of primary importance. From a negative standpoint, it is equally important for the leader to resist the natural tendency of groups to exert conformity pressures—as we will see in Chapter 11. With these group phenomena in mind, one psychologist has outlined what a committee chairman, to be effective, should do:

1. "Identify the problem, consider the available facts, ask each member for his views about the important factors;
2. focus on disagreements in the group, and try to arrive at a creative solution;
3. evaluate different solutions in relation to criteria if these can be agreed upon;
4. ask stimulating questions to make the group question its approach or consider other aspects;
5. divide a problem into sub-problems, which are taken in turn;
6. get the group to consider two possible solutions—it has been found that the second one is often superior to the first."

[Argyle, 1969, pp. 256–257.]

By identifying the overall problem, considering available information, and dividing the problem into subproblems, the chairman brings some organization into the group's activities. By focusing on the disagreements in the group, by trying to use an objective basis for evaluating the ideas presented, and by considering at least two possible solutions, the chairman may overcome the group's tendency to conform to an emerging consensus or to accept uncritically what high-status members of the group say.

The Relative Effectiveness of Leadership Styles

You have to observe only a few leaders casually to note that their styles of exercising influence vary in a number of dimensions. Some are friendly, others cold. Some supervise very closely; others allow their subordinates more autonomy. The list could go on and on. In this section we shall consider two aspects of leadership style, which have been studied intensively: (1) the democratic versus authoritarian style and (2) the people-centered versus the task-centered style.

Is a democratic style of leadership more effective than an authoritarian one? To answer this question, a pioneering study was done in the late 1930s, when Fascism was on the rise in Hitler's Germany and this question was very much in the news (Lewin, Lippitt, and White, 1939). To assess the effects of leadership styles, the investigators randomly assigned ten-year-old boys to one of three after-school groups engaged in hobby activities (such as making papier-mâché theater masks). Each group was led by an adult who behaved in either an authoritarian, democratic, or laissez-faire manner.

In the authoritarian condition the leader determined the group's policy, gave step-by-step directions so that the boys were uncertain about future actions, dictated each boy's particular task, assigned children to work with one another, was subjective in his praise of the children's work, and stayed aloof from group participation. In contrast, the democratic leader allowed the boys to participate in setting group policy, gave the boys a general idea of the steps involved in the project, suggested alternative procedures, allowed them to work with whomever they wished, evaluated them in a fair and objective manner, and tried to be a member of the group. In the laissez-faire condition the leader gave the group complete freedom to do as they wished, supplied material or information only when the boys asked for it, and refrained almost completely from commenting on the boys' work.

As you might expect, the style of leadership had a marked effect on the boys' reactions to one another and to the group. The boys in the authoritarian condition showed significantly more aggression toward one another and were much more discontented than the boys in the democratic condition. Leadership style also influenced the group's production. Although there was a tendency for the subjects in the authoritarian condition to produce a slightly larger quantity of work, the work produced by the subjects in the democratic group was judged to be of a higher quality than that produced by the subjects in either of the other two groups.

A number of subsequent studies have also shown that authoritarian leadership styles are associated with lowered morale and lowered member satisfaction. But is it true that authoritarian leadership always results in group discontent? The setting in which the original study was done is one in which the boys may have expected freedom. There is something incongruous about a goose-stepping authoritarian leader in a group making theater masks. Further, the subjects, American schoolchildren, may have been more accustomed to democratic procedures and therefore preferred them.

Under other circumstances and with other subjects, an authoritarian leader might be preferred. The frequency of dictators in underdeveloped, emerging nations suggests that under highly stressful circumstances people may prefer more directive leadership (Bass, 1960). This hypothesis has been supported by the results of several studies. For instance, when half of a group of independent grocers were told that a supermarket would be opening near them, they preferred a stronger leader than grocers who had not been threatened (Mulder and Stemerding, 1963). Also, in situations in which speed and action are urgently needed, an authoritarian form of leadership may be preferred (Gibb, 1969). We saw earlier that the form of leadership preferred varies with different types of subjects.

Is a task-centered style of leadership more effective than a people-centered one? Or can both types of leadership be effective—given the appropriate circumstances? The results of an extended series of studies by Fiedler and his associates suggest that whether task-centered or people-centered leadership is more effective depends on the situation (Fiedler, 1967).

The first step in assessing the effects of leadership style was to devise a test to measure the leader's basic orientation. On one of the scales, the so-called Least Preferred Co-worker test, leaders were asked to rate the most incompetent person they had ever worked with on a number of traits, such as pleasantness, helpfulness, and cooperativeness. Thinking that a leader who is primarily people-centered would be reluctant to say unpleasant things about any fellow worker, even the worst one he had ever known, the investigator hypothesized that a leader who rated his least preferred co-worker relatively highly would be a people-centered leader. On the other hand, the task-oriented leader would feel free to evaluate negatively someone who was incompetent and so would give a low rating to his least preferred co-worker. Thus a leader with a high LPC score would be people-centered and one with a low LPC score would be task-centered.

After LPC scores were obtained for a number of leaders, the next question was whether or not one style of leadership was consistently better than the other. Do people-centered leaders, for instance, have more productive groups? Studies were done to correlate the LPC test scores with group productivity, and no consistent differences were found. Sometimes task-centered leaders had more productive groups, sometimes people-centered leaders did.

Since neither style showed an overall superiority across all leadership situations, the investigator hypothesized that differences in the situations determined the relative effectiveness of the two styles. Thus the next step was to devise some way of classifying situations.

One obvious way in which situations differ is in the degree to which they are favorable to the leader. Fiedler argued that three characteristics of a group situation primarily determine how favorable it is to leadership: (1) the leader's personal relations with the group, the extent to which the leader is liked and respected, (2) the task structure, the extent to which the work roles of the group members are spelled out in detail, and (3) the leader's legitimate power, the extent to which he has access to rewards and punishments for the members of his group.

It was hypothesized that in situations very favorable to leadership, the task-centered leader would be more effective than the people-centered leader. For instance, if the leader initially has the support of the group, the task is clear, and the leader has a lot of power, the members of the group may not resent his focus on the task. Similarly, in situations that are extremely unfavorable for leadership—say one in which the leader has a bad relationship with the other members of the group, the task is vague, and the leader has little official power—a task-centered leader would also be more effective. Since the situation is so bad, the leader would have to be primarily concerned about the task in order to get anything done.

If the situation is moderately favorable, however, the person-centered leader would be more effective than the task-centered leader. In a situation, for instance, in which the leader's relationship with his subordinates is relatively poor, the task is structured, and his power position is strong, a people-centered leader would try to build better relationships with his subordinates, whereas a task-oriented leader would not be as concerned about this.

Although not all of the results have been consistent with Fiedler's hypotheses (e.g., Graen, Orris, and Alvares, 1971), the bulk of them have supported his predictions. In general, task-oriented leaders have been found to be more effective in either highly favorable or highly unfavorable leadership situations, and person-oriented leaders have been shown to be more effective in moderately favorable circumstances (Fiedler, 1967).

Thus both task-centered and people-centered leaders can be effective—provided they are in the right situation. This finding has important implications for assigning leaders to different situations. In the past large companies have tended to rely on either experience or training to make men better managers—neither of which has yet been proved scientifically to be successful. (See Box 6.) Fiedler's results suggest that, instead of this approach, management would do better to try to match the particular leader's style of leadership to the demands of the situation. If he is people-oriented, place him in a leadership situation of medium difficulty. If he is task-oriented, give him either very difficult or very easy assignments (Fiedler, 1971).

Although Fiedler's model and research have made a very substantial contribution to our understanding of the effects of leadership style, one can question some of his assumptions. First, is it true, as is assumed with the LPC scale, that a leader must be primarily oriented toward either people or tasks? Although Fiedler is careful to note that the LPC score is an index of which is more important to the leader, people

or tasks, we can wonder whether or not the two are equally important to some leaders.

Some theorists have urged that if a leader is to be maximally effective, he should be highly concerned about both people and tasks (Blake and Mouton, 1964). The results of several recent experiments support the hypothesis that a focus on both people and tasks may not only be possible but may be more productive than a focus on either tasks or people alone (Misumi, Takeda, and Seki, 1967).

Further, one might question Fiedler's system for classifying situations in terms of their favorableness to leadership. Of the three variables he discussed, he assumed that the personal relationship between followers and leaders was the most important determinant. Is this always the case? In situations in which leaders have life-and-death power over their followers, personal relationships may pale in comparison with the effect exerted by the power variable. Further, we can wonder if other variables, in addition to the three mentioned in the model, might not influence the degree to which a given situation is favorable to leadership. For instance, the heterogeneity of the people in the group may, under some circumstances, influence the ease or the difficulty with which the group can be led.

Summary In this section we have seen that leadership includes a variety of behaviors, which vary from situation to situation. In discussion groups, for instance, leadership behavior may be classified as behavior relating to the task or as behavior relating to the social-emotional relationships within a group. In other types of situations different varieties of leadership behavior have been found to emerge.

Since leadership behavior varies from situation to situation, it may be that what works well in one situation may not work well in another. The results of a number of studies support this hypothesis. Although democratic leadership may be the best for a group of boys meeting after school to make theater masks, in other, more stressful situations, it may not be. Similarly, although a person-centered form of leadership may be better in a situation moderately favorable to leadership, it may not be in situations that are either very favorable or very unfavorable to leadership.

SUMMARY

In this chapter we have focused on three main topics: (1) group formation, (2) group structure, and (3) leadership.

1. Group Formation Physical proximity alone is not sufficient to make a collection of people a group. For a group to exist its members must interact with a *common goal* in mind. In general, both groups and subgroups tend to be formed when their formation best serves the purposes of their members. Groups are usually formed to attain work goals or to meet the emotional needs of the group members. People, of course, may not always be aware of their reasons for joining a group. Further, the reasons for belonging to a particular group may vary from member to member.

Given that specific individuals have some motivation toward a common goal, then their evolution into a group may be made more likely by the presence of three other variables: their *physical proximity,* their *similarity,* and their being in a *highly stressful situation.* There are limits to the group-inducing effects of stress, however. If the level of stress is too high or if the individual feels that he can better fend for himself alone, he may be more likely to remain independent of others.

2. Group Structure *Roles, norms,* and *status* emerge in groups, just as they do in dyads. The form that group structure assumes is determined by (1) the requirements for efficient group performance, (2) the abilities and motives of the group members, and (3) the physical and social environment of the group. Does the structure of groups go through predictable stages in its development? There are conflicting theories and evidence on this point. One theorist has contended that *any* group, irrespective of its setting, will go through the following four phases: (1) initial orientation to interpersonal and task behaviors, (2) intragroup conflict, (3) development of group cohesiveness, roles, and norms, and (4) use of group structure to perform the tasks required of the group. In contrast, recurrent cycles theories of group development hold that groups are concerned with basic issues that may never become fully resolved. Once a group structure emerges, it is somewhat independent of the group members. Even when the membership of a group changes, the structure tends to remain the same once it has emerged.

Groups vary widely in *cohesiveness,* or the overall level of attraction of the members to the group. Although cohesiveness may be measured in a number of ways, the most frequently used technique is to assess the attraction of the group members toward each other, a technique known as sociometry. However, other measures have been evolved in an attempt to focus on the individual's attraction to the whole group rather than to the individual members.

Once members have been admitted to an organization, their level of attraction to the group is determined by the extent to which the group meets (1) the interpersonal needs of those who belong, and (2) the goals for which it was formed. The extent to which a group meets *interpersonal and affiliative needs* is influenced by such variables as the attractiveness of the members and their relative similarity in values, interests, and beliefs. Generally, people are more attracted to groups with a democratic participatory form of leadership. Groups with a pleasant, warm, accepting feeling, or atmosphere, may be more likely to be cohesive. And as the size of a group increases, its cohesive-

ness decreases. The influence of *goal accomplishment* on group cohesiveness can be evidenced by the cohesiveness shown in a winning team. Under some circumstances, however, the members of a losing team may be highly attracted to their group.

Threats also increase the level of group cohesiveness. A common threat to all members may make them realize that the group represents their best chance for survival. Or threat may increase cohesiveness by making the members more aware of their ingroup identity.

Members of highly cohesive groups are more pleased about their membership, communicate more often and in a more cooperative manner with one another, and have much more social influence on each other than the members of groups low in cohesiveness. Members of highly cohesive groups participate more frequently in group activities. Also, being a member of a highly cohesive group has personal consequences for the members; they have been observed, for example, to feel less nervous or jumpy on their jobs than members of groups low in cohesiveness.

Cohesive groups exert strong influences on their members. All social groups may create a pressure toward uniformity. In addition to the level of cohesiveness, the intensity of these conformity pressures is influenced by (1) the extent of deviation in initial opinions and (2) the relevance of the issue to the group. The usual reaction to deviance is rejection. Since we all know this, the more a person cares about others' liking him, the more motivated he is to agree with them. The more relevant the topic is to the group, the more grating disagreement will be to the group, and the more likely the others will be to try to elicit the individual's agreement.

The *physical environment* influences social interaction. Both individuals and groups tend to assume possessive rights about objects in the environment, or to feel that they have established a given area as their *territory*. People will go to considerable lengths to defend their territory, and being in one's own territory when competing with others seems to provide one with an advantage. When people interact with one another, they are very careful to maintain appropriate *distance* between themselves. Studies of how people arrange themselves in physical space (small-group ecology) have shown that the intimacy of the interpersonal relationship, the need for cooperative action, cultural differences, and stress may influence interpersonal spacing. *Furniture arrangement* also influences social interaction. People have preferences for certain types of seating arrangements. These preferences have been found to depend largely on: (1) the social background of those involved, (2) the environmental setting, and (3) the activity that the group is performing.

When opportunities for communication are restricted, the pattern of communication opportunities, or the *communication network,* has an important impact on member satisfaction with the group, the way the group processes information, and the emergence of leadership. Limiting the opportunity for a member of a group to communicate with other members decreases his satisfaction with the group. In centralized networks information is funneled from all of the group members to the central person, who then distributes the information to the other members. Further, the person who occupies the central position in the communication network is frequently named by the group as the leader. In decentralized networks all the available information is transmitted evenly to all of the group members.

3. Leadership Leadership is an important element in the effective functioning of a group. The term is customarily defined as the exerting of greater influence than the other members of the group. *Clear leadership structure is much more likely to emerge when the group size is large, the discussion time is brief, the task is complex, and the act is either very important or extremely trivial.*

What determines who the leader will be? One answer is that some people possess characteristics that make their rise to leadership in any group situation almost inevitable. Studies done in an attempt to find *trait characteristics* common to leaders in all situations have had limited success, however. This is understandable in view of the widely differing demands on leaders in different situations.

The contemporary approach to leadership determinants is an *interaction approach.* This approach holds that to predict who will assume leadership in a particular group, one must take into account the characteristics of the group

members, the structure of the group, the situation, and the nature of the task facing the group, as well as the personal characteristics that may make one person more likely to emerge as a leader. The person or persons who are most visible and are seen by themselves and by the other members of the group as most apt to move the group toward its goals will assume leadership. Thus if the situation changes, the person who is acknowledged as the leader of the group will change.

However, *if the situation remains basically the same, the group leaders will tend to possess common traits.* Thus people rated as high in *executive potential* share common traits: They have been found to be highly motivated to advance in their company, to possess good interpersonal skills, to withstand stress, to have good insight and financial comprehension, and to have good intellectual ability. Although there is very little evidence on the traits of *politicians,* one study found that men who had initiated their own political activity were significantly higher than average in their desire for power and achievement.

In certain situations people who are willing to use any tactics that work—however unprincipled—may gain influence over those who are not so willing. A test has been devised to measure the extent to which people endorse *Machiavellian* views—a so-called Mach scale. People who obtain high Mach scores are more likely to use exploitative and manipulative tactics when dealing with others. However, high Machs do not always win. Only in ambiguous, emotionally arousing, and face-to-face situations do high Machs exert more influence.

A number of variables in the *situation* influence the emergence of leadership. When people outside the group appoint one person as a leader, the appointed individual's chances of being accepted by the group as a leader are increased. The *cultural context* also influences who assumes leadership. Some group members may possess characteristics that are valued by the group members in question. The *organizational context* of the group is also an important determinant. Informal leaders may be selected primarily because they are seen as liking the other members of a group, while a formal leader's power may be based on his influence with those in the upper levels of the organization. The *pattern of personalities* present in the group influences both the group's preference for particular individuals as leaders and its preference for the kind of leadership exerted. Potential leaders cannot be too different from the other members of the group. The *relative competency and success of the group members* in attaining the group's goals also influence the emergence of leaders.

Perhaps, most important, the sheer *frequency of communication* by the group's members is a major determinant of relative influence. People who talk a lot are very likely to emerge as leaders. But sheer frequency of communication is no guarantee of leadership. People who participate frequently but make negative comments about the group's effectiveness do not emerge as leaders.

Once leadership emerges, a lot of energy goes into maintaining the status quo. Although there is relatively little evidence on the tactics leaders use to maintain power, observation suggests that they use a number of strategies. For example, they may buy loyalty through the promise of favors, or they may use intimidation tactics.

Leadership includes a variety of behaviors, which differ from situation to situation. Two predominant themes of leadership behaviors in Air Force crews were: (1) consideration, the extent to which the leader was characterized by warmth and trust in his personal relationships, and (2) initiating structure, the extent to which the leader organized the work done by the group. In discussion groups leadership behavior may be classified as behavior relating to the task or as behavior relating to the social-emotional relationships within the group. In other types of situations different varieties of leadership have been found to emerge. Since leadership behavior varies from situation to situation, what works well in one situation may not work well in another. Although democratic leadership may be the best for a group of boys meeting after school to make theater masks, in other, more stressful conditions, it may not be. Similarly, although a person-centered form of leadership may be better in situations moderately favorable to leadership, it may not be best in situations either very favorable or very unfavorable to leadership.

DISCUSSION QUESTIONS

1. List the goals of all the groups you belong to. Include both informal groups, such as groups of friends, and formal groups, such as organizations.
2. Analyze the roles, norms, status relationships, and level of cohesiveness in one group you belong to.
3. Give an example of the permanency of some aspect of group structure that is no longer functional.
4. Why do cohesive groups exert so much influence on their members?
5. Why do you think restricting an individual's access to communication with the other members of his group decreases his satisfaction with the group?
6. Analyze the behavior of the leader in one group you belong to.
7. Indicate a procedure that you think would validly measure an individual's reason or reasons for joining a particular group.
8. Do you think that all group structures evolve through forming, storming, norming, and performing stages? Give evidence to support your answer.
9. Why do you think that the level of cohesiveness is lower in larger groups than in small groups?
10. Stand ten feet away from a friend while you converse with him. Note his reactions.
11. Have you ever interacted with someone you consider to be a high Mach? If so, what tactics did the high Mach use to win his point?
12. Under what circumstances do you think that group leadership would not go to those who talk the most? Support your answer with observational evidence.

13. Assuming that specific individuals have some motivation to obtain a common goal, we listed three variables that increase the chances of their evolving into a group. Can you think of any additional variables that facilitate group formation?

14. Design a study to test the effects of varying one of the antecedents of cohesiveness discussed in this chapter. State your hypothesis, procedure, manipulation of the independent variable, measurement of the dependent variable, and predicted results.

15. Diagram the furniture arrangements in a room to be occupied by four people that would be maximally conducive to: (1) conversation, (2) independent work, (3) work that requires their joint cooperation, and (4) competition between the four people. Indicate for each diagram the pieces of furniture to be used, the distances separating them, and their orientation toward each other.

16. The results of contemporary research suggest that there may be at least three kinds of situations in which leaders are likely to possess common traits: business, politics, and situations in which manipulative interpersonal bargaining pays off. Do you think there are any other situations in which leaders possess common traits? Indicate how you could test your hypothesis.

17. List a set of training procedures for increasing the effectiveness of business executives as leaders.

18. Why would you expect a person-centered leader to be most effective in situations that are moderately favorable to leadership and a task-centered leader to be maximally effective in situations that are either very favorable or very unfavorable to leadership? Have you had a chance to observe the relative effectiveness of person-centered versus task-centered leaders in different situations? If you have, are your observations consistent with Fiedler's theory?

GROUPS
IN ACTION

11

Once it has been formed and evolved its own structure and leadership, how does a group function? Since so large a proportion of most people's time is spent interacting in groups, the question of how they

function is very important and practical. For instance, how does an individual's behavior change as a result of his being in a group? How effective are groups—both in terms of material productivity and in terms of meeting the social-emotional needs of their members?

In this chapter we will first discuss some of the classic ways in which groups exert their influence on individual performance, with special emphasis on conformity pressures. We will then analyze those factors that determine the relative level of effectiveness of a group compared to the level of effectiveness of the same number of people working individually. Our discussion will distinguish work-directed groups (with special emphasis on the recently studied phenomenon of "groupthink") from other groups (such as communes and encounter groups) that focus more on the fulfillment of social and emotional needs.

Group Functioning

Before beginning our discussion, we should note that even though group members change as a result of interacting with one another in a group setting, each member retains his individuality to a certain degree. Powerful as group forces are, each member considers the other members from the perspective of his own past experience and his own particular motives. Each continues to have his own separate way of processing information, his own ideas, and his own behaviors. Thus if four different people are brought together, four different points of view and sets of behavior exist.

Nevertheless, it is a common observation and a thoroughly documented finding that individuals coming together in groups are influenced by the group and accordingly behave in a manner somewhat different from the way they behave

alone. (See Figure 11-1.) To see some of the effects of social interaction at work, let us consider the following examples.

1. A basketball player finds it difficult to concentrate on his game when practicing alone, but feels a surge of excitement and plays much better when he practices with the other members of his team.

2. A business executive has to make a decision about his company's expansion plans. After considering the plans by himself, he arrives at a conservative judgment. The next day, however, he discusses the issue with a group of his colleagues and changes his opinion to favor a more risky course of action.

3. A crowd of 200 students is watching a fellow student who has threatened to commit suicide and shouts for him to jump, taunting him for his reluctance (UPI release, September 23, 1967. In Zimbardo, 1969, p. 245).

4. A college student develops a thorough dislike for his noisy roommate but stifles his hostility until he sees another student arguing with his roommate. Then he becomes very aggressive toward his roommate.

In each of these cases, being with others has influenced the individual's behavior. However, different psychological processes are at work in these situations, and these different processes have been separately labeled and studied.

Social facilitation and social interference

The basketball player who performs better with other people than he does when he is alone illustrates a common effect of groups on individual performance. When several people are

FIGURE 11-1 A group of volunteers removing an oil slick from an ocean inlet. To what extent do you think the behavior of each volunteer is being influenced by interaction with others? (Howard Harrison/Jeroboam)

working together on the same task at the same time, even when they are not interacting with one another or overtly competing against each other, their performance may be better than when each individual works alone. This phenomenon has been termed "social facilitation" (Allport, 1920).

Experimental interest in this topic goes back to 1898, when it was the subject of the first laboratory experiment in the newly emerging discipline (Triplett, 1898). The investigator, a great enthusiast of bicycle racing, noticed that the speed of racers varied according to the type of competition. Times were fastest when several riders competed directly against one another; they were the next fastest for paced races, in which one rider tried to beat a record with a somewhat faster vehicle setting the pace; and they were the slowest for unpaced races, in which a lone rider tried to beat an established record. (See Figure 11-2.)

Theorizing that the mere presence of other

people released a special energy enabling an individual to perform at a higher rate than he could alone, Triplett timed the rates at which children performed a task when they worked alone and when they competed with others. As predicted, the competitive conditions produced significantly higher rates.

The results of a number of subsequent studies confirmed the social facilitation effect. Even when attempts were made to minimize the competitive element and to test the effect of the sheer physical presence of other people, the sight and sounds of others were found to improve performance on a variety of simple tasks. For instance, when subjects had to perform a task that they had thoroughly mastered, their performance in front of an audience was significantly better than when they performed alone (Travis, 1925). Moreover, in coacting groups—that is, groups of subjects who performed the same task but did not interact at all—a social facilitation effect was also obtained. In one study, subjects were asked to write down as many words as they could think of in a given period of time. Fourteen of the fifteen subjects worked faster when they were in a room with other students engaged in the same task than when they were alone (Allport, 1920).

You may have noticed this effect yourself when taking written exams. When you take the final exam for a large lecture class, the sight of several hundred other students busily working away may make the competitive aspects of the situation very clear and stimulate you. But in some cases it may also interfere with your performance. The distractions provided by the other students' shifting and moving may prevent you from concentrating as well as you might if you were alone. Further, if you are not particularly sure of yourself, the sight and sound of hundreds of other, competent-appearing students may make you anxious and so may interfere with your ability to perform as well as you could if you were alone.

If you were trying to master a new task, the presence of others might also interfere significantly. Imagine, for instance, that you were called upon in a class to work out on a blackboard a highly complicated statistical formula that you were completely unfamiliar with. You would probably be concerned about how others were reacting to your work. If you couldn't work the problem out immediately, your thoughts about how cloddish and stupid you looked might interfere markedly with your performance on this highly complex task.

The results of a number of studies have shown that the "social interference" effect can be an outgrowth of group functioning. Subjects have been found to take significantly longer to learn new material when working in front of an audience than when working alone (Pessin, 1933). When students were asked for ideas, the level of creativity was lower among students working in groups than it was among students working alone (Wapner and Alper, 1952).

Thus sometimes the presence of other people has been found to facilitate performance and sometimes it has been found to interfere. Although this is an accurate summary of the research findings, it doesn't help one to predict whether facilitation or interference will occur in a particular situation. For instance, if several volunteers are stuffing envelopes for a political campaign, would you expect them to be more productive working separately or in a group?

One psychologist has tried to explain the facilitation-interference findings by distinguishing between learning and performance (Zajonc, 1965). He theorized that the performance of well-learned responses is facilitated by the presence of other people, but the acquisition of new responses is impaired by their presence.

The presence of other people increases the general level of motivation, or "drive." In one study, for instance, subjects reported that when they were with others, they experienced a greater arousal of general emotional excitement than when they were alone (Kelley and Thibaut, 1969). According to drive theory, increasing the individual's general level of drive results in the

FIGURE 11-2 Racers leaving the starting blocks. From Triplett's observations we would predict that the winner of this race will probably record a faster time than if he were running alone against a specified time deadline. (George W. Gardner)

emission of the dominant responses. During the early stages of learning, the wrong responses are usually dominant, so that increasing the level of drive will make the individual more likely to make errors. After the individual has mastered the task, however, the dominant responses will be the correct responses. The theorized effect of an audience is to enhance the emission of a dominant response.

The results of a number of recent studies support this hypothesis. For example, in one experiment subjects were asked to learn material that was either easy or difficult. Half of the subjects learned alone, and the other half learned in front of two other students. As predicted, the subjects learned the easy material better when they worked before an audience than they did when they worked alone. In contrast, the difficult material was learned better when the audience was absent (Cottrell, Rittle, and Wack, 1967).

Although the theory that social contacts are drive-arousing is an interesting one that has received considerable empirical support, there is still the question of whether *all* social contacts or only certain types of social contact are drive-arousing. As we saw in Chapter 5, the results of Schachter's work would suggest that the presence of other people can sometimes have a calming effect on frightened people by providing them with social comparison and emotional support. In your own experience you may have observed that some social interactions make you more tense, and others calm you.

The problem, then, is to specify which types of social contact are arousing. One such type of contact may occur in situations where the individual anticipates evaluation from his audience (Cottrell, 1968). If you think someone is sizing you up as you talk, you may feel uptight and stimulated, whereas if you don't feel that evaluation is in the air, you may be quite relaxed. The results of several studies support this hypothesis (e.g., Paulus and Murdoch, 1971; Martens and Landers, 1972).

Thus whether being with others facilitates or interferes with performance depends on: (1) whether or not the performance in question has been thoroughly learned, or is dominant, and (2) whether the social contact increases or decreases the person's level of overall excite-ment, or drive. If you are in the process of learning and the social contact is arousing, as the presence of an audience that you feel is evaluating you might be, then social interference would be expected to occur. If the response is well learned, the presence of a potentially evaluative audience would result in social facilitation.

Diffusion of responsibility

In the second of our four examples the executive was willing to advocate a riskier solution after he had discussed the issue with other executives. Although a few studies have had inconsistent results (e.g., Zajonc, Wolosin, Wolosin, and Sherman, 1968), many laboratory studies have shown that, on the average, individuals are willing to advocate a solution involving greater risk after participating in a group discussion than before (Clark, 1971). Appropriately enough, this phenomenon has come to be called the "risky shift." See Box 1.

Why does this occur? There are a number of possible answers. One is that during the process of group discussion, the individuals become more familiar with the issues, and their increased familiarity makes them become more willing to take risks on that issue. Or it may be that taking risks is valued more than being conservative and that people want to see themselves as being as willing as the other people in the group to take risks. Still another answer is that group discussion frees the individual from full responsibility for his actions (Clark, 1971). If one man in an organization recommends a particular action and it turns out badly, he alone must bear the responsibility. In contrast, if a committee recommends an action that does not succeed, all of the members of the group share the responsibility, so that each member absorbs less of the blame. Thus when an individual is with other people, he may not feel quite so much on the spot for his own actions.

Diffusion of responsibility minimizes the possibility for individual failure as well as the opportunity for individual achievement or success. In societies in which saving face is a highly desirable goal, elaborate steps may be taken to diffuse responsibility. In Japan, for example, virtually all decision making involves

BOX 1 ARE GROUP DECISIONS ALWAYS RISKIER THAN INDIVIDUAL DECISIONS?

In almost all of the research on the risky shift, one standard procedure has been used—the "choice-dilemma questionnaire" (Kogan and Wallach, 1964). The subjects are asked to give advice in hypothetical situations in which people are faced with a choice between two alternative courses of action, one of which is highly safe but less attractive, the other of which is more chancy and more attractive. For instance, in one experiment the subjects were asked whether an engineer should remain at his present, well-paying job at a stable company or join a new company where his long-range security would be somewhat unsure but he would have the potential of attaining a much higher income than he has in his present job.

In a typical experiment twelve such choices are presented. First, each subject specifies individually the lowest odds of success he would require before recommending the risky alternative. Then, after indicating his advice, each subject discusses the alternatives with some other subjects, and then gives his advice again. Almost inevitably, the subjects made riskier choices after the group discussion.

However, some recent findings raise the question of whether or not the reactions obtained with the choice-dilemma procedure provide a valid measure of risk taking in other situations. These recent studies have shown that the experimental instructions given to the subjects in the choice-dilemma procedure may influence the occurrence of the risky shift. When the subjects are told to indicate the lowest probability of success they would consider acceptable for the hypothetical person to choose the riskier alternative, the directions may focus the subjects' attention on the risk component and so may be responsible for the later shift. If this hypothesis is correct, one would predict that when the subjects are simply told to choose between the alternatives, the risky shift will disappear. This hypothesis has been confirmed in several studies (e.g., Willems and Clark, 1969).

Additionally, in the relatively few studies in which subjects have been faced with real, not hypothetical choices, sometimes the risky shift has occurred, and sometimes it has not. For instance, in one study subjects were given $10 and told to make eight telephone contacts with a person who could be at one of two different places. Since a person-to-person call cost $1.20, the safe option was to make all of the calls person-to-person calls. The subject would then have $.40 left. Station-to-station calls cost $.75, so the riskier but potentially more advantageous solution was to call station-to-station. Subjects making their decisions in groups opted significantly more often to pursue the riskier, station-to-station procedure (Malamuth and Feshbach, 1972).

In another study involving real choices, however, no risky shift occurred. When college students were asked to select one of eight alternative examination schedules (rated by students in a previous class in terms of riskiness), the schedule selected by the group was more conservative than that selected by individual students (Clement and Sullivan, 1970).

It may be argued that when real choices are involved, whether or not the risky shift occurs depends on the importance of the issue. The choice between earning or not earning $.40 in the telephone call study is certainly not as important to a student as making sure that he has an examination schedule that ensures his not getting a lower grade than he thinks he deserves.

---

multiple channels of responsibility, so that no one person can be held responsible. One Japanese businessman reported that in his organization, several higher-ups have to authorize each letter of importance before it can be mailed. Of course, this is inefficient, but the Japanese compensate for this sharing of responsibility by working more hours, taking little time off, and employing more people. Thus they attain a high level of output without the threat of individual failure (Zimbardo, 1972, personal communication).

Further, the diffusion of responsibility caused by the presence of other people may inhibit the individual from taking any action at all—as we saw in our discussion of the bystander effect in Chapter 7. For example, in one experiment subjects were seated in a small waiting room and asked to complete a questionnaire. As they worked, a stream of smoke began to waft into the room through a wall vent. When tested alone, 75 percent of the subjects reported the smoke during the six-minute period of the experiment. However, when three subjects were tested together, in only 38 percent of the groups did even one subject report the smoke. And when one naïve subject was accompanied by two experimental confederates who ignored the smoke, only 10 percent of the subjects reported the smoke. (See Figure 11-3.) As we saw in Chapter 7, when everyone in a situation is in a position to act, no one individual feels that he alone is responsible, so very few take any action. Further, the calmness of the confeder-

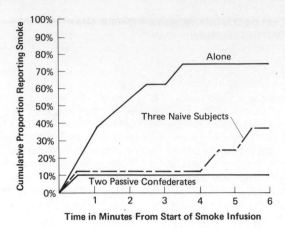

FIGURE 11-3 Cumulative proportion of subjects reporting the smoke over time. (Adapted from Latané and Darley, 1968, p. 218.)

ates may have reassured the subjects that the situation was not serious (Latané and Darley, 1968).

Deindividuation

In our example of a crowd of students encouraging their fellow student to commit suicide, we see people becoming temporarily deindividuated. Not many students alone would bait a potential suicide. But in the excitement and anonymity of the crowd situation, the individual can become immersed in the group and his inner restraints against immoral behavior may be reduced, so that together with others he can engage in highly pathological and aggressive behavior. (See Figure 11-4.)

What is deindividuated behavior like? One recent theoretical account holds that it is highly emotional and impulsive, self-reinforcing and therefore difficult to terminate, highly influenced by what others in the situation are doing, and, in general, very destructive (Zimbardo, 1969). Perhaps the police riot at the 1968 Democratic Convention in Chicago will best illustrate the qualities of deindividuated behavior:

The ones who actually got arrested seemed to have gotten caught up among the police, like a kind of human medicine ball, being shoved and knocked back and forth from one cop to the next with what was

obviously *mounting* fury. And this was a phenomenon somewhat unexpected, which we were to observe consistently throughout the days of violence—that rage seemed to engender rage; the bloodier and more brutal the cops were, the more their fury increased.

[Zimbardo, 1969, p. 244.]

This description of deindividuated behavior sounds very similar to some of the excesses and highly destructive acts engaged in by mobs. One of the earliest theories in social psychology held that when people come together, they lose their distinctive personalities and become a homogeneous and highly emotional mass—one that operates collectively and is manipulated by a "group mind" (Le Bon, 1896). However, a group mind is not necessary to account for the mindless and irrational behavior of crowds. Another explanation is that many of the conditions existing in crowds are conducive to deindividuated behavior, such as anonymity; diffused responsibility; large group size, with the attendant noise, excitement, and arousal; physically involving acts; and altered states of consciousness.

We have seen the effect of anonymity on increasing aggression. The protection a large crowd offers from any possible punishment is obviously much greater than that offered by a hood worn in an experimental laboratory. In situations in which all those surrounding you are engaging in antisocial acts, your own responsibility for such acts may be greatly diminished. That others are "in the same boat" may make the action seem acceptable and may make you feel that it is highly unlikely you will be punished. If you do feel that you may be punished, you may seek to deindividuate yourself, but if rewards are forthcoming in the situation, you are likely to want to stand out, to be unique, and to individuate yourself (Maslach, 1972). As we shall see in the next section, the deindividuating effects of the presence of others may be particularly likely to influence actions about which you are in conflict.

In the noise, excitement, and involvement of the group, you may be so caught up in the action that your independent thinking processes are temporarily suspended. Much like a hypnotic subject, you are carried along by what others do. The physiological arousal created by the emotional excitement, coupled with the use of drugs or alcohol to alter your state of consciousness, may make you more likely to become submerged in the group. As you are carried along, your own independent judgment can become so submerged that you do whatever the group does. When others are looting, burning, and hitting each other, you join in. Further, many of the acts that crowds engage in are in themselves highly involving. The action itself precludes critical thought. When a crowd is in the process of rocking a car back and forth to turn it over, the action of rocking so absorbs the members that they become totally immersed in the activity. Further, in the anonymity of the crowd, there are no counterpressures to make you aware of what you are doing. Everybody else is rocking the car, so that the common experience unifies the group and totally absorbs the mind.

As fascinating as the model of deindividuation is and as clearly as it seems to account for an important group phenomenon, relatively little work has been done to test the model. As has been mentioned, we have evidence that anonymity does increase the incidence of aggression, and in Chapter 6 we saw that a subject's engaging in a physically involving act, such as smashing a car with a sledge hammer, resulted in highly aggressive behavior.

Further, there is some evidence suggesting that people are more attracted to groups in which they can become deindividuated (Festinger, Pepitone, and Newcomb, 1952). Thus a cyclical relationship between deindividuation and attraction to the group may be established. Once the conditions in a group are such that they permit the deindividuation of the group members, the members may be more attracted to the group and thus more liable to lose their identity. However, there is no evidence that an opportunity for deindividuation contributes to the permanency of a group. The attracting power of the opportunity for deindividuation may be a transient attraction. In order for a group to survive, it must also provide opportunities for individuation.

The deindividuation model includes a number of variables that may lead to deindividuated behavior—several of which relate indirectly to the effects of other people. The presence of other people automatically means a diffusion of responsibility and an excitement generated by the sounds they make.

Imitation and contagion

As we have seen repeatedly, whenever people interact, whether in a dyad or a crowd, they tend to imitate what they see other people doing. (See Figure 11-5.) Our example of the college student suppressing his hostility against his roommate until he sees another acting out that hostility illustrates this imitative response. In Chapter 7 we saw that persons who have observed altruistic models are more likely to act in an altruistic manner.

Of course, imitation isn't limited to aggression or altruism; people can and do copy almost any response. Children imitate their parents and peers. People imitate the speech dialects and hand gestures of those with whom they interact. Prejudiced behavior is frequently caused by the individual's copying the behavior of those he observes. The examples could go on and on. Imitation is so pervasive that we often copy the behavior of others without even being aware that we are doing so. For instance, in one study in which subjects were found to

529
**Groups
in Action**

FIGURE 11-4 In scenes such as this, where policemen and rioters confront each other in highly emotional, confused settings, participants tend to lose their identities as separate individuals, to abandon their usual self-restraints, and to engage in highly aggressive behaviors. (Stephen Shames)

imitate the behavior of an experimental collaborator, the subjects were completely unaware that the confederate's behavior had influenced what they did. Under certain conditions subjects tended to leave an experiment shortly after the collaborator did, but they did not know that the collaborator's leaving had influenced their own (Stephenson and Fielding, 1971).

A recent theory has proposed that not all cases of behavior copying are mediated by the same internal processes (Wheeler, 1966b). In one type, known as "simple imitation," there is no conflict about the individual's performing the act in question. A student's imitating the swings of a golf pro might be a good example of this type of simple imitation. Other examples are the conscious and unconscious forms of model imitation that we reviewed extensively in Chapters 6 and 7.

In a second type of copying, which has been termed "behavioral contagion," the individual is initially in conflict about whether or not to perform a certain response. Thus an individual living in an impoverished community might want to take a television set from a local appliance store, but he might be afraid of the consequences. If he sees others looting, however, his own internal restraints against looting may be reduced (Wheeler, 1966b).

FIGURE 11-5 "Why do you only laugh when the laugh track does?"

Since deindividuated behavior is usually thought to involve immoral and irrational acts, behavioral contagion may be a highly important causative factor in deindividuated behavior in crowd settings. Seeing others engaging in an irrational act makes it seem appropriate for a number of reasons. The sight and sound of what the others are doing is stimulating; their presence automatically diffuses responsibility; their performing the act legitimizes it. If others are doing it, it must be right. Thus the theory of contagion provides an important part of the deindividuation explanation of crowd behavior.

For instance, contagion theory predicts that the contagion process will occur when the individual is in conflict about whether or not to perform a given act. Of course, conflict can come from a number of sources. The individual may be in conflict about a particular act because of his own moral standards. Thus an adolescent girl may be in conflict about whether or not to have sexual relations with a date. However, if she has reason to believe that her peers are engaging in sexual relations, she may feel that their activity endorses sex and makes it all right for her. For instance, it has been suggested that adolescents are more likely to engage in sexual activities while double dating than on a single date (Bandura and Walters, 1959).

Further, it might follow that the better you know the other person, the greater the effect of his performing an act that you are in conflict about. If an experimenter asks you to shock another person, seeing a friend deliver intense shocks would make you more likely to deliver shocks yourself. Confirmation for this hypothesis has been obtained (Zabrack and Miller, 1972). Thus if the people in a crowd know one another, the supportive effects of mutually stimulating one another to greater and greater excesses may obtain more readily.

A person can also be in conflict about a particular act because he is afraid he will be punished if he performs the act. He may not steal television sets because he is afraid he will be arrested if he does. But if hundreds of people are rushing about in a riot, his fear of individual detection may be decreased. Thus the protection from a potential punisher provided by anonymity may be a crucial determinant of whether or not behavior is contagious. Confirmation for this hypothesis has also been obtained (Baron, 1970).

Summary

In this section we have reviewed the evidence on four different group processes. First, we saw that being with others can either facilitate or interfere with performance. Whether social interaction helps or hurts performance seems to depend on: (1) whether or not the task to be performed has been thoroughly learned and (2) whether the social contact increases or decreases one's level of overall excitement, or drive. If you are in the process of learning and the social contact is arousing, social interference would be expected to occur. If the response is well learned, the presence of a potentially evaluative audience would result in social facilitation.

Second, diffusion of responsibility can occur in a group. If a person is fearful about the consequences of a particular action, the anonymity of the group may enable him to act more as he would like to act. Further, in a group an individual may be less likely to act at all.

Third, in the excitement and anonymity of a group setting, particularly in a crowd situation, the individual can become immersed in the group, and his inner restraints against immoral behavior may be reduced, so that together with others he can engage in highly pathological and aggressive behaviors.

Fourth, if an individual sees others performing a particular act, he is likely to do as they do. People can and do copy almost any response. However, one theorist has proposed that not all cases of behavior copying are mediated by the same internal processes. In one type, known as simple imitation, there is no conflict about the individual's performing the act in question. In a second type, which has been termed behavioral contagion, the individual is initially in conflict about whether or not to perform a certain response. But seeing others engaging in the act makes it seem appropriate for a number of reasons. The sight and sound of others acting is stimulating; their presence automatically diffuses responsibility; and their performing the

act legitimatizes it. This behavioral contagion may also be an extremely important determinant of whether or not deindividuated behavior occurs.

Conformity

By far the most widely observed and researched aspect of group behavior is the pressure to modify what you say and do to make it correspond with what others say and do—or "conformity" pressure. Because of its importance, we will devote an entire section to this subject, with particular emphasis on: (1) the strength of the tendency to conform, (2) explanations of why people conform, (3) the situational determinants of conformity, (4) personality characteristics related to conformity, and (5) a critique of the work in this area.

The strength of the conformity tendency

Assume that you and eight other students, acquaintances of yours, are participating in an experiment on perceptual judgment. The experimenter places two cards on the blackboard sill in the front of the classroom. The card on the left has a single line, and the one on the right has three lines, one of which is the same length as the line on the card at the left. You and the other subjects are asked to call out the line on the right card that is the same length as the line on the left card. (See Figure 11-6 for a typical set of lines used in this experiment.)

The experiment starts off very routinely. The discriminations are simple, since in each case one of the comparison lines is clearly the same as the standard line. On the first two trials you and the other subjects in the experiment monotonously call out the same judgments, and you sit back and begin to relax. With the third pair of cards, however, the boredom is broken. Everyone except you clearly and confidently indicates that the second comparison line is the same as the line on the left. To you, however, the first comparison line clearly seems to be the one that matches. Perplexingly, this disagreement happens again. On seven out of the twelve

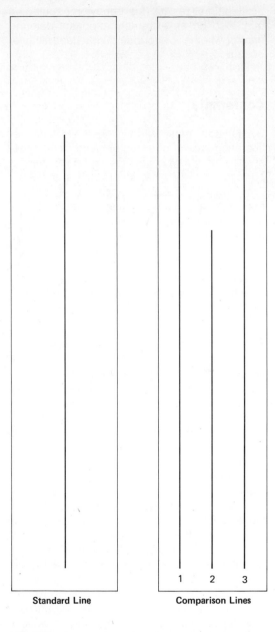

Standard Line   Comparison Lines

FIGURE 11-6 A sample set of cards used in the classic experiment on conformity. The line at the left is 4^1/$_2$ inches long; the lines at the right are 4^1/$_2$, 3^1/$_2$, and 5^1/$_2$ inches long, respectively. In the experiment, each line was ^{3}/$_8$ of an inch thick, and they appeared on cards that measured 17^1/$_2$ by 6 inches. The standard line was shown in the center of one card, and the three comparison lines, separated by a distance of 1^3/$_4$ inches, were centered on the other card. (Figure modified from Asch, 1952, Figure 9, p. 452.)

trials, the others unanimously select a line that differs from your own judgment.

What's happening? You don't understand why you should see the lines differently from the others. All of your life you have depended on your senses. You drive a car confident that things are as you see them. But you have also come to rely on other people as an important source of information. When reality has been at all ambiguous, you have relied on the judgments of others, as we have seen repeatedly in our discussions of social comparison theory. Further, you may be concerned about the way the others will feel about you if your answers differ from theirs. You know that people who deviate are sometimes not very popular, and you are therefore concerned with what the others will think of you. Moreover, disagreeing on something as simple as this will make you stick out like a sore thumb, thus making you embarrassed.

Actually, all of the other subjects are confederates of the experimenter. They have agreed that on seven of the twelve trials they will unanimously give clearly incorrect judgments, choosing lines that vary from the correct line by as much as 1^3/$_4$ inch.

But you don't know this. You try to figure out what could be responsible for the discrepancy. You may check with the experimenter or another subject to make sure that you have understood the directions correctly. Probably you think that there is something wrong with your judgment. You may think that the location of your seat prevents you from getting an accurate view of the cards. Or if you wear glasses, you may think that your prescription needs changing. You begin to look much more closely at the lines. If you're brave, you might even get up and walk over to the cards to get a closer look. Above all, you're probably going to begin to doubt the correctness of your own judgments. As one subject said:

A little doubt came into my mind, but it was before my eyes, and I was determined to say what I saw. Even though in your mind you know you are right, you wonder why everybody else thinks differently. I was doubting myself and was puzzled.

[Asch, 1952, p. 464.]

And you might begin to worry about what the others are going to think of you:

After reading about the Asch procedure, you may be feeling a little sorry for the subject. After all, he's been deceived, and if he conformed, he may be feeling embarrassed at his own plasticity.

But are all subjects so gullible that they accept the Asch procedure without question? Obviously, if some subjects become suspicious, the validity of the Asch procedure as a genuine conformity dilemma is greatly diminished. Thus assessing the frequency of the occurrence of suspicion among the subjects is of great importance. Unfortunately, relatively few studies have been done on the occurrence of suspicion, and the results of those that have been done are exceedingly mixed. Percentages of suspicion among subjects in the Asch procedure have varied all of the way from 2 percent (Vaughan, 1964) to 75 percent (Glinski, Glinski, and Slatin, 1970).

What might make subjects become suspicious? In one study in which junior and senior college students were used and a 75 percent rate of suspicion was obtained, a number of reasons emerged (Glinski, Glinski, and Slatin, 1970). Some of the students had prior knowledge of the Asch procedure. As one psychology student said, "I read this one, therefore I wasn't susceptible to the 'Asch' phenomenon." Aspects of the procedure itself seemed to raise the subjects' suspicion. Out of twenty-eight subjects tested with a unanimous majority, twenty-six were suspicious of the prolonged unanimity of the majority. They felt that a consistent majority was simply incredible. Some students were suspicious because of information they had received from others who had already participated in the study. Although the usual request not to discuss the experiment with other students was made, five of the twenty-eight subjects "admitted that they had been given some information about the experiment" (p. 482).

Although the percentage of suspicious subjects among these advanced college students may be higher than that found in most conformity studies, the problem cannot be solved simply by using less "sophisticated" subjects. Conformity studies using high-school students have also shown high percentages of suspicious subjects. In one study 55.7 percent of the boys tested and 38.8 percent of the girls tested were suspicious (Stricker, Messick, and Jackson, 1967). The current emphasis on group conformity in the mass media may be alerting precollege subjects.

More work is needed to assess whether or not the high percentage of suspicion found in these two conformity studies is typical. However, the results do suggest that when future studies are done using the Asch procedure, investigators will have to be more concerned with the problem of the suspicious student. If students conform less when they are suspicious (Glinski, Glinski, and Slatin, 1970) and suspicion has been more widespread than commonly thought, the true incidence of conformity may be even higher than that reported in the literature.

I felt disturbed, puzzled, separated, like an outcast from the rest. Every time I disagreed I was beginning to wonder if I wasn't beginning to look funny.

[Asch, 1952, p. 465.]

When the time comes again for you to call out your judgment, what do you think you will do? Will you say what you see or go along with the majority? If you are like the other college students who have participated in this procedure, the majority of the time you will call the judgments as you see them: 66.8 percent of all of the judgments given by the subjects were correct and independent. But the rest of the time you will conform and give incorrect answers. And the difficulty of the judgments will not account for your giving incorrect answers. In a control condition, in which subjects were tested alone and asked to make exactly the same judgments, only 7.4 percent of the judgments given were incorrect, but in the conformity setting 33.2 percent of the judgments given were inaccurate (Asch, 1952).

Of course, not all subjects react in the same manner. As you might expect, some conform much more often than others. Twenty percent of those tested were independent on all of the trials, and 10 percent went along with the majority either on all of the trials or on all but one. Further, conformity occurred more frequently on some trials than others. Subjects seemed to yield more on the trials in which longer lines were involved (Asch, 1952).

Thus through the simple procedure of having a unanimous group of people say something that is obviously incorrect, a person can be made to modify what he says to conform to the majority opinion. See Box 2. If one-third of the judgments can be influenced when the situation is as clear as this one was, how much more conformity would obtain in areas that are not as cut-and-dried?

Although individuality is officially admired in college circles, you have only to look about you to see numerous instances of conformity. (See Figure 11-7.) For instance, is the remarkable similarity of dress in the college classroom a coincidence? Sight unseen, you could probably predict with considerable accuracy the relative number of girls wearing dresses and jeans in a particular class. In fact, one approach to conformity has been to do just this. When behaviors have been classified according to the extent to which they adhere to a norm, it has been found that most behaviors do adhere, a few deviate slightly, and even fewer deviate significantly (Allport, 1934; Walker and Heyns, 1962).

But people may adhere to a norm for a number of reasons. College students may prefer jeans because they are less expensive or because they are readily obtainable. Thus rather than cataloging the incidence of adherence to existing norms, it might be more interesting to study the processes by which people are made to modify their behavior and beliefs so that they conform to the majority—as the subjects sometimes did in the Asch experiment.

That behavior can be modified by peer pressure is hardly news. Many studies have shown that peer pressure can influence an individual's judgments in an impressively wide range of areas (Allen and Levine, 1971a). You can see this as you observe your fellow college students. The opinion of others markedly influences behavior and beliefs in areas as disparate as philosophy of life, clothing, and even the decision to smoke marijuana. In one recent study of middle-class college graduates who had tried marijuana, the majority reported that curiosity and the desire to go along with friends were the major reasons (Keeler, 1968). Even sex isn't immune to peer group pressure. As one female Yale sophomore wrote, in a setting in which sexual activity is the norm, virginity can be an embarrassment:

I—the one who slept alone, the one whose only pills were vitamins and aspirin—I was the embarrassed one.

[Maynard, 1972, p. 259.]

Thus conformity is a pervasive phenomenon in groups, whether we like it or not and whether or not we are willing to admit its existence. The

FIGURE 11-7 Jeans seem to be the unofficial uniform on many campuses. (Jean Raisler)

FIGURE 11-8 "Well, heck! If all you smart cookies agree, who am I to dissent?" (Drawing by Handelsman © 1972, *The New Yorker Magazine*, Inc.)

real question, then, is not whether or not it occurs, but why?

Why do people conform?

When the evidence of their senses provided information inconsistent with that given by an incorrect majority, why did the subjects in the Asch experiment conform as often as they did? Reviewing the reactions of our hypothetical subject suggests that the unanimous majority exerted its power through roughly two different forms of pressure: (1) informational pressure and (2) normative pressure (Kelley, 1952).

Informational Pressures Toward Conformity What we know of reality is basically determined by two sources of information: our direct sensory experience of what exists and what other people say. Whenever the evidence from our senses is at all ambiguous—and it frequently is—we look primarily to what others say and do to define reality. (See Figure 11-8.) If you are driving with the sun in your eyes and cannot determine whether a traffic light is red or green, you may watch to see what others do and follow

their lead. Similarly, if in your social psychology class you are given an assignment that is completely new to you, you may check with others to see how they interpret the assignment and what they are doing. Examples of the information provided by others could go on and on. As we saw in Chapter 2, even your definition of your own identity is, in large part, determined by how certain others react to you.

An "informational" approach to the way in which the individual is influenced by the majority would focus on the fact that the subjects in the Asch conformity experiment yielded because they thought the majority was correct. And we saw examples of this trust in the wisdom of the majority in our hypothetical subject's reactions. Thus the less clear physical reality is, the greater the impact of the majority would be expected to be. As we shall see, a number of studies support this hypothesis.

Normative Pressures Toward Conformity In addition to exerting influence through their informational function, groups may pressure individuals to conform in order to avoid punishment, to win group acceptance, and to avoid the embarrassment of being "different"—since to be different usually means that attempts will be made to bring you back in line. (See Figure 11-9.) For instance, a pro-Nixon student might suppress his feelings among anti-Nixon students for fear that the others would ridicule and reject him, that he would stand out as being different, and that the others would try to convert him to their political beliefs.

That the deviant's concern about mistreatment seems to be well founded has been shown in a number of studies. For instance, in a recent series of studies subjects who were made to feel different were uncomfortable and worried about being mistreated, and it seems that their worries were somewhat realistic. When nondeviants were asked to select either a deviant or a nondeviant as a target for aggression, the deviants were selected significantly more often (Freedman and Doob, 1968).

In addition to a deviant's concern about punishment for nonconformity, normative pressures toward conformity may be exerted more subtly. A person may conform because he wishes to avoid the embarrassment of being different. In a restaurant where you don't know anyone, spill-ing your coffee all over your lap may be extremely embarrassing because it makes you stand out and destroys your image in front of other people. The specter of losing face in front of other people may be sufficient to motivate a great deal of conformity. When others are present and in a position to evaluate your performance, you may adhere to what you know is "appropriate" conduct simply to avoid the embarrassment of being different (Modigliani, 1971).

A "normative" understanding of conformity, then, would hold that subjects conform because they are afraid of what will happen to them if they do not conform. From this approach it would follow that any factors in the situation that heighten the group's ability to identify and punish deviance can be expected to increase conformity. As we shall see when we examine some situational variables, there is a considerable amount of evidence in support of this hypothesis.

Situational determinants of conformity

Numerous replications of the Asch conformity experiment have shown that a number of aspects of the situation can influence the relative incidence of conformity. We shall discuss the effects of several situational variables that have been shown consistently to have a marked influence on conformity, but this review is not intended to be all-inclusive.

Our description of these variables will be organized into two parts: (1) those that seem to increase the informational power of the group and (2) those that seem to increase its normative potential. However, this separation is at best approximate. Most of the conformity research has focused exclusively on the effects of situational variations that influence the *incidence* of conformity; explanations of these effects have been left largely to speculation.

Informational Aspects of the Situation An informational approach to conformity would predict that the probability of an individual's conforming to the group would increase as one or more of the following variables increased: (1) the difficulty or ambiguity of the task, (2) the per-

FIGURE 11-9 "Meet young Doctor Hennessey, gentlemen. He's a great believer in socialized medicine. I'm sure you'll have a lot to talk about."

ceived competence of the majority in relation to the subject, (3) the size of the group (a majority of three is significantly more influential than a majority of two), and (4) the amount of agreement in the group.

DIFFICULTY AND AMBIGUITY The results of a number of studies have shown that the more difficult the task is or the more ambiguous the judgment is, the greater the incidence of conformity. In the Asch conformity situation, for instance, when the differences between the length of lines decreased, the subjects conformed more frequently (Asch, 1952). When subjects were asked to make judgments from their memory of the two cards, there was a higher incidence of conformity than when the cards were in front of them (Deutsch and Gerard, 1955). These findings fit very neatly into social comparison theory. The more ambiguous reality is, the more likely one is to depend on others for information.

RELATIVE COMPETENCY OF THE SUBJECT AND THE GROUP   Again as social comparison theory would predict, the more competent the majority seems to be or the less competent the subject is made to feel, the more likely he is to conform (Hollander and Willis, 1967). Again, the results of a number of studies support this hypothesis. For instance, in one recent study it was found that subjects who saw themselves as less competent than the other members of the group were more likely to conform than those who perceived themselves as more competent than the other members of the group (Ettinger et al., 1971). The more confident one is in his own judgment, the less likely is he to rely on judgments provided by others.

GROUP SIZE The results of a number of laboratory studies suggest that the majority does not have to be very large to exert its maximal effect. In Asch's original experiment a majority consisting of either eight or sixteen persons did not exert a significantly greater effect than one consisting of four people (Asch, 1952). However, the results of a subsequent study indicated that the incidence of conformity was significantly higher when the majority numbered six or seven people than when it consist-

ed of three or four (Gerard, Wilhelmy, and Connolley, 1968).

In real life, though, there may be a different relationship between the size of the majority and the incidence of conformity. Some have argued that as group size increases, so will conformity (Krech, Crutchfield, and Ballachey, 1962). In larger groups punishment for deviance may be easier. But one could also argue that in real life even smaller numbers of people may exert maximal conformity pressure. In the intensive relationship of two close friends, any deviation may be very painful and so may be resisted.

GROUP UNANIMITY If the unanimity of the majority is broken, the incidence of conformity decreases significantly. When, in a variation of the Asch procedure, one of the confederates was instructed to give the correct answer, the incidence of conformity dropped sharply (Asch, 1952). Subsequent work has confirmed the importance of the subject's having social support in reducing the incidence of conformity. Even if the social support emanates from someone who is wearing extremely thick glasses (which would cast some doubt on his ability to judge comparison lines), his agreement with the subject's judgment will reduce the incidence of the subject's conforming to the remainder of the group (Allen and Levine, 1971b).

Why does social support reduce conformity so significantly? There are a number of possible explanations. First, Asch felt that the fact that the consensus of the majority was broken showed that a variety of opinions and answers was possible. Second, having a partner meant that the subject did not stand alone as an isolated deviant who might be rejected by the group. Third, and perhaps most important, social support provides the subject with an independent source of information, to which he can compare his own views of reality. From this hypothesis it would follow that the more valid the information provided by the "ally," the less likely the subject will be to conform to the majority. This result has been obtained in a recent study (Allen and Levine, 1971b).

Normative Pressures in the Situation As the normative approach to conformity would predict, pressure toward individual conformity to the group will be enhanced by: (1) the degree to which the individual is attracted to the group, (2) within limits, the extent to which he feels insecure about his standing in the group, (3) the amount of publicity given to his judgments, and (4) the extent to which he lacks commitment to an independent judgment.

COHESIVENESS AND CONFORMITY The more the individual is attracted to the group, the more likely he is to conform. In one Asch type of situation subjects were told that the members of the group making the fewest errors would be given theater tickets. When the members of the group were working for this common goal, they were much more likely to conform than when they were not united in search of a common goal (Deutsch and Gerard, 1955). In another study there was significantly more conformity in groups composed of people who knew one another than in groups of strangers (Thibaut and Strickland, 1956).

Several interpretations of these findings are possible. One is that the more the individual is concerned with maintaining his relationship with the other members of the group, the more punishing a rejection would be. He is therefore more motivated to conform in order to avoid rejection and the embarrassment of being different. Another is that conditions that make a group more attractive to an individual may also make the other members of the group more likely to punish deviance. For instance, if the members of a group are working toward a prize, they may be more likely to punish deviance, since it jeopardizes their getting what they want. Or as the results of one recent study suggest, it may be that the potential for embarrassment is higher when people expect to continue interacting with others (Brown and Garland, 1971).

STATUS AND CONFORMITY Although the evidence is somewhat complicated, it seems that persons of medium status are most likely to conform. Persons who have very high status and are confident that the other members of the group like them may be free to deviate. The leader of a group probably knows that he won't be rejected for one deviation. Persons with very low status are also free to deviate. With their low position in the group, they may feel that they have nothing to lose. Further, the very reason for the person's low status may be his general tendency to deviate from the group. Individuals of medium status, however, may not be free to deviate. They have enough status to care about what others in the group think of them, but not enough to risk losing any. There is some evidence in support of this hypothesized relationship between status and conformity. In one study, for instance, it was found that subjects who were either very low or very high in group acceptance conformed significantly less than did subjects of moderate status (Dittes and Kelley, 1956).

PUBLICITY AND CONFORMITY As would be predicted by a normative approach, it has been shown repeatedly that the more the identity of the subject is made public, the more likely he is to conform. For instance, in an Asch type of experiment subjects who gave their judgments face-to-face with the majority conformed significantly more often than did subjects who gave their judgments anonymously behind partitions (Deutsch and Gerard, 1955).

When the individual's responses are anonymous, the other people in the group may never know that he deviated, so that any possibility of group retaliation for deviance is eliminated. Even if the group members should find out somehow that he deviated, in the anonymity of his booth he is safe from immediate reprisals and so may feel freer to deviate. Further, when he is alone, the individual's deviance may be less embarrassing to him. In fact, some have theorized that embarrassment can occur only when other people are present (Modigliani, 1971).

Thus it may be that only when the potential normative pressures from other people are removed can one test to see if the individual has privately accepted what the group says. As long as other people are present and aware of what the individual is saying, it is impossible to know whether the individual is simply publicly complying while believing something else or whether he has really accepted what the group says. If the individual is only publicly complying, he may do what he pleases when group pressure is removed. This has been clearly shown in a real-life study. The investigator interviewed a group of physicians to assess their attitudes toward new drugs and then examined the prescriptions they had written to see how well their words corresponded to their actions. Interestingly, their publicly stated attitudes were much more modern than their privately written prescriptions would have led one to expect (Menzel, 1957).

Much of the conformity research has involved situations where the subjects were not anonymous. Thus it could be said to have focused primarily on the determinants of public compliance. In contrast, as we saw in Chapter 4, much of the work on the determinants of attitude change has involved questionnaire responses, which are relatively private. Attitude change and private acceptance in a conformity situation clearly involve common processes (Kiesler and Kiesler, 1969). If an individual changes his attitude because of something he is told, he has internalized a different reaction, and if an individual internalizes the majority reaction, that too involves some of the same processes. Since common processes are involved in conformity and attitude change, the findings in one area may yield interesting hypotheses to be tested in the other. For example, in Chapter 4 we saw that both the similarity and the expertness of the communicator influenced his effectiveness in changing the subjects' attitudes. One could also test the relative contribution of these two variables in a conformity situation.

COMMITMENT The more an individual commits himself to a position, the less likely he is to conform to group pressures. If the subject in an Asch type of procedure were to announce his judgment publicly before hearing what the majority had to say, he would be less likely to conform, since the others would be aware of his allowing himself to be influenced by group pressure. Thus if he wanted to maintain his image in front of the others, he would not be as free to conform.

Even if his commitment were private, he would be less free to conform. If the subject wrote down his own initial judgment before hearing what the others had to say and then changed his response, he would know that he was conforming. Given the negative connotations of conformity for most people, the individual's own knowledge that he is conforming

would be upsetting and perhaps embarrassing. If he makes no commitment, he is much freer to change. He can always pretend to himself that he wasn't really sure or that he changed his reaction after a more careful reflection on the matter.

From these arguments it would follow that the more committed the individual is—either publicly or privately—the less likely he is to conform. Support for this hypothesis has been obtained in an Asch type of procedure in which four different types of commitment were obtained. Some subjects made no public or private statement of their judgments until they had heard the judgments of the majority. Other subjects made a minimal private commitment by writing their answers down on a so-called magic pad, a writing surface made up of a piece of cellophane over a layer of graphite. Erasing the magic pad was easy, since all the subject had to do was lift the cellophane. In a third condition subjects wrote down their judgments on a piece of paper, without signing their names. In a fourth condition subjects wrote down their judgments and signed their names.

As the degree of commitment increased, the incidence of conformity decreased significantly. Although 24.7 percent of the subjects who had made no commitment conformed, the percentage was only 16.3 percent in the magic pad condition and only 5.7 percent in the two conditions where the judgments had been written (Deutsch and Gerard, 1955).

Personal characteristics of the individual

We have considered conformity in terms of variations in the situation. But are certain persons more likely to conform in any situation? Are women, for instance, more likely to conform than men? Are intelligent people less likely to conform? You may be able to think of a number of variables that you would expect to be related to conformity. Commonsensical notions about conformity would seem to hold that some kinds of people are more likely to conform than others.

Commonsensical as the notions may seem, attempts to specify characteristics that are consistently related to conformity have not been very successful (Hollander and Willis, 1967). True, some characteristics have been found to correlate significantly in some studies; but often the correlations have not been very large, and the results have often been inconsistent. People who conform more in one situation may not do so in another situation. In fact, in one study it was found that only 20 percent of the subjects studied showed any consistency in their conformity behavior across four different situations (Vaughan, 1964).

As an illustration of how complexly personal characteristics can interact with the situation, let us examine sexual differences in conformity behavior. It has been shown repeatedly that in our culture women conform significantly more than men in almost all situations (Nord, 1969). Considering the historical passivity of the feminine sex role in our culture, you may feel that this is a highly predictable finding. However, some recent work suggests that whether or not women conform more than men depends very much on the demands of the particular situation. If the conformity task is one that is more familiar and interesting to women, they conform significantly less than men do (Sistrunk and McDavid, 1971). Whether women conform more or less than men may really depend on the level of their interest in the task as well as the level of their sophistication in the matter at hand.

The weakness and inconsistency of the findings concerning other personal characteristics may also be a product of the impact of the situation. In the attempt to specify characteristics that apply to leaders in all situations, we saw that what characterizes a particular leader may depend on the situation, and the same may be true of the conformer. Thus the general findings that persons who are more intelligent tend to conform less may be influenced by the situation (Nord, 1969). If conformity is essential to obtain something that the individual wants and needs, the intelligent person may see the need for conformity before someone who is less intelligent. Similarly, the general finding that people who are likely to conform have low self-confidence and low self-esteem may vary in certain situations (Nord, 1969). Even if a person has a generally low opinion of his own skills, he may resist group pressures in an area in which he feels expert.

Thus as one reviewer has noted, personality factors may be more important as they interact with situational factors. Rather than attempting to specify characteristics of people who will conform in all situations, it may be more fruitful to study those characteristics that make conformity in particular situations more likely (Hunt, 1965).

Again, forever Asch?

Just as research on impression formation has tended to focus almost exclusively on Asch's technique, so research in conformity has centered mainly on Asch's conformity procedure or mechanized simulations of it. Although Asch's technique is exciting and the studies using this technique have provided valuable information on the incidence and determinants of conformity, one can ask whether the preoccupation with the Asch conformity paradigm has resulted in an undue emphasis on the situation of one person who is required to make a verbal judgment when confronted with a unanimous majority. Clearly, in real life there are many other social influence situations.

Behavioral Conformity Occasionally, a person is pressured to act, rather than to give a verbal judgment. For example, a group of your friends may try to talk you into seeing a film that you don't want to see. Some of Milgram's work on obedience provides some interesting insights into this kind of conformity. In one variation on his basic procedure (in which, you will recall, an experimenter instructs subjects to administer what they think is a painful shock to an experimental confederate), a third of the subjects were tested with two experimental confederates who refused to administer the shocks; another third were tested with two confederates who agreed to give the shocks; and another third were tested alone with the experimenter.

As might be expected, the rate of compliance was significantly lower when the confederates refused to administer the shock than when the subjects were tested alone. Surprisingly, though, there was no significant difference in the rate of compliance between subjects tested alone and those tested with the confederate who was willing to administer the shocks (Milgram, 1965a). Apparently, in this situation the influence exerted by the experimenter's request was so powerful that the addition of peer group pressure did not contribute materially to compliance.

Are the determinants of behavioral conformity the same or different from those shown in the Asch type of conformity situation? Since so little work has been done on behavioral conformity, the answer to this question is not clear. However, one might speculate that slightly different variables may be involved. Since behavior may require more effort than a verbal response, stronger pressures may be required to induce conformity. For instance, it may be easier to get an antiblack person to modify his questionnaire response to indicate less prejudice than to get him to take some form of pro-black action.

Power of a Consistent Minority In real life one person or a subgroup of persons holding views that are highly divergent from those held by the majority may eventually persuade the majority to accept their views. History provides numerous examples of such cases. When Freud originally introduced his work around the turn of the century, the reaction of the scientific community was hardly enthusiastic. He was either damned or ignored by most of his colleagues. Today, some of his theories are accepted by the scientific community as truisms.

There is clearly more to social influence than the deviant's either slavishly accepting or remaining independent of the majority's view. When not all of the members of a group agree, social influence can work both ways; the majority can influence the minority, or the minority can influence the majority. As we saw in Chapter 9, in the forming of norms, all of the judgments given by the group members influence the reactions of the other members. Each person takes the judgments given by the others into account, so that the final norm is the result of a series of "reciprocal concessions" (Moscovici and Faucheux, 1972). Reaching consensus may be more essential on matters important to the members of the group—such as beliefs about physical reality—than on attitudes, values, or tastes. Disagreement on important issues may threaten the group's survival or its ability to think and perform rationally.

If the attempt to move toward consensus is common to all social influence situations, then if a minority consistently gives answers that deviate from those expressed by the majority,

the only way for the majority to move toward consensus may be to move toward the minority opinion. Just this reaction has been shown in a series of studies (Moscovici and Faucheux, 1972). In fact, it has been found that a consistent minority can even modify the color perception of naïve subjects. All of the subjects were shown thirty-six slides that were clearly blue (as shown by the responses given by subjects in a control group). Each experimental group consisted of six people, four naïve subjects and two confederates who consistently said—slide after slide—that the slides were green. Each subject was asked to indicate the color of the slide being shown. Even though all of the slides were clearly blue, 32 percent of the subjects identified at least one of the slides as green, and 8.42 percent of the total responses given by all of the subjects agreed with the minority view.

To see whether the effect of the consistent minority on the subjects' perception persisted after the confederates ceased responding, the investigators had the naïve subjects participate in a subsequent study in which they were shown colored disks, some of which were clearly blue or green and others of which could be labeled as either blue or green. Subjects who had been exposed to the "green-saying" confederates saw more of the ambiguous chips as green than did a control group of subjects who had not been exposed to a green-saying minority. In fact, the impact of the consistent minority was even greater in this exercise than it had been in the slide-labeling experiment.

How does a minority influence the judgments of the majority? Several possibilities have been suggested. First, if the minority's responses are coherent and consistent, the members of the majority are faced with the dilemma of a conflicting opinion. Having no reason to suspect the authenticity of the minority position, the majority may try to understand the minority position and to see the basis for the minority judgments. The "cognitive work" involved in trying to understand the minority position may thus have been the reason for the modification of the subjects' perception of the stimuli. Second, in a situation in which there is a deviant point of view and a consistent majority, most of the communications are directed toward the deviants (Schachter, 1951). Thus the deviants may have a greater number of persuasion opportunities than the members of the majority. Finally, the minority subgroup or individual may act as a model of independence, so that each member of the group may come to value *his* individual answers more.

Of course, the majority does not always move toward the consistent minority's point of view. Even though Gus Hall, the American Communist party leader, has been reasonably consistent in his views, we can doubt that he has converted many people in Nixon's silent majority. Sometimes deviants are rejected, as we saw earlier. Sometimes, if the deviant point of view is retained, its presence may polarize both the minority and the majority reactions. And sometimes deviant views may be accepted by the majority even though the original holders of those views remain deviants. The determinants of these possible outcomes present a fascinating area for future research work on social influence.

542

Social Psychology and Modern Life

Summary

In this section we have seen the power and pervasiveness of group pressure. Although individuality is officially admired in college circles, you have only to look about you to see numerous instances of conformity. Conformity has been demonstrated repeatedly in laboratory studies. When, in the classic Asch experiment, subjects were confronted with a situation in which the answers given by a majority were incorrect, one-third of their judgments were conforming and incorrect. Thus the *Asch experiment* has shown that through the simple procedure of having a unanimous group of people say something that is obviously incorrect, college students can occasionally be made to modify what they say to conform to the majority opinion.

How does the group exert its pressure on the individual? First, other people are an important source of *information*. Whenever reality is at all ambiguous, we look primarily to what others say and do to define reality. *Any variations in the situation that are likely to make the individual think the majority is correct will increase the incidence of conformity.* The more difficult and ambiguous the task is, the more competent the majority is in relation to the subject, and the larger the group is (a majority of three is significantly more influential than one of one or two), the greater the probability that the subject will conform. Further, the subject is more likely to conform when the group is unanimous than when the unanimity is broken.

Normative pressures may also make an individual conform. People may conform in order to avoid punishment for deviancy, to win group acceptance, or to avoid the embarrassment of being different—since to be different usually means that attempts will be made to bring you back in line. From the normative approach to conformity, it would follow that *any factors in the situation that heighten the group's ability to identify and punish deviance would be expected to increase conformity.* There is a considerable amount of evidence in support of this hypothesis. The more the individual is attracted to the group, the less secure he is about his standing in the group (within limits), the more publicity his judgments are given, and the less committed he is to an independent judgment, the more likely he is to conform.

In addition to discussing situational determinants of conformity, we considered the question of whether or not certain persons are more likely to conform in any situation. We saw that *attempts to specify characteristics that are consistently related to conformity have not been very successful.*

Finally, we saw that research in the area of conformity has centered mainly on Asch's classic procedure. Although this is an exciting procedure, one can ask whether the preoccupation with his paradigm has resulted in an undue emphasis on one type of social influence situation: the case of one person who is required to make a verbal judgment when confronted with a unanimous majority.

In real life there are many *other social influence situations*. Occasionally, a person is pressured to make his actions coincide with what others are doing. Milgram's obedience work provides some interesting insights into this kind of *behavioral obedience*. Also, in real life *one person or a subgroup of persons holding views that are divergent from those held by the majority sometimes persuades the majority to accept its views.* Just this reaction has been shown in a number of studies.

Group Effectiveness: An Overview

We have seen how groups are formed, how they evolve a structure, which may include leadership roles, and how they function. We now come to an issue of great practical importance—the effectiveness of a group.

There are two main ways of evaluating a group's effectiveness. One approach, which has dominated most of the research, is to focus on the extent to which a group accomplishes its work goals. According to this "productivity" approach, a group's effectiveness is gauged solely by the amount of work it achieves.

Another approach is to assess the extent to which a group meets the social and emotional needs of its members. As we saw in Chapter 5, feelings of loneliness and alienation are common in today's rootless society. Loneliness may have replaced sex as contemporary man's area of greatest deprivation. Thus according to a "social" measure of effectiveness, an effective group would be one that lessens the loneliness of its members.

We can ask if the productivity and social measures of effectiveness are necessarily in conflict. Might not the most effective groups—both from the members' point of view and on an objective basis of productivity—be those that are highly satisfying to their members? If a group is highly cohesive and the group norm is to work hard, the members of the group may be much more motivated and work much harder than they would if they didn't value their group membership as much.

In some situations, however, personal-social requirements can interfere with a group's accomplishing its work goals. If a work group evolves a norm about the appropriate level of productivity, strong social pressure can be brought to bear on the members of the group to adhere to that norm, thus limiting the productivity of those who could produce more. This was shown very clearly in a classic study of the productivity of a group of workers who were paid on a piece-rate basis—so much money for each unit produced. A norm concerning the amount of work each person should do per day had evolved, and even though each worker could have made more money by working harder, each agreed to slack off after he had met the socially approved daily quota.

Obviously, anyone who produced more than the normative rate would make the others look bad in the eyes of their superiors, so that very intense pressures were exerted against rate busters—people who exceeded the norms. If you have ever worked in a factory, you may have experienced some of these not-too-subtle pressures. The other members of the group feel free to make their negative feelings known, and they ostracize anyone who produces too much. The pressures applied may even take a direct physical form. In this study a socially acceptable form of punishment evolved. People who produced too much were "binged"—hit sharply on the upper arm—and were not allowed to hit back. Thus the blow not only hurt the deviant but also gave the group members a very concrete way of expressing their disapproval (Homans, 1965).

From findings such as these, the view emerged that meeting the social-emotional needs of the group members interfered with their productivity, and this view persisted in the "human relations" approach to industry for quite a while. Since production was the main concern, most of the research focused on the antecedents of productivity and neglected the determinants of social-emotional effectiveness. Thus as we shall see, much more is known about the conditions that create an effective work group, a fact that shows something about the entrepreneurial bias permeating our society.

The Effective Work Group

Which do you think is more effective—working alone or with other people? Obviously, the question of the relative effectiveness of the individual and of the group is one of great practical importance. If the high frequency of committee meetings in business, education, government, and social organizations is any reflection of current assumptions, it seems that the popular wisdom is that "two heads are better than one." Of course, there may be other reasons for the high frequency of work done by committees besides a belief in the productivity of committees. People may prefer committees because they wish to avoid the personal responsibility involved in individual decision making. Or without necessarily realizing that they are doing so, they may set up committees simply to be with other people. Work may be a great cover for socializing.

The question of whether or not a group is more effective than an individual can be separated into two different questions: (1) Is a group of people more effective than any one member of that group would be working alone? (2) Is a group of people working together more effective than the same people would be if they spent the same amount of time working separately?

One person versus a group

The answer to the first question is fairly clear. Generally, a group of people will be more effective than any one person would be working alone. (See Figure 11-10.) Groups of people can accomplish physical tasks that would be impossible for any one person working alone. Obviously, building a house would be very difficult for one person working by himself. Divided between twelve people, the same task would be much easier. The same general superiority in numbers applies to intellectual tasks. The results of a number of studies have shown that there is superiority in numbers (Davis, 1969). There are at least two reasons why this should occur. With a greater number of judgments, there is less variability and more chance for errors to correct themselves. If the task is a complicated one, there is a greater chance that at least one person will have the needed skills.

However, there may be exceptions to the general rule of group superiority. If an individual is extremely gifted, he may be more effective alone than a group of other, less gifted persons. For instance, Freud might not have been able to evolve his controversial theories had he been bogged down in endless committee meetings with contemporary physicians. If time is very limited, an individual may be superior to a group. A number of studies have consistently shown that groups are much slower than individuals (Kelley and Thibaut, 1969). Further, if a task requires a very high degree of coordination and organization, an individual may be superior to a group, since he can better organize his activities. And, of course, as we saw in the preceding section, people in groups are subjected to very intense social pressures, so that once a group norm emerges—no matter how nonsensical—conformity may subvert the efforts of gifted members of a group.

Working together or working separately

Generally, however, the group is superior to the individual in terms of productivity. The more interesting question is whether the same people are more effective working separately or together. (See Figure 11-11.) For instance, assume that your social psychology instructor said he was going to distribute a take-home final one week before the examination and that groups of five students would be assigned to prepare the answers. You would have the option of working independently and then pooling your work or meeting as a committee. Which would

FIGURE 11-10 "Many hands make light the work." (Drawing by O'Brien © 1971, *The New Yorker Magazine*, Inc.)

FIGURE 11-11 TOGETHER . . .

. . . **OR SEPARATELY?** (R. Lynn Goldberg)

be the more efficient way to use your time? Would it be more productive for you and each of the other students assigned to the committee to work alone for six hours and then pool your answers? Or would it be more productive to meet with the other five students and work for six hours together?

This decision might not be easy for you to make. At their best committees can be very productive. With an effective chairman, who coordinates the activities of the members, and competent committee members, who possess complementary skills and information, a committee working as a group can be extremely effective. The summation and coordination of individual strengths may result in a final group product that is superior to what any one member of a committee could have evolved alone. If you were not very clear on attribution theory, for instance, another member of the committee might be more knowledgeable in that area. The presence of a number of different perspectives can also provide a better balance of views and a chance to correct each other's errors. Simply having to verbalize your thoughts may make you think more clearly than you would alone. The ideas of others in the group might stimulate thoughts you would not have had alone (Jones and Gerard, 1967).

If the task is one that can be readily divided, a committee may also be much more effective than individuals working separately at the same task. Each member of the committee could work on that aspect of the exam that he knew best.

Further, if the group members like one another and are all deeply involved in the assignment, the committee members may be much more highly motivated than they would be if they were working alone. If you like the others and a norm has evolved to work hard, you may feel much more pressure to perform than you would if only your course grade were involved.

But, on the other hand, committees can be just awful. You may have been involved with committees that had endless and unproductive meetings, which were spent trying to organize the group and make assignments. The members of the group may be more concerned with maintaining or creating good relationships with the others on the committee than with the examination. More time may be spent rapping than in discussing social psychology. People

may be reluctant to criticize anyone who isn't working effectively. As the apocryphal saying that a camel is a horse designed by a committee would suggest, once group norms emerge, the group members may be afraid to deviate— no matter how foolish the norm.

Moreover, since a committee's usual focus is on its collective product rather than on the sum of its individual products, no one person is solely responsible for his work or lack of work. Thus the support provided by the group may make its members feel free not to work. After all, if the committee doesn't prepare the answers for the examination well, there will be at least four other people to share the blame. Further, if no one emerges to organize and coordinate the activities, the committee members may not work as hard because they may not be sure of what they are expected to do. If the chairman fails to direct the group, verbose and not-too-bright members of the committee may dominate the discussion. To add to the group's problems, a struggle for status among the group members may distract them from their work. In summary, committee meetings can sometimes be lessons in communal mediocrity. See Box 3, page 548.

Thus your answer to the question of whether it is better to work separately or in a group might be that *it depends on a lot of other variables*. This is basically the answer provided by the results of hundreds of studies comparing the relative effectiveness of a set number of individuals working separately and of the same number of individuals working in groups. Sometimes interacting groups have been found to be more effective than the same number of people have been when they worked alone and then pooled their work products; sometimes interacting groups have not been found to be more effective (Shaw, 1971).

Variables that influence group productivity

Whether or not a group is more effective than a collection of individuals working separately and pooling their work depends on a very large number of variables. We shall now cover the evidence concerning some of the more important variables that have been researched: (a) the task, (b) group cohesiveness, (c) the communication patterns in the group, (d) the size of the group, (e) the group composition, and (f) the members' identification with the group goal. Because of the large volume of work in this area, our review will be selective in nature and will treat only those findings that have had general support.

The Task The task that has to be done is a major determinant of whether groups or individuals are more effective. As you might expect, there is a higher potential for productivity in groups when *tasks can be easily subdivided*. If there were ten questions on the take-home final and each member of our social psychology committee was assigned two questions in the areas in which the committee found him to be the most competent, then the group product would probably be superior to that of any one individual who prepared answers to the entire set of questions or to that of a nominal group, in which subjects worked separately and were randomly assigned the various questions. But if the assignments were made on any basis other than relative competency, group productivity could be disastrously low (Steiner, 1972).

With *unitary tasks,* tasks that cannot be subdivided easily, whether an interacting group or a nominal group is more effective depends on the complexity of the task. If the task is one that requires few steps and the correct answer—once it is reached—is obvious to all of the members of the group, the group may perform at the level of its most effective member. If the task is so simple that the distractions of a social setting will not interfere with the ability of the more competent members of the group, and the answer is obviously correct to all of the members of the group after it has evolved, then groups neither add nor subtract to the level of performance of the more able members (Kelley and Thibaut, 1969).

If the unitary task involves putting together multiple pieces of information, as in recalling the details of an event, groups may be more effective than individuals. The memories of the various group members can be pooled and cross-checked for accuracy. If, however, solving the problem requires a very high degree of organization and an orderly progression

through a complicated series of steps, with an application of what is learned in the earlier steps to the later stages, then individuals may perform better alone than they do in a group setting. Imagine trying to write a term paper in a committee! If different members had alternative views of how the paper should be organized and which studies should be covered, they would simply confuse one another (Kelley and Thibaut, 1969).

Group Cohesiveness The relationship between productivity and group cohesiveness is even more complex. Research in this area has provided inconsistent findings. Sometimes groups high in cohesiveness have been found to be more effective (e.g., Van Zelst, 1952), sometimes less effective (e.g., Schachter et al., 1951), and sometimes there has been no significant relationship between cohesiveness and productivity (e.g., Bridgeman, 1972).

Perhaps an example will illustrate some of the complexities of the cohesiveness-work relationship. Assume that your social psychology instructor has set up two committees to prepare the answers for a take-home final. The students on one committee happen to like each other a great deal, and the students on the other committee do not like each other very much. Which group will be more effective? The answer to this question may seem obvious: Those who like each other will be able to get along better, will coordinate their activities more closely, will be more involved with the group, and so will do a better job. This has been found in some studies. For instance, teams of carpenters and bricklayers comprised of friends were found to be more productive than teams that were assigned without regard to sociometric choices (Van Zelst, 1952).

If you've ever worked on a committee composed of friends, however, you may know that cohesiveness can have its price in productivity. Studies have shown this too (e.g., Schachter et al., 1951). If we consider some of the characteristics of highly cohesive groups, we can see clearly why this result can occur also. The members of cohesive groups are highly concerned about maintaining their relationships with the other members of the group. Thus they may spend more time talking with the others than working. The "business" meetings of a highly cohesive social psychology committee may deteriorate into rap sessions between friends. In a highly cohesive group people may be very reluctant to criticize anyone who is not doing his job for fear of alienating him.

As we have seen, the pressures toward conformity are much more intense in highly cohesive groups. If a norm limiting productivity evolves, the members of a highly cohesive group are more likely to adhere to it and produce less. In a highly cohesive committee, for instance, if the norm evolves that each person should spend the minimum amount of time necessary to do the work, the members will be highly likely to go along. In a low cohesiveness committee, however, if someone indicated that he didn't plan to spend much time, his enemies might begin working harder just to show him up. But, of course, if the norm evolves in the highly cohesive group that the members should work as hard as they can so the whole group can do the best job in the class, that norm, too, will be enforced. Thus the effect of cohesiveness on productivity may depend, in large part, on the norms that evolve in the group.

Communication Patterns   As we saw in Chapter 10, a number of studies have confirmed what businessmen have long suspected—that the patterns of communication have important effects on group functioning. However, the precise effects of varying the many possible communication networks are still somewhat debatable. Because there are a number of inconsistent findings in the literature, it is not possible to make generalizations about the effect of particular patterns of communication in all situations (Collins and Raven, 1969).

However, the majority of the studies would support the hypothesis that when the task is a simple one, say one that merely requires the assembling of all of the information held by the various members of the group, then the more centralized networks (such as the Y and the wheel) are the most efficient (e.g., Leavitt, 1951). When simple tasks are being done, the speed and coordination offered by the centralized networks may make them more effective. However, for more complicated tasks, such as mathematical problems, the more decentralized networks are more efficient (Shaw, 1971). When more complicated tasks are being done,

BOX 3

Management by committee is a fact of life in most American corporations. According to a number of studies, up to 50 percent of most managers' time is spent in meetings (Golde, 1972). But if managers are meeting more, there's evidence that they're liking it less. About 75 percent of one group of managers surveyed indicated that they thought most of the meetings they attended were a waste of time—too long, too disorganized, too dull, and too inefficient (Golde, 1972).

If the managers are correct and most meetings are exercises in communal mediocrity, what can be done to improve them? One approach is to have managers analyze case histories of meetings so that they will become more aware of the potential problems in meetings and thus be able to attempt to correct them. An excerpt from one such case history appears below.

Shortly before Jeff Parks, the general manager of a business, was to hold a weekly meeting with four immediate

subordinates, his supervisor told him to get "immediate action" on a layoff report. The main item on the agenda, therefore, was this report. As you read the following excerpt from the beginning of the meeting, try to spot the weaknesses in this meeting:

Parks: Come in. . . (continuing with his work while the . . . managers seat themselves in front of his desk. . .) Hi Carl . . . Pete . . . Tom. How goes it?

Tom: I'm fine, Jeff, 'cept I'm putting a little weight on. How's your diet, Carl?

Carl: I haven't lost a pound yet.

Pete: At times I think I'm in the middle of a weight watchers club here.

Tom: You bet your life you are.

Parks (looking up): All fun and games, fellas. . . . Well, we've got lots of problems today. The most important one I want to get started on is the layoff situation. . . . Tom, you want to kick off?

Tom: Well, everything in my department is just fine and dandy. The men we

hired and sent out to the coast are doing a great job. And boy, we're right on the six-month projections we made. And I really couldn't be more pleased.

Parks: And people?

Tom: People are fine. Morale is great. Everybody is putting out 100%.

Parks: Numbers of people?

Tom: We've still got 'em, and each guy is holding right to his quota.

Parks: Pete?

Pete: That new reporting system just isn't going to work. (He turns to Joe.) My middle managers do not have the time to sit down and fill out that report in detail.

Joe (with irritation): Pete, it is just going to take a little time to work out the bugs, but—

Pete (interrupts): These are line managers. You cannot ask them to spend maybe more than half an hour a week at doing this sort of thing. Besides, at present most of them aren't interested in it and we have to motivate them. And that is hard enough to start with. . . . In any case, I'm going to have a big morale problem because I've severely underestimated the amount of space, and as you know, that report is due next week. I don't really know what to do on that subject right now.

Parks: Pete, don't you think the layoffs that you're going to be required to make will help your space situation?

Pete: I don't think that will necessarily help the space situation at all. Most of these men have been with us a long time. I have very little exterior space. As a matter of fact, I'm very short of space, perhaps as much as 15% to 20%—

Parks (interrupts): Pete, we'll have to work that out later. Joe?

Joe: Well, I met with the auditors, and we worked on the depreciation policy. (A long silence follows.)

Parks: Carl?

Carl: I've completed the two-year pro-

jection with the exception of verifying the numbers for the last quarter. I've got a memo going out now to the department managers to verify those numbers. I imagine I'll be having a reply in about three days.

Parks: What kind of people input do you expect?

Carl: At the present time I'm going on the staff we have now—

(Parks's telephone intercom buzzes.)

Parks: Yes?

Secretary: Mr. Norton is here—in from Cleveland. Could you see him for a moment?

Parks (reflects): Tell him I'll be out in a minute, please. (He turns to his managers.) I've got to see him, gentlemen. I'll be right back. Excuse me. (He walks out of the office.)

[Golde, 1972, pp. 70–72. Except for Parks, last name references have been changed to first name references.]

What did you think of this meeting? The general reaction of 200 executives who evaluated it while participating in a management development workshop was that it was not very effective, but, interestingly, that it was "about as good as most they had attended." Many of the managers felt that the meeting wasn't sufficiently structured. Parks, the chairman, had no formal agenda and didn't keep the meeting focused on the major problem—the layoff report. Further, the executives thought the atmosphere of the meeting was too tense and formal. Parks didn't seem receptive to the problems of the managers and didn't try to put them at ease. As you will recall, Parks didn't even stop working when the men came into his office. Further, by leaving the meeting without a more complete explanation and with no suggestions as to how the meeting should progress in his absence, he contributed both to the negative atmosphere and to the lack of structure (Golde, 1972).

the greater opportunity for communication between the members may offer more opportunities for various solutions to be proposed and incorrect solutions to be rejected.

Group Size   Would a committee of ten be more effective than one with five members? Existing evidence on the effects of size on productivity yields no simple answers. This evidence has been very carefully reviewed by Steiner (1972), and his findings are summarized here.

In studies in which productivity has increased with the size of the group, the increments in productivity have tended to be smaller as more people were added to the group. Thus in one study the increase in accuracy from one person to a three-person group was 74 percent, whereas the increase in accuracy from a three-person to a six-person group was only 9 percent (Ziller, 1957).

Why aren't larger groups inevitably more productive? For most jobs there is a greater potential for productivity as a group increases in size. If the task can be subdivided easily, there is less work for any one individual when there are more people. If there are ten questions on a take-home final, each member of a committee of ten would have only one question to answer, whereas each member in a group of five would have two questions to do. Moreover, if the task cannot be divided and the most competent person in the group will provide the answer, there is a greater chance of there being some highly competent people in a larger group. If the final exam question consisted of one very difficult question, it is more likely that at least one person could answer it in a group of ten than in a group of five (Steiner, 1972).

However, although the potential for productivity increases with size, so do the interpersonal problems in a group. As you know, it is much harder to coordinate and organize larger groups. Simply deciding who is going to do what and how the group will proceed is more difficult. Also, keeping track of what others are doing becomes difficult in larger groups. In groups of more than eight or ten members, maintaining contact with the others in the group may be highly difficult. This difficulty in coordinating larger groups may account for the observation that real-life groups outside the laboratory seldom include more than seven persons (James, 1951).

Further, as the size of the group increases, the individual members may tend to be less involved with the group. In one study, which compared the level of member motivation in groups of two to five members with that of member motivation in groups of six to eight persons, it was found that the level of involvement with the group was significantly higher in the smaller groups (Shaw, 1960).

Why do people tend to be more involved with, and work harder in, small groups? There are a number of reasons. In smaller groups each member may feel that he has greater control over the outcome of the group. Or he may be afraid to slack off in a smaller group, since each person's contribution can be more easily checked in small groups (Thelen, 1949). Further, in smaller groups there is more of an opportunity for the members to participate and to be heard.

Although member motivation appears to increase as the size of the group decreases, there are limits to the relationship. If a group is so small that it obviously cannot do the job assigned to it, the members may become disenchanted. Two policemen assigned to patrol all of Manhattan would probably get discouraged pretty quickly.

If excessive bigness or smallness can kill member motivation, what is the optimal number of people? Although the best number obviously depends on the task to be done, there is some evidence suggesting that for study committees it may be five. When college students were assigned to study committees that varied in number from two to seven and then asked to evaluate their group, the members of the five-person committee were the most satisfied with their committee's size. In larger groups the students complained of problems in organizing the committee and of its general inefficiency. In the very small groups, particularly the two-man committee, the members seemed to be so concerned with maintaining a good relationship with the other persons or person that their efficient functioning was seriously hampered. The students in the five-man committee seemed to feel that their size was large enough to contain a good diversity of skills but small enough to preclude the problems of bigger groups (Slater, 1958). Also, in further support of the virtue of the number five, it has been observed that most real-life decision-making groups contain at least five members (James, 1951). The question, of course, is whether or not subsequent studies will confirm the magic of the number five in other settings or even replicate the effectiveness of the number five under similar circumstances. Nevertheless, the possibility of determining the optimal work group number for a given task illustrates a highly practical area for further research.

Group Composition The make-up of a group will obviously influence its productivity. As you might expect, groups of *intelligent* and *able* people will generally be more effective than groups made up of incompetents. A take-home exam committee composed of all "A" students in social psychology is probably going to have more highly developed intellectual skills and more creative ideas about preparing the social psychology exam than a committee composed of "D" students. By and large, this is what research in this area has shown (e.g., Davis, 1969).

Attempts to predict group productivity on the basis of *personality characteristics* have been less successful. Intuitively, it would seem clear that a committee composed of immature, maladjusted, overly sensitive people would be less effective than one made up of less disturbed people. In a committee of maladjusted people each person might be so preoccupied with his own personal problems and imagined slights that he would have difficulty focusing on the work to be done. So far, however, no strong or consistent relationship has been found (McGrath and Altman, 1966). Before you conclude that personality doesn't have an effect on performance, however, it should be noted that the absence of significant relationships to date does not mean that there are no relationships. Instead, it may be that the present personality tests are not adequate to detect relationships that do, in fact, exist. Personality measures that are more immediately related to various social orientations might yield more significant relationships (Hall and Williams, 1971).

Another aspect of group composition that influences group productivity is the *degree to which the members of a group are similar or dissimilar.* Suppose you could choose between the following two compositions for your final exam committee: one made up of one "A" student, three "B" students, and one "C" student or one composed of five "B" students. Which one would be the better one to select?

There is no simple answer to this question. Whether a homogeneous or a heterogeneous group is more effective depends on the characteristic in question, the nature of the task, and the way in which a particular group functions (as Steiner, 1972, has noted). In some cases heterogeneity in abilities can clearly add to the group's potential for productivity. If the job is one that only one person in the group can perform, then having a greater diversity may result in a more competent performance. If the exam was a short one, the "A" student on the "A"–"C" committee could prepare the answers, whereas the best single person on the all-"B" committee is obviously a "B" student. If the exam was composed of a series of questions that differed in difficulty, the members' ability and the tasks could be matched more closely in the heterogeneous group. Further, if the members of the committee differed in their areas of greatest competency within the field of social psychology, each could be assigned to the area that he knew best.

But with the greater potential for productivity in groups with heterogeneous ability comes also the potential for more interpersonal difficulties. In a heterogeneous group the majority of the members may not recognize the more talented members and may overwhelm them. Even if the "A" student's answer is objectively better, the other members of the group may not accept it. If the talent is recognized, it may make the other, less competent members uncomfortable and perhaps even jealous. The highly competent person may become dissatisfied. He may be irritated at the slowness of the other members and try to escape from the committee as soon as he can. Or if he remains, he may want to be given disproportionate credit for the final product, since he may feel that he has contributed more than the others (Homans, 1958), which could irritate the other, less talented members.

Identification with the Group's Goal If a group is to be successful, its members must accept the group's goal and work for it. Groups in which the members are more worried about their own personal concerns or are competing with one another are obviously handicapped. If the members of the exam committee spend more time trying to "win points" with one another by showing off and putting down other members of the group, they won't have much of a chance to do a good job on the exam.

These commonsensical suppositions have been substantiated in several studies. For instance, when seventy-two business conference groups were rated on the extent to which the members were motivated primarily toward satisfying their own personal needs "regardless of the effect on attainment of the group goal," it was found that groups with a high frequency of self-oriented behavior were significantly less productive than groups with a lower frequency (Fouriezos, Hutt, and Guetzkow, 1950).

This result is hardly surprising. In groups in which the members are primarily concerned with themselves, the group's goal is neglected. Interpersonal hostilities may emerge as the high frequency of self-oriented behavior becomes obvious. Any member of the group who was genuinely concerned with the group's goal may give up. He may think, if everybody else is being selfish, why shouldn't I be?

If getting the group members to be involved with the group's goal is so important to group success, how can it be accomplished? A number of variables have been found to influence member involvement. First, the *task* itself is important. Obviously, if the group's goal coincides with the individual's own goals, the group member is much more likely to be involved with the group. Thus if an individual is concerned about developing his own potential as a person, meeting the requirements of a job that is challenging and stimulating and that allows creativity will also contribute to his own personal growth. But, of course, if a job doesn't meet these specifications and the person is concerned with his self-actualization, he may become alienated from it. Evidence from a recent study suggests that the "blue-collar blues"—the disenchantment a large number of Americans feel with their jobs—is caused by the fact that the work doesn't contribute to the worker's self-actualization (Seashore and Barnowe, 1972).

Second, the *payoff* is important. If the individual knows that the only way he can get what he wants is to work with the other members and they seem to be able to do the task, he will become involved in the group. However, if he is rewarded according to how much he alone does—with no dependence on what the others do—his involvement with the group will be minimal. This result has been obtained repeatedly in studies comparing the relative effectiveness of groups in which the members are competing with one another and groups in which the members are cooperating. For instance, in one study the relative effectiveness of competitive and cooperative groups in discussing solutions for a series of human relations problems was compared. All of the students met in five-member committees over a period of six weeks to satisfy part of the requirements of their psychology course. Half of the students, those in the cooperative groups, were told that group solutions would be graded and that each person in the group would receive the same individual course grade as the grade given to his group. The other half of the students, those in the competitive groups, were told that each person's grade would depend on his own contributions.

As might be expected, the cooperative groups were more productive. Without worrying about outperforming the other members of the group, each member was more cooperative and friendly to the other members of his group, seemed more open to their ideas, and helped divide the work up fairly and sensibly. In the competitive groups the members may never have seen any need to cooperate with the other members of the group (Deutsch, 1949).

Third, the degree to which an individual feels that he is *involved in making decisions* about what his group does influences his level of involvement. If you feel that "things are happening that you have no control over"—the cry on American campuses in the late 1960s—you may not identify very much with the group. Again, a series of studies has shown that participation in decision making is related to involvement.

In a study in an industrial setting, the investigators manipulated the level of the subjects' participation in the decision to change a number of work rules and time allowances. Previous observations in this setting had shown that generally any changes in routine were greatly resisted. To overcome this resistance, the investigators tried three different approaches: (1) *direct participation,* in which the workers discussed the reason for change and then helped in designing precisely what form the changes should take, (2) *representative participation,* in which the workers chose representatives, who then followed the same procedures as all of the workers had in the direct participation condition, and (3) a *control group* in which the change was announced to the workers with no opportunity for them to be involved.

As you might expect, the workers that were most directly involved in the change resisted it the least. After the change was introduced, workers in the total participation group quickly upped their production to their prechange levels and then began to improve their performance beyond that level. In the representative participation condition, the workers were adversely affected by the change, but after eighteen days their performance returned to prechange levels. In the control, no participation condition, however, the workers were still producing at a very low level thirty-two days after the change had been introduced (Coch and French, 1948).

Why does participating in the planning of a change decrease resistance to it? As anyone knows who has ever been involved in an attempt to persuade people to change some traditional way of behaving—say an attempt to persuade a traditional elementary-school principal to replace his first- and second-grade classrooms with a nongraded classroom—change is extremely threatening to many, if not most, people. No matter how bad what you're doing now is, at least it has the virtue of familiarity. With change, you don't know what to expect.

Through a person's participation, however, a number of the sources of his resistance to change may be overcome. Participation gives the individuals involved in the change an opportunity to ask questions and to understand the need for the change and precisely how it will work. Increased information may dispel anxiety about the unknown. Just as a surgical patient

who has been given some idea of what to expect may be less upset during his postoperative period (Janis, 1958), so people who know what the future will bring may be less afraid and better able to deal with it when it comes. Further, during the process of discussing the changes, each individual in the group sees the other's reactions to the proposed change. If they seem to be in favor of it, then social pressures—both informational and normative—are likely to make the individual go along. And, finally, if, during the discussion, the individual commits himself as favoring the change, this commitment may make him feel obligated to support the change once it occurs (Bennett, 1955), as we saw in Chapter 4.

Of course, participation in decision making is no panacea for solving all group-involvement problems. If management so dominates the situation that those involved know they are just going through the motions, participation will not improve involvement—it may lower it. Perhaps you have been in a situation in which another person pretended to be involving you in a decision although he really had no intention of considering what you said. Involvement and affection may not have been the emotions you experienced.

Summary

In this section we have considered some of the conditions related to the effectiveness of a work group. We saw that, generally, a group of people is more effective than any one member of the group working alone would be, since the group usually has more resources to accomplish a task than an individual does.

Whether people are more effective working separately or together is dependent on a number of variables:

1. *Task.* When tasks can be subdivided easily or when they are unitary and fairly simple, groups tend to be more effective than individuals working separately.

2. *Cohesiveness.* Since the members of cohesive groups have a strong tendency to follow the group norm, the relative productivity of a cohesive group and a nominal group of the

FIGURE 11-12 Characterization of groupthink.

same people depends on whether the group favors high or low productivity.

3. *Communication patterns.* When the task is a simple one, the more centralized networks are the most efficient. For more complicated tasks the decentralized networks are more efficient.

4. *Size.* There is no clear relationship between group size and productivity. Larger groups have a greater potential for productivity, but they also have a higher frequency of interpersonal problems.

5. *Group composition.* The potential for group productivity depends on the potential for productivity of each of the group's members. However, whether a homogeneous or a heterogeneous group will be more effective depends on

the characteristic in question, the nature of the task, and the way a particular group functions.

6. *Identification with the group's goal.* Groups in which the members are more worried about their own personal concerns than the group's goals are less effective than groups in which the members work toward the common group goal. Involvement with the group's goal is more probable if the goal coincides with the individual's own goals, if the individual's and the group's payoff coincides, and if the individual feels that he is involved in making decisions.

Not all of the variables that may influence the relative productivity of interacting groups and of people working alone have been discussed here. If you consider groups that you have worked with, you may be able to think of other variables. Just to mention a few possibilities, individual differences may influence group and individual productivity. Some people may consistently prefer to work alone and be more effective when working alone, and others may prefer group settings and so work better when they are in the company of others (Davis, 1969).

Groupthink

So far we have talked about variables that may make groups either more or less effective. In this section we will consider a set of reactions found in highly cohesive, decision-making groups that are so preoccupied with maintaining group consensus that all critical thought is obliterated: a phenomenon known as "groupthink" (Janis, 1972). (See Figure 11-12.)

How does groupthink work? Although there are many historical examples to choose from, perhaps the most thoroughly documented evidence of the phenomenon is the policy-making process that led to the ill-fated Bay of Pigs invasion in 1961. In that expedition 1,400 badly armed Cuban exiles invaded the coast of Cuba at the Bay of Pigs, and within three days they were captured by 20,000 of Castro's army. (See Figure 11-13.) Nothing went right. The Cuban air force, which was supposed to have been wiped out in a surprise American attack, escaped and dominated the invasion site, sinking American ships and bombing the landings. A second American air strike was called off. Instead of overthrowing Castro, as President John Kennedy and his advisers had thought it would, the Bay of Pigs invasion resulted in deep embarrassment for the United States and a rap-

FIGURE 11-13 Prisoners captured by Castro's militia during the Bay of Pigs attempt to invade Cuba. These men were among twelve hundred prisoners taken by Castro's forces who were later ransomed by the United States government for $53 million in food and drugs. (From Janis, 1972.) (World Wide Photos)

prochement between the Soviet Union and Cuba, which led to an eventual Russian attempt to place atomic missiles in Cuba (Janis, 1972).

As President Kennedy said, "How could we have been so stupid?" (Janis, 1971). Certainly, it looked stupid. Any plan can go badly if the enemy acts unpredictably or if chance events damage timing. But the Bay of Pigs invasion was based on a whole set of assumptions that were almost laughably nonsensical if examined in the light of the evidence available to the United States government. So many facts were inconsistent with the basic assumptions of the plan that even a cursory questioning and a quick consideration of other options would have revealed its fallacies. The question is: Why didn't the president and his advisers check more thoroughly?

One possible answer is that the people involved in making the decision were stupid, but given the caliber of John F. Kennedy and his advisers, this seems a highly unsatisfactory answer. Irrespective of whether people supported or opposed President Kennedy, few accused him of stupidity. And the advisers who were involved in making the Bay of Pigs decision were also highly able men—men who had the ability to make a critical analysis of a proposal as transparently weak as the Bay of Pigs. Just to list the names of some of those involved is sufficient to make the point that the decision was not made by a group of dolts: Robert Kennedy, the president's brother and a highly able politician in his own right; Arthur Schlesinger, Jr., an outstanding Harvard historian; and Robert McNamara, the man with a mind like a computer. All in all, a dazzling array of talent was involved in planning the Bay of Pigs invasion.

But if they were so bright, why did they endorse such a stupid plan? The answer—according to an insightful analysis by Irving Janis, who has studied thousands of pages of documents of the Bay of Pigs and other policy decisions made by American and foreign groups—is that they were victims of groupthink, *a mode of thinking that persons in highly cohesive groups engage in when they become so preoccupied with seeking and maintaining unanimity of thought that their critical thinking is rendered ineffective.* Independent analytical thought, the testing of alternatives, the weighing of pros and cons, the consideration of moral issues—all of the requirements for carefully reasoned decisions became subverted in an attempt to maintain the consensus of the highly cohesive group.

Characteristics of groupthink

By examining the way in which the decision to invade Cuba was made, Janis has identified a number of characteristics of groupthink. These characteristics are summarized below and, for continuity, will be discussed and illustrated in relation to the Bay of Pigs decision.

Invulnerability   The illusion that the group cannot fail and that, whatever the apparent risks, the group's actions are bound to succeed is a fundamental symptom of groupthink. As one of President Kennedy's advisers wrote:

Everything had broken right for him since 1956. He had won the nomination and the election against all the odds in the book. Everyone around him thought he had the Midas touch and *could not lose*.

[Schlesinger, 1965, p. 259, in Janis, 1972, p. 36; italics added.]

The illusion of invulnerability was so powerful that even when the American press began to leak out news of the impending invasion, President Kennedy and his advisers clung to the impossible notion that somehow the United States' involvement in the Cuban operation could be kept secret. The possibility of an adverse world-wide reaction to the United States' plan never entered their discussions.

Rationale   Victims of groupthink also construct rationalizations to justify their actions and to enable themselves to ignore any evidence that is inconsistent with their plans. President Kennedy, as well as his closest advisers, thought that the Cuban people would rally to the exiles' invasion and rebel against Castro. A survey showing Castro's popularity was widely circulated among a number of government bureaus, but it was ignored by Kennedy and his advisers.

Morality   Since all of the members of a group suffering from groupthink believe in the inherent morality of their group, questions of the morality of the group's decisions become irrelevant. The only immorality is to deviate from what the group has accepted. In the Bay of Pigs escapade there was never any thorough discussion of whether the invasion of a small, neighboring country was right or wrong. Apparently, Arthur Schlesinger, Jr., wrote a memorandum expressing doubts about the morality of the proposed plan, and William Fulbright was also known to have moral reservations. These concerns, however, were never fully discussed by the advisory group.

Stereotypes Victims of groupthink talk of their opposition in simplistic and stereotyped terms. Instead of taking into account what is known about the enemy and attempting to predict the enemy's reaction, they persist "in conveying to each other the cliché and oversimplified images of political enemies embodied in long-standing ideological stereotypes" (Janis, 1972, p. 38). Usually, these stereotypes include three components: The enemy is immoral, weak, and stupid.

Just as in a clichéd Western, the assumption is that the group is all good and will always win, and that the opposition, the bad guys, must inevitably lose. It is interesting how many of the assumptions underlying the Bay of Pigs invasion fit into this pattern. For instance, it was assumed that the Cuban air force was so ineffective that it could be eliminated in a surprise attack by a small group of obsolete American B-26s. Castro was assumed to be so stupid that he would not take any steps to round up potential supporters of the invading exiles. His army was assumed to be so ineffective that a very small group of invaders could hold it off. All three of these assumptions proved to be incorrect.

Conformity Pressure For victims of groupthink social pressures are even stronger than usual. Unanimity is the rule, and any critical questioning of the group's assumptions, stereotypes, or plans is discouraged.

Pressure to conform is supplemented by one-sided information. Although President Kennedy was more critical of the invasion plan than the other members of the group, he manipulated the group's agenda—perhaps without being aware that he was doing so—so that most of the information presented supported the plan:

At each meeting, instead of opening up the agenda to permit a full airing of the opposing considerations, he allowed the CIA representatives to dominate the entire discussion. The President permitted them to refute immediately each tentative doubt that one of the others might express, instead of asking whether anyone else had the same doubt or wanted to pursue the implications of the new worrisome issue that had been raised.

[Janis, 1972, p. 43.]

Self-censorship The pressures toward conformity in a groupthink situation are so pervasive that the individual censors his own divergent thoughts. Although Schlesinger had presented his written objection to the Bay of Pigs plan, he reported that he suppressed his objections at the actual face-to-face meetings:

In the months after the Bay of Pigs I bitterly reproached myself for having kept so silent during those crucial discussions in the cabinet room. . . . I can only explain my failure to do more than raise a few timid questions by reporting that one's impulse to blow the whistle on this nonsense was simply undone by the *circumstances of the discussion*.

[Schlesinger, 1965, p. 255; in Janis, 1972, p. 40.]

Mindguards From members of a group practicing groupthink, there will often emerge certain, self-appointed "mindguards"—persons who suppress information inconsistent with the group's decision and who reproach anyone who deviates. In the Bay of Pigs decision-making group, Robert Kennedy gradually assumed the role of mindguard. For instance, on one occasion Schlesinger, who had sometimes opposed the invasion plan, was told by Robert Kennedy:

You may be right or you may be wrong, but the President has made his mind up. Don't push it any further. Now is the time for everyone to help him all they can.

[Janis, 1972, p. 42.]

Illusion of Unanimity Even if some of the group members have serious doubts about the wisdom of the group's decision, there will, nevertheless, be an illusion of unanimity in groupthink decisions. Partly because of the very

BOX 4 YOU'RE IN GOOD HANDS WITH THE UNITED STATES POST OFFICE

The following memo, distributed in 1969, is still the directive for what employees at the National Labor Relations Board in Washington, D.C., should do in the event of enemy attack.

```
National Labor Relations Board
          Washington, D.C.
       Administration Bulletin

TO: All Employees
SUBJECT: Post-attack Registration of Federal Employees

  Civil Service Commission instructions require that government
agencies remind all employees annually of their responsibilities
under the Commission-operated registration system.
  In the event of an attack all National Labor Relations Board em-
ployees should follow the procedure outlined below:
  If you are prevented from going to your regular place of work be-
cause of an enemy attack, or if you are prevented from reporting to
an emergency location
--Go to the nearest Post Office, ask the Postmaster for a Federal
Employee Emergency Registration Card, fill it out and return it to
him.
  He will see that it is forwarded to the office of Civil Service
Commission which will maintain a registration file for your area.
When your card is received the Civil Service Commission will notify
us and we can then decide where and when you should report back for
work.
  Another important reason for mailing your Registration Card as soon
as possible is that it will enable us to keep you on the roster of
active employees and enable us to forward your pay. Even though you
complete your Registration Card promptly, it may be a while before
you are put back to work.  In the meantime, you would be expected to
volunteer your services to the Civil Defense authorities.

Approved for issuance:
  C.S.W.
```

[Peters and Adams, 1970, pp. 248–249.]

strong conformity pressures in operation, anyone having doubts is extremely reluctant to express them. Witness Schlesinger's reluctance to express his misgivings on the Bay of Pigs decision in the group discussions. The others in the group, hearing no objections, assume that the plan has the support of all of the members of the group. As long as the agreement is unanimous, the members of the group can feel complacent about the truth and righteousness of their proposal. As we shall see, if the members of a group begin to express doubts, the others can no longer take shelter in a retreat to unanimity as a definition of truth, and each must confront the agonizing doubts about the correctness of the group's action.

Frequency of groupthink

We have seen that groupthink occurred in as talented a group as President Kennedy and his advisers. When you consider the enormous number of colossal blunders resulting from group decisions in industry, education, and government, you may begin to wonder about the prevalence of groupthink. Unfortunately, at this point no one knows how widespread groupthink is. Simply classifying a decision as a blunder is not enough evidence to show that it was a product of groupthink. There are lots of other reasons for failures. Chance events may cause the most carefully reasoned plan to misfire. Or just one person may have made the foolish decision.

We do know, however, that groupthink is not a uniquely American phenomenon. Analyses of European fiascos—such as the French military high command's resolutely ignoring the German plan to outflank France during World War I —show that Europeans are capable of the same shallowness of thinking (Janis, 1972).

On the basis of the small number of historical case studies that have been analyzed, groupthink does appear to be a major contributor to disastrous decisions. Of course, to obtain a precise estimate of the frequency of groupthink, a large sample of governmental, business, and educational decisions would have to be analyzed. Until that is done, we can only speculate. However, after looking at Box 4, you may think that groupthink is present in a number of miscalculated executive decisions. How could any thought process but groupthink account for these directions for action in the event of attack, which have been in effect at the National Labor Relations Board since 1969?

When and why groupthink occurs

Although some people are probably more susceptible than others, Janis believes that given the appropriate circumstances, most people could fall into groupthink. If this is true and group decision making is as frequent as it appears to be, an understanding of the circumstances that make groupthink possible is of great potential value. So far three conditions have been hypothesized to encourage group-

think: (1) *high cohesiveness* of the decision-making group, (2) *insulation* of the decision-making group from other, more balanced information, and (3) *endorsement of the policy by the leader.*

In the policy-making meetings leading to the Cuban invasion, all three of these situational variables were present. Kennedy and his advisers were a highly cohesive group. They liked and respected one another, and many of them had worked together over a period of years. Information concerning other possible options in the Cuban situation and criticisms of the planned invasion were kept from the decision-making group. Some of the governmental agencies that were best qualified to advise President Kennedy and his advisers—such as the experts on Cuba in the State Department—were excluded from the discussions. And finally, President Kennedy, though he himself occasionally criticized the plan, clearly communicated his endorsement and ran the meetings in a way that biased the information that was made available. The great majority of the material released was in favor of the CIA-endorsed Bay of Pigs plan.

Why are these three situational factors— cohesiveness, insulation, and biased leadership—so important? They work together to make a group more likely to evolve a consensus, and once that consensus has evolved, to make the members support it. One could theorize as follows. Making a decision is painful, especially if you know that the decision is very important or if you realize that the decision may conflict with some of your own morals. You may wonder whether or not you're doing the right thing.

Perhaps without consciously realizing that they are doing so, the members of a group faced with a difficult and important decision may be inclined to try to suppress any dissension. Although the desire to use group unanimity to escape from the pressures of decision making may be present in all groups, when the group is cohesive, isolated from others, and led by someone who obviously endorses the policy, the desire to escape may be actualized. As we have seen, members of cohesive groups are more subject to the social pressures from the other members of their group. If the members of a cohesive group sense that the others want uncritical support, they are more likely to pro-

BOX 5 AVOIDING GROUPTHINK

What should the members of a group do to avoid groupthink? Janis believes that the following nine procedures may help a group's members retain their critical independence.

1. "The leader of a policy-forming group should assign the role of critical evaluator to each member, encouraging the group to give high priority to open airing of objections and doubts. This practice needs to be reinforced by the leader's acceptance of criticism of his own judgments in order to discourage members from soft-pedaling their disagreements and from allowing their striving for concurrance to inhibit critical thinking.

2. "When the key members of a hierarchy assign a policy-planning mission to any group within their organization, they should adopt an impartial stance instead of stating preferences and expectations at the beginning. This will encourage open inquiry and impartial probing of a wide range of policy alternatives.

3. "The organization should routinely set up several outside policy-planning and evaluation groups to work on the same policy question, each deliberating under a different leader. This can prevent the insulation of an ingroup.

4. "At intervals before the group reaches a final consensus, the leader should require each member to discuss the group's deliberations with associates in his own unit of the organization—assuming that these associates can be trusted to adhere to the same security regulations that govern the policy makers—and then to report their reactions back to the group.

5. "The group should invite one or more outside experts to each meeting on a staggered basis and encourage the experts to challenge the views of the core members.

6. "At every general meeting of the group, whenever the agenda calls for an evaluation of policy alternatives, at least one member should play devil's advocate, functioning as a good lawyer in challenging the testimony of those who advocate the majority position.

7. "Whenever the policy issue involves relations with a rival nation or organization, the group should devote a sizable block of time, perhaps an entire session, to a survey of all warning signals from the rivals and should write alternative scenarios on the rivals' intentions.

8. "When the group is surveying policy alternatives for feasibility and effectiveness, it should from time to time divide into two or more subgroups to meet separately, under different chairmen, and then come back together to hammer out differences.

9. "After reaching a preliminary consensus about what seems to be the best policy, the group should hold a "second-chance" meeting at which every member expresses as vividly as he can all his residual doubts, and rethinks the entire issue before making a definitive choice."

[Janis, 1971, p. 76.]

As Janis has pointed out, until these suggestions for avoiding groupthink can be empirically tested, they remain just that: untested suggestions. However, it should be noted that after the Bay of Pigs President Kennedy incorporated several of these techniques into his consultations with his advisers—including encouragement of skepticism and diversity, and the occasional absence of the leader. Following these techniques, basically the same group of men that was previously involved in the Bay of Pigs fiasco resolved the Cuban missile crisis in a much more effective way in 1962.

---

vide it. Isolation from other information reinforces the conforming effects caused by cohesiveness. With no outside, contradictory information, the members have little reason not to go along. And the pressure provided by the leader who favors a particular policy completes the picture. When the members of the group feel a strong emotional attachment to their leader, they may want to believe that what he says is correct. To doubt the wisdom of the leader is a form of disloyalty that the members of the group will not allow themselves.

Preventing groupthink

The results of groupthink are usually undesirable. It is therefore necessary to find ways to prevent its occurrence. One possible way would be to leave all decisions to one person. If President Kennedy alone had made the decision about invading Cuba, his decision would not have been molded by his desire to please and agree with his advisers. Simple as this solution sounds, it too involves problems. A lone individual has weaknesses and biases.

Without the perspective provided by other people, a single person might be more likely to make errors than a group of people expressing and arguing out the merits of various plans.

A better way of preventing groupthink is to change the way in which decision-making groups function in order to counter the powerful pressures toward groupthink. The trick for making a group productive is to set up procedures that counter the negative, debilitating forces that can subtract from a group's potential productivity. In overcoming groupthink the problem is to set up conditions that promote independent thinking. After contrasting the procedures followed in a number of groups in which groupthink prevailed with those in which it did not, Janis has made nine recommendations about tactics that may avoid groupthink. See Box 5.

Indeed, the results of a recent experiment suggest that persons can be trained to avoid groupthink and thus to perform more effectively. After giving one group some guidelines for approaching a problem—including the statement that differences in opinion are desirable and that agreement should not be reached simply to avoid argument—the investigator compared the problem-solving performance of this group with a group given no directions. As predicted, the instructions were effective: The group that had received instructions was significantly more effective in solving problems (Hall, 1971). Apparently, groups can be taught to accept divergence of opinion and thus to avoid groupthink.

Studying groupthink

On the basis of observations of real-life groups and the analysis of thousands of pages of highly regarded historical documents, Janis has identified an important phenomenon and has advanced a series of exciting hypotheses about its causes and methods of control. Until experimental testing can be more fully developed, these must remain speculative. Although Janis (1972) has used a number of highly reliable historical accounts of decisions, there are inevitable problems with this kind of evidence. Accounts of what occurred may conflict. Verbatim records of decision-making meetings

and informal conversations—if they exist—are rarely made public. Thus one seeking to understand what happened must rely chiefly on the accounts of those who participated—some of which may be written with an eye to protecting the writer's own reputation. Because of its importance, experimental evidence on the groupthink phenomenon will probably be forthcoming shortly.

Summary

In this section we have seen evidence concerning the existence of groupthink—a mode of thinking that persons engage in when they become so highly preoccupied with seeking and maintaining the unanimity in their group that their critical thinking is rendered ineffective. Eight characteristics of groupthink have been identified: (1) illusions of invulnerability, (2) evolution of a rationale, (3) belief in the morality of the group's decisions, (4) stereotyped views of the enemy, (5) conformity pressures, (6) self-censorship of critical thoughts, (7) mindguards, who enforce group unanimity, and (8) illusions of unanimity.

Although at this point its prevalence is not clear, groupthink is thought to be especially likely to occur when: (1) the decision-making group is highly cohesive; (2) the group is insulated from other, more balanced information; and (3) the leader has preconceived notions of the correct policy to follow.

It has been suggested that to prevent groupthink conditions should be arranged so that independent thought is encouraged. In general, steps that encourage member skepticism and diversity of opinion may counter the strong pressures toward consensus. Indeed, the results of one recent study suggest that groups can be trained to overcome groupthink and so be made more effective.

The Effective Social-Emotional Group

All the lonely people—
Where do they all come from?

[Lennon and McCartney, 1966.]

The main problem for many people today is to escape from feelings of loneliness. As we saw

FIGURE 11-14 Loneliness may be an especially severe problem for older people. (Charles Gatewood)

in Chapter 5, people have strong needs to feel loved, accepted, and close to and companionable with other people. As we also saw in Chapter 5, the social groups in our society do not seem to be meeting these needs for many of the members of our society. Many people hunger for close and authentic relationships. As one authority has said, "individuals nowadays are probably more aware of their inner loneliness than has ever been true before in history" (Rogers, 1970, p. 106). (See Figure 11-14.)

American ingenuity at solving the loneliness problem

American ingenuity isn't limited to material productivity. In the 1960s and early 1970s, when loneliness emerged as a clearly articulated social problem, various attempts were made to

find a solution. Two of these—communes and sensitivity groups—are especially important.

Communes, one way of "getting back together" (Houriet, 1971), began to increase rapidly in the late 1960s. Although no one knows exactly how many communes there are, it has been estimated that from 1965 to 1970 between 2,000 and 3,000 were established (Houriet, 1971). Spontaneously, groups of people went back to the land together. Although communes varied enormously in structure and people— from the loosely organized "crash pads" of hippie college dropouts to the highly organized groups of executive dropouts—an underlying theme in the whole commune social movement was one of strong unification and group feeling among the commune members.

An even more prevalent way of fighting loneliness is the encounter group. See Box 6. In their search for a way to relate meaningfully with other people and to be accepted by them, countless thousands have participated in such a group. (How many of your friends have been involved in a sensitivity, encounter, or T group—the various names for this sort of experience?) With little institutional encouragement from universities and scanty government funding, encounter groups exploded in the United States as a major force in therapeutic circles in the 1960s. It has been estimated that at least 5,000,000 people in the United States have participated in encounter groups since they became popular several years ago (King, 1973). In fact, the encounter group movement has been labeled by one of its supporters as "the most rapidly spreading *social* invention of the century, and probably the most potent" (Rogers, 1970, p. 1).

If communes and encounter groups meet the social-emotional needs of their members so well, people who really want to alleviate their loneliness could simply join either of these two different forms of groups. But here, too, there are problems. Although joining a commune may make a person feel less lonely, the disadvantages of the commune life-style may outweigh the benefits. For instance, if a person joins a commune, he may not be able to do the other things that are important to him; his sense of privacy may be limited; and he may become bored with the preoccupation with interpersonal relationships that characterizes so many com-

BOX 6 WHAT HAPPENS IN AN ENCOUNTER GROUP?

Although encounter groups vary in terms of the exact procedures followed, one outstanding practitioner in this area has described a number of stages through which most encounter groups progress (Rogers, 1970). Obviously, there is no direct progression through these various steps, and there is a great deal of overlap.

1. *Milling around and resisting opening up.* After the leader, or trainer, makes it clear that the members of the group must set up their own structure, there is usually a period during which the members relate to one another with either silence, frustration, or superficial conversation. Initially, most of the members are very hesitant to reveal anything but their most public selves to the other persons in the group.

2. *Gradual opening up.* Although the members are fearful and ambivalent about talking about their emotions, gradually the participants begin to discuss their feelings. Usually, this first takes the form of discussing how they felt in the past or discussing their current negative feelings—either about other group members or the trainer. Only after the group members have "tested" one another by talking about material less involving and threatening to themselves does a sense of trust in the other members and the trainer emerge, so that they can express more personally relevant material.

3. *Expressing emotionally relevant material.* This may take the form of the members' revealing highly personal material about themselves. For instance, in one encounter group a seemingly confident man confessed that he had "never had a single *friend* in his life" (Rogers, 1970, p. 20). Or the feelings may relate to the members' immediate reactions to the others in the group.

4. *The development of the healing capacity in the members of the group.* As the members of the group reveal personal information about themselves and their reactions to the others in the group, the other members of the group try to be helpful and to ease the psychic pain of those expressing emotionally relevant material. This support may occur both inside and outside the formal sessions.

5. *The basic encounter.* Throughout all of the other developments in the group there runs the basic theme of the group—the encounter. That intensive, involving, interpersonal contact among the members has been theorized to be the unique aspect of the experience that makes possible any therapeutic gains that emerge from the group.

6. *Cracking of façades and self-acceptance.* Either willingly or through the demands of the other members of the group, the façades of the members of the group begin to crack. An individual may volunteer some "horrible" aspect of himself, or the other group members may demand that a particular individual cease being hypocritical and admit to some negative feeling or trait. Through the acceptance of the other members of the group and the trainer, the individual begins to accept his own self.

7. *Feedback and confrontation.* As the members of the group interact and talk about their reactions to the other members of the group, each finds out how the others react to him. This feedback can be both positive and negative, and these reactions give the individual realistic and constructive information about how others see him. Sometimes, when one person really "levels with," or "confronts," another, the feedback can be very negative. However, in the context of trust, helpfulness, and caring that has developed in the sensitivity group, it is theorized that feedback—even when extreme—gives realistic and constructive information to the individual about how he is perceived by others.

---

munes. The fact that communes are not noted for their longevity would seem to indicate that there are a number of disadvantages and problems in membership.

Of course, there's always encounter groups. The popularity of these groups boomed during the 1960s and early 1970s, and a widespread increase in the availability of these might solve the nation's problem. If most people are starved for authentic relationships, then make the product more available in the transitory, noninvolving setting of an encounter group. There Americans can have their instant intimacy at a bargain psychological price. According to Carl Rogers (1968), we may all have to develop an ability for instant intimacy. He feels that in our highly mobile society the ability to invest meaningfully in brief interpersonal encounters and to relinquish these easily may be necessary for psychic survival.

But the massive use of encounter groups to solve the nation's loneliness problems seems a little like using a Band-Aid for a hemorrhage. Although encounter groups may make people feel good temporarily, they can hardly change the quality of day-to-day social experience. One weekend per month spent at a "psych resort" would hardly seem sufficient to suc-

BOX 7 ENCOUNTER GROUPS—MORE THAN FUN AND GAMES

"Last year, she and some friends decided that 'the cocktail party is out' and gave a series of parties that, she said, incorporated the encounter group into the social situation."

[*The New York Times*, February 18, 1971, p. 39, in Back, 1972, p. 131.]

As this hostess's comments reflect, some people think that encounter groups are a new form of social entertainment. For some people, participating in an encounter group can lead to an intensive and highly pleasant feeling of unity with a group and may produce, under some circumstances, beneficial personality and behavioral changes. In one study it was found that about a third of those who had participated in an encounter group benefited from the experience (Lieberman, Yalom, and Miles, 1973). But—like any other procedure powerful enough to create such marked effects—encountering also has possible dangers.

Although statistics are difficult to obtain, there is evidence to show that at least some people do *break down* completely. One long-term study found that 9 percent of those participating became psychiatric casualties as a result of their experience and some had to be hospitalized (Lieberman, Yalom, and Miles, 1973). Anecdotal summaries illustrate clearly the extent of the psychological damage that can be caused.

"As a matter of fact, I am personally familiar with a program manager . . . who was sent by one of the . . . companies to one of these programs. He was stripped of all of his strength and left with nothing. He is now in the Veterans Administration Hospital and is a total wreck."

[Back, 1972, p. 220.]

The incidence of *minor emotional damage* may be considerably higher than that of psychotic breakdowns. One authority has estimated, "We are concerned that 25 to 40 percent of persons sent to sensitivity gain nothing and very possibly lose some highly valuable behavioral assets" (Rodney Luther, 1967, in Back, 1972, p. 221).

If, even knowing the possible dangers, one is still interested in participating in an encounter group, how can he protect himself? First, if you are contemplating joining a group, you should know exactly what procedures will be followed in the particular group. Encounter group procedures vary from the relatively conservative, in which the participants are free to become as involved as they wish and few far-out procedures are followed, to the more far-out groups, which may be conducted in the nude or in which highly aggressive behavior is encouraged.

Second, find out something about the credentials of the leader of your group. With the rapid increase in the popularity of encounter groups, persons who are not adequately trained may decide to conduct groups. One way to make sure that your trainer has been adequately trained is to write to the one organization that examines and accredits trainers: The International Association of Applied Social Science, 1755 Massachusetts Ave., NW, Washington, D.C. 20036.

Third, if the trainer is accredited, check with him in advance to discuss the possibility of your having a harmful reaction to the procedure. Screening out people who might possibly be harmed would seem to be a procedure that should be followed in all cases, but at present it is rarely done. If the trainer doesn't screen everyone, you can make sure that at least you get screened.

At the present time, despite the possible advantages of participating in encounter groups, the old adage "let the buyer beware" is very appropriate.

cessfully offset a general life-style of alienation and loneliness.

And, of course, the encounter groups themselves have inherent problems. First of all, there is considerable controversy about whether or not sensitivity groups cause any long-range changes in their participants. Although some studies have yielded encouraging results (see Aronson, 1972, pp. 258–263), others have yielded no significant differences between those participating in encounter groups and those not involved (see Cooper and Mangham, 1971). In view of some of the problems connected with research in this area, inconsistent results are hardly surprising. In many of the studies the "changes" in those who participated in the group experience were not compared to members of a control group who had not participated in the group experience. Since theorists disagree about exactly what types of changes should be expected, a wide variety of measurements has been used, which makes comparison of the results of the various studies difficult (Campbell and Dunnette, 1968). Further, whether or not participating in encounter groups produces any long-range improvement, there is considerable evidence that in some cases it may be dangerous. See Box 7.

If joining a sensitivity group or a commune is not a feasible way for everyone to fight loneliness, then another approach is to examine some of the procedures followed in communes and encounter groups to provide some leads about how other groups could be structured to meet the social-emotional needs of their members. Since these two very different ways of combating loneliness are obviously popular, it is safe to assume that they are meeting some of the needs of those participating in them. However, it should be noted that our discussion is very speculative. As we said earlier, curiously little is known about the characteristics of a group that can meet the needs of its members to belong and to feel wanted. After hundreds of studies we can say that centralized communication networks are more efficient for the performing of simple tasks; but we have no knowledge of what properties of a group enable it to make its members feel less lonely.

Characteristics of communes and encounter groups

Although the great variety in communes and in encounter groups, as well as the substantial differences between these two types of groups, makes generalizing very hazardous, it does seem that most of these groups possess the following characteristics: (1) the general characteristics necessary for the formation and survival of all groups, (2) the possibility of intense and warm relationships among the members, (3) the expression of affection by touch, (4) the expression of authentic feelings and reactions by the members, (5) the physical isolation of the group from other people, (6) a limited number of people, and (7) rituals of solidarity and deindividuation. In this section we will try to determine how each of these characteristics operates to reduce loneliness and to provide for the social-emotional needs of group members.

General Requirements for Group Formation and Survival If a group is to meet effectively the social-emotional needs of its members, it must first be formed and then survive. As we saw in

Chapter 10, a *common goal* is necessary to transform a collection of separate individuals into a group. The degree to which all of the members seek the same goal may influence the degree to which the group is unified. In an encounter group the members share a common goal: to get to know themselves, to see how others see them, and to see how they are affected by others. In search of this common goal the members share a common task—relating authentically to each other—and a common tradition about how they are expected to behave. The more the members of a group have in common, the more unified they may be.

Communes may also be cemented together by the members' sharing common goals, traditions, and work. Although the precise goals of communes vary from group to group, the general goal is to maintain close, authentic relationships with others who care about the group and its members. Traditions vary from commune to commune, but the usual stimulus toward unity has been found to be either a common religious belief, a shared faith in the efficacy of drugs to move the individual to higher levels of experience, or a common belief in the need to get back to nature and to rebel against what the members consider a degrading, commercialized, and dehumanized society whose institutions are failing. Finally, when the members share common tasks, the shared work can be highly unifying. As one member of a commune said, "In those days, the hard work brought us together" (Houriet, 1971, p. 158). (See Figure 11-15.)

To survive, a group must continue to meet the needs of its members. In a weekend sensitivity group, whose length of existence is determined by schedule, this is much less of a problem than in the commune. Survival has been a problem for most communes, which have been rather short-lived. Since breaking away from society at large has been the main focus of many communes, little time or energy has been spent on other goals. Without structure, leadership, and a provision for privacy, many communes have foundered. And the personalities of the members themselves have frequently destroyed the groups. Just as many noncommune-dwelling Americans have difficulty in communicating, cooperating, and loving others in any but a sexual way, so, too, do many of the

FIGURE 11-15 Sharing work chores in a commune can bring the members closer together. (Dennis Stock/Magnum)

commune members. Selfishness and impersonal sex are all-too-familiar American substitutes for genuine interpersonal involvement. It is just as easy for members of a commune to use those substitutes as it is for other Americans.

In groups that do survive, however, a number of characteristics seem to enable them to make their members less lonely. The rest of this section will be devoted to a discussion of these characteristics.

Intensive and Caring Relationships Groups in which the relationships between the members are characterized by concern, care, and trust may make their members feel loved and in genuine contact with the other members of the group. That genuine love and concern for others is needed in order for each person not to feel lonely seems so obvious that it doesn't need to be said. But in many contemporary social interactions, concern and care seem to be absent from the relationships. Impersonal and opportunistic "friendliness" is more the general rule than the exception. People may smile and be friendly, but you may have the feeling that they're doing so without any recognition of you as a unique person.

In contrast, both communes and encounter groups are frequently characterized by concerned, loving, and caring relationships. Indeed, one of the most noticeable features of a sensitivity session—no matter how brief—is how the participants come to be involved with and care for one another. As one member of a sensitivity session, a woman who was having marital difficulties and who was feeling very depressed, wrote:

I have felt needed, loving, competent, furious, frantic, anything and everything but just plain *loved*. You can imagine the flood of gratitude, humility, release that swept over me. I wrote with considerable joy, "I actually felt *loved*." I doubt that I shall soon forget it.

[Rogers, 1970, p. 34.]

Touching For others to care for you is not enough. You have to be shown that they care. Concern, obviously, can be expressed in a number of ways. People can verbally express their concern; they can do nice things for you. And they can touch you.

In the general course of social interactions, touch has but one meaning: sex. As we saw in Chapter 5, however, there is some evidence to indicate that for human infants, physical contact conveys love and is necessary for healthy psychological development. Touching may be just as crucial for the continued health of adults. In our society, by literally cutting ourselves off from all physical human contact except that provided through sexual outlets, we may be depriving ourselves of something we need badly—warm, loving, physical contact. You may have felt this need yourself when you've been emotionally upset—the desire to have someone hug and comfort you.

Touch and bodily contact are used extensively in both encounter groups and communes. (See Figure 11-16.) As one college student who attended a weekend encounter group wrote:

Verbal communication; so necessary; but words are also a barrier; can be used particularly to fend off contact. And if I want to express things, myself, in another way, what can I do? Can I reach you, reach out to you? With eyes, touch, smile?

We all walk around trying not to bump into people; so much energy expended in avoidance.

But there is nothing so beautiful and beautifully human as to be held, hugged, loved. To feel the warmth and sincerity of another person. To give, in turn, comfort, strength. Words can often deceive; but an embrace—the truth is conveyed by something other than sound.

[Rogers, 1970, p. 63.]

Touching is also used extensively to express affection and concern in communes:

Walking up the road to the farm, I felt I was coming home. Emily hugged me. Roland wrapped his arms around me and his beard brushed my face—the first time it felt natural to embrace another man. "You came back!" said Laura.

[Houriet, 1971, p. 129.]

Allowing Authenticity In most social interactions, as we saw in Chapter 2, people hide behind socially acceptable façades. Since we are afraid that no one will like us if we show how really terrible we are, we present to the world what we think it wants. People are so thoroughly trained in mendacity that honesty in social interaction may be the exception rather than the rule. For instance, if you were to count up all of the comments you've made to others today, how many would reflect how you really felt? How often have you been polite to someone you

really didn't like? How often have you feigned interest in a topic that was really boring? But mendacity has its price, as we also saw in Chapter 2. When we reveal only our socially laundered selves to other people, we may feel that others know only our façade and that the real, essential, and unacceptable part of us is left utterly and terribly alone. The expression of such feelings is very common in sensitivity groups. Many of the members express feelings of loneliness and pain that have resulted from their living behind a façade.

Authenticity is demanded in both encounter groups and communes. The norm in both groups is for members to say what they feel about themselves and the others in the group. In an encounter group, for instance, after a period of tentatively trying out the reactions of others to their secret thoughts and gradually learning that others will not reject them for being honest, the members come to express their heretofore hidden selves and, in so doing, find acceptance for themselves as they truly are:

I had really buried under a layer of concrete many feelings I was afraid people were going to laugh at or stomp on which, needless to say, was working all kinds of hell on my family and on me. I had been looking forward to the workshop with my last few crumbs of hope. It was really a needle of trust in a

FIGURE 11-16 A sensitivity session on touch and love. (Sylvia Plachy)

large haystack of despair. . . . The real turning point for me was a simple gesture on your part of putting your arm around my shoulder one afternoon when I had made some crack about you not being a member of the group—that no one could cry on your shoulder.

[Rogers, 1970, p. 34.]

Authenticity and honesty in communication are the norms in communes, too. In one commune, for instance, there was a ritual of "Sharing"—recounting events in the past and present that troubled the members. Further, in contrast to an encounter group, it is more difficult to turn authenticity off in a commune. In an encounter group people may be candid in the session, but revert to the usual social hypocrisies outside the session. In the twenty-four-hour-a-day intensive contact of a commune, you're "on" all the time. Potentially, every exchange is an encounter.

Physical Separation of the Group from Other People In everyday life we belong to a number of groups among which we move freely. We may be in a social psychology class in the morning, in a rap session with friends in the afternoon, and in still another group in the evening. In contrast, many of the groups that seem to meet the social-emotional needs of their members are physically isolated from everyone except the members of the group. For instance, army units, which have been noted to be highly cohesive, are physically separated from all family and friends outside the other men in the unit. Sensitivity groups are usually held in places where contact with anyone other than fellow sensitivity group members is limited. Many rural communes are isolated from their neighbors.

Isolation may make the members feel more like a part of the group in several ways. When the group is isolated, each member must depend more on the others—either for physical or for emotional survival—so that all are mutually interdependent. As long as those in the group meet each other's needs, the members rapidly learn to trust one another. Further, in the absence of all other people, the members of the group become very dependent on one another for information.

Limited Number of People The number of members in both communes and sensitivity groups is usually small. Typically, sensitivity groups vary in size from ten to twenty people (Aronson, 1972). Although statistics on the size of communes are more difficult to obtain, many of the American communes reported in one recent account were limited to between twenty and thirty members (Houriet, 1971). In larger groups the members may not be able to sustain the intensity of involvement with all of the other members that is necessary to alleviate loneliness. Imagine the psychological strain in trying to care deeply about and respond authentically to each of the other members of a group of fifty!

Rituals of Solidarity and Deindividuation It is not enough for the members of the group to care about one another, to be interested in and concerned about one another, and to allow the others to express themselves authentically. Concrete expressions of the group's unity and provision for a temporary loss of each person's identity may be necessary for a group to meet completely the social-emotional needs of its members.

In ordinary social interactions such rituals and provisions for deindividuation are relatively rare. However, rituals of solidarity, concrete ways in which the members express the unity of their group, are common in both sensitivity groups and communes. In communes rituals of solidarity take a variety of forms. Some members drop their "straight" names and adopt new ones when they enter the commune. The members' sharing of possessions can also be an expression of the group's unity. Rituals of regularly scheduled periods of meditation can also express the oneness of the group. One such ritual in an encounter group was described as follows:

Somehow at the end of our first evening session . . . we all moved into the center of the room, a tight mass of bodies, with our arms around each other, and swayed back and forth with our eyes closed. It was a remarkable feeling, and by the next day we all felt more free to be in physical contact when we wanted to be.

[Rogers, 1970, p. 62.]

In both encounter groups and communes the members can become so immersed in the group that they can temporarily lose their sense of separateness. Indeed, some have theorized that for a group to be truly satisfying to its members, it must provide for this kind of deindividuation (Festinger, Pepitone, and Newcomb, 1952). Encounter groups and communes provide for this kind of experience. In the commune deindividuation can also occur with the unified movement of the members of the group:

We got higher and noisier. Elaine was in a frenzy, turning like a whirling dervish, making inarticulate sounds. People tripped and were caught, embraced and pulled back into the dance. I recalled how the Shakers, another communal sect, had gotten their name from the dances that sent them into ecstasies. We shook with the same frenzy. It came from within, unprompted by drugs, in a bare shed set in a valley of muddy roads, dark woods, prowling coyotes. I looked at the faces. Here were plain simple folk who had found each other. It was inconceivable we could ever have been apart.

[Houriet, 1971, p. 105.]

Conclusion

What are the practical implications of what we have been discussing? We know that many people are lonely. The question is whether or not the preceding discussion has any practical implications for decreasing their loneliness.

The answer, unfortunately, is that utopia is not yet in sight. First, as we said earlier, there is so little evidence on the characteristics that enable a group to meet the social-emotional needs of its members that whether or not the traits discussed in this section are, in fact, related to this type of effectiveness is highly speculative.

But—the important question of empirical verification aside—let's suppose for a moment that it had been shown that belonging to groups with these characteristics did make people feel less lonely. Would the loneliness problem be solved? Again, the pessimistic answer is that even this information wouldn't automatically solve the problem. There's a big gap between knowing the essential characteristics of warm and loving groups and creating groups that have these characteristics.

Many Americans are caught in a paradox. Although they want warmth and love from others, they cannot give it themselves and do not want the involvement that accompanies it. If

you are a member of a group in which the others meet the criteria of loving concern, you have to reciprocate, and that takes a lot of time, effort, and ability. In fact, you may have had the cynic-making experience of thinking that you have discovered just such a group only to find that the group has evaporated when you need it. Many people may not be willing to spend the time required to support others on a regular basis.

If the spontaneous evolution of groups that possess these loneliness-easing characteristics seems like less than a totally hopeful solution, what about giving formal instruction to groups to act in a warm, supporting, and accepting manner? Some adherents of sensitivity groups have proposed that the application of general sensitivity procedures would have highly beneficial effects in real-life settings. For instance, Rogers (1970) has proposed that an "open, problem-solving climate" be implemented throughout industrial organizations. Effective as this sounds in theory, unless those concerned are motivated to implement the spirit of the change, such changes may be limited in scope and have only superficial effects. To the façade of plastic plants in industrial concerns will be added the façades of "concern" and "openness." These façades may make people feel lonelier than the less hypocritical reality of self-concern and self-interest.

So what can be concluded from all of this? Even if the discipline of social psychology could provide a neat list of the characteristics of an effective social-emotional group, whether or not such a group could be implemented would depend on the motives of those involved. Repeatedly, throughout this text we have seen examples of findings that have not been applied to solve social problems. For instance, we saw that there is a lot of evidence suggesting that interracial contact among young (three- and four-year-old) children might reduce racial prejudice. But what is being done to utilize this finding? We saw evidence showing that highly aggressive films may increase the incidence of violence in some cases. But since violence brings crowds to the box office, blood and gore continue to be shown.

The same limitations apply to implementing these characteristics in groups so that they can better meet the social-emotional needs of their members. However, the fact that under some circumstances people can open up and that many people genuinely want warm and interpersonal contact may have a gradual impact on changing the norms of our society about interpersonal contact. If people are made aware of the fact that others are like them, that others also want warmth and authenticity in their interpersonal relationships, it may make them consider their own interpersonal relationships more analytically in order to see the extent to which they meet their social-emotional needs.

Further, a knowledge of some possible characteristics of groups that can effectively meet social-emotional needs may suggest ways in which your groups can be made to meet your social-emotional needs more effectively. For instance, if you have a close group of friends that meets your social-emotional needs to some extent, incorporating some of the characteristics discussed in this section may make the group even more effective in making you feel accepted. The knowledge that the expression of affection by touch may be an important way to make people feel accepted may decrease the social inhibitions against showing nonsexual affection through touch. Or a knowledge of the unifying effects of rituals of solidarity may make you try to introduce these in groups that you belong to.

Although knowledge does not inevitably lead to effective action, it is more likely to do so than ignorance. Perhaps our discussion has given you some ideas about how you might modify your own behavior and that of your friends so that your relationships might better meet your social-emotional needs.

Summary

The main problem for many people today is to escape from feelings of loneliness. In the 1960s and early 1970s, when loneliness emerged as a clearly articulated social problem, two solutions—communes and sensitivity groups—emerged as popular ways to combat feelings of loneliness.

Examining some of the procedures followed in communes and encounter groups provides some leads about how other groups could be structured to meet the social-emotional needs of their members. Most communes and sensitivity groups seem to possess the following characteristics: (1) the general characteristics necessary for the formation and survival of all groups, (2) the possibility of intense and warm relationships among the members, (3) the expression of affection by touch, (4) the expression of authentic feelings and reactions by the members, (5) the physical isolation of the group from other people, (6) a limited number of people, and (7) rituals of solidarity and deindividuation. However, this list is not intended to be exhaustive.

Does our discussion have any practical implications for decreasing loneliness? The answer, unfortunately, is that utopia is not yet in sight. There is so little evidence on the characteristics that enable a group to meet the social-emotional needs of its members that whether or not the traits discussed in this section are, in fact, related to this type of effectiveness is highly speculative. Even if it had been shown that belonging to groups with these characteristics did make people feel less lonely, this information wouldn't automatically solve the problem. There is a big gap between knowing the essential characteristics of warm and loving groups and creating groups that have these characteristics. However, knowing some possible characteristics of groups that may make them more effective in meeting the social-emotional needs of their members may suggest ways in which groups could be modified so that they would better meet the social-emotional needs of their members.

SUMMARY

Since so large a proportion of most people's time is spent interacting in groups, the question of how they function is very important and practical.

1. Group Functioning *Being with others can either facilitate or interfere with performance.* Whether social interaction helps or hurts performance seems to depend on: (1) whether or not the task to be performed has been thoroughly learned and (2) whether the social contact increases or decreases one's level of overall excitement, or drive. If you are in the process of learning and the social contact is arousing, social interference would be expected to occur. If the response is well learned, the presence of a potentially evaluative audience would result in social facilitation.

Diffusion of responsibility can occur in a group. If a person is fearful about the consequences of a particular action, the anonymity of the group may enable him to act more as he would like to act. On the other hand, the reduction in personal responsibility in a group may make any one group member less likely to take any action than if he were alone. Further, in the excitement and anonymity of a group setting, particularly in a crowd situation, the individual can become immersed in the group, or *deindividuated,* and his inner restraints against immoral behavior may be reduced, so that together with others he can engage in highly pathological and aggressive behaviors.

If an individual sees others performing a particular act, he is likely to *imitate* them. People can and do copy almost any response. However, one theorist has proposed that not all cases of behavior copying are mediated by the same internal processes. In one type, known as *simple imitation,* there is no conflict about the individual's performing the act in question. In a second type of copying, which has been termed *behavioral contagion,* the individual is initially in conflict about whether or not to perform a certain response. But seeing others engaging in the act makes it seem appropriate. The sight and sound of others acting is stimulating; their presence automatically diffuses responsibility; and their performing the act legitimatizes it.

Behavioral contagion may also be an extremely important determinant of whether or not deindividuated behavior will occur.

2. Conformity Although individuality is officially admired in college circles, you have only to look about you to see numerous instances of conformity. Conformity has been demonstrated repeatedly in laboratory studies. When, in the classic Asch experiment, subjects were confronted with a situation in which the answers given by a majority were incorrect, one-third of their judgments were conforming and incorrect. Thus the Asch experiment has shown that through the simple procedure of having a unanimous group of people say something that is obviously incorrect, college students can occasionally be made to modify what they say to conform to the majority opinion.

How does the group exert its pressure on the individual? First, other people are an important source of *information.* Whenever reality is at all ambiguous, we look primarily to what others say and do to define reality. *Any variations in the situation that are likely to make the individual think that the majority is correct will increase the incidence of conformity.* The more difficult and ambiguous the task is, the more competent the majority is in relation to the subject, and the larger the group is (a majority of three is significantly more influential than one of one or two), the greater the probability that the subject will conform. Further, the subject is more likely to conform when the group is unanimous than when the unanimity is broken.

Normative pressures may also make an individual conform. People may conform in order to avoid punishment for deviancy, to win group acceptance, or to avoid the embarrassment of being different—since to be different usually means that attempts will be made to bring you back in line. From the normative approach to conformity, it would follow that *any factors in the situation that heighten the group's ability to identify and punish deviance would be expected to increase conformity.* There is a considerable amount of evidence in support of this hypothesis. The more the individual is attracted to the group and the less secure he is about his standing in the group (within limits), the more likely he is to conform. Further, the more publicly the individual's judgments are given and the less committed he is to an independent judgment, the more likely he is to agree with the group.

In addition to discussing situational determinants of conformity, we considered the question of whether or not certain persons are more likely to conform in any situation. We saw that *attempts to specify characteristics that are consistently related to conformity have not been very successful.*

Research in the area of conformity has centered mainly on Asch's classic procedure. Although this is an exciting procedure, one can ask whether the preoccupation with his paradigm has resulted in an undue emphasis on one type of social influence situation: the case of one person who is required to make a verbal judgment when confronted with a unanimous majority.

In real life there are many other social influence situations. Occasionally, a person is pressured to make his actions coincide with what others are doing. Milgram's obedience work provides some interesting insights into this kind of *behavioral obedience.* Also, in real life *one person or a subgroup of persons holding views that are divergent from those held by the majority sometimes persuades the majority to accept its views.* Just this reaction has been dramatically shown in a series of studies in which a consistent minority could make a sizable proportion of the majority change their color perception.

3. Group Effectiveness: An Overview   There are two main ways of evaluating a group's effectiveness. One approach, which has dominated most of the research, is to focus on the *extent to which a group accomplishes its work goals.* Another approach is to assess the extent to which a *group meets the social and emotional needs of its members.* As we saw in Chapter 5, feelings of loneliness and alienation are common in today's rootless society. We can ask if these two productivity measures of effectiveness are necessarily in conflict. In some cases they are not. However, if a work group evolves a norm about the appropriate level of productivi-

ty, strong social pressures can be brought to bear on the members of the group to adhere to that norm, thus limiting the productivity of those who could produce more. From findings such as these, the view emerged that meeting the social-emotional needs of the group members interferes with their effectively meeting work goals. Since production was the main concern, most of the research focused on the antecedents of productivity and neglected the determinants of social-emotional effectiveness.

4. The Effective Work Group   Generally, a group of people is more effective than any one member of the group working alone would be, since the group usually has more resources to accomplish a task than does an individual. *Whether people are more effective working separately or together is dependent on a number of variables:*

a. Task. When tasks can be subdivided easily or when they are unitary and fairly simple, groups tend to be more effective than individuals working separately.

b. Cohesiveness. Since the members of cohesive groups have a strong tendency to follow the group norm, the relative productivity of a cohesive group and a nominal group of the same people depends on whether the group favors high or low productivity.

c. Communication patterns. When the task is a simple one, the more centralized networks are the most efficient. For more complicated tasks the decentralized networks are more efficient.

d. Size. There is no clear relationship between group size and productivity. Larger groups have a greater potential for productivity, but they also have a higher frequency of interpersonal problems.

e. Group composition. The potential for group productivity depends on the potential for productivity of each of the group's members. However, whether a homogeneous or a heterogeneous group will be more effective depends on the characteristic in question, the nature of the task, and the way a particular group functions.

f. Identification with the group's goal. Groups in which the members are more worried about their own personal concerns than the group's goals are less effective than groups in which the members work toward the common group goal. Involvement with the group's goal is more probable if the goal coincides with the individual's own goals, if the individual's and the group's payoff coincides, and if the individual feels involved in making decisions.

5. Groupthink Groupthink is a mode of thinking that persons engage in when they become so highly preoccupied with seeking and maintaining the unanimity of their group that their critical thinking is rendered ineffective. Eight characteristics of groupthink have been identified: (1) illusions of invulnerability, (2) evolution of a rationale, (3) belief in the morality of the group's decisions, (4) stereotyped views of the enemy, (5) conformity pressures, (6) self-censorship of critical thoughts, (7) enforcers of group unanimity, or mindguards, and (8) illusions of unanimity.

Although at this point its prevalence is not clear, groupthink is thought to be especially likely to occur when: (1) the decision-making group is highly cohesive; (2) the group is insulated from other, more balanced information; and (3) the leader has preconceived notions of the correct policy to follow.

It has been suggested that to prevent groupthink conditions should be arranged so that independent thought is encouraged. In general, steps that encourage member skepticism and diversity of opinion may counter the strong pressures toward consensus. Indeed, the results of one recent study suggest that groups can be trained to overcome groupthink and so be made more effective.

6. The Effective Social-Emotional Group The main problem for many people today is to escape from feelings of loneliness. In the 1960s and early 1970s, when loneliness emerged as a clearly articulated social problem, two solutions—communes and sensitivity groups—emerged as popular ways to combat feelings of loneliness.

Examining some of the procedures followed in communes and encounter groups provides some leads about how other groups could be structured to meet the social-emotional needs of their members. Most communes and sensitivity groups appear to possess the following characteristics: (1) the general characteristics necessary for the formation and survival of all groups, (2) the possibility of intense and warm relationships among the members, (3) the expression of affection by touch, (4) the expression of authentic feelings and reactions by the members, (5) the physical isolation of the group from other people, (6) a limited number of people, and (7) rituals of solidarity and deindividuation.

There is little evidence on the characteristics that enable a group to meet the social-emotional needs of its members. Whether or not the traits discussed in this chapter are, in fact, related to this type of effectiveness is highly speculative. Further, even if these characteristics really do make people feel less lonely, there is a big gap between simply knowing about them and implementing them in specific groups. Nevertheless, even a little knowledge in this area is better than nothing. Knowing some of the characteristics of groups that may make them meet more effectively the social-emotional needs of their members may motivate people to try to implement some of these characteristics in the groups they belong to so that they will feel less lonely.

DISCUSSION QUESTIONS

1. Have you observed instances of either social facilitation or social interference in your own behavior or that of others? Under what circumstances does the presence of others facilitate performance? When does it interfere?

2. How do you think your friends would react to you if you strongly supported a position that the majority of them opposed? Have you ever been in this situation? Which pressures—informational or normative—do you think would be stronger?

3. Have you ever been a member of an inefficient committee? If you have, what do you think caused the inefficiency?

4. Have you seen any evidence of the blue-collar blues—the disenchantment that a large number of Americans feel with their jobs?

5. Can you think of any examples of groupthink at work?

6. Of all of the groups you belong to, which one makes you feel the most accepted and cared for? How does this group differ from others in which you feel less accepted?

7. Under what circumstances do you think the risky shift occurs? When do you think groups would make more conservative decisions than individuals?

8. Observe and record the relative frequency of jeans and other types of trousers worn by fifty male college students in the college library. Is one type worn more frequently than another?

9. Under what circumstances do you think a consistent minority can convert a majority? When do you think a deviating minority might result in a majority's supporting its original position more vigorously?

10. Why do you think so much work is done in business settings by committees? Give evidence to support your answer.

11. Seven characteristics that may make groups more effective in meeting the social-emotional needs of their members were listed in the text. On the basis of your observations and your experience, can you think of any additional variables?

12. Try to show how the model of deindividuation could explain the various behaviors occurring in a rioting crowd. Does deindividuation explain all of the phenomena, or are other concepts necessary?

13. Much of the conformity work has involved the Asch paradigm. Devise another way to manipulate conformity pressures, and then design an experiment to test the effects of manipulating one variable on the incidence of conformity. State your hypothesis, your independent variable, procedure, dependent variable, and expected results.

14. On the basis of the material discussed in this chapter and your own observations of effective committees, specify the exact conditions under which a committee of students could prepare the answers for a final examination in social psychology in an efficient manner. Include recommendations about such variables as the spatial arrangement of the members, tasks to be performed, cohesiveness, communication patterns, leadership functions, size, group composition, and identification with the group goal. How would you manipulate conditions so that you could obtain the optimal level of each variable you specified?

15. Three variables thought to increase the frequency of groupthink were listed in this chapter. Can you think of any additional ones? How could you verify your hypothesis?

16. Design a training program to counter the powerful pressures toward groupthink. State exactly what you would do and why.

17. In your opinion, what is the best solution for the American problem of loneliness?

GLOSSARY

acculturation theory of prejudice The theory that if a culture provides racist information as well as pressures to conform to these teachings, people will tend to accept prejudice simply as a means for effectively functioning in a racist society and with others who are racist. One prominent social psychologist has estimated that roughly three out of every four white Americans who are prejudiced are simply reflecting their culture.

activist research An approach to research that argues that social psychologists should focus even more actively than the proponents of relevant research on making research relevant to social problems and to applying that knowledge even more intensively. Further, some feel that social psychologists should become more involved in "action" research by applying their laboratory-tested hypotheses to design and to evaluate real social problems.

affiliation The desire to be with other people. A basic social motive.

affiliation motivation The intensity of an individual's desire to be with other people. In general, people scoring high in the need to affiliate have been found to be first- or only-born children, to be sensitive to social cues, and to engage in a variety of affiliative behaviors. See "affiliation motivation."

aggression Alternately used in an emotional, a motivational, or a behavioral sense. Aggression is popularly thought to be an outgrowth of the emotion of anger. It is also common to focus on the motives behind an act of violence: An act is aggressive when it is intended to hurt another. However, because of the difficulty of determining people's emotions and motives, most psychologists have tended to focus more on observable behavior. Under a behavioral view, aggression is simply a response that injures another.

alienation A general sense of meaninglessness, helplessness, and loneliness.

altruism May be defined either by focusing on the motives or reasons for performing a helping act or on the behavior of helping. Under a motivational definition, a helping act is altruistic when it is motivated primarily by an anticipation of its positive consequences for another individual. Under a behavioral view, altruism is defined as any conduct that helps another, regardless of the helper's motives. The behavioral definition is the one most commonly used in the scientific literature since it has the advantage of being easier to measure objectively.

anchoring effect The interrelating of a number of attitudes in such a way that an attack on any one attitude in the structure will threaten the whole structure and thus produce an especially high level of resistance.

antecedents Causes of a phenomenon. For example, one "antecedent" of the level of group cohesiveness is the level of severity of the initiation into a group.

anxiety The emotion aroused by innocuous stimuli that are subjectively upsetting, but not related to objectively dangerous stimuli in the environment. If for no explicable reason, you suddenly began to feel very upset, you would be experiencing anxiety. In contrast, fear is the emotion aroused when a person is confronted with something that is objectively dangerous.

area sampling A technique which involves the random sampling of geographical areas rather than the random sampling of all the individuals in the population.

artifact An experimental finding that does not reflect the true state of affairs in a social situation and is caused by some confounding in the experimental situation. The "Rosenthal effect" is one example of an experimental artifact.

A-S scale A questionnaire used in the study of the authoritarian personality to measure anti-Semitism—a generally negative attitude toward Jews. One sample item from the scale: "One trouble with Jewish businessmen is that they stick together and connive, so that a Gentile doesn't have a fair chance in competition."

Asch's theory of interpersonal perception The theory that as we use the separate pieces of information to form an overall, consistent picture of another person, each trait influences the way we interpret the others, and the total impression is not one that could be predicted from the individual traits alone. Some traits exert more of an influence than others, since they influence the way other traits are interpreted. However, the whole context determines the meaning of any particular trait.

atmosphere See "group atmosphere."

attitude An overall, learned core disposition that guides thoughts, feelings, and actions toward specific others and objects. Three components have generally been found to be common to all attitudes: (1) cognitive (or beliefs), (2) emotional (or feelings), and (3) behavioral (or action). A concept is generally considered to be an attitude only if it possesses, to at least some degree, each of these three components.

attitude change Any significant modification in the direction of an individual's attitude. Attitude change is influenced by: (1) the communicator, (2) the channel of communication, (3) the communication, and (4) characteristics of the audience.

attitude formation The process of forming an attitude. Our own personal experiences, the influences of others, and our own emotional reactions are the three main determinants of our attitudes.

attribution theory The theory that without our necessarily being aware that we are doing so, we use a series of "tests" to determine whether another person's words and deeds reflect his underlying characteristics or are forced responses to the given situation. The four major criteria used to verify impressions of others are: (1) consistency, (2) consensus, (3) freedom from external pressures, and (4) prior expectancy of a behavior's occurring.

authoritarian leadership A form of leadership in which the leader makes all group decisions, is aloof from the members of the group, and treats group members in a negative, punitive manner.

authoritarian personality A set of attitudes and personality characteristics found to occur in highly prejudiced people. People who were anti-Semitic were also ethnocentric and possessed several common personality traits—highly conventional, obsessed with power, subservient to power, and unanalytical. Although the original study had some methodological flaws, a number of replications have found the original pattern of relationships. However, the question of accounting for the pattern of relationships is still very much an open one. The Berkeley interpretation was that the authoritarian syndrome is caused by repressed hostility, created by overdemanding and unloving parents, which expresses itself in prejudice, a particular personality, and a rigid cognitive style. However, since authoritarians come from homes described as authoritarian, they may have simply imitated their parents.

autokinetic phenomenon A visual illusion in which a stationary point of light shown in a completely dark room appears to move, although it is very difficult for the person watching the light to estimate exactly how far it seems to move.

balance theory A theory that people prefer to hold consistent, compatible beliefs and to avoid inconsistent, incompatible beliefs. Cognitive dissonance theory is an example of one balance theory.

Bales' theory of leadership roles The theory that there are two distinct and separate leadership roles. One, a task specialist, is devoted to commenting on the specific problem at hand, to giving and asking for opinions and suggestions for ways to approach the problem. The other, a social-emotional specialist, focuses on overcoming interpersonal problems in the group, showing the solidarity of the group, and releasing tension through humor. If a group is to be effective, both of these roles must be filled.

basic research An approach to psychological research that focuses on repeated studies of theoretically important issues in order to derive a systematic and integrated understanding of social processes.

behavioral component of an attitude How the person acts in relation to an object or a group. Whether beliefs and emotions are translated into consistent behaviors depends on a number of variables, including the accuracy with which a person's beliefs are measured, his attitudes about other aspects of the situation, his fear of punishment, and the extent to which he feels he is able to act on his attitudes and is personally involved with the issue.

behavioral contagion A type of imitation in which the individual is initially in conflict about whether or not to perform a certain response. However, if he sees others performing the act about which he is in conflict, his internal restraints are reduced and he imitates the others. See "imitation."

behavioral measure Allowing the subjects an opportunity to perform some action to assess the effects of the independent variable.

behavioristic psychology One which focuses exclusively on stimuli and responses, makes extensive use of animal subjects, and generally assumes an "empty organism."

behavioroid measure Measuring the subject's intention to perform some action to assess the effects of the independent variable.

bias An error or an inaccuracy. For example, a bias in perception is that generally perceptions of ourselves are particularly kind.

biased sample A sample that is unrepresentative of a population because of biases in its selection. For example, interviewing a number of students who were studying in the college library would not produce a sample representative of all of the students at the particular college.

"blue-collar blues" The disenchantment that some Americans who perform dull, repetitive tasks feel about their jobs.

body accessibility The openness of arms and legs.

body language Body gestures.

body orientation The degree to which a person's shoulders and legs are turned toward another person.

"boomerang effect" The members of the audience changing their attitude in a direction opposite from that being advocated.

brainwashing See "Chinese brainwashing."

"bystander effect" The finding that people are much less likely to help in an emergency—or indeed to take action of any sort—when they are with others than when they are alone. Being with others sometimes results in the group members defining the situation as less critical than they would if they were alone. Also being with others diffuses the responsibility for helping. However, variations in the situation—such as making the need for help very clear—can counter the bystander effect.

catharsis The theory that once aggressive impulses are aroused, only aggressing will produce a decrease in tension. If an individual feels aggressive but cannot act out his feelings directly on the cause of his frustration, aggressing indirectly, phantasizing about aggression, or viewing or reading about aggression will decrease his aggressive impulses. Thus a catharsis view of the effect of viewing televised violence holds that it would decrease the level of aggressive behavior of the viewer.

central traits Traits that exert more of an influence than other traits in influencing the way other traits are interpreted.

centralized communication network One in which one person has access to the majority of the other members of a group. See "Y communication network" and "wheel communication network."

chain communication pattern A communication pattern in which three people in a five-person group have access to two persons in the group; the other two have access to only one person. Since no one member of the group has access to a majority of the other members, this network—as well as the circle network—is referred to as a "decentralized communication network."

channel of communication How the information is delivered—whether in face-to-face communication, by films, printed materials, etc.

charisma A "personal magnetism" popularly thought to be possessed by some leaders.

Chinese brainwashing The systematic application of a wide variety of persuasive techniques, along with a great emphasis on the use of fellow prisoners as indoctrinators. Physical, psycho-

logical, and social pressures are all effectively used.

circle communication network A communication pattern in which each person has access to the two persons on either side of him and no access to the remaining two members of the group. Since no one member has access to a majority of the other group members, this network—as well as the chain network—is referred to as a "decentralized communication network."

classical conditioning A procedure in which a previously neutral stimulus (the "conditioned stimulus") is associated with a stimulus (the "unconditioned stimulus") that has the power to elicit particular responses (the "unconditioned response"). After a number of associations the conditioned stimulus acquires the power to elicit a response very similar to the unconditioned response in the absence of the unconditioned stimulus. This learning process is to be distinguished from instrumental conditioning and operant conditioning.

clinical approach in police interrogation The interrogator's playing upon the suspect's guilts and anxieties that are unrelated to the crime. For instance, some people have deep-seated guilts about real or imagined crimes committed during their childhood, and these can be relieved by confession. After a suspect has been fully upset by these unrelated guilts, he may be relieved to change the topic to his alleged crime.

coacting group A group in which two or more people are working on the same task at the same time but are not allowed to talk with one another or interact in any other way. Experimental instructions are given that the members of the group are not competing against one another. By trying to eliminate interaction and competition, it is hoped that the "pure" effects of the presence of others on performance can be assessed. However, whether competition could be eliminated from subjects strongly trained to compete is questionable. See "interacting group."

coalition A subgroup of people acting jointly to improve the outcome of their activities at the expense of others in the group. For example, in a group of five card players two may unite to gain mutual advantage over the other, uncoordinated players.

cognition The knowledge, beliefs, thoughts, and ideas that an individual has about himself and his environment. Also, "cognition" may be used to refer to all of the mental processes through which knowledge is acquired—including perception, memory, and thinking. See "cognitive dissonance theory."

cognitive component of an attitude An individual's beliefs about the attitudinal object.

cognitive dissonance An unpleasant state induced by an individual's simultaneously believing two inconsistent ideas (or cognitions) at the same time.

cognitive dissonance theory The theory that simultaneously believing two ideas or opinions ("cognitions") that are psychologically inconsistent arouses cognitive dissonance. Because dissonance is unpleasant, we try to reduce it by removing the inconsistency. To achieve consistency (or "consonance"), we may change one of the beliefs to make it consistent, or we may add others.

cognitive-mediational hypothesis Consistent emotions and behaviors follow from beliefs about attitudinal objects.

cognitive theory of emotional reaction The theory that no matter what emotion is aroused, the physiological reactions are very similar. To make sense out of your physiological arousal, you look to the situation to decide what emotion is being experienced. Then you attach a label to the emotional reaction.

cohesiveness See "group cohesiveness."

commitment Has been operationally defined in three ways: (1) getting a person to take some action consistent with his attitude, (2) getting a person to make his attitudes public, or (3) making a person feel that his attitudes are irrevocable.

commune Although communes vary enormously in structure and people—from the loosely organized "crash pads" of hippie college dropouts to the highly organized groups of executive dropouts—an underlying theme in communes is a sense of strong unification and group feeling among the commune members. Most communes seem to possess the following characteristics: (1) the general characteristics necessary for the formation and survival of all groups, (2) the possibility of intense and warm relationships among the members, (3) the expression of affection by touch, (4) the expression of authentic feelings and reactions by the members, (5) the physical isolation of the group from other people, (6) a limited number of people, and (7) rituals of solidarity and deindividuation.

communication network The pattern of communication opportunities. Members of a group who are free to communicate with a number of persons are generally more satisfied with the group than those who can only interact with one other person. For examples of networks, see "circle communication network," "chain communication network," "Y communication network," and "wheel communication network."

communicator credibility Generally thought to consist of two main components: expertness (how much the source knows) and trustworthiness (how honest he is about it).

comparative function of a reference group The process by which a group provides information about reality to its members—including information about themselves.

competition Working against others in order to obtain possessions, money, prestige, etc. Rivalry.

complementarity Someone's possessing traits that go nicely with your own.

conceptual replication A way to eliminate alternative explanations of the results of a prior study by devising an experimental procedure that differs in as many ways as possible from the original while still testing the same conceptual variable.

conditioning See "instrumental conditioning," "operant conditioning," and "classical conditioning."

conformity The tendency of a member of a group to modify what he says and does in order to correspond with what the others in the group say and do. "Conformity" has also sometimes been defined as the extent to which people adhere to a norm. When behaviors have been classified as to the extent to which they adhere to a norm, it has been found that most behaviors do adhere, a few deviate slightly, and even fewer deviate significantly.

confounded experiment An experiment in which the effects of other variables are varying in an unsystematic and unplanned way along with the independent variable. Other terms are used to mean roughly the same thing as confounded, such as "lack of control," or "lack of internal validity." Note confounding is completely different from an interaction in a factorial design. When confounding occurs, there are no ways to assess the relative contribution of the independent and the uncontrolled variable.

consequences Effects of a phenomenon. For example, one "consequence" of a high level of group cohesiveness is a high frequency of communication and cooperation among the group members.

consideration A dimension of leadership behavior that refers to the extent to which a leader is characterized by warmth and trust in his personal relationships, and is willing to explain his actions to his subordinates and to allow them to participate in decision making. See "initiating structure."

consonance A pleasant state induced when an individual's beliefs are consistent. See "cognitive dissonance theory."

contingency theory of leadership See "Fiedler's 'contingency' theory of leadership."

control Intentionally creating conditions in an experiment so that nothing systematically varies except the independent variable. Includes such tactics as holding variables constant, randomly assigning subjects to experimental conditions, eliminating the effects of variables (such as experimenter expectancy, etc.), and equating variables. Sometimes "control" is confused with the term "control group." However, the presence of a control group is not necessary to maintain control. See "control group."

control group A group that shares all characteristics and treatments with the experimental group except that the independent variable is not manipulated. For example, in an experiment on the effects of severity of initiation on subjects' liking for a group, there might be two conditions: (1) an experimental group that went through a severe initiation, and (2) a control group that was not subjected to any initiation at all. However, the presence of a control group is not necessary to maintain experimental control. See "control."

controlled experiment A research technique in which an experimenter manipulates one or more variables (called "independent variable(s)") in order to see the effect produced on one or more other variables (called "dependent variable(s)"). Through the process of attempting to control all other, extraneous variables that might influence the relationship, the investigator seeks to assure that any effects observed are due only to variations in the independent variable.

Cook's interracial contact theory The theory that the effectiveness of integration can be directly related to specific variables in the situation, the type of person involved, and the things that that person does. For example, integration would be expected to be effective when the following factors are present in a situation of interracial contact: (1) equality of status, (2) need for cooperation, (3) dissimilarity of the black person from the social stereotype, (4) intimacy of interaction, and (5) antiprejudice social norms.

cooperation Working with others in order to obtain a common goal. See "competition."

coping The extent to which a person knows what to do, feels he can do it, and feels it would be effective.

correlation A research technique in which measures are obtained on two (or more) variables and then the extent to which they are related is assessed. The better one score predicts the other score, the higher the correlation. No matter how high the correlation, however, it does not allow one to infer correctly the direction of cause and effect.

cost analysis of helping The theory that the incidence of helping behavior in a particular situation will depend completely on the relationship between the costs of and the rewards for helping. Costs would be the negative consequences to the individual; rewards, the positive consequences.

"cover story" A false rationale provided to cover the true purpose of an experiment and to provide a reasonable explanation for all of the experimental procedures.

culture The shared beliefs, values, and expectations about the appropriate ways to behave in certain situations.

curvilinear relationship One in which both very low levels and very high levels of a variable are less effective than moderate levels of a variable. For example, both too much and too little discrepancy are ineffective; maximum persuasiveness comes with moderately discrepant communications.

debriefing See "dehoaxing."

decentralized communication network One in which no one group member has access to a majority of the other group members. See "circle communication network" and "chain communication network."

dehoaxing (or "debriefing") the subjects Revealing any deceptions which were involved in the experiment.

dehumanization Thinking of other people as not being human—which may result in reducing one's normal inhibitions against acting aggressively toward such people. Not to be confused with "deindividuation."

deindividuation Loss of a sense of separate identity generally resulting in a reduction of inner restraints within the individual.

demand characteristics of an experiment The extent to which the experimental procedures make explicit what the experimenter is trying to prove and thereby influence the subjects to perform as expected.

democratic leadership A form of leadership in which the leader allows the group members to participate fully in making group decisions, participates in the group's activities, and treats the group members in a friendly manner.

579

Glossary

dependent variable(s) The variable(s) measured in a controlled experiment in order to assess the effects of the independent variable(s) in that experiment. For example, in an experiment on the effects of the level of stress on affiliation, the amount of affiliation in the various experimental groups would be the dependent variable.

displacement Directing aggression at a target other than the original source of frustration. Aggression may be displaced to persons about whom very unfavorable stereotypes persist, persons who are not able to retaliate, persons toward whom aggression is sanctioned by the individual's friends, persons who are believed to be partially responsible for a particular frustration, or persons who seem similar to the source of frustration.

dissonance See "cognitive dissonance theory."

double-barrelled questionnaire item An item that refers to two different matters in the question.

dyad A two-person group. A great deal of social interaction takes place on a one-to-one basis; many of the most intensive, most influential relationships take place on a one-to-one basis; and dyadic interactions have important differences from interactions in larger groups.

effective social-emotional group Any group that helps to fulfill the affiliative needs of its members and to overcome their negative feelings about themselves or their society. For example, during the 1960s and early 1970s, when loneliness became a clearly articulated social problem, communes and encounter groups emerged as popular ways to combat feelings of loneliness and to offer the possibility of intense relationships among group members.

emotional component of an attitude The emotional reaction to the attitudinal object.

empathy Experiencing the thoughts, feelings, and motives of others vicariously.

empirical approach The collection of factual information to ascertain the true state of affairs.

encounter group (sometimes termed "sensitivity group" or "T group") A group whose main goal is to have its members relate meaningfully with other people and to be accepted by them. Although encounter groups vary in terms of the exact procedures followed, most go through the following stages: (1) milling around and resisting opening up; (2) gradual opening up; (3) expressing emotionally relevant material; (4) the development of a healing capacity in the members of the group; (5) the basic encounter—the intensive, involving, interpersonal contact among the members; (6) cracking façades and self-acceptance; and (7) feedback and confrontation.

environmental blocking Frustration that occurs as a result of either a physical object or a person blocking you from something you want.

equity theory The theory that people attempt to maintain "equitable relationships" in which the proportion of each member's contributions and benefits is equal to that of the others. Should you injure another person, you do something nice for him, which is roughly equivalent to the injury done, to make up for the injury. The reciprocity norm is one example of the general tendency toward equity in social relationships.

E scale A questionnaire used in the study of the authoritarian personality to measure ethnocentrism—a general dislike of all people who are different from the white middle-class norm. One sample item from the scale: "Certain religious sects who refuse to salute the flag should be forced to such a patriotic action or else be abolished."

ethologists Scientists studying life in its natural habitat.

exact replication A repetition of a study in which research procedures are either as similar to the original as possible or vary in some specified, relatively minor way (such as using students at a different university as subjects).

excessive affiliation effect The finding that when groups of people are confined together over an extended period of time, they react with withdrawal, irritation, and boredom.

experiment See "controlled experiment."

experimenter effects Experimental results due to variations in the experimenter's behavior rather than the independent variable. See "Rosenthal effect."

explicit form of communication Presenting evidence in support of a particular conclusion and then explicitly drawing the conclusions from your evidence.

eye contact Looking another person in the eye.

face work The ritualization of social interactions that allows for mutual enhancement of one's public image, or "face," and the avoidance of honest self-disclosures.

factorial design An experiment involving more than one independent variable. If the effect of one of the independent variables changes according to the level of the other, an "interaction" is said to have occurred and there are statistical procedures to test for its existence. Obtaining an interaction does not preclude assessing the effects of each independent variable separately.

fear The emotion aroused when a person is confronted with something that is objectively dangerous and likely to produce pain. In contrast, anxiety is typically aroused by innocuous stimuli that are subjectively upsetting but not related to objectively dangerous stimuli in the environment.

fear-arousing communications Communications that frighten the members of the audience. Scare appeals.

Festinger's theory of communication and social influence The theory that all social groups create a pressure toward uniformity and that the extent to which the members of a group attempt to reach consensus is determined by: (1) the extent of the differences in initial opinions, (2) the cohesiveness of the group, and (3) the relevance of the issue to the group.

Fiedler's "contingency" theory of leadership The theory that whether task-centered or people-centered leadership is more effective depends on the situation. In situations that are either very favorable or very unfavorable to leadership, the task-centered leader is more effective than the people-centered leader. However if the situation is moderately favorable, the people-centered leader is more effective than the task-centered leader.

field experiment One performed in a natural setting.

"foot-in-the-door" technique The finding that if you want someone to do something big for you, get him to do something small but committing first.

forewarning Telling a person in advance that you are going to try to persuade him.

"forming, storming, norming, and performing" theory of the emergence of group structure The theory that *any* group, irrespective of its setting, will go through the following four phases: (1) initial orientation to interpersonal and task behaviors ("forming"); (2) intragroup conflict ("storming"); (3) the development of group cohesiveness, roles, and norms ("norming"); and (4) use of group structure to perform the tasks required of the group ("performing").

frustration In general, any interference with, or blocking of, a goal-directed behavior. Five variables have been found to influence the amount of aggression elicited by frustration and the form which the aggression will take: (1) environmental blocking versus attack; (2) arbitrariness of the frustration; (3) expectations; (4) cues from the situation; and (5) anticipated results of aggression.

frustration-aggression theory As the theory was initially proposed, the only cause of aggression is frustration: Frustration inevitably leads to some form of aggression, and whenever aggression occurs, some form of frustration is responsible. The strength of the aggressive impulse is proportional to the intensity of frustration. Expression of the aggressive impulse is determined by the expected rewards and punishments. If an individual expects an act of aggression aimed directly at that which is frustrating him to result in punishment, he will express his aggression in a modified way—either indirectly or by displacing it to other, "safe," nonpunishing objects. In some situations, frustration-aggression may be expressed through attitudes about the members of minority groups. However, research has shown that in addition to aggression, frustration can produce a variety of other behaviors. The contemporary approach to the frustration-aggression hypothesis has been to isolate those aspects of a frustration situation that lead to aggression.

F scale A questionnaire used in the study of the authoritarian personality to measure the individual's potentiality for fascism—implicit antidemocratic trends. On the basis of Freudian theory and their previous survey and clinical work, the investigators hypothesized that the potential fascist would be highly conventional, obsessed with power, subservient to authority, and unanalytical.

gains-and-losses theory of interpersonal attraction The theory that increases in rewarding behavior from another person have more impact on interpersonal attraction than constant, invariant rewards from that person.

galvanic skin response (GSR) A measure of changes in the skin's electrical conductivity caused by changes in the amount of perspiration. Sometimes used to assess levels of prejudice.

group A number of people interacting with a common goal in mind. In more permanent groups, other characteristics may emerge, including: (1) identification of the members with the group; (2) a structure, including leadership; (3) strong conformity pressures; and (4) changes in the behavior of the individual members as a result of their membership in the group.

group atmosphere The property of a social situation as a whole. For example, cohesive groups often exude a warm, pleasant, accepting feeling or atmosphere.

group cohesiveness The degree of the total attraction of all of the individual members to the group. Groups in which the members are highly attracted to the group are said to be high in cohesiveness; those in which the members are not highly attracted to the group are said to be low in cohesiveness. The technique most frequently used to measure cohesiveness is sociometry. (See "sociometry.")

group effectiveness The extent to which a group accomplishes its goals. There are two main ways of evaluating a group's effectiveness. One approach, which has dominated most of the research, is to focus on the extent to which a group accomplishes its work goals. Another approach is to assess the extent to which a group meets the social and emotional needs of its members. See "effective social-emotional group."

group formation Transformation of a collection of separate individuals into a group. When some motivation toward a common goal exists among a given number of individuals, their evolution into a group is made more likely by three other variables: their physical proximity, their similarity, and their being in a highly stressful situation.

group sanctions for evil Rationalizations and social support provided by members of a group for violent activities.

group structure See "structure."

groupthink A mode of thinking that persons in highly cohesive groups engage in when they become so preoccupied with seeking and maintaining unanimity of thought that their critical thinking is rendered ineffective. Independent analytical thought, the testing of alternatives, the weighing of pros and cons, the consideration of moral issues—all of the requirements for carefully reasoned decisions become subverted in an attempt to maintain the consensus of the highly cohesive ingroup. Eight characteristics of groupthink have been identified: (1) illusions of invulnerability; (2) evolution of a rationale; (3) belief in the morality of the group's decisions; (4) stereotyped views of the enemy; (5) conformity pressures; (6) self-censorship of critical thoughts; (7) mindguards, who enforce group unanimity; and (8) illusions of unanimity.

guilt-helping effect When an individual harms others, he feels disturbed, troubled, and guilty. To make restitution, he attempts to compensate somehow for his wrongdoing. Confession and penance lead to absolution which then redresses the person's transgressions against God, society or whomever he has injured and "cleans the slate," allowing the individual to be reinstated within the body of accepted individuals.

humanistic psychology One which is self-oriented, uses human subjects, is interested in topics such as social dynamics and personality, and makes a certain amount of use of speculation and intuition.

identification The process by which one person takes on some of the characteristics of another. For example, children who internalize the altruism of their parents are "identifying" with their parents.

identification with a group A feeling of commitment by the members to the group as well as a feeling of involvement with the group.

identity A unified, coherent self.

image seeking The processes involved in people trying to present their own best image, including such tactics as avoiding potentially uncomfortable social interactions and disguising their own feelings to show feelings that are socially acceptable.

imitation Copying what others do. It has been theorized that there are two types of imitation: (1) Simple imitation in which there is no conflict about the individual's performing the act in question. A student's imitating the swings of a golf pro might be a good example of simple imitation. (2) Behavioral contagion in which the individual is initially in conflict about whether or not to perform a certain response. However, if he sees others performing the act about which he is in conflict, his internal restraints are reduced and he imitates the others. For example, an individual living in an impoverished community might want to take a television set from a local appliance store, but he might be afraid of the consequences. If he sees others looting, however, his own internal restraints against looting may be reduced and he may join the others in looting.

implicit form of communication Presenting evidence in support of a particular conclusion and then stopping, hoping that the audience will draw the conclusion you want it to.

"implicit theory of personality" Everyday assumptions of what traits go together. For example, we may tend to think that people who are warm will also tend to be sociable, generous, and popular.

imprinting A form of learning that occurs very early in life, does not involve reinforcement of the response, and has a lasting effect on the organism. An example of imprinting was the exposure of the goslings to a moving stimulus during a "critical" period of their life and their resulting "social" responses to that object—no matter what it was.

incentive theory of role playing A theory that predicts that the greater the reward for role playing, the better job the person does, the more persuasive are the arguments he amasses, and the more attitude change will occur (a maximum-reward effect). In contrast, dissonance theory predicts that increasing the reward for role playing will decrease the predicted attitude change (a minimal-reward effect).

inconsistency model of attitude change The theory that the only way an attitude can be changed is by introducing inconsistent material that is difficult for the target person to dismiss. For example, to persuade a group of automobile drivers to drive more safely, you might ask each to play the role of someone who has been hospitalized because of an automobile accident. Each might be asked to act out a number of scenes: being visited in the hospital by family members, having his driver's license suspended, being told that his insurance was cancelled, and so forth.

independent variable(s) The variable(s) manipulated in a controlled experiment in order to see the effect produced on one or more other variables (called "dependent variable(s)"). Through the process of attempting to control all other, extraneous variables that might influence the relationship, the investigator seeks to assure that any effects observed are due only to variations in the independent variable. For example, in an experiment on the effects of the level of stress on affiliation, the level of stress would be the independent variable.

individuation Standing out from the other members of the group; trying to make yourself appear different from the others in the group. See "deindividuation."

ingratiation Attempts by another person to make you like him for some ulterior motive.

initiating structure A dimension of leadership behavior that refers to the extent to which a leader organizes the work done by the group, sets standards for performance, follows routines, and makes sure that the relationship between himself and his subordinates is clearly understood. See "consideration."

injury-justification effect People have a need to believe they live in a just world in which deserving people are rewarded and the undeserving are appropriately deprived or punished. Given this need, when people are exposed to those who are suffering through no fault of their own, they experience a conflict. They can either decide that the world is not such a fair place after all—which disturbs their basic assumption and makes them uncomfortable, or they can justify the victim's suffering through a variety of rationalizations—the injury-justification effect.

innate behavior Behavior that is instinctively determined. Behavior that is not learned.

inoculation theory A theory that providing an individual with a weakened counterargument which allows him to build up effective refutations is the most effective way of making an individual resistant to counterpropaganda. To take our safe-driving example, you might acknowledge that there is an argument holding engineering design flaws as being primarily responsible for automobile accidents, but you would then point out weaknesses in that argument. Then, when your audience is exposed to the faulty design argument, it will be more resistant to this argument because of your "attitudinal inoculation."

instinct Behavior that is primarily determined by maturation rather than learning. Common in lower animals, but extremely rare in human beings.

institutional racism Racially prejudiced behavior that is not consciously practiced but is rather a function of an institution (corporation, government, church, school, etc.) doing business as usual when the usual patterns in fact discriminate.

instrumental conditioning A procedure in which an organism must perform a certain response in order either to obtain a reward (or reinforcement) or to terminate or prevent a punishment. See "classical conditioning" and "operant conditioning."

interacting group A group in which the subjects are free to interact. See "coacting group."

interaction A situation in a factorial design in which the effect of one of the independent variables changes according to the level of the other. Not to be confused with a "confounded experiment."

interaction approach to leadership The theory that to predict who will assume leadership in a particular group, one must take into account the characteristics of the group members, the structure of the group, the situation, and the nature of the task facing the group, as well as the personal characteristics that may make one person more likely to emerge as a leader. See "trait approach to leadership."

interactive person perception Person perception situations in which we are being perceived—and we know it—at the same time that we are perceiving others. In the process of interaction, we act on the basis of our perceptions of others and our perception of their views of us. Our reactions to others can modify the way they, in turn, react to us. See "static person perception."

internal-external test A measure of the generalized expectancies of people concerning the degree to which they control their behavior. People who indicate that they themselves primarily determine their acts have been termed "internals." Those who feel that their actions are mainly determined by external forces are called "externals."

internalized attitude change Private acceptance of a message since you think the information is correct.

"just world" belief The belief that the world is a just one in which people get what they deserve.

"kernel of truth" theory of stereotypes The belief that there may be some accuracy—some "kernel of truth"—in at least a few stereotypes. Although many stereotypes have been found to be inaccurate, not all are. Some evidence suggests that when people have an opportunity for contact, under some conditions their impressions of group differences may reflect real differences.

laissez-faire leadership A form of leadership in which the leader is very passive and permissive—allowing complete freedom for the members to do as they wish.

leaderless group test A test for assessing leadership in which an individual is put into an unstructured situation with a group of other people to discuss a topic, and at the conclusion of the meeting all of the members of the group rate the leadership shown by the other members of the group.

leadership Has been defined in a number of ways, including: (1) an individual's possession of personal leadership characteristics, (2) an individual's possession of a leadership office within a group, (3) an individual's possession of the highest level of skill for the task at hand, and (4) someone's performing the leadership functions—such as someone who plans the group's activities. Although each of these definitions emphasizes a different aspect of leadership, it can be argued that all of them include the common element of someone who exerts more influence than the other members of the group. Indeed, this is the definition that has been used most frequently in the literature.

Least Preferred Co-worker (LPC) test A test to measure whether a leader is people-centered or task-centered. Leaders are asked to rate the most incompetent person they have ever worked with on a number of traits, such as pleasantness, helpfulness, and cooperativeness. Thinking that a leader who is primarily people-centered would be reluctant to say unpleasant things about any fellow workers, even the worst one he had ever known, the investigator who devised the test hypothesized that a leader who rated his least preferred co-worker relatively highly would be a people-centered leader. On the other hand, the

task-oriented leader would feel free to evaluate negatively someone who was incompetent and so would give a low rating to his least preferred co-worker. Thus a leader with a high LPC score would be people-centered and one with a low LPC score would be task-centered.

level of aspiration The standard by which a person evaluates his own performance. This is generally determined by what the individual would like to achieve as well as by his own past performance.

"looking-glass" concept of the origin of the self The theory that a child's self-concept is determined by his imitation of the reactions of significant others and by their reactions toward him.

Mach scale A test that measures the extent to which people endorse Machiavellian views—the endorsement of the use of impersonally opportunistic tactics in controlling others, a belief in the baseness of most people, and a feeling that there are no absolute moral standards. (Persons who endorse a high number of Machiavellian statements are referred to as "high Machs"; persons who endorse a low number of Machiavellian statements are referred to as "low Machs.")

marital choice theory Murstein has theorized that a couple progresses through three stages before deciding to marry: (1) a so-called stimulus stage in which people are attracted on the basis of what can be seen, (2) a value stage in which the couple is concerned with evolving compatible values, and (3) a role stage in which the partners are concerned about the adequacy of the "fit" between themselves. What draws the couple together, obviously, varies from stage to stage.

matching hypothesis" of dating In actual dating, when the possibility of rejection is present, the level of physical attractiveness of the dating couple should match.

modeling Imitating what another (the "model") does. See "imitation."

motivation A need—generally social or psychological—that directs the individual to seek a particular goal.

"Mutt-and-Jeff approach" A tactic used in police interrogations in which an interrogator who seems pleasant is switched with a cruel, relentless interrogator to increase the suspect's belief in the friendly interrogator's sincerity.

normative function of a reference group The process by which a group evaluates its members and applies pressure on them to conform to the group's "norms" (i.e., its accepted patterns of behavior).

norms Accepted and expected patterns of behavior and belief that are established—either formally or informally—by a group. When norms are formed, all of the reactions given by the group members influence the reactions of the other members. Each person takes the judgments given by the others into account, so that the final norm is the result of a series of reciprocal concessions. Once formed, rewards are usually administered by other members of the group to individuals who adhere to the norms, and sanctions are usually applied for deviation from the norms. Although roles and norms refer to different phenomena, there is some overlap between them. The expectation that a wife will be primarily responsible for cleaning the house may be seen either as an aspect of her role or as a marital norm. See "roles."

objectivity An observation that can be made repeatedly by a number of different observers. See "reliability."

one-sided communication A communication that contains only the arguments supporting your position. In a two-sided communication, arguments in favor of your recommendations are presented along with some arguments that support the opposing view.

operant conditioning A procedure in which the rate of an already occurring response is either increased or decreased through the administration or withholding of reinforcement. See "classical conditioning" and "instrumental conditioning."

operational definition Going from (or "translating") the general hypothesis to experimental procedures so as to make the hypothesis "operational." For example, in the initiation experiment cited in Chapter 1, the "embarrassment test," reading a list of dirty words and paragraphs, was the operational definition of the independent variable, severity of initiation.

paradigm A general plan of research, such as Asch's procedure of presenting lists of adjectives to subjects and asking them to react to the person described. Or "paradigm" may be used to describe a general way of analyzing information—such as a reinforcement approach to learning.

participant observation A technique, in which the observers become an accepted part of the group being measured, used to minimize the reactive effect of measurement. See "reactive effect of measurement."

participation Extent to which an individual feels that he is involved in making decisions about what his group does. If you feel that "things are happening that you have no control over," you may not identify very much with the group.

people-centered leader One who focuses on the people in the group rather than on the work to be done by the group. See "Fiedler's 'contingency' theory of leadership."

person perception The processes involved when people form their impressions of others. Throughout these processes, various abilities, attitudes, and motivations are being attributed to the other person, and an attempt is made to bring all of these impressions into a cohesive whole..

personal space The area around a person that he feels belongs uniquely to him. The size of the personal space differs in various social interactions. Invading another person's personal space produces a variety of negative reactions, ranging from simple avoidance to strong retaliatory actions, depending on the situation and the people involved.

phenomenological method A study of conscious experience.

population See "random sample."

prejudice An attitude in which a distinct combination of beliefs, emotions, and behaviors—usually negative—has led us to a fixed way of thinking about a person or an object (a bias) that does not readily change on the basis of newly acquired information or experiences.

primacy effect The greater impact of information presented first rather than last. (When information presented last has greater impact, a recency effect is said to have occurred.)

primary reinforcement An event—such as giving food—that reinforces an individual or animal without the need for prior training. In contrast, a secondary reinforcement is an event that becomes reinforcing as a result of having been associated with a primary reinforcement on a number of occasions.

principle of reinforcement The theory that responses which are rewarded tend to occur more frequently. See also "instrumental conditioning" and "operant conditioning."

prisoner's dilemma game This game, widely used to study interpersonal bargaining, is based on an old detective-movie cliché situation in which two suspects have been apprehended by the police, are being questioned separately, and have the option of either confessing or not confessing to the crime that they are accused of, but both could be convicted of other minor crimes (mutual cooperation result). If one prisoner confesses and the other remains silent, the one who has confessed will be released for turning state's evidence, and the other prisoner will receive the maximum penalty (competition/cooperation result). If both prisoners confess, both will be convicted, but they will be given some leniency (mutual competition result). Typically, the game is played over several trials, and points are either awarded to or taken away from each player after each trial depending on the result. A player who confesses can gain the maximum number of points in a competition/cooperation result on one trial, but over several trials both players would make more points from mutual cooperation than from either competition/cooperation or from mutual competition. The dilemma for each player then is to decide whether to remain silent (thus creating the best condition for maximizing the points over several trials for both players) or to confess repeatedly (thus focusing on the greater immediate gain of the cooperation/competition result).

projection A defense mechanism by which a person, when confronted with an ambiguous situation, tends to interpret that situation in terms of his personal anxieties. For example, in viewing a picture of two students studying in their room, a person who is lonely will tend to see signs of loneliness. See "Thematic Apperception Test (TAT)."

proximity Geographical closeness. A powerful determinant of interpersonal attraction.

psychoanalytic theory A theory, originated by Freud, that emphasizes the study of unconscious mental processes. Also a theory of personality and a method of psychotherapy that seeks to treat anxiety and other neurotic symptoms by bringing unconscious material into consciousness. In his theoretical writings in the 1920s, Freud saw aggression as an innate primary motive.

psychological reactance The unpleasant emotion that an individual experiences when his freedom to act is reduced. Once reactance is aroused, the person experiences: (1) a decrease in the attractiveness of the forced activity; (2) emotional dissatisfaction, and (3) less involvement and poorer performance at the forced task.

psychological significance The importance of a particular result. Not to be confused with statistical significance.

psychologically compelling situation One in which the demands to enact a certain role are extremely strong and generally of long duration.

"puffing" A bargaining tactic in which one inflates one's initial demands over what one will ultimately accept.

p value The probability that a given event could have occurred by chance alone. Reported in decimal form on a scale from 0 to 1.00. See "statistical significance."

Q Sort measure of self-esteem The most frequently used measure of self-esteem in which subjects are first asked to sort characteristics along a continuum ranging from "like me" to "unlike me." Then, the individual is asked to rate the same characteristics in terms of whether he would like to possess or not to possess those characteristics. The discrepancy between what the individual thinks he is and what he would like to be yields a measure of self-esteem.

questionnaire A self-report measure in which questions are presented to and answered by respondents in writing.

quota sampling A technique which involves selecting a sample so that it represents the basic attributes of the population.

radical behaviorism The theory that unless our thoughts are very clearly articulated, we infer our own attitudes from the observation of what we say and do.

random sample A small group (or sample) selected from the group to which the results are to be generalized (the population) in such a manner that every member of the population has an equal chance of being included in the sample. For very large populations, it is difficult to obtain a random sample so that other sampling methods—such as area sampling and quota sampling—are frequently used.

reactance See "psychological reactance."

reactive effect of measurement (or the "guinea pig effect") The distorting effect of observation when the subjects are aware that they are being observed. A variety of techniques, such as concealment, participant observation, and unobtrusive measures, have been used to minimize the effect of the known observer.

recency effect The greater impact of information presented last rather than first. (When information presented first has a greater impact, a primacy effect is said to have occurred.)

reciprocal perspectives In interactive person perception, in addition to perceiving another person and forming an impression of how he sees you, you tend to form an impression of what he thinks you think of him at the same time that he forms an impression of what you think he thinks of you—or reciprocal perspectives. For example, playing a simple game in which another person has to decide whether to hide a coin in his right hand or his left hand illustrates how complex all of this can get. Each of you forms guesses about what the other is thinking and about what the other thinks you are thinking. What you do is determined by these reciprocal views.

reciprocity norm Norm that an individual should

treat another as that person has treated him. See "equity theory."

reference group theory The individual identifies with the standards and beliefs of certain groups—termed "reference groups"—and then uses these as a standard against which he defines and evaluates himself. For most people the groups to which they actually belong ("membership groups") serve as the measuring standard or reference group. Reference groups may serve both a normative and a comparative function.

reinforcement See "principle of reinforcement" and "instrumental conditioning."

relevant research An approach to psychological research that focuses actively on making research relevant by studying those problems that have a strong and immediate human concern.

reliability The extent to which measures are consistent. Reliability may be considered in two ways: (1) the consistency of responses given by an individual (or "intrapersonal reliability"); and (2) the amount of agreement between two different people evaluating the same information (or "interpersonal reliability").

reward-cost formulation of interpersonal attraction The theory that we like people whose behavior is rewarding to us or who have been associated with pleasant events or rewards.

reward imbalance A situation in which another person likes you more than you like him.

rhetorical questions Questions asked for their dramatic effect and not with any real expectation of receiving an answer.

risky shift The finding that in many laboratory studies people are willing to advocate a solution involving greater risk after participating in a group discussion than before. However, in the relatively few studies in which subjects have been faced with real, non-hypothetical choices, sometimes the risky shift has occurred, and sometimes it has not. Whether or not the risky shift occurs may depend on the importance of the issue to the group.

role playing Acting the part of another person or putting yourself in another situation. A very effective technique to change attitudes.

roles Doing what people in their positions are "supposed to do."

romantic love Although the term has been defined in many ways, it is generally regarded as having two components: an intense, affectionate concern and an intense sexual desire. See Box 2 in Chapter 9 for a number of definitions and a test of romantic love.

Rosenthal effect The fact that in some cases, a person's beliefs about what he expects to happen in various situations may lead him to behave differently toward people so that his expectations become self-fulfilling prophecies.

"running the subjects" Conducting the experiment.

scapegoating The displacement of aggression to less powerful groups or groups that are "socially acceptable" for attack when the original source of frustration is not open to attack.

scientific approach The collection of data, by observation, interview-questionnaire, correlation, controlled experiment and other methods, to ascertain the nature of reality.

secondary reinforcement An event that becomes reinforcing as a result of having been associated with a primary reinforcement on a number of occasions.

selective exposure theory The hypothesis that people deliberately seek out information that supports their point of view and avoid information that does not support their views. Laboratory experiments on selective exposure have had very mixed results.

self That part of our experience which we regard as essentially us. Aspects of the self experienced by many within Western culture include: (1) the material self, any material objects about which the person cares deeply; (2) the actual psychological self, what you think of when you think of your self; (3) the self as a thinking and emotional process, one's own experience of the process of experiencing; (4) the social self, in large part a consequence of the various roles an individual plays; and (5) the ideal self, what the person would like to be.

self-actualization Defined either as an individual's attempt to attain his ideal self or as an individual's attempt to obtain a healthy, optimal form of psychological functioning.

self-disclosure A person's honestly revealing aspects of himself to others. Jourard has theorized that the only way we can peel back the false images of ourselves and force ourselves to be honest in our self-knowledge is to disclose ourselves to others.

self-esteem The individual's own assessment of his adequacy and competency. If a person feels that he is worthy, that he can control events, that his work is worthwhile, he is said to have a high level of self-esteem. In contrast, if a person feels that the work of others is better than his, that he doesn't count for much, and that his efforts usually produce poor results, his self-esteem is low.

self-fulfilling prophecies (or the "Rosenthal ef-

fect") The finding that people can make others act as they expect them to act without even being aware that they are doing so.

self-report measures Measures that involve asking the subject (or respondent) to report information. The two self-report measures most frequently used are the questionnaire and the interview. In a questionnaire, the questions are presented and answered in writing; in an interview, they are asked in a two-person conversation.

sensitivity group See "encounter group."

sensory deprivation effect The finding that when people are deprived of outside stimulation, they experience a variety of negative reactions, including restlessness, boredom, impairment in the ability to concentrate, daydreaming, and in some rare cases, hallucinations.

significance See "psychological significance" and "statistical significance."

similarity-attraction relationship Finding that people generally prefer people who are similar to themselves.

simple imitation A type of imitation in which there is no conflict about the individual's performing the act in question. See "imitation."

"sleeper effect" Although usually the effect of a persuasive communication is maximal immediately after exposure and then declines gradually until it is no longer significant, sometimes the effect is greater after a time delay—a so-called "sleeper effect."

small-group ecology How people arrange themselves in physical space. For example, the intimacy of an interpersonal relationship is a major determinant of what is the appropriate interpersonal distance to be observed in that relationship.

social comparison theory The theory that people need to evaluate their opinions and abilities, and when no objective means are available, they do so by comparing their reactions with those of other people. The more uncertain people are, the stronger is their need for social comparison. In order to evaluate their reactions, people seek out others who are similar to themselves. Once individuals in a group begin comparing themselves with others, there are strong pressures toward uniformity.

social context All of the cues present in a social situation. The social roles of the people present, the perceiver's own interests and motives, and the reactions of others to the person being judged, are all part of the social context. For example, if everyone at a party acts as though they like your date, you yourself may be more favorably impressed than you would if others were not present and reacting favorably.

social desirability A bias introduced in self-report measures by the subject's tendency not to say unpleasant things about himself and to make socially acceptable responses. For example, even if a particular person has a low level of self-esteem, he may not give an honest answer to a question on his self-esteem for fear of making himself look bad.

social determinants theories of the self Theories that our self concept is to a great extent formed by comparing ourselves to others who matter to us, by absorbing the reactions of those significant others to us, and by seeing ourselves as we see them seeing us. However, the social determinants theories differ in their emphasis on who and what is crucial in this development, and give different emphasis to the processes by which the development occurs.

social engineering A technology of a planned control of behavior.

social exchange theory The theory that all of an individual's actions are determined by the rewards he thinks his actions will bring. While a few people who are "virtually saints" may work without thought of reward, most people require an incentive, such as the expectation of reciprocal or anticipated benefits, or the social approval of others, if they are to help others.

social facilitation The finding that when several people are working together on the same task at the same time, even when they are not interacting with one another or overtly competing against each other, their performance may be better than when each individual works alone. However, the presence of others does not always facilitate performance. See "social interference."

social interference The finding that sometimes the presence of other people interferes with the individual's performance. One theory is that the performance of well-learned responses is facilitated by the presence of other people, but the acquisition of new responses is impaired by their presence.

social psychology The psychological field of study concerned with the effects of other people on an individual's behavior.

social reinforcers Reinforcements that involve the approval or affection of others. Someone's smiling, nodding, or saying such things as "good" are examples of social reinforcers. Many, if not most, reinforcements at the human level are social reinforcers.

social responsibility norm The norm that a dependent individual should be helped.

socialization The process of internalization by the individual of the values, beliefs, and acceptable patterns of behavior in a group. Also, may be used to refer to the various ways, such as reinforcement, imitation, etc., by which the socialization process occurs.

sociogram See "sociometry."

sociometry A technique frequently used to measure group cohesiveness. Each person is asked to indicate the other person he would most prefer as an associate for various activities. Then the proportion of people chosen from among the group members is compared to the proportion of persons chosen from outside the group. When the number of people chosen from among the group members is significantly higher than the number chosen from outside the group, the group is said to be highly cohesive. (The graphic representation of these choices is known as a sociogram.)

"static person perception" Interpersonal perception in which a perceiver forms an impression of another person without the perceiver's being observed by the other person or interacting with him. See "interactive person perception."

"statistical" approach to interpersonal perception According to this theory impressions are derived from the separate ratings given to each trait. Among adherents of this "statistical" approach, controversy has centered on the best way of combining the ratings given to the traits. According to the averaging approach, the overall impression is determined best by summing the values of all the component traits and dividing by the total number of traits. However, according to an additive approach, the impression is determined by the total number of positive points in a particular description. Although a considerable amount of research has been done to test the relative validity of the additive and averaging approaches, conclusive evidence is not yet available. Many of the inconsistent findings can best be explained by an averaging model in which some traits are counted more heavily than others—a so-called weighted-average model.

statistical significance A statistically based means of assessing the probability that the experimental results might be due to chance factors, such as sampling variation. To assess statistical significance, a number of tests are used. While the procedures involved differ, all of these tests have the common purpose of deriving the probability that the findings could have occurred by chance. The exact value of the probability that chance alone could have produced the results is reported in decimal form and is read accordingly. While conventions vary among investigators, the usual practice is to consider any results that meet a .05 level of probability or

better as being statistically significant.

statistical test A mathematical test done to derive the probability that a particular set of results could have occurred by chance alone. See "statistical significance."

status Relative power in a group. In a marital dyad, the term is equated with conjugal power. Some theorists have speculated that there are three main bases for conjugal power: (1) acceptance of cultural roles and norms about conjugal power, (2) relative ability to provide rewards and punishments, and (3) relative expertise.

stereotype Frequently defined as an inaccurate, irrational overgeneralization, which, once formed, persists even in the presence of contradictory evidence and is used to justify discriminatory behavior. While this definition has been shown to apply to many stereotypes, not all are inaccurate overgeneralizations. See "'kernel of truth' theory of stereotypes."

structure The regular patterns of behavior that emerge in a group. Includes status, roles, and norms. In addition, regular patterns of communication and the use of space and time may also appear. In any group the structure that is likely to emerge is determined chiefly by: (1) the requirements for efficient group performance, (2) the abilities and motives of the group members, and (3) the group's physical and social environment.

subculture of violence A group, existing within a larger culture, which shares beliefs, values, symbols, and response styles that make violence socially acceptable. In such subcultures of violence, all of the factors of usual social interaction press the individual toward acceptance of the cultural norms that violence is acceptable and is positively valued.

subgroup A small group formed within an existing larger group. For example, in a classroom setting small committees of students may be formed because communication is more efficient than in the overall class setting.

subject roles Behaviors which the subjects believe are expected of them in the experimental situation and which may become confounded with the independent variable. Four such roles have been described. One of them is that of the "good subject," the subject who tries to give responses which he thinks will validate the experimenter's hypothesis. Another role is that of the apprehensive subject—one who tries to make sure that his responses are socially acceptable. Subjects may also adopt a "negativistic role"—doing the opposite of what the subject thinks the experimenter wants—or the role of the "faithful" subject—one who scrupulously follows experimental instructions.

subjects The people or animals that participate in an experiment.

"swinging" A variation on traditional monogamy which involves a couple's having sexual relations with at least one other person.

sympathy A feeling of compassion for an injured person.

taking the other person's role Trying to see the interaction from the other person's point of view.

task-centered leader One who focuses on the work to be done by the group rather than on the people in the group. See "Fiedler's 'contingency' theory of leadership."

T group See "encounter group."

territoriality The assumption by people of possessive rights about objects in the environment, even when they have no legal right to feel that they own them. For example, even when students are not assigned seats and when they obviously have no legal claim to them, many college students tend to sit in the same seat class after class. If another student sits in "their" chair, they may be upset, and if they feel strongly enough, they may ask the other person to move.

Thematic Apperception Test (TAT) A projective test based on the assumption that what a person sees in an ambiguous situation reveals his own personality. In the TAT the subject is required to make up imaginative stories in response to a series of pictures that can be interpreted in a variety of ways. The stories are then analyzed to reveal the subject's motives.

theory A system of ideas containing concepts, hypotheses about the way in which the concepts are interrelated, and ways of linking the concepts to observable behavior.

theory of multiple selves Although many self theorists believe that the self is an enduring object, not all agree. Some have argued that an individual does not have one stable self, but rather is composed of a number of separate selves, which vary according to the other person in the situation, the demands of the situation itself, and the individual's motives. For example, in a business negotiation, a man may see himself as a shrewd bargainer while when out on a date, he may see himself as a playboy.

trait A relatively enduring personality characteristic.

trait approach to leadership The theory that the main determinant of leadership is the possession of unique leadership traits. See "interaction approach to leadership."

transactional aggression Interpersonal aggression that grows out of a sequence of escalating violence in which both parties contribute at least to some extent. If neither one breaks the chain, acts of extreme violence can occur. Transactional aggression has been found to follow a fairly standard pattern: (1) provocation by one or the other of the individuals, and (2) escalation and confrontation.

two-sided communication A communication that contains arguments in favor of your recommendations along with some arguments that support the opposing view. In a one-sided communication, only arguments in favor of your position are presented.

two-step flow of communication The fact that people may pass information they obtain from the media on to other people.

unconscious emotions and attitudes The theory that attitudes can be an expression of an individual's own unconscious desires. The Freudian approach to prejudice is best illustrated by the Berkeley study of the authoritarian personality.

unobtrusive measures Measures which may be obtained without the individual's awareness and thus minimize the reactive effect of measurement. For example, the popularity of museum exhibits has been measured by comparing the relative wear on the flooring materials around the exhibits. See "reactive effect of measurement."

validity The extent to which a measure accurately assesses what it appears to be measuring.

wheel communication network A communication pattern in a five-person group in which the person in the center of the wheel has contact with all members of the group, and the remaining four members have contact only with the person in the center. Since one person in this network has access to all of the others, this network—as well as the Y communication network—is referred to as a "centralized communication network."

"Who am I?" test of the self concept A test that involves asking the subjects to write fifteen different answers to the question "Who am I?" in no more than six or seven minutes. An analysis of the different answers reveals the actual components of the subject's self-representations.

Y communication network A communication pattern in a five-person group in which three persons have only one-person access; the person at the center of the Y has access to three persons; and one subject has access to two persons. Since one person in this group has access to the majority of the others, this network—as well as the wheel communication network—is referred to as a "centralized communication network."

REFERENCES

ABELSON, R. Computers, polls, and public opinion: Some puzzles and paradoxes. *Trans-Action,* 1968, **5,** 20–27.

ABELSON, R., and MILLER, J. Negative persuasion via personal insult. *Journal of Experimental Social Psychology,* 1967, **3,** 321–333.

ADAMS, J. Inequity in social exchange. In L. Berkowitz (Ed.), *Advances in experimental social psychology.* Vol. 2. New York: Academic Press, 1965. Pp. 267–299.

ADAMS, J., and JACOBSON, P. Effects of wage inequities on work quality. *Journal of Abnormal and Social Psychology,* 1964, **69,** 19–25.

ADDINGTON, D. Effect of mispronunciations on general speaking effectiveness. *Speech Monographs,* 1965, **32,** 159–163.

ADERMAN, D. Elation, depression, and helping behavior. *Journal of Personality and Social Psychology,* 1972, **24,** 91–101.

ADORNO, T., FRENKEL-BRUNSWIK, E., LEVINSON, D., and SANFORD, R. *The authoritarian personality.* New York: Harper and Row, 1950.

AHLSTROM, W., and HAVIGHURST, R. *400 losers: Delinquent boys in high school.* San Francisco: Jossey-Bass, 1971.

AIELLO, J., and JONES, S. Field study of the proxamic behavior of young school children in three subcultural groups. *Journal of Personality and Social Psychology,* 1971, **19,** 351–356.

AJZEN, I., and FISHBEIN, M. Attitudes and normative beliefs as factors influencing behavioral intentions. *Journal of Personality and Social Psychology,* 1972, **21,** 1–9.

ALBERT, S., and DABBS, J. M., Jr. Physical distance and persuasion. *Journal of Personality and Social Psychology,* 1970, **15,** 265–270.

ALLEE, W. *Animal aggregations: A study in general sociology.* Chicago: University of Chicago Press, 1931. Cited by F. L. Ruch and P. G. Zimbardo, *Psychology and life.* (8th ed.) Glenview, Ill.: Scott, Foresman and Co., 1971. P. 463.

ALLEN, H. An exploratory study into bystander intervention and helping behavior in the subway. Unpublished doctoral dissertation, New York University, 1970. Cited by J. Darley and B. Latané, Norms and normative behavior: Field studies of social interdependence. In J. Macaulay and L. Berkowitz (Eds.), *Altruism and helping behavior: Social psychological studies of some antecedents and consequences.* New York: Academic Press, 1970. Pp. 93–96.

ALLEN, V., and LEVINE, J. Social pressure and personal preference. *Journal of Experimental Social Psychology,* 1971, **7,** 122–124. (a)

ALLEN, V., and LEVINE, J. Social support and conformity: The role of independent assessment of reality. *Journal of Experimental Social Psychology,* 1971, **7,** 48–58. (b)

ALLPORT, F. H. The influence of the group upon association and thought. *Journal of Experimental Psychology,* 1920, **3,** 159–182.

ALLPORT, F. H. The J-curve hypothesis of conforming behavior. *Journal of Social Psychology,* 1934, **5,** 141–183.

ALLPORT, G. *Becoming.* New Haven: Yale University Press, 1955.

ALLPORT, G., and CANTRIL, H. Judging personality from the voice. *Journal of Social Psychology,* 1934, **5,** 37–55.

ALLPORT, G., and POSTMAN, L. *The psychology of rumor.* New York: Holt, 1947.

ALLPORT, G., and ROSS, J. Personal religious orientation and prejudice. *Journal of Personality and Social Psychology,* 1967, **5,** 432–443.

ALPER, W., and LEIDY, T. The impact of information transmission through television. *The Public Opinion Quarterly,* 1970, **33,** 556–562.

ALTMAN, D., LEVINE, M., NADIEN, M., and VILLENA, J. Unpublished paper, Graduate Center, The City University of New York. P. 1463 in S. Milgram, The experience of living in cities. *Science,* 1970, **167,** 1461–1468.

ALTMAN, I., and HAYTHORN, W. The ecology of isolated groups. *Behavioral Science,* 1967, **12,** 169–182.

ALTMAN, I., TAYLOR, D., and WHEELER, L. Ecological aspects of group behavior in social isolation. *Journal of Applied Social Psychology,* 1971, **1,** 76–100.

ANDERSON, D. Dancing Harry and Earl the Pearl. *The New York Times,* January 6, 1973, p. 35.

ANDERSON, N. Averaging versus adding as a stimulus-combination rule in impression formation. *Journal of Experimental Psychology,* 1965, **70,** 394–400.

ANDERSON, N. Likableness ratings of 555 personality-trait words. *Journal of Personality and Social Psychology,* 1968, **9,** 272–279. (a)

ANDERSON, N. A simple model for information integration. In R. Abelson, E. Aronson, W. McGuire, T. Newcomb, M. Rosenberg, and P. Tannenbaum (Eds.), *Theories of cognitive consistency: A sourcebook.* Chicago: Rand McNally and Co., 1968. Pp. 731–743. (b)

ANDERSON, N., and HUBERT, S. Effects of concomitant recall on order effects in personality impression formation. *Journal of Verbal Learning and Verbal Behavior,* 1963, **2,** 379–391.

ANISFELD, M., BOGO, N., and LAMBERT, W. Evaluation reactions to accented English speech. *Journal of Abnormal and Social Psychology,* 1962, **65,** 223–231.

ARGYLE, M. *Social interaction.* New York: Aldine-Atherton, 1969.

ARGYLE, M., and McHENRY, R. Do spectacles really affect judgments of intelligence? *British Journal of Social and Clinical Psychology,* 1971, **10,** 27–29.

ARONFREED, J. The socialization of altruistic and sympathetic behavior: Some theoretical and experimental analyses. In J. Macaulay and L. Berkowitz (Eds.), *Altruism and helping behavior: Social psychological studies of some antecedents and consequences.* New York: Academic Press, 1970. Pp. 103–126.

ARONSON, E. Avoidance of inter-subject communication. *Psychological Reports,* 1966, **19,** 238. (a)

ARONSON, E. Threat and obedience. *Trans-Action,* 1966, **3,** 25–27. (b)

ARONSON, E. Some antecedents of interpersonal attraction. In W. Arnold and D. Levine (Eds.), *Nebraska Symposium on Motivation,* 1969, **17,** 143–173. (a)

ARONSON, E. The theory of cognitive dissonance: A current perspective. In L. Berkowitz (Ed.), *Advances in experimental social psychology.* Vol. 4. New York: Academic Press, 1969. Pp. 1–34. (b)

ARONSON, E. *The social animal.* San Francisco: Freeman, 1972.

ARONSON, E., and CARLSMITH, J. Performance expectancy as a determinant of actual performance. *Journal of Abnormal and Social Psychology,* 1962, **65,** 178–182.

ARONSON, E., and CARLSMITH, J. The effect of the severity of threat on the devaluation of forbidden behavior. *Journal of Abnormal and Social Psychology,* 1963, **66,** 584–588.

ARONSON, E., and CARLSMITH, J. Experimentation in social psychology. In G. Lindzey and E. Aronson (Eds.), *The handbook of social psychology.* (2nd ed.) Vol. 2. *Research methods.* Reading, Mass.: Addison-Wesley, 1968. Pp. 1–79.

ARONSON, E., and COPE, V. My enemy's enemy is my friend. *Journal of Personality and Social Psychology,* 1968, **8,** 8–12.

ARONSON, E., and LINDER, D. Gain and loss of esteem as determinants of interpersonal attractiveness. *Journal of Experimental Social Psychology,* 1965, **1,** 156–171.

ARONSON, E., and METTEE, D. Dishonest behavior as a function of differential levels of induced self-esteem. *Journal of Personality and Social Psychology,* 1968, **9**(2, Pt. 1), 121–127.

ARONSON, E., and MILLS, J. The effects of severity of initiation on liking for a group. *Journal of Abnormal and Social Psychology,* 1959, **59,** 177–181.

ARONSON, E., and ROSS, A. The effect of support and criticism on interpersonal attractiveness. Unpublished paper, University of Minnesota, 1964.

ARONSON, E., TURNER, J., and CARLSMITH, M. Communicator credibility and communicator discrepancy as determinants of opinion change. *Journal of Abnormal and Social Psychology,* 1963, **67,** 31–36.

ARONSON, E., WILLERMAN, B., and FLOYD, J. The effect of a pratfall on increasing interpersonal attractiveness. *Psychonomic Science,* 1966, **4,** 227–228.

ARROWOOD, A. Personal communication. Cited by J. E. Singer, Social comparison: Progress and issues. *Journal of Experimental Social Psychology Supplement,* 1966, **1**(Pt. 1), 103–110.

ASCH, S. Forming impressions of personality. *Journal of Abnormal and Social Psychology,* 1946, **41,** 258–290.

ASCH, S. *Social psychology.* New York: Prentice-Hall, 1952.

ASHENFELTER, O. Changes in labor market discrimination over time. *Journal of Human Resources,* 1970, **5,** 403–430.

ASHER, S., and ALLEN, V. Racial preference and social comparison processes. *The Journal of Social Issues,* 1969, **25,** 157–165.

ATKINSON, J., HEYNS, R., and VEROFF, J. The effect of experimental arousal of the affiliation motive on thematic apperception. *Journal of Abnormal and Social Psychology,* 1954, **49,** 405–410.

BACH, G., and WYDEN, P. *The intimate enemy: How to fight fair in love and marriage.* New York: William Morrow, 1969.

BACK, K. *Beyond words: The story of sensitivity training and the encounter movement.* New York: Russell Sage Foundation, 1972.

BAKAN, D. *On method: Toward a reconstruction of psychological investigation.* San Francisco: Jossey-Bass, 1969.

BAKER, R. No business like *what* business. *The New York Times,* April 18, 1971, sec. E, p. 13.

BALDWIN, J. *Tell me how long the train's been gone.* New York: Dell, 1969.

BALES, R. F. How people interact in conferences. *Scientific American,* 1955, **192,** 31–35.

BALES, R. F. *Personality and interpersonal behavior.* New York: Holt, Rinehart & Winston, 1970.

BALES, R. F., and BORGATTA, E. Size of group as a factor in the interaction profile. In A. Hare, E. Borgatta, and R. Bales (Eds.), *Small groups: Studies in social interaction.* New York: Knopf, 1955. Pp. 396–413.

BANDURA, A., and MISCHEL, W. Modification of self-imposed delay of reward through exposure to live and symbolic models. *Journal of Personality and Social Psychology,* 1965, **2,** 698–705.

BANDURA, A., and ROSENTHAL, T. Vicarious classical conditioning as a function of arousal level. *Journal of Personality and Social Psychology,* 1966, **3,** 54–62.

BANDURA, A., ROSS, D., and ROSS, S. Transmission of aggression through imitation of aggressive models. *Journal of Abnormal and Social Psychology,* 1961, **63,** 575–582.

BANDURA, A., and WALTERS, R. *Adolescent aggression.* New York: Ronald Press, 1959.

BANTA, T., and HETHERINGTON, M. Relations between needs of friends and fiances. *Journal of Abnormal and Social Psychology,* 1963, **66,** 401–404.

BARBER, T., and CALVERLEY, D. Hypnotizability, suggestibility and personality: IV. A study with the Leary interpersonal checklist. *British Journal of Social and Clinical Psychology,* 1964, **3,** 149–150.

BARBER, T., and SILVER, M. Fact, fiction, and the experimenter bias effect. *Psychological Bulletin,* 1968, **70**(6, Pt. 2), 1–29.

BARKER, R., DEMBO, T., and LEWIN, K. Frustration and regression. *University of Iowa Studies in Child Welfare,* 1941, **18,** No. 1.

BARON, R. Anonymity, deindividuation and aggression. Unpublished doctoral dissertation, University of Minnesota, 1970.

BARRIE, J. M. *The admirable Crichton.* In *English drama in transition.* Indianapolis: Pegasus, 1968.

BARTELL, G. *Group sex: A scientist's eyewitness report on swinging in the suburbs.* New York: Wyden, 1971.

BASS, B. An analysis of the leaderless group discussion. *Journal of Applied Psychology,* 1949, **33,** 527–533.

BASS, B. *Leadership, psychology and organizational behavior.* New York: Harper and Row, 1960.

BATCHELOR, J., and GOETHALS, G. Spatial arrangements in freely formed groups. *Sociometry,* 1972, **35,** 270–279.

BAUMRIND, D. Some thoughts on ethics of research: After reading Milgram's "Behavioral study of obedience." *American Psychologist,* 1964, **19,** 421–423.

BECKER, G. Affiliate perception and the arousal of the participation-affiliation motive. *Perceptual and Motor Skills,* 1967, **24,** 991–997.

BELL, G., and FRENCH, R. Consistency of individual leadership position in small groups of varying membership. *Journal of Abnormal and Social Psychology,* 1950, **45,** 764–767.

BEM, D. Self-perception: An alternative interpretation of cognitive dissonance phenomena. *Psychological Review,* 1967, **74,** 183–200.

BEM, D. *Beliefs, attitudes and human affairs.* Belmont, Calif.: Brooks/Cole, 1970.

BENNETT, E. Discussion, decision commitment, and consensus in "group decision." *Human Relations,* 1955, **8,** 251–274.

BENNIS, W., SCHEIN, E., and STEELE, F. *Interpersonal dynamics: Essays and readings in human interaction.* (Rev. ed.) Homewood, Ill.: Dorsey Press, 1968.

BENNIS, W., and SHEPARD, H. A theory of group development. *Human Relations,* 1956, **9,** 415–437.

BERDIE, R. Playing the dozens. *Journal of Abnormal and Social Psychology,* 1947, **42,** 120–121.

BERELSON, B., LAZARSFELD, P., and McPHEE, W. *Voting: A study of opinion formation in a presidential election.* Chicago: University of Chicago Press, 1954.

BERKOWITZ, L. Anti-Semitism and the displacement of aggression. *Journal of Abnormal and Social Psychology,* 1959, **59,** 182–188.

BERKOWITZ, L. *Aggression.* New York: McGraw-Hill, 1962.

BERKOWITZ, L. Responsibility, reciprocity, and social distance in help-giving: An experimental investigation of English social class differences. *Journal of Experimental Social Psychology,* 1968, **4,** 46–63.

BERKOWITZ, L. The self, selfishness, and altruism. In J. Macaulay and L. Berkowitz (Eds.), *Altruism and helping behavior: Social psychological studies of some antecedents and consequences.* New York: Academic Press, 1970. Pp. 143–151.

BERKOWITZ, L. Social norms, feelings, and other factors affecting helping and altruism. In L. Berkowitz (Ed.), *Advances in experimental social psychology.* Vol. 6. New York: Academic Press, 1972. Pp. 63–108.

BERKOWITZ, L., and DANIELS, L. Responsibility and dependency. *Journal of Abnormal and Social Psychology,* 1963, **66,** 429–436.

BERKOWITZ, L., and DANIELS, L. Affecting the salience of the social responsibility norm: Effects of past help on the response to dependency relationships. *Journal of Abnormal and Social Psychology,* 1964, **68,** 275–281.

BERKOWITZ, L., and FRIEDMAN, P. Some social class differences in helping behavior. *Journal of Personality and Social Psychology,* 1967, **5,** 217–225.

BERKOWITZ, L., and GEEN, R. Film violence and the cue properties of available targets. *Journal of Personality and Social Psychology,* 1966, **3,** 525–530.

BERKOWITZ, L., KLANDERMAN, S., and HARRIS, R. Effects of experimenter awareness and sex of subject and experimenter on reactions to dependency relationships. *Sociometry*, 1964, **27,** 327–337.

BERKOWITZ, L., and KNUREK, D. Label-mediated hostility generalization. *Journal of Personality and Social Psychology,* 1969, **13,** 200–206.

BERKOWITZ, L., and LePAGE, A. Weapons as aggression-eliciting stimuli. *Journal of Personality and Social Psychology,* 1967, **7,** 202–207.

BERLYNE, D. E. *Conflict, arousal and curiosity.* New York: McGraw-Hill, 1960.

BERMANN, E., and MILLER, D. The matching of mates. In R. Jessor and S. Feshbach (Eds.), *Cognition, personality and clinical psychology.* San Francisco: Jossey-Bass, 1967. Pp. 90–111.

BERSCHEID, E. Opinion change and communicator-communicatee similarity and dissimilarity. *Journal of Personality and Social Psychology,* 1966, **4,** 670–680.

BERSCHEID, E. Personal communication. 1972.

BERSCHEID, E., DION, K., WALSTER, E., and WALSTER, G. Physical attractiveness and dating choice: A test of the matching hypothesis. *Journal of Experimental Social Psychology,* 1971, **7,** 173–189.

BERSCHEID, E., and WALSTER, E. When does a harm-doer compensate a victim? *Journal of Personality and Social Psychology,* 1967, **6,** 435–441.

BERSCHEID, E., and WALSTER, E. Beauty and the best. *Psychology Today,* 1972, **5**(10), 42–46, 74.

BERSCHEID, E., and WALSTER, E. Physical attractiveness. In L. Berkowitz (Ed.), *Advances in experimental social psychology.* Vol. 7. New York: Academic Press, in press. (a)

BERSCHEID, E., and WALSTER, E. A little bit about love. In T. L. Huston (Ed.), *Perspectives on interpersonal attraction.* New York: Academic Press, in press. (b)

BERSCHEID, E., WALSTER, E., and CAMPBELL, R. Grow old along with me. Mimeograph copies available from the authors, 1972.

BERSCHEID, E., and WALSTER, G. Liking reciprocity as a function of perceived basis of proffered liking. Cited in E. Berscheid and E. Walster, *Interpersonal attraction.* Reading, Mass.: Addison-Wesley, 1969. Pp. 58–59.

BETTINGHAUS, E. Operation of congruity in an oral communication setting. *Speech Monographs,* 1961, **28,** 131–142.

BETTLEHEIM, B. Individual and mass behavior in extreme situations. *Journal of Abnormal and Social Psychology,* 1943, **38,** 417–452.

BICKMAN, L. The effect of another bystander's ability to help on bystander intervention in an emergency. *Journal of Experimental Social Psychology,* 1971, **7,** 367–379.

BICKMAN, L. Social influence and diffusion of responsibility in an emergency. *Journal of Experimental Social Psychology,* 1972, **8,** 438–445.

BIENVENU, M. J., Sr. Measurement of marital communication. *Family Coordinator,* 1970, **19**(1), 26–31.

BION, W. R. *Experiences in groups.* New York: Basic Books, 1959.

BLAKE, R., and MOUTON, J. Loyalty of representatives to ingroup positions during intergroup competition. *Sociometry,* 1961, **24,** 177–183.

BLAKE, R., and MOUTON, J. *The managerial grid: Key orientations for achieving production through people.* Houston: Gulf Publishing Co., 1964.

BLAKE, R., MOUTON, J., BARNES, J., and GREINER, L. Breakthrough in organization development. *Harvard Business Review,* 1964, **42,** 133–155.

BLANK, J. Rescue on the freeway. *Reader's Digest,* 1970, **96**(577), 73–77.

BLAU, E. New work, new living set-ups: A new nuns' story. *The New York Times,* January 8, 1973, p. 41.

BLAU, P. M. Social exchange. In D. L. Sills (Ed.), *International encyclopedia of the social sciences.* Vol. 7. New York: Macmillan, 1968. Pp. 452–457.

BLOCK, H., and NIEDERHOFFER, A. *The gang: A study in adolescent behavior.* New York: Philosophical Library, 1958. Quoted in F. L. Ruch and P. Zimbardo, *Psychology and life.* (8th ed.) Glenview, Ill.: Scott, Foresman, 1971.

BLUMBERG, H. H. Communication of interpersonal evaluations. *Journal of Personality and Social Psychology,* 1972, **23,** 157–162.

BOSSARD, J. Residential propinquity as a factor in mate selection. *American Journal of Sociology,* 1932, **38,** 219–224.

BOURNE, P. G. *Men, stress, and Vietnam.* Boston: Little, Brown, 1970.

BOVARD, E. Group structure and perception. *Journal of Abnormal and Social Psychology,* 1951, **46,** 389–405.

BOWERS, J., and OSBORN, M. Attitudinal effects of selected types of concluding metaphors in persuasive speech. *Speech Monographs,* 1966, **33,** 147–155.

BOWLBY, J. The nature of the child's tie to his mother. *International Journal of Psycho-Analysis,* 1958, **39,** 350–373.

BOWMAN, C. C. Loneliness and social change. *American Journal of Psychiatry,* 1955, 194–198.

BOYANOWSKY, E., NEWTSON, D., and WALSTER, E.

Effects of murder on movie preference. *Proceedings of the 80th Annual Convention of the American Psychological Association*, 1972, 235–236.

BRADSHAW, J. The information conveyed by varying the dimensions of features in human outline faces. *Perception and Psychophysics*, 1969, **6**, 5–9.

BRADY, J. Emotional behavior. In J. Field, H. Magoun, and E. Hall (Eds.), *Handbook of Physiology*. Vol. 3. Washington, D. C.: American Physiological Society, 1960.

BRAGINSKY, D. Machiavellianism and manipulative interpersonal behavior in children. *Journal of Experimental Social Psychology*, 1970, **6,** 77–99.

BRAMEL, D. Selection of a target for defensive projection. *Journal of Abnormal and Social Psychology*, 1963, **66**, 318–324.

BRAY, D., and GRANT, D. The assessment center in the measurement of potential for business management. *Psychological Monographs*, 1966, **80**(17, Whole No. 625).

BREHM, J. Post-decision changes in desirability of alternatives. *Journal of Abnormal and Social Psychology*, 1956, **52**, 384–389.

BREHM, J. *A theory of psychological reactance.* New York: Academic Press, 1966.

BREHM, J., and COHEN, A. *Explorations in cognitive dissonance.* New York: Wiley, 1962.

BREHM, J., and COLE, A. Effect of a favor which reduces freedom. *Journal of Personality and Social Psychology*, 1966, **3**, 420–426.

BREHM, J., GATZ, M., GOETHALS, G., McCROMMON, J., and WARD, L. Psychological arousal and interpersonal attraction. Mimeograph copies available from the authors, 1970.

BREHM, J., and WICKLUND, R. Regret and dissonance reduction as a function of postdecision salience of dissonant information. *Journal of Personality and Social Psychology*, 1970, **14,** 1–7.

BREHM, M., and BACK, W. Self image and attitudes toward drugs. *Journal of Personality*, 1968, **36,** 299–314.

BRIDGEMAN, W. Student attraction and productivity as a composite function of reinforcement and expectancy conditions. *Journal of Personality and Social Psychology*, 1972, **23,** 249–258.

BRIGHAM, J. Ethnic stereotypes. *Psychological Bulletin*, 1971, **76,** 15–38.

BRISLIN, R., and LEWIS, S. Dating and physical attractiveness: Replication. *Psychological Reports*, 1968, **22,** 976.

BROCK, T. Communicator-recipient similarity and decision-change. *Journal of Personality and Social Psychology*, 1965, **1,** 650–654.

BROCK, T., and BECKER, L. "Debriefing" and susceptibility to subsequent experimental manipu-

lation. *Journal of Experimental Social Psychology*, 1966, **2,** 314–323.

BROCK, T., and BUSS, A. Dissonance, aggression and evaluation of pain. *Journal of Abnormal and Social Psychology*, 1962, **65,** 192–202.

BROWN, B. Saving face. *Psychology Today*, 1971, **4**(12), 55–59, 86.

BROWN, P., and ELLIOT, R. Control of aggression in a nursery-school class. *Journal of Experimental Child Psychology*, 1965, **2,** 103–107.

BROWN, R. *Social psychology.* New York: Free Press, 1965.

BROWN, R., and GARLAND, H. The effects of incompetency, audience acquaintanceship, and anticipated evaluative feedback on face-saving behavior. *Journal of Experimental Social Psychology*, 1971, **7,** 490–502.

BRYAN, J. Children's reactions to helpers: Their money isn't where their mouths are. In J. Macaulay and L. Berkowitz (Eds.), *Altruism and helping behavior: Social psychological studies of some antecedents and consequences.* New York: Academic Press, 1970. Pp. 61–73.

BRYAN, J., and DAVENPORT, M. Donations to the needy: Correlates of financial contributions to the destitute. Unpublished study, 1968. Educational Testing Services, Princeton, N. J. Cited on p. 104 in L. Berkowitz, Social norms, feelings, and other factors affecting helping and altruism. In L. Berkowitz (Ed.), *Advances in experimental social psychology*. Vol. 6. New York: Academic Press, 1972, Pp. 63–108.

BRYAN, J., and TEST, M. Models and helping: Naturalistic studies in aiding behavior. *Journal of Personality and Social Psychology*, 1967, **6,** 400–407.

BUGENTAL, D., KASWAN, J., and LOVE, L. Perception of contradictory meanings conveyed by verbal and nonverbal channels. *Journal of Personality and Social Psychology*, 1970, **16,** 647–655.

BURGESS, E., and WALLIN, P. *Engagement and marriage.* Philadelphia: Lippincott, 1953.

BURLINGHAM, D., and FREUD, A. *Young children in war-time.* London: Allen & Unwin, 1943.

BURNEY, C. *Solitary confinement.* New York: Coward-McCann, 1952.

BURNSTEIN, E., and McRAE, A. Some effects of shared threat and prejudice in racially mixed groups. *Journal of Abnormal and Social Psychology*, 1962, **64,** 257–263.

BURROUGHS, W. A. A study of white females' voting behavior toward two black female corroborators in a modified leaderless group discussion. *Dissertation Abstracts International*, 1970, **30**(11-A), 5063.

BUSS, A. *The psychology of aggression.* New York: Wiley, 1961.

BUSS, A. Instrumentality of aggression, feedback, and frustration as determinants of physical aggression. *Journal of Personality and Social Psychology,* 1966, **3,** 153–162.

BYHAM, W. Assessment centers for spotting future managers. *Harvard Business Review,* 1970, **48,** 150–160, 162–167.

BYRD, R. E. *Alone.* London: Neville Spearman, 1938.

BYRNE, D. Anxiety and the experimental arousal of affiliation need. *Journal of Abnormal and Social Psychology,* 1961, **63,** 660–662.

BYRNE, D. *The attraction paradigm.* New York: Academic Press, 1971.

BYRNE, D., CLORE, G., and WORCHEL, P. The effect of economic similarity-dissimilarity on interpersonal attraction. *Journal of Personality and Social Psychology,* 1966, **4,** 220–224.

BYRNE, D., ERVIN, C., and LAMBERTH, J. Continuity between the experimental study of attraction and real-life computer dating. *Journal of Personality and Social Psychology,* 1970, **16,** 157–165.

BYRNE, D., GRIFFITT, W., and STEFANIAK, D. Attraction and similarity of personality characteristics. *Journal of Personality and Social Psychology,* 1967, **5,** 82–90.

BYRNE, D., NELSON, D., and REEVES, K. Effects of consensual validation and invalidation on attraction as a function of verifiability. *Journal of Experimental Social Psychology,* 1966, **2,** 98–107.

CAFFREY, B., ANDERSON, S., and GARRISON, J. Changes in racial attitudes of white southerners after exposure of the atmosphere of a southern university. *Psychological Reports,* 1969, **25,** 555–558.

CALHOUN, J. Population density and social pathology. *Scientific American,* 1962, **206,** 139–148.

CAMPBELL, A. Factors associated with attitudes toward Jews. In T. M. Newcomb and E. L. Hartley (Eds.), *Readings in social psychology.* New York: Holt, 1947. Pp. 518–527.

CAMPBELL, A., and KATONA, G. The sample survey: A technique for social-science research. In L. Festinger and D. Katz (Eds.), *Research methods in the behavioral sciences.* New York: Dryden Press, 1953. Pp. 15–55.

CAMPBELL, D. Factors relevant to the validity of experiments in social settings. *Psychological Bulletin,* 1957, **54,** 297–312.

CAMPBELL, D. Ethnocentrism and other altruistic motives. In D. Levine (Ed.), *Nebraska Symposium on Motivation,* 1965, **13.**

CAMPBELL, D. Stereotypes and the perception of group differences. *American Psychologist,* 1967, **22,** 817–829.

CAMPBELL, E. Some social psychological correlates of direction in attitude change. *Social Forces,* 1958, **36,** 335–340.

CAMPBELL, J., and DUNNETTE, M. Effectiveness of T group experiences in managerial training and development. *Psychological Bulletin,* 1968, **70,** 73–104.

CAMPBELL, J., DUNNETTE, M., LAWLER, E., III, and WEICK, K., Jr. *Managerial behavior, performance, and effectiveness.* New York: McGraw-Hill, 1970.

CANON, L., and MATHEWS, K. E., Jr. Concern over personal health and smoking-relevant beliefs and behavior. *Proceedings of the 80th Annual Convention of the American Psychological Association,* 1972, 271–272.

CANTRIL, H. *The invasion from Mars.* Princeton: Princeton University Press, 1940. (Republished; New York: Harper Torchbooks, 1966)

CANTRIL, H., and ALLPORT, G. *The psychology of radio.* New York: Harper, 1935.

CARLSMITH, J., COLLINS, B., and HELMREICH, R. Studies in forced compliance: I. The effect of pressure for compliance on attitude change produced by face-to-face role playing and anonymous essay writing. *Journal of Personality and Social Psychology,* 1966, **4,** 1–13.

CARLSMITH, J., and GROSS, A. Some effects of guilt on compliance. *Journal of Personality and Social Psychology,* 1969, **11,** 232–240.

CARTER, L. Leadership and small group behavior. In M. Sherif and M. Wilson (Eds.), *Group relations at the crossroads.* New York: Harper, 1953. Pp. 257–284.

CARTER, L., HAYTHORN, W., SHRIVER, B., and LANZETTA, J. The behavior of leaders and other group members. *Journal of Abnormal and Social Psychology,* 1950, **46,** 589–595.

CARTER, R. Some effects of the debates. In S. Kraus (Ed.), *The great debates.* Bloomington: Indiana University Press, 1962. Pp. 253–270.

CARTWRIGHT, D. The nature of group cohesiveness. In D. Cartwright and A. Zander (Eds.), *Group dynamics: Research and theory.* (3rd ed.) New York: Harper & Row, 1968.

CARTWRIGHT, D., and ZANDER, A. The structural properties of groups: Introduction. In D. Cartwright and A. Zander (Eds.), *Group dynamics: Research and theory.* (3rd ed.) New York: Harper & Row, 1968. Pp. 485–502.

Casebook on ethical standards of psychologists. Washington, D. C.: American Psychological Association, 1967.

CASTORE, C., and DeNINNO, J. Role of relevance in the selection of comparison others. *Proceedings of the 80th Annual Convention of the American Psychological Association,* 1972, 201–202.

CENTERS, R., RAVEN, B., and RODRIGUES, A. Conjugal power structure: A re-examination. *American Sociological Review,* 1971, **36,** 264–278.

CHAFFEE, S., and McLEOD, J. Adolescents, parents, and television violence. Paper presented at the annual meeting of the American Psychological Association, Washington, D.C., September, 1971.

CHAPANIS, N., and CHAPANIS, A. Cognitive dissonance: Five years later. *Psychological Bulletin,* 1964, **61,** 1–22.

CHERTKOFF, J. The effects of probability of future success on coalition formation. *Journal of Experimental Social Psychology,* 1966, **2,** 265–277.

CHERTKOFF, J., and BAIRD, S. Applicability of the big lie technique and the last clear chance doctrine to bargaining. *Journal of Personality and Social Psychology,* 1971, **20,** 298–303.

CHRISTIE, R. Scale construction. In R. Christie, F. Geis, et al., *Studies in Machiavellianism.* New York: Academic Press, 1970. Pp.10–34.

CHRISTIE, R., and GEIS, F. The ten dollar game. In R. Christie, F. Geis, et al., *Studies in Machiavellianism.* New York: Academic Press, 1970. Pp. 161–172.

CHRISTIE, R., GEIS, F., et al. *Studies in Machiavellianism.* New York: Academic Press, 1970.

CHRISTIE, R., and JAHODA, M. (Eds.) *Studies in the scope and method of "The authoritarian personality."* New York: Free Press, 1954.

CHURCH, J. (Ed.) *Three babies: Biographies of cognitive development.* New York: Random House, 1966. (Vintage Books ed., 1968)

CIALDINI, R. Attitudinal advocacy in the verbal conditioner. *Journal of Personality and Social Psychology,* 1971, **17,** 350–358.

CLAPARÈDE, E. Note sur la localisation du moi. *Archives de Psychologie,* 1924, **19,** 172–182.

CLARK, J. V. A preliminary investigation of some unconscious assumptions affecting labor efficiency in eight supermarkets. Unpublished doctoral dissertation, Harvard University, Graduate School of Business Administration, 1958.

CLARK, K. *Prejudice and your child.* Boston: Beacon Press, 1955.

CLARK, K. *Dark ghetto.* New York: Harper & Row, 1965.

CLARK, K., and CLARK, M. Racial identification and preference in Negro children. In T. Newcomb and E. Hartley (Eds.), *Readings in social psychology.* New York: Holt, 1947. Pp. 169–178.

CLARK, R. A. Leadership in rifle squads on the Korean front line. Human Resources Research Unit No. 2, COMARC, Fort Ord, Calif., 1955.

CLARK, R. D., III. Group-induced shift toward risk: A critical appraisal. *Psychological Bulletin,* 1971, **76,** 251–270.

CLARK, R. D., III, and WORD, L. Why don't bystanders help? Because of ambiguity? *Journal of Personality and Social Psychology,* 1972, **24,** 392–400.

CLEMENT, D., and SULLIVAN, D. No risky shift effect without real groups and real risks. *Psychonomic Science,* 1970, **18,** 243–245.

CLIFFORD, M., and WALSTER, E. The effect of physical attractiveness on teacher expectation. *Sociology of Education,* 1973, **46,** 248.

CLINE, M. The influence of social context on the perception of faces. *Journal of Personality,* 1956, **24,** 142–158.

COBB, S., and LINDEMANN, E. Symposium on management of Coconut Grove burns at Massachusetts General Hospital: Neuropsychiatric observations. *Annals of Surgery,* 1943, **117,** 814–824. Cited on p. 48 in I. Janis, G. Mahl, J. Kagan, and R. Holt, *Personality: Dynamics, development, and assessment.* New York: Harcourt, Brace, and World, 1969.

COCH, L., and FRENCH, J. R. P., Jr. Overcoming resistance to change. *Human Relations,* 1948, **1,** 512–532.

COFER, C., and APPLEY, M. *Motivation: Theory and research.* New York: Wiley, 1964.

COLE, D. Affiliative behavior at the time of the president's assassination. *Psychological Reports,* 1965, **16,** 326.

COLEMAN, J. *The adolescent society.* New York: Free Press, 1961.

COLLINS, B., and RAVEN, B. Psychological aspects of structure in the small group: Interpersonal attraction, coalitions, communication, and power. In G. Lindzey and E. Aronson (Eds.), *The handbook of social psychology.* (2nd ed.) Vol. 4. *Group psychology and phenomena of interaction.* Reading, Mass.: Addison-Wesley, 1969. Pp. 102–204.

COLMEN, J. A discovery of commitment. In J. Parmer (Ed.), The Annals of the American Academy of *Political and Social Science.* Vol. 365. *The Peace Corps.* Philadelphia: American Academy of Political and Social Science, 1966. Pp. 12–20.

Commission on Obscenity and Pornography. *The report.* Washington: Government Printing Office, 1970.

COOK, S. Motives in a conceptual analysis of attitude-related behavior. In W. Arnold and D. Levine (Eds.), *Nebraska Symposium on Motivation,* 1969, **17,** 179–231.

COOLEY, C. *Human nature and the social order.* New York: Scribner's, 1902.

COOPER, C., and MANGHAM, I. Before and after the T-group. In C. Cooper and I Mangham, *T-groups: A survey of research.* New York: Wiley-Interscience, 1971. Pp. 25–63.

COOPER, J., and WORCHEL, S. Role of undesired consequences in arousing cognitive dissonance. *Journal of Personality and Social Psychology*, 1970, **16,** 199–206.

COOPERSMITH, S. *The antecedents of self-esteem.* San Francisco: Freeman, 1967.

COSER, L. A. *The functions of social conflict.* Glencoe, Ill.: Free Press, 1956.

COTTRELL, N. Performance expectancy as a determinant of actual performance: A replication with a new design. *Journal of Personality and Social Psychology*, 1965, **2,** 685–692.

COTTRELL, N. Performance in the presence of other human beings, mere presence, audience and affiliation effects. In E. Simmel, R. Hoppe, and G. Milton (Eds.), *Social facilitation and imitative behavior.* Boston: Allyn and Bacon, 1968. Pp. 91–110.

COTTRELL, N., RITTIE, R., and WACK, D. The presence of an audience and list type (competitional or noncompetitional) as joint determinants of performance in paired-associates learning. *Journal of Personality*, 1967, **35,** 425–437.

COUCH, A., and KENISTON, K. Yeasayers and naysayers: Agreeing response set as a personality variable. *Journal of Personality and Social Psychology*, 1960, **60,** 151–174.

COWAN, P., and WALTERS, R. Studies of reinforcement of aggression. Part I: Effects of scheduling. *Child Development*, 1963, **34,** 543–552.

COWAN, T., and STRICKLAND, D. The legal structure microsociety (A report on the cases of Penthouse II and III). Internal working paper No. 34, Space Sciences Lab., Social Sciences Project, University of California, Berkeley, August, 1965. Page 379 in S. Smith, *Studies of small groups in confinement;* pp. 374–403 in J. Zubek (Ed.), *Sensory deprivation: Fifteen years of research.* New York: Appleton-Century-Crofts, 1969.

COX, D., and SIPPRELLE, C. Coercion in participation as a research subject. *American Psychologist*, 1971, **26,** 726–728.

COX, K. Changes in stereotyping of Negroes and whites in magazine advertisements. *The Public Opinion Quarterly*, 1970, **33,** 603–606.

CRONBACH, L. Processes affecting scores on "understanding of others" and "assumed similarity." *Psychological Bulletin*, 1955, **52,** 177–193.

CULBERTSON, F. Modification of an emotionally held attitude through role playing. *Journal of Abnormal and Social Psychology*, 1957, **54,** 230–234.

DANIÉLOU, J., and MARROU, H. (Trans. by V. Cronin). *The Christian centuries.* Vol. I: *The first six hundred years.* New York: McGraw-Hill, 1964.

DARLEY, J., and ARONSON, E. Self-evaluation vs. direct anxiety reduction as determinants of the fear-affiliation relationship. *Journal of Experimental Social Psychology Supplement*, 1966, **1,** 66–79.

DARLEY, J., and BATSON, D. ". . . From Jerusalem to Jericho": A study of situational and dispositional variables in helping behavior. *Journal of Personality and Social Psychology*, 1973, **27,** 100–108.

DARLEY, J., and BERSCHEID, E. Increased liking caused by the anticipation of personal contact. *Human Relations*, 1967, **20,** 29–40.

DARLEY, J., and LATANÉ, B. Norms and normative behavior: Field studies of social interdependence. In J. Macaulay and L. Berkowitz (Eds.), *Altruism and helping behavior: Social psychological studies of some antecedents and consequences.* New York: Academic Press, 1970. Pp. 83–101.

DAVAGE, R. Effect of achievement-affiliation motive patterns on yielding behavior in two-person groups. *Dissertation Abstracts*, 1958, **18,** 1506.

DAVENPORT, W., BROOKER, G., and MUNRO, N. Factors in social perception: Seating position. *Perceptual and Motor Skills*, 1971, **33,** 747–752.

DAVIS, J. *Group performance.* Reading, Mass.: Addison-Wesley, 1969.

DAVIS, K., and JONES, E. Changes in interpersonal perception as a means of reducing cognitive dissonance. *Journal of Abnormal and Social Psychology*, 1960, **61,** 402–410.

DAYTON, L. Instructions and affiliation as factors in the categorizations of love and anger. *Dissertation Abstracts*, 1967, **27**(8-B), 2868.

DeCHARMS, R., and WILKINS, E. Some effects of verbal expression of hostility. *Journal of Abnormal and Social Psychology*, 1963, **66,** 462–470.

de FLEUR, M., and WESTIE, F. Verbal attitudes and overt acts: An experience on the salience of attitudes. *American Sociological Review*, 1958, **23,** 667–673.

DEMBER, W. Birth order and need affiliation. *Journal of Abnormal and Social Psychology*, 1964, **68,** 555–557.

DEUTSCH, M. An experimental study of the effects of co-operation and competition upon group process. *Human Relations*, 1949, **2,** 199–232.

DEUTSCH, M. Trust, trustworthiness, and the F scale. *Journal of Abnormal and Social Psychology*, 1960, **61,** 138–140.

DEUTSCH, M. Socially relevant science: Reflections on some studies of interpersonal conflict. *American Psychologist*, 1969, **24,** 1076–1092.

DEUTSCH, M., CANAVAN, D., and RUBIN, J. The effects of size of conflict and sex of experimenter upon interpersonal bargaining. *Journal of Experimental Social Psychology*, 1971, **7,** 258–267.

DEUTSCH, M., and GERARD, H. A study of normative and informational influence upon individual judgment. *Journal of Abnormal and Social Psychology,* 1955, **51,** 629–636.

DEUTSCH, M., and KRAUSS, R. Studies of interpersonal bargaining. *Journal of Conflict Resolution,* 1962, **4,** 52–76.

DIBIASE, W., and HJELLE, L. Body-image stereotypes and body-type preferences among male college students. *Perceptual and Motor Skills,* 1968, **27**(3, Pt. 2), 1143–1146.

DICHTER, E. *Handbook of consumer motivations.* New York: McGraw-Hill, 1964.

DICKOFF, H. Reactions to evaluations by another person as a function of self evaluation and the interaction context. Unpublished doctoral dissertation, Duke University, 1961.

DIEBOLD, P. Eye contact and gaze aversion in an aggressive encounter. *Dissertation Abstracts International,* 1971, **31**(11-B), 6924–6925.

DIENSTBIER, R., and MUNTER, P. Cheating as a function of the labeling of natural arousal. *Journal of Personality and Social Psychology,* 1971, **17,** 208–213.

DIETRICH, J. The relative effectiveness of two modes of radio delivery in influencing attitudes. *Speech Monographs,* 1946, **13,** 58–65.

DION, K. Physical attractiveness and evaluations of children's transgressions. *Journal of Personality and Social Psychology,* 1972, **24,** 207–213. Quoted in E. Berscheid and E. Walster, Beauty and the best. *Psychology Today,* 1972, **5**(10), 42–46, 74.

DION, K., and BERSCHEID, E. Physical attractiveness and social perception of peers in preschool children. Mimeographed research report available from the authors, 1972.

DION, K., BERSCHEID, E., and WALSTER, E. What is beautiful is good. *Journal of Personality and Social Psychology,* 1972, **24,** 285–290.

DITTES, J. Attractiveness of a group as a function of self-esteem and acceptance by group. *Journal of Abnormal and Social Psychology,* 1959, **59,** 77–82.

DITTES, J., and KELLEY, H. Effects of different conditions of acceptance upon conformity to group norms. *Journal of Abnormal and Social Psychology,* 1956, **53,** 100–107.

DOLLARD, J. Hostility and fear in social life. *Social Forces,* 1938, **17,** 15–26.

DOLLARD, J., DOOB, L., MILLER, N., MOWRER, O., and SEARS, R. *Frustration and aggression.* New Haven: Yale University Press, 1939.

DOLLARD, J., and MILLER, N. *Personality and psychotherapy: An analysis in terms of learning, thinking, and culture.* New York: McGraw-Hill, 1950.

DOMINIAN, J. *Marital breakdown.* Harmondsworth, Middlesex, England: Penguin Books, 1968.

DOOB, A., CARLSMITH, J., FREEDMAN, J., LANDAUER, T., and TOM, S. Effect of initial selling price on subsequent sales. *Journal of Personality and Social Psychology,* 1969, **11,** 345–350.

DOOB, A., and ECKER, B. Stigma and compliance. *Journal of Personality and Social Psychology,* 1970, **14,** 302–304.

DORRIS, J. Reactions to unconditional cooperation: A field study emphasizing variables neglected in laboratory research. *Journal of Personality and Social Psychology,* 1972, **22,** 387–397.

DOSEY, M., and MEISELS, M. Personal space and self-protection. *Journal of Personality and Social Psychology,* 1969, **11,** 93–97.

DOWNS, R. Study in megalomania, Adolf Hitler: Mein Kampf. In *Books that changed the world.* New York: Mentor, 1956. Chapter 10.

DRISCOLL, R., DAVIS, K., and LIPETZ, M. Parental interference and romantic love: The Romeo and Juliet effect. *Journal of Personality and Social Psychology,* 1972, **24,** 1–10.

DUSTER, T. Conditions for guilt-free massacre. In N. Sanford and C. Comstock (Eds.), *Sanctions for evil.* San Francisco: Jossey-Bass, 1971. 25–36.

EDWARDS, A. *The social desirability variable in personality assessment and research.* New York: Holt, 1957.

EELLS, K. Marijuana and LSD: A survey of one college campus. *Journal of Counseling Psychology,* 1968, **15,** 459–467.

EHRLICH, H., and GRAEVEN, D. Reciprocal self-disclosure in a dyad. *Journal of Experimental Social Psychology,* 1971, **7,** 389–400.

EISENHOWER, M., et al. Commission statement on violence in television entertainment programs. Washington, D.C.: National Commission on the Causes and Prevention of Violence, 1969.

EISMAN, B. Some operational measures of cohesiveness and their correlations. *Human Relations,* 1959, **12,** 183–189.

EKMAN, P. Body position, facial expression, and verbal behavior during interviews. *Journal of Abnormal and Social Psychology,* 1964, **68,** 295–301.

EKMAN, P., and FRIESEN, W. Nonverbal leakage and clues to deception. *Psychiatry,* 1969, **32,** 88–106.

EKMAN, P., and FRIESEN, W. Constants across cultures in the face and emotion. *Journal of Personality and Social Psychology,* 1971, **17,** 124–129.

EKMAN, P., FRIESEN, W., and ELLSWORTH, P. *Emotion in the human face: Guidelines for research and an integration of findings.* New York: Pergamon Press, 1972.

EKMAN, P., FRIESEN, W., and TOMKINS, S. Facial affect scoring technique (FAST) : A first validity study. *Semiotica,* 1971, **3,** 37–58.

ELDERSVELD, S., and DODGE, R. Personal contact or mail propaganda? An experiment in voting turnout and attitude change. In D. Katz, D. Cartwright, S. Eldersveld, and A. Lee (Eds.), *Public opinion and propaganda.* New York: Dryden Press, 1954. Pp. 532–542.

ELLSWORTH, P., and CARLSMITH, J. Effects of eye contact and verbal content on affective response to a dyadic interaction. *Journal of Personality and Social Psychology,* 1968, **10,** 15–20.

ELLSWORTH, P., CARLSMITH, J., and HENSON, A. The stare as a stimulus to flight in human subjects: A series of field experiments. *Journal of Personality and Social Psychology,* 1972, **21,** 302–311.

EMSWILLER, R., DEAUX, K., and WILLITS, J. Similarity, sex, and requests for small favors. *Journal of Applied Social Psychology,* 1971, **1,** 284–291.

EPSTEIN, R., and KOMORITA, S. Childhood prejudice as a function of parental ethnocentrism, punitiveness, and outgroup characteristics. *Journal of Personality and Social Psychology,* 1966, **3,** 259–264.

EPSTEIN, S., and TAYLOR, S. Instigation to aggression as a function of degree of defeat and perceived aggressive intent of the opponent. *Journal of Personality,* 1967, **35,** 265–289.

ERIKSON, E. H. *Childhood and society.* New York: Norton, 1950.

ERIKSON, E. H. *Identity: Youth and crisis.* New York: Norton, 1968.

ETTINGER, R., MARINO, C., ENDLER, N., GELLER, S., and NATZIUK, T. Effects of agreement and correctness on relative competence and conformity. *Journal of Personality and Social Psychology,* 1971, **19,** 204–212.

EXLINE, R. Effects of need for affiliation, sex and the sight of others upon initial communications in problem solving groups. *Journal of Personality,* 1962, **30,** 541–556. (a)

EXLINE, R. Need affiliation and initial communication behavior in problem-solving groups characterized by low interpersonal visibility. *Psychological Reports,* 1962, **10,** 79–89. (b)

EYSENCK, H. *The phychology of politics.* London: Routledge and Kegan Paul, 1954.

FANNIN, L., and CLINARD, M. Differences in the conception of self as a male among lower and middle class delinquents. *Social Problems,* 1965, **13,** 205–214.

FEFFER, M., and SUCHOTLIFF, L. Decentering implications of social interactions. *Journal of Personality and Social Psychology,* 1966, **4,** 415–422.

FELDMAN, R. Response to compatriot and foreigner who seek assistance. *Journal of Personality and Social Psychology,* 1968, **10,** 202–214.

FELIPE, N., and SOMMER, R. Invasions of personal space. *Social Problems,* 1966, **14,** 206–214.

FELLNER, C., and MARSHALL, J. Kidney donors. In J. Macaulay and L. Berkowitz (Eds.), *Altruism and helping behavior: Social psychological studies of some antecedents and consequences.* New York: Academic Press, 1970. Pp. 269–281.

FENICHEL, O. The counterphobic attitude. *International Journal of Psychoanalysis,* 1939, **20,** 263–274.

FESHBACH, S. The drive-reducing function of fantasy behavior. *Journal of Abnormal and Social Psychology,* 1955, **59,** 3–11.

FESHBACH, S. The function of aggression and the regulation of aggressive drive. *Psychological Review,* 1964, **71,** 257–272.

FESHBACH, S. Dynamics and morality of violence and aggression: Some psychological considerations. *American Psychologist,* 1971, **26,** 281–292.

FESHBACH, S., and SINGER, R. *Television and aggression.* San Francisco: Jossey-Bass, 1971.

FESTINGER, L. Informal social communication. *Psychological Review,* 1950, **57,** 271–282.

FESTINGER, L. A theory of social comparison processes. *Human Relations,* 1954, **7,** 117–140.

FESTINGER, L. Social psychology and group processes. *Annual Review of Psychology,* 1955, **6,** 187–216.

FESTINGER, L. *A theory of cognitive dissonance.* Stanford: Stanford University Press, 1957.

FESTINGER, L. Cognitive dissonance. *Scientific American,* 1962, **207**(4), 93–107.

FESTINGER, L. Behavioral support for opinion change. *The Public Opinion Quarterly,* 1964, **28,** 404–417.

FESTINGER, L., and CARLSMITH, J. Cognitive consequences of forced compliance. *Journal of Abnormal and Social Psychology,* 1959, **58,** 203–210.

FESTINGER, L., and MACCOBY, N. On resistance to persuasive communications. *Journal of Abnormal and Social Psychology,* 1964, **68,** 359–366.

FESTINGER, L., PEPITONE, A., and NEWCOMB, T. Some consequences of deindividuation in a group. *Journal of Abnormal and Social Psychology,* 1952, **47,** 382–389.

FESTINGER, L., SCHACHTER, S., and BACK, K. *So-*

Social Psychology and Modern Life

cial pressures in informal groups: A study of human factors in housing. New York: Harper & Row, 1950.

FIDELL, L. Empirical verification of sex discrimination in hiring practices in psychology. *American Psychologist,* 1970, **25,** 1094–1098.

FIEDLER, F. *A theory of leadership effectiveness.* New York: McGraw-Hill, 1967.

FIEDLER, F. Leadership experience and leader performance: Another hypothesis shot to hell. *Organizational Behavior and Human Performance,* 1970, **5,** 1–14.

FIEDLER, F. *Leadership.* New York: General Learning Press, 1971.

FIEDLER, F., and CHEMERS, M. Group performance under experienced and inexperienced leaders: A validation experiment. Group effectiveness research laboratory technical report. University of Illinois, 1968.

FINE, M., HIMMELFARB, M., and JELENKO, M. (Eds.) *American Jewish Year Book,* 1972, **73,** 274–277.

FISCHER, W. Sharing in preschool children as a function of amount and type of reinforcement. *Genetic Psychological Monographs,* 1963, **68,** 215–245.

FISHBEIN, M., and HUNTER, R. Summation versus balance in attitude organization and change. *Journal of Abnormal and Social Psychology,* 1964, **69,** 505–510.

FISHMAN, C. Need for approval and the expression of aggression under varying conditions of frustration. *Journal of Personality and Social Psychology,* 1965, **2,** 809–816.

FISHMAN, D. Need and expectancy as determinants of affiliative behavior in small groups. *Journal of Personality and Social Psychology,* 1966, **4,** 155–164.

FLACKS, R. The liberated generation: An exploration of the roots of student protest. *The Journal of Social Issues,* 1967, **23,** 52–75.

FLEISHMAN, E., and HARRIS, E. Patterns of leadership behavior related to employee grievances and turnover. *Personnel Psychology,* 1962, **15,** 43–56.

FLEISHMANN, E., HARRIS, E., and BURTT, H. *Leadership and supervision in industry: An evaluation of a supervisory training program.* Columbus: Ohio State University, Bureau of Educational Research, 1955. Cited in L. Festinger, Behavioral support for opinion change. *The Public Opinion Quarterly,* 1964, **28,** 404–417.

FLEMING, W. *Atkinson study of utilization of student resources.* Toronto: Ontario College of Education, 1958.

FOURIEZOS, N., HUTT, M., and GUETZKOW, H. Measurement of self-oriented needs in discussion groups. *Journal of Abnormal and Social Psychology,* 1950, **45,** 682–690.

FRASER, S., and FUJITOMI, I. Perceived prior compliance, psychological reactance, and altruistic contributions. *Proceedings of the 80th Annual Convention of the American Psychological Association,* 1972, 247–248.

FREEDMAN, J. Attitudinal effects of inadequate justification. *Journal of Personality,* 1963, **31,** 371–385.

FREEDMAN, J. Role playing: Psychology by consensus. *Journal of Personality and Social Psychology,* 1969, **13,** 107–114.

FREEDMAN, J., and DOOB, A. *Deviancy: The psychology of being different.* New York: Academic Press, 1968.

FREEDMAN, J., and FRASER, S. Compliance without pressure: The foot-in-the-door technique. *Journal of Personality and Social Psychology,* 1966, **4,** 195–202.

FREEDMAN, J., LEVY, A., BUCHANAN, R., and PRICE, J. Crowding and human aggressiveness. *Journal of Experimental Social Psychology,* 1972, **8,** 528–548.

FREEDMAN, J., and SEARS, D. Selective exposure. In L. Berkowitz (Ed.), *Advances in experimental social psychology.* Vol. 1. New York: Academic Press, 1965. Pp. 58–98. (a)

FREEDMAN, J., and SEARS, D. Warning, distraction and resistance to influence. *Journal of Personality and Social Psychology,* 1965, **1,** 262–265. (b)

FRENCH, E., and CHADWICK, I. Some characteristics of affiliation motivation. *Journal of Abnormal and Social Psychology,* 1956, **52,** 296–300.

FRENCH, J. R., Jr. The disruption and cohesion of groups. *Journal of Abnormal and Social Psychology,* 1941, **36,** 361–377.

FRENCH, J. R., Jr., and RAVEN, B. The bases of social power. In D. Cartwright (Ed.), *Studies in social power.* Ann Arbor: University of Michigan Press, 1959. Pp. 150–167.

FREUD, S. The most prevalent form of degradation in erotic life. In E. Jones (Ed.), *Collected papers.* Vol. 4. London: Hogarth, 1925. Pp. 203–216.

FREUD, S. *New introductory lectures on psychoanalysis.* London: Hogarth, 1949. (Originally published in 1933)

FRIEDMAN, N. *The social nature of psychological research: The psychological experiment as a social interaction.* New York: Basic Books, 1967.

FRIJDA, N. Recognition of emotion. In L. Berkowitz (Ed.), *Advances in experimental social psychology.* Vol. 4. New York: Academic Press, 1969. Pp. 167–223.

FROMKIN, H. Affective and valuational consequence of self-perceived uniqueness deprivation. Unpublished doctoral dissertation, Ohio State University, 1968.

FROMM, E. *Escape from freedom.* New York: Rinehart, 1941.

FROMM, E. *The art of loving.* New York: Harper and Row, 1956.

FUCHS, D. Election-day radio-television and western voting. *The Public Opinion Quarterly,* 1966, **30,** 226–236.

GALLO, P., FUNK, S., and LEVINE, J. Reward size, method of presentation, and number of alternatives in a prisoner's dilemma game. *Journal of Personality and Social Psychology,* 1969, **13,** 239–244.

GARFINKEL, H. Trust and stable action. In O. Harvey (Ed.), *Motivation and social interaction.* New York: Ronald Press, 1963.

GEEN, R. Effects of frustration, attack, and prior training in aggressiveness upon aggressive behavior. *Journal of Personality and Social Psychology,* 1968, **9,** 316–321.

GEIS, F., and CHRISTIE, R. Overview of experimental research. In R. Christie, F. Geis, et al., *Studies in Machiavellianism.* New York: Academic Press, 1970. Pp. 285–313.

GEIS, F., KRUPAT, E., and BERGER, D. Taking over in group discussion. Unpublished paper, New York University, 1965.

GEIS, F., WEINHEIMER, S., and BERGER, D. Playing legislature: Cool heads and hot issues. In R. Christie, F. Geis, et al., *Studies in Machiavellianism.* New York: Academic Press, 1970. Pp. 190–209.

GERARD, H., and MATHEWSON, G. The effects of severity of initiation on liking for a group: A replication. *Journal of Experimental Social Psychology,* 1966, **2,** 278–287.

GERARD, H., and RABBIE, J. Fear and social comparison. *Journal of Abnormal and Social Psychology,* 1961, **62,** 586–592.

GERARD, H., WILHELMY, R., and CONNOLLEY, E. Conformity and group size. *Journal of Personality and Social Psychology,* 1968, **8,** 79–82.

GERBNER, G., Violence in television drama: Trends and symbolic functions. In G. Comstock and E. Rubinstein (Eds.), *Television and social behavior.* Vol. 1. *Content and control.* Washington: D.C.: Government Printing Office, 1971.

GERGEN, K. Interaction goals and personalistic feedback as factors affecting the presentation of self. *Journal of Personality and Social Psychology,* 1965, **1,** 413–424.

GERGEN, K. *The concept of self.* New York: Holt, Rinehart and Winston, 1971.

GERGEN, K. Multiple identity. *Psychology Today,* 1972, **5**(12), 31–35, 64, 66.

GERGEN, K., and GERGEN, M. Encounter: Research catalyst for general theories of social behavior. Unpublished manuscript, Swarthmore College, 1971.

GERGEN, K., MASLACH, C., ELLSWORTH, P., and SEIPEL, M. Obligation, donor resources, and reactions to receiving aid in three nations. *Journal of Personality and Social Psychology,* in press.

GERGEN, K., and TAYLOR, M. Social expectancy and self-presentation in a status heirachy. *Journal of Experimental Social Psychology,* 1969, **5,** 79–92.

GERGEN, K., and WISHNOV, B. Other's self-evaluations and interaction anticipation as determinants of self-presentation. *Journal of Personality and Social Psychology,* 1965, **2,** 348–358.

GIBB, C. Leadership. In G. Lindzey and E. Aronson (Eds.), *The handbook of social psychology.* (2nd ed.) Vol. 4. *Group psychology and phenomena of interaction.* Reading, Mass.: Addison-Wesley, 1969. Pp. 205–282.

GIBBINS, K. Communication aspects of women's clothes and their relation to fashion ability. *British Journal of Social and Clinical Psychology,* 1969, **8,** 301–312.

GIL, D. Incidence of child abuse and demographic characteristics of persons involved. In R. Helfer and C. Kempe (Eds.), *The battered child.* Chicago: University of Chicago Press, 1968. Pp. 19–40.

GLASS, D., SINGER, J., and FRIEDMAN, L. Psychic cost of adaptation to an environmental stressor. *Journal of Personality and Social Psychology,* 1969, **12,** 200–210.

GLINSKI, R., GLINSKI, B., and SLATIN, G. Nonnaivety contamination in conformity experiments: Sources, effects, and implications for control. *Journal of Personality and Social Psychology,* 1970, **16,** 478–485.

GOETHALS, G. Consensus and modality in the attribution process: The role of similarity and information. *Journal of Personality and Social Psychology,* 1972, **21,** 84–92.

GOFFMAN, E. On face-work: An analysis of ritual elements in social interaction. *Psychiatry,* 1955, **18,** 213–231.

GOFFMAN, E. *Encounters.* Indianapolis: Bobbs-Merrill, 1961.

GOFFMAN, E. *Interaction ritual: Essays in face-to-face behavior.* Chicago: Aldine, 1967.

GOFFMAN, E. The inmate world. In C. Gordon and K. Gergen (Eds.), *The self in social interaction.* New York: Wiley, 1968. Pp. 267–274.

GOLD, A., FRIEDMAN, L., and CHRISTIE, R. The anatomy of revolutionists. *Journal of Applied Social Psychology,* 1971, **1,** 26–43.

GOLDE, R. Are your meetings like this one? *Harvard Business Review,* 1972, **50,** 68–77.

GOLDSEN, R., ROSENBERG, M., WILLIAMS, R., and SUCHMAN, E. *What college students think.* Princeton: Van Nostrand, 1960.

GOLLIN, E. Forming impressions of personality. *Journal of Personality,* 1954, **23,** 65–76.

GOLLOB, H., and DITTES, J. Different effects of manipulated self-esteem on persuasibility depending on the threat and complexity of the communication. *Journal of Personality and Social Psychology,* 1965, **2,** 195–201.

GOODALL, K. Tie line. *Psychology Today,* 1972, **6**(6), 42–49.

GOODSTADT, M. Helping and refusal to help: A test of balance and reactance theories. *Journal of Experimental Social Psychology,* 1971, **7,** 610–622.

GORANSON, R., and BERKOWITZ, L. Reciprocity and responsibility reactions to prior help. *Journal of Personality and Social Psychology,* 1966, **3,** 227–232.

GORDON, A. Friends, strangers, and manipulated stress. *Dissertation Abstracts International,* 1971, **31**(9-A), 4886.

GORDON, B. Influence, social comparison and affiliation. *Dissertation Abstracts,* 1965, **26**(4), 2366.

GORDON, B. Influence and social comparison as motives for affiliation. *Journal of Experimental Social Psychology Supplement,* 1966, **1,** 55–65.

GORDON, C. Self-conceptions: Configurations of content. In C. Gordon and K. Gergen (Eds.), *The self in social interaction.* New York: Wiley, 1968. Pp. 115–136.

GORDON, C., and GERGEN, K. Introduction to Volume I. In C. Gordon and K. Gergen (Eds.), *The self in social interaction.* New York: Wiley, 1968. (a)

GORDON, C., and GERGEN, K. (Eds.) *The self in social interaction.* New York: Wiley, 1968. (b)

GORDON, S., and SIZER, N. Why people join the Peace Corps, 1963, Washington, D.C., Contract PC-W-136, Institute for International Service, out of print. Cited by J. Colmen, A discovery of commitment, pp. 14–17. In J. Parmer (Ed.), *The Annals of the American Academy of Political and Social Science.* Vol. 365. *The Peace Corps.* Philadelphia: American Academy of Political and Social Science, 1966.

GORE, P., and ROTTER, J. A personality correlate of social action. *Journal of Personality,* 1963, **31,** 58–64.

GOULDNER, A. The norm of reciprocity: A preliminary statement. *American Sociological Review,* 1960, **25,** 161–178.

GRAEN, G., ORRIS, J., and ALVARES, K. Contingency model of leadership effectiveness: Some experimental results. *Journal of Applied Psychology,* 1971, **55,** 196–201.

GRAHAM, B. Loneliness: How it can be cured. *Reader's Digest,* October, 1969, pp. 135–138.

GRANET, R. Unpublished study. Cited on pp. 92–93 by J. Darley and B. Latané, Norms and normative behavior: Field studies of social interdependence. In J. Macaulay and L. Berkowitz (Eds.), *Altruism and helping behavior. Social psychological studies of some antecedents and consequences.* New York: Academic Press, 1970.

GRIFFITT, W. Environmental effects on interpersonal affective behavior: Ambient effective temperature and attraction. *Journal of Personality and Social Psychology,* 1970, **15,** 240–244.

GRINKER, R., and SPIEGEL, J. *Men under stress.* Philadelphia: Blakiston, 1945.

GROESBECK, B. Toward description of personality in terms of configuration of motives. In J. Atkinson (Ed.), *Motives in fantasy, action, and society.* New York: Van Nostrand, 1958. Pp. 383–399.

GRUSEC, J. Demand characteristics of the modeling experiment: Altruism as a function of age and aggression. *Journal of Personality and Social Psychology,* 1972, **22,** 139–148.

GRUVER, G. College students as therapeutic agents. *Psychological Bulletin,* 1971, **76,** 111–127.

GUMPERT, P., DEUTSCH, M., and EPSTEIN, Y. Effect of incentive magnitude on cooperation in the prisoner's dilemma game. *Journal of Personality and Social Psychology,* 1969, **11,** 66–69.

GUSTAV, A. Students' attitudes toward compulsory participation in experiments. *Journal of Psychology,* 1962, **53,** 119–125.

HAALAND, G., and VENKATESEN, M. Resistance to persuasive communications: An examination of the distraction hypothesis. *Journal of Personality and Social Psychology,* 1968, **9,** 167–170.

HAAS, H., FINK, H., and HARTFELDER, G. Das Placebo-problem, *Fortschritte der Arzneimittelforchung,* 1959, **1,** 279–454. (*Psychopharmacology·Service Center Bulletin,* 1963, **8,** 1–65)

HAGEN, H. Crew interaction during a thirty-day simulated space flight. Technical Report 61–66. U. S. Air Force, School of Aerospace Medicine, June, 1961.

HAIRE, M. Role-perceptions in labor-management relations: An experimental approach. *Industrial and Labor Relations Review,* 1955, **8,** 204–216.

HAIRE, M., and GRUNES, W. Perceptual defenses: Processes protecting an organized perception of another personality. *Human Relations,* 1950, **3,** 403–412.

HAKMILLER, K. Threat as a determinant of downward comparison. *Journal of Experimental Social Psy-*

603

chology Supplement, 1966, **1,** 27–31.

HALL, E. A system for the notation of proxemic behavior. *American Anthropologist,* 1963, **65,** 1003–1026.

HALL, E. Silent assumptions in social communication. *Disorders of Communication,* 1964, **42,** 41–55.

HALL, E., and POTEETE, R. Do you, Mary and Anne, and Beverly, and Ruth, take these men . . . : A conversation with Robert H. Rimmer about Harrad, group marriage, and other loving arrangements. *Psychology Today,* 1972, **5**(8), 57–64, 78, 80, 82.

HALL, J. Decisions, decisions, decisions. *Psychology Today,* 1971, **5**(6), 51–54, 86.

HALL, J., and WILLIAMS, M. Personality and group encounter style: A multivariate analysis of traits and preferences. *Journal of Personality and Social Psychology,* 1971, **18,** 163–172.

HALLORAN, R. Crime in Tokyo: A minor problem. *The New York Times,* October 3, 1971, p. 6.

HALPIN, A., and WINER, B. *The leadership behavior of the airplane commander.* Ohio State University Research Foundation, 1952.

HALSELL, G. *Soul sister.* Greenwich, Conn.: Fawcett Crest, 1969.

HAMBLIN, R. Leadership and crisis. *Sociometry,* 1958, **21,** 322–335.

HAMPTON, J. The beautiful American. *Volunteer,* 1971, **9**(3–4), 12–15.

HARBURG, E. *Finian's rainbow.* 1947. (Musical comedy, music by B. Lane)

HARDING, J., PROSHANSKY, H., KUTNER, B., and CHEIN, I. Prejudice and ethnic relations. In G. Lindzey and E. Aronson (Eds.), *The handbook of social* psychology. (2nd ed.) Vol. 5. *Applied social psychology.* Reading, Mass.: Addison-Wesley, 1969. Pp. 1–76.

HARE, A. *Handbook of small group research.* New York: The Free Press of Glencoe, 1962.

HARLOW, H. The nature of love. *American Psychologist,* 1958, **13,** 673–685.

HARLOW, H. Love in infant monkeys. *Scientific American,* 1959, **200,** 68–74.

HARLOW, H., and HARLOW, M. The effect of rearing conditions on behavior. *Bulletin of the Menninger Clinic,* 1962, **26,** 213–224.

HARLOW, H., and SUOMI, S. Nature of love—simplified. *American Psychologist,* 1970, **25,** 161–168.

The Harris survey: Race stereotypes continue in U. S. *The Washington Post,* October 4, 1971.

HARRISON, A., and CRANDALL, R. Heterogeneity-homogeneity of exposure sequence and the attitudinal effects of exposure. *Journal of Personality and Social Psychology,* 1972, **21,** 234–238.

HARTMANN, D. Influence of symbolically modeled instrumental aggression and pain cues on aggressive behavior. *Journal of Personality and Social Psychology,* 1969, **11,** 280–288.

HARVEY, O. Personality factors in resolution of conceptual incongruities. *Sociometry,* 1962, **25,** 336–352.

HASHIM, S., and VAN ITALLIE, T. Studies in normal and obese subjects with a monitored food-dispensing device. *Annals of the New York Academy of Science,* 1965, **131,** 654–661.

HAWLEY, P. What women think men think: Does it affect their career choice? *Journal of Counseling Psychology,* 1971, **18,** 193–199.

HAYTHORN, W., and ALTMAN, I. Together in isolation. *Trans-Action,* 1967, **4,** 18–23.

HEBB, D., and THOMPSON, W. The social significance of animal studies. In G. Lindzey and E. Aronson (Eds.), *The handbook of social psychology.* (2nd ed.) Vol. 2. *Research methods.* Reading, Mass.: Addison-Wesley, 1968. Pp. 729–774.

HEIDER, F. *The psychology of interpersonal relations.* New York: Wiley, 1958.

HEIDER, F., and SIMMEL, E. A study of apparent behavior. *American Journal of Psychology,* 1944, **57,** 243–259.

HELFER, R., and KEMPE, C. Introduction. In R. Helfer and C. Kempe (Eds.), *The battered child.* Chicago: University of Chicago Press, 1968. Pp. ix–xi.

HELM, B., BONOMA, T., and TEDESCHI, J. Counteraggression as a function of physical aggression: Reciprocity for harm done. *Proceedings of the 79th Annual Convention of the American Psychological Association,* 1971, **6**(Pt. 1), 237–238.

Help Line Telephone Center. Release, New York, 1970.

HEMPHILL, J. Relations between the size of the group and the behavior of "superior" leaders. *Journal of Social Psychology,* 1950, **32,** 11–22.

HENDRICK, C., BIXENSTINE, V., and HAWKINS, G. Race versus belief similarity as determinants of attraction: A search for a fair test. *Journal of Personality and Social Psychology,* 1971, **17,** 250–258.

HERBERS, J. Summer's urban violence stirs fears of terrorism. *The New York Times,* September 21, 1971, pp. 1, 34.

HERSH, S. *My Lai 4: A report on the massacre and its aftermath.* New York: Vintage Books, 1970.

HESS, E. Imprinting. *Science,* 1959, **130,** 133–141.

HESS, R., and TORNEY, J. *The development of political attitudes in children.* Chicago: Aldine, 1967.

HETHERINGTON, E. A developmental study of the effects of sex of the dominant parent on sex-role performance, identification, and imitation in children. *Journal of Personality and Social Psychology,* 1965, **2,** 188–194.

HEWITT, J. Liking and the proportion of favorable evaluations. *Journal of Personality and Social Psychology,* 1972, **22,** 231–235.

HILGARD, J. Anniversary reactions in parents precipitated by children. *Psychiatry,* 1953, **16,** 73–80. Quoted on pp. 92–93 by D. Bakan, *On method: Toward a reconstruction of psychological investigation.* San Francisco: Jossey-Bass, 1969.

HILL, R., and BONJEAN, C. News diffusion: A test of the regularity hypothesis. *Journalism Quarterly,* 1964, **41,** 336–342.

HILSMAN, R. *To move a nation.* Garden City, N. Y.: Doubleday, 1967.

HITLER, A. *Mein Kampf.* (Trans. by E. Dugdale) Cambridge, Mass.: Riverside Press, 1933.

HOFLING, C., BROTZMAN, E., DALRYMPLE, S., GRAVES, N., and PIERCE, C. An experimental study in nurse-physician relationships. *Journal of Nervous and Mental Disease,* 1966, **143,** 171–180.

HOKANSON, J., and BURGESS, M. Effects of status, type of frustration and aggression on vascular processes. *Journal of Abnormal and Social Psychology,* 1962, **65,** 232–237. (a)

HOKANSON, J., and BURGESS, M. Effects of three types of aggression on vascular processes. *Journal of Abnormal and Social Psychology,* 1962, **64,** 446–449. (b)

HOKANSON, J., and SHETLER, S. The effect of overt aggression on physiological arousal level. *Journal of Abnormal and Social Psychology,* 1961, **63,** 446–448.

HOLLANDER, E., and JULIAN, J. Studies in leader legitimacy, influence, and innovation. In L. Berkowitz (Ed.), *Advances in experimental social psychology.* Vol. 5. New York: Academic Press, 1970. Pp. 33–69.

HOLLANDER, E., and WILLIS, R. Some current issues in the psychology of conformity and nonconformity. *Psychological Bulletin,* 1967, **68,** 62–76.

HOLLES, E. Navy unrest laid to communication gap. *The New York Times,* December 12, 1972, p. 26.

HOLT, L. Resistance to persuasion on explicit beliefs as a function of commitment to and desirability of logically related beliefs. *Journal of Personality and Social Psychology,* 1970, **16,** 583–591.

HOLZBERG, J., GEWIRTZ, H., and EBNER, E. Changes in moral judgment and self-acceptance as a function of companionship with hospitalized mental patients. *Journal of Consulting Psychology,* 1964, **28,** 299–303.

HOLZMAN, P. On hearing one's own voice. *Psychology Today,* 1971, **5**(6), 67–69, 98.

HOMANS, G. *The human group.* New York: Harcourt, 1950.

HOMANS, G. Social behavior as exchange. *American Journal of Sociology,* 1958, **63,** 597–606.

HOMANS, G. *Social behavior: Its elementary forms.* New York: Harcourt, Brace, and World, 1961.

HOMANS, G. Group factors in worker productivity. In H. Proshansky and L. Seidenberg (Eds.), *Basic studies in social psychology.* New York: Holt, 1965. Pp. 592–604.

HOOD, T., and BACK, K. Self-disclosure and the volunteer: A source of bias in laboratory experiments. *Journal of Personality and Social Psychology,* 1971, **17,** 130–136.

HORNSTEIN, H. The influence of social models on helping. In J. Macaulay and L. Berkowitz (Eds.), *Altruism and helping behavior: Social psychological studies of some antecedents and consequences.* New York: Academic Press, 1970. Pp. 29–41.

HORNSTEIN, H., FISCH, E., and HOLMES, M. Influence of a model's feelings about his behavior and his relevance as a comparison on other observers' helping behavior. *Journal of Personality and Social Psychology,* 1968, **10,** 222–226.

HOROWITZ, E., and HOROWITZ, R. Development of social attitudes in children. *Sociometry,* 1938, **1,** 301–338.

HOROWITZ, I. Effect of choice and locus of dependence on helping behavior. *Journal of Personality and Social Psychology,* 1968, **8,** 373–376.

HOROWITZ, I., and ROTHSCHILD, B. Conformity as a function of deception and role playing. *Journal of Personality and Social Psychology,* 1970, **14,** 224–226.

HOURIET, R. *Getting back together.* New York: Coward, McCann and Geoghegan, 1971.

HOVLAND, C., HARVEY, O., and SHERIF, M. Assimilation and contrast effects in communication and attitude change. *Journal of Abnormal and Social Psychology,* 1957, **55,** 242–252.

HOVLAND, C., JANIS, I., and KELLEY, H. *Communication and persuasion.* New Haven: Yale University Press, 1953.

HOVLAND, C., LUMSDAINE, A., and SHEFFIELD, F. *Experiments on mass communication.* Princeton: Princeton University Press, 1949.

HOVLAND, C., and MANDELL, W. An experimental comparison of conclusion-drawing by the communicator and the audience. *Journal of Abnormal and Social Psychology,* 1952, **47,** 581–588.

HOVLAND, C., and WEISS, W. The influence of source credibility on communication effectiveness. *The Public Opinion Quarterly,* 1951, **15,** 635–650.

How the polls made out: The way people voted and why. *U. S. News & World Report,* November 20, 1972, p. 18.

HOWELL, R., and JORGENSON, E. Accuracy of judging emotional behavior in a natural setting: A replication. *Journal of Social Psychology,* 1970, **81,** 269–270.

HOWELLS, L., and BECKER, S. Seating arrangement and leadership emergence. *Journal of Abnormal and Social Psychology,* 1962, **64,** 148–150.

HOYT, M., HENLEY, M., and COLLINS, B. Studies in forced compliance: Confluence of choice and consequence on attitude change. *Journal of Personality and Social Psychology,* 1972, **23,** 205–210.

HRABA, J., and GRANT, G. Black is beautiful: A reexamination of racial preference and identification. *Journal of Personality and Social Psychology,* 1970, **16,** 398–402.

HUNT, J. Traditional personality theory in the light of recent evidence. *American Scientist,* 1965, **53,** 60–96.

HYMAN, H. The psychology of status. *Archives of Psychology,* 1942, No. 269.

HYMAN, H. Social psychology and race relation. In I. Katz and P. Gurin (Eds.), *Race and the social sciences.* New York: Basic Books, 1969. Pp. 3–48.

HYMAN, H., and SHEATSLEY, P. "The authoritarian personality": A methodological critique. In R. Christie and M. Jahoda (Eds.), *Studies in the scope and method of "The authoritarian personality."* New York: Free Press, 1954. Pp. 50–122.

INBAU, F., and REID, J. *Criminal interrogation and confessions.* Baltimore: Williams and Wilkins, 1962.

INDIK, B. Organization size and member participation: Some empirical tests of alternative explanations. *Human Relations,* 1965, **18,** 339–350.

INSKO, C., and CIALDINI, R. A test of three interpretations of attitudinal verbal reinforcement. *Journal of Personality and Social Psychology,* 1969, **12,** 333–341.

ISEN, A. Success, failure, attention and reactions to others: The warm glow of success. *Journal of Personality and Social Psychology,* 1970, **15,** 294–301.

IZZETT, R. Authoritarianism and attitudes toward the Vietnam War as reflected in behavioral and self-report measures. *Journal of Personality and Social Psychology,* 1971, **17,** 145–148.

JACKSON, E. *Understanding grief: Its roots, dynamics, and treatment.* New York: Abingdon Press, 1957.

JACOBS, J. *Adolescent suicide.* New York: Wiley-Interscience, 1971.

JACOBS, R., and CAMPBELL, D. The perpetuation of an arbitrary tradition through several generations of a laboratory microculture. *Journal of Abnormal and Social Psychology,* 1961, **62,** 649–659.

JACOBSEN, A. Conflict of attitudes toward the roles of husband and wife in marriage. *American Sociological Review,* 1952, **17,** 146–150.

JACQUET, C., Jr. (Ed.) *Year book of American churches for 1971.* New York: Council Press, 1971.

JAFFEE, C., and LUCAS, R. Effects of rates of talking and correctness of decision on leader choice in small groups. *Journal of Social Psychology,* 1969, **79,** 247–254.

JAMES, J. A preliminary study of the size determinant in small group interaction. *American Sociological Review,* 1951, **16,** 474–477.

JAMES, W. *Psychology: The briefer course.* New York: Holt, 1910.

JANIS, I. Psychodynamic aspects of adjustment to army life. *Psychiatry,* 1945, **8,** 159–176.

JANIS, I. *Air war and emotional stress.* New York: McGraw-Hill, 1951.

JANIS, I. Personality correlates of susceptibility to persuasion. *Journal of Personality,* 1954, **22,** 504–518.

JANIS, I. *Psychological stress.* New York: Wiley, 1958.

JANIS, I. Effects of fear arousal on attitude change: Recent developments in theory and experimental research. In L. Berkowitz (Ed.), *Advances in experimental social psychology.* Vol. 3. New York: Academic Press, 1967. Pp. 167–224.

JANIS, I. Groupthink. *Psychology Today,* 1971, **5**(6), 43–46, 74–76.

JANIS, I. *Victims of groupthink: A psychological study of foreign-policy decisions and fiascoes.* Boston: Houghton Mifflin, 1972.

JANIS, I., and FESHBACH, S. Effects of fear-arousing communications. *Journal of Abnormal and Social Psychology,* 1953, **48,** 78–92.

JANIS, I., and FESHBACH, S. Personality differences associated with responsiveness to fear-arousing communications. *Journal of Personality,* 1954, **23,** 154–166.

JANIS, I., and FIELD, P. Sex differences and personality factors related to persuasibility. In C. Hovland and I. Janis (Eds.), *Personality and Persuasibility.* New Haven: Yale University Press, 1959. Pp. 55–68.

JANIS, I., and GILMORE, B. The influence of incentive conditions on the success of role playing in modifying attitudes. *Journal of Personality and Social Psychology,* 1965, **1,** 17–27.

JANIS, I., KAYE, D., and KIRSCHNER, P. Facilitating effects of "eating-while-reading" on responsiveness to persuasive communications. *Journal of Personality and Social Psychology,* 1965, **1,** 181–186.

JANIS, I., and MANN, L. A conflict-theory approach to attitude change and decision making. In

A. Greenwald, T. Brock, and T. Ostrom (Eds.), *Psychological foundations of attitudes.* New York: Academic Press, 1968. Pp. 327–360.

JANIS, I., and RIFE, D. Persuasibility and emotional disorder. In C. Hovland and I. Janis (Eds.), *Personality and persuasibility.* New Haven: Yale University Press, 1959. Pp. 121–140.

JELLISON, J., and MILLS, J. Effect of public commitment upon opinions. *Journal of Experimental Social Psychology,* 1969, **5,** 340–346.

JENNINGS, H. *Leadership and isolation.* (2nd ed.) New York: Longmans, Green, 1959.

JENNINGS, M., and NIEMI, R. The transmission of political values from parent to child. *American Political Science Review,* 1968, **62,** 169–184.

JOHNSON, H., and SCILEPPI, J. Effects of ego-involvement conditions on attitude change to high and low credibility communicators. *Journal of Personality and Social Psychology,* 1969, **13,** 31–36.

JOHNSON, H., and STEINER, I. The effects of source on responses to negative information about one's self. *Journal of Social Psychology,* 1968, **74,** 215–224.

JOHNSON, M., and EWENS, W. Power relations and affective style as determinants of confidence in impression formation in a game situation. *Journal of Experimental Social Psychology,* 1971, **7,** 98–110.

JONES, E. *Ingratiation: A social psychological analysis.* New York: Appleton-Century-Crofts, 1964.

JONES, E., and DAVIS, K. From acts to dispositions: The attribution process in person perception. In L. Berkowitz (Ed.), *Advances in experimental social psychology.* Vol. 2. New York: Academic Press, 1965. Pp. 219–266.

JONES, E., DAVIS, K., and GERGEN, K. Role playing variations and their informational value for person perception. *Journal of Abnormal and Social Psychology,* 1961, **63,** 302–310.

JONES, E., and deCHARMS, R. Changes in social perception as a function of the personal relevance of behavior. *Sociometry,* 1957, **20,** 75–85.

JONES, E., and GERARD, H. *Foundations of social psychology.* New York: Wiley, 1967.

JONES, E., GERGEN, K., and DAVIS, K. Some determinants of reactions to being approved or disapproved as a person. *Psychological Monographs,* 1962, **76**(Whole No. 521).

JONES, E., WORCHEL, S., GOETHALS, G., and GRUMET, J. Prior expectancy and behavioral extremity as determinants of attitude attribution. *Journal of Experimental Social Psychology,* 1971, **7,** 59–80.

JONES, R., and BREHM, J. Persuasiveness of one- and two-sided communications as a function of awareness there are two sides. *Journal of Experi-* *mental Social Psychology,* 1970, **6,** 47–56.

JONES, R., and WELSH, J. Ability attribution and impression formation in a strategic game: A limiting case of the primacy effect. *Journal of Personality and Social Psychology,* 1971, **20,** 166–175.

JONES, S., and SCHNEIDER, D. Certainty of self-appraisal and reactions to evaluations from others. *Sociometry,* 1968, **31,** 395–403.

JONES, S., and SHRAUGER, J. Reputation and self evaluation as determinants of attractiveness. *Sociometry,* 1970, **33,** 276–286.

JOURARD, S. *The transparent self: Self-disclosure and well-being.* Princeton, N. J.: Van Nostrand, 1964.

JOURARD, S. *Self-disclosure: An experimental analysis of the transparent self.* New York: Wiley-Interscience, 1971.

JOURARD, S., and LASAKOW, P. A research approach to self-disclosure. *Journal of Abnormal and Social Psychology,* 1958, **56,** 91–98.

JULIAN, J., BISHOP, D., and FIEDLER, F. Quasi-therapeutic effects of intergroup competition. *Journal of Personality and Social Psychology,* 1966, **3,** 321–327.

JULIAN, J., HOLLANDER, E., and REGULA, C. Endorsement of the group spokesman as a function of his source of authority, competence, and success. *Journal of Personality and Social Psychology,* 1969, **11,** 42–49.

KAHN, A., and TICE, T. Returning a favor and retaliating harm: The effects of stated intentions and actual behavior. *Journal of Experimental Social Psychology,* 1973, **9,** 43–56.

KAHN, H. *On escalation.* New York: Praeger, 1965.

KAHN, M. Nonverbal communication as a factor In marital satisfaction. *Dissertation Abstracts International,* 1970, **30**(10-B), 4794.

KAHN, R. Who buys bloodshed and why. *Psychology Today,* 1972, **6**(1), 47–48, 82–84.

KAPLAN, E. Personal communication. 1970. Cited by L. Fidell, Empirical verification of sex discrimination in hiring practices in psychology. *American Psychologist,* 1970, **25,** 1094–1098.

KARDINER, A., and OVESEY, L. *The mark of oppression: Explorations in the personality of the American Negro.* New York: World Publishing Company, 1968. (Originally published in 1951)

KARLINS, M., COFFMAN, T., and WALTERS, G. On the fading of social stereotypes: Studies in three generations of college students. *Journal of Personality and Social Psychology,* 1969, **13,** 1–16.

KATZ, D. The functional approach to the study of attitude. *The Public Opinion Quarterly,* 1960, **24,** 163–204.

KATZ, D., SARNOFF, I., and McCLINTOCK, C. Ego-defense and attitude change. *Human Relations*, 1956, **9,** 27–45.

KATZ, E. The two-step flow of communication: An up-to-date report on an hypothesis. *The Public Opinion Quarterly*, 1957, **21,** 61–78.

KATZ, I., and COHEN, M. The effects of training Negroes upon cooperative problem solving in biracial teams. *Journal of Abnormal and Social Psychology*, 1962, **64,** 319–325.

KATZ, I., and GURIN, P. Race relations and the social science: Overview and further discussion. In I. Katz and P. Gurin (Eds.), *Race and the social sciences*. New York: Basic Books, 1969. Pp. 342–378.

KATZ, W. *The black west.* New York: Doubleday, 1971.

KEASEY, C., and TOMLINSON-KEASEY, C. Petition signing in a naturalistic setting. *Journal of Social Psychology,* 1973, **89,** 313–314.

KEATING, J., and LATANÉ, B. Distorted television reception, distraction, and attitude change. *Proceedings of the 80th Annual Convention of the American Psychological Association,* 1972, 141–142.

KEELER, M. Motivation for marihuana use: A correlate of adverse reaction. *American Journal of Psychiatry,* 1968, **125,** 386–390.

KELLEY, H. The warm-cold variable in first impressions of persons. *Journal of Personality,* 1950, **18,** 431–439.

KELLEY, H. Two functions of reference groups. In G. Swanson, T. Newcomb, and E. Hartley (Eds.), *Readings in social psychology.* (2nd ed.) New York: Holt, Rinehart and Winston, 1952. Pp. 410–414.

KELLEY, H. Attribution theory in social psychology. In D. Levine (Ed.), *Nebraska Symposium on Motivation,* 1967, **15,** 192–238.

KELLEY, H., and STAHELSKI, A. The inference of intention from moves in the prisoner's dilemma game. *Journal of Experimental Social Psychology,* 1970, **6,** 401–419.

KELLEY, H., and THIBAUT, J. Group problem solving. In G. Lindzey and E. Aronson (Eds.), *The handbook of social psychology.* (2nd ed.) Vol. 4. *Group psychology and phenomena of interaction.* Reading, Mass.: Addison-Wesley, 1969. Pp. 1–101.

KELMAN, H. Processes of opinion change. *The Public Opinion Quarterly,* 1961, **25,** 57–78.

KELMAN, H. Human use of human subjects: The problem of deception in social psychological experiments. *Psychological Bulletin,* 1967, **67,** 1–11.

KELMAN, H., and HOVLAND, C. "Reinstatement" of the communicator in delayed measurement of opinion change. *Journal of Abnormal and Social Psychology,* 1953, **48,** 327–335.

KELMAN, H., and LAWRENCE, L. Violent man: American response to the trial of Lt. William L. Calley. *Psychology Today,* 1972, **6**(1), 41–45, 78–82.

KEMPH, J., BERMANN, E., and COPPOLILLO, H. Kidney transplant and shifts in family dynamics. *American Journal of Psychiatry,* 1969, **125,** 1485–1490.

KENKEL, W. Influence differentiation in family decision making. *Sociology and Social Research,* 1957, **42,** 18–25.

KENKEL, W. Dominance, persistence, self-confidence, and spousal roles in decision-making. *Journal of Social Psychology,* 1961, **54,** 349–358.

KENNEDY, J., KOSLIN, B., SCHRODER, H., BLACKMAN, S., RAMSEY, J., and HELM, C. Cognitive patterning of complex stimuli: A symposium. *Journal of General Psychology,* 1966, **74,** 25–49.

KENNY, D. An experimental test of the catharsis hypothesis of aggression. Ann Arbor, Mich.. University Microfilms, 1953.

KEPHART, W. Some correlates of romantic love. *Journal of Marriage and the Family,* 1967, **29,** 470–474.

KEPKA, E., and BRICKMAN, P. Consistency versus discrepancy as clues in the attribution of intelligence and motivation. *Journal of Personality and Social Psychology,* 1971, **20,** 223–229.

KIESLER, C. *The psychology of commitment: Experiments linking behavior to belief.* New York: Academic Press, 1971.

KIESLER, C., COLLINS, B., and MILLER, N. *Attitude change: A critical analysis of theoretical approaches.* New York: Wiley, 1969.

KIESLER, C., and JONES, J. The interactive effects of commitment and forewarning: Three experiments. Summarized in C. Kiesler, *The psychology of commitment: Experiments linking behavior to belief.* New York: Academic Press, 1971. Pp. 94–108.

KIESLER, C., and KIESLER, S. *Conformity.* Reading, Mass.: Addison-Wesley, 1969.

KIESLER, C., MATHOG, R., POOL, P., and HOWENSTINE, R. Commitment and the boomerang effect: A field study. Summarized in C. Kiesler, *The psychology of commitment: Experiments linking behavior to belief.* New York: Academic Press, 1971. Pp. 74–85.

KIESLER, C., and SAKUMURA, J. A test for a model for commitment. *Journal of Personality and Social Psychology,* 1966, **3,** 349–353.

KILLIAN, L. The significance of multiple-group membership in disaster. *American Journal of Sociology,* 1952, **57,** 309–314.

KING, B., and JANIS, I. Comparison of the effectiveness of improvised versus non-improvised role-playing in producing opinion changes. *Human Relations*, 1956, **9,** 177–186.

KING, L. *Confessions of a white racist*. New York: Viking Press, 1971.

KING, S. Encounter study assesses groups. *The New York Times*, February 12, 1973, p. 47.

KISSEL, S. Stress-reducing properties of social stimuli. *Journal of Personality and Social Psychology,* 1965, **2,** 378–384.

KISSEL, S. Anxiety, affiliation and juvenile delinquency. *Journal of Clinical Psychology,* 1967, **23,** 173–175.

KLECK, R., ONO, H., and HASTORF, A. The effects of physical deviance upon face-to-face interaction. *Human Relations,* 1966, **19,** 425–436.

KOGAN, N., and WALLACH, M. *Risk taking: A study in cognition and personality*. New York: Holt, Rinehart and Winston, 1964.

KOHLBERG, L. Stage and sequence: The cognitive-developmental approach to socialization. In D. Goslin (Ed.), *Handbook of socialization theory and research*. Chicago: Rand McNally, 1969. Pp. 347–480.

KOHLBERG, L. *Stages in the development of moral thought and action*. New York: Holt, Rinehart and Winston, in press.

KONEČNI, V. Some effects of guilt on compliance: A field replication. *Journal of Personality and Social Psychology,* 1972, **23,** 30–32.

KOOCHER, G. Swimming, competence, and personality change. *Journal of Personality and Social Psychology,* 1971, **18,** 275–278.

KORTEN, F., COOK, S., and LACEY, J. (Eds.) *Psychology and the problems of society*. Washington, D.C.: American Psychological Association, 1970.

KOTHANDAPANI, V. Validation of feeling, belief, and intention to act as three components of attitude and their contribution to prediction of contraceptive behavior. *Journal of Personality and Social Psychology,* 1971, **19,** 321–333.

KOZEL, N. Perception of emotion: Race of expressor, sex of perceiver, and mode of presentation. *Proceedings of the 77th Annual Convention of the American Psychological Association,* 1969, **4**(Pt. 1), 39–40.

KOZEL, N., and GITTER, A. Perception of emotion: Differences in mode of presentation, sex of perceiver, and role of expressor. *Technical Report* No. 18, Boston University, 1968.

KRAMER, E. Judgement of personal characteristics and emotions from nonverbal properties of speech. *Psychological Bulletin,* 1963, **60,** 408–420.

KREBS, D. Empathically-experienced affect and altruism. Unpublished doctoral dissertation, Harvard University, 1970.

KRECH, D., CRUTCHFIELD, R., and BALLACHEY, E. *Individual in society: A textbook of social psychology*. New York: McGraw-Hill, 1962.

KRESGE, P. The human dimension of sex discrimination. *American Association of University Women Journal,* 1970, **64**(2), 6–9.

KRUGLANSKI, A., and YINON, Y. Threat, temptation and the magnitude of the incentive as affecting the evaluation of an immoral act. Unpublished manuscript, Tel-Aviv University, n.d.

KUPERMAN, A. Relations between differential constraints, affect, and the origin-pawn variable. Unpublished doctoral dissertation, Washington University, 1967. Cited by R. deCharms, *Personal causation: The internal affective determinants of behavior*. New York: Academic Press, 1968. P. 343.

LAING, R. *The divided self: An existential study in sanity and madness*. Baltimore: Penguin Books, 1965.

LAING, R., PHILLIPSON, H., and LEE, A. *Interpersonal perception: A theory and a method of research*. New York: Springer, 1966.

LAMALE, H. Methodology of the survey of consumer expenditures in 1950. Unpublished paper, University of Pennsylvania, 1959.

LANDIS, C. The interpretation of facial expression in emotion. *Journal of General Psychology,* 1929, **2,** 59–72.

LANSING, J., and BLOOD, D. *The changing travel market*. Monograph No. 38. Ann Arbor, Mich.: Survey Research Center, 1964.

LANZETTA, J., and DRISCOLL, J. Preference for information about an uncertain but unavoidable outcome. *Journal of Personality and Social Psychology,* 1966, **3,** 96–102.

LA PIERE, R. Type-rationalizations of group anti-play. *Social Forces,* 1936, **15,** 232–237.

LASSWELL, H. The structure and function of communication in society. In L. Bryson (Ed.), *Communication of ideas*. New York: Harper, 1948. Pp. 37–51.

LATANÉ, B. Studies in social comparison: Introduction and overview. *Journal of Experimental Social Psychology Supplement,* 1966, **1,** 1–5.

LATANÉ, B., and DARLEY, J. Group inhibition of bystander intervention in emergencies. *Journal of Personality and Social Psychology,* 1968, **10,** 215–221.

LATANÉ, B., and DARLEY, J. Bystander "apathy." *American Scientist,* 1969, **57,** 244–268.

LATANÉ, B., and RODIN, J. A lady in distress: Inhibiting effects of friends and strangers on bystander intervention. *Journal of Experimental Social Psychology,* 1969, **5,** 189–202.

609
References

LATANÉ, B., and WHEELER, L. Emotionality and reactions to disaster. *Journal of Experimental and Social Psychology Supplement,* 1966, **1,** 95–102.

LAVERY, J., and FOLEY, P. Altruism or arousal in the rat? *Science,* 1963 **140,** 172–173.

LAWRENSON, H. The feminine mistake. *Esquire,* January, 1971, pp. 82–85, 146–147, 153–154.

LAWSON, E. Hair color, personality, and the observer. *Psychological Reports,* 1971, **28,** 311–322.

LEAVITT, H. Some effects of certain communication patterns on group performance. *Journal of Abnormal and Social Psychology,* 1951, **46,** 38–50.

LE BON, G. *The crowd.* London: Unwin, 1896. (Trans. from *Psychologies des foules.* Paris: Oleon, 1895)

LE COMPTE, W., and ROSENFELD, H. Effects of minimal eye contact in the instruction period on impressions of the experimenter. *Journal of Experimental Social Psychology,* 1971, **7,** 211–220.

LEDERER, W., and JACKSON, D. *The mirages of marriage.* New York: Norton, 1968.

LEFCOURT, H., BARNES, K., PARKE, R., and SCHWARTZ, F. Anticipated social censure and aggression-conflict as mediators of response to aggression induction. *Journal of Social Psychology,* 1966, **70,** 251–263.

LELYVELD, J. How civilians get killed in Vietnam. *The New York Times,* December 16, 1969, pp. 1, 26. Quoted by E. Opton, Jr., It never happened and besides they deserved it. Page 66 in N. Sanford and C. Comstock (Eds.), *Sanctions for evil.* San Francisco: Jossey-Bass, 1971. Pp. 49–70.

LENNON, J., and McCARTNEY, P. *Eleanor Rigby.* New York: Capitol Records, 1966.

LERNER, M. The desire for justice and reactions to victims. In J. Macaulay and L. Berkowitz (Eds.), *Altruism and helping behavior: Social psychological studies of some antecendents and consequences.* New York: Academic Press, 1970. Pp. 205–229.

LEVENTHAL, H. Findings and theory in the study of fear communications. In L. Berkowitz (Ed.), *Advances in experimental social psychology.* Vol. 5. New York: Academic Press, 1970. Pp. 119–186.

LEVENTHAL, H., and NILES, P. Persistence of influence for varying durations of exposure to threat stimuli. *Psychological Reports,* 1965, **16,** 223–233.

LEVENTHAL, H., and SINGER, R. Affect arousal and positioning of recommendations in persuasive communications. *Journal of Personality and Social Psychology,* 1966, **4,** 137–146.

LEVENTHAL, H., SINGER, R., and JONES, S. The effects of fear and specificity of recommendation upon attitudes and behavior. *Journal of Personal-*

ity and Social Psychology, 1965, **2,** 20–29.

LEVINE, A. G. Marital and occupational plans of women in professional schools: Law, medicine, nursing, teaching. Unpublished doctoral dissertation, Yale University, 1968.

LEVINE, A. S. Prolonged isolation and confinement: A problem for Naval Medical Research. *Navy Magazine,* January, 1965, pp. 26–28, 44–45.

LEVINGER, G., and BREEDLOVE, J. Interpersonal attraction and agreement: A study of marriage partners. *Journal of Personality and Social Psychology,* 1966, **3,** 367–372.

LEVISON, P., and FLYNN, J. The objects attacked by cats during stimulation of the hypothalamus. *Animal Behavior,* 1965, **13,** 217–220.

LEVY, L., and HOUSE, W. Perceived origins of beliefs as determinants of expectancy for their change. *Journal of Personality and Social Psychology,* 1970, **14,** 329–334.

LEVY, P., LUNDGREN, D., ANSEL, M., FELL, D., FINK, B., and McGRATH, J. Bystander effect in a demand-without-threat situation. *Journal of Personality and Social Psychology,* 1972, **24,** 166–171.

LEWIN, K. Group decision and social change. In T. Newcomb and E. Hartley (Eds.), *Readings in social psychology.* New York: Holt, 1947. Pp. 330–344.

LEWIN, K., LIPPITT, R., and WHITE, R. Patterns of aggressive behavior in experimentally created "social climates." *Journal of Social Psychology,* 1939, **10,** 271–299.

LIEBERMAN, M., YALOM, I., and MILES, M. Encounter: The leader makes a difference. *Psychology Today,* 1973, **6**(10), 69–72, 74, 76.

LIEBHART, E. Empathy and emergency helping: The effects of personality, self-concern, and acquaintanceship. *Journal of Experimental Social Psychology,* 1972, **8,** 404–411.

LIFTON, R. "Thought reform" of western civilians in Chinese prisons. *Psychiatry,* 1956, **19,** 173–195.

LIFTON, R. *Thought reform and the psychology of totalism: A study of "brainwashing" in China.* (Paperback ed.) New York: Norton, 1963. (Originally published in 1961)

LINCOLN, A., and LEVINGER, G. Observers' evaluations of the victim and the attacker in an aggressive incident. *Journal of Personality and Social Psychology,* 1972, **22,** 202–210.

LIPPMANN, W. *Public opinion.* New York: Harcourt, Brace, 1922.

The listeners. *Time,* August 1, 1969, p. 56.

LITTLE, K. Personal space. *Journal of Experimental Social Psychology,* 1965, **1,** 237–247.

LOGAN, D. An empirical investigation of the cultural determinants of basic motivational patterns. *Dissertation Abstracts,* 1967, **27**(8-B), 2874–2875.

LOMBARDO, J., WEISS, R., and BUCHANAN, W.

Reinforcing and attracting functions of yielding. *Journal of Personality and Social Psychology,* 1972, **21,** 359–368.

LONDON, P. The rescuers: Motivational hypotheses about Christians who saved Jews from the Nazis. In J. Macaulay and L. Berkowitz (Eds.), *Altruism and helping behavior: Social psychological studies of some antecedents and consequences.* New York: Academic Press, 1970. Pp. 241–250.

LOOMIS, C., and BEEGLE, J. *Rural social systems.* New York: Prentice-Hall, 1950.

LORENZ, K. Der Kumpan in der Umvelt des Vogels. Der Artgenosse als auslösendes Moment sozialer Verhaltungsweisen. *Journal of Ornithology,* 1935, **83,** 137–213.

LORENZ, K. *On aggression.* New York: Harcourt, Brace, and World, 1966.

LOTT, A., APONTE, J., LOTT, B., and McGINLEY, W. The effect of delayed reward on the development of positive attitudes toward persons. *Journal of Experimental Social Psychology,* 1969, **5,** 101–113.

LOTT, A., and LOTT, B. Group cohesiveness, communication level, and conformity. *Journal of Abnormal and Social Psychology,* 1961, **62,** 408–412.

LOTT, A., and LOTT, B. Group cohesiveness as interpersonal attraction: A review of relationships with antecedent and consequent variables. *Psychological Bulletin,* 1965, **64,** 259–309.

LUCHINS, A. Primacy-recency in impression formation. In C. Hovland, W. Mandell, E. Campbell, T. Brock, A. Luchins, A. Cohen, W. McGuire, I. Janis, R. Feierabend, and N. Anderson, *The order of presentation in persuasion.* New Haven: Yale University Press, 1957. Pp. 33–61. (a)

LUCHINS, A. Experimental attempts to minimize the impact of first impressions. In C. Hovland, W. Mandell, E. Campbell, T. Brock, A. Luchins, A. Cohen, W. McGuire, I. Janis, R. Feierabend, and N. Anderson, *The order of presentation in persuasion.* New Haven: Yale University Press, 1957. Pp. 62–75. (b)

LUCHINS, A., and LUCHINS, E. The effects of order of presentation of information and explanatory models. *Journal of Social Psychology,* 1970, **80,** 63–70.

LULL, P. The effectiveness of humor in persuasive speeches. *Speech Monographs,* 1940, **7,** 26–40.

LUMSDAINE, A., and JANIS, I. Resistance to "counter-propaganda" produced by one-sided and two-sided "propaganda" presentations. *The Public Opinion Quarterly,* 1953, **17,** 311–318.

LUNDY, R. Self perceptions regarding masculinity-femininity and descriptions of same and opposite sex sociometric choices. *Sociometry,* 1958, **21,** 238–246.

LUTHER, R. Sensitivity training panel of the 1967 meeting of the Personnel Association of Southern California. Transcript, quoted on p. 221 in K. Back, *Beyond words: The story of sensitivity training and the encounter movement.* New York: Russell Sage Foundation, 1972.

MACAULAY, J. A shill for charity. In J. Macaulay and L. Berkowitz (Eds.), *Altruism and helping behavior: Social psychological studies of some antecedents and consequences.* New York: Academic Press, 1970. Pp. 43–59.

MACCOBY, N., ROMNEY, A., ADAMS, J., and MACCOBY, E. "Critical periods" in seeking and accepting information. Stanford, Calif.: Institute for Communication Research, 1962. Summarized in L. Festinger, Behavioral support for opinion change. *The Public Opinion Quarterly,* 1964, **28,** 404–417.

MACHIAVELLI, N. *The prince* (Trans. by Luigi Ricci). New York: Oxford University Press, 1906. (Originally published 1532)

MADDI, S. *Personality theories: A comparative analysis.* Homewood, Ill.: The Dorsey Press, 1968.

MADISON, P. *Personality development in college.* Reading, Mass.: Addison-Wesley, 1969.

MAEROFF, G. The fight for a fair shake on campus. *The New York Times,* October 8, 1972, The News of the Week in Review, p. 10.

MALAMUTH, N., and FESHBACH, S. Risky shift in a naturalistic setting. *Journal of Personality,* 1972, **40,** 38–49.

MALIVER, B. Anti-Negro bias among Negro college students. *Journal of Personality and Social Psychology,* 1965, **2,** 770–775.

MANDELBAUM, D. *Soldier groups and Negro soldiers.* Berkeley: University of California Press, 1952.

MANN, F., and BAUMGARTEL, H. *Absences and employee attitudes in an electric power company.* Ann Arbor, Mich.: Institute for Social Research, 1952.

MANN, L. Effects of a commitment warning on children's decision behavior. *Journal of Personality and Social Psychology,* 1971, **17,** 74–80.

MANN, L., and JANIS, I. A follow-up study on the long-term effects on emotional role playing. *Journal of Personality and Social Psychology,* 1968, **8,** 339–342.

MANN, L., ROSENTHAL, R., and ABELES, R. Early election returns and the voting behavior of adolescent voters. *Journal of Applied Social Psychology,* 1971, **1,** 66–75.

MANN, L., and TAYLOR, V. The effects of commitment and choice difficulty on pre-decision processes. *Journal of Social Psychology,* 1970, **82,** 221–230.

MANN, R. A review of the relationship between personality and performance in small groups. *Psychological Bulletin,* 1959, **56,** 241–270.

MANN, R., GIBBARD, S., and HARTMAN, J. *Interpersonal styles and group development.* New York: Wiley, 1967.

MANNHEIM, B. Reference groups, membership group and the self image. *Sociometry,* 1966, **29,** 265–279.

MANZ, W., and LUECK, H. Influence of wearing glasses on personality ratings: Cross-cultural validation of an old experiment. *Perceptual and Motor Skills,* 1968, **27**(3, Pt. 1), 704.

MARGOLIS, C. The black student in political strife. *Proceedings of the 79th Annual Convention of the American Psychological Association,* 1971, **6,** 395–396.

MARLOWE, D., GERGEN, K., and DOOB, A. Opponent's personality, expectation of social interaction, and interpersonal bargaining. *Journal of Personality and Social Psychology,* 1966, **3,** 206–213.

MARQUIS, D., GUETZKOW, H., and HEYNS, R. A social psychological study of the decision-making conference. In H. Guetzkow (Ed.), *Groups, leadership and men.* Pittsburgh: Carnegie Press, 1951. Pp. 55–67.

MARSHALL, S. *Men against fire.* Washington, D.C.: Combat Forces Press, 1951.

MARTENS, R., and LANDERS, D. Evaluation potential as a determinant of coaction effects. *Journal of Experimental Social Psychology,* 1972, **8,** 347–359.

MARTIN, J., and WESTIE, F. The tolerant personality. *American Sociological Review,* 1959, **24,** 521–528.

MARTINDALE, D. Territorial dominance behavior in dyadic verbal interactions. *Proceedings of the 79th Annual Convention of the American Psychological Association,* 1971, 305–306.

MASLACH, C. The "truth" about false confessions. *Journal of Personality and Social Psychology,* 1971, **20,** 141–146.

MASLACH, C. Social and personal bases of individuation. *Proceedings of the 80th Annual Convention of the American Psychological Association,* 1972, 213–214.

MASLING, J. Birth order and the need for affiliation. *Psychological Reports,* 1965, **16,** 631–632.

MASLOW, A. *Motivation and personality.* New York: Harper and Row, 1954.

MASLOW, A. Peak experiences as acute identity-experiences. *American Journal of Psychoanalysis,* 1961, **21,** 254–260.

MASLOW, A. *Toward a psychology of being.* New York: Van Nostrand, 1962.

MASLOW, A. *Farther reaches of human nature.* Esalen Institute Book-Publishing Program. New York: Viking Press, 1971. Quoted in a book review by J. Bugental, *Psychology Today,* 1972, **5**(11), 18.

MATHEWS, V., and MIHANOVICH, C. New orientations on marital maladjustment. *Marriage and Family Living,* 1963, **25,** 300–304.

MATTHEWS, E., and TIEDEMAN, D. Attitudes toward career and marriage in the development of life styles of young women. *Journal of Counseling Psychology,* 1964, **11,** 375–384.

MAYNARD, J. The embarrassment of virginity. *Mademoiselle,* August, 1972, pp. 258–259, 411.

MAZLISH, B. Psychohistory and Richard Nixon. *Psychology Today,* 1972, **6**(2), 77–80, 90.

McARTHUR, L., KIESLER, C., and COOK, B. Acting on an attitude as a function of self-percept and inequity. *Journal of Personality and Social Psychology,* 1969, **12,** 295–302.

McCALL, G., McCALL, M., DENZIN, N., SUTTLES, G., and KURTH, S. *Social relationships.* Chicago: Aldine, 1970.

McCLELLAND, D. Methods of measuring human motivation. In J. Atkinson (Ed.), *Motives in fantasy, action, and society.* New York: Van Nostrand, 1958. Pp. 7–42.

McCLELLAND, D., ATKINSON, J., CLARK, R., and LOWELL, E. *The achievement motive.* New York: Appleton-Century-Crofts, 1953.

McCLINTOCK, C. Personality factors in attitude change. *Dissertation Abstracts,* 1958, **18,** 1865.

McCROSKEY, J., LARSON, C., and KNAPP, M. *An introduction to interpersonal communication.* Englewood Cliffs, N.J.: Prentice-Hall, 1971.

McGHEE, P., and TEEVAN, R. Conformity behavior and need for affiliation. *Journal of Social Psychology,* 1967, **72,** 117–121.

McGINNIES, E. Studies in persuasion: III. Reactions of Japanese students to one-sided and two-sided communications. *Journal of Social Psychology,* 1966, **70,** 87–93.

McGINNISS, J. *The selling of the President 1968.* New York: Pocket Books, 1970.

McGRATH, J., and ALTMAN, I. *Small group research.* New York: Holt, 1966.

McGREW, W. Group density and children's behavior. Unpublished paper. Cited by J. Freedman, A. Levy, R. Buchanan, and J. Price, Crowding and human aggressiveness. *Journal of Experimental Social Psychology,* 1972, **8,** 528–548.

McGUIRE, W. Order of presentation as a factor in "conditioning" persuasiveness. In C. Hovland (Ed.), *Order of presentation in persuasion.* New Haven: Yale University Press, 1957. Pp. 98–114.

McGUIRE, W. Some impending reorientations in social psychology: Some thoughts provoked by Kenneth Ring. *Journal of Experimental Social Psychology,* 1967, **3,** 124–139.

McGUIRE, W. Theory of the structure of human thought. In R. Abelson, E. Aronson, W. McGuire, T. Newcomb, M. Rosenberg, and P. Tannenbaum (Eds.), *Theories of cognitive consistency: A sourcebook.* Chicago: Rand McNally, 1968. Pp. 140–162.

McGUIRE, W. The nature of attitudes and attitude change. In G. Lindzey and E. Aronson (Eds.), *The handbook of social psychology.* (2nd ed.) Vol. III. *The individual in a social context.* Reading, Mass.: Addison-Wesley, 1969. Pp. 136–314. (a)

McGUIRE, W. Suspiciousness of experimenter's intent. In R. Rosenthal and R. Rosnow (Eds.), *Artifact in behavioral research.* New York: Academic Press, 1969. Pp. 13–57. (b)

McGUIRE, W., and MILLMAN, S. Anticipatory belief lowering following forewarning of a persuasive attack. *Journal of Personality and Social Psychology,* 1965, **2,** 471–479.

McGUIRE, W., and PAPAGEORGIS, D. The relative efficacy of various types of prior belief-defense in producing immunity against persuasion. *Journal of Abnormal and Social Psychology,* 1961, **62,** 327–337.

McINTYRE, A. Social comparison and dependency as motives for affiliation in an anxiety-arousing situation. *Dissertation Abstracts International,* 1971, **32**(1-B), 542.

McKEACHIE, W. Lipstick as a determiner of first impressions of personality. *Journal of Social Psychology,* 1952, **36,** 241–244.

McKUEN, R. *Stranyan Street and other sorrows.* New York: Random House, 1970.

McLUHAN, M., and FIORE, Q. *The medium is the message.* New York: Bantam, 1967.

MEAD, G. The genesis of the self and social control. *International Journal of Ethics,* 1925, **35,** 251–273.

MEAD, G. *Mind, self, and society: From the standpoint of a social behaviorist.* Chicago: University of Chicago Press, 1934.

MEAD, M. *Sex and temperament in three primitive societies.* New York: Morrow, 1935.

MEHRABIAN, A. Orientation behaviors and nonverbal attitude communication. *Journal of Communication,* 1967, **17,** 324–332.

MEHRABIAN, A. Inference of attitude from the posture, orientation, and distance of a communicator. *Journal of Consulting and Clinical Psychology,* 1968, **32,** 296–308.

MEHRABIAN, A. *Nonverbal communication.* Chicago: Aldine-Atherton, 1972.

MEHRABIAN, A., and DIAMOND, S. Effects of furniture arrangement, props, and personality on social interaction. *Journal of Personality and Social Psychology,* 1971, **20,** 18–30.

MEHRABIAN, A., and FRIAR, J. Encoding of attitude by a seated communicator via posture and position cues. *Journal of Consulting and Clinical Psychology,* 1969, **33,** 330–336.

MEHRABIAN, A., and WILLIAMS, M. Nonverbal concomitants of perceived and intended persuasiveness. *Journal of Personality and Social Psychology,* 1969, **13,** 37–58.

MENZEL, H. Public and private conformity under different conditions of acceptance in the group. *Journal of Abnormal and Social Psychology,* 1957, **55,** 398–401.

MEREI, F. Group leadership and institutionalization. *Human Relations,* 1949, **2,** 23–29.

MERTON, R. Bureaucratic structure and personality. *Social Forces,* 1940, **57,** 560–568.

MERTON, R. *Social theory and social structure.* (Rev. ed.) Glencoe, Ill.: Free Press, 1957.

METTEE, D. Rejection of unexpected success as a function of the negative consequences of accepting success. *Journal of Personality and Social Psychology,* 1971, **17,** 332–341.

METTEE, D., and WILKINS, P. When similarity "hurts": Effects of perceived ability and a humorous blunder on interpersonal attractiveness. *Journal of Personality and Social Psychology,* 1972, **22,** 246–258.

MEYER, T. Effects of viewing justified and unjustified real film violence on aggressive behavior. *Journal of Personality and Social Psychology,* 1972, **23,** 21–29.

MEZEI, L. Perceived social pressure as an explanation of shifts in the relative influence of race and belief on prejudice across social interactions. *Journal of Personality and Social Psychology,* 1971, **19,** 69–81.

MICHENER, H., and LAWLER, E. Revolutionary coalition strength and collective failure as determinants of status reallocation. *Journal of Experimental Social Psychology,* 1971, **7,** 448–460.

MIDDLEBROOK, P. Love ten years later. Unpublished paper, Central Connecticut State College, 1972.

MIDDLETON, M. Ex con. *Christian Science Monitor Series.* In P. Zimbardo, C. Haney, W. Banks, and D. Jaffe, The psychology of imprisonment: Privation, power, and pathology. Unpublished paper, Stanford University, 1972.

MILGRAM, S. Behavioral study of obedience. *Journal of Abnormal and Social Psychology,* 1963, **67,** 371–378.

MILGRAM, S. Issues in the study of obedience: A reply to Baumrind. *American Psychologist,* 1964, **19,** 848–852.

MILGRAM, S. Liberating effects of group pressure. *Journal of Personality and Social Psychology,* 1965, **1,** 127–134. (a)

MILGRAM, S. Some conditions of obedience and disobedience to authority. *Human Relations,* 1965, **18,** 57–76. (b)

MILGRAM, S. The experience of living in cities. *Science,* 1970, **167,** 1461–1468.

MILGRAM, S., and SHOTLAND, R. *Television and anti-social behavior: Field experiments.* New York: Academic Press, 1973.

MILLER, A. Role playing: An alternative to deception? A review of the evidence. *American Psychologist,* 1972, **27,** 623–636.

MILLER, N., and BUGELSKI, R. Minor studies of aggression: II. The influence of frustrations imposed by the in-group on attitudes expressed toward out-groups. *Journal of Psychology,* 1948, **25,** 437–452.

MILLER, N., and CAMPBELL, D. Recency and primacy in persuasion as a function of the timing of speeches and measurements. *Journal of Abnormal and Social Psychology,* 1959, **59,** 1–9.

MILLER, N., and ZIMBARDO, P. Motives for fear-induced affiliation: Emotional comparison or interpersonal similarity? *Journal of Personality,* 1966, **34,** 481–503.

MILLETT, K. *Sexual politics.* New York: Doubleday, 1970.

MILLS, D., and ABELES, N. Counselor needs for affiliation and nurturance as related to liking for clients and counseling process. *Journal of Counseling Psychology,* 1965, **12,** 353–358.

MILLS, J., and JELLISON, J. Effect on opinion change of how desirable the communication is to the audience the communicator addressed. *Journal of Personality and Social Psychology,* 1967, **6,** 98–101.

MILLS, J., and MINTZ, P. Effect of unexplained arousal on affiliation. *Journal of Personality and Social Psychology,* 1972, **24,** 11–13.

MINAS, J., SCODEL, A., MARLOWE, D., and RAWSON, H. Some descriptive aspects of two-person non-zero-sum games, II. *Journal of Conflict Resolution,* 1960, **4,** 193–197.

MINOR, M. Experimenter-expectancy effect as a function of evaluation apprehension. *Journal of Personality and Social Psychology,* 1970, **15,** 326–332.

Minorities in social studies textbooks: NAACP unit issues new multi-racial history syllabus. *Negro History Bulletin,* 1970, **33,** 167.

MISUMI, J., TAKEDA, T., and SEKI, F. An empirical study of the effects of managerial and supervisory behavior of PM pattern on productivity and morale, particularly need for achievement, in a hierarchical organization. *Japanese Journal of Educational and Social Psychology,* 1967, **1,** 27–42.

MIYAMOTO, S., and DORNBUSCH, S. A test of interactionist hypotheses of self conception. *American Journal of Sociology,* 1956, **61,** 399–403.

MODIGLIANI, ANDRE. Embarrassment, facework, and eye contact: Testing a theory of embarrassment. *Journal of Personality and Social Psychology,* 1971, **17,** 15–29.

MOORE, J. Loneliness: Personality, self-discrepancy, and demographic variables. Unpublished doctoral dissertation, York University, Toronto, Canada, April, 1972.

MOREHOUS, L. One-play, two-play, five-play, ten-play runs of prisoner's dilemma. *Journal of Conflict Resolution,* 1966, **10,** 354–362.

MORENO, J. *Who shall survive?* (2nd ed.) Beacon, N. Y.: Beacon House, 1953.

MORLAND, J. A comparison of race awareness in northern and southern children. In M. GoldSchmid (Ed.), *Black Americans and white racism: Theory and research.* New York: Holt, Rinehart and Winston, 1970. Pp. 25–32.

MORRIS, C., and HACKMAN, J. Behavioral correlates of perceived leadership. *Journal of Personality and Social Psychology,* 1969, **13,** 350–361.

MORSE, S. Help, likeability, and social influence. *Journal of Applied Social Psychology,* 1972, **2,** 34–46.

MORSE, S., and GERGEN, K. Social comparison, self-consistency, and the concept of self. *Journal of Personality and Social Psychology,* 1970, **16,** 148–156.

MOSCOVICI, S., and FAUCHEUX, C. Social influence, conformity bias, and the study of active minorities. In L. Berkowitz (Ed.), *Advances in experimental social psychology.* Vol. 6. New York: Academic Press, 1972. Pp. 150–202.

MULDER, M., and STEMERDING, A. Threat, attraction to group and need for strong leadership. *Human Relations,* 1963, **16,** 317–334.

MUNN, N. The effect of knowledge of the situation upon judgement of emotion from facial expressions. *Journal of Abnormal and Social Psychology,* 1940, **35,** 324–338.

MURSTEIN, B. A theory of marital choice and its applicability to marriage adjustment. In B. Murstein (Ed.), *Theories of attraction and love.* New York: Springer, 1971. Pp. 100–151.

MURSTEIN, B. Physical attractiveness and marital choice. *Journal of Personality and Social Psychology,* 1972, **22,** 8–12.

MURTAGH, J., and HARRIS, S. *Cast the first stone.* New York: Pocket Books, 1958.

NATIONAL COMMISSION ON MARIHUANA AND DRUG ABUSE. *Marihuana: A signal of misunderstanding. The official report.* New York: The New American Library, 1972.

NATIONAL COMMISSION ON THE CAUSES AND

PREVENTION OF VIOLENCE. *To establish justice, insure domestic tranquility: The final report.* New York: Praeger, 1970.

NAVRAN, L. Communication and adjustment in marriage. *Family Process,* 1967, **6,** 173–184.

Negro in America. *Newsweek,* November 20, 1967, pp. 32–65.

NESBITT, P. The effectiveness of student canvassers. *Journal of Applied Social Psychology,* 1972, **2,** 252–258.

NEUMANN, S. Unpublished study. Cited by L. Berkowitz, Factors affecting helping and altruism, p. 84. In L. Berkowitz (Ed.), *Advances in experimental social psychology.* Vol. 6. New York: Academic Press, 1972. Pp. 63–108.

The new talk jockeys. *Time,* May 22, 1972, p. 79.

NEWCOMB, T. *Personality and social change.* New York: Dryden, 1943.

NEWCOMB, T., KOENIG, K., FLACKS, R., and WARWICK, D. *Persistence and change: Bennington College and its students after 25 years.* New York: Wiley, 1967.

The New York Times Encyclopedic Almanac 1971. Edited by L. Foster and M. Harth. New York: *The New York Times,* 1970.

The New York Times Encyclopedic Almanac 1972. Edited by M. Harth and T. Bernstein. New York: *The New York Times,* 1971.

NEWMAN, O. *Defensible space: Crime prevention through urban design.* New York: Macmillan, 1972.

NIEBURG, H. *Political violence: The behavioral process.* New York: St. Martin's Press, 1969.

NIERENBERG, G. *The art of negotiating.* New York: Hawthorn Books, 1968.

NIERENBERG, G., and CALERO, H. *How to read a person like a book.* New York: Hawthorn Books, 1971.

NIETZSCHE, F. *The birth of tragedy.* New York: Doubleday, 1956. (Originally published 1872)

NILES, P. The relationships of susceptibility and anxiety to acceptance of fear-arousing communications. Unpublished doctoral dissertation, Yale University, 1964.

NISBETT, R., LEGANT, P., and MARECEK, J. The causes of behavior as seen by actor and observer. Unpublished manuscript, Yale University, 1971. Cited by E. Jones and R. Nisbett, *The actor and the observer: Divergent perceptions of the causes of behavior.* New York: General Learning Press, 1971. P. 5.

NISBETT, R., and Schachter, S. Cognitive manipulation of pain. *Journal of Experimental Social Psychology,* 1966, **2,** 227–236.

NISSEN, H., and CRAWFORD, M. A preliminary study of food-sharing behavior in young chimpanzees.

Journal of Comparative Psychology, 1936, **22,** 383–419.

NIZER, L. *My life in court.* New York: Pyramid, 1961.

NORD, W. Social exchange theory: An integrative approach to social conformity. *Psychological Bulletin,* 1969, **71,** 174–208.

NOVACK, D., and LERNER, M. Rejection as a consequence of perceived similarity. *Journal of Personality and Social Psychology,* 1968, **9,** 147–152.

OAKES, W. External validity and the use of real people as subjects. *American Psychologist,* 1972, **27,** 959–962.

O'DELL, J. Group size and emotional interaction. *Journal of Personality and Social Psychology,* 1968, **8,** 75–78.

O'NEILL, E. *The iceman cometh.* New York: Random House, 1940. Cited by H. Fingarette, *Self-deception.* London: Routledge and Kegan Paul, 1969.

O'NEILL, N., and O'NEILL, G. *Open marriage: A new life style for couples.* New York: M. Evans, 1972.

OPTON, E., Jr. "It never happened and besides they deserved it." In N. Sanford and C. Comstock (Eds.), *Sanctions for evil.* San Francisco: Jossey-Bass, 1971. Pp. 49–70.

ORBACH, J., TRAUB, A., and OLSON, R. Psychophysical studies of body image: II. Normative data on the adjustable body-distorting mirror. *Archives of General Psychiatry,* 1966, **4,** 41–47.

ORNE, M. On the social psychology of the psychological experiment: With particular reference to demand characteristics and their implications. *American Psychologist,* 1962, **17,** 776–783.

ORSO, D. Comparison of achievement and affiliation arousal on nAch. *Journal of Projective Techniques and Personality Assessment,* 1969, **33,** 230–233.

OSGOOD, C. *An alternative to war or surrender.* Urbana: University of Illinois Press, 1962.

OSKAMP, S., and KLEINKE, C. Amount of reward in a variable in the prisoner's dilemma game. *Journal of Personality and Social Psychology,* 1970, **16,** 133–140.

OSTERHOUSE, R., and BROCK, T. Distraction increases yielding to propaganda by inhibiting counterarguing. *Journal of Personality and Social Psychology,* 1970, **15,** 344–358.

OSTROM, T. The relationship between the affective, behavioral and cognitive components of attitude. *Journal of Experimental Social Psychology,* 1969, **5,** 12–30.

OTTO, H. Communes: The alternative life-style. *Saturday Review,* 1971, **54,** 16–21.

OWENS, J. *Blackthink: My life as black man and white man.* New York: Pocket Books, 1971.

PACKARD, V. *The hidden persuaders.* New York: McKay, 1957.

PACKARD, V. *A nation of strangers.* New York: McKay, 1972.

PAGE, M. Modification of figure-ground perception as a function of awareness of demand characteristics. *Journal of Personality and Social Psychology,* 1968, **9,** 59–66.

PALLAK, M., and HELLER, J. Interactive effects of commitment to future interaction and threat to attitudinal freedom. *Journal of Personality and Social Psychology,* 1971, **17,** 325–331.

PALLAK, M., MUELLER, M., DOLLAR, K., and PALLAK, J. Effect of commitment on responsiveness to an extreme consonant communication. *Journal of Personality and Social Psychology,* 1972, **23,** 429–436.

PAPAGEORGIS, D., and McGUIRE, W. The generality of immunity to persuasion produced by pre-exposure to weakened counterarguments. *Journal of Abnormal and Social Psychology,* 1961, **62,** 475–481.

PARKE, R., EWALL, W., and SLABY, R. Hostile and helpful verbalizations as regulators of nonverbal aggression. *Journal of Personality and Social Psychology,* 1972, **23,** 243–248.

PARRY, H., and Crossley, H. Validity of responses to survey questions. *The Public Opinion Quarterly,* 1950, **14,** 61–80.

PARSONS, T., and BALES, R. *Family socialization and interaction process.* Glencoe, Ill.: Free Press, 1955.

PAULUS, P., and MURDOCH, P. Anticipated evaluation and audience presence in the enhancement of dominant responses. *Journal of Experimental Social Psychology,* 1971, **7,** 280–291.

PEARSON, K., and LEE, A. On the laws of inheritance in man: I. Inheritance of physical characters. *Biometrika,* 1903, **2,** 357–462.

PELZ, D. Leadership within a hierarchical organization. *The Journal of Social Issues,* 1951, **7,** 49–55.

PEPITONE, A. An experimental analysis of self dynamics. In C. Gordon and K. Gergen (Eds.), *The self in social interaction.* New York: Wiley, 1968. Pp. 347–354.

PEPITONE, A., and REICHLING, G. Group cohesiveness and the expression of hostility. *Human Relations,* 1955, **8,** 327–337.

PESSIN, J. The comparative effects of social and mechanical stimulation on memorizing. *American Journal of Psychology,* 1933, **45,** 263–270.

PETERS, C., and ADAMS, T. *Inside the system: A Washington monthly reader.* New York: Praeger, 1970.

PETERS, R. Primary friendships in the college community: A study of the association of male students. *Dissertation Abstracts International,* 1969, **29**(7-A), 2359.

PETERSON, P., and KOULACK, D. Attitude change as a function of latitudes of acceptance and rejection. *Journal of Personality and Social Psychology,* 1969, **11,** 309–311.

PETTIGREW, T. Regional differences in anti-Negro prejudice. *Journal of Abnormal and Social Psychology,* 1959, **59,** 28–36.

PETTIGREW, T. Social evaluation theory: Convergences and applications. In D. Levine (Ed.), *Nebraska Symposium on Motivation,* 1967, **15,** 241–311.

PETTIGREW, T. Race relations. In R. Merton and R. Nisbet (Eds.), *Contemporary social problems.* New York: Harcourt Brace Jovanovich, 1971. Pp. 407–466.

PHARES, E. Differential utilization of information as a function of internal-external control. *Journal of Personality,* 1968, **36,** 649–662.

PHILLIS, J. Children's judgments of personality on the basis of voice quality. *Developmental Psychology,* 1970, **3**(3, Pt. 1), 411.

PILIAVIN, I., RODIN, J., and PILIAVIN, J. Good samaritanism: An underground phenomenon? *Journal of Personality and Social Psychology,* 1969, **13,** 289–299.

PILIAVIN, J., and PILIAVIN, I. Effects of blood on reactions to a victim. *Journal of Personality and Social Psychology,* 1972, **23,** 353–361.

Political pulse-taking: How the pollsters do it. *U. S. News and World Report,* October 16, 1972, p. 26.

PORIER, G., and LOTT, A. Galvanic skin responses and prejudice. *Journal of Personality and Social Psychology,* 1967, **5,** 253–259.

PORTER, L., and LAWLER, E., III. Properties of organization structure in relation to job attitudes and job behavior. *Psychological Bulletin,* 1965, **64,** 23–51.

POSAVAC, E. Dimensions of trait preferences and personality type. *Journal of Personality and Social Psychology,* 1971, **19,** 274–281.

PRICE, J. The effects of crowding on the social behavior of children. Unpublished doctoral dissertation, Columbia University, 1971.

PRITCHETT, V. *New York proclaimed.* New York: Harcourt, Brace, and World, 1964.

PROSHANSKY, H., ITTELSON, W., and RIVLIN, L. Freedom of choice and behavior in a physical setting. In H. Proshansky, W. Ittelson, and L. Rivlin (Eds.), *Environmental psychology: Man and his physical setting.* New York: Holt, Rinehart and Winston, 1970. Pp. 173–183.

PROVENCE, S., and LIPTON, R. *Infants in institutions.* New York: International Universities Press, 1962.

PRUITT, D. Reciprocity and credit building in a laboratory dyad. *Journal of Personality and So-*

cial Psychology, 1968, **8,** 143–147.

PRUITT, D., and DREWS, J. The effects of time pressure, time elapse, and the opponent's concession rate on behavior in negotiation. Journal of Experimental Social Psychology, 1969, **5,** 43–60.

QUARANTELLI, E., and DYNES, R. When disaster strikes. Psychology Today, 1972, **5**(9), 66–70.

RABBIE, J. Differential preference for companionship under stress. Journal of Abnormal and Social Psychology, 1963, **67,** 643–648.

RABBIE, J., and HORWITZ, M. Arousal of Ingroup-outgroup bias by a chance win or loss. Journal of Personality and Social Psychology, 1969, **13,** 269–277.

RADKE-YARROW, M., and LANDE, B. Personality correlates of differential reactions to minority groups belonging. Journal of Social Psychology, 1953, **38,** 253–272.

RADLOFF, R. Opinion and affiliation. Unpublished doctoral dissertation, University of Minnesota, 1959.

RAPOPORT, A., and CHAMMAH, A. Sex differences in factors contributing to the level of cooperation in the prisoner's dilemma game. Journal of Personality and Social Psychology, 1965, **2,** 831–838.

RAVEN, B., and FRENCH, J. Legitimate power, coercive power, and observability in social influence. Sociometry, 1958, **21,** 83–97.

RAWLINGS, E. Reactive guilt and anticipatory guilt in altruistic behavior. In J. Macaulay and L. Berkowitz (Eds.), Altruism and helping behavior: Some social psychological studies of some antecedents and consequences. New York: Academic Press, 1970. Pp. 163–177.

RAZRAN, G. Conditioned response changes in rating and appraising sociopolitical slogans. Psychological Bulletin, 1940, **37,** 481.

REEDER, L., DONOHUE, G., and BIBLARZ, A. Conceptions of self and others. American Journal of Sociology, 1960, **66,** 153–159.

REGAN, D., WILLIAMS, M., and SPARLING, S. Voluntary expiation of guilt: A field experiment. Journal of Personality and Social Psychology, 1972, **24,** 42–45.

REGAN, J. Guilt, perceived injustice, and altruistic behavior. Journal of Personality and Social Psychology, 1971, **18,** 124–132.

REID, E. Mafia. New York: The New American Library, Inc., 1952. Cited on p. 109 by H. Nieburg, Political violence: The behavioral process. New York: St. Martin's Press, 1969.

REIK, T. Masochism in modern man. New York: Farrar, Strauss, 1941.

REYNOLDS, G. A primer of operant conditioning. Glenview, Ill.: Scott, Foresman, 1968.

RHINE, R., and SEVERANCE, L. Ego-involvement, discrepancy, source credibility, and attitude change. Journal of Personality and Social Psychology, 1970, **16,** 175–190.

RICE, G., and GAINER, P. "Altruism" in the albino rat. Journal of Comparative and Physiological Psychology, 1962, **55,** 123–125.

RICHARDSON, H. Studies of mental resemblance between husbands and wives and between friends. Psychological Bulletin, 1939, **36,** 104–120.

RIESMAN, D. The lonely crowd. New Haven: Yale University Press, 1950.

RING, K. Some determinants of interpersonal attraction in hierarchical relationships: A motivational analysis. Journal of Personality, 1964, **32,** 651–665.

RING, K. Experimental social psychology: Some sober questions about some frivolous values. Journal of Experimental Social Psychology, 1967, **3,** 113–123.

ROBERTS, A., and ROKEACH, M. Anomie, authoritarianism, and prejudice: A replication. American Journal of Sociology, 1956, **61,** 355–358.

ROETHLISBERGER, F., and DICKSON, W. Management and the worker. Cambridge: Harvard University Press, 1939.

ROGERS, C. Interpersonal relationships U. S. A. 2000. Journal of Applied Behavioral Science, 1968, **4,** 268–269.

ROGERS, C. Carl Rogers on encounter groups. New York: Harper, 1970.

ROGERS, R., and THISTLETHWAITE, D. An analysis of active and passive defenses in inducing resistance to persuasion. Journal of Personality and Social Psychology, 1969, **11,** 301–308.

ROHRER, J., BARON, S., HOFFMAN, E., and SWANDER, D. The stability of autokinetic judgments. Journal of Abnormal and Social Psychology, 1954, **49,** 595–597.

ROKEACH, M. The open and closed mind: Investigations into the nature of belief systems and personality systems. New York: Basic Books, 1960.

ROKEACH, M. Long-range experimental modification of values, attitudes, and behavior. American Psychologist, 1971, **26,** 453–459.

ROKEACH, M., and KLIEJUNAS, P. Behavior as a function of attitude-toward-object and attitude-toward-situation. Journal of Personality and Social Psychology, 1972, **22,** 194–201.

ROKEACH, M., and MEZEI, L. Race and shared belief as factors in social choice. Science, 1966, **151,** 167–172.

ROKEACH, M., and ROTHMAN, G. The principle of belief congruence and the congruity principle as models of cognitive interaction. *Psychological Review,* 1965, **72,** 128–142.

ROLL, S., and VERINIS, J. Stereotypes of scalp and facial hair as measured by the semantic differential. *Psychological Reports,* 1971, **28,** 975–980.

ROSE, A. Generalizations in the social sciences. *American Journal of Sociology,* 1953, **59,** 49–58.

ROSE, P. Student opinion on the 1956 presidential election. *The Public Opinion Quarterly,* 1957, **21,** 371–376.

ROSEN, B., and EINHORN, H. Attractiveness of the "middle of the road" political candidate. *Journal of Applied Social Psychology,* 1972, **2,** 157–165.

ROSENBAUM, M., and LEVIN, I. Impression formation as a function of the relative amounts of information presented by high and low credibility sources. *Psychonomic Science,* 1968, **12**(8), 349–350.

ROSENBERG, M. Cognitive reorganization in response to the hypnotic reversal of attitudinal effect. *Journal of Personality,* 1960, **28,** 39–63.

ROSENBERG, M. When dissonance fails: On eliminating evaluation apprehension from attitude measurement. *Journal of Personality and Social Psychology,* 1965, **1,** 28–42.

ROSENBERG, M. Psychological selectivity in self-esteem formation. In C. Gordon and K. Gergen (Eds.), *The self in social interaction.* New York: Wiley, 1968. Pp. 339–346.

ROSENBERG, M. The conditions and consequences of evaluation apprehension. In R. Rosenthal and R. Rosnow (Eds.), *Artifact in behavioral research.* New York: Academic Press, 1969. Pp. 279–349.

ROSENFELD, H. Effect of an approval-seeking induction on interpersonal proximity. *Psychological Reports,* 1965, **17,** 120–122.

ROSENFELD, H. Relationships of ordinal position to affiliation and achievement motives: Direction and generality. *Journal of Personality,* 1966, **34,** 467–479.

ROSENHAN, D. Some origins of concern for others. In P. Mussen, J. Langer, and M. Covington (Eds.), *Trends and issues in developmental psychology.* New York: Holt, Rinehart and Winston, 1969.

ROSENHAN, D. The natural socialization of altruistic autonomy. In J. Macaulay and L. Berkowitz (Eds.), *Altruism and helping behavior: Social psychological studies of some antecedents and consequences.* New York: Academic Press, 1970. Pp. 251–268.

ROSENKRANTZ, P., and CROCKETT, W. Some factors influencing the assimilation of disparate information in impression formation. *Journal of Personality and Social Psychology,* 1965, **2,** 397–402.

ROSENTHAL, A. *Thirty-eight witnesses.* New York: McGraw-Hill, 1964.

ROSENTHAL, R. The volunteer subject. *Human Relations,* 1965, **18,** 389–406.

ROSENTHAL, R. *Experimenter effects in behavioral research.* New York: Appleton-Century-Crofts, 1966.

ROSENTHAL, R., and FODE, K. The effect of experimental bias on the performance of the albino rat. *Behavioral Science,* 1963, **8,** 183–189.

ROSENTHAL, R., and JACOBSON, L. *Pygmalion in the classroom: Teacher expectation and pupils' intellectual development.* New York: Holt, Rinehart and Winston, 1968.

ROSENTHAL, R., PERSINGER, G., MULRY, R., VIKAN-KLINE, L., and GROTHE, M. Emphasis on experimental procedure, sex of subjects, and the biasing effects of experimental hypotheses. *Journal of Projective Techniques and Personality Assessment,* 1964, **28,** 470–473.

ROSNOW, R., and ROBINSON, E. "Channel." In R. Rosnow and E. Robinson (Eds.), *Experiments in persuasion.* New York: Academic Press, 1967. Pp. 369–378.

ROSS, L., RODIN, J., and ZIMBARDO, P. Toward an attribution therapy: The reduction of fear through induced cognitive-emotional misattribution. *Journal of Personality and Social Psychology,* 1969, **12,** 279–288.

ROSSI, A. Status of women in graduate departments of sociology: 1968–1969. *American Sociologist,* 1970, **5,** 1–12.

ROTTER, J. Generalized expectancies for internal versus external control of reinforcement. *Psychological Monographs,* 1966, **80**(1, Whole No. 609).

ROTTER, J., and STEIN, D. Public attitudes toward the trustworthiness, competence, and altruism of twenty selected occupations. *Journal of Applied Social Psychology,* 1971, **1,** 334–343.

ROYKO, M. *Boss: Richard J. Daley of Chicago.* New York: Dutton, 1971.

RUBIN, I. Increased self-acceptance: A means of reducing prejudice. *Journal of Personality and Social Psychology,* 1967, **5,** 233–238.

RUBIN, Z. *Liking and loving: An invitation to social psychology.* New York: Holt, Rinehart and Winston, 1973.

RUBIN, Z., and MOORE, J., Jr. Assessment of subjects' suspicions. *Journal of Personality and Social Psychology,* 1971, **17,** 163–170.

RUBOVITS, P., and MAEHR, M. Pygmalion analyzed: Toward an explanation of the Rosenthal-Jacobson findings. *Journal of Personality and Social Psychology,* 1971, **19,** 197–203.

RUCH, F., and ZIMBARDO, P. *Psychology and life.* (8th ed.) Glenview, Ill.: Scott, Foresman, 1971.

RUFUS, P. Interaction of personality and political systems in decisions to run for office. *The Journal of Social Issues,* 1968, **24,** 93–109.

RUTHERFORD, E., and MUSSEN, P. Generosity in nursery school boys. *Child Development,* 1968, **39,** 755–765.

RYCHLAK, J. The similarity, compatability, or incompatability of needs in interpersonal selection. *Journal of Personality and Social Psychology,* 1965, **2,** 334–340.

RYDER, R. Husband-wife dyads versus married strangers. *Family Process,* 1968, **7,** 233–238.

SAHLINS, M. On the sociology of primitive exchange. In *The relevance of models for social anthropology.* ASA Monographs, I. London: Tavistock Publications, 1965.

SALANCIK, J., and KIESLER, C. Behavioral commitment and retention of consistent and inconsistent attitude word-pairs. In C. Kiesler, *The psychology of commitment: Experiments linking behavior to beliefs.* New York: Academic Press, 1971. Pp. 109–121.

SALES, S. Need for stimulation as a factor in social behavior. *Journal of Personality and Social Psychology,* 1971, **19,** 124–134.

SALES, S. Economic threat as a determinant of conversion rates in authoritarian and nonauthoritarian churches. *Journal of Personality and Social Psychology,* 1972, **23,** 420–428.

SANFORD, F. Research on military leadership. In J. Flanagan (Ed.), *Psychology in the world emergency.* Pittsburgh: University of Pittsburgh Press, 1952.

SANFORD, N. Will psychologists study human problems? *American Psychologist,* 1965, **20,** 192–202.

SANFORD, N., COMSTOCK, C., and ASSOCIATES. *Sanctions for evil.* San Francisco: Jossey-Bass, 1971.

SARASON, S. *The culture of the school and the problem of change.* Boston: Allyn and Bacon, 1971.

SARBIN, T., and ALLEN, V. Role theory. In G. Lindzey and E. Aronson (Eds.), *Handbook of social psychology.* (2nd ed.) Vol. I. *Historical introduction—Systematic positions.* Reading, Mass.: Addison-Wesley, 1969. Pp. 488–567.

SARNOFF, I. Identification with the aggressor: Some personality correlates of anti-Semitism among Jews. Unpublished doctoral dissertation, University of Michigan, 1951.

SARNOFF, I. The experimental evaluation of psychoanalytic hypotheses. *Transactions of the New York Academy of Sciences,* 1965, **28,** 272–290.

SARNOFF, I., and ZIMBARDO, P. Anxiety, fear and social affiliation. *Journal of Abnormal and Social Psychology,* 1961, **62,** 356–363.

SCHACHTER, S. Deviation, rejection, and communication. *Journal of Abnormal and Social Psychology,* 1951, **46,** 190–207.

SCHACHTER, S. *The psychology of affiliation.* Stanford: Stanford University Press, 1959.

SCHACHTER, S., ELLERTSON, N., McBRIDE, D., and GREGORY, D. An experimental study of cohesiveness and productivity. *Human Relations,* 1951, **4,** 229–238.

SCHACHTER, S., GOLDMAN, S., and GORDON, A. Effects of fear, food deprivation, and obesity on eating. *Journal of Personality and Social Psychology,* 1968, **10,** 91–97.

SCHACHTER, S., and GROSS, L. Manipulated time and eating behavior. *Journal of Personality and Social Psychology,* 1968, **10,** 98–106.

SCHACHTER, S., and LATANÉ, B. Crime, cognition and the autonomic nervous system. In D. Levine (Ed.), *Nebraska Symposium on Motivation,* 1964, **12,** 221–273.

SCHACHTER, S., and SINGER, J. Cognitive, social, and physiological determinants of emotional state. *Psychological Review,* 1962, **69,** 379–399.

SCHACHTER, S., and WHEELER, L. Epinephrine, chlorpromazine, and amusement. *Journal of Abnormal and Social Psychology,* 1962, **65,** 121–128.

SCHAPS, E. Cost, dependency, and helping. *Journal of Personality and Social Psychology,* 1972, **21,** 74–78.

SCHEIBE, K. College students spend eight weeks in mental hospital: A case report. *Psychotherapy: Theory, Research, and Practice,* 1965, **2,** 117–120.

SCHELL, J. *The military half.* New York: Random House, 1968.

SCHERER, D. Attribution of personality form voice: A cross-cultural study on interpersonal perception. *Proceedings of the 79th Annual Convention of the American Psychological Association,* 1971, **6**(Pt. 1), 351–352.

SCHLESINGER, A., Jr. *A thousand days.* Boston: Houghton Mifflin, 1965. Quoted on pp. 36, 40, and 42 by I. Janis, *Victims of groupthink: A psychological study of foreign-policy decisions and fiascoes.* Boston: Houghton Mifflin, 1972.

SCHOENINGER, D., and WOOD, W. Comparison of married and ad hoc mixed-sex dyads negotiating the division of a reward. *Journal of Experimental Social Psychology,* 1969, **5,** 483–499.

SCHOOLER, C. Birth order effects: Not here, not now! *Psychological Bulletin,* 1972, **78,** 161–175.

SCHOPLER, J. An investigation of sex differences on the influence of dependence. *Sociometry,* 1967, **30,** 50–63.

SCHOPLER, J. An attribution analysis of some determinants of reciprocating a benefit. In J. Macaulay and L. Berkowitz (Eds.), *Altruism and helping behavior: Social psychological studies of some antecedents and consequences.* New York: Academic Press, 1970. Pp. 231–238.

SCHOPLER, J., and BATESON, N. A dependence interpretation of the effects of a severe initiation. *Journal of Personality,* 1962, **30,** 633–649.

SCHOPLER, J., and THOMPSON, V. Role of attribution processes in mediating amount of reciprocity for a favor. *Journal of Personality and Social Psychology,* 1968, **10,** 243–250.

SCHRODER, H., DRIVER, M., and STREUFERT, S. *Human information processing: Individuals and groups functioning in complex social situations.* New York: Holt, Rinehart and Winston, 1967.

SCHUMAN, H. Social change and the validity of regional stereotypes in East Pakistan. *Sociometry,* 1966, **29,** 428–440.

SCHWARTZ, S. Moral decision making and behavior. In J. Macaulay and L. Berkowitz (Eds.), *Altruism and helping behavior: Social psychological studies of some antecedents and consequences.* New York: Academic Press, 1970. Pp. 127–141.

SCHWARTZ, S., and CLAUSEN, G. Responsibility, norms, and helping in an emergency. *Journal of Personality and Social Psychology,* 1970, **16,** 299–310.

SCOTT, J., and FREDERICSON, E. The causes of fighting in mice and rats. *Physiological Zoology,* 1951, **24,** 273–309.

SCOTT, M., and LYMAN, S. Accounts. *American Sociological Review,* 1968, **33,** 46–62.

SEARS, D. The paradox of de facto selective exposure without preference for supportive information. In R. Abelson, E. Aronson, W. McGuire, T. Newcomb, M. Rosenberg, and P. Tannenbaum (Eds.), *Theories of cognitive consistency: A sourcebook.* Chicago: Rand McNally, 1968. Pp. 777–787.

SEARS, D., and FREEDMAN, J. Effects of expected familiarity of arguments upon opinion change and selective exposure. *Journal of Personality and Social Psychology,* 1965, **2,** 420–425.

SEARS, R., MACCOBY, E., and LEVIN, H. *Patterns of child rearing.* Evanston, Ill.: Row, Peterson, 1957.

SEASHORE, S. *Group cohesiveness in the industrial work group.* Ann Arbor, Mich.: Institute for Social Research, 1954.

SEASHORE, S., and BARNOWE, J. Collar color doesn't count. *Psychology Today,* 1972, **6**(3), 52–54, 80, 82.

SEEMAN, J. Deception in psychological research. *American Psychologist,* 1969, **24,** 1025–1028.

SEEMAN, M. Alienation: A map of its principal territories. *Psychology Today,* 1971, **5**(3), 82–84, 94–95. (a)

SEEMAN, M. The urban alienations: Some dubious theses from Marx to Marcuse. *Journal of Personality and Social Psychology,* 1971, **19,** 135–143. (b)

SELLTIZ, C., JAHODA, M., DEUTSCH, M., and COOK, S. *Research methods in social relations.* New York: Holt, Rinehart and Winston, 1959.

SELZNICK, G., and STEINBERG, S. *The tenacity of prejudice: Anti-Semitism in contemporary America.* New York: Harper Torchbooks, 1969.

SENN, D. Attraction as a function of similarity-dissimilarity in task performance. *Journal of Personality and Social Psychology,* 1971, **18,** 120–123.

SENN, D., and SAWYER, J. Institutional racism: A problem for psychology? *American Psychologist,* 1971, **26,** 671–674.

SENSENIG, J., and BREHM, J. Attitude change from an implied threat to attitudinal freedom. *Journal of Personality and Social Psychology,* 1968, **8,** 324–330.

SERMAT, V. Is game behavior related to behavior in other interpersonal situations? *Journal of Personality and Social Psychology,* 1970, **16,** 92–109.

SERMAT, V. Personal communication to the author. 1972.

SERMAT, V., COHEN, M., and POLLACK, H. Helping freshmen adjust to the university: Orientation groups with an interpersonal emphasis. Internal Report No. 25, April, 1970. York University, Toronto.

SERMAT, V., and SMYTH, M. Content analysis of verbal communication in the development of a relationship: Conditions influencing self-disclosure. *Journal of Personality and Social Psychology,* 1973, **26,** 332–346.

SHAPIRO, A., and SWENSEN, C. Patterns of self-disclosure among married couples. *Journal of Counseling Psychology,* 1969, **16**(2, Pt. 1), 179–180.

SHARP, H., and McCLUNG, T. Effect of organization on the speaker's ethos. *Speech Monographs,* 1966, **33,** 182–183.

SHAW, M. Some effects of unequal distribution of information upon group performance in various communication nets. *Journal of Abnormal and Social Psychology,* 1954, **49,** 547–553.

SHAW, M. A note concerning homogeneity of membership and group problem solving. *Journal of Abnormal and Social Psychology,* 1960, **60,** 448–450.

SHAW, M. *Group dynamics: The psychology of small group behavior.* New York: McGraw-Hill, 1971.

SHEATSLEY, P., and FELDMAN, J. The assassination of President Kennedy: A preliminary report on public reactions and behavior. *The Public Opinion Quarterly,* 1964, **28,** 189–215.

SHERIF, C., SHERIF, M., and NEBERGALL, R. *Attitude and attitude change.* Philadelphia: Saunders, 1965.

SHERIF, M. A study of some social factors in perception. *Archives of Psychology,* 1935, No. 187.

SHERIF, M. *The psychology of social norms.* New York: Harper and Row, 1936.

SHERIF, M. *Social interaction: Processes and products.* Chicago: Aldine, 1967.

SHERIF, M., HARVEY, O., WHITE, B., HOOD, W., and SHERIF, C. *Intergroup conflict and cooperation: The robbers cave experiment.* Norman: Institute of Group Relations, University of Oklahoma, 1961.

SHERIF, M., and SHERIF, C. *Social psychology.* New York: Harper and Row, 1969.

SHERMAN, S. Effects of choice and incentive on attitude change in a discrepant behavior situation. *Journal of Personality and Social Psychology,* 1970, **15,** 245–252.

SHIPLER, D. City unit sees violence pattern by whites against minorities. *The New York Times,* December 12, 1972, pp. 1, 54.

SHIPLEY, W. The demonstration in the domestic guinea pig of a process resembling classical imprinting. *Animal Behaviour,* 1963, **11,** 470–474.

SIEGEL, A., and KOHN, L. Permissiveness, permission, and aggression: The effect of adult presence or absence on aggression in children's play. *Child Development,* 1959, **30,** 131–141.

SIGALL, H., ARONSON, E., and VAN HOOSE, T. The cooperative subject: Myth or reality. *Journal of Experimental Social Psychology,* 1970, **6,** 1–10.

SIGALL, H., and LANDY, D. Radiating beauty: The effects of having a physically attractive partner on person perception. *Journal of Personality and Social Psychology,* in press.

SILVERMAN, I. On the resolution and tolerance of cognitive inconsistency in a natural-occurring event: Attitudes and beliefs following the Senator Edward M. Kennedy incident. *Journal of Personality and Social Psychology,* 1971, **17,** 171–178.

SILVERMAN, I., SHULMAN, A., and WIESENTHAL, D. Effects of deceiving and debriefing psychological subjects on performance in later experiments. *Journal of Personality and Social Psychology,* 1970, **14,** 203–212.

SIMMEL, M. Developmental aspects of the body scheme. *Child Development,* 1966, **37,** 83–95.

SIMMONS, C., and LERNER, M. Altruism as a search for justice. *Journal of Personality and Social Psychology,* 1968, **9,** 216–225.

SINGER, D. The impact of interracial classroom exposure on the social attitudes of fifth grade children. Unpublished study, 1964. Cited on p. 49 by J. Harding, H. Proshansky, B. Kutner, and I. Chein, Prejudice and ethnic relations. In G. Lindzey and E. Aronson (Eds.), *The handbook of social psychology.* (2nd ed.) Vol. 5. *Applied social psychology.* Reading, Mass.: Addison-Wesley, 1969. Pp. 1–76.

SINGER, J. Social comparison: Progress and issues. *Journal of Experimental Social Psychology Supplement,* 1966, **1,** 103–110.

SISTRUNK, F., and McDAVID, J. Sex variable in conforming behavior. *Journal of Personality and Social Psychology,* 1971, **17,** 200–207.

SKINNER, B. F. *Beyond freedom and dignity.* New York: Knopf, 1971.

SKOLNICK, P. Reaction to personal evaluations: A failure to replicate. *Journal of Personality and Social Psychology,* 1971, **18,** 62–67.

SLATER, P. Contrasting correlates of group size. *Sociometry,* 1958, **21,** 129–139.

SMART, R. Social-group membership, leadership, and birth order. *Journal of Social Psychology,* 1965, **67,** 221–225.

SMART, R. Subject selection bias in psychological research. *Canadian Psychologist,* 1966, **7a,** 115–121.

SMITH, D. Use of LSD in the Haight-Asbury: Observations of a neighborhood clinic. *California Medicine,* 1969, **110,** 472–476.

SMITH, D., and ROSE, A. A case study of the Charles Manson group marriage commune. *Journal of the American Society of Psychosomatic Dentistry and Medicine,* 1970, **17,** 99–106.

SMITH, G. Personality correlates of cigarette smoking in students of college age. *Annals of the New York Academy of Sciences,* 1967, **142,** 308–321.

SMITH, H., and ROSEN, E. Some psychological correlates of world mindedness and authoritarianism. *Journal of Personality,* 1958, **26,** 170–183.

SMITH, S., and HAYTHORN, W. Effects of compatability, crowding, group size, and leadership seniority on stress, anxiety, hostility, and annoyance in isolated groups. *Journal of Personality and Social Psychology,* 1972, **22,** 67–79.

SMITH, V. Nonpersuasively induced dissonance-reducing covert altruistic action. *Psychological Reports,* 1969, **25,** 228.

SMITH, W. Observations over the lifetime of a small isolated group: Structure, danger, boredom, and vision. *Psychological Reports,* 1966, **19,** 475–514.

SOMMER, R. *Personal space: The behavioral basis of design.* Englewood Cliffs, N. J.: Prentice-Hall, 1969.

SOMMER, R., and BECKER, F. Territorial defense and the good neighbor. *Journal of Personality and Social Psychology,* 1969, **11,** 85–92.

SOROKIN, P. *Society, culture, and personality: Their structure and dynamics.* New York: Harper, 1947.

STAATS, A. Experimental demand characteristics and the classical conditioning of attitudes. *Journal of Personality and Social Psychology,* 1969, **11,** 187–192.

STAFFORD-CLARK, D. Morale and flying experience: Results of a war-time study. *Journal of Mental Science,* 1949, **95,** 10–50.

STAR, S., WILLIAMS, R., Jr., and STOUFFER, S. Negro infantry platoons in white companies. In H. Proshansky and B. Seidenberg (Eds.), *Basic studies in social psychology.* New York: Holt, Rinehart and Winston, 1965. Pp. 680–685.

STEIN, A., and FRIEDRICH, L. Television content and young children's behavior. In J. Murray, E. Rubinstein, and G. Comstock (Eds.), *Television and social learning.* Washington: Government Printing Office, 1971.

STEINER, I. Perceived freedom. In L. Berkowitz (Ed.), *Advances in experimental social psychology.* Vol. 5. New York: Academic Press, 1970. Pp. 187–248.

STEINER, I. *Group process and productivity.* New York: Academic Press, 1972.

STEINER, I., and JOHNSON, H. Authoritarianism and "tolerance of trait inconsistency." *Journal of Abnormal and Social Psychology,* 1963, **67,** 388–391.

STEPHENSON, G., and FIELDING, G. An experimental study of the contagion of leaving behavior in small gatherings. *Journal of Social Psychology,* 1971, **84,** 81–91.

STEPHENSON, W. Some observations on Q-technique. *Psychological Bulletin,* 1952, **6,** 483–498.

STEVENSON, H., and HILL, K. Rise of rate as a measure of response in studies of social reinforcement. *Psychological Bulletin,* 1966, **66,** 321–326.

STEWART, R. Effects of continuous responding on the order effect in personality impression formation. *Journal of Personality and Social Psychology,* 1965, **1,** 161–165.

STOGDILL, R. Validity of leader behavior description. *Personnel Psychology,* 1969, **22,** 153–158.

STOGDILL, R., and KOEHLER, K. *Measures of leadership structure and organization change.* Columbus: Ohio State University Research Foundation, 1952.

STOTLAND, E., THORLEY, S., THOMAS, A., COHEN, A., and ZANDER, A. The effects of group expectations and self-esteem upon self-evaluation. *Journal of Abnormal and Social Psychology,* 1957, **54,** 55–63.

STREUFERT, S., and STREUFERT, S. C. Effects of conceptual structure, failure, and success on

attribution of causality and interpersonal attitudes. *Journal of Personality and Social Psychology,* 1969, **11,** 138–147.

STRICKER, L. The true deceiver. *Psychological Bulletin,* 1967, **68,** 62–76.

STRICKER, L., MESSICK, S., and JACKSON, D. Suspicion of deception: Implications for conformity research. *Journal of Personality and Social Psychology,* 1967, **5,** 379–389.

STRICKLAND, L. Surveillance and trust. *Journal of Personality,* 1958, **26,** 200–215.

STRODTBECK, F., and HOOK, L. The social dimensions of a twelve man jury table. *Sociometry,* 1961, **24,** 397–415.

STRODTBECK, F., JAMES, R., and HAWKINS, C. Social status in jury deliberations. In E. Maccoby, T. Newcomb, and E. Hartley (Eds.), *Readings in social psychology.* New York: Holt, 1958. Pp. 379–388.

STRUENING, E. Antidemocratic attitudes in a midwestern university. In H. Remmers (Ed.), *Antidemocratic attitudes in American schools.* Evanston: Northwestern University Press, 1963. Ch. 9.

STRÜMPFER, D. Fear and affiliation during a disaster. *Journal of Social Psychology,* 1970, **82,** 263–268.

STUKÁT, K. *Suggestibility: A factorial and experimental study.* Stockholm: Almquist and Wiksell, 1958.

SUEDFELD, P. Attitude manipulation in restricted environments: I. Conceptual structure and response to propaganda. *Journal of Abnormal and Social Psychology,* 1964, **68,** 242–247.

SUEDFELD, P., BOCHNER, S., and MATAS, C. Petitioner's attire and petition signing by peace demonstrators: A field experiment. *Journal of Applied Social Psychology,* 1971, **1,** 278–283.

SUEDFELD, P., BOCHNER, S., and WNEK, D. Helper-sufferer similarity and a specific request for help: Bystander intervention during a peace demonstration. *Journal of Applied Social Psychology,* 1972, **2,** 17–23.

SWINGLE, P. (Ed.) *The structure of conflict.* New York: Academic Press, 1970.

SYKES, G., and MATZA, D. Techniques of neutralization: A theory of delinquency. *American Sociological Review,* 1957, **22,** 664–670.

TANKARD, J. Effects of eye position on person perception. *Perceptual and Motor Skills,* 1970, **31,** 883–893.

TAYLOR, D. Some aspects of the development of inter-personal relationships: Social penetration processes. Naval Medical Research Institute, Washington, 1965.

TAYLOR, D. The development of interpersonal relationships: Social penetration processes. *Journal* of Social Psychology, 1968, **75,** 79–90.

TAYLOR, D., ALTMAN, I., and SORRENTINO, R. Interpersonal exchange as a function of rewards and costs and situational factors: Expectancy confirmation-disconfirmation. *Journal of Experimental Social Psychology,* 1969, **5,** 324–339.

TAYLOR, S., and METTEE, D. When similarity breeds contempt. *Journal of Personality and Social Psychology,* 1971, **20,** 75–81.

TEDESCHI, J., LINDSKOLD, S., HORAI, J., and GAHAGAN, J. Social power and the credibility of promises. *Journal of Personality and Social Psychology,* 1969, **13,** 253–261.

Television and growing up: The impact of televised violence. Report to the Surgeon General, United States Public Health Service from the Surgeon General's Scientific Advisory Committee on Television and Social Behavior. Washington: U. S. Department of Health, Education, and Welfare, 1972.

TESSER, A. Differential weighting and directed meaning as explanations of primacy in impression formation. *Psychonomic Science,* 1968, **11,** 299–300.

TESSER, A., and BRODIE, M. A note on the evaluation of a "computer date." *Psychonomic Science,* 1971, **23,** 300.

TESSER, A., GATEWOOD, R., and DRIVER, M. Some determinants of gratitude. *Journal of Personality and Social Psychology,* 1968, **9,** 233–236.

THAYER, S., and SCHIFF, W. Stimulus factors in observer judgment of social interaction: Facial expression and motion pattern. *American Journal of Psychology,* 1969, **82,** 73–85.

THELEN, H. Group dynamics in instruction: Principles of least group size. *School Review,* 1949, **57,** 139–148.

THEODORSON, G. Elements in the progressive development of small groups. *Social Forces,* 1953, **31,** 311–320.

THIBAUT, J., and COULES, J. The role of communication in the reduction of interpersonal hostility. *Journal of Abnormal and Social Psychology,* 1952, **47,** 770–777.

THIBAUT, J., and FAUCHEUX, C. The development of contractual norms in a bargaining situation under two types of stress. *Journal of Experimental Social Psychology,* 1965, **1,** 89–102.

THIBAUT, J., and KELLEY, H. *The social psychology of groups.* New York: Wiley, 1959.

THIBAUT, J., and STRICKLAND, L. Psychological set and social conformity. *Journal of Personality,* 1956, **25,** 115–129.

THISTLETHWAITE, D., de HAAN, H., and KAMENETZKY, J. The effects of "directive" and "nondirective" communication procedures on attitudes. *Journal of Abnormal and Social Psychology,*

1955, **51,** 107–113.

THOMAS, E., and FINK, C. Effects of group size. *Psychological Bulletin,* 1963, **60,** 371–384.

THOMAS, R. The future of the American family: Despite all, Dr. Brothers sees hope. *The New York Times,* August 11, 1971, p. 32.

THORNTON, D., and ARROWOOD, A. Self-evaluation, self-enhancement, and the locus of social comparison. *Journal of Experimental Social Psychology Supplement,* 1966, **1,** 40–48.

TILKER, H. Socially responsible behavior as a function of observer responsibility and victim feedback. *Journal of Personality and Social Psychology,* 1970, **14,** 95–100.

TIPPETT, J., and SILBER, E. Autonomy of self-esteem: An experimental approach. *Archives of General Psychiatry,* 1966, **14,** 372–385.

TOCH, H. The social psychology of violence. In E. Megargee and J. Hokanson (Eds.), *The dynamics of aggression: Individual, group, and international analyses.* New York: Harper and Row, 1970.

TOCH, H. *Violent men: An inquiry into the psychology of violence.* Chicago: Aldine, 1969.

TOGNOLI, J. Reciprocity and reactance in game-playing behavior. *Bulletin of the British Psychological Society,* 1968, **21**(70), 39.

TRAESTER, J. Army chaplain decorated for bravery in Vietnam. *The New York Times,* June 6, 1968, p. 4.

TRAVIS, L. The effect of a small audience upon eye-hand coordination. *Journal of Abnormal and Social Psychology,* 1925, **20,** 142–146.

TRIANDIS, H. *Attitude and attitude change.* New York: Wiley, 1971.

TRIANDIS, H., and DAVIS, E. Race and belief as determinants of behavioral intentions. *Journal of Personality and Social Psychology,* 1965, **2,** 715–726.

TRIANDIS, H., and VASSILIOU, V. Frequency of contact and stereotyping. *Journal of Personality and Social Psychology,* 1967, **7,** 316–328.

TRIANDIS, H., VASSILIOU, V., and NASSIAKOU, M. Three cross-cultural studies of subjective culture. *Journal of Personality and Social Psychology,* 1968, **8**(4, Pt. 2), 1–42.

TRILLIN, C. U. S. Journal: Manhattan. The ordeal of Fats Goldberg. *The New Yorker,* July 3, 1971, pp. 57–58, 62–63.

TRIPLETT, N. The dynamogenic factors in pace making and competition. *American Journal of Psychology,* 1898, **9**(4), 507–533.

TUCKMAN, B. Developmental sequence in small groups. *Psychological Bulletin,* 1965, **63,** 384–399.

TURK, H. Instrumental and expressive ratings reconsidered. *Sociometry,* 1961, **24,** 76–81.

623

References

TURNER, C., and BERKOWITZ, L. Identification with film aggressor (covert role taking) and reactions to film violence. *Journal of Personality and Social Psychology,* 1972, **21,** 256–264.

TURNER, R. Role-taking, role standpoint, and reference-group behavior. *American Journal of Sociology,* 1956, **61,** 316–328.

UPI release, September 23, 1967. Quoted on p. 245 by P. Zimbardo, The human choice: Individuation, reason, and order versus deindividuation, impulse, and chaos. In W. Arnold and D. Levine (Eds.), *Nebraska Symposium on Motivation,* 1969, **17,** 237–307.

U. S. Department of Commerce, Bureau of the Census. *The social and economic status of Negroes in the United States, 1970.* DLS Report No. 394; Current population reports, series P-23, No. 38.

U. S. Department of Commerce, Bureau of the Census. *Marital status and living arrangements.* Washington, D. C.: Government Printing Office, March, 1971, No. 225, p. 20.

VALIEN, B. *The Saint Louis story: A study of desegregation.* New York: Anti-Defamation League, 1956. Quoted on p. 7 by H. Hyman, Social psychology and race relations. In I. Katz and P. Gurin (Eds.), *Race and the social sciences.* New York: Basic Books, 1969. Pp. 3–48.

VALINS, S. Cognitive effects of false heart-rate feedback. *Journal of Personality and Social Psychology,* 1966, **4,** 400–408.

VAN ZELST, R. Validation of a sociometric regrouping procedure. *Journal of Abnormal and Social Psychology,* 1952, **47,** 299–301.

VAUGHAN, G. The trans-situational aspect of conforming behavior. *Journal of Personality,* 1964, **32,** 335–354.

VERINIS, J., and ROLL, S. Primary and secondary male characteristics: The hairiness and large penis stereotypes. *Psychological Reports,* 1970, **26,** 123–126.

Volunteer kidney. *Newsweek,* March 4, 1963, p. 76.

VREELAND, R. Is it true what they say about Harvard boys? *Psychology Today,* 1972, **5**(8), 65–68.

WAGNER, C., and WHEELER, L. Model, need, and cost effects in helping behavior. *Journal of Personality and Social Psychology,* 1969, **12,** 111–116.

WAHL, C. Some antecedent factors in the family histories of 109 alcoholics. *Quarterly Journal of Studies on Alcohol,* 1956, **17,** 643–654.

WALKER, E., and HEYNS, R. *An anatomy for conformity.* Englewood Cliffs, N. J.: Prentice-Hall, 1962.

WALKER, M. Organizational type, rites of incorporation, and group solidarity: A study of fraternity hell week. *Dissertation Abstracts,* 1968, **29**(2-A), 689–690.

WALLACE, J. Role reward and dissonance reduction. *Journal of Personality and Social Psychology,* 1966, **3,** 305–312.

WALSTER, E. Did you ever see a beautiful conservative? A note. Mimeographed report available from the author, 1971. (a)

WALSTER, E. Passionate love. In B. Murstein (Ed.), *Theories of attraction and love.* New York: Springer, 1971. Pp. 85–99. (b)

WALSTER, E., ARONSON, E., and ABRAHAMS, D. On increasing the persuasiveness of a low prestige communicator. *Journal of Experimental Social Psychology,* 1966, **2,** 325–342.

WALSTER, E., ARONSON, V., ABRAHAMS, D., and ROTTMANN, L. Importance of physical attractiveness in dating behavior. *Journal of Personality and Social Psychology,* 1966, **4,** 508–516.

WALSTER, E., BERSCHEID, E., ABRAHAMS, D., and ARONSON, V. Effectiveness of debriefing following deception experiments. *Journal of Personality and Social Psychology,* 1967, **6**(4, Pt. 1), 371–380.

WALSTER, E., BERSCHEID, E., and BARCLAY, A. A determinant of preference among modes of dissonance reduction. *Journal of Personality and Social Psychology,* 1967, **7,** 211–216.

WALSTER, E., and FESTINGER, L. The effectiveness of "overheard" persuasive communications. *Journal of Abnormal and Social Psychology,* 1962, **65,** 395–402.

WALSTER, E., and WALSTER, G. Effect of expecting to be liked on choice of associates. *Journal of Abnormal and Social Psychology,* 1963, **67,** 402–404.

WALTERS, R. Implication of laboratory studies of aggression for the control and regulation of violence. *Annals of the American Academy of Political and Social Science,* 1966, **364,** 60–72.

WAPNER, S., and ALPER, T. The effect of an audience on behavior in a choice situation. *Journal of Abnormal and Social Psychology,* 1952, **47,** 222–229.

WARR, P., and KNAPPER, C. *The perception of people and events.* New York: Wiley, 1968.

WARREN, J. Birth order and social behavior. *Psychological Bulletin,* 1966, **65,** 38–49.

WASMAN, M., and FLYNN, J. Directed attack elicited from the hypothalamus. *Archives of Neurology,* 1962, **6,** 220–227.

WEATHERLY, D. Anti-Semitism and the expression of fantasy aggression. *Journal of Abnormal and Social Psychology,* 1961, **62,** 454–457

WEBB, E., CAMPBELL, D., SCHWARTZ, R., and SECHREST, L. *Unobtrusive measures: Nonreac-*

Social Psychology and Modern Life

tive research in the social sciences. Chicago: Rand McNally, 1966.

WEBBER, R. Perceptions of interactions between superiors and subordinates. *Human Relations,* 1970, **23,** 235–248.

WEBER, S., and COOK, T. Subject effects in laboratory research: An examination of subject roles, demand characteristics, and valid inference. *Psychological Bulletin,* 1972, **77,** 273–295.

WEICK, K., and GILFILLAN, D. Fate of arbitrary traditions in a laboratory microculture. *Journal of Personality and Social Psychology,* 1971, **17,** 179–191.

WEITZ, S. Attitude, voice, and behavior: A repressed affect model of interracial interaction. *Journal of Personality and Social Psychology,* 1972, **24,** 14–21.

What was that? *Time,* October 18, 1971, p. 80.

Whatever happened to the . . . Super Peace Corps: More aid now to more people. *U. S. News and World Report,* November 27, 1972, pp. 86, 87.

WHEELER, H. A moral equivalent for riots. *Saturday Review,* May 11, 1968, pp. 19–22.

WHEELER, L. Motivation as a determination of upward comparison. *Journal of Experimental Social Psychology Supplement,* 1966, **1,** 27–31. (a)

WHEELER, L. Toward a theory of behavioral contagion. *Psychological Review,* 1966, **73,** 179–192. (b)

WHITE, E., and THURBER, J. *Is sex necessary?* New York: Harper and Row, 1973.

WHITE, P. Bare handed battle to cleanse the Bay. *National Geographic,* 1971, **139,** 866–881.

WHITE, R. Motivation reconsidered: The concept of competence. *Psychological Review,* 1959, **66,** 297–334.

WHITMORE, P., Jr. A study of school desegregation: Attitude change and scale validation. *Dissertation Abstracts,* 1957, **17**(A-4), 891–892.

WHYTE, W. Corner boys: A study of clique behavior. *American Journal of Sociology,* 1941, **46,** 647–664.

WHYTE, W. *Street corner society.* Chicago: University of Chicago Press, 1943.

WICHMAN, H. Effects of isolation and communication on cooperation in a two-person game. *Journal of Personality and Social Psychology,* 1970, **16,** 114–120.

WICKER, A. Attitudes versus actions: The relationship of verbal and overt behavioral responses to attitude objects. *The Journal of Social Issues,* 1969, **25,** 41–78.

WIEBE, G. Two psychological factors in media audience behavior. *The Public Opinion Quarterly,* 1970, **33,** 523–536.

WIGGINS, J., WIGGINS, N., and CONGER, J. Correlates of heterosexual somatic preference. *Journal of Personality and Social Psychology,* 1968, **10,**

82–90.

WILLEMS, E., and CLARK. R., III. Dependency of risky shift on instructions: A replication. *Psychological Reports,* 1969, **25,** 811–814.

WILLERMAN, B., and SWANSON, L. Group prestige in voluntary organizations. *Human Relations,* 1953, **6,** 57–77.

WILLIAMS, J., Jr. Regional differences in authoritarianism. *Social Forces,* 1966, **45,** 273–277.

WILLIAMS, J. E. Connotation of racial concepts and color names. In M. Goldschmid (Ed.), *Black Americans and white racism: Theory and research.* New York: Holt, Rinehart and Winston, 1970. Pp. 38–48.

WILLIS, R., and BULATAO, R. Belief and ethnicity as determinants of friendship and marriage acceptance in the Philippines. Paper presented at the meeting of the American Psychological Association, Washington, D. C., September 1967.

WILSON, W., and MILLER, H. Repetition, order of presentation, and timing of arguments and measures as determinants of opinion change. *Journal of Personality and Social Psychology,* 1968, **9,** 184–188.

WILSON, W., and MILLER, N. Shifts in evaluation of participants following intergroup competition. *Journal of Abnormal and Social Psychology,* 1961, **63,** 428–432.

WINCHESTER, J. Volunteer firemen: Heroes without pay. *Popular Science,* 1969, **194,** 94–97.

WINWAR, F. *American giant: Walt Whitman and his times.* New York: Harper, 1941.

WISHNER, J. Reanalysis of "impressions of personality." *Psychological Review,* 1960, **67,** 96–112.

WISPÉ, L., AWKWARD, J., HOFFMAN, M., ASH, P., HICKS, L., and PORTER, J. The Negro in America. *American Psychologist,* 1969, **24,** 142–150.

WOFFORD, J. Factor analysis of managerial behavior variables. *Journal of Applied Psychology,* 1970, **54,** 169–173.

WOLFGANG, M. *Patterns in criminal homicide.* Philadelphia: University of Pennsylvania Press, 1958.

WOLFGANG, M., and FERRACUTI, F. *The subculture of violence: Towards an integrated theory in criminology.* London: Social Science Paperbacks in association with Tavistock Publications, 1967.

WORCHEL, S., and BREHM, J. Direct and implied social restoration of freedom. *Journal of Personality and Social Psychology,* 1971, **18,** 294–304.

WORTHY, M., GARY, A., and KAHN, G. Self disclosure as an exchange process. *Journal of Personality and Social Psychology,* 1969, **13,** 59–63.

WRIGHT, B. Altruism in children and the perceived conduct of others. *Journal of Abnormal and Social Psychology,* 1942, **37,** 218–233.

WRIGHTSMAN, L. Effects of waiting with others on changes in level of felt anxiety. *Journal of Abnormal and Social Psychology,* 1960, **61,** 216–222.

WUEBBEN, P. Honesty of subjects and birth order. *Journal of Personality and Social Psychology,* 1967, **5,** 350–352.

WYER, R., Jr. The effects of information redundancy on evaluation of social stimuli. *Psychonomic Science,* 1968, **13**(4), 245–246.

WYLIE, R. *The self concept: A critical survey of pertinent research literature.* Lincoln: University of Nebraska Press, 1961.

WYLIE, R. Self-ratings, level of ideal-self ratings, and defensiveness. *Psychological Reports,* 1965, **16,** 135–150.

YARROW, L. Maternal deprivation. *Psychological Bulletin,* 1961, **58,** 459–490.

ZABRACK, M., and MILLER, N. Group aggression: The effects of friendship ties and anonymity. *Proceedings of the 80th Annual Convention of the American Psychological Association,* 1972, 211–212.

ZAJONC, R. Social facilitation. *Science,* 1965, **149,** 269–274.

ZAJONC, R. Attitudinal effects of mere exposure. *Journal of Personality and Social Psychology,* 1968, **9**(2, Pt. 2), 1–27.

ZAJONC, R., SHAVER, P., TAVRIS, C., and VAN KREVELD, D. Exposure, satiation, and stimulus discriminability. *Journal of Personality and Social Psychology,* 1972, **21,** 270–280.

ZAJONC, R., WOLOSIN, R., WOLOSIN, M., and SHERMAN, S. Individual and group risk-taking in a two-choice situation. *Journal of Experimental Social Psychology,* 1968, **4,** 89–106.

ZANDER, A., and HAVELIN, A. Social comparison and interpersonal attraction. *Human Relations,* 1960, **13,** 21–32.

ZANNA, M., KIESLER, C., and PILKONIS, P. Positive and negative attitudinal effect established by classical conditioning. *Journal of Personality and Social Psychology,* 1970, **14,** 321–328.

ZILLER, R. Group size: A determinant of the quality and stability of group decisions. *Sociometry,* 1957, **20,** 165–173.

ZILLMANN, D. Rhetorical elicitation of agreement in persuasion. *Journal of Personality and Social Psychology,* 1972, **21,** 159–165.

ZIMBARDO, P. The effect of effort and improvisation on self-persuasion produced by role-playing. *Journal of Experimental Social Psychology,* 1965, **1,** 103–120.

ZIMBARDO, P. Physical integration and social segregation of northern Negro college students (1953, 1963 and 1965). Paper presented at the Eastern Psychological Association, 1966.

ZIMBARDO, P. The human choice: Individuation, reason, and order versus deindividuation, impulse, and chaos. In W. Arnold and D. Levine (Eds.), *Nebraska Symposium on Motivation,* 1969, **17,** 237–307.

ZIMBARDO, P. The psychology of police confessions. In *Readings in social psychology today.* Del Mar, Calif.: CRM Books, 1970. Pp. 101–107.

ZIMBARDO, P. Freaks, hippies, and voters: The effects of deviant dress and appearance on political persuasion processes. Symposium presented at the meeting of the Eastern Psychological Association, New York City, April 1971. (a)

ZIMBARDO, P. The psychological power and pathology of imprisonment. A statement prepared for the U. S. House of Representatives Committee on the Judiciary. (Subcommittee No. 3. Robert Kastenmeyer, Chairman: hearings on prison reform.) Unpublished paper, Stanford University, 1971. (b)

ZIMBARDO, P. Personal communication to the author. 1972.

ZIMBARDO, P., and FORMICA, R. Emotional comparison and self esteem as determinants of affiliation. *Journal of Personality,* 1963, **31,** 141–162.

ZIMBARDO, P., HANEY, C., BANKS, W., and JAFFE, D. The psychology of imprisonment: Privation, power, and pathology. Unpublished paper, Stanford University, 1972.

ZIMBARDO, P., SNYDER, M., THOMAS, J., GOLD, A., and GURWITZ, S. Modifying the impact of persuasive communications with external distraction. *Journal of Personality and Social Psychology,* 1970, **16,** 669–680.

ZIMBARDO, P., WEISENBERG, M., FIRESTONE, I., and LEVY, B. Communicator effectiveness in producing public conformity and private attitude change. *Journal of Personality,* 1965, **33,** 233–255.

ZIMBARDO, P., WEISENBERG, M., FIRESTONE, I., and LEVY, B. Changing appetites for eating fried grasshoppers. In P. Zimbardo (Ed.), *The cognitive control of motivation.* Chicago: Scott, Foresman, 1969. Pp. 44–54.

ZLUTNICK, S., and ALTMAN, I. Crowding and human behavior. Unpublished study. Cited by J. Freedman, A. Levy, R. Buchanan, and J. Price, Crowding and human aggressiveness. *Journal of Experimental Social Psychology,* 1972, **8,** 528–548.

ZUBEC, J. (Ed.) *Sensory deprivation: Fifteen years of research.* New York: Appleton-Century-Crofts, 1969.

ZUCKERMAN, M., PERSKY, H., LINK, K., and BASU, G. Experimental and subject factors determining responses to sensory deprivation, social isolation, and confinement. *Journal of Abnormal Psychology,* 1968, **73,** 183–194.

NAME INDEX

SUBJECT INDEX

About the Author

Dr. Patricia Niles Middlebrook is presently Associate Professor of Psychology at Central Connecticut State College, where she has taught since 1963. A Phi Beta Kappa graduate of Swarthmore College, she acquired her M.S. and Ph.D. at Yale University in 1959 and 1964, respectively. As a Graduate Teaching Fellow, Dr. Middlebrook taught two years at Yale Divinity School. She has co-authored several journal articles.